THE BEST RECIPE

THE

Best Recipe

BY THE EDITORS OF

COOK'S ILLUSTRATED

ILLUSTRATIONS BY JOHN BURGOYNE

PHOTOGRAPHY BY CARL TREMBLAY

BOSTON COMMON PRESS

BROOKLINE, MASSACHUSETTS

Boston Common Press
17 Station Street
Brookline, Massachusetts 02445

ISBN 0-936184-38-8
Library of Congress Cataloging-in-Publication Data
The Editors of *Cook's Illustrated*
The Best Recipe: Would you make 38 versions of Crème Caramel to find the absolute best version?
We did. Here are 700 exhaustively tested recipes plus no-nonsense kitchen tests and tastings.
1st edition

ISBN 0-936184-38-8 (hardback): $29.95
I. Cooking. I. Title
1999

Manufactured in the United States of America

Distributed by Boston Common Press, 17 Station Street, Brookline, MA 02445.

Designed by Amy Klee
Edited by Jack Bishop

CONTENTS

ACKNOWLEDGMENTS

THIS BOOK CONTAINS THE BEST RECIPES that have appeared in the pages of *Cook's Illustrated* since the charter issue was published in 1993. We would like to thank the following authors for their contributions to the magazine over the years: Katherine Alford, Pam Anderson, Melanie Barnard, Sharon Kebschull Barrett, Douglas Bellow, Jack Bishop, Mark Bittman, Stephana Bottom, Todd Butcher, Phyllis M. Carey, Lauren Chattman, Elaine Corn, Elizabeth Gunas Crampton, Julia della Croce, Brooke Dojny, Maryellen Driscoll, Gene Freeland, Sarah Fritschner, Elizabeth Germain, Sam Gugino, Melissa Hamilton, Cynthia Hizer, Steve Johnson, Eva Katz, Christopher Kimball, Deborah Krasner, Bridget Lancaster, Susan Logozzo, Stephanie Lyness, Nick Malgieri, Alice Medrich, Judy Monroe, Jamie Morris, Jessika Bella Mura, Gail Nagele-Hopkins, Marie Piraino, Susan G. Purdy, Kay Rentschler, Adam Ried, Chris Schlesinger, Stephen Schmidt, Regina Schrambling, Diana Shaw, A. Cort Sinnes, Karen Tack, Fred Thomas, Anne Marie Weiss-Armush, John Willoughby, Eric Wolff, Dede Wilson, Anne Yamanaka, Dawn Yanagihara, Lisa Yockelson, and Mark Zanger.

A book of this scope could not have come together as quickly and easily as this one did without a fabulous editor and a talented art director. Special thanks to Jack Bishop and Amy Klee for handling those roles, respectively.

In addition, we would like to thank the myriad art, editorial, and production staff who produced this book, including Barbara Bourassa, Rich Cassidy, Sheila Datz, Daniel Frey, India Koopman, Nate Nickerson, Jim McCormack, Livia McRee, and Marcia Palmater. Special thanks to John Burgoyne, our illustrator, for his beautiful drawings, and to Carl Tremblay, our photographer, for his wonderful work. And, last but not least, thanks to Angela Miller of The Miller Agency.

INTRODUCTION

ONE MIGHT COMMENT THAT ANY COOKBOOK titled *The Best Recipe* has a great deal to prove. On the face of it, the notion that any one cookbook has the "best" recipes seems far-fetched, even outrageous. Yet, in choosing this title, our intent was to convey the process by which the editors of *Cook's Illustrated* magazine develop recipes. We start with a stated goal—the "best" meatloaf or the "best" chocolate pudding—and then proceed to a blind taste test in which a half-dozen or so recipes are sampled from various cookbooks. We then set out what, for us, is the ideal version of the recipe under consideration and proceed to develop it through a long, arduous process of testing and research. This does not mean that reasonable folks can't disagree on what defines the ideal chocolate chip cookie or the perfect roast chicken or that we always achieve our goals. Yet this group process does rule out methods that are less successful and recipes that are less than foolproof. In fact, this process has led us to the conclusion that much of cooking is indeed objective. One can say something definitive about roasting temperatures for different cuts of meat; one can clearly taste the difference between butter and vegetable shortening in cakes and cookies. These discoveries are the foundation of good cooking, on which one can layer elements of personal taste.

This collection of recipes comes from the pages of *Cook's Illustrated* magazine and represents the editors' picks from 1993 to the present. For those of you not familiar with *Cook's Illustrated,* we are a bimonthly publication (that is, produced six times a year) on home cooking that does not accept advertising. Our goal is to investigate why a recipe works and how to make it better. Some efforts are more successful than others, but everyone at *Cook's* loves the process. We have discovered most of our closely held opinions to be either wrong or, at best, not totally accurate, and that kitchen testing almost always leads to unexpected places. We have come to love the journey itself, not just the end result, and enjoy sharing our discoveries with readers. We also test and rate cookware, foods, and cookbooks in our pages, and, because we do not accept advertising, we can share our honest results with you.

Our hope is that you not only find the recipes in this book appealing and trustworthy but that you enjoy reading about the process: why we brine turkey and chicken before roasting or grilling, why we chose one baking chocolate over another, or why cake flour is preferred to all-purpose for a particular cake or cookie. This is not just a collection of recipes but a collection of investigations into the very heart of cooking, an exploration of what makes one recipe better than another.

If you enjoy this approach to cooking, you can contact us at **www.cooksillustrated.com** to purchase a subscription or one of our other books or just to say hello.

Christopher Kimball
Editor and Publisher
Cook's Illustrated

1

SOUPS

TWO KINDS OF SOUP ARE EXAMINED IN THIS chapter—soups that rely on homemade chicken or beef stock and soups that are made with water or canned broth. How do you know which soups should be made with homemade stock and which can be made successfully with canned broth or water?

In general, we find that brothy soups with few ingredients must be made with homemade stock. Chicken noodle soup made with canned broth is not nearly as good as the same soup made with homemade stock. To save time and work, we have developed recipes for chicken and beef stock that also yield meat that can be used in soups.

On the other hand, we find that soups with complex seasonings (such as Asian noodle soups loaded with fish sauce and ginger) or soups with richly flavored ingredients (such as onion soup with caramelized onions and cheese croutons) can be made with canned broth or water. In these cases, we have successfully devised methods for punching up the flavor of the liquid. Of course, you can use homemade stock in these recipes. However, when we find that the quality of a soup made without homemade stock is quite high, we are happy to take this shortcut.

CHICKEN STOCK

MOST STANDARD CHICKEN STOCKS ARE NOT flavorful enough for a robust chicken soup. They are fine if ladled into risotto, but we wanted a broth that really tastes like chicken. We knew that the conventional method—simmering chicken parts and aromatics, such as onions, carrots, and celery, in water for hours—was part of the problem. This method takes too long (at least three hours) to extract flavor from the chicken. We wanted to see if we could do better, and in less time.

We tried blanching a whole chicken under the theory that blanching keeps the chicken from releasing foam during cooking. The blanched chicken was then partially covered with water and placed in a heatproof bowl over a pan of simmering water. Cooked this way, the chicken never simmered, and the resulting broth was remarkably clear, refined, and full-flavored. The only problem: it took four hours

for the broth to take on sufficient flavor. We also noted that our four-pound chicken was good for nothing but the garbage bin after being cooked for so long.

A number of recipes promote roasting chicken bones or parts and then using them to make stock. The theory, at least, is that roasted parts will flavor stock in minutes, not hours. We gave it a try several times, roasting chicken backs, necks, and bones—with and without vegetables. We preferred the roasted stock with vegetables, but the actual chicken flavor was too tame.

Finally, we tried a method described by Edna Lewis in her book *In Pursuit of Flavor* (Knopf, 1988). She sautés a chicken that's been hacked into small pieces with an onion until the chicken loses its raw color. The pot is then covered and the chicken and onion cook over low heat until they release their rich, flavorful juices, which takes about 20 minutes. Only at that point is the water added, and the broth is simmered for just 20 minutes longer.

We knew we were onto something as we smelled the chicken and onions sautéing, and the finished broth confirmed what our noses had detected. The broth tasted pleasantly sautéed, not boiled. We had some refining to do, though. For once, we had made too strong a broth.

We substituted chicken backs and wing tips for the whole chicken and used more water. The broth was less intense, but just the right strength to make a base for some of the best chicken soup we've ever tasted. We made the stock twice more—once without the onion and once with onion, celery, and carrot. The onion added a flavor dimension we liked; the extra vegetables neither added nor detracted from the final soup, so we left them out.

After much trial and error, we had a master recipe that delivered liquid gold in just 40 minutes. While this recipe requires more hands-on work (hacking up parts, browning an onion, then chicken parts), it is ready in a fraction of the time required to make stock by traditional methods.

So where do you find the useless chicken parts necessary for this stock? The Buffalo chicken wing fad has made wings more expensive than legs and thighs. For those who can buy chicken backs, this is clearly an inexpensive way to make stock for soup.

Our local grocery store usually sells them for almost nothing, but in many locations they may be difficult to find.

Luckily, we found that relatively inexpensive whole legs make incredibly full-flavored broths for soup. In a side-by-side comparison of a stock made from backs and from whole legs, we found the whole leg broth was actually more full-flavored than the all-bone stock. Just don't try to salvage the meat from the legs. After 5 minutes of sautéing, 20 minutes of sweating, and another 20 minutes of simmering, the meat is void of flavor.

If you are making a soup that needs some chicken meat, use a whole chicken as directed in the recipe Chicken Stock with Sautéed Breast Meat. The breast is removed in two pieces, sautéed briefly, and then added with the water to finish cooking. The rest of the bird—the legs, back, wings, and giblets—is sweated with the onions and discarded when the stock is done. However, the breast meat is perfectly cooked, ready to be skinned and shredded when cool. We particularly liked the tidiness of this method: one chicken yields one pot of soup.

One note about this method. We found it necessary to cut the chicken into pieces small enough to release their flavorful juices in a short period of time. A meat cleaver, a heavy-duty chef's knife, or a pair of heavy-duty kitchen shears makes the task fairly simple. Cutting up the chicken for stock doesn't require precision. The point is to get the pieces small enough to release their flavorful juices in a short period of time.

To cut up a whole chicken, start by removing the whole legs and wings from the body; set them aside. Separate the back from the breast, then split the breast and set the halves aside. Hack the back crosswise into three or four pieces, then halve each of these pieces. Cut the wing at each joint to yield three pieces. Leave the wing tip whole, then halve each of the remaining joints. Because of their larger bones, the legs and thighs are most difficult to cut. Start by splitting the leg and thigh at the joint, then hack each to yield three to four pieces.

Master Recipe for Chicken Stock

MAKES ABOUT 2 QUARTS

A cleaver will quickly cut up the chicken parts, although a chef's knife or kitchen shears will work, albeit more slowly.

1	tablespoon vegetable oil
1	medium onion, cut into medium dice
4	pounds chicken backs and wing tips or whole legs, hacked with cleaver into 2-inch pieces
2	quarts boiling water
2	teaspoons salt
2	bay leaves

1. Heat oil in large stock pot or soup kettle. Add onion; sauté until colored and softened slightly, 2 to 3 minutes. Transfer onion to large bowl.

2. Add half of chicken pieces to pot; sauté until no longer pink, 4 to 5 minutes. Transfer cooked chicken to bowl with onion. Sauté remaining chicken pieces. Return onion and chicken pieces to pot. Reduce heat to low, cover, and cook until chicken releases its juices, about 20 minutes.

3. Increase heat to high; add boiling water, salt, and bay leaves. Return to simmer, then cover and barely simmer until broth is rich and flavorful, about 20 minutes.

4. Strain broth and discard solids. Skim fat and reserve for later use in soups or other recipes, if desired. (Broth can be covered and refrigerated up to 2 days or frozen for several months.)

➤ VARIATION
Chicken Stock with Sautéed Breast Meat

Choose this broth when you want to have some breast meat to add to soup. This recipe starts with a whole chicken, rather than just backs or legs.

1	tablespoon vegetable oil
1	whole chicken (about 3½ pounds), breast removed, split, and reserved; remaining chicken hacked with cleaver into 2-inch pieces
1	medium onion, cut into medium dice
2	quarts boiling water
2	teaspoons salt
2	bay leaves

1. Heat oil in large stock pot or soup kettle. When oil shimmers and starts to smoke, add chicken breast halves; sauté until brown on both sides, about 5 minutes. Remove chicken breast pieces and set aside. Add onion to the pot; sauté until colored and softened slightly, 2 to 3 minutes. Transfer onion to large bowl.

2. Add half of chicken pieces to pot; sauté until no longer pink, 4 to 5 minutes. Transfer cooked chicken to bowl with onion. Sauté remaining chicken pieces. Return onion and chicken pieces (excluding breasts) to pot. Reduce heat to low, cover, and cook until chicken releases its juices, about 20 minutes.

3. Increase heat to high; add boiling water, chicken breasts, salt, and bay leaves. Return to simmer, then cover and barely simmer until chicken breasts are cooked through and broth is rich and flavorful, about 20 minutes.

4. Remove chicken breasts from pot; when cool enough to handle, remove skin from breasts, then remove meat from bones and shred into bite-sized pieces; discard skin and bone. Strain broth into separate container and discard solids. Skim fat and reserve for later use in soups or other recipes. (The shredded chicken and broth can be covered and refrigerated separately up to 2 days.)

Chicken Noodle Soup

SERVES 6 TO 8

Once we figured out how to make good chicken stock (see page 14), making chicken noodle soup was incredibly easy.

2	tablespoons chicken fat (reserved from making stock) or vegetable oil
I	medium onion, cut into medium dice
I	large carrot, peeled and sliced ¼-inch thick
I	celery stalk, sliced ¼-inch thick
½	teaspoon dried thyme leaves
I	recipe Chicken Stock with Sautéed Breast Meat (page 15)
2	cups (3 ounces) wide egg noodles
¼	cup minced fresh parsley leaves
	Ground black pepper

1. Heat chicken fat in soup kettle over medium-high heat. Add onion, carrot, and celery; sauté until softened, about 5 minutes. Add thyme, along with stock and shredded chicken meat; simmer until vegetables are tender and flavors meld, 10 to 15 minutes.

2. Add noodles and cook until just tender, about 5 minutes. Stir in parsley and pepper to taste, adjust seasonings, and serve.

➤ VARIATIONS

Chicken Soup with Orzo and Spring Vegetables

Follow recipe for Chicken Noodle Soup, replacing onion with 1 medium leek, rinsed thoroughly, quartered lengthwise, then sliced thin crosswise. Substitute ½ cup orzo for egg noodles. Along with orzo, add ¼ pound trimmed asparagus, cut into 1-inch lengths, and ¼ cup fresh or frozen peas. Substitute 2 tablespoons minced fresh tarragon leaves for parsley.

Chicken Soup with Shells, Tomatoes, and Zucchini

Follow recipe for Chicken Noodle Soup, adding 1 medium zucchini, cut into medium dice, along with onion, carrot and celery, and increase sautéing time to 7 minutes. Add ½ cup chopped tomatoes (fresh or canned) along with stock. Substitute 1 cup small shells or macaroni for egg noodles and simmer until noodles are cooked, about 10 minutes. Substitute an equal portion of fresh basil for parsley. Serve with grated Parmesan, if you like.

BEEF STOCK

BEEF STOCK SHOULD TASTE LIKE BEEF—ALMOST as intense as pot roast jus or beef stew broth—and be flavorful enough to need only a few vegetables and a handful of noodles or barley to make a good soup. We didn't want a broth that demanded a trip to the butcher, nor did we want to spend all day making it.

We began our testing by making a traditional stock using four pounds of beef bones fortified with a generous two pounds of beef, as well as celery, carrot, onion, tomato, and fresh thyme, all covered with four quarts of water. Our plan was to taste the stock after 4, 6, 8, 12, and 16 hours of simmering.

At hours 4, 6, and even 8, our stock was weak and

tasted mostly of vegetables. And while the texture of the 12- and 16-hour stocks was richly gelatinous, the flavors of vegetables and bones (not beef) predominated. Not willing to give up on this method quite yet, we found a recipe that instructed us to roast and then simmer beef bones, onions, and tomatoes—no celery and carrots—for 12 hours. During the last three hours of cooking, three pounds of beef were added to the pot. This, we thought, could be our ideal—a stock with great body from the bones, minimal vegetable flavor, and generous hunks of beef to enhance the rich, reduced stock. Once again, however, the stock was beautifully textured, but with very little flavor; the vegetal taste was gone, but there was no real, deep beef flavor in its place. Time to move on.

Knowing now that it was going to take more meat than bones to get great flavor, we started our next set of tests by making broths with different cuts of meat, including chuck, shank, round, arm blade, oxtail, and short ribs. We browned two pounds of meat and one pound of small marrowbones (or three pounds bone-in cuts like shank, short ribs, and oxtails), along with an onion. We covered the browned ingredients and let them "sweat" for 20 minutes. We added only a quart of water to each pot and simmered them until the meat in each pot was done.

With so little added water, these broths were more braise-like than broth-like. But because more traditional methods yielded bland broths, we decided to start with the flavor we were looking for and add water from there.

After a 1½-hour simmer, our broths were done, most tasting unmistakably beefy. Upon a blind tasting of each, we all agreed that the shank broth was our favorite, followed by the marrowbone-enhanced brisket and chuck. Not only was the broth rich, beefy, and full of body, the shank meat was soft and gelatinous, perfect for shredding and adding to a pot of soup. Because it appeared that our broth was going to require a generous amount of meat, brisket's high price ($3.99 per pound compared with $1.99 for both the shank and chuck) knocked it out of the running.

Though not yet perfect, this broth was on its way to fulfilling our requirements. First, it didn't require a trip to the butcher. It could be made from common supermarket cuts like shank, chuck, and marrowbones. Second, it didn't take all day. This broth was done in about two and one-half hours and was full-flavored as soon as the meat was tender. Unlike traditional stocks, which require a roasting pan, stock pot, oven, and burner, this was a one-pot, stove top-only affair. Finally, this broth didn't require a cornucopia of vegetables to make it taste good. To us, the more vegetables, the weaker the beef flavor. At this point, our recipe called for one lone onion.

What we sacrificed in vegetables, however, we were apparently going to have to compensate for in meat. Our two pounds of meat were yielding only one quart of broth. But now that we had a flavor we liked, we decided to see if we could achieve an equally beefy broth with less meat.

To stretch the meat a bit further, we increased the amount of meat and bones by 50 percent and doubled the amount of water. Unfortunately, the extra water diluted the meat flavor, and though this broth was better than many we had tried, we missed the strong beef flavor of our original formula. To intensify flavor, we tried adding a pound of ground beef to the three pounds of meat, thinking we would throw away the spent meat during straining. But ground beef only fattened up the broth, and its distinctive hamburger flavor muddied the waters. Also, fried ground beef does not brown well, and this burger-enhanced broth confirmed that browning not only deepened the color but beefed up the flavor as well.

We went back to the original proportions, doubling both the meat and bones as well as the water. Not surprisingly, the broth was deeply colored, richly flavored, and full-bodied. We were finally convinced that a good beef broth requires a generous portion of meat. Though our broth required more meat than was necessary for the soup, the leftover beef was delicious, good for sandwiches and cold salads.

At this point our richly flavored broth needed enlivening. Some broth recipes accomplished this with a splash of vinegar, others with tomato. Although we liked tomatoes in many of the soups we developed, they didn't do much for our broth. And although vinegar was an improvement, red wine made the broth even better. We ultimately fortified our broth with a modest one-half cup of red wine, adding it to the kettle after browning the meat.

We had followed our method for making chicken broth without giving it much thought—browning then sweating a generous portion of meat and bones, adding water just to cover, and simmering for a relatively short time. We knew the ratio of meat to water was right, but we questioned whether sweating the meat for 20 minutes before adding the water was really a necessary step. Side-by-side tests proved that sweating the meat did result in a richer-flavored broth. Moreover, the sweated meat and bones did not release foamy scum, thus eliminating the need to skim.

After much testing, we came to this inescapable conclusion: If you want to make beef soup right, you just can't skimp on the meat.

Master Recipe for Rich Beef Stock

MAKES SCANT 2 QUARTS

If using shanks for your broth, cut the meat away from the bone in the largest possible pieces. Both meat and bones contribute flavor to the final product. You only need half of the meat for use either any of the soup recipes that follow. Refrigerate the remaining meat in an airtight container and use it in sandwiches or cold salads.

2	tablespoons vegetable oil
6	pounds of shank, meat cut from bone in large chunks, or 4 pounds chuck and 2 pounds of small marrowbones
1	large onion, halved
½	cup dry red wine
½	teaspoon salt

1. Heat 1 tablespoon oil in a large soup kettle or Dutch oven over medium-high heat; brown meat, bones, and onion halves on all sides in batches, making sure not to overcrowd the pan, and adding additional oil to the pan if necessary. Remove kettle contents and set aside. Add red wine to empty kettle; cook until reduced to a syrup, 1 to 2 minutes. Return browned bones, meat, and onion to kettle. Reduce heat to low, then cover and sweat meat and onion until they have released about ¾ cup dark, very intensely flavored liquid, about 20 minutes. Increase heat to medium-high, add 2 quarts water

and salt; bring to a simmer, reduce heat to very low, partially cover, and barely simmer until meat is tender, 1½ to 2 hours.

2. Strain broth, discard bones and onion, and set meat aside, reserving half of the meat for other use. (At this point, broth and remaining meat that will be used in soup can be cooled to room temperature and covered and refrigerated up to 5 days.) Let broth stand until fat rises to the top; skim and discard fat. When the meat is cool enough to handle, shred into bite-sized pieces for use in soup recipe.

SCIENCE: So Much Beef, So Little Broth

Before we actually began testing, we would not have believed how much meat was required to make a rich, beefy-flavored broth. Why, we wondered, did a good beef soup require six pounds of beef and bones when a mere three-pound chicken could beautifully flavor the same size pot of soup?

Though we had always thought of beef as the heartier-flavored meat, we began to understand chicken's strength when making broths for this soup. In one of our time-saving beef broth experiments, we used the four pounds of beef called for in the recipe, but substituted two pounds of quicker-cooking hacked-up chicken bones for the beef bones. The result was surprising. Even with twice as much meaty beef as chicken bones, the chicken flavor predominated.

So what's happening here? Appearances aside, the flavor compounds in chicken are very strong, possibly stronger than those of beef. It's the browning or searing that contributes much of the robust beefy flavor to a good steak or stew. (Think how bland boiled beef tastes.) Skin and bones may be another reason why less chicken is required to flavor a broth. Chicken skin, predominantly fat, tastes like the animal. Beef fat, on the other hand, tastes "rich," but not beefy, as evidenced by French fries cooked in beef tallow. In addition, chicken bones, filled with rich, dark marrow, also contribute flavor. Beef bones, on the other hand, lend incredible body to stocks and broths, but their flavor is predominantly and unmistakably that of bone, not of beef.

Finally, according to the U.S. Department of Agriculture, chicken contains more water than beef—61 percent in chuck compared with 77 percent in drumsticks and 73 to 74 percent for wings and backs. This means that when simmered, chicken is releasing 11 to 16 percent more liquid—and flavor—into the pot.

Beef Noodle Soup

SERVES 6

Our beef stock is the basis of this quick noodle soup.

1	tablespoon vegetable oil
1	medium onion, cut into medium dice
2	medium carrots, cut into medium dice
1	celery stalk, cut into medium dice
½	teaspoon dried thyme or 1½ teaspoons minced fresh thyme leaves
½	cup canned tomatoes, cut into medium dice
1	recipe Rich Beef Stock, strained and skimmed of fat, and 2 cups meat shredded into bite-sized pieces
2	cups (3 ounces) wide egg noodles
¼	cup minced fresh parsley leaves
	Salt and ground black pepper

1. Heat oil over medium-high heat in a soup kettle or Dutch oven. Add onion, carrots, and celery; sauté until softened, about 5 minutes. Add thyme and tomatoes, then beef broth and meat; bring to simmer. Reduce heat to low; simmer until vegetables are no longer crunchy and flavors have blended, about 15 minutes.

2. Add noodles; simmer until fully cooked, about 5 minutes longer. Stir in parsley, adjust seasonings, including salt and pepper to taste, and serve.

➤ VARIATION

Beef Barley Soup with Mushrooms and Thyme

2	tablespoons vegetable oil
1	medium onion, cut into medium dice
2	medium carrots, cut into medium dice
12	ounces domestic or wild mushrooms, stems removed, wiped clean, and sliced thin
½	teaspoon dried thyme or 1½ teaspoons minced fresh thyme leaves
½	cup canned tomatoes, cut into medium dice
1	recipe Rich Beef Stock, strained and skimmed of fat, and 2 cups meat shredded into bite-sized pieces
½	cup pearl barley
¼	cup minced fresh parsley leaves
	Salt and ground black pepper

Heat oil over medium-high heat in a soup kettle or Dutch oven. Add onion and carrots; sauté until almost soft, 3 to 4 minutes. Add mushrooms; sauté until softened and liquid is almost completely evaporated, 4 to 5 minutes longer. Add thyme and tomatoes, then beef broth, meat, and barley; bring to simmer. Reduce heat to low; simmer until barley is just tender, 45 to 50 minutes. Stir in parsley, adjust seasonings, including salt and pepper to taste, and serve.

FRENCH ONION SOUP

MAKING TRADITIONAL FRENCH ONION SOUP is easily a two-day affair, one day making the beef stock and another toiling over the onions to finish the soup. And there's no guarantee that it will turn out right. We had many crocks of flavorless onions floating in hypersalty beef bouillon and topped with globs of greasy melted cheese. We also had weak, watery soups. French onion soup should have a dark, rich broth, intensely flavored by a plethora of seriously cooked onions, covered by a crouton that is broth-soaked beneath and cheesy and crusty on top.

The first obstacle to success is the broth. This soup is most commonly made with homemade beef stock. If the right stock is used (see our Master Recipe for Rich Beef Stock on page 18), the results can be delicious. But making beef stock takes at least three hours. We wondered if there was a way to get around this step.

We tested soups made with chicken stock, both homemade (which takes considerably less time to prepare than beef stock) and canned. Both were, well, too chicken-y and just not right. Soups made with canned beef broth were terrible. Canned beef broth does not have enough flavor to carry the day alone. After experimentation, we devised a formula for what we call "cheater" broth. By combining canned beef and chicken broths with red wine (the secret ingredient here), we came up with a broth that has enough good, rich flavor to make an excellent soup base.

The next obvious step was to examine the onion factor. After a crying game of slicing many onions of several varieties and then sautéing away, we found Vidalias to be disappointingly bland and boring, white onions to be candy-sweet and one-dimensional, and yellow onions to be only mildly flavorful, with just a slight sweetness. Red onions ranked supreme. They were intensely onion-y, sweet but not cloying, with subtle complexity and nuance.

It was exasperating that the onions took so long—nearly an hour—to caramelize. On top of that, they required frequent stirring to keep them from sticking to the bottom of the pot and burning. We found that adding salt to the onions as they began to cook helped draw out some of the water and shaved about 10 minutes off the cooking time. But we wondered if it was necessary for the onions to be so caramelized. We tried, as one recipe suggested, sautéing them until just softened and colored, but they didn't brown enough to contribute much flavor to the soup. Maybe, we thought, a vigorous sauté over high heat to achieve deep browning might do the trick. Not so. Onions cooked that way did not lose enough liquid and made the soup watery and bland. Besides, there is something wrong with onions in onion soup that have even an iota of crunch. We also tried roasting the onions, thinking that the even, constant heat of the oven might be the answer. Wrong again. Going in and out of the oven to stir the onions is an incredible hassle.

It was inattentiveness that caused us to let the drippings in the pot of a batch of onions go a little too far. The onions themselves weren't thoroughly caramelized, but all the goo stuck on the pot was.

We were sure that the finished soup would taste burnt, but we were surprised to find that it was, in fact, as sweet, rich, and flavorful as the soups we had been making with fully caramelized onions. To refine the technique we had stumbled on, we decided that medium-high heat was the way to go and that the drippings should be very, very deeply browned. There's no way around frequent stirring, but this method cut about another 10 minutes off the onion-cooking time, bringing it down to just over 30 minutes.

With all those wonderful, tasty drippings stuck on the bottom of the pot, the deglazing process of adding the liquid and scraping up all the browned bits is crucial. Once the broth is added to the onions, we found that a simmering time of 20 minutes is needed to allow the onion flavor to permeate the broth and for the flavors to meld.

Many French onion soup recipes call for herbs. A couple of sprigs of fresh parsley, some thyme, and a bay leaf simmered in the soup rounded out the flavors and imparted freshness. We also tried just a smidgen of garlic, but its flavor is far too distinct in a soup where onions should take center stage.

Finally, we tried a little flour as a thickener, stirring it into the onions after they were cooked. It added body to the soup, but it also bogged down its flavor and muddied its appearance, just as we thought it would. The soup was excellent without it. Having

SCIENCE: Cry Me A River

Every now and then, something will prompt you to think of a particular song. In the *Cook's* test kitchen, that something occurred every time we had to slice another batch of onions for another pot of soup, and the song that came to mind, of course, was Arthur Hamilton's "Cry Me a River." As we started humming it for the umpteenth time, we began to wonder if we could change our tune to Johnny Nash's "I Can See Clearly Now."

Over the past couple of years, we have compiled more than 20 ideas from reader correspondence, books, and conversations with colleagues all aimed at reducing our tears while cutting onions. What better time than now, we thought, to put all those ideas to the test?

The problem, it turns out, is caused by the sulfuric compounds in onions. When an onion is cut, the cells that are damaged in the process release sulfuric compounds as well as various enzymes, notably one called sulfoxide lyase. Those compounds, which are separated in the onion's cell structure, activate and mix to form the real culprit, a volatile new compound called thiopropanal sulfoxide. When thiopropanal sulfoxide evaporates into the air, it irritates the eyes, causing us to cry.

The two general methods that we found worked best were to protect our eyes by covering them with goggles or contact lenses or to introduce a flame near the cut onions. The goggles and contact lenses form a physical barrier that keeps the gases from irritating our eyes. The flame, which can be produced by either a lit candle or a gas burner, changes the activity of the thiopropanal sulfoxide by completely oxidizing it.

arrived at a soup that was rich, well-balanced, and full of fabulous onion flavor, it was time to move on to the crouton and the cheese, much to our tasters' delight.

Some recipes call for placing the crouton in the bottom of the bowl and ladling the soup over it. We disagree. We opt to set the crouton on top, so that only its bottom side is moistened with broth while its top side is crusted with cheese. The crouton can then physically support the cheese and prevent it from sinking into the soup. To keep as much cheese as possible on the surface, we found it best to use two croutons, instead of only one, to completely fill the mouth of the bowl. A baguette can be cut on the bias as necessary to secure the closest fit in the bowl.

Traditionally, French onion soup is topped with Swiss, Gruyère, or Emmentaler. We also ventured across the border to try Parmesan, Asiago, mozzarella, and fontina. Plain Swiss cheese was neither outstanding nor offensive. It was gooey, bubbly, and mild in characteristic Swiss flavor. Both Gruyère and Emmentaler melted to perfection and were sweet, nutty, and faintly tangy, but they also were very strong and pungent, overwhelming many tasters' palettes. We surprised ourselves by favoring the subdued Italian Asiago. Its flavor, like that of Gruyère and Emmentaler, was sweet and nutty, but without the pungent quality. Parmesan, too, was good, with a pleasant sweetness and saltiness, but without the nuttiness of Asiago. The big losers were mozzarella and fontina. The first was extremely bland, too chewy, rubbery, and suggestive of pizza topping; the latter was very soft, almost wet and slippery, with no distinctive character.

Both Asiago and Parmesan are dry, not "melting," cheeses, so although we were leaning toward them in flavor, we were left wanting in texture. The obvious answer was to combine cheeses. We tried a layer of Swiss topped with a grating of Asiago. A winning combination, hands down, of chewy goodness and nutty sweetness.

The final coup that weakens knees and makes French onion soup irresistible is a browned, bubbly, molten cheese crust. The quickest way to brown the cheese is to set the bowls on a baking sheet under the broiler, so heat-safe bowls are essential. Bowls or crocks with handles make maneuvering easier. This is no soup for fine china.

French Onion Soup

SERVES 6

For a soup that is resplendent with deep, rich flavors, use 8 cups of Rich Beef Stock (page 18) in place of the canned chicken and beef broths and red wine. Tie the parsley and thyme sprigs together with kitchen twine so they will be easy to retrieve from the soup pot. Slicing the baguette on the bias will yield slices shaped to fill the mouths of the bowls.

FOR THE SOUP

- 2 tablespoons unsalted butter
- 5 medium red onions (about 3 pounds), sliced thin
-    Salt
- 6 cups low-sodium canned chicken broth
- 1¾ cups low-sodium canned beef broth
- ¼ cup dry red wine
- 2 sprigs fresh parsley
- 1 sprig fresh thyme
- 1 bay leaf
- 1 tablespoon balsamic vinegar
-    Ground black pepper

FOR THE CHEESE-TOPPED CRUST

- 1 baguette, cut on the bias into ¾-inch slices (2 slices per serving)
- 4½ ounces Swiss cheese, sliced ¹/₁₆ inch thick
- 3 ounces Asiago cheese, grated

1. FOR THE SOUP: Melt butter in large soup kettle or Dutch oven over medium-high heat; add sliced onions and ½ teaspoon salt and stir to coat onions thoroughly with butter. Cook, stirring frequently, until onions are reduced and syrupy and inside of pot is coated with very deep brown crust, 30 to 35 minutes. Stir in the chicken and beef broths, red wine, parsley, thyme, and bay leaf, scraping pot bottom with wooden spoon to loosen browned bits, and bring to simmer. Simmer to blend flavors, about 20 minutes, and discard herbs. Stir in balsamic vinegar and adjust seasonings with salt and pepper. (Can be cooled to room temperature and refrigerated in airtight container up to 2 days; return to simmer before finishing soup with croutons and cheese).

2. FOR THE CRUST: Adjust oven rack to upper-

middle position; heat broiler. Set serving bowls on baking sheet; fill each with about 1½ cups soup. Top each bowl with two baguette slices and divide Swiss cheese slices, placing them in a single layer, if possible, on bread. Sprinkle with about 2 tablespoons grated Asiago cheese and broil until well-browned and bubbly, about 10 minutes. Cool 5 minutes and serve.

SCIENCE: Blue Onion Soup?

Red onions may be the best choice in terms of flavor, but they can turn the soup an unappetizing bluish-gray color. This is because they contain anthocyanin, a water-soluble pigment that also causes red cabbage to discolor when cooked. This pigment is present in some other reddish fruits and vegetables as well, such as cherries and radishes.

When the fruit or vegetable is cooked in liquid, the anthocyanin leaches out. If the liquid is alkaline (as is the case with our soup), the anthocyanin becomes blue. Adding some acid, either lemon juice or vinegar, to the soup at the end helps it to regain its reddish color. This may sound improbable, but when we stirred in one tablespoon of balsamic vinegar, the soup returned to a deep reddish brown. The vinegar also brightens the flavors in the soup.

HAM AND SPLIT PEA SOUP

OLD-FASHIONED RECIPES FOR HAM AND SPLIT pea soup start with the bone from a large roast ham that has been nearly picked clean. The bone and some split peas are thrown in a pot with some water and cooked until the meat falls off the bone. By that time, the fat has discreetly melted into the broth, and the peas have become creamy enough to thicken the soup.

We love split pea soup made with ham broth, but times have changed. Except for the occasional holiday, most cooks rarely buy a bone-in ham, opting more often for the thin-sliced deli meat. We wondered if we could duplicate this wonderful soup without buying a huge ham.

To confirm or disprove our belief that ham broth is crucial to split pea soup, we made several pork broths and pork-enhanced canned chicken broths. In addition to making broth the old-fashioned way

from a meaty ham bone, we made broths from smoked pork necks, pork hocks (fresh and smoked), and smoked ham shanks. We also made cheater broths: kielbasa simmered in canned chicken broth, kielbasa simmered in water, bacon simmered in chicken broth, and bacon simmered in water.

Broths made with hocks—fresh as well as smoked—were more greasy than flavorful. In addition, the hocks gave up very little meat, making it necessary to purchase an additional portion of ham to fortify the soup. Ham shanks, which include the hock, made a pleasant but lightweight broth that was a tad greasy and salty—both fixable problems had the broth been stellar. Pork necks, which are not widely available, made a fairly flavorful but salty broth. All four cheater broths failed. Both the kielbasa- and bacon-enhanced chicken broths tasted strongly of overly processed meat, while the water-based versions tasted weak.

Not surprisingly, the broth made from the bone of a big ham was the winner. It was meaty and full-flavored, rich but not greasy, nicely seasoned without being overly salty, and smoky without tasting artificial. Unlike any of the other broths, this one sported bits of meat. And not just good meat—*great* meat. The tender pieces of ham that fell away from the bone during cooking were not just a nice byproduct of the broth. They were the glory of our split pea soup.

But was there a way around buying half a ham (with an average weight of about 8 pounds) just to make a pot of soup?

After checking out the ham and smoked pork cases at several different stores, we discovered the picnic from the pork shoulder. Unlike what we generally refer to as ham, which comes from the back legs of the animal, the picnic comes from the shoulder and front legs. Smaller than a ham, the half-picnic weighs only 4½ pounds. After making a couple more pots of soup, we found that the picnic pork shoulder—with its bones, fat, rind, and meat—made outstanding stock, and after two hours of simmering, the meat was meltingly tender yet still potently flavorful.

Since we did not need the full picnic half for our pot of soup, we pulled off and roasted two of its meatier muscles and used the remaining meat, bone, fat, and rind to make the soup. At around 99 cents a pound, a picnic shoulder is usually cheaper than a ham, and often cheaper than pork hocks, shanks, and neck bones as well. Here, we thought, was the modern solution. Rather than buy a ham for eating (and eating and eating) with a leftover bone for soup, instead purchase a picnic for soup, and roast the remaining couple of pounds for eating.

There are several ways to make ham and split pea soup. You can throw all the ingredients—ham bone, peas, and diced vegetables—into a pot and simmer until everything is tender. Or you can sauté the vegetables, then add the remaining ingredients and cook the soup until the ham and peas are tender. Alternatively, you can cook the ham bone and peas (or give the ham bone a little bit of a head start) until ham and peas are tender and then add raw, sautéed, or caramelized vegetables to the pot, continuing to cook until the vegetables are tender and the flavors have blended.

Although we had hoped to keep the soup a straightforward one-pot operation, we found out pretty quickly that dumping everything in at the same time resulted in gloppy, overcooked peas and tired, mushy vegetables by the time the ham was tender. For textural contrast in this smooth, creamy soup, we ultimately preferred fully—not overly—cooked vegetables.

Our best soups were those in which the vegetables spent enough time in the pot for their flavors to blend but not so long that they had lost all of their individual taste. Of the soups with vegetables added toward the end of cooking, we preferred the one with the caramelized vegetables. The sweeter vegetables gave this otherwise straightforward meat and starch soup a richness and depth of flavor that made the extra step and pan worth the trouble.

Many pea soup recipes call for an acidic ingredient—vinegar, lemon juice, fortified wines such as sherry or Madeira, Worcestershire sauce, or sour cream—to bring balance to an otherwise rich, heavy soup. After tasting all of the above, we found ourselves drawn to balsamic vinegar. Unlike any of the other ingredients, balsamic vinegar's mildly sweet, mildly acidic flavor perfectly complemented the soup.

Ham and Split Pea Soup
SERVES 6

Use a small 2½-pound smoked picnic portion ham if you can find one. Otherwise, buy a half-picnic ham and remove some meat, which you can save for use in sandwiches, salads, or omelets.

1	piece (about 2½ pounds) smoked, bone-in picnic ham
4	bay leaves
1	pound (2½ cups) split peas, rinsed and picked through
1	teaspoon dried thyme
2	tablespoons extra-virgin olive oil
2	medium onions, chopped medium
2	medium carrots, chopped medium
2	medium celery stalks, chopped medium
1	tablespoon butter
2	medium garlic cloves, minced
	Pinch sugar
3	small new potatoes, scrubbed and cut into medium dice
	Ground black pepper
	Minced red onion (optional)
	Balsamic vinegar

1. Bring 3 quarts water, ham, and bay leaves to boil, covered, over medium-high heat in large soup kettle. Reduce heat to low and simmer until meat is tender and pulls away from bone, 2 to 2½ hours. Remove ham meat and bone from broth; add split peas and thyme and simmer until peas are tender but not dissolved, about 45 minutes. Meanwhile, when ham is cool enough to handle, shred meat into bite-sized pieces and set aside. Discard rind and bone.

2. While ham is simmering, heat oil in large skillet over high heat until shimmering. Add onions, carrots, and celery; sauté, stirring frequently, until most of the liquid evaporates and vegetables begin to brown, 5 to 6 minutes. Reduce heat to medium-low; add butter, garlic, and sugar. Cook vegetables, stirring frequently, until deeply browned, 30 to 35 minutes; set aside.

3. Add sautéed vegetables, potatoes, and shredded ham to soup; simmer until potatoes are tender and peas dissolve and thicken soup to the consistency of

light cream, about 20 minutes more. Season with ground black pepper. Ladle soup into bowls, sprinkle with red onion, if using, and serve, passing balsamic vinegar separately.

> VARIATION

Ham and Split Pea Soup with Caraway
Toast 1½ teaspoons caraway seeds in a small skillet over medium-high heat, stirring frequently, until fragrant and browned, about 4 minutes. Follow recipe for Ham and Split Pea Soup, substituting toasted caraway seeds for dried thyme.

PUREED VEGETABLE SOUPS WITHOUT CREAM

WE ENJOY THE SMOOTH, SILKY TEXTURE OF creamed vegetable soups, but we often find the flavor to be lacking. The dairy elements (usually lots of butter and cream) mask the taste of the vegetables. Instead of an intense carrot flavor in a creamy base, for example, we usually taste cream with carrots in the background.

We wanted to see if there was a way to make a pureed soup that tasted more like vegetables. We wanted a creamy carrot soup reminiscent of the sweetest carrots, a broccoli soup that really had the flavor of broccoli. However, we were not willing to sacrifice anything in terms of consistency. Pureed vegetable soups must be silky. Otherwise there is no point in pureeing them.

Cream soups usually begin in one of two ways. The first method calls for making a white sauce (flour cooked in butter and lightened with milk or cream) and then adding vegetables and more dairy. In addition to the dairy products, the vegetables must compete with the flour, which can sometimes give these soups a gummy or starchy quality.

We wanted to experiment with this technique further and decided to use carrots as our model and then test other vegetables once we had developed a basic recipe. We started out with other starches (cornstarch and potato starch) but found the results to be similar to soups made with flour. The texture was still too thick and gummy, and the vegetables were not the primary flavor. We had also seen recipes using potatoes or rice as thickeners, usually cooked right along with the vegetables in broth. When we tried this, though, the potatoes and rice detracted from the carrot flavor and caused the color of the soup to fade.

The second classic technique for making cream soups begins by sautéing vegetables, adding some broth and seasonings, and finally adding cream, which is then cooked down to create the proper texture. We found that the elimination of the starch improved the texture of the soup, but the dairy component still dominated. We liked the idea of starting with the vegetables, though it seemed to us that the best idea might be to use a larger quantity of vegetables and puree them for texture.

Most recipes for pureed vegetable soup use equal amounts of vegetables and liquid, or in some cases slightly more liquid than vegetables. We decided to alter this ratio in a big way and cook four cups of carrots in two cups of stock. We figured we would get more vegetable flavor and could use the vegetables themselves as a thickener.

This change resulted in an immediate improvement. By the time the vegetables were cooked, the mixture was thick enough to create a puree with good body. In fact, the pureed carrots and broth were actually a little too thick. Instead of adding cream to the vegetables as they cooked, we now needed to add cream to the blender to thin out the pureed carrots.

We used about one cup of cream to get the right consistency, but this was too much dairy fat for our tastes. Next we tried substituting half-and-half as well as whole and low-fat milk. We found that whole milk provided just the right amount of dairy fat to improve the texture, providing smoothness and a creamy mouthfeel without overwhelming the carrot flavor. Adding skim milk or 2 percent milk was like adding more broth, and not at all satisfying. Half-and-half was good, but a tad too rich.

Now that we had successfully developed a bright orange carrot soup that tasted like good, sweet carrots, we wondered which other vegetables might take to this technique. Watery vegetables refused to work. Mushrooms, for instance, don't have enough fiber and bulk to work as their own thickening agent. Spinach and asparagus are also poor candidates for this technique, which works best with tubers, roots, and hearty winter vegetables.

Pureed Carrot Soup with Nutmeg

SERVES 4 TO 6

Either chicken or vegetable stock can be used in this recipe. Canned broths may be used, if desired. Add enough water to one 14.5-ounce can to make the necessary two cups. If you intend to serve any of these soups cold, use oil; unlike butter, it will not congeal when chilled.

2	tablespoons unsalted butter, extra-virgin olive oil, or vegetable oil
1	medium onion, 3 medium shallots, or 1 medium leek (white and light green parts only), chopped
2	tablespoons dry sherry or white wine
1½	pounds (about 8 medium) carrots, peeled, halved lengthwise, and sliced thin (about 4 cups)
2	cups chicken or vegetable stock
1	teaspoon salt
	Ground white pepper
	Pinch freshly grated nutmeg
1–1¼	cups whole milk
2	teaspoons minced fresh tarragon, mint, chive, or parsley leaves

1. Heat butter or oil in large saucepan over medium-high heat. Add onion; sauté until golden, about 5 minutes. Add sherry and carrots; stir-cook until sherry evaporates, about 30 seconds.

2. Add stock, salt, pepper to taste, and nutmeg to saucepan; bring to boil. Reduce heat to simmer; cover and cook until carrots are tender, about 20 minutes.

3. Ladle carrot mixture into blender. Add 1 cup milk; blend until very smooth. Return soup to saucepan; cook over low heat until warmed through. If soup is too thick, stir in additional milk to thin consistency. Adjust seasonings. (Soup can be refrigerated for 3 days and reheated just before serving.)

4. Ladle soup into individual bowls. Garnish with minced herb and serve immediately.

> VARIATIONS

Pureed Broccoli Soup with Basil

Follow recipe for Pureed Carrot Soup with Nutmeg, replacing carrots with 2 pounds broccoli, stalks discarded and florets cut into bite-sized pieces to yield 5 cups. Omit nutmeg and cook broccoli until tender, about 10 minutes. Thin with ½ to ¾ cup milk and garnish soup with 2 tablespoons minced fresh basil leaves.

Pureed Butternut Squash Soup with Ginger

Follow recipe for Pureed Carrot Soup with Nutmeg, replacing carrots with 1 medium butternut squash (about 2½ pounds), which has been halved, seeded,

---

EQUIPMENT: Blenders

The texture of a pureed soup should be as smooth and creamy as possible. With this in mind, we tried pureeing these soups in a food mill, a food processor, a handheld immersion blender, and a regular countertop blender.

Forget using the food mill for this purpose. We tried all three blades (coarse, medium, and fine), and, in each case, the liquid ran right through the blade as we churned and churned only to produce baby food of varying textures. The liquid and pureed solids were separated and could not be combined with a whisk.

The food processor does a decent job of pureeing, but some small bits of vegetables can be trapped under the blade and remain unchopped. Even more troubling is the tendency of a food processor to leak hot liquid. Fill the workbowl more than halfway and you are likely to see liquid running down the side of the food processor base. Even small quantities of soup must be pureed in batches, and that's a hassle.

The immersion blender has more appeal since this tool can be brought directly to the pot and there is no ladling of hot ingredients. However, we found that this kind of blender also leaves some chunks behind. If you don't mind a few lumps, use an immersion blender.

For perfectly smooth pureed soups, use a standard blender. As long as a little headroom is left at the top of the blender, there is never any leaking, and the blade on the blender does an excellent job with soups because it pulls ingredients down from the top of the container. No stray bits go untouched by the blade. The recipes we've presented here can be pureed in a single batch in a standard seven-cup blender.

peeled, and cut into ½-inch cubes to yield 5 cups. Substitute 1 teaspoon ground ginger for nutmeg and cook squash until tender, about 15 minutes. Thin with ¾ to 1 cup milk and garnish with minced fresh chives or parsley.

Pureed Cauliflower Soup with Coriander

Follow recipe for Pureed Carrot Soup with Nutmeg, replacing carrots with 1 medium head cauliflower (about 2 pounds), stems discarded and florets cut into bite-sized pieces to yield 5 cups. Replace nutmeg with 1 teaspoon ground coriander and cook cauliflower until tender, about 12 minutes. Thin with ½ to ¾ cup milk and garnish with minced chives or parsley.

Creamy Potato Soup with Chives

Follow recipe for Pureed Carrot Soup with Nutmeg, replacing carrots with 2 large russet potatoes (about 1½ pounds), peeled and cut into ½-inch dice to yield 4 cups. Omit nutmeg and cook potatoes until very tender, about 20 minutes. Thin with 1 to 1¼ cups milk and garnish with minced chives.

MINESTRONE

MINESTRONE IS NOT A LIGHT UNDERTAKING. Any way you cut it, there is a lot of dicing and chopping. Given the amount of preparation, we thought it was important to discover which steps and ingredients were essential and which we could do without. Could we just add everything at once to the pot, or would precooking some of the vegetables be necessary? Was stock essential, or could we use water, as many traditional Italian recipes do? How many vegetables were enough? And which ones?

While we wanted to pack the soup with vegetables, we were also determined to create a harmonious balance of flavors. Minestrone should be a group effort, with each element pulling equal weight. From the start, we decided to jettison vegetables that were too bold (such as broccoli) as well as those that were too bland and would contribute no flavor to the soup (such as mushrooms).

But before tackling the issue of ingredients (we had come up with a list of more than 35 to test), we wanted to devise a basic technique. Our research turned up two possible paths. The majority of recipes dump the vegetables into a pot with liquid and simmer them until everything is tender. A smaller number of recipes call for sautéing some or most of the vegetables before adding the liquid along with any vegetables, such as spinach, that would not benefit from cooking in fat.

Although we expected the soup with sautéed vegetables to be more flavorful, it wasn't. We then prepared three more pots without sautéing any of the vegetables. We added homemade vegetable stock to one pot, homemade chicken stock to a second, and water and the rind from a wedge of Parmesan cheese to a third.

The results were unexpected. The soup made with vegetable stock tasted one-dimensional and overwhelmingly sweet; because the vegetables were already sweet, using vegetable stock, which is also fairly sweet, did not help to balance the flavors. We realized we wanted the liquid portion of the soup to add a layer of complexity that would play off the vegetables. The soup made with chicken stock seemed to fit the bill. It was rich, complex, and delicious. However, the chicken flavor overwhelmed the vegetables. Diluting the stock with water wasn't the answer; this resulted in a rather bland soup. Ultimately, we preferred the soup made with water and the cheese rind. The cheese gave the broth a buttery, nutty flavor that contrasted nicely with the vegetables without overshadowing them.

We wanted the vegetables to soften completely but not lose their shape, and an hour of gentle simmering accomplished this. Much longer and the vegetables began to break down. Any less time over the flame and the vegetables were too crunchy. We liked the concentrating effect of simmering without the lid on.

We also saw several recipes that added some fresh vegetables at the end of the cooking time. It sounded like a nice idea, but the fresh peas and green beans added 10 minutes before the soup was done tasted uncooked and bland compared with the vegetables that had simmered in the flavorful broth for an hour. For maximum flavor, all the vegetables, even ones that usually require brief cooking times, should be added at the outset.

The addition of the cheese rind to the soup was an interesting find. During our research we also turned up two other flavor boosters that could be added to the soup up front—rehydrated porcini mushrooms and their soaking liquid, and pancetta, unsmoked Italian bacon. We made a batch of soup with the porcini but felt that, like the chicken stock, the flavor of the addition was so strong it reduced the role of the vegetables to a bit part.

Pancetta must be sautéed to render its fat and release its flavor. We cooked a little pancetta until crisp in some olive oil, then added the water and vegetables. Like the cheese rind, the pancetta contributed depth. While the soup made with the cheese rind was buttery and nutty, the soup with pancetta had a very subtle pork and spice flavor. We tried regular American bacon as well. It was a bit stronger and lent the soup a smoky element. We preferred the subtler flavor of the pancetta, but either pancetta or smoked bacon is a significant improvement over water alone.

Up until this point, we had focused on ingredients that went into the soup pot at the start. But many traditional Mediterranean recipes stir in fresh herbs or herb pastes just before the soup is served. Pesto is the most common choice. The first time we added pesto we were hooked. The heat of the soup releases the perfume of the basil and garlic and creates another delicious layer of flavor. A simple mixture of minced fresh rosemary, garlic, and extra-virgin olive oil was also delicious. As with the pesto, the oil adds some fat to a soup that is otherwise very lean. The rosemary and garlic combo is very strong and must be used in smaller quantities than pesto.

Varying the Vegetables in Minestrone

Our recipe for minestrone contains seven kinds of vegetables, tomatoes, and cannellini beans. The aromatics—leeks, carrots, onions, and celery—are essential, as are the tomatoes. We like to add starchy potatoes, sweet zucchini, and leafy spinach, but this list is fairly subjective.

What follows are some notes on other vegetables that were tested in this soup. Bell peppers and broccoli were too distinctive, while eggplant and white mushrooms added little flavor, so none of those four vegetables is recommended.

When making substitutions, keep in mind that our minestrone recipe has 2½ cups of solid vegetables (potatoes and zucchini) and three cups of leafy spinach. Follow similar proportions when using the vegetables below.

As for the beans, white kidney beans, called cannellini beans in Italy, are the classic choice. But other white beans may be used, as well as red kidney, cranberry, or borlotti beans, all of which appear in various Italian recipes for minestrone.

VEGETABLE	TESTING NOTES	HOW TO USE
Cauliflower	While broccoli is too intense for minestrone, milder cauliflower can blend in.	Cut into tiny florets and use in place of potatoes or zucchini.
Escarole	This slightly bitter green works well with white beans and pasta.	Chop and use in place of spinach.
Green Beans	A standard ingredient in French versions of this soup.	Cut into ½-inch pieces and use in place of zucchini.
Kale	This assertive green can be overwhelming on its own, but when combined with spinach it gives the soup a pleasant edge.	Remove ribs and chop. Use up to 1½ cups in place of 1½ cups of the spinach.
Peas	The delicate flavor of fresh peas is wasted in this soup, so use frozen.	Add up to ½ cup in place of ½ cup of the zucchini or white beans.
Savoy Cabbage	Adds an earthy note.	Shred finely and use in place of spinach.
Swiss Chard	Similar to spinach, with a slightly more earthy flavor.	Remove ribs and chop. Use in place of spinach.
Turnips	Modest bitter edge helps balance the sweetness of some of the other vegetables.	Peel and dice. Use in place of potatoes.
Winter Squash	Butternut squash is sweet, but in small quantities it is especially colorful and delicious.	Peel and dice. Use in place of potatoes or zucchini.

Minestrone

SERVES 6 TO 8

One secret to this soup is adding the rind from a wedge of Parmesan cheese, preferably Parmigiano-Reggiano. It brings complexity and depth to a soup made with water instead of stock. Remove the rind from a wedge of fresh Parmesan. (Rinds from which all the cheese has been grated can be stored in a zipper-lock bag in the freezer to use as needed.) To use different vegetables or beans, see chart on page 27.

2   small leeks (or 1 large), washed thoroughly, white and light green parts sliced thin crosswise (about ¾ cup)

2   medium carrots, peeled and cut into small dice (about ¾ cup)

2   small onions, peeled and cut into small dice (about ¾ cup)

2   medium celery stalks, trimmed and cut into small dice (about ¾ cup)

1   medium russet potato, peeled and cut into medium dice (about 1¼ cups)

1   medium zucchini, trimmed and cut into medium dice (about 1¼ cups)

3   cups stemmed spinach leaves, cut into thin strips

1   can (28 ounces) whole tomatoes packed in juice, drained, and chopped

1   Parmesan cheese rind, about 5 x 2 inches
    Salt

1   can (15 ounces) cannellini beans, drained and rinsed

¼   cup basil pesto (from recipe on page 103) or 1 tablespoon minced fresh rosemary mixed with 1 teaspoon minced garlic and 1 tablespoon extra-virgin olive oil
    Ground black pepper

1. Bring vegetables, tomatoes, 8 cups water, cheese rind, and 1 teaspoon salt to boil in a soup kettle or pot. Reduce heat to medium-low; simmer, uncovered and stirring occasionally, until vegetables are tender but still hold their shape, about 1 hour. (Soup can be refrigerated in airtight container for 3 days or frozen for 1 month. Defrost if necessary and reheat before proceeding with recipe.)

2. Add beans and cook just until heated through, about 5 minutes. Remove pot from heat. Remove and discard cheese rind. Stir in pesto (or rosemary-garlic mixture). Adjust seasonings, adding pepper and more salt, if necessary. Ladle soup into bowls and serve immediately.

➤ VARIATIONS

Minestrone with Pancetta

Pancetta, unsmoked Italian bacon, can be used in place of a cheese rind to boost flavor in the soup. Because it has been smoked, American bacon can overwhelm the vegetables. Try cooking American bacon strips in simmering water for one minute to wash away some of the smokiness.

Mince 2 ounces thinly sliced pancetta (or an equal amount of blanched American bacon) and sauté in 1 tablespoon extra-virgin olive oil in soup kettle until crisp, 3 to 4 minutes. Proceed with recipe for Minestrone, adding vegetables, tomatoes, and water but omitting cheese rind.

Minestrone with Rice or Pasta

Adding pasta or rice makes this soup hearty enough to have as a dinner. If the soup seems too thick after adding the pasta or rice, stir in a little water. Pasta and rice do not hold up well when refrigerated or frozen, so serve this soup as soon as the pasta or rice is tender.

Follow recipe for Minestrone or Minestrone with Pancetta until vegetables are tender. Add ½ cup arborio rice or small pasta shape, such as elbows, ditalini, or orzo, and continue cooking until rice is tender but still a bit firm in the center of each grain, about 20 minutes, or until pasta is al dente, 8 to 12 minutes, depending on the shape. Add beans and continue with recipe.

NEW ENGLAND CLAM CHOWDER

WE WANTED TO DEVELOP A DELICIOUS, traditional chowder that was economical, would not curdle, and could be prepared quickly. Before testing chowder recipes, we explored our clam options. Chowders are typically made with hard-shell clams, so we purchased (from smallest to largest) cockles, littlenecks, cherrystones, and chowder clams, often called quahogs.

Although they made delicious chowders, we

eliminated littlenecks and cockles, both of which were just too expensive to toss into a chowder pot. Chowders made with the cheapest clams, however, weren't really satisfactory, either. The quahogs we purchased for testing were large (four to five inches in diameter), tough, and strong flavored. Their over-sized bellies (and the contents therein) gave the chowder an overbearing mineral taste, detracting from its smooth, rich flavor.

Though only a little more expensive, cherry-stones offered good value and flavor. The chowder made from these slightly smaller clams was distinctly clam-flavored, without an inky aftertaste. Because there are no industry sizing standards for each clam variety, you may find some small quahogs labeled as cherrystones or large cherrystones labeled as qua-hogs. Regardless of designation, clams much over three inches in diameter will deliver a distinctly metallic, inky-flavored chowder.

Steaming clams open is far easier than shucking them. Five minutes over simmering water, and the clams open as naturally as budding flowers. Ours did not toughen up as long as we pulled them from the pot as soon as they opened and didn't let them cook too long in the finished chowder.

The extra step of purging or filtering hard-shell clams is unnecessary. All of the hard-shells we tested were relatively clean, and what little sediment there was sank to the bottom of the steaming liquid. Getting rid of the grit was as simple as leaving the last few tablespoons of broth in the pan when pour-ing it from the pot. If you find that your clam broth is gritty, strain it through a coffee filter.

Older recipes call for thickening clam chowder with crumbled biscuits; bread crumbs and crackers are modern stand-ins.

Standard bread crumb-thickened chowders failed to impress. We wanted a smooth, creamy soup base for the potatoes, onions, and clams, but no matter how long the chowder was simmered, bread crumbs or crackers never completely dissolved into the cooking liquid. Heavy cream alone, by contrast, did not give the chowder enough body. We discovered fairly quickly that flour was necessary, not only as a thickener but as a stabilizer, because unthickened chowders separate and curdle. Of the two flour methods, we opted to thicken at the beginning of cooking rather than at the end. Because our final recipe was finished with cream, we felt the chowder didn't need the extra butter that would be required to add the flour in a paste to the finished soup.

Because chowders call for potatoes, some cooks suggest that starchy baking potatoes, which tend to break down when boiled, can double as a thickener. But the potatoes did not break down sufficiently, and instead simply became soft and mushy. Waxy red boiling potatoes are best for chowders.

Should the chowder be enriched with milk or cream? We found that so much milk was required to make it look and taste creamy that the chowder started to lose its clam flavor and became more like mild bisque or the clam equivalent of oyster stew. Making the chowder with almost all clam broth (five cups of the cooking liquid from the steaming clams), then finishing the stew with a cup of cream gave us what we were looking for—a rich, creamy chowder that tasted distinctly of clams.

New England Clam Chowder
SERVES 6

You can replace the bacon with 4 ounces of salt pork if you prefer.

7	pounds medium-sized hard-shell clams, such as cherrystones, washed and scrubbed clean
4	slices thick-cut bacon (about 4 ounces), cut into ¼-inch pieces
I	large Spanish onion, diced medium
2	tablespoons flour
3	medium boiling potatoes (about 1½ pounds), scrubbed and diced medium
I	large bay leaf
I	teaspoon fresh thyme leaves or ¼ teaspoon dried thyme
I	cup heavy cream
2	tablespoons minced fresh parsley leaves
	Salt and ground black or white pepper

1. Bring clams and 3 cups water to boil in large, covered soup kettle. Steam until clams just start to open, 3 to 5 minutes. Transfer clams to large bowl; cool slightly. Open clams with a paring knife, hold-ing clams over a bowl to catch any juices. With knife,

sever muscle that attaches clam to shell and transfer meat to cutting board. Mince clams; set aside. Pour clam broth into 2-quart Pyrex measuring cup, holding back last few tablespoons of broth in case of sediment; set clam broth aside. (Should have about 5 cups.) Rinse and dry kettle; return to burner.

2. Fry bacon in kettle over medium-low heat until fat renders and bacon crisps, 5 to 7 minutes. Add onion to bacon; sauté until softened, about 5 minutes. Add flour; stir until lightly colored, about 1 minute. Gradually whisk in reserved clam broth. Add potatoes, bay leaf, and thyme; simmer until potatoes are tender, about 10 minutes. Add clams, cream, parsley, and salt (if necessary) and ground pepper to taste; bring to simmer. Remove from heat and serve.

➤ VARIATION
Quick Pantry Clam Chowder
From late summer through winter, when clams are plentiful, you'll probably want to make fresh clam chowder. But if you're short on time or find clams scarce and expensive, we've found that the right canned clams and bottled clam juice deliver a chowder that's at least three notches above canned soup in quality. We tested seven brands of minced and small whole canned clams. We preferred Doxsee Minced Clams teamed with Doxsee brand clam juice. Doxsee clams were neither too tough nor too tender, and they had a decent natural clam flavor.

Follow recipe for New England Clam Chowder, substituting for the fresh clams 4 cans (6.5 ounces each) minced clams, juice drained and reserved, along with 1 cup water and 2 bottles (8 ounces each) clam juice in medium bowl, and clam meat reserved in small bowl. Add reserved clam meat and juice at same points as when fresh clam meat and juice would be added.

ASIAN NOODLE SOUPS
ASIAN NOODLE SOUPS MADE IN GOOD Vietnamese or Thai restaurants start with homemade beef, chicken, or fish stock. Knowing this full well, we still wanted to develop a recipe that would not call for the long cooking times most homemade stocks demand. We wanted a simple recipe that could be made up as an everyday, home-cooked,

one-pot meal. But we wanted it to taste anything but everyday.

Faced with this dilemma when cooking a Western-style soup, we can usually substitute canned broth, even though it doesn't taste homemade and we don't particularly like the taste that it does have. Western-style soups are typically set up something like a stew—sauté aromatics, add broth and whatever major ingredient, season with herbs, and simmer at least half an hour to cook the ingredients through and marry the flavors—so that by the time the soup is cooked, the flavor of the broth has been substantially transformed by the ingredients cooked in it. In fact, we can often dispense with the canned broth entirely and use just water because the soup-making process itself is similar to that for making a quick stock from scratch.

Soups made in Southeast Asia rely on a different technique. In contrast with the simmering and marrying that characterizes most Western soups, these Asian soups are collections of raw and cooked ingredients—one or several different proteins, noodles, vegetables, handfuls of fresh herbs and other aromatics—that are combined in the hot broth like a garnish at the last minute, with little or no secondary cooking. So whereas a leek and potato soup cooks leeks, potatoes, and chicken stock together until the edges of the flavors soften and merge, Asian soups are structured in a way that allows the flavorings to remain distinct and separate.

These Asian soups are tremendously flavorful despite their short cooking time because the ingredients themselves are so potent. The minimal cooking allows the flavors to remain clean and bright, just as they do in a stir fry. Clearly, canned broth alone could not stand up to such a soup. We would have to use strong flavorings to punch up the pallid flavor of the broth.

Simmering crushed garlic and ginger with the broth for 20 minutes improved its flavor immeasurably. Soy and fish sauces added much-needed body and depth of flavor; fish sauce, in particular, added just the right combination of salt and a musky sweetness. Cinnamon sticks and star anise give the broth an exotic and authentic flavor that works well with beef. Lime juice in the broth works especially well with shrimp, which calls for more fish sauce than a soup made with beef.

Fresh herbs are crucial in these soups and are more effective in whole leaf than chopped. Finally, because the rice noodles used in these soups are so bland and smooth, some crunchy vegetables, such as bean sprouts and Asian cabbages, are needed for texture.

Quick Vietnamese-Style Broth

MAKES ABOUT 5 CUPS

The beef noodle soup that follows uses this broth as is; the broth should be tailored to suit the flavors in the shrimp soup recipes. Make the broth while the noodles are soaking, noting the adjustments to the broth in the ingredient list of the shrimp soup recipe.

- 5 cups canned low-sodium chicken broth
- 4 medium garlic cloves, smashed and peeled
- 1 piece fresh gingerroot, about 2 inches long, peeled, cut into 1/8-inch rounds, and smashed with handle of chef's knife
- 2 cinnamon sticks, each about 3 inches long
- 2 pods star anise
- 2 tablespoons Asian fish sauce
- 1 tablespoon soy sauce
- 1 tablespoon sugar

Bring all ingredients to boil in medium saucepan over medium-high heat. Reduce heat to low; simmer partially covered to blend flavors, about 20 minutes. Remove solids with slotted spoon and discard. Cover and keep hot over low heat until ready to serve.

Vietnamese-Style Beef Noodle Soup

SERVES 4

For this soup and the one that follows, be sure to have all the vegetables and herbs ready at hand.

- 8 ounces thick rice noodles
- 1 recipe Quick Vietnamese-Style Broth
  Salt
- 12 ounces sirloin steak, sliced crosswise into 1/4-inch strips
  Ground black pepper
- 1 tablespoon vegetable oil
- 2 cups bean sprouts (about 5 ounces)
- 1 jalapeño chile, sliced thin
- 2 scallions, white and green parts, sliced thin on an angle
- 1/3 cup loose-packed basil leaves, torn in half if large
- 1/2 cup loose-packed fresh mint leaves, torn in half if large
- 1/2 cup loose-packed fresh cilantro leaves
- 2 tablespoons chopped roasted unsalted peanuts
  Lime wedges

INGREDIENTS: Dried Rice Noodles

Dried rice noodles are sold in two different styles: a thick, flat, fettuccine-width noodle and a very thin, thread-like noodle. It's confusing to try to buy these noodles by name. Because they're used in several Asian cuisines (including Chinese, Thai, and Vietnamese), they're marketed under several different Asian names. The English names are no more helpful because they're not standardized; you'll find the thicker noodles sold as "rice sticks" and the thread-like noodles sold as both "rice sticks" and "vermicelli." To further confuse matters, thin cellophane noodles made from mung beans are also marketed as "vermicelli." So don't bother with the names, just look for the shape of the noodle—all of the packages we've seen have been obligingly transparent.

The literature we read indicates that rice noodles are made from rice flour and water. But some of the packages we've seen list cornstarch in the ingredients as well as rice flour. In the fabrication of the noodles, rice flour may be stretched with or completely replaced by cornstarch, a cheaper ingredient. Noodles made with cornstarch break apart and stick together more readily than noodles made only with rice flour, so, if you have a choice, buy noodles made without cornstarch.

We found that boiled noodles have a tendency to get mushy and, if left in the soup for any length of time, to break apart. So we tried soaking for 15 minutes and then briefly submerging in boiling water. This worked better but required two pots. Ultimately, we settled on soaking alone (in very hot water) because it was less complicated and worked just as well. We simply drained the noodles when they had softened to the point that they were tender but still had tooth. The only problem was that the noodles sometimes stuck together and then failed to soften properly. We were able to prevent this dilemma by stirring the noodles occasionally, especially at the beginning.

1. Bring 4 quarts water to boil in large pot. Off heat, add rice noodles, and let sit, stirring occasionally, until tender, 10 to 15 minutes. Drain and distribute among four individual serving bowls.

2. Meanwhile, make Quick Vietnamese-Style broth, seasoning with salt if necessary.

3. Season steak with salt and pepper. Heat oil in medium skillet over medium-high heat until shimmering. Add half of steak slices in single layer and sear until well-browned, 1 to 2 minutes on each side; set aside. Repeat with remaining slices.

4. Divide sprouts, chile slices, scallions, and meat among bowls with noodles. Ladle broth into bowls. Divide herbs and peanuts among bowls. Serve immediately with lime wedges passed separately.

Hot and Sour Noodle Soup with Shrimp and Tomato

SERVES 4

Lemon grass is an essential ingredient in Southeast Asian cooking; it lends a subtle fragrant lemon essence without harsh citrus notes. Use fresh lemon grass if you can find it. Bruise the lemon grass with the back of a chef's knife before adding it to the broth to speed release of its flavorful juices. If you can't find fresh lemon grass, substitute two pieces of water-packed lemon grass, bruised, or ½ teaspoon grated lemon zest. See right for more information on lemon grass.

6	ounces thin rice noodles
1	recipe Quick Vietnamese-Style Broth (page 31), cinnamon omitted, Asian fish sauce increased to 3 tablespoons, sugar decreased to 1 teaspoon
1	stalk lemon grass, bruised
12	ounces shrimp, shelled, shells reserved
1	jalapeño chile, sliced thin
¼	cup juice from 4 or 5 limes
	Salt
2	cups bean sprouts (about 5 ounces)
1	medium tomato, cut into 12 wedges
2	scallions, white and green parts, sliced thin on an angle
½	cup loose-packed fresh mint leaves, torn in half if large
½	cup loose-packed fresh cilantro leaves

1. Bring 4 quarts water to boil in large pot. Off heat, add rice noodles, and let sit, stirring occasionally, until tender, 5 to 10 minutes. Drain and distribute among four individual serving bowls.

2. Meanwhile, make Quick Vietnamese-Style Broth, simmering lemon grass and reserved shrimp shells with broth for 15 minutes. Add jalapeño and simmer 5 minutes longer; strain, return broth to pot, and bring back to simmer over medium heat. Add shrimp and simmer until opaque and cooked through, about 2 minutes. Remove with slotted spoon; set aside. Add lime juice, and season broth to taste with additional salt if necessary. Cover and keep hot over low heat.

3. Divide sprouts, tomatoes, scallions, and shrimp among bowls with noodles. Ladle broth into bowls. Divide herbs among bowls. Serve immediately.

INGREDIENTS: Lemon Grass

Lemon grass is an integral part of Southeast Asian cooking, imparting a rich, ethereal, lemony essence to many dishes. Most often it is trimmed to the lower third, the tough outer leaves stripped away, and the soft inner core chopped or minced. Or, if it is eventually to be removed, as in a broth, the stalk—leaves and all—can simply be bruised and used as is. This is the approach that we took, for example, in making the broth for Hot and Sour Noodle Soup with Shrimp and Tomato.

Fresh lemon grass is a staple in many Asian grocery stores, but it is not always available everywhere. We did find it in both dried and water-packed form at our local grocer, however, and decided to investigate. We cooked them into broths and compared them with broths made with fresh lemon grass and lemon zest. Here are our findings.

Fresh lemon grass was the most aromatic, infusing the broth with a delicate, lemony freshness that made it the clear favorite. The next best was the water-packed lemon grass. Although it lacked the crispness and clarity of fresh, this version still maintained lemon grass characteristics. Grated lemon zest finished a remote third. Better zest than dried lemon grass, though. While the broth made with lemon zest was flat and one-dimensional compared with those made with fresh or water-packed lemon grass, it was still, at the very least, lemony. Dried lemon grass was the dog, with a dull, "off" herbal quality; the broth made with it lacked not only freshness but any lemon flavor.

SALADS

WHAT DO SALADS MADE WITH LEAFY GREENS have in common with potato salad or coleslaw? The answer is dressing. There are two main types of cold sauces typically used to dress salads. Vinaigrette is a relatively thin emulsion made of oil, vinegar, and seasonings. Mayonnaise is a thick, creamy emulsion of egg yolk and oil with a little acid and some seasonings.

An emulsion is a mixture of two things that don't ordinarily mix, such as oil and water or oil and vinegar. The only way to mix them is to stir or whisk so strenuously that the two ingredients break down into tiny droplets. Many of these droplets will continue to find each other and recoalesce into pure fluid. (This is what happens when the emulsion breaks.) Eventually one of the fluids (usually the less plentiful one) will break entirely into droplets so tiny that they remain separated by the opposite fluid, at least temporarily.

The liquid in the droplet form is called the dispersed phase (vinegar in a vinaigrette, oil in mayonnaise) because the droplets are dispersed throughout the emulsion. The liquid that surrounds the droplets is the continuous phase (oil in a vinaigrette, egg in mayonnaise). Because the continuous phase forms the surface of the emulsion, that's what the mouth and tongue feel and taste first.

VINAIGRETTE

VINAIGRETTE IS THE MOST COMMON DRESSing for salads, used with leafy greens as well as vegetables, grains, and beans. While it is possible to dress a salad with vinegar and then oil, the results are quite different when these ingredients are combined before being poured over greens.

To demonstrate this difference, try this test. Dress a simple green salad first with oil, then a mixture of vinegar, salt, and pepper. The result will be harsh, with an extremely prominent vinegar bite. Next, take another batch of greens and the same dressing ingredients. Mix the salt and pepper into the vinegar and then whisk in the oil until the dressing is translucent. When this emulsified dressing is poured over greens, the flavor will be smoother, with a greater emphasis on the oil.

The science of emulsions explains why the same ingredients can taste so different. In the first oil-then-vinegar salad, the oil and vinegar don't mix, so both race up the tongue. The less viscous vinegar wins, hence this salad tastes more acidic. In the emulsion, the oil is whipped into tiny molecules that surround dispersed droplets of vinegar. The oil is the continuous phase and is tasted first. Your tongue is coated with fat droplets that cushion the impact of the acid.

The correct ratio of oil to vinegar is open to much discussion and can depend on the acidity of the vinegar as well as the flavor of the oil. In general, we prefer a ratio of four parts oil to one part acid, but this can vary, especially when using citrus juices and rice wine vinegar, which are much less acidic than common vinegars.

In terms of forming a vinaigrette, either a fork or small whisk will generate the whipping action necessary to break up the oil and vinegar into small droplets. With either tool, the emulsion will break rather quickly, so rewhisk the dressing just before pouring it over salad greens. We found that adding the salt and pepper to the vinegar is best because the vinegar mutes these flavors a bit and prevents them from becoming overpowering. On the other hand, we prefer to add herbs and some other seasonings to the finished dressing to maximize their impact.

Master Recipe for Vinaigrette

MAKES ABOUT ¹/₂ CUP, ENOUGH TO DRESS 4 QUARTS (8 SERVINGS) OF SALAD GREENS

Salt and pepper are mixed first with the vinegar for subtlety. If you like, you can adjust the seasonings after the salad has been dressed by sprinkling additional salt and/or pepper directly onto the greens. Extra dressing can be refrigerated for several days. Variations that contain fresh herbs should be used within several hours for maximum freshness.

1 ¹/₂	tablespoons red wine vinegar
¹/₄	teaspoon salt
¹/₈	teaspoon ground black pepper
6	tablespoons extra-virgin olive oil

Combine vinegar, salt, and pepper in bowl with fork. Add oil, then whisk or mix with fork until smooth, about 30 seconds. The dressing will separate after 5 or 10 minutes, so use immediately or cover and refrigerate for several days and mix again before tossing with greens.

➤ VARIATIONS

Balsamic Vinaigrette

Follow Master Recipe for Vinaigrette, reducing red wine vinegar to 1½ teaspoons and combining with 1½ tablespoons balsamic vinegar.

Mediterranean Vinaigrette

Follow Master Recipe for Vinaigrette, replacing vinegar with 2¼ teaspoons lemon juice, increasing pepper to ¼ teaspoon, and decreasing oil to 4 tablespoons. Whisk 1 tablespoon drained and minced capers, 1 tablespoon minced fresh parsley leaves, 1 teaspoon minced fresh thyme leaves, and 1 medium garlic clove, minced fine, into finished dressing.

Walnut Vinaigrette

Follow Master Recipe for Vinaigrette, replacing vinegar with 2 tablespoons lemon juice and replacing olive oil with 4 tablespoons canola oil mixed with 2 tablespoons walnut oil.

Mixed Herb Vinaigrette

Follow Master Recipe for Vinaigrette, adding 1 tablespoon minced fresh basil leaves, 1½ teaspoons minced fresh parsley leaves, and 1 teaspoon minced fresh oregano leaves to finished dressing. Use dressing within several hours for optimum freshness.

INGREDIENTS: Common Oils and Vinegars

The following oils and vinegars are used in recipes throughout this book. To keep oils from becoming rancid, store bottles in a cool, dark pantry and buy small quantities that will be used up within a few months. Storing oils in the refrigerator will prolong their freshness.

EXTRA-VIRGIN OLIVE OIL This is our standard choice for most salads. In blind tastings, we could not tell the difference between extra-virgin oil that cost $10 per liter and $80 per liter. However, cheaper pure and "light" oils are characterless and decidedly inferior in salads, although they may be fine for some cooking. An inexpensive supermarket extra-virgin oil, such as Berio or Colavita, is our recommendation for salads.

WALNUT OIL This oil has a warm, nutty flavor that works well in salads with fruits and/or toasted nuts. Like other nut oils, walnut oil tends to go rancid quickly and is best stored in the refrigerator.

ASIAN SESAME OIL With its dark brown color and rich aroma, toasted sesame oil adds a distinctive Asian flavor to salad dressings. Use it in moderation. More than a tablespoon or two will overwhelm other ingredients.

CANOLA OIL This bland oil is best used to soften a particularly strong oil, especially sesame or walnut. Alone, its flavor is unremarkable. But in combination with a potent nut or seed oil, canola can be part of a good dressing.

RED WINE VINEGAR Red wine vinegar is the most versatile choice in salads. Its flavor is sharp but clean. Domestic brands tend to have an acidity around 5 percent, while imported brands often contain as much as 7 percent. In our tasting of red wine vinegars, Heinz beat other domestic brands as well as imports, some of which cost ten times as much.

WHITE WINE VINEGAR Similar to red wine vinegar but often not quite as complex. Our choice when a pink vinaigrette made with red wine vinegar might seem odd.

BALSAMIC VINEGAR A rich, sweet, oaky vinegar that is best used in combination with red wine vinegar in salads. Real balsamic vinegar is aged many years and costs at least $10 per bottle. Cheap supermarket versions are nothing more than caramel-colored red wine vinegar. They are usually harsh and unpleasant tasting. Given the small quantities of balsamic vinegar needed to transform a salad, it's worth investing in the real thing. In our tasting, we liked vinegars from Cavalli, Fiorucci, Fini, and Masserie di Sant'Eramo.

SHERRY VINEGAR This Spanish vinegar is usually quite strong (often with 7 percent acidity) but has a rich, oaky, nutty flavor.

CITRUS JUICES Orange, lime, and lemon juices can all be used in salad dressing. They add acidity (although not as much as most vinegars) as well as flavor. Lemon and lime juices are more acidic and can stand on their own. Orange juice is usually combined with vinegar. To add more citrus flavor without disturbing the ratio of acid to oil, stir in some grated zest.

RICE WINE VINEGAR A natural choice in Asian dressings, this low-acidity (about 4.5 percent), clear vinegar is quite mild. Use it when you want to keep acidity in check but want to avoid the distinctive flavor of citrus juices.

Creamy Mustard Vinaigrette

MAKES ABOUT ⅔ CUP

Follow Master Recipe for Vinaigrette, replacing red wine vinegar with 1 tablespoon white wine vinegar. Combine vinegar, salt, and pepper with 1 tablespoon lemon juice and 2 teaspoons Dijon mustard. Reduce oil to 4 tablespoons. Whisk 2 tablespoons sour cream or plain yogurt into finished dressing.

Orange-Sesame Vinaigrette

MAKES ABOUT ⅔ CUP

Follow Master Recipe for Vinaigrette, replacing red wine vinegar with 1 tablespoon rice wine vinegar. Combine vinegar, salt, and pepper with 1 teaspoon grated orange zest, 2 tablespoons orange juice, and 1 tablespoon minced fresh gingerroot. Replace olive oil with 4 tablespoons canola oil mixed with 1 tablespoon Asian sesame oil.

Tarragon-Mustard Vinaigrette

MAKES ABOUT ⅔ CUP

Follow Master Recipe for Vinaigrette, replacing red wine vinegar with 2 tablespoons white wine vinegar. Increase salt to ½ teaspoon and pepper to ¼ teaspoon. Combine vinegar, salt, and pepper with 1 tablespoon Dijon mustard. Whisk in oil and then 1 tablespoon minced fresh tarragon leaves. Use dressing within several hours for optimum freshness.

MAYONNAISE

MAYONNAISE IS USED TO DRESS VEGETABLE salads—especially potato salad and coleslaw. It acts as a creamy binder and adds richness to any salad. The science of mayonnaise is fairly complex and unusual. Whisking transforms three thin liquids—vegetable oil, lemon juice, and egg yolk—into a thick, creamy sauce. In mayonnaise, the egg yolk and lemon juice are the continuous phase (that's why something that is 95 percent oil doesn't taste greasy) and the oil is the dispersed phase that must be broken into tiny droplets.

Mayonnaise works because an egg yolk is such a good emulsifier and stabilizer. But sometimes mayonnaise can "break," as the ingredients revert back to their original liquid form. To keep mayonnaise from breaking, it is first necessary to whisk the egg yolk and lemon juice thoroughly (the egg yolk itself contains liquid and fat materials that must be emulsified). It is equally important to add the oil slowly to the egg yolk. Remember, two tablespoons of yolk and lemon juice must be "stretched" around ¾ cup of oil.

We like the flavor of corn oil in our basic mayonnaise. It produces a dressing that is rich and eggy with good body. Canola oil makes a slightly lighter, more lemony mayo. We find that extra-virgin olive oil can be harsh and bitter, especially if used alone in mayonnaise. While pure olive oil produces a mellower mayonnaise, it costs more than corn or canola oil and does not deliver better results.

While homemade mayonnaise is a delicious addition to salads, many cooks prefer the convenience and safety of commercial brands made without raw eggs. In our tasting of major brands, Hellmann's came out on top. Among light or reduced-calorie brands, Hellmann's again beat out Kraft, which is its main competition in the marketplace.

Master Recipe for Mayonnaise

MAKES ABOUT ¾ CUP

Each time you add oil, make sure to whisk until it is thoroughly incorporated. It's fine to stop for a rest or to measure the next addition of oil. If the mayonnaise appears grainy or beaded after the last addition of oil, continue to whisk until smooth.

1	large egg yolk
¼	teaspoon salt
¼	teaspoon Dijon mustard
1½	teaspoons lemon juice
1	teaspoon white wine vinegar
¾	cup corn oil

1. Whisk egg yolk vigorously in medium bowl for 15 seconds. Add all remaining ingredients except for oil and whisk until yolk thickens and color brightens, about 30 seconds.

2. Add ¼ cup oil in slow, steady stream, continuing to whisk vigorously until oil is incorporated completely and mixture thickens, about 1 minute. Add another ¼ cup oil in the same manner, whisking until incorporated completely, about 30 seconds more. Add

MAKING MAYONNAISE

1. An easy way to drizzle oil into mayonnaise slowly and evenly is to punch a small hole in the bottom of a paper cup and use it to add the oil to the egg yolk and lemon juice.

2. Pour the oil into the cup while holding your finger over the hole, then hold the cup above the bowl and remove your finger. To keep the bowl stable while whisking, set it on a wet dishcloth.

last ¼ cup oil all at once and whisk until incorporated completely, about 30 seconds more. Serve. (Can be refrigerated in airtight container for several days.)

➤ VARIATIONS

Lemon Mayonnaise

Follow Master Recipe for Mayonnaise, adding 1½ teaspoons grated lemon zest along with lemon juice.

Dijon Mayonnaise

Follow Master Recipe for Mayonnaise, whisking 2 tablespoons Dijon mustard into finished mayonnaise.

Tarragon Mayonnaise

Follow Master Recipe for Mayonnaise, stirring 1 tablespoon minced fresh tarragon leaves into finished mayonnaise.

Food Processor Mayonnaise

MAKES ABOUT 1½ CUPS

Use 1 whole large egg and double quantities of other ingredients in Master Recipe for Mayonnaise. Pulse all ingredients except oil in workbowl of food processor fitted with metal blade three or four times to combine. With machine running, add oil in thin steady stream through open feed tube until incorporated completely. (If food pusher has small hole in bottom, pour oil into pusher and allow to drizzle down into machine while motor is running.)

LEAFY SALADS

LEAFY SALADS START WITH GREENS OF SOME sort. Most greens have a short shelf life, so it's especially important to buy specimens that look healthy at the market. Greens with stems and roots will stay fresher longer and should be purchased when possible. Also, look for any rot among bunches as you shop. Decay can spread quickly, so it's best to avoid greens on which this process has already begun. If you get greens home and notice a few slimy leaves, pick them out immediately rather than waiting until you make salad. If you wait, the rot may well spread throughout the bunch.

Because they are mostly water, greens should be stored in the crisper drawer of the refrigerator, where the humidity is the highest. But while moist air will help prolong their freshness, excessive amounts of water won't. Therefore, don't wash lettuces until you are ready to use them, and drain off any standing water in bags before refrigerating greens.

Because they grow so close to the ground, salad greens are often quite sandy. Thorough washing in a deep bowl or sink filled with cold water is a must. Swish the greens in the water to loosen any sand. Once the bottom of bowl is free of grit (you may need to drain the bowl and add clean water several times), dry greens in a salad spinner and then use paper or kitchen towels to blot off any remaining moisture. It's imperative to remove all visible moisture. Dressing will slide off damp greens and pool up at the bottom of the salad bowl. Washed and dried greens can be refrigerated in a dry zipper-lock bag for several hours.

While whole leaves can be washed and dried in advance, do not tear lettuce until ready to dress the salad. Tearing the leaves leads to oxidation and browning. This process happens quite quickly in delicate greens, such as arugula, but can take several hours in tougher greens like romaine. Whatever you do, don't take a knife to salad greens. The more violently they are cut, the quicker they will brown. Gentle tearing of large leaves by hand is best.

Nothing is worse than a limp, soggy salad with too much dressing. Dressed greens should glisten. We find that ¼ cup of vinaigrette is sufficient to dress 2 quarts of salad greens, enough for four servings. We lightly pack a 4-cup plastic measure to portion out greens.

INGREDIENTS: Salad Greens

The following glossary starts with the four main varieties of lettuce and then covers the most commonly available specialty greens. When substituting one green for another, try to choose greens with a similar intensity. For example, peppery arugula could be used as a substitute for watercress or dandelion greens, but not for red leaf lettuce, at least not without significantly altering the flavor of the salad.

BUTTERHEAD LETTUCES Boston and Bibb are among the most common varieties of these very mild-tasting lettuces. A head of butterhead lettuce has a nice round shape and loose outer leaves. The color of the leaves is light to medium green (except, of course, in red-tinged varieties) and the leaves are extremely tender.

LOOSELEAF LETTUCES Red leaf, green leaf, red oakleaf, and lolla rossa are the most common varieties. These lettuces grow in a loose rosette shape, not a tight head. The ruffled leaves are perhaps the most versatile because their texture is soft yet still crunchy and their flavor is mild but not bland.

ROMAINE LETTUCE The leaves on this lettuce are long and broad at the top. The color shades from dark green in outer leaves (which are often tough and should be discarded) to pale green in the thick, crisp heart. Also called Cos lettuce, this variety has more crunch than either butterhead or looseleaf lettuces and a more pronounced earthy flavor. Romaine lettuce is essential in Caesar salad, when the greens must stand up to a thick, creamy dressing.

ICEBERG LETTUCE Iceberg is the best known variety of crisphead lettuce. Its shape is perfectly round and the leaves are tightly packed. A high water content makes iceberg especially crisp and crunchy but also robs it of flavor.

ARUGULA Also called rocket, this tender, dark green leaf can be faintly peppery or downright spicy. Larger, older leaves tend to be hotter than small, young leaves, but the flavor is variable, so taste arugula before adding it to a salad. Try to buy arugula in bunches with the stems and roots still attached—they help keep the leaves fresh. Arugula bruises and discolors quite easily. Try to keep stemmed leaves whole. Very large leaves can be torn just before they are needed.

WATERCRESS With its small leaves and long stalks, watercress is easy to spot. It requires some patience in the kitchen because the stalks are really quite tough and must be removed one at a time. Like arugula, watercress usually has a mildly spicy flavor.

DANDELION GREENS Dandelion greens are tender and pleasantly bitter. The leaves are long and have ragged edges.

The flavor is similar to that of arugula or watercress, both of which can be used interchangeably with dandelion. Note that tougher, older leaves that are more than several inches long should be cooked and not used raw in salads.

MIZUNA This Japanese spider mustard has long, thin, dark green leaves with deeply cut jagged edges. Sturdier than arugula, watercress, or dandelion, it can nonetheless be used interchangeably with these slightly milder greens in salads when a strong peppery punch is desired. Note that larger, older leaves are better cooked, so choose small "baby" mizuna for salads.

TATSOI This Asian green has thin white stalks and round, dark green leaves. A member of the crucifer family of vegetables that includes broccoli and cabbage, tatsoi tastes like a mild Chinese cabbage, especially bok choy. However, the texture of these miniature leaves is always delicate.

RADICCHIO This most familiar chicory was almost unknown in this country two decades ago. The tight heads of purple leaves streaked with prominent white ribs are now a supermarket staple. Radicchio has a decent punch but is not nearly as bitter as other chicories, especially Belgian endive.

BELGIAN ENDIVE With its characteristic bitter chicory flavor, endive is generally used sparingly in salads. Unlike its cousin radicchio, endive is crisp and crunchy, not tender and leafy. The yellow leaf tips are usually mild-flavored, while the white, thick leaf bases are more bitter. Endive is the one salad green we routinely cut rather than tear. Remove whole leaves from the head and then slice crosswise into bite-sized pieces.

CHICORY Chicory, or curly endive, has curly, jagged leaves that form a loose head that resembles a sunburst. The leaves are bright green and their flavor is usually fairly bitter. The outer leaves can be somewhat tough, especially at the base. Inner leaves are generally more tender.

ESCAROLE Escarole has smooth, broad leaves bunched together in a loose head. With its long ribs and softly ruffled leaves, it looks a bit like leaf lettuce. As a member of the chicory family, escarole can have an intense flavor, although not nearly as strong as that of endive or chicory.

SPINACH Of all the cooking greens, spinach is the most versatile in salads because it can be used in its miniature or full-grown form. Flat-leaf spinach is better than curly-leaf spinach in salads because the stems are usually less fibrous and the spade-shaped leaves are thinner, more tender, and sweeter. Curly spinach is often dry and chewy, while flat-leaf spinach, sold in bundles rather than in cellophane bags, is usually tender and moist, more like lettuce than a cooking green.

Once a leafy salad is dressed, the clock is ticking. Waiting even 15 minutes to eat the salad may cause some loss in freshness and crispness. The longer salad greens sit under a coating of dressing, the less appetizing they become, as the salt in the dressing draws moisture out of the greens and causes them to become limp.

Master Recipe for Leafy Green Salad

SERVES 4

We like a hint of garlic in our basic salad but find the flavor is too bitter when minced garlic is added directly to the dressing. For garlic aroma without any harshness, we rub the salad bowl with a halved clove.

- ½ medium garlic clove, peeled
- 2 quarts washed and dried mild salad greens, such as romaine, Boston, Bibb, or other leaf lettuces
- ¼ cup Vinaigrette or any variation (page 34)

Rub bottom and sides of large salad bowl (at least 4-quart) with garlic clove; discard garlic. Place greens in large salad bowl. Drizzle dressing over greens and toss to coat. Serve immediately.

➤ VARIATIONS

Tri-Color Salad with Balsamic Vinaigrette

Dress 4 cups arugula, 1 small head radicchio, cored and leaves torn, and 2 small heads Belgian endive, stems trimmed and leaves cut crosswise into thirds, with ¼ cup Balsamic Vinaigrette.

Asian Baby Greens with Orange-Sesame Vinaigrette

Dress 2 quarts baby spinach, mizuna, tatsoi, and/or other spicy Asian greens with ¼ cup Orange-Sesame Vinaigrette.

Arugula Salad with Walnut Vinaigrette and Toasted Walnuts

Dress 2 quarts arugula and 3 tablespoons toasted and coarsely chopped walnuts with ¼ cup Walnut Vinaigrette.

SPINACH SALAD

WHEN CHOOSING SPINACH FOR SALADS, WE find it especially important to select a flavorful, tender variety. The dried-out curly leaves packaged in cellophane are fine for pasta fillings or side dishes. However, when used raw, they often make a tough, tasteless salad.

A better option is the flat-leaf spinach sold in bundles at most supermarkets. The spade-shaped leaves tend to have thin, less fibrous stems, which are often edible. The leaves themselves are not as stringy as curly spinach leaves, and their flavor is far superior, sweeter and with more mineral and earthy notes. In addition, and most important in terms of salads, flat-leaf spinach is not as dry or chewy. The leaves are tender and moist, more like lettuce.

One drawback is perishability. Unlike curly spinach, flat-leaf varieties will wilt and become slimy very quickly. In tests, we found that wrapping the root ends in damp paper towels and keeping the spinach in an open plastic bag can prolong freshness an extra day or two in the refrigerator.

When you're ready to use the spinach, pinch off and discard the stems as needed, based on their thickness and toughness. We found that the portion of the stem near the leaf is usually quite tender and just a little crunchy. In really fresh bundles that come with the pink rootlets attached, the entire plant—leaves, stems, and pink crowns—may be eaten.

As you trim the stems, drop the leaves into a bowl, sink, or salad spinner full of cold water. Swish the leaves around and continue washing in several changes of water until there is no grit on the bottom of the container you are using. Spinach should be spun dry in a salad spinner and then laid out over paper towels to blot off any remaining water. Spinach leaves can be prepped to this point and then refrigerated in zipper-lock plastic bags for several hours.

In addition to selling flat-leaf spinach in bundles, many supermarkets now sell baby spinach in bulk. Look for it near the mesclun. These tender leaves have no stems and are usually fairly clean. One wash and a thorough drying are all that is required.

The substantial salads that follow are designed to serve four as a lunch entrée or light dinner. They will also feed six as a first course.

Spinach Salad with Mushrooms, Croutons, and Warm Lemon Dressing

SERVES 4

Homemade croutons are better than any you can buy and are a good use for stale bread. Cut a hunk of leftover baguette or country white bread into small cubes and fry them in olive oil until crisp. We prefer slightly woodsy cremini mushrooms in this salad, but regular white mushrooms are fine.

½ pound flat-leaf spinach, stemmed, washed, dried, and torn into large pieces (about 9 cups, tightly packed)

½ pound fresh cremini or white mushrooms, cleaned, stems trimmed, sliced thin

½ cup extra-virgin olive oil

3 cups stale French or Italian-style bread, cut into ¾-inch cubes

2 medium garlic cloves, minced

¼ cup juice from 2 medium lemons
Salt and ground black pepper

1. Place spinach and mushrooms in large bowl; set aside.

2. Heat oil in large skillet over medium-high heat until shimmering. Add bread; fry, turning several times with slotted spoon, until crisp and golden, about 3 minutes. Transfer to paper towel–lined plate. Off heat, let remaining oil cool slightly, about 1 minute. Add garlic; cook until lightly colored, about 2 minutes. Whisk in lemon juice and salt and pepper to taste. Pour warm dressing over salad; toss. Add croutons; toss again. Serve immediately.

Spinach Salad with Shrimp, Mango, and Red Onion

SERVES 4

To save time, buy shrimp that has been peeled and cooked. If you want to boil the shrimp yourself, buy slightly more than 1 pound with the shells on.

1½ pounds flat-leaf spinach, stemmed, washed, dried, and torn into large pieces (about 9 cups, tightly packed)

1 pound cooked medium shrimp

1 large ripe mango, peeled, pitted, and cut into thin strips

½ small red onion, sliced thin

2 tablespoons rice wine vinegar

1 teaspoon grated zest and 2 tablespoons juice from 1 orange

1 tablespoon minced fresh gingerroot

¼ cup canola or other mild vegetable oil

1 tablespoon Asian sesame oil
Salt and ground black pepper

1. Place spinach, shrimp, and mango in large bowl. Set aside.

2. Place onion and 1 tablespoon of vinegar in small bowl; macerate until onions are bright pink, about 5 minutes.

3. Whisk orange zest and juice, gingerroot, and remaining vinegar, as well as salt and pepper to taste, in small bowl. Gradually whisk in oils.

4. Add onion to salad bowl. Pour dressing over salad; toss and serve immediately.

Spinach and Avocado Salad with Chili-Flavored Chicken

SERVES 4

A creamy yogurt dressing spiked with lemon and garlic is a good match for the strong flavors in this salad.

2 teaspoons chili powder

1 teaspoon ground cumin
Salt

1 pound boneless, skinless chicken breasts, trimmed

2 teaspoons vegetable oil

1½ pounds flat-leaf spinach, stemmed, washed, dried, and torn into large pieces (about 9 cups, tightly packed)

4 ripe plum tomatoes, cored and cut into wedges

1 Haas avocado, halved, pitted, peeled, and cut into thin strips

3 tablespoons juice from 1 large lemon

¾ cup plain yogurt

2 tablespoons extra-virgin olive oil

1 large garlic clove, minced

1. Heat broiler or light grill. Mix chili powder,

cumin, and ½ teaspoon salt in small bowl. Rub vegetable oil then spice mixture into both sides of each chicken breast. Broil or grill, turning once, until cooked through, about 10 minutes. Set aside.

2. Place spinach and tomatoes in large bowl. Sprinkle avocado with 1 tablespoon of the lemon juice; add to salad bowl.

3. Whisk yogurt, olive oil, garlic, remaining lemon juice, and salt to taste, in small bowl.

4. Slice chicken crosswise into ¾-inch-wide strips and add to salad bowl. Pour dressing over salad; toss and serve immediately.

Caesar Salad

AS ORIGINALLY CONCEIVED BY CAESAR CARDINI, a restaurant owner in Tijuana, Mexico, Caesar salad was a tableside creation. A waiter would first place leaves of romaine lettuce in a large bowl, then lightly dress them with olive oil. Salt, pepper, more oil, lemon juice, and Worcestershire sauce were added along with two eggs that had been boiled for one minute and then cracked right into the bowl. In went the cheese and garlicky croutons and after much mixing and showmanship, the salad was transferred to a chilled plate and eaten immediately.

This recipe became a restaurant sensation in the 1920s, and, unlike other classics of that era, Caesar salad has grown in popularity ever since. We wanted to recapture the flavors of the original recipe while simplifying the technique, so the dressing can be in the refrigerator when guests arrive.

We first focused on the lettuce and croutons. Tasters could not tell the difference between bagged romaine hearts and leaves taken from the hearts of whole heads of romaine, so feel free to choose either one. Just make sure that you end up with 10 cups of torn lettuce leaves, which should be enough for four to six first-course servings.

The croutons were also fairly straightforward. We found that bread cut into half-inch cubes was the right size for this salad and that two cups of cubed bread made plenty of croutons. After trying six basic methods for making croutons, we ended up preferring those tossed with garlic oil and then baked in a 350-degree oven.

Using a simple version of the original dressing recipe, with extra-virgin olive oil, lemon juice, Worcestershire sauce, salt, and pepper, we set out to explore the role of the egg, which we consider the central question of this singular dressing.

We tried one and two raw eggs as well as one egg coddled for 45 seconds, 1 minute, and 2 minutes. Two eggs caused the dressing to separate; one was enough for this recipe. We liked the effect coddling has on the egg. The heat unleashes the thickening powers of the egg and results in a smoother, creamier dressing. However, coddling for more than 45 seconds can present some problems. As the egg continues to cook, the white will solidify and start sticking to the shell. When you go to crack an egg that has been coddled for two minutes, the shell shatters and can end up in the dressing. We prefer to coddle the egg for just 45 seconds. The shell still cracks neatly, and although a little of the white is opaque, most of the egg slides right into the bowl with the dressing.

We also decided to explore various options for those who do not wish to use a raw or coddled egg in their dressing because of fear of salmonella. We had seen several recipes for "modern" Caesar dressing made with a hard-boiled egg. Although the egg does an excellent job of thickening the dressing, it leaves behind that unmistakable sulfur smell of cooked eggs. We also detected a little grittiness, even when we made this dressing in the food processor.

Finally, we tried replacing the egg with a little soft tofu. We had seen this suggestion in several health foods cookbooks and were skeptical. However, tofu is the perfect thickener for this dressing because it is bland and smooth. There's no grittiness, and the flavors are basically the same as in our original recipe. Use the food processor, because it completely incorporates the tofu into the dressing. Our eggless Caesar dressing has a lighter color and slightly thicker texture than the traditional recipe.

Final tests revolved around seasonings. Although we wanted to remain faithful to the classic recipe, we missed the garlic and anchovy hit we now associate with Caesar salad. Without these ingredients, the dressing tastes more lemony, but also a bit flat. One small garlic clove (put through a press) and four minced anchovies add sufficient zing without becoming overpowering.

Caesar Salad

SERVES 4 TO 6

If you don't own a garlic press, chop the garlic for both the croutons and dressing by hand; sprinkle it with the salt and then continue mincing it until it is almost pureed. The garlic and anchovies in the dressing are optional but strongly recommended.

GARLIC CROUTONS

2 large garlic cloves, peeled and pressed through a garlic press

¼ teaspoon salt

3 tablespoons extra-virgin olive oil

2 cups ½-inch white bread cubes (from a baguette or country loaf)

CAESAR SALAD

1 large egg

3 tablespoons juice from 1 medium lemon

1 teaspoon Worcestershire sauce

¼ teaspoon salt

8 grindings fresh black pepper

1 small garlic clove, pressed (¼ teaspoon)

1½ teaspoons anchovy paste or 4 anchovy fillets, minced very fine

⅓ cup extra-virgin olive oil

2 medium heads romaine lettuce (large outer leaves removed) or 2 large romaine hearts; washed, dried, and torn into 1½-inch pieces (about 10 cups, lightly packed)

⅓ cup grated Parmesan cheese

1. FOR THE CROUTONS: Adjust oven rack to center position and heat oven to 350 degrees. Mix garlic, salt, and oil in small bowl; set aside for 20 minutes. Spread bread cubes out over small baking sheet. Drizzle oil through fine-mesh strainer evenly onto bread; toss to coat. Bake until golden, about 12 minutes. Cool on baking sheet to room temperature. (Croutons can be stored in airtight container for up to 1 day.)

2. FOR THE DRESSING: Bring water to boil in small saucepan over high heat. Carefully lower whole egg into water; cook 45 seconds. Remove with slotted spoon. When cool enough to handle, crack egg into small bowl with all other dressing ingredients except oil; whisk until smooth. Add oil in slow, steady stream, whisking constantly until smooth. Adjust seasonings. (Dressing may be refrigerated in airtight container for 1 day; shake before using.)

3. To mix the salad: Place lettuce in large bowl; drizzle with half of dressing, then toss to coat lightly. Sprinkle with cheese, remaining dressing, and croutons; toss to coat well. Divide among individual plates; serve immediately.

➤ VARIATIONS

Caesar Salad with Tofu Dressing

This eggless dressing will keep for a week in the refrigerator.

Follow recipe for Caesar Salad, substituting 2 ounces soft tofu, drained and crumbled (about ⅓ cup), for egg. Process dressing ingredients except oil in food processor workbowl fitted with steel blade, scraping down sides as needed, until tofu is incorporated fully and mixture is smooth, about 1 minute. With motor running, add oil in slow, steady stream until smooth.

Grilled Chicken Caesar Salad

SERVES 4 AS MAIN COURSE

Brush two boneless, skinless chicken breasts (about ¾ pound) with 1 tablespoon olive oil and sprinkle with salt and pepper to taste. Grill or broil, turning once, until cooked through, about 10 minutes. Cool chicken to room temperature and slice crosswise into ½-inch-wide strips. Follow recipe for Caesar Salad, adding chicken to the salad along with the cheese.

COLESLAW

DESPITE ITS SIMPLICITY, COLESLAW HAS always bothered us for two reasons: the pool of watery dressing that appears at the bottom of the bowl after a few hours, and the salad's sharp flavor, no matter what kind or quantity of vinegar is used. Our slaw always seemed to taste better when we tried it again the next day, but by then the dressing was the consistency of milk.

While most recipes instruct the cook to toss the shredded cabbage immediately with dressing, a few add an extra step. Either the shredded (or merely quartered) cabbage is soaked in ice water for crisping and refreshing, or it is salted, drained, and allowed to wilt.

Cabbage soaked in ice water was crisp, plump, and fresh. If looks were all that mattered, this cabbage would have scored high next to the limp, salted cabbage in the neighboring colander. But its good looks were deceiving. Even though we drained the cabbage and dried it thoroughly, the dressing didn't really adhere. Furthermore, within minutes, the cabbage shreds started to lose their recently acquired water, making for not a small but a large puddle of water to dilute the creamy dressing. The stiff cabbage shreds were strawlike, making them difficult to fork and even more difficult to get into the mouth without leaving a creamy trail.

Quite unlike the ice-water cabbage, the salted shreds lost most of their liquid while sitting in the salt, leaving the cabbage wilted but pickle-crisp. Since the cabbage had already lost most of its own liquid, there was little or no liquid for the salt in the dressing to draw out. We had found the solution to the problem of watery dressing. In addition, we found that this cabbage, having less water in it, took on more of the dressing's flavors, and unlike the stiff, icy shreds, this limp cabbage was also easier to eat.

We did discover that the salting process leaves the cabbage a bit too salty, but a quick rinse washes away the excess salt. After the cabbage has been rinsed, just pat it dry with paper towels and refrigerate until ready to combine it with the dressing. If the coleslaw is to be eaten immediately, rinse it quickly in ice water rather than tap water, then pat it dry. Coleslaw, at least the creamy style, should be served cold.

Having figured out how to keep the cabbage from watering down the dressing, we were ready to tackle the problem of acidity in the dressing. We found a few creamy coleslaw recipes in which the cabbage was tossed with sour cream only, or a combination of mayonnaise and sour cream—no vinegar. Although we were looking for ways to tone down the tang, a mix of sour cream and mayonnaise proved too mild for our taste. Other recipes called for lemon juice rather than vinegar. Although the lemon juice–flavored coleslaw was pleasantly tart, it lacked the depth that vinegar could offer. We decided to give low-acidity rice wine vinegar a try. We drizzled a bit of rice vinegar over the mayonnaise-tossed cabbage and found its mild acidity to be perfect for coleslaw.

Although there are several styles of coleslaw, the two that follow are classics—one mild and creamy, the other sweet-and-sour. Adjust either recipe to your taste. If sour cream is a must for your creamy slaw, then substitute it for some or all of the mayonnaise. Add green pepper or celery, red onions, or apples. Try caraway seeds or fresh dill, radishes or nuts.

Creamy Coleslaw
SERVES 4

If you like caraway or celery seed in your coleslaw, you can add one-quarter teaspoon of either with the mayonnaise and vinegar. You can shred, salt, rinse, and pat the cabbage dry a day ahead, but dress it close to serving time.

1	pound (about $\frac{1}{2}$ medium head) red or green cabbage, shredded fine or chopped (6 cups)
1	large carrot, peeled and grated
2	teaspoons kosher salt or 1 teaspoon table salt
$\frac{1}{2}$	small onion, minced
$\frac{1}{2}$	cup mayonnaise
2	tablespoons rice wine vinegar
	Ground black pepper

SCIENCE: Where There's Salt, There's Water

Vegetables that soak in ice water crisp up, while salted and drained vegetables go limp. These phenomena result from the cell structure of most foods, including vegetables. Cells are filled with liquid, but cell walls are semipermeable, allowing liquid to flow into and out of the cell. Depending on where the salt quantity is greater, that's where the water flows.

Cabbage is a pretty tough vegetable, but when soaked in ice water, its shreds become even stiffer and crisper. In this case, the cabbage cells contain more salt than the ice water. The ice water is drawn into the cabbage cells, causing the shreds to plump up. Watching a scored radish blossom into a radish rose when soaked in ice water is an even more dramatic example of this principle.

When shredded cabbage is salted, on the other hand, there is more salt outside the cabbage than there is contained in the cells. The cell water is drawn out by the clinging salt. This partially dehydrated cabbage is limp but still crisp.

1. Toss cabbage and carrots with salt in colander set over medium bowl. Let stand until cabbage wilts, at least 1 hour and up to 4 hours.

2. Dump wilted cabbage and carrots into the bowl. Rinse thoroughly in cold water (ice water if serving slaw immediately). Pour vegetables back into colander, pressing, but not squeezing, them to drain. Pat dry with paper towels. (Can be stored in a zipper-lock bag and refrigerated overnight.)

3. Pour cabbage and carrots back again into bowl. Add onion, mayonnaise, and vinegar; toss to coat. Season with pepper to taste. Cover and refrigerate until ready to serve.

Sweet-and-Sour Coleslaw

SERVES 4

Since rice wine vinegar tends to mellow, you may want to use cider vinegar if making the slaw a day ahead. The presence of the sugar in this recipe keeps you from having to rinse off salt from the cabbage, as is ordinarily the case.

1	pound (about ½ medium head) red or green cabbage, shredded according to illustrations below (6 cups)
1	large carrot, peeled and grated
½	cup sugar
2	teaspoons kosher salt or 1 teaspoon table salt
¼	teaspoon celery seed
6	tablespoons vegetable oil
¼	cup rice wine vinegar
	Ground black pepper

1. Toss cabbage and carrots with sugar, salt, and celery seed in colander set over medium bowl. Let stand until cabbage wilts, at least 1 hour and up to 4 hours.

2. Pour draining liquid from bowl; rinse bowl and dry. Dump wilted cabbage and carrots into bowl.

3. Add oil and vinegar; toss to coat. Season with pepper to taste. Cover and refrigerate until ready to serve. (Can be refrigerated for 2 days.)

➤ VARIATION

Curried Coleslaw with Apples and Raisins

SERVES 6

Follow recipe for Sweet-and-Sour Coleslaw, adding 1 teaspoon curry powder, 1 medium apple, peeled and cut into small dice, and ¼ cup raisins (optional) with oil and vinegar.

POTATO SALAD

POTATO SALADS COME IN NUMEROUS STYLES. Though recipes may seem dramatically different, most have four things in common—potatoes (of course), fat (usually bacon, olive oil, or mayonnaise); an acidic ingredient to perk things up; and flavorings for distinction. Though these salads may be very different in character, the issues affecting all of them, as it turns out, are much the same.

We first wanted to know what type of potato should be used and how it should be cooked. Recipe writers seemed split down the middle between starchy and waxy potatoes, with starchy praised for being more absorbent and waxy admired for their

SHREDDING CABBAGE

1. Cut a whole head of cabbage into quarters. Remove the piece of the core attached to each quarter.

2. Separate the cabbage quarters into stacks of leaves that flatten when pressed lightly.

3. To shred by hand, use a chef's knife to cut each stack of cabbage diagonally into long, thin pieces.

4. To shred in a food processor (which is best for larger jobs), roll the stacked leaves crosswise to fit them into the feed tube.

sturdiness. We have always just boiled potatoes with the skin on, but steaming, microwaving, roasting, or baking are all options.

Next, when should the potato be peeled? On the assumption that hot potatoes are more absorbent, some thought it worth scorching fingertips to get the cooked potatoes peeled and cut immediately. Other recipe writers were more casual—"peel when cool enough to handle." Still others suggested refrigerating the cooled potatoes, then peeling and cutting the next day. And of course you wonder whether you really need to peel them at all.

Finally, should potatoes be seasoned when still warm, assuming that they do absorb flavorings better in this state? Is it worth the two-step process of seasoning the potatoes with vinegar (or vinaigrette), salt, and pepper first? Or should you toss everything together at the same time?

After boiling, steaming, baking/roasting, and microwaving four different varieties of potatoes—Red Bliss, russet, all-purpose, and Yukon Golds—we found that Red Bliss is the potato of choice and that boiling is the cooking method of choice. High-starch potatoes—russet, all-purpose, and Yukon Gold—are not sturdy enough for salad making. They fell apart when cut and looked sloppy in salad form.

Before giving up on high-starch potatoes for salad making, we wanted to test their absorption power, a selling point for many cooks. A number of French, German, and American potato salad recipes suggested an initial drizzling of vinegar over warm or hot salad potatoes, so that they would taste seasoned from within as well as dressed from without.

We found that high-starch potatoes are indeed more absorbent than the lower-starch varieties—to a fault. When tossed with vinegar, the high-starch potato salads tasted dry, sucking up all the vinegar and asking for more. These mealy high-starch potatoes, we determined, were great for mashing or baking, but not for salad. The low-starch boiling potatoes successfully absorbed the vinegar but they remained firm and creamy.

Next we wanted to see if we could boost flavor at the cooking stage by boiling the potatoes in chicken broth and in water heavily seasoned with bay leaves and garlic cloves. The chicken stock may as well have been water—there wasn't even a hint of evidence

that the potatoes had been cooked in stock. The bay leaves and garlic smelled wonderful as the potatoes cooked, but while the potato skin smelled faintly of garlic, the potato itself was still bland.

The fact that nothing seemed to penetrate the potato got us wondering: Does the potato skin act as a barrier? We performed yet another experiment by cooking two batches of unpeeled potatoes, the first in heavily salted water and the second in unsalted water. We rinsed them quickly under cold running water and tasted. Sure enough, both batches of potatoes tasted exactly the same. We tried boiling potatoes without the skin, but they were waterlogged compared with their skin-on counterparts. In salad form all the potatoes had a sloppy, broken look and tasted watery. Our conclusion: Potatoes should be boiled skin-on in unsalted water.

Although we might not want to eat the skin of a boiled russet in a salad, we found the paper-thin skin of the boiled red potato not unpleasant to taste and certainly pleasant to look at in what is often a monochromatic salad. Although this saved the peeling step, we found the skin tended to rip when cutting the potato. Since this was especially true when the potatoes were very hot, we solved the problem in two ways. First, we cut the potatoes with a serrated knife, which minimized ripping, and second, we found it wasn't necessary to cut them when they were hot, since warm ones are just as absorbent.

At this point we had learned that warm potatoes absorb vinegar, but we weren't necessarily sure where we wanted the acidity: Should it be in the potato, in the dressing, or in both? To find out, we made three mayonnaise-based salads. In the first, we drizzled all the vinegar on the potato; in the second, half the vinegar went on the potato and the other half was mixed with the mayonnaise; and in the third salad, we mixed all the vinegar with the mayonnaise. The results were clear. Too much vinegar on the potatoes makes them taste pickled. The other extreme produced a zesty salad dressing, with creamy but bland potatoes. Using vinegar in moderation both on the potatoes and in the dressing provided the right balance.

To sum up: Use low-starch potatoes; boil them in their skins; don't salt the water; don't peel them unless you really want to; and use a serrated knife to cut the potatoes after boiling, once they have cooled down slightly. Then, while the potatoes are still warm, drizzle them with a splash of vinegar. After this, proceed with one of the salad recipes we've developed. If you prefer to add your own vegetables or seasonings, follow our basic technique.

Boiled Potatoes for Salad
MAKES ENOUGH POTATOES FOR
1 SALAD RECIPE

These boiled potatoes can be used in any of the three potato salad recipes that follow.

2   pounds Red Bliss or new potatoes (about 6 medium or 18 new), rinsed; scrubbed if you will not be peeling them

1. Place potatoes in a 4- to 6-quart pot; cover with water. Bring to a boil, cover, and simmer, stirring once or twice to ensure even cooking, until a thin-bladed paring knife or a metal cake tester inserted into the potato can be removed with no resistance (25 to 30 minutes for medium potatoes and 15 to 20 minutes for new potatoes).

2. Drain; cool potatoes slightly and peel if you like. Cut potatoes (use a serrated knife if they have skins) while still warm, rinsing knife occasionally in warm water to remove gumminess. Proceed as directed in one of the following recipes.

American-Style Potato Salad with Eggs and Sweet Pickles
SERVES 6 TO 8

Use sweet pickle, not relish, for the best results. Use homemade (page 36) or store-bought mayonnaise as you like in this recipe.

1   recipe Boiled Potatoes for Salad, cut into 1-inch cubes
2   tablespoons red wine vinegar
1/2   teaspoon salt
1/2   teaspoon ground black pepper
3   hard-boiled eggs, peeled and cut into small dice
2   large scallions, sliced thin
1   small celery stalk, cut into small dice
1/4   cup sweet pickles, cut into small dice

1/2   cup mayonnaise
2   tablespoons Dijon mustard
1/4   cup minced fresh parsley

1. Layer warm potato cubes in medium bowl, sprinkling with vinegar, salt, and pepper as you go. Refrigerate while preparing remaining ingredients.

2. Mix in remaining ingredients; refrigerate until ready to serve, up to 1 day.

French-Style Potato Salad with Tarragon Vinaigrette
SERVES 6

If fresh tarragon is not available, increase the parsley to three tablespoons and use tarragon vinegar in place of the white wine vinegar both for drizzling and in the dressing.

1   recipe Boiled Potatoes for Salad, cut into 1/4-inch slices
2   tablespoons white wine vinegar
1/2   teaspoon salt
1/2   teaspoon ground black pepper
2/3   cup Tarragon-Mustard Vinaigrette (page 36)
1   medium shallot, minced
2   tablespoons minced fresh parsley

1. Layer warm potato slices in medium bowl, sprinkling vinegar and the salt and pepper as you go. Let stand at room temperature while preparing dressing.

2. Whisk dressing and shallot together in small bowl. Pour over potatoes; toss lightly to coat. Refrigerate salad until ready to serve, up to 1 day. Bring to room temperature; stir in parsley, and serve.

German-Style Potato Salad with Bacon and Balsamic Vinegar
SERVES 6

Smaller new potatoes are more attractive in this recipe. The slices are smaller and tend not to break up, as do the bigger potatoes. Cider vinegar is traditional here, but we like the sweeter, fuller flavor of balsamic vinegar.

1   recipe Boiled Potatoes for Salad, cut into 1/4-inch slices
1/4   cup balsamic or cider vinegar

½	teaspoon salt
½	teaspoon ground black pepper
4–5	slices bacon (about 4 ounces), cut crosswise into ¼-inch strips
1	medium onion, cut into medium dice
2	tablespoons vegetable oil, if needed
½	cup beef broth
¼	cup minced fresh parsley

1. Layer warm potato slices in a medium bowl, sprinkling with 2 tablespoons vinegar and the salt and pepper as you go. Let stand at room temperature while preparing dressing.

2. Fry bacon in a medium skillet over medium heat until bacon is brown and crisp and fat is rendered, 7 to 10 minutes. Transfer bacon with a slotted spoon to bowl of potatoes. Add onion to bacon drippings; sauté until softened, 4 to 5 minutes. If bacon is fairly lean, onion will absorb most of drippings, so you will need to add up to 2 tablespoons vegetable oil to yield 2 tablespoons unabsorbed fat.

3. Add beef broth to onion and bring to a boil; add remaining 2 tablespoons vinegar. Remove from heat and pour mixture over potatoes. Add parsley; toss gently to coat. Serve warm or tepid.

PASTA SALAD

SINCE PASTA SALADS MAKE THE MOST SENSE as a side dish for a summer meal, we've always found it odd that many recipes are heavy and creamy. A good pasta salad should be light and refreshing, with a fair amount of vegetables. (We find little bits of salami a greasy and distressing addition to deli pasta salads.) The dressing should help convey flavors and keep the pasta moist, not weigh it down. Vinaigrette (rather than mayonnaise) is the obvious choice.

Almost every deli in America sells a pasta salad dressed with vinaigrette. Often made with fusilli (tri-color fusilli in trendier markets), this salad invariably looks unappetizing. The pasta is so mushy you can see it falling apart through the glass deli case. And the vegetables are tired and sad. The broccoli has faded to drab olive green and the shredded carrots that most markets add (a weird Americanization) have wilted. And as for the flavor—these unattractive salads usually look better than they taste.

The problem with most of these pasta salads is that the acid causes the pasta to soften and dulls the color and flavor of many vegetables, especially green ones. But leave out the lemon juice or vinegar and the salad tastes flat. We wanted to develop a light, vinaigrette-dressed vegetable pasta salad that looked good and tasted even better.

We started by making salads with four very simple vinaigrettes. Each contained a different acidic liquid, along with olive oil, salt, and pepper. Each was used to dress a simple pasta salad with blanched and cooled broccoli. The salads made with red wine vinegar and balsamic vinegar dyed the pasta and tasted too sharp. The salad made with white wine vinegar looked fine but tasted too acidic. The salad made with lemon juice was clearly the best. It had a nice bright flavor but was not puckery or sour. After half an hour, we noticed that the broccoli in the three salads with vinegar was turning olive green and starting to fall apart. But even after several hours, the broccoli in the salad with lemon juice was green and crunchy.

With lemon juice now our choice of acid, we focused on the sequence of assembling the pasta salad. Would hot vegetables absorb more dressing and taste better? Should we run the vegetables under cold water after cooking to set their color? Neither idea panned out. We found that green vegetables like broccoli are most susceptible to the effects of acid when they are hot. Letting them cool to room temperature helped stem any color loss, but unfortunately you can't speed up the process by running them under cold water. No matter how well we drained them, the vegetables tasted waterlogged after being rinsed in cold water. The best method is to let the vegetables rest in the colander for at least 20 minutes, or until barely warm to the touch, before tossing them with the pasta and dressing.

At this point, we had a master recipe that we liked pretty well, but it needed some other flavors. An herb—we chose basil, but almost anything will work—perked things up. Olives (or sun-dried tomatoes) made everything more lively by adding some acidity and saltiness to a dish that otherwise was a bit bland.

When we turned our attention to other vegetables, we discovered that, as we had suspected, other cooking methods added more flavor than blanching. A pasta salad made with roasted asparagus tasted better than one made with blanched asparagus, for example. Grilling also gave the vegetables a lot of flavor and made a better pasta salad.

Pasta Salad with Broccoli and Olives

SERVES 6 TO 8

If you prefer, increase the hot red pepper flakes or replace them with a few grindings of black pepper.

> Salt
> 3 pounds broccoli (about 2 small heads), florets cut into bite-sized pieces (about 7 cups)
> ¼ cup juice and ½ teaspoon grated zest from 2 lemons
> 1 medium garlic clove, minced
> ½ teaspoon hot red pepper flakes
> ½ cup extra-virgin olive oil
> 1 pound short, bite-sized pasta, such as fusilli, farfalle, or orecchiette
> 20 large black olives, such as kalamata or other brine-cured variety, pitted and chopped
> 15 large fresh basil leaves, shredded

1. Bring 4 quarts water to boil in large pot over high heat. Bring several quarts water to boil in large saucepan. Add salt to taste and broccoli to saucepan and cook until crisp-tender, about 2 minutes. Drain and cool to room temperature.

2. Meanwhile, whisk lemon juice and zest, garlic, ¾ teaspoon salt, and red pepper flakes in large bowl; whisk in oil in slow, steady stream until smooth.

3. Add pasta and 1 tablespoon salt to boiling water. Cook until pasta is al dente and drain. Whisk dressing again to blend; add hot pasta, cooled broccoli, olives, and basil; toss to mix thoroughly. Cool to room temperature, adjust seasonings, and serve. (Can be covered with plastic wrap and refrigerated for 1 day; return to room temperature before serving.)

Pasta Salad with Eggplant, Tomatoes, and Basil

SERVES 6 TO 8

The eggplant can be broiled until golden brown if you prefer not to grill them.

> 2 medium eggplant (about 1 pound total), cut into ½-inch-thick rounds
> ½ cup extra-virgin olive oil, plus extra for brushing on eggplant
> Salt and ground black pepper
> ¼ cup juice and ½ teaspoon grated zest from 2 lemons
> 1 medium garlic clove, minced
> ½ teaspoon hot red pepper flakes
> 1 pound short, bite-sized pasta, such as fusilli, farfalle, or orecchiette
> 2 large tomatoes, cored, seeded, and cut into ½-inch dice
> 15 large fresh basil leaves, shredded

1. Light grill. Bring 4 quarts water to boil in large pot over high heat.

2. Lightly brush eggplant with oil and sprinkle with salt and pepper to taste. Grill, turning once, until marked with dark stripes, about 10 minutes. Cool and cut into bite-sized pieces.

3. Meanwhile, whisk lemon juice and zest, garlic, ¾ teaspoon salt, and red pepper flakes in large bowl; whisk in oil in slow, steady stream until smooth.

4. Add pasta and 1 tablespoon salt to boiling water. Cook until pasta is al dente and drain. Whisk dressing again to blend; add hot pasta, cooled eggplant, tomatoes, and basil; toss to mix thoroughly. Cool to room temperature, adjust seasonings, and serve. (Can be covered with plastic wrap and refrigerated for 1 day; return to room temperature before serving.)

Pasta Salad with Asparagus and Red Peppers

SERVES 6 TO 8

If you prefer, roast the vegetables in a 425-degree oven. The asparagus will need about 10 minutes of cooking time; the peppers about 15 minutes. You can substitute fresh mint, parsley, or basil for the chives.

1½ pounds asparagus, tough ends snapped off

3 large red bell peppers, cored, seeded, and cut into 1½-inch wedges

½ cup extra-virgin olive oil, plus extra for brushing on vegetables

Salt and ground black pepper

¼ cup juice and ½ teaspoon grated zest from 2 lemons

1 medium garlic clove, minced

1 pound short, bite-sized pasta, such as fusilli, farfalle, or orecchiette

3 tablespoons snipped fresh chives

⅓ cup grated Parmesan cheese

1. Light grill. Bring 4 quarts water to boil in large pot over high heat.

2. Lightly brush asparagus and peppers with oil and sprinkle with salt and pepper to taste. Grill, turning once, until streaked with light grill marks, 6 to 8 minutes. Cool and cut into bite-sized pieces.

3. Meanwhile, whisk lemon juice and zest, garlic, ¾ teaspoon salt, and pepper to taste in large bowl; whisk in oil in slow, steady stream until smooth.

4. Add pasta and 1 tablespoon salt to boiling water. Cook until pasta is al dente and drain. Whisk dressing again to blend; add hot pasta, cooled asparagus and peppers, chives, and cheese; toss to mix thoroughly. Cool to room temperature, adjust seasonings, and serve. (Can be covered with plastic wrap and refrigerated for 1 day; return to room temperature before serving.)

Pasta Salad with Fennel, Red Onions, and Sun-Dried Tomatoes

SERVES 6 TO 8

If you prefer, roast the lightly oiled fennel and onions in a 425-degree oven until tender and light brown on both sides, 15 to 20 minutes.

2 large fennel bulbs, stalks discarded, bulbs halved through core and cut into ½-inch wedges

2 large red onions, cut into ½-inch-thick rounds

½ cup extra-virgin olive oil, plus extra for brushing on vegetables

Salt and ground black pepper

¼ cup juice and ½ teaspoon grated zest from 2 lemons

1 medium garlic clove, minced

1 pound short, bite-sized pasta, such as fusilli, farfalle, or orecchiette

½ cup oil-packed sun-dried tomatoes, sliced thin

15 large fresh basil leaves, shredded

1. Light grill. Bring 4 quarts water to boil in large pot over high heat.

2. Lightly brush fennel and onions with oil and sprinkle with salt and pepper to taste. Grill, turning once, until marked with dark stripes on both sides, about 15 minutes. Cool and cut fennel and onions into bite-sized pieces.

3. Meanwhile, whisk lemon juice and zest, garlic, ¾ teaspoon salt, and pepper to taste in large bowl; whisk in oil in slow, steady stream until smooth.

4. Add pasta and 1 tablespoon salt to boiling water. Cook until pasta is al dente and drain. Whisk dressing again to blend; add hot pasta, cooled fennel and onions, sun-dried tomatoes, and basil; toss to mix thoroughly. Cool to room temperature, adjust seasonings, and serve. (Can be covered with plastic wrap and refrigerated for 1 day; return to room temperature before serving.)

BREAD SALAD

TO THE PEOPLES OF THE MEDITERRANEAN, bread is holy; it is almost unthinkable to throw it away. It is not surprising, then, that there are so many uses for bread throughout the Mediterranean. One of the most delightful and surprising dishes that evolved in this part of the world is the use of stale bread for salads.

Such thrifty salads are superb dishes because they allow flavorful and fresh tomatoes to be fully experienced, along with fragrant mint, parsley, and fresh cilantro. Another crucial ingredient is high-quality, extra-virgin olive oil. Because the dry bread so readily absorbs moisture, much of the flavor of the dish is derived from the dressing.

Last but not least, fundamental to the success of these salads is the quality of bread. Sliced white bread, or airy supermarket bread that is highly refined and becomes rock-hard within a few days simply won't do. Ideally, bread used in bread salads should not contain sugar or sweeteners of any kind, which would conflict with the savory nature of the ingredients. Nor should it include such ingredients as raisins or nuts. What the bread should have is a sturdy texture and good wheaty flavor.

Depending on how stale the bread is, it may need to be dampened with a little water. The extent of dampening is determined by the dryness of the bread; if the bread receives too much dampening, it will collapse into a soggy mess from the anointment of water or dressing. Therefore, assemble the salad, see how much the bread softens, and then adjust the texture by sprinkling lightly with water.

Because the bread becomes soggy fairly quickly, none of these salads should be made very much in advance of serving. The best approach is to assemble all of the salad ingredients in advance, then combine the ingredients just before serving.

Bread Salad with Tomatoes, Herbs, and Red Onions

SERVES 4

Sturdy bread is important here—commercial white breads will fall apart when dressed with oil and vinegar.

1	pound day-old coarse peasant bread or sturdy Italian-style bread, crusts removed, cut or torn into 1-inch cubes (about 6 cups)
½	cup extra-virgin olive oil
3	tablespoons red wine vinegar
2	large, vine-ripened tomatoes or 4 plum tomatoes, cored, seeded, and cut into medium dice
½	red onion, sliced paper thin
2	tablespoons torn fresh basil or mint leaves
2	teaspoons whole fresh oregano leaves
1	tablespoon minced fresh Italian parsley leaves
½	teaspoon salt
¼	teaspoon ground black pepper

Place bread cubes in shallow bowl. Mix oil, vinegar, tomatoes, onion, and half of herbs in medium bowl. Let stand until flavors develop, about 10 minutes, then add to bread, along with remaining herbs, and toss well. Season with salt and pepper to taste. If bread still seems dry, sprinkle with 1 or 2 tablespoons water to rehydrate it a bit. Serve. (If sturdy bread is used, salad can be covered and set aside up to 2 hours.)

Pita Bread Salad with Cucumbers, Tomatoes, and Fresh Herbs

SERVES 6

Fattoush is a Lebanese salad that is dressed with the juice of fresh lemons instead of vinegar. While draining the cucumbers is an extra step, it keeps the salad from becoming soggy.

½	seedless cucumber (skin intact) or 1 regular cucumber (peeled and seeded), cut into small dice
	Salt and ground black pepper
1	foot-length Syrian flat bread or four 6-inch pita breads, several days old, torn into ½-inch pieces
1	pint cherry tomatoes, halved, or 2 large vine-ripened tomatoes, chopped coarse
6	scallions, trimmed and sliced thin, including 2 inches of green part
¼	cup minced fresh mint leaves
¼	cup minced fresh cilantro or parsley leaves
½	cup extra-virgin olive oil
6	tablespoons juice from 2 large lemons

1. Heat oven to 375 degrees. Put cucumber in colander; sprinkle with ¼ teaspoon salt. Place weight (such as zipper-lock bag filled with water) over cucumbers; drain to release most of liquid, about 1 hour.

2. Put bread pieces on baking sheet; bake until crisp but not browned, 5 to 7 minutes. Transfer to large bowl; add cucumber, tomatoes, scallions, and herbs, and toss well. In small bowl, combine oil, juice, and salt and pepper to taste. Add to large bowl, toss again, and serve immediately.

Bread Salad with Roasted Peppers and Olives

SERVES 4 TO 6

Sourdough or a sturdy peasant bread is needed for this salad. Airy, unsubstantial bread will become soggy very quickly.

1	pound sturdy Italian bread, crusts removed, cut or torn into 1-inch cubes (about 6 cups)
2	bell peppers, one red and one yellow, roasted (page 85), stemmed, seeded, and cut into ½-inch strips

½ cup extra-virgin olive oil

¼ cup cider vinegar

1 small red or white onion, quartered and sliced thin

1 medium scallion, trimmed and sliced thin, including 2 inches of green part

3 tablespoons pitted and sliced green olives

1 tablespoon minced fresh oregano leaves

½ teaspoon salt

¼ teaspoon ground black pepper

1. Mix bread cubes and pepper strips in large bowl; set aside.

2. Mix oil, vinegar, onion, scallion, olives, oregano, salt, and pepper in medium bowl; let stand for flavors to develop, about 10 minutes. Add dressing to bread and peppers; toss to combine. If bread still seems dry, sprinkle with 1 or 2 tablespoons water to rehydrate it a bit. Serve. (If sturdy bread is used, salad can be covered and set aside up to 2 hours.)

TABBOULEH

PERHAPS THE BEST-KNOWN ARAB DISH IN the United States is tabbouleh. However, the tabbouleh typically served here is very different from the original. In its Middle Eastern home, this dish is basically a parsley salad with bulghur, rather than the bulghur salad with parsley that is frequently found here.

In addition to finely minced parsley, a perfect tabbouleh includes morsels of bulghur—crushed, parboiled wheat—tossed in a penetrating, minty lemon dressing with bits of ripe tomato. While these principal ingredients remain the same, a variety of preparation techniques exist, each Arab cook being convinced that his or her method produces the finest version.

The variety of parsley used in the Arab Mediterranean is the flavorful, flat-leafed plant that is usually labeled "Italian parsley" in American markets. The other option is curly-leafed parsley, which is more delicately flavored and less fragrant than flat-leafed. Either will make an acceptable salad. If you particularly like the parsley flavor to shine through, use flat-leafed; if you don't mind a more mellow tabbouleh in which the flavors blend together, the curly is a good choice.

One advantage of curly-leafed parsley is that its tougher leaves can be minced—with care—in the food processor. To do so, snip off and discard the crisp stems. Fill the bowl of your machine lightly with the leaves, and briefly pulse. Instead of packing in a large quantity of parsley, it is better to repeat this step two or three times until all the parsley is lightly minced. Unless you have removed every bit of stem before processing, some noticeable lengths will remain. These should be removed. Contrary to popular belief, the stems are not more bitter than the leaves, but they are much more fibrous and can create an unpleasant texture in the salad.

Flat-leafed parsley, more delicate than the curly variety, should be chopped by hand in the traditional manner. Simply pinch off the leaves and mince them.

The bulghur used in tabbouleh in the Middle East is an earthy homemade product, boiled until it is just about to crack open, then set out to dry on sheets in the hot sun. A more commercial version of bulghur can be found in ethnic groceries and natural food stores throughout the United States, as well as in supermarkets in many parts of the country. When buying this product for use in tabbouleh, be sure to look for fine grain (often labeled #1). Medium grain (labeled #2) is an acceptable substitute. Just be sure that you do not get the coarse version, which needs to be cooked rather than just soaked. Medium bulghur is about the same size as couscous, while fine is even smaller. Never substitute cracked wheat, which is an uncooked and totally dissimilar grain. Similarly, avoid boxed tabbouleh mixes, which usually consist of irregularly sized bits of bulghur with a few flecks of dried parsley.

Arab cooks have developed many different methods of processing the bulghur for tabbouleh, each method sworn to by its adherents as the only acceptable one. We tried processing the bulghur in the five most commonly used ways. First we rinsed the grain, combined it with the minced tomato, and set it aside to absorb the tomato juices. With this method, the bulghur remained unacceptably crunchy.

Next we marinated the bulghur in lemon juice and olive oil dressing. This approach produced bulghur that was tasty but slightly heavy. The third method, soaking the grain in water until fluffy and then squeezing out the excess moisture, produced an equally acceptable—but equally heavy—nutty-flavored wheat.

Next we learned that by first soaking the wheat in water for about five minutes, then draining the liquid and replacing it with the lemon–olive oil dressing, the wheat's texture was good and the flavor superior.

But the all-out winner came as a surprise. We first rinsed the bulghur, then mixed it with fresh lemon juice. We then set the mixture aside to allow the juice to be absorbed. When treated in this way, bulghur acquires a fresh and intense flavor, but without the heaviness that the added olive oil produces.

To complete the dish, combine the bulghur with the parsley, finely chopped scallions, fresh mint, and tomatoes. Toss with the remaining dressing ingredients and serve within a few hours. Letting the mixture sit for an hour or so blends the flavors nicely, but after five or six hours the scallions tends to become too strong and overpower the other flavors.

The final question is the proportion of parsley to bulghur. Although some Lebanese restaurateurs present a 9 to 1 ratio of parsley to bulghur, we find that the wholesome goodness of the wheat is lost unless it is in a more harmonious balance. We recommend that the finished dish contain 5 parts parsley to 3 or 4 parts wheat.

Tabbouleh

SERVES 4 TO 6

Middle Eastern cooks frequently serve this salad with crisp inner leaves of romaine lettuce, using them as spoons to scoop the salad from the serving dish. Fine-grain bulghur is best in this recipe, but medium-grain will work; avoid coarse-grain bulghur, which must be cooked.

½	cup fine-grain bulghur wheat, rinsed under running water and drained
⅓	cup juice from 2 lemons
⅓	cup extra-virgin olive oil
	Salt
⅛	teaspoon Middle Eastern red pepper or cayenne (optional)
2	cups minced fresh parsley
2	medium tomatoes, halved, seeded, and cut into very small dice
4	medium scallions, green and white parts, minced
2	tablespoons minced fresh mint leaves (or 1 rounded teaspoon dried mint)

1. Mix bulghur wheat with ¼ cup lemon juice in medium bowl; set aside until grains are tender and fluffy, 20 to 40 minutes, depending on age and type of bulghur.

2. Mix remaining lemon juice, olive oil, salt to taste, and red pepper if desired in small bowl. Mix bulghur, parsley, tomatoes, scallions, and mint; add dressing and toss to combine. Cover and refrigerate to let flavors blend, 1 to 2 hours. Serve.

TOMATO SALAD

A BONUS OF SUMMER TOMATO SALADS IS THAT the mildly acidic juices from the tomatoes themselves provide a delicious base for a dressing, so very little additional acid is needed in the dressing. To make this work, you need to extract a little of the juice from the tomatoes before you make the salads. This is easily done. Simply cutting the tomatoes into wedges and letting them sit for fifteen minutes provides enough time for the juices to exude. Salting the cut tomatoes helps this process and seasons the tomatoes and their juices at the same time.

Some cooks recommend peeling the tomatoes, but we find the skin on local vine-ripened tomatoes to be thin and unobtrusive. If home-grown or locally grown tomatoes are unavailable, substitute halved cherry tomatoes.

Tomato Salad with Canned Tuna, Capers, and Black Olives

SERVES 6

Oil-packed tuna is more in tune with the Mediterranean flavors in this salad, but you may use water-packed tuna if you prefer.

4–5	large vine-ripened tomatoes (about 1½ pounds)
½	teaspoon salt
3	tablespoons extra-virgin olive oil
1	tablespoon juice from 1 lemon
3	tablespoons capers, chopped
12	large black olives, such as kalamata or other brine-cured variety, pitted and chopped

¼ cup finely chopped small red onion

2 tablespoons chopped fresh parsley leaves

Ground black pepper

1 6-ounce can tuna, drained

1. Core and halve tomatoes, then cut each half into 4 or 5 wedges. Toss wedges with salt in large bowl; let rest until small pool of liquid accumulates, 15 to 20 minutes.

2. Meanwhile, whisk oil, lemon juice, capers, olives, onion, parsley, and pepper to taste in small bowl. Pour mixture over tomatoes and accumulated liquid; toss to coat. Set aside to blend flavors, about 5 minutes.

3. Crumble tuna over tomatoes; toss to combine. Adjust seasonings and serve immediately.

Tomato Salad with Arugula and Shaved Parmesan

SERVES 6

Use a vegetable peeler to remove thin shavings from the hunk of cheese.

4–5 large vine-ripened tomatoes
(about 1½ pounds)

½ teaspoon salt

2 tablespoons extra-virgin olive oil

1 tablespoon balsamic vinegar

1 small garlic clove, minced or put through garlic press

Ground black pepper

1 small bunch arugula, cleaned and chopped coarse (about 1 cup)

1 small chunk (about 2 ounces) Parmesan cheese, shaved into strips

1. Core and halve tomatoes, then cut each half into 4 or 5 wedges. Toss wedges with salt in large bowl; let rest until small pool of liquid accumulates, 15 to 20 minutes.

2. Meanwhile, whisk oil, vinegar, garlic, and pepper to taste in small bowl. Pour mixture over tomatoes and accumulated liquid; toss to coat. Set aside to blend flavors, about 5 minutes.

3. Add arugula and Parmesan; toss to combine. Adjust seasonings and serve immediately.

Tomato Salad with Feta and Cumin-Yogurt Dressing

SERVES 6

Draining the yogurt in a fine sieve gives it a creamier, denser texture, which is better suited to use in a dressing.

4–5 large vine-ripened tomatoes
(about 1½ pounds)

½ teaspoon salt

¼ cup plain yogurt, drained in fine sieve about 30 minutes (discard liquid)

1 tablespoon extra-virgin olive oil

1 tablespoon juice from 1 lemon

1 small garlic clove, minced or put through garlic press

1 teaspoon ground cumin

3 small scallions, white and green parts, sliced thin

1 tablespoon chopped fresh oregano leaves

Ground black pepper

1 small chunk (about 3 ounces) feta cheese

1. Core and halve tomatoes, then cut each half into 4 or 5 wedges. Toss wedges with salt in large bowl; let rest until small pool of liquid accumulates, 15 to 20 minutes.

2. Meanwhile, whisk drained yogurt, oil, lemon juice, garlic, cumin, scallions, oregano, and pepper to taste in small bowl. Pour mixture over tomatoes and accumulated liquid; toss to coat. Set aside to blend flavors, about 5 minutes.

3. Crumble feta over tomatoes; toss to combine. Adjust seasonings and serve immediately.

Israeli Tomato and Cucumber Salad

SERVES 6

Thin-skinned English cucumbers, with or without the peel, work well in this salad.

4–5 large vine-ripened tomatoes
(about 1½ pounds)

½ teaspoon salt

3 tablespoons extra-virgin olive oil

3 tablespoons juice from 1 lemon

¼ cup finely chopped red onion

¼   cup chopped fresh mint leaves
        Ground black pepper
2   medium cucumbers, peeled, quartered, seeded,
        cut into ¼-inch pieces, tossed with
        2 teaspoons salt in strainer or colander set over
        bowl, and drained about 1 hour (discard liquid)

1. Core and halve tomatoes, then cut each half into 4 or 5 wedges. Toss wedges with salt in large bowl; let rest until small pool of liquid accumulates, 15 to 20 minutes.

2. Meanwhile, whisk oil, lemon juice, red onion, mint, and pepper to taste in small bowl. Pour mixture over tomatoes and accumulated liquid and toss to coat. Let rest to blend flavors, about 5 minutes.

3. Add drained cucumber pieces; toss to combine. Adjust seasonings and serve immediately.

CUCUMBER SALAD

MORE OFTEN THAN NOT, BY THE TIME YOU eat a cucumber salad, the cucumbers have gone soft and watery, losing their appealing texture and diluting the dressing to near tastelessness. This made the primary goal of our testing simple: Maximize the crunch.

The standard recommendation for ridding watery vegetables such as cucumbers, zucchini, and eggplant of unwanted moisture is to salt them. The salt creates a higher concentration of ions (tiny, charged particles) at the surface of the vegetable than exists deep within its cells. To equalize the concentration levels, the water within the cells is drawn out through permeable cell walls. In the case of cucumbers, this leaves them wilted, yet very crunchy. Of course, some culinary questions remain: How much salt should be used? Should the cucumber slices be weighted, or pressed, to squeeze out the liquid? How long should they drain?

To find out if pressing salted cucumbers really squeezes out more liquid, we trimmed and seeded six cucumbers to eight ounces each, sliced them on the bias, and tossed each batch with one teaspoon of salt in its own colander set over a bowl. Three of them had zipper-lock freezer bags filled with water placed on top of them; no additional weight was added to the other three. Then we left them all to drain, measuring the liquid each had released after 30 minutes and after 1, 2, 3, and 12 hours. At each time point, the weighted cucumbers had released about 1 tablespoon more liquid than the unweighted cucumbers; 3 versus 2 after 30 minutes, 4 versus 3 after 1 hour, and so on. Interestingly, the weighted cukes gave off no more liquid after 12 hours than they had after 3 hours (7 tablespoons at both points). So weighting the cucumbers is worthwhile, but forget about draining the cucumbers overnight; it's not necessary.

At the one-hour mark, we could not detect an

SALTING CUCUMBERS

1. Peel and halve each cucumber lengthwise. Use a small spoon to remove the seeds and surrounding liquid from each cucumber half.

2. Lay the cucumber halves flat side down on a work surface and slice them on the diagonal into ¼-inch-thick pieces.

3. Toss the cucumbers and salt (1 teaspoon for each cucumber) in a colander set in a bowl. Place a gallon-sized plastic bag filled with water on top of the cucumbers to weigh them down and force out the liquid. Drain for at least 1 hour and up to 3 hours.

appreciable difference in flavor or texture between weighted and unweighted cukes. But we wanted to see how they would perform in salads with different types of dressings. We mixed one batch each of the weighted and unweighted cucumbers with three types of sauces—creamy, oil-based, and water-based—and allowed each to sit at room temperature for one hour. This is where the true value of better-drained cucumbers became obvious; every single taster preferred the salads made with pressed cucumbers for their superior crunch and less diluted dressings.

As for the amount of salt, some cooks recommend simply using the quantity with which you would normally season the cucumber, while others say you should use more, up to two tablespoons per cucumber, and then rinse off the excess before further use. We tried a few cucumbers, prepared exactly as those described above except with two tablespoons of salt. The cucumbers with two tablespoons did give up about one more tablespoon of liquid within the first hour than those drained with one teaspoon had, but they also required rinsing and blotting dry with paper towels. And despite this extra hassle, they still tasted much too salty in the salads. We would advise forgoing the extra salt.

Sesame Lemon Cucumber Salad
SERVES 4

Mild rice wine vinegar works well in this Asian-inspired dressing. Toast sesame seeds in a small skillet set over medium heat, shaking the pan occasionally, until they are fragrant and golden, 4 to 5 minutes.

¼	cup rice wine vinegar
1	tablespoon juice from 1 small lemon
2	tablespoons Asian sesame oil
2	teaspoons sugar
⅛	teaspoon dried red pepper flakes plus more to taste
1	tablespoon sesame seeds, toasted
3	medium cucumbers, sliced, salted, and drained (see illustrations on page 54)

Whisk all ingredients except cucumbers in medium bowl. Add cucumbers; toss to coat. Serve chilled or at room temperature.

Sweet-and-Tart Cucumber Salad
SERVES 4

Based on a common Thai relish served with saté, this salad is also great with grilled salmon or grilled chicken breasts.

½	cup rice wine vinegar
2½	tablespoons sugar
3	medium cucumbers, sliced, salted, and drained (see illustrations on page 54)
½	medium red onion, sliced very thin
2	small jalapeño chiles, seeded and minced (or more, to taste)

1. Bring ⅔ cup water and vinegar to boil in small nonreactive saucepan over medium heat. Stir in sugar to dissolve; reduce heat and simmer 15 minutes. Cool to room temperature.

2. Meanwhile, mix cucumbers, onion, and jalapeños in medium bowl. Pour dressing over cucumber mixture; toss to coat. Serve chilled.

Creamy Dill Cucumber Salad
SERVES 4

Salting and draining the onion along with the cucumbers in this recipe removes the sharp sting of raw onion.

1	cup sour cream
3	tablespoons cider vinegar
1	teaspoon sugar
¼	cup minced fresh dill
	Salt and ground black pepper
3	medium cucumbers, sliced, salted, and drained (see illustrations on page 54)
½	medium red onion, sliced very thin, salted and drained with cucumbers

Whisk sour cream, vinegar, sugar, dill, and salt and pepper to taste in medium bowl. Add cucumbers and onion; toss to coat. Serve chilled, adjusting seasonings if necessary.

Yogurt Mint Cucumber Salad

SERVES 4

Known as raita, this creamy salad is traditionally served as a cooling contrast to curry dishes.

I	cup plain low-fat yogurt
2	tablespoons extra-virgin olive oil
¼	cup minced fresh mint leaves
2	small garlic cloves, minced
	Salt and ground black pepper
3	medium cucumbers, sliced, salted, and drained (see illustrations on page 54)

Whisk yogurt, oil, mint, garlic, and salt and pepper to taste in medium bowl. Add cucumbers; toss to coat. Serve chilled, adjusting seasonings if necessary.

CHICKEN SALAD

CLASSIC CHICKEN SALAD CONSISTS OF tender breast meat, pulled apart by hand rather than cubed with a knife, and bound loosely with mayonnaise. There's a little celery for texture, some parsley or tarragon for flavor, and a squeeze of lemon juice for freshness. We often make this salad from leftover roast or poached chicken, and we put it together by taste and sight.

So what didn't we know about chicken salad? After a little thought, we had only one question. When making the classic version from scratch, and not from leftover meat, how should we cook the chicken?

Although there were many choices, they basically fell into two camps, wet cooking and dry cooking. The wet cooking methods included poaching, steaming, roasting in foil, and, in a method new to us, dropping the chicken into simmering aromatic water and then removing it from heat and letting it cool to room temperature.

Unfortunately, chicken cooked by each of these methods had a bland, unmistakably boiled flavor. Chicken cooked in the microwave also had that wet-cooked taste.

Roast chicken, which is cooked with dry heat, was a very different matter. Even after the skin and bones were removed, the meat tasted roasted and the resulting chicken salad was superb.

Roast Chicken Breasts for Salad

MAKES ABOUT 5 CUPS WHEN SHREDDED, ENOUGH FOR I SALAD RECIPE

Once the chicken breasts have cooled to room temperature, remove and discard the skin. At this point, you may wrap and refrigerate the breasts or make salad.

2	large whole bone-in, skin-on chicken breasts (at least 1½ pounds each)
I	tablespoon vegetable oil
	Salt

Adjust oven rack to middle position and heat oven to 400 degrees. Set breasts on small, foil-lined jelly-roll pan. Brush with oil and sprinkle generously with

SHREDDING CHICKEN BREASTS

  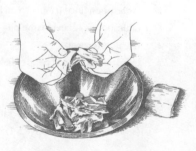

1. Slice along the center bone to separate the two pieces of breast meat. Insert your fingers into the cut made by the knife and gently pry the breast meat off the bone in two pieces.

2. Cut each breast piece into thirds.

3. Use your hands to pull apart each breast piece and shred it into small chunks.

salt. Roast until meat thermometer inserted into thickest part of breast registers 160 degrees, 35 to 40 minutes. Cool to room temperature, remove skin, and continue with one of salad recipes that follow. (Can be wrapped in plastic and refrigerated for 2 days.)

Classic Creamy Chicken Salad
SERVES 6

In addition to the parsley leaves, you can flavor the salad with 2 tablespoons of minced fresh tarragon or basil leaves. You may use leftover meat from a roast chicken if desired.

1	recipe Roast Chicken Breasts for Salad, skinned and boned, meat shredded according to illustrations on page 56 (about 5 cups)
2	medium celery stalks, cut into small dice
2	medium scallions, white and green parts, minced
¾	cup mayonnaise
2	tablespoons juice from 1 small lemon
2	tablespoons minced fresh parsley leaves
	Salt and ground black pepper

Mix all salad ingredients together in large bowl, including salt and pepper to taste. Serve. (Can be covered and refrigerated overnight.)

VARIATIONS

Waldorf Chicken Salad

Follow recipe for Classic Creamy Chicken Salad, adding 1 large crisp apple, cored and cut into medium dice, and 6 tablespoons chopped toasted walnuts.

Curried Chicken Salad with Raisins and Honey

Follow recipe for Classic Creamy Chicken Salad, adding 6 tablespoons golden raisins, 2 teaspoons curry powder, and 1 tablespoon honey. Replace parsley with equal amount of cilantro.

EGG SALAD

EGG SALAD IS ONE OF THOSE SIMPLE, spur-of-the-moment comfort foods that should be easy to make. However, sometimes it turns out to be too pasty. The overall flavor can be drab. The mayonnaise excessive. The onions too biting. The hardest part, though, is cooking the eggs properly.

We have always considered hard-cooking an egg to be a crapshoot. There's no way to watch the proteins cook under the brittle shell of an uncracked egg, and you certainly can't poke it with an instant-read thermometer, as you would with so many other foods. Often eggs are overcooked, with rubbery whites and chalky yolks. Of course, undercooked eggs without fully set yolks are even more problematic, especially when trying to make egg salad.

There are two general methods for boiling eggs—starting them in cold water and bringing them to a simmer, and lowering them into already simmering water. The first method is not terribly precise. When do you start the clock—when the eggs go into the water, when the water starts to boil? Also, what temperature is right for simmering? Everyone knows what boiling water looks like (and the temperature is always 212 degrees at sea level), but simmering water can be 180, 190, or even 200 degrees. We never developed a reliable timing mechanism with this technique.

Lowering eggs into simmering water is not easy either, because the eggs are likely to crack. Some sources suggest poking a thumb tack through the large end of the egg where the air hole typically sits, but we had inconsistent results with this "trick." Again, the issue of defining "simmering water" proved problematic.

Not satisfied with either method, we tried a third method—starting the eggs in cold water, bringing the water to a boil, and then turning off the heat. The pan is covered and the eggs are set aside to cook by residual heat for 10 minutes. There's no need to define "simmer" with this method. As long as you can recognize when water is at a boil and can time 10 minutes, you are guaranteed hard-boiled eggs with bright, creamy yolks and tender whites.

With our eggs perfectly boiled, it was time to make salad. We quickly found that both a fork and a pastry blender mashed the eggs so much that, when blended with mayonnaise, they became unpleasantly pasty. In addition to being reminiscent of baby food, this egg salad was quick to ooze out from between the slices of bread in a sandwich. After experimenting with various options, we found that eggs diced into small cubes (just under one-half inch) gave the salad the full mouthfeel we had been seeking and also held up well in a sandwich.

Although most egg salad recipes call for binding the eggs with mayonnaise, we found recipes that called for combining the mayonnaise with cream cheese, yogurt, light cream, cottage cheese, sour cream, or even buttermilk. Thankfully, we liked plain mayonnaise the best. Some lemon brightened things up, while a bit of mustard added depth. We preferred the sweetness of a red onion for the classic recipe but also liked scallions and shallots for some of the variations. Yellow onion was simply too harsh. Minced celery and parsley added an element of freshness, and we finally had an egg salad that was truly a source of comfort rather than disappointment.

Foolproof Boiled Eggs for Salad

MAKES ENOUGH FOR I SALAD RECIPE

You may double or triple this recipe as long as you use a pot large enough to hold the eggs in a single layer, covered by an inch of water.

6   large eggs

Place eggs in medium saucepan, cover with 1 inch of water, and bring to boil over high heat. Remove pan from heat, cover, and let sit for 10 minutes. Meanwhile, fill a medium bowl with 1 quart water and 1 tray of ice cubes (or equivalent). Transfer eggs to ice bath with slotted spoon; let sit 5 minutes. Tap eggs all over against the counter surface to crack surface, then roll it gently back and forth a few times. Begin peeling from the air pocket end. The shell should come off in spiral strips attached to the thin membrane.

Classic Egg Salad

MAKES ABOUT 2¹/₂ CUPS, ENOUGH
FOR 4 SANDWICHES

A mozzarella slicer turns a boiled egg into perfect ³/₈-inch cubes. Place the egg in the slicer and cut through it lengthwise. Turn the egg a quarter turn and slice it crosswise. Now, rotate the egg 90 degrees and slice it widthwise.

I	recipe Foolproof Boiled Eggs for Salad, peeled and diced medium
¹/₄	cup mayonnaise
2	tablespoons minced red onion
I	tablespoon minced fresh parsley leaves
¹/₂	medium celery stalk, chopped fine
2	teaspoons Dijon mustard
2	teaspoons juice from I lemon
¹/₄	teaspoon salt
	Ground black pepper

Mix all ingredients together in medium bowl, including ground black pepper to taste. Serve. (Can be covered and refrigerated overnight.)

> VARIATIONS

Egg Salad with Radish, Scallions, and Dill

Follow recipe for Classic Egg Salad, substituting 1 tablespoon minced fresh dill for parsley, 1 medium thin-sliced scallion for red onion, and adding 3 medium radishes, minced.

Curried Egg Salad

Follow recipe for Classic Egg Salad, substituting 1 tablespoon minced fresh cilantro for parsley and adding 1½ teaspoons curry powder. Omit salt.

Creamy Egg Salad with Capers and Anchovies

Follow the recipe for Classic Egg Salad, adding 1 small garlic clove, minced, 2 tablespoons chopped capers, and 1 minced anchovy fillet. Omit salt.

Creamy Egg Salad with Bacon, Shallots, and Watercress

In medium skillet over medium heat, fry 4 slices bacon (about 4 ounces, cut into ¼-inch pieces), until brown and crisp, about 5 minutes. Transfer bacon with slotted spoon to plate lined with paper towel; pour off all but 1 tablespoon of fat from pan. Add 2 large shallots, chopped medium, and sauté until softened and browned, about 5 minutes. Follow recipe for Classic Egg Salad, omitting celery and salt, substituting sautéed shallots for red onion, and adding bacon and ¼ cup watercress leaves, chopped coarse.

3

VEGETABLES

ASPARAGUS

ASPARAGUS PRESENTS ONLY ONE PREPARATION issue—should the spears be peeled, or is it better to discard the tough, fibrous ends entirely? In our tests, we found that peeled asparagus have a silkier texture, but we preferred the contrast between the crisp peel and tender inner flesh. Peeling also requires a lot of work. We prefer to simply snap off the tough ends and proceed with cooking.

We investigated moist-heat cooking methods and found that boiling and steaming yielded similar results. The delicate tips remained a bit crisper when the asparagus was steamed, so that's our preferred method.

A second option for asparagus is stir-frying. The spears must be cut into smaller pieces—about one-and-a-half inches is right. We found that there is no reason to precook asparagus before stir-frying. As long as you use a skillet large enough to hold the asparagus in a single layer, they will soften after about four minutes of stir-frying. Adding a fairly liquidy sauce (which will reduce quickly to a syrup) helps finish the cooking process.

A third option, and one that most cooks don't consider, is grilling or broiling. The intense dry heat concentrates the flavor of the asparagus, and the exterior caramelization makes the spears especially sweet. The result is asparagus with a heightened, and we think, delicious flavor.

SNAPPING OFF TOUGH ENDS FROM ASPARAGUS

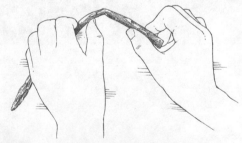

In our tests, we found that the tough, woody part of the stem will break off in just the right place if you hold the spear the right way: Hold the asparagus about halfway down the stalk; with the other hand, hold the cut end between the thumb and index finger about an inch or so up from the bottom, then bend the stalk until it snaps.

Master Recipe for Steamed Asparagus
SERVES 4

A large sauté pan or Dutch oven is the best pot for steaming asparagus. Steamed asparagus is rather bland, so we prefer to toss it with a flavorful vinaigrette as in the variations.

1½	pounds asparagus, tough ends snapped off (see illustration below)

Fit wide saucepan with steamer basket. Add water, keeping water level below basket. Bring water to boil over high heat. Add asparagus to basket. Cover and steam until asparagus spears bend slightly when picked up and flesh at cut end yields when squeezed, 3 to 4 minutes for asparagus under ½ inch in diameter, 4 to 5 minutes for jumbo asparagus. Remove asparagus from basket and season as directed in variations.

VARIATIONS
Steamed Asparagus with Lemon Vinaigrette

1½	tablespoons lemon juice
½	teaspoon Dijon mustard
¼	teaspoon Tabasco sauce
2	tablespoons extra-virgin olive oil
	Salt and ground black pepper
1	recipe Steamed Asparagus

1. Whisk lemon juice, mustard, and Tabasco together in small bowl. Whisk in oil until dressing is smooth. Season with salt and pepper to taste.

2. Prepare asparagus and place on platter when cooked. Rewhisk dressing and drizzle over asparagus. Serve warm or at room temperature.

Steamed Asparagus with Ginger-Hoisin Vinaigrette

2½	tablespoons rice wine vinegar
1½	tablespoons hoisin sauce
2½	teaspoons soy sauce
1½	teaspoons minced fresh gingerroot
1½	tablespoons canola oil
1½	teaspoons Asian sesame oil
1	recipe Steamed Asparagus

1. Whisk vinegar, hoisin sauce, soy sauce, and ginger together in small bowl. Whisk in oils until dressing is smooth.

2. Prepare asparagus and place on platter when cooked. Rewhisk dressing and drizzle over asparagus. Serve warm or at room temperature.

❧

Master Recipe for Stir-Fried Asparagus

SERVES 4

Really thick spears should be halved lengthwise, then cut into 1½-inch pieces to ensure that the center cooks through.

½	cup chicken stock or low-sodium canned broth
½	teaspoon salt
¼	teaspoon ground black pepper
1½	tablespoons plus 1 teaspoon peanut oil
1½	pounds asparagus, tough ends snapped off (see illustration on page 60) and cut on the bias into 1½-inch pieces
3	medium garlic cloves, minced

1. Combine stock, salt, and pepper in small bowl and set aside.

2. Heat 12-inch nonstick skillet over high heat until quite hot, 2 to 3 minutes. Add 1½ tablespoons oil and swirl to coat pan evenly (oil should shimmer in pan immediately). Add asparagus in single layer and stir-fry, tossing every 45 seconds, until well browned, about 4 minutes.

3. Clear center of pan, add garlic, and drizzle with remaining 1 teaspoon oil. Mash garlic with back of spatula. Cook 10 seconds and mix garlic with asparagus. Add chicken broth mixture and cook until sauce is syrupy, about 30 seconds. Serve immediately.

➢ VARIATIONS

Thai-Style Stir-Fried Asparagus with Chiles, Garlic, and Basil

2	tablespoons soy sauce
1	tablespoon water
1	tablespoon sugar
1½	tablespoons plus 1 teaspoon peanut oil
1½	pounds asparagus, tough ends snapped off (see illustration on page 60) and cut on the bias into 1½-inch pieces
3	medium garlic cloves, minced
1	tablespoon minced fresh jalapeño or serrano chile
¼	cup chopped fresh basil leaves

1. Combine soy sauce, water, and sugar in small bowl and set aside.

2. Heat 12-inch nonstick skillet over high heat until quite hot, 2 to 3 minutes. Add 1½ tablespoons oil and swirl to coat pan evenly (oil should shimmer in pan immediately). Add asparagus in single layer and stir-fry, tossing every 45 seconds, until well browned, about 4 minutes.

3. Clear center of pan, add garlic and chile, and drizzle with remaining 1 teaspoon oil. Mash garlic with back of spatula. Cook 10 seconds and mix garlic with asparagus. Add soy sauce mixture and cook until sauce is syrupy, about 30 seconds. Off heat, stir in basil. Serve immediately.

Stir-Fried Asparagus with Black Bean Sauce

3	tablespoons dry sherry
2	tablespoons chicken stock or low-sodium canned broth
1	tablespoon soy sauce
1	tablespoon Asian sesame oil
1	tablespoon fermented black beans
1	teaspoon sugar
¼	teaspoon ground black pepper
1½	tablespoons plus 1 teaspoon peanut oil
1½	pounds asparagus, tough ends snapped off (see illustration on page 60) and cut on the bias into 1½-inch pieces
3	medium garlic cloves, minced
1½	teaspoons minced fresh gingerroot
2	scallions, thinly sliced

1. Combine sherry, stock, soy sauce, sesame oil, beans, sugar, and pepper in small bowl and set aside.

2. Heat 12-inch nonstick skillet over high heat until quite hot, 2 to 3 minutes. Add 1½ tablespoons oil and swirl to coat pan evenly (oil should shimmer in pan immediately). Add asparagus in single layer and stir-fry, tossing every 45 seconds, until well browned, about 4 minutes.

3. Clear center of pan, add garlic and ginger, and drizzle with remaining 1 teaspoon oil. Mash garlic with back of spatula. Cook 10 seconds and mix gar-

lic with asparagus. Add sherry mixture and cook until sauce is syrupy, about 30 seconds. Off heat, add scallions. Serve immediately.

Master Recipe for Grilled or Broiled Asparagus

SERVES 4

Thick spears will burn on the surface before they cook through. Use spears no thicker than ⅝ inch.

1½	pounds asparagus, tough ends snapped off (see illustration on page 60)
1	tablespoon extra-virgin olive oil
	Salt and ground black pepper

1. Either light grill or preheat broiler. Toss asparagus with oil in medium bowl, or, if broiling, on rimmed baking sheet.

2. Grill asparagus over medium heat, turning once, until tender and streaked with light grill marks, 5 to 7 minutes. If broiling, line up spears in single layer on baking sheet and place pan about 4 inches from broiler. Broil, shaking pan once halfway through cooking to rotate spears, until tender and browned in some spots, 5 to 7 minutes. Season asparagus with salt and pepper to taste and serve hot, warm, or at room temperature.

➤ VARIATIONS

Grilled or Broiled Asparagus with Peanut Sauce

1	tablespoon Asian sesame oil
1	tablespoon smooth peanut butter
1	tablespoon water
1½	teaspoons rice wine vinegar
1½	teaspoons soy sauce
1	medium garlic clove, minced
1½	teaspoons minced fresh gingerroot
	Salt and ground black pepper
1½	pounds asparagus, tough ends snapped off (see illustration on page 60)
1	tablespoon minced fresh cilantro leaves

1. Either light grill or preheat broiler. Whisk oil, peanut butter, water, vinegar, soy sauce, garlic, ginger, and salt and pepper to taste in small bowl. Toss asparagus with half of peanut butter mixture in medium bowl, or, if broiling, on rimmed baking sheet.

2. Grill asparagus over medium heat, turning once, until tender and streaked with light grill marks, 5 to 7 minutes. If broiling, line up spears in single layer on baking sheet and place pan about 4 inches from broiler. Broil, shaking pan once halfway through cooking to rotate spears, until tender and browned in some spots, 5 to 7 minutes.

3. Whisk cilantro into remaining peanut butter mixture. Toss with cooked asparagus and adjust seasonings. Serve hot, warm, or at room temperature.

Grilled or Broiled Asparagus with Rosemary and Goat Cheese

2	tablespoons extra-virgin olive oil
1	tablespoon lemon juice
1	medium garlic clove, minced
½	teaspoon minced fresh rosemary
	Salt and ground black pepper
1½	pounds asparagus, tough ends snapped off (see illustration on page 60)
1	ounce goat cheese, crumbled

1. Either light grill or preheat broiler. Whisk oil, lemon juice, garlic, rosemary, and salt and pepper to taste together in small bowl. Toss asparagus with 1 tablespoon dressing in medium bowl, or, if broiling, on rimmed baking sheet.

2. Grill asparagus over medium heat, turning once, until tender and streaked with light grill marks, 5 to 7 minutes. If broiling, line up spears in single layer on baking sheet and place pan about 4 inches from broiler. Broil, shaking pan once halfway through cooking to rotate spears, until tender and browned in some spots, 5 to 7 minutes.

3. Toss cooked asparagus with remaining dressing. Adjust seasonings and sprinkle with goat cheese. Serve hot, warm, or at room temperature.

BROCCOLI

BROCCOLI REQUIRES A MOIST-HEAT COOKING method to keep the florets tender and to cook through the stalks. We tested boiling, blanching then sautéing, and steaming. Boiled broccoli is soggy-tasting and mushy, even when cooked for just two minutes. The florets absorb too much water. We found the same thing happened when we blanched the broccoli for a minute and then finished cooking it in a hot skillet.

Delicate florets are best cooked above the water in a steamer basket. We found that the stalk may be cooked along with the florets as long as it has been peeled and cut into small chunks. Broccoli will be fully cooked after about five minutes of steaming. At this point, it may be tossed with a flavorful dressing. A warning: Cook broccoli just two or three minutes too long and chemical changes cause this vegetable to lose color and texture.

We tried stir-frying broccoli without precooking and found that the florets started to fall apart long before the stems were tender. While blanching and then stir-frying helped the broccoli to cook more evenly, the florets were soggy. We found that partially cooking the broccoli in the steamer basket and then adding it to a stir-fry pan works best. This technique is best when you want to sauce broccoli rather than dress it with vinaigrette.

Master Recipe for Steamed Broccoli

SERVES 4

For maximum absorption, toss steamed broccoli with the dressings listed in the variations when hot. The broccoli may be served immediately or cooled to room temperature.

| 1½ | pounds broccoli (about 1 medium bunch), prepared according to illustrations below |

Fit wide saucepan with steamer basket. Add water, keeping water level below basket. Bring water to boil over high heat. Add broccoli to basket. Cover and steam until broccoli is just tender, 4½ to 5 minutes. Remove broccoli from basket and season as directed in variations.

➤ VARIATIONS

Steamed Broccoli with Spicy Balsamic Dressing and Black Olives

2	teaspoons balsamic vinegar
2	teaspoons red wine vinegar
1	medium garlic clove, minced
½	teaspoon hot red pepper flakes
¼	teaspoon salt
¼	cup extra-virgin olive oil
1	recipe Steamed Broccoli
12	large black olives, pitted and quartered

PREPARING BROCCOLI

1. Place head of broccoli upside down on a cutting board and trim off the florets very close to their heads with a large knife.

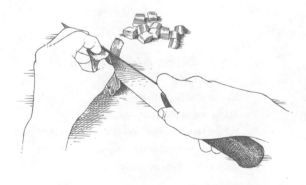

2. The stalks may also be trimmed and cooked. Stand each stalk up on the cutting board and square it off with a large knife. This will remove the outer ⅛ inch from the stalk, which is quite tough. Now cut the stalk in half lengthwise and into bite-sized pieces.

1. Whisk vinegars, garlic, hot red pepper flakes, and salt together in small bowl. Whisk in oil.

2. Prepare broccoli and place in serving bowl when cooked. Rewhisk dressing and toss with broccoli and olives. Serve warm or at room temperature.

Steamed Broccoli with Orange-Ginger Dressing and Walnuts

1	tablespoon peanut oil
1	tablespoon soy sauce
1	tablespoon honey
1	tablespoon grated orange zest
3	tablespoons orange juice
1	medium garlic clove, peeled
1	piece fresh gingerroot, about 1 inch, peeled
1/2	teaspoon salt
1	recipe Steamed Broccoli
2/3	cup walnuts, toasted and chopped
2	medium scallions, thinly sliced

1. Place oil, soy sauce, honey, orange zest and juice, garlic, ginger, and salt in workbowl of food processor. Process until smooth.

2. Prepare broccoli and place in serving bowl when cooked. Rewhisk dressing and toss with broccoli, walnuts, and scallions. Serve warm or at room temperature.

Master Recipe for Stir-Fried Broccoli

SERVES 4

Instead of steaming broccoli until tender and tossing it with a dressing, it may be partially steamed and then stir-fried with seasonings.

1/2	cup chicken stock or low-sodium canned broth
1/2	teaspoon salt
	Ground black pepper
1 1/2	tablespoons plus 1 teaspoon peanut oil
1	recipe Steamed Broccoli (page 63), cooked just 2 1/2 minutes and removed from steamer
1	tablespoon minced garlic

1. Mix together chicken stock, salt, and pepper to taste in small bowl.

2. Heat 12-inch nonstick skillet over high heat until quite hot, 2 to 3 minutes. Add 1 1/2 tablespoons oil and swirl to coat bottom of pan (oil should shimmer immediately). Add broccoli and cook, stirring every 30 seconds, until fully cooked and heated through, about 2 1/2 minutes.

3. Clear center of pan, add garlic, and drizzle with remaining 1 teaspoon oil. Mash garlic with back of spatula. Cook 10 seconds and then mix garlic with broccoli. Add chicken stock mixture and cook until sauce is syrupy, about 30 seconds. Serve immediately.

➤ VARIATION

Stir-Fried Broccoli with Orange Sauce

1 1/2	teaspoons grated orange zest
3	tablespoons orange juice
1 1/2	tablespoons chicken stock or canned low-sodium broth
2	teaspoons soy sauce
1/4	teaspoon sugar
	Ground black pepper
1 1/2	tablespoons plus 1 teaspoon peanut oil
1	recipe Steamed Broccoli (page 63), cooked just 2 1/2 minutes and removed from steamer
1	medium garlic clove, minced
1	teaspoon minced fresh gingerroot
1	medium scallion, thinly sliced

1. Mix together orange zest and juice, chicken stock, soy sauce, sugar, and pepper to taste in small bowl.

2. Heat 12-inch nonstick skillet over high heat until quite hot, 2 to 3 minutes. Add 1 1/2 tablespoons oil and swirl to coat bottom of pan (oil should shimmer immediately). Add broccoli and cook, stirring every 30 seconds, until fully cooked and heated through, about 2 1/2 minutes.

3. Clear center of pan, add garlic, ginger, and scallion, and drizzle with remaining 1 teaspoon oil. Mash garlic with back of spatula. Cook 10 seconds and then mix garlic mixture with broccoli. Add orange juice mixture and cook until sauce is syrupy, about 30 seconds. Serve immediately.

BROCCOLI RABE

A PERFECT PLATE OF BROCCOLI RABE SHOULD be intensely flavored but not intensely bitter. You want to taste the other ingredients and flavors in the dish. So we set our sights on developing a dependable, quick method of cooking this aggressive vegetable that would deliver less bitterness and a rounder, more balanced flavor.

Parcooking any bitter greens helps to carry off some of the bitter flavor. We found that steaming produced little change in the broccoli rabe—it was still very intense. When blanched in a small amount of salted boiling water (1 quart of water for about 1 pound of broccoli rabe), the rabe was much better. But the bitterness was still overwhelming, so we increased the boiling salted water to three quarts.

Sure enough, the broccoli rabe was delicious; it was complex, mustardy, and peppery as well as slightly bitter, and the garlic and olive oil added later complemented rather than competed with its flavor. Depending on personal taste, you can reduce the amount of blanching water for stronger flavor or, to really to tone down the bitterness, increase it.

After considerable testing, we found that the lower two inches or so of the stems were woody and tough, while the upper portions of the stems were tender enough to include in the recipes. When we used only the upper portions, there was no need to go through the laborious task of peeling the stems. Cutting the stems into pieces about one inch long made them easier to eat and allowed them to cook in the same amount of time as the florets and the leaves.

EQUIPMENT: Chef's Knives

A good chef's knife is probably the most useful tool any cook owns. Besides chopping vegetables, it can be used for myriad tasks, including cutting up poultry, mincing herbs, and slicing fruit. So what separates a good knife from an inferior one? To understand the answer to this question, it helps to know something about how knives are constructed.

The first pieces of cutlery were made about 4,000 years ago with the discovery that iron ore could be melted and shaped into tools. The creation of steel, which is 80 percent iron and 20 percent other elements, led to the development of carbon steel knives—the standard for 3,000 years. Although this kind of steel takes and holds an edge easily, it also stains and rusts. Something as simple as cutting an acidic tomato can corrode carbon steel.

In this century, new alloys have given cooks better options. Stainless steel, made with at least 4 percent chromium and/or nickel, will never rust. Used for many cheap knives, stainless steel is also very difficult to sharpen. The compromise between durable but dull stainless steel and sharp but corrosive carbon steel is something called high-carbon stainless steel. Used by most knife manufacturers, this blend combines durability and sharpness.

Until recently, all knives were "hot drop forged"—that is, the steel was heated to 2,000 degrees, dropped into a mold, given four or five shots with a hammer, and then tempered (cooled and heated several times to build strength). This process is labor-intensive (many steps must be done by hand), which explains why many chef's knives cost almost $100.

A second manufacturing process feeds longs sheets of steel through a press that punches out knife after knife, much like a cookie cutter slicing through dough. Called stamped blades, these knives require some hand finishing but are much cheaper to produce since a machine does most of the work.

While experts have long argued that forged knives are better than stamped ones, our testing did not fully support this position. We liked some forged knives and did not like others. Likewise, we liked some stamped knives and did not like others. The weight and shape of the handle (it must be comfortable to hold and substantial but not too heavy), the ability of the blade to take an edge, and the shape of the blade (we like a slightly curved blade, which is better suited to the rocking motion often used to mince herbs or garlic than a straight blade) are all key factors in choosing a knife.

When shopping, pick up the knife and see how it feels in your hand. Is it easy to grip? Does the weight seem properly distributed between the handle and blade? In our testing, we liked knives made by both Henckels and Wüsthof. An inexpensive knife by Forschner, with a stamped blade, also scored well.

Buying a good knife is only half the challenge. You must keep the edge sharp. To that end, we recommend buying an electric knife sharpener. Steels are best for modest corrections and all knives will require more substantial sharpening at least several times a year, if not more often if you cook a lot. Stones are difficult to use since they require that you maintain a perfect 20 degree angle between the stone and blade. An electric knife sharpener (we like models made by Chef's Choice) takes the guesswork out of sharpening and allows you to keep those edges sharp and effective.

Master Recipe for Blanched Broccoli Rabe

SERVES 4

Using a salad spinner makes easy work of drying the cooled, blanched broccoli rabe.

- 1 bunch broccoli rabe (about 14 ounces), washed, bottom 2 inches of stems trimmed and discarded, remainder cut into 1-inch pieces
- 2 teaspoons salt

1. Bring 3 quarts water to boil in large saucepan. Stir in broccoli rabe and salt and cook until wilted and tender, about 2½ minutes. Drain broccoli rabe and set aside.

2. Cool empty saucepan by rinsing under cold running water. Fill cooled saucepan with cold water and submerge broccoli rabe to stop the cooking process. Drain again; squeeze well to dry and proceed with one of the following variations.

➤ VARIATIONS

Broccoli Rabe with Garlic and Red Pepper Flakes

This variation and the following one can be turned into main course pasta dishes. Increase the oil to 4 tablespoons and toss the broccoli rabe with 1 pound of pasta, cooked al dente. Season to taste with salt and ground black pepper, and serve with grated Parmesan cheese.

- 2 tablespoons extra-virgin olive oil
- 3 medium garlic cloves, minced
- ¼ teaspoon red pepper flakes
- 1 recipe Blanched Broccoli Rabe
   Salt

Heat oil, garlic, and red pepper flakes in medium skillet over medium heat until garlic begins to sizzle, about 3 to 4 minutes. Increase heat to medium high, add blanched broccoli rabe, and cook, stirring to coat with oil, until heated through, about 1 minute. Season to taste with salt; serve immediately.

Broccoli Rabe with Sun-Dried Tomatoes and Pine Nuts

- 2 tablespoons extra-virgin olive oil
- 3 medium garlic cloves, minced
- ¼ teaspoon red pepper flakes
- ¼ cup oil-packed sun-dried tomatoes, cut into thin strips
- 1 recipe Blanched Broccoli Rabe
- 3 tablespoons pine nuts, toasted
   Salt

Heat oil, garlic, red pepper flakes, and sun-dried tomatoes in medium skillet over medium heat until garlic begins to sizzle, about 3 to 4 minutes. Increase heat to medium high, add blanched broccoli rabe and pine nuts, and cook, stirring to coat with oil, until broccoli rabe is heated through, about 1 minute. Season to taste with salt; serve immediately.

CABBAGE AND BRUSSELS SPROUTS

THE LARGE GREEN CABBAGE AND THE SMALL Brussels sprout have similar cooking properties. Both become waterlogged when boiled. Steaming leaves cabbage and Brussels sprouts less soggy, but the flavor is wan and listless. Cabbage and Brussels sprouts need a cooking method that will add some flavor as well as counter their strong mustardy smell.

We found that braising shredded cabbage in a mixture of butter and chicken stock adds flavor. As long as the amount of liquid is quite small, the texture will still be a bit crunchy and delicious. Cabbage can also be braised in other fats (bacon drippings) and liquids (apple juice, wine). Cream combines fat and liquid and may be used alone.

Because of their shape and size, we found that Brussels sprouts could easily be cooked, drained, and then sautéed in seasonings. (This method is too awkward with shredded cabbage but works with the small, round sprouts.) We tested steaming the sprouts as well as braising them in a little salted water. The sprouts benefited greatly from cooking with some salt, so braising is our preferred cooking method. As with cabbage, Brussels sprouts may also be braised in cream and served as is.

Master Recipe for Braised Cabbage

SERVES 4

This recipe uses about 6 cups of shredded cabbage. See page 44 for more details on shredding cabbage.

1	tablespoon unsalted butter
1	tablespoon chicken stock or low-sodium canned broth
½	large head green cabbage (about 1½ pounds), cored and cut into ¼-inch shreds
¼	teaspoon dried thyme
1	tablespoon minced fresh parsley leaves
	Salt and ground black pepper

Heat butter in large skillet over medium heat. Add stock, then cabbage and thyme. Bring to simmer; cover and continue to simmer, stirring occasionally, until cabbage is wilted but still bright green, 7 to 9 minutes. Sprinkle with parsley and season with salt and pepper to taste. Serve immediately.

➤ VARIATIONS

Cream–Braised Cabbage with Lemon and Shallots

Follow recipe for Braised Cabbage, replacing butter and chicken stock with ¼ cup heavy cream, 1 teaspoon lemon juice, and 1 small minced shallot. Omit thyme and parsley.

Braised Cabbage with Caraway and Mustard

Follow recipe for Braised Cabbage, replacing stock with 1 tablespoon apple juice and ½ teaspoon Dijon mustard and substituting 1 tablespoon caraway seeds for parsley.

Braised Cabbage with Bacon and Onion

4	strips bacon
½	small onion, minced
1	tablespoon chicken stock or low-sodium canned broth
½	large head green cabbage (about 1½ pounds), cored and cut into ¼-inch shreds
¼	teaspoon dried thyme
1	tablespoon minced fresh parsley leaves
	Salt and ground black pepper

1. Fry bacon in large skillet over medium heat until crisp, about 5 minutes. Remove bacon from pan with slotted spoon and drain on paper towels. Pour off all but 1 tablespoon bacon drippings.

2. Add onion to remaining drippings and sauté until lightly colored, about 1 minute. Add stock, then cabbage and thyme. Bring to simmer; cover and continue to simmer, stirring occasionally, until cabbage is wilted but still bright green, 7 to 9 minutes. Sprinkle with parsley and season with salt and pepper to taste.

3. Transfer cabbage to serving bowl. Crumble bacon over cabbage and serve immediately.

Master Recipe for Braised Brussels Sprouts

SERVES 3 TO 4

You can toss Brussels sprouts with a little butter and season them with ground black pepper, or make one of the variations that follow. In our testing, we found no benefit to cutting an X into the bottom of each sprout. (Some sources claim that this promotes even cooking.) Simply trim the bottom of the stem and remove any discolored leaves before cooking.

1	pound small Brussels sprouts, stems trimmed and any discolored outer leaves removed
½	teaspoon salt

Bring sprouts, ½ cup water, and salt to boil in large skillet over heat. Lower heat to medium, cover, and simmer (shaking pan once or twice to redistribute sprouts) until knife tip inserted into center of sprout meets little resistance, 8 to 10 minutes. Drain well and season as directed in variations below or note above.

➤ VARIATIONS

Brussels Sprouts Braised in Cream

Follow recipe for Braised Brussels Sprouts, substituting 1 cup heavy cream for water. Increase cooking time to 10 to 12 minutes. Season with pinch grated nutmeg and ground black pepper and serve without draining.

Brussels Sprouts with Garlic and Pine Nuts

Prepare Braised Brussels Sprouts and set aside. Heat 2 tablespoons extra-virgin olive oil in large skillet over medium heat. Add ¼ cup pine nuts and cook, stirring occasionally, until nuts begin to brown, about 2 minutes. Add 2 minced garlic cloves and cook until softened, about 1 minute. Stir in cooked Brussels sprouts. Cook, stirring occasionally, until heated through, 3 to 4 minutes. Season with salt and pepper to taste and serve immediately.

Brussels Sprouts with Tarragon–Mustard Butter

The mustard sauce may separate and appear curdled after the sprouts are added. If so, continue cooking and it should come back together.

Prepare Braised Brussels Sprouts and set aside. Melt 4 tablespoon unsalted butter in large skillet over medium heat. Whisk in 2 tablespoons Dijon mustard until smooth. Add 1 teaspoon dried tarragon leaves. Cook, stirring constantly, until bubbly, about 30 seconds. Stir in cooked Brussels sprouts, coating well with sauce. Cook, stirring frequently, until heated through, 3 to 4 minutes. Season to taste with salt and pepper and serve immediately.

CARROTS

CRISP, RAW CARROTS ARE UNIVERSAL FAVORITES, but when carrots are cooked, people often turn away. They seem to be used more to provide an accent with their brilliant color than for their distinctive taste. Admittedly, carrots can be mushy and earthy-tasting if overcooked, but when treated properly, they are wonderful, having just a hint of sweetness and a crisp-tender texture.

In our tests, we found that boiling and steaming (the methods used by most cooks to prepare carrots) do nothing to bring out the flavor of the carrots. Sautéing works wonders with the flavor, but it takes quite a while for the carrots to soften, and the butter (which is our preferred fat with carrots) tends to burn. Braising (cooking the carrots in a little water and then sautéing them) seemed like the way to go.

Just put the carrots in a pan with some water and butter, and cook with the lid on until they are crisp-tender. At this point, we remove the lid to let the water cook off. (There is no need to drain the car-

rots.) The carrots finish cooking in the remaining fat. To improve their flavor, we found it helpful to add salt and sugar to the butter and water.

Master Recipe for Quick-Cooked Carrots
SERVES 3 TO 4

Once the water evaporates, make sure to sauté the carrots for a minute or two to flavor them with butter and bring out their sweetness.

1	pound carrots, peeled, ends trimmed, and sliced on the diagonal, ¼ inch thick
2	tablespoons unsalted butter
1	teaspoon sugar
½	teaspoon salt
	Ground black pepper
1	tablespoon minced fresh parsley leaves

In 10-inch skillet, bring carrots, 2 tablespoons water, butter, sugar, and salt to boil over medium-high heat. Cover and cook 3 minutes. Uncover skillet; continue to cook over medium-high heat until remaining water evaporates, about 1 minute. Sauté carrots until tender, 1 to 2 minutes longer. Season to taste with pepper, sprinkle with fresh parsley leaves, and serve.

➤ VARIATIONS
Quick-Cooked Carrots with Orange and Pistachios

Follow recipe for Quick-Cooked Carrots, substituting ¼ cup fresh orange juice and 1 teaspoon orange zest for the water and increasing sugar from 1 teaspoon to 1 tablespoon. Once liquid has evaporated, add ¼ cup toasted pistachio nuts and continue with recipe.

Quick-Cooked Carrots with Mustard–Brown Sugar Glaze

Follow recipe for Quick-Cooked Carrots, omitting sugar. Once liquid has evaporated, stir in 2 packed tablespoons dark or light brown sugar and 1½ tablespoons Dijon mustard. Continue cooking until carrots are tender and glazed, about 2 minutes longer. Substitute 2 tablespoons snipped fresh chives for the parsley.

Quick-Cooked Carrots with Vinegar and Thyme

Follow recipe for Quick-Cooked Carrots. Once liquid has evaporated, add 2 tablespoons red wine vinegar and ¼ teaspoon dried thyme leaves. Cook until carrots are tender and glazed, about 2 minutes longer. Stir in parsley.

CAULIFLOWER

CAULIFLOWER IS VERY POROUS, WHICH CAN be an advantage or a disadvantage depending on the cooking medium being used. For instance, we found that boiled cauliflower, even when underdone, always tastes watery. Steaming is a much better cooking method, producing a clean, bright, sweet flavor and a crisp-tender, not soggy, texture.

To confirm our sensory observations, we weighed cauliflower before and after cooking and noticed a 10 percent increase in weight when the cauliflower was boiled (the extra weight was all water) and no change in weight when the cauliflower was steamed. After steaming, cauliflower may be dressed with a vinaigrette or sautéed briefly in a flavorful fat.

A second option is braising, which takes advantage of cauliflower's ability to absorb liquid. We found that it is best to sauté the cauliflower first—browning intensifies the naturally mild flavor of this vegetable and adds a layer of sweetness—and then add a flavorful liquid. Browned cauliflower takes well to aggressive seasonings, such as soy sauce, Indian spices, and even chiles.

Master Recipe for Steamed Cauliflower

SERVES 4

Mild seasonings such as dill, basil, nuts, and citrus are the best complement to the fresh, delicate flavor of steamed cauliflower. You may toss steamed cauliflower with extra-virgin olive oil or butter and salt and serve as is, or follow any of the simple variations.

I	medium head cauliflower (about 2 pounds), trimmed, cored, and cut into florets (see illustrations on page 70)

Fit wide saucepan with steamer basket. Fill with enough water to reach just below bottom of basket. Bring water to boil over high heat. Add cauliflower to basket. Cover and steam until cauliflower is tender but still offers some resistance to the tooth when sampled, 7 to 8 minutes. Remove cauliflower from basket and season as directed in variations or note above.

➤ VARIATIONS

Steamed Cauliflower with Dill-Walnut Vinaigrette

I	tablespoon red wine vinegar
I	tablespoon lemon juice
I	teaspoon Dijon mustard
½	shallot or scallion, minced
2	tablespoons minced fresh dill
2	tablespoons extra-virgin olive oil
	Salt and ground black pepper
I	recipe Steamed Cauliflower
½	cup walnuts, toasted and chopped

1. Whisk vinegar, lemon juice, mustard, shallot, dill, oil, and salt and pepper to taste together in small bowl.

2. Prepare cauliflower and place in serving bowl when cooked. Rewhisk dressing and toss with cauliflower and walnuts. Adjust seasonings and serve warm or at room temperature.

Steamed Cauliflower with Curry-Basil Vinaigrette

I	tablespoon lemon juice
I	tablespoon white wine vinegar
I ½	teaspoons honey
I	teaspoon curry powder
¼	teaspoon salt
⅛	teaspoon ground black pepper
3	tablespoons extra-virgin olive oil
2	tablespoons chopped fresh basil leaves
I	recipe Steamed Cauliflower

1. Whisk lemon juice, vinegar, honey, curry powder, salt, and pepper together in small bowl. Whisk in oil until dressing is smooth. Stir in basil.

2. Prepare cauliflower and place in serving bowl when cooked. Rewhisk dressing and toss with cauliflower. Adjust seasonings and serve warm or at room temperature.

Browned and Braised Cauliflower with Asian Flavors

SERVES 4

The stronger flavor of browned cauliflower stands up well to bolder, more complex flavor combinations, such as the garlic, ginger, sesame oil, and soy sauce in this recipe.

2	tablespoons soy sauce
2	tablespoons rice wine vinegar
1	tablespoon dry sherry
1½	tablespoons canola oil
1	medium head cauliflower, trimmed, cored, and cut into florets (see illustrations below)
2	medium garlic cloves, minced
2	tablespoons minced fresh gingerroot
1	teaspoon Asian sesame oil
2	medium scallions, sliced thin
	Ground black pepper

1. Combine soy sauce, vinegar, sherry, and ¼ cup water in small bowl and set aside.

2. Heat large skillet over medium-high heat until pan is very hot, 3 to 4 minutes. Add canola oil, swirling pan to coat evenly. Add florets and sauté, stirring occasionally, until they begin to brown, 6 to 7 minutes.

3. Clear center of pan, add garlic and ginger, and drizzle with sesame oil. Mash garlic-ginger mixture with back of spatula and cook until fragrant, about 1 minute. Stir to combine garlic-ginger mixture with cauliflower. Sauté for 30 seconds.

4. Reduce heat to low and add soy sauce mixture. Cover and cook until florets are fully tender but still offer some resistance to the tooth when sampled, 4 to 5 minutes. Add scallions and toss lightly to distribute. Season with pepper to taste and serve immediately.

Browned and Braised Cauliflower with Indian Flavors

SERVES 4

Yogurt creates a rich and satisfying sauce that tames and blends the flavors of the spices. If you like, add ½ cup thawed frozen green peas along with cilantro.

¼	cup plain yogurt
1	tablespoon lime juice
1½	tablespoons canola oil
1	medium head cauliflower, trimmed, cored, and cut into florets (see illustrations below)
½	medium onion, sliced thin
1	teaspoon ground cumin
1	teaspoon ground coriander
1	teaspoon ground turmeric
¼	teaspoon hot red pepper flakes
¼	cup chopped fresh cilantro leaves
	Salt and ground black pepper

1. Combine yogurt, lime juice, and ¼ cup water in small bowl and set aside.

2. Heat large skillet over medium-high heat until pan is very hot, 3 to 4 minutes. Add oil, swirling pan to coat evenly. Add florets and sauté, stirring occasionally, until they begin to soften, 2 to 3 minutes. Add onion; continue sautéing until florets begin to brown and onion softens, about 4 minutes.

CUTTING CAULIFLOWER INTO FLORETS

1. Start by pulling off the outer leaves and trimming off the stem near the base of the head.

2. Turn the cauliflower upside down so the stem is facing up. Using a sharp knife, cut around the core to remove it.

3. Separate the individual florets from the inner stem using the tip of a chef's knife.

4. Cut the florets in half or quarters if necessary so that individual pieces are about 1 inch square.

3. Stir in cumin, coriander, turmeric, and pepper flakes; sauté until spices begin to toast and are fragrant, 1 to 2 minutes. Reduce heat to low and add yogurt mixture. Cover and cook until flavors meld, about 4 minutes. Add cilantro, toss to distribute, cover, and cook until florets are fully tender but still offer some resistance to the tooth when sampled, about 2 minutes more. Season with salt and pepper to taste and serve immediately.

CORN

DESPITE FARMSTAND SIGNS ACROSS THE country announcing "Butter and Sugar" corn for sale, no one actually grows old-time butter and sugar corn anymore. Nor does anybody grow most of the other old-fashioned nonhybrid varieties. Bygone varieties of corn have mostly disappeared for a reason. They converted sugar into starch so rapidly that people literally fired up their kettles before going out to pick the corn. Corn has since been crossbred to make for sweeter ears that have a longer hold on their fresh flavor and tender texture.

Basically, there are three hybrid types: normal sugary, sugar enhanced, and supersweet. Each contains dozens of varieties, with fancy names such as Kandy Korn, Double Gem, and Mystique. Normal sugary types, such as Silver Queen, are moderately sweet, with traditional corn flavor. Its sugars convert to starch rapidly after being picked. The sugar-enhanced types are more tender and somewhat sweeter, with a slower conversion of sugar to starch.

Supersweet corn has heightened sweetness, a crisp texture, and a remarkably slow conversion of sugar to starch after it is picked. It is a popular type for growers who supply to distant markets and require a product with longer shelf life. So it is most likely that any corn sold in your supermarket during the off-season is a variety of supersweet.

Beyond the above generalization, it's impossible to tell which kind of corn you have unless you taste it. With that in mind, we developed cooking methods that would work with all three kinds of corn hybrids. Boiling is probably the most all-purpose cooking method. We tried adding milk to the water but found it muddied the corn flavor. Salt toughens the corn up a bit and is best added at the table. Sugar can be added to the water to bring out the corn's sweetness, but when we tried this with supersweet corn the results were corn that tasted too sweet, almost like dessert.

Grilling is our other preferred method. Grilled corn should retain the juiciness of boiled without sacrificing the toasty caramelization and smoke-infused graces of the grill. We started our tests with the bare ear cooked directly over a medium-high fire. The outcome seemed too good to be true. The lightly caramelized corn was still juicy, but with a toasty hit of grilled flavor and a sweet essence to chase it down. In fact, it *was* too good to be true. The variety of corn we used was fittingly called Fantasy, which is a supersweet. When we tried grilling a normal sweet corn variety with the husk off, the outcome was a flavorless, dry, gummy turn-off. The end result was no better with sugar-enhanced corn. The direct heat was just too much for the fleeting flavors and tender texture of the normal sweet and sugar-enhanced corn types.

We went on to test another popular grilling technique: throw the whole ear on the grill, husk and all, as is. We tried this with all three sweet corn types at various heat levels. Half of the ears of corn were soaked beforehand; the other half were not. In sum, the husk-on method makes for a great-tasting ear of corn, and a particularly crisp, juicy one. But if it were not for the sticky charred husks that must be awkwardly peeled away at the table if you are to serve the corn hot, you would think you were eating boiled corn. The presoaked corn in particular just steams in the husk and picks up absolutely no grilled flavor.

Since grilling with the husk off was too aggressive for non-supersweet varieties and grilling with the husk on was no different from boiled corn, we turned to a compromise approach. We peeled the husk totally off except for the final layer that wrapped around the ear. This layer is much more moist and delicate than the outer layers, so much so that you can practically see the kernels through the husk. When cooked over a medium-high fire, this gave the corn a jacket heavy enough to prevent dehydration yet light enough to allow a gentle toasting of the kernels. After about eight minutes (rolling the corn one-quarter turn every two minutes) we could be certain that the corn was cooked just right, because the husk picked up a dark silhouette of the kernels and began to pull back at the corn's tip.

Master Recipe for Boiled Corn

SERVES 6

If you want to serve more corn, bring a second pot of water to a boil at the same time, or cook the corn in batches in just one pot. If you know that you have supersweet corn, omit the sugar. Serve boiled corn with butter, salt, and pepper.

    4   teaspoons sugar, optional
    6   ears of corn, husked

Bring 4 quarts of water and sugar, if using, to a boil in a large pot. Add corn; return to boil and cook until tender, 5 to 7 minutes. Drain and serve immediately.

Master Recipe for Grilled Corn

SERVES 6

The following recipe will work for all types of sweet corn. If you are certain you have a supersweet variety, it can be grilled with the husk off over a medium-high fire. To test the intensity of the fire, hold your hand 5 inches above the grill surface. If you can keep your hand there for three seconds (but no more), you have a medium-high fire.

    6   ears of corn

1. Light grill. Remove all but last layer of husk from each ear of corn, so that the kernels are covered but you can practically see them through the last thin layer of husk. Snip the straggling silk ends at the tip.

2. Grill semihusked ears of corn over medium-high fire, turning every 1½ to 2 minutes until husk begins to peel away at tip, exposing some kernels, and husk is charred a deep, dark brown, 8 to 10 minutes.

S C I E N C E : Corn Storage

While the general rule of thumb is to buy and eat corn the same day it has been harvested (as soon as the corn is harvested the sugars start converting to starches and the corn loses sweetness), most of us have been guilty of trying to break that rule for one reason or another. We tried a variety of methods for overnight storage using Silver Queen corn, one of the more perishable varieties. We found that the worst thing you can do to corn is to leave it sitting out on the counter. Throwing it into the refrigerator without any wrapping is nearly as bad. Storing in an airtight bag helps, but the hands-down winner entailed wrapping the corn (husk left on) in a wet paper bag and then in a plastic bag (any shopping bag will do). After 24 hours of storage we found the corn stored this way to be juicy, sweet, not starchy, and fresh tasting.

EGGPLANT

THE BIGGEST CHALLENGE THAT CONFRONTS the cook when preparing eggplant is excess moisture. While the grill will evaporate this liquid and allow the eggplant to brown nicely, this won't happen under the broiler or in a hot pan. Instead, the eggplant will steam in its own juices. The result is an insipid flavor and mushy texture.

Salting is the classic technique for drawing some moisture out of the eggplant before cooking. We experimented with both regular table salt and kosher salt and preferred kosher salt because the crystals are large enough to wipe away after the salt has done its job. Finer table salt crystals dissolve into the eggplant flesh and must be flushed out with water. The eggplant must then be thoroughly dried, which adds more prep time, especially if the eggplant has been diced for sautéing. (We prefer to dice eggplant that will be sautéed to increase the surface area that can brown and absorb flavorings.)

Eggplant destined for the broiler should be sliced very thin (about ¼ inch thick) so that the salt can work quickly. The salt will take more time to penetrate thicker slices and will in the end be less effective. However, when grilling, you want thicker slices that won't fall apart on the cooking grate. We found ¾-inch rounds to be perfect for grilling.

Master Recipe for Sautéed Eggplant

SERVES 4

Very small eggplants (less than 6 ounces each) can be cooked without salting. However, we found that large eggplants generally have a lot of moisture, which is best removed before cooking.

1	large eggplant (about 1½ pounds), ends trimmed and cut into ¾-inch cubes
1	tablespoon kosher salt
2	tablespoons extra-virgin olive oil
	Ground black pepper
1	medium garlic clove, minced
2–4	tablespoons minced fresh parsley or finely shredded basil leaves

1. Place eggplant in large colander and sprinkle with salt, tossing to coat evenly. Let stand 30 minutes. Using paper towels or large kitchen towel, wipe salt off and pat excess moisture from eggplant.

2. Heat oil in heavy-bottomed 12-inch skillet until it shimmers and becomes fragrant over medium-high heat. Add eggplant cubes and sauté until they begin to brown, about 4 minutes. Reduce heat to medium-low and cook, stirring occasionally, until eggplant is fully tender and lightly browned, 10 to 15 minutes. Stir in pepper to taste, and add garlic. Cook to blend flavors, about 2 minutes. Off heat, stir in herb, adjust seasonings, and serve immediately.

➤ VARIATIONS

Sautéed Eggplant with Crisped Bread Crumbs

Melt 2 tablespoons unsalted butter in small skillet. Add ½ cup plain dried bread crumbs and toast over medium-high heat until deep golden and crisp, stirring frequently, about 5 to 6 minutes. Follow recipe for Sautéed Eggplant, adding toasted bread crumbs with herb.

Sautéed Eggplant with Asian Garlic Sauce

1	large eggplant (about 1½ pounds), ends trimmed and cut into ¾-inch cubes
1	tablespoon kosher salt
2	tablespoons peanut or vegetable oil
	Ground black pepper
1	medium garlic clove, minced
2	teaspoons minced fresh gingerroot
2	tablespoons soy sauce
2	tablespoons rice wine vinegar
1	teaspoon sugar
2	tablespoons minced fresh cilantro leaves
2	tablespoons thinly sliced scallions

1. Place eggplant in large colander and sprinkle with salt, tossing to coat evenly. Let stand 30 minutes. Using paper towels or large kitchen towel, wipe salt off and pat excess moisture from eggplant.

2. Heat oil in heavy-bottomed 12-inch skillet until it shimmers and becomes fragrant over medium-high heat. Add eggplant cubes and sauté until they begin to brown, about 4 minutes. Reduce heat to medium-low and cook, stirring occasionally, until eggplant is fully tender and lightly browned, 10 to 15 minutes. Stir in pepper to taste, and add garlic and ginger. Cook to blend flavors, about 1 minute.

3. Combine soy sauce, vinegar, and sugar in small bowl. Add to pan and cook until eggplant absorbs liquid, about 1 minute. Off heat, stir in cilantro and scallions, adjust seasonings, and serve immediately.

Master Recipe for Broiled Eggplant

SERVES 4

For broiling, it's best to slice the eggplant very thin.

1	large eggplant (about 1½ pounds), ends trimmed and sliced crosswise into ¼-inch-thick rounds
1	tablespoon kosher salt
3	tablespoons extra-virgin olive oil
2	to 3 tablespoons minced fresh parsley or finely shredded basil leaves
	Ground black pepper

1. Place eggplant in large colander and sprinkle with salt, tossing to coat evenly. Let stand 30 minutes. Using paper towels or large kitchen towel, wipe salt off and pat excess moisture from eggplant.

2. Preheat broiler. Arrange eggplant slices on foil-

lined baking sheet. Brush both sides with oil. Broil eggplant slices 4 inches from heat source until tops are mahogany brown, 3 to 4 minutes. Turn slices over and broil until other side browns, another 3 to 4 minutes.

3. Remove eggplant from oven and sprinkle with herb. Season with pepper to taste and serve hot, warm, or at room temperature.

> VARIATION

Broiled Eggplant with Parmesan Cheese

Delicious on its own or perfect as vegetarian main course for two when served with a basic tomato sauce.

Follow recipe for Broiled Eggplant through step 2. Sprinkle cooked eggplant with ½ cup grated Parmesan cheese. Return eggplant to broiler until cheese melts and becomes bubbly and browned, 2 to 3 minutes. Sprinkle with parsley or basil, sprinkle with pepper to taste, and serve immediately.

Master Recipe for Grilled Eggplant

SERVES 4

There's no need to salt eggplant destined for the grill. The intense grill heat will vaporize excess moisture.

- 3　tablespoons extra-virgin olive oil
- 2　medium garlic cloves, minced
- 2　teaspoons minced fresh thyme or oregano leaves
- 　Salt and ground black pepper
- 1　large eggplant (about 1½ pounds), ends trimmed and cut crosswise into ¾-inch rounds

1. Light grill. Combine oil, garlic, herbs, and salt and pepper to taste in small bowl. Place eggplant on platter and brush both sides with oil mixture.

2. Grill eggplant, turning once, until both sides are marked with dark stripes, 8 to 10 minutes. Serve hot, warm, or at room temperature.

> VARIATION

Grilled Eggplant with Ginger and Soy

- 2　tablespoons soy sauce
- 1½　tablespoons honey
- 1　tablespoon rice wine vinegar
- 1　tablespoon water
- 1　teaspoon Asian sesame oil
- 3　tablespoons peanut oil
- 2　teaspoons minced fresh gingerroot
- 　Ground black pepper
- 1　large eggplant (about 1½ pounds), ends trimmed and cut crosswise into ¾-inch rounds
- 2　medium scallions, thinly sliced

1. Light grill. Combine soy sauce, honey, vinegar, and water in small skillet. Bring to boil over medium-high heat and simmer until slightly thickened, about 2 minutes. Remove from heat and add sesame oil. Set mixture aside.

2. Combine peanut oil, ginger, and pepper to taste in small bowl. Place eggplant on platter and brush both sides with oil mixture.

3. Grill eggplant, turning once, until both sides are marked with dark stripes, 8 to 10 minutes. Drizzle thickened soy mixture over eggplant and sprinkle with scallions. Serve hot, warm, or at room temperature.

FENNEL

UNLIKE MOST VEGETABLES, RAW FENNEL HAS a long history of use in salads and antipasti. Italians often put out strips of fennel along with a bowl of fine olive oil and salt as a quick antipasto. The fennel is simply dipped in the oil, sprinkled with salt, and enjoyed with cocktails. Raw fennel can also be cut into thin strips or diced and used in salads. Add a handful of diced fennel to a leafy salad or use thin strips of fennel in a citrus salad.

When it comes to cooking, we find that fennel generally responds best to dry-heat methods. Sautéing and roasting cause the natural sugars in the fennel to caramelize, thereby enhancing its flavor. The exception to the "dry heat is best" rule is braising. This method involves wet heat, with the fennel absorbing flavors from the cooking liquid (usually stock or wine) and, therefore, delivering very good results as well.

Fairly slow cooking is the key to achieving uniform tenderness in each piece. Sautéing over medium heat for a considerable period (about 15 minutes), braising for 30 minutes, and roasting for 35 minutes all worked beautifully. Our attempts to hurry fennel along by using faster methods such as boiling and microwaving did not succeed; the fennel became mushy with both methods, and boiling also washed out much of its flavor. Steaming was time consuming and turned the fennel a bit mushy, and, because it did not brown the fennel, it did little to elicit or enhance its sweet flavor.

Braised Fennel with White Wine and Parmesan

SERVES 4

In this recipe, the fennel cooks slowly in butter and white wine until tender, then receives a dusting of cheese just before serving. This rich side dish works well with beef or veal.

> 3   tablespoons butter
> 3   small fennel bulbs (about 2¼ pounds), stems and fronds discarded, blemished portions of bulb trimmed, and bulb cut vertically into ½-inch thick slices
>   Salt and ground black pepper
> ⅓   cup dry white wine
> ¼   cup grated Parmesan cheese

1. Heat butter over medium heat in sauté pan large enough to hold fennel in almost single layer. Add fennel and sprinkle with salt and pepper to taste. Add wine and cover pan. Simmer over medium heat 15 minutes. Turn slices and continue to simmer, covered, until fennel is quite tender, has absorbed most of pan liquid, and starts to turn golden, about 10 minutes longer. Turn fennel again and continue cooking until fennel starts to color on other side, about 4 minutes longer.

2. Sprinkle fennel with cheese. Transfer to platter or individual plates and serve immediately.

Sautéed Fennel with Garlic and Parsley

SERVES 4

Sautéing causes the anise flavor of fennel to fade but concentrates the natural sugars in the vegetable. This side dish complements seafood and poultry particularly well.

> 2   medium fennel bulbs (about 2 pounds), stems and fronds removed, 1 tablespoon minced fronds reserved and stems discarded

> 3   tablespoons olive oil
> 4   medium garlic cloves, minced
>   Salt and ground black pepper
> 2   tablespoons minced fresh parsley leaves

1. Remove any blemished portions from fennel bulb. Halve bulb through base. Use a paring knife to remove the pyramid-shaped piece of core attached to each half. With cut side down and knife parallel to work surface, slice each fennel half crosswise to yield ½-inch slices. Then, with knife perpendicular to work surface, cut each fennel half lengthwise into long thin strips.

2. Heat oil in large skillet. Add garlic; sauté over medium heat until lightly colored, about 1 minute. Add fennel strips; toss to coat with oil. Cook, stirring often, until fennel has softened considerably but still offers some resistance, about 15 minutes.

3. Season generously with salt and pepper to taste. Stir in minced fronds and parsley. Serve immediately.

Roasted Fennel with Red Onions and Carrots

SERVES 4

Drizzle a tablespoon of balsamic vinegar over the vegetables during the last minutes of roasting to highlight their sweetness. Serve this fennel as a side dish with chicken or veal.

> 1   large or two small fennel bulbs (about 1½ pounds), stems and fronds discarded, blemished portions of bulb trimmed
> 1   medium red onion, peeled and cut lengthwise into 8 wedges
> 2   medium carrots, peeled, halved lengthwise, and cut into 2-inch lengths
> 2   tablespoons extra-virgin olive oil
>   Salt
> 1   tablespoon balsamic vinegar

1. Heat oven to 425 degrees. Remove any blemished portions from fennel bulb. Halve bulb through base. Use paring knife to remove pyramid-shaped piece of core attached to each half. With cut side down and knife parallel to work surface, slice each fennel half crosswise to yield ½-inch slices. Then, with knife perpendicular to work surface, cut each

fennel half lengthwise into long thin strips.

2. Toss fennel, onion, and carrots in large roasting pan with oil. Season generously with salt. Roast 30 minutes, turning vegetables once after 20 minutes.

3. Drizzle vinegar over vegetables and toss gently. Continue roasting until vegetables are richly colored and tender, about 5 minutes longer. Adjust seasonings. Serve hot or warm.

GREEN BEANS

WE FIND THAT GREEN BEANS RESPOND better to boiling than to steaming. A pound of beans in a standard steamer basket will not cook evenly— the beans close to the steaming water cook more quickly than the beans at the top of the pile. Stirring the beans once or twice as they cook solves this problem, but it is somewhat dangerous to stick your hand into the hot pot. Boiling is simpler—just add the beans and cook until tender—and permits the addition of salt during cooking.

Unlike other vegetables, green beans do not become soggy when boiled, because their thick skins keep them crisp and firm. Leave beans whole when boiling; cut beans will become waterlogged. Boiled beans can be flavored with some butter or oil, dressed with a vinaigrette, or sautéed briefly in a flavorful fat.

A second cooking option is braising. We found that the thick skin on most beans means that they are fairly slow to absorb flavorful liquids like cream or stock. For this reason, we had the best success when we braised the beans for a full 20 minutes.

Braised beans lose their bright green color. Older, tougher beans benefit from long cooking, but really fresh green beans are best boiled and then seasoned, so as to retain as much of their flavor and texture as possible.

Master Recipe for Boiled Green Beans

SERVES 4

The freshness and thickness of the beans can greatly affect cooking time. Thin, farm-fresh beans—not much thicker than a strand of cooked linguine—may be done in just 2 minutes. Most supermarket beans are considerably thicker and have traveled some distance, hence the 5-minute cooking time recommended below. Dress the beans with a drizzle of extra-virgin olive oil or a pat of butter as well as a generous sprinkling of salt and pepper. Or make one of the variations.

I	pound green beans, ends snapped off
I	teaspoon salt

Bring 2½ quarts of water to boil in large saucepan. Add beans and salt and cook until tender, about 5 minutes. Drain and season as directed in variations below or note above.

➤ VARIATIONS

Green Beans with Toasted Walnuts and Tarragon

Nuts other than walnuts, especially pine nuts or hazelnuts, and herbs such as parsley or basil, may be used in this recipe.

Follow recipe for Boiled Green Beans, placing drained beans in large serving bowl. Add ¼ cup chopped and toasted walnuts and 1½ tablespoons minced fresh tarragon leaves. Drizzle with 1½ tablespoons walnut or extra-virgin olive oil and toss gently to coat. Sprinkle with salt and pepper to taste and serve warm or at room temperature.

Green Beans with Fresh Tomato, Basil, and Goat Cheese

Follow recipe for Boiled Green Beans, placing drained beans in large serving bowl. Add ½ cup chopped fresh tomato, 2 tablespoons chopped fresh basil leaves, and 1 ounce crumbled goat cheese. Drizzle with 2 tablespoons extra-virgin olive oil and 1 teaspoon balsamic vinegar and toss gently to coat. Season with salt and pepper to taste and serve warm or at room temperature.

Green Beans with Bacon and Onion

4	strips bacon, cut into ½-inch pieces
I	medium onion, minced
I	pound green beans, ends snapped off
	Salt and ground black pepper

1. Fry bacon in large skillet over medium heat until crisp, about 5 minutes. Remove bacon from pan with slotted spoon and drain on paper towels. Pour off all but 2 tablespoons bacon drippings. Add onion and sauté until softened, about 5 minutes.

2. Meanwhile, bring 2½ quarts of water to boil in large saucepan. Add beans and salt and cook until tender, about 5 minutes.

3. Drain and add to skillet with onion. Toss to heat through, 1 to 2 minutes. Add bacon and season with salt (sparingly) and pepper to taste. Serve immediately.

Braised Green Beans, Italian Style

SERVES 4

The beans lose their bright green color but gain flavor from cooking in a tomato sauce.

2	tablespoons extra-virgin olive oil
I	small onion, diced
2	medium garlic cloves, minced
I	cup chopped canned tomatoes
I	pound green beans, ends snapped off
	Salt and ground black pepper
2	tablespoons minced fresh parsley leaves

1. Heat oil in large sauté pan over medium heat. Add onion and cook until softened, about 5 minutes. Add garlic and cook for 1 minute. Add tomatoes and simmer until juices thicken slightly, about 5 minutes.

2. Add green beans, ¼ teaspoon salt, and a few grindings of pepper to pan. Stir well, cover, and cook, stirring occasionally, until beans are tender but still offer some resistance to bite, about 20 minutes. Stir in parsley and adjust seasonings. Serve immediately.

Braised Green Beans, Asian Style

SERVES 4

The braising liquid—chicken stock, soy sauce, and rice wine vinegar—cooks down to a concentrated, very flavorful sauce, which is especially delicious over rice.

2	tablespoons peanut oil
4	medium scallions, thinly sliced
2	medium garlic cloves, minced
¾	cup chicken stock or low-sodium canned broth
3	tablespoons soy sauce
I	tablespoon rice wine vinegar
2	teaspoons sugar
I	pound green beans, ends snapped off
	Ground black pepper
2	tablespoons minced fresh basil leaves

1. Heat oil in large sauté pan over medium heat. Add scallions and cook until softened, 2 to 3 minutes. Add garlic and cook for 1 minute. Add stock, soy sauce, vinegar, and sugar and simmer until liquid thickens slightly, about 5 minutes.

2. Add green beans and a few grindings of pepper to pan. Stir well, cover, and cook, stirring occasionally, until beans are tender but still offer some resistance to bite, about 20 minutes. Stir in basil and adjust seasonings. Serve immediately.

GREENS

MANY COOKS THINK THEY CAN TREAT ALL leafy greens the same way, even though some are delicate enough for salads while others seem as tough as shoe leather. After cleaning, stemming, and cooking more than 100 pounds of leafy greens, we found that they fell into two categories, each of which is handled quite differently.

Spinach, beet greens, and Swiss chard are tender and rich in moisture. They require no additional liquid during cooking. They taste of the earth and minerals but are still rather delicate. Kale as well as mustard, turnip, and collard greens are tougher and require the addition of some liquid as they cook. Their flavor is much more assertive, even peppery in some cases, and can be overwhelming.

We tested boiling, steaming, and sautéing tender greens. Boiling produced the most brilliantly colored greens, but they were also very mushy and bland. The water cooked out all their flavor and texture. Steamed greens were less mushy, but clearly these tender greens did not need any liquid. Damp greens that were tossed in a hot oil (which could be flavored with aromatics and spices) wilted in just two or three minutes in a covered pan. Once wilted, we found it best to remove the lid so the liquid in the pan would evaporate. This method has the advantage of flavoring the greens as they cook.

Tougher greens don't have enough moisture to be wilted in a hot pan; they scorch before they wilt.

Steaming these greens produces a better texture but does nothing to tame their bitter flavor. Tough greens benefit from cooking in some water, which will wash away some of their harsh notes.

We tested boiling two pounds of greens in an abundant quantity of salted water and what might be called shallow blanching in just two quarts of salted water. We found that cooking the greens in lots of water diluted their flavor too much. Shallow blanching removes enough bitterness to make these assertive greens palatable, but not so much as to rob them of their character. Blanched greens should be drained and then briefly cooked with seasonings.

Master Recipe for Sautéed Tender Greens

SERVES 4

To stem spinach and beet greens, simply pinch off the leaves where they meet the stems. A thick stalk runs through each Swiss chard leaf, so it must be handled differently; see illustration below for information on this technique. A large, deep Dutch oven or even a soup kettle is best for this recipe.

3   tablespoons extra-virgin olive oil
2   medium garlic cloves, minced
2   pounds damp tender greens, such as spinach, beet greens, or Swiss chard, stemmed, washed in several changes of cold water, and coarsely chopped
     Salt and ground black pepper
     Lemon wedges (optional)

Heat oil and garlic in Dutch oven or other deep pot and cook until garlic sizzles and turns golden, about 1 minute. Add wet greens, cover, and cook over medium-high heat, stirring occasionally, until greens completely wilt, about 2 to 3 minutes. Uncover and season with salt and pepper to taste. Cook over high heat until liquid evaporates, 2 to 3 minutes. Serve immediately, with lemon wedges if desired.

➤ VARIATIONS

Sautéed Tender Greens with Raisins and Almonds

3   tablespoons extra-virgin olive oil
3   medium garlic cloves, minced
¼   teaspoon hot red pepper flakes
2   pounds damp tender greens, such as spinach, beet greens, or Swiss chard, stemmed, washed in several changes of cold water, and coarsely chopped
⅓   cup golden raisins
½   teaspoon minced lemon zest
     Salt and ground black pepper
3   tablespoons toasted slivered almonds

Heat oil, garlic, and hot pepper flakes in Dutch oven or other deep pot and cook until garlic sizzles and turns golden, about 1 minute. Add wet greens and raisins, cover, and cook over medium-high heat, stirring occasionally, until greens completely wilt, about 2 to 3 minutes. Uncover and add lemon zest and season with salt and pepper to taste. Cook over

PREPARING LEAFY GREENS

1. To prepare Swiss chard, kale, collards, and mustard greens, hold each leaf at the base of the stem over a bowl filled with water and use a sharp knife to slash the leafy portion from either side of the thick stem.

2. Turnip greens are most easily stemmed by grasping the leaf between your thumb and index finger at the base of the stem and stripping it off by hand.

3. When using this method with turnip greens, the very tip of the stem will break off along with the leaves. It is tender enough to cook along with the leaves.

high heat until liquid evaporates, 2 to 3 minutes. Stir in almonds and serve immediately.

Sautéed Tender Greens with Indian Spices

2	tablespoons vegetable oil
1	medium onion, minced
2	medium garlic cloves, minced
1	teaspoon minced fresh gingerroot
½	fresh jalapeño chile, stemmed, seeded if desired, and minced
2	teaspoons curry powder
½	teaspoon ground cumin
2	pounds damp tender greens, such as spinach, beet greens, or Swiss chard, stemmed, washed in several changes of cold water, and coarsely chopped
	Salt and ground black pepper
¼	cup heavy cream
2	teaspoons brown sugar
	Lime wedges (optional)

1. Heat oil, onion, and garlic in Dutch oven or other deep pot and cook until onion and garlic sizzle and turn golden, about 1 minute. Add ginger, chile, curry powder, and cumin. Cook until fragrant, about 2 minutes.

2. Add wet greens, cover, and cook over medium-high heat, stirring occasionally, until greens completely wilt, about 2 to 3 minutes. Uncover and season with salt and pepper to taste. Cook over high heat until liquid evaporates, 2 to 3 minutes. Stir in cream and sugar. Cook, uncovered, until cream thickens, about 2 minutes. Serve immediately, with lime wedges if desired.

Sautéed Tender Greens with Asian Flavors

1½	tablespoons soy sauce
1	tablespoon Asian sesame oil
2	teaspoons rice wine vinegar
2	teaspoons sugar
	Ground black pepper
2	tablespoons vegetable or peanut oil
2	medium garlic cloves, minced
½	teaspoon hot red pepper flakes
2	pounds damp tender greens, such as spinach, beet greens, or Swiss chard, stemmed, washed in several changes of cold water, and coarsely chopped
2	teaspoons toasted sesame seeds

1. Combine soy sauce, sesame oil, vinegar, sugar, and ground black pepper to taste in small bowl.

2. Heat oil, garlic, and pepper flakes in Dutch oven or other deep pot and cook until garlic sizzles and turns golden, about 1 minute. Add wet greens, cover, and cook over medium-high heat, stirring occasionally, until greens completely wilt, about 2 to 3 minutes.

3. Uncover and cook over high heat until liquid evaporates, 2 to 3 minutes. Add soy mixture and simmer until liquid almost evaporates, about 1 minute. Garnish with sesame seeds and serve immediately.

Master Recipe for Quick-Cooked Tough Greens
SERVES 4

With the exception of turnip greens, all tough greens can be stemmed by the method outlined in illustration 1 on page 78. See illustrations 2 and 3 when working with turnip greens. Shallow-blanched greens should be shocked in cold water to stop the cooking process, drained, and then braised.

	Salt
2	pounds tough greens, such as kale, collards, mustard, or turnip, stemmed, washed in several changes of cold water, and coarsely chopped
2	large garlic cloves, sliced thin
¼	teaspoon hot red pepper flakes
3	tablespoons extra-virgin olive oil
⅓–½	cup chicken stock or low-sodium canned broth
	Lemon wedges (optional)

1. Bring 2 quarts water to boil in soup kettle or other large pot. Add 1½ teaspoons salt and greens and stir until wilted. Cover and cook until greens are just tender, about 7 minutes. Drain in colander. Rinse kettle with cold water to cool, then refill with cold water. Pour greens into cold water to stop cooking process. Gather handful of greens, lift out of water, and squeeze until only droplets fall from them. Repeat with remaining greens.

2. Heat garlic, red pepper flakes, and oil in large sauté pan over medium heat until garlic starts to sizzle, about 1 minute. Add greens and stir to coat with oil. Add ⅓ cup stock, cover, and cook over medium-high heat, adding more stock if necessary, until

greens are tender and juicy and most of stock has been absorbed, about 5 minutes. Adjust seasonings, adding salt and red pepper flakes to taste. Serve immediately, with lemon wedges if desired.

➤ VARIATIONS

Quick-Cooked Tough Greens with Prosciutto

Follow recipe for Quick-Cooked Tough Greens, adding 1 ounce thin-sliced prosciutto that has been cut into thin strips along with garlic and red pepper flakes. Proceed as directed, stirring in ¼ teaspoon grated lemon zest just before serving.

Quick-Cooked Tough Greens with Red Bell Pepper

Follow recipe for Quick-Cooked Tough Greens through step 1. Sauté ½ thinly sliced red bell pepper in oil until softened, about 4 minutes. Add garlic and red pepper flakes and proceed as directed.

Quick-Cooked Tough Greens with Black Olives and Lemon Zest

Follow recipe for Quick-Cooked Tough Greens, adding ⅓ cup pitted and chopped black olives, such as kalamatas, after garlic starts to sizzle. Add greens and proceed as directed, stirring in ¼ teaspoon grated lemon zest just before serving.

LEEKS

THE UNIQUE, ONION-LIKE SWEETNESS OF leeks makes them a delicious vegetable side dish, equally good whether served hot or cold. Most sources suggest boiling leeks, but we wondered if this was the best way to preserve and enhance their flavor.

We found that boiling and braising tend to wash away some of the leek flavor. If you use a flavorful cooking liquid, such as chicken stock, this can compensate for the duller leek flavor. However, we did like the silky texture of leeks that were boiled or braised. In search of stronger leek flavor, we tried baking but found that the texture suffered—the leeks were too dry and chewy. The same thing happened when we tested sautéing and grilling. The center of each leek was not tender enough and the exterior

had actually cooked too much and was a bit dry.

The last method that we tried turned out to be the hands-down winner. When we steamed leeks, the results were full-flavored, moist, and tender. Steamed leeks had the same supple texture as leeks that were boiled or braised but with a stronger and sweeter onionlike flavor. Steaming turned out to be not only an excellent method of cooking leeks but also a very useful first step when cooking leeks by other methods. The steaming softens the leeks and leaves them better suited to sautéing, grilling, braising, or baking.

Master Recipe for Steamed Leeks

SERVES 4

Once the leeks have been steamed, they may be dressed with vinaigrette or briefly sautéed with seasonings. See the variations for specific ideas.

4   leeks (preferably small to medium thickness)

1. Trim leeks about 2 inches beyond the point where leaves start to darken. Trim root end, keeping base intact. Slit leek lengthwise upward through the leaves, leaving the base intact. Soak trimmed leeks in bowl of cold water to loosen dirt, then rinse leeks under cold running water, pulling apart the layers with your fingers in order to expose any clinging dirt.

2. Arrange leeks in a single layer in a steamer basket or steamer insert. Carefully place basket over pot of vigorously boiling water; cover and steam until tip of knife inserted in thickest part of leek meets no resistance, about 10 minutes for leeks ¾ inch thick, about 12 minutes for leeks 1¼ inches thick.

➤ VARIATIONS

Steamed Leeks with Mustard Vinaigrette

I	tablespoon cider vinegar
I	tablespoon Dijon mustard
½	teaspoon salt
⅛	teaspoon ground black pepper
I	teaspoon sugar
¼	cup extra-virgin olive oil
I	recipe Steamed Leeks, warm or chilled

1. Whisk vinegar, mustard, salt, pepper, and sugar together in small bowl until well blended; slowly whisk in oil so that vinaigrette emulsifies.

2. Arrange leeks on individual plates or serving platter; drizzle with vinaigrette and serve.

Steamed Leeks Glazed with Crunchy Seeds

1	tablespoon red wine vinegar
2	teaspoons sugar
¼	teaspoon salt
⅛	teaspoon ground black pepper
1	teaspoon yellow mustard seeds
½	teaspoon fennel seeds
1	teaspoon sesame seeds
3	tablespoons unsalted butter
1	recipe Steamed Leeks

1. Mix vinegar, sugar, salt, pepper, mustard seeds, fennel seeds, and sesame seeds together in small bowl; set aside.

2. Heat butter in large skillet over medium-high heat. Add leeks and spice mixture. Cook, shaking skillet constantly and turning leeks to coat all sides, until mixture thickens to glaze, about 2 minutes.

3. Arrange leeks on individual plates or serving platter; pour remaining glaze over leeks and serve.

MUSHROOMS

WHITE MUSHROOMS HAVE A LOUSY REPUTAtion. Cooks who ooh and aah over porcini, portobellos, shiitakes, and other exotic mushrooms often find the white mushroom, also called the button, to be beneath their consideration. But button mushrooms are inexpensive and almost always available (they are the only choice in some markets), which gives them at least some appeal. We figured there must be a way of cooking them that would bring out the deep, rich, earthy flavors for which their tonier cousins are so highly prized.

The most common method of cooking mushrooms is sautéing. The sautéing time seemed crucial, so we cut a handful of mushrooms into uniform ⅜-inch slices and sautéed them in a bit of oil over medium-high heat for times ranging from three minutes to eight minutes, removing one slice from the pan every minute. We preferred those cooked for six minutes, since at this point the mushrooms were moist all the way through—a condition we had learned to recognize as indicating doneness—and slightly browned but not burned on the exterior. Much of the moisture had been cooked out and had evaporated, but some still remained in the pan. These mushrooms also tasted pretty good, with a fairly deep, somewhat complex, nutty flavor from the exterior

---

SCIENCE: To Wash or Not to Wash Mushrooms

Common culinary wisdom dictates that mushrooms should never, ever be washed. Put these spongy fungi under the faucet or in a bowl, the dictum goes, and they will soak up water like a sponge.

Like most cooks, we had always blindly followed this precept. But when we learned that mushrooms were over 80 percent water, we began to question their ability to absorb yet more liquid. As we so often do in situations like this, we consulted the works of food scientist and author Harold McGee. Sure enough, in his book *The Curious Cook* (North Point Press, 1990) we found an experiment he had devised to test this very piece of accepted mushroom lore. We decided to duplicate McGee's work in our test kitchen.

We weighed out six ounces of white mushrooms and put them into a bowl, then added water to cover and let them sit. After five minutes we shook off the surface water and weighed them again. Our results replicated McGee's—the total weight gain for all the mushrooms together was one-quarter ounce, which translates to about 1½ teaspoons of water.

We suspected that even this gain represented mostly surface moisture rather than absorption, so we repeated the experiment with six ounces of broccoli, which no one would claim is an absorbent vegetable. The weight gain after a five-minute soak was almost identical—one-fifth of an ounce—suggesting that most of the moisture was clinging to the surface of both vegetables rather than being absorbed by them.

So, as it turns out, mushrooms can be cleaned in the same way as other vegetables are—rinsed under cold water. However, it's best to rinse them just before cooking and to avoid rinsing altogether if you are using them uncooked, since the surfaces of wet mushrooms turn dark and slimy when they're exposed to air for more than four or five minutes.

browning. The texture, however, was not ideal; while tender, the mushrooms were also a bit rubbery.

We tried sautéing the mushrooms until they exuded no more liquid, as suggested in several cookbooks. This took about 12 minutes, though, and by that time the mushrooms had acquired a dark, almost burned taste, and again were slightly rubbery. Not terrible, but not great either.

We decided to try roasting to see if we could improve upon the flavor and texture delivered by sautéing. Roasted mushrooms were not only moist all the way through but had a deep, rich, pronounced flavor that seemed at once meaty and nutty. This was the real mushroom flavor that we had been trying to coax from this everyday mushroom.

Master Recipe for Roasted Mushrooms

SERVES 4

This basic recipe can be flavored in numerous ways. See the variations for specific ideas.

1	pound white mushrooms, washed and halved if small, quartered if medium, cut into sixths if large
2	tablespoons olive oil
	Salt and ground black pepper

1. Adjust oven rack to lowest position and heat oven to 450 degrees.

2. Toss mushrooms with olive oil and salt and pepper to taste in medium bowl. Arrange in a single layer on a large low-sided roasting pan or jelly-roll pan. Roast until released juices have nearly evaporated and mushroom surfaces facing pan are browned, 12 to 15 minutes. Remove pan from oven and turn mushrooms with a metal spatula. Continue to roast until mushroom liquid has completely evaporated and mushrooms are brown all over, about 5 to 10 minutes longer. Serve.

➤ VARIATIONS
Roasted Mushrooms with Garlic, Olives, and Thyme

1	small garlic clove, minced
1	tablespoon minced fresh thyme leaves
12	brine-cured black olives, pitted and chopped coarse

1	recipe Roasted Mushrooms
1	tablespoon balsamic vinegar

Mix garlic, thyme, and olives in medium bowl. Add roasted mushrooms and vinegar; toss to coat. Serve hot, warm, or at room temperature.

Roasted Mushrooms with Warm Spices

1	pound white mushrooms, washed and halved if small, quartered if medium, cut into sixths if large
2	tablespoons olive oil
1	teaspoon paprika
¾	teaspoon salt
½	teaspoon ground black pepper
¼	teaspoon ground cinnamon
¼	teaspoon ground nutmeg
¼	teaspoon ground cumin
¼	teaspoon minced garlic
1½	tablespoons lemon juice

1. Adjust oven rack to lowest position and heat oven to 450 degrees.

2. Toss mushrooms with olive oil and salt and pepper to taste in medium bowl. Arrange in a single layer on a large low-sided roasting pan or jelly-roll pan. Roast until released juices have nearly evaporated and mushroom surfaces facing pan are browned, 12 to 15 minutes.

3. Meanwhile, mix paprika, salt, pepper, cinnamon, nutmeg, cumin, and garlic in medium bowl. Remove pan from oven, sprinkle spice mixture over mushrooms, and turn mushrooms with a metal spatula to coat evenly. Continue to roast until mushroom liquid has completely evaporated and mushrooms are brown all over, about 5 minutes longer.

4. Return mushrooms to bowl used for spice mixture. Add lemon juice and toss to coat. Serve hot, warm, or at room temperature.

PEAS

THERE ARE THREE VARIETIES OF PEAS SOLD in most markets—shell peas, sugar snap peas, and snow peas. We find that shell peas are generally mealy and bland. Frozen peas are usually sweeter and better-tasting, but given the other fresh options (namely, sugar snap and snow peas) that are almost always available, we prefer not to use frozen peas for side dishes.

The flat, light green snow pea has a long history, especially in the Chinese kitchen. The peas are immature and the pod is tender enough to eat. Sugar snap peas are a relatively recent invention, which date back just 20 years. They are a cross between shell peas and snow peas. The sweet, crisp pod is edible and holds small, juicy peas.

Sugar snap and snow peas should be cooked quickly so that they retain some crunch and color. Stir-frying works well with snow peas, which have a fairly sturdy pod. However, sugar snap peas are too delicate for such intense heat. We found the pods will become mushy by the time the peas inside are actually heated through.

Both kinds of peas can be steamed, but we found that they respond better to blanching in salted water. The salt balances some of their sweetness and brings out their flavor. Blanched peas tend to shrivel or pucker as they cool. To solve this problem, we plunge the cooked peas into ice water as soon as they are drained. This also helps sets their bright color.

Once cooled, the peas can be drained, patted dry, and briefly sautéed in butter or oil to heat them through and add flavor.

Master Recipe for Blanched Sugar Snap Peas or Snow Peas

SERVES 4

Sugar snap and snow peas may be cooked and seasoned the same way. The only difference is the cooking time; snow peas should be blanched an extra 30 seconds or so. The string that runs along the top of the snow pea is fairly tough and should be pulled off before cooking. Have a bowl of ice water ready to shock the drained peas and prevent further softening and shriveling. The peas should be seasoned and reheated as directed in variations.

1   teaspoon salt
4   cups loosely packed sugar snap peas or snow peas (about 1 pound), tips pulled off and strings removed if necessary

Bring 6 cups water to boil in large saucepan. Add salt and peas and cook until crisp-tender, 1½ to 2 minutes for sugar snap peas or about 2½ minutes for

snow peas. Drain peas, shock in ice water, drain again, and pat dry. (Peas can be set aside for 1 hour before seasoning.)

➤ VARIATIONS

Peas with Hazelnut Butter and Sage

2   tablespoons chopped hazelnuts
2   tablespoons unsalted butter
1   recipe Blanched Sugar Snap Peas or Snow Peas
2   tablespoons chopped fresh sage leaves
     Salt and ground black pepper

1. Toast nuts in small skillet over medium heat, shaking pan often to promote even cooking, just until fragrant, 3 to 4 minutes. Set nuts aside.

2. Heat butter in medium sauté pan over medium heat until it turns to the color of brown sugar and smells nutty, about 5 minutes. (Take care not to burn butter.) Add peas, sage, and nuts. Toss to combine and cook until peas are heated through, 1 to 1½ minutes. Adjust seasonings, adding salt and pepper to taste, and serve immediately

Peas with Ham and Mint

1   tablespoon unsalted butter
½   cup country or smoked ham, cut into ¼-inch dice
1   recipe Blanched Sugar Snap Peas or Snow Peas
2   tablespoons chopped fresh mint
     Salt and ground black pepper

Melt butter in medium sauté pan over medium heat. When foam subsides, add ham and sauté for 1 minute. Add peas and mint. Toss to combine and cook until peas are heated through, 1 to 1½ minutes. Adjust seasonings, adding salt and pepper to taste, and serve immediately.

Peas with Lemon, Garlic, and Basil

2   tablespoons extra-virgin olive oil
     Zest of 1 medium lemon, minced, plus
       1 tablespoon juice
1   medium garlic clove, minced
1   recipe Blanched Sugar Snap Peas or Snow Peas
8   fresh basil leaves, chopped
     Salt and ground black pepper

Heat oil in medium sauté pan over medium heat.

Add zest and garlic and sauté until garlic is golden, about 2 minutes. Add peas, lemon juice, and basil. Toss to combine and cook until peas are heated through, 1 to 1½ minutes. Adjust seasonings, adding salt and pepper to taste, and serve immediately.

Master Recipe for Stir-Fried Snow Peas

SERVES 4

Snow peas are sturdier than sugar snap peas and hold up well when stir-fried.

¼	cup chicken stock or canned low-sodium broth
¼	teaspoon salt
	Ground black pepper
1	tablespoon plus 1 teaspoon peanut oil
4	cups loosely packed snow peas (about 1 pound), tips pulled off and strings removed
1½	teaspoons minced garlic
1½	teaspoons minced fresh gingerroot

1. Mix chicken stock, salt, and pepper to taste in small bowl.

2. Heat 12-inch nonstick skillet over high heat until quite hot, 2 to 3 minutes. Add 1 tablespoon oil and swirl to coat bottom of pan (oil should shimmer immediately). Add snow peas and cook for 2 minutes, tossing peas every 30 seconds.

3. Clear center of pan, add garlic and ginger, and drizzle with remaining 1 teaspoon oil. Mash garlic and ginger with back of spatula. Cook for 10 seconds and then mix with snow peas. Off heat, add chicken stock mixture (it should immediately reduce down to a glaze). Serve immediately.

➤ VARIATIONS

Stir-Fried Snow Peas with Spicy Orange Sauce

3	tablespoons dry sherry
1	tablespoon soy sauce
1	tablespoon Asian sesame oil
2	teaspoons red wine vinegar
½	teaspoon sugar
½	teaspoon ground black pepper
¼	teaspoon salt
1	tablespoon plus 1 teaspoon peanut oil
4	cups loosely packed snow peas (about 1 pound), tips pulled off and strings removed
1½	teaspoons minced garlic
1½	teaspoons minced fresh gingerroot
1	tablespoon grated orange zest
¼	teaspoon hot red pepper flakes

1. Mix sherry, soy sauce, sesame oil, vinegar, sugar, pepper, and salt in small bowl.

2. Heat 12-inch nonstick skillet over high heat until quite hot, 2 to 3 minutes. Add 1 tablespoon peanut oil and swirl to coat bottom of pan (oil should shimmer immediately). Add snow peas and cook for 2 minutes, tossing peas every 30 seconds.

3. Clear center of pan, add garlic, ginger, orange zest, and hot red pepper flakes, and drizzle with remaining 1 teaspoon peanut oil. Mash garlic mixture with back of spatula. Cook for 10 seconds and then mix with snow peas. Off heat, add sherry mixture (it should immediately reduce down to a glaze). Serve immediately.

Stir-Fried Snow Peas with Oyster Sauce

3	tablespoons dry sherry
2	tablespoons oyster sauce
1	tablespoon Asian sesame oil
1	tablespoon soy sauce
¼	teaspoon ground black pepper
1	tablespoon plus 1 teaspoon peanut oil
4	cups loosely packed snow peas (about 1 pound), tips pulled off and strings removed
1½	teaspoons minced garlic
1½	teaspoons minced fresh gingerroot

1. Mix sherry, oyster sauce, sesame oil, soy sauce, and pepper in small bowl.

2. Heat 12-inch nonstick skillet over high heat until quite hot, 2 to 3 minutes. Add 1 tablespoon peanut oil and swirl to coat bottom of pan (oil should shimmer immediately). Add snow peas and cook for 2 minutes, tossing peas every 30 seconds.

3. Clear center of pan, add garlic and ginger, and drizzle with remaining 1 teaspoon peanut oil. Mash garlic and ginger with back of spatula. Cook for 10 seconds and then mix with snow peas. Off heat, add oyster sauce mixture (it should immediately reduce down to a glaze). Serve immediately.

PEPPERS

THE ROASTING OF BELL PEPPERS HAS BECOME very popular, and for very good reasons. When roasted, sweet red bell peppers assume a whole new layer of complex, smoky flavor. In testing the many different methods of roasting peppers, we sought the most efficient way to achieve a tender but not mushy flesh, smoky flavor, and skin that would peel off easily.

After flaming (over a gas burner), broiling, baking, and steaming dozens of peppers, we found that oven broiling is clearly superior. It's neater and faster, and the peppers are delicious.

To reach this conclusion, we roasted dozens of peppers. We found that you must take care not to overroast the peppers. When the skin of the pepper just puffs up and turns black, you have reached the point at which flavor is maximized and the texture of the pepper flesh is soft but not mushy. After this point, continued exposure to heat will result in darkened flesh that is thinner, flabbier-textured, and slightly bitter.

Broiling peppers does present some challenges. The broiler element in most ovens is approximately three inches away from the upper rack, which means that whole peppers usually touch the element. A lower rack level takes too long and cooks the flesh too much. The answer, then, is to cut the peppers.

Unless you have asbestos fingers, roasted peppers need time to cool before handling, and steaming during this time does make the charred skin a bit easier to peel off. The ideal steaming time is 15 minutes—any less and the peppers are still too hot to work with comfortably. The best method is to use a heat-resistant bowl (glass, ceramic, or metal) with a piece of plastic wrap secured over the top to trap the steam.

Seeding the peppers before roasting makes it possible to peel the pepper without having to rinse them to wash away the seeds. If you are still tempted to rinse, notice the rich oils that accumulate on your fingers as you work. It seems silly to rinse away those oils rather than savoring them later with your meal.

The way peppers are treated after they are peeled will determine how long they keep. Unadorned and wrapped in plastic wrap, peppers will keep their full, meaty texture only about two days in the refrigera-

ROASTING PEPPERS

1. Slice ¼ inch from the top and bottom of the pepper. Then gently remove the stem from the top lobe.

2. Pull the core out of the pepper.

3. Make a slit down one side of the pepper, then lay it flat, skin side down. Use a sharp knife to remove all the ribs and seeds.

4. Arrange the strips of peppers and the top and bottom lobes on a baking sheet, skin-side up. Flatten the strips with the palm of your hand.

5. Adjust the oven rack to its top position. If the rack is more than 3½ inches from the heating element, set a jelly-roll pan, bottom up, on the rack under the baking sheet.

6. Roast until the skin of the peppers is charred and puffed up like a balloon but the flesh is still firm. You may steam the peppers at this point or not, as you wish. Start peeling where the skin has charred the most.

tor. Drizzled with a generous amount of olive oil and kept in an air-tight container, peppers will keep about one week without losing texture or flavor. Completely covered with olive oil, peppers will last in the fridge three to four weeks.

Most cooks are familiar with roasting bell peppers for salads, sauces, or dips. However, peppers may also be sliced and cooked by other means as a vegetable side dish. Green peppers are unripe and generally quite bitter. Red, yellow, and orange peppers are all fully ripe and much sweeter. Avoid purple peppers, which turn a drab green color when cooked and cost much more than green peppers.

We tested sautéing and stir-frying first and found that both methods yield lightly seared peppers that are still fairly crisp. The peppers were good, but we missed the silky smoothness of roasted peppers. We tried cooking the peppers more but found that the exterior charred by the time the pepper was fully cooked.

We decided to see what would happen if we put the cover on the skillet after searing them. As we hoped, the peppers steamed in their own juices and became especially tender. We found that the moisture from the peppers is enough to keep them from scorching in the covered pan. We also realized that we now had an opportunity to add another liquid for juicier, seasoned peppers. A little vinegar balances the intense sweetness of the peppers and works especially well.

Master Recipe for Roasted Red Bell Peppers

MAKES 4 ROASTED PEPPERS

Cooking times vary, depending on the broiler, so watch the peppers carefully as they roast. You will need to increase the cooking time slightly if your peppers are just out of the refrigerator instead of at room temperature. Yellow and orange peppers roast faster than red ones, so decrease their cooking time by 2 to 4 minutes.

> 4   red medium-to-large bell peppers (6 to 9 ounces each), prepared according to illustrations 1 through 4 on page 85

1. Adjust oven rack to top position. Turn broiler on. With oven door closed, let oven heat for 5 minutes. Oven rack should be 2½ to 3½ inches from heating element. If not, set a jelly-roll pan, turned upside down, on oven rack to elevate pan (see illustration 5 on page 85). Place prepared room-temperature peppers on a foil-lined 17 x 11-inch baking sheet and flatten peppers with palm of your hand. Broil peppers, with oven door closed, until spotty brown, about 5 minutes. Reverse pan in oven; roast until skin is charred and puffed but the flesh is still firm, 3 to 5 minutes longer.

2. Remove pan from oven; let peppers sit until cool enough to handle; peel and discard skin from each piece (see illustration 6 on page 85). To facilitate peeling, peppers can be transferred right out of oven to a large heat-resistant bowl, covered with plastic wrap, and steamed for 15 minutes before peeling skin.

Master Recipe for Sautéed Bell Peppers

SERVES 4

A mixture of yellow, orange, and red peppers delivers the sweetest and best results. You can use one green pepper, but these unripe peppers are much less sweet and should not be used in greater amounts.

> 2   tablespoons extra-virgin olive oil
> 4   medium bell peppers (about 1¾ pounds), cored, seeded, and cut into ¼-inch-wide strips
> 1   medium garlic clove, minced
> 1   tablespoon chopped fresh oregano, basil, or parsley leaves
>   Salt and ground black pepper

1. Heat oil in large skillet over medium-high heat. Add peppers and sauté, tossing occasionally, until peppers begin to brown on edges, about 5 minutes.

2. Add garlic and cook for 1 minute. Reduce heat to low, cover pan, and cook until peppers are tender, 4 to 5 minutes. Remove cover and stir in herb. Season with salt and pepper to taste. Serve hot, warm, or at room temperature.

➤ VARIATIONS

Sautéed Bell Peppers with Red Onion and Balsamic Vinegar

Follow recipe for Sautéed Bell Peppers, cooking 1 small red onion, thinly sliced, with bell peppers. Just before covering pan, add 3 tablespoons balsamic vinegar. Use parsley as herb.

Sautéed Bell Peppers with Black Olives and Feta Cheese

Follow recipe for Sautéed Bell Peppers, adding 2 tablespoons red wine vinegar to pan just before covering. Use oregano as herb and add 8 pitted and chopped black olives at the same time. Just before serving, crumble 2 ounces feta cheese over peppers.

POTATOES

DOZENS OF POTATO VARIETIES ARE GROWN in this country, and at any time you may see as many as five or six in your supermarket. Some potatoes are sold by varietal name (such as Yukon Gold), but others are sold by generic name (baking, all-purpose, etc.). To make sense of this confusion, we find it helpful to group potatoes into three major categories, based on the ratio of solids (mostly starch) to water. The categories are high-starch/low-moisture potatoes, medium-starch potatoes, and low-starch/high-moisture potatoes.

The high-starch/low-moisture category includes baking, russet, and white creamer potatoes. (The formal name for the russet is russet Burbank potato, named after its developer, Luther Burbank of Idaho. This type of potato is also known as the Idaho. In all of our recipes, we call them russets.) These potatoes are best for baking and mashing. The medium-starch category includes all-purpose, Yukon Gold, Yellow Finn, and purple Peruvian potatoes. These potatoes can be mashed or baked, but are generally not as fluffy as the high-starch potatoes. The low-starch/high-moisture category includes Red Bliss, red creamer, new, white rose, and fingerling potatoes. These potatoes are best roasted or boiled and used in salad.

BAKED POTATOES

WE BAKED ALL-PURPOSE POTATOES, YUKON Golds, and russets and found that russets produce the fluffiest and, to our mind, the best baked potato. We baked russets at temperatures ranging from 350 to 500 degrees and discovered that traditional slow-baking is best, mainly because of the effect it has on the skin. The skin of a potato baked at 350 degrees for an hour and 15 minutes simply has no peer. Just under the skin, a well-baked potato will develop a substantial brown layer. This is because the dark skin absorbs heat during cooking, and the starch just inside the skin is broken down into sugar and starts to brown. If you love baked potato skin, this is definitely the best method.

If slow-baking is essential to good skin, the consistency of the flesh also requires some attention. Letting the potato sit awhile after baking without opening it up will steam the potato and cause the flesh to become more dense. For fluffy potatoes, create a wide opening as soon as the potatoes come out of the oven to let steam escape.

Master Recipe for Baked Potatoes
SERVES 4

We found no benefit or harm was done to the potatoes by poking them with the tines of a fork before putting them in the oven. Do use a fork to open the skin as soon as potatoes come out of the oven.

4   medium russet potatoes (7 to 8 ounces each), scrubbed

Heat oven to 350 degrees. Place potatoes on middle rack and bake for 75 minutes. Remove from oven and pierce with fork to create dotted X on top of each potato. Press in at ends of each potato to push flesh up and out.

TWICE-BAKED POTATOES

THIS SIMPLE DISH—ESSENTIALLY JUST BAKED russet potatoes from which the flesh has been removed, mashed with dairy ingredients and seasonings, mounded back in the shells, and baked again—offers a good range of both texture and flavor in a single morsel. Done well, the skin is chewy and substantial without being tough, with just a hint of crispness to play off the smooth, creamy filling. In terms of flavor, cheese and other dairy ingredients make the filling rich and tangy, a contrast to the mild, slightly sweet potato shell.

Because twice-baked potatoes are put in the oven

twice, we found it best to bake them for just an hour, rather than the usual seventy-five minutes. Oiling the skins before baking promotes crispness, not something you necessarily want in plain baked potatoes but a trait we came to admire in creamy twice-baked potatoes.

The baked potato recipe underscored the importance of opening the potatoes right after baking to release as much steam as possible. However, we found that the potatoes are significantly easier to handle once they have cooled for a few minutes; because the flesh is mixed with wet ingredients, any compromise to the texture from unreleased moisture is negligible.

Once the potato halves had been emptied of their flesh, we noticed they got a little flabby sitting on the counter waiting to be stuffed. Because the oven was still on and waiting for the return of the stuffed halves, we decided to put the skins back in while we prepared the filling. That worked beautifully, giving the shells an extra dimension of crispness.

Pleased with our chewy, slightly crunchy skins, we now had to develop a smooth, lush, flavorful filling that would hold up its end of the bargain. (Lumpy, sodden, and dull-tasting would not do.) Dozens of further tests helped us refine our filling to a rich, but not killer, combination of sharp cheddar, sour cream, buttermilk, and just two tablespoons of butter. We learned to season the filling aggressively with salt and pepper; for herbs, the slightly sharp flavor of scallions or chives was best.

With the filling mixed and mounded back into the shells, our last tests centered on the final baking. We wanted to do more than just heat the filling through; we aimed to form an attractive brown crust on it as well. We found that using the broiler was the easiest and most effective method. After 15 minutes, the potatoes emerged browned, crusted, and ready for the table.

Twice-Baked Potatoes

SERVES 6 TO 8

To vary the flavor a bit, try substituting other types of cheese, such as Gruyère, fontina, or feta, for the cheddar. Yukon Gold potatoes, though slightly more moist than our ideal, gave our twice-baked potatoes a buttery flavor and mouthfeel that everyone liked, so we recommend them as a substitution for the russets.

4 medium russet potatoes (7 to 8 ounces each), scrubbed, dried, and rubbed lightly with vegetable oil
4 ounces sharp cheddar cheese, shredded (about 1 cup)
½ cup sour cream
½ cup buttermilk
2 tablespoons unsalted butter, room temperature
3 medium scallions, thinly sliced
½ teaspoon salt
 Ground black pepper

1. Adjust oven rack to upper-middle position and heat oven to 400 degrees. Bake potatoes on foil-lined baking sheet until skin is crisp and deep brown and skewer easily pierces flesh, about 1 hour. Setting baking sheet aside, transfer potatoes to wire rack and let cool slightly, about 10 minutes.

2. Using an oven mitt or folded kitchen towel to handle hot potatoes, cut each potato in half so that long, blunt sides rest on work surface. Using a small spoon, scoop flesh from each half into medium bowl, leaving a ⅛- to ¼-inch thickness of flesh in each shell. Arrange shells on lined sheet and return to oven until dry and slightly crisped, about 10 minutes. Meanwhile, mash potato flesh with fork until smooth. Stir in remaining ingredients, including ground black pepper to taste, until well combined.

3. Remove shells from oven and increase oven setting to broil. Holding shells steady on pan with oven mitt or towel-protected hand, spoon mixture into crisped shells, mounding slightly at the center, and return to oven. Broil until spotty brown and crisp on top, 10 to 15 minutes. Allow to cool for 10 minutes. Serve warm.

➤ VARIATIONS

Twice-Baked Potatoes with Pepperjack Cheese and Bacon

Fry 8 strips (about 8 ounces) bacon, cut crosswise into ¼-inch pieces, in medium skillet over medium heat until crisp, 5 to 7 minutes. Remove bacon to paper towel–lined plate to drain; set aside. Follow recipe for Twice-Baked Potatoes, substituting pepperjack cheese for cheddar and stirring reserved bacon into filling mixture.

Twice–Baked Potatoes with Smoked Salmon and Chives

This variation makes a fine brunch dish.

Follow recipe for Twice-Baked Potatoes, omitting cheese and scallions and stirring 4 ounces smoked salmon, cut into ½-inch pieces, and 3 tablespoons minced fresh chives into filling mixture. Sprinkle finished potatoes with additional chopped chives as garnish just before serving.

ROASTED POTATOES

THE PERFECT ROASTED POTATO IS CRISP AND deep golden brown on the outside, with moist, velvety, dense interior flesh. The potato's slightly bitter skin is intact, providing a contrast to the sweet, caramelized flavor that the flesh develops during the roasting process. It is rich, but never greasy, and it is accompanied by the heady taste of garlic and herbs.

To start, we roasted several kinds of potatoes. We liked high-starch/low-moisture potatoes (we used russets) the least. They did not brown well, their dry, fluffy texture was more like baked than roasted potatoes, and their flavor reminded us of raw potatoes. The medium-starch all-purpose potatoes (we used Yukon Golds) produced a beautiful golden crust, but the interior flesh was still rather dry. The best roasting potatoes came from the low-starch/high-moisture category (we used Red Bliss). These potatoes emerged from the oven with a light, delicate crust and a moist, dense interior that had a more complex, nutty flavor than the others, with hints of bitterness and tang.

After choosing the Red Bliss potatoes, we began to test oven temperatures. At 425 degrees, the result was an even-colored, golden-brown potato with a thin, crisp crust and an interior that was soft and dense, although still slightly dry.

While researching, we came across some recipes that called for parboiling the potatoes before roasting them. Hoping that this approach would produce a texturally superior potato that retained more of its moisture after cooking, we tried boiling the potatoes for seven minutes prior to roasting. This produced a potato closer to our ideal, but required considerable attention owing to the additional step.

We then tried covering the potatoes for a portion of their roasting time. We were especially drawn to this technique because it provided a way to steam the potatoes in their own moisture that required little extra effort on the cook's part. The results were perfect. The crisp, deep golden-brown crust was perfectly balanced by a creamy, moist interior. These potatoes had a sweet and nutty caramelized flavor, with just a hint of tang from the skin. This simplest of methods had produced the very best potatoes.

The next step in the process was figuring out how to add garlic flavor, which makes a good variation on the standard roasted potatoes. When we added minced garlic during the last five minutes of cooking, it burned almost instantly; coating the pota-

---

EQUIPMENT: Vegetable Peelers

You might imagine that all vegetable peelers are pretty much the same. Not so. In our research, we turned up 25 peelers, many with quite novel features. The major differences were the fixture of the blade, either stationary or swiveling; the material of the blade, either carbon stainless steel, stainless steel, or ceramic; and the orientation of the blade to the handle, either straight in line with the body or perpendicular to it. The last arrangement, with the blade perpendicular to the handle, is called a harp or Y peeler because the frame looks like the body of a harp or the letter Y. This type of peeler, which is popular in Europe, works with a pulling motion rather than the more prevalent shucking motion of most American peelers.

To test the peelers, we recruited several cooks and asked them to peel carrots, potatoes, lemons, butternut squash, and celery root. In most cases, testers preferred the Oxo Good Grips peeler, which has a sharp stainless steel blade that swivels. Peelers with stationary blades are fine for peeling carrots, but they have trouble hugging the curves on potatoes.

The Y-shaped peelers tested well, although they removed more flesh with the skin on potatoes, lemons, and carrots and therefore did not rate as well as the Oxo Good Grips. The one case where this liability turned into an asset was on butternut squash, where these Y-shaped peelers took off the skin as well as the greenish-tinged flesh right below the skin in one pass. With the Oxo Good Grips, it was necessary to go over the peeled flesh once the skin had been removed.

toes with garlic-infused oil failed to produce the strong garlic flavor that we were after; and roasting whole, unpeeled garlic cloves alongside the potatoes and squeezing the pulp out afterwards to add to the potatoes was too tedious. The best method turned out to be both very simple and very flavorful. You can just mash raw garlic into a paste, place it in a large stainless steel bowl, put the hot roasted potatoes into the bowl, and toss. This method yields potatoes with a strong garlic flavor yet without the raw spiciness of uncooked garlic.

Master Recipe for Roasted Potatoes

SERVES 4

To roast more than 2 pounds of potatoes at once, use a second pan rather than crowding the first. If your potatoes are as small as new potatoes, cut them in halves instead of wedges and turn them cut-side up during the final 10 minutes of roasting.

> 2 pounds Red Bliss or other low-starch potatoes, scrubbed clean, dried, halved, and cut into ¾-inch wedges
> 3 tablespoons extra-virgin olive oil
> Salt and ground black pepper

1. Adjust oven rack to middle position and heat oven to 425 degrees. Toss potatoes and olive oil in medium bowl to coat; season generously with salt and pepper and toss again to blend.

2. Place potatoes flesh side down, in a single layer, on shallow roasting pan; cover tightly with aluminum foil and cook about 20 minutes. Remove foil; roast until side of potato touching pan is crusty golden brown, about 15 minutes more. Remove pan from oven and carefully turn potatoes over using metal spatula. (Press spatula against metal as it slides under potatoes to protect crusts.) Return pan to oven and roast until side of potato now touching pan is crusty golden brown and skins have raisinlike wrinkles, 5 to 10 minutes more. Remove from oven, transfer potatoes to serving dish (again, using metal spatula and extra care not to rip crusts), and serve warm.

✒ VARIATION
Roasted Potatoes with Garlic and Rosemary

Follow recipe for Roasted Potatoes. While potatoes roast, mince two medium garlic cloves; sprinkle with ⅛ teaspoon salt and mash with flat side of chef's knife blade until paste forms. Transfer garlic paste to large bowl; set aside. In last 3 minutes of roasting time, sprinkle 2 tablespoons chopped fresh rosemary evenly over potatoes. Immediately transfer potatoes to bowl with garlic; toss to distribute, and serve warm.

MASHED POTATOES

ALTHOUGH YOU CAN MASH ANY TYPE OF potato, the variety you choose does make a significant difference in the ultimate quality of the dish. Potatoes are composed mostly of starch and water. The starch is in the form of granules, which in turn are contained in starch cells. The higher the starch content of the potato, the fuller the cells. In high-starch potatoes, the cells are completely full—they look like plump little beach balls. In medium- or low-starch potatoes, the cells are more like underinflated beach balls. The space between these less-full cells is mostly taken up by water.

The full starch cells of high-starch potatoes are most likely to maintain their integrity and stay separate when mashed, giving the potatoes a delightfully fluffy, full texture. In addition, the low water content of these potatoes allows them to absorb milk, cream, and/or butter without becoming wet or gummy. Starch cells in lower-starch potatoes, on the other hand, tend to clump when cooked and break more easily, allowing the starch to dissolve into whatever liquid is present. The broken cells and dissolved starch tend to make sticky, gummy mashed potatoes.

Be careful not to overcook potatoes you plan to mash, because the starch cells will break down and create a sticky mash. Cook them just until a thin-bladed knife meets a bit of resistance. It is also important to drain the potatoes well after cooking; again, excess water combining with starch produces gumminess.

We prefer to force cooked potatoes through a ricer, which turns the potatoes into fine, thin shreds. With the potatoes already mashed, you can blend in butter and milk with a wooden spoon or a stiff whisk, which is gentle on those starch cells and therefore helps ensure consistently fluffy mashed potatoes.

The more traditional mashers are usually of two types: a disk with large holes in it or a curvy wire loop. We found the disk to be more efficient for reducing both mashing time and the number of lumps in the finished product. If you choose one of these mashers, don't use a spoon to blend in the other ingredients, as recommended with the ricer, but blend and mash at the same time to minimize stickiness. We recommend mashing a little, then stirring a bit, then mashing, and so on, finishing with a brisk stirring.

Many recipes call for heating milk before adding it and justify this by saying that cold milk makes mashed potatoes sticky. But our repeated experiments have demonstrated that this is not true. Cold milk does cool the potatoes, which you really don't want to do, but the stories about the milk forming strange, gummy substances are poppycock. (Adding boiling milk, however, does tend to make mashed potatoes sticky, because the additional heat breaks up the starch cells.) Our choice is to use warm milk, but only because it keeps the potatoes up to temperature. Similarly, when adding butter to mashed potatoes, be sure that it is softened to room temperature so that it melts quickly.

Mashed Potatoes

SERVES 6

This recipe delivers spectacularly smooth, fluffy potatoes, not too rich and not too assertively flavored. Russet potatoes make slightly fluffier mashed potatoes, but Yukon Golds have an appealing buttery flavor.

2	pounds russet or Yukon Gold potatoes, peeled, eyes and blemishes removed, cut into 2-inch chunks
¾	teaspoon salt
6	tablespoons butter, softened
I	cup whole milk or half-and-half, warm Ground black pepper

1. Put potatoes in a large saucepan; add cold water to cover and ½ teaspoon salt. Bring to boil and continue to cook over medium heat until potatoes are tender when pierced with a knife, 15 to 20 minutes.

2. Drain potatoes well and return pan to low heat.

Rice potatoes into pan and use whisk or wooden spoon to blend in butter, then warm milk. Or, return potatoes to saucepan; mash over low heat with a potato masher, adding butter as you mash and stirring in warm milk.

3. Season mashed potatoes with ¼ teaspoon salt and a pinch of black pepper, and serve immediately.

FRENCH FRIES

THE IDEAL FRENCH FRY IS LONG AND CRISP, with right-angle sides, a nice crunch on the outside, and an earthy potato taste. Its bass flavor note should be rustic, like a mushroom, and its high note should hint of the oil in which it was created. It should definitely not droop, and its coloring should be two-tone, blond with hints of brown.

Obviously, a good french fry requires the right potato. Would it be starchy or waxy? We tested two of the most popular waxy potatoes, and neither was even close to ideal, both being too watery. During the frying, water evaporated inside the potato, leaving hollows that would fill with oil, so the finished fries were greasy.

Next we tested the starchy potato most readily available nationwide, the russet. This potato turned out to be ideal, frying up with all the qualities that we were looking for.

Because these are starchy potatoes, it is important to rinse the starch off the surface after you cut the potato into fries. To do this, simply put the cut fries into a bowl, place the bowl in the sink, and run cold water into it, swirling with your fingers until the water runs clear. This might seem like an unimportant step, but it makes a real difference. When we skipped the starch rinse, the fries weren't quite right, and the oil clouded.

At this point, you take the second crucial step: Fill the bowl with clear water, add ice, and refrigerate the potatoes for at least 30 minutes. That way, when the potatoes first enter the hot oil, they are nearly frozen; this allows a slow, thorough cooking of the inner potato pulp. When we tried making fries without this chilling, the outsides started to brown well before the insides were fully cooked.

We prefer to peel the potatoes. A skin-on fry keeps the potato from forming those little airy blisters that we prefer. Peeling the potato also allows home cooks to see—and remove, if they want to—

any imperfections and greenish coloring.

What is the right fat for making perfect french fries?

To find out, we experimented with lard, vegetable shortening, canola oil, corn oil, and peanut oil. Lard and shortening make great fries, but we figured that many cooks wouldn't want to use these products. We moved on to canola oil, the ballyhooed oil of the '90s, now used in a blend with safflower oil by McDonald's, which produces 4 million pounds of finished fries a day. But we were unhappy with the results: bland, almost watery fries.

Corn oil was the most forgiving oil in the test kitchen. It rebounded well from temperature fluctuations and held up very well in subsequent frying, and the fries tasted marvelous. A potato fried in peanut oil is light, and the flavor is rich but not dense. The earthy flavor of the potato is there, as with corn oil, but is not overbearing. At this point, we were very close, and yet there was still something missing. The high flavor note, which is supplied by the animal fat in lard, was lacking.

We tried a dollop of strained bacon grease in peanut oil, about two generous tablespoons per quart of oil. The meaty flavor came through, but without its nasty baggage.

So bacon grease appeared to be the fat of choice. To be certain of this, we added bacon grease to each of the oils, with these results: canola oil, extra body, but still short on flavor; corn oil, more body, more flavor, nearly perfect; peanut oil, flavor, bite, body, bass notes, high notes galore. At last, an equivalent to lard.

So now it was time to get down to the frying, which actually means double-frying. First, we parfried the potatoes at a relatively low temperature to release their rich and earthy flavor. The potatoes are then quick-fried at a higher temperature until nicely browned and immediately served.

The garden variety cookbook recipe calls for parfrying at 350 degrees and final frying at 375 to 400 degrees. But we found these temperatures to be far too aggressive. We prefer an initial frying at 325 degrees, with the final frying at 350 degrees. Lower temperatures allowed for easier monitoring; with higher temperatures the fries can get away from the cook.

For the sake of convenience, we also attempted a single, longer frying. Like many cooks before us, we found that with standard french fries (as opposed to the much thinner shoestring fries), we could not both sear the outside and properly cook the inside with a single visit to the hot fat. When we left them in long enough to sear the outside, we wound up with wooden, overcooked fries.

French Fries

SERVES 4

For those who like it, flavoring the oil with a few tablespoons of bacon grease adds a subtle, meaty flavor to the fries. Their texture, however, is not affected if the bacon grease is omitted. Once you've peeled the potatoes, you can cut them with a mandolin or V-slicer instead of doing it by hand. To prepare steak fries, cut the potatoes 1/3- to 1/2-inch thick, and increase the cooking time to 10 to 12 minutes during the initial frying and just a few seconds longer in the final fry.

4   large russet potatoes, peeled and cut into
     1/4 x 1/4-inch-thick lengths
2   quarts peanut oil
4   tablespoons strained bacon grease (optional)
     Salt and ground black pepper

1. Rinse cut fries in large bowl under cold running water until water turns from milky colored to clear. Cover with at least 1 inch of water, then cover with ice. Refrigerate at least 30 minutes. (Can be refrigerated up to 3 days ahead.)

2. In 5-quart pot or Dutch oven fitted with clip-on-the-pot candy thermometer, or in larger electric fryer, heat oil over medium-low heat to 325 degrees. As oil heats, add bacon grease. Oil will bubble up when you add fries, so be sure you have at least 3 inches of room at top of cooking pot.

3. Pour off ice and water, quickly wrap potatoes in a clean tea towel, and thoroughly pat dry. Increase heat to medium-high and add fries, a handful at a time, to hot oil. Fry, stirring with Chinese skimmer or large-hole slotted spoon, until potatoes are limp and soft and start to turn from white to blond, 6 to 8 minutes. (Oil temperature will drop 50 to 60 degrees during this frying.) Use skimmer or slotted spoon to transfer fries to brown paper bag to drain; let rest at least 10 minutes. (Can stand at room temperature up to 2 hours.)

4. When ready to serve fries, reheat oil to 350 degrees. Using paper bag as a funnel, pour potatoes into hot oil. Discard bag and set up second paper bag. Fry potatoes, stirring fairly constantly, until golden brown and puffed, about 1 minute. Transfer to paper bag and drain again. Season to taste with salt and pepper or seasoned salt. Serve immediately.

SCIENCE: Stress-Free Spud Storage

Since potatoes seem almost indestructible compared with other vegetables, little thought is generally given to their storage. But because various problems can result from inadequate storage conditions, we decided to find out how much difference storage really made. We stored all-purpose potatoes in five environments: in a cool (50–60 degrees), dark place; in the refrigerator; in a basket near a sunlit window; in a warm (70–80 degrees), dark place; and in a drawer with some onions at room temperature. We checked all the potatoes after four weeks.

As expected, the potatoes stored in the cool, dark place were firm, had not sprouted, and were crisp and moist when cut. There were no negative marks on the potatoes stored in the refrigerator, either; although some experts say that the sugar level dramatically increases in some potato varieties under these conditions, we could not see or taste any difference between these potatoes and the ones stored in the cool, dark, but unrefrigerated environment.

Our last three storage tests produced unfavorable results. The potatoes stored in sunlight, in warm storage, and with onions ended up with a greenish tinge along the edges. When potatoes are stressed by improper storage, the level of naturally occurring toxins increases, causing the greenish tinge known as solanine. Because solanine is not destroyed by cooking, any part of the potato with this greenish coloring should be completely cut away before cooking.

The skin of the potatoes stored in sunlight became gray and mottled, while the potatoes stored in a warm place and those stored with onions sprouted and became soft and wrinkled. Sprouts also contain increased levels of solanine and should be cut away before cooking.

HASH BROWNS

HASH BROWNS ARE BEST DEFINED AS THIN, crisply sautéed potato cakes made with grated or chopped potatoes, raw or precooked. We tested various kinds of potatoes and found that the high-starch

russet yielded the best overall results. It adhered well, browned beautifully, and had the most pronounced potato flavor.

Our next challenge was to decide between raw and precooked potatoes. Precooked potatoes tasted good, but when cut into chunks they did not stay together in a cohesive cake, and when grated they needed to be pressed very hard to form a cake. Unfortunately, this meant they ended up having the mouthfeel of fried mashed potato. Although this is an acceptable alternative if you have leftover cooked potatoes, we preferred using raw, grated potatoes. We also liked the more textured interior, the pronounced potato taste, and the way the raw shreds of potatoes formed an attractive, deeply browned crust.

Choosing the best method for cutting the potatoes was easy. Grating the potatoes on the large-hole side of a box grater or with the shredding disk on a food processor yielded hash browns that form a coherent cake when cooked.

Hash browns can be made into one or more individual servings or one large portion that can be cut into wedges. No matter how you choose to present the hash browns, make sure you serve them steaming hot.

Hash Browns

SERVES 4

To prevent potatoes from turning brown, grate them just before cooking. For individual servings, simply divide the grated potatoes into four equal portions and reduce cooking time to 5 minutes per side. To vary flavor, add 2 tablespoons grated onion, 1 to 2 tablespoons herb of choice, or roasted garlic to taste to the raw grated potatoes. You can also garnish the cooked hash browns with snipped chives or scallion tops just before serving.

1	pound high-starch potatoes such as russets, peeled, washed, dried, grated coarse, and squeezed dry in kitchen towel (1½ cups loosely packed grated potatoes)
¼	teaspoon salt
	Ground black pepper
1	tablespoon butter

1. Toss fully dried grated potatoes with salt and pepper in a medium bowl.

[handwritten marginalia: √G could have been more seasonal 3/22/15 make again. check salt to make sure have right amount.]

2. Meanwhile, heat half the butter in a 10-inch skillet over medium-high heat until it just starts to brown, then scatter potatoes evenly over entire pan bottom. Using a wide spatula, firmly press potatoes to flatten; reduce heat to medium and continue cooking until dark golden brown and crisp, 7 to 8 minutes.

3. Invert hash browns, browned side up, onto a large plate; add remaining butter to pan. Once butter has melted, slide hash browns back into pan. Continue to cook over medium heat until remaining side is dark golden brown and crisp, 5 to 6 minutes longer.

4. Slide hash browns onto plate or cutting board, cut into wedges, and serve immediately.

POTATO GRATIN

POTATO GRATIN—ALSO KNOWN AS FRENCH dauphinois or Yankee scalloped potatoes—consists of thinly sliced potatoes covered by a liquid and baked in a wide, shallow baking pan until the potatoes are tender and the top gets a burnished crust. Most recipes follow the same procedure: Rub an ovenproof dish with garlic, brush it with butter, layer it with sliced potatoes, add seasonings and just enough liquid to cover the potatoes, and bake.

We tried all the major varieties of potatoes, including all-purpose whites, boilers, yellow-fleshed, and new potatoes. All made tasty gratins, but we did find subtle variations in flavor or texture—waxy potatoes ended up firmer, for example, while floury baking potatoes were more tender. However, the differences were relatively slight, and we began to suspect that the way the potato is sliced is more significant than which type is used.

We found potatoes cut into ¹⁄₁₆-inch slices soaked up the cooking liquid and melted into a cakelike texture. When sliced ⅛-inch thick, however, they kept their shape nicely throughout baking but still melded together. However, when sliced too thick (¼ inch or more), the potato slices did not properly meld together in the oven.

The pan in which you make a gratin is an important consideration. A standard gratin dish is oval, 10 to 12 inches long and 6 to 8 inches wide. As it turns out, the dimensions of the pan are more important than the material it's made of. We cooked successful gratins in a variety of dishes, from classic enamel to earthenware to ovenproof glass—the key is that they were all shallow. Two to three layers of potatoes should come about three-quarters of the way up the sides of the pan so they cook evenly and have a broad surface area to brown.

We found 350 degrees to be the best oven temperature. At higher temperatures, the slices on the top of the gratin tended to dry out and become tough. We also discovered that it helps to baste the top slices once or twice during the cooking so they stay moist and brown evenly.

We made gratins using a variety of liquids, including whole milk, low-fat milk, half-and-half, heavy cream, meat broths, and water. The heavy cream had a tendency to break up and become greasy, particularly at higher temperatures. The low-fat milk, on the other hand, was insipid, while the whole milk was almost completely soaked up by the potatoes, leaving only a light curd between the layers. Our favorite all-purpose, dairy cooking medium turned out to be half-and-half cooked at 350 degrees for about an hour. Gratins made this way had just the right balance of saturated potato and saucy liquid, without overwhelming the taste of the potato. They were also easy to prepare.

Until this point, we had tried pouring cold liquids over the layered potatoes and baking them. We wondered if we could cut the cooking time by heating the potatoes and liquid beforehand. We placed a pound of sliced potatoes, enough liquid to barely cover them, salt, and pepper into a saucepan and brought the liquid to a boil, stirring occasionally so the potatoes didn't scorch or stick. We next lowered the heat and simmered the mixture until the liquid thickened. Finally we poured the potatoes into a baking dish and finished them in a 350-degree oven.

This method turned out to possess many benefits. The cooking time was reduced, the assembly of the gratin took less time, and, because the seasoning was added to the liquid, the final product was evenly seasoned.

There are several ways to enhance the crust from which these dishes get their name (the French word gratin means "crust"). Dotting the top with butter makes for a golden crust, as does cheese. A nice finish can also be achieved by pouring a thin layer of cream over the top of the gratin for the final 20 or 30 minutes of baking. This cap of cream browns evenly without greasy edges.

Potato Gratin

SERVES 4 TO 6

Russet potatoes will produce a more tender gratin; slices of waxy new potatoes will be firmer. Use either, depending on your personal preference. For a more pronounced crust, sprinkle three tablespoons of heavy cream or grated Gruyère cheese on top of the potatoes after forty-five minutes of baking.

I	large garlic clove, peeled and smashed
I	tablespoon butter, softened
2¼	cups half-and-half
1¼	teaspoons salt
⅛	teaspoon ground black pepper
	Pinch grated nutmeg
	Pinch cayenne pepper (optional)
2	pounds potatoes, peeled and sliced ⅛-inch thick

1. Adjust oven rack to center position and heat oven to 350 degrees. Rub bottom and sides of 5- to 6-cup gratin dish or shallow baking dish with garlic. Mince remaining garlic and set aside. Once garlic in dish has dried, about 2 minutes, spread dish with half the butter.

2. Bring half-and-half, salt, pepper, nutmeg, cayenne (if desired), potatoes, and reserved garlic to boil in medium saucepan over medium-high heat, stirring occasionally with wooden spoon (liquid will just barely cover potatoes). Reduce heat and simmer until liquid thickens, about 2 minutes.

3. Pour potato mixture into prepared dish; shake dish or use fork to distribute potatoes evenly. Gently press down potatoes until submerged in liquid; dot with remaining butter.

4. Bake until top is golden brown (basting once or twice during first 45 minutes), about 75 minutes. Let rest 5 minutes and serve.

EQUIPMENT: Mandolins and V-Slicers

The consistently thin, even potato slices that make great gratins are easy to achieve using a slicing device known as a mandolin. To determine the performance differences between the more and less expensive models, we sliced potatoes and lemons on a top-of-the-line French Bron mandolin costing $150, a $30 German Boerner V-Slicer, and a $5.50 Feemster Vegetable Slicer made in the United States.

First, it is important to purchase a slicer with a safety guard, which guides food onto—and protects your hands from—the blade. Whether expensive or not, all of these contraptions have razor-sharp blades, and a slip of the finger could be dangerous. While the Feemster, for example, makes respectable slices and has a wide adjustment range, it does not have a safety guard and is light and flimsy. We do not recommend it.

The expensive Bron mandolin is the heaviest and most solid. It has a safety guard and adjusts infinitely between ⅟₁₆ and ½ inch for slicing, thick and thin julienning, and waffle cutting. It sliced well, though we felt the blade on our brand new test model might be a bit dull. If durability tops your priority list and cost is less important, this model is a good choice. Many restaurant kitchens use it and consider it a workhorse for slicing.

The best of the three slicers we tested, however, was the Boerner V-Slicer. Though it is made of plastic and therefore probably less durable than a stainless-steel model, it does have a safety guard that spears the food to hold it in place and also plunges it toward the blade, enabling you to safely slice the entire piece as the slicing action decreases its size. This feature helps minimize waste. Also, the edges of the safety guard are ridged, so you'll be able to feel them with your fingers even if you glance away. Another advantage of the V-Slicer is the angle of its blades. Food hits an angled blade less abruptly than it does a straight blade and is exposed to more blade area for a cleaner, easier slice. We found this to be a significant advantage. The V-Slicer has only two adjustments for slicing—thick (one-quarter inch) and thin (between one-eighth and one-sixteenth inch)—but that should be sufficient for most home cooking.

ZUCCHINI AND SUMMER SQUASH

THE BIGGEST PROBLEM THAT CONFRONTS THE cook when preparing zucchini and yellow summer squash is their wateriness. Both are about 95 percent water and will become soupy if just thrown into a hot pan. If they cook in their own juices, they won't brown. And since both are fairly bland, they really benefit from some browning. Clearly, some of the water must be removed before sautéing.

We tested salting to draw off some water and found that sliced and salted zucchini will shed about 20 percent of its weight after sitting for 30 minutes. (Summer squash performed the same in all of our tests.) One pound of sliced zucchini threw off almost three tablespoons of liquid, further confirmation that salting works. We tested longer periods and found that little moisture is extracted after 30 minutes.

Given that you don't always have 30 minutes, we wanted to develop quicker methods for cooking zucchini. We tried shredding the zucchini on the large holes of a box grater and then squeezing out excess water by hand. We were able to reduce the weight of shredded zucchini by 25 percent by wrapping it in paper towels and squeezing until dry. Because sliced zucchini has so much less surface area than shredded zucchini, the process works much more efficiently with shredded zucchini.

SHREDDING ZUCCHINI

1. For quick indoor cooking, shred trimmed zucchini or squash on the large holes of a box grater or in a food processor fitted with the shredding disk.

2. Wrap the shredded zucchini or squash in paper towels and squeeze out excess liquid. Proceed immediately with sautéing.

Another quick-prep option is the grill. The intense heat quickly expels excess moisture in zucchini, and that moisture harmlessly drops down on the coals rather than sitting in the pan. We found that so much evaporation occurs during grilling that salting or shredding is not necessary.

Master Recipe for Shredded Zucchini or Summer Squash Sauté

SERVES 4

This recipe is best when you're pressed for time and want to cook zucchini indoors.

- 3   tablespoons extra-virgin olive oil
- 5   medium zucchini or summer squash (about 2 pounds), trimmed, shredded, and squeezed dry (see illustrations below)
- 3   medium garlic cloves, minced
- 2   tablespoons minced fresh parsley, basil, mint, tarragon, or chives
  Salt and ground black pepper

Heat oil in large nonstick skillet over medium-high heat. Add zucchini or squash and garlic and cook, stirring occasionally, until tender, about 7 minutes. Stir in herb and salt and pepper to taste. Serve immediately.

VARIATION

Creamed Zucchini or Summer Squash

Follow recipe for Shredded Zucchini or Summer Squash Sauté, substituting an equal amount of butter for oil. Omit garlic and add ⅓ cup heavy cream with herb; simmer briefly until cream is absorbed.

Master Recipe for Sautéed Zucchini or Summer Squash

SERVES 4

If you like browned zucchini or squash, you must salt it before cooking. Salting drives off excess water and helps the zucchini or squash sauté rather than stew in its own juices. Coarse kosher salt does the best job of driving off liquid and can be wiped away without rinsing. Do not add more salt when cooking or the dish will be too salty.

4   medium zucchini or summer squash (about
    1½ pounds), trimmed and sliced crosswise
    into ¼-inch rounds
1   tablespoon kosher salt
3   tablespoons extra-virgin olive oil
1   small onion or 2 large shallots, minced
1   teaspoon grated lemon zest
1   tablespoon lemon juice
1 to 2   tablespoons minced fresh parsley, basil, mint,
    tarragon, or chives
    Ground black pepper

1. Place zucchini or squash slices in colander and sprinkle with salt. Set colander over bowl until about ⅓ cup water drains from zucchini or squash, about 30 minutes. Remove zucchini from colander and pat dry with clean kitchen towel or several paper towels, wiping off any remaining crystals of salt.

2. Heat oil in large skillet over medium heat. Add onion or shallots and sauté until almost softened, about 2 minutes. Increase heat to medium-high and add zucchini or squash and lemon zest. Sauté until zucchini or squash is golden brown, about 10 minutes. Stir in lemon juice and herb and season with pepper to taste. Serve immediately.

➤ VARIATIONS

Sautéed Zucchini or Summer Squash with Walnuts and Herbs

Follow recipe for Sautéed Zucchini or Summer Squash, omitting lemon zest and juice and adding 2 tablespoons toasted chopped walnuts along with herb.

Sautéed Zucchini or Summer Squash with Olives and Lemon

Follow recipe for Sautéed Zucchini or Summer Squash, adding ¼ cup pitted and chopped black olives along with lemon juice and using 2 teaspoons minced fresh thyme or oregano as herb.

Sautéed Zucchini or Summer Squash with Pancetta and Parsley

Follow recipe for Sautéed Zucchini or Summer Squash, omitting oil and lemon zest and juice. After salting zucchini or squash, cook 2 ounces diced pancetta or bacon in skillet. When fat renders, add onion and continue with recipe. Use parsley as herb.

Master Recipe for Grilled Zucchini or Summer Squash

SERVES 4

Excess water evaporates over hot coals so no salting of zucchini or squash is necessary before cooking.

4   medium zucchini or summer squash (about
    1½ pounds), trimmed and sliced lengthwise
    into ½-inch-thick strips
2   tablespoons extra-virgin olive oil
    Salt and ground black pepper

1. Light grill. Lay zucchini or squash on large baking sheet and brush both sides with oil. Sprinkle generously with salt and pepper.

2. Place zucchini or squash on grill. Cook, turning once, until marked with dark stripes, 8 to 10 minutes. Remove from grill and serve hot, warm, or at room temperature.

➤ VARIATION

Grilled Zucchini or Summer Squash with Capers and Oregano

1   tablespoon red wine vinegar
1   tablespoon capers, chopped
1   medium garlic clove, minced
4   tablespoons extra-virgin olive oil
    Salt and ground black pepper
4   medium zucchini or summer squash (about
    1½ pounds), trimmed and sliced lengthwise
    into ½-inch-thick strips
1   tablespoon chopped fresh oregano leaves

1. Light grill. Whisk vinegar, capers, and garlic together in small bowl. Whisk in 2 tablespoons oil until smooth and season with salt and pepper to taste.

2. Lay zucchini or squash on large baking sheet and brush both sides with remaining 2 tablespoons oil. Sprinkle generously with salt and pepper. Place zucchini or squash on grill. Cook, turning once, until marked with dark stripes, 8 to 10 minutes.

3. Remove zucchini or squash from grill and cool slightly. Cut into 1-inch pieces and toss with dressing and oregano. Serve warm or at room temperature.

GRILLED VEGETABLES

GRILLING VEGETABLES SOUNDS SIMPLE, BUT a number of issues immediately arise. Do you have to precook the vegetables? How thick should each vegetable be sliced? What's the best temperature for grilling them?

Vegetables don't respond well to blazing fires—incineration is a real possibility. We found that most vegetables are best cooked over a medium fire. What does a "medium" fire mean? To gauge the temperature, hold your hand about five inches above the fire. If you can keep your hand there for four seconds, the fire is medium. For medium-low, you should be able to keep your hand above the fire for six seconds.

The best way to add flavor is to brush vegetables with a flavored oil just before grilling. (Marinating is not advised because the acids will make vegetables soggy.) Make sure the oil is a good-quality olive oil. Try adding fresh herbs, garlic, and/or grated citrus zest to the oil, or purchase one that is already flavored. Seasoning with salt and pepper both before and after grilling is another way to maximize flavor.

A lot of equipment exists out there for grilling, much of it designed for vegetables. We tried grilling vegetables in a hinged metal basket and felt that this tool was not very practical since some vegetables are ready to be turned before others. Large vegetables (everything from asparagus spears to sliced zucchini) are best cooked right on the grill grate.

You can skewer smaller items (like cherry tomatoes and white mushrooms) to prevent them from falling onto the coals, but our favorite tool for handling small items is a vegetable grid. We used a tightly woven grid with handles that can be set down right onto the grate. A piece of fine mesh, like that used in a window screen, also works well. And the small items are easy enough to turn with a pair of metal tongs. (We've always found flipping skewers to be a tricky business). A grid is also good for grilling onion rings that otherwise might fall through grate openings.

Grilling Vegetables at a Glance

Use this chart as a guide to grilling the following vegetables. Lightly toss the vegetables or brush them on both sides with olive oil, preferably extra-virgin, before grilling. Unless otherwise specified, vegetables should be cooked over a medium fire.

VEGETABLE	PREPARATION	GRILLING DIRECTIONS
Asparagus	Snap off tough ends.	Grill over medium-low fire, turning once, until tender and streaked with light grill marks, 5 to 7 minutes.
Corn	Remove all but last layer of husk.	Grill, turning every 1½ to 2 minutes, until husk chars and begins to peel away at tip, exposing some kernels, 8 to 10 minutes.
Eggplant	Remove ends. Cut into ¾-inch-thick rounds or ¾-inch-thick strips.	Grill, turning once, until flesh is darkly colored, 8 to 10 minutes.
Endive	Cut in half lengthwise through stem end.	Grill, flat side down, until streaked with dark grill marks, 6 to 8 minutes.
Fennel	Remove stalks and fronds. Slice vertically through base into ½-inch-thick pieces.	Grill, turning once, until streaked with dark grill marks and quite soft, 10 to 15 minutes.
Mushrooms, white and cremini	Clean with a damp towel and trim thin slice from stems.	Grill on a vegetable grid, turning several times, until golden brown, 6 to 7 minutes.
Mushrooms, portobello	Clean with a damp towel and remove stems.	Grill, with gill-like underside facing up, until cap is streaked with grill marks, 8 to 10 minutes.
Onions	Peel and cut into ½-inch-thick slices.	Grill, turning occasionally, until lightly charred, about 5 to 6 minutes.
Peppers	Core, seed, and cut into large wedges.	Grill, turning once, until streaked with dark grill marks, 9 to 10 minutes.
Tomatoes, cherry	Remove stems.	Grill on vegetable grid, turning several times, until streaked with dark grill marks, about 3 minutes.
Tomatoes, plum	Cut in half lengthwise and seed.	Grill, turning once, until streaked with dark grill marks, about 8 minutes.
Zucchini and Summer Squash	Remove ends. Slice lengthwise into ½-inch-thick strips.	Grill, turning once, until streaked with dark grill marks, 8 to 10 minutes.

4
PASTA

COOKING PASTA SEEMS SIMPLE—AFTER ALL, who can't boil water—but there are a number of fine points that can make the difference between decent pasta dishes and great ones. Let's start with buying the pasta itself.

While many sources tout the superiority of Italian pasta, our blind taste tests have shown this to be a myth. American brands of spaghetti scored just as well as Italian brands, and Ronzoni, which is made by Hershey Foods, topped the rankings. While Italian brands offer a greater variety of shapes—such as the earlike orecchiette or the bow-tie shape of farfalle—the quality differences that once existed between domestic and Italian pasta have largely disappeared. (Note: We do prefer Italian lasagne; see page 117.)

As for flavored pasta, we find that saffron, beet, and tomato pasta look great but that the difference in flavor is subtle, if not undetectable. Even spinach pasta has only the mildest spinach flavor, and it's hard to detect once the noodles have been sauced. Buy flavored pastas if you like, but don't spend extra money thinking they will taste better than plain wheat pasta.

Fresh pasta, either made at home or at a local pasta shop, is our first choice for lasagne or ravioli. It's also wonderful when cut into fettuccine and then tossed with a cream sauce (the eggs in fresh pasta work well with dairy sauces in general). However, for most uses, dried pasta, which contains just flour and water, is the best choice. Dried pasta has a sturdier texture better suited to many sauces, especially those with vegetables or other large chunks. Dried pasta is also much more convenient than fresh because it has an almost unlimited shelf life. If you do use fresh pasta, don't buy packages from the refrigerator case in the supermarket. These brands are soft and mushy and have none of the delicacy and subtle egg flavor of fresh pasta made at home or in a pasta shop.

While the brand of pasta may not make much difference, the way you cook the pasta does. First and foremost, start with enough water (at least four quarts for a pound of pasta). Cooking pasta in enough water is the single most important factor in preventing sticking. Pasta swells as it rehydrates, and if there is not enough room, the result is a sticky mess.

Some cookbooks suggest adding oil to the cooking water to keep the pasta from sticking together. In our tests, we have found that abundant water will do this job. Oil will make the pasta slick and therefore less receptive to the sauce and should not be added to the cooking water. While we leave oil out of the cooking pot, salt is a must. Pasta cooked without salt is bland, no matter how salty the sauce is. Add at least 1 tablespoon once the water comes to a boil, remembering that most of the salt goes down the drain with the cooking water.

There are no tricks to tell when pasta is al dente, or cooked "to the tooth." (We tried them all, including throwing strands against the ceiling or refrigerator; we couldn't tell when that pasta was done, but did we end up with a messy kitchen.) When properly cooked, pasta should be resilient but not chewy. Cooking times on packages or in cookbooks are often inaccurate because each stove works differently, so tasting pasta is a must. Keep in mind that the pasta will soften a bit more once drained.

Nothing is worse than a soggy, watery bowl of pasta. However, there is no need to shake the pasta bone-dry either. A little pasta water dripping from the noodles helps thin and spread the sauce. In fact, in many recipes we suggest reserving a little of the cooking water and using it as needed with oil-based sauces that may not moisten the pasta quite enough.

In Italy there is a fine art to matching pasta shapes and sauces. However, we find that there is only one important consideration—the texture of the sauce. A very chunky sauce is better with shells or rigatoni than spaghetti because the former shapes can trap and hold pieces of the sauce, while large chunks of vegetables, for instance, would just sit on top of long, thin strands. The idea is to eat the sauce and pasta in the same mouthful.

We think that one pound of pasta will serve four as a main course. Of course, if the sauce is particularly rich, if there are kids at the table, or if there are a lot of other foods being served, you may be able to get five or six servings. As a first course in the Italian style, a pound of pasta will yield six to eight servings.

One last note—about grated cheese: Parmesan cheese is a ubiquitous accompaniment to pasta in this country, not so in Italy. Italians would never serve cheese with seafood and often omit it with oil-based vegetable sauces. Of course, you can do as you like. We find that grated cheese (Parmesan is usually our first choice, but when we want a stronger cheese flavor we choose Pecorino Romano) works best when the sauce is fairly liquid, made with either cream or tomatoes. Otherwise, the cheese may stick to the pasta and make it seem dry.

GARLIC AND OIL SAUCES

IF YOU HAVE GARLIC AND OLIVE OIL ON hand, you have the makings of a basic sauce for pasta. Italians call this sauce aglio e olio, garlic and oil, and they prepare it for late-night snacks or quick dinners when the refrigerator is bare.

Although this pantry sauce is easy to make, we did have a number of questions. How much garlic is right for a pound of pasta, and how should it be prepared and/or cooked to keep it from burning? How much oil will coat a pound of pasta? Is extra-virgin oil necessary?

After several tests, we determined that one-third cup of oil was enough to sauce a pound of spaghetti. (Oil-based sauces are best with long, thin pasta shapes. They coat the long strands from end to end, and the sauce does not pool up on the noodles and become greasy, as can happen with stubby pasta shapes.) We found an extra-virgin oil to be worth the extra pennies. The sauces we made with pure olive oil were bland and severely downgraded by tasters. As for the garlic, four medium cloves deliver enough flavor without overwhelming the pasta.

The next task was to fully cook the garlic to tame its sharpness but at the same time avoid burning it, which turns it bitter. This is not necessarily easy, since in hot oil garlic can go from perfectly golden to burned in seconds.

We tried preparing the garlic several ways, including slicing, crushing, mincing, pressing, and pureeing. The larger the pieces, the more likely they were to burn and become acrid. Putting peeled cloves through a press is the best way to get the pieces very small. If you don't own a press, you can mince the garlic by hand, sprinkle it with salt, and continue mincing and pressing on the garlic until it forms a smooth puree.

As an added precaution against burning, we found it helpful to dilute the pressed or pureed gar-lic with a little bit of water, a tip we discovered when cooking spices to make curry. We also found it imperative to heat the oil and garlic together, rather than heating the oil first and then adding the garlic. Letting the garlic gradually heat up ensures even cooking, as does the use of medium-low heat.

Because there is so little sauce, and that sauce may be just barely warm, these pastas tend to cool off very quickly. Heating pasta bowls in a 200-degree oven for 10 minutes keeps the pasta warm, right down to the last noodle. Just make sure to warn everyone that the bowls are hot, and use oven mitts to bring them to the table.

Spaghetti with Garlic and Olive Oil
SERVES 4

The garlic is quickly and easily pureed with a garlic press. Alternatively, you can mince it with a chef's knife, sprinkle with ¼ teaspoon salt, and continue to mince to a paste, but be sure to reduce the amount of salt cooked with the oil and garlic to ½ teaspoon. Diluting the garlic with a bit of water before sautéing ensures a mild, even garlic flavor and helps to prevent burning. Although not a pantry item, parsley adds a fresh herbal flavor and should be used if you have some on hand. If you like, cook ¼ teaspoon red pepper flakes (or more to taste) along with the garlic and oil for this recipe only (not for the variations).

- ⅓ cup extra-virgin olive oil
- 4 medium garlic cloves, peeled, processed through a garlic press, and mixed with 1 teaspoon water (see note above)
  Salt
- 1 pound spaghetti or linguine
- ¼ cup minced fresh parsley leaves (optional)
  Ground black pepper

1. Heat oil, garlic, and ¾ teaspoon salt in small skillet over medium-low heat. Cook, stirring frequently, until garlic turns golden but not brown, about 5 minutes; remove pan from heat.

2. Meanwhile, bring 4 quarts water to a boil in a large pot. Add 1 tablespoon salt and pasta; cook until al dente. Reserving ¼ cup cooking water, drain pasta and return it to pot. Add garlic mixture, reserved pasta

cooking water, and optional parsley; toss well to coat. Adjust seasoning with salt and pepper to taste. Serve immediately.

➤ VARIATIONS

Linguine with Lemon and Pine Nuts

Toast ¼ cup pine nuts in small dry skillet over medium heat, stirring frequently, until golden and fragrant, about 5 minutes; set aside. Follow recipe for Spaghetti with Garlic and Olive Oil, adding pine nuts and 1 teaspoon grated lemon zest to pasta along with garlic mixture.

Linguine with Pecorino and Black Pepper

Follow recipe for Spaghetti with Garlic and Olive Oil, reducing salt to ½ teaspoon and adding ½ cup grated Pecorino Romano cheese and 2 teaspoons lemon juice to pasta along with garlic mixture. Omit parsley and season with 1 teaspoon ground black pepper.

Linguine with Walnuts, Garlic, and Oil

The finely chopped walnuts, sautéed with the garlic and oil, make for an especially rich sauce.

Follow recipe for Spaghetti with Garlic and Olive Oil, cooking ⅔ cup finely chopped walnuts along with garlic.

Spaghetti with Green and Black Olives

Follow recipe for Spaghetti with Garlic and Olive Oil, reducing salt to ½ teaspoon and adding ⅓ cup each pitted and chopped green and black olives and 1 tablespoon lemon juice to cooked garlic mixture.

PESTO SAUCE

IN OUR EXPERIENCE WITH PESTO, THE BRIGHT herbal fragrance of basil always hinted at more flavor than it really delivered. Also, although we love garlic, the raw article can have a sharp, acrid taste that overwhelms everything else in the sauce. So our goals were clear when developing a recipe for this simple sauce—heighten the flavor of the basil and subdue the garlic.

Traditionally, pesto is made in a mortar and pestle,

which yields an especially silky texture and intense basil flavor. The slow pounding of the basil leaves (it takes 15 minutes to make pesto this way) releases their full flavor. By comparison, blender and food-processor pestos can seem dull or bland. We prefer a food processor to the blender for several reasons. Ingredients tend to bunch up near the blender blade and do not become evenly chopped. Also, to keep solids moving in a blender, it is necessary to add more oil than is really needed to make pesto.

Since most Americans don't own a mortar and pestle (and those who do are unlikely to invest 15 minutes of pounding when the sauce can be made in seconds), we decided to focus on improving flavor in food-processor pesto. We tested chopping, tearing, and bruising basil leaves to release more of their flavor. In the end, we settled on packing basil leaves in a plastic bag and bruising them with a meat pounder or rolling pin.

The other main issue with pesto is taming the acrid, overpowering garlic flavor. We tested roasting, sautéing, and infusing oil with garlic flavor but found all these methods lacking. However, blanching tamed the harsh garlic notes and loosened its skin for easy peeling. To save time, we found it helpful to blanch the garlic in the pot of water which we eventually used to cook the pasta. Skewering the garlic cloves makes them easy to retrieve.

To bring out the full flavor of the nuts, we found it best to toast them in a dry skillet before processing. Almonds are relatively sweet but are fairly hard, so they give pesto a coarse, granular texture. Walnuts are softer but still fairly meaty in texture and flavor. Pine nuts yield the smoothest, creamiest pesto. The choice is yours.

Once basic basil pesto is mastered, other variations can be tried, including those with mint, arugula, parsley (flat Italian leaves have the best flavor), and even ricotta cheese. All of these sauces should be thinned with some pasta cooking water to facilitate good distribution throughout the pasta, to soften flavors, and to highlight creaminess.

Pasta with Pesto Sauce

SERVES 4

Basil usually darkens in homemade pesto, but you can boost the green color by adding the optional parsley. For sharper flavor, substitute 1 tablespoon finely grated Pecorino Romano cheese for 1 tablespoon of the Parmesan. Serve with long, thin pasta or a shape, like fusilli, that can trap bits of the pesto. Pasta with pesto can be served immediately or allowed to cool and eaten at room temperature.

3	medium garlic cloves, threaded on a skewer
¼	cup pine nuts, walnuts, or almonds
2	cups packed fresh basil leaves
2	tablespoons fresh parsley leaves (optional)
7	tablespoons extra-virgin olive oil
	Salt
¼	cup finely grated Parmesan cheese
1	pound pasta (see note above)

1. Bring 4 quarts of water to a boil in a large pot. Lower skewered garlic into water; boil for 45 seconds. Immediately run garlic under cold water. Remove from skewer; peel and mince. Keep water on stove for cooking pasta.

2. Meanwhile, toast nuts in small, heavy skillet over medium heat, stirring frequently, until just golden and fragrant, 4 to 5 minutes.

3. Place basil and parsley in heavy-duty, quart-size, zipper-lock bag; pound with flat side of meat pounder until all leaves are bruised.

4. Place all ingredients except cheese in work bowl of food processor; process until smooth, stopping as necessary to scrape down sides of bowl. Transfer mixture to small bowl, stir in cheese, and add salt to taste. (Cover surface of pesto with sheet of plastic wrap or thin film of oil and refrigerate for up to 5 days.)

5. Add 1 tablespoon salt and pasta to boiling water. Cook until al dente. Reserving ½ cup cooking water, drain pasta and return it to pot. Stir ¼ cup pasta cooking water into pesto. Toss pasta with thinned pesto, adding remaining reserved cooking water as needed. Serve immediately, or let cool to room temperature.

➤ VARIATIONS

Pasta with Mint Pesto

Follow recipe for Pasta with Pesto Sauce, replacing basil with equal amount of mint leaves and omitting parsley.

Pasta with Arugula Pesto

Follow recipe for Pasta with Pesto Sauce, replacing basil with 1 cup packed fresh arugula leaves and increasing parsley to 1 cup packed. Reduce Parmesan to 2 tablespoons and add ⅓ cup ricotta cheese at same time as Parmesan.

EQUIPMENT: Cheese Graters

In the old days, you grated cheese on the fine teeth of a box grater. Now, cheese graters come in several distinct designs. Unfortunately, many of them don't work all that well. With some designs you need Herculean strength to move the cheese over the teeth with sufficient pressure for grating; with others you eventually discover that a large portion of the grated cheese has remained jammed in the grater instead of sitting where it belongs, on your food. Whether you are dusting a plate of pasta or grating a full cup of cheese to use in a recipe, a good grater should be easy to use and efficient.

We rounded up 15 different models and set about determining which was the best grater. We found five basic configurations. Four-sided box graters have different size holes on each side to allow for both fine grating and coarse shredding. Flat graters consist of a flat sheet of metal that is punched through with fine teeth and attached to some type of handle. With rotary graters, you put a small chunk of cheese in a hopper and use a handle to press it down against a crank-operated grating wheel. Porcelain dish graters have raised teeth in the center and a well around the outside edge to collect the grated cheese. We also found a model that uses an electric motor to push and rotate small chunks of cheese against a grating disk.

After grating more than 10 pounds of Parmesan, we came to some conclusions. Success, we learned, was due to a combination of sharp grating teeth, a comfortable handle or grip, and good leverage for pressing the cheese onto the grater. Our favorite model was a flat grater based on a small, maneuverable wood-working tool called a rasp. Shaped like a ruler but with lots and lots of tiny, sharp raised teeth, the Cheese Grater (as it is called) can grate large quantities of cheese smoothly and almost effortlessly. The black plastic handle, which we found more comfortable than any of the others, also earned high praise. Other flat graters also scored well. *(Continued on next page.)*

What about traditional box graters? Box graters can deliver good results and can do more than just grating hard cheese. However, if grating hard cheese is the task at hand, a box grater is not our first choice.

We also had good results with rotary graters made from metal, but did not like flimsy versions made from plastic. A metal arm is rigid enough to do some of the work of pushing the cheese down onto the grating drum. The arms on the plastic models we tested flexed too much against the cheese, thus requiring extra pressure to force the cheese down. Hand strain set in quickly. A rotary grater can also chop nuts finely and grate chocolate.

The two porcelain dish graters we tested were duds. The teeth were quite ineffective. And the electric grater was a loser of monumental proportions. True, the grating effort required was next to nothing, but so were the results. A child could have grated cheese faster and more efficiently.

TOMATO SAUCE

DAY IN, DAY OUT, WE FIND THAT CANNED tomatoes make the best sauce. (The exception might be at the height of the local tomato season, but even then good canned tomatoes can compete.) To make our sauce we wanted to use the fewest ingredients possible, so we selected the key players—tomatoes, oil, garlic, and salt—and eliminated nonessentials, such as carrots, meat, wine, and so forth. This immediately eliminated a whole category of longer-cooked, full-bodied Italian sauces. The sauce we were looking for also had to be easy to make—done in 20 minutes or less from pantry to table. Finally, it had to taste first and foremost of tomatoes, with a nice hint of acidity and a light, fresh flavor.

With this fairly limited mission statement formed, a number of fundamental issues came to mind. What sort of canned tomatoes are best: whole, chopped, or crushed, packed in puree or juice? How do you get a nice hint of garlic without overpowering the sauce? How does cooking time affect flavor? Do you need sugar to boost tomato flavor? And what about tomato paste?

To get a better sense of the possibilities, we went into the kitchen and cooked a batch of different sauces from our favorite Italian cooks. To our surprise, there was considerable agreement among the staff as to what worked and what didn't. Butter tend-

ed to dull the bright, slightly acidic flavor of the tomatoes. Nobody was enthusiastic about the rather one-dimensional flavor of tomato paste. More than two cloves of garlic and three tablespoons of olive oil for one 28-ounce can of tomatoes was too much.

In general, shorter cooking times of 10 to 15 minutes produced a fresher, brighter tomato flavor. A large sauté pan was preferred to a saucepan because it hurried up the cooking.

We also came to some conclusions about overall flavor. The sauces we preferred tasted predominantly of tomatoes, not garlic, basil, or any other ingredient. The better recipes also had a nice balance between sweetness and acidity to give the sauce some depth. Sauces made with a little sugar (no more than ¼ teaspoon) tasted more complex and had a better balance between sweet and tart.

With these decisions made, we compiled a master recipe using one teaspoon of minced garlic, three tablespoons of olive oil, one can of diced tomatoes, eight chopped basil leaves, one-quarter teaspoon of sugar, and salt to taste. This was to make enough to sauce one pound of pasta.

We also tested whether all of the olive oil should be added at the beginning of cooking or some withheld and added at the end to provide a nice burst of fresh flavor. As we suspected, it was best to use two tablespoons of olive oil for cooking and a third tablespoon at the end to finish the sauce. Not surprisingly, we preferred a high-quality, extra-virgin oil because it delivered a pleasant hint of fresh olives.

Now we were ready to taste the sauce on pasta. Much to our surprise, we found that it did not properly cling to the pasta. Our first fix was to add back a quarter cup of pasta cooking water to the drained pasta once it had been returned to its original pot. This dramatically improved the consistency of the sauce and, to our great surprise, also improved the flavor. As a final note, we found that adding the tomato sauce, stirring to coat the pasta, and then heating everything for one minute was the most effective saucing method, giving the sauce better distribution and overall consistency.

Pasta and Quick Tomato Sauce

SERVES 4

If you use whole canned tomatoes, avoid those packed in sauce or puree, which results in a dull, relatively flavorless sauce without the interplay of sweetness and acidity. If you choose Muir Glen Diced Tomatoes instead, use the can's entire contents, without discarding any liquid. The pasta and sauce quantities can be doubled, but you will have to simmer the sauce for an extra five or six minutes to thicken it. If you do not have a garlic press, mince the garlic very fine.

1	28-ounce can diced or whole tomatoes (not packed in puree or sauce)
2	medium garlic cloves, peeled
3	tablespoons extra-virgin olive oil
3	tablespoons coarsely chopped fresh basil leaves (about 8 leaves)
¼	teaspoon sugar
	Salt
1	pound pasta (any shape)

1. If using diced tomatoes, go to step 2. If using whole tomatoes, drain and reserve liquid. Dice tomatoes either by hand or in workbowl of food processor fitted with metal blade (three or four ½-second pulses). Tomatoes should be coarse, with ¼-inch pieces visible. If necessary, add enough reserved liquid to tomatoes to total 2⅔ cups.

2. Process garlic through garlic press into small bowl (or mince very fine); stir in 1 teaspoon water. Heat 2 tablespoons oil and garlic in 10-inch sauté pan over medium heat until fragrant but not brown, about 2 minutes. Stir in tomatoes; simmer until thickened slightly, about 10 minutes. Stir in basil, sugar, and ½ teaspoon salt.

3. Meanwhile, bring 4 quarts of water to a boil in large pot. Add 1 tablespoon salt and the pasta and cook until al dente. Reserve ¼ cup cooking water; drain pasta and return it to pot. Mix in reserved cooking water, sauce, and remaining oil; cook together over medium heat for 1 minute, stirring constantly, and serve immediately.

➤ VARIATIONS

Pasta and Tomato Sauce with Bacon and Parsley

In 10-inch skillet, fry 4 ounces sliced bacon, cut into ½-inch pieces, over medium-high heat until crisp and brown, about 5 minutes. Transfer with slotted spoon to paper towel–lined plate; pour off all but 2 tablespoons fat from pan. Follow recipe for Pasta and Quick Tomato Sauce, omitting olive oil from sauce and heating garlic and ½ teaspoon dried red pepper flakes in bacon fat until fragrant but not brown, about 2 minutes. Continue with recipe, substituting 2 tablespoons chopped fresh parsley leaves for basil and adding reserved bacon along with parsley.

Pasta and Tomato Sauce with Anchovies and Olives

Follow recipe for Pasta and Quick Tomato Sauce, increasing garlic to 3 cloves and adding ½ teaspoon dried red pepper flakes and 3 minced anchovy fillets

---

INGREDIENTS: Canned Tomatoes

As we continued testing variant after variant of our simple sauce, a key issue began to emerge: What is the best type of canned tomato to use? In a blind tasting of canned crushed tomatoes, we established that Progresso, Muir Glen, and Redpack were our favorites. But we were disappointed when made our sauce with these tomatoes. They did not taste as fresh or complex as we wanted, no doubt because crushed tomatoes are made with a high percentage of tomato puree for body. Tomato puree is a cooked product that has little tomato freshness.

Whole tomatoes were far superior in our simple tomato sauce. Our favorite brands were Muir Glen and Progresso. The thick puree used in the Redpack brand we found unappealing for this particular recipe, although the tomatoes themselves are high quality. We decided that it is important to drain the tomatoes first, reserving the liquid, to prevent the tendency of the quick-cooked sauce to be too thin.

We then stumbled onto what was to be our clear favorite in canned tomato products, Muir Glen Diced Tomatoes. To begin with, they were very convenient because the entire contents of the can could be used without draining or chopping. Even better, the flavor was fresh and bright with a good balance of sweet and acid. Incidentally, Muir Glen also sells ground tomatoes, which we did not like as much given that they had a flatter, duller flavor. This supported our finding that overly processed sauces tend to have less flavor.

along with garlic puree and oil. Substitute ¼ cup minced fresh parsley leaves for basil. Add ¼ cup pitted, sliced kalamata olives and 2 tablespoons drained capers along with parsley.

Pasta and Tomato Sauce with Vodka and Cream

Follow recipe for Pasta and Quick Tomato Sauce, adding ¼ teaspoon dried red pepper flakes along with garlic. Halfway through the 10-minute simmering time, add ½ cup vodka. Continue with recipe, adding 1 cup heavy cream and ground black pepper to taste along with remaining seasonings. Transfer sauce to workbowl of food processor fitted with a steel blade; pulse to a coarse puree. Return sauce to pan; simmer over medium heat to thicken, 2 to 3 minutes.

SPAGHETTI AND MEATBALLS

THE PROBLEM WITH MOST MEATBALLS IS THAT they are too dense and heavy. Serving meatballs over thin, long noodles is already a bit awkward. If the meatballs are compact, overcooked little hamburgers, the dish can be leaden.

Many cooks think of meatballs as hamburgers with seasonings (cheese, herbs, garlic, etc.) and a round shape. This is partly true. However, unlike hamburgers, which are best cooked rare or medium-rare, meatballs are cooked through until well-done. At this point, the ground beef and seasonings will form dry, tough hockey pucks. Meatballs require additional ingredients to keep them moist and to lighten their texture. Meatballs also require binders to keep them from falling apart in tomato sauce.

We tested eggs, dried bread crumbs, fresh bread crumbs, ground crackers, and bread soaked in milk. The egg was a welcome addition; meatballs made

---

INGREDIENTS: Jarred Tomato Sauce

We wondered if any tomato sauce from a jar could complete with our simple recipe. We assembled a sampling of 11 leading brands of marinara-style sauces containing tomatoes, garlic, herbs (usually basil and/or oregano), and sometimes onions and tasted them blind against our sauce.

While tasters clearly expressed varied preferences when it came to the ideal consistency of the sauces, they all agreed on the driving component—freshness of flavor. In this department, our homemade sauce was the only one considered to taste "extremely fresh" and the only one that tasters really liked. Several jarred sauces were deemed acceptable, the rest we judged not worth eating.

We found several probable reasons for the stale taste of most of the jarred sauces. Apart from those which placed first and third (Barilla and Classico, respectively), all of the supermarket jarred tomato sauces listed tomato puree as their main ingredient and diced tomatoes second. We find that tomato puree diminishes the fresh tomato flavor. This results from the fact that puree is a concentrate requiring higher temperatures and longer cooking times to process than simple cooked tomatoes, whether whole or diced.

The freshness and purity of other ingredients in a sauce also contribute to the success of the final product. Barilla, a market leader in pasta and jarred sauces in Italy, uses primarily fresh ingredients that are diced at the plant. Some other producers use dried spices and even dried vegetables. Barilla's sauce is minimally cooked, really just enough to prevent the growth of bacteria. The problem for many manufacturers, however, is not excessive cooking but the prolonged time that a sauce stays hot before it is jarred and cooled. To avoid this, Barilla expedites the final stage by rapidly cooling the sauce and filling the jars.

A few of the sauces tried to make up for their deficiency in tomato flavor with excessive sweetness. These efforts failed. Our tasters typically labeled these sauces as "kids' food." Notably, Barilla and Classico were the only supermarket brands to put onions before sugar (or corn syrup in some cases) on their lists of ingredients.

Many of the higher-priced sauces found at specialty food stores contained neither tomato puree nor a morsel of added sugar. Tasters found that these products lacked flavor or that what flavor they had was undesirable. This was not surprising, since we found when developing our sauce recipe that a small amount of sugar was important in reducing sour notes and heightening the tomato flavor.

with an egg were moister and lighter. We found that bread and cracker crumbs soaked up any available moisture and compounded the problems caused by cooking meatballs to the well-done stage. In comparison, the meatballs made with bread soaked in milk were moister, creamier, and richer. Clearly, milk was important part of the equation.

We liked the milk but wondered if we could do better. We tried adding yogurt (which works well in meat loaf, see page 219) but had to thin it with some milk in order to mix it with the bread. Meatballs made with thinned yogurt were even creamier and more flavorful than those made with plain milk. We also tried buttermilk and the results were just as good, with no need to thin the liquid.

With the dairy now part of our working recipe, we found the meatball mixture a tad sticky. Eliminating the egg white (the yolk has all the fat and emulsifiers that contribute smoothness) worked just fine.

We experimented with meats next. Ground round was too lean; we preferred fattier chuck in this recipe. We tested blending in some ground veal but felt it was too bland and not worth the bother. Ground pork was another matter. It added another flavor dimension.

With our ingredients in order, it was time to test cooking methods. We tried roasting, broiling, and the traditional pan-frying. Roasting yielded dry, crumbly meatballs, and broiling was extremely messy and also tended to produce dry meatballs. Pan-frying produced meatballs with a rich, dark crust and moist texture.

We wondered if we could save some cleanup time and add flavor by building the tomato sauce in the same pan used to fry the meatballs. We emptied out the vegetable oil used to fry the meatballs (olive oil is too expensive for this task and doesn't add much), added a little fresh olive oil, and started to make sauce. Not only did this method prove convenient, but it gave depth to the sauce as the browned bits that formed as the meatballs were fried loosened from the pan bottom and dissolved in the sauce.

Meatballs need a thick, smooth sauce—the kind produced by canned crushed tomatoes. We discovered that sauces made with whole tomatoes are too chunky and more liquidy, so they don't blend well with the meatballs and tend to make them soggy.

Spaghetti and Meatballs

SERVES 4 TO 6

If you like, you can shape the meatballs and refrigerate them on a large plate, covered loosely with plastic wrap, for several hours. Fry the meatballs and make the sauce at the last minute.

MEATBALLS

- 2 slices white sandwich bread (crusts discarded), torn into small pieces
- 1/2 cup buttermilk or 6 tablespoons plain yogurt thinned with 2 tablespoons whole milk
- 1 pound ground meat (preferably 3/4 pound ground chuck and 1/4 pound ground pork)
- 1/4 cup freshly grated Parmesan cheese
- 2 tablespoons finely minced fresh parsley leaves
- 1 large egg yolk
- 1 teaspoon finely minced garlic
- 3/4 teaspoon salt
  Ground black pepper
  About 1 1/4 cups vegetable oil for pan-frying

SMOOTH TOMATO SAUCE

- 2 tablespoons extra-virgin olive oil
- 1 teaspoon minced garlic
- 1 28-ounce can crushed tomatoes
- 1 tablespoon minced fresh basil leaves
  Salt and ground black pepper

- 1 pound spaghetti
  Grated Parmesan cheese

1. FOR THE MEATBALLS: Combine bread and buttermilk in small bowl, mashing occasionally with fork, until smooth paste forms, about 10 minutes.

2. Place ground meat, cheese, parsley, egg yolk, garlic, salt, and pepper to taste in medium bowl. Add bread-milk mixture and combine until evenly mixed. Shape 3 tablespoons of mixture into 1½-inch round meatball. (When forming meatballs use a fairly light touch. If you compact the meatballs too much, they can become dense and hard.) You should be able to form about 14 meatballs.

3. Pour vegetable oil into 10- or 11-inch sauté pan to depth of 1/4 inch. Turn flame to medium-high. After several minutes, test oil with edge of meatball.

When oil sizzles, add meatballs in single layer. Fry, turning several times, until nicely browned on all sides, about 10 minutes. Regulate heat as needed to keep oil sizzling but not smoking. Transfer browned meatballs to plate lined with paper towels and set aside.

4. Meanwhile, bring 4 quarts of water to a boil in a large pot for cooking pasta

5. FOR THE SAUCE: Discard oil in pan but leave behind any browned bits. Add olive oil for tomato sauce along with garlic and sauté, scraping up any browned bits, just until garlic is golden, about 30 seconds. Add tomatoes, bring to boil, and simmer gently until sauce thickens, about 10 minutes. Stir in basil and salt and pepper to taste. Add meatballs and simmer, turning them occasionally, until heated through, about 5 minutes. Keep warm over low flame.

6. Meanwhile, add 1 tablespoon salt and pasta to boiling water. Cook until al dente, drain, and return to pot. Ladle several large spoonfuls of sauce (without meatballs) over spaghetti and toss until noodles are well-coated. Divide pasta among individual bowls and top each with a little more tomato sauce and 2 to 3 meatballs. Serve immediately, with grated cheese passed separately.

BOLOGNESE SAUCE

THERE ARE SCORES OF DELICIOUS MEAT-based sauces made in Italy and elsewhere, but slow-simmering Bolognese (it comes from the city of Bologna, hence the name) is perhaps the best. Unlike other meat sauces in which tomatoes dominate (think jars of spaghetti sauce with flecks of meat in a sea of tomato puree), Bolognese sauce is about the meat, with the tomatoes in a supporting role. Bolognese also differs from many tomato-based meat sauces in that it contains dairy—butter, milk, and/or cream. The dairy gives the meat an especially sweet, appealing flavor.

Bolognese sauce is not hard to prepare (the hands-on work is less than 30 minutes), but it does require hours of slow simmering. The sauce must be worth the effort. Bolognese should be complex, with a good balance of flavors. The meat should be first and foremost, but there should be sweet, salty, and acidic flavors in the background.

All Bolognese recipes can be broken down into three steps. First, vegetables are sautéed in fat. Ground meat is then browned in the pan. The final step is the addition of liquids and slow simmering over very low heat.

After an initial round of testing in which we made five different styles of Bolognese, we had a recipe we liked pretty well. We preferred using only onions, carrots, and celery as the vegetables, and we liked them sautéed in butter rather than oil. We also discovered that a combination of ground beef, veal, and pork made this sauce especially complex and rich tasting. The veal adds finesse and delicacy to the sauce, while the pork makes it sweet.

Settling on the liquid element of the recipe, however, proved more difficult.

The secret to a great Bolognese sauce is the sequential reduction of various liquids over the sautéed meat and vegetables. The idea is to build flavor and tenderize the meat, which has toughened during the browning phase. Many recipes insist on a particular order for adding these liquids. The most common liquid choices we uncovered in our research were milk, cream, stock, wine (both red and white), and tomatoes (fresh, canned whole, crushed, or paste). We ended up testing numerous combinations to find the perfect balance.

Liquids are treated in two ways. In the earlier part of the cooking process, liquids are added to the pan and simmered briskly until fully evaporated, the point being to impart flavor rather than to cook the meat and vegetables. Wine is always treated this way; if the wine is not evaporated the sauce will be too alcoholic. Milk and cream are often but not always treated this way. Later, either stock or tomatoes are added in greater quantity and allowed to cook off very slowly. These liquids add flavor, to be sure, but they also serve as the "cooking medium" for the sauce during the slow simmering phase.

We tested pouring wine over the browned meat first, followed by milk. We also tried them in the opposite order, milk and then wine. We found that the meat cooked in milk first was softer and sweeter. As the bits of meat cook, they develop a hard crust that makes it more difficult for them to absorb liquid. Adding the milk first, when the meat is just barely cooked, works better. The milk penetrates more easily, tenderizing the meat and making it especially sweet.

We tried using cream instead of milk but felt that the sauce was too rich. Milk provides just enough dairy flavor to complement the meat flavor. (Some recipes finish the sauce with cream. We found that cream added just before the sauce was done was also overpowering.)

So we settled on milk as the first liquid for the sauce. For the second liquid, we liked both white and red wine. White wine was a bit more delicate and is our choice for the basic recipe.

Now we moved on to the final element in most recipes, the cooking liquid. We did not like any of the recipes we tested with stock. As for the tomato paste, we felt that it had little to offer; with none of the bright acidity of canned whole tomatoes and no fresh tomato flavor, it produced a dull sauce.

We tried tomatoes three more ways—fresh, canned whole, and canned crushed. Fresh tomatoes did nothing for the sauce and were a lot of work since we found it necessary to peel them. (If not peeled, the skins would separate during the long cooking process and mar the texture of the sauce.) Crushed tomatoes were fine, but they did not taste as good as the canned whole tomatoes that we chopped. Whole tomatoes have an additional benefit—the packing juice. Since Bolognese sauce simmers for quite a while, it's nice to have all that juice to keep the pot from scorching.

Our recipe was finally taking shape, with all the ingredients in place. But we still wanted to know if it was necessary to cook Bolognese sauce over low heat and, if so, how long the sauce must simmer. When we tried to hurry the process by cooking over medium heat to evaporate the tomato juice more quickly, the meat was too firm and the flavors were not melded. Low simmering over the lowest possible heat—a few bubbles may rise to the surface of the sauce at one time, but it should not be simmering all over—is the only method that allows enough time for flavor to develop and for the meat to become especially tender.

As for the timing, we found that the sauce was too soupy after two hours on low heat and the meat was still pretty firm. At three hours, the meat was much softer, with a melt-in-the-mouth consistency. The sauce was dense and smooth at this point. We tried simmering the sauce for four hours but found no benefit. In fact, some batches cooked this long over-reduced and scorched a bit.

Fettuccine with Bolognese Sauce

SERVES 4

Don't drain the pasta of its cooking water too meticulously when using this sauce; a little water left clinging to the noodles will help distribute the very thick sauce evenly over the noodles, as will adding two tablespoons of butter along with the sauce. If doubling this recipe, increase the simmering times for the milk and the wine to 30 minutes each, and increase the simmering time once the tomatoes are added to 4 hours.

5	tablespoons unsalted butter
2	tablespoons minced onion
2	tablespoons minced carrot
2	tablespoons minced celery
¾	pound meatloaf mix or ¼ pound each ground beef chuck, ground veal, and ground pork
	Salt
1	cup whole milk
1	cup dry white wine
1	can (28 ounces) whole tomatoes packed in juice, chopped fine, with juice reserved
1	pound fresh or dried fettuccine
	Grated Parmesan cheese

1. Heat 3 tablespoons butter in large, heavy-bottomed Dutch oven over medium heat; add onion, carrot, and celery and sauté until softened but not browned, about 6 minutes. Add ground meat and ½ teaspoon salt; crumble meat with edge of wooden spoon to break apart into tiny pieces. Cook, continuing to crumble meat, just until it loses its raw color but has not yet browned, about 3 minutes.

2. Add milk and bring to simmer; continue to simmer until milk evaporates and only clear fat remains, 10 to 15 minutes. Add wine and bring to simmer; continue to simmer until wine evaporates, 10 to 15 minutes longer. Add tomatoes and their juice and bring to simmer; reduce heat to low so that sauce continues to simmer just barely, with an occasional bubble or two at the surface, until liquid has evaporated, about 3 hours (if lowest burner setting is too high to allow such a low simmer, use a flame tamer). Adjust seasonings with extra salt to taste. Keep sauce warm. (Can be refrigerated in an airtight con-

tainer for several days or frozen for several months. Warm over low heat before serving.)

3. Bring 4 quarts of water to a boil in a large pot. Add 1 tablespoon salt and pasta. Cook until al dente. Drain pasta, leaving some water dripping from noodles. Toss with sauce and remaining 2 tablespoons butter. Distribute among individual bowls and serve immediately, with cheese passed separately at the table.

➤ VARIATIONS

Fettuccine with Beef Bolognese Sauce

There is something very appealing about the simplicity of an all-beef sauce; while it may lack some of the finesse and sweetness of the master recipe, its pure beef flavor is uniquely satisfying.

Follow recipe for Fettuccine with Bolognese Sauce, substituting ¾ pound ground beef chuck for meatloaf mix.

Fettuccine with Beef, Pancetta, and Red Wine Bolognese Sauce

All ground beef works best with the pancetta in this sauce. If you can't find pancetta, use prosciutto, but don't use American bacon, which is smoked and will overwhelm the beef. Last, we found that red wine stands up to the more robust flavors in this sauce better than the white wine.

Follow recipe for Fettuccine with Bolognese Sauce, adding 2 ounces minced pancetta to butter along with vegetables, substituting ¾ pound ground beef chuck for meatloaf mix, and substituting an equal amount of red wine for white wine.

EQUIPMENT: Flame Tamer

A flame tamer (or heat diffuser) is a metal disk that can be fitted over an electric or a gas burner to reduce the heat output. This device is especially useful when trying to keep a pot at the barest simmer. If you don't own a flame tamer (it costs less than $10 and is stocked at most kitchenware stores), you can fashion one from aluminum foil. Take a long sheet of heavy-duty foil and shape it into a 1-inch-thick ring that will fit on your burner. Make sure that the ring is an even thickness so that a pot will rest flat on it. A foil ring elevates the pot slightly above the flame or electric coil, allowing you to keep a pot of Bolognese sauce at the merest simmer.

CLAM SAUCE

TOO OFTEN, SPAGHETTI WITH CLAM SAUCE is a soggy mess of canned clams tossed with some overcooked pasta. We knew we could do better, especially if we used fresh clams.

First we decided to identify the best clams and figure out the best way to cook them. In Italy, tiny clams are often used for this dish, but we couldn't find these clams unless we begged them from chefs. So we began by buying the tiniest littlenecks we could find. This helped somewhat, but with clams selling for about $5 a dozen, regardless of size, a simple pasta dish for four quickly became an extravaganza.

We tried the larger cherrystones and even giant quahogs (they're all the same species, just increasingly bigger specimens), lightly steamed and chopped into pieces. But no matter how long or short we cooked them, they were tough, and they lacked the distinctive, fresh brininess of littlenecks. However, we did learn something: Large, less palatable, and far less expensive clams gave us the same kind of delicious clam juice—the backbone of this dish—as small clams.

Then we found some cockles, which are almost as small as the baby clams you find in Italy. Because they are sold by the pound, not the dozen, and because they are small, cockles are less expensive than littlenecks. They are also quite delicious. Unfortunately, they're not nearly as widely available as littlenecks. The alternative is littlenecks, the littler the better, and at least six (preferably eight or more) per person.

Because we still favored using all littlenecks, our dish remained quite expensive. So we resolved that if we were going to pay a small fortune for the dish, we would make sure that it would be uniformly wonderful each time we cooked it. There were three problems with our original recipe, we thought. One was that the clam meat tended to become overcooked in the time it took to finish the sauce; the other was that there was often not enough clam juice; finally, we thought that the sauce itself could use another dimension of flavor.

Solving the first problem was easy: We cooked the clams first, just until they gave up their juices. Then we recombined the clams with the sauce at the last minute, just enough to reheat them.

Next we turned to the occasional dearth of clam juice. When we were too cheap to buy enough lit-

110

tlenecks, or couldn't find cockles, we combined a couple of dozen littlenecks with about six large quahogs, which we could often buy for just a couple of dollars. Because it was the juice we were after—not the clam meat—this worked out fine; we simply discarded the quahog meat after cooking it.

We liked the flavor of white wine mixed with clam juice, but we did not like using more than one-half cup or so, because its distinctive flavor was somewhat overwhelming. Cutting back on the wine, though, robbed the dish of needed acidity. We experimented with lemon juice, but felt that the flavor was too strong. Vinegar, of course, was even worse. Finally, we added just a little bit of diced plum tomato, barely enough to color the sauce. The benefits were immediate: Not only was the flavor balanced, but another welcome texture was added to the dish.

Satisfied at last, we pronounced ourselves done. With the final recipe, you can steam the clams open while bringing the pasta water to a boil and preparing the other ingredients. Once the clams are done, begin browning the garlic; five minutes later, put in the pasta and finish the sauce. The timing is perfect, and perfectly easy.

Pasta with Fresh Clam Sauce

SERVES 4

You can save money by using large, inexpensive quahogs, which provide plenty of liquid for a briny, brothy dish, for about half the price of littlenecks. Because quahogs are so cheap, discard the steamed meat without guilt and dine on the sweet, tender littlenecks with the pasta.

24	littleneck clams (the smaller the better), scrubbed thoroughly
6	quahog or chowder clams (the larger the better), scrubbed thoroughly
½	cup dry white wine
	Pinch cayenne
¼	cup extra-virgin olive oil
2	medium garlic cloves, minced
I	large or 2 small plum tomatoes, peeled, seeded, and minced
	Salt
I	pound spaghetti, linguine, or other long-strand pasta
¾	cup chopped fresh parsley leaves

1. Bring 4 quarts water to a boil in a large pot for cooking pasta.

2. Bring clams, wine, and cayenne to boil in deep, 10- to 12-inch covered skillet over high heat. Boil, shaking pan occasionally, until littlenecks begin to open, 3 to 5 minutes. Transfer littlenecks with slotted spoon to medium bowl; set aside. Re-cover pan and continue cooking quahogs until their liquid is released, about 5 minutes longer. Discard quahogs; strain liquid in pan through paper towel–lined sieve into large measuring cup. Add enough water to make 1 cup; set aside.

3. Heat oil and garlic in cleaned skillet over medium-low heat until garlic turns pale gold, about 5 minutes. Add tomatoes, raise heat to high and sauté until tomatoes soften, about 2 minutes longer. Add littlenecks and cover; cook until all clams open completely, 1 to 2 minutes longer.

4. Meanwhile, add 1 tablespoon salt and pasta to boiling water; cook until al dente, 7 to 9 minutes. Drain pasta; transfer to skillet and toss. Add reserved clam liquid and cook until flavors meld, about 30 seconds. Stir in parsley, adjust seasonings, and serve immediately.

PORCINI MUSHROOM SAUCES

PORCINI MUSHROOMS CREATE HEARTY, ROBUST pasta sauces. Available fresh in Italy, they are magnificent shaved over simple pasta. Unfortunately, fresh porcini are rarely sold in this country. Dried porcini re-create the flavor but require some preparation.

After a number of tests, we concluded that hot tap water extracts plenty of flavor from dried porcini without making them mushy. Boiling water works quickly but can result in listless texture, while lukewarm water does not soften the mushrooms quickly enough. Soaking times need not be precise. We found 20 minutes to be the minimum time necessary for proper softening in hot water, but another 5 or 10 minutes does no harm. One cup of water per ounce of dried mushrooms is enough to cover them completely without diluting their flavor.

Perhaps more important than soaking technique is straining. Dried porcini are often packaged with foreign matter, such as twigs. Lifting the mushrooms from the soaking liquid with a fork helps keep the grit in the bowl. If the mushrooms feel gritty, then wash them under cold running water.

The soaking liquid should never be discarded. The recipes below utilize this brown, fragrant liquid, and it can also be added to stock for mushroom soup or risotto. The best way to remove the grit at the bottom of the bowl is to pour the soaking liquid through a small mesh strainer that has been lined with a single paper towel. The towel traps the dirt and absorbs a minimum of the precious liquid.

Proper handling can do nothing for inferior specimens. Although most dried porcini in markets are fine, some are nothing more than mushroom dust. Look for dried porcini that are large, thick, and tan or brown in color, rather than black. Also avoid packages with a lots of dust or crumbled pieces mixed in.

Fettuccine with Porcini Cream Sauce

SERVES 4

This intensely flavored sauce works best with fresh pasta.

2	ounces dried porcini mushrooms
3	tablespoons unsalted butter
1	medium onion, minced
	Salt and ground black pepper
6	tablespoons heavy cream
3	tablespoons minced fresh parsley leaves
1	pound fresh or dried fettuccine
½	cup grated Parmesan cheese, plus more for the table

1. Place porcini in small bowl, cover with 2 cups hot water, and soak until softened, about 20 minutes. Lift porcini from water with fork. If they feel gritty, rinse under cold water. Chop porcini. Strain soaking liquid through sieve lined with paper towel and reserve separately.

2. Bring 4 quarts of water to a boil in a large pot for cooking pasta.

3. Heat butter in large sauté pan over medium heat. Add onion; sauté until edges begin to brown, about 7 minutes. Add porcini and salt and pepper to taste; sauté to release flavors, 1 to 2 minutes. Increase heat to medium-high. Add soaking liquid; simmer briskly until liquid has reduced by half, about 10 minutes. Stir in cream; simmer until sauce just starts to thicken, about 2 minutes. Stir in parsley, adjust seasonings, and keep warm.

4. Meanwhile, add 1 tablespoon salt and pasta to boiling water. Cook until al dente. Drain and toss with sauce and cheese. Serve immediately, with more cheese passed at the table.

Spaghetti with Tomato-Porcini Sauce

SERVES 4

Fusilli can be used in place of spaghetti if you like.

1	ounce dried porcini mushrooms
3	tablespoons extra-virgin olive oil
1	medium onion, minced
1	celery stalk, minced
1	small carrot, peeled and minced
	Salt
1	can (28 ounces) whole tomatoes packed in juice, drained, seeded, and chopped
3	tablespoons minced fresh parsley leaves
1	pound spaghetti
	Grated Parmesan cheese

1. Place porcini in small bowl, cover with 1 cup hot water, and soak until softened, about 20 minutes. Lift porcini from water with fork. If they feel gritty, rinse under cold water. Chop porcini. Strain soaking liquid through sieve lined with paper towel and reserve separately.

2. Bring 4 quarts of water to a boil in a large pot for cooking pasta.

3. Heat oil in large sauté pan over medium heat. Add onion, celery, and carrot; sauté until vegetables soften, 8 to 10 minutes. Add porcini and salt; sauté to release flavors, 1 to 2 minutes. Increase heat to medium-high; add tomatoes and soaking liquid. Bring sauce to boil, lower heat, then simmer until sauce thickens, about 15 minutes. Stir in parsley, adjust seasonings, and keep warm.

4. Meanwhile, add 1 tablespoon salt and pasta to boiling water. Cook until al dente. Drain and toss with sauce. Serve immediately, with cheese passed at the table.

VEGETABLE SAUCES

THERE ARE TWO MAIN CONSIDERATIONS when preparing vegetable sauces for pasta. First, the vegetables must be cut into small enough pieces that they will not overwhelm the pasta. For example, broccoli must be trimmed into very small florets and mushrooms sliced. The other major issue is moisture.

Some vegetables, such as mushrooms, are fairly watery and will help create their own sauce. Other vegetables, like broccoli, need some help. Possible choices include tomatoes, cream, and oil. Tomatoes are low in fat but can obscure delicate vegetable flavors. Cream has the same problem, with additional concern about fat. Olive oil is probably the best all-purpose solution because its flavor complements that of most vegetables, but care must be taken to keep the pasta from becoming too greasy.

While it is certainly possible to use more than ½ cup of oil in a vegetable sauce meant for tossing with one pound of pasta (many traditional Italian recipes do so), we think it's better to keep the oil under ½ cup. If you want to keep oil use to a minimum, rely on a little of the pasta cooking water to moisten and stretch the sauce.

Orecchiette with Broccoli-Anchovy Sauce

SERVES 4

This recipe can be made with cauliflower, broccoli rabe, kale, turnip greens, or collards. Simply adjust blanching time to ensure that the vegetable is cooked only until crisp-tender or slightly wilted. The hot red pepper flakes can be omitted from the basic recipe or any of the variations for a milder sauce. Serve with orecchiette or shells if using broccoli or cauliflower. When made with leafy greens, this sauce works well with fusilli or penne.

1	medium head broccoli (about 1 ½ pounds), florets cut into bite-sized pieces (about 6 cups) and stalks discarded
	Salt
⅓	cup extra-virgin olive oil
4	medium garlic cloves, minced
1	2-ounce can anchovy fillets, drained and minced
½	teaspoon hot red pepper flakes
1	pound orecchiette or small shells

1. Bring 4 quarts of water to a boil in a large pot. Add broccoli and 1 tablespoon salt to boiling water. Cook until crisp-tender, 2 to 3 minutes. Retrieve broccoli with slotted spoon and set aside.

2. Heat oil, garlic, and anchovies in medium sauté pan over medium heat until garlic is fragrant but not brown, about 2 minutes. Stir in hot red pepper flakes and then broccoli. Cook, stirring often, until broccoli is heated through, about 2 minutes. Adjust seasonings and keep sauce warm.

3. Meanwhile, add pasta to boiling water and cook until al dente. Reserve ¼ cup pasta cooking water. Drain pasta and toss with broccoli sauce, adding reserved cooking water as needed to moisten sauce. Serve immediately.

➤ VARIATIONS

Orecchiette with Broccoli Rabe, Garlic, Raisins, and Pine Nuts

Follow recipe for Orecchiette with Broccoli-Anchovy Sauce, replacing broccoli with 6 cups broccoli rabe cut into 1-inch pieces and cook until tender, 1 to 2 minutes. Omit anchovies. Add ¼ cup yellow or dark raisins and 2 tablespoons pine nuts along with hot red pepper flakes, and cook for 30 seconds before adding blanched broccoli rabe.

Orecchiette with Cauliflower, Onion, and Bacon Sauce

1	medium head cauliflower (about 1 ½ pounds), florets cut into bite-sized pieces (about 6 cups) and stalks discarded
	Salt
4	ounces pancetta or bacon, cut into ½-inch dice
	Extra-virgin olive oil as needed
1	medium onion, minced
4	medium garlic cloves, minced
1	pound orecchiette or small shells
¼	cup minced fresh parsley leaves

1. Bring 4 quarts of water to a boil in a large pot. Add cauliflower and 1 tablespoon salt to boiling water. Cook until crisp-tender, 3 to 4 minutes. Retrieve cauliflower with slotted spoon and set aside.

2. Cook pancetta in medium sauté pan over medium heat until crisp, about 7 minutes. Remove with

slotted spoon; add enough oil to pan to yield ⅓ cup total fat. Add onion and sauté until golden, about 6 minutes. Add garlic and cook until fragrant, about 1 minute. Stir in cauliflower and pancetta and cook until heated through, about 2 minutes. Stir in parsley, adjust seasonings, and keep sauce warm.

3. Meanwhile, add pasta to boiling water and cook until al dente. Reserve ¼ cup pasta cooking water. Drain pasta and toss with cauliflower sauce, adding reserved cooking water as needed to moisten sauce. Serve immediately.

Linguine with Braised Fennel and Kale Sauce

SERVES 4

The natural sweetness of fennel makes it a good partner for bitter greens like kale, mustard, turnip, and beet. Flowering purple kale adds color as well as earthy flavor and should be used if possible.

¼	cup extra-virgin olive oil
1	medium onion, minced
1	medium fennel bulb (about 1 pound), fronds removed, minced, and reserved (about 1 tablespoon); stems discarded; and bulb trimmed, halved, cored, and sliced thin
	Salt and ground black pepper
¾	pound kale or other bitter greens, stemmed, washed, and chopped coarse
2	tablespoons balsamic vinegar
1	pound linguine or spaghetti
¼	cup grated Parmesan cheese, plus more for table

1. Bring 4 quarts of water to a boil in a large pot for cooking pasta.

2. Heat oil in large sauté pan or skillet with cover. Add onion; sauté over medium heat until softened, about 5 minutes. Stir in fennel and cook until golden, about 10 minutes.

3. Add ½ cup water and salt and pepper to taste. Stir in kale and cover. Simmer over medium-low heat until fennel is tender and greens are fully cooked, about 10 minutes. Stir in vinegar and simmer to blend flavors, about 1 minute. Adjust seasonings and keep sauce warm.

4. Meanwhile, add 1 tablespoon salt and pasta to

boiling water. Cook until al dente. Reserve ¼ cup pasta cooking water. Drain pasta and toss with sauce and cheese, adding reserved cooking water as needed to moisten sauce. Serve immediately, garnishing bowls with minced fennel fronds and passing more cheese at the table.

Penne with Portobello Mushroom Ragu

SERVES 4

A ragu is a thick tomato sauce, usually made with meat. Here, hearty portobello mushrooms take the place of the meat and add an earthy, woodsy flavor.

3	tablespoons extra-virgin olive oil
1	medium onion, minced
2	medium portobello mushrooms (about ½ pound), stems discarded; caps halved and cut crosswise into ¼-inch strips
1	teaspoon minced fresh rosemary leaves
	Salt and ground black pepper
½	cup dry red wine
1½	cups chopped canned whole tomatoes
1	pound penne
	Grated Parmesan cheese

1. Bring 4 quarts of water to a boil in a large pot for cooking pasta.

2. Heat oil in large skillet. Add onion and sauté over medium heat until translucent, about 5 minutes. Add mushrooms and cook, stirring occasionally, until quite tender and starting to shed their liquid, about 5 minutes. Stir in rosemary and salt and pepper to taste, and cook for 30 seconds.

3. Add wine and simmer until it reduces by half, about 3 minutes. Add tomatoes and simmer until sauce thickens considerably, 10 to 15 minutes. Adjust seasonings and keep sauce warm.

4. Meanwhile, add 1 teaspoon salt and pasta to boiling water. Cook until al dente. Reserve ¼ cup pasta cooking water. Drain pasta and toss with sauce, adding reserved cooking water as needed to moisten sauce. Serve immediately, with cheese passed separately at the table.

LASAGNE

WE DECIDED TO EXPLORE THE CLASSIC MEAT-and-tomato lasagne—the most popular kind of lasagne in this country—in an attempt to come up with a great recipe that didn't require backbreaking effort. We also wanted to create a lasagne that avoids the unhappy sight of mushy noodles swimming in a sea of red sauce and cheese.

Our first task was to make sense of the cheese component. Various recipes call for mozzarella, ricotta (sometimes mixed with whole eggs or egg yolks), and/or a hard grating cheese (usually Parmesan, but sometimes Pecorino). After trying the various combinations, we realized that ricotta was responsible for what we call "lasagne meltdown"—the loss of shape and distinct layering. Even with the addition of whole eggs or yolks as a thickener, we found that ricotta was too watery to use in lasagne and usually leads to a sloppy mess.

Mozzarella provides more than enough creaminess, and its stringiness binds the layers to each other and helps keep them from slipping apart when served. Most American recipes call for shrink-wrapped mozzarella in lasagne, and after a few disastrous attempts with fresh mozzarella, we now know why. Fresh mozzarella has too much moisture to be effective. When it melts, it releases so much liquid that the lasagne becomes mushy and watery. In addition, the delicate flavor of expensive fresh mozzarella is lost in the baking. We also found that a small amount of either Parmesan or Pecorino provides a pleasantly sharp contrast to the somewhat bland mozzarella.

With the cheese question resolved, we next focused on the sauce. Most lasagne recipes in American cookbooks call for a tomato sauce built on browned ground beef. When we tried these sauces, we thought the beef tasted bland and washed out. We wanted the beef presence to be stronger and better seasoned. We wondered if our meatball recipe (see page 116) would work. Instead of rolling out real meatballs, which would be too large to rest snugly between the layers of pasta, we pinched off small bits of the meatball mixture directly into hot oil. These free-form mini-meatballs don't require tedious shaping (in fact, if some fall apart that's fine) and are cooked in just a few minutes. As we hoped, these meatballs made a great addition to lasagne.

Since our aim was to simplify matters, we decided to add the drained meatballs to a quick-cooking tomato sauce made with crushed tomatoes. (We tried canned whole tomatoes but they made a sauce that was fairly chunky. Lasagne really needs a smooth, thick sauce that will coat the noodles evenly.)

With the sauce and cheese combinations down, we focused on the choice of noodles and layering tricks. After much experimentation, we realized that some noodles are far superior to others. Choosing either imported noodles or fresh sheets of pasta (purchased or homemade) guarantees thin, delicate layers in your lasagne. (See page 117 for more information.)

In terms of the actual layering procedure, we find it helpful to grease the baking pan with cooking spray. (Use a 13 by 9-inch metal, glass, or ceramic dish with square corners that the pasta can easily rest against.) Spread a small amount of tomato sauce without large chunks of meat over the pan to moisten the bottom layer of pasta. Then lay down the first layer of noodles (choose large, whole noodles for this layer). Spread sauce and meatballs evenly over the noodles, cover this with shredded mozzarella, then sprinkle on grated Parmesan. Build four more layers using this same process, putting any broken noodles in the middle where they won't be seen. The tomato sauce and meatballs tend to dry out when not covered by pasta, so the sixth and final layer is covered only by the two cheeses, which brown during baking to give an attractive appearance.

Lasagne should be baked just until the top turns golden brown in spots and the sauce is bubbling, 20 to 25 minutes at 400 degrees. If you have any doubts about it being done, stick a knife deep into the center of the pan and hold it there for two seconds. When you remove it, the tip of the blade should be quite hot.

When the lasagna is cooked, remove it from the oven and let it rest for five minutes before serving. This gives everything a chance to cool slightly and solidify a little. (Cover the pan with foil if you need to hold the baked lasagne for more than five minutes.) To serve, use a sharp knife to cut squares of no more than three inches; larger pieces are almost impossible to extract intact from the pan. A flexible plastic spatula is the best way to dig underneath the lasagne and lift the pieces out.

Lasagne with Herbed Meatballs, Tomato Sauce, and Mozzarella

SERVES 8

If you want to prepare lasagne in advance, complete the layering process and then wrap the pan tightly with plastic wrap and refrigerate it for up to one day. To cook it, take the chilled lasagne directly from the refrigerator, unwrap the pan, and place it in a preheated oven. Uncooked lasagne can also be wrapped in plastic and then covered with aluminum foil and frozen for up to a month, but you'll need to move the lasagne to the refrigerator at least 12 hours before baking. Allow it to defrost slowly, and then transfer it directly to a preheated oven.

MEATBALLS

2   slices white sandwich bread (crusts discarded), torn into small pieces
½   cup buttermilk or 6 tablespoons plain yogurt thinned with 2 tablespoons whole milk
I   pound ground meat (preferably ¾ pound ground chuck and ¼ pound ground pork)
¼   cup freshly grated Parmesan cheese
2   tablespoons finely minced fresh parsley leaves
I   large egg yolk
I   teaspoon finely minced garlic
¾   teaspoon salt
    Ground black pepper
    About 1¼ cups vegetable oil for pan-frying

SMOOTH TOMATO SAUCE

2   tablespoons extra-virgin olive oil
I   teaspoon minced garlic
I   28-ounce can crushed tomatoes
I   tablespoon minced fresh basil leaves
    Salt and ground black pepper

I   tablespoon salt
I   pound fresh pasta sheets or 18 dried lasagne noodles
I   pound mozzarella cheese, shredded
I   cup grated Parmesan or Pecorino Romano cheese (4 ounces)

1. FOR THE MEATBALLS: Combine bread and buttermilk in small bowl, mashing occasionally with fork, until smooth paste forms, about 10 minutes.

2. Place ground meat, cheese, parsley, egg yolk, garlic, salt, and pepper to taste in medium bowl. Add bread-milk mixture and combine until evenly mixed.

3. Heat about ¼ inch of oil in large skillet. Take a handful of meat mixture, and, working directly over skillet, pinch off pieces no larger than a small grape and flatten them slightly. Cooking in batches to avoid overcrowding, carefully drop them into hot oil. Fry, turning once, until evenly browned, 3 to 4 minutes. Use a slotted spoon to transfer meatballs to a paper towel on a platter.

4. FOR THE SAUCE: Heat oil with garlic in medium saucepan over medium heat. When garlic starts to sizzle, add tomatoes, basil, and salt and pepper to taste. Simmer until sauce thickens slightly, about 10 minutes. Stir in meatballs and adjust seasonings.

5. Meanwhile, bring 6 quarts of water to a boil in a large soup kettle. Add 1 tablespoon salt. If cooking fresh pasta, cook three or four noodles at a time until al dente. Gently retrieve them with a large slotted spoon and transfer them to a bowl of ice-cold water for thirty seconds. Then drain the noodles and lay them out on kitchen towels for up to one hour. Repeat the process with three or four more noodles and a fresh bowl of ice-cold water. If cooking dried pasta, add all noodles at once and boil until al dente. Drain and soak noodles for 30 seconds in a bowl of ice-cold water, drain them again, and lay them out on kitchen towels for up to one hour.

6. Grease a 13 by 9-inch pan with cooking spray. Smear several tablespoons of tomato sauce (without meatballs) across pan bottom. Line pan with a layer of pasta, making sure that noodles touch but do not overlap. (If using fresh noodles, cut them to fit with a pair of scissors.) Spread ¾ cup of tomato sauce and meatballs evenly over pasta. Sprinkle evenly with ⅔ cup mozzarella and 2½ tablespoons Parmesan. Repeat layering of pasta, tomato sauce and meatballs, and cheeses four more times. For the sixth and final layer, cover pasta with remaining 1 cup mozzarella and sprinkle with remaining 3½ tablespoons Parmesan. (Assembled lasagne can now be wrapped with plastic and refrigerated overnight or wrapped in plastic and aluminum foil and frozen for up to 1 month.)

7. Adjust oven rack to center position and heat

oven to 400 degrees. Bake until cheese on top turns golden brown in spots and sauce is bubbling, 20 to 25 minutes (25 to 35 minutes for chilled lasagne). Remove pan from oven and let lasagne rest for 5 minutes. Cut and serve.

INGREDIENTS: Lasagne Noodles

There is a seemingly endless number of choices when it comes to lasagne noodles—domestic and imported dried noodles, dried no-boil noodles, fresh no-boil noodles, purchased fresh pasta sheets, and homemade pasta. After making a hundred lasagne recipes, we have some clear recommendations.

There is no doubt that fresh noodles (either homemade or store-bought) make the best lasagne. Sheets of fresh pasta are now available in many Italian delicatessens, gourmet stores, and even some of the better supermarkets. (Check with the deli manager to see if fresh noodles must be ordered in advance.) While labels on some of these refrigerated noodles claim that cooking is not necessary, we recommend that you treat them as you would homemade.

If for reasons of convenience or availability you use dried noodles, be aware that their quality varies considerably. Some are quite good, others are quite wretched. The key is thinness. Every American brand we tested was too thick. Italian noodles are generally thinner and better approximate the delicate texture of fresh pasta. The best way to judge dried noodles is by counting the number of sheets per pound. Most domestic brands have eighteen or twenty noodles in a one-pound box. In contrast, a box of our favorite Italian brand, DeCecco, has twenty-eight noodles in a pound. This brand, which is the most widely available imported Italian pasta, has shorter, wider noodles that fit just right when laid crosswise in a standard lasagne pan. This makes for a much neater lasagne than longer noodles, which never seem quite long enough to fit a 13 by 9-inch pan.

We tested no-boil dried lasagne noodles and found that they made a credible lasagne with some modifications to our recipe. These precooked and dried noodles need to be cooked with extra liquid so they rehydrate and soften in the oven. This means layering them with a liquidy sauce and covering the pan with foil to trap steam. Our recipe can be adapted to use no-boil noodles by stirring ½ cup water into our smooth tomato sauce before adding the meatballs, covering the pan with foil and baking as directed with foil for 25 minutes, and then uncovering the pan and baking until the cheese turns golden brown in spots, 10 to 15 minutes more.

MACARONI AND CHEESE

THERE ARE TWO DISTINCT STYLES OF MACaroni and cheese. The more common variety is béchamel-based, in which macaroni is blanketed with a cheese-flavored white sauce, usually topped with crumbs, and baked. The other variety is custard-based. In this style, a mixture of egg and milk is poured over layers of grated cheese and noodles. As the dish bakes, the eggs, milk, and cheese set into a custard. This macaroni and cheese is also topped with bread crumbs and baked.

Even though macaroni and cheese is a wonderful, satisfying dish, many of the recipes we tested were tired, leaden, and uninspired. Others attempted to perk up the dish with canned green chiles, scallions, or olives. And, of course, there were attempts to lighten it. No one seemed to really love the dish enough to give it the care it deserves.

Then we ran across a recipe in John Thorne's *Simple Cooking* (Penguin, 1989). "As it happens," he begins, "I'm very fond of macaroni and cheese, and keep a special spot in my heart for cooks who genuinely love it: they are not that many." After reading his four-page essay, we suspected that his recipe for macaroni and cheese was the real one, the others mere shadows.

Making the dish confirmed what we suspected to be true. John Thorne's macaroni and cheese was the best. His recipe starts with macaroni cooked just shy of al dente. The hot, drained macaroni is then tossed with butter in a heatproof pan or bowl. Evaporated milk, hot red pepper sauce, dry mustard, eggs, and a large quantity of cheese are stirred into the noodles. The combination is baked for 20 minutes, with cheese and milk additions and a thorough stir every 5 minutes. Frequent stirrings allow the eggs to thicken without setting, which results in an incredibly silky sauce. During cooking, the sauce settles into the tubular openings of the pasta, offering a burst of cheese with each new bite.

Out of curiosity, we baked the two styles of macaroni and cheese defined earlier: one with a cheese-flavored béchamel sauce, the other thickened with eggs, milk, and cheese. Neither compared to Thorne's dish. The béchamel-based version was grainy and tasted exactly as Thorne predicted: not like macaroni and cheese, but "macaroni with cheese sauce." In terms of texture, Thorne's macaroni and cheese was smooth silk while the béchamel dish was thick velvet.

If we had to choose between the two baked macaroni and cheeses, however, we would pick the cheesier-flavored custard version. Because this custard-based macaroni and cheese was simply a baked version of Thorne's recipe, we thought we might offer it as an alternative to his stirred version. A side-by-side tasting proved the two dishes to be very different, however, and the stirred version remained superior in our minds. The stirred macaroni had a luxuriously silky cheese sauce, while the baked egg, milk, and cheese formed an unappealingly dry custard that set around the noodles.

The competition ruled out, we moved forward to study Thorne's recipe a little more closely. We wondered if the dish really required evaporated milk or if this was an idiosyncrasy of the late 1930s, when the recipe was first published in *The Home Comfort Cook Book* (Wrought Iron Range Company, 1937). Wouldn't regular milk or half-and-half work equally well? What other cheeses, besides sharp cheddar, would taste good?

Although Thorne's recipe was virtually perfect, we had thought of a few possible refinements. First, we found that at the end of the 20 minutes of baking, the dish was hot, but hardly piping. By the time a person had consumed his or her portion, the cheese sauce had cooled and set a bit.

After testing the recipe with whole and low-fat milks and half-and-half, we realized that evaporated milk was indeed an important ingredient. All the macaroni and cheese dishes made with fresh milk curdled a bit, resulting in a chalky, grainy texture. The one made with evaporated milk remained silky smooth. The evaporation and sterilization process stabilizes the milk, which in turn stabilizes the macaroni and cheese.

After making the dish with Vermont, New York, and Wisconsin cheddars, we preferred the less sharp Wisconsin variety. Because the recipe calls for such a large quantity, a slightly milder cheese is preferable. Further testing confirmed this point. Macaroni and cheese made with Gruyère was so strong we couldn't even eat it. To our surprise, highly processed cheeses like American performed quite well in this dish. Much like evaporated milk, the more processing, the more stable the cheese and the more creamy the dish. For flavor, use cheddar; for texture, buy American. We also found the dish did not suffer when prepared with only 12 ounces of cheese as opposed to the pound called for in the original recipe.

The problem of the dish's lukewarm temperature, we learned, could not be remedied by leaving it in the oven much longer than the suggested 20 minutes. To do so meant running the risk of curdling the eggs, and the dish starts to develop a subtle grainy texture. We wondered if we could cook the macaroni and cheese on top of the stove instead of in the oven. We found that by using a heavy-bottomed pot and cooking over low heat, it was possible to make the macaroni and cheese on top of the stove in less than five minutes. Not only was this method quicker, it kept the macaroni and cheese piping hot.

Stovetop Macaroni and Cheese

SERVES 4 AS A MAIN COURSE OR
6 TO 8 AS A SIDE DISH

If you're in a hurry or prefer to sprinkle the dish with crumbled crackers (saltines aren't bad), you can skip the bread crumb step.

TOASTED BREAD CRUMBS

I	cup fresh bread crumbs from French or Italian bread
	Pinch salt
I ½	tablespoons melted unsalted butter

CREAMY MACARONI AND CHEESE

2	large eggs
I	can (12 ounces) evaporated milk
¼	teaspoon hot red pepper sauce
2	teaspoons salt
¼	teaspoon ground black pepper
I	teaspoon dry mustard, dissolved in I teaspoon water
½	pound elbow macaroni
4	tablespoons unsalted butter
12	ounces sharp Wisconsin cheddar, American, or Monterey Jack cheese, grated (about 3 cups)

1. FOR THE BREAD CRUMBS: Heat oven to 350 degrees. Mix bread crumb ingredients together in

small baking pan. Bake until golden brown and crisp, 15 to 20 minutes; set aside.

2. FOR THE MACARONI AND CHEESE: Meanwhile, mix eggs, 1 cup evaporated milk, pepper sauce, ½ teaspoon salt, pepper, and mustard mixture in small bowl; set aside.

3. Meanwhile, bring 2 quarts water to a boil in a large heavy-bottomed saucepan or Dutch oven. Add remaining 1½ teaspoons salt and macaroni; cook until almost tender but still a little firm to the bite. Drain and return to pan over low heat. Add butter; toss to melt.

4. Pour egg mixture over buttered noodles along with three-quarters of the cheese; stir until thoroughly combined and cheese starts to melt. Gradually add remaining milk and cheese, stirring constantly, until mixture is hot and creamy, about 5 minutes. Serve immediately, topped with toasted bread crumbs.

➤ VARIATION
"Baked" Macaroni and Cheese

This dish is the answer for those who prefer their macaroni and cheese topped with crumbs and served out of a baking dish. Smooth and creamy like the stovetop version, this one is broiled just long enough to brown the crumb topping.

BREAD CRUMB TOPPING

2	tablespoons unsalted butter
I	cup fresh bread crumbs from French or Italian bread
	Pinch salt
I	ounce sharp Wisconsin cheddar, American, or Monterey Jack cheese, grated (about ¼ cup)

CREAMY MACARONI AND CHEESE

2	large eggs
I	can (12 ounces) evaporated milk
¼	teaspoon hot red pepper sauce
2	teaspoons salt
¼	teaspoon ground black pepper
I	teaspoon dry mustard, dissolved in I teaspoon water
½	pound elbow macaroni
4	tablespoons unsalted butter
II	ounces sharp Wisconsin cheddar, American, or Monterey Jack cheese, grated (about 2¾ cups)

1. FOR THE BREAD CRUMBS: Heat butter in large skillet over medium heat until foam subsides. Add 1 cup bread crumbs; cook, tossing to coat with butter, until crumbs just begin to color. Season to taste with salt; set aside. When cool, stir in cheese.

2. FOR THE MACARONI AND CHEESE: Mix eggs, 1 cup evaporated milk, pepper sauce, ½ teaspoon salt, pepper, and mustard mixture in small bowl; set aside. Adjust oven rack so it is about 6 inches from broiler; heat broiler.

3. Meanwhile, bring 2 quarts water to a boil in a large heavy-bottomed saucepan or Dutch oven. Add 1½ teaspoons salt and macaroni; cook until almost tender but still a little firm to the bite. Drain and return to pan over low heat. Add butter; toss to melt.

4. Pour egg mixture over buttered noodles along with three-quarters of the cheese; stir until thoroughly combined and cheese starts to melt. Gradually add remaining milk and cheese, stirring constantly, until mixture is hot and creamy, about 5 minutes.

5. Pour cooked macaroni and cheese into 9-inch-square baking dish (or another heatproof dish of similar surface area). Spread crumbs evenly over top. Broil until crumbs turn deep brown, 1 to 2 minutes. Let stand to set a bit, about 5 minutes, and serve immediately.

TURKEY TETRAZZINI

TURKEY TETRAZZINI CAN BE AN INTEREST-ing blend of toasted bread crumbs, silky sauce, and a modicum of turkey meat, all bound together by one of our favorite foods, spaghetti. Or it can taste like cafeteria food. The downside of most casseroles—in which the fusion of individual tastes and textures diminishes them—was true here as well. We then wondered if a basic noodle casserole could be reengineered so that this eminently practical American dish could be made worthy of a well-laid table.

A bit of culinary sleuthing solved the most pressing problem, the fact that the ingredients are double-cooked. (Most casserole recipes are two-step affairs: Cook the ingredients, mix them together, and then bake them in a casserole.) In *American Cookery* (Little, Brown & Co., 1972), James Beard suggests using a shallow baking dish rather than a deep casserole. Paired with a very hot (450-degree) oven, this reduces the baking time to a mere 15 minutes, a fraction of the time suggested by most cookbooks. Tasted against longer baking times and slower ovens, this quick method won hands down; with its fresher-tasting vegetables, it easily avoided the wretched, overcooked dullness of cafeteria cuisine.

Next we adjusted the sauce. The traditional choice is béchamel, a sauce in which milk is added to a roux. We decided to use a velouté, a sauce based on chicken stock, instead. This brightened up both the texture and the flavor, since dairy tends to dampen other flavors. We also played around a bit with the amount of sauce, trying larger and smaller quantities, and found that more sauce overran the taste of the other ingredients. In this case, less was more. It still needed a burst of flavor, however, so we spruced it up with a shot of sherry and a little lemon juice and nutmeg; a bit of Parmesan cheese provided tang and bite; and a full two teaspoons of fresh thyme also helped freshen the overall impression.

Most recipes do not toast the bread crumbs before baking. Doing so does complicate things by adding an extra step (in a pinch, you can skip the toasting), but it is well worth it. Tossing the toasted bread crumbs with a bit of grated Parmesan also helps to boost the flavor.

Turkey Tetrazzini

SERVES 8

Tetrazzini is also great with leftover chicken. Using a shallow baking dish without a cover and a very hot oven benefits both texture and flavor. Don't skimp on the salt and pepper; this dish needs aggressive seasoning.

BREAD CRUMB TOPPING

- ½ cup fresh bread crumbs
  Pinch salt
- 1½ tablespoons unsalted butter, melted
- 1 ounce Parmesan cheese, grated (about ¼ cup)

FILLING

- 6 tablespoons unsalted butter, plus extra for baking dish
- 8 ounces white button mushrooms, cleaned and sliced thin
- 2 medium onions, chopped fine
  Salt and ground black pepper
- ¾ pound spaghetti or other long-strand pasta, strands snapped in half
- ¼ cup flour
- 2 cups chicken stock or canned low-sodium chicken broth
- 3 tablespoons dry sherry
- 3 ounces Parmesan cheese, grated (about ¾ cup)
- ¼ teaspoon grated nutmeg
- 2 teaspoons juice from 1 small lemon
- 2 teaspoons minced fresh thyme leaves
- 2 cups frozen peas
- 4 cups leftover cooked boneless turkey or chicken meat, cut into ¼-inch pieces

1. FOR THE TOPPING: Adjust oven rack to middle position and heat oven to 350 degrees. Mix bread crumbs, salt, and butter in small baking dish; bake until golden brown and crisp, 15 to 20 minutes. Cool to room temperature and mix with ¼ cup grated Parmesan in small bowl. Set aside.

2. FOR THE FILLING: Increase oven temperature to 450 degrees. Heat 2 tablespoons butter in large skillet over medium heat until foaming subsides; add mushrooms and onions and sauté, stirring frequently, until onions soften and mushroom liquid evaporates, 12 to 15 minutes. Season with salt and ground black pepper to taste; transfer to medium bowl and set aside.

3. Meanwhile, bring 4 quarts of water to a boil in large pot. Add 1 tablespoon salt and pasta and cook until al dente. Reserve ¼ cup cooking water, drain spaghetti, and return to pot with reserved liquid.

4. Melt remaining 4 tablespoons butter in cleaned skillet over medium heat. When foam subsides, whisk in flour and cook, whisking constantly, until flour turns golden, 1 to 2 minutes. Whisking constantly, gradually add chicken stock. Adjust heat to medium-high and simmer until mixture thickens, 3 to 4 minutes. Off heat, whisk in sherry, Parmesan, nutmeg, lemon juice, thyme, and ½ teaspoon salt. Add sauce, sautéed vegetables, peas, and meat to spaghetti and mix well; adjust seasonings to taste.

5. Turn mixture into a buttered 13 x 9-inch baking dish (or other shallow, ovenproof dish of similar size), sprinkle evenly with reserved breadcrumbs, and bake until breadcrumbs brown and mixture is bubbly, 13 to 15 minutes. Serve immediately.

5

BEANS AND GRAINS

THIS CHAPTER COVERS THE TWO MOST popular grains in the American kitchen—rice and cornmeal—as well as two popular legumes, black beans and lentils.

When buying rice, it is imperative that you pay attention to the size of the grains. Rice can be classed as either long-, medium-, or short-grain. Long-grain rice is about four times as long as it is wide. Medium-grain rice is twice as long as it is wide. Short-grain rice is round. In general, long grain rice cooks up fluffy and separate, while medium and short grain rices tend to cling or become starchy. This is due to the ratio of the two main starches in rice, amylose and amylopectin.

Long-grain rice contains between 23 and 26 percent amylose, a starch that does not gelatinize during cooking. With such a high amylose content, properly cooked long-grain rice remains dry and separate. Medium-grain has an average amylose content between 18 and 26 percent, and short grain falls between 15 and 20 percent. As these numbers indicate, individual lots of rice will behave differently, and our tests with different brands proved this.

We found medium-grain rice a favorite for risotto, where we want some starchiness but not too much. When making plain steamed rice or pilafs, we prefer long-grain rice because individual grains cook up separately.

Cornmeal also comes in three different styles: fine-, medium-, and coarse-grind. We prefer medium-grind cornmeal (about the texture of granulated sugar) when making polenta, but like the silky quality that fine-grind cornmeal (about the texture of table salt) gives spoon bread.

The chapter concludes with recipes for black beans and a variety of lentils. Other dried beans may be prepared like black beans—no soaking, seasoning with salt from the start—although you will need to adjust the cooking times.

WHITE RICE

FEW FOODS ARE AS SATISFYING AS PERFECTLY cooked rice. But this elemental food can be temperamental—it can resist the cook and be a pot of true grit or dissolve to an unpleasant, gummy mess. Advertisements stress perfect rice, but package instructions are unreliable when you want a tasty bowl of fluffy rice with nicely separate grains. We wanted to find an easy method for making really great long-grain white rice.

We started our tests by following the package directions on four brands of long-grain rice. The technique was a variation on a simmer-covered method, with 1 cup rice to 2–2½ cups water. Some of the instructions called for salt, some didn't, and there were recipes with and without butter. All the recipes were disappointing, the results mostly insipid, with mushy, frayed grains. There was gritty rice, there was fatty rice, but there was no rice we liked.

Next we tried a method popular with both French and Indian cooks—boiling the rice in a generous quantity of salted water as if cooking pasta. Cooked this way, all types of rice came to the table evenly done, with separate kernels, but also waterlogged and bland.

Then we experimented with baking the rice in casseroles, with 1¾ to 2½ parts water to 1 part rice, some with butter, salted and unsalted. Boiling water was poured over the rice, then the vessels were sealed with foil and baked for 25 to 30 minutes. The rice made with less water and salt was better. This result was somewhat beside the point, however, because baked rice, while slightly creamy, did not have the well-defined grains we wanted.

We next tried a routine advocated by Asian cooks, a combination of uncovered boiling and covered steaming. For this technique the quantity of water is gauged by the length of a finger joint over the rice, or one-half to three-quarters of an inch. First the water is boiled until it evaporates to the level of the grains, then the heat is turned down to low, the pot is covered, and cooking continues over low heat for 10 to 16 minutes. The four varieties took unevenly to this method, some better than others, but the rice was always sticky—easier to handle with chopsticks but not the distinct grains that we were after.

The perfect method still eluded us, but we had discerned a pattern: Less water and an even, gentle heat worked better. So we tried a pilaf method, because pilaf recipes generally use less water and produce distinct grains of rice. First we sautéed the rice in two teaspoons of butter or oil, with water varying from one to two cups. After the water came to a boil, we covered the pan and let the rice simmer for 15

INGREDIENTS: White Rice

Essentially, white rice is brown rice made convenient. Developed thousands of years ago, the technique of stripping the germ and bran layers from brown rice to get white rice saves 30 minutes in cooking time. In today's busy world, that can make a big difference. Yet rice manufacturers have made cooking long-grain white rice even more of a snap with five-minute instant varieties and boil-in-bag options. We could not help but wonder whether so much convenience could still taste good. We decided to find out with a blind taste test.

To avoid comparing apples to oranges, we limited the candidates in our tasting to nationally distributed brands or major regional brands of plain, nonaromatic, long-grain white rice products. This gave us a lineup of 13 products, including standard, instant, converted, and boil-in-bag.

To understand the differences in these products, it helps to first know what they have in common. To begin with, all the rices in our tasting were long-grain, which means that each kernel is about four times longer than its width when uncooked. (Other common types of rice include medium- and short-grain.) Long-grain white rice is characteristically "fluffy" and is the least sticky of the white rices. In part, this is because it contains a high percentage of amylose, a starch that keeps grains separate after cooking.

All the rices were also milled using the standard milling process in which the hull is removed and the grains are then rubbed together by machine to remove the bran and germ. (Rice with bran and germ left intact is brown rice.) These two processes create standard white rice. Converted and instant rice, however, are subjected to more processing.

The additional processing for converted rice is done before the milling. The unmilled rice is soaked in hot water, then steamed and dried in the husk. This technique is far from modern, dating back about 1,500 years in India, where rice was put in large pots of water, soaked, steamed, and laid out in the sun to dry. Still practiced today in rural parts of India, this method makes it easier to remove the hull. For modern cooks the primary advantage of this processing is that the rice remains firmer and more separate when it's cooked. Some of the starch in the outer portion of the kernel becomes gelatinized when it's steamed in the husk. The rice kernel then dries harder than its original state, and nutrients are retained as they seep from the bran into the kernel. The harder starch makes it more difficult for water to penetrate, so it takes about five minutes more time for converted rice to cook. The result is not only firmer, more separate rice but rice with a tan-yellow tint and a stronger flavor than standard rice.

On the opposite end of the spectrum is instant rice. To make it, milled rice is fully precooked and then dried very fast. This creates cracks or channels that facilitate the movement of water into the kernel as it cooks on the stove. You can actually see this if you look closely at kernels of instant rice, which tend to be light and porous, like miniature puffed rice. This process makes cooking rice as effortless as making instant soup—stir into boiling water, cover, and let rest off heat for five minutes.

The compromise between the firm, separate kernels of converted rice and the convenience of instant rice seems to be boil-in-bag products. These modern innovations are made by precooking converted rice. In other words, these rices are parboiled prior to hulling, then precooked and dried after hulling and the removal of the bran and germ. The idea is that the parboiling will create rice grains with a firmer texture resistant to breaking down and turning mushy, so that even though they are also precooked they will remain firm and separate during their final 10 minutes of cooking.

When it came to tasting, our panel decided that in the case of white rice, less is definitely more. Most of the top ratings went to standard rices that had not been subjected to any special processing to make them cook faster or end up with grains that were unusually separate.

This result was not unexpected. What really surprised us, though, was the second-place finish of Uncle Ben's Boil-in-Bag rice, along with the sixth-place showing of Kraft's Boil-in-Bag. In both cases, the idea behind the dual processing of these rices really paid off. Testers found the grains of Uncle Ben's, in particular, to be firm, perfectly unbroken, and nicely moist.

The converted rices, on the other hand, did not fare as well, with testers downgrading them on both flavor and texture. As for instant rices, our tasters found these products unpalatably mushy, and they noted that the individual kernels tended to fall apart and fray. We also detected off flavors.

So if you aren't opposed to preparing your rice in a plastic pouch, a boil-in-bag rice might be the best option when you're looking for convenience. The trade-off, however, is that you get less rice for your dollar and you cannot cook these rices along with other seasonings or ingredients. The recommended standard long-grain white rices take a total of only 30 to 35 minutes to prepare (including resting time) and require minimal attention, so the rest of your meal can be prepared as they cook.

minutes, then removed it from the heat and let it rest a bit prior to serving. With this method, the rice cooked up light and tender but not mushy, with individual grains, and the sautéing added a rich dimension of flavor.

No matter the variety of rice, we preferred the ratio of 1 cup rice to 1½ cups water. The kernels should be sautéed and stirred until some become milky white. For stronger, nutty flavors, the raw rice can be fried to a toasted golden brown.

Fine-tuning the method produced different nuances in the grain. In repeated tests we found the rice was less starchy when the pan was swirled to incorporate all the ingredients instead of stirred with a fork. But, surprisingly, the rice added to boiling water turned out stickier than the rice added to cold water and then heated to a boil.

We were curious to try the same formula (1 cup rice, 1½ cups water, ½ teaspoon salt) without sautéing. Fluffed with a fork, rice cooked in this manner was almost as fluffy as the pilaf-method rice, with a mild flavor that brings out the subtly floral, "ricey" aromatics. At a small sacrifice of texture, this is the ideal rice for many chicken stews and fish dishes.

There was some flexibility in cooking time, as long as the rice was allowed to rest, covered, after cooking. We got the most consistent results with a cooking time of 15 to 18 minutes from when the pot was sealed to the time the rice was done, with a 15-minute rest on the turned-off burner. (Don't pull the cover off the pot to peek.) Before serving, fluff the rice with a fork.

Fluffy White Rice
SERVES 4

This recipe is designed for 1 cup of raw rice in a tight-lidded pot. As you cook more rice, you should reduce the proportion of water. With 2 cups of rice, you can get these results with 2½ to 2¾ cups of water. But it is very hard to get a reliable result with less than a cup of rice, so do not halve this recipe.

2	teaspoons unsalted butter or oil (vegetable or olive)
1	cup long-grain white rice (not converted)
1½	cups water
½	teaspoon salt

1. Heat oil in medium saucepan over medium heat. Add rice; cook, stirring constantly, for 1 to 3 minutes, depending on desired amount of nutty flavor. Add water and salt; bring to boil, swirling pot to blend ingredients.

2. Reduce heat to low, cover tightly, and cook until liquid is absorbed, about 15 minutes.

3. Turn off heat; let rice stand on burner, still covered, to finish cooking, about 15 minutes longer. Fluff with fork and serve.

EQUIPMENT: Two-Quart Saucepan

A medium saucepan (two to two-and-one-half quarts) is the best pot for preparing rice on top of the stove. Many of the jobs suited for a small saucepan (making rice or oatmeal, heating milk for cocoa) involve ingredients that stick and leave a mess in the pan, even when the recipe comes out right. Leave a pot of rice unattended or burn some pastry cream, and you may have to soak the pot for hours and then put in a lot of elbow grease to get it back in shape.

For these reasons, we recommend buying a nonstick two-quart saucepan. Choose a pan with some heft (two to three pounds is ideal for this size pan). Avoid really lightweight pans, which are prone to scorching, as well as heavy copper or enameled cast-iron saucepans, which are hard to maneuver because they weigh too much. Lastly, look for pans with handles that won't become scorching hot. Hollowed-out stainless steel handles (like those on All-Clad pans) or even cheap plastic handles (a saucepan never goes into the oven, so there's no need to buy something ovenproof anyway) are better than solid metal handles, which become hot very quickly.

BROWN RICE

BROWN RICE IS VALUED FOR ITS NUTRIENTS as well as for its satisfying texture and nutty flavor. But the traditional cooking method—in a covered pot on the stove—is unreliable and frequently results in gummy rice and burned pots.

Many cooks avoid brown rice because it takes so long to prepare—45 minutes versus about 20 for white rice—so we first decided to see if we could reduce the cooking time. We tried using "quick cooking" or "precooked" brown rice. In this kind of rice, the bran has been roughed up so that water can penetrate more quickly; it has also been partially cooked and then dried. The results were unsatisfactory—mushy, starchy, and unappealing.

Next we tried presoaking rice for eight hours before cooking. This process cuts 15 minutes off the total cooking time, but doesn't solve the get-dinner-on-the-table-quickly dilemma.

We then moved on to various cooking methods. Looking to cut cooking time and still end up with superior rice, we tried boiling, steaming, microwaving, baking, the traditional stove-top method, and a rice cooker. The cooking times varied considerably, ranging from 25 to 60 minutes. The differences in time, however, paled in significance when the differences in taste and convenience were compared.

Treating rice like pasta—boiling and draining it in a colander—is relatively quick (35 minutes), but the rice turns out mushy and tastes waterlogged. Steaming it (about 45 minutes) is gentler and yields separate grains that are nicely al dente. The problem is that most steamer setups run dry before the rice is cooked—adding boiling water is a nuisance, and the probability of ruining a good pot is quite high (we did it).

Microwaving saves little time (it takes about 40 minutes) and involves changing the power from high to medium after 5 minutes. More important, microwaved brown rice tends to be sticky. Baking rice in a covered casserole was quite good, and easy enough, but it takes about an hour. We recommend it only if you are using the oven for something else anyway.

This left the conventional method and the rice cooker. Traditional recipes say to bring rice and water to a boil, reduce heat to low, cover, and simmer until water is absorbed, about 45 minutes. Simmering at a higher temperature can cut cooking time by 5 minutes but increases the risk of sticky rice. Very low heat generally works better, but we still had less-than-perfect results. Try as we might, we could not develop a foolproof variation on the traditional technique.

As expected, the rice cooker delivered excellent results. But not everyone wants another appliance—no matter how useful—in the kitchen. After rereading our notes, we realized that steaming yielded good results and was problematic only because of the long cooking time and the danger of the pot running dry. We decided to do most of the cooking in boiling water, but to finish rice in the steamer. Boiling the rice until it is almost tender (about 30 minutes), draining it, then steaming it until done (another 5 or 10 minutes) is by far the best stove-top method for brown rice. Steaming dries out boiled rice and gets rid of the watery taste. The slight loss of nutrients in the boiling water makes this method a second choice, behind the rice cooker. However, the superior results place boiling/steaming far ahead of traditional covered cooking.

Brown Rice

SERVES 4

Use long-, medium-, or short-grain rice in this recipe. If you own a rice cooker, follow the variation on page 126, using less fat and salt owing to the reduced quantity of water.

6	cups water
I	cup brown rice
2	teaspoons extra-virgin olive oil or butter
I	teaspoon salt

1. Bring water to boil in a large pot. Stir in rice, oil or butter, and salt. Simmer briskly, uncovered, until rice is almost tender, about 30 minutes.

2. Drain rice into a steamer basket that fits inside the pot. Fill pot with about 1 inch water and return to heat. Place basket of rice in pot; cover and steam until tender, 5 to 10 minutes. Scoop rice into a bowl and fluff gently with a fork.

INGREDIENTS: Brown Rice

Brown rice has volatile bran oils that have been linked to cholesterol reduction in humans. Because these oils can oxidize, brown rice should be purchased in small quantities (as much as you will use in a couple of months) and/or stored in the refrigerator.

Brown rice may contain numerous immature green or broken kernels. Although there is nothing wrong with green or broken grains, they will cook differently and can give a finished dish an uneven texture. Therefore, buy brown rice in clear packages or from bins and make sure that there are few imperfect grains. Top processors limit immature or broken kernels to less than 4 percent.

➤ VARIATION
Brown Rice in a Rice Cooker

Stir 2¼ cups water, 1 cup brown rice, 1 teaspoon oil or butter, and ½ teaspoon salt together in the cooking chamber of a rice cooker. Cover and cook according to manufacturer's directions. If rice remains too crunchy for your taste, add several tablespoons water and restart cooking. Machine will automatically shut off when additional water has been absorbed.

EQUIPMENT: Rice Cooker

Without a doubt, the easiest, most reliable method for preparing brown rice is the rice cooker. Besides turning out the best brown rice (it's fluffy, separate, and still has a nice bite), rice cookers are easy to clean, especially models with a nonstick surface on the cooking pot. (When buying a rice cooker, we consider a nonstick finish a must.)

Besides doing a great job with brown rice, rice cookers are also very good for preparing white rice. However, since white rice cooks more quickly, it is more easily done in a saucepan on top of the stove than brown rice, making the need for a rice cooker not quite as strong.

A rice cooker consists of a large chamber with an electric heating element on the bottom. A cooking pot slips into the holding chamber and is covered with a lid. The heating element brings the rice and water to a boil and maintains a constant temperature. When the temperature inside the cooking chamber rises above 212 degrees—a sign that there is no more steam and that all the water has been absorbed—the rice cooker automatically shuts off. Most models actually switch to a "keep warm" mode, which holds rice for several hours without damage.

BASMATI RICE

IDEALLY, BASMATI RICE HAS A NUTTY, HIGHLY aromatic flavor and cooks up with separate grains that are at once fluffy and firm to the bite. Two major questions surfaced as we researched traditional Indian recipes. Is it necessary to prepare the rice for cooking by soaking or rinsing it, and what is the best cooking method?

In the first series of tests, we examined the tradition of presoaking the rice, which is believed to maximize grain elongation and prevent the rice grains from breaking during and after cooking. We tested basmati rice prepared with a twenty-minute presoak in water as well as rice prepared with just a quick rinse and rice made with neither soaking nor rinsing. To make sure that our tests were not skewed because we had used more water overall with one method than with another, we weighed the rice before and after rinsing and soaking, then subtracted one ounce of water for each ounce of increased rice weight to compensate for absorbed water.

When we ran a taste test on these rice preparation methods, we were surprised. Presoaking resulted in overcooked rice and inconsistently sized grains, ranging from 10 to 15 millimeters, with a mushy texture because of water absorbed during soaking. Contrary to what we had expected from our research, many of the presoaked rice grains broke.

The texture and flavor of the rinsed rice was in the same league as that of the soaked: definitely less aromatic and flavorsome than the unsoaked rice. Grains ranged in length from 10 to 14 millimeters. Despite the claim of some cookbooks that rinsing produces a less sticky product, our tests found the opposite to be true.

Rice that was not soaked or rinsed was fluffy, and the grains were dry and separate with a firm, toothy texture and a consistent grain size of 11 to 12 millimeters. This rice also had the nuttiest flavor and the most intact grains. All in all, we preferred the unsoaked rice with its slightly shorter grain and firmer texture.

In the next series of tests we focused on the cooking method. The three methods we tested were steeped, pilaf, and boiled and drained. In the steeping method, which is the standard way of making rice, water is brought to a boil, rice and salt are added, and the pot is stirred, returned to a simmer, then covered until all the water has been absorbed. In the pilaf method, the rice is first cooked in oil that has been infused with spice and onions, then steeped in water. In the boiled and drained method, the rice is cooked in a large quantity of boiling water and then drained, just as pasta is cooked.

The pilaf and steeped versions each had their merits. With the pilaf, an infusion of flavors resulted in a dish that can truly stand alone. Our preference is for this method because of its dynamic flavors; it also produced more separate grains than the other methods. However, steeped basmati rice is a simpler method for everyday curries and produces a rice with an extremely fresh and nutty flavor. Our least favorite was the boiled and drained version; the nutty flavor was washed out, and the rice ended up bland and waterlogged.

We tried various ratios of water to rice and found 1 cup of rice to 1½ cups of water to be ideal. In terms of timing, we got the most consistent results with 15 to 18 minutes from the moment the pot is sealed to the point when the rice is done.

Basmati Rice, Pilaf Style

SERVES 4

This rice is the ideal accompaniment to curry, but it can be served at any meal where regular white rice might be appropriate.

1	tablespoon canola, vegetable, or corn oil
1	3-inch cinnamon stick, halved
2	whole green cardamom pods
2	whole cloves
¼	cup thinly sliced onion
1	cup basmati rice
1½	cups water
1	teaspoon salt

1. Heat oil in medium saucepan over high heat until almost smoking. Add cinnamon, cardamom, and cloves and cook, stirring until cinnamon unfurls and cardamom and cloves pop, 5 to 10 seconds. Add onion and cook, stirring until translucent, about 2 minutes. Stir in rice and cook, stirring until fragrant, about 1 minute.

2. Add water and salt; bring to boil. Reduce heat, cover tightly, and simmer until all water has been absorbed, about 17 minutes. Let stand, covered, at least 10 minutes, fluff with fork, and serve immediately.

RISOTTO

PERFECT RISOTTO IS LIKE GREAT ART—DIFFICULT to define, but you know it when you see it. Depending on the cook, this classic Italian rice dish may be thick enough to scoop or thin enough to pour, redolent of smoked meat and vegetables or gently seasoned with saffron and a little onion, chock full of chunky vegetables and meat or a simple dish of cooked, seasoned rice.

About the only thing that everyone agrees on is that risotto is an Italian short-grain rice dish. We would add two other criteria that a rice dish must meet to qualify as risotto: First, the cooked rice grains must be discrete but loosely bound by a sauce that appears spontaneously when you cook the rice (this is because starch molecules known as amylopectin are abundant in the rice). Second, risotto must be served al dente, with a substantial firmness.

When it comes to cooking risotto, though, disagreement reigns. Some cookbook authors of stellar reputation insist upon a whole set of immutable rules, while others repudiate these guidelines. So what's the truth?

After extensive testing, we have learned that traditional methods of making the dish are not sacred and can be simplified. But we also found that the best risotto still requires time, at least some (but not constant) stirring, and top-quality ingredients.

The first rule of risotto says that the cook must

INGREDIENTS: Basmati Rice

Basmati rice has been grown in India and Pakistan for nearly 9,000 years. American versions of the aromatic rice can be found under the names of Texmati, Della, and Kasmati. After preparing a batch of each of these, we found that Texmati and Della do have a vague aromatic resemblance to Indian basmati rice, but the grains are bolder and wider and do not fully elongate. Instead, they tend to expand like standard long-grain rice, which grows in length by about 50 percent when cooked, compared to true basmati rice, which doubles in length. Kasmati rice, on the other hand, is a close cousin to Indian basmati. It is not as fluffy as the authentic Indian variety and the grains are somewhat sticky, but the flavor holds its own. Imported basmati is available in well-stocked supermarkets, natural foods stores, and Indian grocery stores. We found it to be superior to and more economical than the American varieties.

begin with a certain type of rice (Arborio) that grows only in northern Italy. Nothing else will do. Arborio designates a short-grain rice. It is not surprising that Italians insist on using Italian rice in an Italian dish, but there are other japonica-type rices that may be substituted in a risotto recipe. Japanese short-grain rice and California-grown medium-grain rice (both widely available in U.S. supermarkets) substitute adequately, if not perfectly, for the more expensive Italian varieties. The taste is a little different, to be sure; these medium- and short-grain rices lack the subtle "grainy" flavor you get from Arborio. Also, because the grains are not the same size as Arborio, they don't turn over in your mouth in exactly the same way, making for a somewhat different aesthetic experience. Finally, these substitute rices are more prone to overcooking, passing through the al dente stage with a much shorter grace period than does Arborio.

The above disclaimers notwithstanding, our conclusion is that, while Arborio is the preferred rice, other japonica varieties will do. We would not hesitate to use the medium-grain rice from the supermarket or the short-grain rice from the Asian grocery.

Tradition calls for a hot liquid to be added to the rice, about one-half cup at a time. The liquid is always flavorful: broth or wine or a combination of both. Adding the liquid in small amounts keeps the risotto under your constant scrutiny, which is crucial because the rice needs to be al dente.

However, the traditional method requires constant stirring to keep the fairly dry rice from scorching. To save work, we prefer a deluge-then-stir method that starts out with a lot of liquid. When the pot dries out, the remaining liquid is added in small increments. An occasional stir as the first batch of liquid evaporates is fine. Only toward the end of the cooking time, when you are adding the liquid in small increments, is constant stirring necessary.

As for the type of liquid to use, we prefer homemade chicken broth to canned broth because its subtlety allows for mistakes—if you reduce homemade broth too fast, it doesn't go tinny or salty on you and ruin the dish, as can happen with some canned broths. If you are going to use canned chicken broth, make sure that you use one that is low in sodium. (See page 277 for more information on choosing canned broth.)

Basic Risotto

SERVES 4 AS A MAIN COURSE OR 6 AS A FIRST COURSE

When the rice is done, stir in a little extra liquid, as the sauce will set up a bit when served. Arborio rice is our first choice for risotto, but you can use another medium- or short-grain rice if you like.

3	tablespoons extra-virgin olive oil
I	medium onion, diced
2-4	ounces country ham, pancetta, prosciutto, or other flavorful cured meat, minced
2	cups Arborio rice
	Salt
5	cups homemade chicken broth (or I can low-sodium broth mixed with 3 cups water), room temperature
½	cup dry white wine
½	cup grated Parmesan or Asiago cheese, plus extra for passing

1. Heat oil in a heavy pot 10 to 12 inches in diameter. Add onions and ham; sauté, stirring occasionally, until onions soften, 3 to 5 minutes. Stir in rice and 1 teaspoon salt or to taste. Add 3 cups broth and bring to boil, stirring occasionally. Reduce heat to simmer and cook, stirring occasionally, until pan bottom is dry when rice is pulled back with spoon, 8 to 10 minutes.

2. Add wine, stirring frequently until absorbed. Then add ½ cup broth at a time, stirring constantly, until each addition is absorbed; cook until rice is creamy but still somewhat firm in center (add water in ½ cup increments if broth runs out), 10 to 12 minutes longer. Stir in cheese. Serve on a wide platter or individual plates with additional cheese passed separately.

➤ VARIATIONS

Risotto with Cabbage and Country Ham

Follow recipe for Basic Risotto, adding ½ small cabbage, shredded, to the pan after the onions have softened. Cover pan and cook over medium heat, stirring occasionally, until cabbage is very soft, limp, and beginning to brown, about 15 minutes. Add rice and salt and proceed as directed.

Risotto with Asparagus and Wild Mushrooms

Heat 2 tablespoons butter in a large skillet. Add 4 ounces fresh wild mushrooms, trimmed and sliced thin, and ½ pound thin asparagus, trimmed and cut into 2-inch pieces; sauté until asparagus pieces are almost tender, about 7 minutes; set aside. Follow recipe for Basic Risotto, omitting ham. When risotto is done, stir in asparagus-mushroom mixture and serve.

Risotto with Tomatoes and Basil

Follow recipe for Basic Risotto, adding 1½ pounds peeled, seeded, and chopped plum tomatoes to pan after onions have softened. Cover and cook over medium heat until tomatoes start to look like a thin sauce, about 10 minutes. Add rice and salt and proceed as directed, sprinkling each serving of risotto with 1 tablespoon shredded fresh basil leaves.

POLENTA

IF YOUR MOTHER EVER COMPLAINED ABOUT slaving over a hot stove, she was probably talking about making polenta. Nothing more than cornmeal mush, polenta is made from dried, ground corn cooked in liquid until the starches in the corn have had enough time to hydrate and swell into soft, balloonlike structures. For many purposes, this soft stage is the most delicious way to serve polenta.

The stiff polenta you often see in restaurants starts out as a soft mass but is spread into a thin layer on a baking sheet or marble surface, cooled until stiff, sliced, and then sautéed, fried, or grilled until it resembles a crouton. These crisp rectangles are rarely more than a garnish, but a smooth, piping hot mound of soft polenta can be a meal. More commonly, soft polenta is used as a filler to stretch out meager game birds like quail or to cut the richness of sausages. Most stews and braised dishes—everything from ratatouille to braised rabbit—can also be ladled over a bowl of soft polenta.

Although making polenta sounds easy, the traditional Italian method for cooking it is a lot of work. The polenta must be slowly added to boiling salted water and then stirred constantly (to prevent scorching) during the entire 30- to 40-minute

cooking time. Within minutes, you'll feel like you've been arm-wrestling Arnold Schwarzenegger. And 30 minutes of such constant stirring can seem like an eternity.

Of course, this assumes that you have avoided the biggest pitfall of all, the "seizing" problem at the beginning of the cooking process. Cornmeal is a starch, and starch thickens when it's mixed with water and heated. If this happens too quickly, the cornmeal seizes up in a solid, nearly immovable mass.

We tested adding cornmeal to cold water, using more water, using less water, and using different grinds of cornmeal, all to no avail. Yes, we learned to prevent seizing (keep the water at a simmer and add the cornmeal very slowly), but we still needed to stir constantly for at least 30 minutes to prevent scorching.

This testing did, however, reveal some important information. We found that medium-grind cornmeal makes the best polenta. Finely ground cornmeal, such as the Quaker brand sold in many supermarkets, is too powdery and makes gummy polenta. Cornmeal with a texture akin to granulated sugar, not table salt, makes the best polenta. We also discovered that a ratio of 4 parts water to 1 part cornmeal delivers the right consistency. As for salt, 1 teaspoon is the right amount for 1 cup of cornmeal.

At this point in our testing, we started to explore alternative cooking methods. The microwave was a bust, yielding sticky, raw-tasting polenta. The pressure cooker was even worse—taking a long time and then sticking firmly to the pot.

We finally hit upon our solution when we prepared polenta in a double boiler. The polenta is cooked over simmering water so it cannot scorch or seize up the way it can when cooked over direct heat. There is only one drawback: the double-boiler method takes twice as long as the constant-stir method. However, since you need only stir the pot once every 10 or 15 minutes, we don't consider this much of a drawback, as long as you are around the kitchen anyway, cooking something else. Perhaps the best reason to use the double boiler to prepare polenta is the end result. To our mind, polenta prepared this way has a softer, lighter texture than polenta prepared according to the traditional recipe. It also tastes sweeter and more like corn.

Double-Boiler Polenta

SERVES 4

When stirring the polenta, there's no need to beat it vigorously; just move the cornmeal around, scraping the sides and bottom of the pan to ensure even cooking. Use this polenta as base for any stew (see chapter 11) or braise, especially lamb shanks (page 255). Sautéed mushrooms or cooked leafy greens also make excellent toppings for soft polenta.

    4   cups boiling water
    I   teaspoon salt
    I   cup medium-grind cornmeal

1. Bring about 2 inches of water to boil in bottom of double boiler; reduce to simmer and maintain throughout cooking process.

2. Set top of double boiler over simmering water, add 4 cups boiling water. Add salt, then gradually sprinkle cornmeal into water, whisking constantly to prevent lump formation.

3. Cover and cook until polenta is very soft and smooth, 1¼ to 1½ hours, stirring for several seconds every 10 to 15 minutes. (Once cooked, polenta can be covered and set aside at room temperature for up to 4 hours. Reheat over simmering water, stirring in a little water if polenta has become too thick.)

➤ VARIATIONS

Polenta with Parmesan and Butter

SERVES 4 AS A FIRST COURSE OR SIDE DISH

Follow recipe for Double-Boiler Polenta, stirring in 4 tablespoons softened butter and ½ cup grated Parmesan cheese when polenta is done. Divide polenta among 4 individual bowls and top each with a small pat of butter. Sprinkle generously with Parmesan cheese to taste and serve immediately.

Polenta with Gorgonzola

SERVES 4 AS A SUBSTANTIAL FIRST COURSE OR LIGHT ENTRÉE

Choose a Dolcelatte Gorgonzola or other mild, creamy blue cheese such as Saga blue. Do not use an aged Gorgonzola for this dish. Other aged blue cheeses will also be too salty, crumbly, and pungent.

Follow recipe for Double-Boiler Polenta, stirring in 2 tablespoons softened butter when polenta is done. Divide polenta among 4 individual bowls and top each with a 1-ounce slice of Gorgonzola cheese. Serve immediately.

Polenta with Italian Sausages and Tomato Sauce

SERVES 4 AS A MAIN COURSE

    I   recipe Double-Boiler Polenta
    2   tablespoons extra-virgin olive oil
    I   pound sweet Italian sausage, cut into
         3-inch lengths
    ½   small onion, chopped
    ½   small carrot, peeled and chopped
    ½   small celery stalk, chopped
    I   can (16 ounces) whole tomatoes, juice reserved
         and tomatoes chopped coarse
         Salt and ground black pepper

1. Prepare polenta.

2. Meanwhile, heat oil in large sauté pan. Add sausage and cook, turning occasionally, until browned on all sides, about 10 minutes. Add onion, carrot, and celery and sauté until vegetables soften, about 5 minutes. Add tomatoes and their juices; simmer gently until sauce thickens, 20 to 25 minutes. Season with salt and pepper to taste.

3. Divide cooked polenta among 4 individual bowls. Top each with a portion of sausage and tomato sauce and serve immediately.

INGREDIENTS: Instant Polenta

After testing dozens of ways to prepare polenta, we still had one question. What about "quick-cooking" or "instant" polenta? We tested several brands (all imported from Italy) and found that instant polenta is a great way to make polenta in a hurry. The flavor is good (although not nearly as good as double-boiler polenta), and it takes no more than 10 minutes.

Quick polenta, like quick grits or instant rice, has been cooked before, then dried out. All you need to do is reconstitute it with boiling water. Quick polenta costs at least three times as much as regular cornmeal and won't have the smooth texture and full corn flavor of double-boiler polenta. However, instant polenta is easy to prepare (just add to boiling water and simmer for several minutes), and the end result is good.

SPOON BREAD

SPOON BREAD IS A SOUTHERN SPECIALTY made from a cornmeal batter that is poured into a baking dish and placed in a hot oven until set. The texture is somewhere between rich cornbread and a soufflé. (Since spoon bread is soft—and must be served with a spoon—it's probably closer to a soufflé.) Spoon bread is a side dish, which can be served in place of rice or potatoes.

To make a spoon bread, you must first whisk cornmeal into a simmering liquid and let it thicken into a "mush," as if you were cooking oatmeal or farina. To the cooled mush you add eggs, salt, butter, and other ingredients. The mixture is poured into a baking dish and baked for 35 to 45 minutes. The resulting dish should be light as air with a tender, rich crumb.

As with many traditional dishes, ingredients and cooking techniques for spoon bread vary enormously. To find the recipe we liked best, we started by figuring out the best way to make the initial corn mush.

The proportion of liquid to solids differed wildly in the recipes we consulted. After trying various ratios, we eventually settled on a medium-thick batter, using 3 cups liquid to 1 cup cornmeal. Heavier mushes made it harder to incorporate beaten egg whites and turned out, well, somewhat heavy. Lighter versions simply did not gel adequately.

The act of stirring cornmeal into simmering milk can be tricky; if you don't do it properly, the meal can separate from the liquid and turn into a bunch of lumps rather than a smooth mush. Plenty of recipes call for the use of a double boiler to prevent lumping, but our suggestion is to turn the focus on the job at hand. Start whisking like crazy and don't stop until the mush is thickened, two to four minutes. It's not much of a time investment when you consider the alternative: 20 to 30 minutes of gentle stirring in a double boiler. Keep the cooking temperature low rather than high because you want the cornmeal to soften as it cooks.

Having settled on the mush-making method, we moved on to consider the individual ingredients of the dish. Spoon bread made with water is like cornbread made with water: lean. Because spoon bread is often an accompaniment to a special meal, we prefer to splurge on the real article and cut fat and calories somewhere else. Half-and-half was our favorite, supplying just the right amount of richness; cream provided too much, and milk not quite enough.

The oldest recipes for spoon bread call for whole eggs, not separated, but in later recipes the eggs are separated and beaten to produce a light, high soufflé. Now we are beginning to see inroads to that procedure, with chemical leaveners compensating for the work eggs used to do. After tasting several dozen spoon breads made with simple ingredients, we found those made with baking powder or soda to taste plainly of chemicals. Beaten whites are the best leavener.

Finally, we considered the important question of what type of cornmeal to use. Yellow corn is more common in the North, and Southerners choose white for the same reason. We found that both made good spoon bread, the major difference being that the white produced a bread that was slightly milder in flavor.

A more important variation, however, came with grinds. We prefer a fine grind because it produces a considerably smoother texture. Yellow Quaker cornmeal has a texture akin to table salt and is the proper grind. If you can't get fine grind cornmeal in your local store, it's no problem. You can approximate a fine grind by putting a medium-grind cornmeal in the food processor or, even better, the blender. The processing will take several minutes, but eventually you will have little clouds of powder-fine meal in the bottom of the bowl.

Spoon Bread

SERVES 6 TO 8

A standard eight-inch soufflé dish works beautifully, but any straight-sided, heavy pan will work, even a cast-iron skillet. Because the spoon bread falls fast from its spectacular height, serve it as quickly as possible; even in its deflated state, though, spoon bread still tastes delicious. Serve leftovers with maple syrup.

3	cups half-and-half
1	teaspoon salt
1	cup fine-grind white or yellow cornmeal
2–3	tablespoons unsalted butter, plus extra for soufflé dish
3	large eggs, warmed to room temperature, then separated

1. Heat oven to 350 degrees. Butter a 1½-quart soufflé dish.

2. Bring half-and-half and salt to simmer in large, heavy saucepan. Reduce heat to low. Slowly whisk in cornmeal. Continue whisking until cornmeal thickens and develops satin sheen, 2 to 4 minutes. Turn off heat and stir in butter; set mush aside.

3. Whisk yolks and 1 to 2 teaspoons water together in small bowl until lemon-colored and very frothy. Stir them into cooled mush, a little at a time to keep yolks from cooking. Beat egg whites to stiff but not dry peaks; gently fold them into mush mixture.

4. Pour mixture into buttered soufflé dish. Bake in oven until spoon bread is golden brown and has risen above dish rim, about 45 minutes. Serve immediately.

➤ VARIATION

Spoon Bread with Cheddar Cheese

Follow recipe for Spoon Bread, adding 1 cup (2 ounces) grated sharp cheddar cheese along with the butter.

BLACK BEANS

BLACK BEANS AS MADE IN LATIN AMERICA are more than a side dish. They are flavorful enough to serve as a main course with rice. We wanted to figure out how to build enough flavor to make beans a satisfying main course. While we focused on flavor, we also paid close attention to texture. The perfect bean was tender without being mushy, with enough tooth to make a satisfying chew.

In pursuit of this perfect texture, we discovered that it was important to cook the beans in enough water; too little water and the beans on the top cooked more slowly than the beans underneath, and the whole pot took forever to cook. (Twelve cups is sufficient water to cook one pound of beans.) We did some further testing by comparing beans that had been soaked overnight to a batch of unsoaked, as well as with a batch softened by a "quick-soak" method in which the beans were brought to a boil, simmered 2 minutes, then covered to let stand 1 hour off the heat. The quick-soak method caused a large percentage of the beans to burst during cooking. This reduced the chew we were after, so we nixed that method. Contrary to our expectations, overnight soaking decreased the cooking time by only about half an hour and didn't improve the texture. Because we are rarely organized enough to soak the night before, we no longer soak.

Next, to test the theory that salting toughens the skin of beans and lengthens the cooking time, we tested beans salted at the end of cooking against those salted three-quarters of the way through, as well as against beans salted at the beginning. In a blind tasting, we couldn't discern any difference in the skins, but only those beans salted from the beginning had enough salt for our taste, so we salt them then.

Now that we had discovered how to cook beans with the texture we wanted, it was time to discover the best way to build more layers of flavor onto this base without drowning the earthy flavor of the beans.

We determined that meat gave the beans a necessary depth of flavor. We tested cooking beans with a ham hock, bacon, ham, and pork loin. We liked all four, and each gave the beans a slightly different flavor; ham hock provided a smooth background taste, while bacon and ham produced a more assertive flavor. Pork loin was the most subtle.

INGREDIENTS: Canned Beans

So what about using canned beans? In recipes where the beans take center stage, we find that there is real difference in flavor and texture between using dried beans that you cook yourself and opening a can. Beans from a can are much less flavorful. They taste of salt and not much else, as compared to beans you cook yourself, which can take on the flavors of the garlic, bay leaves, and other seasonings added to the water. Canned beans also tend to fall apart if simmered for any length of time, as required in our black bean recipe.

However, in recipes where beans are not the focus and the cooking time is short, canned beans are an acceptable shortcut. For instance, canned beans are just fine in our minestrone soup recipe (see page 28).

We tested six leading brands of canned beans—both traditional and organic—and found that creamy, well-seasoned beans were preferred by the majority of tasters. Organic beans tend to be quite firm and chalky and taste underseasoned. By comparison, Green Giant and Goya beans were the top choices of our tasters because they are creamy (but not mushy) and well-seasoned.

In many Caribbean recipes, a sofrito is added to the cooked beans for flavor. Chopped vegetables—usually onion, garlic, and green bell pepper—are sautéed in olive oil until soft and then stirred into the beans. This mixture adds another layer of fresh flavor to beans without overwhelming them.

Some recipes suggest pureeing the sofrito with some of the beans, while others call for mashing some beans with the sofrito. We found that pureeing intensified the flavor of the vegetables enough to almost overwhelm the beans. Simply mashing some beans and the sofrito by hand gets the job done.

We experimented with cumin, the traditional spice for black beans, simmered with the beans or mixed into the sofrito. The flavor of the spice got lost when simmered with the beans; we decided to save the cumin for the sofrito.

Black Beans

SERVES 6

Serve with Fluffy White Rice (page 124) and garnish with a spoonful of sour cream, minced red onion, and a dash or two of hot red pepper sauce.

BEANS

1	pound black beans, picked over and rinsed
1	smoked ham hock (about ⅔ pound), rinsed
1	green bell pepper, stemmed, seeded, and quartered
1	medium onion, minced
6	medium garlic cloves, minced
2	bay leaves
1½	teaspoons salt

SOFRITO

2	tablespoons extra-virgin olive oil
1	medium onion, minced
1	small green bell pepper, stemmed, seeded, and minced
8	medium garlic cloves, minced
2	teaspoons dried oregano
¾	teaspoon salt
1½	teaspoons ground cumin
1	tablespoon juice from 1 medium lime
½	cup chopped fresh cilantro leaves
	Salt and ground black pepper

1. FOR THE BEANS: Bring all bean ingredients to boil in 12 cups of water over medium-high heat in heavy soup kettle or Dutch oven, skimming surface as scum rises. Reduce heat to low and simmer, partially covered, adding more water if cooking liquid reduces to level of beans, until tender but not splitting (taste several, as they cook unevenly), about 2 hours. Remove ham hock from beans. When cool enough to handle, remove ham from bone, discard bone and skin, and cut meat into bite-size pieces; set aside. Remove and discard bay leaves.

2. FOR THE SOFRITO: Meanwhile, heat oil in large skillet over medium heat; add ingredients from onion through salt; sauté until vegetables soften, 8 to 10 minutes. Add cumin; sauté until fragrant, about 1 minute longer.

3. TO FINISH DISH: Scoop 1 cup beans and 2 cups cooking liquid into pan with sofrito; mash beans with potato masher or fork until smooth. Simmer over medium heat until liquid is reduced and thickened, about 6 minutes. Return sofrito mixture and meat from ham hock to bean pot; simmer until beans are creamy and liquid thickens to sauce consistency, 15 to 20 minutes. Add lime juice; simmer 1 minute longer. Stir in cilantro, adjust seasoning with pepper and salt if necessary, and serve hot over white rice.

➤ VARIATIONS

Black Beans with Dry Sherry

Follow recipe for Black Beans, adding 1 teaspoon ground coriander to sofrito along with cumin, substituting dry sherry for lime juice, and omitting cilantro.

Black Beans with Bacon, Balsamic Vinegar, and Sweet Pepper

Fry ½ pound bacon, cut into ½-inch strips, in medium skillet over medium heat until crisp and brown, about 5 minutes. Transfer with slotted spoon to paper towel–lined plate. Follow recipe for Black Beans, omitting ham hock and substituting bacon fat for olive oil and 1 medium red bell pepper for the green pepper in sofrito. Add cooked bacon to beans with sofrito, and substitute 2 teaspoons balsamic vinegar for lime juice.

LENTILS

THE CONVENTIONAL PRACTICE WHEN COOK-
ing lentils is not to add salt or acidic ingredients until
the lentils have softened. We wondered if this restric-
tion was necessary. We set out to test this factor and to
determine the best cooking times for common green
or brown, peeled red, and whole red masoor (red
lentils with the brownish seed coat left on).

Before cooking, all lentils need to be inspected for
stones, seeds, and other unwanted objects. After sort-
ing, lentils should be rinsed in water to remove any
residual dirt. To determine how long it takes the lentils
to cook to tenderness without any graininess, we
cooked half a cup of each kind of cleaned lentil in
three cups of plain water.

As they cooked, each kind of lentil showed its
unique character. Peeled red lentils almost immediately lost their shape and turned into a rough mush;
this explains why these lentils are used in purees. The
common green or brown lentils and the masoors
became tender and creamy in 20 to 25 minutes.

There was a dramatic difference in the tastes of
the different lentils. The common green lentils were
dull and bland; the red lentils had a slight sweetness
to them; the flavor of the whole red masoors was
delightful, with a hint of cumin and coriander.

Our next test was to follow the same procedure but
to add one-half teaspoon of salt to the water. The
lentils all cooked in about the same amount of time as
they had in plain water. The taste of each lentil was
much more developed and were clearer.

Next, we cooked each lentil in the same amount of
water, but substituted one tablespoon of vinegar for the
salt. The vinegar had a striking effect on the lentils, doubling their cooking time and giving them a rather
grainy texture. This is because acids interfere with
lentils' ability to bind with water. This causes them to
take longer to soften and to have a rather dry taste.

Indian-Spiced Lentils with Kale

SERVES 4 AS A SIDE DISH

*Use common brown or green lentils or whole red lentils
(called masoor lentils) in this dish.*

1	cup lentils, picked over and rinsed
1	teaspoon salt
1	pound kale, stemmed and chopped
2	tablespoons unsalted butter
1	teaspoon ground coriander
½	teaspoon ground cumin
½	teaspoon ground mustard
¼–½	teaspoon hot red pepper flakes
2	garlic cloves, minced
2	teaspoons minced fresh gingerroot

1. Bring lentils, 6 cups water, and salt to boil in
medium saucepan; boil for 5 minutes. Reduce heat;
simmer until lentils are tender but still hold their shape,
20 to 25 minutes, adding kale during last 5 minutes of
cooking. Drain, reserving 1 cup cooking liquid.

2. Meanwhile, heat butter in large skillet over
medium heat. Add coriander, cumin, mustard, and
hot red pepper flakes; sauté to develop flavors, about
1 minute. Add garlic and ginger; sauté until softened
and fragrant, about 2 minutes. Add lentils and kale
and reserved cooking liquid. Simmer to blend flavors, about 5 minutes. Adjust seasonings and serve.

Red Lentil Puree

SERVES 4 AS A SIDE DISH

Red lentils will dissolve into a thick, spicy puree.

1½	cups red lentils, picked over and rinsed
1½	tablespoons minced fresh gingerroot
2	medium garlic cloves, minced
½	teaspoon turmeric
½	teaspoon salt
2	tablespoons unsalted butter
½	teaspoon cumin seeds
½	teaspoon anise seeds
3	tablespoons juice from 1 lemon
	Ground white pepper

1. Bring first five ingredients plus 4 cups water to
boil in medium saucepan; boil for 5 minutes. Reduce
heat; simmer until lentils lose their shape, 15 to 20
minutes. Whisk lentils to make a puree; set aside.

2. Heat butter in a small sauté pan. Add cumin
and anise seeds; sauté until butter is nutty brown.
Remove from heat; add lemon juice. Stir mixture
into lentil puree. Season with pepper, adjust other
seasonings, and serve immediately.

6

POULTRY

THIS CHAPTER COVERS CHICKEN, CORNISH hens, turkey, duck, and goose. The goal in cooking all these birds is to produce tender, juicy meat and crisp, nicely browned skin. While all of these birds have a similar bone structure, there are some important distinctions.

Chicken, hens, and turkey are an amalgam of white and dark meat. Breast meat has very little fat and is prone to drying out. Devising strategies to keep delicate white meat juicy is a recurring theme in this chapter. Turning birds and brining (see page 137) are common solutions.

Keeping breast meat tender is not an issue when preparing duck and goose since all the meat on these birds is dark. The biggest challenge when cooking these birds is the fat—there's too much, and the skin can be flabby if duck and goose are not properly cooked.

See chapter 11 for information on chicken stews. Chapter 10 contains information on grilling chicken kebabs, thighs, legs, and breasts, as well as grill-roasting a whole chicken.

SAUTÉED CHICKEN BREASTS

SAUTÉING A BONELESS, SKINLESS CHICKEN breast sounds easy. But too often the chicken comes out only lightly colored and dry. Ideally, a sautéed chicken breast should have a nicely browned exterior and a tender, juicy interior.

Although there are several keys to sautéing boneless chicken breasts correctly, we found that one is paramount: there must be enough heat. Home cooks often shy away from the smoke and splatters that can accompany strong heat. But a thin, delicate food like boneless chicken must be cooked through quickly. Cooking over low or even moderate heat pushes the meat's moisture to the surface before any browning occurs, and once the juices hit the exterior of the meat, it will not brown at all, unless it is cooked for a long, long time. Furthermore—and this is especially true in a lean piece of meat such as a chicken breast—these same juices provide the lion's share of moisture; expel them, and the result is a tough, leathery piece of meat rather than a tender, moist one.

There are other points to bear in mind, as well. After you have trimmed excess fat from the cutlets and removed the tendon, if desired, rinse them quickly under cool water if they seem sticky or have even the slightest off-scent. (The surface of foods is usually the first part to go bad, and rinsing can do wonders to salvage the flavor.) Then dry the meat thoroughly with paper towels; again, if it is wet, it will not brown. For best flavor, we sprinkle salt and pepper on both sides, using a full teaspoon of salt for four pieces of chicken.

We sautéed both floured and unfloured chicken cutlets to determine any differences in taste, texture, and juiciness. We immediately noticed a more dramatic sizzle when the unfloured cutlet hit the pan. While both cutlets sizzled during cooking, the unfloured cutlet "spit" a bit more. The flour seems to provide a barrier between the fat in the pan and the moisture in the cutlet. The floured cutlet also moved about more freely; while neither version stuck to the skillet, the floured cutlet skated easily when we swirled it about.

When cooked, the floured cutlet displayed a consistently brown crust, almost resembling a skin. The uncoated breast was a spotty brown. Both breasts were equally moist, but the floured cutlet had a better mouthfeel with its contrasting crispy exterior and juicy, tender meat. The floured cutlet, reminiscent of fried chicken, was also more flavorful than its uncoated counterpart. Our advice: Flour those cutlets.

In our tests, we found that a skillet must measure at least nine inches across the bottom in order to comfortably hold four six-ounce chicken cutlets (crowded meat will not brown well), and the bottom should be reasonably heavy, or else the chicken will scorch. We tested nonstick and enamel-coated pans and found them perfectly acceptable, but we prefer bare metal—stainless steel or an alloy—as it seems to yield more intense color.

The best cooking medium for chicken cutlets is a mixture of butter and oil. Butter contains milk solids, which brown during cooking, providing a beautiful rich color; it also contributes mightily to flavor. Adding oil reduces the proportion of burnt milk solids and helps keep the fat from blackening.

We discovered something else about fat in the course of our experiments. In a concession to the reigning wisdom about health, we tried sautéing a batch of cutlets in just the sheerest film of fat. The results were disastrous. The fat burned, the outside of the chicken became dry and stringy, and the crust was very disappointing, nearly blackened in some spots and a strange yellowish color in others. For sautéed food to become crisp and uniformly brown, the entire surface must stay in contact with the fat; meat has an irregular surface, and any part that is not in contact with the cooking medium—in this case, the oil—is steamed by the moisture generated by the cooking meat and, therefore, will not brown. You will need about one-eighth inch of fat in the pan at the start. Assuming that your skillet measures nine inches across the bottom, 1½ tablespoons each of butter and oil is about right. If your skillet is wider, you may need closer to two tablespoons of each.

Place the butter and oil in the skillet and set it over high heat—everyone's stove is different, of course, but most home burners are quite weak, so when we say "high," we mean "high." Hold the skillet by the handle and swirl it a few times until the butter melts. Now you must pay close attention. At first, the butter will foam, and possibly sputter, as the moisture boils out. As the foam subsides, the butter will become fragrant and begin to darken. At just the moment when the butter turns the pale brown color of roasted peanuts, quickly lay in the chicken cutlets, with the tenderloin side down, holding onto the tapered end as you lay the cutlet down flat.

Maintain the heat at the point where the fat remains at a fast sizzle but does not quite smoke. If you see more than just a wisp or two of smoke, immediately slide the pan off the burner, turn down the heat, and wait a few seconds before returning the pan to the flame. Be advised that there will be some spattering.

After cooking, your plump, moist, beautifully brown chicken cutlets may be served just as they are. But it seems a pity to waste the browned bits left in the skillet, when these can so easily be "deglazed" to make a simple, lovely sauce. To make the most basic sauce, pour one-half cup water into the skillet, turn the heat way up, and boil the water until it's reduced by half; use a wooden spoon to scrape up the browned bits. For a more refined and flavorful sauce, replace the water either with wine (virtually any kind), brandy, vinegar, chicken broth, heavy cream,

SCIENCE: How Brining Works

We find that delicate white meat is best protected by soaking chicken, hens, and turkey in a saltwater solution before cooking. Whether we are roasting a turkey or grilling chicken parts, we have consistently found that brining keeps the meat juicier. Brining also gives delicate (and sometimes mushy) poultry a meatier, firmer consistency and seasons the meat down to the bone.

To explain these sensory perceptions, we ran some tests. We started by weighing several 11-pound turkeys after they had been brined for 12 hours and found an average weight gain of almost ¾ pound. Even more impressive, we found that brined birds weighed six to eight ounces more after roasting than a same-sized bird that had not been brined. Our taste buds were right: brined birds are juicier.

So why does brining work? Brining actually promotes a change in the structure of the proteins in the muscle. The salt causes protein strands to become denatured, or unwound. This is the same process that occurs when proteins are exposed to heat, acid, or alcohol. When protein strands unwind, they get tangled in one another and trap water in the matrix that forms.

Salt is commonly used to give processed meats a better texture. For example, hot dogs made without salt would be limp.

Depending on the size of the bird, it is necessary to vary the amount of salt in the solution and the brining time. In general, bigger birds require a longer soaking time in a less concentrated solution. A less salty solution will season the meat evenly and prevents the skin and outside layers of meat from becoming too salty in the time it takes to season the meat near the bone. In contrast, chicken parts can be brined in a much saltier solution for less time. Follow the specific directions in the recipes that follow with regards to the proportion of salt to water and the optimum brining time.

In some cases, we have added sugar to the brine. The sugar does not affect the texture of the meat, but it does add flavor. For instance, we find that brining chicken parts in a sugar-salt solution enhances the caramelized flavor that occurs when the parts are grilled. However, a turkey destined for the oven is best brined in a plain saltwater solution; the added sweetness does not work with gravy and stuffing.

or fruit juice. After reducing the liquid, take the pan off the heat and swirl in one or more tablespoons of softened butter to give the sauce added richness.

If you wish to use butter to thicken a deglazing sauce—in addition to enriching its flavor—you must observe these rules: The sauce must be slightly syrupy and be well-reduced; it takes about three tablespoons of butter to thicken one-third cup of sauce. Add the butter off the heat, and do not return the pan to the heat once the butter is incorporated, or the sauce will separate and thin out. Finally, swirl the pan by the handle, or stir very gently until the butter is incorporated and the sauce thickened. Note also that acidic deglazing sauces—those made with a high proportion of lemon juice or vinegar or wine—are more stable and thicker than others.

Master Recipe for Sautéed Chicken Breast Cutlets

SERVES 4

Serve the chicken breast cutlets plain or with any of the sauces that follow this recipe. If making a pan sauce, turn the oven to 200 degrees before you start this recipe and place the cooked cutlets in the warm oven while making the pan sauce.

4	chicken breast cutlets (1½ pounds), trimmed, tendons removed, rinsed, and thoroughly dried
	Salt and ground black pepper
¼	cup all-purpose flour
1½	tablespoons unsalted butter
1½	tablespoons vegetable oil or olive oil

1. Sprinkle 1 teaspoon salt and ¼ to ½ teaspoon pepper on both sides of the cutlets. Measure flour onto a plate or pie tin. Working with one cutlet at a time, press both sides into flour. Make sure tenderloin is tucked beneath and fused to main portion of breast. Pick up cutlet from tapered end; shake gently to remove excess flour.

2. Heat butter and oil in a heavy-bottomed skillet measuring at least 9 inches across bottom. Swirl skillet over high heat until butter has melted. Continue to heat skillet until butter stops foaming and has just begun to color. Lay cutlets in skillet, tenderloin side down.

3. Maintain medium-high heat, so fat sizzles but does not smoke, and sauté cutlets until browned on one side, about 4 minutes. Turn cutlets with tongs (a fork will pierce meat); cook on other side until meat feels firm when pressed and clotted juices begin to emerge around tenderloin, 3 to 4 minutes. Serve immediately, or, if making one of the sauces, transfer cutlets to a plate, keep warm in 200-degree oven, and continue with one of the recipes that follow.

PAN SAUCES FOR CHICKEN

THE CONCEPT OF A PAN SAUCE IS SIMPLE. The juices that escape from the meat (in this case, chicken) during cooking reduce, caramelize, and sometimes harden. These bits, which are basically caramelized proteins that chefs refer to as "fond," provide a concentrated flavor on which to build a sauce. The flavors are created by a process known as the Maillard reaction. Named for a French chemist, this reaction (also more simply known as browning) takes place whenever a carbohydrate and a protein are heated together. The molecules break apart as they are heated, then combine and recombine over and over, forming hundreds of distinctly flavored compounds.

To release these flavors into a sauce, a liquid is used to wash and dissolve these bits off the bottom of the pan. This "deglazing" can be done with many different liquids—wine, water, juice, brandy, stock, vinegar, or a combination. The liquids are then boiled and reduced to thicken the sauce.

Lemon-Caper Sauce

ENOUGH FOR 4 CHICKEN BREAST CUTLETS

1	shallot or scallion, minced
1	cup chicken stock or low-sodium canned broth
¼	cup juice from 1 large lemon
2	tablespoons small capers, drained
3	tablespoons unsalted butter, softened

Follow Master Recipe for Sautéed Chicken Breast Cutlets. Without discarding fat, set skillet over medium heat. Add shallot; sauté until softened, about 1 minute. Increase heat to high, add stock, and scrape skillet bottom with wooden spatula or spoon to loosen browned bits. Add lemon juice and capers; boil until liquid reduces to about ⅓ cup, 3 to 4 minutes. Add any accumulated chicken juices; reduce sauce again to ⅓ cup. Off heat, swirl in softened butter until it melts and thickens sauce. Spoon sauce over cutlets and serve immediately.

Sherry-Cream Sauce With Mushrooms

ENOUGH FOR 4 CHICKEN BREAST CUTLETS

2	shallots or scallions, minced
8	ounces mushrooms, sliced thin (about 2½ cups)
⅓	cup sherry, preferably cream or amontillado
½	cup chicken stock or low-sodium canned broth
1	cup heavy cream
2	tablespoons minced parsley leaves
	Pinch of ground mace
	Salt and ground black or white pepper
1	small piece of lemon

Follow Master Recipe for Sautéed Chicken Breast Cutlets. Without discarding fat, set skillet over medium heat. Add shallots; sauté until softened, about 1 minute. Increase heat to high, add mushrooms, sauté until limp and brown, 2 to 3 minutes. Add sherry; boil until sherry completely evaporates, about 1 minute. Add stock and cream; boil, stirring frequently, until sauce reduces to about ⅓ cup and is thick enough to lightly coat a spoon, about 5 to 6 minutes. Add any accumulated chicken juices; reduce sauce to previous consistency. Stir in parsley and mace and season to taste with salt, pepper, and drops of lemon juice. Spoon sauce over cutlets and serve immediately.

Oaxacan-Style Sauce with Cloves and Cinnamon

ENOUGH FOR 4 CHICKEN BREAST CUTLETS

1	small onion, minced
2	large or 3 small jalapeño chiles, stemmed, seeded, and minced
2	medium garlic cloves, minced
½	teaspoon ground cinnamon
¼	teaspoon (scant) ground cloves
½	cup chicken stock or low-sodium canned broth
1	tablespoon cider vinegar
½	cup unsweetened crushed pineapple, undrained
⅓	cup pimiento-stuffed green olives, sliced thin crosswise
¼	cup currants or chopped raisins
¼	cup canned crushed tomatoes
1½	tablespoons minced fresh cilantro leaves
3	tablespoons pine nuts, toasted (optional)

1. Follow Master Recipe for Sautéed Chicken Breast Cutlets. Without discarding fat, set skillet over medium heat. Add onion and jalapeños and sauté until softened, about 1 minute. Stir in garlic, cinnamon, and cloves, and cook until garlic softens, about 30 seconds longer. Add stock and vinegar and bring mixture to a boil, scraping bottom of skillet with a wooden spoon to incorporate browned bits. Add pineapple, olives, currants, and tomatoes, increase heat to high, and boil sauce, stirring, until thick, about 3 minutes.

2. Return cutlets to pan, spoon sauce over cutlets. Cover and let cutlets stand over very low heat to blend flavors, about 5 minutes. Adjust seasonings; transfer cutlets to a plate, spoon sauce over cutlets, and sprinkle with cilantro and optional pine nuts; serve immediately.

Tomato-Basil Sauce with Capers

ENOUGH FOR 4 CHICKEN BREAST CUTLETS

2–3	shallots or scallions, minced (about ⅓ cup)
3–4	garlic cloves, minced (about 2 tablespoons)
2	medium-large tomatoes, seeded and chopped (about 2 cups)
¼	cup dry white wine or 3 tablespoons dry vermouth
2	tablespoons small capers, drained
2	tablespoons shredded basil leaves or minced parsley leaves
	Salt and ground black pepper

Follow Master Recipe for Sautéed Chicken Breast Cutlets. Without discarding fat, set skillet over medium heat. Add shallots and sauté until softened, about 1 minute. Stir in garlic, then tomatoes.

Increase heat to high and cook, stirring frequently, until tomatoes have given up most of their juice, forming a lumpy puree, about 2 minutes. Add wine, capers, and any accumulated chicken juices; boil sauce until thick enough to mound slightly in a spoon, about 2 minutes. Stir in herb and season with salt and pepper. Spoon sauce over chicken and serve immediately.

Asian-Style Sweet and Sour Sauce
ENOUGH FOR 4 CHICKEN BREAST CUTLETS

2–3	garlic cloves (1½ tablespoons), minced
2	teaspoons minced fresh ginger
¼	teaspoon crushed red pepper flakes
¼	cup dark brown sugar, packed firm
¼	cup distilled white vinegar
2	tablespoons soy sauce
½	teaspoon anchovy paste or Thai or Vietnamese fish sauce
4	medium scallions, including the tender green parts, sliced thin

Place garlic, ginger, and pepper flakes on a cutting board; mince further to pulverize the pepper. Follow Master Recipe for Sautéed Chicken Breast Cutlets. Without draining fat, return skillet to medium heat; add garlic mixture and sauté until softened, about 1 minute. Increase heat to high; add next 4 ingredients and accumulated pan juices; boil, stirring to loosen browned bits from pan bottom until mixture thickens to a light syrup, less than a minute. Pour sauce over chicken cutlets, scatter scallions on top, and serve immediately.

Mustard and Cream Sauce with Endive and Caraway
ENOUGH FOR 4 CHICKEN BREAST CUTLETS

1	medium head endive, cut diagonally into ¼-inch slices
2	medium shallots, minced
2	tablespoons cider vinegar
1	teaspoon caraway seeds
½	cup chicken stock or low-sodium canned broth
½	cup heavy cream
1	teaspoon Dijon mustard
	Salt and ground black pepper

Follow Master Recipe for Sautéed Chicken Breast Cutlets. Without draining fat, return skillet to medium heat; add endive and shallots; sauté until softened and lightly browned, 3 to 4 minutes. Add cider vinegar and bring to boil, scraping up browned bits from bottom of skillet with wooden spoon. Add caraway seeds, stock, and cream; increase heat to medium-high and boil, stirring occasionally, until slightly thickened and reduced to generous ½ cup, about 5 minutes. Stir in Dijon mustard; season to taste with salt and pepper. Pour sauce over cutlets and serve immediately.

Peach Salsa
ENOUGH FOR 4 CHICKEN BREAST CUTLETS

2	small peaches or nectarines, peeled and cut into small dice (about 1 cup)
½	large cucumber (5 to 6 ounces), peeled, seeded, and cut into small dice (about ⅔ cup)
1	plum tomato, seeded and cut into small dice (about ¼ cup)
2	tablespoons chopped red onion
1	serrano or jalapeño chile, seeded and minced
4	teaspoons juice from 1 lime
	Salt
1	cup chicken stock or low-sodium canned broth
2	teaspoons juice from 1 small lemon (or additional lime juice)

1. Mix peaches, cucumber, tomato, onion, chile, and lime juice in a medium bowl. (Can cover and refrigerate up to 24 hours.) Shortly before serving, season the salsa with ¼ teaspoon salt or to taste; set aside at room temperature and follow Master Recipe for Sautéed Chicken Breast Cutlets.

2. Pour off any remaining chicken fat, set skillet over high heat; add stock and boil until it reduces to ⅓ cup, scraping up browned bits from pan bottom. Add any accumulated chicken juices and reduce sauce to previous consistency; stir in lemon juice. Pour sauce over cutlets. Spoon salsa alongside chicken and serve immediately.

ROAST CHICKEN

COOKING A CHICKEN APPEARS TO BE A SIMPLE task at first. The meat is not tough by nature. The dark meat is relatively forgiving in terms of cooking time. The breast meat is not particularly thick, which means that the outer layers are less likely to dry out while you are attempting to properly cook the center of the bird.

Yet when you are served a perfectly roasted chicken, the experience is not only unusual, it is extraordinary. The skin is perfectly crisp and well-seasoned. The white meat is juicy and tender, but with a hint of chew. The dark meat is fully cooked all the way to the bone. There is clearly more to chicken cookery than we at first imagined because most home-cooked chickens are either grossly overcooked or so underdone that they resemble an avian version of steak tartare.

To solve this problem once and for all, we decided to devise a series of tests based on a few simple observations. The first observation is that chicken is made up of two totally different types of meat: white and dark. The white meat is inevitably overcooked and dry even as the dark meat is still little more than raw next to the bone. The second observation is that chicken, unlike beef, has skin, which should be nicely browned and crispy. As we found during the testing process, crisp skin is not always consistent with perfectly cooked meat. Finally, chicken is an odd amalgam of meat and bones. The drumsticks and wings stick out, the thigh meat is on the side of the bird, and the breast meat is on the top (at least when the chicken is roasted). The home cook is dealing with a complex three-dimensional structure, quite different from a brisket or a pot roast. These anatomical realities require a more complex set of cooking instructions. In search of these instructions, we ended up roasting chickens 14 different ways.

We started our tests with the most pertinent question: What is the best oven temperature for roasting a chicken? Our first bird went into a 450-degree oven and cooked for 44 minutes. When it emerged, the skin was dark and crispy, but we encountered the classic problem with high-heat meat cookery: While the dark meat was fine, the outer portion of the white meat was overcooked and on the tough side even as the internal thigh temperature registered 160 degrees, the temperature we generally consider best for white meat. (Dark meat really tastes best cooked to at least 165 or 170 degrees.)

We then went to the other extreme and tested a bird in a 275-degree oven for an hour and 35 minutes, raising the heat to 425 degrees for the last 10 minutes to crisp up the skin. The white meat was not quite as juicy as the dark, but not dry either. The skin, however, was a light gold, not a rich sienna, and it was chewy and not very tasty—obviously, not browned enough.

EQUIPMENT: Roasting Racks

A rack keeps a roast above pan juices and grease, which helps prevent the exterior from cooking up soft or fatty. A rack also allows air to circulate underneath so the bottom of a chicken or other roast can brown without burning or overcooking, which often happens when meat rests directly on a hot pan.

There are several types of roasting racks, each with a different use. In our tests, we found that a U-shaped basket rack cradles a chicken perfectly, keeping the wings and legs in good position so birds are easy to turn. We also found that a perforated nonstick finish conducts heat better than other racks, so that skin browns especially well. Basket racks are solid and stable, but too small to accommodate turkeys or geese.

For these larger birds, a nonadjustable V-rack is recommended. Unlike adjustable V-racks, the nonadjustable version is made from thick metal bars, not flimsy wires. We found that this kind of rack stays put in the pan and doesn't bend when holding heavy birds. While you can use a V-rack to roast a chicken, the wings and/or legs may slip through the bars. When you go to turn the bird, you may have to lift the dangling limbs back over the bars.

Basket and V-racks keep birds well above the roasting pan so that the skin on the underside browns well. In our tests, we found that a vertical rack doesn't lift the chicken far enough off the pan to brown the skin on the bottom end of the bird. A vertical rack also splatters fat all over the oven.

For other recipes, you simply need to keep the meat out of the rendered fat and juices. A regular flat roasting rack is fine for prime rib, ham, or leg of lamb. Look for special roasting racks that are small enough to fit in most pans.

Finally, we tried a simple, classic approach: we roasted the bird at 375 degrees for one hour. The skin was golden and slightly crispy. At 160 degrees internal temperature, the juices ran clear, but the dark meat was still not properly cooked near the bone. We continued cooking to an internal temperature of about 170 degrees (thigh meat), and the white meat was still juicy (the breast meat was close to 180 degrees). This was an interesting discovery. While the breast meat of chicken roasted at 450 degrees was a bit dry when the thigh registered 160 degrees, the bird roasted at 375 degrees still had juicy breast meat when the thigh registered close to 170 degrees. We also found that "until the juices run clear" is an imprecise measure of doneness—the white meat will be cooked, but the dark meat can still be a little bloody at the bone, a sight that we would prefer to leave to B movies rather than a dinner plate.

We then tried starting the oven out at a higher temperature (450 degrees), putting in the chicken, and then immediately turning the oven down to 350 degrees. The bird cooked in 53 minutes, and the skin was a pale gold and slightly chewy—not much difference from the chicken roasted at 375 degrees and not quite as good overall. So the winner was the simpler method, a constant 375 degrees.

Using the 375-degree method, we set out to determine if basting is a good idea or just another one of those hand-me-down cookbook directions that make no sense. We started with butter and basted every 15 minutes. The results were appalling. Despite a nice brown color, the skin was chewy and greasy. The next bird was basted with oil, which turned out a crispier skin, but the color was off—a pale gold. We then brushed a bird with butter before roasting and shoved it in the oven without any further basting. This was the best method. Great color and great crispy texture.

Basting may have made sense when cooking a large piece of meat on a spit over an open fire. The outer layers would easily get overcooked, and the basting may have prevented burning or scorching. However, a three-pound chicken in a 375-degree oven is a different matter entirely. The skin will not scorch or burn (in fact, if you leave it alone, it will cook rather nicely on its own), and the basting liquid is not going to penetrate the meat, making it more tender. Juiciness has nothing to do with the external application of liquid. In fact, neither stew meat nor braised meat absorbs any liquid. The only reason, therefore, to brush a chicken with butter is to advance the color of the skin. The oven heat turns the milk solids brown and, in the process, also provides added flavor.

EQUIPMENT: Instant-Read Thermometer

A thermometer is a key piece of kitchen equipment, essential for producing a roast chicken (or any roast) that is cooked properly. We recommend an instant-read thermometer over the traditional meat thermometers, which are inserted in foods before they go into the oven. An instant-read thermometer can be inserted into almost any food—everything from a roast to a custard for ice cream—and will display the internal temperature within seconds. Unlike traditional meat thermometers, instant-read thermometers are not designed to be left in the oven. Prolonged exposure of the whole unit to heat will destroy the measuring mechanism.

There are two types of instant-read thermometers on the market—dial face and digital. Though pocket-size dial face thermometers are less expensive than digitals, they are less precise, and most read temperatures in a narrower range. Our favorite thermometer registers temperatures from below 0 to 500 degrees.

Another important difference between digital and dial thermometers is the location of the temperature sensor. On dial face thermometers, the sensors are roughly 1½ inches from the tip of the stem. The sensors on digital thermometers are usually located at the very tip of the stem. What this means is that the stem of the dial face thermometer must be stuck deep into the meat or other food. A digital thermometer will deliver a more accurate reading in thin cutlets or shallow liquids.

There is one last factor to consider when buying an instant-read thermometer. In our testing of nine models, we found that some models responded in just 10 seconds, while others took as long as 30 seconds to record the correct temperature. There is no point keeping the oven door open longer than is necessary, so choose a fast-responding model such as the Owen Instruments Thermapen or Taylor Digital Pocket.

Next we turned to trussing. We trussed a bird according to the best French method and cooked it for what seemed a long time, 1½ hours (this was a larger bird weighing in at 3.42 pounds). The white meat was overcooked at this point, but the dark meat was just right. It was also interesting to note that the cooking time was so long. We concluded that trussing makes it more difficult to properly cook the inner part of the thigh—because it is less exposed to the heat, it needs more oven time. Voilà! Overcooked white meat. A 3.11-pound bird took only one hour at 375 degrees without trussing, and the white and dark meat were both nicely cooked.

Incidentally, we also made an odd discovery after we had roasted a half-dozen birds with the basic 375-degree method. The thigh that was facing up during the second 20 minutes of roasting ended up lower in temperature than the thigh that started off facing up. At first we thought this was just a random occurrence, but after measuring the temperature in four or five birds, it became clear that this was a trend. After thinking about this phenomenon for a few days, we seem to have figured it out. The thigh that started off facing the roasting pan was facing a cold pan that reflected little heat. When the thigh that started by facing up was turned face down, the pan was hot and was radiating plenty of heat. So, to even things out, preheat the roasting pan.

Having figured out that continuous basting and trussing were both unnecessary, we were hoping to find that the bird need not be turned, either. But even cooking is crucial to chicken cookery, and a couple of tests were in order.

First, we roasted a bird for 20 minutes on each side and then put it on its back. This 3.21-pound chicken took just 50 minutes to cook. The skin was golden and crunchy, the white and dark meat perfectly cooked, and the overall presentation superb. To make this process a bit easier, we tried roasting another bird breast side down for 20 minutes and then turned it breast side up. This chicken was good, but the skin was less crispy, and, at the point at which the white meat was perfect, the dark meat was a bit undercooked. Thus, unfortunately, two turns proved crucial.

We had heard a lot of good things about clay roasters and had tried La Cloche, a bell-shaped clay cooker for bread that works well with other recipes.

We followed the directions and roasted the bird enclosed in the clay cooker in a 425-degree oven. The directions suggested cooking for 90 minutes (with no specification of how large a bird to use), which seemed absurd—the bird was done in just an hour (the internal temperature of the thigh registering 168 degrees), and this was a 3.4-pound chicken. The good news was that the white and dark meat cooked equally, and the meat was quite juicy. The bad news was that the skin was pale and, although moist, chewy rather than crispy. So this is a good

SCIENCE: When Is It Done?

As we have discovered when cooking red meat, internal temperatures are relative, not absolute. That is, 160 degrees means one thing when the food being measured has been roasted at 375 degrees and something quite different when that food has been roasted at 200 degrees. In other words, it's how you get there that matters. Many experts advise cooking the dark meat to 160 degrees, the initial premise we used for our testing. Forget it. The dark meat just isn't going to be fully cooked at the bone. You need the dark meat (don't measure the breast meat, since the dark meat has to be cooked properly or it is inedible) between 165 and 170 degrees. However, if you slow-cook at 200 degrees, you can cook the dark meat up to 175 to 180 degrees without a problem.

Why the difference? Because at higher oven temperatures, the outer layers of meat will end up at much higher internal temperatures. That is, while the middle of the chicken breast may register 160 degrees whether slow- or fast-roasted, the outer layer of meat may reach 200 degrees if roasted at a high temperature but only 170 degrees if roasted at a low temperature. So, although the exact center of the meat may be the same with both methods, a serving of chicken breast will also contain overcooked meat when roasted at high temperatures. Slow-roasting guarantees even cooking as well as more consistent internal temperatures.

We also tested the notion of the internal temperature rising after the chicken is removed from the oven, as it does with a beef roast. This simply does not happen. We removed a chicken from the oven and inserted an instant-read thermometer into the breast. It started out at 155 degrees and immediately started to fall, ending at 140 degrees after 15 minutes. Although resting for 20 minutes makes the meat juicier, the bird will not continue to cook.

method for even cooking, but not a first choice if you are a skin fanatic.

Fourteen chickens later, we had finally arrived at the best method: Roast the chicken on its side untrussed at 375 degrees in a preheated pan, turning it on its other side after 20 minutes, then breast side up after another 20 minutes, and cooking until the thigh has reached an internal temperature of 165 to 170 degrees. Easy, straightforward, and guaranteed (or as guaranteed as cooking methods can be) to produce a truly satisfying roast chicken.

Easy Roast Chicken

SERVES 4

A 3½-pound bird should roast in 55 to 60 minutes, while a 4½-pound bird requires 60 to 65 minutes. If using a basket or V-rack, be sure to grease it so the chicken does not stick to it. If you don't have a basket or V-rack, set the bird on a regular rack and use balls of aluminum foil to keep the roasting chicken propped up on its side.

1   **roasting chicken (about 3 pounds), giblets removed and reserved for another use, chicken rinsed and patted dry with paper towels**

2   **tablespoons unsalted butter, melted**
     Salt and ground black pepper
     Oil for basket or V-rack

1. Place shallow roasting pan in oven and heat oven to 375 degrees. Brush chicken with butter and sprinkle liberally with salt and pepper.

2. Remove heated pan from oven and set oiled basket or V-rack in it. Place chicken on rack, wing side up. Roast 20 minutes, then rotate chicken, other wing side up. Roast 20 minutes, then rotate chicken, breast side up. Roast until instant-read thermometer inserted in breast registers 160 degrees and in thigh registers between 165 and 170 degrees, 10 to 15 minutes longer. Transfer chicken to cutting board; let rest 20 minutes. Carve and serve.

FRIED CHICKEN

OUR GRANDMOTHERS FRIED CHICKEN IN A cast-iron skillet and covered the pan with a lid while the chicken cooked. The result was crispy yet somehow smothered fried chicken. In recent years, most home cooks have followed the lead of fast-food restaurants and now deep-fry chicken in a Dutch oven. This chicken has a crisper, more brittle coating.

We wondered if pan-fried chicken was better than deep-fried chicken or if we were just romanticizing the past. But frying chicken involves more than just using the right pan. There are other issues to consider. What size chickens are best? Should the chicken parts be soaked before frying and, if so, in what? What fat or combination of fats is best for frying chicken? Is all-purpose flour the best coating? We wanted to develop the best recipe for pan-fried chicken we could and then test it against deep-fried chicken.

We've always thought pan-frying chicken to be a time-consuming project, mainly because it had to be cooked in two batches. We discovered, though, that if the bird is small enough and the pan big enough, you can fry a whole chicken at one time. Birds weighing 2½ to 3 pounds work best, but these smaller birds are often not easy to find. Call your butcher or grocery meat department to check on availability.

We wanted to like the 13⅜-inch cast-iron skillet we had specially purchased for this fried chicken, because it was large enough to hold all the pieces of chicken in one frying. But we soon found that its size was a handicap because the perimeter of the pan sat off the burner. Getting the fat temperature right for frying chicken around the edge of the pan meant scorching the chicken in the center, while properly cooking the chicken in the center of the pan meant blond-skinned, greasy chicken around the edges. The skillet we came to prefer was a 12-inch cast-iron skillet (a modest $15 investment), though any heavy-bottomed 12-inch skillet would work.

Of all the stages—buying, butchering, seasoning, coating, and frying—we found the greatest recipe diversity in the soaking period. After testing 13 different soaking methods, we discovered that dairy-soaked chicken displayed the most beautifully textured and richly colored skin.

This is not surprising. Since milk is thicker than water, dairy-based soaking liquids tend to cling better to the slippery, raw chicken parts, which, in turn, attract more flour during dredging. The end result is a thick, even coating. Lactose, the sugar found in milk, caused the chicken to develop a deep mahogany color during frying. Heavy cream also coated the chicken beautifully, but the resulting fried chicken was too rich. The milk and lemon juice combination gave the chicken a clean, heightened flavor, but since it was thinner it didn't adhere as well and offered a less impressive coat. The buttermilk, on the other hand, was as viscous as cream and as tangy as the milk with lemon juice, with none of the lia-

bilities. This became our favorite soaking medium.

With the soaking issue resolved, we moved on to coatings. We tried all-purpose flour, self-rising flour, cornmeal, cornstarch, whole-wheat flour, corn flour, bread crumbs, and various combinations of these ingredients. Plain all-purpose flour produced the best crust, nicely browned and crisp.

Several recipes recommended drying the chicken on a rack for a couple of hours to allow the flour to adhere. We found that this extra step produced a brittle, thin, shell-like crust, not unpleasant but certainly not worth the wait. On the other hand, if you

CUTTING UP A CHICKEN

Every cook should know how to cut a chicken into eight parts—two wings, two thighs, two drumsticks, and two breasts. Buying a whole chicken is much cheaper than buying parts. In addition, buying chicken parts restricts your choices at the supermarket. In tastings, we consistently have preferred premium chickens—organic, free-range, or kosher birds—to mass-market brands. Generally, premium chickens are only sold whole. If you buy chicken parts, they are likely to have come from a lower-quality bird.

Cutting up a whole chicken takes less than five minutes. You must own a sharp chef's knife, and we like to use poultry shears to separate the back from the breast (but you can also complete this step with a chef's knife). The cook who takes the time to butcher a chicken at home is rewarded with backs that can be frozen and used to make stock.

1. With a sharp chef's knife, cut through the skin around the leg where it attaches to the breast.

2. Using both hands, pop the leg out of its socket.

3. Use your chef's knife to cut through the flesh and skin to detach the leg from the body.

4. A line of fat separates the thigh and drumstick. Cut through the joint at this point. Repeat steps 1 through 4 with the other leg.

5. Bend the wing out from the breast and cut to remove the wing. Repeat with the other wing.

6. Using poultry shears, cut down along the ribs between the back and the breast to totally separate the back from the breast.

7. Place a chef's knife directly on the breast bone, then apply pressure to cut through the bone and separate the breast into two halves.

want to coat your chicken and let it sit for a couple of hours before frying, it certainly won't hurt it.

We were also intent on finding the best way to get the coating on the chicken. We compared dredging the chicken parts in a flour-filled pie tin to shaking the chicken and flour in a brown paper bag. After only one try with each, we quickly declared the bag method the winner in the categories of both consistency of coating and ease of cleanup. We have to add, however, that after shaking a thin dusting of flour over the kitchen floor and watching heavy chicken parts threaten to break the bag, we quickly switched to a double brown bag.

We tested every conceivable fat and combination of fats for frying, and found less dramatic results in this area. Lard produced gorgeous, deeply tanned chicken, but we disliked the heavy, porky smell it produced during frying. Also, while this fat seemed to enforce and enhance the chicken's meatiness, it overpowered the skin and crust. We appreciated its rich, heavy taste, but tired of it after only a few bites. Even when we cut the lard with shortening, the crust remained tainted with a distinctive lard flavor.

Chicken fried in a combination of butter and vegetable oil was sweet and mild, but too rich. It was also lighter in color than any of the other chickens we fried, and the fat foamed nonstop during frying. This combination is also more perishable, making it difficult to store and use again, as can be done with other fats. Plain vegetable oil worked only relatively well; the resulting chicken, although pleasant and fast-food-like, was a bit splotchy.

Our overall preference turned out to be straight shortening. Chicken fried in this medium had a consistent mahogany color, and shortening also turned out to be the most odor-free of all the fats. A few recipes called for flavoring the shortening with bacon drippings. We tried this but were unimpressed. Although we could distinctly smell bacon as the chicken was frying, we could barely identify it during tasting.

It was now time to test pan-frying against deep-frying. We fried chicken both ways, and the results were surprisingly clear: pan-frying produces superior fried chicken. Deep-fried chicken, simultaneously attacked on all sides by hot oil, quickly develops a brittle, protective shell right down to the meat. Pan-fried chicken, on the other hand, is more complex.

It has the same crunchy exterior, but when the pan is covered, the half of the meat not submerged in oil is exposed to a sort of steaming process. This creates a moist sublayer that offers a nice contrast to the crisp exterior.

Although we liked the chicken cooked in a covered pan, we wondered if the lid was really necessary, so we cooked the chicken both with and without the lid. The point of covering the pan during frying is to trap moisture; the chicken we left uncovered during the entire frying time did not develop the soft undercoating we came to like. Yet we found that covering the chicken during the entire process created too much steam, leaving the coating too soft. In some cases the oversteaming caused the skin to separate from the meat and fall into the hot oil. Covering the chicken during the first half of the cooking time allows the chicken to steam and fry; leaving it uncovered for the second half keeps the already browned side from getting soggy.

Chicken drained on paper towels gets soggy faster than chicken drained on a paper bag, but both were inferior to a wire rack set over a jelly-roll pan. The pan and wire rack mimic the draining system used by many fast-food restaurants. In the prefrying stage, the rack offers the ideal resting place for the coated chicken. After frying, the same rack (which has been washed in hot soapy water and dried) keeps the chicken grease-free and crisp. The pan and rack sit safely on a stovetop as well as in a warm oven—not true for either paper towels or bags.

~

Buttermilk Fried Chicken
SERVES 4

We find it best to cut each breast piece in half crosswise so that the breasts are not so large and will cook through at the same rate as the other parts. The result is 10 pieces—two wings, two thighs, two drumsticks, and four breast pieces.

1	whole chicken (2½ to 3 pounds), cut into 8 pieces (see illustrations on page 145), breast pieces halved crosswise
1½	cups buttermilk
	Salt and ground black pepper
2	cups all-purpose flour
3–4	cups vegetable shortening for frying

1. Place chicken pieces in a gallon-sized zipper-lock bag. Mix buttermilk with 1 teaspoon salt and ½ teaspoon pepper. Pour mixture over chicken; seal bag, then refrigerate for at least 2 hours and up to 24 hours.

2. Measure flour, 1 teaspoon salt, and ½ teaspoon pepper into a large double brown paper bag; shake to combine. Drop half of chicken pieces into flour mixture and shake thoroughly to completely coat with flour. Remove chicken from bag, shaking excess flour from each piece. Place coated chicken pieces on a large wire rack set over a jelly-roll pan until ready to fry. Repeat coating with remaining chicken pieces.

3. Meanwhile, spoon enough shortening to measure ½ inch deep into a 12-inch skillet; heat to 350 degrees. Place chicken pieces, skin side down, into hot oil; cover with lid or cookie sheet and cook for 5 minutes. Lift chicken pieces with tongs to make sure chicken is frying evenly; rearrange if some pieces are browning faster than others. Cover again and continue cooking until chicken pieces are evenly browned, about 5 minutes longer. (Be sure oil continues to bubble; oil temperature at this point should be between 250 and 300 degrees, and should be maintained at this level until chicken is done.) Turn chicken over with tongs and cook, uncovered, until chicken is browned all over, 10 to 12 minutes longer. Remove chicken from skillet with tongs and return to wire rack set over jelly-roll pan.

➤ VARIATION
Skinless Fried Chicken

We fried three skinless chickens, one simply dusted with seasoned flour; one dipped in flour, then buttermilk, then back in flour; and finally one simply soaked in buttermilk, then dipped in flour, as in the recipe for Buttermilk Fried Chicken. The meat of the simple flour-coated chicken fried up leathery; there just wasn't enough coating to protect the meat from the boiling oil. The flour-buttermilk-flour treatment formed a tough, leathery protective coating. Although it adhered to the chicken, it ballooned during frying and separated from the meat. We determined that simply coating the buttermilk-soaked chicken with flour provided just the right coating and protection for the skinned meat. Many of those participating in taste tests did not detect the missing skin, and those who noticed didn't really miss it.

Follow recipe for Buttermilk Fried Chicken, removing skin from each piece before soaking it in buttermilk.

SCIENCE: Frying in Vegetable Shortening
Remember the old commercial: "It all comes back but one tablespoon"? We put this claim to the test and found it to be absolutely true. We heated three cups of fat to 350 degrees in a 12-inch skillet, pan-fried a whole chicken, and poured back almost exactly three cups of fat after frying. We conducted the test a number of times to confirm our findings, and each time we ended up with virtually the same amount of fat before and after.

If the water in the food you are frying is kept above the boiling point (212 degrees), the outward pressure of the escaping water vapor keeps oil from soaking into the food. If the frying oil is not hot enough, on the other hand, it will seep into the food, making it greasy. The key is to start cooking with the oil hot enough (we found that 350 degrees worked well) so that you maintain a temperature (between 250 and 300 degrees) that keeps the moisture in the food, in essence, boiling.

We discovered another interesting thing about shortening in the course of frying dozens of chickens—it's far less likely to make your kitchen smell greasy. Shortening is a much more carefully refined fat than vegetable oil. Since it has to be good enough for baking, it is essential that it be unflavored and odorless. Many of the odor-causing compounds are refined out of shortening. We also noticed that the chicken fried in vegetable oil frequently fried up a bit spotty compared with the consistently colored shortening-fried chicken. This again may be the result of the more intense refinement that shortening undergoes.

OVEN-FRIED CHICKEN
WE'VE ALWAYS THOUGHT OF OVEN-FRIED chicken as ersatz fried chicken—only for those who were afraid to mess up their kitchen or consume too much fat or who had to cook for a large crowd. Although there was certainly nothing wrong with this chicken, there often wasn't a lot that was right with it, either. Depending on the liquid or crumb coating, this chicken could be bland, soggy, rubbery-skinned, greasy, artificially flavored, dry, or crumbly. Was it possible, we wondered, to make oven-fried chicken that had real crunch and good flavor, a quick weeknight alternative to the real thing?

After looking at scores of recipes, it seemed that good oven-fried chicken depends on the right flavorings, oven temperature, and baking time. But most crucial of all are the coatings—both the moist one that helps the crumbs stick and the dry one that provides texture and crunch.

Since the moist coating comes first, we started there. A review of oven-fried chicken recipes revealed that this first coat could be as lean as water or milk, as rich as cream or butter, and as thick as mayonnaise, yogurt, or even sour cream. Before testing, we assumed this wet dunk did little more than help the crumbs adhere to the chicken. After testing, however, it became clear that this initial coat plays a larger role. A good first coat, we discovered, should offer flavor, season the meat without tasting too obvious, attract the right proportion of crumbs to form an impressive uniform crust, and, finally, help the crust stay crunchy during baking.

To find the best moist coating, we baked 13 drumsticks. Keeping the dry coating constant while varying the moist coating: water, whole milk, evaporated milk, cream, buttermilk, yogurt, sour cream, milk beaten with egg, egg beaten with lemon juice, and egg with Dijon mustard. In addition, we tried legs coated with ranch dressing, mayonnaise, and butter.

Since many oven-fried chicken recipes start by rolling chicken parts in butter, we thought the fat coatings would perform well. Not so. All of them— butter, mayonnaise, and ranch dressing—created a slick surface that prevented the crumbs from adhering properly. In addition, none of the fats did anything to crisp up the crumbs.

With the exception of buttermilk and evaporated milk, moreover, none of the dairy coatings impressed us. Buttermilk and evaporated milk did attract decent crusts and give a subtle flavor dimension to the chicken, but they didn't result in the crispness we wanted.

The egg beaten with lemon did result in a crisp coating. Unfortunately, it also contributed too much lemon flavor, with an overcooked egg aftertaste. But a change of just one ingredient made all the difference. Chicken coated with beaten egg and Dijon mustard was our favorite. This not-too-thick, not-too-thin moistener not only attracted a uniform, impressive layer of crumbs, it also gave the meat a wonderfully subtle flavor. Unlike many of the wet coatings, which made the crumbs either soggy or barely crisp, this one took the crumbs to an almost crunchy level.

For consistency, we had used dry breadcrumbs in all of the moist coating tests, but we constantly remarked on their lackluster texture and flavor. Now it was time to put those dry breadcrumbs to the test. Considering that there's an oven-fried chicken recipe on the back of many boxes of crackers and most good-for-you cereals, we had scores of options. We started with 20 dry coatings or combinations, all from published recipes.

After baking and tasting them all, there wasn't a single one we thought was perfect. Of the cereal coatings, cornflakes made the best, offering good color and crunch but too much sweet corn flavor for our taste. Ditto for bran flakes, but its distinct flavor was even more pronounced. Unprocessed bran looked like kitty litter, while Grape-Nuts looked (worse) like hamster food. Oatmeal tasted raw and chewy.

Crackers didn't work, either. Both saltines and Ritz were too soft; the Ritz, in addition, were too sweet. Cracker meal delivered a bland blond shell. In the bread department, stuffing mix scored well in crunch but struck out in flavor. Fresh bread crumbs, on the other hand, tasted great but lacked the crunch we had come to like. The addition of Parmesan cheese did nothing to improve the texture.

The meals and flours, as to be expected, did not show well. Cornmeal tasted raw, and it chipped off the chicken like flecks of old paint. Our grocery store's house brand of Shake 'n Bake was vile, tasting of liquid smoke and bad hot dogs. To be fair, we tried the real thing, but it was only a step up from bad.

Although this first round of tests did not produce a strong winner, it did help us to clarify what it was that we wanted—a coating that was crunchy (not just crisp) and flavorful (but not artificial tasting) and that baked up a rich copper brown.

With a clear ideal in mind, we found a whole new range of coating possibilities in the specialty/international cracker section of my grocery store. Melba toast, pain grillé (French crisp toast), Swedish crisps, lavash (crisp flat bread), two varieties of bread sticks, two brands of bagel chips, Italian toasts, and pita chips presented new options. We also located some almost plain croutons and dry bread cubes for stuffing.

This series of tests delivered oven-fried chicken that was much closer to our ideal. Many of the coatings were good but not great, offering good flavor or texture or color, but only one was consistently good. The rather surprising winner, it turned out, was Melba toast. It scored the best in all three major categories—texture, flavor, and color.

Over the course of testing, we found that we much preferred legs and thighs to breasts because they don't dry out as quickly. For chicken breast lovers, however, egg and mustard/Melba toast coatings work well. We also discovered that we didn't like the skin on oven-fried chicken. Unlike fried chicken, in which hot oil causes the fat to render and the skin to crisp up, oven heat simply softens the skin and makes it rubbery. We remove the skin before coating the pieces.

Oven temperature was a simple matter. We started baking at 400 degrees, and all our chicken parts were cooked through and rich golden brown in about 40 minutes. As a check, we baked one batch at 375 degrees and another at 425 degrees. At the lower oven temperature the chicken was too blond, and at the higher oven temperature the chicken looked and tasted overly brown by the time it was done.

A wire rack set over a foil-covered jelly-roll or shallow baking pan allows heat to circulate around the chicken during baking, resulting in crisp chicken without turning. The foil, of course, protects the pan, making cleanup a breeze.

Oven-Fried Chicken

SERVES 4

For those who like breast meat, use a whole cut-up chicken instead of drumsticks and thighs. To make Melba toast crumbs, place the toasts in a heavy-duty plastic freezer bag, seal, and pound with a meat pounder or other heavy blunt object. Leave some crumbs in the mixture the size of pebbles, but most should resemble coarse sand. Be careful not to over-crush the Melba toast; crumbs that are too fine will leave the chicken wanting in crunchiness. If you own a spray bottle for oil (see below), skip the step of tossing the Melba toast crumbs in oil. Instead, once the chicken is coated with crumbs, spray the pieces evenly with oil.

¼	cup vegetable oil
1	box (about 5 ounces) plain Melba toast, crushed (see above)
2	large eggs
1	tablespoon Dijon mustard
1	teaspoon dried thyme
¾	teaspoon salt
½	teaspoon ground black pepper
½	teaspoon dried oregano
¼	teaspoon garlic powder
¼	teaspoon cayenne (optional)
4	whole chicken legs, separated into drumsticks and thighs, skin removed, and patted dry with paper towels

1. Adjust oven rack to upper-middle position and

EQUIPMENT: Oil Misters

When challenged to find the most effective way to evenly coat the chicken pieces with oil, we tested four different oil sprayers: Quick-Mist and Misto (two of the newer air-pumped sprayers), a plastic spray bottle, and vegetable oil Pam. All the refillable sprayers were filled with vegetable oil.

The Quick-Mist fared the best. Only 15 pumps were necessary to create the pressure needed to keep the oil at a constant spray. The mist of oil created was the finest, making it easy to coat the chicken evenly. Conveniently, the Quick-Mist also held a mist for the longest period of time, making the task of pumping less repetitive. Pam came in a distant second. While no pumping is necessary, the spray produced tended to be very concentrated in the center, with splatters of oil on the outside.

The Misto, the other air-pumped sprayer we tested, gave us results that were surprisingly different from the Quick-Mist. While the number of pumps required to pressurize the sprayer was the same, the spray did not last as long, requiring more frequent pumping. It was also difficult to produce a fine mist, and once again the spray was concentrated in the center and splotched on the outside.

The worst of the bunch was the ordinary spray bottle. The spray was the most uneven of all, and to ensure coverage we had to overspray. The constant squeezing of the bottle caused our hands to fatigue quickly, and the nozzle tip gave us little control of the mist.

heat oven to 400 degrees. Line sheet pan with foil and set large flat wire rack over sheet pan.

2. Drizzle vegetable oil over Melba toast crumbs in a shallow dish or pie plate; toss well to coat. Mix eggs, mustard, thyme, salt, pepper, oregano, garlic powder, and optional cayenne with a fork in a second shallow dish or pie plate.

3. Working one piece at a time, coat chicken on both sides with egg mixture. Set chicken in Melba crumbs, sprinkle crumbs over chicken, and press to coat. Turn chicken over and repeat on other side. Gently shake off excess and place on rack. Bake until chicken is deep nutty brown and juices run clear, about 40 minutes.

BUTTERFLIED CHICKEN

REMOVING THE BACKBONE FROM A WHOLE chicken—a process known as butterflying—may seem like an unnecessary and time-consuming process. But we have found that this relatively quick and simple procedure, because it leaves the bird with a more even thickness, provides many benefits.

A flattened three-pound chicken cooks in half an hour or less, versus 55 minutes for a traditionally roasted bird. In addition, since the breast isn't sticking out exposed to the heat while the legs are tucked under away from it, all the parts of a flattened bird get done at the same time. Finally, unlike a whole roasted chicken, the butterfly cut is a breeze to separate into sections. One cut down the breast with the kitchen shears, a quick snip of the skin holding the legs, and the job is done.

Won over by the virtues of this technique, we set out to test various methods by which butterflied chicken could be cooked. Our purpose was to work out the kinks in each method and determine if there were some general rules that applied to all of them.

We began our research with the butterflying technique itself. To find out if the chicken should be split at the breast or the back, we prepared one each way for roasting. From the start, the breast-split chicken looked unnatural. The back, now the center of the bird, was flanked by two towering chicken breasts. During cooking, the bird bowed and the breasts overshadowed the back, which caused the juices to puddle in the middle and prevented the chicken from browning evenly. The bird split down the back was much more attractive; it stayed flat during cooking and browned evenly.

We also discovered that tucking the chicken legs under was worth the effort, if only for visual appeal. This was particularly true for the roasted and broiled chicken, where holding the legs in place with weights was not possible. Chickens cooked with untucked legs tended to bow and warp. In any case, tucking the chicken legs makes the presentation nicer. Even the weighted birds looked more attractive with tucked legs.

We thought pounding the chicken might decrease cooking time, but it made no noticeable difference. However, it was easier to weight a chicken that had been pounded to a uniform thickness. We also liked the look of the really flattened chicken. We recommend buying a mallet with a flat side for this purpose, but whatever tool you use, make sure it is has a smooth face. A rough-textured mallet will make a mess of things.

Seasoning the outside of the chicken with herbs or garlic, regardless of the cooking method, proved to be pointless. Because each technique required high heat, the herbs charred and the garlic burned. But butterflied chickens are especially easy to season under the skin. Since the backs had been removed, access to the legs and thighs was easy. In fact, stuffing the seasoning under the skin worked beautifully for all the cooking techniques. We included salt and pepper in the seasoning mixture, and also started by adding a bit of oil or butter, but soon realized that this wasn't necessary. Garlic gave the seasoning mixture the pasty quality necessary for easy spreading. And once the cooking process began, there was enough fat from the skin and juice from the meat to moisten and transport the flavorings.

Roasting is the simplest of the cooking methods for butterflied chicken. Once the chicken is butchered (and rubbed with seasonings, if you like), it goes in the oven, and you can forget about it until it's done.

Many of the recipes for grilling, broiling, and sautéing butterflied chicken were a bit more complicated, calling for turning the chicken several times. If possible, we wanted to turn the bird just once (especially the weighted birds).

Cooking chicken with only one turn in a skillet was a bit tricky. Our first attempts produced skin that was too dark and meat that was too pink near the bone. Two things overcame these problems. First, not heating the skillet too high before putting in the chicken (it has, after all, 30 minutes to brown); and second, reducing the heat from medium-high to a strong medium, which allowed the chicken to cook through before it became too brown.

We also decided to explore the effect of weighting the birds during cooking, so we cooked two chickens—one weighted, the other simply covered. The weighted chicken browned more evenly and got done a few minutes faster than the unweighted bird.

Most recipes recommended using bricks or a large can to weight the bird. But there had to be a better solution than scrounging the basement for dirty bricks or searching the cabinets for 10 pounds of cans. We found we could use a pot of water to weight the cooking chicken. We used a soup kettle with a diameter slightly smaller than the skillet, covered its bottom with foil to protect it from spattering fat, and filled it with five quarts of water (about 10 pounds). Not only was the soup kettle easier to find than bricks or cans, but it was simple to use. When it came time to turn the chicken, we just lifted the pot by its handles, flipped the bird, and returned the pot to its spot.

Unless you have an old pot that you don't mind getting smoke-damaged, you'll have to resort to bricks or stones for grilling. We used a beat-up jelly-roll pan and two bricks. Since the chicken was to cook over direct heat, we thought grease fires might be a problem, but we cooked a half dozen chickens this way without a single flare-up. We suspect the combination of the grill lid and the jelly-roll pan prevented oxygen from feeding the fire. As with the sautéing, we found that one turn was enough—12 minutes breast side up, and about 15 minutes breast side down produced a stunning-looking chicken.

Broiling is another method that took some fine-tuning. Our first attempts set off smoke alarms all over the place. After experimenting, we found that the key to good chicken broiling is oven rack position. The chicken must be far enough from the heating element to cook through without burning, which means the top of the chicken must be about 8 inches from the heat source (so the oven rack should be about 12 inches away to take into account broiler pan height).

As with grilling and sautéing, only one turn is necessary. If you want a bread-crumb or Parmesan cheese coating, though, you do have to give it one more flip to sprinkle them on and brown them.

The following recipes provide an example of each cooking technique, but they're just to get you started. Virtually any chicken recipe (excluding boneless, skinless chicken breast) can be tailored to one of these cooking methods.

Charcoal-Grilled Butterflied Chicken with Rosemary, Lemon, and Garlic
SERVES 4

We tested this recipe several times with a 3-pound (gross weight) chicken. Although grilling conditions vary, each time we cooked the chicken, it was done in less than a half hour—12 minutes on the skin side and 12 to 15 minutes on the other side. Avoid checking the chicken except when turning, or the coals will cool, increasing the grilling time. Besides, cooking a chicken this way is like grilling a steak—one turn should do it.

1	teaspoon minced zest from ½ lemon
1	teaspoon minced fresh rosemary
1	large clove garlic, minced
½	teaspoon salt
¼	teaspoon ground black pepper
1	3-pound chicken, butterflied (see illustrations on page 153)
3	tablespoons juice from 1 lemon
3	tablespoons extra-virgin olive oil

1. Mix lemon zest, rosemary, garlic, salt, and pepper in small bowl. Rub this paste under skin. Place chicken in gallon-sized zipper-lock bag with lemon juice and olive oil. Seal and refrigerate from 2 to 24 hours; return to room temperature before cooking.

2. Build a single-level fire (see page 258). Set grill rack in place, cover grill with lid, and let rack heat up, about 5 minutes.

3. Place chicken, skin side down, on grill rack. Set a jelly-roll or other flat pan on top of chicken; put 2 bricks in jelly-roll pan. Cover and grill until chicken skin is deep brown and shows grill marks, about 12 minutes. Turn chicken with tongs. Replace jelly-roll

pan, bricks, and grill lid, and continue cooking until chicken juices run clear, about 15 minutes more.

4. Remove chicken from grill; cover with foil and let rest 10 to 15 minutes. To carve, use kitchen shears to cut along breastbone and split chicken in half. Snip skin to separate each leg and thigh portion from each breast and wing portion. Serve.

➤ VARIATION

Gas-Grilled Butterflied Chicken with Rosemary, Lemon, and Garlic

Follow recipe for Charcoal-Grilled Butterflied Chicken, making the following changes: Turn all burners to high and preheat with lid down until very hot, about 15 minutes. Turn all burners to medium. Grill as directed in charcoal recipe.

Broiled Butterflied Chicken with Parmesan, Lemon, and Red Pepper Flakes
SERVES 4

1	teaspoon minced zest from ½ lemon
1	large garlic clove, minced
	Salt and ground black pepper
¼	teaspoon hot red pepper flakes
1	3-pound chicken, butterflied (see illustrations on page 153)
1	teaspoon vegetable oil
2	tablespoons grated Parmesan cheese
1	tablespoon dried bread crumbs

1. Mix lemon zest, garlic, ½ teaspoon salt, and red pepper flakes in small bowl. Rub this paste under skin. Transfer chicken to broiler pan, skin side up; brush with oil and lightly season with salt and pepper; let stand while broiler heats. Mix cheese and bread crumbs; set aside.

2. Adjust oven rack so that chicken is a minimum of 8 inches from heating element. Broil chicken until skin is rich brown, about 12 minutes. Turn chicken over; continue to broil until juices run clear, about 15 minutes longer. Remove from oven, turn skin side up, brush with pan drippings, then sprinkle with cheese mixture. Return to oven; broil until topping turns golden brown, about 3 minutes longer.

3. Remove chicken from oven, cover with foil, and let rest 10 to 15 minutes. To carve, use kitchen shears to cut along breastbone and split chicken in half. Snip skin to separate each leg and thigh portion from each breast and wing portion. Serve.

Sautéed Butterflied Chicken with Mushroom-Sage Pan Sauce
SERVES 4

4	teaspoons minced fresh sage
1	medium garlic clove, minced
	Salt and ground black pepper
1	3-pound chicken, butterflied (see illustrations on page 153)
1	tablespoon vegetable oil
2	medium shallots, minced
5	ounces assorted wild mushrooms, sliced (about 2 cups)
2	tablespoons dry vermouth
½	cup chicken stock or low-sodium canned broth
1	tablespoon unsalted butter

1. Mix 2 teaspoons of the sage, the minced garlic, ½ teaspoon salt, and ¼ teaspoon pepper in small bowl. Rub this paste under skin. Lightly season chicken with salt and pepper. Let stand at room temperature about 15 minutes to allow flavors to meld.

2. Heat oil in an 11- or 12-inch sauté pan. Cover bottom of soup kettle that has a diameter slightly smaller than sauté pan with foil and fill with 5 quarts water. Lay chicken, skin side down, in sauté pan. Set kettle on top to hold flat; cook over strong medium heat until skin is nicely browned, about 12 minutes. Remove soup kettle; turn chicken skin side up. Replace kettle and continue cooking until juices run clear, about 18 minutes. Transfer chicken to plate; cover with foil while making sauce.

3. Remove all but 1 tablespoon fat from pan; return pan to burner and increase heat to medium-high. Add shallots; sauté until softened, about 2 minutes. Add mushrooms; sauté until juices release and mushrooms soften, about 2 minutes. Add vermouth; cook until liquid has almost evaporated, about 1 minute. Add chicken stock; simmer until thickened,

about 2 minutes. Stir in remaining sage. Remove from heat and swirl in butter. To carve, use kitchen shears to cut along breastbone and split chicken in half. Snip skin to separate each leg and thigh portion from each breast and wing portion. Serve with pan sauce.

Roast Butterflied Chicken with Tarragon–Mustard Pan Sauce

SERVES 4

Roasting the chicken in an ovenproof sauté pan makes it easier to make a stove-top sauce right in the cooking pan. If you don't have an ovenproof sauté pan, you can substitute a roasting pan, using two burners to make the sauce.

2	teaspoons minced fresh tarragon leaves
1	medium garlic clove, minced
	Salt and ground black pepper
1	3-pound chicken, butterflied (see illustrations below)
1	teaspoon vegetable oil

1	cup chicken stock or low-sodium canned broth
1	tablespoon Dijon mustard
1	tablespoon unsalted butter, softened

1. Mix tarragon, garlic, ½ teaspoon salt, and ¼ teaspoon pepper in small bowl. Rub this paste under skin. Heat oven to 500 degrees. Transfer chicken to a large ovenproof sauté pan, skin side up; rub with oil and lightly season with salt and pepper. Let stand at room temperature while oven heats.

2. Roast chicken until skin is nicely browned and juices run clear, about 30 minutes. Transfer to plate, cover with foil, and let rest while making sauce.

3. Spoon off all fat from sauté pan. Place pan on burner set at medium-high; add stock and simmer until reduced by half, scraping up drippings that have stuck to bottom, 3 to 4 minutes. Whisk in mustard, then swirl in butter. To carve, use kitchen shears to cut along breastbone and split in chicken half. Snip skin to separate each leg and thigh portion from each breast and wing portion. Serve with pan sauce.

BUTTERFLYING CHICKEN

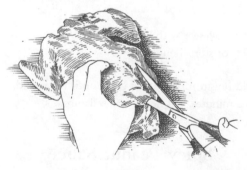

1. With the breast side down and the tail of the chicken facing you, use kitchen shears to cut along one side of the backbone down its entire length.

2. With the breast side still down, turn the neck end to face you and cut along the other side of the backbone and remove it.

3. Turn the chicken breast side up; open the chicken out on the work surface. Use the palm of your hand to flatten it.

4. Make half-inch slits on either side of each breast about 1 inch from the tip; tuck the legs into these openings.

5. Use the smooth face of a mallet to pound the chicken into an approximately even thickness.

GRILLED CHICKEN WINGS

CHICKEN WINGS ARE BEST COOKED ON THE grill so that their fat is rendered and falls away onto the coals. Cooked in the oven, the wings rest in their own fat and will turn out flabby. But grill wings incorrectly and you have greasy meat, surrounded by a charred, rubbery, thick coating of skin. We wanted to develop a grilling technique that was foolproof, that would produce wings with crisp, thin, caramelized skin, tender and moist meat, and smoky grilled flavor that was well-seasoned throughout. Furthermore, we wanted it to be eater-friendly without being tedious or time-consuming.

Wings are made up of three parts—the meaty, drumstick-like portion that is closest to the breast section of the bird; the two-boned center portion that is surrounded by a band of meat and skin; and the small, almost meatless wingtip. After cutting and grilling wings several different ways, we concluded that wingtips are not worth grilling. They offer almost no meat and char long before the other two parts are even close to being cooked through.

Wingtips discarded, we pushed the meat up the bones of the separated meatier parts to replicate the lollipop-shaped wings favored by traditional chefs. We felt it took too much time and effort. So we decided that the best method for preparing wings is to divide the usable two portions at the joint. The pieces are small enough to be eaten as finger food, and are less awkward to eat than a whole wing.

Our first rounds of grilling tests were disappointing. Grilling the wings directly over the coals at temperatures ranging from high heat to low heat produced wings that were mediocre at best. Those cooked over medium-high and high heat charred quickly, and the skin remained thick and tough. Grilling the wings over medium and medium-low heat produced better wings; the skin was crisper and thinner, but the wings still lacked the great caramelized crust that we desired.

DIPPING SAUCES FOR CHICKEN WINGS

Serve grilled wings with one of the following sauces or with barbecue sauce, either homemade (see page 272) or store-bought.

Hoisin Sesame Dipping Sauce
MAKES ENOUGH FOR 12 WINGS

- 2   tablespoons hoisin sauce
- 1   tablespoon rice wine vinegar
- 1   tablespoon soy sauce
- 1   teaspoon Asian sesame oil
- 1   tablespoon vegetable oil
- 2   tablespoons minced fresh gingerroot
- 2   medium garlic cloves, minced
- 2   tablespoons minced fresh cilantro leaves

1. Mix together hoisin sauce, vinegar, soy sauce, sesame oil, and 2 tablespoons water.

2. Heat vegetable oil in small saucepan over medium heat. Add ginger and garlic and sauté until fragrant but not browned, about 30 seconds. Add hoisin mixture and cook until thickened, 1 to 2 minutes. Off heat, stir in cilantro.

Spicy Peanut Sauce
MAKES ENOUGH FOR 12 WINGS

- 5   tablespoons creamy peanut butter
- 2   tablespoons fish sauce
- 2   tablespoons lime juice
- 1/4 cup unsweetened coconut milk
- 1   tablespoon honey
- 1   tablespoon minced fresh gingerroot
- 2   medium garlic cloves, minced
- 1/2 teaspoon hot red pepper flakes
- 1   teaspoon curry powder (optional)

Combine ingredients in blender until smooth.

It was at this point that we tried the indirect heat method, that is, building a fire on one half of the grill, placing the meat on the opposite side, then covering until cooked through. The result was a nicely moist interior, but the skin was flaccid and had a very unappealing grayish tint.

Gathering information from these initial tests, we concluded that a more sophisticated grilling technique was necessary, perhaps even a second method of cooking was in order. We tried blanching the wings for various amounts of time before throwing them on the grill for crisping and browning, but this technique, while producing thinner, crisper skin, also yielded wings with less flavor and drier meat. It also was time-consuming and added extra clean-up.

So far, the best wings were those cooked directly over the coals at a medium-low heat level (a single layer of charcoal). Although they were acceptable, we felt that the texture and flavor would be greatly improved with a crisper, darker, exterior. At this point we decided to try a two-level fire. We grilled the chicken wings using two different methods. One batch was browned over medium-high heat and then moved to the other side of the grill to continue cooking slowly, while the other was started on medium-low to cook low and slow and then moved to medium-high heat to get a final quick crisping and browning. While both were good, the one cooked over medium-low heat and then moved to medium-high heat was superior. Wings cooked using this method rendered more fat from the skin, resulting in a thin, delicate crust.

Prompted by past experience, we felt that brining might improve the flavor as well as the texture of our chicken wings. We used a brining solution in which equal parts by volume of sugar and kosher salt are added to water. Tasting the wings as they came off of the grill, we happily discovered that the brined chicken wings were not only tasty and well-seasoned throughout but that brining added several unexpected bonuses. The brined chicken meat was noticeably plumper before grilling and more tender after cooking, and the wings had also developed a crisper, more caramelized skin than those that had not been brined.

Charcoal-Grilled Chicken Wings

SERVES 4 TO 6

Chicken wings are made up of three parts—the meaty, drumstick-like portion that is closest to the breast section of the bird; the two-boned center portion that is surrounded by a band of meat and skin; and the small, almost meatless wingtip. Only the two meaty sections are worth eating. Hack off the wing tips with a chef's knife or cleaver; then cut through the remaining joint to separate the two meaty sections. Make sure your grill is large enough to hold all the wings over roughly one-half of the rack surface, and brine the wings while the grill fire heats up to save time. Serve the wings as is, with a squeeze of lemon or lime, or with one of the sauce recipes on page 154.

¾	cup kosher salt or 6 tablespoons table salt
¾	cup sugar
12	whole chicken wings (about 2½ pounds), wingtips discarded and then separated at the remaining joint into 2 pieces
	Ground black pepper

1. In gallon-sized zipper-lock plastic bag, dissolve salt and sugar in 1 quart water. Add chicken; press out as much air as possible from bag and seal; refrigerate until fully seasoned, 30 minutes. Remove from brine, rinse well under running water, dry thoroughly with paper towels, and season with pepper.

2. Meanwhile, build a two-level fire (see page 258). Set grill rack in place, cover grill with lid, and let rack heat up, about 5 minutes.

3. Grill chicken pieces over lower-heat area (with single layer of coals), turning once, until color is light spotty brown, skin has thinned, and fat has rendered, 8 to 10 minutes. Using tongs, move chicken pieces to high-heat side of grill; grill, turning constantly to prevent charring, until wings are dark spotty brown and skin has crisped, 2 to 3 minutes longer. Transfer to serving platter and serve immediately.

➤ VARIATION

Gas-Grilled Chicken Wings

Follow recipe for Charcoal-Grilled Chicken Wings through step 1. Turn all burners to high and preheat with lid down until very hot, about 15 minutes.

Leave one burner on high and turn other burner(s) to medium. Grill as in charcoal recipe but with lid down, placing wings first over cooler part of grill and then sliding wings to hotter part of the grill to crisp them up.

CHICKEN POT PIE

MOST EVERYONE LOVES A GOOD CHICKEN pot pie, though few seem to have the time or energy to make one. Not surprising. Like a lot of satisfying dishes, traditional pot pie takes time. Before the pie even makes it to the oven, the cook must poach a chicken, take the meat off the bone and cut it up, strain the broth, prepare and blanch vegetables, make a sauce, and mix and roll out biscuit or pie dough.

Given the many time-consuming steps it can take to make a pot pie, our goal was to make the best one we could as quickly as possible. Pot pie, after all, is supper food.

Our experiences with making pot pie also made us aware of two other difficulties. First, the vegetables tend to overcook. A filling that is chock-full of bright, fresh vegetables going into the oven looks completely different after 40 minutes of high-heat baking under a blanket of dough. Carrots become mushy and pumpkin-colored, while peas and fresh herbs fade from fresh spring to drab green. We wanted to preserve the vegetables' color as long as it didn't require any unnatural acts to do so.

We had also made a number of pot pies that were too juicy. Before baking, the filling was thick and creamy. When cut into after baking, however, the pie looked like chicken soup en croute. Although we wanted the pie moist and saucy, we also wanted it thick enough to eat with a fork.

We began by determining the best way to cook the chicken. In addition to making pies with roast chicken and poached chicken, we steamed and roasted whole chickens and braised chicken parts.

Steaming the chicken was time-consuming, requiring about one hour, and the steaming liquid didn't make a strong enough broth for the pot pie sauce. Roast chicken also required an hour in the oven, and by the time we took off the skin and mixed the meat in with the sauce and vegetables, the roasted flavor was lost. We had similar results with braised chicken. It lost its delicious flavor once the browned skin was removed, and the sauce made from the braising liquid tasted too pronounced, distracting us from the meat, vegetables, and crust.

Next we tried poaching, the most traditional cooking method. Of the two poaching liquids we tried, we preferred the chicken poached in wine and broth to the one poached in broth alone. The wine infused the meat and made for a richer, more full-flavored sauce. To our disappointment, however, the acidity of the wine-broth sauce caused the green peas and fresh herbs to lose their bright green color in the oven. Vegetables baked in the broth-only sauce kept their bright color, though the bland sauce needed perking up—a problem we'd have to deal with later. Now we were ready to test this method against quicker-cooking boneless, skinless chicken breasts.

Because boneless, skinless breasts cook so quickly, sautéing was another possible cooking method. Before comparing poached parts to breasts, we tried cooking the breasts three different ways. We cut raw breast meat into bite-sized pieces and sautéed them; we sautéed whole breasts, shredding the breast meat once cool enough to handle; and we poached whole breasts in canned broth, also shredding the meat.

Once again, poaching was our favorite method. The resulting tender, irregularly shaped chicken pieces mixed well with the vegetables and, much like textured pasta, caused the sauce to cling. The sautéed chicken pieces, however, floated independently in the sauce, their surfaces too smooth to attract sauce. For simplicity's sake, we had hoped to like the sautéed whole breasts. Unfortunately, sautéing caused the outer layer of meat to turn crusty, a texture we did not like in the pie.

Our only concern with the poached boneless, skinless breasts was the quality of the broth. Though both the parts and the breasts were poached in canned broth, we thought the long-simmered poaching liquid of the parts would be significantly better. But in our comparison of the pies, we found no difference in quality, and we were able to shave half an hour off the cooking time (10 minutes to cook the breasts compared with 40 minutes to cook the parts). For those who like either dark or a mix of dark and white meat in the pie, boneless, skinless chicken thighs can be used as well.

A good pot pie with fresh vegetables, warm pastry, and full-flavored sauce tastes satisfying. One with overcooked vegetables tastes stodgy and old-fashioned. So we made pies with raw vegetables, sautéed vegetables, and parboiled vegetables.

After comparing the pies, we found that the vegetables sautéed before baking held their color and flavor best, the parboiled ones less so. The raw vegetables were not fully cooked at the end of baking time and gave off too much liquid, watering down the flavor and thickness of the sauce.

Our final task was to develop a sauce that was flavorful, creamy, and of the proper consistency. Chicken pot pie sauce is traditionally based on a roux (a mixture of butter and flour sautéed together briefly), which is thinned with chicken broth and often enriched with cream.

Because of the dish's inherent richness, we wanted to see how little cream we could get away with using. We tried three different pot pie fillings, using ¼ cup of cream, ¼ cup of half-and-half, and 1½ cups of milk, respectively. Going into the oven, all of the fillings seemed to have the right consistency and creaminess; when they came out, however, it was a different story. Vegetable and meat juices diluted the consistency and creaminess of the cream and half-and-half sauces. To achieve a creamy-looking sauce, we would have needed to increase the cream dramatically. Fortunately, we didn't have to try it, because we actually liked the milk-enriched sauce. The larger quantity of milk kept the sauce creamy and tasted delicious.

To keep the sauce from becoming too liquid, we simply added more flour. A sauce that looks a little thick before baking will become the perfect consistency after taking on the chicken and vegetable juices that release during baking.

We had worked out the right consistency, but because we had been forced to abandon the wine for the vegetables' sake, the sauce tasted a little bland. Lemon juice, a flavor heightener we had seen in a number of recipes, had the same dulling effect on the color of the vegetables as the wine. We tried sherry, and it worked perfectly. Because sherry is more intensely flavored and less acidic than wine, it gave us the flavor we were looking for without harming the peas and carrots.

Chicken Pot Pie
SERVES 6 TO 8

You can make the filling ahead of time, but remember to heat it on top of the stove before topping it. Mushrooms can be sautéed along with the celery and carrots, and blanched pearl onions can stand in for the onion.

1	recipe pie dough or biscuit topping (page 158)
1½	pounds boneless, skinless chicken breasts and/or thighs
2	cups homemade chicken broth or 1 can (15 ounces) low-sodium chicken broth with water added to equal 2 cups
1½	tablespoons vegetable oil
1	medium-large onion, chopped fine
3	medium carrots, peeled and cut crosswise ¼-inch thick
2	small celery stalks, cut crosswise ¼-inch thick
	Salt and ground black pepper
4	tablespoons unsalted butter
½	cup flour
1½	cups milk
½	teaspoon dried thyme leaves
3	tablespoons dry sherry
¾	cup frozen green peas, thawed
3	tablespoons minced fresh parsley leaves

1. Make pie dough or biscuit topping and refrigerate until ready to use.

2. Adjust oven rack to low-center position; heat oven to 400 degrees. Put chicken and broth in small Dutch oven or soup kettle over medium heat. Cover, bring to simmer; simmer until chicken is just done, 8 to 10 minutes. Transfer meat to large bowl, reserving broth in measuring cup.

3. Increase heat to medium-high; heat oil in now-empty pan. Add onion, carrots, and celery; sauté until just tender, about 5 minutes. Season to taste with salt and pepper. While vegetables are sautéing, shred meat into bite-sized pieces. Transfer cooked vegetables to bowl with chicken; set aside.

4. Heat butter over medium heat in again-empty skillet. When foaming subsides, add flour; cook about 1 minute. Whisk in chicken broth, milk, any accumulated chicken juices, and thyme. Bring to simmer, then continue to simmer until sauce fully thickens,

about 1 minute. Season to taste with salt and pepper; stir in sherry.

5. Pour sauce over chicken mixture; stir to combine. Stir in peas and parsley. Adjust seasonings. (Can be covered and refrigerated overnight; reheat before topping with pastry.) Pour mixture into 13 x 9-inch pan or any shallow baking dish of similar size. Top with desired pastry dough; bake until pastry is golden brown and filling is bubbly, 30 minutes for large pies and 20 to 25 minutes for smaller pies. Serve hot.

Savory Pie Dough Topping

ENOUGH TO COVER ONE 13 X 9-INCH (OR EQUIVALENT) PAN OR SIX 12-OUNCE OVENPROOF BAKING DISHES

This recipe is similar to our American Pie Dough for Fruit Pies, but made without the sugar. (See chapter 19 for more detailed information about handling pie dough.) If you like a bottom crust in your pot pie, you can duplicate that soft crust texture by tucking the overhanging dough down into the pan side rather than fluting it.

1½	cups all-purpose flour
½	teaspoon salt
8	tablespoons (¼ pound) unsalted butter, chilled and cut into ¼-inch pieces
4	tablespoons all-vegetable shortening, chilled
3–4	tablespoons ice water

1. Mix flour and salt in food processor fitted with steel blade. Scatter butter pieces over flour mixture, tossing to coat butter with a little of the flour. Cut butter into flour with five 1-second pulses. Add shortening and continue cutting in until flour is pale yellow and resembles coarse cornmeal, with butter bits no larger than small peas, about four more 1-second pulses. Turn mixture into medium bowl.

2. Sprinkle 3 tablespoons ice water over the mixture. With blade of rubber spatula, use folding motion to mix in. Press down on dough mixture with broad side of spatula until dough sticks together, adding up to 1 tablespoon more ice water if dough will not come together. Shape dough into ball, then flatten into 4-inch-wide disk. Wrap in plastic and refrigerate 30 minutes, or up to 2 days, before rolling.

3. When pie filling is ready, roll dough on floured surface to approximate 15 x 11-inch rectangle, about ⅛-inch thick. If making individual pies, roll dough ⅛-inch thick and cut 6 dough rounds about 1 inch larger than dish circumference. Lay dough over pot pie filling, trimming dough to within ½ inch of pan lip. Tuck overhanging dough back under itself so folded edge is flush with lip. Flute edges all around. Or don't trim dough and simply tuck overhanging dough down into pan side. Cut at least four 1-inch vent holes in large pot pie or one 1-inch vent hole in smaller pies. Proceed with Chicken Pot Pie recipe.

Fluffy Buttermilk Biscuit Topping

ENOUGH TO COVER ONE 13 X 9-INCH (OR EQUIVALENT) PAN OR SIX 12-OUNCE OVENPROOF BAKING DISHES

For more information about biscuit making, see page 379.

1	cup all-purpose flour
1	cup plain cake flour
2	teaspoons baking powder
¼	teaspoon baking soda
1	teaspoon sugar
½	teaspoon salt
8	tablespoons (¼ pound) unsalted butter, chilled, quartered lengthwise and cut crosswise into ¼-inch pieces
¾	cup cold buttermilk, plus 1 to 2 tablespoons extra, if needed

1. Pulse first six ingredients in workbowl of food processor fitted with steel blade. Add butter pieces; pulse until mixture resembles coarse cornmeal with a few slightly larger butter lumps.

2. Transfer mixture to medium bowl; add buttermilk; stir with fork until dough gathers into moist clumps. Transfer dough to floured work surface and form into rough ball, then roll dough ½-inch thick. Using 2½- to 3-inch pastry cutter, stamp out 8 rounds of dough. If making individual pies, cut dough slightly smaller than circumference of each dish. (Dough rounds can be refrigerated on lightly floured baking sheet covered with plastic wrap up to 2 hours.)

3. Arrange dough rounds over warm filling and proceed with Chicken Pot Pie recipe.

VARIATIONS

Chicken Pot Pie with Spring Vegetables

Follow recipe for Chicken Pot Pie, replacing celery with 18 thin asparagus stalks that have been trimmed and cut into 1-inch pieces. Increase peas to 1 cup.

Chicken Pot Pie with Wild Mushrooms

The soaking liquid used to rehydrate dried porcini mushrooms replaces some of the chicken stock used to poach the chicken and then to enrich the sauce. See page 111 for more information about rehydrating dried mushrooms.

Follow recipe for Chicken Pot Pie, soaking 1 ounce dried porcini mushrooms in 2 cups warm tap water until softened, about 20 minutes. Lift mushrooms from liquid, strain liquid, and reserve 1 cup. Use soaking liquid in place of 1 cup of chicken stock. Proceed with recipe, cooking rehydrated porcini and 12 ounces sliced button mushrooms with vegetables. Finish as directed.

Chicken Pot Pie with Corn and Bacon

This Southern variation with corn and bacon works especially well with biscuits.

Follow recipe for Chicken Pot Pie, replacing oil with ¼ pound bacon, cut crosswise into ½-inch-wide strips. Cook over medium heat until fat is rendered and bacon is crisp, about 6 minutes. Remove bacon from pan with slotted spoon and drain on paper towels. Cook vegetables in bacon fat. Add drained bacon to bowl with chicken and cooked vegetables. Proceed with recipe, replacing peas with 2 cups fresh or frozen corn.

SHREDDING CHICKEN

Chicken is best shredded by hand into bite-sized pieces. Do not use a knife. Irregular surfaces caused by hand-shredding help the sauce to coat and cling to the chicken.

CHICKEN AND DUMPLINGS

DESPITE AMERICA'S ONGOING LOVE AFFAIR with comfort food, chicken and dumplings, unlike its baked cousin, chicken pot pie, hasn't made a comeback. After making several dozen batches of dumplings, we think we know why.

As tricky as pie pastry and biscuits are for pot pie, dumplings are far more temperamental. With pot pie, dry oven heat and rich sauce camouflage minor biscuit and pastry flaws, whereas moist, steamy heat highlights gummy or leaden dumplings.

With its meat, vegetables, bread, and sauce, chicken pot pie is a perfect complete meal. But chicken and dumplings is, well, chicken and dumplings. A few hearty vegetables would make it a complete meal—just the selling point to attract today's busy cook.

Our mission in developing a recipe for chicken and dumplings was twofold. First, we wanted a recipe that was as foolproof and complete as that for chicken pot pie. Second, we wanted a dumpling that was light yet substantial, tender yet durable. But which style of dumpling to explore?

In different parts of the country, dumplings come in different shapes. They may be rolled thin and cut into strips, rolled thick and stamped out like biscuits, or shaped into round balls by hand. Could these three styles come from the same dough, or would we need to develop separate doughs to accommodate each style?

Most flour-based dumplings are made of flour, salt, and one or more of the following ingredients: butter, eggs, milk, and baking powder. Depending on the ingredients list, dumplings are usually mixed in one of three ways.

The most common mixing method is a biscuit or pastry style in which cold butter is cut into the dry ingredients, then cold milk and/or eggs are stirred in until just mixed. Other dumplings are made by simply mixing wet into dry ingredients. Many of the eggier dumplings are made pâte à choux-style, adding flour to hot water and butter, then whisking in eggs, one at a time.

We spent a full day making batch after batch of dumplings from some combination of the above ingredients and following one of the three mixing methods. By the end of the day, we hadn't made a single dumpling that we really liked.

We finally made progress after looking at a recipe in *Master Recipes* (Ballantine, 1987) in which author Stephen Schmidt cuts butter into flour, baking powder, and salt. Instead of the usual cold liquid into the dry ingredients, he adds hot liquid to the flour-butter mixture. Dumplings made according to this method were light and fluffy, yet they held up beautifully during cooking. These were the firm yet tender dumplings we were looking for. This type of dumpling is a success because hot liquids, unlike cold ones, expand and set the starch in the flour, keeping it from absorbing too much of the cooking liquid. Now that we had the technique down, it was time to test the formula.

We thought that cake flour dumplings would be even lighter-textured than those made with all-purpose. In fact, just the opposite was true. They were tight, spongy little dumplings with a metallic, acidic aftertaste. The problem lies with the cake flour, not the baking powder. The process by which cake flour is chlorinated leaves it acidic. One of the benefits of acidic flour is that it sets eggs faster in baking, resulting in a smoother, finer-textured cake. This acidic flavor, less distracting in a batter rich with butter, sugar, and eggs, really comes through in a simple dumpling dough.

Although we were pretty sure the dumplings made with vegetable shortening wouldn't taste as good as those made with butter, we had high hopes for the ones made with chicken fat. After a side-by-side test of dumplings made with butter, shortening,

and chicken fat, we selected those made with butter. The shortening dumpling tasted flat, like cooked flour and chicken stock, while the one made with chicken fat tasted like flour and stronger-flavored chicken stock. The butter gave the dumpling that extra flavor dimension it needed.

Liquids were simple. Dumplings made with chicken stock, much like those made with chicken fat, tasted too similar to the broth. Those made with water were pretty dull. Because buttermilk tends to separate and even curdle when heated, buttermilk dumplings felt a little wrong. Whole milk dumplings were tender, with a pleasant biscuity flavor, and were our first choice.

Up to this point, we had made all of our dumplings by cutting the fat into the dry ingredients, then adding hot liquid. Because we were adding hot milk, we questioned why it was necessary to cut in the cold butter. Why couldn't we simply heat the milk and butter together and dump it into the dry ingredients? A side-by-side tasting of dumplings made from the two different mixing techniques made us realize that cutting the butter into the flour was indeed an unnecessary step. The simpler route of adding the hot milk and melted butter to the dry ingredients actually yielded more substantial, better-textured dumplings.

Having decided on dumplings made with all-purpose flour, butter, milk, baking powder, and salt, we tested the formula by shaping them into balls, cutting them into biscuit shapes, and rolling them thin and cutting them into strips. Regardless of shape, we got the same consistent results: tender, sturdy dumplings.

SHAPING DUMPLINGS

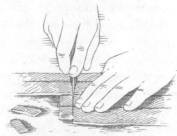

1. For flat, noodlelike dumplings, roll dough to ⅛ inch thick and cut into 2 by ½-inch strips.

2. For biscuitlike dumplings, roll dough to ½ inch thick. Use a 2-inch biscuit cutter or a round drinking glass top to cut dough rounds.

3. For round, puffy dumplings, divide dough into 18 pieces. Roll each piece of dough into a rough round.

After refining the dumpling, we turned our energies to updating the chicken part of the dish. Our first few attempts were disastrous. To make the dish clean and sleek, we left the chicken pieces on the bone, cut the vegetables into long, thin strips, and thickened the broth ever so slightly. As we ate the finished product, we realized that we needed a knife (to cut the chicken off the bone), a fork (to eat the vegetables, dumplings, and meat), and a spoon (for the broth). Although we wanted the dish to look beautiful, it had to be eater-friendly. In order for the dish to work, the chicken had to come off the bone, the vegetables needed to be cut a little smaller, and the broth would have to be reduced and thickened. As the dish evolved, we worked toward making it not only a one-dish, but a one-utensil meal.

While boneless, skinless chicken breasts had been a wonderful timesaving substitute for a whole chicken in chicken pot pie, the breasts just didn't seem right for this dish. We wanted large, uneven chunks of light and dark meat. Only a whole chicken would work. Because we wanted this dish to serve six to eight and because we preferred bigger chunks of meat, we chose the larger oven roasters over the small fryer hens.

Because we had already developed a method for rich, flavorful chicken stock and perfectly poached chicken parts (see page 15), we simply adapted the technique to this recipe.

Our updated chicken and dumplings now needed vegetables, but where and how to cook them? In an attempt to streamline the process, we tried cooking the vegetables along with the poaching chicken parts. After fishing out hot, slightly overcooked vegetables from among the chicken parts and pieces, we decided this little shortcut wasn't worth it. So we simply washed the pot, returned it to the stove, and steamed the vegetables for 10 minutes while removing the meat from the bone, straining the stock, and making the dumpling dough. Because the vegetables would cook again for a short time in the sauce, we wanted them slightly undercooked at this point. Steaming them separately gave us more control.

With our meat poached and off the bone, our stock degreased and strained, and our vegetables steamed to perfection, we were ready to complete the dish, like someone ready to stir-fry. We chose to thicken the sauce at the beginning of this final phase, rather than at the end, because once our chicken, vegetables, and dumplings were added to the pot, thickening became virtually impossible.

To a roux of flour and chicken fat (once again, using every bit of the chicken to make the dish), we added our homemade stock and stirred until thickened. Although we needed six cups of stock to poach the chicken parts, we found this quantity of liquid made the dish much too saucy, more like chicken and dumpling soup. Pouring off two cups of stock to reserve for another use solved the problem.

We added the chicken and vegetables to the thickened sauce, then steamed the dumplings. Not only did the dumplings remain undisturbed, the chicken and vegetables had an opportunity to marry and mingle with one another and the sauce. A few peas and a little parsley made the dish beautiful, and a little dry sherry or vermouth, as we found with chicken pot pie, heightened the flavor. A touch of cream enriches and beautifies, but the dish is equally good without it.

Chicken and Dumplings with Aromatic Vegetables

SERVES 6 TO 8

A touch of heavy cream gives this dish a more refined look and rich flavor, but it can be omitted. If you are in a hurry, you can poach boneless chicken breasts in low-sodium canned broth, then pull the breast into large pieces, and skip step 1 below. This compromise saves time, but the results are not nearly as delicious.

POACHED CHICKEN AND AROMATIC VEGETABLES

1	large roasting chicken (6 to 7 pounds), cut into 2 legs, 2 thighs, and 2 breast pieces, each with skin removed; back, neck, and wings hacked with cleaver into 1- to 2-inch pieces to make stock
1	large onion, cut into large chunks (not necessary to peel)
2	bay leaves
	Salt
3	celery stalks, trimmed and cut into 1 x ½-inch pieces

4   medium carrots, peeled and cut into
    I x ½-inch pieces
6   boiling onions, peeled and halved
4   tablespoons unsalted butter, softened, or
    chicken fat from the cooked chicken
6   tablespoons all-purpose flour
I   teaspoon dried thyme leaves
2   tablespoons dry sherry or vermouth
¼   cup heavy cream (optional)
¾   cup frozen peas, thawed
¼   cup minced fresh parsley leaves
    Ground black or white pepper

BAKING POWDER DUMPLINGS

2   cups all-purpose flour
I   tablespoon baking powder
¾   teaspoon salt
3   tablespoons butter
I   cup milk

1. FOR THE CHICKEN: Heat deep 11- or 12-inch skillet or Dutch oven over medium-high heat. Add hacked-up chicken pieces (back, neck, and wings) and onion chunks; sauté until onion softens and chicken loses its raw color, about 5 minutes. Reduce heat to low, cover, and continue to cook until chicken pieces give up most of their liquid, about 20 minutes. Increase heat to medium-high, add 6 cups hot water, skinned chicken parts (legs, thighs, and breasts), bay leaves, and ¾ teaspoon salt, then bring to simmer. Reduce heat; continue to simmer, partially covered, until broth is flavorful and chicken parts are just cooked through, about 20 minutes longer. Remove chicken parts and set aside. When cool enough to handle, remove meat from bones in 2- to 3-inch chunks. Strain broth, discarding chicken pieces. Skim and reserve fat from broth and set aside 4 cups of broth, reserving extra for another use.

2. Meanwhile, bring ½ inch water to simmer in cleaned skillet fitted with steamer basket. Add celery, carrots, and boiling onions; cover and steam until just tender, about 10 minutes. Remove and set aside.

3. FOR THE DUMPLINGS: Mix flour, baking powder, and salt in medium bowl. Heat butter and milk to simmer and add to dry ingredients. Mix with a fork or knead by hand two to three times until mixture just comes together. Following illustrations on page 160, form dough into desired shape; set aside.

4. Heat butter or reserved chicken fat in cleaned skillet over medium-high heat. Whisk in flour and thyme; cook, whisking constantly, until flour turns golden, 1 to 2 minutes. Whisking constantly, gradually add sherry or vermouth, then reserved 4 cups chicken stock; simmer until gravy thickens slightly, 2 to 3 minutes. Stir in optional cream and chicken and steamed vegetables; return to simmer.

5. Lay formed dumplings on surface of chicken mixture; cover and simmer until dumplings are cooked through, about 10 minutes for strip dumplings and 15 minutes for balls and biscuit rounds. Gently stir in peas and parsley. Adjust seasonings, including generous amounts of salt and pepper. Ladle portion of meat, sauce, vegetables, and dumplings into soup plates and serve immediately.

➤ VARIATION

Chicken and Herbed Dumplings with Aromatic Vegetables

Follow recipe for Chicken and Dumplings with Aromatic Vegetables, adding ¼ cup minced soft fresh herb leaves such as parsley, chives (or scallion greens), dill, and tarragon to dumpling mixture along with dry ingredients. If other herbs are unavailable, all parsley may be used.

CHICKEN AND RICE

ALTHOUGH THERE IS NO SPECIFIC AMERICAN tradition for a dish called "chicken and rice," its appeal is obvious: It's a one-dish supper, it's easy, and it's eminently variable. Yet after having made a dozen attempts at perfecting this recipe, we found two major problems. The white meat tends to dry out before the dark meat is cooked, and the rice is often heavy and greasy.

First, we tackled the problem of overcooked breast meat. It turned out that the solution was rather simple. By adding the breast meat to the dish 15 minutes after the thighs and legs, both cooked perfectly. Of course, one could make this dish with just dark or light meat, but most cooks are more likely to have a whole chicken on hand than just thighs or breasts.

The texture of the rice was a more vexing issue.

Our first thought was to reduce the amount of olive oil in which the chicken and onion are sautéed from two tablespoons to one. But this simply was not enough fat to get the job done, and the resulting rice was only fractionally less greasy. We thought that perhaps the chicken skin was the culprit, but after making this dish with skinless chicken pieces, we were surprised to find that the rice was still heavy and that the chicken, as we had expected, was tough and chewy without the skin to protect it during initial sautéing.

We then thought that perhaps reducing the amount of liquid would produce less-sodden rice. For 1½ cups of long-grain white rice, we were using an equal amount of chicken stock, plus two cups of water. We tried reducing the stock to a mere half cup; the rice was indeed less sodden, but the layer of rice on top was undercooked and dried out. Fortunately, this problem, too, was rather easily solved. We found that stirring the dish once when adding the breast meat, so that the rice on top was stirred into the bottom, produced more even cooking.

Next we made four different batches using different liquids: chicken stock (heavy rice); water (bland and flat tasting); a combination of wine and water (the acidity of the wine cut through the fat, producing clean, clear flavors); and a combination of water, chopped canned tomatoes, and tomato liquid (the acid in the tomatoes punched up and enriched the flavor). Learning from these tests, we tried a combination of white wine, water, chopped canned tomatoes, and tomato liquid, with excellent results.

Finally, we tested different varieties of rice to see which held up best to this sort of cooking. A basic long-grain white rice was fine, with good flavor and decent texture; a medium-grain rice was creamy, with a risotto-like texture and excellent flavor; basmati rice was nutty, with separate, light grains (this was by far the lightest version, but the basmati rice seemed somewhat out of place in such a pedestrian dish; it is, however, well-suited to the variation with Indian spices); and converted rice was absolutely tasteless. So, while medium-grain and basmati rices both provided good results, we preferred basic long-grain white rice for this all-purpose dish.

Chicken and Rice with Tomatoes and White Wine
SERVES 4

If you prefer, substitute 2 pounds of breast meat or boneless thighs for the pieces of a whole chicken.

I	chicken (3 to 4 pounds), rinsed, patted dry, and cut into 8 pieces (see illustrations on page 145), wings reserved for another use
	Salt and ground black pepper
2	tablespoons extra-virgin olive oil
I	medium onion, chopped fine
3	medium garlic cloves, minced very fine
I ½	cups long-grain white rice
I	can (14½ ounces) diced tomatoes, drained (about I cup) and ½ cup liquid reserved
½	cup white wine
I	teaspoon salt
⅓	cup chopped fresh parsley leaves

1. Sprinkle chicken pieces liberally on both sides with salt and ground black pepper. Heat oil until shimmering in large, heavy, nonreactive Dutch oven over high heat. Add chicken pieces skin side down; cook, without moving them, until well-browned, about 6 minutes. Turn chicken pieces over with tongs and cook, again without moving them, until well-browned on second side, about 6 minutes longer. Remove from pot and set aside.

2. Pour all but 2 tablespoons fat from pot; return to burner. Reduce heat to medium; add onion and sauté, stirring frequently, until softened, about 3 to 4 minutes. Add garlic and sauté until fragrant, approximately 1 minute longer. Stir in rice and cook, stirring frequently, until coated and glistening, about 1 minute longer. Add tomatoes with reserved liquid, wine, salt, and 2 cups water, scraping browned bits off pot bottom with wooden spoon. Return chicken thighs and legs to pot; bring to boil. Reduce heat to low, cover, and simmer gently for 15 minutes. Add chicken breast pieces and stir ingredients gently until rice is thoroughly mixed; replace cover and simmer until both rice and chicken are tender, 10 to 15 minutes longer. Stir in parsley, cover pot, and allow dish to rest for 5 minutes; serve immediately.

➤ VARIATIONS

Chicken and Rice with Saffron and Peas

1 chicken (3 to 4 pounds), rinsed, patted dry, and cut into 8 pieces (see illustrations on page 145), wings reserved for another use
  Salt and ground black pepper
2 tablespoons extra-virgin olive oil
1 medium onion, chopped fine
1 medium green bell pepper, cored, seeded, and cut into medium dice
3 medium garlic cloves, minced very fine
4 teaspoons paprika
1/4 teaspoon saffron threads
1 1/2 cups long-grain white rice
1 can (14 1/2 ounces) diced tomatoes, drained (about 1 cup) and 1/2 cup liquid reserved
1/2 cup white wine
1 teaspoon salt
1 cup thawed frozen peas
1/3 cup chopped fresh parsley leaves

1. Sprinkle chicken pieces liberally on both sides with salt and ground black pepper. Heat oil until shimmering in large, heavy, nonreactive Dutch oven over high heat. Add chicken pieces skin side down; cook, without moving them, until well-browned, about 6 minutes. Turn chicken pieces over with tongs and cook, again without moving them, until well-browned on second side, about 6 minutes longer. Remove from pot and set aside.

2. Pour all but 2 tablespoons fat from pot; return to burner. Reduce heat to medium; add onion and bell pepper and sauté, stirring frequently, until softened, about 3 to 4 minutes. Add garlic, paprika, and saffron and sauté until fragrant, approximately 1 minute longer. Stir in rice and cook, stirring frequently, until coated and glistening, about 1 minute longer. Add tomatoes with reserved liquid, wine, salt, and 2 cups water, scraping browned bits off pot bottom with wooden spoon. Return chicken thighs and legs to pot; bring to boil. Reduce heat to low, cover, and simmer gently for 15 minutes. Add chicken breast pieces and stir ingredients gently until rice is thoroughly mixed; replace cover and simmer until both rice and chicken are tender, 10 to 15 minutes longer. Stir in peas and parsley, cover pot, and allow dish to rest for 5 minutes; serve immediately.

Chicken and Rice with Chiles and Lime

1 chicken (3 to 4 pounds), rinsed, patted dry, and cut into 8 pieces (see illustrations on page 145), wings reserved for another use
  Salt and ground black pepper
2 tablespoons extra-virgin olive oil
1 medium onion, chopped fine
2 jalapeño chiles, stemmed, seeded, and minced
3 medium garlic cloves, minced very fine
2 teaspoons ground cumin
2 teaspoons ground coriander
1 teaspoon chili powder
1 1/2 cups long-grain white rice
1 can (14 1/2 ounces) diced tomatoes, drained (about 1 cup) and 1/2 cup liquid reserved
1/2 cup white wine
1 teaspoon salt
1/4 cup chopped fresh cilantro leaves
3 tablespoons lime juice

1. Sprinkle chicken pieces liberally on both sides with salt and ground black pepper. Heat oil until shimmering in large, heavy, nonreactive Dutch oven over high heat. Add chicken pieces skin side down; cook, without moving them, until well-browned, about 6 minutes. Turn chicken pieces over with tongs and cook, again without moving them, until well-browned on second side, about 6 minutes longer. Remove from pot and set aside.

2. Pour all but 2 tablespoons fat from pot; return to burner. Reduce heat to medium; add onion and chiles and sauté, stirring frequently, until softened, about 3 to 4 minutes. Add garlic, cumin, coriander, and chili powder and sauté until fragrant, approximately 1 minute longer. Stir in rice and cook, stirring frequently, until coated and glistening, about 1 minute longer. Add tomatoes with reserved liquid, wine, salt, and 2 cups water, scraping browned bits off pot bottom with wooden spoon. Return chicken thighs and legs to pot; bring to boil. Reduce heat to low, cover, and simmer gently for 15 minutes. Add chicken breast pieces and stir ingredients gently until rice is thoroughly mixed; replace cover and simmer until both rice and chicken are tender, 10 to 15 minutes longer. Stir in cilantro and lime juice, cover pot, and allow dish to rest for 5 minutes; serve immediately.

Chicken and Rice with Indian Spices

1   chicken (3 to 4 pounds), rinsed, patted dry, and cut into 8 pieces (see illustrations on page 145), wings reserved for another use
    Salt and ground black pepper
2   tablespoons extra-virgin olive oil
1   3-inch piece cinnamon stick
1   medium onion, chopped fine
2   green bell peppers, cored, seeded, and diced
3   medium garlic cloves, minced very fine
1   teaspoon ground turmeric
1   teaspoon ground coriander
1   teaspoon ground cumin
1 ½   cups long-grain white rice
1   can (14½ ounces) diced tomatoes, drained (about 1 cup) and ½ cup liquid reserved
½   cup white wine
1   teaspoon salt

1. Sprinkle chicken pieces liberally on both sides with salt and ground black pepper. Heat oil until shimmering in large, heavy, non-reactive Dutch oven over high heat. Add chicken pieces skin side down; cook, without moving them, until well browned, about 6 minutes. Turn chicken pieces over with tongs and cook, again without moving them, until well browned on second side, about 6 minutes longer. Remove from pot and set aside.

2. Pour all but 2 tablespoons fat from pot; return to burner. Reduce heat to medium; add cinnamon stick and sauté, stirring with wooden spoon, until it unfurls, about 15 seconds. Add onion and bell peppers and sauté, stirring frequently, until softened, about 5 to 6 minutes. Add garlic, turmeric, coriander, and cumin and sauté until fragrant, approximately 1 minute longer. Stir in rice and cook, stirring frequently, until coated and glistening, about 1 minute longer. Add tomatoes with reserved liquid, wine, salt, and 2 cups water, scraping browned bits off pot bottom with wooden spoon. Return chicken thighs and legs to pot; bring to boil. Reduce heat to low, cover, and simmer gently for 15 minutes. Add chicken breast pieces and stir ingredients gently until rice is thoroughly mixed; replace cover and simmer until both rice and chicken are tender, 10 to 15 minutes longer. Remove pot from heat and allow dish to rest for 5 minutes; serve immediately.

Chicken and Rice with Anchovies, Olives, and Lemon

1   chicken (3 to 4 pounds), rinsed, patted dry, and cut into 8 pieces (see illustrations on page 145), wings reserved for another use
    Salt and ground black pepper
2   tablespoons extra-virgin olive oil
1   medium onion, chopped fine
5   anchovy fillets, minced
3   medium garlic cloves, minced very fine
1 ½   cups long-grain white rice
1   can (14½ ounces) diced tomatoes, drained (about 1 cup) and ½ cup liquid reserved
½   cup white wine
1   teaspoon salt
⅓   cup chopped fresh parsley leaves
1   teaspoon minced zest and 1 tablespoon juice from 1 small lemon
½   cup imported black olives, pitted and halved

1. Sprinkle chicken pieces liberally on both sides with salt and ground black pepper. Heat oil until shimmering in large, heavy, non-reactive Dutch oven over high heat. Add chicken pieces skin side down; cook, without moving them, until well browned, about 6 minutes. Turn chicken pieces over with tongs and cook, again without moving them, until well browned on second side, about 6 minutes longer. Remove from pot and set aside.

2. Pour all but 2 tablespoons fat from pot; return to burner. Reduce heat to medium; add onion and anchovies and sauté, stirring frequently, until onion has softened, about 3 to 4 minutes. Add garlic and sauté until fragrant, approximately 1 minute longer. Stir in rice and cook, stirring frequently, until coated and glistening, about 1 minute longer. Add tomatoes with reserved liquid, wine, salt, and 2 cups water, scraping browned bits off pot bottom with wooden spoon. Return chicken thighs and legs to pot; bring to boil. Reduce heat to low, cover, and simmer gently for 15 minutes. Add chicken breast pieces and stir ingredients gently until rice is thoroughly mixed; replace cover and simmer until both rice and chicken are tender, 10 to 15 minutes longer. Stir in parsley, lemon zest and juice, and olives, cover pot, and allow dish to rest for 5 minutes; serve immediately.

CHICKEN PARMESAN

CHICKEN PARMESAN—BREADED AND SAUTÉED chicken cutlets topped with cheese and tomato sauce—is not a particularly hard dish to make, but there are a lot of piddly steps that can bog you down if you're in a hurry. First you must prepare and pound the chicken breasts. You must make an egg wash for dipping and a crumb mixture for dredging. You need to make a quick tomato sauce and boil water for pasta, since spaghetti is almost always served with this dish. And, of course, there's an impressive stack of pots, pans, pounders, and plates to wash and dry after dinner.

Since chicken Parmesan is such a family favorite, our goal was to make sure it was the both the best it could be and easy enough to make for a weeknight supper—on the table in less than 30 minutes. We also wanted to avoid a problem that's common to this dish, a soggy cutlet.

Up to this point in our chicken Parmesan making, we had bought and pounded standard (six- to eight-ounce) boneless, skinless breasts. As you can imagine, these full-sized breasts pounded into massive cutlets that demanded one of three choices: batch cooking, which was time-consuming; two skillets, which made an even bigger mess; or oven-frying, which didn't brown the cutlets as well. Semiattached to these large breasts were the extra-tender tenderloin pieces that had a tendency to fall off during pounding or disintegrate when we removed the tendon.

These problems, however, were easily solved once we set our minds to it. Reducing portion size was a step in the right direction. A standard boneless, skinless breast half, when served with a side of spaghetti, a ladle of tomato sauce, and a topping of rich mozzarella and Parmesan cheese is too much for most appetites. One breast half split horizontally with the tenderloin removed was perfect for two people. In addition, we discovered that splitting the breast in this way drastically cut down on the need for pounding.

Specially trimmed chicken breasts—a relatively new product—also worked well for chicken Parmesan. Fully trimmed with tenderloins removed, these boneless, skinless breast halves weigh four to five ounces each and require minimal pounding. Whether you buy boneless, skinless breasts and

split them or use the specially trimmed ones, you will need to do at least some pounding to make them thin enough to cook through before the coating begins to burn. We tried several different pounding gadgets—makeshift as well as purchased—and found that the best chicken breast pounders were relatively lightweight with large flat surfaces. The disk-style pounder with a handle in the center was our favorite. As long as we pounded lightly, its relatively large, round surface quickly and efficiently transformed breasts into cutlets. If you don't have this kind of pounder, we suggest pounding gently with what you have on hand, which is likely heavier than our disk-style pounder.

Pounding the chicken lightly with a flat surface was important, but we also discovered that it mattered which side of the chicken breast we pounded. The pliable cut side of the breast easily flattened to perfection, while the skin side often split, resulting in an unsightly cutlet.

We also found that pounding the breast directly with no protection was messy and damaged the cutlet. We tried wax paper, but it disintegrated during pounding and bits of paper stuck to the breast. Flattening it between two sheets of plastic wrap ensured perfectly shaped cutlets.

With pounded breasts in hand, we moved on to coating. Traditionally, chicken cutlets are dipped in an egg wash before being rolled in the crumb coating. Some recipes go even further, dredging the cutlet in flour before the egg dip. Was this extra flour step necessary? We thought not. Although the coating of the flour-dipped cutlet was thicker, it tended to separate from the cutlet, peeling off in sheets. The simple egg and bread crumb coating formed a skin that was almost inseparable from the meat.

We tried other dips—buttermilk, yogurt, even mayonnaise—but we didn't find anything better than just plain egg. Since one egg perfectly coated four cutlets, we had no need to extend the egg with water or milk, as some recipes did.

Dry bread crumbs were the coating to beat. A crushed potato chip coating was surprisingly good, but too distinctly flavored for chicken Parmesan. Cornflake crumbs were perfectly textured—fine and beautifully crisp—but, like the potato chips, they tasted too pronounced. Matzo meal cutlets were too bland, while those coated with crushed saltines were too soft. Cracker meal rivaled the dry bread crumbs, but it wasn't good enough to warrant a special purchase. Bread crumbs could not be beat, and panko (Japanese-style bread crumbs) turned out to be the favorite in a blind tasting (see page 168).

Of the two cooking options for the cutlets—broiling and sautéing—we preferred sautéing. Broiling resulted in unevenly and unimpressively browned cutlets. Sautéing produced a beautiful, evenly golden-brown color and rich, satisfying flavor. And using the smaller portions of chicken made it possible to cook four cutlets at the same time, eliminating the need for a second pan.

Which fat should be used for sautéing the cutlets? For a full-flavored dish like chicken Parmesan we might have guessed it didn't much matter. We were wrong. Cutlets sautéed in olive oil were markedly better than those sautéed in vegetable oil. Cutlets sautéed in a combination of olive oil and butter were acceptable but not superior to those sautéed in olive oil, and sautéing in all butter produced too rich a flavor.

Some recipes, especially older ones, instruct the reader to top cooked cutlets with mozzarella cheese and bake them on a bed of tomato sauce, covered, until the cheese melts. As far as we are concerned, this step not only added several minutes to the preparation time, it also destroyed the crisp, delicious coating and turned the cutlets into soggy mush. We simply sprinkled the cooked cutlets with mozzarella and Parmesan and broiled them until the cheeses melted and turned spotty brown. After that they were ready for tomato sauce and the accompanying pasta.

So, to conclude: Buying trimmed chicken breasts saves time and preparation (although halving standard-size breasts is almost as easy). The egg dip and bread dredge couldn't be simpler. Buying shredded mozzarella cheese also shaves minutes off preparation time, and using crushed tomatoes renders sauce making almost as simple as opening a can. Chicken Parmesan in half an hour. Now all you need is someone to do the dishes!

Streamlined Chicken Parmesan

SERVES 4

Though not widely available, panko—Japanese bread crumbs—make an excellent coating. They can often be found at Asian markets. See page 168 for more information on various kinds of bread crumbs.

SIMPLE TOMATO SAUCE WITH BASIL AND GARLIC

- 2   medium garlic cloves, peeled and minced
- ¼   cup extra-virgin olive oil
- I   can (28 ounces) crushed tomatoes, preferably Red Pack, Progresso, or Muir Glen Ground Peeled
- ½   teaspoon dried basil
- ¼   teaspoon dried oregano
- ¼   teaspoon sugar
     Salt and ground black pepper

CHICKEN PARMESAN

- 2   large boneless, skinless chicken breasts (8 ounces each), tenderloins removed and breasts halved horizontally, or 4 trimmed chicken breasts (4 to 5 ounces each)
- I   large egg
     Salt and ground black pepper
- ½–I   cup dry bread crumbs
- ¼   cup extra-virgin olive oil
- ¾   cup (3 ounces) grated part-skim mozzarella cheese
- ¼   cup (½ ounce) grated Parmesan cheese, plus extra for passing
- 8   ounces spaghetti or linguine

1. FOR THE SAUCE: In a large saucepan or Dutch oven, heat garlic and oil together over medium-high heat until garlic starts to sizzle. Stir in tomatoes, basil, oregano, sugar, a pinch of salt, and a couple of grinds of pepper; bring to a simmer. Continue to simmer until sauce thickens a bit and flavors meld, 10 to 12 minutes. Taste sauce, adjusting salt if necessary. Cover and keep warm.

2. FOR THE CHICKEN PARMESAN: Place chicken breasts smooth side down on large sheet of plastic wrap. Cover with second sheet of plastic wrap and pound gently to ¼-inch thickness.

3. Bring 2 to 3 quarts of water to boil in a large

soup kettle. Beat egg and a heaping ¼ teaspoon salt in a small pie plate or other shallow dish until completely broken up. Mix bread crumbs, a heaping ¼ teaspoon salt, and a grind or two of pepper in another small pie plate or shallow baking dish.

4. Preheat broiler. Working with one at a time, dip both sides of each cutlet in the beaten egg, then in the bread crumb mixture. Set cutlets on large wire rack set over a jelly-roll pan.

5. Add 2 teaspoons salt and the spaghetti to the boiling water.

6. While pasta is cooking, heat oil over medium-high heat in 12-inch skillet. When oil starts to shimmer, add cutlets and sauté until golden brown on each side, about 5 to 6 minutes total. Wash and dry wire rack and return to jelly-roll pan. Transfer cutlets to wire rack and top each with equal portions of mozzarella and Parmesan cheeses. Place pan of cutlets 4 to 5 inches from heat source and broil until cheese melts and is spotty brown, about 3 minutes. Drain spaghetti.

7. Transfer a chicken cutlet and a portion of spaghetti to each of four plates. Spoon 1 or 2 tablespoons of sauce over part of each cutlet, then sauce the spaghetti as desired. Serve immediately with extra Parmesan passed separately.

INGREDIENTS: Bread Crumbs

To find out which bread crumbs make the best coating, we tested pan-fried chicken cutlets coated with four different brands: Progresso Plain Bread Crumbs, 4C Plain Bread Crumbs, Wel-Pac Panko (Japanese style) Bread Crumbs, and Manischewitz Unsalted Matzo Meal. The chicken cutlets were tasted with and without tomato sauce.

Wel-Pac Panko Bread Crumbs scored the highest of all, owing to what our tasters described as their light, "crisp" texture and "toasty," "wheaty" flavor. They even held up well when doused with tomato sauce, maintaining a nice contrast in texture. The Progresso bread crumbs came in second, receiving higher scores in both flavor and texture than the 4C bread crumbs, which came in third because of their less-than-crisp texture, which "disappears under sauce." Manischewitz Unsalted Matzo Meal received the lowest scores overall. Tasters found this breading "flavorless" and "bland," with an "initial crunch, then sogginess."

ROAST CORNISH HENS

EVEN THOUGH CORNISH HENS ARE CHEAP enough (two for five bucks in our grocery store) and cook quickly enough for a weeknight supper (less than 30 minutes unstuffed), most people think of them as festive fare. And for good reason. They make a stunning presentation and they stuff beautifully.

Cooking a large number of Cornish hens to perfection, however, is not an easy task. As with all poultry, if the hen is roasted breast side up, the breast will surely overcook before the legs and thighs get done. Getting the birds to brown properly with such a short stay in the oven is difficult, too, especially with six in a pan. If you think a 500-degree oven is the answer, think again. Six little birds dripping fat onto an overheated roasting pan automatically sets off the smoke alarms. Roasting these birds at high temperatures also causes their skin to bubble and blister.

Stuffing them presents problems as well. Because the cavity is the last spot to heat up, getting the stuffing to reach a safe internal temperature of 165 degrees means overcooking the meat.

One final problem: After roasting a few batches, we realized that these birds didn't taste superb. Because most Cornish hens are mass-produced and not premium quality, we were faced with the added challenge of trying to deepen their flavor.

We had our mission: to stuff and roast at least six grocery store–quality Cornish hens in such a way as to make them look good and taste great—without overcooking or smoking up the kitchen.

You may as well steam Cornish hens as roast six of them in a high-sided roasting pan. The pan sides shield the birds from oven heat, and their snug fit in the pan further prevents browning. So our first move was to get the birds up out of the roasting pan and onto a wire rack set over the pan. Our second step in the right direction was to space the birds as far apart as possible. Just as chops won't brown if overcrowded in the frying pan, Cornish hens won't brown if arranged too close together on the rack.

From initial testing, we determined that rotating the birds was crucial for moist and juicy breast meat. In a side-by-side taste test of hens roasted breast side up and hens turned during roasting, the turned birds won easily. Though the unturned birds showed off a deeper shade of brown, their breast meat was indeed drier and coarser-textured than that of the birds that were rotated. But because Cornish hens are in the oven for such a relatively short time, and because there are so many of them, multiple turns are out of the question. One turn, from breast side down to breast side up, was our limit.

After roasting Cornish hens at temperatures ranging from 350 degrees to 500 degrees, as well as roasting high and finishing low and roasting low and finishing high, we found that all oven temperatures had their problems. We finally settled on 400 degrees, cranking up the oven to 450 degrees during the last few minutes of roasting. This roasting temperature was high enough to encourage browning while low enough to keep the oven from smoking dramatically. Adding water to the roasting pan once the fat starts to render and the juices start to flow further ensures a smokeless kitchen at both the 400- and 450-degree temperatures. Another perk: The pan is automatically deglazed in the oven. Once the birds are roasted, you can pour the pan juices into a saucepan without having to deglaze the roasting pan over two burners.

Even roasted at a relatively high 400 degrees with a 450-degree finish, our birds still lacked that gorgeous mahogany turkey-skin color. We quickly realized that these expectations were unrealistic. Unlike turkeys, Cornish hens must brown in 45 minutes (and about half that time, with our method, is breast side down). We needed some sort of glaze to fix the color problem.

We roasted six birds, brushing two with soy sauce, two with balsamic vinegar, and two with jam thinned with a little soy sauce right before they were turned, and once after the oven was increased to 450 degrees. Because the high oven heat caramelized the sugar in all of these glazes, all of the birds colored more beautifully than any of our unglazed birds. But the balsamic vinegar glaze finished as our favorite, giving the hens a pleasant spotty brown, barbecued look.

Having roasted the first few birds without brining, we wondered if they tasted good enough to even bother writing about. Although our local grocery store sells premium-quality poussins (baby chickens), all of its Cornish hens are mass-produced. Just two hours in a saltwater bath, however, transformed these mediocre-tasting birds into something we would proudly serve to guests. Much like koshering, brining draws out the blood, giving the bird a clean, fresh flavor. The salt water permeates the birds, making each bite, rather than just the skin, taste seasoned. No matter how you roast your Cornish hens, brining will improve them immensely.

Our final challenge was how to roast these birds, stuffed, without overcooking them. Although we're certain that slightly overcooking a stuffed bird is inevitable, two things help. Starting the birds breast side down keeps the breast meat from drastically overcooking. And heating the stuffing before spooning it into the birds' cavities also reduces oven time. By stuffing the birds with microwave-hot stuffing, we were able to roast birds that registered 172 to 174 degrees in the breast and 176 to 178 degrees in the leg/thigh by the time the stuffing reached 165 degrees. Even though we thought breast meat at this temperature might be borderline dry (160 to 165 is ideal), we found this petite breast tender and juicy. Of course, the leg/thigh meat, which always tastes best at a higher temperature, was perfect.

Although we were aware that trussing would slow down the roasting of the hens' legs and thighs, we knew we had to do something. With their fragile, loose frame and dangling legs, Cornish hens can be a bit unsightly. Stuffing the bird further increases the need to close the cavity. We quickly discovered that simply tying the hens' legs together was all that was needed to improve their looks and secure the stuffing without impeding the roasting.

INGREDIENTS: Cornish Hens and Poussins

These days, it is becoming more and more difficult to find small Cornish hens. Not long ago, these dwarf birds hovered at around a pound, but for economic reasons, producers have started growing them bigger. Now the consumer is lucky to find one under 1½ pounds.

This larger size is perfect for two people, but for individual presentation, seek out the smaller hens or look for poussins, baby chickens sold at many butcher shops. Though a little more expensive, these baby chickens usually weigh about one pound and are perfect for one person. Poussins are likely to come from a smaller producer and generally taste better than mass-produced hens.

STUFFINGS FOR CORNISH HENS

Wild Rice Stuffing with Mushrooms and Thyme

MAKES ABOUT 3 CUPS, ENOUGH TO
STUFF 6 CORNISH HENS

The wild rice blend (a boxed mixture of long-grain and wild rice sold in supermarkets) in this stuffing holds together when pressed with a fork. You can use wild rice alone, but the cooked grains will remain separate.

1	ounce dried porcini mushrooms, rehydrated in 1 cup hot water
1¼	cups chicken stock or low-sodium canned broth, or more if necessary
1	cup wild rice blend
2	tablespoons unsalted butter
1	small onion, minced (½ cup)
1	small carrot, minced (¼ cup)
½	small celery stalk, minced (¼ cup)
4	ounces fresh shiitake mushrooms, stemmed and sliced thin
2	teaspoons minced fresh thyme leaves
2	tablespoons minced fresh parsley leaves
	Salt and ground black pepper

1. Lift rehydrated porcini from liquid, squeeze dry, and chop coarse. Strain rehydrating liquid through sieve lined with paper towel and reserve (should be approximately ¾ cup).

2. Add enough chicken stock to mushroom liquid to equal 2 cups. Bring liquid to boil in medium saucepan, add rice blend, and return to boil. Reduce heat to low, cover, and simmer until rice is fully cooked, 40 to 45 minutes. Turn rice into a medium microwave-safe bowl; fluff with fork.

3. Meanwhile, heat butter in medium skillet over medium heat. Add onions, carrots, and celery; sauté until softened, 3 to 4 minutes. Add shiitake mushrooms; sauté until tender and liquid evaporates. Add porcini mushrooms and thyme; cook, stirring until well-coated and blended with other ingredients, 1 to 2 minutes longer. Add this mixture to rice; toss to combine. Add parsley and season to taste with salt and ground black pepper.

Couscous Stuffing with Currants, Apricots, and Pistachios

MAKES ABOUT 3 CUPS, ENOUGH TO
STUFF 6 CORNISH HENS

Toasted slivered almonds can be substituted for the pistachio nuts.

2	tablespoons unsalted butter
1	small onion, minced (½ cup)
2	medium garlic cloves, minced
¼	teaspoon ground cinnamon
⅛	teaspoon ground ginger
⅛	teaspoon ground turmeric
1	cup plain couscous
1⅓	cups chicken stock or low-sodium canned broth
¼	cup dried apricots (8 to 9 whole), chopped fine
3	tablespoons currants
¼	cup shelled, toasted pistachio nuts, chopped
2	tablespoons minced fresh parsley leaves
1	teaspoon juice from 1 small lemon
	Salt and ground black pepper

Heat butter over medium heat in a medium saucepan. Add onion, garlic, cinnamon, ginger, and turmeric; sauté until onion softens, 3 to 4 minutes. Add couscous; stir until well-coated, 1 to 2 minutes. Add chicken stock, bring to simmer, remove from heat, cover, and let stand until couscous has fully rehydrated, about 5 minutes. Fluff couscous with fork; stir in dried fruit, nuts, and parsley and lemon juice. Season to taste with salt and pepper. Transfer mixture to microwave-safe bowl; set aside.

Roast Stuffed Cornish Hens

SERVES 6

Brining the birds breast side down ensures that the meatiest portions are fully submerged. Pouring a little water into the roasting pan at the 25-minute mark, once the birds have been turned, both prevents them from smoking during cooking and makes instant "jus," eliminating the need to deglaze the pan over two burners on the stove top. To enrich the flavor of the jus and use it as a sauce, pour it into a small saucepan, spoon off the fat that collects on the surface, and simmer it with a little vermouth or white wine.

2 cups kosher or 1 cup table salt

6 Cornish hens (each less than ½ pound, if possible), trimmed of extra fat, giblets removed, rinsed well

1 recipe stuffing (see page 170), heated until very hot

6 tablespoons balsamic vinegar

3 tablespoons extra-virgin olive oil

¼ cup dry vermouth or white wine

1. Dissolve salt in 5 quarts cold water in small clean bucket or large bowl. Add hens breast side down; refrigerate 2 to 3 hours. Remove, rinse thoroughly, pat dry, and prick skin all over breast and legs with point of a paring knife to prevent skin from ballooning.

2. Adjust oven rack to middle position and heat oven to 400 degrees. Whisk balsamic vinegar and oil in small bowl; set aside. Spoon ½ cup hot stuffing into cavity of each hen; tie its legs together with 6-inch piece of kitchen twine. Leaving as much space as possible between each bird, arrange them, breast side down and wings facing out, on large (at least 19 x 13-inch) wire rack, set over equally large roasting or jelly-roll pan. Roast until backs are golden brown, about 25 minutes. Remove pan from oven, brush bird backs with vinegar and oil glaze (reblending before each bird), turn hens breast side up and wings facing out, and brush breast and leg area with additional glaze. Return pan to oven, add 1 cup water, roast until instant read thermometer inserted into the stuffed cavity registers about 150 degrees, about 15 to 20 minutes longer. Remove pan from oven again, brush birds with remaining re-blended

glaze, return pan to oven, add another ½ cup water to pan, and increase oven temperature to 450 degrees. Roast until birds are spotty brown and cavity registers 165 degrees, 5 to 10 minutes longer, depending on bird size. Remove birds from oven and let them rest for 10 minutes.

3. Meanwhile, pour hen "jus" from roasting pan into small saucepan, spoon off excess fat, add vermouth or wine, and simmer over medium-high heat until flavors blend, 2 to 3 minutes. Drizzle about ¼ cup sauce over each hen and serve, passing remaining sauce separately.

ROAST TURKEY

IS IT POSSIBLE TO ROAST A TURKEY PERFECTLY? Usually juicy breast meat comes at a price—shocking pink legs and thighs. You have some leeway with the dark meat, which is almost impossible to dry out during normal roasting times. The problem is that the breast, which is exposed to direct heat and finishes cooking at a lower temperature, becomes parched, while the legs and thighs take their time creeping to doneness. Nearly every roasting method in existence tries to compensate for this; few succeed.

We tested dozens of different methods for roasting a turkey, from traditional to idiosyncratic. Our goals were to end up with an attractive bird, to determine the ideal internal temperature, and to find a method that would finish both white and dark meat simultaneously.

Our first roasting experiments used the method most frequently promoted by the National Turkey Federation, the U.S. Department of Agriculture, and legions of cookbook authors and recipe writers. This method features a moderately low roasting temperature of 325 degrees, a breast-up bird, and an open pan. We tried this method twice, basting one turkey and leaving the other alone. The basted turkey acquired a beautifully tanned skin, while the unbasted bird remained quite pale. Both were cooked to 170 degrees in the leg/thigh. Despite the fact that this was 10 degrees lower than recommended by the USDA and most producers, the breasts still registered a throat-catchingly dry 180 degrees.

We quickly determined that almost all turkeys

roasted in the traditional breast-up manner produced breast meat that was 10 degrees ahead of the leg/thigh meat (tenting the breast with heavy-duty foil was the exception; read on). Because white meat is ideal at 160 degrees, and dark thigh meat just loses its last shades of pink at about 170 degrees, you might conclude, as we did, that roasting turkeys with their breasts up is a losing proposition.

We also discovered that stuffing a bird makes overcooked meat more likely. Because it slows interior cooking (our tests showed a nearly 30-degree difference in internal temperature after an hour in the oven), stuffing means longer oven times, which can translate to bone-dry surface meat. We eventually developed a method for roasting a stuffed turkey (see page 176), but if the turkey is your priority, we recommend cooking the dressing separately.

Of all the breast-up methods, tenting the bird's breast and upper legs with foil, as suggested by numerous authors, worked the best. The foil deflects some of the oven's heat, reducing the ultimate temperature differential between white and dark meat from 10 to 6 degrees. The bird is roasted at a consistent 325-degree temperature, and during the last 45 minutes of roasting the foil is removed, allowing enough time for lovely browning. If you're partial to open-pan roasting and don't care to follow the technique we developed, try the foil shield; it certainly ran second in our tests.

Amidst all these failures and near-successes, some

PREPARING A ROAST TURKEY

 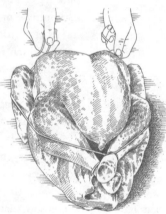 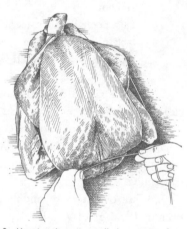

1. Using the center of a 5-foot length of cooking twine, tie the legs together at the ankles.

2. Run the twine around the thighs and under the wings on both sides of the bird and pull it tight.

3. Keeping the twine pulled snug, tie a firm knot around the excess flesh at the neck of the bird. Snip off the excess twine.

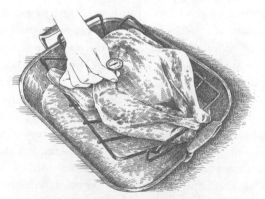 

4. When using an instant-read thermometer, make sure that you measure the temperature of the thickest part of the thigh.

5. This cutaway drawing shows the actual point to which the tip of the thermometer should penetrate.

real winners did emerge. Early on, we became fans of brining turkey in a salt water bath before roasting. When we first removed the brined turkey from the refrigerator, we found a beautiful, milky-white bird. When roasted, the texture of the breast was different from that of the other birds we had cooked; the meat was firm and juicy at the same time. And the turkey tasted fully seasoned; others had required a bite of skin with the meat to achieve the same effect. We experimented with the brining time and found that 8 to 12 hours in the refrigerator produces a nicely seasoned turkey without overly salty pan juices. Brining was our first real breakthrough; we now believe it to be essential to achieving perfect taste and texture. But we had yet to discover the way to roast.

Our most successful attempt at achieving equal temperatures in leg and breast came when we borrowed James Beard's technique of turning the turkey as it roasts. In this method, the bird begins breast side down on a V-rack, then spends equal time on each of its sides before being turned breast side up. The V-rack is important not just to hold the turkey in place but also to elevate it, affording it some protection from the heat of the roasting pan. This combination of rack and technique produced a turkey with a breast temperature that ran only a few degrees behind the leg temperature.

Because we were using smaller turkeys than Beard had used, we had to fine-tune his method. Large turkeys spend enough time in the oven to brown at 350 degrees; our turkeys were in the 12-pound range and were cooking in as little as two hours, yielding quite pale skin. Clearly, we needed higher heat.

Reviewing our notes, we noticed that the basted birds were usually the evenly browned, beautiful ones. So we turned up the heat to 400 degrees, basted faithfully, and got what we wanted. In an effort to streamline, we tried to skip the leg-up turns, roasting only breast side down, then breast side up. But in order for the turkey to brown all over, these two extra turns were necessary. Brining, turning, and basting are work, yes, but the combination produces the best turkey we've ever had.

During our first few tests, we discovered that filling the cavity with aromatic herbs and vegetables made for a subtle but perceptible difference in flavor. This was especially noticeable in the inner meat of the leg and thigh; turkeys with hollow cavities, by contrast, tasted bland. Roasted alongside the turkey, the same combination of carrot, celery, onion, and thyme also did wonders for the pan juices.

Best Roast Turkey
SERVES 10 TO 12

We prefer to roast small turkeys, no more than 14 pounds gross weight, because they cook more evenly than large birds. (If you must cook a large bird, see the variation below.) If you prefer, you can double the amount of salt in the brine and brine for just four hours. This hurry-up brine also works with large turkeys and turkeys destined to be stuffed.

2	cups kosher salt or 1 cup table salt
1	turkey (12 to 14 pounds gross weight), rinsed thoroughly; giblets, neck, and tailpiece removed and reserved to make gravy (see page 175)
3	medium onions, chopped coarse
1½	medium carrots, chopped coarse
1½	celery stalks, chopped coarse
6	thyme sprigs
3	tablespoons unsalted butter, melted

1. Dissolve salt in 2 gallons of cold water in large stockpot or clean bucket. Add turkey and refrigerate or set in very cool (40 degrees or less) spot for 12 hours.

2. Remove turkey from salt water and rinse both cavities and skin under cool running water for several minutes until all traces of salt are gone. Pat dry inside and out with paper towels. Adjust oven rack to lowest position, and heat oven to 400 degrees. Toss one-third of onion, carrot, celery, and thyme with 1 tablespoon of melted butter and place this mixture in body cavity. Bring turkey legs together and perform a simple truss (see illustrations on page 172).

3. Scatter remaining vegetables and thyme over a shallow roasting pan. Pour 1 cup water over vegetables. Set V-rack in pan. Brush entire breast side of turkey with half of remaining butter, then place turkey, breast side down, on V-rack. Brush entire backside of turkey with remaining butter.

4. Roast for 45 minutes. Remove pan from oven (close oven door); baste with juices from pan. With wad of paper toweling in each hand, turn turkey, leg/thigh side up. If liquid in pan has totally evaporated, add additional ½ cup water. Return turkey to

oven and roast for 15 minutes. Remove turkey from oven again, baste, and again use paper toweling to turn other leg/thigh side up; roast for another 15 minutes. Remove turkey from oven for final time, baste, and turn it breast side up; roast until breast registers about 165 degrees and thigh registers 170 to 175 degrees on an instant-read thermometer, 30 to 45 minutes (see illustrations, page 172). Remove turkey from pan and let rest until ready to carve. Serve with gravy.

➤ VARIATION

Large Roast Turkey

SERVES 18 TO 20

Smaller turkeys cook faster and are generally more tender, but sometimes you need a bigger bird for a large holiday crowd. By tinkering with our original recipe, we were able to produce a beautiful large turkey without sacrificing juiciness and flavor. When roasting a large turkey, it's not necessary to roast bird on each side.

Follow recipe for Best Roast Turkey, roasting 18- to 20-pound turkey breast side down in 250-degree oven for 3 hours, basting every hour. Then turn breast side up and roast another hour, basting once or twice. Increase oven temperature to 400 degrees and roast until done, about 1 hour longer.

EQUIPMENT: Roasting Pan

Roasting pans can cost $2 or $200, or even more once you start talking about copper. Most roasting pans are made of aluminum because it heats quickly. Some pans are lined with stainless steel, which is easier to clean than aluminum. We find that material is less important than size, depth, and weight.

You want a roasting pan that is large enough to hold a turkey or leg of lamb. A 13 x 9-inch baking pan is fine for a chicken, but you will need something considerably larger for most roasts. For most recipes in this book, including turkey, a 15 x 12-inch pan will work just fine.

In addition to size, you want a roasting pan that is deep enough to keep fat from splattering onto the walls of the oven. Since many roasts are cooked on racks, a shallow pan may prove problematic. On the other hand, a really deep pan will discourage browning. We find a depth of 2½ inches to be ideal.

We also prefer roasting pans with handles, which make it easy to lift them in and out of the oven. Last, you should consider buying a roasting pan with a heavy bottom. Some recipes, including our recipe for turkey with gravy, end by placing the empty pan on top of the stove for deglazing. A thin pan may buckle or scorch.

We know that many cooks rely on disposable aluminum pans for holiday roasts and birds. They are large and cheap and there is no cleanup. The downside is that these pans are flimsy and can fall apart. If you insist on using them, fit two pans together to support heavy roasts and birds. Also, buy disposable pans with handles and support the bottom of the filled pan when lifting it.

SCIENCE: What's a Safe Internal Temperature?

Industry standards developed by the U.S. Department of Agriculture and the National Turkey Federation call for whole birds to be cooked to an internal thigh temperature of 180 to 185 degrees. The breast temperature, according to these standards, should be 170 degrees. However, our kitchen tests showed that no meat is at its best at a temperature of 180 or 185 degrees. And breast meat really tastes best closer to 160 to 165 degrees.

While the USDA might have us believe that the only safe turkey is a dry turkey, this just isn't true. The two main bacterial problems in turkey are salmonella and Campylobacter jejuni. According to USDA standards, salmonella in meat is killed at 160 degrees, as is campylobacter. Turkey is no different. So why the higher safety standard of 180 degrees?

Part of the problem is that stuffing must reach an internal temperature of 165 degrees to be considered safe. (Carbohydrates such as bread provide a better medium for bacterial growth than do proteins such as meat; hence the extra safety margin of 5 degrees). The USDA also worries that most cooks don't own an accurate thermometer.

The final word on poultry safety is this: As long as the temperature on an accurate instant-read thermometer reaches 160 degrees when inserted in several places, all unstuffed meat (including turkey) should be bacteria-free. Dark meat is undercooked at this stage and tastes better at 170 or 175 degrees. With our turning method, the breast will reach about 165 degrees when the leg is done.

A temperature of 165 degrees also guarantees that stuffed turkeys are safe. But bacteria in meat cooked to 180 or 185 degrees is long gone—as is moistness and flavor.

GRAVY

TO A TRADITIONALIST, THE THOUGHT OF A gravyless Thanksgiving dinner is culinary heresy. Good gravy is no mere condiment; it's the tie that binds. But too often gravy is a last-minute affair, thrown together without much advance preparation or thought. Many of us have experienced the result: either dull, greasy gravy or thin, acidic pan juices that are one-dimensional, lacking the body and stature that we expect from a good American gravy.

So we set out to produce a rich, complex sauce with as much advance preparation as possible to avoid that last-minute time pressure, when space is at a premium and potatoes need to be mashed, turkey sliced, water goblets filled, and candles lit.

We began our tests by experimenting with thickeners. In a blind taste test we tried four different options, including cornstarch, beurre manié (a paste made from equal parts by weight of flour and butter), and two flour-based roux, one regular (a mixture of melted butter and flour stirred together over heat) and one dark (in which the butter-flour paste is cooked until it is dark brown).

Although most tasters were pretty sure before the tasting began that the cornstarch-thickened gravy would have inferior texture and flavor, it actually turned out to be quite good. Admittedly, it was a bit thinner in body and more acidic in flavor than the roux-based sauces, but it was acceptable.

Overall, though, the dark roux proved to be the best thickener. It added a subtle depth and complexity to the sauce not found with the other options. It can also be made ahead of time, a slight advantage because the other methods require last-minute whisking.

To this dark roux, we added turkey stock made from the neck and giblets. Cooking the sauce over low heat for half an hour or more helped develop the flavor, but the resulting gravy was still pale and lacked punch. We then tried using a bulb baster to remove fat from the roasting turkey and using this as the base for the roux, instead of the butter. This tasted fine but was not an improvement over the butter version. We soon discovered, however, that the trick was to take this basic brown sauce—prethickened—and enrich it with pan drippings.

Pan drippings are the source of gravy's allure and also its difficulties. That gorgeous mahogany-colored goo that congeals at the bottom of a roasting pan is one of the best-tasting things on earth, a carnivore's ambrosia. But we found that to get dark brown pan drippings with a complex range of flavors, you need to roast your turkey over aromatic vegetables—chopped onions, carrots, and celery—as well as some fresh thyme sprigs. We also found it necessary to keep an eye on the pan, adding water or stock whenever things started looking too dry.

After deglazing the pan with wine and simmering off the alcohol, we strained the resulting wine sauce into the roux, smashing the remaining herbs and vegetables with a wooden spoon to wring the taste out of them. The result was worth the effort. After a quick simmer and an adjustment of the seasonings, we had an intense and richly flavored sauce that had the familiarity and comfort of traditional American gravy but hinted at the sophistication of a fine French brown sauce.

Giblet Pan Gravy

MAKES ABOUT 6 CUPS

The gravy is best made over several hours. Complete step 1 while the turkey is brining. Continue with step 2 once the bird is in the oven. Start step 3 once the bird has been removed from the oven and is resting on a carving board.

1	tablespoon vegetable oil
	Reserved turkey giblets, neck, and tailpiece
1	onion, unpeeled and chopped
1½	quarts turkey or chicken stock or 1 quart low-sodium canned broth plus 2 cups water
2	thyme branches
8	parsley stems
3	tablespoons unsalted butter
¼	cup flour
1	cup dry white wine
	Salt and ground black pepper

1. Heat oil in soup kettle; add giblets, neck, and tail, then sauté until golden and fragrant, about 5 minutes. Add onion; continue to sauté until softened, 3 to 4 minutes longer. Reduce heat to low; cover and cook until turkey and onion release their juices, about 20 minutes. Add stock and herbs, bring to boil, then adjust heat to low. Simmer, uncovered, skim-

ming any scum that may rise to surface, until broth is rich and flavorful, about 30 minutes longer. Strain broth (you should have about 5 cups) and reserve neck, heart, and gizzard. When cool enough to handle, shred neck meat, remove gristle from gizzard, then dice reserved heart and gizzard. Refrigerate giblets and broth until ready to use.

2. While turkey is roasting, return reserved turkey broth to simmer. Heat butter in large heavy-bottomed saucepan over medium-low heat. Vigorously whisk in flour (roux will froth and then thin out again). Cook slowly, stirring constantly, until nutty brown and fragrant, 10 to 15 minutes. Vigorously whisk all but 1 cup of hot broth into roux. Bring to boil, then continue to simmer until gravy is lightly thickened and very flavorful, about 30 minutes longer. Set aside until turkey is done.

3. When turkey has been transferred to carving board to rest, spoon out and discard as much fat as possible from roasting pan, leaving caramelized herbs and vegetables. Place roasting pan over two burners at medium-high heat (if drippings are not a dark brown, cook, stirring constantly, until they caramelize.) Return gravy to simmer. Add wine to roasting pan of caramelized vegetables, scraping up any browned bits with wooden spoon and boiling until reduced by half, about 5 minutes. Add remaining 1 cup broth, then strain pan juices into gravy, pressing as much juice as possible out of vegetables. Stir giblets into gravy; return to a boil. Adjust seasonings, adding salt and pepper to taste if necessary. Serve with carved turkey.

Roast Turkey with Stuffing

THERE IS SOMETHING UNDENIABLY FESTIVE about a stuffed roasted turkey, and for many people the holidays just aren't the holidays without one. Every year, though, we are warned that for health and safety reasons, turkeys are best roasted unstuffed. Despite these warnings, many cooks continue to stuff their holiday bird. For the sake of flavorful, moist, turkey-infused stuffing, these cooks sacrifice perfectly cooked breast meat and risk food-borne illness from underdone stuffing.

There must be a way, we thought, to safely and successfully roast a stuffed turkey, keeping the breast meat succulent and ensuring that the stuffing is fully cooked. Before we began, we decided to limit our turkey to a maximum of 15 pounds, because it is just too difficult to safely stuff and roast larger birds.

Our objectives were clear. For health reasons, we wanted to find a means of minimizing the amount of time our stuffing would spend in the danger zone of 40 to 140 degrees, in which bacteria grows most quickly. In addition, we sought to coordinate the cooking of the breast and the thigh. We knew that the breast meat cooks faster than the thigh by about 10 degrees, and because the breast is done at 160 degrees and the thigh at 170, this usually results in choke-quality white meat. Introducing stuffing into this equation, we thought, was just asking for trouble; testing had demonstrated that stuffing the turkey slows interior cooking significantly, requiring longer cooking times and producing even drier surface meat.

After a few introductory tests, it became clear that this was exactly the problem we would face. Using high heat or low, the stuffing lagged behind the meat, remaining 5 degrees shy of the 165 we were aiming for, even when both breast and thigh were about 15 degrees higher than we wanted them.

In desperation, we toyed with the idea of sticking hot skewers or a ball of foil into the stuffing in the cavity to help conduct some heat. Suddenly, it occurred to us that if we heated the stuffing for a few minutes in the microwave before filling the cavity, we might give it a head start on cooking. This technique worked for roasting Cornish hens, so why wouldn't it work for a turkey?

We tested the pre-warmed stuffing hypothesis on a turkey that we roasted at a constant 325 degrees. We heated the stuffing in the microwave to about 120 degrees before stuffing the bird. We opted to roast the bird one hour breast down, one hour on each side, then finish with the breast up. As we monitored the temperature of the stuffing, the outlook seemed grim. The stuffing temperature dropped and bottomed out in the first hour at 89 degrees. Gradually it climbed back up and hit 140 degrees, also free of the danger zone, in 2¼ hours, the best time yet. Most impressively, this time we were waiting for thigh to finish cooking, not the stuffing! The breast was long gone at 178 degrees, but we knew we were onto something. This was an enormous improvement over the 3½ hours it had taken for the cold stuffing used in previous tests to dawdle its way to 165, while the breast and thigh meat invariably overcooked.

We pursued the pre-warming technique, and in further tests found that the stuffing usually hits its lowest temperature in the bird at the one-hour mark, dropping approximately 20 degrees. In the microwave we were able to heat it to 130 degrees; starting at such a high temperature helps it get out of the danger zone in 2¼ to 2¾ hours. We checked with food scientists to see if this half an hour differential in times presented a bacterial growth problem. We were told no, since very little occurs above 110 degrees. No longer did we have to wait for the stuffing to finish cooking while the breast and thigh overcooked.

With the stuffing issue resolved, we focused on the best way to roast the turkey. It had become clear to us that high heat and even constant moderate heat wreak havoc on the turkey, resulting in parched breast meat. The low and slow method is, well, too low and slow, and not a safe method for a stuffed turkey. A combination of low heat with high or moderate heat seemed to be the answer.

We also determined that no matter what the cooking temperature, roasting the bird breast down for only one hour was not sufficient. In this position, the breast is shielded and its cooking slowed while the thighs are exposed to the heat needed to speed their cooking. If we rotated the breast up after one or even two hours, the breast was guaranteed to overcook in the remaining time. We abandoned roasting leg side up because it was awkward and ineffective.

We then roasted two turkeys, both started breast down. One cooked at a low 250 degrees for three hours, was rotated breast up, cooked for an additional 15 minutes, and then the temperature was then increased to 400 degrees. The breast overcooked as the thigh crept up to 180 degrees. The other turkey we roasted at 400 degrees for one hour, reduced oven temperature to 250 degrees, flipped breast up after a total of three hours, then turned the heat back up to 400 degrees and roasted until done. This bird

finished as close to perfection as possible: 163 degrees in the breast, 180 degrees in the thigh, and 165 degrees in the stuffing. Clearly, the thigh meat benefited from the initial blast of heat. The only disappointment was the spotty browning of the skin. A few minor adjustments to time spent breast up and we arrived at a safe, perfectly roasted stuffed turkey, one that was flavorful and moist.

Roast Stuffed Turkey
SERVES 10 TO 12

A 12- to 15-pound turkey will accommodate approximately half of the stuffing. Bake the remainder in a casserole dish while the bird rests before carving. Try the gravy recipe on page 175.

2	cups kosher or 1 cup table salt
1	turkey (12 to 15 pounds gross weight), rinsed thoroughly; giblets, neck, and tailpiece removed and reserved to make gravy (see page 175)
2	medium onions, chopped coarse
1	medium carrot, chopped coarse
1	celery stalk, chopped coarse
4	thyme sprigs
12	cups prepared stuffing (pages 180–181)
3	tablespoons unsalted butter, plus extra to grease casserole dish and foil
¼	cup turkey or chicken stock or low-sodium canned broth

1. Dissolve salt in 2 gallons of cold water in large stockpot or clean bucket. Add turkey and refrigerate or set in very cool (40 degrees or less) spot for 12 hours.

2. Remove turkey from salt water and rinse skin and both cavities under cool water for several minutes until all traces of salt are gone. Pat dry inside and out with paper towels; set aside. Adjust oven rack to the lowest position and heat the oven to 400 degrees. Scatter onions, carrot, celery, and thyme over shallow roasting pan. Pour 1 cup water over vegetables. Set V-rack in pan.

3. Place half of stuffing in buttered medium casserole dish, dot surface with 1 tablespoon butter, cover with buttered foil, and refrigerate until ready to use. Microwave remaining stuffing on full power, stirring

CRANBERRY "SAUCES"

THE DISTINCTIVE, TART FLAVOR OF CRANBERRIES HAS LONG MADE THEM A FAVORITE accompaniment for game and fowl, particularly the holiday turkey. You can always follow the directions on the bag of cranberries and boil the fruit with some sugar and water. But why make the same old sauce, which is generally too sweet and one-dimensional in flavor?

Before preparing any of these "sauces," sort through the berries carefully. Leave in any white berries, but discard any that are bruised, bloated, or soft. Freeze berries right in the bag if you like and use thawed berries in any of these recipes.

Cranberry-Red Pepper Relish

MAKES ABOUT 2 1/2 CUPS

2	red bell peppers, cored, seeded, and cut into small dice
2	cups cranberries, picked through and coarsely chopped
1	medium onion, finely chopped
1/2	cup apple cider vinegar
3/4	cup sugar
1	jalapeño chile, stemmed, seeded if desired, and minced
1/4	teaspoon salt
1/4	teaspoon hot red pepper flakes

Mix all ingredients in medium saucepan. Bring to boil, then simmer, uncovered, stirring occasionally, until mixture thickens to the consistency of jam, about 30 minutes. Cool to room temperature. (Can be jarred and refrigerated for at least 2 weeks.)

Cranberry-Onion Confit

MAKES ABOUT 3 CUPS

6	tablespoons unsalted butter
4	large onions, thinly sliced (about 7 cups)
1/2	cup sugar
2	cups whole cranberries, picked through
1	cup red wine
1/4	cup red wine vinegar
3	tablespoons grenadine (optional)
1	teaspoon salt

1. Heat butter in a nonreactive soup kettle or Dutch oven. Add onions; cook over medium-low heat until onions are very soft, about 30 minutes. Increase heat to medium-high and add sugar; cook, stirring frequently, until onions are golden brown and caramelized, about 15 minutes longer.

2. Add remaining ingredients; bring to boil. Simmer, partially covered, until most of liquid is absorbed and mixture has a jamlike consistency, about 25 minutes. Serve warm or at room temperature. (Can be jarred and refrigerated for at least 2 weeks.)

Curried Apple-Cranberry Chutney

MAKES ABOUT 2 1/2 CUPS

2	large Golden Delicious apples, peeled, quartered, cored, and cut into medium dice (about 2 1/2 cups)
1 1/2	cups cranberries, picked through and coarsely chopped
3/4	cup light brown sugar
1/2	cup golden raisins
1/2	medium onion, minced
1	tablespoon minced crystallized ginger
1	tablespoon yellow mustard seeds
2	medium garlic cloves, minced
1	teaspoon zest from 1 small lemon
1	teaspoon curry powder
1/4	teaspoon salt
1/8	teaspoon cayenne pepper

Mix all ingredients in medium saucepan. Bring to boil; cover and simmer, stirring occasionally, until apples are tender and most liquid is absorbed, about 30 minutes. Cool to room temperature. (Can be jarred and refrigerated for at least 2 weeks.)

two or three times, until very hot (120 to 130 degrees), 6 to 8 minutes (if you can handle stuffing with hands, it is not hot enough). Spoon 4 to 5 cups of stuffing into the turkey cavity until very loosely packed (see illustration below). Secure skin flap over the cavity opening with turkey lacers or skewers (see illustration below). Melt remaining 2 tablespoons butter. Tuck wings behind back, brush entire breast side with half of melted butter, then place turkey breast side down on V-rack. Fill neck cavity with remaining heated stuffing and secure skin flap over opening as above (see illustration below). Brush back with remaining butter.

4. Roast 1 hour, then reduce temperature to 250 degrees and roast 2 hours longer, adding additional water if pan becomes dry. Remove pan from oven (close oven door) and with wad of paper toweling in each hand, turn bird breast side up and baste (temperature of breast should be 145 to 150 degrees). Increase oven temperature to 400 degrees; continue roasting until breast registers about 165 degrees, thigh registers 170 to 175 degrees, and stuffing registers 165 degrees on instant-read thermometer, 1 to 1½ hours longer. Remove turkey from oven and let rest until ready to carve.

5. Add ¼ cup stock to dish of reserved stuffing, replace foil, and bake until hot throughout, about 20 minutes. Remove foil; continue to bake until stuffing forms golden brown crust, about 15 minutes longer.

6. Carve turkey; serve with stuffing and gravy.

BREAD STUFFINGS FOR TURKEY

IN OUR TESTS, WE FOUND THAT DRY BREAD cubes are essential when making stuffing because they do a better job of absorbing seasonings and other flavors than fresh cubes. To dry bread, cut a fresh loaf of French or other white bread into half-inch slices, place the slices in a single layer on cookie sheets or cooling racks, and allow the slices to sit out overnight. The next day, cut the slices into half-inch cubes and allow them to dry in a single layer for an additional night.

If you're in a hurry, place half-inch slices of bread in a 225-degree oven for 30 to 40 minutes, or until dried but not browned. Remove the bread from the oven and cut into half-inch cubes. You will need a one-pound loaf of bread to obtain the 12 cups of bread cubes necessary for the following recipes.

All of these stuffings can be covered and refrigerated for one day. Store the mixture in a 13 x 9-inch or comparably sized microwave-safe pan and reheat in a 325-degree oven or microwave until stuffing is heated through before packing it into a bird.

Place any stuffing that won't fit in the bird in a greased eight-inch-square baking dish. Drizzle ¼ cup stock over stuffing, dot with pats of butter, and cover with piece of foil that has been smeared with butter. Bake in 400-degree oven for about 25 minutes, remove the foil, and bake an additional 15 minutes.

STUFFING A TURKEY

1. Use a measuring cup to place the preheated stuffing into the cavity of the bird. Remember, it's imperative that the stuffing be heated before it is placed in the bird.

2. To keep the stuffing in the cavity, use metal skewers (or cut bamboo skewers) and thread them through the skin on both sides of the cavity.

3. Center a 2-foot piece of kitchen twine on the top skewer and then cross the twine as you wrap each end of the string around and under the skewers. Loosely tie the legs together with another short piece of twine.

4. Flip bird over onto its breast. Stuff the neck cavity loosely with approximately 1 cup of stuffing. Pull skin flap over and use a skewer to pin flap to turkey.

Bread Stuffing with Sausage, Pecans, and Dried Apricots

MAKES ABOUT 12 CUPS

High-quality sausage is the key to this recipe. Toast the pecans in a 350-degree oven until fragrant, 6 to 8 minutes.

1	pound sweet Italian sausage, removed from casings and crumbled
6	tablespoons unsalted butter
1	large onion, chopped (about 1½ cups)
4	medium celery stalks, chopped (about 1½ cups)
½	teaspoon each dried sage, dried thyme, dried marjoram
½	teaspoon ground black pepper
½	cup fresh parsley leaves, chopped fine
2	cups pecans, toasted and roughly chopped
1	cup dried apricots, cut into thin strips
1	teaspoon salt
12	cups dried French or other white bread cubes (see page 179)
1	cup chicken stock or low-sodium canned broth
3	large eggs, lightly beaten

1. Cook sausage in large skillet over medium heat until browned, about 10 minutes. Transfer sausage to large bowl with slotted spoon. Discard fat and in same pan melt butter.

2. Add onion and celery and cook, stirring occasionally, over medium heat until soft and translucent, 6 to 7 minutes. Add dried herbs and pepper and cook for another minute. Transfer contents of pan to bowl with sausage. Add parsley, pecans, apricots, and salt and mix to combine. Add bread cubes to bowl.

3. Whisk stock and eggs together in small bowl. Pour mixture over bread cubes. Gently toss to evenly distribute ingredients.

Bread Stuffing with Ham, Pine Nuts, Mushrooms, and Fennel

MAKES ABOUT 12 CUPS

Light brown cremini mushrooms have more flavor than regular white button mushrooms, but the latter can be used in this recipe.

6	tablespoons unsalted butter
1	large onion, chopped (about 1½ cups)
1	large fennel bulb, chopped (about 1½ cups)
10	ounces cremini mushrooms, cleaned and sliced thin
1½	teaspoons dried basil
½	teaspoon ground black pepper
1	cup pine nuts, toasted
¼	pound thinly sliced prosciutto, cut into thin strips
¼	pound thinly sliced smoked ham, cut in half and then crosswise into thin strips
½	cup grated Parmesan cheese
½	cup fresh parsley leaves, chopped fine
½	teaspoon salt
12	cups dried French or other white bread cubes (see page 179)
1	cup chicken stock or low-sodium canned broth
3	large eggs, lightly beaten

1. Melt butter in large skillet or Dutch oven. Add onion and fennel and cook, stirring occasionally, over medium heat until soft and translucent, 6 to 7 minutes. Add mushrooms and cook until liquid they release has evaporated, about 10 minutes. Add basil and pepper and cook for another minute. Transfer contents of pan to large bowl.

2. Add pine nuts, prosciutto, smoked ham, cheese, parsley, and salt to bowl and mix to combine. Add bread cubes.

3. Whisk stock and eggs together in small bowl. Pour mixture over bread cubes. Gently toss to evenly distribute ingredients.

Bread Stuffing with Bacon, Apples, Sage, and Caramelized Onions

MAKES ABOUT 12 CUPS

For the best flavor, make sure to cook the onions until they are a deep golden-brown color.

1	pound bacon, cut crosswise into ¼-inch strips
6	medium onions, sliced thin (about 7 cups)
1	teaspoon salt
2	Granny Smith apples, peeled, cored, and cut into ½-inch cubes (about 2 cups)
½	teaspoon ground black pepper

½ cup fresh parsley leaves, chopped fine

3   tablespoons fresh sage leaves, cut into thin strips

12 cups dried French or other white bread cubes
     (see page 179)

1   cup chicken stock or low-sodium canned broth

3   large eggs, lightly beaten

1. Cook bacon in large skillet or Dutch oven over medium heat until crisp and browned, about 12 minutes. Remove bacon from pan with slotted spoon and drain on paper towels. Discard all but 3 tablespoons of rendered bacon fat.

2. Increase heat to medium-high and add onions and ¼ teaspoon of salt. Cook onions until golden in color, making sure to stir occasionally and scrape sides and bottom of pan, about 20 minutes. Reduce heat to medium and continue to cook, stirring more often to prevent burning, until onions are deep golden brown, another 5 minutes. Add apples and continue to cook another 5 minutes. Transfer contents of pan to large bowl.

3. Add remaining ¾ teaspoon salt, pepper, parsley, and sage to bowl and mix to combine. Add bread cubes.

4. Whisk stock and eggs together in small bowl. Pour mixture over bread cubes. Gently toss to evenly distribute ingredients.

TURKEY BURGERS

A LEAN, FULLY COOKED TURKEY BURGER, seasoned with salt and pepper, is a weak stand-in for an all-beef burger. Simply put, it is dry, tasteless, and colorless. We wanted a turkey burger with beef burger qualities—dark and crusty on the outside and full-flavored and juicy with every bite.

Finding the right meat was crucial to developing the best turkey burger. According to the National Turkey Federation, there are three options—white meat (with 1 to 2 percent fat), dark meat (over 15 percent fat), and a blend of the two (ranging from 7 to 15 percent fat).

At the grocery store, we found multiple variations on the white meat/dark meat theme, including preformed lean patties, higher-fat ground fresh turkey on Styrofoam trays or frozen in tubes like bulk sausage, and lower-fat ground turkey breasts; then there were the individual turkey parts we take home

and grind up ourselves. We bought them all, took them home, and fired up a skillet.

We first tested the preformed lean patties—refrigerated and frozen—and found them mediocre. To varying degrees, the frozen ones had a week-old-roast-turkey taste. A few bites from one of the refrigerated varieties turned up significant turkey debris—tendon, ground-up gristle, and bonelike chips. We moved on to bulk ground turkey.

The higher-fat (15 percent) ground turkey turned out to be flavorful and reasonably juicy with a decent, burgerlike crust. Frankly, these burgers didn't need too much help. On the other hand, we didn't see much point in eating them either. Given that a great beef burger contains only 20 percent fat, a mere 5 percent fat savings didn't seem worth it.

At the other extreme, with only 1 or 2 percent fat, was ground turkey breast. As we were mixing and forming these patties, we knew we had about as much chance of making them look, taste, and feel like real burgers as we did of making vanilla wafers taste like chocolate chip cookies. They needed a binder to keep them from falling apart. They needed extra fat to keep them from parching and extra fat in the pan to keep them from sticking. And they needed flavor to save them from blandness.

With 7 percent fat, lean ground turkey was the most popular style at all the grocery stores we checked. Burgers made from this mix were dry, rubbery-textured, and mild-flavored. With a little help, however, these leaner patties were meaty enough to have real burger potential.

Most flavorful of all and only about 10 percent fat were the boned and skinless turkey thighs we ground ourselves in the food processor. We first tried grinding the skin with the meat but found that it ground inconsistently and we had to pick it out. In the next batch we left it out and found the result to be equally flavorful and much lower in calories. As a matter of fact, our butcher declared our home-ground skinless turkey almost 90-percent lean when he tested it in his Univex Fat Analyzer.

For all the obvious reasons, we had sworn that even if we liked the outcome we weren't going to make grind-your-own-turkey part of the recipe, but these burgers—meaty-flavored with a beeflike chew—were far superior to any we made with the commercially ground turkey. Of course, we had suspected as much, given our liking for grind-your-own-chuck beef burgers (see page 216). If you are willing to take the time, turkey thighs ground up in the food processor cook up into low-fat turkey burgers with great flavor and texture.

For those with little time or energy for this process, we decided to see what we could do to improve the lean commercially ground turkey. To improve texture and juiciness, we started with the obvious—milk-soaked bread. For comparison we also made burgers with buttermilk- and yogurt-soaked bread. All these additions made the burgers feel too much like meat loaf and destroyed whatever meaty flavor there had been, since turkey is mild to start with. The bread and milk lightened the meat's color unpleasantly, while the sugar in both ingredients caused the burgers to burn easily and made it impossible to develop a good thick crust.

We tried other fillers to improve the texture, including cornmeal mush, mashed pinto beans, and minced tempeh, but their flavors were too distinct. Minced, rehydrated, dried mushrooms added a moist, chewy texture that the burgers desperately needed. They also offered an earthy, meaty, yet not overly distinct flavor. However, the real winner—for flavor, texture, and easy availability—was ricotta cheese. Moist and chewy, it gave the burgers the texture boost they needed and required very little effort.

Finally, we decided to experiment a bit with added flavorings. We wanted only those which would enhance a burger's taste without drawing attention to themselves. We tried more than 25 different flavorings—from fermented black beans to olive paste to teriyaki marinade—and found only two that we liked: Worcestershire sauce and Dijon mustard.

Next we turned to the cooking method. Since turkey burgers must be well-done for safety reasons, cooking them can be a bit tricky—too high a heat and they burn before they're done; too low and they look pale and steamed. We tried several cooking methods, from broiling to roasting, but nothing compared in quality and ease with our stove-top method. Browning the burgers in a heavy-bottomed skillet over medium heat, then cooking them partially covered over low heat gave us a rich-crusted burger that was cooked all the way through.

Although our generous cooking times should ensure a fully cooked burger, as an extra precaution you may want to test for doneness by sticking an instant-read thermometer through the side and into the center of one of them. The burger is done at 160 degrees.

Best Turkey Burgers
SERVES 4

We found that the extra step of grinding fresh turkey thighs ourselves made the most flavorful, best-textured burgers. If you can, buy boneless turkey thighs. Pan-frying develops a good, thick crust on the burgers, while grilling (see page 183) gives them a subtle smoky flavor that we love.

1	turkey thigh (about 2 pounds), skinned and boned, or 1 ½ pounds skinless, boneless thighs
½	teaspoon salt
½	teaspoon ground black pepper
2	teaspoons Worcestershire sauce
2	teaspoons Dijon mustard
1	tablespoon vegetable or canola oil

1. Cut skinned and boned thigh into 1-inch chunks and arrange in single layer on baking sheet. Freeze until somewhat firm, about 30 minutes.

2. Working in 3 batches, place semifrozen turkey chunks in workbowl of food processor fitted with steel blade; pulse until largest pieces are no bigger than ⅛ inch, 12 to 14 one-second pulses.

3. Transfer ground meat to medium bowl. Stir in salt, pepper, Worcestershire sauce, and mustard until blended, and divide meat into 4 portions. Lightly toss one portion from hand to hand to form a ball, then lightly flatten ball with fingertips into 1-inch-thick patty. Repeat with remaining portions.

4. Heat a large, heavy skillet (preferably cast iron or stainless steel with an aluminum core) over medium heat until very hot, 4 to 5 minutes. Swirl oil in pan to coat bottom, then add burgers. Cook over medium heat without moving burgers until bottom side of each is dark brown and crusted, about 5 minutes. Turn burgers over; continue to cook until bottom side is light brown but not yet crusted, 4 to 5 minutes longer. Reduce heat to low, position cover slightly ajar on pan to allow steam to escape, and continue to cook 5 to 6 minutes longer, or until cen-

ter is completely opaque yet still juicy or an instant-read thermometer inserted from the side of the burger into the center registers 160 degrees. Remove from pan and serve immediately.

Quicker Turkey Burgers
SERVES 4

By enriching store-bought ground lean turkey with ricotta cheese, you can produce an excellent burger. Ricotta cheese can burn easily, so keep a close watch on the burgers as they cook.

1 ¼	pounds 93 percent lean ground turkey
½	cup ricotta cheese
½	teaspoon salt
½	teaspoon ground black pepper
2	teaspoons Worcestershire sauce
2	teaspoons Dijon mustard
1	tablespoon vegetable or canola oil

1. Combine ground turkey, cheese, salt, pepper, Worcestershire sauce, and mustard in medium bowl until blended. Divide meat into 4 portions. Lightly toss one portion from hand to hand to form a ball, then lightly flatten ball with fingertips into 1-inch-thick patty. Repeat with remaining portions.

2. Heat a large, heavy skillet (preferably cast iron or stainless steel with an aluminum core) over medium heat until very hot, 4 to 5 minutes. Swirl oil in pan to coat bottom, then add burgers. Cook over medium heat without moving burgers until bottom side of each is dark brown and crusted, 3 to 4 minutes. Turn burgers over; continue to cook until bottom side is light brown but not yet crusted, 3 to 4 minutes longer. Reduce heat to low, position cover slightly ajar on pan to allow steam to escape, and continue to cook 8 to 10 minutes longer, flipping once if necessary to promote deep browning, or until center is completely opaque yet still juicy or an instant-read thermometer inserted from the side of the burger into the center registers 160 degrees. Remove from pan and serve immediately.

➤ VARIATION
Grilled Turkey Burgers
Complete recipe for Best Turkey Burgers through step 3, or complete recipe for Quicker Turkey Burgers through step 1. Grill burgers over medium-low fire (you can hold your hand about 5 inches above grill surface for 5 seconds) until dark spotty brown on bottom side, 7 to 9 minutes. Turn burgers over; continue grilling 7 to 9 minutes longer or until bottom side is dark spotty brown and center is completely cooked or instant-read thermometer inserted from the side of the burger registers 160 degrees. Remove from grill and serve immediately.

ROAST DUCK

GOOD DUCKS ARE DELICIOUS, BUT TOO often our pleasure in them is ruined because they are just too greasy. It wasn't always this way. Wild ducks are so lean they need to be covered with bacon to keep them from drying out in the oven. But only hunters encounter this problem. Supermarket shoppers must rely on domesticated Pekin (also called Long Island) ducks. And, boy, are these birds fatty. Although the sticker weight may say 4½ pounds, the final weight after roasting can be less than 2 pounds. No wonder a single duck yields two or maybe three servings.

A knockout duck should have crisp skin and moist, flavorful meat. To achieve this goal, we would have to rid the bird of a lot of fat. At the outset, we decided we wanted an old-fashioned roast duck, cooked through without a trace of pink. Restaurants rely on different duck breeds with large breasts, in particular the muscovy, that can be cooked rare. But consumers must order such ducks by mail, and we wanted to use the duck you find in the supermarket. Since the breast on a Pekin duck is no thicker than half an inch, it can't be cooked rare or medium, especially if you're trying to get the legs to soften up.

Our initial tests demonstrated the need to start getting rid of the fat from the outset. We found that unless the skin rests directly on meat or bone it will never crisp properly. So before cooking even starts, the large clumps of white fat that line the body and neck cavity must be pulled out by hand and discarded. Any loose skin must also be trimmed away, including most of the flap that covers the neck cavity.

Our next tests centered on roasting methods. Every source we consulted agreed that a roasting rack is necessary to keep the duck elevated above the rendered fat. After that, there was little agreement. Many recipes suggest pricking the skin to help fat escape. We used a fork as well as the tip of a paring knife, and both worked moderately well.

One chef told us he always starts duck in a 500-degree oven to render the fat quickly and then turns down the heat to 350 degrees to cook the duck through. Our instincts told us this approach was problematic, and the billows of smoke that filled the kitchen proved that this method can work only in a kitchen equipped with an extremely powerful exhaust.

Next we tried the method advocated by most older sources—cooking in a moderate oven (350 degrees) for two hours, followed by a short burst of higher heat (425 degrees) to crisp the skin. The results were decent. The skin was good and the breast was fine. However, the legs were still too fatty, and the wings were flabby and totally unappetizing. Tasters devoured the breasts, but they ate around the fat in the legs and no one would touch the wings.

Many recent sources tout slow roasting followed by a period of moderate roasting to crisp the skin. Of all the traditional methods that we tried, slow roasting and constant turning (so that the fat drips down from all sides) did the best job of getting rid of fat. However, even after four hours in the oven, the legs were still too fatty to eat with gusto. The internal fat, especially the fat that divides the thigh from the leg, was not melting away. And we noticed that the breast meat (which is hard to overcook because of the fatty skin on top) was actually starting to dry out after so many hours in the oven. We had created a problem that duck wasn't supposed to have. Clearly, it was time to switch gears.

Many Asian recipes for duck start with steaming or boiling. The theory is that moist heat melts some of the fat, and it's true. Because moisture transfers heat more efficiently than dry air, moist cooking methods such as steaming cause more fluid loss than dry cooking methods such as roasting. After steaming or boiling, the duck can be roasted to render the rest of the fat and crisp up the skin. We decided to try a two-step cooking process, with moist heat followed by dry heat.

We bought three ducks and steamed one for an hour (a time suggested by several sources), blanched another for one minute (the method we'd found best for goose; see page 185), and boiled a third for 15 minutes. The steamed and boiled ducks were already

cooked, so we roasted them in a 400-degree oven to crisp the skin. The blanched duck was roasted at a constant 350 degrees for two hours, followed by 425 degrees until the skin was brown and crisp.

The scale told the story here. When we roasted a duck without any treatment with water, we were able to reduce its initial weight by an average of 45 percent. Boiling or blanching pushed this number up to 48 percent and 46 percent, respectively. In contrast, the duck that was steamed lost an astonishing 58% of its weight. This duck also tasted less greasy, especially in the breast, and the skin was the thinnest and the crispest.

One problem remained. We still thought the legs were a bit too fatty. We wanted them to be dense, dark, and meaty, like the best confit. Steaming was melting all the fat right underneath the skin, but domesticated birds have a lot of intermuscular fat in the leg and thigh, which is shielded from the steam and the oven heat by skin, meat, and bone. We tried various steaming times and roasting regimens, but we just couldn't get the legs degreased.

At this point, we decided to cut the bird into six parts—two wings, two leg/thighs, and two breasts. We figured the fat in the leg/thighs would no longer be protected and would render quickly in the oven. And were we ever right. The difference was dramatic.

When we roasted a whole steamed duck for an hour, only two to three tablespoons of fat were rendered. However, when we roasted the parts from a steamed duck for less time and with far less body weight (we were saving the carcass and back for stock), we were able to coax a full one-third cup of fat out of the six parts. The skin was especially crisp and delicious because we were able to cook the parts skin side down directly on the pan, not on a rack. (We found it helpful to spoon off the fat when turning the parts.) The breast was moist, the wings were beautifully browned and very crisp, and we finally had a roast duck with legs that everyone at the table was fighting over.

There is a downside here—you can't bring a whole roasted duck to the table. But the duck tastes better, and we think it's easier to carve it before roasting than to do it with everyone gathered at the table. Also, because the duck is split into parts, you can roast two ducks at once in a regular large roasting pan.

As for the steaming step, we would never roast duck again without doing this first. It doesn't really add any time to the process because the duck roasts for such a short period. It can also be steamed a day in advance. Two-step duck may not be the easiest, but it produces the best results and minimizes last-minute kitchen work. You can roast duck for a small holiday gathering, knowing that every piece of the duck will be delicious—and mercifully free of grease.

Crisp Roast Duck with Port Wine Glaze

SERVES 2 TO 3

Pekin ducks, also called Long Island ducks, are the only choice in most supermarkets. Almost always sold frozen, the duck must defrost in the refrigerator for at least one day before cooking. To feed six people, steam one duck after the other and then roast all the pieces together in an oversized roasting pan or a large jelly-roll pan.

PORT WINE GLAZE

1¼   cups port wine
2   medium garlic cloves, peeled and cut into thin slivers
4   fresh thyme sprigs

CRISP ROAST DUCK

1   whole Pekin duck (about 4½ pounds), neck, giblets, and all visible fat discarded, and rinsed
  Salt and ground black pepper

1. FOR THE GLAZE: Bring all ingredients to boil in small saucepan. Reduce heat to medium–low and simmer until slightly thickened and reduced to scant ¼ cup, 25 to 30 minutes. Remove and discard garlic and thyme; set glaze aside until ready to use.

2. FOR THE DUCK: Meanwhile, set V-rack in large, high-sided roasting pan and position duck, breast side up, on rack. Add water to just below bottom of duck. Bring water to boil over high heat, cover pan tightly with aluminum foil (or pan cover, if available), adjust heat to medium (to maintain a slow, steady boil), and steam, adding more hot water to maintain water level if necessary, until skin has pulled away from at least one leg. For duck with very moist, tender meat and slightly crisp skin once roasted, steam about 40 minutes. Steam 10 minutes longer for somewhat denser meat and very crisp skin after roasting. Transfer duck

to carving board and, when cool enough to handle, cut into six pieces, two wings, two legs, and two breast halves. (Cooled duck, either whole or cut into pieces, can be wrapped in foil and refrigerated overnight. Reserve back and carcass for another use.)

3. Adjust oven rack to bottom position and heat oven to 425 degrees. Season pieces on both sides with salt and pepper to taste and position skin side down in lightly oiled roasting pan. Roast, carefully pouring off fat if more than two tablespoons accumulate in pan, until skin on breast pieces is rich brown color and crisp, about 25 minutes. Transfer breast pieces to platter and cover with foil to keep warm. Again, pour off excess fat from pan, turn leg/thigh and wing pieces skin side up, and continue roasting until skin on these pieces is deep brown and crisp, 15 to 20 minutes longer. Again, pour off excess fat from pan. Return breast pieces to pan and brush both sides of every piece with glaze. Roast until glaze is hot and richly colored on duck pieces, 3 to 4 minutes. Serve immediately.

➤ VARIATION
Crisp Roast Duck with Orange Glaze
The lime juice keeps this thick, syrupy glaze from being too sweet.

Follow recipe for Crisp Roast Duck with Port Wine Glaze, substituting 1 cup fresh squeezed orange juice, 2 tablespoons fresh lime juice, and 2 tablespoons honey for port and omitting garlic and thyme.

ROAST GOOSE
THOSE WHO HAVE NEVER COOKED A GOOSE are in for a treat. The meat is surprisingly firm, almost chewy to the bite, yet it is also moist and not at all tough or stringy. Both the breast and legs are dark, in the manner of duck, but unlike duck, goose has no gamy or tallowy undertones. Actually, the first impression of many people is that goose tastes a lot like roast beef, and perhaps it is this rich, beefy quality that makes the bird so satisfying.

Goose does, however, have a problem. Although the meat itself is not fatty, a thick layer of fat lies just below the skin. As a consequence, the skin, which looks so tempting, often turns out to be too soft and greasy to eat. To make a good roast goose, it is imperative to rid the bird of this fat.

Most cookbooks and chefs suggest periodic basting with chicken stock or wine to dissolve the fat and promote a handsome brown color. But this method does not work. A considerable amount of subcutaneous fat always remains, and, worse, the basting seriously softens goose skin, which should be crackling crisp. We tried a variation on this technique. During the last hour of roasting, we turned the oven heat up to 450 degrees and stopped basting. We were hoping to get crispy skin, but what we actually got was a smoky kitchen. And to no purpose—the skin was still chewy and fatty.

Among all the goose-cooking methods we had read about, we were most intrigued by the steam-roasting and closed-cover techniques recommended by various authorities. Since the best way to render fat is to simmer it in water, steaming sounded like a promising procedure. It had already worked for us in degreasing duck.

So we set a goose on a rack above an inch of water and steamed it on top of the stove in a covered roaster for about an hour. Then we poured the water out of the pan and put the goose into a 325-degree oven, covered. After one hour we checked on the goose, and, seeing that the skin was very flabby and not in the least bit brown, we removed the pan cover and turned the heat up to 350 degrees. Alas, an hour later the skin was still soft and only a little more brown. Even though the goose tested done at this point, we let it stay in the oven for another 30 min-

PREPARING A GOOSE

1. Use tweezers or small pliers to remove any remaining quills from the goose skin.

2. Pull back the skin at the neck end and locate the wishbone. Scrape along the outside of the wishbone with a paring knife until the bone is exposed; then cut the bone free of the flesh.

3. Pull down on the wishbone, freeing it from the carcass; add the bone to the stockpot.

4. With a trussing needle or thin skewer, prick skin all over, especially around breast and thighs, holding the needle parallel to the bird to avoid pricking meat. This helps render the fat during cooking.

5. Using rubber gloves to protect your hands, lower the goose, neck end down, into boiling water, until "goose bumps" appear, about 1 minute. Repeat this process, submerging the goose tail end down.

6. Pack a small handful of stuffing into the neck cavity; sew the opening shut with a trussing needle and heavy white twine.

7. Pack the remaining stuffing in the body cavity, pressing it in firmly with your hands or a large spoon; sew the body vent shut.

utes, but the skin did not improve.

Tasting the goose, we realized that there was yet another problem: steaming had perhaps made the meat a tad juicier, but it had also made the texture a little rubbery and imparted a boiled, stewish flavor. The goose no longer tasted the way we thought goose should. So we abandoned steaming.

Since liquid basting and steaming had both proved unsuccessful, we thought it was time to try a simple dry roast. Some of the geese that we had bought came with instructions to roast at 500 degrees for 30 minutes and then to turn the oven down to 300 degrees and roast several hours longer. We stuffed the goose, dried and pricked the skin, and popped it into the scorching oven. As we should have guessed, within 15 minutes the goose had begun to drip, and the kitchen had filled with smoke. We quickly turned the oven thermostat down to 300 degrees and let the bird roast until it tested done, about three hours. Then we increased the oven temperature to 400 degrees, transferred the goose to a large jelly-roll pan, and returned it to the oven for about 15 minutes to brown and crisp the skin. This method, the simplest of all, yielded a beautifully brown, crisp-skinned bird, with moist meat and surprisingly little unmelted fat.

Dry, open roasting looked like the way to proceed, but we wondered if the technique could be further improved. We thought about adapting a classic technique often used with duck. The duck is immersed in boiling water for one minute and then allowed to dry, uncovered, in the refrigerator for 24 hours. The boiling and drying were supposed to tighten the skin, so that during roasting, the fat would be squeezed out. We tried this method with a goose and loved the results. The skin was papery-crisp and defatted to the point where it could be eaten with pleasure—and without guilt.

Unlike these other birds, the doneness of goose cannot be judged solely by the internal temperature of the meat. The length of the cooking time is also an important factor. Goose generally reaches an internal temperature of 170 degrees in the thigh cavity (the usual indicator of "well done") after less than two hours of roasting. Yet the meat turns out to be tough, especially around the thighs, if the bird is removed from the oven at this point. At least 45 minutes of additional roasting are required to make the meat tender. Since goose has so much fat, there is little chance of the meat drying out. The most reliable indicator of doneness is the feel of the drumsticks. When the skin has puffed and the meat inside feels soft and almost shredded when pressed—like well-done stew meat—the rest of the bird should be just right.

Another good way to test for doneness is to make a small slit in the skin at the base of the thigh, where it joins the body. If the juices are pinkish rather than clear, the bird needs more cooking. If, on the other hand, there are no juices, the goose has been cooked enough and may even be verging on overdone. Don't panic though. One of the nicest things about goose is that it is tolerant of a little overcooking and does not readily dry out and turn stringy. This is because the particular proteins in goose tend to turn soft and gelatinous during cooking, so goose remains moist and tender even when thoroughly cooked.

Roast Goose
SERVES 8 TO 10
Turning the goose in the boiling water is not necessary if you have a stock pot large enough for the goose to be fully submerged.

1   whole goose (10 to 12 pounds gross weight), neck, giblets, wing tips, and excess fat removed, rinsed, patted dry, and reserved in refrigerator to make gravy; wishbone removed and skin pricked all over (see illustrations on page 186)
8   cups Bread Stuffing with Bacon, Apples, Sage, and Caramelized Onions (page 180), heated
    Salt and ground black pepper
1   recipe Giblet Gravy with Red Wine and Sherry (page 188)

1. Heat large stockpot two-thirds full of water to boil. Submerge goose in boiling water (see illustration on page 186). Drain goose and dry thoroughly, inside and out, with paper towels. Set goose, breast side up, on flat rack in roasting pan and refrigerate, uncovered, for 24 to 48 hours.

2. Adjust oven rack to low-center position and heat to 325 degrees. Stuff and truss goose (see illustrations on page 186). Season goose skin liberally with salt and pepper.

3. Place goose, breast down, on heavy-duty V-rack set over roasting pan; roast for 1½ hours. Remove goose from oven and bail out most of fat from roasting pan, being careful not to disturb browned bits at bottom of pan. Turn goose breast up, and return to oven to roast until flesh of drumsticks feels soft and broken up (like well-done stew meat) and skin has puffed up around breast bone and tops of thighs, 1¼ to 1½ hours longer. Increase oven temperature to 400 degrees; transfer goose, still on its rack, to large jelly-roll pan. Return to oven to further brown and fully crisp skin, about 15 minutes longer. Let stand, uncovered, about 30 minutes before carving.

4. Remove trussing, and spoon stuffing into serving bowl. Carve goose; serve with stuffing and gravy.

Giblet Gravy with Red Wine and Sherry

MAKES ABOUT 2 CUPS

This simple gravy starts with the Brown Goose Stock and then uses sherry to deglaze the roasting pan with the browned bits from the goose. Make the stock (steps 1 through 3) while the goose is in the oven, and then start this gravy (step 4) once the goose has been transferred to a carving board.

BROWN GOOSE STOCK

3	tablespoons reserved goose fat, patted dry and chopped
	Reserved goose neck and wing tips, hacked into 1-inch pieces; heart and gizzard left whole, all parts patted dry
1	medium onion, chopped
1	medium carrot, peeled and chopped
1	medium celery stalk, chopped
2	teaspoons sugar
2	cups full-bodied red wine
½	cup chicken stock or low-sodium canned broth
6	large parsley stems
1	large bay leaf
1	teaspoon black peppercorns
½	teaspoon dried thyme

GRAVY

½	cup sweet sherry (cream or amontillado)
½	cup chicken stock or low-sodium canned broth, if needed
2½	tablespoons melted goose fat from the roasting pan
2½	tablespoons all-purpose flour
1	goose liver, cut into small dice
	Salt and ground black pepper

1. Heat fat over medium heat in large saucepan until it melts. Increase heat to medium-high; heat fat until it just begins to smoke. Add goose pieces to fat; sauté, stirring frequently, until meat turns deep mahogany color, about 10 minutes.

2. Add heart and gizzard, onion, carrot, and celery; sauté, stirring frequently, until vegetables brown around edges, about 10 minutes longer. Stir in sugar; continue to cook, stirring continuously, until it caramelizes. Pour in wine, scraping pan bottom with wooden spoon to dissolve browned bits.

3. Add chicken stock, parsley, bay leaf, peppercorns, and thyme. Bring to simmer, then adjust heat so that liquid barely bubbles. Simmer, partially covered, until stock is dark and rich, about 2 hours, adding a little water if solids become exposed.

4. Spoon most of fat out of roasting pan, leaving behind all brown roasting particles. Set pan over two burners on low heat. Add sherry; scrape with wooden spoon until all brown glaze in pan is dissolved. Pour mixture into goose stock; simmer to blend flavors, about 5 minutes.

5. Strain mixture into 4-cup glass measure, pressing down on solids with back of spoon; let liquid stand until fat rises to top. Skim fat, and, if necessary, add enough chicken stock to make up to 2 cups. Rinse out goose stockpot and return strained stock to it. Take heart and gizzard from strainer, cut in tiny dice, and add to goose stock. (Discard remaining solids in strainer.) Return stock to boil.

6. Heat goose fat and flour over medium-low heat in heavy-bottomed medium saucepan, stirring constantly with wooden spoon until roux just begins to color, about 5 minutes; remove from heat. Beating constantly with whisk, pour boiling stock, all at once, into brown roux. Return saucepan to low heat; simmer 3 minutes. Add liver; simmer 1 minute longer. Taste, and adjust seasoning, adding salt and lots of freshly ground black pepper.

7

BEEF

EIGHT DIFFERENT CUTS OF BEEF ARE SOLD AT the wholesale level (see illustration below). From this first series of cuts, known to those in the trade as primal cuts, a butcher (usually at a meat-packing plant in the Midwest but sometimes on-site at your local market) will make the retail cuts that you bring home from the market. How you choose to cook a particular piece of beef depends on where the meat comes from on the cow and how it was butchered.

CHUCK Starting at the front of the animal, the chuck (or shoulder) runs from the neck down to the fifth rib. There are four major muscles in this region, and meat from the chuck tends to be flavorful and fairly fatty, which is why ground chuck makes the best hamburgers. Chuck also contains a fair amount of connective tissue, so when the meat is not ground it generally requires a long cooking time to become tender.

RIB SECTION Moving back from the chuck, the next primal cut along the top half of the animal is the rib section, which extends from the sixth to the twelfth rib. The prime rib comes from this area, as do rib-eye steaks. Rib cuts have an excellent beefy flavor and are quite tender.

LOIN The loin (called the short loin on a cow) extends from the last rib back through the midsection of the animal to the hip area. It contains two major muscles—the tenderloin and the shell. The tenderloin is extremely tender (it is positioned right under the spine) and has a quite mild flavor. This muscle may be sold whole as a roast or sliced crosswise into steaks, called filet mignon. The shell is a much larger muscle and has a more robust beef flavor as well as more fat. Strip steaks (also called shell steaks) come from this muscle and are our favorite. Two steaks from the short loin area contain portions of both the tenderloin and shell muscles. These steaks are called the T-bone and porterhouse, and both are excellent choices.

SIRLOIN The next area is the sirloin, which contains relatively inexpensive cuts that are sold both as steaks and roasts. We find that sirloin cuts are fairly lean and tough. In general, we prefer other parts of the animal, although top sirloin makes a decent roast.

ROUND The rear of the cow is called the round. Roasts and steaks cut from this area are usually sold boneless and are quite lean and can be tough. Again, we generally prefer cuts from other parts of the cow, although top round can be roasted with some measure of success.

SHANK/BRISKET, PLATE, & FLANK The underside of the animal is divided into the shank/brisket (near the front of the animal), the plate, and the flank. Thick boneless cuts are removed from these three parts of the cow. The brisket is rather tough and contains a lot of connective tissue. The plate is rarely sold at the retail level (it is used to make pastrami). The flank is a leaner cut that makes an excellent steak when grilled.

Certain parts of the cow tend to be fatty, others are quite lean. Certain muscles (such as those in the brisket) are used quite frequently (by the cow, that is) and develop a lot of connective tissue that makes them quite tough. These cuts require long, slow cooking to become tender. Other muscles (such as those in the short loin) receive little exercise and as a result are quite tender. These cuts are generally cooked quickly over high heat.

This chapter (and those which follow on pork and on lamb) covers the cuts you are most likely to see in the supermarket. In each case, we have tested various methods for cooking that cut and developed recipes that showcase that best method (or methods) for preparing it. (See chapter 11 for information on using boneless chuck in stews.)

THE EIGHT PRIMAL CUTS OF BEEF

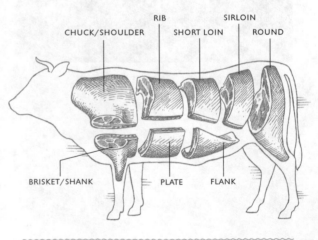

SCIENCE: Do Marinades Work?

Can tough cuts of lamb, beef, and pork yield tender results if marinated long enough? Many cookbooks suggest tenderizing meat in acidic marinades, often for several days. The science here is pretty straightforward. Acids, such as lemon juice, vinegar, and wine, will break apart protein strands and cause the structure of meats to soften over time. Whether this can happen in the refrigerator under real-life conditions is another question. We went into the kitchen to find out.

We took London broil from the round (a particularly lean cut and therefore prone to being tough when cooked), cut it into two-inch cubes, and then marinated the cubes in various solutions for 24 hours. Marinades with little or no acid had no effect on the texture of the meat. When we used more acid, the outer layer of the meat turned gray and dry—it had "cooked." While some might call the texture tender, quite frankly we found the meat to be mushy and the flavor of the acid to be overpowering.

Our conclusion was simple—if you want tender meat you must pay attention to the cut you purchase and the cooking method and forget about tenderizing with marinades.

Although marinades may not tenderize meat, they can give it a delicious flavor, that is, if you soak the food long enough. We marinated cubes of beef, lamb, and pork, as well as chicken parts, flounder, and tuna in low-acid marinades for varying amounts of time.

As might be expected, more delicate fish and chicken picked up flavor rather quickly, in as little as 15 minutes for flounder and 30 minutes for firmer fish like tuna. Chicken was somewhat slower to become fully flavored, about 3 hours for skinless pieces and at least 8 hours for skin-on pieces.

Denser meats required the most time to absorb marinades. It took 8 hours for the flavor to penetrate beyond the surface of beef, lamb, and pork, and meat marinated for 24 hours absorbed even more flavor. After a day, we found that meat gained little extra flavor. Although you can leave meat in a low-acid marinade for days, we don't really see the point.

STEAK

STEAKS GENERALLY COME FROM SIX PLACES on the cow (discussed below; see diagram on page 190). For all cuts of steak, look for meat that has a bright, lively color. Beef normally ranges in color from pink to red, but dark meat probably indicates an older, tougher animal. The external fat as well as the fat that runs through the meat (called intramuscular fat) should be as white as possible. As a general rule, the more intramuscular fat (marbling), the more flavorful and juicy the steak will be. But the marbling should be smooth and fine, running all through the meat, rather than showing up in clumps; smooth marbling melts into the meat during cooking, while knots remain as clumps of fat pockets. Stay away from packaged steaks that show a lot of red juice (known as purge). The purge may indicate a bad job of freezing; your steak will be dry and cottony.

Steaks sport different names depending on locale. We've used industry names that we feel best describe where the steaks lie on the loin; we also include some other common names.

SHOULDER/CHUCK STEAKS Often labeled London broil, steaks from the shoulder of the cow are boneless and consist of a single muscle. Buy a shoulder steak that is 1½ pounds to 2 pounds and slice it thin on the bias after cooking. We find that shoulder steaks offer the best value for cost-conscious shoppers.

RIB STEAKS Rib, rib-eye, and Delmonico steaks can be cut with or without the bone. They are very tender and smooth-textured, with a distinctive, robust, beefy taste. Very rich with good-sized pockets of fat.

SHORT LOIN STEAKS Our favorite steak, the strip, is cut from this region. The strip (also called shell, New York strip, or top loin) has a noticeable grain and a moderate amount of chew. The flavor is excellent and the meat is a bit less fatty than rib steaks. These steaks are slightly more expensive than rib steaks.

The tenderloin and filet mignon are also from the short loin, but we find them overly tender, almost soft. We prefer to cook the tenderloin whole, rather than cut into individual steaks where mushy texture is especially problematic and there are so many better choices. The whole tenderloin is best roasted or grill-roasted (see page 207).

The T-bone and porterhouse contain a nice balance of chewy strip and buttery tenderloin and are a better bet than tenderloin steaks. The tenderloin on the porterhouse is the larger section on this cut, and the grain of the strip piece on a porterhouse is rougher than that on a T-bone because it is closer to the hip. The T-bone cut combines an oblong piece of strip with a round of tenderloin—the tenderloin measures less than 1¼ inches in diameter. Because the grain of the strip piece on the T-bone is finer, it is also more desirable than that of porterhouse.

SIRLOIN STEAKS Sometimes labeled London broil, these steaks are generally quite tough and often overpriced.

ROUND STEAKS Steaks cut from the round are most often called London broil. They are boneless and quite lean. We find them dry and chewy and do not recommend them.

FLANK STEAKS The tender, boneless, single-muscle steak from the flank is fairly thin (no more than an inch thick) and weighs 2 to 2½ pounds. Like shoulder steaks, this cut is less expensive than top quality steaks and still quite good when sliced thin on the bias before serving.

GRILLED STEAK

GRILLED STEAKS HAVE MANY ATTRACTIVE qualities: rich, beefy flavor; a thick, caramelized crust; and almost no prep or cleanup for the cook. But sometimes a small bonfire fueled by steak fat can leave expensive steaks charred and tasting of resinous smoke. And then sometimes the coals burn down so low that the steaks end up with those pale, wimpy grill marks and just about no flavor at all. In those cases you try leaving the steaks on the grill long enough to develop flavor, but they just overcook.

Two of our favorite cuts, porterhouse and T-bone, are especially tricky. Both of these consist of two muscles (strip and tenderloin) with a T-shaped bone in between. When we grill them so that the strip section is perfectly cooked, the lean tenderloin is inevitably overcooked, dry, and flavorless.

So we went to work, promising ourselves we'd figure out how to use the grill to get the results we were after: meat seared evenly on both sides so that the juices are concentrated into a powerfully flavored, dark brown, brittle coating of crust; the juicy inside cooked a little past rare; and the outside strip of rich, soft fat crisped and browned slightly on the edges.

We decided to focus on the steaks from the short loin section of the animal that we think are the best the cow has to offer—the already mentioned T-bone and porterhouse and the strip. (Less expensive cuts are covered on pages 196 through 201.) We figured these steaks were bound to cook pretty much the

same because they were all cut from the same part of the cow.

Early on in our testing, we determined that we needed a very hot fire to get the crust we wanted without overcooking the steak. We could get that kind of heat by building the charcoal up to within 2 or 2½ inches of the grilling grate. But with this arrangement, we ran into problems with the fat dripping down onto the charcoal and flaming. We had already decided that a thick steak—about 1½ inches thick, to be precise—was optimal, because at that thickness we got a tasty contrast between the charcoal flavoring on the outside of the steak and the beefy flavor on the inside. The problem was that we couldn't cook a thick steak over consistently high heat without burning it.

After considerable experimentation, we found the answer to this dilemma: We had to build a fire with two levels of heat. Once we realized that we needed a fire with a lot of coals on one side and far fewer coals on the other, we could sear the steak properly at the beginning of cooking, then pull it onto the cooler half of the grill to finish cooking at a lower temperature. We could also use the dual heat levels to cook thin steaks as well as thick ones properly, and the system also provided insurance against bonfires—if a steak flared up, we simply moved it off the high heat.

We found we could be sure we had the right levels of heat on both sides of the fire by holding a hand about five inches over the cooking grate: When the hot side of the grill was hot enough for searing, we could hold a hand over the grill only for about two seconds. For the cooler side of the grill, we could count four to five seconds. (This is how we adapted our recipes for a gas grill, using burners set to high and low.)

We found that if we grilled the steak with the tenderloin toward the cooler side of the fire, it cooked more slowly and reached proper doneness at the same time as the strip. We could even engineer it so the tenderloin came off the grill rare while the strip was cooked to medium-rare.

But one question kept bugging us. The literature that came with the kettle grill we were using recommended grilling covered. Most cooking professionals we spoke to, however, were not in favor of covered grilling. So we ran a test comparing the taste of steak grilled covered with that grilled uncovered. We found that, depending on the type of charcoal used, steak cooked with the lid on picked up a mild to unpleasant smoky, resinous flavor. Grilling steak uncovered, on the other hand, allowed us to avoid that resinous taste, as well as to control any flare-ups by moving the steak off the hotter side of the grill. (This is not an issue on gas grills, so we put the cover down to speed up the cooking time and to ensure the formation of a thick brown crust.)

Common cooking wisdom suggests that bringing meat to room temperature before grilling will cause it to cook more evenly and that letting it rest for five minutes after taking it off the grill will both preserve the juices and provide a more even color. We tested the first of these theories by simultaneously grilling two similar steaks, one straight from the refrigerator and a second that stood at room temperature for one hour. We noticed no difference in the cooked steaks except that the room temperature steak cooked a couple of minutes faster than the other. The second test was more conclusive. Letting a cooked steak rest for five minutes does indeed help the meat retain more juices when sliced and promotes a more even color throughout the meat.

We tried lightly oiling steaks before grilling to see if they browned better that way, as well as brushing with butter halfway through grilling to see if the flavor improved. Although the oiled steaks browned a tiny bit better, the difference wasn't significant enough to merit the added ingredient. As for the butter, we couldn't taste any difference.

Charcoal-Grilled Strip Steaks

SERVES 4

Strip steaks, on or off the bone, are our first choice for individual steaks. A steak that's between 1¼ to 1½ inches thick gives you a solid meat flavor as well as a little taste of the grill; cut any thicker and the steak becomes too thick for one person to eat. If your guests are more likely to eat only an eight-ounce steak, grill two one-pounders, slice them, and serve each person a half steak. You may want to use the same method to cook rib-eye steaks. The most accurate way to judge doneness is to stick an instant-read thermometer through the side of the steak deep into the meat, so that most of the shaft is embedded in the steak.

4   strip steaks with or without bone, 1¼ to
1½ inches thick (12 to 16 ounces each),
patted dry
Salt and ground black pepper

1. Build a two-level fire (see page 258). Set grill rack in place, cover grill with lid, and let rack heat up, about 5 minutes.

2. Meanwhile, sprinkle both sides of each steak with salt and pepper to taste.

3. Position steaks over higher-level (hotter) fire. Grill, uncovered, until well-browned on one side, 2 to 3 minutes. Turn each steak over with tongs; grill until well-browned on second side, 2 to 3 minutes longer. (If steaks start to flame, pull them to lower, cooler level or extinguish flames with a squirt bottle.)

4. Once steaks are well-browned on both sides, slide each one to lower level; continue cooking to desired doneness, 5 to 6 more minutes for rare (120 degrees), 6 to 7 minutes for medium-rare on the rare side (125 degrees), 7 to 8 more minutes for medium-rare on the medium side (130 degrees), or 8 to 9 more minutes for medium (135 to 140 degrees). Let steaks rest 5 minutes, then serve immediately.

➤ VARIATIONS
Grilled Porterhouse or T-Bone Steaks

We prefer the robust taste and tooth of other steaks to filet mignon, which is cut from the tenderloin. On a porterhouse or T-bone steak, however, the buttery, delicate tenderloin suddenly makes sense. How can you argue with a steak that gives you two different tastes and textures in one cut, plus the bone? Since these steaks are so large, it's best to have the butcher cut them thick (1½ inches) and let one steak serve two people. Sliced, as in the recipe below, these steaks make a more elegant meal than individual strip steaks (until four people start to fight over the two bones).

2   porterhouse or T-bone steaks, each 1½ inches
thick (about 3½ pounds total)
Salt and ground black pepper

Follow recipe for Charcoal-Grilled Strip Steaks, positioning 2 porterhouse or T-bone steaks on the grill so the tenderloin pieces are over the lower-level (cooler) fire. Grill exactly as in recipe for Charcoal-Grilled Strip Steaks, browning steaks over the higher (hotter) level, then sliding the steaks to the cooler level to finish cooking. Cooking times remain the same. Once steaks have rested 5 minutes, cut the strip and filet pieces off bones and slice them each crosswise about ⅓ inch thick. Serve immediately.

Gas-Grilled Steaks

Follow recipe for Charcoal-Grilled Strip Steaks or Grilled Porterhouse or T-Bone Steaks, making the following changes: Turn all burners to high and preheat with lid down until very hot, about 15 minutes. Turn one burner to medium. Grill as in charcoal recipes but with lid down, placing steaks first over burner left on high and then sliding steaks to cooler part of the grill to cook through.

PAN-FRIED STEAKS

WE THINK STEAK MUST BE COOKED SO THAT the entire surface caramelizes to form a rich, thick crust. The intense heat of the grill makes it easy to obtain such a crust (see page 192). But about when the weather makes grilling impractical? We wanted to get the same result from pan-frying.

This task turned out to be harder than we thought. Sometimes we did get the great crust we were looking for, but sometimes we didn't. It seemed like our cast-iron pan worked particularly well, but we had never tested it against pans made from other materials. So we set to work to establish a foolproof technique for pan-frying steak. Along with the technique, we figured we also would need to determine which pans were best suited to the job.

We decided to focus on the boneless steak we

EQUIPMENT: Cast-Iron Skillet

Cast-iron pans are cheap, widely available (almost every hardware store stocks them), and will last a lifetime if cared for properly. This last caveat causes much confusion and is the reason why many cooks would rather own a stainless steel or anodized aluminum pan that costs four or five times as much as a common cast-iron pan.

Nothing causes so much confusion about cast-iron pans as the question of how to season them. To find the best method, we spoke to Billie Hill, customer service manager at Lodge Manufacturing Company, a major manufacturer of cast-iron cookware.

Because the main component of cast iron is iron, which combines more easily with oxygen than other metals, cast iron rusts quickly. One object of what's known as seasoning the pan, therefore, is to penetrate the pores of the iron with fat to protect the metal from the water and food that will rust it. Another, lesser-known reason, however, is to create a temporary nonstick surface: When fat is heated at a certain temperature for a particular length of time, it polymerizes. In other words, the fat breaks down into units that like to hook up with other units to create very stable chains; these chains make a fairly durable coating on the pan that acts much like Teflon. Heating the pan while seasoning, therefore, is necessary for two reasons: First, as explained above, heat is needed for the creation of polymers. Heating also expands the metal and seals in the fat.

Armed with this knowledge, we proceeded to test two sea-

soning methods, one from Lodge and one recommended by Barbara Tropp in The Modern Art of Chinese Cooking (Morrow, 1982) for seasoning a wok. Instructions attached to Lodge's pans recommend coating the pan with solid vegetable shortening (liquid oils go rancid, according to Hill) and baking upside down (upside down so that the fat doesn't collect as sticky gunk on the bottom of the pan) on an oven rack (over a baking sheet to collect drips) for an hour at 350 degrees. Tropp's directions call for heating the pan over high heat on top of the stove until a bead of water evaporates immediately upon hitting the pan, then wiping the inside of the pan with a wad of paper towels dipped in liquid oil, wiping out the excess and repeating as needed. A new pan will need several rounds of this.

We tried both methods, and there was no contest: Lodge's was lengthy and still left gunk in the pan, while Tropp's was brilliantly simple and quick and left the pan smooth and glossy. Nor did we find over several weeks of testing that liquid oil caused any rancid flavor in food cooked in the pan.

So here is the way to season: Heat the pan over high heat until a drop of water sizzles immediately upon contact. Dunk a wad of paper towels in cooking oil and wipe the entire inside of the pan with the oil. Then use another wad of toweling to rub the oil into the metal and wipe out any excess. Use another clean wad if needed. Repeat three to four times for a new pan until it blackens. If your pan has rusted from misuse, scrub off the rust with soap and an abrasive pad, and then season.

liked so much in our grill testing—the strip. (Bone-in steaks really should be grilled because the bone, rather than the meat, is the part of the steak that is actually in contact with the pan. The result is poor coloring and no crust development.)

It was obvious to us from the beginning that the key to browning the steaks was going to be preheating the pan, so that when the steak hit the pan, the surface would already be hot enough to sear the steak before it overcooked. (We also found out the hard way that the steak may stick if the pan isn't well heated, leaving the delicious seared flavor in the pan, not on the steak.) In this regard, we had two questions: Do different types of pans heat and cook differently? And does it make more sense to brown quickly over a high heat and then finish over a low heat, or to cook the steaks over a constant high heat?

We started all our testing with two pans: a 10½-inch and a 12-inch cast-iron pan, figuring that, at $10 to $15 a pop (as opposed to $100-plus for many sauté pans), these were the pans most folks were likely to own or want to own. We used 1-inch- to 1¼-inch-thick boneless strip steaks to begin, but ultimately found that there was no difference in technique between cooking strip and rib steaks.

We tried preheating the pan for various lengths of time at different temperatures. After several tests, we found that our favorite method was to preheat the pan at a medium temperature for about 10 minutes before cooking the steak. (If you're using a powerful professional gas range, however, cut the time to 5 minutes.) This method allowed us to cook the steak all the way through, turning it once, without having to adjust the heat. When we started with a higher heat, lowering it once the steak had browned, the process required more attention without producing better results, while the splattering, a problem to be reckoned with even on medium heat, was much worse.

In fact, a splatter screen is a must for pan-frying, even on the lower heat. (A splatter screen is a round mesh screen with attached handle that is set over the pan like a lid to keep grease inside without causing the meat to steam, as it would if covered with a lid.)

We then went on to try this same technique with an All-Clad stainless steel pan with an aluminum core, a Calphalon anodized aluminum pan, an All-Clad nonstick pan, and a thin, inexpensive stainless steel pan of the type many of us have sitting in a back drawer somewhere. The All-Clad stainless steel and the cast-iron pans held the heat and browned the steaks better than the other two.

Using our two favorite pans, we tested for the optimal amount and type of fat. We fried steaks in two tablespoons, one tablespoon, two teaspoons, and one teaspoon of oil. As these cuts of steaks give off some fat as they cook, two tablespoons made more mess and didn't brown better than one. One teaspoon browned spottily; two teaspoons and one tablespoon browned equally well without outrageous splattering. We decided to stick with one tablespoon because it's simpler to measure; at any rate, the goal is to lightly coat the pan with oil.

Then we tested one tablespoon each of peanut, corn, canola, and half-and-half butter and canola oil. As we expected, the butter burned immediately, even with the oil. The other three oils browned equally well.

In our research on grilled steaks, we had determined that five minutes of resting gave the meat even color; the same held true for pan-frying. Any longer than that, and the steak gets cold. Chances are that it will be about that long before you actually cut into the steak at the table anyway.

Pan-Fried Steaks

SERVES 2

Covering the skillet with a splatter screen will reduce the mess that pan-frying inevitably makes. Serve the steaks as is or with one of the sauces or condiments that follow.

2	boneless strip or rib-eye steaks, or 1 sirloin, 1 to 1¼ inches thick (8 to 10 ounces each)
	Salt and ground black pepper
1	tablespoon vegetable oil

1. Heat 11- to 12-inch skillet (preferably cast-iron or stainless steel with an aluminum core) for 10 minutes over medium heat. Generously sprinkle each side of each steak with salt and pepper.

2. Add oil to pan; swirl to coat bottom. Add steaks, cover pan with splatter screen, and cook until

well-browned on one side, 5 minutes. Turn steaks; cook 3 more minutes for rare, 4 minutes for medium-rare, or 5 minutes for medium. Remove steaks from pan; let rest 5 minutes or while making pan sauce or condiment, then serve immediately.

> VARIATIONS

Pan-Fried Steaks with Roquefort Butter

Use a fork to mash together 1 tablespoon softened butter, ½ ounce crumbled Roquefort cheese, and ¼ teaspoon brandy in small bowl. Season with salt and pepper to taste. Follow recipe for Pan-Fried Steaks. Top each cooked steak with portion of flavored butter and serve immediately.

Pan-Fried Steaks with Horseradish Cream

Stir together 2 tablespoons each sour cream and prepared horseradish. Season with salt and pepper to taste. Follow recipe for Pan-Fried Steaks. Serve dollop of sauce alongside each cooked steak.

Pan-Fried Steaks with Mustard Sauce

Follow recipe for Pan-Fried Steaks. Cook steaks as directed and remove from pan. Wipe fat from skillet; add ¾ cup chicken stock, then boil until reduced by one-half. Stir in 1½ tablespoons Dijon mustard and 1 tablespoon butter as well as salt and pepper to taste; spoon portion of sauce over each cooked steak.

EQUIPMENT: Splatter Screen

Pan-frying can deliver great results, but the cleanup can be a real chore. Whether cooking steaks or soft-shell crabs in hot fat, we find that a splatter screen reduces the mess and also protects exposed skin on your arms and face from splattering grease. The mesh screen keeps spitting grease in the pan but allows heat and moisture to escape so that foods don't steam. (A cover may protect against splattering, but it traps moisture and will ruin the crust on pan-fried foods.) Look for a large splatter screen (a diameter of 11 to 12 inches is best) with heavy-gauge mesh and a long handle. This item costs just $3 or $4 at most cookware shops and is worth every penny.

LONDON BROIL

LONDON BROIL IS A RECIPE, NOT A PARTICUlar cut of meat. You take a thick steak (steaks labeled London broil are usually taken from the shoulder or round); grill, broil, or pan-grill it; then slice it thin on the bias across the grain. This process makes the most of relatively inexpensive cuts of beef.

It was for flank steak that the tradition of preparing steak this way originated. Since flank steak has some marbling and is not a supertough cut, it is ideal for this purpose. (See page 198 for more details on cooking flank steak.) However, now that flank steak costs $7 a pound, it's not such an inexpensive cut anymore, especially since cuts from the round or shoulder that are often labeled "London broil" can cost just

SCIENCE: Can You Deglaze a Cast-Iron Pan?

Common cooking lore says that if you deglaze a cast-iron pan with an acidic liquid such as wine, the sauce will taste funny. Given that information, we questioned whether even the mustard in one of our sauces might cause a reaction. Some experts had told us yes. Others claimed they regularly make tomato sauces in cast iron to no ill effect. What was the deal here?

To find out, we tested both the mustard sauce above and a red wine pan sauce in a seasoned cast-iron pan. The mustard sauce collected some tiny black flecks from the pan, but because the mustard was in the pan for only seconds, the taste was fine. We'd certainly make this sauce in cast iron. The red wine sauce, however, tasted distinctly "off": not metallic, surprisingly, but unpleasantly sour. Finally, we tested a quick tomato sauce (roughly chopped canned tomatoes, garlic, basil, olive oil, and salt, cooked 10 minutes to thicken). It tasted perfect.

Confused by the results, we talked to several food scientists to find out why we should have had better luck with a tomato sauce than a red wine sauce, when both cooked for approximately the same length of time and both were high in acid. They explained that while iron reacts quite easily with acid to cause a metallic taste, 10 minutes isn't long enough to produce this reaction. The sour taste in the red wine sauce was due to the reaction of the tannins in the wine to the iron. Therefore, don't deglaze with red wine or red wine vinegar, but feel free to do quick pan sauces based on stock, water, and even tomato.

$2 or $3 a pound. We wanted to figure out how to cook these cheap cuts, many of which are quite lean and pose numerous challenges for the cook.

Before narrowing down the cuts, we decided to settle on the cooking technique. We wanted a London broil with a nice crisp crust and rare-to-medium-rare interior. (Because they are so lean, London broil cuts will become intolerably dry and tough if cooked to medium or beyond. If you don't like a pink steak, try a cut with more fat, such as rib-eye steak.)

Broiling a thick London broil at home doesn't really work all that well. The broiler on most home ovens doesn't generate enough heat to brown the exterior of a thick steak before the interior becomes overcooked. We had far better luck on the grill. In fact, a London broil can be cooked much like a thick T-bone or porterhouse steak on the grill—sear both sides on the hottest part of the grill and then slide to a cooler part of the grill to cook through. We needed an alternative for indoor cooking, and pan-grilling was the obvious solution.

Cooking such a thick cut in a cast-iron skillet is not easy. When we got a cast-iron skillet blazing hot and threw the steak in, the kitchen quickly filled with smoke. Lower heat yielded a steak with a poor crust. After fiddling with various heat levels on top of the stove, we decided to see how the oven might work. We thought we would use a technique championed by many restaurant chefs—sear the meat on top of the stove and then put the pan in a hot oven to finish cooking it through.

After much experimentation, we got this to work perfectly. We set the oven rack at the lowest position and turned the heat in the oven up to 500 degrees. When the oven was hot, we preheated a cast-iron skillet on the stove for several minutes. We added the steak and immediately moved the skillet into the oven, using double potholders to protect our hands. After three or four minutes, we turned the steak and finished cooking. The smoke problem was virtually eliminated, and we had a fairly crusty steak cooked indoors. As a further refinement, we preheated a pizza stone (a ceramic baking stone; see page 334) in the oven for 30 minutes and placed the hot skillet on the stone to finish cooking. The stone transferred more heat to the bottom of the skillet and produced a better crust.

Having settled on a cooking method, we began comparing the different cuts. To work as London broil, a cut must be made up of one muscle; otherwise it simply falls apart when you slice it. There are only a few cuts of beef that meet this criterion. We eliminated one of them, the tri-tip cut, because it is too difficult for most consumers to find. We put top sirloin out of the running along with the flank because they are too expensive. Eye of round has the wrong shape for steaks, while bottom round is almost always used for roasts.

That left us two cuts—the top round and the shoulder. When we began investigating them, we quickly made an important discovery. Although supermarkets tend to sell top round and shoulder the same way (as thick steaks labeled London Broil), the cuts are very different.

If you treat a 1- or 1½-inch-thick shoulder steak like flank steak, you get good results—a chewy, flavorful steak. Not only is shoulder the least expensive steak you can buy, it also has a little bit of fat, which you want. If, however, you cook a thick cut of top round like a flank steak, you will be disappointed. The round is lean and tight-grained, with a liverlike flavor that is almost disgusting in quickly cooked muscle meat. Shoulder has a robust beef flavor and a reasonably tender texture that are far superior.

"Oven-Grilled" London Broil

SERVES 4

Using a pizza stone in the oven helps superheat the bottom of the skillet, but this method works without the stone, too.

I   boneless shoulder steak (1½ to 2 pounds),
     cut about 1½ inches thick, patted dry
     Salt and ground black pepper

1. Adjust oven rack to lowest position; position pizza stone, if using, on rack and heat oven to 500 degrees for at least 30 minutes.

2. Heat large, heavy, ovenproof skillet, preferably cast iron or stainless steel with aluminum core, for at least 3 minutes over high heat. Generously sprinkle both sides of meat with salt and pepper to taste; add meat to pan. As soon as steak smokes, about 5 seconds, carefully transfer pan to oven; cook 3½ to 4

minutes, then flip steak and cook until well-seared and meat is medium-rare (125 degrees on instant-read thermometer), 3½ to 4 minutes longer. Transfer steak to cutting board; let rest for 5 minutes. Slice very thin on bias against grain, adjusting seasoning with additional salt and pepper. Serve immediately with meat juices.

Charcoal-Grilled London Broil
SERVES 4
Because the shoulder steak is so thick, it must be grilled over a two-level fire. Do not cook past medium-rare or this lean cut will be unpalatably dry.

1½–2   **pounds boneless shoulder steak,
         about 1½ inches thick
         Salt and ground black pepper**

1. Build a two-level fire (see page 258). Set grill rack in place, cover grill with lid, and let rack heat up, about 5 minutes.

2. Meanwhile, sprinkle both sides of steak with salt and pepper to taste. Grill, uncovered, until well-browned on one side, 2 to 3 minutes. Turn steak; grill until well-browned on second side, 2 to 3 minutes.

3. Once steak is well-browned on both sides, slide to cooler part of grill. Continue grilling over medium fire to desired doneness, 5 to 6 minutes more for rare (120 degrees on instant-read thermometer), 6 to 7 minutes for medium-rare on the rare side (125 degrees), or 7 to 8 minutes for medium-rare on the medium side (130 degrees). Let steak rest 5 minutes, slice thin on bias, and serve immediately.

➤ VARIATION
Gas-Grilled London Broil
Follow recipe for Charcoal-Grilled London Broil, making the following changes: Turn all burners to high and preheat with lid down until very hot, about 15 minutes. Turn one burner to medium. Grill as in charcoal recipe but with lid down, placing steak first over burner left on high and then sliding steak to cooler part of the grill to cook through.

FLANK STEAK
THANKS TO FAJITAS, FLANK STEAK HAS become the darling of Tex-Mex fans from New York to California and everywhere in between. But there are good reasons for the popularity of flank steak in addition to mere culinary fashion. Like other steaks cut from the chest and side of the cow, flank has a rich, full, beefy flavor. Also, because it is very thin, it cooks quite quickly. Flank steak is too large to fit in a pan, so grilling makes the most sense for this cut.

Although this is a pretty straightforward proposition, we still had some questions about what was exactly the best way to go about it. All of them were directed at the achievement of two very simple goals: getting a good sear on the outside of this thin cut of meat before overcooking on the inside, and keeping it tender. We wondered whether the meat should be marinated or rubbed with spices, how hot the fire should be, and how long the meat should be cooked.

Virtually every recipe we found for flank steak called for marinating. Most sources ballyhooed the marinade as a means of tenderizing the meat as well as adding flavor. We found that marinades with a lot of acid eventually made this thin cut mushy and unappealing. If we left out the acid, we could flavor the meat, but this took at least 12 hours. As for tenderness, when the cooked steaks were sliced thin against the grain, there was virtually no difference between those which were marinated and those which were not.

With marinades out, we turned to spice rubs. We rubbed one steak with a spice rub 8 hours before cooking it, one an hour before cooking it, and one just before we put it over the flames. One more steak was cooked exactly like the others, but with no spice rub at all.

Again, the results were not unexpected. The three spice-rubbed steaks all had about the same amount of flavor, and all developed almost identical dark brown, very flavorful crusts. The plain steak did not develop nearly as nice a crust but cooked in approximately the same amount of time. We noticed no differences in tenderness among the steaks.

Since spice rubs create an excellent crust with plenty of intense flavor, they are our first choice for flank steaks. However, they are not good for folks who like their steak medium, because if you leave the steak on long enough to get it that done, the spices burn. You even have to be a bit careful to keep them from burning if you like your steak medium-rare. But if you don't mind exercising that small degree of care, we recommend spice rubs highly.

Every source we checked is in the same camp about cooking and resting flank steak, and it is the right camp. These steaks should be cooked over high heat for a short period of time. We tried lower heat and longer times, but inevitably the meat ended up being tough.

Flank steak is too thin to effectively check its temperature with a meat thermometer, so you need to resort to the most primitive (but ultimately the most effective) method of checking for doneness: Cut into the meat and see if it is done to your liking. Remember that carryover heat will continue to cook the steak after it comes off the grill. So if you want the steak medium-rare, take it off the heat when it looks rare, and so on. (Because cooking flank steak beyond medium-rare toughens it, we advise against it. In fact, if you like your meat more than medium, you might want to choose another cut.)

As for resting the meat after it comes off the heat, this final step is as important for flank steak as it is with all red meats. During cooking, the heat drives the juices to the center of the meat. This phenomenon is particularly noticeable with a high-heat cooking method such as grilling. If you cut the meat right after it comes off the heat, much more of the juice spills out than if you allow the meat to rest, during which time the blood becomes evenly distributed throughout the meat once again. This is common wisdom among cooks, but to be sure it was correct, we cooked two more flank steaks, sliced one up immediately after it came off the fire, and allowed the second to rest for five minutes before slicing it. Not only did the first steak exude almost twice as much juice when sliced as the second, it also looked grayer and was not as tender. So in this case, it is crucial to follow conventional wisdom: Give your steak a rest.

Charcoal-Grilled Flank Steak

SERVES 4 TO 6

Flank steak is best when cooked rare, or medium-rare at most. Because flank is a thin cut, it is very important for the meat to rest after it comes off the grill.

I   flank steak (about 2½ pounds)
      Salt and ground black pepper

1. Build a two-level fire (see page 258), but pile all coals over half of grill and leave other half of grill empty. Set grill rack in place, cover grill with lid, and let rack heat up, about 5 minutes.

2. Generously sprinkle both sides of steak with salt and pepper; cook over coals until well-seared and dark brown on first side, 5 to 7 minutes. Flip steak using tongs; continue grilling on second side until interior of meat is slightly less done than you want it to be when you eat it, 2 to 5 minutes more for medium rare (depending on heat of fire and thickness of steak). Transfer meat to cutting board; cover loosely with foil, and let rest for 5 minutes. Slice very thin on bias against the grain; adjust seasoning with additional salt and pepper and serve immediately.

➤ VARIATIONS

Gas-Grilled Flank Steak

Follow recipe for Charcoal-Grilled Flank Steak, making the following changes: Turn all burners to high and preheat with lid down until very hot, about 15 minutes. Grill as in charcoal recipe but with lid down.

Grilled Flank Steak Rubbed with Latin Spices

Mix 2 tablespoons each ground cumin and chili powder, 1 tablespoon each ground coriander and kosher salt (or 1½ teaspoons table salt), 2 teaspoons ground black pepper, and ½ teaspoon each ground cinnamon and hot red pepper flakes in small bowl. Follow recipe for either Charcoal-Grilled or Gas-Grilled Flank Steak, rubbing steak all over with spice mixture before cooking and watching meat carefully to ensure that spice rub darkens but does not burn.

Grilled Flank Steak with Sweet and Sour Chipotle Sauce

If you can't find chipotles, substitute a mixture of ½ teaspoon liquid smoke, 2 minced jalapeño chiles, and 3 tablespoons ketchup.

¼	cup honey
2	tablespoons vegetable oil
3	chipotle peppers
2	tablespoons balsamic vinegar
2	tablespoons grainy mustard
½	cup juice from 4 medium limes
2	medium garlic cloves, minced
I	teaspoon ground cumin
2	tablespoons chopped fresh cilantro leaves
I	teaspoon kosher salt or ½ teaspoon table salt
	Ground black pepper
I	recipe Charcoal-Grilled or Gas-Grilled Flank Steak (page 199)

1. Combine honey, oil, chipotles, vinegar, mustard, lime juice, garlic, and cumin in blender jar or workbowl of food processor fitted with steel blade; puree or process until smooth. Transfer to small bowl, stir in cilantro, salt, and pepper to taste; set aside. (Sauce can be covered and refrigerated for up to 3 days.)

2. Generously brush both sides of meat with sauce after grilling but before resting. Pass remaining sauce separately with sliced steak.

Grilled Flank Steak with Spicy Parsley Sauce

This simple, thick, almost spreadable sauce lets the flavor of the flank come through.

I	cup minced fresh parsley leaves (about I medium bunch parsley)
3	medium garlic cloves, minced
I	medium jalapeño chile, minced
½	cup extra-virgin olive oil
3	tablespoons red wine vinegar
	Salt and ground black pepper
I	recipe Charcoal-Grilled or Gas-Grilled Flank Steak (page 199)

1. Mix parsley, garlic, chile, olive oil, vinegar, and salt and pepper to taste in small bowl. (Sauce can be

covered and refrigerated up to 3 days).

2. Serve sauce, passing separately, with sliced steak.

Classic Fajitas
SERVES 8

Although it was originally made with skirt steak (a fattier cut with more flavor), this combination of flank steak and vegetables grilled and then wrapped in warm tortillas is the dish that put flank steak on the culinary map in the United States. The ingredients go on the grill in order as the fire dies down: steak over a hot fire, vegetables over a medium fire, and tortillas around the edge of the medium to low fire just to warm them. Alternately, the tortillas can be wrapped together in a clean, damp dish towel and warmed in a microwave oven for about 3 minutes at full power; keep them wrapped until you're ready to use them.

I	recipe Charcoal-Grilled or Gas-Grilled Flank Steak, steak sprinkled with ¼ cup lime juice and salt and pepper to taste before cooking
I	very large onion, peeled and cut into ½-inch rounds
2	very large red or green bell peppers, cored, seeded, and cut into large wedges
16	10-inch flour tortillas
I	recipe Classic Red Table Salsa (recipe follows)
I	recipe Chunky Guacamole (recipe follows)

1. Follow recipe for either Charcoal-Grilled or Gas-Grilled Flank Steak, sprinkling steak with lime juice and salt and pepper to taste before cooking.

2. While meat rests and charcoal fire has died down to medium or gas grill burners have been adjusted to medium (you can hold your hand 5 inches above grill surface for 4 seconds), grill onions and peppers, turning occasionally, until onions are lightly charred, about 6 minutes, and peppers are streaked with dark grill marks, about 10 minutes. Remove from grill and cut into long, thin strips; set aside. Arrange tortillas around edge of grill; heat until just warmed, about 20 seconds per side. (Take care not to dry out tortillas or they will become brittle; wrap tortillas in towel to keep warm.) Remove to platter; set aside.

3. Arrange sliced meat and vegetables on large platter; serve immediately with tortillas, salsa, and guacamole passed separately.

Classic Red Table Salsa

MAKES ABOUT 5 CUPS

Our favorite Mexican-style salsa, equally good with faji-
tas or chips. To reduce the heat in the salsa, seed the chile.

3	large, very ripe tomatoes (about 2 pounds), cored and diced small
½	cup tomato juice
1	small jalapeño or other fresh chile, stemmed, seeded if desired, and minced
1	medium red onion, diced small
1	medium garlic clove, minced
½	cup chopped fresh cilantro leaves
½	cup juice from 4 medium limes
	Salt

Mix all ingredients, including salt to taste, in
medium bowl. Cover and refrigerate to blend flavors, at least 1 hour and up to 5 days.

Chunky Guacamole

MAKES 2½ TO 3 CUPS

To minimize the risk of discoloration, prepare the minced
ingredients first so they are ready to mix with the avocados as
soon as they are cut. Ripe avocados are essential here. To test
for ripeness, try to flick the small stem off the end of the avo-
cado. If it comes off easily and you can see green underneath
it, the avocado is ripe. If it does not come off or if you see
brown underneath after prying it off, the avocado is not ripe.

3	medium, ripe avocados (preferably pebbly-skinned Haas)
2	tablespoons minced onion
1	medium garlic clove, minced
1	small jalapeño chile, minced
¼	cup minced fresh cilantro leaves
¼	teaspoon salt
½	teaspoon ground cumin (optional)
2	tablespoons juice from 1 lime

1. Halve one avocado, remove pit, and scoop flesh
into medium bowl. Mash flesh lightly with onion,
garlic, chile, cilantro, salt, and cumin (if using) with
tines of a fork until just combined.

2. Halve and pit remaining two avocados. Make

½-inch cross-hatch incisions in flesh of each avocado half with dinner knife, cutting down to but not
through skin. Separate diced flesh from skin using
spoon inserted between skin and flesh, gently scooping out avocado cubes. Add cubes to bowl with
mashed avocado mixture.

3. Sprinkle lime juice over diced avocado and mix
entire contents of bowl lightly with fork until combined but still chunky. Adjust seasonings with salt, if
necessary, and serve. (Can be covered with plastic
wrap, pressed directly onto surface of mixture, and
refrigerated up to 1 day. Return guacamole to room
temperature; remove plastic wrap just before serving.)

INGREDIENTS: Flank, Skirt, and Hanger Steaks

These three recently popular steaks share the distinction of coming from the chest and side of the animal. Hanger and flank both
come from the underside of the cow, while skirt comes from the
area between the abdomen and the chest cavity. In addition to
location, these steaks share certain other basic qualities: all are
long, relatively thin, as well as quite tough and grainy, but with
rich, deep, beefy flavor.

Of course, these flavorful steaks also have their differences.
Hanger, a thick muscle that is attached to the diaphragm,
derives its name from the fact that when a cow is butchered, this
steak hangs down into the center of the carcass. Because it is a
classic French bistro dish, this cut is highly prized by restaurants
and therefore difficult to find in butcher shops. This is no great
loss, however, since the hangers that we sampled had the tough-
est texture and least rich, beefy flavor of these three cuts.

Fortunately, flank steak is quite easy to find in any butcher shop
or supermarket. Easily recognizable by its longitudinal grain, flank
has great beef flavor and is quite tender if cooked to rare or medium rare and sliced thin against the grain. Unfortunately, largely due
to the popularity of fajitas and "London broil," flank has become a
relatively expensive cut, running about $5 a pound in local markets.

The skirt steak, which was the cut originally used in fajitas,
can be hard to locate in supermarkets or butcher shops. This is a
real pity, because the skirt steak is a beefeater's dream. It has
more fat than the hanger or flank, which makes it juicier and
richer; at the same time, it also has a deep, full, beefy flavor that
outdoes either the flank or the hanger. If you can get your hands
on a skirt steak, by all means do so. You will not be sorry. Just season and cook it as directed in the recipes for flank steak.

ROAST BEEF

THE APPEAL OF ROAST BEEF IS CLEAR. TAKE a large, usually inexpensive cut of beef, put it in the oven for a long period of time, and leave it alone. When done, the roast is sliced and served with potatoes (usually mashed) and gravy. Unfortunately, roast beef is often tough and dry. So tough and dry that only a lot of gravy can save the meal. We wondered why this is so. Is it just the cut of beef? Is it the internal temperature of the meat when it's considered "done"? Is it the cooking method?

For our first test, we cooked five separate bottom round roasts, each at a different oven temperature, ranging from 300 to 500 degrees. The results were disappointing, but we learned two things. First, the lowest oven temperature was best. The meat that was roasted at 500 degrees became dry, with most of the outer layers of the meat overcooked. The roast cooked at 300 degrees, however, was more tender and more juicy, and it had better internal flavor. Second, and most important, we found that the internal temperature of the meat does not necessarily determine the juiciness or texture of the roast. A roast cooked at 300 degrees until it reaches an internal temperature of 120 degrees is definitely more tender and juicier than meat cooked to the same internal temperature in a 500-degree oven. In other words, it's not just where you are going but how you get there.

Why is this true? To fully understand what was happening inside the meat, we prepared four different roasts at different temperatures—250, 350, 400, and 500 degrees. All were cooked to the same internal temperature—130 degrees—and allowed to sit for 10 minutes after they were removed from the oven. The roasts were then cut in half and photographed, so we would have a physical record we could study. When we compared the photographs, the answer was immediately apparent. The 500-degree roast was almost entirely overcooked.

That is, the center was still red, but 70 percent of the remainder was gray and unappealing. By comparison, the roast cooked at 250 degrees was light red throughout, with only 10 percent of the outer layer gray and overcooked. The roasts cooked at the in-between oven temperatures varied between these two extremes. It's simply a matter of physics. Lower oven temperatures allow sufficient time for the even conduction of heat to the center of the roast from the outer layers. At higher oven temperatures, the outside and inside of the roast have a much larger temperature differential.

In doing these tests, however, we found a problem with roasting at low temperatures: There is little flavor development on the exterior of the meat. To remedy this situation, we compared two new oven methods with the winner thus far, a constant 250 degrees.

In the first test, we tried roasting at 400 degrees for 15 minutes, then reducing the heat to 200 degrees until the roast reached an internal temperature of 130 degrees. This method was not bad, resulting in a juicy roast with good texture and flavor inside. But the outer layers of meat were still overcooked.

Finally we tried roasting at 250 degrees until the meat reached an internal temperature of 110 degrees, then increasing the oven heat to 500 degrees and cooking another 15 minutes or so until the internal temperature of the roast reached 130 degrees. This technique provided the best of both worlds—terrific flavor development on the exterior and an even, juicy, tender roast on the interior. The contrast of texture and taste between the inside and the outside was wonderful.

We had finally found the best method. But we still wanted to go back and make sure we were cooking the meat to the proper internal temperature. So we cooked five more bottom round roasts to different internal temperatures, starting at 120 degrees and ending at 160 degrees. We found that 130 degrees still delivered the most flavor, the best texture, and the most juice. At 120 degrees, the roast lacked flavor; at 140 degrees, it was a bit chewy; and at 150 degrees internal temperature, it was dry, overcooked, and tough.

When we repeated these tests with chuck roasts, we did find some difference from the bottom round roasts. While the chuck was also best when cooked to 130 degrees, this fattier cut was acceptable cooked to somewhat higher internal temperatures because the fat kept it more flavorful and moist than a round roast.

In fact, the chuck is on all counts the best cheap

cut for slow roasting. In our tests, we found that, generally speaking, the chuck is more tender and flavorful than cuts from the lean and relatively tough round. The sirloin is a mixed bag; the bottom rump roast is not as good as the better round roasts, but the top sirloin and top rump roasts are indeed better than roasts from the round.

Now that we had determined the best oven temperature, internal temperature, and type of roast, we decided to investigate some slightly less crucial elements involved in roasting beef, including how long to let it rest after cooking and whether aging the beef would make a real difference in the end product.

We wanted to determine the optimum amount of time a roast should sit after coming out of the

INGREDIENTS: Cuts for Roast Beef

Expensive cuts of beef, such as the tenderloin, can be roasted at very high heat with excellent results. Cheaper cuts, however, are best when roasted at low oven temperatures. We had heard various recommendations for cheap cuts and wondered which among them was actually the very best for slow roasting.

There is no lack of choices here. A side of beef is initially cut into eight sections that are generally referred to as "primal" cuts (see the diagram on page 190). The less expensive boneless beef roasts come from one of three of these primal cuts: the chuck, the sirloin, or the round. Generally speaking, the chuck is both fattier and more tender than any cut from the round, which is lean and relatively tough. The sirloin falls in between the two.

We roasted 10 different cuts: 5 from the chuck, 2 from the sirloin, and 3 from the round. Although we tend to prefer the juicier, fattier meat from the chuck, the top round and the top sirloin were actually quite good.

CUTS FROM THE CHUCK

In general, cuts from the chuck provide more flavor and better texture than roasts from the round or sirloin.

BLADE ROAST This was the best roast in the taste test—flavorful, juicy, and tender. However, it does contain connective tissue, which, though unattractive, is not unpleasant to eat. The term "blade" refers to the shoulder blade, which is part of the chuck. A "blade roast" refers to the "top blade" muscle, which is similar to the muscle on your back over your shoulder blade.

CHUCK-EYE ROAST This is a boneless rib roast that is cut from the center of the first five ribs (the term "eye" always refers to a center-cut piece of meat). The meat has good marbling throughout, which adds both flavor and moisture. This chuck is an extremely tender, juicy, and fatty piece of meat. It would have won first place in our tasting but was marked down for excessive fat content.

CHUCK FILLET OR CHUCK TENDER ROAST Made from the "mock tender" muscle located next to the top blade muscle, this cut is tougher, stringier, and less flavorful than chuck-eye. However, many supermarkets mislabel this cut as chuck-eye. If the roast is cone-shaped, it is probably the mock tender muscle and therefore an inferior chuck cut.

SHOULDER ROAST Formerly referred to as an arm roast because it consists of the muscle at the top of the arm by the shoulder, this cut of beef is chewy and its texture grainy. Moreover, it is not the most flavorful chuck cut.

UNDER BLADE ROAST This is the muscle underneath the shoulder blade. It is quite similar to a blade roast, with lots of connective tissue and lots of flavor.

CUTS FROM THE ROUND

Roasts from the round tend to be lean and relatively tough compared with chuck roasts. Generally speaking, it is recommended that they be sliced very thin for serving. (We did not test the sirloin tip muscle, which is roughly equal to the top round in terms of flavor and texture.)

TOP ROUND Not quite as good as the top sirloin but has good flavor, texture, and juiciness.

EYE OF THE ROUND Less juicy and flavorful than the chuck roasts.

BOTTOM ROUND The least tender of all the cuts. Mediocre flavor as well.

CUTS FROM THE SIRLOIN

There are three important cuts for roasts from the sirloin: the top sirloin and the top and bottom rump roast, which are very similar.

TOP SIRLOIN Relatively juicy, flavorful, and tender. Good coloration on both the outside (dark brown) and inside (bright red). The clear winner among roasts from the sirloin or round.

BOTTOM RUMP ROAST Juicy and with good flavor but not as tender as either the top sirloin or the top round roast.

TOP RUMP ROAST Similar to bottom rump roast, with slightly superior flavor and texture.

oven. We let a roast sit for 30 minutes, testing it every 5 minutes until reaching the 30-minute point. Twenty minutes—the amount of time suggested by most cooks—turned out to be the proper waiting period. At that point, the roast was succulent, tender, and juicy, with more flavor than it had in previous tastings. Additional sitting time did not prove helpful to texture or flavor.

Next we tested the effect that a moderate amount of aging would have on the meat. (For more information on aging beef, see page 209.) We placed a large eye round roast in the refrigerator, uncovered, on a rack above a pan. Each day we sliced off a piece, browned it for five minutes in two tablespoons of olive oil, and then roasted it in a 200-degree oven until the meat reached an internal temperature of 130 degrees. We found that the process does indeed have a tremendous effect on texture and flavor. To achieve this effect for the size and cut of roast we were testing, though, the meat needed to sit for four days. Aging the roast for more days did not seem to improve taste, texture, or juiciness.

Slow-Roasted Beef with Red Wine Pan Juices
SERVES 6 TO 8

Buy a blade chuck roast or top sirloin roast if possible. (For more information on buying a roast, see page 203.) If you have time, refrigerate the roast on a wire rack set over a paper towel-covered plate for four days. This aging process delivers a tender, more flavorful roast. Make sure, however, that before roasting you trim off the parts of the roast that have dehydrated and turned leathery. Tying the roast makes it compact and evenly shaped. Leftovers from a roasted cut of round, by the way, make excellent roast beef sandwiches.

I	boneless beef roast (3 to 4 pounds), aged if possible (see note, above), tied crosswise with twine every inch, then tied lengthwise once or twice
	Salt and ground black pepper
2	tablespoons olive oil
1/3	cup full-flavored red wine
I	cup low-sodium chicken or beef broth

SCIENCE: How Roasting Works

Natural proteins, such as those found in beef, consist of many separate, coiled molecules. Bonds across the coils hold the proteins together in a single unit. When the proteins are heated, however, some of these bonds break, causing the protein molecules to pop loose and unwind (this process is called denaturing). Almost immediately, these unwound proteins bump into each other and bond together. This process is the essence of cooking proteins. It is perhaps easiest to witness when you fry an egg and the white, which is translucent when raw, becomes opaque as it cooks. This change in appearance is caused by the denatured proteins. In their natural, raw state, the proteins leave plenty of room for light to pass through; when these proteins become denatured in the heated state, they coagulate (join together) to create a dense, opaque structure.

The relevance of this process to the cooking of meat is that during cooking, these proteins also coagulate, or shrink. The way in which they shrink depends on how hot they are. Under 120 degrees, muscle proteins contract in width; over 120 degrees, these proteins start to shrink in length, expelling juices. Because more water is lost when the proteins shrink in length than when they shrink in width, meat tends to dry out rapidly as it is heated above 120 degrees. The process is much like the wringing of a wet towel. The meat proteins get shorter and tighter, expelling more and more water. And because meat is 75 percent water, there is a dramatic change in texture and juiciness during the cooking process from raw all the way to well-done. A roast can lose 30 to 40 percent of its weight by the time it reaches an internal temperature of 170 degrees, the point at which the meat is inedible and no additional liquid will be lost. (Cut into a piece of well-done meat, for example, and you'll notice that it will exude no juices.)

The good news, however, is that during cooking the connective tissue (collagen) in the meat starts to turn soft and jellylike and act as a lubricant. So as the meat cooks, it is getting both more tender and more tough at the same time. The trick is to find the point at which the tissue softening is maximized and the juice loss is minimized. The maximum benefit in terms of texture occurs when fatty beef, for example, is cooked to a final temperature of 130 to 140 degrees, the temperature at which the connective tissue starts to gelatinize but relatively little juice has been squeezed from the meat.

1. Heat oven to 250 degrees. Sprinkle roast with salt and pepper as desired. Heat oil over medium-high heat in Dutch oven or large, heavy, ovenproof pot. Add roast; sear until brown, about 4 minutes each side.

2. Transfer pot to oven and cook, uncovered, until meat thermometer inserted into thickest part of roast registers 110 degrees, 45 minutes to 1 hour. Increase oven temperature to 500 degrees and cook until internal temperature reaches 130 degrees, about 15 minutes longer. (Cooking times will vary depending on size and shape of roast.) Remove roast from pot; let stand 20 minutes before carving.

3. Meanwhile, set pot over medium-high heat; spoon all but 1 tablespoon fat from pot. Add wine, stirring pan bottom with wooden spoon to loosen brown bits; simmer until wine reduces to glaze—about 2 minutes. Add broth; simmer until sauce reduces and thickens slightly, 1 to 2 minutes longer. (For pan juices with a little extra body, juices can be thickened at this point with 1 teaspoon cornstarch dissolved in 1 tablespoon water.) Cut roast into thin slices, adding meat juices to pan juices. Serve immediately, with sauce passed separately.

BEEF TENDERLOIN

WHILE INEXPENSIVE ROASTS FROM THE chuck, round, or sirloin must be slow-cooked for the best results, a beef tenderloin, which comes from the short loin, starts out very tender and can be cooked at a high oven temperature. This elegant roast cooks quickly and its rich, buttery slices are fork-tender.

Despite its many virtues, however, beef tenderloin is not without its liabilities. Price, of course, is the biggest. Even at a local warehouse-style supermarket, the going rate for a whole beef tenderloin is $7.99 a pound—making for an average sticker price of about $50.

There is good reason for the tenderloin's hefty price. Because it sits up under the spine of the cow, it gets no exercise at all and is therefore the most tender piece of meat. It is one of the two muscles in the ultra-premium steaks known as the porterhouse and T-bone, so when it is removed from the cow as a whole muscle, it is going to go for ultra-premium prices—a

fact we confirmed by heading to the supermarket and the local butcher and purchasing $550 worth of beef tenderloin—which bought us just 11 roasts.

A whole beef tenderloin can be purchased "unpeeled," with an incredibly thick layer of exterior fat left attached, but it's usually sold "peeled," or stripped of its fat. Because of our many bad experiences with today's overly lean pork and beef, we purchased six of the 11 roasts unpeeled, determined to leave on as much fat as possible. However, after a quick examination of the unpeeled roasts, we realized that the excessively thick layer of surface fat had to go. Not only would such a large quantity of rendering fat smoke up the kitchen, it would also prohibit a delicious crust from forming on the meat. We dutifully peeled the thick layer of fat from the six tenderloins, but even after removing the sheaths of fat, there were still large pockets of fat and significant surface fat.

So does it make sense to buy an unpeeled roast and trim it yourself? We think not. We paid $6.99 a pound at the butcher for our unpeeled tenderloins, each weighing about eight pounds. After cleaning them up, the peeled tenderloins weighed about five pounds, a whopping three pounds of waste. We purchased peeled tenderloins of similar quality from another source for only $7.99 per pound. Clearly the unpeeled tenderloins were more expensive, with no benefits. And although we don't like tenderloins that have been picked clean, right down to the meat, we recommend buying peeled roasts, with their patches of scattered fat, and letting them be.

The tenderloin's sleek, boneless form makes for quick roasting, but its torpedo-like shape—thick and chunky at one end, gradually tapering at the other end—naturally roasts unevenly. For those looking for a range of doneness, this is not a problem, but for cooks who want a more evenly cooked roast, something must be done.

Folding the tip end of the roast under and tying it bulks up the tenderloin center to almost the same thickness as the more substantial butt tender. This ensures that the tenderloin cooks more evenly. (Even so, the tip end is always a little more well-done than the butt end.) Tying the roast at approximately 1½-inch intervals further guarantees a more uniformly shaped roast and consequently more even slices of beef. Snipping the silver skin (the translucent sheath that encases certain cuts of beef) at several points also prevents the meat from bowing during cooking. This occurs when the silver skin shrinks more than the meat to which it is attached.

After cooking many roasts—beef, pork, and poultry—we've come to like slow-roasting for large roasts. The lower the heat, we've found, the more evenly the roast cooks. To develop a rich brown crust or skin on these slow-roasted larger cuts, we either pan-sear them up front, increase the oven temperature for the last few minutes of roasting, or do both.

But a beef tenderloin is a different proposition. Though relatively large, its long, thin shape would seem to dictate a relatively quick cooking time. To determine the ideal roasting temperature, we started at the two extremes, roasting one tenderloin at 200 degrees, the other at 500. As expected, the roast cooked at 500 degrees not only created a very smoky kitchen from the rendering fat, it was also overcooked at each end and around the outside perimeter. However, the high oven heat had formed a thick, flavorful crust. A good crust is crucial to this rich yet mild-tasting roast, whose flavor is sometimes barely recognizable as beef. Despite the even, rosy pink interior of the beef cooked at 200 degrees, this roast lacked the all-important meat crust. Neither oven temperature was ideal, so we kept roasting.

Since the higher roasting temperature provided the rich flavor this roast desperately needed, we decided to roast it at as high a temperature as possible. A 450-degree oven still gave us smoke and uneven cooking, so we moved down to 425 degrees.

For comparison, we roasted another tenderloin at 200 degrees, this time increasing the oven temperature to 425 degrees at the end to develop a crust. Both roasts emerged from the oven looking quite beautiful, and their meat looked and tasted almost identical. Since the tenderloin roasted at 425 degrees was done in just 45 minutes (compared with the slow-roasted tenderloin, which took just about twice as long), we chose the high-heat method.

Although all roasts should rest 15 to 20 minutes after cooking, we found that beef tenderloin improves dramatically if left uncarved even longer. If cut too soon, its slices are soft and flabby. A slightly longer rest—we decided on 30 minutes—allows the meat to firm up into a texture we found much more appealing. Before carving, we preferred removing the big pockets of excess fat, which become more obvious at warm and room temperatures.

Roast Beef Tenderloin

SERVES 10 TO 12

To give the tenderloin a more pronounced pepper crust, increase the amount of pepper to 6 tablespoons and use a mixture of strong black and white and mild pink and green peppercorns. Be sure to crush the peppercorns with a mortar and pestle or with a heavy-bottomed saucepan or skillet. Do not use a coffee or spice grinder, which will grind the softer green and pink peppercorns to a powder before the harder black and white peppercorns begin to break up. See the illustrations below for more information on preparing the tenderloin.

PREPARING A BEEF TENDERLOIN

1. To ensure that the tenderloin roasts more evenly, fold the thin tip end of the roast under about 6 inches.

2. For more even cooking and evenly sized slices, use 12-inch lengths of kitchen twine to tie the roast every 1½ inches.

3. Set the meat on a sheet of plastic wrap and rub it all over with oil. Sprinkle with salt and pepper, then lift the plastic wrap up and around the meat to press on the excess. This method guarantees even coverage and can be used with the pepper crust as well.

1   whole beef tenderloin, peeled (5 to 6 pounds),
    thoroughly patted dry
2   tablespoons olive oil
1   tablespoon kosher salt or 2 teaspoons table salt
2   tablespoons coarse-ground black pepper

1. Remove tenderloin from refrigerator 1 hour before roasting to bring meat to room temperature. Use a sharp knife to carefully nick the silver skin on the side opposite the tip with shallow slashes at 1½-inch intervals. Tuck tip end under and tie roast crosswise, knotting at 1½-inch intervals.

2. Adjust oven rack to upper-middle position and heat oven to 425 degrees. Set meat on a sheet of plastic wrap and rub all over with oil. Sprinkle with salt and pepper; then lift plastic wrap up and around meat to press on excess.

3. Transfer prepared tenderloin from wrap to wire rack on shallow roasting pan. Roast until instant-read thermometer inserted into the thickest part of the roast registers about 125 degrees (meat will range from medium-rare to medium in different areas of the roast), about 45 minutes. Let stand for about 30 minutes before carving. (Can be wrapped in plastic, refrigerated up to 2 days, sliced, and served chilled.)

4. Cut meat into ½-inch thick slices. Arrange on a serving platter and serve.

➤ VARIATION

Roast Beef Tenderloin with Parsley, Cornichons, and Capers

1   recipe Roast Beef Tenderloin
¾   cup minced fresh parsley leaves
12   cornichons, minced (6 tablespoons), plus
     1 teaspoon cornichon juice
¼   cup capers, chopped coarsely
2   medium scallions, white and light green parts,
     minced
     Pinch salt
¼   teaspoon ground black pepper
½   cup extra-virgin olive oil

Prepare and cook tenderloin as directed. While roast is resting, mix parsley, cornichons, capers, scallions, salt, pepper, and oil in medium bowl. Slice roast and serve with sauce.

Grill-Roasted Beef Tenderloin
SERVES 10 TO 12

We found that a beef tenderloin cooks perfectly on a grill over indirect heat in 35 to 40 minutes. To build a nice thick crust on the meat, let the charcoal fire initially get fairly hot— about 375 degrees is ideal. We tried turning the roast but found that opening the lid caused the fire to lose heat and that the roast was browning evenly anyway. Once the roast is cooked to an internal temperature of 125 degrees (the optimum temperature if you like your meat cooked medium-rare), it should be pulled off the grill and allowed to rest; the internal temperature will rise by at least 5 degrees.

1   whole beef tenderloin, peeled (5 to 6 pounds),
    thoroughly patted dry, silver skin cut, tip end
    tucked under (see illustration 1 on page 206)
    and tied (see illustration 2)
2   3-inch wood chunks or 2 cups wood chips and
    heavy-duty aluminum foil
2   tablespoons olive oil
1   tablespoon kosher salt or 2 teaspoons table salt
2   tablespoons coarse-ground black pepper

1. Remove tenderloin from refrigerator 1 hour before grill-roasting to bring meat to room temperature.

2. Soak wood chunks in cold water to cover for 1 hour and drain, or place wood chips on 18-inch square of aluminum foil, seal to make packet, and use fork to create about six holes to allow smoke to escape (see illustrations on page 271).

3. Set roast on sheet of plastic wrap and rub all over with oil. Sprinkle with salt and pepper and then lift wrap to press on excess.

4. Meanwhile, light chimney filled with charcoal briquettes. Transfer coals from chimney to one side of kettle grill, piling them up in a mound three briquettes high. Keep bottom vents completely open. When coals are covered with light gray ash, lay wood chunks or packet with chips on top of charcoal. Put cooking grate in place, open grill lid vents completely and cover, turning lid so that vents are opposite wood chunks or chips to draw smoke through grill. Let grate heat for 5 minutes, clean with wire brush, and roll tenderloin off plastic and onto grate opposite fire so that long side of fillet is perpendicu-

lar to grill rods. Initial temperature will be about 375 degrees. Grill-roast tenderloin, covered, until instant-read thermometer inserted into thickest part of roast registers about 125 degrees, 35 to 40 minutes.

5. Let stand about 30 minutes before carving. (Can be wrapped in plastic, refrigerated up to 2 days, sliced, and served chilled.) Cut roast into slices ½-inch thick and serve.

➤ VARIATIONS

Grill-Roasted Beef Tenderloin on a Gas Grill

Follow recipe for Grill-Roasted Beef Tenderloin, making the following changes: Place foil tray with soaked wood chips (see illustrations on page 271) on top of primary burner (see illustration on page 268). Turn all burners to high and preheat with lid down until chips are smoking heavily, about 20 minutes. Leave primary burner on high and turn off other burner. (If using grill with three burners, turn off middle burner and leave others on high.) Position tenderloin over cool part of grill. Grill-roast for 30 to 35 minutes. (Temperature inside grill should average between 375 to 400 degrees; adjust lit burner as necessary.)

Grill-Roasted Beef Tenderloin with Pepper Crust

Follow recipe for Grill-Roasted Beef Tenderloin (charcoal or gas grill variation), increase pepper to 6 tablespoons, and use mixture of strong white and black as well as mild pink and green peppercorns. Coarsely crush peppercorns with mortar and pestle or with heavy saucepan or skillet.

Grill-Roasted Beef Tenderloin with Garlic and Rosemary

Studding the tenderloin with slivered garlic and fresh rosemary gives it an Italian flavor.

Follow recipe for Grill-Roasted Beef Tenderloin (charcoal or gas grill variation), making following changes: After tying roast, use paring knife to make several dozen shallow incisions around surface of roast. Stuff a few fresh rosemary needles and 1 thin sliver of garlic into each incision. (You will need a total of 1 tablespoon rosemary and 3 large garlic cloves, slivered.) Oil as directed. Sprinkle with salt,

pepper, and additional 2 tablespoons rosemary. Proceed as directed.

PRIME RIB

A PRIME RIB IS A LITTLE LIKE A TURKEY: You probably cook only one a year, usually for an important occasion, almost always for a crowd. Although you know there are alternative cooking methods that might deliver a better roast, they're too risky. You don't want to be remembered as the cook who carved slices of almost raw standing rib, or the host who delayed dinner for hours waiting for the roast to get done. Rather than chance it, you stick with the standard 350 degrees for X minutes per pound. A roast cooked this way, you decide, will at least not embarrass you.

Other than using general terms like juicy and tender, we weren't exactly sure how to define perfect prime rib when we started testing, so we had no preconceived ideas about what techniques or methods would deliver a superior roast. In addition to our normal cookbook research, we decided to interview a few of the thousands of chefs who cook prime rib every day. Between what we found in books and what we learned from these chefs, we came up with a dozen or so fairly different methods. Although there were minor issues, such as whether the roast needed to be tied or whether it should be roasted on a rack, one big question needed answering: At what temperature should prime rib be roasted?

We started with oven temperatures. Suggested roasting temperatures ranged from a bold 425 degrees to a tepid 200. Other recipes recommended an initial high-temperature sear (450 to 500 degrees), then reducing the oven temperature to a more moderate temperature (350 degrees) for actual roasting. Testing the full range, we roasted prime ribs at temperatures ranging from 200 to 500 degrees.

All prime ribs roasted at oven temperatures exceeding 300 degrees were pretty much the same. Each slice of carved beef was well done around the exterior, medium toward the center, and a beautiful medium-rare pink at the center. We might have been tempted to report that roasting temperature doesn't much matter if we hadn't tried cooking prime rib at oven temperatures under 300 degrees. Certainly, the ribs cooked at 300 degrees and above all looked quite acceptable before carving, especially when compared with the low-temperature prime ribs. We ended up with a surprise, however.

It's funny that we should end up preferring the prime rib roasted at 200 degrees because it certainly wasn't love at first sight. About halfway through this roast's cooking time, we wrote in our notes, "Though the meat looks virtually raw, the internal temperature registers a surprising 110 degrees, and very little of its fat has rendered." But we changed our minds quickly as soon as we carved the first slice. This roast was as beautiful on the inside as it was anemic on the outside. Unlike the roasts that cooked at higher temperatures, this one was rosy pink from the surface to the center—the juiciest and most tender of all the roasts we cooked. This was restaurant prime rib at its best.

Besides being evenly cooked, the prime rib roasted in a 200-degree oven had another thing going for it: Its internal temperature increased only a degree or two during its resting period. (Roasts are allowed to rest when they come out of the oven both to distribute the heat evenly and to allow the juices to reabsorb back into the outer layers of the meat.) A roast cooked to 128 degrees, for example, moved only to 130 degrees after a 45-minute rest.

Not so with the roasts cooked at higher temperatures. Their internal temperatures increased much more dramatically out of the oven. As a matter of fact, we noticed a direct correlation between oven temperature and the roast's post-cooking temperature increase. Prime ribs roasted at more moderate temperatures (325 to 350) increased, on average, 14 degrees during resting. In other words, if pulled from the oven at a rare 126-degree internal temperature,

---

SCIENCE: Aging Beef

Traditionally, butchers have hung carcasses in the meat locker to age their beef. Meat is aged to develop its flavor and improve its texture. This process depends on certain enzymes, whose function while the animal is alive is to digest proteins. After the animal is slaughtered, the cells that contain these enzymes start to break down, releasing the enzymes into the meat where they attack the cell proteins and break them down into amino acids, which have more flavor. In addition, the enzymes also start to break down the muscles, so the tissue becomes softer. This process can take from one to several weeks. (To age meat for more than a week, however, it must be done under carefully controlled conditions—it should not be done at home.)

Today, some beef is still aged on hooks (this process is called dry aging), but for the most part beef is wet-aged in sealed Cryovac packets. We wondered if it was worth searching for dry-aged beef, so we ordered both a dry-aged and wet-aged prime rib roast from a restaurant supplier in Manhattan. The differences between the two roasts were clear-cut.

Like a good, young red wine, wet-aged beef tasted pleasant and fresh on its own. When compared with the dry-aged beef, though, we realized its flavors were less concentrated. The meat tasted washed out. The dry-aged beef, on the other hand, engaged the mouth. It was stronger, richer, and gamier-tasting, with a pleasant tang. The dry-aged and wet-aged beef were equally tender, but the dry-aged beef had an added buttery texture.

Unfortunately, most butchers don't dry-age beef anymore because hanging quarters of beef take up too much refrigerator space for too long. During the aging process, dry-aged beef also dehydrates (loses weight) and requires trimming (loses more weight). That weight loss means less beef costs more money. Wet-aged beef loses virtually no weight during the aging process, and it comes prebutchered, packaged, and ready to sell. Since beef is expensive to begin with, most customers opt for the less expensive wet-aged beef. So why does dry aging work better than wet aging? The answer is simple: air. Enclosed in Cryovac, wet-aged beef is shut off from oxygen—the key to flavor development and concentration.

Since availability and price pose problems, you may simply want to age beef yourself. It's just a matter of making room in the refrigerator and remembering to buy the roast ahead of time, up to one week before you plan on roasting it. When you get the roast home, pat it dry and place it on a wire rack set over a paper towel-lined cake pan or plate. Set the racked roast in the refrigerator and let it age until you are ready to roast it, up to seven days. (Aging begins to have a dramatic effect on the roast after three or four days, but we detected some improvement in flavor and texture after just one day of aging.) Before roasting, shave off any exterior meat that has completely dehydrated. Between the trimming and dehydration, count on a seven-pound roast losing a pound or so during a week's aging.

these roasts moved up to a solid medium (140 degrees) by the end of the resting period. Furthermore, the prime rib roasted at 425 degrees increased a whopping 24 degrees (from 119 to 143) during its rest. Those roasted at a lower 250 degrees crept up only 5 degrees before carving. We considered this smaller increase a definite advantage. It let us pull the roast from the oven at the temperature we wanted instead of having to speculate on how many degrees the roast would jump during resting.

In addition to its more stable internal temperature, the prime rib roasted at 200 degrees also lost less weight during cooking than those roasted at higher temperatures. A 6¾-pound roast cooked in a 200-degree oven weighed just over 6¼ pounds when it came out of the oven, a loss of less than half a pound. By contrast, similar roasts cooked in a 325-degree oven lost just over a pound, while the roast cooked at 350 degrees lost 1½ pounds. The prime rib cooked at 425 degrees lost a shocking 2 pounds. Part of the weight loss is fat, but certainly a good portion is juice. This test confirmed our sense that the beef roasted at 200 degrees was indeed juicier than those roasted at the higher temperatures.

Because members of the Beef Council would not endorse an oven-roasting temperature below 300 degrees, we decided to check the safety of this low-heat method before getting too sold on it. After conversations with a number of food scientists across the country, we determined that low-temperature roasting is as safe a cooking method as higher-temperature roasting. And though the odds of finding bacteria inside a prime rib roast are virtually nonexistent, the only way to guarantee a bacteria-free slab of prime rib is to cook it to an internal temperature of 160 degrees, no matter what cooking method is used, low temperature or high. Unfortunately, at 160 degrees, the meat is gray, tough, and unappetizing.

The only thing that bothered us about the slow-roasted prime rib was its raw-looking, unrendered fatty exterior. By searing the meat on top of the stove before low-roasting it, though, we solved the problem of the unattractive look.

As unclear a term as "perfect prime rib" had been to us at the beginning, it was crystal clear the moment we carved off that first slab from our 200-degree roasted prime rib. We immediately recognized it as the beef you get at a great prime rib restaurant. As it turns out, many prime rib restaurants slow-roast their meat. They use special ovens that roast the meat at 250 degrees until it reaches an internal temperature of 120 degrees. At that time, the oven heat is decreased to 140 degrees, causing the meat's internal temperature to increase to 130 degrees and remain there until ready to serve (up to 24 hours later). Unfortunately, few home cooks can use this method since most home oven thermostats do not go below 200 degrees. But by following our recipe, home cooks can very closely approximate the superb prime rib served in the country's best restaurants.

Prime Rib

SERVES 6 TO 8

Butchers tend to cut a rib roast, which consists of ribs 6 through 12 if left whole, into two distinct cuts. The more desirable of the two cuts consists of ribs 10 through 12. Since this portion of the roast is closer to the loin end, it is sometimes called the "loin end." Other butchers call it the "small end" or the "first cut." Whatever it is called, it is more desirable because it contains the large, single rib-eye muscle and is less fatty. A less desirable cut, which is still an excellent roast, consists of ribs 6 to 9, closer to the chuck end, and sometimes called the second cut. The closer to the chuck, the more multimuscled the roast becomes. Since muscles are surrounded by fat, this also means a fattier roast. While some cooks may prefer this cut because the fat adds flavor, in general, the more tender and more regularly formed loin end is considered the best.

Even if you don't purchase the roast a week ahead of time as the instructions suggest, even a day or two of aging in the refrigerator will help. (See page 209 for more information on aging.)

1   3-rib standing rib roast (7 pounds), aged up to
      1 week, set at room temperature for 3 hours,
      and tied with kitchen twine at both ends, twine
      running parallel to bone (see illustration on
      page 211)
      Salt and ground black pepper

1. Remove roast from refrigerator 2 to 3 hours before roasting to bring meat to room temperature. Adjust oven rack to low position and heat oven to

200 degrees. Heat large roasting pan over two burners set at medium-high heat. Place roast in hot pan and cook on all sides until nicely browned and about ½ cup fat has rendered, 6 to 8 minutes.

2. Remove roast from pan. Set wire rack in pan, then set roast on rack. Generously season with salt and pepper.

3. Place roast in oven, and roast until meat registers 130 degrees (for medium-rare), about 3½ hours (or about 30 minutes per pound). Let stand 20 minutes (a bit longer is fine) before serving.

4. To carve, remove the twine and set the roast on a cutting board, rib bones perpendicular to the board. Using a carving fork to hold the roast in place, cut along the rib bones to sever the meat from the bones. Set the roast cut side down; carve the meat across the grain into thick slices.

TYING UP PRIME RIB

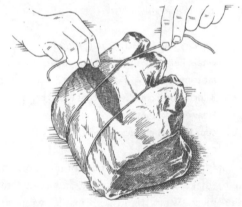

It is imperative to tie prime rib before roasting. If left untied, the outer layer of meat will pull away from the rib-eye muscle and overcook. To prevent this problem, tie the roast at both ends, running string parallel to the bone.

BRISKET

OUR FAVORITE WAY TO COOK BRISKET IS ON the barbecue. When prepared correctly, the meat picks up a great smoky flavor and the meat is fork-tender. Unfortunately, many a barbecued brisket ends up burned, tough, or chewy.

The main reason it's so hard to cook brisket right is that it starts out as a very tough cut of meat. Unless brisket is fully cooked, the meat is very chewy and practically inedible. Because a brisket is so large, cooking the meat fully can take many hours. Our goal was to make the meat as tender as possible as quickly as possible.

So what does "fully cooked" mean when talking about brisket? To find out, we roasted four small pieces to various internal temperatures. The pieces cooked to 160 and 180 degrees were dry and quite tough. A piece cooked to 200 degrees was slightly less tough, although quite dry. A final piece cooked to 210 degrees had the most appealing texture and the most pleasant chew, despite the fact that it was the driest.

So what's going on here? Heat causes muscle proteins to uncoil and then bond together, which drives out juices in the same way that wringing removes moisture from a wet cloth. This process starts in earnest at around 140 degrees, and by the time meat reaches 180 degrees most juices have been expelled. This explains why a medium-rare steak (cooked to 130 degrees) is much juicier than a well-done steak (cooked to 160 degrees).

With tender cuts, like steak, the lower the internal temperature of the meat, the juicier and less tough the meat will be. However, with cuts that start out tough, like brisket, another process is also at work. Brisket is loaded with waxy looking connective tissue called collagen, which makes the meat chewy and tough unless fully cooked. Only when the collagen has been transformed into gelatin will the meat be tender. Collagen begins to convert to gelatin at 130 to 140 degrees, but the conversion process occurs most rapidly at temperatures above 180 degrees.

When cooking brisket, the gelatinization of collagen must be the priority. Thus, the meat should be cooked as fully as possible, or to an internal temperature of 210 degrees. The muscle juices will be long gone (that's why the sliced meat is served with barbecue sauce), but the meat will be extremely tender because all the collagen will have been converted to gelatin.

It is important to point out that moist-heat cooking methods (such as braising) are appropriate for cooking meats to such high internal temperatures because water is a more efficient conductor of heat than air. Meats cooked in a moist environment heat up faster and can be held at high internal temperatures without burning or drying out.

Given the fact that brisket must be fully cooked and that the meat is so big (a full brisket can weigh 13 pounds), the meat needs 10 to 12 hours of barbecuing to reach the fork-tender stage. Even when butchers separate the brisket into smaller pieces, as is often the case, the cooking time is astronomical. Most cooks are not prepared to keep a fire going that long.

To get around this all-day-long-tending-the-fire problem, we found it necessary to commit barbecue heresy. After much testing, we decided to start the meat on the grill but then finish in the oven, where it could be left to cook unattended. We wondered how long the meat would have to stay on the grill to pick up enough smoke flavor. In our testing, we found that two hours allowed the meat to absorb plenty of smoke flavor and created a dark brown, crusty exterior.

At this point, the meat is ready for the oven. We found it best to wrap the meat in foil to create a moist environment. (Unwrapped briskets cooked up drier, and the exterior was prone to burning.) After barbecuing, a whole brisket requires three hours or so in a 300-degree oven to become fork-tender. Barbecue purists might object to the use of the oven, but this method works and doesn't require a tremendous commitment of hands-on cooking time.

Some further notes about our testing. Although many experts recommend basting a brisket regularly as it cooks on the grill to ensure moistness, we disagree. Taking the lid off wreaked havoc with our charcoal fire, and the meat didn't taste any different despite frequent basting with sauce. Likewise, we don't recommend placing a pan filled with water (we also tried beer) on the grill. Some barbecue masters believe that the liquid adds moisture and flavor to the meat, but we couldn't tell any difference between brisket cooked with and without the pan of liquid.

Brisket comes with a thick layer of fat on one side. We tried turning the brisket as it cooks, thinking this might promote even cooking. However, we had better results when we barbecued the brisket fat side up the entire time. When positioned this way, the fat slowly melts, lubricating the meat below.

Barbecued Beef Brisket
SERVES 18 TO 24

Cooking a whole brisket, which weighs at least 10 pounds, may seem like overkill. However, the process is easy, and the leftovers keep well in the refrigerator for up to four days. (Leave leftover brisket unsliced, and reheat the foil-wrapped meat in a 300-degree oven until warm.) Don't worry if your brisket is a little larger or smaller; split-second cooking times are not critical since the meat is eaten very well-done. Still, if you don't want to bother with a big piece of meat, barbecuing brisket for less than a crowd is easy to do. Simply ask your butcher for either the point or flat portion of the brisket, each of which weighs about half as much as the whole brisket. Then follow this recipe, reducing the spice rub by half and barbecuing for just 1½ hours. Wrap the meat tightly in foil and reduce the time in the oven to 2 hours. No matter how large or small a piece you cook, it's a good idea to save the juices the meat gives off while in the oven to enrich the barbecue sauce. Hickory and mesquite are both traditional wood choices with brisket.

¾	cup Dry Rub for Barbecue (page 272)
1	whole beef brisket (9 to 11 pounds), fat trimmed to ¼-inch thickness
2	3-inch wood chunks or 2 cups wood chips Heavy-duty aluminum foil
2	cups Barbecue Sauce (page 272)

1. Apply rub liberally to all sides of meat, pressing down to make sure spices adhere and completely obscure meat. Wrap tightly in plastic wrap and refrigerate for 2 hours. (For stronger flavor, refrigerate brisket for up to 2 days.)

2. One hour prior to cooking, remove brisket from refrigerator, unwrap, and let come to room temperature. Soak wood chunks in cold water to cover for 1 hour and drain, or place wood chips on 18-inch square of aluminum foil, seal to make packet, and use fork to create about six holes to allow smoke to escape (see illustrations on page 271).

3. Meanwhile, light about 40 charcoal briquettes in chimney. Transfer coals from chimney to one side of kettle grill, piling them up in a mound two or three briquettes high. Keep bottom vents completely open. When coals are covered with light gray ash, lay wood chunks or packet with chips on top of char-

coal. Put cooking grate in place, open grill lid vents completely, and cover, turning lid so that vents are opposite wood chunks or chips to draw smoke through grill. Let grate heat for 5 minutes, clean with wire brush, and position brisket, fat side up, on grate opposite fire. Barbecue without removing lid for 2 hours. (Initial temperature will be about 350 degrees and will drop to 250 degrees after 2 hours.)

4. Adjust oven rack to middle position and preheat oven to 300 degrees. Attach two 48-inch-long pieces of heavy-duty foil by folding edges together two or three times, crimping tightly to seal well, to form an approximately 48 x 36-inch rectangle. Position brisket lengthwise in center of foil. Bring short edges over brisket and fold down, crimping tightly to seal. Repeat with long sides of foil to seal brisket completely. Place brisket on jelly-roll pan; bake until meat is fork-tender, 3 to 3½ hours.

5. Remove brisket from oven, loosen foil at one end to release steam, and let rest for 30 minutes. If you like, drain juices into large bowl and defat juices in gravy skimmer.

6. Unwrap brisket and place on cutting board. Separate into two sections and carve against grain on diagonal into long, thin slices. Serve with plain barbecue sauce or with barbecue sauce that has been flavored with up to 1 cup of defatted brisket juices.

➤ VARIATION
Barbecued Beef Brisket on a Gas Grill
Follow recipe for Barbecued Beef Brisket, making the following changes: Place foil tray with soaked wood chips (see illustrations on page 271) on top of primary burner (see illustration on page 268). Turn all burners to high and preheat with lid down until chips are smoking heavily, about 20 minutes. Turn primary burner down to medium, turn off burner(s) without chips, and clean grill with wire brush. Position brisket, fat side up, over cool part of grill. Barbecue for 2 hours. (Temperature inside grill should be constant 275 degrees; adjust lit burner as necessary.) Proceed with recipe as directed.

CORNED BEEF AND CABBAGE

CORNED BEEF AND CABBAGE, THE VENERABLE one-pot meal composed of boiled corned beef, cabbage, and other winter vegetables (also known in parts of the country as New England boiled dinner), has struck us less as a dish with big flavor and genuine dinner-table appeal than as a symbol of the stalwart Yankee ethics of hard work and thrift. That misconception, however, was the first of several to be busted during our testing. In the course of tasting umpteen dishes of corned beef and cabbage, we came to realize that this dish needn't be mushy, overwhelmingly salty, or one-dimensional, as it had always seemed. Instead, it can be a full-flavored medley of meaty, tender, well-seasoned beef, subtle spice, and sweet, earthy vegetables, each distinct in flavor and texture.

We commenced our research and testing with the usual spate of recipes, most of which were based on a four- to six-pound piece of corned beef. The term "corned" refers to the curing of meat with salt, often used as a method of preservation before refrigeration became widespread. Legend has it that the salt grains were roughly the same size as corn kernels, hence the name "corned beef." The cut of beef most commonly corned is boneless brisket, which is a trimmed, 12- or 13-pound piece taken from the front part of the cow's breast. For retail sale, the whole brisket is usually split into two parts, called the first, or flat, cut and second, or point, cut. Of the two, the point cut is thicker, fattier, and, to our tastes, both more flavorful and more tender than the flat cut. Both of these cuts can be trimmed further into smaller pieces of meat, and both are available as commercially corned beef.

At the supermarket, we found more commercial corned beef options than we had anticipated from reading the recipes we had researched. In addition to "low-sodium" corned beef, there were regular and "gray," each in both flat and point cuts in sizes ranging from three to six pounds. We were told by a representative from Mosey's, a national producer of corned beef, that the gray style is popular only in, and therefore limited to, New England. The difference between regular and gray is made clear on the package. The brine for gray corned beef contains only water and salt, whereas the "regular" corned beef brine also contains sodium nitrite, which helps the meat retain its red color by reacting with purple color pigments and turning them to pink and red.

We brought home an example of each type and took to the stove. Cooking directions on the packages and in our research recipes did not vary by much. Generally, instructions were to cover the meat with one to three inches of water and simmer until tender, anywhere from 2½ to 3½ hours, depending on the size of the brisket.

To our surprise, the regular corned beef choices disappointed us across the board. Though they remained an appealing pink even when cooked, our tasters described the flavor of both the full- and low-salt versions as "sharp and somewhat chemical," most likely from the nitrite. In addition, the texture was deemed to be grainy, with a noticeably chalky mouthfeel. By comparison, the gray corned beef

looked, well, gray, because it lacked the color boost given to regular brisket by the nitrite. The flavor, however, was superior, and for that, we'll gladly trade the pink color. Whereas the chemical qualities we noted in the regular versions obscured the flavor of the beef, the gray corned beef tasted cleaner and beefier. The salt had a stronger presence than we preferred, and the spice we look for in ideal corned beef was nonexistent, but we knew we wanted to stick with the gray for further testing.

But because the gray corned beef we preferred is a product limited to a small region of the country, we decided to try corning our own brisket. We figured that this would also make it easier to control the saltiness. Our research turned up two methods of corning your own beef—the wet cure and the dry cure. Both methods require close to a week, but they are also mindlessly easy. All you need to do is prepare the meat and its cure. Beyond that, there is no work whatsoever. Of course, we tested each method, using

Vegetables for Corned Beef and Cabbage

The vegetables listed below are some of our favorites. However, if you love potatoes but cannot abide parsnips, choose vegetables to suit your tastes. To make sure that the vegetables are evenly cooked, we trim them all to sizes appropriate for their density and cooking characteristics and add them to the pot in two batches.

CATEGORY 1
Once the meat has been removed from the pot, add the desired selection and quantity of vegetables from this category. Return the liquid to a boil and simmer for 10 minutes before adding vegetables from category 2.

VEGETABLE	PREPARATION
Carrots	Peeled and halved crosswise; thin end halved lengthwise, thick end quartered lengthwise.
Rutabagas (small)	Peeled and halved crosswise; each half cut into six chunks.
White turnips (medium)	Peeled and quartered.
New potatoes (small)	Scrubbed and left whole.

CATEGORY 2
At the 10-minute mark, add selected vegetables from this category, return cooking liquid to boil, then continue to simmer until all vegetables are just tender, 10 to 15 minutes longer.

Boiling onions	Peeled and left whole.
Green cabbage, uncored (small head)	Blemished leaves removed and cut into six to eight wedges.
Parsnips	Peeled and halved crosswise; thin end halved lengthwise, thick end quartered lengthwise.
Brussels sprouts	Blemished leaves removed, stems trimmed, and left whole.

five-pound fresh briskets in both flat and point cut.

Because meat preservative is readily available in drugstores in the form of the potassium nitrate called saltpeter, we still had the option of producing regular and gray corned beef. Even in our home-corned beef, though, the preservative added a harshness to the flavor that competed with the taste of the beef. Because the color of the meat was less important to us than the flavor, we dropped the saltpeter from further testing.

Testing the wet method on our gray corned beef involved tasting briskets cured in a brine of two cups of salt and three quarts of water for 14, 12, 10, 7, and 5 days. Among all of them, we liked the 5-day brisket best, noting a pleasing saltiness alongside the distinctive flavor of beef. We also confirmed our preference for the fattier point cut of brisket. Fat carries flavor in all cuts of meat, and beef brisket is no different. The flat cut is especially lean and therefore less flavorful and moist than the point cut.

At this point, we also gave the dry-cure method a go. Adapting a recipe from Julia Child's *The Way to Cook* (Knopf, 1989), we rubbed our six-pound, point-cut brisket with one-half cup of salt and a few crushed herbs and spices, placed it in a huge, two-gallon zipper-lock bag, weighted the meat with a brick, and let it sit for five days in the fridge. Lo and behold, the result was the best corned beef of them all, even better than the five-day wet-cured corned beef, with a concentrated beef flavor, assertive yet not overpowering salt, and a pleasant spiciness. Curing the brisket for two extra days, seven in total, brought out the flavor of the spices a little more, without affecting the saltiness. Julia Child's recipe suggested desalting the dry-cured meat by soaking it in several changes of water for at least twenty-four hours or up to three days, depending on the size of the brisket. To be honest, we initially overlooked this step; we simply rinsed the surface of the meat to remove shards of crumbled bay leaf and cracked peppercorns and went ahead with the cooking. When we finally did try the full desalting, we found that the meat tasted slightly richer because of the diminished salt presence, but not so much better that it justified a twenty-four-hour soak versus a quick rinse.

With the corned beef tasting just the way we wanted, we turned our attention to the cooking method, then to the vegetables. Though most recipes call for cooking corned beef and cabbage on the stove, we did try a couple of tests in the oven. Our advice is to stick to the stove, on which the meat cooked faster and was easier to monitor. Also, we found that adding the vegetables and adjusting the heat to compensate was easier with the pot on top of the stove.

On the stove, we noticed that the meat emerged from the pot tender and flaky if cooked at a lively simmer, as opposed to tight and tough when cooked at a full boil. We also preferred to cook the meat covered to prevent water evaporation and a resulting overconcentration of salt in the broth. We experimented with different quantities of water in the pot, covering the corned beef by one-half inch to three inches, and found that it makes no difference in terms of the meat or vegetables. The amount of water does matter to the broth, though. The broth produced from covering the meat by one-half to one inch (8–10 cups over a 4½ pound brisket in our eight-quart pot) and cooking it with the pot lid on was nicely seasoned and suitable for use on its own or in another soup.

The last, though not insignificant, variable was the vegetables. We tested a wide variety of vegetables from the appropriate to the exotic and settled on the traditional green cabbage, with the added interest of carrots, parsnips, potatoes, turnips, rutabagas, onions, and Brussels sprouts, all borrowed from the New England boiled dinner, as our favorites. We tried cooking the vegetables along with the meat, but there were two distinct disadvantages to this approach. First, it made it too difficult to judge when the vegetables were properly done. Second, it would require a pot larger than any that we had in the test kitchen or in our own homes.

The best method turned out to be removing the meat from the broth when done, then cooking the vegetables in the broth. This not only benefited the vegetables, giving them a full, round flavor from the salt and rendered fat in the broth, but it also allowed us time to let the meat rest before cutting.

Home-Corned Beef Brisket and Cabbage, New England Style

SERVES 8 WITH LEFTOVERS

If you prefer a leaner piece of meat, feel free to use the flat cut. In fact, we found more flat cut than point cut briskets in supermarket meat cases, so you'll probably have to ask the meat department attendant or butcher to bring you a point cut. Leave a bit of fat attached for better texture and flavor.

The meat is cooked fully when it is tender, the muscle fibers have loosened visibly, and a skewer slides in with minimal resistance. Serve this dish with horseradish, either plain or mixed with whipped or sour cream, or with grainy mustard.

½	cup kosher salt
I	tablespoon black peppercorns, cracked
¾	tablespoon ground allspice
I	tablespoon dried thyme
½	tablespoon paprika
2	bay leaves, crumbled
I	fresh beef brisket (4 to 6 pounds), preferably point cut, trimmed of excess fat, rinsed and patted dry
7–8	pounds prepared vegetables of your choice (see page 214)

1. Mix salt and seasonings in small bowl.

2. Spear brisket about 30 times per side with meat fork or metal skewer. Rub each side evenly with salt mixture; place in 2-gallon-size zipper-lock bag, forcing out as much air as possible. Place in pan large enough to hold it (a jelly-roll pan works well), cover with second, similar-size pan, and weight with two bricks or heavy cans of similar weight. Refrigerate 5 to 7 days, turning once a day. Rinse meat and pat dry.

3. Bring brisket to boil with water to cover by ½ to 1 inch in large soup kettle or stockpot (at least eight quarts), skimming any scum that rises to surface. Cover and simmer until skewer inserted in thickest part of brisket slides out with ease, 2 to 3 hours.

4. Heat oven to 200 degrees. Transfer meat to large platter, ladling about 1 cup cooking liquid over it to keep it moist. Cover with foil and set in oven.

5. Add vegetables from category 1 to kettle and bring to boil; cover and simmer until vegetables begin to soften, about 10 minutes. Add vegetables from category 2 and bring to boil; cover and simmer until all

vegetables are tender, 10 to 15 minutes longer.

6. Meanwhile, remove meat from oven and cut across the grain into ¼-inch slices.

7. Transfer vegetables to meat platter, moisten with additional broth, and serve.

HAMBURGERS

MOST HAMBURGERS SEEM MERELY TO SATISFY hunger, rather than give pleasure. Too bad, because making an exceptional hamburger isn't hard or time-consuming. We're sure fast-food chains have good reasons for not offering hand-formed, 100 percent ground-chuck burgers, but home cooks do not.

If you have the right ground beef, the perfect hamburger can be ready in under 15 minutes, assuming you season, form, and cook it properly. The biggest difficulty for many cooks, though, may be finding the right beef.

In order to test which cut or cuts of beef cook into the best burger, we ordered chuck, round, rump, sirloin, and hanging tenderloin, all ground to order with 20 percent fat. (Although we would question fat percentages in later testing, we needed a standard for these early tests. From our experience this percentage seemed right.) After a side-by-side taste test, we quickly concluded that most cuts of ground beef are pleasant but bland when compared with the robust, beefy-flavored ground chuck. Pricier ground sirloin, for example, cooked up into a particularly boring burger.

So pure ground chuck—the cut of beef that starts where the ribs end and moves up to the shoulder and neck, ending at the foreshank—was the clear winner. We were ready to race ahead to seasonings, but before moving on we stopped to ask ourselves, "Will cooks buying ground chuck from the grocery store agree with our choice?" Our efforts to determine whether grocery store ground chuck and ground-to-order chuck were even remotely similar took us along a culinary blue highway from kitchen to packing plant, butcher shop, and science lab.

According to the National Live Stock and Meat Board, beef's fat percentage is checked and enforced at the retail level. If a package of beef is labeled 90 percent lean, then it must contain no more than 10 percent fat, give or take a point. Retail stores are required to test each batch of ground beef, make the necessary adjustments, and keep a log of the results. Local inspectors routinely pull ground beef from a store's meat case for a fat check. If the tested meat is not within 1 percent of the package sticker, the store is fined.

Whether a package labeled ground chuck is, in fact, 100 percent ground chuck is a different story. First, we surveyed a number of grocery store meat department managers, who said that what was written on the label did match what was in the package. For instance, a package labeled "ground chuck" would contain only chuck trimmings. Same for sirloin and round. Only "ground beef" would contain mixed beef trimmings.

We got a little closer to the truth, however, by interviewing a respected butcher in the Chicago area, who spoke candidly. Of the several grocery stores and butcher shops he had worked at over the years, he had never known a store to segregate meat trimmings. In fact, in his present butcher shop, he sells only two kinds of ground beef: sirloin and chuck. He defines ground sirloin as ground beef (mostly but not exclusively sirloin) that's labeled 90 percent lean, and chuck as ground beef (including a lot of chuck trimmings) that's labeled 85 percent lean.

Only meat ground at federally inspected plants is guaranteed to match its label. At these plants an inspector checks that labeled ground beef actually comes from the cut of beef named on the label and that the fat percentage is correct. To most retailers, though, specific cuts of ground beef can only be guaranteed to equal specific fat percentages.

Since retail ground beef labeling is deceptive, we suggest buying a chuck roast and having the butcher grind it for you. Even at a local grocery store, the butcher was willing to grind to order. Some meat always gets lost in the grinder, so count on losing a bit (2 to 3 percent).

Because mass-ground beef can also be risky, it made theoretical sense to recommend grinding beef at home for those who want to reduce further their odds of eating beef tainted with E. coli. It doesn't make much practical sense, though. Not all cooks own a grinder. And even if they did, we thought that home grinding demanded far too much setup,

cleanup, and effort for a dish meant to be so simple.

To see if there was an easier way, we tried chopping by hand and grinding in the food processor. The hibachi-style, hand-chopping method was just as time-consuming and more messy than the traditional grinder. The meat must be sliced thin, then cut into cubes—before you go at it with two chef's knives. The fat doesn't evenly distribute, meat flies everywhere, and unless your knives are razor sharp, it's difficult to chop through the meat. What's worse, you can't efficiently chop more than two burgers at a time. And the resulting cooked burger could have been mistaken for chopped steak.

The food processor performed a surprisingly good meat-grinding job. We thought the steel blade would raggedly chew the meat, but to our surprise, it was evenly chopped and fluffy.

For those who buy a chuck roast for grinding, we found the average chuck roast to be about 80 percent lean. To check its leanness, we bought a chuck roast—not too fatty, not too lean—and ground it in the food processor. We took our ground chuck back to the grocery store for the butcher to check its fat content in the Univex Fat Analyzer, a machine the store uses to check each batch of beef it grinds. A plug of our ground beef scored an almost perfect 21 percent fat when tested in the fat analyzer.

Up to this point, all of our beef had been ground with approximately 20 percent fat. A quick test of burgers with less and more fat helped us to decide that 20 percent fat, give or take a few percentage points, was good for burgers. Any higher fat percentage, and it's left in the pan. Any lower, and you start compromising the beef's juicy, moist texture.

Working with fresh-ground chuck, we now moved into shaping and cooking. To defy the overpacking and overhandling warning you see in many recipes, we thoroughly worked a portion of ground beef before cooking it. The well-done burger exterior was nearly as dense as a meat pâté, and the less well-done interior was compact and pasty.

It's pretty hard to overhandle a beef patty, though, especially if you're trying not to. Once the meat has been divided into portions, we found tossing the meat from one hand to another helped bring it together into a ball without overworking it. From there, pressing the ball of meat into a patty with the fingertips not only gave it surface texture, it also flattened it, again without overworking the meat.

For our taste, a four-ounce burger seemed a little skimpy. A five-ounce portion of meat patted into a nice size burger: a scant four inches in diameter and just shy of one inch thick. Just the right size for a bun.

No cooking method surpasses grilling, but we were awfully fond of the thick-crusted burgers we were able to cook in a well-seasoned cast-iron skillet. We didn't need any fat in the pan to keep the burgers from sticking. Like a good loaf of bread, the perfect burger should display a crisp, flavorful crust that protects a moist, tender interior. Both grilling and pan-searing delivered this kind of burger. Broiling did not offer the contrast in texture we were looking for.

Whether you are grilling or pan-searing, we make two suggestions. First, make sure the grill rack or pan is hot before adding the meat. If not, the hamburger will not develop that crucial crusty exterior. Second, avoid the temptation to continually flip the burger during cooking. Follow the cooking times in the recipe below, setting a timer if you like. When the buzzer goes off, flip the burger. When the buzzer goes off again, pull that burger confidently from the heat.

For those who like their burgers well-done, we found that poking a small hole in the center of the patty before cooking helped the burger center to get done before the edges dried out. And for those who love cheese, we liked grating it into the raw beef as opposed to melting it on top. Since the cheese was more evenly distributed, a little went much further than the big hunk on top.

Hamburgers

SERVES 4

You can grill these burgers or pan-sear them in a 12-inch cast-iron skillet.

1¼	pounds 100 percent ground chuck
¾	teaspoon salt
¼	teaspoon ground black pepper
	Buns and desired toppings

1. Break up chuck to increase surface area for seasoning. Sprinkle salt and pepper over meat; toss lightly with hands to distribute seasoning. Divide meat into four equal portions (5 ounces each); with cupped hands, toss one portion of meat back and forth to form loose ball. Pat lightly to flatten into 1-inch-thick burger, 3½ to 4 inches across, using fingertips to create pocked, textured surface. Repeat with remaining portions of meat.

2. IF GRILLING: Heat enough coals to make hot fire. When coals are hot and covered with white ash, spread them in single layer. Position grill rack and lid; heat until rack is very hot, about 5 minutes. (If using gas grill, turn all burners to high and preheat for 15 minutes.) Place burgers on rack and grill, turning once, to desired doneness as follows: 3 minutes per side for rare, 4 minutes per side for medium-rare, 5 minutes on first side and 4 minutes on second side for medium, and 5 minutes per side for well-done.

3. IF PAN-SEARING: Heat skillet over medium-high heat. When skillet is hot (drops of water flicked into it evaporate immediately), add patties and cook, turning once, to desired doneness, using same times as if grilling. Serve immediately with buns and desired toppings.

EQUIPMENT: Food Processor as Grinder
Even though we have a meat grinder in the kitchen, we don't regularly grind meat ourselves. The setup, breakdown, and washing up for a two-pound chuck roast is just not worth the effort. Besides, hamburgers are supposed to be impromptu, fast, fun food. To our surprise, though, the food processor does a respectable grinding job, and it's much simpler than a grinder. The key is to make sure the roast is cold, that it is cut into small chunks, and that it is processed in small batches. For a two-pound roast, cut the meat into one-inch chunks. Divide the chunks into four equal portions. Place one portion of meat in the workbowl of a food processor fitted with the steel blade. Pulse the cubes until the meat is ground, 15 to 20 one-second pulses. Repeat with the remaining portions of beef. Then shape the ground meat as directed, into six patties.

MEAT LOAF

NOT ALL MEAT LOAVES RESEMBLE MAMA'S. In fact, some ingredient lists look like the work of a proud child or defiant adolescent. Canned pineapple, cranberry sauce, raisins, prepared taco mix, and even goat cheese have all found their way into published recipes. Rather than feud over flavorings, though, we decided to focus on the meatier issues.

To begin with, we narrowed our testing to red meat. We had plenty of questions to answer: What meat or mix of meats delivers good mouthfeel and flavor? Which fillers offer unobtrusive texture? Should the loaf be cooked free-form or in a standard loaf pan, or are the new perforated pans designed for meat loaves worth the money? Should the loaf be topped with bacon, ketchup, both, or neither? Is it better to sauté the onions and garlic before adding them to the meat mix, or are they just as good raw and grated?

To determine which ground meat or meat mix makes the best loaf, we used a very basic meat loaf recipe and made miniature loaves with the following meat proportions: equal parts beef chuck and pork; equal parts veal and pork; equal parts beef chuck, pork, and veal; two parts beef chuck to one part ground pork and one part ground veal; three-quarters beef chuck and one-quarter ground bacon; equal parts beef chuck and ham; all ground beef chuck; and all ground veal.

We found out that meat markets haven't been selling meat loaf mix (a mix of beef, pork, and veal, usually equal proportions of each) all these years for nothing. As we expected, the best meat loaves were made from the combinations of these three meats. Straight ground veal was tender but overly mild and mushy, while the all-beef loaf was coarse-textured, liver-flavored, and tough. Though interesting, neither the beef/ham nor the beef/bacon loaves looked or tasted like classic meat loaf. Both were firm, dense, and more terrinelike. Also, as bacon lovers, we preferred the bacon's smoky flavor and crispy texture surrounding, not in, the loaf.

Although both of the beef/pork/veal mixtures were good, we preferred the mix with a higher proportion of ground chuck. This amount gave the loaf a distinct but not overly strong beef flavor. The extra beef percentage also kept the loaf firm, making it easier to cut. Mild-tasting pork added another flavor dimension while the small quantity of veal kept it tender. For those who choose not to special-order this mix or mix it themselves at home, we recommend the standard meat loaf mix of equal parts beef, pork, and veal.

After comparing meat loaves made with and without fillers or binders, we realized that starch in a meat loaf offers more than economy. Loaves made without filler were coarse-textured, dense, and too hamburger-like. Those with binders, on the other hand, had that distinctive meat loaf texture.

But which binder to use? Practically every hot and cold cereal box offers a meat loaf recipe using that particular cereal. We made several meat loaves, each with a different filler. Though there was no clear-cut winner, we narrowed the number from 11 down to 3.

After tasting all the meat loaves, we realized that a good binder should help with texture but not add distinct flavor. Cracker crumbs, quick-cooking oatmeal, and fresh bread crumbs fit the bill.

Just as we found that we liked the less distinctly flavored fillers, so we preferred sautéed—not raw—onions and garlic in the meat mix. Because the meat loaf only cooks to an internal temperature of 160 degrees, raw onions never fully cook. Sautéing the vegetables is a five-minute detour well worth the time.

We found our meat loaves need some added liquid to moisten the filler. Without it, the filler robs the meat dry. As with the fillers, we ran across a host of meat loaf moisteners and tried as many as made sense.

Tomato sauce made the loaf taste like a meatball with sauce. We liked the flavor of ketchup, but ultimately decided that we preferred it baked on top rather than inside.

Beer and wine do not make ideal meat moisteners, either. The meat doesn't cook long enough or to a high enough internal temperature to burn the alcohol off, so the meat ends up with a distinctly raw alcohol taste.

As with many other aspects of this home-cooked favorite, we found that there is a good reason that the majority of meat loaf recipes call for some form of dairy product for the liquid—it's the best choice. We tried half-and-half, milk, sour cream, yogurt, skim and whole evaporated milk, and even cottage cheese. Whole milk and plain yogurt ended up as our liquids of choice, with the yogurt offering a complementary subtle tang to the rich beef.

Cooks who don't like a crusty exterior on their meat loaf usually prefer to bake it in a loaf pan. We found that the high-sided standard loaf pan, however, causes the meat to stew rather than bake. Also, for those who like a glazed top, there is another disadvantage: The enclosed pan allows the meat juices to bubble up from the sides to dilute and destroy the glaze. Similarly, bacon placed on top of the meat loaf curls and doesn't properly attach to the loaf, and if tucked inside the pan, the bacon never crisps.

For all these reasons, we advise against the use of a standard loaf pan. If you prefer a crustless, soft-sided meat loaf, you should invest in a meat loaf pan with a perforated bottom and accompanying drip pan. The enclosed pan keeps the meat soft while the perforated bottom allows the drippings to flow to the pan below. While still not ideal for a crispy bacon top, it at least saves a glaze from destruction.

We ultimately found that baking a meat loaf freeform in a shallow baking pan gave us the results we wanted. The top and sides of the loaf brown nicely, and, as an additional advantage, basting sauces, like the brown sugar and ketchup sauce we developed, glaze the entire loaf, not just the top. Bacon, too, covers the whole loaf. And because its drippings also fall into the pan, the bacon crisps up nicely.

Meat Loaf with Brown Sugar–Ketchup Glaze

SERVES 6 TO 8

If you like, you can omit the bacon topping from the loaf. In this case, brush on half of the glaze before baking and the other half during the last 15 minutes of baking. If you choose not to special-order the mix of meat below, we recommend the standard meat loaf mix of equal parts beef, pork, and veal, available at most grocery stores.

BROWN SUGAR-KETCHUP GLAZE

- ½   cup ketchup or chili sauce
- 4   tablespoons brown sugar
- 4   teaspoons cider or white vinegar

MEAT LOAF

- 2   teaspoons vegetable oil
- 1   medium onion, chopped
- 2   garlic cloves, minced
- 2   large eggs
- ½   teaspoon dried thyme leaves
- 1   teaspoon salt
- ½   teaspoon ground black pepper
- 2   teaspoons Dijon mustard
- 2   teaspoons Worcestershire sauce
- ¼   teaspoon hot red pepper sauce
- ½   cup whole milk or plain yogurt
- 2   pounds meat loaf mix (50 percent ground chuck, 25 percent ground pork, 25 percent ground veal)
- ⅔   cup crushed saltine crackers (about 16) or quick oatmeal or 1⅓ cups fresh bread crumbs
- ⅓   cup minced fresh parsley leaves
- 6–8   ounces thin-sliced bacon (8 to 12 slices, depending on loaf shape)

1. For the glaze: Mix all ingredients in small saucepan; set aside.

2. For the meat loaf: Heat oven to 350 degrees. Heat oil in medium skillet. Add onion and garlic; sauté until softened, about 5 minutes. Set aside to cool while preparing remaining ingredients.

3. Mix eggs with thyme, salt, pepper, mustard, Worcestershire sauce, pepper sauce, and milk or yogurt. Add egg mixture to meat in large bowl along with crackers, parsley, and cooked onion and garlic; mix with fork until evenly blended and meat mixture does not stick to bowl. (If mixture sticks, add additional milk or yogurt, a couple tablespoons at a time, until mix no longer sticks.)

4. Turn meat mixture onto work surface. With wet hands, pat mixture into approximately 9 x 5-inch loaf shape. Place on foil-lined (for easy cleanup) shallow baking pan. Brush with half the glaze, then arrange bacon slices, crosswise, over loaf, overlapping slightly and tucking only bacon tip ends under loaf.

5. Bake loaf until bacon is crisp and internal temperature of loaf registers 160 degrees, about 1 hour. Cool at least 20 minutes. Simmer remaining glaze over medium heat until thickened slightly. Slice meat loaf and serve with extra glaze passed separately.

PORK

UP UNTIL WORLD WAR II, PIGS WERE RAISED as much for their fat as for their meat—a pig with four to five inches of exterior fat (equivalent to about 60 pounds of lard) at slaughter was the norm. After the war, vegetable sources of fat (oil, shortening, margarine) became the fats of choice, and lard was no longer an asset. Coupled with the health trends of the past two decades, this forced the industry to "lean up" its pork, largely through genetic engineering. Today, many processors penalize producers for pigs with more than a mere ⅕-inch layer (or less than eight pounds) of exterior fat.

Industry's success at eliminating the pig's surface fat, however, has resulted in the loss of its intramuscular fat as well. Known as marbling, this fat traps and retains juices during cooking and gives the meat flavor and body.

This problem is greatest in the loin, the area that extends from the back of the shoulder down to the hip. Chops come from this part of the pig, as do the crown roast of pork as well as the tenderloin. These cuts are generally very lean. The main issue confronting the cook when preparing cuts from the loin is how to keep the meat from becoming tough and chewy.

Although health experts recommend cooking all meat (including pork) to an internal temperature of 160 degrees, we find that most pork cuts cooked to this temperature are dry and tough. An internal temperature of 145 to 150 degrees is our preference. At this temperature the meat, when cut, is ivory in color

and reveals a distinct grain, but the juices still run pale pink.

Fear of trichinosis should not prompt anyone to overcook pork chops: the trichina parasite is killed at 137 degrees, when the pork is still medium-rare. If you are unalterably opposed to pinkish pork juices (or are concerned about salmonella), you should cook pork to 160 degrees, but you will find that the meat is markedly drier and harder.

Drying out is not so much an issue when cooking cuts from the other three primal cuts—the shoulder, belly, and leg. Meat from these areas tends to be much fattier and tough, requiring long, slow cooking to make them fork-tender. The shoulder is divided into two cuts, the picnic roast and Boston butt. The leg is sold as ham, and the belly is where bacon and spareribs come from.

The recipes in this chapter cover the cuts most home cooks are likely to encounter at the market and offer strategies for getting the best results when cooking each. See chapter 11 for information on using boneless pork shoulder in stews.

PORK CHOPS

ALL TOO OFTEN, COOKED PORK CHOPS TURN out tough and dry. You can avoid this by selecting the right type of chop (see page 225) and by choosing the right cooking method.

We first attempted to broil pork chops. But no matter how close or far from the heating element they were placed, the chops came out hard and dry. This has always been our experience with broiling pork chops, and we are thoroughly convinced that it is simply a bad idea.

We had much better results when we tried the grill. Because chops are so thick, they require cooking over two levels of heat. We tried searing the chops on both sides over high heat (about 6 minutes total) and then sliding them over to a cooler part of the grill to cook through for about 10 minutes. The chops developed a nice caramelized crust but were not completely cooked through. We tried lengthening the cooking times over both high and lower heat, but the result was dry chops that had charred on the exterior. The solution (which we first learned

THE FOUR PRIMAL CUTS OF PORK

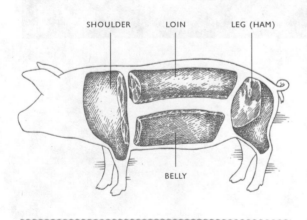

SHOULDER   LOIN   LEG (HAM)

BELLY

to use with chicken parts) was to cover the chops with a disposable aluminum pan as they cook over a cool fire. This concentrates the heat and creates an ovenlike effect, cooking through the chops quickly and efficiently.

We were pleased with our grilling results but also wanted to develop an indoor cooking method. Baking the chops uncovered on a flat tray proved little better than broiling, which we had already dismissed. The chops did not brown at either low or high oven temperatures, and at the higher temperature they turned leathery.

Then there is braising. Formerly, when pork was more fatty, braising was the cooking method of choice. The long, slow cooking in liquid served to melt out some of the fat, and the fat that remained prevented the pork from being dry, especially when served with a flavorful gravy made from the pan juices. But today's leaner pork does not take well to braising: it simply becomes fibrous and dry. Actually, even old-fashioned fatty pork had a tendency to become fibrous rather than truly tender, though its fat helped to camouflage that.

At this point, we were pretty sure that sautéing was going to be our preferred indoor cooking method. While honing in on a specific technique, we wanted to test some precooking notions we had run across, such as marinating and freezing pork chops. To test various preparation and sautéing techniques, we bought an entire pork loin and had it cut into 20 chops one inch thick. This way we could be sure that differences in results would be caused by the way we handled the chops rather than by variations in the meat itself.

We began by investigating the tenderizing effects of various marinades. We prepared one marinade with white wine, aromatic vegetables, and herbs and another with lemon juice and garlic. We poured the marinades into self-sealing plastic bags and added three chops to each. After 12 hours, we cooked one chop from each bag; a day later we cooked one more of each, and three days after putting them in the marinade, we prepared the remaining ones. Predictably, we found that the longer the chops marinated, the more strongly flavored they became, and the less we liked them. The effect of the marinade on texture was more complicated. The chops that were

marinated for a day or less did not seem appreciably more tender. Those marinated for a full three days struck us as a being a little softer, but they also had a mushy, mealy quality. So we still don't recommend marinating pork.

Some sources suggest that freezing pork before cooking yields a more tender final result. We tried this technique twice. Our first test followed standard practice: the chops were allowed to thaw slowly before cooking, so as to minimize juice loss. Defrosted in this manner, the chops seemed no more tender than others that we had not frozen. So we ran the test again, this time defrosting the chops in sealed plastic bags immersed in hot water. There was no difference. Freezing is not the answer for pork.

Having found limited value in all these precooking strategies, we turned to sautéing techniques for our remaining experiments. To say that pork chops belong in a skillet is to tell only part of the story, for they require skillet cooking of a specific kind. First you should brown them over high heat for a minute on each side. When browning is done, cover the chops and cook them relatively slowly for about 10 minutes more, turning the chops only once.

We also tried cooking chops following this general method but leaving the skillet uncovered and was surprised by the difference it made. The chops cooked through before the meat around the bones was completely done. Worse still, the chops were tough.

Pork chops will toughen if the cooking temperature is too high or too low, so listen carefully as they sauté. Loud sputtering and hissing indicate that the heat is too high; remove the skillet from the burner for a minute, counting this as part of the cooking time. If cooking noises subside to a bare murmur, turn up the heat a bit, or the chops will poach in their own juices.

Sautéed Pork Chops with White Wine Pan Sauce

SERVES 4

When the chops feel firm but not hard, they are done to our taste—an internal temperature of 145 to 150 degrees. If the chops still feel a little squishy, particularly near the bone, at the end of the cooking time, or if you prefer them done to the point where the juices run clear, cook them another minute or two until the juices begin to collect on top of the chops and spill into the pan. At this point, the temperature is nearing the 160-degree mark. Don't cook beyond this point, or the meat will surely be tough.

4	center loin or center rib pork chops, each 1 inch thick (about 2 pounds), patted dry with paper towels
1/2	teaspoon salt
1/2	teaspoon ground black pepper
1	tablespoon unsalted butter
1	tablespoon vegetable oil
2	large shallots, minced (1/4 cup)
1	medium garlic clove, minced
1/3	cup dry white wine or 1/4 cup dry vermouth
1/2	cup chicken stock or low-sodium canned broth
2–3	tablespoons unsalted butter, cut into pieces and softened
1	small wedge lemon

1. Season pork chops with salt and pepper. Melt 1 tablespoon butter in a 10- to 12-inch skillet over a strong medium-high heat. Add oil; swirl skillet occasionally until fat turns nut brown and just begins to smoke.

2. Lay pork chops in skillet, bony side facing toward center of skillet; sauté until browned on one side, about 1 minute. Turn chops with tongs and sauté until browned on other side, about 1 minute. Reduce heat to medium; cover and cook chops 4 minutes. Turn chops; cover and cook until firm but not hard when pressed with a finger, about 5 minutes longer. Transfer chops to a plate; set aside in a warm spot while preparing sauce.

3. Spoon all but 1 tablespoon of the fat from the skillet. Add shallots; sauté until softened, about 1 minute. Add garlic; sauté until fragrant, about 30 seconds. Add wine; boil until reduced by half, about 1 minute, scraping skillet with wooden spoon to dislodge browned bits. Pour in stock and accumulated juices from around chops; boil to a thin syrupy texture (about 1/3 cup), 2 to 3 minutes. Off heat, scatter butter pieces over sauce; swirl skillet until butter melts and sauce thickens slightly. Squeeze a few drops of lemon juice over sauce and swirl in. Adjust seasonings. Spoon over chops and serve.

VARIATIONS

Sautéed Pork Chops with Mustard and Capers

Follow recipe for Sautéed Pork Chops with White Wine Pan Sauce, making the following change: In step 3, reduce stock and accumulated juices to a total of about 1/4 cup, and whisk in 2 tablespoons Dijon mustard and 2 tablespoons drained small capers. Proceed as directed.

Sautéed Pork Chops with Pineapple Salsa

A moist, flavorful salsa takes the place of a pan sauce in this recipe. A light spice coating works well with the salsa.

1	teaspoon ground cinnamon
1/2	teaspoon ground cumin
1/2	teaspoon salt
1/2	teaspoon ground black pepper
1	tablespoon unsalted butter
1	tablespoon vegetable oil
4	center loin or center rib pork chops, each 1 inch thick (about 2 pounds), patted dry with paper towels
1/3	cup dark rum
1/3	cup chicken stock or low-sodium canned broth
1	teaspoon sugar
1	recipe Pineapple Salsa (page 228)

1. Combine cinnamon, cumin, salt, and pepper in small bowl. Rub spice mixture over chops and refrigerate for 2 hours.

2. Melt 1 tablespoon butter in a 10- to 12-inch skillet over a strong medium-high heat. Add oil; swirl skillet occasionally until fat turns nut brown and just begins to smoke.

3. Lay pork chops in skillet, bony side facing toward center of skillet; sauté until browned on one side, about 1 minute. Turn chops with tongs and

sauté until browned on other side, about 1 minute. Reduce heat to medium; cover and cook chops 4 minutes. Turn chops; cover and cook until firm but not hard when pressed with a finger, about 5 minutes longer. Transfer chops to a plate; set aside in a warm spot while preparing sauce.

4. Pour off and discard fat from skillet. Add rum and boil, scraping skillet with wooden spoon to dislodge browned bits, until reduced by half, about 1 minute. Add stock and accumulated juices from around chops; boil to a thin syrupy texture (about ⅓ cup), 2 to 3 minutes. Add sugar and cook briefly until dissolved. Spoon over chops and serve with pineapple salsa.

INGREDIENTS: Pork Chops

When buying pork chops, always look for chops that are solidly pink rather than streaked with white—the white is not fat but connective tissue, mostly elastin, which does not break down in cooking. Also be sure to buy chops that are about an inch thick. Thinner chops always become overcooked, and thus hard and dry, no matter how careful you are.

There are five different types of chop to choose from. The two "center-cut" chops, so named because they are taken from the center of the loin, are usually considered the top choices. These two are the center rib chop, which looks like a miniature beef rib, and the center loin chop, which looks like a miniature T-bone or porterhouse steak.

The cuts you do not want are generally from the ends of the loin. The first of these is called the sirloin end chop. Cut from the sirloin, or hip, area, this chop contains a slice of hip bone, and the meat appears broken into bundles.

The second undesirable end cut is the rib end blade chop, which comes from the shoulder. It is easily identified because it contains a section of the long, thin blade bone and also shows many muscle separations.

There is, however, one end cut that you might want to consider, the so-called "rib-end" pork chop. Taken from the part of the rib that lies closest to the shoulder, the rib-end chop looks much like a center rib chop, but the rib-eye meat is smaller, as well as coarser, fattier, and darker. Rib-end chops are also less compact and uniform in shape than center-cut rib chops. While rib ends are a little chewy, they also tend to be juicier than center-cut rib chops.

Charcoal-Grilled Pork Chops
SERVES 4

The chops can be seasoned only with salt and pepper, but we prefer them when coated with a spice or herb rub (page 226) and served with salsa (page 228).

4 center loin or center rib pork chops, each 1 inch thick (about 2 pounds total)
2 tablespoons extra-virgin olive oil
   Salt and ground black pepper

1. Build a two-level fire (see page 258). Set grill rack in place, cover grill with lid, and let rack heat up, about 5 minutes.

2. Rub chops with oil and sprinkle with salt and pepper to taste. Grill over medium-hot fire, turning once, until both sides are browned, about 6 minutes.

3. Slide chops to cooler part of fire and cover with disposable aluminum roasting pan. Grill over medium-low fire, turning once, until meat is tinged with pink in center, 8 to 10 minutes. Serve immediately.

VARIATION
Gas-Grilled Pork Chops

Follow recipe for Charcoal-Grilled Pork Chops, making the following changes: Turn all burners to high and preheat with lid down until very hot, about 15 minutes. Turn one burner to medium. Grill as in charcoal recipe but with lid down, placing chops first over burner left on high and then sliding chops to cooler part of the grill to cook through. (With lid down, there's no need to use disposable roasting pan.)

PORK TENDERLOIN

PORK TENDERLOIN HAS MANY CHARMS. IT IS exceptionally lean and tender, and, because it usually weighs between 12 and 24 ounces, it cooks very quickly, which makes it perfect for weeknight dinners.

The tenderloin is a small, boneless, torpedo-shaped muscle nestled against the rib bones in the loin section, which is roughly equivalent to a position deep inside the midback on a human being. The cut is notable for its remarkable lack of marbling, those ribbons of intramuscular fat that run through meat. While this is a virtue in terms of fat intake, it also presents a pitfall in that the tenderloin is particularly vulnerable to overcooking, which can lead to dry meat. To protect the tenderloin's characteristic tenderness, we prefer that it be cooked medium-well, so it is slightly rosy inside. This translates to an internal temperature of 145 to 150 degrees. If you prefer to cook pork well-done and gray-white throughout, this may not be the cut for you. We also realized from the outset that the tenderloin's lack of fat leaves it in need of a flavor boost, perhaps in the form of a dry spice rub, a paste, or a sauce.

After perusing many recipes, we saw that we had three basic options in terms of cooking technique: broiling, grilling, and roasting. Broiling practically turned the pan drippings to carbon and gave the meat an overly chewy texture. Grilling the tenderloin smeared with a spice paste or rub produced a fabulous seared crust cloaking potently flavored, tender, juicy meat within. As with chops, we found it best to sear the tenderloins over high heat and then cook them over low heat with the help of a disposable aluminum roasting pan to concentrate the heat.

With our grilling method set, we turned our attention indoors to roasting. We knew from our success on the grill that the tenderloin required searing to optimize its flavor. Roasting presented us with three choices for achieving a good sear in a short time. We could pan-sear the tenderloin on the stove top and finish cooking it in the oven; sear it in the oven at a high temperature and then lower the temperature to finish the cooking; or start the meat at a low temperature, cranking the temperature up to sear near the end of the cooking time.

Searing in a preheated pan on the stove top

TWO RUBS FOR PORK

Pork chops and tenderloin benefit from assertive seasonings, especially when they will be grilled and there is no opportunity to make a pan sauce. These two rubs are especially well suited to pork.

Spice Rub for Pork

ENOUGH FOR 4 CHOPS OR
2 TENDERLOINS

Because this rub contains sugar, make sure to turn the pork often to keep the sugar from burning.

I	tablespoon fennel seeds
I	tablespoon cumin seeds
I	tablespoon coriander seeds
¾	teaspoon ground cinnamon
I ½	teaspoons dry mustard
I ½	teaspoons brown sugar

Toast seeds in small skillet over medium heat, shaking pan occasionally to prevent burning, until first wisps of smoke appear, 3 to 5 minutes. Cool to room temperature, mix with remaining ingredients, and grind to powder in spice grinder. Rub mixture over oiled and seasoned pork before grilling.

Herb Rub for Pork

ENOUGH FOR 4 CHOPS OR
2 TENDERLOINS

The salt is added directly to this rub to help break down the spices into powder when ground.

I ½	teaspoons dried thyme
I ½	teaspoons dried rosemary
I ½	teaspoons black peppercorns
2	bay leaves, crumbled
2	whole cloves or allspice berries
I	teaspoon salt

Grind ingredients in spice grinder to powder. Rub mixture over oiled but unseasoned pork (do not sprinkle pork with salt or pepper) before grilling.

before placing the meat in the oven shrank the meat excessively and sacrificed too much tenderness. So we tried using the oven for the entire cooking time, experimenting with different temperatures as well as different combinations of both low and high heat to see if we could oven-sear at either the beginning or the end of the cooking time. Of these options, the most promising seemed to be starting the meat at 325 degrees in a preheated pan, cooking it to an internal temperature of 110 degrees, and then increasing the oven to 450 degrees to sear. Usually, we got a reasonable crust, tender meat, and nicely caramelized pan drippings from which to make a sauce.

But not 100 percent of the time. Catching the meat at 110 degrees meant frequent checks in the oven with an instant-read thermometer. More often than not, the meat reached 120 or 130 by mistake, which robbed it of valuable high-temperature searing time on its way to a final internal temperature of 145 to 150 degrees. Once the temperature had been increased, we had to go back into the oven several times to turn the meat so it would sear on all sides. Worst of all, these hurried trips into and out of the oven transformed our cooking process from simple to complicated and finicky.

It was at this point that we realized we hadn't yet tried slicing the tenderloin and sautéing it on the stove top, avoiding the oven altogether. So we cut the tenderloin into one-inch slices and pounded them down to three-quarters of an inch with the flat side of a chef's knife (to increase the surface area for searing), then sautéed them in a bit of sizzling oil for about one minute per side. At the end, every single slice was seared beautifully on both sides, pan drippings were perfectly caramelized and ready to deglaze for a flavorful, simple sauce, and we had shaved about 10 minutes off the cooking process. The whole operation, from refrigerator to table, took only 15 minutes. Beneath the seared crust on each slice was juicy, succulent meat that met all our expectations for this extra-tender cut.

While testing and retesting our chosen method, we came up with a few pointers to help ensure successful sautéing. First, trim the pearlescent membrane, called the silver skin, from the tenderloin before cutting the medallions. (We like to remove

the silver skin before grilling as well since it prevents bowing.) If left on, the silver skin shrinks in the heat of the pan, pulling the meat up and out of the hot fat, thereby inhibiting browning. Second, do not overcook the meat. There should be just a tinge of pink when you peek into a piece with the tip of a paring knife. The meat will not be completely cooked at the end of the searing time, but that is fine because you later return it to the pan to reheat and meld with the sauce.

There is one drawback to sautéing. We found that sautéing four batches of medallions (the amount derived from two tenderloins) in the same pan caused the pan drippings to burn. We found it best to sauté just two batches of medallions (the amount that one tenderloin yields) and then make the pan sauce. For this reason, sautéing is ideal when cooking for three. You may cook medallions from two tenderloins in two sauté pans at the same time and then make pan sauces in each pan, but grilling is probably easier when trying to cook pork tenderloin for a crowd.

Sautéed Pork Tenderloin Medallions

SERVES 3 (3 OR 4 SLICES PER PERSON)

To promote even cooking, cut your slices to a uniform thickness. If it helps, lay a ruler in front of the loin and slice at the one-inch marks. If you've got one, cover the pan with a splatter screen to keep the fat from splattering out of the pan. Serve with one of the pan sauce variations that follow.

1	teaspoon salt
½	teaspoon ground black pepper
1	pork tenderloin (about 1 pound), silver skin removed, cut into 1-inch slices, each pounded to ¾-inch thick with flat side of chef's knife blade
2	tablespoons olive oil

Sprinkle salt and pepper over both sides of pork slices. Heat oil until shimmering in heavy-bottomed pan, at least 10 inches across bottom, over medium-high heat, swirling pan to distribute oil. Working in batches of no more than six slices to avoid overcrowding, sear medallions without moving them until brown on one side, about 80 seconds (oil should sizzle, but not smoke). Turn medallions with tongs to avoid scraping off the sear; sear until meat is mostly opaque at sides, firm to the touch, and well-browned, about 80 seconds. Transfer pork to plate; continue with pan sauce recipe using drippings in pan.

➤ VARIATIONS

Sautéed Pork Tenderloin Medallions with Port, Dried Cherries, and Rosemary

1	recipe Sautéed Pork Tenderloin Medallions
1/3	cup port
1/2	cup dried cherries
2/3	cup chicken stock or low-sodium canned broth
2	teaspoons minced fresh rosemary leaves
	Salt and ground black pepper

1. Prepare pork as directed and transfer to plate.

2. Set pan in which pork was cooked over medium-high heat; add port and cherries. Boil, scraping pan bottom with wooden spatula to loosen browned bits, until liquid reduces to about 2 tablespoons, 2 to 3 minutes. Increase heat to high; add stock or broth, rosemary, and any accumulated pork juices; boil until liquid reaches consistency of maple syrup, about 2 minutes. Add salt and pepper to taste.

3. Reduce heat to medium; return pork to pan, turning meat to coat. Simmer to heat pork through and blend flavors, about 3 minutes. Adjust seasonings, adding salt and pepper to taste. Transfer pork to serving plate and spoon sauce over meat. Serve immediately.

TWO SALSAS FOR PORK

Sweet salsas complement the flavor of sautéed or grilled pork. Moist, juicy salsas also keep pork from tasting dry.

Pineapple Salsa

MAKES ABOUT 2 1/2 CUPS

See page 508 for information on cutting up a pineapple.

1/4	small pineapple, peeled, cored, and cut into 3/8-inch dice (about 1 1/4 cups)
1	small barely ripe banana, peeled and cut into 3/8-inch dice
1/2	cup seedless green grapes, halved or quartered
1/2	firm avocado, peeled and cut into 3/8-inch dice
4	teaspoons lime juice
1	jalapeño chile, stemmed, seeded, and minced
1	teaspoon minced fresh oregano leaves
	Salt

Combine all ingredients including salt to taste in medium bowl. Let stand at room temperature for 30 minutes. (Banana and avocado will darken if salsa is prepared much further in advance.) Serve alongside chops or grilled pork tenderloin.

Peach Salsa

MAKES ABOUT 2 1/2 CUPS

Mangoes or nectarines can be substituted for peaches if desired.

2	ripe but not mushy peaches, pitted and chopped coarse
1	small red bell pepper, cored, seeded, and diced
1	small red onion, diced
1/4	cup chopped fresh parsley leaves
1	medium garlic clove, minced
1/4	cup pineapple juice
6	tablespoons lime juice
1	jalapeño or other fresh chile, stemmed, seeded, and minced
	Salt

Combine all ingredients including salt to taste in medium bowl. Cover and refrigerate to blend flavors, at least 1 hour or up to 4 days. Serve alongside chops or grilled pork tenderloin.

Sautéed Pork Tenderloin Medallions with Cream, Apples, and Sage

1	recipe Sautéed Pork Tenderloin Medallions
1	tablespoon unsalted butter
1	Granny Smith or other firm apple, peeled, cored, and cut into 12 slices
½	medium onion, sliced thin (about ½ cup)
⅓	cup apple cider
3	tablespoons applejack or brandy
½	cup chicken stock or low-sodium canned broth
2	tablespoons minced fresh sage leaves
¼	cup heavy cream
	Salt and ground black pepper

1. Prepare pork as directed and transfer to plate.

2. Melt butter in pan in which pork was cooked over medium-high heat, swirling to distribute. Add apple and onion; sauté until apple starts to brown, about 4 minutes. Add cider and applejack or brandy; boil, scraping pan bottom with wooden spatula to loosen browned bits, until liquid reduces to a glaze, about 2½ minutes. Increase heat to high; add stock or broth, sage, and any accumulated pork juices; boil until liquid reaches consistency of maple syrup, about 3 minutes. Add cream; boil until reduced by half, about 2 minutes.

3. Reduce heat to medium; return pork to pan, turning meat to coat. Simmer to heat pork thoroughly and blend flavors, about 3 minutes. Adjust seasonings, adding salt and pepper to taste. Transfer pork to serving plate and spoon sauce over meat. Serve immediately.

Sautéed Pork Tenderloin Medallions with Vinegar, Spices, and Raisins

1	recipe Sautéed Pork Tenderloin Medallions
½	teaspoon ground cinnamon
¼	teaspoon ground cloves
⅛	teaspoon ground cayenne pepper
2	teaspoons sugar
1	tablespoon olive oil
1	medium onion, sliced thin (about 1 cup)
¼	cup dry sherry
¼	cup red wine vinegar
½	cup chicken stock or low-sodium canned broth
¼	cup raisins
	Salt

1. Prepare pork as directed and transfer to plate.

2. Mix cinnamon, cloves, cayenne, and sugar in small bowl; set aside. Heat oil in pan in which pork was cooked over medium heat, swirling to distribute. Add onion; sauté until softened and starting to color, about 2 minutes. Add spice mixture, sherry, and vinegar; boil, scraping pan bottom with wooden spatula to loosen browned bits, until liquid reduces to a glaze, about 2½ minutes. Increase heat to high and add stock or broth, raisins, and any accumulated pork juices; boil until liquid reaches consistency of maple syrup, about 3 minutes.

3. Reduce heat to medium; return pork to pan, turning meat to coat. Simmer to heat pork thoroughly and blend flavors, about 3 minutes. Adjust seasonings, adding salt to taste. Transfer pork to serving plate and spoon sauce over meat. Serve immediately.

Sautéed Pork Tenderloin Medallions with Orange, Fennel, and Green Olives

1	recipe Sautéed Pork Tenderloin Medallions
1	tablespoon olive oil
½	medium fennel bulb, sliced thin (about 1 cup)
2	medium garlic cloves, minced (about 1 tablespoon)
⅓	cup juice and 1 teaspoon zest from 1 large orange
⅔	cup chicken stock or low-sodium canned broth
¼	cup pitted green olives, sliced
2	tablespoons chopped fresh parsley leaves
	Salt and ground black pepper

1. Prepare pork as directed and transfer to plate.

2. Heat oil in pan in which pork was cooked over

PREPARING PORK TENDERLOIN

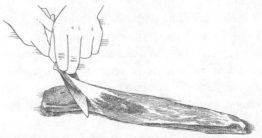

1. To remove the silver skin, slip a paring knife between the silver skin and the muscle fibers. Angle the knife slightly upward and use a gentle back-and-forth sawing action.

medium heat, swirling to distribute. Add fennel; sauté until softened and starting to color, about 2 minutes. Add garlic; sauté 1 minute more. Add juice; boil, scraping pan bottom with wooden spatula to loosen browned bits, until liquid reduces to a glaze, about 2½ minutes. Increase heat to high and add stock or broth and any accumulated pork juices; boil until liquid reaches consistency of maple syrup, about 3 minutes.

3. Reduce heat to medium; return pork to pan with zest, olives, and parsley, turning meat to coat. Simmer to heat pork thoroughly and blend flavors, about 3 minutes. Adjust seasonings, adding salt and pepper to taste. Transfer pork to serving plate and spoon sauce over meat. Serve immediately.

Charcoal-Grilled Pork Tenderloins

SERVES 4 TO 6

Tenderloins come two to a package, each weighing a little less than a pound and serving four to six depending on the side dishes. Invariably one tenderloin is smaller than the other and will require 2 or 3 minutes less time on the grill. Season with salt and pepper as directed below or coat with a spice or herb rub (see page 226). Either way, serve with a salsa (see page 228) to make the meat seem moist.

- 2   pork tenderloins (about 2 pounds total), silver skin removed
- 2   tablespoons extra-virgin olive oil
     Salt and ground black pepper
- 1   recipe Salsa for Pork (page 228)

1. Build a single-level fire (see page 258). Set grill rack in place, cover grill with lid, and let rack heat up, about 5 minutes.

2. Rub tenderloins with oil and sprinkle with salt and pepper to taste. Grill over medium–hot fire, turning several times to make sure all four sides are browned, about 4 minutes per side. Cover tenderloins with disposable aluminum roasting pan. Cook, turning once, until meat is tinged with pink in center or internal temperature registers 150 degrees, 5 to 7 minutes. Let tenderloins rest for 5 minutes, slice crosswise into 1-inch-thick pieces, and serve immediately with salsa.

> VARIATION

Gas-Grilled Pork Tenderloins

Follow recipe for Charcoal-Grilled Pork Tenderloins, making the following changes: Turn all burners to high and preheat with lid down until very hot, about 15 minutes. Turn both burners to medium. Grill, with lid down, turning tenderloins several times to make sure all four sides are browned, about 5 minutes per side. (With lid down, there's no need to use disposable roasting pan.)

PORK ROAST

FOR QUICK WEEKNIGHT MEALS, CHOPS OR tenderloin are the cuts most cooks will turn to. But we also wanted to develop a recipe for a large pork roast. We starting working with a crown roast of pork. That large, crowd-pleaser of a cut consists of two center-cut pork loins trussed together to form a ring. The "frenched" rib bones ("frenching" refers to removing the meat from between each rib with a paring knife) around the perimeter and stuffing in the shallow cavity make this roast a truly coronal comestible.

But after cooking eight crown roasts at a range of oven temperatures (200 to 400 degrees) and to varying internal temperatures (145 to 160 degrees), we finally concluded that we didn't like this roast enough to serve it for weeknight supper, much less for a memorable dinner party. Devoid of fat, the center loin was tasteless and unsatisfying. Even roasted to a low 145 degrees, this lean cut was at once watery and dry, much like white tuna packed in water. The problem was compounded by the roast's shape. Because the ribs formed the outside of the crown, only the bones browned, while the loin itself steamed rather than roasted.

Disappointed with every crown roast of pork we had cooked, we went back to the butcher shop for advice. Our local butcher suggested we switch from a crown roast to a "rack of pork." In this case, two pork loins are roasted separately, then presented at the table with frenched ribs crossed.

Because this cooking arrangement allowed the loins to roast independently of each other, browning on all sides was ensured. Cutting roasts from the rib end rather than the center or loin end of the whole loin also made for a big improvement. Located close to the more flavorful shoulder, this part of the loin is multimuscled, with much-needed fat separating the muscles.

Bones also add flavor to meat. To make the loins bend into a crown roast, the chine bone (the backbone) has to be removed, thus further robbing the meat of much-needed flavor. A rack of pork, however, does not require complete removal of the chine bone, so the loin can roast on the bone.

To further improve the roast's flavor, we decided to mimic the pork industry's meat-marinating technique. Using a gadget we found at a local cooking shop, we injected each of three roasts with a different flavor. Dying each mixture blue so that it could be tracked as it traveled through the meat, we made one of salt and water; one of salt, sugar, and water; and one of salt, water, and oil. We roasted these three roasts along with one seasoned only on the surface.

The results were quite amazing. The injected flavorings permeated the roasts, gravitating to the center and making the loin muscle much more flavorful and juicy than the surface-seasoned roast. This instant marinating step takes about 10 minutes, and the results make it worth the effort.

We still had one more test up our sleeves. From our previous work with corned beef, we knew that dry curing (rubbing meat with salt and aging it in the refrigerator) could improve the flavor of beef (see page 209). It seemed to us that pork might react the same way. So we bought a second roast, coated each rack with two tablespoons kosher salt, and put them on a wire rack over a paper towel-lined plate set in the refrigerator for one week. After thoroughly brushing off all the remaining salt and removing thin slices of dried-out pork from each end of the roast, we roasted this rack. The flavor and texture of this roast was even better than the injected one. Even though it was a little too salty, this roast tasted like real pork, with a smooth, buttery texture. Reducing the salt the second time around gave us still better results.

For those who buy their rack of pork the afternoon before they want to serve it, we recommend the injection method. For those who think even three or four days ahead, salting and refrigerating the roast is the ticket. Personally, we look forward to the day when producers figure out how to marble pork

again, without the surface fat. Until then, we're sticking close to the shoulder, hoarding the bones, infusing the meat with a little fat and flavor, and roasting it slow and low.

Roast Cured Rack of Pork

SERVES 6 TO 8

Dry curing requires only that you make space in the refrigerator and purchase the meat three to five days prior to serving it. If you don't have that much time, try the optional marinade below. If you're in a real rush, skip both, knowing that choosing the right roast and cooking it according to the suggested method will deliver better-than-average results.

So that the bones will cross at presentation, have the butcher remove the tip of chine. So that chops can easily be carved from the roast, have the butcher cut the chine bone between each rib. For festive presentation, remove meat from between each rib with a paring knife—a process called frenching.

2	pork loin roasts (5 to 6 ribs each) from the rib end of the whole loin, tip of chine removed, chine bone cut between each rib, and "frenched" (see illustrations on page 232)
2	tablespoons kosher or I tablespoon table salt
3	medium garlic cloves, minced
2	teaspoons ground black pepper
2	tablespoons minced fresh thyme, sage, or rosemary leaves
2	tablespoons olive oil, plus extra for tossing vegetables
I	small carrot, cut into I-inch chunks
I	small onion, chopped coarse
3	tablespoons Madeira

1. Scrape rib bones with paring knife to remove any scraps of meat or fat butcher might have missed until bones are absolutely clean. Rinse roasts and pat dry with paper towels.

2. Rub 1 tablespoon kosher or 1½ teaspoons table salt evenly over each roast. Place on wire rack set over paper towel–lined baking or roasting pan and refrigerate, uncovered, for five days.

3. Adjust oven rack to lower-middle position and heat oven to 250 degrees. Brush salt from roasts and shave off very thin exterior layer of hardened, dehy-

drated meat. Mix garlic, pepper, herbs, and olive oil in small bowl to make thick paste, and rub half evenly over each roast. Scatter vegetables in roasting pan, toss lightly with oil, place loins on large roasting rack, and set in pan over vegetables. Roast until loins register internal temperature of 120 to 130 degrees on instant-read thermometer, 1¼ to 1½ hours. Increase oven temperature to 425 degrees. When drippings turn brown and just start to smoke, 8 to 10 minutes, add one cup water to roasting pan. Continue roasting until meat registers 145 degrees, about 20 minutes longer.

4. Transfer loins to serving platter, arranging so that ribs cross (see illustration 6 below). Cover loosely with foil. To make sauce, strain pan drippings into measuring cup, pressing on vegetables to release liquid, and spoon off excess fat. Add more water, if necessary, to equal 1 cup. Transfer to small saucepan, add Madeira, and simmer to blend flavors, about 5 minutes. Carve roast, cutting between each rib, and serve with sauce passed separately.

➤ VARIATION
Roast Marinated Rack of Pork

After curing, the next best (and at just 10 minutes, significantly speedier) way to improve the flavor and mouthfeel of the meat is to inject it with this simple marinade. The injector looks like a large doctor's syringe, somewhat shocking in appearance but very effective. (Look for this item in kitchenware shops.) For a hint of sweetness in the meat, dissolve 1 tablespoon brown sugar along with the salt in the marinade.

Follow recipe for Roast Cured Rack of Pork, omitting step 2 and instead dissolving 2 teaspoons salt in ⅓ cup lukewarm water in lidded container. Add ¼ cup flavorless oil, such as canola or corn; shake to emulsify. Fill syringe and inject each loin, shaking injector occasionally to ensure that oil and water do not separate (oil alone is difficult to inject). Rub ½ teaspoon salt, then garlic-herb paste, evenly over each rack. Continue with roasting instructions for Roast Cured Rack of Pork.

PREPARING A PORK ROAST

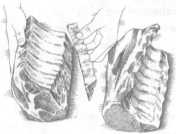

1. Select a roast from the rib end of the pork loin. (Whole roast is at right.) To make it possible to cross the bones at the table, have the butcher remove the tip of the chine (as seen on left).

2. So that chops can be easily carved from the roast, have the butcher cut the chine bone between each rib. When you pull the roast apart, you should be able to see the cuts between the individual chops.

3. Before the ribs can be frenched, the fatty piece that covers the ribs must be removed. Ask your butcher to do this, or do it yourself.

4. Use a paring knife to remove the meat from between each rib. Again, have the butcher do this, if possible.

5. Scrape the bones to remove any remaining pieces of meat or fat. The butcher should do this, unless you are frenching the bones yourself.

6. For a dramatic presentation, arrange roasted loins on a serving platter so that ribs cross.

Ham

HAM IS MADE FROM THE HIND QUARTER OF a pig. There are two general categories, which are referred to by butchers and people in the business as country and city hams. Country hams are salted and aged by a process known as dry-curing. City hams are brined in a salt solution (like pickles) by a process known as wet-curing. The former method results in salty, firm, dry meat, like prosciutto or the famed serrano ham of Spain. The latter process is used to make moister slicing hams, the kind sold in supermarkets.

Most country hams are made in small batches on farms in Virginia, the Carolinas, Kentucky, and Tennessee. Unless you live in the South, you won't see country hams in markets, but they can be ordered by mail or through your local butcher.

Country hams are cured in salt or a mixture of salt and sugar for several weeks, usually about five. During this dry-curing period, the meat must lose at least 18 percent of its fresh weight. (Many country hams shed 25 percent of their weight, for an even saltier, more concentrated ham flavor.) By law, a country ham must also absorb at least 4 percent salt. At this level, the salt acts as a preservative and prevents any bacterial growth during the long aging process that follows.

Once a country ham has been cured, it's smoked (over hardwoods like hickory or apple) for 2 to 6 days, rubbed with black pepper, and then aged, at least 60 days and up to a year or more in some cases. Country ham can be eaten raw (it's fully preserved), but the custom in the United States is to cook ham. The most famous country hams come from the small Virginia town of Smithfield. By law, Smithfield hams must be dry-cured and then aged a minimum of six months.

The flavor of a country ham is always intense and often quite salty. Good country ham has a complex smoky flavor with hints of blue cheese, nuts, wood, and spice. In general, the longer a ham has been aged, the stronger the flavors will be. When buying country ham, decide how strong and intense a flavor you like and then buy according to age. Most novices will find a 15-month ham overpowering and are probably better off with a shorter-cure ham. Southerners who grew up on good country ham may find a three-month ham insipid.

Many people believe that soaking a country ham is essential to its final edibility. The theory is that soaking causes the meat to lose some of the salt with which it was cured, as the salt naturally moves from places of greater concentration (in the ham) to places of lesser concentration (the soaking water). As salt migrates out of the ham, water replaces some of it, a process that helps soften the ham's texture and prevents excessive dryness.

Our testing supported this theory but also showed that the process doesn't happen as quickly as you might think. Only when we soaked a year-old ham for a full 36 hours could we detect any change in texture compared with a similar ham that was not soaked. The soaked ham was just a bit less dry and a bit less salty.

In our tests, we found that hams subjected to cures of less than six months are rarely so salty that they need soaking. But a ham cured for more than a year needs at least three days in cold water before cooking to become edible. Hams cured for 6 to 12 months need to be soaked for 36 hours.

Many recipes suggest adding ingredients, especially sweeteners, to the soaking liquid. We found that sugar, Coca-Cola, and white vinegar (all recommended by various sources) have no effect on the ham.

The next step is to cook the ham. We tried baking the ham in a 325-degree oven and liked the results quite a lot. The ham was dry and salty. However, this method is for ham lovers only. Many ham novices were put off by the strong flavor. Simmering the ham tames some of the salt and is the best bet when preparing ham for a holiday crowd. Simmering also adds a little moisture to the ham, making it easier to carve in thin slices. (Country ham is too rich and salty to be sliced into thick slabs like a city ham.)

We tried all kinds of simmering regimens and found that cooking the ham at the barest simmer is better than boiling. Gentle heat ensures that the outside layers of meat don't cook too fast. As for the timing, we found that 10 minutes per pound is a decent barometer. Better still, use an instant-read thermometer and pull the ham out of the pot when it reaches 120 degrees.

At this point, the rind and most of the fat need to be removed. The ham can then be scored, glazed, and put into the oven just to set the glaze, the best option when serving the ham as the centerpiece of a holiday meal. A simmered country ham can also be cooled, boned, weighted, and then sliced in very thin

---

TWO GLAZES FOR HAM

We don't like to chew on whole cloves so we don't stud the ham; we prefer adding the flavor of cloves to the glaze. Don't baste the ham with any of the pan juices. They are too salty and intense.

Orange Juice and Brown Sugar Glaze for Ham

MAKES ABOUT I CUP

For a sweeter, glossier glaze, brush ham with a little honey about 30 minutes before it is ready to come out of the oven.

1 ¼	cups packed light brown sugar
3	tablespoons fresh squeezed orange juice
½	teaspoon ground cloves

Mix sugar, orange juice, and cloves together in medium bowl to form thick paste. Set mixture aside until ready to glaze ham.

Mustard and Brown Sugar Glaze for Ham

MAKES ABOUT I CUP

For a sweeter, glossier glaze, brush ham with a little maple syrup about 30 minutes before it is ready to come out of the oven.

1 ¼	cups packed light brown sugar
¼	cup Dijon mustard
½	teaspoon ground cloves

Mix sugar, mustard, and cloves together in medium bowl to form thick paste. Set mixture aside until ready to glaze ham.

---

chunks and served as part of a buffet with biscuits.

Many cooks would rather skip the scrubbing, soaking, and simmering steps that a country ham often requires. They would also prefer a ham that can be carved into thick, moist slices. Wet-cured city hams are the answer. City hams are smoked like country hams but not aged. Unlike country hams, brined hams are not actually preserved and must be refrigerated like fresh meat.

There are several types of city hams. Some hams are labeled "boneless," others "bone-in." Boneless hams are usually made by pressing together various pieces of meat. There is no muscle definition and the "skin" is often made by a machine that scores the exterior and then paints it with food coloring. We prefer bone-in city hams, in which the large hip bone that runs the length of the ham has been left intact but some or all of the small bones that can make carving a country ham so tricky have been removed.

The other issue regarding the purchase of city hams is the water content. Many large commercial outfits inject the meat with brine to increase its weight and cost (hams are usually sold by the pound), sometimes by as much as 25 percent. Hams that are actually brined instead of injected taste stronger and are more economical, since you are not paying for water weight that the ham will lose when cooked. If you see the words "with natural juices" or "water added," the ham has been injected and will probably cook up moister, less smoky, and much lighter. If you want a really mild ham flavor, you might consider a water-added ham. However, our recommendation is to stick with a no-water-added ham. They are chewy rather than squishy and have some of the character of a country ham without all the bother and the salt.

Some city hams are sold with a partial rind and some fat that must be trimmed, just like a country ham. However, most city hams have very little fat and cannot even be scored. If you have a choice, buy a ham with some fat on it. You can then remove as much fat as you like and score whatever remains.

To serve a city ham, simply glaze and bake. We recommend buying a city ham that is labeled "ready to eat" or "fully cooked." (Most city hams are sold this way.) If the ham has been fully cooked at the plant, you need only warm it in the oven to an internal temperature of 140 degrees. If you happen to buy a ham labeled "partially cooked" or "cook before eating," it must baked to an internal temperature of 160 degrees, and you will need to adjust the cooking times in our recipe.

Baked Country Ham

SERVES ABOUT 30

We tested nine brands of mail-order country hams. All but one of the hams was deemed good or excellent. We particularly liked the Wigwam ham from S. Wallace Edwards & Sons (800-222-4267). Any size dry-cured ham can be adapted to this recipe; just adjust the cooking time as needed to reach the internal temperatures listed below. Country ham is best served in very thin slices in biscuits or rolls. It's too rich and salty to serve in thick slices. Leftover bits of ham can be used to flavor greens, eggs, pasta, or rice. If removing the hock, save it to flavor soup or beans.

I   country ham, 14 to 15 pounds
I   cup glaze of choice (page 234)

1. Scrub mold off. Remove hock with hacksaw (see illustration below). If ham has been aged less than six months, proceed with step 2. If ham has been aged more than six months, place ham in large stockpot filled with cool water. Place pot in cool place and change water once a day. Hams aged 6 to 12 months should be soaked for 36 hours. Hams aged more than a year should be soaked for 3 days. Drain ham and scrub again.

2. Place ham in large stockpot and cover with fresh water. Bring to boil, reduce heat, and simmer until instant-read thermometer inserted into thickest part of ham registers 120 degrees, 2 to 3 hours.

Transfer ham from pot to large cutting board. (Liquid can be reserved and used to cook greens or rice or to flavor soup.)

3. Preheat oven to 325 degrees. When ham has cooled just enough to handle, peel away rind and most of fat. Score remaining fat (see illustration below).

4. Place ham on flat rack in large roasting pan lined with double layer of aluminum foil. Pour 2 cups water into pan. Smear glaze onto exterior of ham using rubber spatula. Bake until instant-read thermometer inserted in several places in ham registers 140 degrees, about 1 hour. Transfer ham to cutting board and let rest about 15 minutes. Carve into very thin slices and serve.

Baked City Ham

SERVES 6 TO 20, DEPENDING ON SIZE OF HAM

Any brined or wet-cured ham can be cooked according to this recipe. A whole ham can weigh as much as 16 pounds. However, many companies sell portions of the leg, which can weigh as little as 5 pounds. Cook the ham according to internal temperature rather than time, and use more or less glaze depending on the size of the ham. Try to buy a ham with some fat so that it can be scored.

I   wet-cured, fully cooked bone-in ham
    (5 to 16 pounds)
½–I   cup glaze of choice (page 234)

PREPARING A HAM

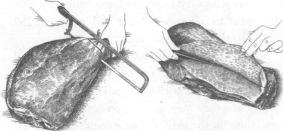  

1. If using a country ham, use a hacksaw to remove the hock so that the ham will fit into a large stockpot.

2. If using a country ham, simmer ham as directed in recipe. As soon as the ham is removed from the simmering water, remove the skin and most, but not all, of the fat. Slice into the rind with a sharp knife.

3. If using a country ham, peel back the rind and discard. With knife, trim remaining fat to thickness of about ¼ inch. If using a city ham, perform this step if the ham has rind and/or is covered with a thick layer of fat.

4. Use a paring knife to cut down into the fat, making sure not to cut into meat. Cut parallel lines across ham, spacing them about 1½ inches apart. Make a series of perpendicular lines to create a diamond pattern.

1. Let ham sit at room temperature for at least 3 hours. Adjust oven rack to lowest position. Heat oven to 325 degrees.

2. Remove wrapping. If ham is covered with jelly-like layer, rinse and pat dry. If necessary, remove rind and trim fat to thickness of ¼ inch (see illustration on page 235). Most wet-cured hams don't have enough fat for scoring. However, if ham is covered with even layer of fat, score ham (see illustration on page 235).

3. Place ham on flat rack in large roasting pan lined with double layer of aluminum foil. Pour 2 cups water into pan. Bake ham until instant-read thermometer inserted in several places in ham registers 120 degrees, 1 to 3 hours, depending on size of ham. Smear glaze onto exterior of ham using rubber spatula. Continue baking until instant-read thermometer registers 140 degrees, about 1 hour longer. Let ham rest for about 15 minutes. Carve perpendicular to bone into ½-inch-thick slices.

BARBECUED RIBS

WE WANTED TO KNOW WHETHER IT IS POSsible to produce "authentic" ribs (the kind you get at a barbecue joint) at home. We started by cooking ribs—for us, this means pork spareribs—three different ways. One slab was cooked over indirect heat, one parboiled and then grilled over direct heat, and the third cooked on a rotisserie attachment to our grill—we were reluctant to use this unusual bit of equipment but, in the name of science, thought we should give it a shot. All three tests were conducted over charcoal with hickory chips in a covered grill.

The ribs cooked over indirect heat were the hands-down favorite. Those cooked on the rotisserie were not nearly as tender, and the parboiled ribs retained the unappealing flavor of boiled meat. While the indirect method needed some refinement, we were convinced it is the best way to cook ribs at home. It also came closest to replicating the method used by barbecue pit masters.

There are several kinds of pork ribs available in most markets. Spareribs come from the underbelly, or lower rib cage, of the pig. A full slab contains 13 ribs and weighs about three pounds. Baby back ribs don't come from a young pig. Rather, they are from the upper end of the rib cage and are smaller than spareribs. Country-style ribs also come from the upper side of the rib cage, but from the end of the loin (opposite the lean tenderloin).

We prefer regular spareribs to either baby back ribs or country-style ribs. The latter ribs are leaner, but the extra fat on spareribs helps keep the meat tender and moist during the long cooking process. Baby back ribs are especially prone to drying out, as are country-style ribs.

We tested a number of popular techniques for barbecuing ribs. Some experts swear by placing some source of moisture in the grill, most often an aluminum pan filled with water or beer. We filled a pan with water and put it next to the coals to create some steam. We couldn't taste the difference between ribs cooked with or without the water.

Next, we tested turning and basting. We found that for the even melting of the fat, it is best to turn the ribs every half-hour. Turning also ensures even cooking. When turning, work as quickly as possible to conserve heat in the grill; don't leave the lid off and wander away to find a pair of tongs. Basting proved to be a bust. Tomato-based sauces burn over the long cooking time, and we didn't find the meat any moister after basting.

Under normal weather conditions, we found the ribs to be done in two to three hours. Signs of doneness include the meat starting to pull away from the ribs (if you grab one end of an individual rib bone and twist it, the bone will actually turn a bit and separate from the meat) and a distinct rosy glow on the exterior. Since the ribs require a relatively short cooking time, there is no need to replenish the coals. A fire that starts out at 350 degrees will drop back to around 250 degrees by the end of two hours.

At this point in our testing, we had produced good ribs, but they were not quite as moist and tender as some restaurant ribs. We spoke with several pit masters, and they suggested wrapping the ribs when they come off the grill. We wrapped the ribs in foil and then placed them in a brown paper bag to trap any escaping steam. After an hour, we unwrapped the ribs and couldn't believe the difference. The flavor, which was great straight off the grill, was the same, but the texture was markedly improved. The wrapped ribs literally fell off the bone.

We spoke with several food scientists who explained that as the ribs rest, the juices are evenly distributed back through the meat and the ribs become more moist and tender. In fact, our ribs are so flavorful and tender that we consider sauce optional.

Barbecued Ribs

SERVES 4

Spareribs are our first choice for this recipe. Hickory is the traditional wood choice with ribs, but some of our tasters liked mesquite as well.

    2   full slabs pork spareribs (about 6 pounds total)
    ¾   cup Dry Rub for Barbecue (page 272)
    2   3-inch wood chunks or 2 cups wood chips
         Heavy-duty aluminum foil
         Brown paper grocery bag
    2   cups Barbecue Sauce (page 272), optional

1. Rub both sides of ribs with dry rub and let stand at room temperature for 1 hour. (For stronger flavor, wrap rubbed ribs in double layer of plastic and refrigerate for up to 1 day.)

2. Soak wood chunks in cold water to cover for 1 hour and drain, or place wood chips on 18-inch square of aluminum foil, seal to make packet, and use fork tines to create about six holes to allow smoke to escape (see illustrations on page 271).

3. Meanwhile, light about 40 charcoal briquettes in chimney. Transfer coals from chimney to one side of kettle grill, piling them up in a mound two or three briquettes high. Keep bottom vents completely open. When coals are covered with light gray ash, lay wood chunks or packet with chips on top of charcoal. Put cooking grate in place, open grill lid vents completely, and cover, turning lid so that vents are opposite wood chunks or chips to draw smoke through grill. Let grate heat for 5 minutes, clean with wire brush, and position ribs over cool part of grill. (Initial temperature will be about 350 degrees and will drop to 250 degrees after 2 hours.)

4. Barbecue, turning ribs every 30 minutes, until meat starts to pull away from ribs and has rosy glow on exterior, 2 to 3 hours. Remove ribs from grill and completely wrap each slab in foil. Put foil-wrapped slabs in brown paper bag and crimp top of bag to seal tightly. Allow to rest at room temperature for 1 hour.

5. Unwrap ribs and brush with barbecue sauce if desired or serve with sauce on side.

➤ VARIATION

Barbecued Ribs on a Gas Grill
If working with a small grill, cook the second slab of ribs on the warming rack.

Follow recipe for Barbecued Ribs, making the following changes: Place foil tray with soaked wood chips (see illustrations on page 271) on top of the primary burner (see illustration on page 268). Turn all burners to high and preheat with lid down until chips are smoking heavily, about 20 minutes. Turn primary burner down to medium, turn off burner(s) without chips, and clean grill with wire brush. Position ribs over cool part of grill. Barbecue, turning ribs every 30 minutes, until done, 2 to 3 hours. (Temperature inside grill should be constant 275 degrees; adjust lit burner as necessary.) Wrap, rest, and brush ribs with barbecue sauce as directed in charcoal recipe.

BARBECUED PULLED PORK

PULLED PORK, ALSO CALLED PULLED PIG OR sometimes just plain barbecue, is slow-cooked pork roast, shredded and seasoned, and then served on a hamburger bun (or sliced white bread) with just enough of your favorite barbecue sauce, a couple of dill pickle chips, and a topping of coleslaw.

Our goal was to devise a procedure for cooking this classic Southern dish that was at once both doable and delicious. The meat should be tender, not tough, and moist but not too fatty. Most barbecue restaurants use a special smoker. We wanted to adapt the technique for the grill. We also set out to reduce the hands-on cooking time, which can stretch to eight hours of constant fire tending in some recipes.

There are two pork roasts commonly associated with pulled pork sandwiches: the shoulder roast and the fresh ham. In their whole state, both are massive roasts, anywhere from 14 to 20 pounds. Because they are so large, most butchers and supermarket meat departments cut both the front and back leg roasts into more manageable sizes: The part of the front leg containing the shoulder blade is usually sold as either a pork shoulder roast or a Boston butt and runs from 6 to 8 pounds. The meat from the upper portion of the front leg is marketed as a picnic roast and runs about the same size. The meat from the rear leg is often segmented into three or four separate boneless roasts called a fresh ham or boneless fresh ham roast.

For barbecue, we find it best to choose a cut of meat with a fair amount of fat, which helps keep the meat moist and succulent during long cooking and adds considerably to the flavor. For this reason, we think the pork shoulder roast, or Boston butt, is the best choice. We found that picnic roasts and fresh hams will also produce excellent results, but they are our second choice.

To set our benchmark for quality, we first cooked a Boston butt using the traditional low-and-slow barbecue method. Using a standard 22-inch kettle grill, we lit about 30 coals and cooked the roast with indirect heat, adding about eight coals every half-hour or so. It took seven hours to cook a seven-pound roast. While the meat was delicious, tending a grill fire for seven hours is not very practical.

In our next test we tried a much bigger initial fire, with about five pounds of charcoal. After the coals were lit, we placed the pork in a small pan and set it on the grate. The trick to this more intense method is not to remove the lid for any reason until the fire is out three hours later. Because you start with so many coals, it is not necessary to add charcoal during the cooking time. Unfortunately, the high initial heat charred the exterior of the roast and the interior was still tough and not nearly "fork-tender" when we took it off the grill.

Next, we tried a combination approach: a moderate amount of charcoal (more than the low-and-slow method but less than the no-peek procedure), cooking the pork roast for three hours on the grill and adding additional coals four times. We then finished the roast in a 325-degree oven for two hours. This method produced almost the same results as the traditional barbecue but in considerably less time and with nine fewer additions of charcoal.

As with ribs (and all barbecue), we find it helpful to let the finished roast rest in a sealed paper bag for an hour. The meat reabsorbs the flavorful juices. In addition, the sealed bag produces a steaming effect that helps break down any remaining tough collagen. The result is a much more savory and succulent roast. Don't omit this step; it's the difference between good pulled pork and great pulled pork.

As with all barbecue, pork roast benefits from being rubbed with a ground spice mixture. However, because the roast is so thick, we find it best to let the rubbed roast "marinate" in the refrigerator for at least three hours and preferably overnight. The salt in the rub is slowly absorbed by the meat and carries some of the spices with it. The result is a more evenly flavored piece of meat.

Barbecued Pulled Pork

SERVES 8

Preparing pulled pork requires little effort but lots of time. Plan on nine hours from start to finish: three hours with the spice rub, three hours on the grill, two hours in the oven, and one hour to rest. Hickory is the traditional choice with pork, although mesquite may be used if desired. Serve the pulled pork on plain white bread or warmed buns with the classic accompaniments of dill pickle chips and cole slaw.

¾	cup Dry Rub for Barbecue (page 272)
I	bone-in pork roast, preferably Boston butt, 6 to 8 pounds
4	3-inch wood chunks or 4 cups wood chips
	Heavy-duty aluminum foil
	Disposable aluminum roasting pan (about 8 x 10-inch)
	Brown paper grocery bag
2	cups Barbecue Sauce (page 272)

1. If using fresh ham or picnic roast, remove skin. Massage dry rub into meat. Wrap tightly in double layer of plastic wrap and refrigerate for at least 3 hours. (For stronger flavor, roast can be refrigerated for up to 3 days.)

2. At least 1 hour prior to cooking, remove roast from refrigerator, unwrap, and let come to room temperature. Soak wood chunks in cold water to cover for 1 hour and drain, or place wood chips on 18-inch square of aluminum foil, seal to make packet, and use fork to create about six holes to allow smoke to escape (see illustrations on page 271).

3. Meanwhile, light about 40 charcoal briquettes

in chimney. Transfer coals from chimney to one side of kettle grill, piling them up in a mound two or three briquettes high. Keep bottom vents completely open. When coals are covered with light gray ash, lay wood chunks or packet with chips on top of charcoal. Put cooking grate in place. Set unwrapped roast in disposable pan and place on grate opposite fire. Open grill lid vents three-quarters of the way and cover, turning lid so that vents are opposite wood chunks or chips to draw smoke through grill. Cook, adding about 8 briquettes every hour or so to maintain average temperature of 275 degrees, for 3 hours.

4. Adjust oven rack to middle position and preheat oven to 325 degrees. Wrap pan holding roast with heavy-duty foil to cover completely. Place pan in oven and bake until meat is fork-tender, about 2 hours.

5. Slide foil-wrapped pan with roast into brown bag. Crimp top shut; let roast rest for 1 hour. Transfer roast to cutting board and unwrap. When cool enough to handle, "pull" pork by separating roast into muscle sections, removing fat if desired, and tearing meat into thin shreds with fingers. Place shredded meat in large bowl; toss with 1 cup barbecue sauce, adding more to taste. Serve with remaining sauce passed separately.

➤ VARIATION

Barbecued Pulled Pork on a Gas Grill

Follow recipe for Barbecued Pulled Pork, making the following changes: Place foil tray with soaked wood chips (see illustrations on page 271) on top of primary burner (see illustration on page 268). Turn all burners to high and preheat with lid down until chips are smoking heavily, about 20 minutes. Turn primary burner down to medium and turn off burner(s) without chips. Position pan with roast over cool part of grill. Barbecue for 3 hours. (Temperature inside grill should be constant 275 degrees; adjust lit burner as necessary.) Proceed with charcoal recipe as directed.

BACON

MANY HOME COOKS NOW USE THE MICROwave to cook bacon, while others still fry bacon in a skillet. In restaurants, many chefs "fry" bacon in the oven. We decided to compare these three techniques in our test kitchen to learn which is best.

For each cooking technique, we varied temperature, timing, and material, cooking both a typical store-bought bacon and a thick-cut mail-order bacon. The finished strips were compared in terms of flavor, texture, and appearance, while the techniques were compared for consistency, safety, and ease.

While the microwave would seem to have the apparent advantage of ease—stick the pieces in and forget about them—it turned out that this was not the case. The microwave produced such a narrow window of doneness that extreme care had to be taken, leaving very little margin for error. Strips were still raw at 90 seconds; at two minutes they were medium-well-done in most spots, but still uneven; but by two minutes and 30 seconds the strips were hard and flat and definitely overcooked.

In addition, the finished product didn't warrant the investment of time it would take to figure out the perfect number of seconds. The texture of microwave bacon is not crisp, the color is pink/gray even when well-done, and we really felt that the taste was bland—less bright, smoky, and sweet-when compared with that afforded by the other methods.

The skillet made for a significantly better finished product than the microwave. The bacon flavors were much more pronounced than in the nuked version, the finished color of the meat was a more appealing brick red, and the meat had a pleasing crispness. There were, however, a number of drawbacks to pan-frying. In addition to the functional problems of grease splatter and the number of 11-inch strips you can fit into a 12-inch round shape, there were problems of consistency and convenience. Because all of the heat comes from below the meat, the strips brown on one side before the other. Moreover, even when using a cast-iron pan, as we did, heat is not distributed perfectly evenly across the bottom of the pan. This means that to get consistent strips of bacon you have to turn them over and rotate them in the pan. In addition, when more strips are added to an already-hot pan, they tend to wrinkle up, making for raw or burned spots in the finished product.

The best results in a pan came when we lowered the heat from medium to medium-low—just hot enough to sizzle. The right temperature allowed the strips to render their grease more slowly, with a lot less curling and spitting out of the pan. Of course, this added to cooking time somewhat, and it did not alleviate the need for vigilance. We even tried pouring off two-thirds of the grease halfway through cooking, but it did nothing to speed the cooking time or to improve the crispness of the finished strips.

Oven-frying seemed to combine the advantages of the microwave and pan-frying techniques while eliminating most of the problems. We tried cooking three strips in a preheated 400-degree oven on a 9 by 12-inch cookie sheet with a raised lip to contain the grease. Bacon was medium-well-done after 9 to 10 minutes and crispy after 11 to 12 minutes. The texture was more like a seared piece of meat than a brittle cracker, the color was that nice brick red, and all of the flavors were just as bright and obvious as when pan-cooked. Oven-frying also provided a greater margin of timing error than either of the other methods, and, surprisingly, it was just about as easy as microwaving, adding only the steps of preheating and draining. Finally, the oven-fried strips of bacon were more consistently cooked throughout, showing no raw spots, and requiring no turning or flipping during cooking, because the heat hits the strip from all sides, and curly areas cook as quickly as flat ones.

Our last test was to try 12 strips of bacon—a pretty full tray—in a preheated oven. This was also quite successful. The pieces were very consistent, the only difference being between those in the back and those in the front of the oven; this inconsistency was corrected by one rotation of the tray during cooking. That was about the limit of our contact with the hot grease. Thick-cut bacon also did well in the oven.

So, when is it worth it to use the oven, as opposed to the pan? Clearly, the added cooking time is a drawback. However, when cooking more than a few strips of bacon, that issue becomes irrelevant—you can add more strips to the oven without significantly increasing cooking time. For crisp, evenly cooked bacon that you have to pay virtually no attention to during cooking, the oven is definitely the way to go.

Oven-Fried Bacon

SERVES 4 TO 6

Use a large, rimmed baking sheet, such as a jelly-roll pan, that is shallow enough to promote browning, yet tall enough (at least ¾ inch in height) to contain the rendered bacon fat. To save time, you can add the bacon to the oven before it reaches 400 degrees, but exact cooking time will vary from oven to oven. If cooking more than one tray of bacon, exchange their oven positions once about halfway through the cooking process.

12   slices bacon, thin- or thick-cut

Adjust oven rack to middle position and heat oven to 400 degrees. Arrange bacon slices in a large jelly-roll pan or other shallow baking pan. Roast until fat begins to render, 5 to 6 minutes; rotate pan front to back. Continue roasting until bacon is crisp and brown, 5 to 6 minutes longer for thin-sliced bacon, 8 to 10 minutes for thick-cut. Transfer with tongs to paper towel-lined plate, drain, and serve.

INGREDIENTS: Bacon

We tested a range of bacons, including 9 leading supermarket brands, a preservative-free "natural" brand, and 2 premium mail-order brands. Tasters were asked to rate all 12 brands based on flavor, balance of lean to fat, and overall quality. Our tasting showed that both the flavor of the meat itself and the flavors provided by the curing process were crucial factors in judging bacon.

We found a surprising difference in the "pork" flavor in the brands we tested. Different manufacturers use different parts of the pork belly to make their bacon. The best bacon comes from the center of the belly. The top portion of the belly is quite lean, while the bottom portion is very fatty.

In terms of flavors provided by curing, tasters preferred a strong balance of salt and sugar. We found that most bacons have only a mild smoky flavor, no doubt because the smoking process in most modern processing plants is just six to eight hours.

The one bacon with a real smoked flavor was one of the mail-order varieties. This bacon was smoked for 24 hours and was clearly in a class by itself. Among supermarket brands, Oscar Mayer took top honors, followed by John Morrell and Hillshire Farm. The one brand cured without preservatives landed at the bottom of the rankings owing to its rubbery texture and excessive sweetness.

9

LAMB

LIKE BEEF, LAMB HAS A RICH RED COLOR, but the meat is generally stronger tasting. This is because the muscle itself is quite tasty and because lamb fat has a particularly strong flavor. In fact, lamb fat can be overpowering, which is why lamb cuts are generally well trimmed before cooking.

Most lamb sold in the supermarket has been slaughtered when 6 to 12 months old. (When the animal is slaughtered past the first year, the meat must be labeled mutton.) Generally, younger lamb has a milder flavor that most people prefer. The only indication of slaughter age at the supermarket is size. A whole leg of lamb weighing nine pounds is likely to have come from an older animal than a whole leg weighing just six pounds.

Lamb is divided into five primal cuts. The shoulder area extends from the neck through the fourth rib. Meat from this area is flavorful, although it contains a fair amount of connective tissue and can be tough. Chops, roasts, and boneless stew meat (for information on making lamb stew, see chapter 11) all come from the shoulder.

The rib area is directly behind the shoulder and extends from the fifth to the twelfth rib. The rack (all eight ribs from this section) is cut from the rib. When cut into individual chops, the meat is called rib chops. Meat from this area has a fine, tender grain and a mild flavor.

The loin extends from the last rib down to the hip area. Several roasts popular with restaurant chefs, such as the saddle, come from this region. For con-

sumers, the loin chop is the most familiar cut from this part of the sheep. Like the rib chop, it is tender and has a mild, somewhat sweet lamb flavor.

The leg portion runs from the hip area down to the hoof. It may be sold whole or broken into smaller roasts and shanks (one comes from each hind leg). These roasts may be sold with the bones in, or the roasts may be butterflied and sold boneless.

The final primal cut is from the underside of the animal and is called the foreshank and breast. This area includes the two front legs (each yields a shank) as well as the breast, which is rarely sold in supermarkets.

LAMB CHOPS

LAMB CHOPS DON'T HAVE TO BE A RARE (and expensive) treat. True, loin and rib chops (together, the eight rib chops form the cut known as rack of lamb) can cost upward of $12 a pound. But we love the meaty flavor and chewy (but not tough) texture of shoulder chops. We also like the fact that they cost just $4 per pound.

In a side-by-side taste test, we grilled loin, rib, and shoulder chops to medium-rare and let them stand about 5 minutes before tasting. The rib chop was the most refined of the three, with a mild, almost sweet flavor and tender texture. The loin chop had a slightly stronger flavor, and the texture was a bit firmer (but not chewier) than the rib chop. The shoulder chop had a distinctly gutsier flavor than the other two. While it was not at all tough, it was chewier. If you like the flavor of lamb (and we do) and are trying to keep within a budget, then try shoulder chops.

We also tried a second test in which we grilled the chops to medium, a stage at which many people prefer lamb. Both the rib and loin chops were dry and less flavorful and juicy than they were at medium-rare. The shoulder chop held its own, in both taste and texture, displaying another advantage besides price.

Shoulder chops can range in thickness from half an inch to an inch. We prefer the thicker chops, and you should ask your butcher to cut them for you if necessary. Loin and rib chops are usually thicker, often close to 1½ inches. The added thickness means that these chops should be cooked over a two-level

THE FIVE PRIMAL CUTS OF LAMB

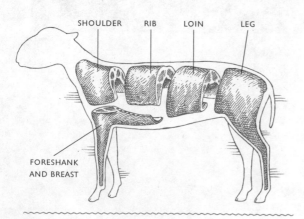

SHOULDER   RIB   LOIN   LEG

FORESHANK AND BREAST

fire to bring the inside up to temperature without charring the exterior.

A two-level fire also makes sense because lamb tends to flame and the cooler part of the grill is the perfect place to let flames die down. Even when making a single-level fire for thinner shoulder chops, we leave part of the grill bottom uncovered with coals so that we have a place to slide the chops if the flames become too intense.

In our tests, we found that grilling is the best method for cooking lamb chops. They are too fatty for broiling (unless, of course, your kitchen has a professional ventilation system); our kitchen filled with smoke every time we tried this technique. Sautéing is not much better. The chops render so much fat that they are swimming in grease in no time, and do not brown all that well since the edges tend to curl up as the chops cook. For the best results, we prefer to grill lamb chops.

There is one exception to this rule. Somewhat chewy shoulder chops respond well to braising. (Don't braise rib or loin chops; they lose their distinctive flavor when braised and are too expensive to serve any way other than grilled.) Our first test in this arena was a simple stovetop braise using a minimal amount of liquid that could be quickly reduced and thickened for a sauce. We browned the chops with sliced onion in a deep sauté pan large enough to hold the chops in a single layer. Then we deglazed with white wine, herbs, a little tomato, and water to barely cover the chops and simmered the whole thing, covered, for an hour and a half, until the meat was tender. We were surprised at how long the relatively thin chops took to cook, and the results were disappointing. The lamb had a sticky, gummy quality that we attributed to the scant quantity of liquid.

Next time we switched to red wine (and more of it) and braised the chops just to medium. We decided to try this experiment after it occurred to us that if the grilled chops were tender, we needn't actually stew the meat at all—just cook it through. The red wine improved the flavor, and cooking the meat to a lesser degree of doneness vastly shortened the cooking time. Using chops about ¾ inch thick, we found that we now had a delicious stovetop braise that cooked in just 15 to 20 minutes—a true weeknight supper dish for the winter months.

Charcoal-Grilled Shoulder Lamb Chops
SERVES 4

Grill shoulder lamb chops over a very hot fire. Half-inch-thick chops, which many supermarkets sell, require about 30 seconds less cooking time per side. See page 244 for information about the different kinds of shoulder chops.

    4   shoulder lamb chops (blade or round bone), about ¾ inch thick
    2   tablespoons extra-virgin olive oil
         Salt and ground black pepper

1. Build a single-level fire (see page 258), but pile all coals over half of grill and leave other half of grill empty. Set grill rack in place, cover grill with lid, and let rack heat up, about 5 minutes.

2. Rub chops with oil and sprinkle with salt and pepper to taste. Cook over coals until bottom of each chop is well-browned, about 2 minutes. (If chops start to flame, pull off heat for a moment or extinguish flames with squirt bottle.) Turn each chop and cook about 2 minutes more for medium-rare or 2½ minutes for medium. Serve immediately.

➤ VARIATIONS
Gas-Grilled Shoulder Lamb Chops
Follow recipe for Charcoal-Grilled Shoulder Lamb Chops, making the following changes: Turn all burners to high and preheat with lid down until very hot, about 15 minutes. Grill as directed in charcoal recipe, but with lid down.

Grilled Lamb Chops with Garlic-Rosemary Marinade
Stir 2 large garlic cloves, put through a press or pureed, 1 tablespoon minced fresh rosemary leaves, and pinch cayenne into oil. Rub chops with paste; let stand at least 30 minutes. (Chops can be refrigerated overnight.) Grill as directed.

Grilled Lamb Chops with Soy-Shallot Marinade
Stir ¼ cup minced shallot or scallion, 2 tablespoons each minced fresh thyme and parsley leaves, 3 tablespoons lemon juice, and 2 tablespoons soy sauce into

oil. Marinate chops in mixture for at least 20 minutes, or up to 1 hour. Grill as directed.

Charcoal-Grilled Loin or Rib Lamb Chops

SERVES 4

Because loin and rib chops are thicker than shoulder chops, they must first be seared over a hot fire and then cooked through on a cooler part of the grill. These chops are smaller than shoulder chops, and you will need two for each serving. If you like, use either the garlic-rosemary or soy-shallot marinade (see page 243) with these chops.

> 8   loin or rib lamb chops, each about 1¼ inches thick
> 2   tablespoons extra-virgin olive oil
>   Salt and ground black pepper

1. Build a two-level fire (see page 258). Set grill rack in place, cover grill with lid, and let rack heat up, about 5 minutes.

2. Rub chops with oil and sprinkle with salt and pepper to taste. Grill over hot fire, turning once, for 4 minutes. (If chops start to flame, pull off heat for a moment or extinguish flames with squirt bottle.) Move chops to cooler part of grill and continue grilling over medium fire, turning once, until desired doneness, about 6 minutes for rare, 8 minutes for medium, and 10 minutes for well-done. Serve immediately.

➢ VARIATION
Gas-Grilled Loin or Rib Lamb Chops

Follow recipe for Charcoal-Grilled Loin or Rib Lamb Chops, making the following changes: Turn all burners to high and preheat with lid down until very hot, about 15 minutes. Leave one burner on high and turn other burner(s) to medium. Grill as directed in charcoal recipe but with lid down.

Braised Lamb Shoulder Chops with Tomatoes and Red Wine

SERVES 4

Because they are generally leaner, round bone chops, also called arm chops, are preferable for this braise. If available, however, lean blade chops also braise nicely. See below for more information on different shoulder chops.

> 4   shoulder lamb chops, about ¾ inch thick, trimmed of external fat
>   Salt and ground black pepper
> 2   tablespoons olive oil
> 1   small onion, chopped fine
> 2   small garlic cloves, minced
> ⅓   cup dry red wine
> 1   cup canned tomatoes packed in puree, chopped
> 2   tablespoons minced fresh parsley leaves

1. Sprinkle chops with salt and pepper to taste.
2. Heat 1 tablespoon of the oil in 12-inch heavy-

INGREDIENTS: Shoulder Lamb Chops

Lamb shoulder is sliced into two different cuts, blade and round bone chops. You'll find them sold in a range of thicknesses (from about one-half inch to more than one inch thick), depending on who's doing the butchering. (In our experience, supermarkets tend to cut them thinner, while independent butchers cut them thicker.) Blade chops are roughly rectangular in shape, and some are thickly striated with fat. Each blade chop includes a piece of the chine bone (the backbone of the animal) and a thin piece of the blade bone (the shoulder blade of the animal).

Round bone chops, also called arm chops, are more oval in shape and as a rule are substantially leaner than blade chops. Each contains a round cross-section of the arm bone so that the chop looks a bit like a mini–ham steak. In addition to the arm bone, there's also a tiny line of riblets on the side of each chop.

As to which chop is better, we didn't find any difference in taste or texture between the two types except that the blade chops generally have more fat. We grill both blade and round bone chops. We like the way the fat in the blade chop melts on the grill, flavoring and moistening the meat, and we love the grilled riblets from the round bone chop. For braising, though, we always prefer round bone chops because they add less fat to the sauce. That said, blade chops vary quite a bit in fat content; those with little intermuscular fat will work fine if well trimmed.

bottomed nonreactive skillet over medium-high heat. Cooking in batches if necessary to avoid over-crowding, add chops; sauté until brown on both sides, 4 to 5 minutes. Remove from pan; set aside.

3. Pour fat from pan; return pan to medium heat, adding remaining tablespoon of oil. Add onion; sauté until softened, about 4 minutes. Add garlic; cook until fragrant, about 1 minute longer. Add wine; simmer until reduced by half, scraping browned bits from pan bottom with wooden spoon, 2 to 3 minutes. Stir in tomatoes, then return chops to pan. Reduce heat to low; cover and simmer until chops are cooked through but tender, 15 to 20 minutes.

4. Transfer chops to each of four plates. Stir parsley into braising liquid; simmer until sauce thickens, 2 to 3 minutes. Adjust seasonings, spoon portion of sauce over each chop, and serve.

➤ VARIATIONS

Braised Lamb Shoulder Chops with Tomatoes, Rosemary, and Olives

Follow recipe for Braised Lamb Shoulder Chops with Tomatoes and Red Wine, adding 1 tablespoon minced fresh rosemary along with garlic and stirring in ⅓ cup pitted and sliced kalamata olives along with tomatoes.

Braised Lamb Shoulder Chops with Red Peppers, Capers, and Balsamic Vinegar

Follow recipe for Braised Lamb Shoulder Chops with Tomatoes and Red Wine, adding 1 medium red bell pepper, seeded and diced, along with onion and stirring in 2 tablespoons drained capers and 2 tablespoons balsamic vinegar along with parsley.

Braised Lamb Shoulder Chops with Figs and North African Spices

⅓	cup stemmed dried figs
4	shoulder lamb chops, about ¾ inch thick, trimmed of external fat
	Salt and ground black pepper
2	tablespoons olive oil
1	small onion, chopped fine
2	small garlic cloves, minced
1	teaspoon ground coriander
½	teaspoon ground cumin
½	teaspoon ground cinnamon
⅛	teaspoon cayenne pepper
1	cup canned tomatoes packed in puree, chopped
2	tablespoons honey
2	tablespoons minced fresh parsley leaves

1. Place figs and ⅓ cup warm water in bowl and soak for 30 minutes. Drain and reserve water. Cut figs into quarters and reserve.

2. Sprinkle chops with salt and pepper to taste.

3. Heat 1 tablespoon of the oil in 12-inch heavy-bottomed nonreactive skillet over medium-high heat. Cooking in batches if necessary to avoid over-crowding, add chops; sauté until brown on both sides, 4 to 5 minutes. Remove from pan; set aside.

4. Pour fat from pan; return pan to medium heat, adding remaining tablespoon of oil. Add onion; sauté until softened, about 4 minutes. Add garlic and spices; cook until fragrant, about 1 minute longer. Add reserved liquid from soaking figs; simmer until reduced by half, scraping browned bits from pan bottom with wooden spoon, 2 to 3 minutes. Stir in tomatoes and honey, then return chops to pan. Reduce heat to low; cover and simmer until chops are cooked through but tender, 15 to 20 minutes.

5. Transfer chops to each of four plates. Stir parsley into braising liquid; simmer until sauce thickens, 2 to 3 minutes. Adjust seasonings, spoon portion of sauce over each chop, and serve.

RACK OF LAMB

THE WORD "MOUTHWATERING" MUST HAVE been invented to describe rack of lamb. The meat is ultratender and luscious tasting, more refined in flavor than almost any other cut of lamb, but no less satisfying.

But, at $17 to $18 a pound, there's hardly a cut of meat more expensive. And like other simple but fabulous dishes (roast chicken comes to mind), there's nothing to cooking it except that there's no disguising imperfection. You want the meat to be perfectly pink and juicy, the outside intensely browned to boost flavor and provide contrasting texture, and the fat to be well enough rendered to encase the meat in a thin, crisp, brittle shell.

With all of this in mind, we set out to find a foolproof way to roast this extravagant cut. And because it's such a good choice for a party, we wanted a sauce to serve with it. A traditional jus is easy to make from pan drippings if your butcher gives you bones from butchering and trimming the rack. But you don't get bones if you buy a rack from a supermarket or one that's been packaged in Cryovac, and two racks on their own, cooked only to medium-rare, just don't produce enough jus to feed four people. We had to figure out a new way to make a sauce.

Since good exterior caramelization is critical to the taste of any roast meat, we needed to find out whether the rack would brown adequately in the oven or would need to be browned on top of the stove first. We hoped for the former; we like the ease of simply shoving the rack into the oven. So we decided to test four racks that had been trimmed and frenched (rib bones cleaned of meat and fat for an attractive presentation) at four different temperatures in a preheated oven: 425 degrees, 475 degrees, 500 degrees, and, finally, 200 degrees.

Unfortunately, none of the high oven temperatures gave us the quality of crust we were looking for, even when we preheated the roasting pan. We knew that the conditions of our remaining test—roasting at 200 degrees—would not make for a nicely browned lamb; the meat wouldn't form a crust at such a low temperature. So we started this test by searing the fat side of the rack in a little vegetable oil in a skillet on top of the stove to get a crust before putting it in a 200-degree oven. The slow-roast technique was a bust: the meat was no more tender than when cooked at a high heat, it had a funny, murky taste and mushy texture that we didn't

like, and it took much too long to cook. But the searing technique was terrific. The only refinement we needed was to find a way to brown the strip of eye meat that lies below the bones on the bony side of the rack. After some experimentation we came up with the system of leaning two racks upright one against the other in the pan; this allowed us to brown all parts of the meat before roasting.

Now we went back to testing oven temperatures. Once the rack was seared, we roasted it at 350, 425, and 475 degrees. We ended up taking the middle road. At 425 degrees, the lamb tastes at least as good as (if not better than) it does when cooked at a lower temperature, and there was more room for error than when cooked at a higher heat.

But now we were running into an unexpected problem. Surprisingly, the racks were too fatty. They looked great when they came out of the oven, but once carved, the chops were covered with a layer of fat that was browned only on the exterior. Some chops also had a second layer of internal fat, separated by a thin piece of meat, called the cap, that didn't get browned at all. We didn't want to forfeit this little flap of meat (particularly at the price we paid for it), but there seemed no help for it: We needed to get rid of some of the fat. So we trimmed the flap and all the fat underneath it, leaving only a minimal amount at the top and covering the bones.

The meat tasted great, needing only one final adjustment: we removed the silver skin that we had exposed in trimming the fat. (The silver skin is the pearlescent membrane found on certain cuts of meat. It is very tough and, if not removed, can cause meat to curl during cooking.)

PREPARING THE RACK OF LAMB

1. Using a boning or paring knife, scrape the ribs clean of any scraps of meat or fat.

2. Trim off the outer layer of fat, the flap of meat underneath it, and the fat underneath that flap.

3. Remove the silver skin by sliding the boning knife between the silver skin and the flesh.

Satisfied with our roasting technique, we were now ready to work on a sauce. We wanted a separate sauce, ready just as soon as the lamb was done, so that we weren't starting from scratch with the pan drippings at the last minute. First we made a separate jus (a very concentrated, reduced stock made with meat, onions, carrots, garlic, and a little water), using lamb stew pieces on the bone bought separately at the supermarket. The jus tasted good, but making it was too much work.

So we went back to the pan drippings. If we transferred the rack to a second pan after browning on top of the stove, we could make a pan sauce while the lamb roasted. As it turned out, we got the best results by preheating the roasting pan in the oven so that it was hot when the lamb hit it.

Roasted Rack of Lamb

SERVES 4 TO 6

Have your butcher french the racks (that is, remove excess fat from the rib bones) for you; inevitably, the ribs will need some cleaning up, but at least the bulk of the work will be done. Should you choose to make one of the accompanying pan sauces, have all the ingredients ready before browning the lamb on the stove top and start to make the sauce just as the lamb goes into the oven.

2	racks of lamb (each 8 to 9 ribs, weighing 1¼ to 1½ pounds), rib bones frenched, and meat trimmed of fat and silver skin (see illustrations on page 246)
	Salt and ground black pepper
2	tablespoons vegetable oil

1. Adjust oven rack to lower-middle position, place shallow roasting pan or jelly-roll pan on oven rack, and heat oven to 425 degrees.

2. Season lamb with salt and pepper. Heat oil in heavy-bottomed 12-inch skillet over high heat until shimmering. Place racks of lamb in skillet, meat-side down, in the center of the pan, with ribs facing outwards; cook until well-browned and nice crust has formed on surface, about 4 minutes. Using tongs, stand racks up in skillet, leaning them against each other to brown the bottoms; cook until bottom sides have browned, about 2 minutes longer.

3. Transfer lamb to preheated roasting pan. (Begin pan sauce, if making.) Roast until instant-read thermometer inserted into the center of each rack registers about 135 degrees, 12 to 15 minutes, depending on size of rack. Cover meat loosely with foil and let rest about 10 minutes. Carve, slicing between each rib into individual chops, and serve immediately with an additional sprinkling of salt and pepper or with one of the following sauces.

➤ VARIATIONS

Roasted Rack of Lamb with Red Wine Pan Sauce and Rosemary

1	recipe Roasted Rack of Lamb
2	medium shallots, minced
1	cup dry red wine
2½	teaspoons minced fresh rosemary leaves
1	cup chicken stock or low-sodium canned broth
2	tablespoons butter, softened
	Salt and ground black pepper

1. Prepare lamb as directed.

2. After transferring browned lamb to roasting pan, pour off all but 1½ tablespoons fat from skillet. Add shallots and place skillet over medium heat. Sauté shallots until softened, about 1 minute. Add red wine and rosemary; increase heat to medium-high and simmer until dark and syrupy, about 7 minutes. Add chicken stock; simmer until reduced to about ¾ cup, about 5 minutes longer. Off heat, swirl in butter; season to taste with salt and pepper, and serve with lamb.

Roasted Rack of Lamb with Orange Pan Sauce and Middle Eastern Spices

1	recipe Roasted Rack of Lamb
2	medium shallots, minced
1	teaspoon ground cumin
¼	teaspoon ground black pepper
¼	teaspoon ground cinnamon
¼	teaspoon ground cardamom
⅛	teaspoon cayenne
2	teaspoons sugar
3	tablespoons red wine vinegar
¼	cup juice from 1 medium orange
1½	cups chicken stock or low-sodium canned broth
1	tablespoon minced fresh cilantro leaves
	Salt

1. Prepare lamb as directed.

2. After transferring browned lamb to roasting pan, pour off all but 1½ tablespoons fat from skillet. Add shallots and place skillet over medium heat. Sauté shallots until softened, about 1 minute. Stir in cumin, pepper, cinnamon, cardamom, cayenne, and sugar; cook until fragrant, about 1 minute. Stir in vinegar, scraping up browned bits on bottom of pan. Add orange juice, increase heat to medium-high, and simmer until very thick and syrupy, about 2 minutes. Add chicken stock and simmer until slightly thickened and reduced to about ¾ cup, 8 to 10 minutes. Off heat, stir in cilantro, season to taste with salt and serve with lamb.

Roasted Rack of Lamb with Sweet and Sour Mint Sauce

This simple sauce should be made before you begin cooking the lamb so the sugar has time to dissolve while the lamb cooks.

½	cup loosely packed fresh mint leaves, chopped
¼	cup red wine vinegar
1	tablespoon sugar
	Salt
1	recipe Roasted Rack of Lamb

1. Stir together mint, vinegar, and sugar in small bowl. Let stand about 20 minutes to allow sugar to dissolve. Season to taste with salt.

2. Prepare lamb as directed. Serve lamb, passing sauce separately at the table.

ROAST LEG OF LAMB

THE MAIN PROBLEM WE HAVE HAD WITH roast leg of lamb is that it cooks unevenly. In the past, no matter what we have tried, the outer part became dry and gray, while the meat around the bone remained almost raw. The uneven thickness of the leg is the most formidable obstacle to even cooking. At the thicker sirloin end, the meat surrounding the flat, twisting hipbone is very thin. The center of the leg, which consists of the top half of the thigh, is fleshy, but the thigh then tapers dramatically toward the knee joint, and the shank itself is a mere nub of meat.

The only way to deal with this problem is to remove the hipbone and aitchbone entirely and then tie the leg into as compact a shape as possible. Boning and tying, however, do not by themselves guarantee even cooking. Special procedures must be followed in roasting the leg to ensure that all parts are exposed to the same amount of heat and will thus reach similar internal temperatures at the same time.

We started out by roasting a 7½-pound leg at 400 degrees, with the meat resting directly on the roasting pan. After approximately one hour, the top of the leg, which had been facing up, registered 120 degrees on a meat thermometer, which to our taste is underdone for leg of lamb. The meat around the thigh bone, meanwhile, was practically raw, while the bottom of the leg, which had been resting on the hot pan, had reached a temperature of around 135 degrees, which is a little overcooked for our taste.

We have always resisted roasting on a rack because, when cooked only to rare or medium-rare, meat produces virtually no brown bits for gravy unless it rests directly on the pan. With leg of lamb, however, we surmised that a rack might be useful, for it would protect the downward-facing side of the leg from becoming overcooked by the heat of the pan.

To test this theory, we rack-roasted another leg. After cooking at 500 degrees for 30 minutes (high initial heat promotes browning) and then at 300 degrees for about 45 minutes longer, the leg was done on the top side; the thermometer registered a consistent 130 degrees whether inserted sideways, into the exterior portion of the top side, or poked deep into the middle. Alas, the bottom side of the roast proved undercooked. Evidently the rack had been too effective in keeping the bottom of the leg cool.

But this experiment, while only partially successful, pointed toward a solution. Perhaps turning the leg during cooking would promote more even cooking by allowing the top and the bottom sides equal exposure to both the cool rack and the hot oven roof. We further reasoned that setting the pan on the bottom shelf of the oven would slightly heat up the rack side, which was too cool, while mitigating the glare from the oven roof.

This is how we roasted our next lamb leg, and the results were near perfect. The outermost slices were a little closer to medium than to medium-rare and the bone meat was still a bit underdone, but most of the roast was the way we wanted it, deep pink and juicy.

TWO SAUCES FOR ROAST LEG OF LAMB

You can serve lamb plain or with mint jelly, but we find that these two sauces are far superior.

Piquant Caper Sauce

MAKES ENOUGH TO ACCOMPANY
I LEG OF LAMB

If making this sauce, ask the butcher for the hipbone and aitchbone and reserve any meat scraps that have come off the lamb during the cleaning process. Make sure to remove the fat from these scraps. You can also use the hinged part of the shank bone. To accommodate the hipbone, you will need a wide saucepan or deep sauté pan. Start the sauce as soon as the lamb goes into the oven.

I	tablespoon olive oil
	Lamb bones and meat scraps
I	medium onion, chopped coarse
3	cups chicken stock or low-sodium canned broth
⅓	cup dry white wine or dry vermouth
2	tablespoons unsalted butter, softened
2	tablespoons all-purpose flour
⅓	cup (3 ounces) small capers, drained, bottling liquid reserved
I	teaspoon balsamic vinegar

1. Heat oil in large, heavy-bottomed saucepan set over medium heat. Add reserved bones and meat scraps and onion. Sauté, turning bones several times, until well browned, about 10 minutes. Add broth, scraping pan bottom to loosen browned bits; bring to boil. Reduce heat to low; simmer, partially covered, until bones and meat have given up their flavor to broth, about 1 hour. Add a little water if bones are more than half exposed during cooking.

2. While roasted leg of lamb is resting, set empty pan used to roast lamb over medium heat. Add wine and scrape with wooden spoon until brown bits dissolve. Pour mixture into lamb stock, then strain everything into 2-cup glass measure. Let sit until fat rises, then skim. Add water, if necessary, to make 1½ cups of liquid. Pour liquid back into saucepan and bring to boil.

3. Mix butter and flour to smooth paste. Gradually whisk butter-flour mixture into stock. Stir in capers, vinegar, and any juices lamb throws off while resting. Simmer to blend flavors, about 3 minutes. Add more vinegar or caper bottling liquid to achieve piquant, subtly sharp-sweet sauce. Serve with lamb.

Mint Sauce

MAKES ENOUGH TO ACCOMPANY
I LEG OF LAMB

This sauce has a refreshing mint flavor without the cloying sweetness of mint jelly. The texture is much thinner than jelly, similar to maple syrup. This sauce is remarkably easy to make and does not require any bones since no stock is necessary. If making this sauce, eliminate the rosemary from the lamb recipe and just rub the meat with olive oil and salt and pepper and stud with garlic. Chop the mint right before adding it to the sauce to preserve its fresh flavor.

I	cup white wine vinegar
6	tablespoons sugar
¼	cup minced fresh mint leaves

1. Heat vinegar and sugar in medium saucepan over medium heat. Bring to boil and simmer until slightly syrupy, 8 to 10 minutes. (Liquid should be reduced to about ½ cup.)

2. Remove pan from heat, let cool for 5 minutes, and stir in mint. Pour sauce into bowl and cover with plastic wrap. Set aside for at least 1 hour. (Sauce can be set aside for one day.) Serve at room temperature with lamb.

Roast Leg of Lamb

SERVES 8 TO 12, DEPENDING ON
SIZE OF LEG

Legs come in a variety of sizes. Our recipe starts with a semiboneless (the butcher should remove the hipbone and aitchbone) leg that weighs between six and eight pounds. (The weight of the whole, untrimmed leg is about 1½ pounds more.) Smaller legs have a sweeter, milder flavor, so you may want to search for a petite leg if you don't like a strong "sheepy" flavor. If roasting a smaller leg, reduce the cooking time at 325 degrees by at least 10 minutes.

We find it best to cook lamb by internal temperature. We like our lamb medium-rare, or about 135 degrees when carved. Since the internal temperature will rise while the lamb rests, pull the leg out of the oven when the temperatures reaches 130 degrees. If you like lamb on the rarer side, pull it out of the oven at 120 degrees (the tempera-ture will rise to 125 degrees by carving time). If you like lamb more well done, pull it out at 135 degrees (the temperature will rise above 140 degrees).

Salt and ground black pepper

1   teaspoon finely minced fresh rosemary leaves or ½ teaspoon dried rosemary, finely crushed (omit if making Mint Sauce on page 249)

1   semiboneless leg of lamb (6 to 8 pounds), excess fat removed and discarded (see illustrations below)

3   medium garlic cloves, peeled and cut into thin slivers

2   tablespoons olive oil

1. Mix 2 teaspoons salt, 2 teaspoons pepper, and rosemary in small bowl.

2. Sprinkle portion of rosemary mixture over

PREPARING A LEG OF LAMB FOR ROASTING

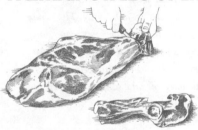

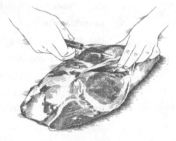

1. The butcher should remove the aitchbone and hipbone (right front); you should save the bones so you can make stock. If the shank bone has been partially detached by the butcher, remove it with a knife and save it, too, for stock.

2. Lamb fat is strong-flavored and unpleasant to chew. Remove large pieces of fat, using a knife and your hands to cut and then pull the fat off the leg. It's fine to leave a few streaks of fat to moisten the roast.

3. The strong-tasting lymph node (a ½-inch round, grayish nodule) and surrounding fat should be removed. Set the leg meaty side up and cut into the area that separates the broad, thin flap of meat on one side of the leg with the thick, meaty lobe.

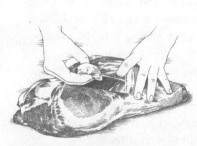

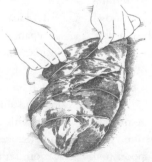

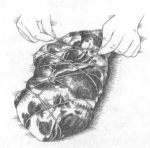

4. Use both hands and the knife to widen the incision, exposing the lymph node and surrounding fat. Reach in and grasp the nugget of fat. Pull while cutting the connective tissue, being very careful not to cut into the gland itself. Pull the fat and other matter free.

5. Set the leg meaty side up and smooth the flap of meat at the sirloin end so that it folds over and neatly covers the tip of the thigh bone. Tie several short lengths of twine around the leg, placing each piece of twine parallel to the next.

6. Tie several more short lengths of twine around the leg, running pieces of twine perpendicular to those in step 5.

inner surface of cleaned and boned meat. Tie lamb according to illustrations on page 250. Cut slits into roast with tip of paring knife. Poke garlic slivers inside. Brush exterior with oil, then rub remaining seasoning onto all surfaces of meat. Place leg, meaty side up, on roasting pan fitted with flat rack; let stand 30 minutes. Adjust oven rack to lowest position and heat oven to 450 degrees.

3. Pour ½ cup water into bottom of roasting pan. Roast lamb for 10 minutes. With wad of paper toweling in each hand, turn leg over. Roast 10 minutes longer. Lower oven temperature to 325 degrees. Turn leg meaty side up and continue roasting, turning leg every 20 minutes, until instant-read thermometer inserted in several locations registers 130 degrees, 60 to 80 minutes longer. Transfer roast to another pan; cover with foil and set aside in warm spot to complete cooking and to allow juices to reabsorb into meat, 15 to 20 minutes. Reserve roasting pan if making Piquant Caper Sauce.

4. When sauce is ready, remove string from roast and carve by cutting slices parallel to bone, each about ¼-inch thick. When meat on top has been removed, flip leg over and carve bottom in same fashion. To facilitate carving side of leg, grasp narrow end of leg and hold it perpendicular to work surface and slice as before. Serve sliced lamb with sauce.

GRILLED LEG OF LAMB

A LEG OF LAMB CAN BE GRILLED IF THE LEG is boned and then butterflied (a technique in which several cuts are made in the boned flesh to open and flatten the leg so that its uneven topography is smoothed to an even thickness). A butterflied leg of lamb is a large, unwieldy piece of meat, about ¾-inch thick and covered with a thin layer of fat.

For our first test, we used a kettle grill and our preferred fuel—hardwood charcoal—to build a two-level fire. We seasoned the meat with salt and pepper and, wary of flaming, used no oil. We placed the meat fat-side-down over the coals, intending to brown it quickly over direct heat and then finish it over indirect.

The results dismayed us. The leg flamed and blackened. It was difficult to maneuver on the grill because of its size. The connective tissue in the shank retracted and curled so badly that eventually we had

to cut it off and cook it longer. The rest of the leg cooked unevenly and tasted oily as well as scorched from the flame. Because it was so thin, it was difficult to carve into attractive slices.

We made up our minds to start from scratch and find out the best way to grill a leg of lamb. We had several questions: First, is butterflying really necessary, and, if so, what's the best way to do it? Is there a way to grill the shank attached to the leg, or must we always cut it off? Direct heat chars the leg more than we like, but how else can we grill it? Do we need to cover the grill to control the flaming? And is it necessary to carve a leg of lamb against the grain for the sake of tenderness?

Our goal was to come up with a butchering technique that would yield an easy-to-manage piece of meat, thick enough to carve into attractive slices. And, as always when grilling, we wanted a crust that was caramelized but not blackened and a moist, tender interior.

To start, it helps to understand the structure of the leg, which consists of six different muscles: the meaty, dome-shaped top and smaller bottom rounds; the small, cylindrical eye of round; the flat, trapezoidal hip; the round knuckle; and the oblong shank. Restaurant chefs sometimes separate the muscles from one another (they pull apart very easily) and then cook and carve each separately, because that allows each muscle to be cooked perfectly and carved against the grain into large slices for optimal tenderness. (After the meat is butterflied, the grain runs every which way, and it's impossible to carve against the grain.)

LEG OF LAMB: THE BONES

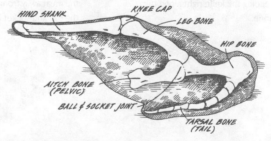

When butterflying a leg of lamb (see step-by-step illustrations on page 254), it is helpful to know the inner skeletal structure. In particular, note where all the bones come together in the center of the leg at the large ball and socket joint.

Cooking the muscles separately doesn't make sense for a home cook, particularly since people tend to turn to this cut when planning for a crowd. But we tried to adapt this technique by boning the leg and cooking it as is—with all the muscles intact and unbutterflied—planning to cut the muscles apart after cooking and carve each one separately. This time, to solve the flaming problem, we cooked the lamb entirely over indirect heat. It browned beautifully and didn't flame, but after 40 minutes it was clear that there wasn't enough heat to cook through the larger muscles (the top round and knuckle).

BONING A LEG OF LAMB

1. Using a tip of a boning knife, make the first cut at the top of the shank, cutting around the knee cap, and continuing down one side of the leg bone.

2. Cut straight down to the leg bone with the tip of the knife, and, using the bone as a guide, cut until you reach the hipbone and must stop. Repeat on the other side.

3. Cut under and around the knee cap and along the side of the leg bone, loosening the meat from the bone as you go.

4. Cut around the hip bone to loosen the meat from the bone.

5. Using the tip of the knife, cut the meat away from the aitchbone (or pelvic bone). Use the tip of the knife to scrape the meat away from the bone.

6. At this point, the meat should be free from the leg bone (center), the aitchbone (lower left center), and the hip bone (lower right). The ball and socket joint is in the center.

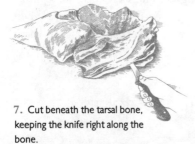

7. Cut beneath the tarsal bone, keeping the knife right along the bone.

8. Lift the tarsal bone and continue scraping the meat away from the bone until you reach the ball and socket joint.

9. With the tip of the knife, scrape along and beneath the ball and socket joint to loosen it from the meat, and cut between ball and socket to loosen.

10. Snap the ball and socket apart and pull the tail-, hip-, and aitchbones away from the leg bone (save this piece for stock or discard).

11. Continue to cut beneath the leg bone, lifting it from the meat as you cut.

12. Lift the leg bone and cartilage around the knee cap to totally separate the leg and shank portion (if the leg came shank attached) and remove (save for stock or discard).

We knew from previous experience that using the grill cover for anything other than very long cooking would impart an unwanted "off" flavor, so we decided to see if we could solve the problem in the butchering stage.

We were familiar with two methods of butterflying. One calls for cutting straight down into the meat and then spreading the meat open on either side of the cut. The second technique is to cut into the meat horizontally and then open it out like a book. We tried both and found that a combination of the two techniques worked best (see page 254). The butterflied leg was very large, however, so we cut it in half along a natural separation between the muscles. That not only made it easier to fit the meat on the limited grill space, it also enabled us to turn it with a single pair of tongs rather than struggling with a pair of tongs in each hand. It was also more practical to buy, since you can freeze half if you are cooking for only four.

Satisfied with our butchering technique, we returned to the cooking. Working again over indirect heat, we grilled the butterflied leg, cut side up, for five minutes. Then we turned it 180 degrees and cooked it five more minutes to ensure that it cooked evenly all around. After 10 minutes the leg was well-browned on the skin side, so we turned it over and repeated the procedure, cooking it another 10 minutes until it registered 130 degrees on a meat thermometer. We let the meat rest 10 minutes and then sliced into it. The outside crust was perfect but inside we still had problems. While the meat in the center was a beautiful medium-rare, the perimeter of the leg was still pale because it had needed more time to rest. And the shank was still undercooked.

The problem with the shank was easy enough to solve; we decided to cut it off and save it for another use. (Some supermarkets also sell the leg without the shank.) Then we tested resting times, letting the meat rest 15, 20, and 25 minutes, and found that 20 minutes was ample time for the juices to be redistributed through the leg. Finally, we experimented with carving to test for tenderness: We carved the meat into thin slices on an angle (to produce slices as large as possible) and disregarded the grain. As it turned out, this was a good decision: Although the different muscles varied in taste and texture, they were all plenty tender.

Charcoal-Grilled Butterflied Leg of Lamb
SERVES 10

On those occasions when we want to cook only half a leg of lamb, we prefer the sirloin end.

1	7-pound leg of lamb, boned, butterflied, and halved between the eye and the bottom round (see illustrations on pages 252 and 254)
1½	tablespoons extra-virgin olive oil
	Salt and ground black pepper

1. Open all grill vents. Build a fire large enough to cover half a large charcoal grill and come within 1½ inches of the grill rack, about 5 pounds of hardwood charcoal. Allow charcoal to burn down until the flames have died and all the charcoal is covered with a layer of fine gray ash, about 20 minutes. Return grill rack to position, open lid vents, cover grill with lid, and let rack heat for 5 minutes.

2. Rub olive oil onto all sides of both pieces of lamb and sprinkle with salt and pepper. Place lamb pieces, fat side down, on the side of the rack that is not directly over the coals. Lamb should sizzle when it hits the grill.

3. Grill lamb, uncovered, for 5 minutes. Fat side still down, rotate meat so that outside edges are now closest to the fire; grill, uncovered, until fat side of lamb is a rich dark brown, 3 to 5 minutes longer. With tongs or a large meat fork, turn both pieces over; repeat grilling procedure described above, rotating lamb to ensure even cooking, until an instant-read thermometer inserted into the thickest part of each piece registers 130 degrees for medium rare, about 10 minutes longer. Transfer meat to a large platter or cutting board, tent with foil, and let rest 20 minutes. Slice on an angle and serve.

➤ VARIATION
Gas-Grilled Butterflied Leg of Lamb
Follow recipe for Charcoal-Grilled Butterflied Leg of Lamb, making the following changes: Turn all burners to high and preheat with lid down until very hot, about 15 minutes. Leave one burner on high and turn other burner(s) to medium. Grill as directed in charcoal recipe over medium burners but with lid down.

BUTTERFLYING A LEG OF LAMB

1. To butterfly, lay a large chef's knife flat on the center of the meat, at the thinnest part, parallel to the top round.

2. Keeping the knife blade parallel to the board, begin slicing through the muscle. Cut horizontally about 1 inch.

3. Begin to unroll the meat (it's like unrolling a carpet) with your other hand as you continue to cut into the muscle, always keeping the knife blade parallel to the board, cutting about 1 inch at a time, and unrolling as you cut.

4. Stopping about 1 inch from the end, unfold the edge of the meat and flatten it.

5. The butterflied muscle should be even in thickness.

6. Turn the board around and cut the knuckle muscle on the other side, using the same method as in steps 1 through 4.

7. Near the center of the bottom round, locate a hard thick section of fat. Using the tip of the boning knife, cut into the fat to locate the lymph node (a ½-inch round, grayish flat nodule). Carefully remove and discard.

8. Divide the butterflied meat in half by cutting between the eye and the bottom round.

9. Turn the pieces of meat over and use a boning knife to cut away the thick pieces of fat, leaving about ⅛-inch thickness for self-basting during grilling.

LAMB SHANKS

ONE OF THE GREAT PLEASURES OF COOKING is to take a relatively tough cut of meat and turn it into a meltingly tender dish. Among the most richly flavored of these tougher cuts is the lamb shank, which is simply the bottom portion of the fore or hind leg of a lamb.

Like other cuts of meat that come from the joints of animals, such as oxtails or short ribs, lamb shanks are extremely flavorful when properly cooked. This is because they contain a high proportion of connective tissue and fat, which break down during cooking and add flavor to the meat.

However, the presence of all this connective tissue and fat means that shanks can only be cooked using a long, slow, moist cooking method that will disintegrate the connective tissue and render the fat without drying out the meat. The only practical cooking method to achieve this goal is braising, which means cooking the meat partially covered in liquid, usually in a closed container. Braising keeps the temperature of the meat relatively low—around the boiling point of water—for a long period of time, which is exactly what is needed to convert the tough collagen to tender gelatin.

While satisfactory results can be obtained by braising shanks on top of the stove, we prefer braising in an oven because of its heating properties. With the heat coming from all directions, the meat cooks more evenly. This is a particular advantage given that many pans have "hot spots" that cause them to heat unevenly on a burner.

Because of the high fat content of this cut, several straightforward precautions are necessary to keep the level of fat in the final product to a minimum.

First, if your butcher has not already done so, it is very helpful to take the time to trim the lamb shanks of the excess fat that encases the meat. Even a long, slow braise will not successfully render all of the exterior fat on a lamb shank. Trimming it helps you get a jump on that potential problem.

Browning the shanks well before braising them also helps render some of the exterior fat. Browning also has the advantage of adding a great deal of flavor to the dish. Be sure to drain the fat from the pan after browning.

The third important step is to remove the fat from the braising liquid after the shanks have been cooked. To do this, take the shanks out of the braising liquid, strain out the vegetables, and allow the sauce to rest undisturbed for a short while. Then, using a ladle, carefully skim the fat that has risen to the surface and discard it. This process can be facilitated by transferring the sauce to a taller, narrower container before setting it aside to rest. Further, if the braise is prepared well in advance of serving, you may refrigerate the braising liquid and then simply lift the solidified fat from the top of the liquid.

The braising liquid, along with the aromatics you include in it, will greatly enhance the flavor of the entire dish. Stock is traditionally the braising liquid because it adds a textural richness as well as depth of flavor. We recommend that you use chicken stock in the braise rather than either beef or veal stock, because these heartier stocks compete too much with the flavor of the lamb and tend to make the sauce overly rich. A good chicken stock will complement the flavor

of the lamb shanks.

Wine is a particularly good addition to the braising liquid, adding complexity and acid to the sauce. The acid is particularly important because of the richness of the lamb. Too little acid creates a dull, rather flat-tasting dish. On the other hand, too much acid results in a rather harsh, off-putting flavor. After trying different ratios, we find that two parts wine to three parts stock gives the best flavor.

Either white wine or red works well, the difference being that red wine will give you a richer, deeper finish. You may also vary the choice of herbs and spices according to your taste, and in the following recipes we have included several suggestions.

Whatever liquid you use for braising, it should cover all but the top inch of the shanks. This differs somewhat from classical braising, in which only a small amount of liquid is used. We adopted this method after leaving some shanks braising in the oven, then returning some time later to find that the liquid had boiled away and the shanks were burned. Unless you are using a true braising pan with an extremely tight-fitting lid, a fair amount of liquid will escape. Using more liquid prevents the pan from drying out, no matter how loose the seal is.

Lamb Shanks Braised in Red Wine with Herbes de Provence

SERVES 6

If you cannot locate herbes de Provence, substitute a mixture of one teaspoon each of dried thyme, rosemary, and marjoram. If you're using smaller shanks than the ones called for in this recipe, reduce the braising time from 1½ hours to 1 hour. Serve braised shanks over mashed potatoes, polenta, rice, or couscous.

6 lamb shanks (¾ to 1 pound each), trimmed of excess fat
 Salt
1 tablespoon canola oil
2 medium onions, sliced thick
3 medium carrots, peeled and cut crosswise into 2-inch pieces
2 celery stalks, cut crosswise into 2-inch pieces
4 medium garlic cloves, peeled
2 tablespoons tomato paste
1 tablespoon herbes de Provence

2 cups dry red wine
3 cups chicken stock or low-sodium canned broth
Ground black pepper

1. Heat oven to 350 degrees. Sprinkle shanks with salt. Heat oil in a large, nonreactive sauté pan over medium-high heat. Add shanks to pan, in batches if necessary to avoid overcrowding. Sauté until browned on all sides, 5 to 7 minutes. Using tongs, transfer shanks to a plate as they brown.

2. Drain all but 2 tablespoons of fat from pan; add onions, carrots, celery, garlic, tomato paste, 1 teaspoon of herbes de Provence, and a light sprinkling of salt; sauté vegetables to soften slightly, 3 to 4 minutes. Add wine, then stock, stirring with wooden spoon to loosen browned bits from bottom of pan. Bring liquid to simmer; transfer vegetables and liquid to deep braising pan large enough to hold shanks in a single layer. Add shanks; season with salt, pepper, and remaining 2 teaspoons herbes de Provence.

3. Cover pan and transfer to oven; braise shanks for 1½ hours. Uncover and continue braising until shank tops are browned, about 30 minutes. Turn shanks and braise until other side is browned and shanks are fall-off-the-bone tender.

4. Remove pan from oven; let shanks rest for at least 15 minutes. With tongs, carefully transfer shanks to each of 6 plates. Arrange a portion of vegetables around each shank. Skim excess fat from braising liquid and adjust seasonings. Spoon braising liquid over each shank and serve.

➤ VARIATION
Braised Lamb Shanks with Lemon and Mint

6 lamb shanks (¾ to 1 pound each), trimmed of excess fat
  Salt
1 tablespoon canola oil
2 medium onions, sliced thick
3 medium carrots, peeled and cut crosswise into 2-inch pieces
2 celery stalks, cut crosswise into 2-inch pieces
4 medium garlic cloves, peeled
2 tablespoons tomato paste
2 tablespoons minced fresh mint leaves
1 lemon, zest removed and minced, lemon quartered
2 cups dry white wine
3 cups chicken stock or low-sodium canned broth
  Ground black pepper

1. Heat oven to 350 degrees. Sprinkle shanks with salt. Heat oil in a large, nonreactive sauté pan over medium-high heat. Add shanks to pan, in batches if necessary to avoid overcrowding. Sauté until browned on all sides, 5 to 7 minutes. Using tongs, transfer shanks to a plate as they brown.

2. Drain all but 2 tablespoons of fat from pan; add onions, carrots, celery, garlic, tomato paste, 1 tablespoon mint, quartered lemon (but not zest), and a light sprinkling of salt; sauté vegetables to soften slightly, 3 to 4 minutes. Add wine, then stock, stirring with wooden spoon to loosen browned bits from bottom of pan. Bring liquid to simmer; transfer vegetables and liquid to deep braising pan large enough to hold shanks in a single layer. Add shanks and season with salt and pepper.

3. Cover pan and transfer to oven; braise shanks for 1½ hours. Uncover and continue braising until shank tops are browned, about 30 minutes. Turn shanks and braise until other side is browned and shanks are fall-off-the-bone tender.

4. Remove pan from oven; let shanks rest for at least 15 minutes. With tongs, carefully transfer shanks to each of 6 plates. Arrange a portion of vegetables around each shank. Skim excess fat from braising liquid, stir in lemon zest and remaining 1 tablespoon mint, and adjust seasonings. Spoon braising liquid over each shank and serve.

10

GRILLING AND BARBECUING

COOKING FOOD OUTDOORS OFTEN DELIVERS the best results, but it can be a challenge for the cook because grilling (quick cooking with a hot fire) and barbecuing (long, slow cooking with a cooler fire) are so imprecise. As long as the thermostat on your oven is properly calibrated, you should have no trouble following recipes that call for roasting at a particular temperature. Cooking over a charcoal or gas fire is more complicated.

To take as much of the guesswork out of the process as possible, we have developed a long list of tips, which are assembled here. The following pages cover the basics, everything from buying a grill and lighting charcoal to using wood chips on a gas grill. We suggest that you read this material before preparing any of the recipes that follow.

This chapter includes three chicken recipes that demonstrate three different ways of cooking outdoors. Boneless kebabs are grilled quickly and directly over a single-level fire. Thicker, bone-in parts are grilled over a two-level fire; that is they are first seared on the hot part of the grill and then cooked through on the cooler part of the grill. Finally, a whole chicken is cooked by indirect heat (the fire is contained to one part of the grill and the chicken is placed over

the part of the grill without any coals). This process is slow and permits the food to be flavored with smoke from wood chunks or chips as it cooks.

The techniques that these three recipes illustrate are used throughout this book. You will want to refer to these recipes and the other information in this chapter when preparing many of the recipes in the meat, seafood, poultry, and vegetable chapters.

GRILLING

GRILLING IS NOT A SCIENCE. FIRE IS A LIVING, changing entity that requires constant attention and rapid response to current conditions. All the grilling recipes in this book were tested on a kettle-style grill using hardwood lump charcoal.

Hardwood lump charcoal contains no additives (it's just burned pieces of wood) and burns very hot. (In contrast, briquettes are often made from sawdust and other scraps.) We find that lump charcoal burns down more quickly than briquettes, perhaps because some of the pieces are tiny; but, given that it starts very quickly (more quickly than briquettes), it's possible to resurrect a waning fire within 5 to 10 min-

CHARCOAL FIRE BASICS

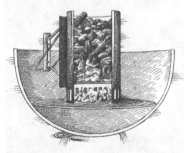

LIGHTING A CHARCOAL FIRE
Our favorite way to start a charcoal fire is with a chimney starter, also known as a flue starter. To use this simple device, fill the bottom section with crumpled newspaper, set the starter on the grill grate, and fill the top with charcoal. When you light the newspaper, flames will shoot up through the charcoal, igniting it. When the coals are well-lit and covered with a layer of gray ash, dump them onto the charcoal grate. (If you need more than five quarts of charcoal, add some unlit charcoal. Continue heating until all the coals are gray.)

BUILDING A SINGLE-LEVEL FIRE
Once the lit charcoal is in the grill, the coals can be arranged in an even layer to create a single-level fire. This kind of fire delivers even heat and is best for quick searing at a moderate temperature.

BUILDING A TWO-LEVEL FIRE
Another option is to build a two-level fire, which permits searing over very hot coals and slower cooking over medium coals to cook through thicker cuts. To build a two-level fire, spread some of the lit coals in a single layer over half the grill. Leave the remaining coals in a pile that rises to within 2 or 2½ inches of the cooking grate. If necessary, you may add some unlit charcoal on the hot side of the grill. Wait 10 minutes or so for these coals to become hot.

utes with just one or two handfuls of fresh charcoal thrown directly on the coals in the grill. Lump charcoal is substantially more expensive than briquettes, but because a thin layer burns very hot, you won't need as much.

Many cooks stint on the fuel when grilling and never get the temperature high enough. There's no point spending $30 on steaks and then steaming them over an inadequate fire. The size of your grill, the amount of food being cooked, and the desired intensity of the fire are all factors in deciding how much charcoal to use. In the end, you want a fire that is slightly larger than the space on the cooking grate occupied by food. Remember that you can always let the fire die down a bit if the heat is too intense. It's possible to add more charcoal if the fire is too weak, but this involves lifting up the hot cooking grate, which is awkward and inconvenient.

For most jobs, we light one chimney full of charcoal, dump it into the grill bottom when lit, add another chimney of unlit charcoal, and then let the second batch heat up. Five pounds of charcoal (or more when a blazing hot fire is needed for cooking more than six or eight steaks) is not an unreasonable amount.

There are two basic types of charcoal fire you can build in a grill. When the coals are lit, they may be spread out evenly across the bottom of the grill. A single-level fire delivers even heat across the cooking grate, usually at a moderate temperature because the coals are fairly distant from the cooking grate. We cook chicken kebabs, vegetables, and shrimp over this kind of fire.

A second option, one that we employ in most instances when cooking meat or chicken parts, is a two-level fire. Once the coals are lit, some of the coals should be raked off the pile and spread out in a single layer across half the grill bottom. The remaining coals stay piled up on the other side of the grill so that they are closer to the cooking grate. (On a gas grill, the burners are adjusted to create a two-level fire.)

There are several advantages to a two-level fire. The heat above the pile of coals is quite hot, perfect for searing. The heat above the single layer of coals is less intense, perfect for cooking thicker foods once they are well-browned. This cooler part of the fire also comes in handy if flames engulf food. Simply

---

EQUIPMENT: Charcoal Grills

We find that a round kettle-style grill is the best all-purpose choice for outdoor cooking. (The other charcoal option is the hibachi, which is generally quite small.) The large cooking grate (usually at least 16 inches across and often as much as 22 inches) allows you to prepare a good amount of food at one time. The deep bowl shape allows air to circulate, and the high lid accommodates even tall foods like a roast. Also, the deep kettle holds a lot of charcoal, so you can build a big, hot fire. Some charcoal grill grids have hinged sections that make it much easier to add coals to the fire during cooking. If you have a choice, buy a grill with this feature.

We use the Weber kettle grill, which is the most common (and often the only) charcoal option in hardware stores. We recommend that you buy the 22-inch grill, which is large enough to accommodate a couple of racks of ribs, 8 or 10 steaks, and a dozen or more chicken parts. On smaller grills, the "cool" part of the grill will be too cramped to accommodate a large brisket or two slabs of ribs when barbecuing.

There is one drawback to this grill. Over time, soot and resinous compounds can build up on the inside of a kettle grill cover. For this reason, we don't use the cover when grilling since we find that it often imparts a slightly "off" taste, which we can best describe as resembling the odor of stale smoke. We prefer to use a disposable aluminum roasting or pie pan to cover foods that require some buildup of heat to cook them through.

When barbecuing, however, the lid must be used to trap heat. We find that any off or smoky taste that the lid may impart is overwhelmed by the smoky flavor the food absorbs from wood chips or chunks, which are a given in all barbecuing recipes.

We find that a chimney starter (also called a flue starter) is the best way to light charcoal. (See the illustration on page 258.) A chimney starter is foolproof, and it eliminates the need for lighter fluid, which can impart off flavors to delicate foods such as fish, poultry, and vegetables.

A charcoal grill may not be as convenient to use as a gas grill, but we think the results are better. Foods usually taste a bit smokier and are better seared when grilled over charcoal rather than gas. In addition, a charcoal grill is far less expensive than a good gas grill, Lastly, we like the challenge and fun of cooking over a live fire.

drag the food to the cooler part of the grill, and the fire will usually subside.

In general, it's best to use moderately thick steaks, fish fillets, and chops when grilling. This is because they will be well-seared by the time the inside is properly cooked. Very thin steaks, chops, and fish fillets are harder to keep moist, especially if you like a crisp exterior. When shopping, you may need to ask the butcher or fishmonger to cut meat or fish to fit your needs.

Cooking over a live fire is not like cooking in a precisely calibrated oven. Be prepared to adjust timing, especially if grilling in cool or windy weather. Using an instant-read thermometer (grilling recipes in this book cite optimum internal temperatures) or taking the meat off the grill and peeking inside with the tip of a knife are the best ways of telling when food is cooked to your liking.

We find that beef, pork, and fish are more flavorful and juicier when cooked short of well done, either rare, medium-rare, or medium, depending on the item in question. If you are worried about killing possible bacteria, you should cook all meat and seafood to an internal temperature of at least 160 degrees. Of course, chicken must be fully cooked to at least 160 degrees both because of taste and safety considerations.

TAKING THE TEMPERATURE OF THE FIRE

Once the coals have been spread out in the bottom of the grill, put the cooking grate in place, and put the cover on for five minutes to heat up the grate. Before cooking, determine the intensity of the fire by holding your hand five inches above the cooking grate. When the fire is hot, you should be able to keep your hand in place for no more than two seconds. For a medium-hot fire, the time extends to three or four seconds; for a medium fire, five or six seconds; and for a medium-low fire, seven seconds.

GRILLED CHICKEN KEBABS

GRILLED CHICKEN KEBABS SHOULD BE SUC-culent and well-seasoned, and they should really taste like they've been cooked over an open fire. They must be complemented by fruits and vegetables that are equally satisfying: grill-marked but juicy, cooked all the way through but not incinerated or shrunken. When we started our testing, we figured it would be simple. After all, skewered chicken is a standby of every street-corner grill cook from here to China.

But after some early attempts, we found that the difficulties in cooking and flavoring kebabs often result in skewers that look better than they taste. When we simply threaded the chicken and veggies on skewers, brushed them with a little oil, and sprinkled them with salt and pepper, we were always disappointed. Sometimes the components cooked at different rates, resulting in dry meat and under-cooked vegetables. Even when they were nicely grilled, the quick-cooking kebabs didn't absorb much flavor from the fire and were bland. White meat seemed to lose moisture as it cooked, so that by the time it was safe to eat it was too dry to enjoy. With its extra fat, dark meat was invariably juicier than white meat, but still needed a considerable flavor boost before it could be called perfect.

We decided to attack the flavor problem first, reasoning that once we could produce well-seasoned, juicy chicken chunks, we could then work out the kinks of cooking chicken, fruits, and vegetables at the same time. Having committed ourselves to dark meat, we started with the simplest solution—using a spice rub before cooking. The results were disappointing. The skinless chunks looked and tasted dry. A spice rub works far better on chicken parts with skin attached.

Wanting to add a little moisture, we turned to "wet" preparations. We mixed a simple marinade of lemon juice, olive oil, garlic, and herbs and soaked the chicken in it for three hours. We liked the glossy, slightly moist grilled crust that the marinade produced and the way the garlic and herb flavors had penetrated the meat. But we found the flavor of the lemon juice, refreshing on larger pieces of chicken, to be overpowering on the smaller chunks. A more serious problem was the way the acid-based marinade "tenderized" the chicken. Even with shorter

EQUIPMENT: Gas Grills

Gas grills are increasing in popularity, and the reasons are clear: the fire is easy to light and control. While there are few options when buying a charcoal grill, there are dozens and dozens of gas grills on the market. We tested six moderately priced grills from the leading manufacturers and came to the following conclusions.

In general, we found that you get what you pay for. Inexpensive gas grills, priced at $200 or less, are generally inferior. If you are willing to spend more money (about $400), you can buy a gas grill that works extremely well, with results that can compete with the charcoal grill.

There are several features and design elements that separate a good grill from a poor one. A built-in thermometer that registers real numbers (not just low, medium, and hot) is essential. A gauge that tells you how much gas is left in the tank is also a plus.

As you might expect, a large grill offers the cook more possibilities. Unless the cooking surface has an area of at least 400 square inches, you will need to cook one slab of ribs at a time. (If the grill comes with a warming rack, you may cook a second slab there.)

In addition to size, the number of burners is critical. It's not possible to cook indirectly on a grill with only one burner, because the burner is usually positioned in the center of the grill and the "cool" parts of the grill are too small to fit most foods. You must use a grill with at least two burners. With one burner on and one burner off, at least half of the grill will be cool enough for slow cooking.

The heat should be evenly distributed across the entire surface of the grill. We found that most gas grills are plenty hot. In fact, in our testing we found that some gas grills can actually run just as hot as charcoal. A bigger problem is that gas grills are often unable to sustain temperatures low enough for barbecuing. Many of the cheaper grills we tested were unable to barbecue a brisket without burning the exterior before the meat was tender. A good grill will heat up to 600 degrees and maintain a temperature of 250 degrees when the lid is down and just one burner is lit and turned to low.

Perhaps the most shocking conclusion we came to during our testing of gas grills concerns the cause of flare-ups. We found that lava rocks soak up dripping fat and will catch fire as soon as there is some sort of flare-up. Several times we moved flaming chicken parts to the cool side of the grill (without a lit burner), and they still flamed from below for several minutes. It wasn't the chicken that was on fire, rather, the lava rocks had caught fire even though the burner underneath those rocks was cool.

Lava rocks are not the sole reason for flare-ups. Poor design that traps grease on the bottom of the grill doesn't help either. We consider a drainage system mandatory. The bottom of the cooking chamber should be sloped so that fat runs through an opening in the center and into a drain pan below.

Weber gas grills do not have lava rocks. Bars, made from steel coated with porcelain-enamel and shaped like an upside down V, channel fat down into the bottom of the grill and eventually into a drip pan attached to the underside of the cooking chamber. We find this drainage system is far superior to the other options.

If you entertain a lot, you will want the bigger and more expensive Weber Genesis with three burners. If your needs (or budget) are more modest, the Weber Spirit in an excellent choice.

The recipe instructions in this book give the proper heat level, which is determined by the length of time you can hold your hand five inches above the cooking grate (see the illustration on page 260). If using a gas grill, adjust the dials as necessary to produce the correct temperature.

Most gas grills come with two temperature controls, each regulating a separate burner. You can use the dials to change the heat level on the entire grill, turning it from high to medium once food has been seared. The dials can also be manipulated to create two heat levels on the cooking surface at the same time. For instance, you may set one burner at high for searing and set the other at medium to cook foods through or to have a place to move foods if they ignite.

One final note about gas grills. Unlike charcoal grills, the inside of the cover stays fairly clean. Since there is no buildup of resinous smoke, the grill cover (rather than a disposable aluminum pan) can be used in recipes, such as grilled chicken breasts, where a cover is needed to cook foods through.

To make sure a gas grill is good and hot, always preheat with all burners turned to high and the lid down for 15 minutes. Then adjust the burners as directed in recipes, scrape the grill surface clean with wire-bristle brush, and place the food on the grill to cook.

Unless you know you are going to need it, you may want to remove the warming rack before lighting the grill. On most grills, the rack is very close to the cooking surface and it can be hard to reach foods on the back of the grill without burning your hands on the hot metal.

marinating times (we tried one hour and one-half hour), the chunks were mushy after cooking.

Was there a way to season the chicken all the way through and keep it moist on the grill without the acid? We ruled out brining because it would make the small skinless chicken chunks much too salty. But since we wanted the juiciness and flavor that brining imparts, we decided to try soaking the chicken in a lightly salted, acid-free marinade. We prepared two batches of acid-free olive oil marinade, one with salt and one without. We let the chunks sit in the mari-nade for three hours before grilling. The results were what we had hoped for. The salted marinade produced plump, well-seasoned kebabs. The chicken marinated without salt was drier and seemed to absorb less flavor from the garlic and herbs.

Fine-tuning the method, we settled on one teaspoon of salt (this quantity seasons the chicken without making it overly salty) for 1½ pounds of chicken and a marinating time of at least three hours. (During testing, chicken marinated for less time did not absorb enough of the marinade flavorings.)

MARINADES FOR GRILLED CHICKEN KEBABS

Master Recipe for Garlic and Herb Marinade

MAKES SCANT ¾ CUP, ENOUGH TO COAT 1½ POUNDS CHICKEN CHUNKS

½   cup extra-virgin olive oil
6   small garlic cloves, minced
     (about 2 tablespoons)
¼   cup snipped chives, minced fresh basil,
     parsley, tarragon, oregano, cilantro, or mint
     leaves or 2 tablespoons minced fresh thyme
     or rosemary
1   teaspoon salt
     Ground black pepper to taste

Whisk all ingredients in small bowl.

➤ VARIATIONS

Curry Marinade
Follow Master Recipe, using ¼ cup minced fresh cilantro or mint leaves and adding 1 teaspoon curry powder to marinade.

Caribbean Marinade
Follow Master Recipe, using ¼ cup minced fresh parsley leaves and adding 1 teaspoon cumin, 1 teaspoon chili powder, ½ teaspoon allspice, ½ teaspoon black pepper, and ¼ teaspoon ground cinnamon to marinade.

Middle Eastern Marinade
Follow Master Recipe, using ¼ cup minced fresh mint or parsley leaves, alone or in combination, and adding ½ teaspoon cinnamon, ½ teaspoon allspice, and ¼ teaspoon cayenne to marinade.

Southwestern Marinade
Follow Master Recipe, using ¼ cup minced fresh cilantro leaves, decreasing salt to ½ teaspoon, and adding 1 teaspoon cumin, 1 teaspoon chili powder, 1 teaspoon turmeric, and 1 medium chile, such as jalapeño, seeded and minced.

Asian Marinade

MAKES GENEROUS ¾ CUP, ENOUGH TO COAT 1½–2 POUNDS CHICKEN CHUNKS

6   tablespoons vegetable oil
2   tablespoons Asian sesame oil
¼   cup soy sauce
6   small garlic cloves, minced
     (about 2 tablespoons)
¼   cup minced fresh cilantro leaves
1   piece (about 1 inch) fresh gingerroot,
     minced (about 1 tablespoon)
2   medium scallions, white and green parts,
     sliced thin

Whisk all ingredients in small bowl.

Because there is no acid in the marinade and thus no danger of breaking down the texture of the meat, the chicken can be soaked for up to 24 hours before cooking.

Since it was clear early on that cooking chicken, fruits, and vegetables together enhances the flavor of all three, we now needed to figure out how to prepare the fruits and vegetables so they would cook at the same rate as the chicken. We eliminated items like potatoes and yams, which need precooking. We also decided against marinating fruits and vegetables, partly because the chicken was already highly flavored from the marinade, and partly because we did not like the way some of them lost their characteristic flavor after just a short dip. We found that simply tossing the fruits and vegetables with a little olive oil, salt, and pepper produced the best texture and flavor.

In general, resilient (but not rock-hard) vegetables such as zucchini, eggplant, and bell peppers cook thoroughly but stay moist and lend good flavor and crunch to chicken skewers. Cherry tomatoes, on the other hand, tend to disintegrate by the time the chicken is done. Firm-textured fruits like apples, pears, and pineapples grill beautifully, holding their shape while cooking all the way through. Fruits that tend toward softness when overripe, like peaches or nectarines, will work fine if still firm. Softer fruits like mangoes or grapes turn to mush over the fire, no matter what size you cut them.

As for the fire, medium is best (you should be able to keep your hand five inches above the fire for five seconds). A hotter fire chars the outside before the inside is done; a cooler fire won't give you those appetizing grill marks and may dry out the chicken. For the juiciest chicken with the strongest grilled flavor, cook skewers of dark meat for about nine minutes; if you prefer white meat, cook it for eight minutes. In both cases the grill should be uncovered.

After experimenting with various sizes and shapes of chicken, we decided on 1- to 1½-inch chunks, small enough for easy eating but big enough to pick up some good grilled flavor. With smaller chunks or thin strips there's no margin for error; a few seconds too long on the grill and you'll wind up with a dry-as-dust dinner.

A final note on skewering itself. Chicken and vegetables simply skewered through the center may spin around when you try to turn them on the grill, inhibiting even cooking. We tried out some heavy-gauge twisted metal skewers designed to prevent this problem, but in the end found that threading the ingredients through two thinner skewers at once was more effective. We prefer thin but sturdy metal skewers that can fit two at a time through the kebabs but won't bend under the weight of the food.

Charcoal-Grilled Chicken Kebabs

MAKES 8 KEBABS (4 SERVINGS)

This recipe is a good example of how to build and grill over a single-level fire. Although white breast meat can be used, we prefer the juicier, more flavorful dark thigh meat for these kebabs. Whichever you choose, do not mix white and dark meat on the same skewer, since they cook at slightly different rates.

Cut peeled eggplant and onions into half-inch cubes and zucchini into half-inch rounds; button mushrooms can be skewered whole, but portobello caps should be cut into half-inch chunks; seeded bell peppers work best as inch-wide wedges, while peeled shallots can be skewered whole; apples and pears should be cored and cut into one-inch cubes, peaches pitted and cut into six sections, and pineapples peeled, cored, and cut into one-inch cubes.

1	recipe marinade of choice (see page 262)
1½	pounds skinless boneless chicken breasts or thighs, cut into 1- to 1½-inch chunks
3	cups vegetables and/or fruit, prepared according to above directions
2	tablespoons olive oil to coat vegetables and fruit
	Salt and ground black pepper for vegetables and fruit

1. Mix marinade and chicken in gallon-sized zipper-lock plastic bag; seal bag and refrigerate, turning once or twice, until chicken has marinated fully, at least 3 and up to 24 hours.

2. Build a single level-fire (see page 258). Set grill rack in place, cover grill with lid, and let rack heat up, about 5 minutes. If necessary, let grill cool down until fire is medium-low (you can hold your hand 5 inches above grill surface for 5 seconds).

3. Meanwhile, lightly coat vegetables and/or fruit

by tossing in medium bowl with oil and salt and pepper to taste.

4. Remove chicken chunks from bag; discard marinade. Use one hand to hold two skewers about ½ inch apart, then thread a portion of chicken and vegetables on both skewers at once for easy turning on the grill. Repeat with remaining chicken and vegetables to make 8 sets of double skewers.

5. Grill, turning each kebab one quarter turn every 2 minutes, until chicken and vegetables and/or fruit are lightly browned and meat is fully cooked, about 8 minutes total for white meat and 9 minutes total for dark meat. Check for doneness by cutting into one piece when it looks opaque on all sides. Remove kebabs from grill when there is no pink at the center. Serve immediately.

➤ VARIATION
Gas-Grilled Chicken Kebabs
Follow recipe for Charcoal-Grilled Chicken Kebabs through step 1. Turn all burners to high and preheat with lid down until very hot, about 15 minutes. Turn all burners to medium and proceed as directed.

GRILLED CHICKEN PARTS
GRILLED CHICKEN PARTS SHOULD HAVE RICHLY caramelized, golden brown (but not burned) skin and moist, juicy meat. As soon as our testing started, we realized we needed to develop slightly different methods for dark and white meat parts. The higher fat content in thighs and legs makes flare-ups a greater problem, while the breasts have a tendency to dry out and need special handling. (Wings are covered with a lot of skin and have a tendency to be flabby; as such they require a completely different cooking technique. See page 154 for details.)

We soon dismissed partially cooking before or after grilling, and we found that poaching or microwaving beforehand yielded dry, cottony meat. Finishing grilled parts in a hot oven is cumbersome, and the grill flavor is not strong enough.

Clearly, we needed to use a two-level fire. We tried the method recommended by the manufacturers of many covered grills: searing chicken over a hot fire, then moving it to a medium fire, putting the cover on, and cooking until done. This method works well, but the residue on the inside of the cover

imparts an undesirable flavor.

Next, we tried searing the chicken over a medium-hot fire and then moving it to a medium fire to finish cooking. This approach was fine for the thinner thighs and legs. However, we found that breasts need to be moved to an area with no coals and covered with a disposable pan (no off flavors here) to cook through.

Marinating the chicken does not add much flavor and causes constant flare-ups during the initial searing period. Rubbing the chicken with a spice rub prior to grilling proved far more satisfactory. Barbecue sauces often contain some sweetener and can burn if brushed on the chicken before cooking. We found it best to brush them on when cooking was almost done, serving extra sauce at the table if desired. As a final test, we tried brining the chicken before grilling it. The brine penetrated the chicken, seasoning it and slightly firming up its texture before grilling.

You can grill dark and white meat parts together, if you like. Set up a three-level fire with most of the coals on one side of the grill, some coals in the middle, and no coals on the opposite side. Sear all the chicken parts over the hottest part of the fire, finish cooking the legs and thighs over the medium fire in the middle, and move the seared breasts to the coolest part of the grill and cover with a disposable pan.

Charcoal-Grilled Chicken Thighs or Legs
SERVES 4
This recipe is a good example of how to build and grill over a two-level fire. Brining improves the chicken's flavor, but if you're short on time, skip step 1 and season the chicken generously with salt and pepper before cooking. Add flavorings before or during cooking: Rub the chicken parts with a spice rub or paste (page 265) before they go on the grill, or brush them with barbecue sauce (page 272) during the final 2 minutes of cooking.

8	chicken thighs or 4 whole legs
¾	cup kosher salt or 6 tablespoons table salt
¾	cup sugar
	Ground black pepper

1. Trim overhanging fat and skin from chicken pieces; this will prevent burning. In gallon-sized zip-

RUBS AND PASTES FOR GRILLED CHICKEN PARTS

Rubs are made with ground dry spices and are best applied with your fingers. Pastes contain some sort of liquid and can be applied with your fingers or a brush. If you have decided to skip brining, make sure to season the parts with salt.

Pantry Spice Rub for Chicken

MAKES ABOUT ½ CUP, ENOUGH TO COAT A SINGLE RECIPE OF EITHER DARK OR WHITE MEAT PARTS

2	tablespoons ground cumin
2	tablespoons curry powder
2	tablespoons chili powder
1	tablespoon ground allspice
1	tablespoon ground black pepper
1	teaspoon ground cinnamon

Combine all ingredients in small bowl. Rub mixture over brined and dried chicken parts before grilling.

Garam Masala Spice Rub for Chicken

MAKES ABOUT ½ CUP, ENOUGH TO COAT A SINGLE RECIPE OF EITHER DARK OR WHITE MEAT PARTS

2	tablespoons fennel seeds
2	tablespoons anise seeds
2	tablespoons cardamom pods
2	tablespoons black peppercorns
1	teaspoon whole cloves
1	cinnamon stick, broken into several pieces

Toast ingredients in dry skillet until fragrant, about 2 minutes. Grind to powder in spice grinder. Rub mixture over brined and dried chicken parts before grilling.

Citrus and Cilantro Spice Paste for Chicken

MAKES ABOUT ⅓ CUP, ENOUGH TO SEASON A SINGLE RECIPE OF EITHER DARK OR WHITE MEAT PARTS

1	teaspoon ground cumin
1	teaspoon chili powder
1	teaspoon paprika
1	teaspoon ground coriander
2	tablespoons orange juice
1	tablespoon lime juice
1	tablespoon olive oil
1	garlic clove, peeled
2	tablespoons fresh cilantro leaves

Puree all ingredients in food processor or blender until smooth. Rub paste over brined and dried chicken parts before grilling.

Asian Spice Paste for Chicken

MAKES ABOUT ⅓ CUP, ENOUGH TO SEASON A SINGLE RECIPE OF EITHER DARK OR WHITE MEAT PARTS

2	tablespoons soy sauce
2	tablespoons peanut oil
1	tablespoon minced fresh jalapeño or other chile
1	tablespoon chopped fresh gingerroot
1	garlic clove, peeled
2	tablespoons fresh cilantro leaves

Puree all ingredients in food processor or blender until smooth. Rub paste over brined and dried chicken parts before grilling.

per-lock plastic bag, dissolve salt and sugar in 1 quart of water. Add chicken, seal bag, and refrigerate until fully seasoned, about 1½ hours.

2. Build a two-level fire (see page 258). Set grill rack in place, cover grill with lid, and let rack heat up, about 5 minutes.

3. Meanwhile, remove chicken from brine, rinse well, dry thoroughly with paper towels, and season with pepper to taste or one of the spice rubs or pastes on page 265.

4. Cook chicken, uncovered, over hotter part of grill until seared, about 1 to 2 minutes on each side. Move chicken to cooler part of grill; continue to grill, uncovered, turning occasionally, until dark and fully cooked, 12 to 16 minutes for thighs, 16 to 20 minutes for whole legs. To test for doneness, either peek into thickest part of chicken with tip of small knife (you should see no redness near the bone), or check internal temperature at thickest part with instant-read thermometer, which should register 165 degrees. Transfer to serving platter. Serve warm or at room temperature.

➤ VARIATION

Gas-Grilled Chicken Thighs or Legs
Follow recipe for Charcoal-Grilled Chicken Thighs or Legs through step 1. Turn all burners to high and preheat with lid down until very hot, about 15 minutes. Leave one burner on high and turn other burner(s) to medium. Grill as in charcoal recipe but with lid down, placing chicken first over burner on high and then sliding chicken to cooler part of the grill to cook through.

Charcoal-Grilled Bone-In Chicken Breasts

SERVES 4

This recipe is a good example of how to build and grill over a modified two-level fire, with all the coals banked to one side of the grill. If the fire flares because of dripping fat or a gust of wind, move the chicken to the area without coals until the flames die down. Brining improves the chicken's flavor, but if you're short on time, skip step 1 and season the chicken generously with salt and pepper before cooking. Add flavorings before or during cooking: Rub the chicken parts with a spice rub or paste (page 265) before

they go on the grill or brush them with barbecue sauce (page 272) during the final 2 minutes of cooking.

¾	cup kosher salt or 6 tablespoons table salt
¾	cup sugar
4	split chicken breasts (bone-in, skin-on), 10 to 12 ounces each
	Ground black pepper

1. In gallon-size zipper-lock plastic bag, dissolve salt and sugar in 1 quart of water. Add chicken, seal bag, and refrigerate until fully seasoned, about 1½ hours.

2. Build a two-level fire (see page 258), but pile all coals over half of grill and leave other half of grill empty. Set grill rack in place, cover grill with lid, and let rack heat up, about 5 minutes.

3. Meanwhile, remove chicken from brine, rinse well, dry thoroughly with paper towels, and season with pepper to taste or one of the spice rubs or pastes on page 265.

4. Cook chicken, uncovered, over hotter part of the grill until well browned, 2 to 3 minutes per side. Move chicken to area with no fire and cover with disposable aluminum roasting pan; continue to cook, skin side up, 10 minutes. Turn and cook 5 minutes more. To test for doneness, either peek into thickest part of chicken with tip of small knife (you should see no redness near the bone) or check internal temperature at thickest part with instant-read thermometer, which should register 160 degrees. Transfer to serving platter. Serve warm or at room temperature.

➤ VARIATION

Gas-Grilled Bone-In Chicken Breasts
Follow recipe for Charcoal-Grilled Bone-In Chicken Breasts through step 1. Turn all burners to high and preheat with lid down until very hot, about 15 minutes. Leave one burner on high and turn other burner(s) to medium. Grill as in charcoal recipe but with lid down, placing chicken first over burner on high and then sliding chicken to cooler part of the grill to cook through. (With lid down, there's no need to use disposable roasting pan.)

BARBECUING AND GRILL-ROASTING

MOST COOKS INTUITIVELY UNDERSTAND how to grill. You build the biggest fire possible and place the food—meat, seafood, chicken, or vegetables—right over the coals. Steaks, chops, and other relatively thin foods can be grilled this way because the interior will be cooked by the time the exterior is nicely browned.

But what about a thick pork roast or brisket? If grilled this way, the exterior will be charred and ashen well before the interior of such a large piece of meat has a chance to cook through. Same thing for a whole chicken. The solution is indirect cooking, with the lid down (not up, as in grilling) to trap heat and create a regulated cooking environment much like that of an oven.

While grilling calls for filling the grill with charcoal or lighting all the gas burners, indirect cooking on the grill relies on a smaller fire. The lit coals are banked on one side of the grill, or one of the gas burners is turned off. Foods cooked by indirect heat are placed over the "cool" part of the grill. Since there is no direct heat, the exterior of the food cooks slowly without flare-ups. With the lid on, the heat of the fire is trapped, and it cooks the food slowly and evenly.

Why bother with indirect cooking on the grill when you can roast in the oven? The smoky flavor we associate with ribs or pulled pork comes only from the grill. Even foods that we don't normally consider grilling—a whole turkey or side of salmon—taste better when wood flavor is added.

Two kinds of indirect cooking are possible on a covered grill. Barbecuing is the traditional low- and slow-cooking method used with ribs, pulled pork (shredded Boston butt), and brisket. Because the goal is to impart as much smoke flavor as possible, a long cooking time over a relatively low fire is required.

USING A CHARCOAL GRILL FOR INDIRECT COOKING

Before starting, empty the grill of any old ashes, which may block air circulation and prolong cooking times when barbecuing or grill-roasting. Some experts recommend banking the coals on either side of the grill and leaving the center open for indirect cooking. They believe that having the coals on both sides of the grill promotes even heating. When we tried this method, we found that the edges of large pieces of food, such as ribs and brisket, can burn. We prefer to bank all the coals on one side of the grill, leaving half of the grill free of coals and providing a large space for foods to cook without danger of burning. Since the lid is down, the heat from the coals is distributed just as well as with two piles of charcoal.

1. Fill the bottom section of a chimney starter with crumpled newspaper, set the starter on the bottom grate in a kettle grill, fill the main compartment with as much charcoal as directed in individual recipes, and light the newspaper. When the coals are well-lit and covered with a layer of gray ash, dump them onto the charcoal grate, piling the coals up on one half of the grill and leaving the other half free of coals. If necessary, use long-handled tongs to move the briquettes into place.

2. Place soaked and drained wood chunks or a foil packet filled with wood chips on top of the coals. Set the top grate in position, heat briefly, and then scrape the grate clean with a wire brush. You are now ready to cook over the cool part of the fire.

3. A grill thermometer inserted through the vents on the lid can tell you if the fire is too hot or if the fire is too cool and it's time to add more charcoal. You can control the heat level to some extent by adjusting the vents on the lid and base of the grill. Opening the vents gives the fire more oxygen and will cause the coals to burn hotter at first, but then the fire will cool down more quickly as the coals peter out. Closing the vents partially (don't close the vents all the way or the fire will die) lowers the heat but keeps the coals from burning too fast.

Barbecuing also provides ample time for fatty, tough cuts to become more tender.

Although there is much debate among barbecue experts as to the proper cooking temperature, we found that barbecuing should take place between 250 and 300 degrees. While some pit masters might argue that ribs are best barbecued at 180 degrees, we found it very difficult to maintain such a low fire. Also, low temperatures allow bacteria to multiply and increase the risk of food-borne illnesses.

Once the sustained (or average) temperature during the cooking period exceeds 300 degrees, we believe (and most experts concur) that the process becomes grill-roasting, the other method of indirect cooking. The grill setup is the same, there's just more heat.

Grill-roasting is best for foods that are already tender and that don't require low and slow cooking. Birds are especially well-suited to grill-roasting (at lower temperatures the skin remains soft and flabby), as are tender cuts of meat (like beef tenderloin) that need to develop a crisp crust during their relatively short cooking time. Grill-roasting occurs at temperatures between 300 and 400 degrees.

Our preference when grilling is to use charcoal. We like the way it heats up and the flavor that food absorbs from hardwood charcoal (our favorite fuel for most recipes). However, when doing indirect cooking—barbecuing or grill-roasting—many of the advantages that charcoal grills have over gas grills disappear.

Hardwood charcoal, also called natural or lump charcoal, tends to burn too quickly. It's too hot to be practical when cooking by indirect heat. We like the intense fire this charcoal makes when searing steaks, but when using it to barbecue brisket, you have to open the grill and add charcoal much more often than you'd like. Also, because the fire can run hotter at the outset, there is a greater risk of burning the edges of large foods (such as turkeys and ribs) that may be close to the coals. For indirect cooking, we prefer regular charcoal briquettes, which burn cooler and more slowly.

Briquettes don't have as much flavor as hardwood charcoal, but they do give foods a more smoky flavor than a gas grill. Whether grilling over briquettes or gas, wood chunks or chips must do the real flavoring work. In our testing, we consistently found that foods cooked over charcoal had a smokier flavor than those cooked over gas. That's because a charcoal fire does a better job of getting the wood (which is sitting right in the fire) to smolder and smoke. Although we eventually devised a method for maximizing the smoke from chips used in a gas grill, the smoke flavor is not as strong as it is in foods cooked over charcoal. If you like really smoky foods and are using a gas grill, you might consider using more chips at the outset when grill-roasting or adding more chips to the foil tray partway through the cooking time when barbecuing.

Intense smoky flavor aside, gas grills do have some advantages over charcoal when cooking by indirect heat. It's easier to regulate the heat on a gas grill. Just turn the dial and the temperature immediately responds. Also, there is no need to add charcoal during the long cooking process, so there is less hassle and mess. Gas grills are also more convenient to use during rainy weather.

USING A GAS GRILL FOR INDIRECT COOKING

To set up a gas grill for indirect cooking, remove all warming shelves attached to the hood or the back of the grill. (Leave the racks in place when making ribs on a small grill.) Place a foil tray with soaked wood chips (see illustrations on page 271) on top of the primary burner. (With some gas grills, one burner must be turned on first. This is the primary burner. With other grills, you may designate a primary burner yourself.) Make sure the tray is resting securely over the burner and will not tip. Replace the grill rack. Light all burners and cover the grill. When you see a lot of smoke (this will take about 20 minutes), turn off the burner(s) without the chips and place the food over these off burners. If the chips start to flame, douse the fire with water from a squirt bottle.

Finally, our tasters felt that foods cooked over gas were juicier than foods cooked over charcoal. The reason for this is simple. Smoke makes foods taste great but causes them to dehydrate. Since gas grilling generates less smoke, foods retain more moisture.

In the end, we found that cooking with charcoal or gas each produce excellent, if somewhat different, results. For your convenience, each recipe in this book for grilling, barbecuing, or grill-roasting includes direction for both charcoal and gas.

The chicken recipe on this page illustrates the technique of grill-roasting. The setup is the same for barbecuing, although most recipes will use fewer coals (for a cooler fire), and you may need to add coals more often to keep the fire going longer.

GRILL-ROASTED CHICKEN

GRILL-ROASTING A CHICKEN—COOKING IT in a covered grill over indirect heat at a temperature between 350 and 400 degrees—is an impressive feat. As with a conventionally roasted chicken, we wanted the meat to remain moist and tender while the skin becomes bronzed and crisp. We also wanted the bird to pick up a good amount of smoke flavor.

We conducted several tests to see if turning and basting were necessary. We found that starting the bird breast side down and then turning it halfway through the cooking time kept the breast juicy and was worth the effort. Rotating the bird 180 degrees, so that the opposite side faces the fire, promotes even cooking. We tested two more turns—putting the bird on either side and then breast side up—but too much heat was lost from the grill and we had to add more charcoal. More important, the chicken did not taste any juicier for the extra effort.

As for basting, we found that basting with butter before grilling can speed the browning of the skin. We tried basting again during the cooking time but found that this was not necessary. Also, opening the grill too often will cause the fire to die out, and the chicken may not cook properly.

An oven-roasted chicken is likely to remain moist if properly cooked, but grill-roasted birds tend to dry out. For this reason, as with grilled chicken parts (see page 264), we recommend brining a whole chicken before grill-roasting if you have the time.

One final note: we found that birds cooked over charcoal absorb more smoke flavor but were also slightly drier. (Brining birds destined for charcoal grills mitigates this problem.) Birds cooked over gas were slightly moister but also don't absorb as much smoke.

Grill-Roasted Chicken

SERVES 4

Although brining is not essential, it is recommended, especially when cooking over charcoal. Mix 4 quarts water with 1 cup kosher salt or ½ cup table salt and refrigerate the bird, breast side down, in this mixture for 6 to 8 hours. Remove the chicken from the brine and rinse inside and out under cool running water for several minutes until all traces of salt are gone. Pat chicken dry, inside and out, with paper towels. If brining, omit the salt in step 2 below.

2   3-inch wood chunks or 2 cups wood chips and heavy-duty aluminum foil

I   whole chicken (about 3½ pounds), giblets discarded, chicken rinsed and patted dry with paper towels

2   tablespoons unsalted butter, melted
    Salt and ground black pepper

1. Soak wood chunks in cold water to cover for 1 hour and drain, or place wood chips on 18-inch square of aluminum foil, seal to make packet, and use fork to create about six holes to allow smoke to escape (see illustrations on page 271).

2. Brush chicken, including cavity, with butter, and sprinkle with salt and pepper to taste.

3. Meanwhile, fill chimney with charcoal briquettes and light. Transfer coals from chimney to one side of kettle grill, piling them up in a mound three briquettes high. Keep bottom vents halfway open. When coals are covered with light gray ash, lay wood chunks or packet with chips on top of charcoal. Put cooking grate in place, open grill lid vents halfway and cover, turning lid so that vents are opposite wood chunks or chips to draw smoke through grill. Let grate heat for 5 minutes, clean with wire brush, and position chicken, breast side down, on grate opposite fire. (Initial temperature will be about 375 degrees.) Grill-roast chicken, covered, for about 30 minutes.

4. Using heavy-duty tongs, remove chicken from grill and place it in large roasting pan. Working as

quickly as possible, remove grill rack, push foil packet aside (if using), add 12 more briquettes, stir them into pile, return foil packet (if using), and place grill rack back in position. Return chicken to grill, breast side up, so the side of chicken that was facing away from fire is now facing coals. Quickly replace lid and continue grill-roasting until instant-read thermometer inserted into thigh and breast registers between 165 and 170 degrees, 30 to 40 minutes longer, depending on grill temperature. Remove chicken from grill, let rest for 10 minutes, carve, and serve.

➤ VARIATIONS

Grill-Roasted Chicken on a Gas Grill

Follow recipe for Grill-Roasted Chicken, making the following changes: Soak wood chips in cold water for 15 minutes. Place foil tray with soaked wood chips (see illustrations on page 271) on top of primary burner (see illustration on page 268). Turn all burners to high and preheat with lid down until chips are smoking heavily, about 20 minutes. Leave primary burner on high and turn off other burner. (If using grill with three burners, turn off middle burner and turn others to medium.) Position chicken, breast side down, over cool part of grill. Grill-roast, turning as directed, for 50 to 60 minutes. (Temperature inside grill should be 350 to 375 degrees; adjust lit burner(s) as necessary.)

Grill-Roasted Chicken with Barbecue Sauce

Follow recipe for Grill-Roasted Chicken or gas grill variation, brushing chicken with ¼ cup Barbecue Sauce (page 272) during last 10 minutes of cooking. Continue as directed, watching grill carefully to make sure sauce does not burn.

Grill-Roasted Chicken with Spice Rub

Follow recipe for Grill-Roasted Chicken or gas grill variation, omitting butter and coating skin with ¼ cup of either spice rub on page 272. Sprinkle with salt to taste and grill-roast as directed.

SMOKE

One of the best reasons to barbecue or grill-roast is to flavor foods with smoke. Charcoal itself has some flavor (gas adds none), but the real smoky flavor of good ribs or brisket comes from wood chunks or chips. Chips will work on either a charcoal or gas grill, but chunks are suited to charcoal fires only, since they must rest in a pile of lit coals to work. (If placed on the bottom of a gas grill they will not get hot enough to smoke.)

Hickory is the most traditional wood used for outdoor cooking, but there are other choices. In our tests, we found that any hardwood chunks or chips can be used. Frankly, the differences in flavor are minimal, especially if the food has been coated with spices. We have noted traditional pairings (such as ribs and hickory or salmon and alder) throughout the book, but feel free to use whatever wood is available.

Wood chunks are the easiest way to add smoke flavor when cooking over charcoal.

Ideally, the chunks should smolder slowly, releasing smoke for as long as possible. We found that soaking chunks adds enough moisture to the wood to prevent it from catching fire as soon as it is placed on the charcoal. Soak as many three-inch chunks as directed in each recipe in cold water to cover for one hour. Drain the chunks and place them directly on the lit pile of charcoal.

If you can't find wood chunks, small wood chips may be used. To keep the chips from burning up too quickly, we found it best to wrap them in a foil packet. (There's no need to soak these chips; the foil protects them from catching fire too quickly.) We tried soaking the chips and throwing them directly onto the coals, but they caught fire immediately.

If using wood chips, follow the illustrations on page 271 to wrap chips in heavy-duty aluminum foil. Note that regular foil does not offer enough protection and the chips can catch fire rather than smoke.

Chips are the only choice for gas grills. We prefer to place the chips in an open foil tray. (See the illustrations on page 271 for information on constructing a foil tray.) The tray (which can be made from heavy-duty aluminum foil) shields the chips from direct contact with the burner but is open on top to allow the smoke to flow freely. The tray also allows you to spread out the chips so that they are not piled on top of each other, as they are inside a smaller foil packet. More chips can also be added to the tray throughout the cooking process. When we placed unsoaked chips in the tray they caught fire immediately. Soaking the chips for 15 minutes prevents them from igniting and allows them to smolder slowly and produce a lot of smoke.

BARBECUE RUBS AND SAUCES

SPICE RUBS AND BARBECUE SAUCES ADD flavor to barbecued and grill-roasted foods. Rubs and sauces each have a different function and are used at different times in the cooking process.

Rubbed onto the outside of foods, spice blends encourage the formation of a deeply browned crust filled with complex, concentrated flavors. Like marinades, spice rubs add flavor to foods, but they have several advantages over their wet counterparts.

Since they are composed almost solely of spices, they provide stronger flavors than marinades, which typically contain oil, an acidic liquid, and spices. Rubs also stick better to the surface of foods than marinades, which, again, gives them an edge when it comes to intensifying flavor. Finally, marinades almost always contain oil and cause flare-ups on the grill. Spice rubs are ideal for foods that will be barbecued or grill-roasted since they can be left on foods for many hours without causing fires.

Spice rubs can be used with virtually any type of food, and in general you can mix and match rubs and foods with abandon. However, there are a couple of guidelines to follow. You might consider matching the strength of the rub with the strength of the food being rubbed. For example, earthier spices are better with meat, lighter spices with fish and chicken. Also keep in mind that spices like cumin and paprika are good "bulk" spices, while aromatic spices like cinnamon and cloves should be used lightly.

USING WOOD CHIPS ON A CHARCOAL GRILL

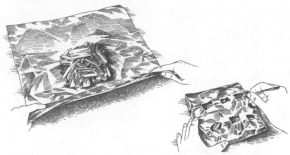

1. Place the amount of wood chips called for in the recipe in the center of an 18-inch square of heavy-duty aluminum foil. Fold in all four sides of foil to encase the chips.

2. Turn the foil packet over. Tear six large holes (each the size of a quarter) through the the foil packet with a fork to allow smoke to escape. Place the packet, with holes facing up, directly on a pile of lit charcoal.

We find that bare hands—not brushes—are the best tools for applying spice rubs. Use a bit of pressure to make sure the spices actually adhere to the food. Although rubs can be applied right before cooking, we found that the flavor of the spices penetrates deeper into the food if given some time. In general, we like to refrigerate rubbed meats for a few hours to allow the flavors to develop.

Barbecue sauce is best added to grilled foods at the table. When we added the sauce earlier, we found that the sugars and fat in most sauces caused foods to burn. You can brush barbecue sauce on some foods during the final minutes of grill-roasting, if you like.

USING WOOD CHIPS ON A GAS GRILL

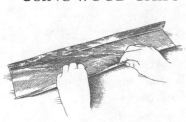   

1. Start with a 12 x 18-inch piece of heavy-duty foil. Make a 1-inch fold on one long side. Repeat three more times and turn the fold up to create a sturdy side. Repeat on the other long side.

2. With a short side facing you, fold in both corners as if wrapping a gift.

3. Turn up the inside inch or so of each triangular fold to match the rim on the long sides of the foil tray.

4. Lift the pointed end of the triangle over the rim of foil and fold down to seal. Repeat the process on the other short side. Place soaked wood chips in tray.

For instance, you may want to glaze a chicken with sauce, applying it during the last 10 minutes of grill time to set the sauce as a light crust.

Barbecue Sauce
MAKES ABOUT 3 CUPS

Barbecue sauce should be brushed on foods at the very end of the grilling time or used as dipping sauce at the table.

2	tablespoons vegetable oil
1	medium onion, minced
1	cup tomato sauce
1	28-ounce can whole tomatoes with their juice
¾	cup distilled white vinegar
¼	cup packed dark brown sugar
2	tablespoons molasses
1	tablespoon sweet paprika
1	tablespoon chili powder
2	teaspoons liquid smoke (optional)
1	teaspoon salt
2	teaspoons ground black pepper
¼	cup orange juice

1. Heat oil in large, heavy-bottomed saucepan over medium heat. Add onion and sauté until golden brown, 7 to 10 minutes. Add remaining ingredients. Bring to boil, reduce heat to lowest possible setting, and simmer, uncovered, until thickened, 2 to 2½ hours. Cool slightly.

2. Puree sauce, in batches if necessary, in blender or workbowl of food processor. (Sauce can be refrigerated in airtight container for up to 2 weeks.)

> VARIATIONS

Barbecue Sauce with Mexican Flavors
This sauce is good with beef or chicken.

Follow recipe for Barbecue Sauce, adding 1½ teaspoons ground cumin, 1½ teaspoons chili powder, 6 tablespoons lime juice, and 3 tablespoons chopped fresh cilantro leaves to completed and cooled sauce.

Barbecue Sauce with Asian Flavors
This variation is especially good with chicken or pork.

Follow recipe for Barbecue Sauce, adding 1 tablespoon minced fresh gingerroot, 6 tablespoons soy sauce, 6 tablespoons rice wine vinegar, 3 tablespoons sugar, and 1½ tablespoons Asian sesame oil to completed and cooled sauce.

Dry Rub for Barbecue
MAKES ABOUT 1 CUP

This rub works well with ribs or brisket and with Boston butt if you want to make pulled pork.

4	tablespoons sweet paprika
2	tablespoons chili powder
2	tablespoons ground cumin
2	tablespoons dark brown sugar
2	tablespoons salt
1	tablespoon dried oregano
1	tablespoon granulated sugar
1	tablespoon ground black pepper
1	tablespoon ground white pepper
1–2	teaspoons cayenne pepper

Mix all ingredients in small bowl. (Can be stored in airtight container for several weeks.)

Dry Rubs for Poultry
MAKES ABOUT ½ CUP

These rubs are not as potent as the Dry Rub for Barbecue, making them well suited to the mild flavor of poultry.

INDIAN SPICE RUB

3	tablespoons curry powder
3	tablespoons chili powder
1½	tablespoons ground allspice
1½	teaspoons ground cinnamon

AROMATIC RUB

1½	tablespoons ground cardamom
1½	tablespoons ground ginger
1½	tablespoons ground black pepper
1	tablespoon ground turmeric
1	tablespoon ground cumin
1	tablespoon ground coriander
1½	teaspoons ground allspice
½	teaspoon ground cloves

Mix ingredients in small bowl. (Can be stored in airtight container for several weeks.)

11

STEWS

WHEN SUCCESSFUL, STEW IS ONE OF THOSE dishes that is more than the sum of its parts. Slow, long cooking transforms proteins, vegetables, and liquids into a hearty dish that is satisfying and intensely flavored.

So what exactly is stew and how does it differ from soup? There is some disagreement in the food world, but for our purposes a stew consists of small chunks of meat, chicken, seafood, and/or vegetables cooked in liquid, which is usually thickened and served as a sauce. A stew is a one-dish meal that can be eaten with a fork and without a knife.

Soup may contain the same ingredients (small bits of protein and vegetables in a liquid base), but it contains much more liquid than a stew, and the liquid is generally not thickened. Soup is eaten with a spoon.

At the opposite end of the spectrum, a braise usually contains less liquid than a stew, and the protein and vegetables are cut into much larger pieces or even left whole, as in a pot roast. The meat in a braise often contains bones (stews are usually boneless), and the vegetables are there more for flavoring the meat and juices than for eating. Finally, a braise is eaten with a fork but usually requires a knife as well.

INGREDIENTS: Wine

We found in our testing that the quality of the wine used in a stew matters. "Cooking wine"—the dreadful, usually oxidized stuff sold in supermarkets—does not cut it when it comes to a stew that relies on wine for much of its flavor. However, there is no reason to overcompensate. Pouring a $30 bottle of good burgundy into the pot is not advisable either. We have found that as long as the wine tastes good enough to drink, it will make delicious stew. Therefore, we recommend inexpensive, young wines in the $7 to $9 range when making stew. In general, fruity reds such as Chianti, zinfandel, young cabernets from California, and many of the hearty wines from southern France are best in stew. As for white wines, avoid wines that are very dry or heavily oaked. A crisp, fruity Sauvignon Blanc, Pinot Blanc, or a young Chardonnay is ideal.

MEAT STEW

MEAT STEWS, MADE WITH BEEF, LAMB, OR pork, should be rich and satisfying. Our goal in developing a master recipe was to keep the cooking process simple without compromising the stew's deep, complex flavor. We focused on the following issues: What cut or cuts of meat respond best to stewing? Is it the same cut from different animals? How much and what kind of liquid should you use? When and with what do you thicken the stew? And where should the stew be cooked, in the oven or on top of the stove, or does it matter? We decided to start our tests with beef and then see if our findings held true for lamb and pork.

At the outset, we made several decisions. We tried several recipes with homemade meat stock. They were delicious but require much more effort than stews made with canned broth or other liquids. At the other extreme, we rejected recipes that call for dumping meat, vegetables, and liquid into a pot to simmer for a couple of hours. Browning the meat and some of the vegetables, especially onions, adds flavor, and this step is too important to skip.

So how does browning work? The sugars in the vegetables (and meat and chicken) caramelize during browning. Deglazing the pan with wine or stock loosens flavorful browned bits from the bottom of the pan, which in turn dissolve and flavor the stew liquid.

We discovered that, contrary to popular belief, browning does not seal in juices in stew meat. As the internal temperature of the meat rises, more and more juices are expelled. By the time the meat is fork-tender, it has shed most of its juices. As odd as it sounds, this is the beauty of a stew or braise, since the surrounding liquid, which will be served as a sauce, is enriched by these juices.

Stew meat remains edible because slow cooking turns the collagen and connective tissue found in tough cuts of meat, such as the shoulder, into gelatin. This gelatin makes meat tender; it also helps thicken the stew liquid.

Experts tout different cuts as being ideal for stewing. We browned 12 different cuts of beef, marked them for identification, and stewed them in the same pot. Chuck proved to be the most flavorful, tender, and juicy. Most other cuts were either too stringy, too chewy, too dry, or just plain bland. The exception was rib eye steak, which made good stew meat but is too expensive a cut to use for this purpose.

Our advice is to buy a steak or roast from the chuck and cube it yourself instead of buying precut stewing beef. The reason is simple: Prepackaged stewing beef is often made up of irregularly shaped end pieces from different muscles that cannot be sold retail as steaks or roasts because of their uneven appearance. Because of the differences in origin, pre-cut stewing cubes in the same package may have inconsistent cooking, flavor, and tenderness qualities. If you cut your own cubes from a piece of chuck, you are assured that all the cubes will cook in the same way and have the flavor and richness of chuck.

So why does chuck make the best stew? The intramuscular fat and connective tissue in chuck is well suited to long, slow, moist cooking. When cooked in liquid, the connective tissue melts down into gelatin, making the meat tender. The fat in the meat helps, too, in two important ways. Fat carries the chemical compounds that our taste buds receive as beef flavor, and it also melts when cooked, lubricating the meat fibers as it slips between the cells, increasing tenderness.

Having settled on our cut of beef, we started to explore how and when to thicken the stew. Dredging meat cubes in flour is a roundabout way of thickening stew. The floured beef is browned, then stewed. During the stewing process, some of the flour from the beef dissolves into the liquid, causing it to thicken. Although the stew we cooked this way thickened up nicely, the beef cubes had a "smothered steak" look.

We also tried two thickening methods at the end of cooking—a beurre manié (softened butter mixed with flour) and cornstarch mixed with water. Either method is acceptable, but the beurre manié lightened the stew's color, making it look more like pale gravy than rich stew juices. Also, the extra fat did not improve the stew's flavor enough to justify its addition. For those who prefer thickening at the end of cooking, we found that cornstarch dissolved in water did the job without compromising the stew's dark, rich color.

Ultimately, though, we opted for thickening the

EQUIPMENT: Dutch Oven

We find that a Dutch oven (also called a lidded casserole) is almost essential to making a stew. You can try to use a large pasta pot or soup kettle. However, these pots are probably too narrow and too tall. Also, many are quite light, thin, and cheap—designed to heat up water quickly but not meant for browning. Since most stew recipes begin by browning to develop flavor, it's imperative to use a pot with a heavy bottom.

A Dutch oven is nothing more than a wide, deep pot with a cover. It was originally manufactured with "ears" on the side (small, round tabs used to pick up the pot) and a top that had a lip around the edge. The latter design element was important because a Dutch oven was heated through coals placed both underneath and on top of the pot. The lip kept the coals on the lid from falling off. One could bake biscuits, cobblers, beans, and stews in this pot. It was, in the full sense of the word, an oven. And this "oven" was a key feature of chuck wagons and essential in many American households, where all cooking occurred in the fireplace. As for the "Dutch" in the name, it seems that the best cast iron used to come from Holland; the pots made in this style were therefore referred to as Dutch ovens.

Now that everyone in America has an oven, the Dutch oven is no longer used to bake biscuits or cobblers. However, it is essential for dishes that start on top of the stove and finish in the oven, like stew. To make some recommendations about buying a modern Dutch oven, we tested 12 models made by leading cookware companies.

In our testing, we found that a Dutch oven should have a capacity of at least six quarts to be useful. Eight quarts is even better. As we cooked in the pots, we came to prefer wider and shallower Dutch ovens because it's easier to see and reach inside them, and they offer more bottom surface to accommodate larger batches of meat for browning. This reduces the number of batches required to brown a given quantity of meat, and, with it, the chances of burning the flavorful pan drippings. Ideally, a Dutch oven should have a diameter twice as wide as its height.

We also preferred pots with a light-colored interior finish, such as stainless steel or enameled cast iron. It is easier to judge the caramelization of the drippings at a glance in these pots. Dark finishes can mask the color of the drippings, which may burn before you realize it. Our favorite pot is the eight-quart All-Clad Stainless Stockpot (despite the name, this pot is a Dutch oven). The seven-quart Le Creuset Round French Oven, which is made of enameled cast iron, also tested well. These pots are quite expensive, costing at least $150, even when on sale. A less expensive alternative is the seven-quart Lodge Dutch Oven, which is made from cast iron. Although it is extremely heavy (making it a bit hard to maneuver), it must be seasoned regularly, and the dark interior finish is not ideal, this pot browns quite well and costs just $45.

stew with flour at the beginning—stirring it into the sautéing onions and garlic, right before adding the liquid. Stew thickened this way was not any better, but it was easier. There's no last-minute work; once the liquid starts to simmer, the cook is free to do something else.

We next focused on stewing liquids. We tried water, wine, low-sodium canned beef broth, low-sodium chicken broth, as well as combinations of these liquids. Stews made with water were bland and greasy. Stews made with all wine were too strong. All stock was good, but we missed the acidity and flavor provided by the wine. In the end, we preferred a combination of chicken stock and red wine.

We prefer to add the vegetables partway through the cooking process. They don't fall apart this way, but they still have enough time to meld with the other stew ingredients. There is one exception to this rule. Peas should be added just before serving the stew to preserve their fresh color and texture.

In our testing, we found the temperature of the stewing liquid to be crucial. We found it is essential to keep the temperature of the liquid below 212 degrees. Boiled meat stays tough, and the outside becomes especially dry. Keeping the liquid at a simmer (rather than a boil) allows the internal temperature of the meat to rise slowly. By the time it is actually fork-tender, much of the collagen will have turned to gelatin.

We have found that putting a covered Dutch oven in a 250-degree oven ensures that the temperature of the stewing liquid will remain below the boiling point, at about 200 degrees. (Ovens are not totally effective at transferring heat; a temperature of 250 degrees recognizes that some heat will be lost as it penetrates through the pot and into the stew.)

Now that we had developed a stew recipe using beef chuck, we wondered if the same technique and ingredients would work with other meats. We tested various cuts of pork and lamb and found that shoulder cuts respond best to stewing. Like chuck, these cuts have enough fat to keep the meat tender during the long cooking process.

Pork shoulder is often called Boston butt or Boston shoulder in markets. We generally bought a boneless Boston butt or pork shoulder roast and cut it into cubes ourselves. A lamb shoulder roast can be hard to find. We often bought inexpensive bone-in lamb shoulder chops and cut the meat off the bone and into chunks.

For the most part, the beef recipe worked fine with these cuts of pork and lamb. However, lamb tends to cook a bit more quickly. Beef and pork require a total cooking time of 2½ to 3 hours. Lamb needs just 2 to 2½ hours to soften up. All times will vary depending on the addition of slow-cooking vegetables, such as potatoes and carrots, as the meat cooks.

Master Recipe for Meat Stew
SERVES 6 TO 8

Make this stew in a large, ovenproof Dutch oven, preferably a pot with a capacity of 8 quarts but nothing less than 6 quarts. In either case, choose a Dutch oven with a wide bottom; this will allow you to brown the meat in two batches.

3	pounds beef chuck, lamb shoulder, or pork shoulder, trimmed and cut into 1½-inch cubes
1½	teaspoons salt
1	teaspoon ground black pepper
3	tablespoons vegetable oil
2	medium-large onions, chopped coarse (about 2 cups)
3	medium garlic cloves, minced
3	tablespoons flour
1	cup full-bodied red wine
2	cups chicken stock or low-sodium canned chicken broth
2	bay leaves
1	teaspoon dried thyme
4	medium boiling potatoes, cut into 1-inch cubes
4	large carrots, peeled and sliced ¼-inch thick
1	cup frozen peas (about 6 ounces), thawed
¼	cup minced fresh parsley leaves

1. Heat oven to 250 degrees. Place beef cubes in large bowl. Sprinkle with salt and pepper; toss to coat. Heat 2 tablespoons oil over medium-high heat in large ovenproof Dutch oven. Add half of meat and brown on all sides, about 5 minutes. Remove meat and set aside on plate. Repeat process with remaining oil and meat.

2. Add onions to empty Dutch oven and sauté

until softened, 4 to 5 minutes. Add garlic and continue to cook for 30 seconds. Stir in flour and cook until lightly colored, 1 to 2 minutes. Add wine, scraping up any browned bits that may have stuck to pot. Add stock, bay leaves, and thyme, and bring to a simmer. Add meat and return to a simmer. Cover and place pot in oven. Cook for 1 hour.

3. Remove pot from oven and add potatoes and carrots. Cover and return to oven. Cook just until meat is tender, 1 to 1½ hours for lamb and 1½ to 2 hours for beef and pork. Remove pot from oven. (Can be cooled, covered, and refrigerated up to 3 days. Reheat on top of the stove.)

4. Add peas, cover, and allow to stand for 5 minutes. Stir in parsley, discard bay leaves, adjust seasonings, and serve.

INGREDIENTS: Canned Broth

Homemade stock makes delicious stews. However, we find that canned products will work quite well, and they greatly simplify the process. There is no reason not to use homemade stock if you have some on hand, but beef, lamb, and pork stews will taste just fine if made with canned broth.

You might think that meat stews, especially those with beef, would taste better when made with canned beef broth. However, canned beef broths simply do not deliver full-bodied, beefy flavor. We tested 11 commercial beef broths and bouillon cubes. Some had a subtle suggestion of beef, but most begged the question, "Where's the beef?"

Current government regulations require that beef broth need only contain 1 part protein to 135 parts moisture. That translates into less than an ounce of meat to flavor a gallon of water. Most manufacturers use salt, monosodium glutamate (MSG), and yeast-based hydrolyzed soy protein to give this watery concoction some flavor and mouthfeel. Does any canned beef broth or powdered beef bouillon cube taste like the real thing? Our panel shouted a resounding no.

By comparison, canned chicken broths are far superior. While they rarely taste like homemade stock, several of the 11 brands that we tested had some decent chicken flavor. In stews, even those made with beef, we have found that canned chicken broth is superior to canned beef broth. So which canned broths do we recommend? In our tasting, reduced- and low-sodium broths made by Campbell's and Swanson (both brands are owned by the same company) topped the list.

➤ VARIATIONS

Beef Stew with Bacon, Mushrooms, and Pearl Onions

This hearty stew is our version of boeuf bourguignonne. It calls for equal amounts of red wine and chicken stock. This stew is delicious over mashed potatoes.

3	pounds beef chuck, trimmed and cut into 1½-inch cubes
1½	teaspoons salt
1	teaspoon ground black pepper
4	ounces sliced bacon, cut into ½-inch pieces
1	tablespoon vegetable oil
2	medium-large onions, chopped coarse (about 2 cups)
3	medium garlic cloves, minced
3	tablespoons flour
1½	cups full-bodied red wine
1½	cups chicken stock or low-sodium canned chicken broth
2	bay leaves
1	teaspoon dried thyme
1	pound white button mushrooms, quartered
1	cup frozen pearl onions, cooked according to package directions
¼	cup minced fresh parsley leaves

1. Heat oven to 250 degrees. Place beef cubes in large bowl. Sprinkle with salt and pepper; toss to coat. Fry bacon in large ovenproof Dutch oven over medium heat until golden brown, about 7 minutes. Drain bacon, reserving bits and drippings separately. Increase heat to medium-high and heat 2 tablespoons bacon drippings in Dutch oven. Add half of meat and brown on all sides, about 5 minutes. Remove meat and set aside on plate. Repeat process with another tablespoon of bacon drippings and remaining meat.

2. Add onions to empty Dutch oven and sauté until softened, 4 to 5 minutes. Add garlic and continue to cook for 30 seconds. Stir in flour and cook until lightly colored, 1 to 2 minutes. Add wine, scraping up any browned bits that may have stuck to pot. Add stock, bay leaves, and thyme, and bring to a simmer. Add meat and bacon bits and return to a simmer. Cover and place pot in oven. Cook until meat is almost tender, 2 to 2½ hours.

3. Meanwhile, heat 2 tablespoons bacon drippings

in large skillet. Add mushrooms and sauté over high heat until browned, 5 to 7 minutes. Transfer mushrooms to large bowl. Add cooked pearl onions and sauté until lightly browned, 2 to 3 minutes. Add onions to bowl with mushrooms.

4. Add mushrooms and onions to stew when meat is almost tender. Cover and return pot to oven. Cook until meat is completely tender, 20 to 30 minutes. (Can be cooled, covered, and refrigerated up to 3 days. Reheat on top of the stove.)

5. Stir in parsley, discard bay leaves, adjust seasonings, and serve.

Beef Goulash

The sour cream is optional but adds a nice color and richness to this stew. Serve over egg noodles.

3	pounds beef chuck, trimmed and cut into 1½-inch cubes
1½	teaspoons salt
1	teaspoon ground black pepper
4	ounces sliced bacon, cut into ½-inch pieces
2	medium-large onions, chopped coarse (about 2 cups)
1	medium red bell pepper, stemmed, seeded, and chopped
6	medium garlic cloves, minced
2	tablespoons sweet paprika
3	tablespoons flour
1	cup white wine
2	cups chicken stock or low-sodium canned broth
2	bay leaves
1	teaspoon dried thyme
4	large carrots, peeled and sliced ¼-inch thick
¼	cup minced fresh parsley leaves
½	cup sour cream

1. Heat oven to 250 degrees. Place beef cubes in large bowl. Sprinkle with salt and pepper; toss to coat. Fry bacon in large ovenproof Dutch oven over medium heat until golden brown, about 7 minutes. Drain bacon, reserving bits and drippings separately. Increase heat to medium-high and heat 2 tablespoons bacon drippings in Dutch oven. Add half of meat and brown on all sides, about 5 minutes. Remove meat and set aside on plate. Repeat process with another tablespoon of bacon drippings and remaining meat.

2. Add onions and red bell pepper to empty Dutch oven and sauté until softened, 4 to 5 minutes. Add garlic and continue to cook for 30 seconds. Stir in paprika and flour and cook until lightly colored, 1 to 2 minutes. Add wine, scraping up any browned bits that may have stuck to pot. Add stock, bay leaves, and thyme, and bring to a simmer. Add meat and bacon bits and return to a simmer. Cover and place pot in oven. Cook for 1 hour.

3. Remove pot from oven and add carrots. Cover and return pot to oven. Cook just until meat is tender, 1½ to 2 hours. Remove pot from oven. (Can be cooled, covered, and refrigerated up to 3 days. Reheat on top of the stove.)

4. Stir in parsley and sour cream, discard bay leaves, adjust seasonings, and serve. (Once sour cream has been added, do not let stew simmer or boil or sour cream will curdle.)

Lamb Stew with Tomatoes, Chickpeas, and Spices

This North African stew uses canned tomatoes in place of wine. Because no vegetables are added partway through the cooking, the stewing time is just 2 hours. Serve over couscous.

3	pounds lamb shoulder, trimmed and cut into 1½-inch cubes
1½	teaspoons salt
1	teaspoon ground black pepper
3	tablespoons vegetable oil
2	medium-large onions, chopped coarse (about 2 cups)
4	medium garlic cloves, minced
3	tablespoons flour
1½	cups chicken stock or low-sodium canned broth
1½	cups chopped canned tomatoes with their juice
2	bay leaves
1½	teaspoons ground coriander
1	teaspoon ground cumin
¾	teaspoon ground cinnamon
½	teaspoon ground ginger
1	15-ounce can chickpeas, drained and rinsed
¼	cup minced fresh parsley or cilantro leaves

1. Heat oven to 250 degrees. Place lamb cubes in large bowl. Sprinkle with salt and pepper; toss to coat. Heat 2 tablespoons oil over medium-high heat

in large ovenproof Dutch oven. Add half of lamb and brown on all sides, about 5 minutes. Remove meat and set aside on plate. Repeat process with remaining oil and lamb.

2. Add onions to empty Dutch oven and sauté until softened, 4 to 5 minutes. Add garlic and continue to cook for 30 seconds. Stir in flour and cook until lightly colored, 1 to 2 minutes. Add stock, scraping up any browned bits that may have stuck to pot. Add tomatoes, bay leaves, coriander, cumin, cinnamon, and ginger, and bring to a simmer. Add meat and return to a simmer. Cover and place pot in oven. Cook until meat is almost tender, 1¾ to 2¼ hours.

3. Remove pot from oven and add chickpeas. Cover and return pot to oven. Cook until meat is tender and chickpeas are heated through, about 15 minutes. Remove pot from oven. (Can be cooled, covered, and refrigerated up to 3 days. Reheat on top of the stove.)

4. Stir in parsley, discard bay leaves, adjust seasonings, and serve.

Lamb Stew with Rosemary and White Beans

In this Italian stew, cannellini or other white beans take the place of potatoes. Since this dish contains beans, it can be served as is or perhaps with some bread, but it does not require any other starch.

3	pounds lamb shoulder, trimmed and cut into 1½-inch cubes
1½	teaspoons salt
1	teaspoon ground black pepper
3	tablespoons vegetable oil
2	medium-large onions, chopped coarse (about 2 cups)
3	medium garlic cloves, minced
3	tablespoons flour
1	cup white wine
2	cups chicken stock or low-sodium canned chicken broth
2	bay leaves
1	tablespoon minced fresh rosemary
3	large carrots, peeled and cut into ⅜-inch dice
1	15-ounce can white beans, drained and rinsed
¼	cup minced fresh parsley leaves

1. Heat oven to 250 degrees. Place lamb cubes in large bowl. Sprinkle with salt and pepper; toss to coat. Heat 2 tablespoons oil over medium-high heat in large ovenproof Dutch oven. Add half of lamb and brown on all sides, about 5 minutes. Remove meat and set aside on plate. Repeat process with remaining oil and lamb.

2. Add onions to empty Dutch oven and sauté until softened, 4 to 5 minutes. Add garlic and continue to cook for 30 seconds. Stir in flour and cook until lightly colored, 1 to 2 minutes. Add wine, scraping up any browned bits that may have stuck to pot. Add stock, bay leaves, and rosemary, and bring to a simmer. Add meat and return to a simmer. Cover and place pot in oven. Cook for 1 hour.

3. Remove pot from oven and add carrots. Cover and return to oven. Cook just until meat is almost tender, 1 to 1¼ hours. Remove pot from oven and add white beans. Cover and return to oven and cook until meat is tender and beans are heated through, about 15 minutes. Remove pot from oven. (Can be cooled, covered, and refrigerated up to 3 days. Reheat on top of the stove.)

4. Stir in parsley, discard bay leaves, adjust seasonings, and serve.

Pork Stew with Prunes, Mustard, and Cream

This French stew features prunes soaked in brandy. The liquid is enriched with cream. If you like, use Armagnac in place of the brandy. Ladle this stew over buttered noodles.

6	ounces dried prunes, halved and soaked in ⅓ cup brandy until softened, about 20 minutes
3	pounds pork shoulder, trimmed and cut into 1½-inch cubes
1½	teaspoons salt
1	teaspoon ground black pepper
3	tablespoons vegetable oil
2	medium-large onions, chopped coarse (about 2 cups)
3	medium garlic cloves, minced
3	tablespoons flour
1	cup white wine
2	cups chicken stock or low-sodium canned chicken broth
2	bay leaves

1	teaspoon dried thyme
½	cup heavy cream
3	tablespoons Dijon mustard
¼	cup minced fresh parsley leaves

1. Heat oven to 250 degrees. Place pork cubes in large bowl. Sprinkle with salt and pepper; toss to coat. Heat 2 tablespoons oil over medium-high heat in large ovenproof Dutch oven. Add half of pork and brown on all sides, about 5 minutes. Remove meat and set aside on plate. Repeat process with remaining oil and pork.

2. Add onions to empty Dutch oven and sauté until softened, 4 to 5 minutes. Add garlic and continue to cook for 30 seconds. Stir in flour and cook until lightly colored, 1 to 2 minutes. Add wine, scraping up any browned bits that may have stuck to pot. Add stock, bay leaves, and thyme, and bring to a simmer. Add meat and return to a simmer. Cover and place pot in oven. Cook for 2 hours.

3. Add prunes, brandy, and cream. Cover and return to oven. Cook just until meat is tender, 30 to 45 minutes. Remove pot from oven. (Can be cooled, covered, and refrigerated up to 3 days. Reheat on top of the stove.)

4. Stir in mustard and parsley, discard bay leaves, adjust seasonings, and serve.

CHICKEN STEW

CHICKEN STEW IS A BIT HARD TO DEFINE. Say beef stew and most everyone can imagine large, boneless chunks of browned beef floating in a rich, dark sauce along with some vegetables. But what exactly is chicken stew? Is it a cut-up chicken that is browned and then braised? Is it a cut-up chicken that is stewed (to make homemade stock) and then cooled in order to tear the meat from the bones? Is it boneless breasts or thighs cut into chunks and browned and stewed like beef?

To get our bearings, we tested a number of possible dishes that might be called chicken stew. We started by preparing a variation of our favorite chicken and dumpling recipe, minus the dumplings. This dish starts with a whole chicken that is cut up, browned, and then simmered in water to make stock. The liquid is strained and the meat is removed from the breasts, legs, and thighs. Like meat stew, this preparation produced a stew without bones, and the homemade stock was a nice bonus. But the dish required a lot of effort (pulling the meat off each piece is very tedious), and the results were good but not great.

Our next thought was to follow our Master Recipe for Meat Stew but use a cut-up chicken (two wings, two thighs, two drumsticks, and two breasts) instead of cubes of boneless beef, lamb, or pork. We encountered several problems with this method. The skin is nice and crisp after browning but becomes flabby and not very appealing after stewing in liquid for the necessary half hour or so. In addition, the wings are very unappetizing—they contain mostly inedible skin and very little meat. You couldn't really ladle out a portion of stew that contained just a wing and some vegetables. Also, the breast pieces were way too large to fit into a bowl (each piece would have to be cut in half crosswise), and they had dried out during the stewing process.

At this point in our testing, we concluded that dark meat pieces, with their extra fat and connective tissue, are better suited to stewing. They have much more flavor, and their texture is more appealing. In addition, our tasters preferred the meatier thighs to the drumsticks, which tend to have more bone. The thighs are also easier to eat than the drumsticks, with the meat easily separating from the bones. We decided to abandon the breasts and drumsticks and concentrate on a stew made with thighs only.

We discovered that removing the skin after the parts were browned was a must. The stew liquid was much less fatty, and, since the skin was very soft and flabby and not really edible, there seemed little reason to serve it to people. We wondered if we should just start with boneless, skinless thighs—it certainly would be easier to eat a stew without bones. Unfortunately, when we browned boneless, skinless thighs, the outer layer of meat became tough and dry. Also, the skinless thighs tended to stick to the pan, even when we added quite a bit of oil. The skin acts as a cushion between the meat and pan. We prefer to use bone-in, skin-on thighs and then strip off the skin after the parts have been browned. If you really object to a stew with bones, use boneless, skinless thighs but note that the meat will be a bit tough around the edges.

In either case, don't skip the browning step. Although it might seem like a lot of work for just one tablespoon of drippings, we found that the rendered chicken fat and browned bits that cling to the bottom of the pot really add flavor to this dish.

We had decided on the style of chicken stew and for the most part liked the Master Recipe for Meat Stew adapted to chicken thighs. But we found that we could not simply take the meat stew recipe wholesale and just add chicken instead of beef, lamb, or pork.

First of all, meat stews often taste best with red wine, while chicken generally matches up better with white wine. Also, because chicken requires less cooking time, we found a stew made with one cup of wine and two cups of stock (as suggested in our meat stew recipes) too alcoholic. Cutting the wine back to half a cup and increasing the stock by a half a cup keeps the stew from being too boozy. We also found that chicken's milder flavor calls for less aggressive seasoning.

Finally, we wondered if chicken stew was best simmered in the oven, like meat stew, or if it could stay on top of the stove. Like meat stew, we found that chicken stew responds best to subsimmer temperatures, which are easier to maintain in a low oven. However, when we put the chicken in a 250-degree oven it took almost the entire cooking time for the liquid to come up to temperature. We tried raising the oven temperature to 300 degrees and found that the stew was ready 25 minutes after the chicken is added back to the liquid. Although this higher temperature would eventually cause the stew temperature to rise to the boiling point, we found that the temperature was just about 200 degrees when the chicken was done.

Because chicken requires so much less cooking time than meat, vegetables are added before the chicken, not after. For instance, the carrots and potatoes get a 10 minute start on the chicken to make sure they will be tender by the time the chicken is cooked through.

Master Recipe for Chicken Stew

SERVES 6 TO 8

We recommend using regular chicken thighs in this recipe. As a second option, you may use boneless, skinless chicken thighs, although the outer layer of meat will toughen during the cooking process. If using boneless, skinless thighs, add a few more tablespoons of vegetable oil during the sauté process to keep them from sticking to the pan. You may need to use a metal spatula to loosen browned skinless thighs from the pan.

8	bone-in, skin-on chicken thighs (about 3 pounds)
½	teaspoon salt
¼	teaspoon ground black pepper
2	tablespoons vegetable oil
I	large onion, chopped coarse
2	medium garlic cloves, minced
3	tablespoons flour
½	cup white wine
2½	cups chicken stock or low-sodium canned chicken broth
I	bay leaf
½	teaspoon dried thyme
4	large carrots, peeled and sliced ¼-inch thick
4	medium boiling potatoes, cut into ½-inch cubes
I	cup frozen peas (about 6 ounces), thawed
¼	cup minced fresh parsley leaves

1. Heat oven to 300 degrees. Sprinkle chicken with salt and pepper. Heat oil over medium-high heat in large ovenproof Dutch oven. Add half of chicken, skin side down, and brown, about 4 minutes. Turn chicken and brown on other side, about 4 minutes. Remove chicken and set aside on plate. Repeat process with remaining chicken. Drain and discard all but 1 tablespoon fat from pot. When chicken has cooled, remove and discard skin.

2. Add onion to empty Dutch oven and sauté until softened, 4 to 5 minutes. Add garlic and continue to cook for 30 seconds. Stir in flour and cook until lightly colored, 1 to 2 minutes. Add wine, scraping up any browned bits that may have stuck to pot. Add stock, bay leaf, and thyme, and bring to a simmer. Add carrots and potatoes and simmer for 10

minutes. Add chicken, submerging it in liquid, and return to a simmer. Cover and place pot in oven. Cook for 30 minutes. Remove pot from oven. (Can be cooled, covered, and refrigerated up to 3 days. Reheat on top of the stove.)

3. Add peas, cover, and allow to stand for 5 minutes. Stir in parsley, discard bay leaf, adjust seasonings, and serve.

➤ VARIATIONS

Chicken Stew with Peppers, Tomatoes, and Rosemary

This classic Italian stew contains bell peppers, tomatoes, and rosemary. Ladle this stew over a mound of polenta. Serves six to eight.

8	bone-in, skin-on chicken thighs (about 3 pounds)
1/2	teaspoon salt
1/4	teaspoon ground black pepper
2	tablespoons vegetable oil
1	large onion, chopped coarse
2	medium bell peppers (preferably one red, one yellow), stemmed, seeded, and chopped coarse
4	medium garlic cloves, minced
3	tablespoons flour
1 1/2	cups chicken stock or low-sodium canned chicken broth
1 1/2	cups chopped canned tomatoes with their juice
1	bay leaf
2	teaspoons minced fresh rosemary
1/4	cup minced fresh parsley leaves

1. Heat oven to 300 degrees. Sprinkle chicken with salt and pepper. Heat oil over medium-high heat in large ovenproof Dutch oven. Add half of chicken, skin side down, and brown, about 4 minutes. Turn chicken and brown on other side, about 4 minutes. Remove chicken and set aside on plate. Repeat process with remaining chicken. Drain and discard all but 1 tablespoon fat from pot. When chicken has cooled, remove and discard skin.

2. Add onion and bell peppers to empty Dutch oven and sauté until softened, 4 to 5 minutes. Add garlic and continue to cook for 30 seconds. Stir in flour and cook until lightly colored, 1 to 2 minutes. Add stock, scraping up any browned bits that may

have stuck to pot. Add tomatoes, bay leaf, and rosemary, and bring to a simmer. Simmer for 10 minutes to blend flavors. Add chicken, submerging it in liquid, and return to a simmer. Cover and place pot in oven. Cook for 30 minutes. Remove pot from oven. (Can be cooled, covered, and refrigerated up to 3 days. Reheat on top of the stove.)

3. Stir in parsley, discard bay leaf, adjust seasonings, and serve.

Country Captain Chicken Stew

A Southern favorite. We like this curried chicken stew with fresh mangoes rather than the usual mango chutney. Rice is a good accompaniment to this stew.

8	bone-in, skin-on chicken thighs (about 3 pounds)
1/2	teaspoon salt
1/4	teaspoon ground black pepper
2	tablespoons vegetable oil
2	large onions, chopped coarse
1	green bell pepper, stemmed, seeded, and chopped
2	medium garlic cloves, minced
1 1/2	tablespoons sweet paprika
1	tablespoon curry powder
1/4	teaspoon cayenne pepper
3	tablespoons flour
1 1/2	cups chicken stock or low-sodium canned chicken broth
1 1/2	cups chopped canned tomatoes with their juice
1	bay leaf
1/2	teaspoon dried thyme
1/2	cup raisins
1	ripe mango, peeled, pitted, and cut into 1/4-inch dice
1/4	cup minced fresh parsley leaves

1. Heat oven to 300 degrees. Sprinkle chicken with salt and pepper. Heat oil over medium-high heat in large ovenproof Dutch oven. Add half of chicken, skin side down, and brown, about 4 minutes. Turn chicken and brown other side, about 4 minutes. Remove chicken and set aside on plate. Repeat process with remaining chicken. Drain and discard all but 1 tablespoon fat from pot. When chicken has cooled, remove and discard skin.

2. Add onions and bell pepper to empty Dutch

oven and sauté until softened, 4 to 5 minutes. Add garlic and continue to cook for 30 seconds. Stir in paprika, curry powder, and cayenne and cook until spices are fragrant, about 30 seconds. Stir in flour and cook until lightly colored, 1 to 2 minutes. Add stock, scraping up any browned bits that may have stuck to pot. Add tomatoes, bay leaf, thyme, raisins, and mango, and bring to a simmer. Simmer for 10 minutes to blend flavors. Add chicken, submerging it in liquid, and return to a simmer. Cover and place pot in oven. Cook for 30 minutes. Remove pot from oven. (Can be cooled, covered, and refrigerated up to 3 days. Reheat on top of the stove.)

3. Stir in parsley, discard bay leaf, adjust seasonings, and serve.

FISH STEW

FISH STEW CONSISTS OF THREE COMPONENTS— fish stock, a flavor base (usually made with sautéed vegetables, herbs, and other seasonings), and the fish itself. Unlike meat and chicken stews, which develop flavor during a long simmering process, fish stew is cooked quickly. The stock and flavor base are prepared separately and then combined. The fish is then cooked in the flavorful liquid. In fish stew, it is the components of the recipe that build flavor, not the cooking process.

We started our testing by making a favorite fish stew with homemade fish stock, water, chicken stock, and a cheater stock that started with bottled clam juice. The stew made with homemade fish stock was far superior. Unlike meat or chicken stews, where the protein simmers for some time, fish can cook for a only few minutes before it dries out and falls apart. Since the fish does not have time to flavor the stew liquid, the liquid must start out tasting good. Water made a horrible fish stew. Chicken stock tasted too much like chicken. Bottled clam juice, doctored up with some fresh ingredients, is our second choice if making fish stock is impossible.

The prime flavoring element in many fish stews is a seasoned tomato sauce, or base. The base begins with aromatic vegetables (onions, carrots, and celery), which should be sautéed to bring out their full flavor. White wine brings a much-needed acidic edge to the stew. Other ingredients, such as fresh fennel and Pernod for bouillabaisse, are added to give specific stews their character. Whatever the ingredients, the base should be well seasoned; it will be diluted with fish stock, which is cooked without salt.

We tested bases made with fresh and canned tomatoes and found little difference between them, so don't hesitate to use canned tomatoes. Unlike the stock, the base for the stew doesn't improve with longer cooking. After 20 minutes, the tomatoes begin to lose their freshness. After 30 minutes, the tomato base tastes too acidic and all the fresh tomato flavor is gone. Once the tomatoes are added, we recommend simmering the stew base just long enough to thicken the consistency and blend flavors, 15 to 20 minutes.

Once the base is cooked, it's time to add the stock and bring the mixture to a boil. The fish is then added and cooked briefly. In our testing, we found that overcooking the fish is the biggest problem with most fish stews. We found that three- to four-ounce pieces are best for serving (they are neither too large to eat gracefully nor so small that they fall apart in the stew). Pieces of fish this small, however, will cook very quickly. We tried various simmering and boiling regimens. In the end, we found that cooking the fish in simmering broth for 5 minutes, followed by 5 minutes of indirect cooking with the heat turned off and the lid on the pot, works best.

Any white-fleshed fillet can be used in fish stew. In general, we like firmer fillets, such as red snapper or monkfish. Tender fillets, such as flounder or sole, can be used, but you might want to reduce the simmering time by a minute or two to keep these thinner fillets from overcooking.

FISH STOCK

WE TESTED VARIOUS FISH AND PREFERRED THOSE WITH HEADS AND BONES THAT WILL produce a gelatinous stock. Trimmings (heads, tails, and bones) from blackfish, monkfish, red snapper, and sea bass make exceptionally good stock that is rich and gelatinous. These fish are our first choice. Trimmings from cod, flatfish (such as sole and flounder), haddock, rockfish, and skate also make good stock. Avoid oily fish, such as bluefish, mackerel, pompano, salmon, and smelt. If making a seafood stew, you may use an equal amount of lobster, shrimp, or crab shells instead.

Many recipes suggest sweating fish bones and vegetables before adding water. In our tests, we found that this step was unnecessary, and in fact, yielded an inferior stock. We found that simply adding all the ingredients to the pot, including the water, at the same time, produces a cleaner, brighter tasting stock.

Unlike meat or chicken stock, fish stock is rarely simmered for hours. Some sources warn against simmering for longer than 15 or 30 minutes, suggesting that the trimmings will make the stock bitter if cooked too long. We tested various times and found that fish stock tastes best when simmered for a full hour. Since cooking time is still relatively brief, it is wise to cut vegetables quite small so they release their full flavor. Fish bones, heads, and tails should also be chopped into small pieces.

We made fish stock both with and without wine and found that the wine adds a pleasant acidity. Adding a little lemon adds some acidity, but not enough. We found that adding more than a quarter of a lemon will make the stock taste overly lemony.

Fish Stock

MAKES 2 TO 2½ QUARTS

There was a time when fishmongers would gladly give away bones, heads, and tails. But no longer, so call ahead and reserve what you need.

3	pounds fish trimmings, gills discarded, cut into 3-inch pieces
1	medium onion, diced
2	medium carrots, diced
1	large celery stalk, diced
8	fresh parsley stems, chopped
1	cup dry white wine
¼	lemon
10	whole black peppercorns
2	bay leaves
1	dried chile pepper

1. Put all ingredients in 6- to 8-quart pot. Cover with 2¾ quarts cold water. Bring to boil over medium heat; simmer gently for 1 hour, periodically skimming away scum.

2. Strain stock through double thickness of cheesecloth, pressing out as much liquid as possible with back of spoon. (Stock can be cooled and refrigerated for 3 days or frozen for 3 months.)

Cheater Stock

MAKES ABOUT 4½ CUPS

We found that doctored clam juice can be used in a pinch in place of fish stock. Clam juice is very salty, so don't add any salt to the stew until you have tasted it.

1	small onion, minced
1	medium carrot, minced
2	medium celery stalks, minced
8	sprigs fresh parsley
1	cup dry white wine
3	8-ounce bottles clam juice
3	cups water
2	bay leaves
8	whole black peppercorns
½	teaspoon dried thyme
1	tablespoon lemon juice
1	dried chile pepper

Bring all ingredients to boil in medium saucepan. Simmer to blend flavors (no skimming necessary), about 30 minutes. Strain through cheesecloth, pressing on solids with back of spoon to extract as much liquid as possible. (Can be refrigerated for 3 days.)

Cod Stew with Potatoes and Bacon

SERVES 6 TO 8

This simple New England-style fish stew contains just cod, potatoes, onions, and bacon. Other firm, white-fleshed fish fillets can be used, but cod is the most authentic choice. The stew is delicious as is but can be enriched with a little heavy cream just before serving if you like.

4	ounces sliced bacon, cut into ¼-inch pieces
1	medium onion, diced
½	cup dry white wine
2	cups chopped canned tomatoes with their juice
2	large bay leaves
⅛	teaspoon cayenne pepper, or to taste
	Salt and ground black pepper
4½	cups Fish Stock or Cheater Fish Stock (see page 284)
3	medium boiling potatoes, cut into ½-inch cubes
½	cup heavy cream (optional)
3	pounds cod fillets, rinsed, patted dry, and cut into 3- to 4-ounce pieces
¼	cup minced fresh parsley leaves

1. Fry bacon in large soup kettle over medium heat until nicely browned, about 7 minutes. Remove bacon with slotted spoon and set aside. Add onion to bacon fat and cook over medium heat until softened, about 10 minutes. Add wine and simmer until reduced by half, 2 to 3 minutes. Add tomatoes, bay leaves, cayenne pepper, and salt and pepper to taste. Bring to boil, reduce heat, and simmer until mixture has thickened to tomato sauce consistency, 15 to 20 minutes.

2. Add fish stock and potatoes and bring to boil. Reduce heat and simmer until potatoes are almost tender, 10 to 15 minutes. Add cream, if using. Adjust seasonings with salt, pepper, and cayenne to taste.

3. Add fish pieces and simmer, stirring a few times to ensure even cooking, for 5 minutes. Remove kettle from heat, cover, and let stand until fish is just cooked through, about 5 minutes. Stir in bacon and parsley, discard bay leaves, and serve immediately.

Bouillabaisse

SERVES 8

Red snapper, cod, grouper, monkfish, and sea bass are our favorite choices for this French stew. Serve bouillabaisse in soup plates—wide, shallow bowls—that have been lined with sliced cooked potatoes. Float two slices of toasted French bread dolloped with Roasted Red Pepper Mayonnaise (page 286) in each bowl.

2	tablespoons extra-virgin olive oil
2	medium onions, diced
1	small fennel bulb, tough parts and stalks discarded, diced
6	large garlic cloves, minced
½	cup dry white wine
3	cups chopped canned tomatoes with their juice
¼	teaspoon saffron threads, crumbled
3	tablespoons anise-flavored liqueur such as Pernod
1	teaspoon grated orange zest
2	large bay leaves
⅛	teaspoon cayenne pepper, or to taste
	Salt and ground black pepper
4½	cups Fish Stock or Cheater Fish Stock (see page 284)
1	pound new potatoes
3	pounds white-fleshed fish fillets, rinsed, patted dry, and cut into 3- to 4-ounce pieces
1	recipe Roasted Red Pepper Mayonnaise (page 286)
16	slices ½-inch-thick French bread, toasted
¼	cup minced fresh parsley leaves

1. Heat oil in large soup kettle. Add onions, fennel, and garlic and cook over medium heat until softened, about 10 minutes. Add wine and simmer until reduced by half, 2 to 3 minutes. Add tomatoes, saffron, Pernod, orange zest, bay leaves, cayenne pepper, and salt and pepper to taste. Bring to boil, reduce heat, and simmer until mixture has thickened to tomato sauce consistency, 15 to 20 minutes.

2. Add fish stock and bring to boil. Reduce heat to simmer and adjust seasonings with salt, pepper, and cayenne to taste.

3. Meanwhile, place potatoes in medium saucepan and cover with water. Bring to boil and

simmer until cooked through, 15 to 20 minutes. Drain, cool slightly, and cut into thick slices. Cover and keep potatoes warm.

4. Add fish pieces to stew and simmer, stirring a few times to ensure even cooking, for 5 minutes. Remove kettle from heat, cover, and let stand until fish is just cooked through, about 5 minutes.

5. Spread a dollop of red pepper mayonnaise over each piece of toast. Divide potato slices among soup plates. Stir parsley into stew, discard bay leaves, and ladle stew into soup plates. Float 2 toasts in each soup plate and serve immediately.

Roasted Red Pepper Mayonnaise
MAKES ABOUT I CUP

Spread this French sauce, called rouille, on toasts that you float in bowls of seafood stew. If you like, mix the mayonnaise right into the stew for added flavor. Note that this mayonnaise does contain raw eggs. If you prefer not to eat dishes with raw eggs, replace the egg yolk and olive oil with ¾ cup prepared mayonnaise, adding the mayonnaise with the pepper and saffron and processing until smooth.

I	small red bell pepper
2	large garlic cloves, peeled
I	slice (about ¹/₂-inch thick) French bread
¹/₈	teaspoon saffron threads, crumbled
I	large egg yolk, at room temperature
¹/₂	cup extra-virgin olive oil
	Salt
	Pinch cayenne pepper

1. If using a gas stove, hold pepper with long-handled tongs over flame and roast, turning often, until skin blackens in spots. (If using an electric stove, roast pepper on baking sheet under the broiler, turning often, until skin blackens in spots.) Place roasted pepper in small bowl, cover with plastic wrap, and set aside for 15 minutes. When pepper is cool enough to handle, peel skin with fingers. Core and seed pepper and set aside.

2. With food processor motor running, drop garlic cloves, one at a time, through feed tube. Push garlic down sides of bowl with rubber spatula. Add bread and process to fine crumbs. Add bell pepper, saffron, then egg yolk and process until pureed. With motor still running, slowly add oil until mixture thickens to mayonnaise consistency. Season to taste with salt and cayenne pepper.

CHILI CON CARNE
DEFINED IN THE BROADEST POSSIBLE SENSE, chili con carne consists of meat, dried red chiles, and liquid, more often than not seasoned with garlic, cumin, and oregano. But, of course, it's not that easy. Our research turned up numerous distinct styles of chili, the most prevalent of which were from Texas, New Mexico, the Midwest, and Cincinnati.

Countless variations exist within each style, but, generally speaking, Texas chili depends on either pureed or powdered ancho chile, uses beef, excludes tomato, onion, and beans, and features a high proportion of meat to chiles. We wanted a chili that would be hearty, heavy on the meat, and spicy but not overwhelmingly hot. We wanted a creamy consistency somewhere between soup and stew. The flavors would be balanced so that no single spice or seasoning stood out or competed with the chile.

Because chiles are the heart of chili con carne, we had to learn about the different types. After considerable testing and tasting, we settled on a combination of ancho and New Mexico for the dried chiles, with a few jalapeños added for their fresh flavor and bite.

Chilis made with toasted chiles tasted noticeably fuller and warmer than those made with chiles left untoasted. One caveat, though: Overtoasted chiles can take on a distinctly bitter flavor, so don't let them go too long.

Many of the recipes we looked at in our research suggested that a tablespoon of ground chile per pound of meat was sufficient, but we found these chilis to be bland and watery. Three tablespoons per pound of meat, on the other hand, produced chili with too much punch and richness. Two tablespoons per pound was the way to go. We also discovered that blending the chili powder with water to make a paste keeps it from scorching in the pot; this step is advised.

Since chuck is our favorite meat for stewing, we knew it would work best in chili. Still, there were some aspects of the meat question that had to be settled. Should the chuck be standard hamburger grind, coarser chili grind, hand-cut into tiny cubes, or a combination? The chili made from small cubes of beef was far more appealing than those made from either type of ground beef; they both had a grainy, extruded texture. Most of the recipes we looked at specified that the meat should be cut into ¼-inch cubes. However, we found that larger 1-inch chunks gave chili a satisfying chew.

Next we set out to determine the best type, or types, of liquid for chili. The main contenders were water, chicken stock, beef stock, beer, black coffee, and red wine. We tried each one on its own, as well as in any combination we felt made sense. The surprise result was that we liked plain water best because it allowed the flavor of the chiles to come through in full force.

The acidity of tomato and the sweetness of onion, both in small amounts, add interest and dimension to chili. Garlic is another essential seasoning. We found that bacon provides a subtly sweet, smoky essence to the chili that is most welcome.

Chili is generally thickened to tighten the sauce and make it smoother. Flour, roux, cornstarch, and masa harina (a flour ground from corn treated with lime, or calcium oxide) are the most common options. Dredging the meat in flour before browning and adding a roux along with the liquid were both effective, but these approaches made it more difficult to finesse the consistency of the finished product because both were introduced early in the cooking process. Roux added at the end of the cooking left a faint taste of raw flour. We did prefer thickening at the end of cooking, though, because we could control the consistency by adding thickener gradually until it was right. We like chili thick enough to coat the back of a wooden spoon, like the custard base of homemade ice cream.

Our first choice for thickening was masa harina, added at the end of cooking. Masa both thickened and imparted a slightly sweet, earthy corn flavor to the chili. If masa harina is not available in your grocery store and you'd rather not mail-order it, use a cornstarch and water slurry. It brings no flavor to the chili, but it is predictable, easy to use, and gives the gravy a silky consistency and attractive sheen.

Chili Con Carne

SERVES 6

To ensure the best chile flavor, we recommend toasting whole dried chiles and grinding them in a minichopper or spice-dedicated coffee grinder, all of which takes only 10 (very well-spent) minutes. Select dried chiles that are moist and pliant, like dried fruit.

To toast and grind dried chiles: Place chiles on baking sheet in 350-degree oven until fragrant and puffed, about 6 minutes. Cool, stem, and seed, tearing pods into pieces. Place pieces of the pods in spice grinder and process until powdery, 30 to 45 seconds.

For hotter chili, boost the heat with a pinch of cayenne, a dash of hot pepper sauce, or crumbled pequín chiles near the end of cooking. Serve the chili with any of the following side dishes: warm pinto or kidney beans, corn bread or chips, corn tortillas or tamales, rice, biscuits, or just plain crackers. Top with any of the following garnishes: chopped fresh cilantro leaves, minced white onion, diced avocado, shredded cheddar or jack cheese, or sour cream.

3	tablespoons ancho chili powder, or 3 medium pods (about ½ ounce), toasted and ground
3	tablespoons New Mexico chili powder, or 3 medium pods (about ¾ ounce), toasted and ground
2	tablespoons cumin seeds, toasted in a dry skillet over medium heat until fragrant, about 4 minutes, and ground
2	teaspoons dried oregano, preferably Mexican
½	cup water
I	beef chuck roast, 4 pounds, trimmed of excess fat and cut into 1-inch cubes
2	teaspoons salt, plus extra for seasoning
7–8	slices bacon (about 8 ounces), cut into ¼-inch pieces
I	medium onion, minced (about I cup)
5	medium garlic cloves, minced
4–5	small jalapeño chile peppers, cored, seeded, and minced
I	cup canned crushed tomatoes or plain tomato sauce
2	tablespoons juice from I medium lime
5	tablespoons masa harina or 3 tablespoons cornstarch
	Ground black pepper

1. Mix chili powders, cumin, and oregano in small bowl and stir in ½ cup water to form thick paste; set aside. Toss beef cubes with salt; set aside.

2. Fry bacon in large, heavy soup kettle or Dutch oven over medium-low heat until fat renders and bacon crisps, about 10 minutes. Remove bacon with slotted spoon to paper towel–lined plate; pour all but 2 teaspoons fat from pot into small bowl; set aside. Increase heat to medium-high; sauté meat in four batches until well-browned on all sides, about 5 minutes per batch, adding additional 2 teaspoons bacon fat to pot as necessary. Reduce heat to medium; add 3 tablespoons bacon fat to now-empty pan. Add onion; sauté until softened, 5 to 6 minutes. Add garlic and jalapeño; sauté until fragrant, about 1 minute. Add chili paste; sauté until fragrant, 2 to 3 minutes. Add reserved bacon and browned beef, crushed tomatoes or tomato sauce, lime juice, and 7 cups water; bring to simmer. Continue to cook at a steady simmer until meat is tender and juices are dark, rich, and starting to thicken, about 2 hours.

3. Mix masa harina with ⅔ cup water (or cornstarch with 3 tablespoons water) in a small bowl to form smooth paste. Increase heat to medium; stir in paste and simmer until thickened, 5 to 10 minutes. Adjust seasoning generously with salt and ground black pepper. Serve immediately or, for best flavor, cool slightly, cover, and refrigerate overnight or for up to 5 days. Reheat before serving.

➤ VARIATION
Smoky Chipotle Chili Con Carne
SERVES 6

Grill-smoking the meat in combination with chipotle chiles gives this chili a distinct, but not overwhelming, smoky flavor. Make sure you start with a chuck roast that is at least three inches thick. The grilling is meant to flavor the meat by searing the surface and smoking it lightly, not to cook it.

1. TO PREPARE MEAT: Puree 4 medium garlic cloves with two teaspoons salt. Rub intact chuck roast with puree, and sprinkle evenly with 2 to 3 tablespoons New Mexico chili powder; cover and set aside. Meanwhile, build hot fire. When you can hold your hand 5 inches above grill surface for no more than 3 seconds, spread hot coals to area about the size of roast. Open bottom grill vents, scatter one cup soaked mesquite or hickory wood chips over hot coals, and set grill rack in place. Grill roast over hot coals, opening lid vents three-quarters of the way and covering so that vents are opposite bottom vents to draw smoke through and around roast. Sear meat until all sides are dark and richly colored, about 12 minutes per side. Remove roast to bowl; when cool to the touch, trim and cut into 1-inch cubes, reserving juices.

2. FOR THE CHILI: Follow recipe for Chili Con Carne, omitting the browning of the beef cubes and substituting 5 minced canned chipotle peppers in adobo sauce for jalapeños. Add grilled meat and juice with cooked bacon.

INGREDIENTS: Dried Chiles

For the most part, chili con carne is based on fairly mild chiles. The most common of these are dark, mahogany red, wrinkly-skinned ancho chiles, which have a deep, sweet, raisiny flavor; New Mexico Reds, which have a smooth, shiny, brick-red skin and a crisp, slightly acidic, weedy, earthy flavor; California chiles, which are very similar to New Mexico in appearance but have a slightly milder flavor; and long, shiny, smooth, dark brown pasilla chiles. Pasillas, which are a little hotter than the other three varieties, have grapey, herby flavor notes, and, depending on the region of the country, are often packaged and sold as either ancho or mulato chiles.

We sampled each of these types, as well as a selection of preblended commercial powders, alone and in various combinations in batches of chili. Though the individual chiles tasted much purer and fresher than any of the premixed powders, they nonetheless seemed one-dimensional on their own. When all was said and done, the two-chile combination we favored was equal parts ancho, for its earthy, fruity sweetness and the stunning deep red color it imparted to the chili, and New Mexico, for its lighter flavor and crisp acidity.

Chile heat was another factor to consider. Hotter dried chiles that appear regularly in chili include guajillo, de Arbol, pequín, japonais, and cayenne. Though we did not want to develop a fiery, overly hot chili, we did want a subtle bite to give the dish some oomph. Minced jalapeños, added with the garlic to the chili pot, supplied some heat and a fresh vegetal flavor.

CURRY

OUR GOAL IN CREATING A CURRY RECIPE WAS to translate the many dishes that earn this name (almost any Indian stew can be called a "curry") into a basic formula that could be easily adapted. In the process, we wanted to discover how to keep the flavors bright and clear. So many curries are dull and heavy-tasting.

Like a standard stew, curry begins by heating oil to provide a cooking medium. After that, however, it diverges completely from the traditional Western method. Rather than browning the meat in the oil, you must first sauté the whole spices (cinnamon, cloves, cardamom, peppercorns, and bay leaf), then the onions. This step infuses the oil with the fragrance of the spices, thus flavoring everything else that comes in contact with the oil.

Next, you stir in equal volumes of pureed garlic and ginger. Why pureed? With no surfaces to burn, we found that pureed garlic and ginger cooked more evenly than a mince and melted into the sauce for a smooth finish. And because a puree is wet where a mince is dry, this method also helps to guard against burning.

We mixed the ground dried spices (cumin, coriander, turmeric) with enough water to form a paste, then added the paste and the meat to the pan. We cooked this mixture, stirring often, until enough moisture had been cooked out of the ingredients to allow the oil to separate out and pool around the clumps of meat, onion, and spice paste. This is the secret to a well-made curry. The spices must fry in this hot oil, uninhibited by liquid, to release and develop their flavors. Once the final stewing liquid was added, the flavor of the spices would develop no further.

We cooked three curries to determine how long the combined ground spices needed to cook to develop their flavor: We tried 30 seconds, 5 minutes, and 10 minutes after the oil had separated. We found that 30 seconds was all it took. We also determined that the heavy, muddy taste in many curries probably results from spices that have burned and turned bitter as a result of sticking to the bottom of the skillet. When cooked quickly, the spices are less likely to stick. We also learned that the addition of yogurt or tomato to the pan obviates the need to make a paste with the ground spices.

Next we made a curry in which we added the stewing liquid before the oil had separated. Indeed, the curry tasted raw. Use your ear to help you recognize when the spices are frying in pure oil. There is a change from the gentle sound of a simmer to the loud, staccato sound of frying. The idea behind this traditional Indian technique is to release the flavors of the aromatic ingredients into the oil and cook them into the meat. If the meat were browned first, as in a Western stew, the caramelized crust might inhibit the meat from absorbing the flavors.

The ingredients in the recipe are completely interchangeable, depending on what result you're looking for. The whole spice combination (cinnamon, cloves, cardamom, peppercorns, and bay leaf) can be abbreviated to cinnamon and cloves or to cinnamon, cloves, and cardamom, if you like.

Master Recipe for Curry
SERVES 4 TO 6

Gather and prepare all of your ingredients before you begin. Garlic and ginger may be pureed by hand or in a minichop food processor. If pureeing by hand, use a garlic press, or mince the garlic and ginger with a knife on a cutting board, sprinkling with salt to break them down quite a bit. If using a minichopper, process the garlic and ginger with 1 to 2 tablespoons of water until pureed. You can substitute a scant half teaspoon of cayenne pepper for the jalapeño, adding it to the skillet with the other ground dried spices. Feel free to increase the wet (garlic, ginger, jalapeños, and onions) or dry spice quantities. Serve the curry with basmati rice (page 127).

WHOLE SPICE BLEND (OPTIONAL)

1½	3-inch cinnamon sticks
4	cloves
4	green cardamom pods
8	peppercorns
1	bay leaf
¼	cup vegetable or canola oil
1	medium onion, sliced thin
4	large garlic cloves, pureed
1	chunk (1½ inches) fresh gingerroot, peeled and pureed

1 ½   pounds top sirloin or boneless leg of lamb, trimmed and cut into ¾-inch cubes, or 6 chicken thighs, skinned, or 1 ½ pounds shrimp, peeled and deveined

2   teaspoons ground cumin

2   teaspoons ground coriander

1   teaspoon ground turmeric

½   teaspoon salt, plus more to taste

3   canned plum tomatoes, chopped, plus 1 tablespoon juice, or ⅔ cup crushed tomatoes, or ½ cup plain low-fat yogurt

2   bunches (1 ½ pounds) spinach, stemmed, thoroughly washed, and chopped coarse (optional)

1   cup chopped fresh cilantro leaves (optional)

1   jalapeño pepper, stemmed and cut in half through stem end

½   cup Indian split peas, or 4 medium boiling potatoes, peeled and cut into ¾-inch cubes, or 4 medium zucchini, cut into ½-inch cubes, or 1 cup fresh or thawed frozen green peas

2–4   tablespoons chopped fresh cilantro leaves (use the lesser amount if you've already added the optional cilantro)

1. Heat oil in large deep skillet or soup kettle, preferably nonstick, over medium-high heat until hot, but not smoking. If using whole spice blend, add to oil and cook, stirring with wooden spoon until cinnamon stick unfurls and cloves pop, about 5 seconds. Add onion to skillet; sauté until softened, 3 to 4 minutes, or browned, 5 to 7 minutes, as desired. (If omitting whole spice blend, simply add onion to skillet and proceed with recipe.)

2. Stir in garlic, ginger, selected meat (except shrimp), ground spices, ½ teaspoon salt, and tomatoes or yogurt; cook, stirring almost constantly, until liquid evaporates, oil separates and turns orange, and spices begin to fry, 5 to 7 minutes, depending on skillet or kettle size. Continue to cook, stirring constantly, until spices smell cooked, about 30 seconds longer.

3. Stir in optional spinach and/or cilantro. Add 2 cups water and jalapeño and season with salt; bring to simmer. Reduce heat; cover and simmer until meat is tender, 20 to 30 minutes for chicken, 30 to

40 minutes for beef or lamb.

4. Add selected vegetable (except green peas); cook until tender, about 15 minutes. Stir in cilantro. Add shrimp and/or peas if using. Simmer 3 minutes longer and serve.

➤ VARIATIONS

Chicken Curry with Yogurt, Cilantro, and Zucchini

Follow Master Recipe for Curry, choosing optional whole spice blend, chicken, yogurt, optional 1 cup chopped cilantro, and zucchini and omitting optional spinach. Sauté onion until golden brown.

Chicken Curry with Spinach and Fenugreek

Follow Master Recipe for Curry, choosing chicken, tomatoes, optional spinach, and potatoes and omitting optional whole spice blend and optional cilantro. Sauté onion until softened. Add ½ teaspoon fenugreek along with cumin and coriander. Once chicken parts are done, remove and keep warm. Continue to cook sauce over high heat until thickened, about 10 minutes. (The spinach becomes the sauce.)

Shrimp Curry with Yogurt and Peas

Follow Master Recipe for Curry, choosing shrimp, yogurt, optional cilantro, peas, and omitting optional whole spice blend and optional spinach. Sauté onion until golden brown.

Lamb Curry with Whole Spices

Follow Master Recipe for Curry, choosing optional whole spice blend, lamb, tomatoes, and potatoes and omitting optional spinach and optional 1 cup chopped cilantro. Sauté onion until softened.

Lamb Curry with Figs and Fenugreek

Follow Master Recipe for Curry, choosing lamb and tomatoes and omitting optional whole spice blend and optional spinach and cilantro. Sauté onion until softened. Add ½ teaspoon fenugreek along with cumin and coriander and ¼ cup dried figs, chopped coarse, along with water. Omit the optional vegetable.

12

FISH AND SHELLFISH

FISH AND SHELLFISH ARE IN SOME WAYS easy to cook. The actual cooking time for most of the recipes in this chapter is under 10 minutes. That said, keeping seafood moist is a constant challenge. The most important thing you can do to ensure good results is not to overcook fish. While we like most fish cooked through (salmon and tuna are exceptions), fish that is overcooked becomes dry and overly flaky, and overcooked shellfish becomes tough and rubbery.

In some cases, we have resorted to brining (soaking in salted water) before cooking to help seafood retain moisture. (Brining works well with shrimp and with salmon that will be barbecued.) With tuna, which is especially prone to drying out on the grill, we found that marinating steaks in olive oil helped keep them moist. The other solutions are to steam fish (this cooking method is less likely to dry out fish than others) or serve it with some sort of sauce.

A few general points about fish and shellfish. You must buy from a trusted source, preferably one with a high volume that ensures freshness. While cooking can hide imperfections in meat and poultry, there is little the cook can do to salvage a tired piece of salmon or slimy, mushy shrimp. Of course, seafood, especially shellfish, that is past its prime can be dangerous to your health.

So what should you look for at the seafood shop? Shellfish is generally sold alive. This means that lobsters should be moving around in the tank, and oysters, clams, and mussels should be tightly shut. Shrimp is the exception, since it is shipped frozen and generally thawed by your local retailer. (You can buy frozen shrimp, which we find to be quite a good option.)

Buying fish fillets and steaks is a bit more complicated. Fish should smell like the sea, not fishy or sour. The flesh should look bright, shiny, and firm, not dull or mushy. When possible, try to get your fishmonger to slice steaks and fillets to order, rather than buying precut pieces that may have been sitting for some time and lost some fluids. Avoid fish that is shrink-wrapped, since the packaging makes it difficult to examine and smell the fish. No matter how you buy fish, make sure it has been kept chilled until the minute you buy it; get fish home quickly and into the refrigerator.

This chapter is divided mostly by type of fish (salmon, tuna) or shellfish (shrimp, scallops, etc.). We also have included some recipes for sautéing and steaming that can be adapted to most any kind of fish, everything from flounder to red snapper. See chapter 11 for information on using fish and shellfish in stews.

SALMON

SALMON IS AMERICA'S MOST POPULAR "dinner" fish (we consume more tuna, but most of that is canned) for good reason. The flesh is rich and flavorful, and the fish is relatively easy to prepare. An additional advantage lies in the fact that modern fish-farming technology all but guarantees that you can buy excellent-quality salmon any day of the year. Even at the supermarket, where other fish is often not up to our admittedly exacting standards, salmon comes in so fresh and sells out so fast that we are rarely dissatisfied.

Salmon can be purchased in boneless fillets or in steaks. Our preference is for fillets, which are easier to eat since they are boneless. Another distinction you may see at some high-end fish shops is between farmed and wild fish. On the East Coast, you are unlikely to see much wild salmon. In the West, especially the Northwest, you may see wild salmon at certain times of year.

We wondered if there are important differences between farmed and wild salmon and also wondered about any differences that might exist in salmon from various sources around the globe. The most common kind of salmon sold in the United States is Atlantic salmon farmed in pens off the coast of Maine or eastern Canada. (This species is farmed around the world, in Norway, Chile, and the Pacific Northwest.) We taste-tested four farmed salmon fillets sold at the Fulton Fish Market in New York City. One was from Chile, one from Maine, and two from eastern Canada. One of the Canadian fish was Bay of Fundy Certified Quality salmon, a brand name.

We ran pan-seared, grilled, and steamed tests of each fish. The major split developed between the fish farmed in northern versus Chilean waters. In all of the tests we conducted, the Chilean fish was drier even when we cooked it less. The steaming test brought out some subtle differences in texture and flavor that were less obvious when the fish was pan-seared or (almost completely obscured by) grilling: The nonbrand Canadian fish had a slightly mushy texture compared with the silken firm flesh of the branded and Maine fish. Steaming also showed the branded fish to have a rounder, richer flavor than its northern counterparts.

The dryness in Chilean fish was likely due to its lower fat content. Chilean-farmed salmon is leaner than Maine, Canadian, or Norwegian salmon because it's younger. Salmon farmed in warm Chilean water grow to market size faster than when farmed in colder northern water. The older a salmon gets, the more fat it puts on. So, if you're buying farmed fish, steer clear of Chilean.

As for wild salmon, which is sometimes available in high-end fish markets, we found that it has a more complex, less homogeneous flavor than farmed salmon and a meatier texture. However, wild salmon can be dry when cooked. That's because wild salmon has less white fat—you can see the difference. So, if you happen to find some wild salmon, you may want to undercook slightly to ensure that it remains moist.

GRILLED SALMON

SALMON IS OUR FAVORITE FISH TO GRILL. Not only does it taste great but it's firm enough to hold together better than many other fish. That said, salmon grilling has its pitfalls. Many is the time we've put perfect, gleaming fillets on a too-cool grill only to have them stick and tear when we tried to turn them, making the presentation side of the fish look like something the cat dragged in. Too hot and the flesh blackened while the charcoal flamed, ruining the delicate flavor of the fish.

We wanted to find a grilling technique we could depend on. We were after a well-browned crust, crisp skin, firm and succulent flesh, and the light woody flavor that high-heat grilling accomplishes so beautifully; what we did not want was the heavy, smoky flavor that sometimes overpowers grilled food. We wondered how to gauge when the salmon was cooked, what heat was correct, and whether this was a time to use the grill cover to promote gentle, even

cooking. We also wanted to test those baskets they advertise for grilling fish.

We started our testing with boneless, individual-portion farmed salmon fillets with skin, weighing about six ounces each. We used our 22½-inch kettle grill and hardwood charcoal. Whenever possible, we bought center-cut fillets because in farmed salmon the center cut is often almost exactly 1½ inches thick and thus cooks consistently from one piece to the next. Cuts from the tail are thinner and thus easier to overcook, while cuts from the head end are thicker and tend to take too long to cook through.

Our first test was to determine the proper heat. Several tests proved that a medium-high heat (you can hold your hand five inches above the grill for about four seconds) browned without burning and, more important, created the necessary crust so that we could turn the salmon fairly easily after some initial prodding with long-handled tongs or a spatula.

Next, we tested a fillet brushed with vegetable oil against one that was unoiled. We were surprised (and pleased) to find that the untreated fillet detached as easily as the one that had been oiled; we were glad to lose a messy step that, because of the added fat, must surely encourage flaming. We did, however, find it useful to rub the heated grill grate itself with a wad of paper towels dipped lightly in vegetable oil, held by long-handled tongs. (The paper doesn't catch fire.) This extra step not only lubricated the grate but cleaned off lingering residue as well, important given the delicate flavor and light color of a salmon fillet.

Finally, we tested fillets grilled (1) entirely over direct heat, (2) one side over direct and the second

REMOVING PIN BONES FROM SALMON

1. Using the tips of your fingers, gently rub the surface of the salmon to locate any pin bones.

2. If you feel any bones, use a pair of needle-nose pliers or tweezers to pull them out.

over indirect (that is, not directly over the coals), and (3) covered over both direct and indirect heat. There was no difference in taste or texture between the fillets grilled entirely over direct heat and those finished over indirect. Because direct heat cooks faster, we opted for that. That said, we found the direct/indirect method to be an excellent way to cook the thin tail pieces; by the time the flesh has seared enough to turn, the fish is almost cooked through and needs just a minute or so of gentle heat to finish it without overcooking.

As for the tests with the cover, the fillet grilled covered over direct heat looked great and made us feel carefree (like having someone else baby-sit the grill), but the cover infused the flesh with a smoky, fatty flavor that got in the way of the really fresh, direct taste we wanted. So we nixed, with regrets, the cover.

As we grilled the salmon, we remained alert for clues to tell us when it was properly cooked. We like salmon medium-rare in the center, or still slightly translucent. Mostly we found that by the time 1½-inch-thick fillets were well-browned on both sides, the center was perfect—that is, slightly undercooked but close enough to finish cooking the last little bit on the plate. We also developed a tactile test. As the salmon cooks, we pull it off the grill every now and then and squeeze the sides of the fillet gently between the fingertips. Raw salmon feels squishy; medium-rare salmon is firm but not hard. If you're

stumped and want to be really sure, cut into the fillet with a paring knife and look.

Our final test was to compare fillets grilled in a fish grill basket with fillets cooked straight on the grill. A grill basket is a long-handled wire contraption that's shaped something like a sandwich press. The two rectangular halves (each half is a wire grid) sandwich the food between them. The food (in this case salmon) is cooked in the basket on top of the grill grate. Our first attempt was a bust; the fillets browned well but stuck to the basket. So we oiled the basket for the next test, and this method worked beautifully.

A basket takes all the guesswork out of manipulating the fish on a grill. There's no chance it will stick to the grill grate, and it won't fall apart while you turn it or take it off. One word of caution: Remove the fish immediately from the basket once cooked. The skin, particularly, will stick to the wire as it cools. Since most cooks don't have a grill basket, our recipe explains how to cook directly on the cooking grate, but if you have a basket, oil and use it.

Charcoal-Grilled Salmon Fillets
SERVES 4

Whether hot from the grill, at room temperature, or chilled, we usually serve grilled salmon very simply, with a drizzle of lemon juice, salt and pepper, one of the glazes below, or a homemade mayonnaise (page 36). If your fillets are less than 1¼ inches thick, decrease the grilling time by roughly 30 seconds per side. To test fillets for doneness, either peek into the salmon with the tip of a small knife as described below or remove the salmon from the grill and squeeze both sides of the fillet gently with your fingertips (raw salmon is squishy; medium-rare salmon is firm but not hard).

> Vegetable oil for grill grate
> 4   center-cut salmon fillets (each about 6 ounces and 1¼ inches thick), pin bones removed (see illustrations on page 293)
>   Salt and ground black pepper

1. Build a single-level fire (see page 258). Set grill rack in place, cover grill with lid, and let rack heat up, about 5 minutes. Rub cooking grate with oil-dipped wad of paper towels (see illustration at left).

RUBBING GRILL GRATE WITH OIL

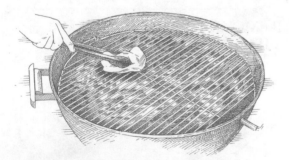

Just before placing fish on grill, dip large wad of paper towels in vegetable oil, grab it with tongs, and wipe grid thoroughly to lubricate and prevent sticking. This will also clean any remaining residue from the grill that might mar the delicate flavor of seafood.

2. Generously sprinkle each side of fillets with salt and pepper. Place fillets skin side down on grill grate; grill until skin shrinks and separates from flesh and turns black, 2 to 3 minutes. Flip fillets gently with long-handled tongs or spatula; grill until fillets are opaque throughout, yet translucent at very center when checked with point of paring knife, 3 to 4 minutes. Transfer to platter and serve.

➤ VARIATIONS

Gas-Grilled Salmon Fillets

Follow recipe for Charcoal-Grilled Salmon Fillets, making the following changes: Turn all burners to high and preheat with lid down until very hot, about 15 minutes. Grill as in charcoal recipe but with lid down, cooking 3 to 4 minutes per side.

Grilled Butterflied Salmon

Follow illustrations below to butterfly salmon fillets; follow cooking instructions for Charcoal-Grilled Salmon Fillets or gas variation.

Grilled Salmon Fillets with Mustard Glaze

Mix 2 tablespoons each dry mustard and sugar and 2 teaspoons water to make thick paste. Follow recipe for Charcoal-Grilled Salmon Fillets or gas variation, spreading mustard mixture over flesh side of fillets

before grilling. Drizzle cooked salmon with extra-virgin olive oil.

Grilled Salmon Fillets with Indian Flavors and Fresh Mango Chutney

FISH

2	tablespoons vegetable oil, plus extra for grill grate
2	tablespoons grated fresh gingerroot
1½	teaspoons ground cumin
1½	teaspoons ground coriander
1½	teaspoons salt
¼	teaspoon cayenne pepper
4	center-cut salmon fillets (each about 6 ounces and 1¼ inches thick), pin bones removed (see illustrations on page 293)

CHUTNEY

1	large ripe mango, peeled, pitted, and cut into ½-inch dice
3	tablespoons lemon juice
1	tablespoon chopped fresh cilantro leaves

1. Mix oil, ginger, cumin, coriander, salt, and cayenne together in large shallow bowl. Add fish and marinate in the refrigerator for no more than 30 minutes.

2. Combine mango, lemon juice, and cilantro in small bowl; set chutney aside.

BUTTERFLYING SALMON FILLETS

Because they are thinner at the edges, salmon fillets do not cook through evenly. We like the gradation from well-done at the edges to rare in the center, but not everyone does. Steaks, which have an even thickness throughout, cook more evenly, but are bony. A better solution than buying steak is to turn fillets into steaks by butterflying them.

This technique is not recommended for skin lovers because the skin is never exposed to the heat, so it never crisps. For those who want to avoid the skin, however, the advantage is that both sides of the flesh get a good sear, so there is twice as much of the brown, flavorful crust.

1. Start by cutting through a 3-inch-wide fillet lengthwise, down to, but not through, the skin.

2. Fold the two flesh pieces out with the skin acting as a hinge.

3. A 3-inch-wide fillet will now look like a steak, but without any bones, and have an even thickness of 1½ inches.

3. Meanwhile, build a single-level fire (see page 258). Set grill rack in place, cover grill with lid, and let rack heat up, about 5 minutes. Rub cooking grate with oil-dipped wad of paper towels (see illustration on page 294).

4. Place fillets skin side down on grill grate; grill until skin shrinks and separates from flesh and turns black, 2 to 3 minutes. Flip fillets gently with long-handled tongs or spatula; grill until fillets are opaque throughout, yet translucent at very center when checked with point of paring knife, 3 to 4 minutes. Transfer to platter and serve with chutney.

PAN-SEARED SALMON

GRILLING MAY BE THE PERFECT WAY TO COOK salmon (excellent result with no smoke or smell in the house), however it's not always practical to cook outdoors. We wanted to develop an almost effortless indoor technique that would exploit salmon's high oil content and natural moistness while also indulging our taste for fish that comes out of the pan with a crisp, even, deeply golden crust. So we zeroed in on pan-cooking over a relatively high heat on the stove top. Requiring little time and equipment, this method heightens the flavor of the fish and produces an appealing contrast in texture.

Or at least it does when the fish is cooked right. In the past, we have struggled to attain the perfect degree of doneness. Our fish was often overcooked to the point of being dry and chalky as we tried to create a nice, healthy crust, or, in an effort to protect against overcooking, we ended up with a poor crust. Our past travails had shown us what areas to explore. Should we use fat in the pan? If so, what kind and how much? Should the fillets be dredged in flour, bread crumbs, or the like for added crispness? And, of course, we had questions about the type of pan to use, the degree of heat required, and cooking times. Getting all of that right would lead to fish with a crisp, uniform crust and moist, firm flesh within.

The amount and type of fat to use was a real wild card in our research. There were recipes using everything from butter to canola oil in quantities ranging from five tablespoons down to no fat at all for four fillets.

We chose the extreme first, cooking four fillets with no fat in the pan. Though salmon supplies plenty of its own fat and a nonstick pan eliminates sticking problems, these fillets developed uneven, blotchy, unappealing crusts, especially on the skin side. Some fat in the pan, we thought, would improve matters. So we cooked four fillets in amounts ranging from one to three tablespoons of canola oil, moving in one-half tablespoon increments. These larger amounts might work well for lean fish, but for a fatty fish such as salmon even one tablespoon of oil was too much. Eventually, we found that a mere teaspoon of fat in a large skillet was all we needed to promote a deep, even crust on both sides of the fillets.

We also experimented with the different types of fat suggested in our research. Salmon is extremely rich to begin with, so butter simply pushed it over the top, not to mention the fact that it burned. The flavor of olive oil seemed at odds with the fish, and a butter–olive oil combination offered no advantage. Cooking spray was sub-par. Peanut oil worked nicely, as did both canola and vegetable oil. Because these two oils are more of a staple than peanut oil and are neutral in flavor, they were our first choice. Some recipes suggested oiling the fillets themselves instead of the pan, but this practice diminished the crust we were looking for.

While we were at it, we also tried dredging the fish in a coating meant to cook up crisp, including seasoned flour, bread crumbs, and corn meal, but we disliked them all for uneven browning, dull flavor, and pasty texture.

Without a doubt, the type of pan would be an important variable. The good news concerning pans was that every one of the four we tried—including a cheap, thin stainless steel model, heavy-bottomed stainless steel and nonstick models, and our faithful cast-iron skillet—produced a decent crust. Though the nonstick pan ensures easy cleanup and no sticking, the crust it developed was marginally less deep than the others, and the necessary preheating of the pan is not kind to the nonstick finish. The heavy stainless steel and cast-iron pans produced exemplary crusts, while the lighter, cheaper pan scorched almost fatally during cooking. While any one of them will work, our favorites were the heavy stainless steel and cast-iron models. Whichever pan you choose, make sure it is large enough to accommodate the fillets comfortably; the edges of the fillets should not touch, as this can cause steaming, instead of searing, to occur. We found a 12-inch skillet to be just right.

Preheating the pan and choosing the right heat for cooking the fish were also critical. We tried preheating for lengths of time ranging from one to five minutes and found that three minutes over high heat did the trick, regardless of whether the stove is gas or electric. But the high heat was too much once the fish was in the pan, cooking it too fast and producing billows of smoke, so we reduced the heat to medium-high. Because the pan loses some heat when the fish is added, we waited about 30 seconds before reducing the flame so the pan could regain some of the lost heat.

Timing, of course, was also crucial. We did not want to overcook the salmon. Because our fillets were consistently 1¼ inches thick, we decided to start by following the old kitchen maxim of 10 minutes per inch of thickness. The fish overcooked. It overcooked at 10 minutes and at 9 minutes, too. At 8 minutes, though, it undercooked ever so slightly. Fortunately, as with many cuts of meat, we learned that salmon fillets have enough residual heat to continue cooking briefly after they come out of the pan. In fact, we found that a 1-minute rest before serving brought the 8-minute fillets to a perfect medium with no danger of overcooking.

Though many sources suggest shaking the pan after adding the salmon to prevent sticking, we found this step to be unnecessary. Provided that the pan is hot enough and the fat is shimmering, we decided it is best to just drop the fillet in the pan skin side down and leave it be. When the fish turns opaque and milky white from the bottom to about halfway up the fillet, it's time to flip it. Then simply slide a thin, flexible metal spatula between the pan bottom and the skin, and flip it quickly so the flesh side is down; make sure not to move the fish for the first two minutes. After that, you can lift it gently at the corner with the spatula to check the bottom crust. We also suggest peeking inside the fillet with the tip of a paring knife. The center should still show traces of bright, translucent orange. If it is completely opaque and the orange color is a little duller, as it is toward the exterior of the fillet, the fish is overcooked.

Pan-Seared Salmon
SERVES 4

With the addition of the fish fillets, the pan temperature drops; compensate for the heat loss by keeping the heat on high for 30 seconds after adding them. If cooking two or three fillets instead of the full recipe of four, use a 10-inch skillet and medium-high heat for both preheating the pan and cooking the salmon. A splatter screen helps reduce the mess of pan-searing. Serve salmon with chutney (see variation that follows), a fresh salsa, an herb-spiked vinaigrette, or a squirt of lemon or lime.

4   center-cut salmon fillets (each about 6 ounces and 1¼ inches thick), pin bones removed (see illustrations on page 293)
    Salt and ground black pepper
1   teaspoon canola or vegetable oil

1. Heat a 12-inch heavy-bottomed skillet for 3 minutes over high heat. Sprinkle salmon with salt and pepper to taste.

2. Add oil to pan; swirl to coat. When oil shimmers (but does not smoke) add fillets skin side down and cook, without moving fillets, until pan regains lost heat, about 30 seconds. Reduce heat to medium-high; continue to cook until skin side is well-browned and bottom half of fillets turn opaque, 4½ minutes. Turn fillets and cook, without moving them, until they are no longer translucent on the exterior and are firm, but not hard, when gently squeezed: 3 minutes for medium-rare and 3½ minutes for medium. Remove fillets from pan; let stand 1 minute. Pat with paper towel to absorb excess fat on surface, if desired. Serve immediately.

VARIATIONS
Pan-Seared Butterflied Salmon

Following illustrations on page 295, butterfly salmon fillets. Follow cooking instructions for Pan-Seared Salmon, cooking fillets for one minute less on the first side.

Pan-Seared Salmon with Sesame Crust

Spread ¼ cup sesame seeds in a pie plate. Follow recipe for Pan-Seared Salmon, rubbing fillets with 2 teaspoons canola or vegetable oil, sprinkling with salt and pepper to taste, then pressing flesh sides of fillets into sesame seeds to coat. Continue with recipe, being careful not to break sesame crust when removing fillets from pan.

For heightened sesame flavor, rub the fish fillets with Asian sesame oil instead of canola or vegetable. If you pair this variation with butterflied fillets, double the quantity of sesame seeds and coat both sides of each fillet.

Pan-Seared Salmon with Sweet-and-Sour Chutney

A little of this intensely flavored condiment goes a long way.

I	teaspoon fennel seeds
½	teaspoon ground cumin
½	teaspoon ground coriander
¼	teaspoon ground cardamom
¼	teaspoon paprika
¼	teaspoon salt
2	teaspoons olive oil
½	medium onion, chopped fine (about ½ cup)
¼	cup red wine vinegar
I	tablespoon sugar
I	tablespoon minced fresh parsley leaves
I	recipe Pan-Seared Salmon

1. Mix fennel, cumin, coriander, cardamom, paprika, and salt in small bowl; set aside. Heat oil in medium skillet over medium heat; sauté onion until soft, 3 to 4 minutes. Add reserved spice mixture; sauté until fragrant, about 1 minute more. Increase heat to medium-high and add vinegar, sugar, and 2 tablespoons water; cook until mixture reduces by about one-third and reaches a syrupy consistency, about 1½ minutes. Stir in parsley. Set chutney aside.

2. Prepare salmon fillets as directed. Serve with chutney.

HOT-SMOKED SALMON

IS IT POSSIBLE TO MAKE SMOKED SALMON at home without a smoker? We thought it was worth a try and started off trying to make a covered grill act like a cold smoker, using very few coals, adding them as we went along, often putting out the fire with handfuls of wet smoking chips. The results were disappointing; the salmon was lacking in flavor, and the texture was a bit too wet.

Patience is supposed to be a virtue, but in this case impatience turned out to be the key to success. We simply got tired of messing with the process of cold-smoking. In fact, at this point we realized that cold-smoking, which occurs in a range of 75 to 110 degrees and is used by commercial smokers to make smoked salmon, is simply not practical for home cooks. It takes a very long time, requires both skill and patience, and can be disastrous if health precautions are not followed carefully. Therefore, we decided to use a greater number of briquettes in the initial fire. This eliminated the need to add more coals during the smoking process, and the larger fire was less likely to go out when we added more wet smoking chips. This time the results were gratifying. The hotter fire cooked the fish more, giving it a more pleasing and flaky texture.

We continued to refine this method over many months of trial and error. Eventually, we perfected a procedure that yields a salmon that has many of the attributes of good smoked salmon but that is crustier and a whole lot easier to make. Since it is somewhere between classic smoked salmon and traditional barbecue, we call it "hot-smoked." The difference between hot- and cold-smoked salmon is largely one of texture: the cold-smoked salmon is more silky, like lox, whereas hot-smoked salmon will actually flake.

But the drawback of this method—and the reason why salmon is usually cold-smoked—is that it

INGREDIENTS: Alder Wood

For years, alder wood has been the top choice for smoking salmon, a tradition begun eons ago with the American Indians of the Pacific Northwest. Apple wood is often recommended as a close second. (If you use apple wood from your own trees, make sure no chemical pesticides or fungicides have been applied to them). We wondered if you could really taste any difference among various woods.

In a blind tasting, we found that alder wood does taste a bit better on salmon than other woods. But beyond that exception, we think it's darned near impossible to tell the difference between mesquite, hickory, apple, or any other hardwood chips or chunks. Even the difference with alder was very slight, so we recommend that you choose whichever wood is most readily available.

dries out the fish. We figured that brining might help the fish hold onto moisture as it cooked and experimented with various brining times, eventually settling on three to four hours for a fillet weighing 2½ to 3 pounds. Any longer and the flavor of the brine was too intense; any shorter and it didn't produce the desired results as far as texture was concerned. This brined, hot-smoked salmon definitely had the moist texture we had been longing for, but we were still looking for more flavor to complement its smokiness.

To improve the flavor we added some sugar to the brine. We also experimented with various salt/sugar/water ratios; with different brining times (from 2 to 24 hours); and with all manner of smoking woods (alder wood, apple, hickory, and oak). We eventually settled on the recipe below, which calls for three hours of brining in a solution of 1 cup each of sugar and salt to 7 cups of water and which favors alder wood chips for the distinctive flavor they give the fish. The salmon it produces has a moist but flaky texture and is just smoky enough, with the natural flavors of the salmon getting a boost from the brining process.

Hot-smoked salmon can be served warm off the grill as well as chilled, and works as both a traditional hors d'oeuvre and, somewhat surprisingly, an entrée. For hors d'oeuvres it is absolutely delicious as is or accompanied by melba toast (or any other flat bread or cracker), finely chopped white onion, capers, and lemon wedges. If you serve the salmon as an entrée, simple wedges of lemon will suffice, or you might try a sour cream, dill, and cucumber sauce.

Hot-Smoked Salmon
SERVES 4 TO 6

Alder wood is best for this recipe, but apple wood, hickory or mesquite are also fine. The grill rack must be hot and thoroughly clean before you place the salmon on it; otherwise the fish might stick.

1	cup kosher salt (or ½ cup table salt)
1	cup sugar
1	skin-on salmon fillet (about 2½ pounds), pin bones removed (see illustrations on page 293)
2	3-inch wood chunks, or 2 cups wood chips and heavy-duty aluminum foil
2	tablespoons vegetable oil
1½	teaspoons sweet paprika
1	teaspoon ground white pepper

1. Dissolve salt and sugar in 2 cups hot water in gallon-sized zipper-lock plastic bag, about 20 minutes. Add 5 cups cold water and salmon, seal bag, and refrigerate until fish is fully brined, about 3 hours.

2. Meanwhile, soak wood chunks in cold water to cover for 1 hour and drain, or place wood chips on 18-inch square of aluminum foil, seal to make pack-

BARBECUING AND SERVING SALMON

1. Slide the salmon off the foil and onto the grill. To make it easier to remove the salmon from the grill once it is done, position the fillet so that the long side is perpendicular to the grill rods.

2. Use two spatulas to transfer the cooked fish from the grill to a cookie sheet or cutting board.

3. To serve, cut through the pink flesh, but not the skin, to divide into individual portions.

4. Slide a spatula between the fillet and skin to remove individual pieces, leaving the skin behind.

et, and use fork to create about six holes to allow smoke to escape (see the illustrations on page 271).

3. Fill chimney with 4 quarts of charcoal briquettes and light. Transfer coals from chimney to one side of kettle grill, piling them up in a mound three briquettes high. Keep bottom vents completely open. When coals are covered with light gray ash, lay wood chunks or packet with chips on top of charcoal.

4. Meanwhile, remove salmon from brine and blot dry completely with paper towels. Place fillet, skin side down, on 30-inch sheet of heavy-duty foil; rub both sides of fillet, especially skin side, with oil. Dust fillet top with paprika and pepper.

5. Put cooking grate in place, open grill lid vents, and cover, turning lid so that vents are opposite wood chunks or chips to draw smoke through grill. Let grate heat thoroughly for 5 minutes and clean with wire brush. Following illustrations on page 299, slide salmon off foil and onto rack opposite fire so that long side of fillet is perpendicular to grill rods. Barbecue until cooked through and heavily flavored with smoke, 1½ hours.

6. Following illustrations on page 299, use two spatulas to remove salmon from grill. Serve either hot or room temperature, cutting through flesh but not skin to divide into individual portions and sliding spatula between flesh and skin to remove individual pieces, leaving skin behind. (Can be wrapped in plastic and refrigerated up to 2 days.)

➤ VARIATION
Hot–Smoked Salmon on a Gas Grill

Here is a way to mimic the indirect heat method of cooking on a charcoal grill. Since some gas grills require that one burner be ignited before the other(s), make sure that the foil tray containing the wood chips is placed over the burner that will remain on.

Follow recipe for Hot-Smoked Salmon, making the following changes: Soak wood chips for 15 minutes and drain. Following illustrations on page 271, make foil tray for wood chips and position on top of burner that will remain on. Turn all burners to high, close lid, and heat grill until chips smoke heavily, about 20 minutes. Turn off burner(s) without chips. Position salmon over cool part of grill and barbecue until cooked through and perfumed heavily with smoke, 1½ hours. Serve as directed.

GRILLED TUNA

GRILLED TUNA HAS BECOME SUCH A FAMILIAR dish on the American home-cooking scene that it never occurred to us that it might also be a bear to cook. We had assumed that we could get a perfect tuna steak—beautifully seared on the outside, moist and tender on the inside—the same way we get a perfect beef or salmon steak: a quick sear over direct heat to brown and then, if the steak is really thick, a final few minutes over indirect heat to finish it. We also knew that tuna, lacking the fat of salmon, would be particularly susceptible to overcooking, so we would probably need to undercook it.

But a few days of testing proved tuna to be a tougher customer than we'd imagined. No matter what thickness we sliced it or how we cooked it—medium-rare to rare, direct or indirect heat—we were startled to find that steak after steak was almost inedible. Every one was tough and dry and tasted off-puttingly strong and fishy. Clearly more experimenting was in order.

We did all our testing with our standard grill—a 22½-inch kettle grill fired with hardwood charcoal. We worked with ¾- to 1-inch-thick steaks, the cut most available at supermarket fish counters.

First we tried grilling over direct heat, starting with an oiled and salted steak, for 3½ minutes on each side over a medium-hot fire. (We could hold a hand five inches above the grill for about four seconds.) The outside of the tuna was paler than we liked and the inside was overcooked. In successive tests we determined that a hotter fire (one over which we could hold a hand for only two to three seconds) seared better, particularly since the tuna needed to cook only 2½ minutes total for medium, and 3 to 4 minutes for well-done.

While the hotter fire was an improvement, the fish was still drier than we liked, particularly when it was cooked past medium-rare. So we experimented with indirect heat. We now tried searing the tuna 1½ minutes on each side over direct heat, and then pulled it to the side of the grill to finish cooking over indirect heat. The tuna came off the grill with the same texture but was less well seared than before, so we gave up on the indirect heat approach.

We also tested different thicknesses over direct heat and learned that if we wanted the tuna well-seared and rare, it must be cut about 1½ inches thick; the standard supermarket steak, which is thinner, will already be cooked to at least medium-rare after the initial searing on both sides. But while we preferred the moistness of the thick, rare steaks, we were concerned that some folks would not like to eat their tuna rare. In addition, we know that many consumers have difficulty locating thick steaks.

Clearly, the problem wasn't going to be solved in the actual cooking. Something had to be done to the tuna before it hit the grill. Our next inspiration was to test a marinade.

We talked to several restaurant chefs (after all, grilled tuna has become a restaurant classic), and they suggested marinating the tuna in olive oil. We marinated one 1½-inch-thick steak and one ½-inch-thick steak in an herb-flavored oil for three hours, turning every now and then. We then grilled the thick steak to rare, and the thin steak to medium. The results were amazing. Both tunas were subtly flavored with olive oil and herbs, and their texture was moist and luscious. Perhaps most surprisingly, we liked the well-cooked tuna as well as the rare. Later

tests showed that the thick steak, when cooked to rare or medium-rare, needed only brushing with the oil-herb mixture; soaking it in the oil actually made it a bit too moist.

Finally, we ran tests to determine whether the type of oil made a difference and how long a soak was necessary. Comparing extra-virgin and pure olive oils with canola oil, we found that after one hour, only the extra-virgin oil had made a noticeable impact on the tuna. The pure olive oil seemed to catch up after another hour, but it didn't flavor the tuna appreciably until after three hours. The canola oil never affected the taste or the texture of the tuna.

We learned that an oil marinade tenderizes tuna in much the same way that marbling tenderizes beef. The oil coats the strands of protein, allowing a tuna steak to feel moist in the mouth even after most of the moisture has been cooked out of it. The extra-virgin olive oil penetrates the fish more quickly than the other two oils because it is much richer in emulsifiers. Emulsifiers (mono- and diglycerides) have a water-soluble molecule at one end and a fat-soluble

---

INGREDIENTS: Tuna Steaks

Tuna is universally sold in the form of triangular-shaped, boneless steaks. These steaks are sliced from the four quarter sections, called loins, that are cut from the thick central spine when the fish is butchered. Each loin is a triangular quarter, wide at the head end and tapering toward the tail.

Sometimes when you buy a tuna steak, you'll see dark red coloration in the flesh. This is the bloodline, a piece of fibrous tissue heavily laden with blood vessels that runs from the gills to the tail on both sides of the spine. This specialized tissue makes possible the rapid bursts of speed that characterize tuna as they hunt for food: the bloodline fuels these bursts by dispersing oxygen quickly throughout the muscle. It tastes fishier and more bitter than the rest of the meat. We recommend that you cut it off before cooking.

To find out which of the five varieties of tuna available to consumers in the United States would make the tastiest grilled tuna, we held a blind tasting. The good news is that the fresh tuna most readily available, yellowfin, was the clear favorite. So if you're buying fresh tuna, you're probably buying the right one. Here are the results of the taste test.

YELLOWFIN The favorite of almost all tasters, who found it had the best combination of texture and flavor without tasting fishy or having a fatty mouthfeel. In fact, previously frozen yellowfin, which tasters found to have a slightly more fishy flavor, came in second, beating out fresh versions of other tuna varieties.

BIGEYE Although this is the variety most often used for sushi, it was only moderately popular with tasters. Several tasters did mention, however, that it had the most intense flavor of all the tunas. Probably the best choice for those who really love the taste of tuna.

BLUEFIN We could not get fresh bluefin, and the previously frozen version was rated as "good but not outstanding" by most tasters.

ALBACORE Most tasters found this fish dry and quite bland. Perhaps this is not surprising, since it is familiar to our taste buds as the only tuna that can legally be sold in cans as "white-meat tuna."

SKIPJACK The least popular tuna in the tasting, skipjack was thought by almost all tasters to have too strong a flavor and too greasy a mouthfeel.

INGREDIENTS: Canned Tuna

In most of our blind taste tests, taste has predictably reigned. That is, despite the many other characteristics that we assess—aroma, mouthfeel, appearance, texture—if it tastes good, it ranks well. No tough math.

Yet when it came to canned tuna, texture set the pace. Tasters were less concerned with flavor. But how it settled between the teeth—could you chew it, or just gum it?—determined their partiality.

As an inexpensive, readily available source of protein, canned tuna took off during World War I and really came into its own as a postwar lunch-time favorite. Today, it is also the most frequently eaten seafood in the United States. The average American eats 8.5 cans of tuna a year, according to the U.S. Department of Commerce. And there really is no mystery as to why. It's cheap, it's healthy, it's an easy sandwich filler, it keeps—for years and years; and it's almost always on sale.

We set out to determine which supermarket brands would make the best tuna salad, since that is the most popular use of canned tuna. Because there are a number of national brands, each of which makes several varieties, we decided to narrow the tasting down to the two top-selling varieties sold by the five major national brands—the chunk light and solid white varieties packed in water and made by Bumble Bee, Chicken of the Sea, Geisha, StarKist, and 3 Diamonds.

Solid tuna consists of one large piece of loin meat. If the segment is too small to fit perfectly into the can, a piece of another segment can be added. Free flakes broken from the loins can also be added but cannot exceed 18 percent of the total contents.

Chunk tuna consists of several pieces, more than half of which are required to be larger than ½ inch. The rest can consist of flakes, which sometimes makes the consistency mushy. Chunk is the main form in which light-meat tuna is sold, although there are some chunk white-meat tunas, too.

Chunk light was the less expensive of the two varieties in our tasting, costing about 41 cents a can less than solid white. This may explain why it is also the top-selling type of canned tuna. Certainly our tasting results do not explain it, since tasters found only one of the five chunk light samples acceptable. In general, chunk light tuna is made of skipjack tuna or yellowfin tuna or both; skipjack contributes a stronger flavor than yellowfin. These two tuna species are found in warm waters all around the world.

While our tasters were not wild about the more pronounced flavor of chunk light (which often included an aftertaste of the tin can), what really upset the balance between the white and light tunas was the texture. White tuna you could eat, even pierce, with a fork; the light version was more appropriately scooped with a spoon. When blended with mayonnaise, the small flakes of chunk light tuna quickly broke down even further, taking on a texture that reminded many tasters of cat food. It is unusual to find a light tuna sold in solid form because it is lower in fat and more susceptible to breaking down into small pieces than white tuna when exposed to the duress of pressure cooking. Many tasters not only disliked the lack of chew in the light tuna but also found that the small shreds of fish held moisture too well, which created a sopping, mushy consistency.

Solid white, on the other hand, consists of large meaty chunks. In accordance with the U.S. Food and Drug Administration's standards, it is made up exclusively of albacore tuna. Because albacore do not swim in tight schools like yellowfin or skipjack, they have to be caught individually by lines dragging behind a slow-moving boat. This limits the harvest and, because of market forces, makes solid white a more expensive canned tuna.

Though known as "white" tuna, albacore can vary from nearly white to light pink or even beige. Its fat content can also vary, typically ranging from 1 to 5 percent. (The nutrition table on the can's label will indicate the percentage.) The amount of fat depends on where the fish are caught—both the region and the depth. Despite these natural variances, tuna manufacturers are able to produce a relatively consistent product through quality control and special processing methods. Some of the white tuna products promote themselves as "Fancy Albacore" or "Premium Albacore." This is merely a marketing strategy. They do not differ.

With certain brands favored more than others, solid white was the tuna of choice among tasters for its mild flavor, milky-white appearance, and full flakes. (We broke down the large pieces with a fork before serving them to tasters so their consistency in the salad would be similar to chunky tuna.).

Parenthetically, all the tunas in our tasting displayed a dolphin-safe logo, even though the danger of dolphins being caught in fishing nets and drowning applies only to light tuna—specifically, to yellowfin caught in the eastern Pacific Ocean, near Mexico and the United States. Only in this area is this species known to swim in schools beneath schools of dolphin.

So what are our favorite brands? StarKist Solid White Tuna in Water took top honors in our tasting, followed by 3 Diamonds Solid White Tuna in Water and Chicken of the Sea Solid White Tuna in Water. If light tuna is your preference (for reasons of flavor or affordability), we found Geisha Chunk Light Tuna in Water to be the best of the leading brands.

molecule at the other; this double solubility increases their mobility and hence their ability to penetrate protein. Because the filtering process extracts emulsifiers, pure olive oil takes much longer than extra-virgin olive oil to coat the protein strands.

Charcoal-Grilled Tuna, Thin Steaks

SERVES 4

This recipe is designed for relatively thin steaks, the kind you might get at the supermarket. It is difficult to avoid cooking tuna steaks thinner than ¾-inch to medium because the interior cooks almost as quickly as the surface. For this reason, we recommend not getting steaks any thinner than this. Piquant sauces and fresh salsas are natural partners for either thin or thick grilled tuna steaks.

4	tuna steaks (each about 8 ounces and about ¾-inch thick)
3	tablespoons extra-virgin olive oil
	Salt and ground black pepper

1. Place tuna and oil in gallon-sized zipper-lock plastic bag; seal bag and refrigerate until fish has marinated fully, at least 1 and up to 24 hours.

2. Build a single-level fire (see page 258). Set grill rack in place, cover grill with lid, and let rack heat up, about 5 minutes. Rub cooking grate with oil-dipped wad of paper towels (see illustration on page 294).

3. Remove tuna from bag; season both sides of each steak with salt and pepper. Grill over blazing hot fire (you should be able to hold your hand 5 inches above grill surface for 1 to 2 seconds) until well-seared and grill marks appear, about 1½ minutes. Flip steaks over and grill on second side until fish is cooked to medium (opaque throughout, yet translucent at very center when checked with point of paring knife), 1 to 1½ minutes longer. Serve immediately.

➤ VARIATION

Gas-Grilled Tuna, Thin Steaks

Follow recipe for Charcoal-Grilled Tuna, making the following changes: Turn all burners to high and preheat with lid down until very hot, about 15 minutes. Grill as in charcoal recipe but with lid down, cooking 2 to 3 minutes per side.

Grilled Tuna with Herb-Infused Oil

This herb oil may be brushed onto thick tuna steaks before and after grilling as well.

Heat ¼ cup extra-virgin olive oil, 1½ teaspoon grated lemon zest, 1½ teaspoons chopped fresh thyme, 1 minced garlic clove, and ¼ teaspoon hot red pepper flakes in small saucepan until hot. Cool oil and then use as marinade for fish in place of plain oil in step 1 of recipe for Charcoal-Grilled Tuna, Thin Steaks. Proceed as directed.

Charcoal-Grilled Tuna, Thick Steaks

SERVES 4

Whereas thinner tuna steaks cook to medium before you know it, thicker 1- to 1½-inch steaks can easily be cooked to rare or medium-rare. In addition, you need only brush thick steaks with olive oil rather than marinate them because they are less likely to dry out during cooking. Buy two steaks and cut them in half before cooking to yield four individual portions.

2	tuna steaks (each about 1 pound and cut 1½ inches thick)
2	tablespoons extra-virgin olive oil
	Salt and ground black pepper

1. Build a single-level fire (see page 258). Set grill rack in place, cover grill with lid, and let rack heat up, about 5 minutes. Rub cooking grate with oil-dipped wad of paper towels (see illustration on page 294).

2. Brush tuna steaks with oil; season with salt and pepper to taste. Grill over blazing hot fire (you should be able to hold your hand 5 inches above grill surface for 1 to 2 seconds) until well-seared and grill marks appear, about 2½ minutes. Flip steaks over and grill on second side until fish is cooked to rare (opaque near surface and still red at center when checked with point of paring knife), 2½ to 3½ minutes longer. For fish cooked medium-rare (just opaque throughout, yet still pink at very center when checked with point of paring knife), cook 2½ to 3 minutes on first side and 3 to 4 minutes on second side. Serve immediately.

➤ VARIATION

Gas-Grilled Tuna, Thick Steaks

Follow recipe for Charcoal-Grilled Tuna, making the following changes: Turn all burners to high and preheat with lid down until very hot, about 15 minutes. Grill as in charcoal recipe but with lid down, cooking 3 to 3½ minutes per side for rare and 4 minutes per side for medium-rare.

SAUTÉED FISH FILLETS

SAUTÉING IS AN IDEAL WAY TO HANDLE A wide variety of fish. It is particularly well suited to mild flatfish fillets such as flounder, adding a delicate, crispy texture and flavor you can't get with other techniques. But sautéing fish can be intimidating to the uninitiated cook, particularly if the fish sticks to the pan or falls apart.

We wanted to establish a consistent method that we could use with different fish. We limited our tests to filleted, white-fleshed fish. We classified them by thickness: thin, meaning about one-half inch thick, including sole and flounder; medium thick, meaning about three-quarters of an inch thick, including snapper and sea bass; and thick, meaning about one inch thick, including catfish and scrod.

Our first test was to see if the type of pan used made any difference when sautéing. To find out, we sautéed two-ounce pieces of lemon sole in nonstick, stainless steel, cast-iron, and aluminum pans. We knew from past experience that the key was to preheat the pan. When food is added to a cold pan, it is guaranteed to stick and cook unevenly. When choosing a pan for sautéing, it is important that it be of a heavy enough material to conduct the heat uniformly.

We heated the pans for three minutes over moderate heat, or until a drop of water beaded up and evaporated in about 20 seconds, before adding the fat. When ready to sauté, we raised the heat to high, added one teaspoon of canola oil, and then added a small fish fillet. This test confirmed that as long as the pan is heated and the fish cooked with moderate to high heat, there is almost no difference in the end result. Each piece of fish was browned and moist, and none of them stuck to the pan.

There is one thing to keep in mind when working with nonstick pans. Because fat beads up on the surface, it is tempting to add more fat to evenly cover it. To make sure that the fish was lubricated by the fat, we dragged it through the oil before laying it in the lubricated pan. We then tried another approach for adding fat to the nonstick pan. We brushed the fish with the fat, then put the fish into a hot, unlubricated pan. Even with this limited amount of fat, the fish browned and was moist. It was a bit of an odd way to sauté—without the gratifying sound of food sizzling in the pan—but it was ideal for reduced fat cooking.

How much fat do you need if you're not going with the nonstick method? This depends on the size and number of fillets being cooked. For a single fillet about seven to eight inches long and three to four inches wide, in an eight to nine-inch sauté pan, one teaspoon of fat was sufficient. However, when we cooked more than one fillet in the same pan, we discovered we needed about a tablespoon of fat to accommodate them. The weight of the fillets didn't seem to matter as much as the surface area covered by the fish. We found overall that less fat when sautéing was better. Too much fat coming up the sides of the fish made the crust a tough shell and the fish greasy. If you need to add fat while cooking, the best way is to drizzle it down the side of the pan so it doesn't cool things down.

We were also curious to see if the type of fat used made a significant difference. We sautéed the different thicknesses of fish fillets in butter, olive oil, flavorless canola oil, and a combination of butter and oil.

All the fats produced satisfactory results, each with a distinct advantage. Butter was by far the tastiest and gave the fish a gorgeous golden crust. There is a disadvantage to cooking with butter, however: its smoke point is lower than that of vegetable oils, and it can burn easily. This can be problematic when cooking a thick piece of fish. (We found that butter must be used in combination with oil when sautéing fillets thicker than half an inch.) Plain butter is an ideal medium for sautéing thin fillets. To get the best results with butter, heat the pan over moderate heat, then add the butter. It will melt, then foam up. If you add the fish fillet just as the foam subsides, you catch the butter at the proper temperature for sautéing. If the butter burns and smokes, the pan is too hot; wipe out the pan and start again.

Next we tested both pure and extra-virgin olive oils. Both were perfectly suitable for sautéing the fish. Not surprisingly, the extra-virgin complemented the fish with a sweeter, fuller, more complex flavor than the pure. Although the olive oils produced a crust on the fish, they did not provide the same rich appearance as the butter.

The canola oil was the most versatile of the bunch. Its high smoke point allowed it to take prolonged heat, making it suitable for thin or thick fillets. Canola contributes no flavor to the fish, which can be an advantage when pairing it with certain sauces.

When preparing to sauté, make sure that your pan can properly accommodate the fish. The fillets should lie flat and uncrowded in the pan. In our testing, if a fish snuck up the side of the pan, it stuck and fell apart when flipped over. Since some flatfish fillets can be quite large, it is better to cut them before cooking so that they will lie flat. A trick for fitting fillets that taper down to a thin tail is to fold the tail under so the piece is of the same thickness throughout; this avoids overcooking the thinner portion. When sautéing three or four fillets, you may need to use two pans.

Some fish fillets are sold with the skin on. This is helpful when cooking because it holds the fish together while it cooks. However, fish sautéed with the skin on can curl inconveniently. To avoid this, you can score the skin with a sharp knife at 1½-inch intervals. When the fish is cooked on the skin side, press it down with a spatula for 20 seconds or so until it lies flat.

For all fillets, thick or thin, we found it best to cook them first on the smooth, rounded side, not the skin side. The trick is to brown the fillets undisturbed on the first side, in the fresh fat and with assertive heat, until the edges and a thin border on the fillet turn opaque. Resist the temptation to check the fish constantly as it cooks. All that activity cools the food down, meaning that the fish won't brown and will be more likely to stick to the pan. Before turning the fillets over, give the pan a shake to make sure they are free. If a fillet does stick, don't scrape it off the bottom of the pan; instead, let it cook a bit longer. When the fish sticks, it is usually because it hasn't had a chance to form its protective crust. Once the crust is formed, it will shake loose. If you have a troublesome piece, drizzle in a bit of fat and cook it for 30 seconds to a minute more, then briskly slip a spatula under it.

We found that the length of time the fillets spend in the pan plays a big part in the results. With thin pieces, a minute too long, and the fish will flake, fall apart, and be dry. With thick pieces, a minute shy, and they can be raw.

After testing fillets one-half inch thick, we learned that the best method was to brown the fillets over an assertive heat, then flip them over, turn the heat down to moderate, and cook for one minute. Then take the pan off the heat. Cooking will continue with the residual heat of the pan but will be modulated by the cooling as well. The second side may be slightly less brown than the first side, but on very thin fillets, if you crisp both sides, you run the risk of overcooking the fish.

We tried cooking thick fillets by browning them in the fry pan and finishing them in a 350-degree oven, but the crust got soggy. The most successful technique calls for browning the fish over high to medium-high heat, then flipping it over and cooking over medium heat.

To check for doneness, poke the fish with your finger. It should feel firm but should not flake. If the fish falls into dry flakes, it's been overcooked.

After timing more than 25 different fillets, we were surprised to find that the timing was consistent with the Canadian method of 10 minutes cooking per inch of thickness. We thought the fish would overcook in this much time, but cooking over high heat first and then moderating it for the latter part of the cooking did, in fact, cook one-half-inch fillets within 4 to 5 minutes and one-inch-thick fillets within 9 to 11 minutes. To gauge how long to cook the fish, measure it at its thickest point and estimate 8 to 10 minutes per inch. If the fish is held while a pan sauce is made, it is important to remember that it will continue to cook as it rests.

QUICK PAN SAUCES FOR SAUTÉED FISH

Pan sauces are one of the rewards of sautéing. When making them, keep the fats used in the dish complementary; for example, a warm vinaigrette will complement fish sautéed in olive or neutral oils but will fight with fish sautéed in butter. Cream sauces enhance fish sautéed in butter.

Warm Balsamic Vinaigrette with Herbs

MAKES ENOUGH TO SAUCE 4 PORTIONS OF FISH

3	tablespoons balsamic vinegar
1	medium garlic clove, minced
2	tablespoons minced fresh parsley leaves
1	tablespoon minced fresh thyme leaves
¼	teaspoon salt
	Ground black pepper
⅓	cup extra-virgin olive oil

1. Whisk vinegar with garlic, parsley, thyme, and salt, as well as pepper to taste; slowly whisk in olive oil. Set aside.

2. Add vinaigrette to hot pan once fish has been sautéed and removed, and any juices in the pan set aside. Bring to simmer and continue simmering 1 minute. Pour in any reserved juices. Spoon warm sauce over fish and serve.

Horseradish and Cider Cream Sauce

MAKES ENOUGH TO SAUCE 4 PORTIONS OF FISH

1	shallot, minced
	Butter (if necessary for sautéing)
¼	cup cider
4	teaspoons cider vinegar
⅔	cup heavy cream
2 ½	tablespoons prepared horseradish
	Salt and ground black pepper
1	tablespoon minced fresh parsley leaves

Add shallot to warm pan once fish has been sautéed and removed, and any juices in pan set aside; add bit of butter if pan is dry. Sauté over medium heat until almost softened, 1 to 2 minutes. Increase heat to high; add cider and vinegar and reduce to thin syrup, 2 to 3 minutes. Add cream, horseradish, and reserved juices; simmer until sauce thickens, 1 to 2 minutes. Pour in any reserved juices. Season with salt and pepper to taste. Spoon warm sauce over fish, sprinkle with parsley, and serve.

Provençal Tomato Sauce with Basil and Orange

MAKES ENOUGH TO SAUCE 4 PORTIONS OF FISH

2	garlic cloves, minced
½	small onion, minced
	Oil (if necessary for sautéing)
¼	cup white wine
½	teaspoon fennel seeds, cracked
½	teaspoon grated zest from small orange
⅓	cup clam juice or fish stock
⅔	cup tomato puree
	Pinch saffron threads, crumbled
2	tablespoons minced fresh basil leaves
	Salt and ground black pepper

Add garlic and onion to warm pan once fish has been sautéed and removed, and any juices in pan set aside; add bit of oil if pan is dry. Sauté over medium heat until almost softened, about 3 minutes. Add wine, fennel, and zest, then clam juice, puree, saffron, and any reserved juices. Simmer until slightly thickened, 2 to 3 minutes. Stir in basil and season to taste with salt and pepper. Spoon warm sauce over fish and serve.

Sautéed Thin Fish Fillets

SERVES 4

For these thin, flat fillets, such as sole or flounder, you can fold the thin tail end under. This step will enable you to fit all four fillets in one large skillet rather than having to heat up two.

- 1 ½   pounds thin fish fillets, rinsed and dried with paper towels, skin scored at 1 ½-inch intervals if present
- 2   tablespoons unsalted butter and/or oil
     Salt and ground black pepper

Heat one large or two medium skillets over medium heat until drop of water beads up and evaporates, 2 to 3 minutes. Increase heat to medium-high; add butter and/or oil to pan (or 1 tablespoon to each pan). Season fish with salt and pepper to taste. When foaming subsides (if using butter) or oil starts to shimmer, add fillets, skin side up, to pan(s). Cook until golden brown, 2 to 3 minutes, occasionally shaking pan gently to keep fillets from sticking. Turn fish with spatula. If fillets are very thin, turn heat off immediately, allowing residual heat from pan to finish cooking fish. If fish is a little thicker, continue to cook over medium-high heat for 1 minute, then turn off heat and allow residual heat to finish the cooking. Transfer fillets to platter, cover with foil, and make one of the pan sauces on page 306, if desired. When pan sauce is done, serve immediately.

➤ VARIATIONS

Sautéed Medium-Thick Fish Fillets

Medium-thick fish measure about three-quarters inch thick and include fish such as striped bass, sea bass, and snapper.

Follow recipe for Sautéed Thin Fish Fillets, using oil or combination oil and butter and increasing cooking time on first side to 3 to 4 minutes and cooking time on second side to 2 to 3 minutes.

Sautéed Thick Fish Fillets

This category of fish includes those measuring at least one inch thick. Larger flaked fish, such as scrod, tend to fall apart easily during cooking. We found cutting the fillets into individual portions made them easier to turn and therefore less likely to fall apart. If the fillets look like they

will crowd the pan, use two skillets rather than one. You want to make sure that they brown, not steam.

Follow recipe for Sautéed Thin Fish Fillets, using oil or combination butter and oil and increasing cooking time on first side to 5 to 6 minutes over high to medium-high heat and cooking time on second side to 4 to 5 minutes over medium heat.

STEAMED FISH FILLETS AND STEAKS

WE'VE STEAMED ALL TYPES OF FISH AND found it to be a terrific way to cook them. Not only is it easy and quick, but it also keeps the fish moist and its flavor pure. Generally—with the exception of wild striped bass and sturgeon, both of which toughen when steamed—if you like a fish cooked by another technique, you'll enjoy it steamed as well.

Steaming fish is really very easy, but there is one factor that is a bit tricky, and that is timing. In our testing, we hoped to find a simple timing rule that would hold true for all varieties of fish. We were looking for something like the Canadian rule that fish should be cooked 10 minutes per inch of thickness (which did in fact apply when we sautéed fillets). Unfortunately, we discovered no such rule of thumb when it came to steaming. Instead, we found that determining the proper cooking time is a risky business; there are so many variables that no rule can be applied. We did come to the conclusion, however, that certain variables are very important in determining cooking time, while others turned out to be less important than we had expected. By paying attention to the proper variables, a very close approximation of perfect cooking time can be made for each type of fish.

We found the two most important variables affecting steaming time to be the thickness and the texture of the individual fish. Times are more affected by the thickness of the fillet or steak, for example, than by weight or size; as long as they are roughly the same thickness, an eight-ounce salmon fillet and a one-pound salmon fillet take the same amount of time to cook. The texture of the flesh varies considerably among different fish, and this makes a real difference when it comes to cooking time. A flaky cod fillet steams much more quickly, for example, than a meaty monkfish fillet of the same thickness. After a while we got pretty good at estimating what the steaming time of a fillet or steak might be by comparing it with a fish of similar texture for which we already had a steaming time. Using the table below, you should be able to do the same.

When it comes to heat, we have always steamed fish at a rapid simmer rather than a full boil. Steaming at full boil leaves little room for error. There is so much steam that a piece of fish goes from underdone to overdone very quickly. If you reduce the heat to a rapid simmer, there's a slightly longer window of time during which the fish will be perfectly cooked.

Knowing that steam cooks with a relatively low,

moist heat, we wondered whether there was a greater margin for error when steaming fish than when cooking by other methods. Except for oily fish such as bluefish and mackerel, which remained moist even when overcooked, the answer was no; steaming, too, dries out fillets and steaks if they are allowed to overcook. Since the fish continues to cook after it is removed from the steamer, we found it best to take steaks out when they are still medium-rare at the bone; by the time we ate the fish, it had cooked through. Fillets should still be slightly translucent in the center when they're removed from the steamer; if the fish is flaking apart, it's overcooked.

We also found that we could hold the cooked fish in the steamer for a few minutes while we made a

Steaming Times for Fish Fillets and Steaks

Although we have found the cooking times listed here to be very reliable (seven minutes has been perfect for every salmon fillet we have ever steamed, for example), keep in mind that because the temperature, thickness, and perhaps the quality of the fish affect the steaming time, these times should be used as guidelines. We prefer to err on the side of undercooking; check the fish for doneness early and continue steaming if it isn't cooked enough for your taste. You can always cook it a little longer, but once fish is overcooked, it's overcooked.

If you are going to be steaming a fish that is not listed on the chart below, find a fish on the chart that has a similar texture and thickness and use the time shown for it.

SPECIES	TYPE OF CUT	TIME
Arctic Char	Fillet (1 inch thick)	5 minutes
Bluefish	Fillet (¾ to 1 inch thick)	7 to 8 minutes
Cod	Steak (1 inch thick) Fillet (1 inch thick)	6 to 8 minutes 6 minutes
Flounder and Gray Sole	Fillet (¼ to ½ inch thick, folded in half so the tail end is under the wide end)	4 to 6 minutes
Grouper	Fillet (1 to 1½ inches thick)	10 to 12 minutes
Halibut	Steak (1 inch thick)	6 minutes
Monkfish	Fillet (1 inch thick)	10 to 12 minutes
Pompano	Fillet (½ to ¾ inch thick)	6 to 8 minutes
Salmon	Steak (1¼ to 1½ inches thick)	7 to 8 minutes for medium-rare 8 to 9 minutes for medium
Snapper	Fillet (1¼ inches thick)	7 to 8 minutes for medium-rare 8 to 9 minutes for medium
Swordfish	Fillet (¾ inch thick)	5 minutes
Tilefish	Steak (¾ to 1 inch thick)	6 minutes
Tuna	Steak (1 to 1¼ inches thick)	6 to 8 minutes
Wolffish	Steak (¾ to 1 inch thick) Fillet (½ to ¾ inch thick)	2 minutes for rare 4 minutes for medium-rare 5 minutes

QUICK SAUCES FOR STEAMED FISH

Steamed fish is not as wet as poached fish, but as it sits it gives off juices. The juices are welcome if you are just using oil and lemon juice, but they'll dilute a "real" sauce. Blot them with paper towels or drain the fish for a minute on clean cloth towels before putting it on serving plates.

White Wine, Butter, and Caper Sauce

MAKES ENOUGH TO SAUCE
4 SERVINGS OF FISH

This quick, rather thin pan sauce is made with reduced white wine and a little of the liquid used for steaming. It bathes the fish rather than thickly coating it.

- ½ cup white wine
- ¼ cup of liquid used for steaming
- 1 rounded tablespoon capers, drained (¼ teaspoon brine reserved) and coarsely chopped
- 4 tablespoons unsalted butter, chilled and cut into small pieces
- 1 teaspoon chopped fresh parsley leaves
  Salt and ground black pepper

Over high heat, reduce wine to ¼ cup in a small saucepan. Add steaming liquid and reduce combined liquids to ⅓ cup. Add capers and whisk in butter pieces a few at a time to incorporate. When all butter has been added, remove sauce from heat and whisk in caper brine, parsley, salt and pepper to taste. Serve immediately.

Tomato Sauce with Bell Peppers and Balsamic Vinegar

MAKES ENOUGH TO SAUCE
4 SERVINGS OF FISH

Try this simple sauce with cod, salmon, swordfish, tuna, or even shrimp or chicken.

- 1 tablespoon olive oil
- 1 garlic clove, minced
- ½ medium onion, chopped
- ½ red bell pepper, halved, stemmed, cored, and thinly sliced lengthwise
- ½ green bell pepper, halved, stemmed, cored, and thinly sliced lengthwise
- 1½ cups canned tomatoes with juice
- 1 teaspoon balsamic or red wine vinegar
  Salt and ground black pepper

Heat oil over medium heat in medium saucepan; add garlic, onion, and bell peppers. Cover and cook until vegetables soften, about 5 minutes. Add tomatoes and juice; simmer, uncovered, until thickened, about 15 minutes. Stir in vinegar, and season to taste with salt and pepper. Serve.

Black Olive Paste

MAKES ENOUGH TO SAUCE
12 SERVINGS OF FISH

A little of this paste goes a long way. You need only a tablespoon or so per serving of fish, but making a smaller quantity doesn't make sense considering that whatever is left over can be spread on toast rounds and served as appetizers. Only strong-flavored fish such as tuna and bluefish can stand up to this assertive paste.

- 1 cup black olives, such as kalamata or niçoise, pitted
- 1 large garlic clove, chopped coarse
- 2 anchovy fillets (optional)
- 1 tablespoon capers, drained
- ½ teaspoon minced fresh thyme leaves
  Pinch cayenne pepper
- 3 tablespoons extra-virgin olive oil

Place all ingredients in work bowl of a food processor fitted with steel blade; process to a paste. Scrape into a small bowl. (Can be refrigerated in an airtight container for at least 1 month.)

sauce or set the table by turning off the heat and setting the steamer lid at an angle.

Two factors that we expected to influence cooking times—the tightness of the seal on the steamer and the quantity of fish being steamed—turned out to be irrelevant.

When you are dealing with most foods, a steamer with a tight-fitting lid and a tight seal between pot and steamer basket cooks food faster than a steamer with a less effective seal and lid. This is not true, however, when steaming fish; even in a pot covered with foil instead of a lid, the fish steams at the same rate.

The quantity of fish in the pot does not seem to influence the steaming time, either. We discovered that as long as the fish is not jammed up against the side of the pot or the lid and is arranged in a single layer so that the steam can circulate freely, four fillets or steaks take the same amount of time as one fillet or steak.

For a long time our method of moving fish out of the steamer after it was done was to turn off the fire, open the steamer, and, battling the heat of the steam, use a spatula to lift the fish out and onto a serving plate. We finally realized that it was much easier to remove the entire steamer basket or perforated insert from the steamer pot, setting it on a plate to catch the drips, before lifting out the fish itself with a spatula.

We found that steamed fillets of delicate fish like snapper, bluefish, and pompano flake apart when moved. A "tray" made with a single sheet of aluminum foil cut to size and placed under each fillet made it easy to move them. This also kept the fillets from sticking to the steamer and was especially useful when using a rack in a roasting pan to steam the fish. (See below for recommendations on types of steamers—improvised and otherwise.) To move the cooked fish, simply grasp opposite corners of the foil and lift it, with the fillet, out of the steamer. Then, with a spatula, gently slide the fillet onto a plate.

EQUIPMENT: Tools for Steaming

All you really need for steaming is some kind of pot and a perforated steamer rack that stands up off the bottom of the pot so that the fish is above the water. You probably already have something suitable in your kitchen.

We experimented with steaming fish in various pieces of kitchen equipment, some actually marketed as steamers and some just contraptions that we improvised. There are also a number of electric steamers on the market that steam fish beautifully, although they may do so somewhat more slowly than stove-top arrangements.

We found that most nonelectric steamers cook fish at about the same rate, except for bamboo steamers set over a wok, which take quite a bit more time. Since we wanted to give steaming times that would be consistent between steamers, we excluded bamboo steamers from our testing. Here are some options for steaming equipment:

Collapsible steamer baskets: These are useful and convenient for steaming steaks and smallish fillets. They are cheap, easy to wash and store, and are sold everywhere. We prefer to use them in a deep sauté pan rather than a pot because it is easier to get the basket in and out. The disadvantage these baskets have is that they tip easily and are tricky to handle when loaded with fish.

Pasta cookers and stackable steamers: These contraptions both have the same design—a pot with holes in the bottom rests inside a larger pot that holds the steaming liquid. Deep pasta cookers are cheap and readily available, but it's hard to get the fish out of them because there isn't room to maneuver the spatula under the fish. We prefer two-tiered stackable steamers. With its two baskets, this type of steamer can accommodate steaks for up to eight people and even fairly large fillets for four. On the down side, these steamers are large and fairly expensive.

Roasting pan and rack: Our favorite steaming apparatus is an oval, dome-lidded roasting pan (the cheap speckled kind sold at most hardware stores) fitted with an oval roasting rack. We like this set-up because it is multipurpose and very inexpensive, only about $12. It's also large enough to steam four fairly large fillets or six steaks. To use it, simply set the rack on two empty tuna cans to raise it up a bit, thus assuring that the water doesn't touch the fish. You can use any roasting pan as long as it has a rack. The pan needn't have a lid; we have often resorted to covering a pan with aluminum foil. When using this setup, it is best to put the pan over two burners.

Fish poachers: A fish poacher, particularly useful for steaming whole fish, can also be used for steaks and fillets. Raise the rack off the bottom with empty cans and cover the poacher with a lid or with aluminum foil, as when steaming in a roasting pan. Again, it is best to steam over two burners. Unfortunately, a good poacher costs at least $80.

SHRIMP

IT'S SAFE TO SAY THAT ANY SHRIMP YOU BUY have been frozen (and usually thawed by the retailer), but not all shrimp are the same—far from it. The Gulf of Mexico supplies about 200 million pounds of shrimp annually to the rest of the country, but three times that amount is imported, mostly from Asia and Central and South America.

After tasting all of the commonly available varieties of shrimp several times, we have little trouble declaring two winners: Mexican whites (*Panaeus vannamei*), from the Pacific coast, are usually the best. A close second, and often just as good, are Gulf whites (*P. setiferus*). Either of these may be wild or farm-raised. Unfortunately, these are rarely the shrimp you're offered in supermarkets. The shrimp most commonly found in supermarkets is Black Tiger, a farmed shrimp from Asia. Its quality is inconsistent, but it can be quite flavorful and firm. And even if you go into a fishmonger's and ask for white shrimp, you may get farm-raised shrimp from China—a less expensive but decidedly inferior species (*P. chinensis*). (There are more than 300 species of shrimp in the world and not nearly as many common names.)

All you can do is try to buy the best shrimp available, and buy it right. Beyond choosing the best species you can find, you should also consider some of the other factors affecting quality, described below.

Buy still-frozen shrimp rather than those which have been thawed. Because almost all shrimp are frozen after the catch, and thawed shrimp start losing their flavor in just a couple of days, buying thawed shrimp gives you neither the flavor of fresh nor the flexibility of frozen. We found that shrimp stored in the freezer retain peak quality for several weeks, deteriorating very slowly after that until about the three-month point, when we detected a noticeable deterioration in quality. If you do buy thawed shrimp, they should smell of salt water and little else, and they should be firm and fully fill their shells.

Avoid prepeeled and deveined shrimp; cleaning before freezing unquestionably deprives shrimp of some of their flavor and texture; everyone we asked to sample precleaned shrimp found them to be nearly tasteless. In addition, precleaned shrimp may have added tripolyphosphate, a chemical that aids in water retention and can give shrimp an off flavor.

Shrimp should have no black spots, or melanosis, on their shells, which indicate that a breakdown of the meat has begun. Be equally suspicious of shrimp with yellowing shells or those which feel gritty: either of these conditions may indicate the overuse of sodium bisulfite, a bleaching agent sometimes used to retard melanosis.

Despite the popularity of shrimp, there are no standards for size. Small, medium, large, extra large, jumbo, and other size classifications are subjective and relative. Small shrimp of 70 or so to the pound are frequently labeled "medium," as are those twice that size and even larger. It pays, then, to judge shrimp size by the number it takes to make a pound, as retailers do. Shrimp labeled "16/20," for example, require 16 to 20 (usually closer to 20) individual specimens to make a pound. Those labeled "U-20" require fewer than 20 to make a pound. Shrimp of 15 or 20 to about 30 per pound usually yield the best combination of flavor, ease of peeling (peeling tiny shrimp is a nuisance), and value (really big shrimp usually cost more than $10 per pound).

Once shrimp are purchased, they should be prepared before cooking. Should they be peeled? Should the vein that runs down the back of each shrimp be removed?

We found that the issue of peeling depends on the cooking method. After some initial tests, we concluded that shrimp must be prepared differently when cooked by dry and moist heat. We found that when shrimp are grilled or pan-seared, the shell shields the meat from the intense heat and helps to keep the shrimp moist and tender. Try as we might, we found it impossible to grill or pan-sear peeled shrimp without overcooking them and making the meat dry and tough, especially the exterior layers. The only method that worked was to intentionally undercook the shrimp; but that left the inside a little gooey, something that almost no one enjoyed.

When shrimp are cooked in liquid the tables turn, and it is best to peel them first. The exterior of shrimp cooked in liquid are not as prone to drying out, and the shells can be simmered in the liquid to increase its flavor. Also, it is nearly impossible to peel shrimp cooked in hot liquid. While the shell separates easily from grilled or pan-seared shrimp, it becomes firmly attached to the meat when the shrimp are cooked in liquid.

In addition to peeling, the issue of deveining generates much controversy, even among experts. Although some people won't eat shrimp that has not been deveined, others believe that the "vein"—actually the animal's intestinal tract—contributes flavor and insist on leaving it in. In our tests, we could not detect an effect (either positive or negative) on flavor when we left the vein in. The vein is generally so tiny in most medium-sized shrimp that it virtually disappears after cooking. Out of laziness, we leave it alone. In very large shrimp, the vein is usually larger as well. Very large veins can detract from the overall texture of the shrimp and are best removed before cooking.

PAN-SEARED, GRILLED, OR BROILED SHRIMP

COOKING SHRIMP IN A HOT SKILLET, OVER hot coals, or under a broiler would seem to be an easy undertaking—as soon as the shrimp turn pink, they are done. And while it is fairly easy, we did find that shrimp exposed to dry heat (the issues when pan-searing, grilling, or broiling are basically the same, so they are considered here together) have a tendency to dry out. We discovered that brining the shrimp in a salt solution, which works so well with poultry (see page 137 for details), also works with shrimp. Brining causes shrimp to become especially

plump (we found they may gain as much 10 percent in water weight) and firm.

The science is fairly simple. Salt causes protein strands in the shrimp to unwind, allowing them to trap and hold onto more moisture when cooked. At its most successful, brining turns mushy shrimp into shrimp with the chewy texture of a lobster tail. Even top-quality shrimp are improved by this process. We tested various concentrations of salt and brining times and in the end settled on soaking shrimp in a strong salt solution (3 cups kosher salt dissolved in 5½ cups water) for 20 to 25 minutes.

Once the shrimp has been brined, it can be dumped into a hot skillet or threaded onto skewers and grilled or broiled. Unpeeled shrimp is easy to cook either way. As soon as the meat turns pink, the shrimp are done. We found that shrimp should be cooked quickly to prevent them from toughening. This means using a very hot skillet, a hot grill fire, or a preheated broiler.

When pan-searing, it's easy enough to make a quick pan sauce once the shrimp have been cooked and transferred to a bowl. Just add some oil and seasonings (garlic, shallots, lemon juice, herbs, spices) to the empty pan and cook briefly. The sauce can then be tossed with the shrimp in the shell to coat them. When grilling or broiling, we like to coat the shrimp with a paste or marinade before cooking. With all three cooking methods, the flavorings adhere to the shell beautifully. When you peel the shrimp at the table, the seasonings stick to your fingers and they are in turn transferred directly to the meat as you eat it. Licking your fingers also helps.

PREPARING BRINED SHRIMP FOR COOKING

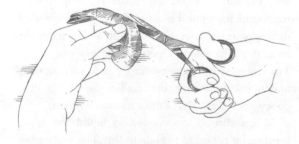

When cooked with dry heat (pan-searing, grilling, or broiling), shrimp are best cooked in their shells. The shells hold in moisture and also flavor the shrimp as they cook. However, eating shrimp cooked in its shell can be a challenge. As a compromise, we found it helpful to slit the back of the shell with a manicure or other small scissors with a fine point. When ready to eat, each person can quickly and easily peel away the shell.

Brined Shrimp

MAKES ENOUGH TO SERVE 4 TO 6

When pan-searing, grilling, or broiling, we recommend that you brine the shrimp first to make them especially plump and juicy. When poaching shrimp for cocktail (page 316), brining is not necessary—the shrimp remain nice and plump when cooked in liquid.

3   cups kosher salt or 1½ cups table salt
2   pounds large shrimp (21 to 25 count per pound)

Pour 2 cups boiling water into large bowl. Add

salt, stirring to dissolve, and cool to room temperature. Add 3½ cups ice water and shrimp and let stand 20 to 25 minutes. Drain and rinse thoroughly under cold running water. Open shells with manicure scissors and devein if desired.

➤ VARIATION

Brined Frozen Shrimp

In many ways, uncooked frozen shrimp offers consumers the best quality, since the shrimp are frozen at sea and then thawed at home, not at the market, as is the case with almost all the "fresh" shrimp sold at the retail level. However, because frozen shrimp are generally sold in five-pound blocks, these shrimp can be difficult to handle. Rather than trying to saw through a block of ice, we recommend running the frozen block of shrimp under cold running water and pulling off individual shrimp as they become free. When you have the desired amount of shrimp (in this recipe, two pounds), place the remaining portion of the block back in the freezer and proceed with brining the partially thawed shrimp.

Follow recipe for Brined Shrimp, using frozen shrimp and 3½ cups cold (not ice) water, since shrimp themselves are still partially frozen. Proceed as directed with brining.

Pan-Seared Shrimp

SERVES 4 TO 6

This recipe delivers shrimp in its simplest and purest form. The variations add some other flavors but are also remarkably simple. To keep burnt bits from ending up in the sauce, rinse the pan and wipe clean after the shrimp has been cooked.

1	recipe Brined Shrimp (page 312)
½	lemon

1. Heat large nonstick or cast-iron skillet over high heat until very hot. Place single layer of shrimp in pan. Cook until shrimp shells turn spotty brown, 1 to 2 minutes. Turn shrimp as they brown; cook until remaining side turns spotty brown, 1 to 2 minutes longer. As shrimp are done, transfer them to medium bowl. Repeat process with remaining shrimp.

2. Squeeze lemon juice over shrimp and serve warm or at room temperature.

➤ VARIATIONS

Pan-Seared Shrimp with Shallots and Tarragon

1	recipe Brined Shrimp (page 312)
1	tablespoon extra-virgin olive oil
1	large shallot, minced
1½	tablespoons sherry vinegar
1½	tablespoons minced fresh tarragon leaves
	Salt and ground black pepper

1. Heat large nonstick or cast-iron skillet over high heat until very hot. Place single layer of shrimp in pan. Cook until shrimp shells turn spotty brown, 1 to 2 minutes. Turn shrimp as they brown; cook until remaining side turns spotty brown, 1 to 2 minutes longer. As shrimp are done, transfer them to medium bowl. Repeat process with remaining shrimp.

2. Rinse and wipe out pan with paper towel. Heat oil in skillet over medium heat. Add shallot and sauté until softened and just beginning to brown, 1 to 1½ minutes; add to bowl with shrimp. Add vinegar, tarragon, and salt and pepper to taste to bowl. Toss to combine. Serve warm or at room temperature.

Pan-Seared Shrimp with Southwestern Flavors

1	recipe Brined Shrimp (page 312)
1	tablespoon extra-virgin olive oil
1	large garlic clove, minced
2	teaspoons chili powder
¾	teaspoon ground cumin
2½	tablespoons lime juice
2	tablespoons minced fresh cilantro leaves
	Salt and ground black pepper

1. Heat large nonstick or cast-iron skillet over high heat until very hot. Place single layer of shrimp in pan. Cook until shrimp shells turn spotty brown, 1 to 2 minutes. Turn shrimp as they brown; cook until remaining side turns spotty brown, 1 to 2 minutes longer. As shrimp are done, transfer them to medium bowl. Repeat process with remaining shrimp.

2. Rinse and wipe out pan with paper towel. Heat oil in skillet over medium heat. Add garlic, chili powder, and cumin and sauté until garlic is fragrant and lightens in color, 30 to 45 seconds; add to bowl with

shrimp. Add lime juice, cilantro, and salt and pepper to taste to bowl. Toss to combine. Serve warm or at room temperature.

Charcoal-Grilled Shrimp with Spicy Garlic Paste

SERVES 4 TO 6

To keep the shrimp from dropping through the grill rack onto the hot coals, thread them onto skewers (see illustration below). You can cook shrimp loose on a perforated grill grid that rests right on the cooking grate. The problem with this method is that each shrimp must be turned individually with tongs rather than in groups, as with skewered shrimp (see illustration below). The shrimp are more likely to cook unevenly on a grid because it takes so long to turn them all.

I	large garlic clove, peeled
I	teaspoon salt
½	teaspoon cayenne pepper
I	teaspoon paprika
2	tablespoons olive oil
2	teaspoons lemon juice
I	recipe Brined Shrimp (page 312)
	Lemon wedges

1. Build a single-level fire (page 258). Mince garlic with salt into smooth paste. Mix garlic and salt with cayenne and paprika in small bowl. Add oil and lemon juice to form thin paste. Toss shrimp with paste until evenly coated. (Can be covered and refrigerated for up to 1 hour). Thread shrimp onto skewers.

2. Grill shrimp over medium-hot fire, turning once, until shells are bright pink, 2 to 3 minutes per side. Serve hot or at room temperature with lemon wedges.

➤ VARIATIONS

Gas-Grilled Shrimp

Follow recipe for Charcoal-Grilled Shrimp with Spicy Garlic Paste, making the following changes: Turn all burners to high and preheat with lid down until very hot, about 15 minutes. Grill as in charcoal recipe but with lid down.

Broiled Shrimp

Follow recipe for Charcoal-Grilled Shrimp with Spicy Garlic Paste, adjusting oven rack to top position and preheating broiler. Place skewered shrimp in jelly-roll or other shallow pan and broil, turning once, until shells are bright pink, 2 to 3 minutes per side.

Charcoal-Grilled Shrimp with Asian Flavors

Unlike the garlic paste (which adheres beautifully to the shrimp as they cook), this seasoning mixture is fairly liquidy and falls off. We found that letting the shrimp sit in this mixture for at least half an hour (but no more than an hour) flavors them nicely. This recipe can be adapted to the gas grill or the broiler.

SKEWERING SHRIMP

1. Thread shrimp on skewers by passing the skewer through the body near the tail, folding the shrimp over, and passing the shrimp through the body again near the head. Threading each shrimp twice keeps it in place (it won't spin) and makes it easy to cook shrimp on both sides.

2. Long-handled tongs make it easy to turn hot skewers on the grill. Lightly grab onto a single shrimp to turn the entire skewer.

1 ½	tablespoons soy sauce
2	teaspoons rice wine vinegar
¾	teaspoon Asian sesame oil
1 ½	teaspoons sugar
½	teaspoon grated fresh gingerroot
1	large garlic clove, minced
2	medium scallions, sliced thin
1	recipe Brined Shrimp (page 312)

1. Build a single-level fire (page 258). Combine all ingredients except for shrimp in medium bowl. Add shrimp and toss well. Refrigerate for 30 to 60 minutes. Thread shrimp onto skewers.

2. Grill shrimp over medium-hot fire, turning once, until shells are bright pink, 2 to 3 minutes per side. Serve hot or at room temperature with lemon wedges.

SHRIMP COCKTAIL

NOTHING IS MORE BASIC THAN SHRIMP cocktail, and given its simplicity, few dishes are more difficult to improve. Yet we set out to do just that, and we believe we succeeded.

Shrimp cocktail, as everyone must know, is "boiled" shrimp served cold with "cocktail" sauce, typically a blend of bottled ketchup or chili sauce spiked with horseradish. It's easy enough to change the basic pattern in order to produce a more contemporary cold shrimp dish; you could, for example, grill shrimp and serve them with a fresh tomato salsa (and many people have done just that). But there is something refreshing and utterly classic about traditional shrimp cocktail, and sometimes it fits the occasion better than anything else.

We saw three ways to challenge the traditional method of preparing shrimp cocktail in order to produce the best-tasting but recognizable version of this dish. One, work on the flavor of the shrimp; two, work on the cooking method for the shrimp; three, produce a great cocktail sauce.

The shrimp in shrimp cocktail can be ice-cold strings of protein, chewy or mushy, or they can be tender, flavorful morsels that barely need sauce. To achieve the latter, you need to start with the best shrimp you can find and give them as much flavor as they can handle without overwhelming them.

If you start with good shrimp and follow a typical shrimp cocktail recipe—that is, simmer the shrimp in salted water until pink—the shrimp will have decent but rarely intense flavor. The easiest way to intensify the flavor of shrimp is to cook them in their shells. But, as we found out, this method has its drawbacks. First of all, it's far easier to peel shrimp when they are raw than once they are cooked in liquid. More important, however, the full flavor of the shells is not extracted during the relatively short time required for the shrimp to cook through. It takes a good 20 minutes for the shells to impart their flavor to the cooking water, and this is far too long to keep shrimp in a pot.

It's better, then, to make shrimp stock, a simple enough process that takes only 20 minutes using just the shrimp shells. To improve on the results of this process, every time you use shrimp for any purpose, place the peels in a pot with water to cover, then simmer them for 20 minutes. Cool, strain, and freeze the resultant stock. Use this stock as the cooking liquid for your next batch of shrimp peels. Naturally, this stock will become more and more intense each time you add to it.

Next, we thought, it would be best to see what other flavors would complement the shrimp without overpowering it. Our first attempt was to use beer and a spicy commercial seasoning, but this was a near disaster; the shrimp for cocktail should not taste like a New Orleans crab boil. Next we tried a court bouillon, the traditional herb-scented stock for poaching fish, but quickly discovered that the game wasn't worth the candle; we wanted a few quick additions to our shrimp stock that would add complexity of flavor without making a simple process complicated.

After trying about 20 different combinations, involving wine, vinegar, lemon juice, and a near-ludicrous number of herbs and spices, we settled on the mixture given in the recipe here. It contains about 25 percent white wine, a dash of lemon juice, and a more or less traditional herb combination. Variations are certainly possible, but we would caution you against adding more wine or lemon juice; both were good up to a point, but after that their pungency became overwhelming.

Although we were pleased at this point with the quality of the shrimp's flavor, we still thought it could be more intense. We quickly learned, however, that the answer to this problem was not to keep pouring flavorings into the cooking liquid; that was self-defeating because we eventually lost the flavor of the shrimp. We decided to try to keep the shrimp in contact with the flavorings for a longer period of time.

We tried several methods to achieve this, including starting the shrimp in cold water with the seasonings and using a longer cooking time at a lower temperature. But shrimp cook so quickly—this is part of their appeal, of course—that these methods only served to toughen the meat. What worked best, we found, was to bring the cooking liquid to a boil, turn it off, and add the shrimp. Depending on their size, we could leave them in contact with the liquid for up to 10 minutes (even a little longer for jumbo shrimp), during which time they would cook through without toughening, while taking on near perfect flavor.

Improving traditional cocktail sauce proved to be a tricky business. We wanted to make a better sauce, but we still wanted it to be recognizable as cocktail sauce. Starting with fresh or canned tomatoes, we discovered, just didn't work. The result was often terrific (some might say preferable), but it was not cocktail sauce. It was as if we had decided to make a better version of liver and onions by substituting foie gras for veal liver—it might be "better," but it would no longer be liver and onions.

We went so far as to make American-style ketchup from scratch, an interesting project but not especially profitable, in that the effect was to duplicate something sold in near-perfect form in the supermarket. Again, there are more interesting tomato-based sauces than ketchup, but they're not ketchup.

So we decided the best thing we could do was to find the bottled ketchup or chili sauce we liked best and season it ourselves. First we had to determine which made the better base, ketchup or chili sauce. The answer to this question was surprising but straightforward: ketchup. Bottled chili sauce is little more than vinegary ketchup with a host of seasonings added. The less expensive chili sauces have the acrid, bitter taste of garlic powder, monosodium glutamate, and other dried seasonings. The more expensive ones have more honest flavors but still did not compare to the cocktail sauce we whipped up in three minutes using basic store-bought ketchup. In addition, chili sauce can be four to eight times as expensive as ketchup.

Our preference in cocktail sauce has always been to emphasize the horseradish. But ketchup and horseradish, we knew, were not enough. Cocktail sauce benefits from a variety of heat sources, none of which overpower the other, and the sum of which still allows the flavor of the shrimp to come through. We liked the addition of chili powder. We also liked a bit of bite from cayenne, but only a pinch. Black pepper plays a favorable role as well (as does salt, even though ketchup is already salty). Finally, after trying high-quality wine vinegar, balsamic vinegar, rice vinegar, sherry vinegar, and distilled vinegar, we went back to lemon, which is the gentlest and most fragrant acidic seasoning. In sum, the keys to good cocktail sauce include ordinary ketchup, fresh lemon juice, horseradish (fresh is best: even month-old bottled horseradish is pathetic compared with a just-opened bottle), and fresh chili powder. Proportions can be varied to taste.

Herb-Poached Shrimp
SERVES 4

When using larger or smaller shrimp, increase or decrease cooking times for shrimp by one to two minutes, respectively.

1	pound very large (16 to 20 per pound) shrimp, peeled, deveined, and rinsed, shells reserved
1	teaspoon salt
1	cup dry white wine
4	peppercorns
5	coriander seeds
½	bay leaf
5	sprigs fresh parsley
1	sprig fresh tarragon
1	teaspoon juice from 1 small lemon

1. Bring reserved shells, 3 cups water, and salt to boil in medium saucepan over medium-high heat; reduce heat to low, cover, and simmer until fragrant, about 20 minutes. Strain stock through sieve, pressing on shells to extract all liquid.

2. Bring stock and remaining ingredients except shrimp to boil in 3- or 4-quart saucepan over high heat; boil 2 minutes. Turn off heat and stir in shrimp; cover and let stand until firm and pink, 8 to 10 minutes. Drain shrimp, reserving stock for another use. Plunge shrimp into ice water to stop cooking, then drain again. Serve shrimp chilled with cocktail sauce.

Cocktail Sauce

MAKES ABOUT I CUP

Use horseradish from a fresh bottle and mild chili powder for the best flavor.

I   cup ketchup
2 ½   teaspoons prepared horseradish
¼   teaspoon salt
¼   teaspoon ground black pepper
I   teaspoon ancho or other mild chili powder
    Pinch cayenne pepper
I   tablespoon juice from I small lemon

Stir all ingredients together in small bowl; adjust seasonings as necessary.

SHRIMP SCAMPI

SHRIMP SCAMPI HAS BEEN A CLASSIC Italian restaurant dish for generations. We think of scampi as sautéed shrimp in an olive oil–based sauce with garlic, herbs, and perhaps some lemon juice. The term "scampi," however, is applied to a wide variety of dishes, everything from batter-dipped, deep-fried shrimp drenched in bad oil to boiled shrimp and tomato sauce on a bed of pasta. For true scampi, the shrimp is lightly cooked and moist, the seasonings are fresh and minimal, and the surrounding liquid is light, plentiful, natural tasting, and delicious.

When it came time to re-create that dish, we found it a challenge to cook the shrimp in a way that produced that wonderful juice, which is so good for dunking bread or for moistening rice or even pasta. We tried adding every liquid we could think of that might fit the bill: white wine (of course), lemon juice, more olive oil, fish stock, chicken stock, even water. The wine and lemon juice added too much acidity; the extra oil made the dish, well, too oily; the stocks and water diluted the flavor of the shrimp. During all of these trial runs, we also played with the heat level. We found that an overly high heat not only caused the garlic to become overdone and bitter but also toughened the shrimp.

As we lowered the heat for cooking, we noticed that the liquid given off by the shrimp lingered in the pan. Could this be the elusive liquid we were searching for? We set out to do everything we could

to focus on these shrimp juices, cooking slowly, as if we were braising in the olive oil and natural juices. In fact, because the goal is to preserve the liquid and the tenderness of the shrimp rather than create crispness, the technique is actually closer to braising than sautéing.

Once we started moving in this direction, everything fell into place. With lower heat, the garlic becomes tender and mild-flavored rather than bitter, the olive oil retains its freshness, and the shrimp remains moist and tender—there's little danger of overcooking. We added the lemon juice and parsley at the last possible minute, almost as a garnish, and both kept their sparkle as well. An unexpected benefit of this technique was that it opened up some great possibilities for variations on the basic recipe.

Finally, a serving suggestion. Although this dish goes very well with rice, it is really at its best with bread. Make it in a cast-iron skillet, and bring the pan to the table; serve the shrimp with a spoon, and use the bread to sop up remaining juices from both plate and skillet—there are few greater pleasures.

Shrimp Scampi

SERVES 4

Cayenne pepper replaces ground black pepper in this recipe, but use it sparingly, only to give the faintest hint of spiciness.

¼   cup extra-virgin olive oil
4   medium garlic cloves, minced
2   pounds large shrimp (21 to 25 per pound), peeled, deveined if desired, and rinsed
¼   cup minced fresh parsley leaves
2   tablespoons juice from I lemon
    Salt
    Cayenne pepper

Heat oil and garlic in 10-inch skillet over medium heat until garlic begins to sizzle. Reduce heat to medium-low and cook until fragrant and pale gold, about 2 minutes. Add shrimp, increase heat to medium and cook, stirring occasionally, until shrimp turn pink, about 7 minutes. Be careful not to overcook or the shrimp will become tough. Off heat, stir in parsley, lemon juice, and salt and cayenne pepper to taste. Serve immediately.

➤ VARIATIONS

Shrimp Scampi with Cumin, Paprika, and Sherry Vinegar

This dish is deeply flavorful but has slightly less heat than either of the other two versions.

Follow recipe for Shrimp Scampi, sautéing 1 teaspoon ground cumin and 2 teaspoons paprika with garlic, substituting an equal amount of sherry vinegar for lemon juice, and omitting cayenne.

Shrimp Scampi with Orange Zest and Cilantro

Because it is spicy, this dish is best served with white rice.

Follow recipe for Shrimp Scampi, sautéing 1 teaspoon finely grated orange zest and ¼ teaspoon hot red pepper flakes with garlic, substituting 2 tablespoons minced fresh cilantro leaves for parsley, and omitting cayenne.

PAN-SEARED SCALLOPS

SCALLOPS OFFER SEVERAL POSSIBLE CHOICES for the cook, both when shopping and when cooking. There are three main varieties of scallops—sea, bay, and calico. Sea scallops are available year-round throughout the country and are the best choice in most instances. Like all scallops, the product sold at the market is the dense, disk-shaped muscle that propels the live scallop in its shell through the water. The guts and roe are usually jettisoned at sea because they are so perishable. Ivory-colored sea scallops are usually at least an inch in diameter (and often much bigger) and look like squat marshmallows. Sometimes they are sold cut up, but we found that they can lose moisture when handled this way and are best purchased whole.

Small, cork-shaped bay scallops (about half an inch in diameter) are harvested in a small area from Cape Cod to Long Island. Bay scallops are seasonal—available from late fall through midwinter—and are very expensive, up to $20 a pound. They are delicious but nearly impossible to find outside of top restaurants.

Calico scallops are a small species (less than half an inch across and taller than they are wide) harvested in the southern United States and around the world. They are inexpensive (often priced at just a few dollars a pound) but generally not terribly good. Unlike sea and bay scallops, which are harvested by hand, calicos are shucked by machine steaming. This steaming partially cooks the scallops and gives them an opaque look. Calicos are often sold as "bays," but they are not the same thing. In our kitchen test, we found that calicos are easy to overcook and often end up with a rubbery, eraser-like texture. Our recommendation is to stick with sea scallops, unless you have access to real bay scallops.

In addition to choosing the right species, you should inquire about processing when purchasing scallops. Most scallops (by some estimates up to 90 percent of the retail supply) are dipped in a phosphate-and-water mixture that may also contain citric and sorbic acids. Processing extends shelf life but harms the flavor and texture of the scallop. Its naturally delicate, sweet flavor can be masked by the bitter-tasting chemicals. Even worse, during processing scallops absorb water, which is thrown off when they are cooked. You can't brown processed scallops in a skillet—they shed so much liquid that they steam.

By law, processed scallops must be identified at the wholesale level, so ask your fishmonger. Also, look at the scallops. Scallops are naturally ivory or pinkish tan; processing turns them bright white. Processed scallops are slippery and swollen and usually sitting in milky white liquid at the store. Unprocessed scallops (also called dry scallops) are sticky and flabby. If they are surrounded by any liquid (and often they are not), the juices are clear, not white.

Besides the obvious objections (why pay for water weight or processing that detracts from their natural flavor?), processed scallops are more difficult to cook. We found that sautéing to caramelize the exterior to a concentrated, nutty-flavored, brown-and-tan crust is the best way to cook scallops. The caramelized exterior greatly enhances the natural sweetness of the scallop and provides a nice crisp contrast with the tender interior.

The most common problem a cook runs into with scallops is getting a nice crust before the scallop overcooks and toughens. We started our tests by focusing on the fat in the pan. Since scallops cook quickly, we knew it would be important to choose a fat that browned efficiently. We tried butter, olive oil, canola oil, a combination of butter and oil, plus cooking in oil with a finish of butter at the end for flavor.

To preserve the creamy texture of the flesh, we cooked the scallops to medium-rare, which means the scallop is hot all the way through but the center still retains some translucence. As a scallop cooks, the soft flesh firms and you can see an opaqueness that starts at the bottom of the scallop, where it sits in the pan, and slowly creeps up toward the center. The scallop is medium-rare when the sides have firmed up and all but about the middle third of the scallop has turned opaque.

The scallops browned well in all the fats we tested, but butter produced the thickest crust and best flavor. The nutty taste of butter complements the sweetness of the scallop without compromising its delicate flavor. We tested various pans, and while the technique worked in both nonstick and regular skillets, we recommend a light-colored regular skillet so you can judge how quickly the butter is browning and regulate the heat if necessary.

Despite the origin of the word sauté, which means "to jump" in French, it's critical for the formation of a good crust to leave the scallop alone once it hits the pan. We found the best method for cooking was to carefully place the scallops in the pan one at a time, with one flat side down for maximum contact with the hot pan. We turned the scallops once and browned the second flat side. The best tool for turning scallops is a pair of tongs, although a spatula can be used in a pinch.

Pan-Seared Scallops

SERVES 4

This recipe was developed for standard sea scallops, about the size of a short, squat marshmallow. If using smaller scallops, turn off the heat as soon as you turn them; they will finish cooking from the residual heat, 15 to 30 seconds longer. For very large scallops, turn the heat to low once they have browned and continue cooking for 1 minute, then turn the scallops, raise the heat to medium, and cook them at least 2 minutes on the second side.

1½	pounds sea scallops (about 30 to a pound), small muscles removed (see illustration at right)
	Salt and ground black pepper
1½	tablespoons unsalted butter

1. Sprinkle scallops on both sides with salt and pepper to taste. Heat large sauté pan over medium-high heat until hot, about 1 minute. Add half the butter; swirl to coat pan bottom. Continue to heat pan until butter begins to turn golden brown.

2. Add half the scallops, one at a time, flat side down. Cook, adjusting heat as necessary to prevent fat from burning, until scallops are well browned, 1½ to 2 minutes. Using tongs, turn scallops, one at a time. Cook until medium-rare (sides have firmed up and all but middle third of scallop is opaque), 30 seconds to 1½ minutes longer, depending on size. Transfer scallops to warm platter; cover with foil. Repeat cooking process using remaining butter and scallops. Serve immediately.

➤ VARIATIONS
Pan-Seared Scallops with Lemon, Shallots, and Capers

1	recipe Pan-Seared Scallops
1	medium shallot, minced
1	cup dry white wine
1	teaspoon grated lemon zest
2	tablespoons unsalted butter
2	tablespoons minced fresh parsley leaves
1	tablespoon lemon juice
1	tablespoon minced capers
	Salt and ground black pepper

After searing scallops and transferring them to warm platter, pour off all but 1 tablespoon butter and sauté shallot in fat until softened, 1 to 2 minutes. Add

REMOVING TENDON FROM A SCALLOP

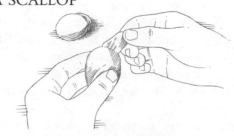

The small, rough-textured, crescent-shaped tendon that attaches the scallop to the shell is often not removed during processing. You can readily remove any tendons that are still attached. If you don't, they will toughen slightly during cooking.

wine and lemon zest and simmer until reduced to about ⅓ cup, 6 to 7 minutes. Off heat, stir in butter, parsley, lemon juice, capers, and salt and pepper to taste. Spoon sauce over scallops and serve.

Pan-Seared Scallops with Sherry, Red Onion, Orange, and Thyme

1	recipe Pan-Seared Scallops
⅓	cup minced red onion
¾	cup sherry
¼	cup orange juice
1	teaspoon grated orange zest
1	teaspoon minced fresh thyme leaves
2	tablespoons unsalted butter
1	tablespoon lemon juice
	Salt and ground black pepper

After searing scallops and transferring them to warm platter, pour off all but 1 tablespoon butter and sauté onion in fat until softened, 1 to 2 minutes. Add sherry, orange juice and zest, and thyme, and simmer until reduced to about ⅓ cup, 6 to 7 minutes. Off heat, stir in butter, lemon juice, and salt and pepper to taste. Spoon sauce over scallops and serve.

STEAMED CLAMS AND MUSSELS

CLAMS AND MUSSELS ARE BOTH BIVALVES, and they can be prepared in the same fashion. The main challenge when preparing clams and mussels is getting rid of the grit. These two-shelled creatures are easy to cook: When they open, they are done. However, perfectly cooked clams and mussels can be made inedible by lingering sand. Straining their juices through cheesecloth after cooking will remove the grit, but it's a pain. Besides being messy, solids such as shallots and garlic are removed. Worse still, careful straining may not remove every trace of grit, especially bits that are still clinging to the clam or mussel meat.

After much trial and error in the test kitchen, we concluded that it is also impossible to remove all the sand from dirty clams or mussels before cooking. We tried various soaking regimens—such as soaking in cold water for two hours, soaking in water with flour, soaking in water with cornmeal, and scrubbing and rinsing in five changes of water. None of these techniques worked. Dirty clams and mussels must be rinsed and scrubbed before cooking, and any cooking liquid must be strained after cooking. Rinsing the cooked clams and mussels is a final guarantee that the grit will be removed, but flavor is washed away as well.

During the course of this testing, we noticed that some varieties of clams and mussels were extremely clean and free of grit. A quick scrub of the shell exterior and these bivalves were ready for the pot. Best of all, the cooking liquid could be served without straining. After talking to seafood experts around the country we came to this conclusion: If you want to minimize your kitchen work and ensure that your clams and mussels are free of grit, you must shop carefully.

Clams can be divided into two categories—hard-shell varieties (such as littlenecks and cherrystones) and soft-shell varieties (such as steamers and razor clams). Hard-shells grow along sandy beaches and bays; soft-shells in muddy tidal flats. A modest shift in location makes all the difference in the kitchen.

When harvested, hard-shells remain tightly closed. In our test, we found that the meat inside was always free of sand. The exterior should be scrubbed under cold running water to remove any caked-on mud, but otherwise these clams can be cooked without further worry about gritty broths.

Soft-shell clams gape in their natural habitat. We found that they almost always contain a lot of sand. While it's worthwhile to soak them in several batches of cold water to remove some of the sand, you can never get rid of it all. In the end, you must strain the cooking liquid. And sometimes you must rinse the cooked clams after shucking as well.

We ultimately concluded that hard-shell clams (that is, littlenecks or cherrystones) are worth the extra money at the market. Gritty clams, no matter how cheap, are inedible. Buying either littlenecks or cherrystones ensures that the clams will be clean.

A similar distinction can be made with mussels based on how and where they are grown. Most mussels are now farmed either on ropes or along seabeds. (You may also see "wild" mussels at the market. These mussels are caught the old-fashioned way—by dredging along the sea floor. In our tests, we found them extremely muddy and basically inedible.) Rope-cultured mussels can be as much as twice the cost of wild or bottom-cultured mussels, but we found them to be free of grit in our testing. Since mussels are generally inexpensive (no more than a few dollars a pound), we think clean mussels are worth the extra money. Look for tags, usually attached to bags of mussels, that indicate how and where the mussels have been grown.

When shopping, look for tightly closed clams and mussels (avoid any that are gaping, which may be dying or dead). Clams need only be scrubbed. Mussels may need scrubbing as well as debearding. Simply grab onto the weedy protrusion and pull it out from between the shells and discard. Don't debeard mussels until you are ready to cook them, as debearding can cause the mussel to die. Mussels or clams kept in sealed plastic bags or under water will also die. Keep them in a bowl in the refrigerator and use them within a day or two for best results.

We tested the four most common cooking methods for clams and mussels: steaming in an aromatic broth (usually with some wine in it), steaming over an aromatic broth, roasting in the oven, and sautéing in some oil on the stove. In our tests, we found that clams or mussels that were sautéed, roasted, or steamed over a broth tasted of pure shellfish, but they also tasted flat and one-dimensional. They cooked in their juices. In contrast, clams and mussels that were steamed in a flavorful broth picked up flavors from the liquid. They became more complex tasting and, in our opinion, better.

With steaming in broth as our preferred all-purpose cooking method, we started to test various amounts and types of liquids, including fish stock, water, wine, and beer. We found white wine to be the best choice, although beer worked nicely with the mussels and is given on page 323 as a recipe variation. The bright acidity of white wine balances the briny flavor of clams and mussels. Fish stock and water (even when seasoned with garlic, herbs, and spices) were dull by comparison. While it is possible to steam four pounds of bivalves in just half a cup of liquid (naturally, the pot must be tightly sealed), we like to have extra broth for soaking into bread or rice. We settled on using two cups of white wine to

cook four pounds of clams or mussels.

We also made some refinements to the cooking broth. Garlic, shallots, and a bay leaf enrich the flavor of the shellfish. Simmering the broth for three minutes before adding the shellfish is sufficient time for these seasonings to flavor the wine broth. The all-purpose broth can be flavored in numerous ways, as the recipe variations demonstrate.

Steamed Clams or Mussels
SERVES 4

The basic flavorings in this recipe work with all kinds of mussels and with either littlenecks or cherrystone clams. (Really large cherrystones may require 9 or 10 minutes of steaming to open.) Variations below may be better suited to the particular flavors of mussels or clams, as indicated.

2	cups white wine
½	cup minced shallots
4	medium garlic cloves, minced
I	bay leaf
4	pounds clams or mussels, scrubbed and debearded if cooking mussels
4	tablespoons unsalted butter
½	cup chopped fresh parsley leaves

1. Bring wine, shallots, garlic, and bay leaf to simmer in large pot. Continue to simmer to blend flavors for about 3 minutes. Increase heat to high and add clams or mussels. Cover and cook, stirring twice, until clams or mussels open, 4 to 8 minutes, depending on size of shellfish and pot.

2. Use slotted spoon to transfer clams or mussels to large serving bowl. Swirl butter into pan liquid to make emulsified sauce. Stir in parsley. Pour broth over clams or mussels and serve immediately with warm bread or rice.

➤ VARIATIONS
Steamed Clams or Mussels with White Wine, Curry, and Herbs

2	cups white wine
½	cup minced shallots
4	medium garlic cloves, minced
I	bay leaf
I	teaspoon curry powder

- 4 pounds clams or mussels, scrubbed and debearded if cooking mussels
- 4 tablespoons unsalted butter
- 2 tablespoons chopped fresh parsley leaves
- 2 tablespoons chopped fresh cilantro leaves
- 2 tablespoons chopped fresh basil leaves

1. Bring wine, shallots, garlic, bay leaf, and curry powder to simmer in large pot. Continue to simmer to blend flavors for about 3 minutes. Increase heat to high and add clams or mussels. Cover and cook, stirring twice, until clams or mussels open, 4 to 8 minutes, depending on size of shellfish and pot.

2. Use slotted spoon to transfer clams or mussels to large serving bowl. Swirl butter into pan liquid to make emulsified sauce. Stir in parsley, cilantro, and basil. Pour broth over clams or mussels and serve immediately with warm bread or rice.

Steamed Clams or Mussels with White Wine, Tomato, and Basil

This can be served over one pound of cooked linguine if desired.

- 1 cup white wine
- 1/2 cup minced shallots
- 4 medium garlic cloves, minced
- 1 bay leaf
- 4 pounds clams or mussels, scrubbed and debearded if cooking mussels
- 2 cups crushed canned tomatoes
- 1/4 cup extra-virgin olive oil
- 1/2 cup minced fresh basil leaves
  Salt and ground black pepper

1. Bring wine, shallots, garlic, and bay leaf to simmer in large pot. Continue to simmer to blend flavors for about 3 minutes. Increase heat to high and add clams or mussels. Cover and cook, stirring twice, until clams or mussels open, 4 to 8 minutes, depending on size of shellfish and pot.

2. Use slotted spoon to transfer clams or mussels to large serving bowl. Add tomatoes and oil to pan liquid and simmer until reduced to sauce consistency, about 10 minutes. Stir in basil and season with salt and pepper to taste. Return clams or mussels to pot, heat briefly, and serve immediately.

Steamed Clams or Mussels with Asian Flavors

- 1 cup chicken stock or low-sodium canned broth
- 2 tablespoons soy or fish sauce
- 2 teaspoons rice wine vinegar
- 1/8 teaspoon cayenne pepper
- 2 tablespoons minced fresh gingerroot
- 4 medium scallions, minced
- 2 tablespoons minced lime zest
- 4 pounds clams or mussels, scrubbed and debearded if cooking mussels
- 4 tablespoons unsalted butter
- 2 tablespoons chopped fresh cilantro leaves
- 1 lime, quartered

1. Bring stock, soy sauce, vinegar, cayenne, ginger, scallions, and lime zest to simmer in large pot. Continue to simmer to blend flavors for about 3 minutes. Increase heat to high and add clams or mussels. Cover and cook, stirring twice, until clams or mussels open, 4 to 8 minutes, depending on size of shellfish and pot.

2. Serve clams and broth, garnishing with cilantro and lime quarters.

Steamed Mussels with Cream Sauce and Tarragon

- 2 cups white wine
- 1/2 cup minced shallots
- 4 medium garlic cloves, minced
- 1 bay leaf
- 4 pounds mussels, scrubbed and debearded
- 3/4 cup heavy cream
- 1/2 cup chopped fresh parsley leaves
- 2 teaspoons minced fresh tarragon leaves
- 1 tablespoon lemon juice

1. Bring wine, shallots, garlic, and bay leaf to simmer in large pot. Continue to simmer to blend flavors for about 3 minutes. Increase heat to high and add mussels. Cover and cook, stirring twice, until mussels open, 4 to 8 minutes, depending on size of shellfish and pot.

2. Use slotted spoon to transfer mussels to large serving bowl. Simmer broth until reduced to 1/2 cup, about 8 minutes. Add cream and simmer until thickened, about 2 minutes. Stir in parsley, tarragon, and

lemon juice. Return mussels to pot, heat briefly, and serve immediately with bread.

Mussels Steamed in Beer

2	cups light-colored beer
½	cup minced onion
4	medium garlic cloves, minced
3	sprigs fresh thyme
I	bay leaf
4	pounds mussels, scrubbed and debearded
4	tablespoons unsalted butter
½	cup chopped fresh parsley leaves

1. Bring beer, onion, garlic, thyme, and bay leaf to simmer in large pot. Continue to simmer to blend flavors for about 3 minutes. Increase heat to high and add mussels. Cover and cook, stirring twice, until mussels open, 4 to 8 minutes, depending on size of shellfish and pot.

2. Use slotted spoon to transfer mussels to large serving bowl. Swirl butter into pan liquid to make emulsified sauce. Stir in parsley. Pour broth over mussels and serve immediately with warm bread or rice.

LOBSTER

AS WITH MOST SEAFOOD, WE FIND THAT knowing how to shop for lobster is just as important as knowing how to cook it. Lobsters must be purchased alive. Choose lobsters that are active in the tank, avoiding listless specimens that may have been in the tank too long. Maine lobsters, with their large claws, are meatier and sweeter than clawless rock or spiny lobsters, and they are our first and only choice. Size is really a matter of preference and budget. We found it possible to cook large as well as small lobsters to perfection as long as we adjusted the cooking time (see page 324).

During our initial phase of testing, we confirmed our preference for steamed lobster rather than boiled. Steamed lobster did not taste better than boiled, but the process was simpler and neater, and the finished product was less watery when cracked open on the plate. Steaming the lobster on a rack or steamer basket kept it from becoming waterlogged. (If you happen to live near the ocean, seaweed makes a natural rack.) We found that neither beer nor wine in the pot improved the lobster's flavor, nor did any herbs, spices, or other seasonings. It seems that nothing can penetrate the hard lobster shell.

As for dry-heat cooking methods, we found the steady, even heat of the oven preferable to broiling, where charring of the meat is a real danger. We found that a high oven temperature of 450 degrees worked the best. You want to cook the lobster quickly. When we roasted lobsters at lower temperatures, the outer layer of meat had dried out by the time the inside was cooked through. To keep the tail from curling during roasting, we found it helpful to run a skewer through it.

Although we had little trouble perfecting these two cooking methods, we were bothered by the toughness of some of the lobster tails we were eating. No matter how we cooked them, most of the tails were at least slightly rubbery and chewy.

We spent six months talking to research scientists, chefs, seafood experts, lobstermen, and home cooks to see how they tackled the problem of the tough tail. The suggestions ranged from the bizarre (petting the lobster to "hypnotize" it and thus prevent an adrenaline rush at death that causes the tail to toughen, or using a chopstick to kill the lobster before cooking) to the sensible (avoiding really old, large lobsters). But after testing every one of these suggestions, we still didn't have a cooking method that consistently delivered a tender tail.

Occasionally, we would get a nice tender tail, but there did not seem to be a pattern. We then spoke with several scientists who said we were barking up the wrong tree. The secret to tender lobster was not so much in the preparation and cooking as in the selection.

Before working on this topic in the test kitchen, the terms "hard-shell" and "soft-shell" lobster meant nothing to us. Unlike crabs, there's certainly no distinction between the two at the retail level. Of course, we knew from past experience that some lobster claws rip open as easily as an aluminum flip-top can, while others require shop tools to crack. We also noticed the small, limp claw meat of some lobsters and the full, packed meat of others. We attributed these differences to how long the lobsters had been stored in tanks. It seems we were wrong. These variations are caused by the particular stage of molting that the lobster was in at the time it was caught.

As it turns out, most of the lobsters we eat during the summer and fall are in some phase of molting. During the late spring, as waters begin to warm, lobsters start to form the new shell tissue underneath their old shells. As early as June off the shores of New Jersey and in July or August in colder Maine and Canadian waters, the lobsters shed their hard exterior shell. Because the most difficult task in molting is pulling the claw muscle through the old shell, the lobster dehydrates its claw (hence the smaller claw meat).

Once the lobster molts, it emerges with nothing but a wrinkled, soft covering, much like that on a soft-shell crab. Within 15 minutes, the lobster inflates itself with water, increasing its length by 15 percent and its weight by 50 percent. This extra water expands the wrinkled, soft covering, allowing the lobster room to grow long after the shell starts to harden. The newly molted lobster immediately eats its old shell, digesting the crucial shell-hardening calcium.

Understanding the molt phase clarifies the deficiencies of soft-shell summer lobster. It explains why it is so waterlogged, why its claw meat is so shriveled and scrawny, and why its tail meat is so underdeveloped and chewy. There is also far less meat in a one-pound soft-shell lobster than in a hard-shell lobster that weighs the same.

During the fall, the lobster shell continues to harden and the meat expands to fill the new shell. By spring, lobsters are at their peak, packed with meat and relatively inexpensive since it is easier for fishermen to check their traps than it is during the winter. As the tail grows, it becomes firmer and meatier and will cook up tender, not tough. Better texture and more meat are two excellent reasons to give lobsters a squeeze at the market and buy only those with hard shells. As a rule of thumb, hard-shell lobsters are reasonably priced from Mother's Day through the Fourth of July.

Steamed Lobsters

SERVES 4

Hard-shell lobsters are much meatier than soft-shell lobsters, which have recently molted. To determine whether a lobster has a hard or soft shell, squeeze the side of the lobster's body. A soft-shell lobster will yield to pressure, while a hard-shell lobster will feel hard, brittle, and tightly packed. Because hard-shell lobsters are packed with more meat than soft-shell lobsters, you may want to buy slightly larger lobsters if the shells appear to be soft.

4	whole lobsters
8	tablespoons unsalted butter, melted until hot (optional)
	Lemon wedges

Bring about 1 inch of water to a boil over high heat in large soup kettle set up with wire rack, pasta insert, or seaweed bed. Add lobsters, cover, and return water to boil. Reduce heat to medium-high and steam until lobsters are done (see table at left). Serve immediately with warm butter and lemon wedges.

Oven-Roasted Lobsters with Herbed Bread Crumbs

SERVES 4

Freezing the lobster for 10 minutes numbs the creature and makes it easier to handle when cutting in half for roasting. Freezing for this short amount of time does not affect the texture or quality of the meat.

| 4 | tablespoons unsalted butter |
| 1/2 | cup dried plain bread crumbs |

Approximate Steaming Times and Meat Yields for Lobster

LOBSTER SIZE	COOKING TIME (IN MINUTES)	MEAT YIELD (IN OUNCES)
1 lb		
SOFT-SHELL	8 to 9	about 3
HARD-SHELL	10 to 11	4 to 4½
1¼ lbs		
SOFT-SHELL	11 to 12	3½ to 4
HARD-SHELL	13 to 14	5½ to 6
1½ lbs		
SOFT-SHELL	13 to 14	5½ to 6
HARD-SHELL	15 to 16	7½ to 8
1¾–2 lbs		
SOFT-SHELL	17 to 18	6¼ to 6½
HARD-SHELL	about 19	8½ to 9

2 tablespoons minced fresh parsley leaves or
1 tablespoon minced fresh tarragon leaves or
snipped chives
4 whole lobsters, prepared according to
illustrations below
Salt and ground black pepper
Lemon wedges

1. Adjust oven rack to middle-high position and heat oven to 450 degrees. Heat 1 tablespoon butter in small skillet over medium heat. When foaming subsides, add bread crumbs and cook, stirring occasionally, until toasted and golden brown, 3 to 4 minutes. Stir in herbs and set aside.

2. Arrange lobsters crosswise on two 17 x 11-inch foil-lined jelly-roll pans, alternating tail and claw ends. Melt remaining butter and brush over body and tail of each lobster; season with salt and pepper to taste. Sprinkle portion of bread crumb mixture evenly over body and tail meat.

3. Roast lobsters until tail meat is opaque and bread crumbs are crisp, 12 to 15 minutes. Serve immediately with lemon wedges.

Soft-Shell Crabs

THERE ARE DOZENS OF SPECIES OF CRABS, but the blue crab, which is found in waters along the East Coast, is the most common variety. Soft-shell crabs are blue crabs that have been taken out of the water just after they have shed their shells. At this brief stage of its life, the whole crab, with its new, soft, gray skin, is almost completely edible and fabulously delicious.

For the cook, soft-shells are a wonderfully immediate experience. Once cleaned, they demand to be cooked and eaten on the spot, so they offer a very direct taste of the sea. Because they must be cooked so quickly after they are killed and cleaned, home

PREPARING LOBSTERS FOR ROASTING

1. Freeze lobster for 10 minutes to numb it. Kill the lobster by plunging a chef's knife into the body at the point where the shell forms a "T." Move the blade down until it touches the head.

2. Turn the lobster over. Position the knife blade so that it faces the tail end. Cut through the body toward the tail, making sure not to cut all the way through the shell.

3. Move your hand down to the lower body and continue cutting through the tail.

4. Holding half of the tail in each hand, crack, but do not break, the back shell to butterfly the lobster.

5. Use a spoon to remove and discard the stomach sac.

6. Remove and discard the intestinal tracts.

7. Remove and discard the green tomalley if you wish.

8. Run a skewer up one side of the lobster tail to keep if from curling during cooking.

cooks have an advantage over restaurants. We're convinced that the best way to enjoy soft-shells is to cook them at home, where you can be sure to eat them within minutes of preparing them.

The whole point of preparing soft-shells is to get them crisp. The legs should crunch delicately, while the body should provide a contrast between its thin, crisp outer skin and the soft, rich interior that explodes juicily in the mouth. Deep-frying delivers these results, but this method is better suited to restaurants. Air pockets and water in the crab cause a lot of dangerous splattering. For optimum safety, soft-shell crabs should be deep-fried in a very large quantity of oil in a very deep pot, which is not practical at home.

We wanted to develop an alternative method for home cooks. We tried roasting, but the crabs did not get crisp enough. Grilling is not always practical and broiling did not work well. In the end, we found that pan-frying produces a satisfyingly crisp crab. Crabs still splatter hot fat when cooked this way, but less fat than when deep-fried. To avoid the mess and danger of the splattering fat, we recommend sliding a splatter screen (see page 327) over the pan as the crabs cook.

A coating of some kind helps crisp the crab. We tried flour, cornmeal, bread crumbs, and even Cream of Wheat coatings, and ended up opting for flour. It's a shame to hide the unique, essential flavor of the crab with a heavy coating, and flour provides a crisp crust without adding flavor. It also has the advantage

of being on hand most of the time.

We also tried soaking the crabs in milk for two hours before applying the coating, since we had read that this process sweetens the crab. To the contrary, we found that milk takes away from the just-out-of-the-water flavor that we like.

The type of fat you use for frying is largely a matter of personal preference. We tried frying floured crabs in whole butter, clarified butter, vegetable and peanut oils, and a combination of whole butter and olive oil. Whole butter gave the crabs a delicious, nutty taste and browned them well. Clarified butter didn't brown them significantly better and was more work, so it offers no advantage over whole butter. Vegetable and peanut oils got the crab a hair crisper than butter and added no flavor; peanut oil crisped the crabs particularly well because it fries very hot without burning. The combination of butter and oil didn't give a better result than either fat used separately, and we were surprised to find that the flavor of butter and even the flavorlessness of the other oils complement the crab better than the olive oil. Our preference is to fry with either peanut oil or butter, depending on the taste we want and the kind of sauce we are making.

Whether you opt for peanut oil, vegetable oil, or butter, the crab fries best in quite a lot of fat. Count on at least one tablespoon of butter per crab depending on the size of the pan; the crabs actually seem to absorb the butter as they cook. When cooking with oil, we add the oil to a depth of one-eighth to one-

CLEANING A SOFT-SHELL CRAB

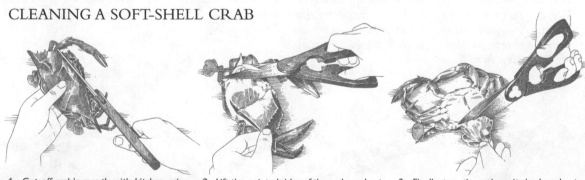

1. Cut off crab's mouth with kitchen scissors; the mouth is the first part of the shell to harden. You can also cut off the eyes at the same time, but this is for purely aesthetic purposes; the eyes are edible.

2. Lift the pointed sides of the crab, and cut out the spongy off-white gills underneath; the gills are fibrous and watery and unpleasant to eat.

3. Finally, turn the crab on its back and cut off the triangular or T-shaped "apron flap."

quarter inch. You can cook in any kind of pan, but a cast-iron pan holds even heat particularly well and practically guarantees a crispy critter.

Once you've cooked the crabs, they should be sauced and served immediately. In a pinch, you can hold crabs for a few minutes in a 300-degree oven, but they're really better eaten practically out of the pan. Therefore, if you're serving a main course for four (count on two crabs per person), you'll need two pans, each at least 11 inches in diameter, if you expect everyone to sit down to eat together. If you've got only one pan, your best bet is to let two people start on the first batch of crabs when they're cooked, while you start cooking the second batch. Or serve crabs as an appetizer—one per person is plenty. Because they're fried, the crabs don't need much of a sauce, just a drizzle of something acidic.

Pan-Fried Soft-Shell Crabs

SERVES 4

A splatter screen is essential if you want to minimize the mess and the danger to your arms and face. For maximum crispness, you should cook the crabs in two pans, each covered with a splatter screen, so you can serve the crabs as soon as they are cooked. If you are working with just one splatter screen and pan, cook four crabs in four tablespoons of butter, transfer them to a platter in a 300-degree oven, wipe out the pan, add 4 more tablespoons of butter, and cook the remaining crabs.

8	medium-to-large soft-shell crabs, cleaned (see illustrations on page 326) and patted dry with paper towels
	All-purpose flour for dredging
10	tablespoons unsalted butter
1/4	cup lemon juice
2	tablespoons minced fresh parsley leaves
	Salt and ground black pepper

1. Dredge crabs in flour; pat off excess. Heat two 11- or 12-inch heavy-bottomed frying pans over medium-high heat until pans are quite hot, about 3 minutes. Add 4 tablespoons butter to each pan, swirling pans to keep butter from burning as it melts. When foam subsides, add four crabs, skins down, to each pan. Cover each pan with splatter screen and

cook, adjusting heat as necessary to keep butter from burning, until crabs turn reddish brown, about 3 minutes. Turn crabs with spatula or tongs and cook until second side is browned, about 3 minutes more. Drain crabs on plate lined with paper towel.

2. Set one pan aside for cleaning. Pour off butter from other pan and remove from heat. Add lemon juice to deglaze empty, hot pan. Cut remaining 2 tablespoons butter into pieces and add to skillet. Swirl pan to melt butter. Add parsley and salt and pepper to taste. Arrange two crabs on each of four plates. Spoon some sauce over each plate and serve immediately.

> VARIATIONS

Pan-Fried Soft-Shell Crabs with Lemon, Capers, and Herbs

The pan sauce is tart and powerfully flavorful; you need only about one tablespoon per serving.

8	medium-to-large soft-shell crabs, cleaned (see illustrations on page 326) and patted dry with paper towels
	All-purpose flour for dredging
10	tablespoons unsalted butter
3	tablespoons lemon juice
2	teaspoons sherry vinegar
1 1/2	teaspoons chopped capers
1	medium scallion, sliced thin
2	tablespoons minced fresh parsley leaves
2	teaspoons minced fresh tarragon
	Salt and ground black pepper

Soy sauce is the most important condiment in Asian cooking. Made from equal parts soybeans and roasted grains (usually wheat), plus water and salt, this fermented sauce is an all-purpose condiment that works with many other flavors. Many Americans confuse soy sauce with tamari. Soy sauce is made with wheat, while tamari contains just soybeans, water, and salt. Tamari is generally saltier and darker and better-suited as a dipping sauce (with sushi, for instance) than as a seasoning in cooking.

There are several kinds of soy sauce commonly sold in supermarkets in this country. For the most part, we prefer regular Chinese soy sauce. It's our choice for marinating meat, seafood, or tofu, or for adding a salty, fermented flavor to sauces. However, when using a larger amount of soy sauce, we prefer to use a light or reduced-sodium brand. For instance, a ginger sauce that contains three tablespoons of soy sauce would be too salty if made with a regular, full-sodium sauce. Unless otherwise noted, recipes were tested with regular soy sauce.

1. Dredge crabs in flour; pat off excess. Heat two 11- or 12-inch heavy-bottomed frying pans over medium-high heat until pans are quite hot, about 3 minutes. Add 4 tablespoons butter to each pan, swirling pans to keep butter from burning as it melts. When foam subsides, add four crabs, skins down, to each pan. Cover each pan with splatter screen and cook, adjusting heat as necessary to keep butter from burning, until crabs turn reddish brown, about 3 minutes. Turn crabs with spatula or tongs and cook

until second side is browned, about 3 minutes more. Drain crabs on plate lined with paper towel.

2. Set one pan aside for cleaning. Pour off butter from other pan and remove from heat. Add lemon juice, vinegar, capers, and scallion to deglaze empty, hot pan. Cut remaining 2 tablespoons butter into pieces and add to skillet. Swirl pan to melt butter. Add parsley, tarragon, and salt and pepper to taste. Arrange two crabs on each of four plates. Spoon some sauce over each plate and serve immediately.

Pan-Fried Soft-Shell Crabs with Orange and Soy

This Asian recipe uses peanut oil rather than butter to cook the crabs.

8	medium-to-large soft-shell crabs, cleaned (see illustrations on page 326) and patted dry with paper towels
	All-purpose flour for dredging
10	tablespoons peanut oil
3	medium garlic cloves, minced
¾	teaspoon minced fresh gingerroot
¼	teaspoon hot red pepper flakes
2	tablespoons orange juice
2	tablespoons rice wine vinegar
1	teaspoon soy sauce
2	medium scallions, sliced thin

1. Dredge crabs in flour; pat off excess. Heat two 11- or 12-inch heavy-bottomed frying pans over

Not surprisingly, considering how perishable they are, soft-shells can be quite difficult to locate. Fresh soft-shells are available only "in season," which used to mean a few short months during the summer. Now the "season" can extend from February all the way through to September and maybe into October, depending on the weather. Frozen crabs may also be available, but they are not nearly as good.

Once you buy the crabs, your fishmonger will probably offer to clean them for you. If you like the crabs juicy, you'll be happier if you clean them yourself. The reason is that a crab, like a lobster, grows by shedding its hard shell periodically. After shedding, the crab swells with water to fill out its new skin, and the skin immediately begins to harden into a new, larger shell. When you clean a live crab, juice pours out of it. The longer the crab sits before cooking, the more liquid it loses. We found that a crab that is cooked immediately after cleaning is much plumper and juicier than a crab cleaned several hours before cooking. To clean a live crab, follow the illustrations on page 326.

We advise against storing soft-shells. Even a live crab won't stay that way very long in your refrigerator; because they can die from the cold temperature in your refrigerator, they're better off at the fish store, where they are kept not cold, but cool.

medium-high heat until pans are quite hot, about 3 minutes. Heat 4 tablespoons oil in each pan. When oil is shimmering, add four crabs, skins down, to each pan. Cover each pan with splatter screen and cook, adjusting heat as necessary to keep fat from burning, until crabs turn reddish brown, about 3 minutes. Turn crabs with spatula or tongs and cook until second side is browned, about 3 minutes more. Drain crabs on plate lined with paper towel.

2. Set one pan aside for cleaning. Pour off oil from other pan and remove pan from heat. Add remaining 2 tablespoons oil to empty pan and return pan to medium heat. Add garlic, ginger, and hot red pepper flakes and sauté until garlic is fragrant and lightened in color, 30 to 45 seconds. Off heat, stir in orange juice, vinegar, soy sauce, and scallions. Arrange two crabs on each of four plates. Spoon some sauce over each plate and serve immediately.

CRAB CAKES

GOOD CRAB CAKES TASTE FIRST AND FORE-most of sweet crabmeat. Too many restaurants serve crab-flecked dough balls. That's why the crab cake is especially suited to home cooking.

Great crab cakes begin with top-quality crabmeat. We tested all the various options, and the differences are stark. Canned crabmeat is horrible; like canned tuna, it bears little resemblance to the fresh product. Fresh pasteurized crabmeat is watery and bland. Frozen crabmeat is stringy and wet. There is no substitute for fresh blue crabmeat, preferably "jumbo lump," which indicates the largest pieces and highest grade. This variety costs a couple of dollars a pound more than other types of fresh crab meat, but, since a one-pound container is enough to make crab cakes for four, in our opinion it's money well spent.

Fresh lump blue crab is available year-round but tends to be most expensive from December to March. The meat should never be rinsed, but it does need to be picked over to remove any shells or cartilage the processors may have missed.

Once we figured out what type of crab to use, our next task was to find the right binder. None of the usual suspects worked. Crushed saltines were a pain to smash into small-enough crumbs, potato chips added too

much richness, and fresh bread crumbs blended into the crabmeat a little too well. We finally settled on fine dry bread crumbs. They have no overwhelming flavor and are easy to mix in. The trickiest part is knowing when to stop; crab cakes need just enough binder to hold them together but not so much that the filler overwhelms the seafood. We started out using three-quarters of a cup of crumbs but ended up reducing that to two tablespoons for our final recipe. Cooks who economize by padding out their pricey seafood with bread crumbs will end up with dough balls, not crab cakes.

Other ingredients we've adopted are equally basic. Good, sturdy commercial mayonnaise (we like Hellmann's) keeps the crabmeat moist (a homemade blend can be too liquid), and a whole egg, unbeaten, makes the crab, crumbs, and seasonings meld together both before and during cooking.

Classic recipes call for spiking crab cakes with everything from Tabasco to Worcestershire sauce, and those are both fine. But we've decided the best blend of tradition and trendiness is Old Bay seasoning combined with freshly ground white pepper and a tablespoon or more of chopped fresh herbs.

Just as essential as careful seasoning is careful mixing. We've found a rubber spatula works best, used in a folding motion rather than stirring. This is important because you want to end up with a chunky consistency. Those lumps aren't cheap.

We were pleased with our basic recipe on most fronts, but we still had trouble keeping the cakes together as they cooked. Our last breakthrough came when we tried chilling the shaped cakes before cooking. As little as half an hour in the refrigerator made an ocean of difference: the cold firmed up the cakes so that they fried into perfect plump rounds without falling apart. We found that formed cakes can be kept, refrigerated and tightly wrapped, for up to 24 hours.

We also tried different cooking methods. After baking, deep-frying, and broiling, we settled on pan-frying in a cast-iron skillet over medium-high heat. This method is fast and also gives the cook complete control over how brown and how crisp the cakes get. We first tried frying in butter, but it burned as it saturated the crab cakes. Cut with vegetable oil, it was still too heavy and made a mess of the pan. The ideal medium turned out to be plain old vegetable oil. It can be heated without burning and smoking, it creates a crisp crust, and it never gets in the way of the crab flavor.

Pan-Fried Crab Cakes

SERVES 4

The amount of bread crumbs you add will depend on the crab-meat's juiciness. Start with the smallest amount, adjust the seasonings, then add the egg. If the cakes won't bind at this point, then add more bread crumbs, one tablespoon at a time.

I	pound jumbo lump crabmeat, picked over to remove cartilage or shell
4	scallions, green part only, minced (about ½ cup)
I	tablespoon chopped fresh herb, such as cilantro, dill, basil, or parsley
I ½	teaspoons Old Bay seasoning
2–4	tablespoons plain dry bread crumbs
¼	cup mayonnaise
	Salt and ground white pepper
I	large egg
¼	cup all-purpose flour
4	tablespoons vegetable oil

1. Gently mix crabmeat, scallions, herb, Old Bay, 2 tablespoons bread crumbs, and mayonnaise in medium bowl, being careful not to break up crab lumps. Season with salt and white pepper to taste. Carefully fold in egg with rubber spatula until mixture just clings together. Add more crumbs if necessary.

2. Divide crab mixture into four portions and shape each into a fat, round cake, about 3 inches across and 1½ inches high. Arrange on baking sheet lined with waxed paper; cover with plastic wrap and chill at least 30 minutes. (Can be refrigerated up to 24 hours.)

3. Put flour on plate or in pie tin. Lightly dredge crab cakes. Heat oil in large, preferably nonstick skil-

let over medium-high heat until hot but not smoking. Gently lay chilled crab cakes in skillet; pan-fry until outsides are crisp and browned, 4 to 5 minutes per side. Serve hot, with Tartar Sauce or Creamy Dipping Sauce.

Tartar Sauce

MAKES GENEROUS ¾ CUP

The classic sauce for crab cakes and fried seafood.

¾	cup mayonnaise
I ½	tablespoons minced cornichons (about 3 large), plus I teaspoon cornichon juice
I	tablespoon minced scallion
I	tablespoon minced red onion
I	tablespoon capers, minced

Mix all ingredients together in small bowl. Cover and refrigerate until flavors blend, at least 30 minutes. (Can be refrigerated for several days.)

Creamy Dipping Sauce

MAKES ABOUT ½ CUP

This sauce is richer and more complex-tasting than tartar sauce.

¼	cup mayonnaise
¼	cup sour cream
2	teaspoons minced chipotle chiles (smoked jalapeños)
I	small garlic clove, minced
2	teaspoons minced fresh cilantro leaves
I	teaspoon juice from I small lime

Mix all ingredients in small bowl. Cover and refrigerate until flavors blend, about 30 minutes. (Can be refrigerated for several days.)

13

PIZZA, FOCACCIA, AND BRUSCHETTA

THIS CHAPTER COVERS THIN YEAST BREADS—pizza and focaccia—as well as bruschetta, Italian toasts made from slices of grilled bread.

Pizza and focaccia (which are in fact both flatbreads) are Italian in origin. Pizza is generally thinner and crisper, while focaccia is thicker, softer, and chewier. In addition, pizza is usually generously topped with cheese, tomato sauce, cooked vegetables, and/or meats. Traditionally, focaccia is more lightly topped, sometimes with just coarse salt, oil, and herbs. This chapter considers thin-crust pizza, cooked both conventionally in the oven and less conventionally on the grill, as well as traditional focaccia.

The challenge when making both pizza and focaccia is to build flavor into the dough while keeping prep time to a minimum. We tested numerous possibilities before hitting on the right solutions. Giving pizza and focaccia the right texture is also difficult. Too many pizza crusts are soggy, while most focaccia are not nearly chewy and soft enough. Finding the right mix of ingredients for the dough as well as using the proper stretching and shaping technique will help you get the right results.

Bruschetta starts with a loaf of bread that you buy or make yourself. Bruschetta is an excellent way to recycle day-old bread. (Leftover slices of our Rustic Country Bread on page 362 make excellent bruschetta.) Thick slices of crusty country bread are toasted, rubbed with garlic, and then brushed with good olive oil. Toppings can be as simple as some salt or minced fresh herbs or slightly more elaborate, such as grilled vegetables or diced fresh tomatoes.

PIZZA DOUGH

THE DOUGH IS PROBABLY THE TRICKIEST part of pizza making at home. While pizza dough is nothing more than bread dough with oil added for softness and suppleness, we found in our testing that minor changes in the ingredients list can yield dramatically different results.

Our goal in testing was threefold. We wanted to develop a recipe that was simple to put together; the dough had to be easy to shape and stretch; and the crust needed to bake up crisp and chewy, not tough and leathery.

After some initial tests, it was clear that bread flour delivers the best texture. Bread flour makes pizza crust that is chewy and crisp. Unbleached all-purpose flour can be used in a pinch, but the resulting crust is less crisp.

The second key to perfect crust is water. We found that using more water makes the dough softer and more elastic. It stretches more easily than a stiffer, harder dough with less water. We prefer to jump-start the yeast in a little warm water for five minutes. We then add more room-temperature water and oil.

When it comes to combining the dry ingredients (flour and salt) with the wet ingredients, the food processor is our first choice. The liquid gets evenly incorporated into the dry ingredients, and the blade kneads the dough in just 30 seconds. Of course, the dough can be kneaded by hand or with a standing mixer. If making the dough by hand, resist the temptation to add a lot of flour as you knead.

Use plastic wrap to cover the oiled bowl with the rising dough. We found that the tight seal offered by plastic wrap keeps the dough moist and protects it from drafts better than the standard damp cloth. We reserve the traditional damp cloth for use when the dough has been divided into balls and is waiting to be stretched out.

To stretch dough to its maximum diameter, let it rest one or two times during the shaping process. Once you feel some resistance from the dough, cover it with a damp cloth, and wait five minutes before going at it again. Fingertips and hands generally do a better job of stretching dough than a rolling pin, which presses out air from the risen dough and makes it tough. Our low-tech method is also superior to flipping dough into the air and other frivolous techniques that may work in a pizza parlor but can lead to disaster at home.

It is possible to flavor pizza dough (we offer several variations) or to change the rising time by using less yeast and/or refrigerating the dough. This way, dough can be made the night before or in the morning and be ready when you need it for dinner.

Even if baking just one medium pizza, make a full dough recipe. After the dough has risen and been divided, place the extra dough in an airtight container and freeze it for up to several weeks. Defrost and stretch the dough when desired.

Master Recipe for Pizza Dough

MAKES ENOUGH FOR 2 LARGE, 4 MEDIUM,
OR 8 INDIVIDUAL PIZZAS

We find that the food processor is the best tool for making pizza dough. However, you can knead this dough by hand or in a standing mixer (see the directions at right). Note that the flavor variations can be used interchangeably with the time and kneading variations. For instance, you can make Eight-Hour Cornmeal Pizza Dough and knead it by hand if you like. This dough requires about two hours of rising time.

½	cup warm water, at about 105 degrees
1	envelope (2¼ teaspoons) active dry yeast
1¼	cups water, at room temperature
2	tablespoons extra-virgin olive oil
4	cups bread flour, plus extra for dusting hands and work surfaces
1½	teaspoons salt
	Vegetable oil or spray for oiling bowl

1. Measure warm water into 2-cup measuring cup. Sprinkle in yeast; let stand until yeast dissolves and swells, about 5 minutes. Add room-temperature water and oil; stir to combine.

2. Pulse flour and salt in workbowl of large food processor fitted with steel blade to combine. Continue pulsing while pouring liquid ingredients (holding back a few tablespoons) through feed tube. If dough does not readily form into ball, add remaining liquid, and continue to pulse until ball forms. Process until dough is smooth and elastic, about 30 seconds longer.

3. Dough will be a bit tacky, so use rubber spatula to turn out dough onto lightly floured work surface; knead by hand with a few strokes to form smooth, round ball. Put dough into deep oiled bowl and cover with plastic wrap. Let rise until doubled in size, about 2 hours. Punch dough down with your fist and turn out onto lightly floured work surface. Divide and shape as directed in master recipe for thin-crust or grilled pizza.

➤ VARIATIONS
Hand-Kneaded Pizza Dough

Follow step 1 of Master Recipe for Pizza Dough. Omit step 2 and instead combine salt and half of flour in deep bowl. Add liquid ingredients and use wooden spoon to combine. Add remaining flour, stirring until cohesive mass forms. Turn dough out onto lightly floured work surface and knead until smooth and elastic, 7 to 8 minutes. Use as little dusting flour as possible while kneading. Form dough into ball, put it into deep oiled bowl, cover with plastic wrap, and proceed with recipe.

Pizza Dough Kneaded in a Standing Mixer

Follow step 1 of Master Recipe for Pizza Dough. Omit step 2 and instead place flour and salt in deep bowl of standing mixer. With paddle attachment, briefly combine dry ingredients on low speed.

EQUIPMENT: Baking Sheets and Peels

Rimless baking sheets and peels make handling pizza dough much easier. For thin-crust pizza, we like to transfer stretched dough to a peel that has been dusted with semolina. The long handle on the peel makes it easy to slide the dough onto tiles or a stone in a hot oven. Although a rimless metal baking sheet can be used in this fashion, the lack of a handle means your hands are that much closer to the oven heat.

When shopping for a pizza peel, note that there are two choices. Aluminum peels with heat-resistant wooden handles are probably the better bet because they can be washed and cleaned easily. Peels made entirely of wood can mildew when washed, so it's best just to wipe them clean. Either way, make sure your peel measures at least 16 inches across so that it can accommodate a large dough round and still have room left around the edges.

For grilled pizzas, we like to put stretched dough rounds on a rimless baking sheet or aluminum peel that has been dusted with flour. We're not comfortable placing a wooden peel so close to an open fire. We also recommend flipping the grilled dough rounds back onto the baking sheet or peel and then topping them (as opposed to topping them right on the grill); this method keeps your hands far away from the intense heat of the grill.

Slowly add liquid ingredients and continue to mix on low speed until cohesive mass forms. Stop mixer and replace paddle with dough hook. Knead until dough is smooth and elastic, about 5 minutes. Form dough into ball, place in deep oiled bowl, cover with plastic wrap, and proceed with recipe.

Twenty-four-Hour Pizza Dough

Follow Master Recipe for Pizza Dough, decreasing yeast to ½ teaspoon. Let covered dough rise in refrigerator for up to 16 hours. Remove from refrigerator and finish rising at room temperature until doubled in size, 6 to 8 hours.

Eight-Hour Pizza Dough

Follow Master Recipe for Pizza Dough, decreasing yeast to ½ teaspoon. Let covered dough rise at cool room temperature (about 68 degrees) until doubled in size, about eight hours.

Cornmeal Pizza Dough

Follow Master Recipe for Pizza Dough, replacing ¾ cup bread flour with equal amount of cornmeal.

Semolina Pizza Dough

Similar to Cornmeal Pizza Dough but slightly lighter and crisper.

Follow Master Recipe for Pizza Dough, decreasing room-temperature water to 1 cup and replacing ¾ cup bread flour with equal amount of semolina.

Whole Wheat Pizza Dough

Whole wheat flour gives dough a hearty flavor but slows down the rising process a bit.

Follow Master Recipe for Pizza Dough, replacing 2 cups bread flour with equal amount of whole wheat flour. Dough may require an extra 30 minutes to double in size while rising.

Garlic-Herb Pizza Dough

Especially good when grilling but excellent in the oven as well.

Heat 2 tablespoons extra-virgin olive oil in small skillet. Add 4 medium minced garlic cloves and 1 teaspoon minced fresh thyme, oregano, or rosemary leaves. Sauté until garlic is golden, 2 to 3 minutes. Cool mixture and use in place of oil in Master Recipe for Pizza Dough.

Fastest Pizza Dough

MAKES 2 LARGE, 4 MEDIUM, OR
8 INDIVIDUAL PIZZAS

Although this dough does not have quite the same texture as our master recipe, it can be prepared after coming home from work to make thin-crust pizza. Rapid-rise yeast makes it possible to serve pizza in a little more than an hour after walking into the kitchen. The sugar speeds up the rising process, as does putting the dough into a warm oven. Bread flour delivers a crisper crust, but all-purpose flour can be used.

1½	cups warm water, at about 105 degrees
1	envelope (2¼ teaspoons) rapid-rise dry yeast
1	tablespoon sugar
2	tablespoons extra-virgin olive oil
4	cups bread or all-purpose flour, plus extra for dusting hands and work surfaces
1½	teaspoons salt
	Vegetable oil or spray for oiling bowl

EQUIPMENT: Baking Tiles or Stone

If you like pizza with a thin, crisp crust, we recommend that you invest fifteen or twenty dollars to line the bottom rack of your oven with unglazed quarry tiles made of terra cotta. These porous tiles absorb heat better than a metal baking sheet and thus transfer more heat to whatever food is cooked on them. Pizza crust becomes especially crisp and well-browned on the bottom when cooked on tiles. In our test kitchen, we have found that these tiles are good for most bread as well. The tiles come in six-inch squares and can be cut at a tile store to fit your oven rack perfectly. Look for half-inch-thick tiles.

A large rectangular pizza stone (circular stones are generally smaller and not recommended) is also a good option. The chief drawback here is size. In most home ovens, you can fit two medium pizzas on a tile-lined rack. However, most pizza stones can accommodate only one pizza at a time. If using a stone, be careful when sliding the pizza into the oven. You don't want part of the pizza to hang off the stone, dumping toppings onto the oven floor.

1. Set oven to 200 degrees for 10 minutes, then turn oven off.

2. Meanwhile, pour water into workbowl of large food processor. Sprinkle yeast and sugar over water and pulse twice. Add oil, flour, and salt, and process until mixture forms cohesive mass. Dough should be soft and just a bit tacky. (If it is very sticky, add 2 tablespoons flour and pulse briefly. If it is stiff and tight, add 1 tablespoon water and pulse briefly.) Process another 30 seconds.

3. Dough will be a bit tacky, so use rubber spatula to turn out dough onto lightly floured work surface; knead by hand with a few strokes to form smooth, round ball.

4. Put dough into deep, lightly oiled bowl and cover with plastic wrap. Place in warm oven. Let rise for 40 minutes or until doubled. Remove from oven, punch dough down, and turn out onto lightly floured work surface. Divide and shape as directed in recipe for thin-crust or grilled pizza.

THIN-CRUST PIZZA

UNLESS YOU BUILD A BRICK OVEN IN YOUR kitchen, it's not possible to duplicate thin pizzeria-style pies at home. Commercial pizza ovens can reach 800 degrees; home ovens just can't compete. That said, homemade thin-crust pizza is delicious, if different, from the pies you get when you eat out. The crust is chewier, crisper, and not nearly as greasy.

While American pizza parlors weigh down their crusts with pounds of toppings, we prefer to follow the Italian method and use a restrained hand when topping a thin-crust pizza. This is partly out of necessity (without the extreme heat of a commercial oven, crusts with too much cheese and sauce will be soggy) and partly because we like pizzas this way. After all, you are making homemade bread, and pizza should be about the crust as well as the cheese and sauce.

In our testing, we found that baking pizza on tiles or a pizza stone is a must. We found that crusts baked on a pizza screen (a perforated pan) or baking sheet were not as crisp and chewy. (See box on page 334 for more information on tiles and stones.)

Our testing revealed that an oven temperature of 450 degrees is your best bet. We could not detect any extra crispness in a pizza cooked in a 500-degree oven. What we did notice was a fair amount of smoke in our kitchen. If your oven works well at 500 degrees without smoking, feel free to bake pizzas at this temperature; you will shave a minute or two off the cooking time.

With its fine, sandy texture, semolina keeps pizza dough from sticking to peels. Cornmeal can be used, but we find that its coarser texture can make the bottom of the crust a bit gritty.

To keep soft cheeses like mozzarella moist and lush, we found it best to add them toward the end of the baking time. When added earlier, mozzarella tends to shrivel up and dry out. Adding it later also gets more impact from less cheese, keeping the fat content to a minimum. Grating cheeses, like Parmesan, may be added at the start or near the end of baking, as desired.

Master Recipe for Thin-Crust Pizza

MAKES 2 LARGE, 4 MEDIUM, OR
8 INDIVIDUAL PIZZAS

Any of the variations on basic pizza dough may be used to make thin-crust pizza. See the illustrations on the next page for more information on stretching and baking pizza. Remember to preheat the oven (and stone, if using one) for at least 30 minutes. Depending on your oven, the type of stone or tiles used, the size of the dough round, and the amount of topping, thin-crust pizzas may be done in as little as 5 or 6 minutes or may take as long as 12 minutes. Larger pies with heavier or juicier toppings may sometimes need closer to 15 minutes in the oven. Don't pull a pizza out of the oven until the edge of the crust is golden brown and the toppings are sizzling.

1 recipe for Pizza Dough, Master (page 333) or
Fastest Pizza Dough (page 334)
Flour for dusting hands and work surfaces
Semolina or cornmeal for dusting peel
Extra-virgin olive oil for brushing on dough
Toppings of choice (see recipes that follow for specific ideas)

1. Prepare dough as directed in dough recipe. Preheat oven to 450 degrees, placing pizza stone on

rack in lower third of oven if not already lined with tiles, for 30 minutes. Turn punched-down dough out onto lightly floured work surface. Use chef's knife or dough scraper to halve, quarter, or cut dough into eighths, depending on the number and size of pizzas desired. Form each piece into ball and cover with damp cloth. Let dough relax at least 5 minutes but not more than 30 minutes.

2. Working with one piece of dough at a time and keeping others covered, flatten ball into disk using palms of hands. Starting at center and working outward, use fingertips to press dough to about ½-inch thick. Use one hand to hold dough in place and other hand to stretch dough outward; rotate dough quarter turn and stretch again. Repeat turning and stretching until dough will not stretch any further.

SHAPING PIZZAS

1. Use a chef's knife or dough scraper to divide the risen and punched-down dough into two, four, or eight pieces. A single dough recipe will make two 14-inch pizzas, four 12-inch pizzas, or eight 8-inch pies.

2. Form each piece of dough into a smooth, round ball and cover it with a damp cloth. Let the dough relax for at least 5 minutes but no more than 30 minutes.

3. Working with one ball of dough at a time and keeping the others covered, flatten the dough ball into a disk using the palms of your hands.

4. Starting at the center of the disk and working outward, use your fingertips to press the dough to about ½ inch thick.

5. Holding center of dough in place, stretch dough outward. Rotate dough a quarter turn and stretch again. Repeat until dough will not stretch any further. Let dough relax for 5 minutes, then continue stretching until it reaches correct diameter.

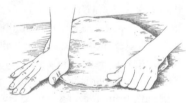

6. Use your palm to press down and flatten the thick edge of the dough.

7. Carefully lift the dough round and transfer it to a peel dusted with semolina or cornmeal. If the dough loses its round shape, adjust it on the peel to return it to the original shape.

8. Brush the entire dough round with a little olive oil. Add the toppings. To make it easier to hold pizza slices when eating, leave a ½-inch border around the edges of the dough uncovered.

9. Use a quick jerking action to slide the topped dough off the peel and onto the hot tiles or stone. Make sure that the pizza lands far enough back so that the front edge does not hang off the tiles or stone.

Let dough relax 5 minutes, then continue stretching until it reaches correct diameter. Dough should be about ¼ inch thick. (For large pizzas, let dough relax another 5 minutes and stretch again.) Use palm to flatten edge of dough. When all dough rounds are done, transfer to pizza peel that has been lightly dusted with semolina or cornmeal.

3. Brush dough rounds very lightly with oil and then add toppings. Cook topped pizzas in preheated oven until crust edges are golden brown, 5 to 12 minutes depending on size of pizzas. Add cheese if using and continue baking until melted, 2 to 3 minutes. Remove pizzas from oven, cut into wedges, and serve immediately.

Pizza Bianca with Garlic and Rosemary

MAKES 2 LARGE, 4 MEDIUM, OR 8 INDIVIDUAL PIZZAS

This simple pizza is best as a snack or bread accompaniment to dinner. Pizza bianca translates as "white pizza" and refers to the fact that there are no tomatoes, just garlic, oil, rosemary, and salt in this recipe.

I	recipe Thin-Crust Pizza (page 335)
¼	cup extra-virgin olive oil, plus extra for brushing on stretched dough
6	medium garlic cloves, minced
4	teaspoons minced fresh rosemary leaves Salt and ground black pepper

1. Prepare dough rounds as directed in Master Recipe for Thin-Crust Pizza through step 2.
2. While preparing dough, combine ¼ cup oil, garlic, rosemary, and salt and pepper to taste in small bowl. Set herb oil aside.
3. Brush plain olive oil evenly over each stretched dough round. Prick each dough round all over with fork to prevent ballooning in the oven.
4. Bake until crusts begin to brown in spots, 5 to 10 minutes. Remove crusts from oven and brush with herb oil. Continue baking 1 to 2 minutes. Remove pizzas from oven, cut into wedges, and serve immediately.

Three-Cheese Pizza

MAKES 2 LARGE, 4 MEDIUM, OR 8 INDIVIDUAL PIZZAS

This classic combination of mozzarella, Parmesan, and Gorgonzola is not a study in excess, as the name might imply. A little of each cheese contributes to a rich, complex flavor. We also recommend adding garlic and olives, although these are optional.

I	recipe Thin-Crust Pizza (page 335) Extra-virgin olive oil for brushing on stretched dough
2	ounces mozzarella cheese, shredded (about ½ cup)
¼	cup grated Parmesan cheese
4	ounces Gorgonzola cheese, crumbled (about I cup)
3	medium garlic cloves, slivered (optional)
¼	cup pitted and quartered oil-cured black olives (optional)

1. Prepare dough rounds as directed in Master Recipe for Thin-Crust Pizza through step 2.
2. Brush oil evenly over each stretched dough round. Prick each dough round all over with fork to prevent ballooning in the oven. Bake until crusts begin to brown in spots, 5 to 10 minutes.
3. Remove crusts from oven and sprinkle evenly with mozzarella and Parmesan, leaving ½-inch border around the edges uncovered. Dot with Gorgonzola, sprinkle with garlic and olives if using, and return pizzas to oven.
4. Bake until cheeses are golden and bubbling, 2 to 3 minutes. Remove pizzas from oven, cut into wedges, and serve immediately.

Classic Tomato Pizza with Mozzarella and Basil

MAKES 2 LARGE, 4 MEDIUM, OR 8 INDIVIDUAL PIZZAS

Known as pizza Margherita, this Neapolitan specialty is Italian cooking at its simplest and best. Ripe tomatoes will make all the difference here. It's imperative that excess moisture be removed from the tomatoes by seeding them. If you don't mind the skins, don't bother peeling the tomatoes.

1   recipe Thin-Crust Pizza (page 335)

2   tablespoons extra-virgin olive oil, plus extra for
    brushing on stretched dough

4   medium ripe tomatoes (about 1 ½ pounds),
    peeled if desired, seeded, and chopped
    Salt and ground black pepper

¼   cup shredded fresh basil leaves

4   ounces mozzarella cheese, shredded
    (about 1 cup)

¼   cup grated Parmesan or Pecorino
    Romano cheese

1. Prepare dough rounds as directed in Master Recipe for Thin-Crust Pizza through step 2.

2. Brush oil evenly over each stretched dough round. Arrange portion of tomatoes over each dough round, leaving ½-inch border around edges uncovered. Season with salt and pepper to taste and scatter portion of basil over tomatoes. Drizzle with 2 tablespoons oil.

3. Bake until crust edges start to brown, 6 to 12 minutes. Sprinkle with cheeses and continue baking until cheeses melt, 2 to 3 minutes more. Remove pizzas from oven, cut into wedges, and serve immediately.

Fresh Tomato Pizza with Arugula and Prosciutto

MAKES 2 LARGE, 4 MEDIUM, OR
8 INDIVIDUAL PIZZAS

The arugula for this pizza is tossed with a little oil to keep it moist, then sprinkled over the baked pizza as soon as it comes out of the oven. The heat from the pizza wilts the arugula without causing it to dry out. Because these topping ingredients are not precooked, this pizza is especially easy to prepare.

1   recipe Thin-Crust Pizza (page 335)

2   tablespoons extra-virgin olive oil, plus extra for
    brushing on stretched dough

3   medium ripe tomatoes (about 1 pound), cored
    and sliced crosswise into thin rounds
    Salt and ground black pepper

4   ounces thin-sliced prosciutto (about 8 slices)

4   ounces mozzarella cheese, shredded
    (about 1 cup)

2   cups stemmed arugula leaves, washed and
    thoroughly dried

1. Prepare dough rounds as directed in Master Recipe for Thin-Crust Pizza through step 2.

2. Brush oil evenly over each stretched dough round. Arrange portion of tomatoes in concentric circles over each dough round, leaving ¼-inch border around edges uncovered. Season with salt and pepper to taste and drizzle with 4 teaspoons oil.

3. Bake until crust edges start to brown, 6 to 12 minutes. Lay prosciutto slices over tomatoes and sprinkle with cheese. Continue baking until cheese melts, 2 to 3 minutes more.

4. Toss arugula with remaining 2 teaspoons oil. Remove pizzas from oven and top each with portion of arugula. Cut pizzas into wedges and serve immediately.

Caramelized Onion Pizza with Oil-Cured Olives and Parmesan

MAKES 2 LARGE, 4 MEDIUM, OR
8 INDIVIDUAL PIZZAS

Although these pizzas are substantial enough for dinner, they are particularly good as an hors d'oeuvre when cooked and then cut into small pieces.

1   recipe Thin-Crust Pizza (page 335)

2   tablespoons extra-virgin olive oil, plus extra for
    brushing on stretched dough

2   medium yellow onions, halved and sliced thin

1   teaspoon fresh thyme leaves
    Salt and ground black pepper

1½ cups No-Cook Tomato Sauce for Pizza
    (page 339)

¼   cup pitted and quartered oil-cured black olives

6   anchovies, chopped coarse (optional)

¼   cup grated Parmesan cheese

1. Prepare dough rounds as directed in Master Recipe for Thin-Crust Pizza through step 2.

2. While preparing dough, heat 2 tablespoons oil in large skillet set over medium-high heat. Add onions and sauté until softened and somewhat caramelized, about 10 minutes. Stir in thyme; season with salt and pepper to taste. Set onions aside.

3. Brush oil evenly over each stretched dough round. Spread portion of tomato sauce over each

dough round, leaving ½-inch border around edges uncovered. Scatter portion of onions over sauce onto each dough round. Sprinkle with olives and anchovies if using.

4. Bake until crust edges start to brown, 6 to 12 minutes. Sprinkle with cheese and continue baking until cheese melts, 2 to 3 minutes more. Remove pizzas from oven, cut into wedges, and serve immediately.

Pepperoni Pizza

MAKES 2 LARGE, 4 MEDIUM, OR
8 INDIVIDUAL PIZZAS

This classic pizzeria favorite is especially easy to prepare because the pepperoni cooks right in the oven with the pizza.

1	recipe Thin-Crust Pizza (page 335) Extra-virgin olive oil for brushing on stretched dough
1½	cups No-Cook Tomato Sauce for Pizza (see recipe at right)
8	ounces pepperoni, peeled and sliced thin
4	ounces mozzarella cheese, shredded (about 1 cup)
¼	cup grated Parmesan cheese

1. Prepare dough rounds as directed in Master Recipe for Thin-Crust Pizza through step 2.

2. Brush oil evenly over each stretched dough round. Spread portion of tomato sauce over each dough round, leaving ½-inch border around edges uncovered. Scatter some pepperoni slices over sauce onto each dough round.

3. Bake until crust edges start to brown, 6 to 12 minutes. Sprinkle with cheeses and continue baking until cheeses melt, 2 to 3 minutes more. Remove pizzas from oven, cut into wedges, and serve immediately.

Sausage and Bell Pepper Pizza with Basil and Mozzarella

MAKES 2 LARGE, 4 MEDIUM, OR
8 INDIVIDUAL PIZZAS

If bulk sausage is not available, buy link sausage, remove the meat from the casings, and then break it into bite-sized pieces.

| 1 | recipe Thin-Crust Pizza (page 335) |

¾	pound bulk sweet Italian sausage, broken into bite-sized pieces
1½	teaspoons extra-virgin olive oil (approximately), plus extra for brushing on stretched dough
1	red or yellow bell pepper, cored, halved, seeded, and cut into thin strips Salt and ground black pepper
1½	cups No-Cook Tomato Sauce for Pizza (below) combined with 2 tablespoons minced fresh basil leaves
4	ounces mozzarella cheese, shredded (about 1 cup)

1. Prepare dough rounds as directed in Master Recipe for Thin-Crust Pizza through step 2.

2. While preparing dough, put sausage and ¼ cup water in large skillet. Cook over medium-high heat until water evaporates and sausage cooks through and browns, about 10 minutes. Remove sausage with slotted spoon and set aside. Add enough oil so that amount of fat in skillet equals 1 tablespoon. Add

No-Cook Tomato Sauce for Pizza

MAKES ABOUT 3 CUPS

We found that the oven heat "cooks" the tomato sauce when making pizza. All you need do to prepare the sauce is combine canned crushed tomatoes, oil, garlic, salt, and pepper, and then spread the mixture on the dough. When shopping for crushed tomatoes, look for a brand that lists tomatoes, not tomato puree, as the first ingredient. In our testing, we have found Muir Glen and Progresso to be excellent products.

1	28-ounce can crushed tomatoes
2	tablespoons extra-virgin olive oil
2	large garlic cloves, minced Salt and ground black pepper

Combine tomatoes, oil, garlic, and salt and pepper to taste in medium bowl. Set aside at room temperature for up to several hours. (Sauce may be refrigerated in airtight container for 3 days.)

bell pepper and sauté until softened slightly, about 5 minutes. Season with salt and pepper to taste. Set bell pepper aside.

3. Brush oil evenly over each stretched dough round. Spread portion of tomato sauce over each dough round, leaving ½-inch border around edges uncovered. Scatter portion of sausage and bell pepper over sauce onto each dough round.

4. Bake until crust edges start to brown, 6 to 12 minutes. Sprinkle with cheese and continue baking until cheese melts, 2 to 3 minutes more. Remove pizzas from oven, cut into wedges, and serve immediately.

Mushroom Pizza with Sage, Fontina, and Parmesan

MAKES 2 LARGE, 4 MEDIUM, OR
8 INDIVIDUAL PIZZAS

Any fresh mushrooms will work in this recipe. Cremini are especially good.

1	recipe Thin-Crust Pizza (page 335)
2	large garlic cloves, minced
2	tablespoons extra-virgin olive oil, plus extra for brushing on stretched dough
1	pound fresh mushrooms, trimmed and sliced thin
1	teaspoon minced fresh sage leaves
	Salt and ground black pepper
1	cup No-Cook Tomato Sauce for Pizza (page 339)
4	ounces fontina cheese, shredded (about 1 cup)
¼	cup grated Parmesan cheese

1. Prepare dough rounds as directed in Master Recipe for Thin-Crust Pizza through step 2.

2. While preparing dough, heat garlic and 2 tablespoons oil in large skillet set over medium-high heat. When garlic begins to sizzle, add mushrooms; sauté until mushrooms are golden brown and juices they release have evaporated, about 7 minutes. Stir in sage and salt and pepper to taste. Set mushrooms aside.

3. Brush oil evenly over each stretched dough round. Spread portion of tomato sauce over each dough round, leaving ½-inch border around edges uncovered. Scatter portion of mushrooms over sauce onto each dough round.

4. Bake until crust edges start to brown, 6 to 12 minutes. Sprinkle with cheeses and continue baking until cheeses melt, 2 to 3 minutes more. Remove pizzas from oven, cut into wedges, and serve immediately.

White Pizza with Spinach and Ricotta

MAKES 2 LARGE, 4 MEDIUM, OR
8 INDIVIDUAL PIZZAS

Ricotta cheese and garlicky sautéed spinach flavor this tomato-less pizza.

1	recipe Thin-Crust Pizza (page 335)
2	tablespoons extra-virgin olive oil, plus extra for brushing on stretched dough
4	medium garlic cloves, slivered
¼	teaspoon hot red pepper flakes
1¼	pounds spinach, stemmed, washed, partially dried, and chopped coarse
	Salt and ground black pepper
1	cup ricotta cheese
¼	cup grated Parmesan cheese

1. Prepare dough rounds as directed in Master Recipe for Thin-Crust Pizza through step 2.

2. While preparing dough, heat 2 tablespoons oil in deep saucepan set over medium heat. Add garlic and pepper flakes and cook until fragrant, about 1 minute. Add damp spinach, cover, and cook, stirring occasionally, until just wilted, about 2 minutes. Season with salt and pepper to taste. Transfer to bowl with slotted spoon, leaving behind any liquid. Set spinach aside.

3. Brush oil evenly over each stretched dough round. Arrange portion of spinach over each round, leaving ½-inch border around edges uncovered. Dot with ricotta and sprinkle with Parmesan.

4. Bake until edges of crusts brown, 6 to 12 minutes. Remove pizzas from oven, cut into wedges, and serve immediately.

White Clam Pizza

MAKES 2 LARGE, 4 MEDIUM, OR
8 INDIVIDUAL PIZZAS

This pizza is a specialty of New Haven, Connecticut, one of the great pizza capitals of America. Traditionally, freshly shucked clams are tossed with garlic, olive oil, and herbs. Canned clams work as well.

1	recipe Thin-Crust Pizza (page 335)
2	tablespoons extra-virgin olive oil, plus extra for brushing on stretched dough
6	medium garlic cloves, minced
1	medium onion, minced
½	teaspoon hot red pepper flakes
2	10-ounce cans baby clams, drained
1	tablespoon fresh thyme or oregano leaves
	Salt and ground black pepper
½	cup grated Parmesan cheese

1. Prepare dough rounds as directed in Master Recipe for Thin-Crust Pizza through step 2.

2. While preparing dough, heat 2 tablespoons oil in large skillet set over medium heat. Add garlic, onion, and pepper flakes and cook until softened and fragrant, 1½ minutes. Stir in clams and thyme or oregano. Season with salt and pepper to taste. Set sauce aside.

3. Brush oil evenly over each stretched dough round. Spread portion of sauce over each round, leaving ½-inch border around edges uncovered. Sprinkle with cheese.

4. Bake until edges of crusts brown, 5 to 10 minutes. Remove pizzas from oven, cut into wedges, and serve immediately.

GRILLED PIZZA

GETTING THE TOPPING HOT IS THE HARDEST challenge when grilling pizza. Toppings have only a few minutes to heat through (any longer and the bottom crust will burn), so they must be kept fairly light. Therefore, we like to get as much flavor from the crust as possible and recommend the Garlic-Herb Pizza Dough (page 334) when grilling. This dough is so flavorful that we often just brush it with olive oil and serve it as an accompaniment to summer meals. Plain dough will work fine on the grill; it just won't taste as good.

Because grilled pizzas are flipped (the bottom of the dough round eventually becomes the top of the pizza), we do not dust peels (use metal only; wooden peels should not go near the grill) or baking sheets with sandy semolina or cornmeal. Flour will keep the dough from sticking yet will not make the crust gritty, as did the semolina and cornmeal in our tests.

We found that heavy toppings or liquidy sauces made grilled pizza very soggy and should thus be avoided. In our tests, raw ingredients that need only to be heated through (fresh tomatoes, cheese, sliced shrimp) or cooked ingredients that are fairly dry (sautéed onions, grilled mushrooms, eggplant) worked best as toppings for grilled pizzas.

We found that oil will help keep grilled pizza dough moist, prevent sticking to the grill, and promote even browning. Keep a brush and small bowl of olive oil nearby when grilling pizzas. We brush some oil on the dough before it is grilled and then again when it is flipped.

Although we prefer to top grilled pizzas on a baking sheet and not on the grill, you will still spend a fair amount of time near the fire. To keep your hands as far away from the grill as possible, use tongs with long, heat-resistant handles to maneuver the dough.

Once the dough has been flipped, it's time to add the toppings. We recommend that you use either the grill cover or small disposable pie pans to concentrate heat and get the toppings hot by the time the bottom crust is nicely browned. If the toppings are not ready and the bottom crust is done, you can slide the pizzas onto a baking sheet and run them under the broiler.

In our testing, we found that larger crusts are hard to flip, so we recommend making only small pizzas on the grill. This necessitates working in batches, so consider grilling pizzas for an informal meal when everyone is gathered in the backyard. As each pizza comes off the grill, serve it immediately. An extra pair of hands to top crusts while you tend the grill is helpful.

If you prefer not to be grilling pizzas to order, the crusts can be grilled until nicely browned on both sides and then slid onto a baking sheet, cooled, covered, and kept at room temperature for several hours. When you are ready to serve the pizzas, brush the top of the grilled pizza rounds with a little oil, add the toppings, and slide the crusts under a preheated broiler for several minutes. While the smoky grill flavor is not quite as intense, this do-ahead method is much easier.

Master Recipe for Grilled Pizza

MAKES 8 INDIVIDUAL PIZZAS

The following grilled pizza recipes will serve four as a light summer meal (two small pizzas per person) or eight as a first course. We particularly like to serve grilled pizzas as a first course or hors d'oeuvre with drinks and then follow with something else from the grill.

1	recipe Garlic-Herb Pizza Dough (page 334) Flour for dusting hands, work surfaces, and baking sheets or metal peels
¼	cup extra-virgin olive oil for brushing on dough Salt

1. Prepare dough as directed in recipe. Light grill. Turn punched-down dough out onto lightly floured work surface. Use chef's knife or dough scraper to cut dough into eighths. Form each piece into ball and cover with damp cloth. Let dough relax at least 5 minutes but not more than 30 minutes.

2. Working with one piece of dough at a time and keeping others covered, flatten ball into disk using palm of hand. Starting at center and working outward, use fingertips to press dough to about ½ inch thick. Use one hand to hold dough in place and other hand to stretch dough outward; rotate dough quarter turn and stretch again. Repeat turning and stretching until dough will not stretch any further. Let dough relax 5 minutes, then continue stretching until it has reached diameter of 7 or 8 inches. Dough should be about ¼ inch thick. Use palm to flatten edge of dough. Transfer dough rounds to baking sheets or metal peels that have been lightly dusted with flour.

3. Check to make sure grill is medium-hot. (You should be able to hold your hand 5 inches above the grill surface for no more than 3 or 4 seconds.) Brush oil evenly over each stretched dough round and sprinkle with salt to taste.

4. Slide your hand under each dough round and gently flip the dough onto the grill, oiled side down. Grill until dark brown grill marks appear, 1 to 2 minutes. Prick any bubbles that develop on top surface with fork. Brush tops with more oil, then flip with long-handled tongs onto clean baking sheet or peel, grilled side up. (If grilling bread without toppings,

simply brush tops with oil and flip back onto grill.)

5. Brush grilled dough surfaces with oil and add toppings, leaving ½-inch border around edges uncovered. Slide pizzas back onto grill. Cover and grill until pizza bottoms are crisp and browned, toppings are hot, and cheese melts, 2 to 3 minutes; serve immediately and repeat with remaining rounds.

➤ VARIATION

Do-Ahead Grilled Pizza

Follow Master Recipe for Grilled Pizza, grilling dough rounds until both sides are crisp and nicely browned, 2 to 3 minutes per side. Repeat with remaining dough rounds. (Grilled dough rounds can be covered and stored at room temperature for up to 6 hours.) When ready to serve, preheat broiler. Brush tops of grilled dough with oil and add toppings, leaving ½-inch border around edges uncovered. Broil until toppings are hot and cheese melts, about 2 minutes. Serve immediately.

Grilled Pizza with Fresh Tomatoes and Basil

MAKES 8 INDIVIDUAL PIZZAS

When tomatoes are at their best and all your cooking is outside on the grill, think of this light pizza, which makes a good lunch for four or a first course for eight.

1	recipe Grilled Pizza (above)
¼	cup extra-virgin olive oil
3	medium ripe tomatoes (about 1 pound), cored and sliced crosswise into thin rounds
½	cup grated Parmesan cheese (optional)
1	cup lightly packed chopped fresh basil leaves Salt and ground black pepper
¼	cup pitted and quartered oil-cured black olives (optional)

1. Grill dough rounds as directed in Master Recipe for Grilled Pizza through step 4.

2. Brush grilled dough surfaces with oil. Arrange portion of tomatoes over each dough round, leaving ½-inch border around edges uncovered. Sprinkle with optional Parmesan, basil, and salt and pepper to taste. Drizzle with remaining oil and dot with olives if using.

3. Continue grilling pizzas, covered, until topping is hot and cheese melts, 2 to 3 minutes. Serve immediately.

Grilled Pizza with Portobello Mushrooms and Onions

MAKES 8 INDIVIDUAL PIZZAS

You can sauté the onions well in advance, but it makes sense to grill the mushrooms right before grilling the pizzas.

I	recipe Grilled Pizza (page 342)
¼	cup extra-virgin olive oil, plus extra for brushing on stretched dough
2	medium onions, halved and sliced thin
2	tablespoons balsamic vinegar
I	teaspoon minced fresh oregano or thyme leaves
	Salt and ground black pepper
4	medium portobello mushrooms (about I pound), stems discarded
½	cup grated Parmesan cheese

1. Prepare dough rounds as directed in Master Recipe for Grilled Pizza through step 2.

2. While preparing dough, heat 2 tablespoons oil in large skillet. Add onions and sauté over medium heat until golden, about 8 minutes. Stir in vinegar and cook until liquid has evaporated, about 1 minute. Stir in oregano or thyme and salt and pepper to taste. Set onions aside.

3. Brush mushrooms with 2 tablespoons oil. Season with salt and pepper to taste and grill, gill sides up, until caps are streaked with dark grill marks, 8 to 10 minutes. Remove mushrooms from grill and cut into ¼-inch strips. Set mushrooms aside.

4. Check grill heat and brush oil evenly over each stretched dough round. Grill, oiled side down, until dark brown grill marks appear, 1 to 2 minutes. Brush tops with more oil, then flip onto clean baking sheet, grilled side up.

5. Brush grilled dough surfaces with oil. Arrange portion of onions and mushrooms over each dough round, leaving ½-inch border around edges uncovered. Sprinkle cheese over vegetables.

6. Continue grilling pizzas, covered, until vegetables are hot and cheese melts, 2 to 3 minutes. Serve immediately.

Grilled Pizza with Fennel, Sun-Dried Tomato, and Asiago

MAKES 8 INDIVIDUAL PIZZAS

The sautéed fennel and onion topping can be prepared a day in advance of grilling the pizza. Bring to room temperature before using to top pizza.

I	recipe Grilled Pizza (page 342)
3	tablespoons extra-virgin olive oil, plus extra for brushing on stretched dough
I	large Spanish onion (about I pound), halved and sliced thin
I	medium fennel bulb (about ¾ pound), stems and fronds discarded; halved, cored, and sliced very thin
4	large garlic cloves, minced
I	tablespoon fresh thyme leaves
I	teaspoon fennel seeds
¼	teaspoon hot red pepper flakes
	Salt
½	cup drained and slivered sun-dried tomatoes
½	cup grated Asiago cheese

1. Prepare dough rounds as directed in Master Recipe for Grilled Pizza through step 2.

2. While preparing dough, heat 3 tablespoons oil in large skillet over medium-high heat. Add onion and fennel and cook, stirring often, until vegetables soften, about 8 minutes. Add garlic and continue cooking, 2 minutes. Stir in thyme, fennel seeds, and pepper flakes. Season with salt to taste. Set onion-fennel mixture aside.

3. Check grill heat and brush oil evenly over each stretched dough round. Grill, oiled side down, until dark brown grill marks appear, 1 to 2 minutes. Brush tops with more oil, then flip onto clean baking sheet, grilled side up.

4. Brush grilled dough surfaces with more oil. Arrange portion of onion-fennel mixture over each dough round, leaving ½-inch border around edges uncovered. Sprinkle tomatoes and cheese over vegetables.

5. Continue grilling pizzas, covered, until tomatoes and onion-fennel mixture are hot and cheese melts, 2 to 3 minutes. Serve immediately.

343

Grilled Pizza with Grilled Eggplant and Goat Cheese

MAKES 8 INDIVIDUAL PIZZAS

Thin rounds of eggplant are brushed with a garlicky basil oil, grilled, and then layered over grilled crusts and sprinkled with goat cheese.

I	recipe Grilled Pizza (page 342)
¼	cup extra-virgin olive oil, plus extra for brushing on stretched dough
6	medium garlic cloves, minced
4	tablespoons minced fresh basil leaves
	Salt and ground black pepper
I	large eggplant (about I pound), cut crosswise into ¼-inch-thick rounds
8	ounces goat cheese, crumbled (about 2 cups)

1. Prepare dough rounds as directed in Master Recipe for Grilled Pizza through step 2.

2. While preparing dough, combine ¼ cup oil, garlic, 2 tablespoons basil, and salt and pepper to taste in small bowl. Set herb oil aside.

3. Brush both sides of eggplant slices with half of herb oil. Grill, turning once, until flesh is darkly colored, 8 to 10 minutes. Set eggplant aside.

4. Check grill heat and brush plain olive oil evenly over each stretched dough round. Grill, oiled side down, until dark brown grill marks appear, 1 to 2 minutes. Brush tops with more plain olive oil, then flip onto clean baking sheet, grilled side up.

5. Brush grilled dough surfaces with remaining herb oil. Arrange portion of eggplant slices over each dough round, leaving ½-inch border around edges uncovered. Sprinkle cheese and remaining 2 tablespoons basil over eggplant.

6. Continue grilling pizzas, covered, until eggplant is hot and cheese melts, 2 to 3 minutes. Serve immediately.

Grilled Pizza with Shrimp and Feta Cheese

MAKES 8 INDIVIDUAL PIZZAS

This pizza is moister than some of the others and works well as a dinner for four when served with a salad.

I	recipe Grilled Pizza (page 342)
¼	cup extra-virgin olive oil, plus extra for brushing on stretched dough
6	medium garlic cloves, minced
4	teaspoons minced fresh oregano leaves
	Salt and ground black pepper
I	pound medium shrimp, peeled and halved lengthwise
8	ounces feta cheese, crumbled (2 cups)

1. Prepare dough rounds as directed in Master Recipe for Grilled Pizza through step 2.

2. While preparing dough, combine ¼ cup oil, garlic, 2 teaspoons oregano, and salt and pepper to taste in small bowl. Set herb oil aside.

3. Check grill heat and brush plain olive oil evenly over each stretched dough round. Grill, oiled side down, until dark brown grill marks appear, 1 to 2 minutes. Brush tops with more plain olive oil, then flip onto clean baking sheet, grilled side up.

4. Arrange portion of shrimp over each dough round, leaving ½-inch border around edges uncovered. Brush some herb oil over each pizza, making sure that shrimp are lightly brushed with oil as well. Sprinkle cheese and remaining 2 teaspoons oregano over shrimp.

5. Continue grilling pizzas, covered, until shrimp are pink and cheese melts, 2 to 3 minutes. Serve immediately.

FOCACCIA

MANY OF THE FOCACCIA RECIPES WE HAVE tried in the past produced a crusty, crisp bread that was only slightly thicker than pizza. These dense, hard breads were often loaded down with toppings. They were more a meal than a snack or an accompaniment to Sunday dinner.

We wanted something quite different. Good focaccia should have a soft, chewy texture and high rise. The crumb should be filled with small to medium-sized air pockets, which will give the bread a good rise and create an overall impression of lightness and chewiness. As for the toppings, they should be minimal. Focaccia is a bread, not a meal.

We began our investigations with a composite

recipe of yeast, warm water, olive oil, flour, and salt that was similar to our pizza dough. After more than a dozen initial tests, we were not much closer to a solution. We tried reducing the salt because it can inhibit the action of the yeast and ended up with a better rise but bland bread. We tried bread flour, all-purpose flour, whole wheat flour, and all possible combinations of these three. Bread flour makes focaccia chewy but also dry and tough. Whole wheat flour is at cross-purposes with our stated goal of a soft texture and high rise. Unbleached all-purpose flour turned out to be the right choice, but we still had a lot of work to do.

We tried milk instead of water and got better browning and a softer dough, but the bread was kind of flat. Increasing the yeast produced a high focaccia, but the flavor of the yeast was too dominant. We tried letting the dough ferment in the refrigerator for a day. This lightened the texture and produced larger holes in the dough but seemed like a lot of work for a relatively small improvement. We wanted to be able to make and enjoy focaccia on the same day.

In our research we ran across two recipes from southern Italy that added riced potatoes to the dough. When we tried a recipe from Carol Field's *The Italian Baker* (Harper & Row, 1985), we liked the moistness, high rise, and soft texture of this bread. However, the crumb was fairly dense and compact like a cake. This bread had several appealing traits but still was not quite what we wanted.

We knew that sponges (relatively thin mixtures of yeast, water, and flour that are allowed to ferment briefly) are often used to lend flavor and create airholes in breads. We were not terribly concerned about flavor. With olive oil, salt, and herbs, we were sure that any flavor boost from a sponge would be hard to detect. But we did want those airholes, so we tried a quick sponge.

We stirred the yeast, half the water, and a small portion of the flour together in a small bowl, covered the bowl with plastic wrap, and let the sponge rest before adding the remaining water, flour, oil, and salt. The difference was quite remarkable. The extra half-hour of fermentation produced wonderfully large bubbles. The result was a bread that rose very high but still had a nice, light texture. We tried longer sponges and found that 30 minutes was enough time

for the yeast to work its magic.

With the sponge having been successful in our basic composite recipe, we now tried it with Carol Field's potato focaccia, which we had liked so much. The result was perfect. The sponge transformed the crumb from dense and cakelike to chewy and airy. The bread rose higher than the version made with just flour, and the crumb was softer and more moist. As a final adjustment, we tried rapid-rise yeast to see if we could cut the rising times. This yeast works fine in this recipe and shaves off more than an hour from the process.

A couple of notes about working with this dough. The moisture from the potatoes helps keep the crumb soft but also makes the dough very sticky. Adding extra flour makes the dough easier to handle, but the results are not as good because the wet dough helps produce bread with air pockets and chewiness.

Sticky doughs are best kneaded in a standing mixer or a food processor. You can make the dough by hand, but you will probably end up incorporating slightly more flour.

When it comes time to shape the dough, moisten your hands with a little water. This will prevent the dough from sticking to your fingers. If trying to stretch the dough into a rectangular pan, you may need to let it rest before completing the final shaping. The dough is quite elastic and will put up a good fight without this rest.

An easier method is to divide the dough in half and shape it into two eight-inch disks on a large, oiled baking sheet. These free-form disks rise and bake on the same pan, thus avoiding the tricky task of transferring such a sticky dough. You may also form disks on wooden peels that have been liberally coated with cornmeal, then slide them onto a pizza stone. The bottom crust is especially thick and chewy when cooked on a stone.

The problem with using a peel is that the dough often sticks, even when the peel is well dusted with cornmeal. When we were able to get the dough onto the stone without incident, however, the results were excellent. For the sake of simplicity, we opted to rise and bake the dough on an oiled metal pan, as described in the recipe below.

An oven temperature of 425 degrees bakes the focaccia quickly without any burning. Lower temperatures produce an inferior crust, and high temperatures can cause the bottom to burn. Keep the focaccia away from the bottom of the oven to prevent the crust from scorching. Once the bread is golden brown, immediately transfer it to a cooling rack to keep the bottom crust from becoming soggy. Focaccia tastes best warm, so wait about 20 minutes and then serve.

Rosemary Focaccia

MAKES ONE 15½ X 10½-INCH RECTANGLE
OR TWO 8-INCH ROUNDS

Rapid-rise yeast reduces the preparation time by more than an hour. If you use an equal amount of regular active dry yeast instead, let the sponge in step 2 develop for 30 minutes rather than 20, and increase the first and second rises to 1½ hours each.

DOUGH

1	medium baking potato (about 9 ounces), peeled and quartered
1½	teaspoons rapid-rise yeast
3½	cups unbleached all-purpose flour
1	cup warm water (105 to 115 degrees)
2	tablespoons extra-virgin olive oil, plus more for oiling bowl and pan
1¼	teaspoons salt

TOPPING

2	tablespoons extra-virgin olive oil
2	tablespoons fresh rosemary leaves
¾	teaspoon coarse sea salt (or 1¼ teaspoons kosher salt)

1. FOR THE DOUGH: Bring 1 quart water to boil in small saucepan; add potato and simmer until tender, about 25 minutes. Drain potato well; cool until it can be handled comfortably and put through fine disk on ricer or grate through large holes on box grater. Reserve 1⅓ cups lightly packed potato.

2. Meanwhile, in large bowl of electric mixer or workbowl of food processor fitted with steel blade, mix or pulse yeast, ½ cup flour, and ½ cup warm water until combined. Cover tightly with plastic wrap (or put workbowl lid on) and set aside until bubbly, about 20 minutes. Add remaining dough

ingredients, including reserved potato. If using mixer, fit with paddle attachment and mix on low speed until dough comes together. Switch to dough hook attachment and increase speed to medium; continue kneading until dough is smooth and elastic, about 5 minutes. For food processor, process until dough is smooth and elastic, about 40 seconds.

3. Transfer dough to lightly oiled bowl, turn to coat with oil, and cover tightly with plastic wrap. Let rise in warm, draft-free area until dough is puffy and doubled in volume, about 1 hour.

4. With wet hands (to prevent sticking), press dough flat into generously oiled 15½ x 10½-inch jelly-roll pan. If the dough resists going into the corners (and it probably will), cover it with a damp cloth and let it relax for 15 minutes before trying to stretch again. Or, if making rounds, halve and flatten each piece of dough into 8-inch round on large (at least 18 inches long), generously oiled baking sheet. Either way, cover dough with lightly greased or oil-sprayed plastic wrap; let rise in warm, draft-free area until dough is puffy and doubled in volume, 45 minutes to 1 hour.

5. Meanwhile, adjust oven rack to lower-middle position and heat oven to 425 degrees. With two wet fingers, dimple risen dough at regular intervals. The dimples (there should be about 2 dozen) should be deep enough to hold small pieces of topping, herbs, and/or pools of olive oil.

6. FOR THE TOPPING: Drizzle dough with oil and sprinkle evenly with rosemary and coarse salt, landing some in pools of oil.

7. Bake until focaccia bottom(s) are golden brown and crisp, 23 to 25 minutes. Transfer to wire rack to cool slightly. Cut rectangular focaccia into squares or round focaccia into wedges; serve warm. (Focaccia can be kept on counter for several hours and reheated just before serving. Or, wrap cooled focaccia in plastic and then foil and freeze for up to 1 month; unwrap and defrost in 325-degree oven until soft, about 15 minutes.

➤ VARIATIONS
Hand-Kneaded Focaccia
Follow recipe for Rosemary Focaccia through step 1. In step 2, mix starter ingredients with wooden spoon in large bowl; cover and let stand 20 minutes. Add 1½

cups flour to starter, then beat with wooden spoon for 5 minutes. Add 1¼ cups flour along with remaining dough ingredients; continue beating until dough comes together. Turn dough onto floured surface; knead in remaining ¼ cup flour until dough is elastic and sticky, 4 to 5 minutes. Transfer dough to oiled bowl as in step 3 and follow remaining instructions.

Sage Focaccia

Follow recipe for Rosemary Focaccia, adding 1 tablespoon chopped fresh sage leaves with other dough ingredients in step 2 and substituting 24 whole fresh sage leaves (one per oil-filled dimple) for rosemary.

Parmesan Focaccia

Follow recipe for Rosemary Focaccia, substituting ⅔ cup grated Parmesan cheese for rosemary and coarse sea salt.

Focaccia with Black Olives and Thyme

Follow recipe for Rosemary Focaccia, substituting 1 teaspoon fresh thyme leaves and 24 pitted large black olives (one per oil-filled dimple) for rosemary.

BRUSCHETTA

AUTHENTIC ITALIAN GARLIC BREAD, CALLED bruschetta, is never squishy or soft. Crisp, toasted slices of country bread are rubbed with raw garlic, brushed with extra-virgin olive oil (never butter), and then slathered with various ingredients. Toppings can be as simple as salt and pepper or fresh herbs. Ripe tomatoes, grilled mushrooms, or sautéed onions make more substantial toppings.

We found that narrow loaves of Italian bread are not suitable for bruschetta. Crusty country loaves that will yield larger slices are preferable. Oblong loaves that measure about five inches across are best, but round loaves will work. As for thickness, we found that about one inch provides enough heft to support weighty toppings and gives a good chew.

Toasting the bread, which can be done over a grill fire or under the broiler, creates little jagged edges that will pull off tiny bits of garlic when the raw clove is rubbed over the bread. For more garlic flavor, rub vigorously.

Oil can be drizzled over the garlicky toast or brushed on for more even coverage. One large piece of toast is enough for a single appetizer serving. Two or three slices will make a good lunch when accompanied by a salad.

Bruschetta with Tomatoes and Basil

MAKES 8 LARGE SLICES

This is the classic bruschetta, although you can substitute other herbs. Decrease the quantity of stronger herbs, such as thyme or oregano.

4	medium ripe tomatoes (about 1⅔ pounds), cored and cut into ½-inch dice
⅓	cup shredded fresh basil leaves
	Salt and ground black pepper
1	12 x 5-inch loaf country bread, sliced crosswise into 1-inch-thick pieces, ends removed
1	large garlic clove, peeled
3	tablespoons extra-virgin olive oil

1. Heat broiler or light grill fire.

2. Mix tomatoes, basil, and salt and pepper to taste in medium bowl. Set aside.

3. Broil or grill bread until golden brown on both sides. Place toast slices on large platter, rub garlic over tops, then brush with oil.

4. Use slotted spoon to divide tomato mixture among toast slices. Serve immediately.

Bruschetta with Fresh Herbs

MAKES 8 LARGE SLICES

Ideal as an accompaniment to meals.

5	tablespoons extra-virgin olive oil
1½	tablespoons minced fresh parsley leaves
1	tablespoon minced fresh oregano or thyme leaves
1	tablespoon minced fresh sage leaves
	Salt and ground black pepper
1	12 x 5-inch loaf country bread, sliced crosswise into 1-inch-thick pieces, ends removed
1	large garlic clove, peeled

1. Heat broiler or light grill fire.

2. Mix oil, herbs, and salt and pepper to taste in small bowl. Set aside.

3. Broil or grill bread until golden brown on both sides. Place toast slices on large platter, rub garlic over tops, brush with herb oil, and serve immediately.

Bruschetta with Red Onions, Herbs, and Parmesan
MAKES 8 LARGE SLICES

The sautéed onions may be prepared in advance and the toasts assembled at the last minute. Because this bruschetta contains cheese, we like to use the broiler rather than the grill. The heat from above (rather than below) melts the cheese more effectively.

6	tablespoons extra-virgin olive oil
4	medium red onions (about 1½ pounds), halved lengthwise and sliced thin
4	teaspoons sugar
1½	tablespoons minced fresh mint leaves
2	tablespoons balsamic vinegar Salt and ground black pepper
1	12 x 5-inch loaf country bread, sliced crosswise into 1-inch-thick pieces, ends removed
1	large garlic clove, peeled
3	tablespoons grated Parmesan cheese

1. Heat 3½ tablespoons of the oil in large skillet set over medium-high heat. Add onions and sugar; sauté, stirring often, until softened, 7 to 8 minutes. Reduce heat to medium-low. Continue to cook, stirring often, until onions are sweet and tender, 7 to 8 minutes longer. Stir in mint and vinegar and season to taste with salt and pepper. Set onion mixture aside. (Can be covered and refrigerated for up to 1 week.)

2. Heat broiler. Place bread on large baking sheet; broil bread until golden brown on both sides.

3. Remove baking sheet from oven. Rub garlic over toast tops. Brush remaining 2½ tablespoons oil over bread. Divide onion mixture among slices, then sprinkle with cheese.

4. Broil until cheese just melts. Transfer bruschetta to large platter and serve immediately.

Bruschetta with Grilled Portobello Mushrooms
MAKES 8 LARGE SLICES

The mushrooms are grilled with the gill-like undersides facing up to prevent loss of juices. For serving, the mushrooms are flipped onto the bread so their juices seep down into the toast.

4	large portobello mushrooms (about 1⅓ pounds), stemmed
6	tablespoons extra-virgin olive oil
1	tablespoon minced fresh rosemary leaves Salt and ground black pepper
1	12 x 5-inch loaf country bread, sliced crosswise into 1-inch-thick pieces, ends removed
1	large garlic clove, peeled

1. Light grill. Place mushroom caps on large baking sheet. Mix 3½ tablespoons of the oil, rosemary, and salt and pepper to taste in small bowl. Brush oil mixture over both sides of mushrooms.

2. Grill mushrooms, gill side up over medium-hot fire, until caps are cooked through and grill-marked, 8 to 10 minutes.

3. Meanwhile, grill bread until golden brown on both sides. Place toast slices on large platter. Rub garlic over tops, then brush with remaining 2½ tablespoons oil.

4. Halve grilled mushrooms; place one half, gill side down, over each slice of toast. Serve immediately.

14

YEAST BREADS

YEAST BREADS FALL INTO TWO BASIC CATE-
gories. European-style loaves are generally made
without dairy (the ingredients may be as basic as
water, flour, yeast, and salt) and are baked directly on
a baking stone or on tiles. (See page 334 for more
information on these helpful baking tools.) The crust
on these loaves is quite thick and crisp, and the
crumb is chewy. American-style loaves usually contain dairy (milk and butter) as well as a sweetener.
This kind of bread is baked in a metal loaf pan. The
crust is thinner and the crumb is richer and more
tender than that on a European loaf.

This chapter begins with an examination of
American sandwich breads. Several simple European-
style breads are considered next, and the chapter concludes with some enriched yeast breads that contain
a lot of butter and sugar as well as eggs. These sweet
breads are more like dessert than bread.

Despite these differences, there are some con-
stants when making all kinds of bread. First of all, the
kind of flour that you choose really matters. (For
more on flour, see page 416.) For strong structure
and optimum chew, we prefer high-protein bread
flour. However, in loaves made with a coarser flour,
such as whole wheat flour and rye flour, or in loaves
with a lot of butter, we use all-purpose flour. Follow
the recommendations in individual recipes.

Although you might find it hard to believe, the
quality of the water that goes into a bread recipe is
also important. We compared loaves of our whole
wheat bread (see page 356) made with tap water versus bottled water. To our great surprise, most tasters
immediately picked out the loaf made with bottled
water as being substantially better, with a sweeter,
fuller flavor. Of course, since many bread recipes call
for two cups or more of water, it makes sense that
the flavor and quality of the water should matter. So
if someone tells you to use good, bottled water for
bread making (or tap water if the local supply is of
high quality), don't immediately assume that person
is a culinary snob.

The third essential ingredient in most bread
recipes is yeast. There are several kinds of yeast available to home cooks. All yeast begins as a small, cul-
tured, purified sample that feeds and multiplies continuously in a liquid medium until it reaches the
desired volume and stage of development. This liquid yeast is sold by the tankerful to commercial food
manufacturers. For bakeries, yeast companies remove
some of the moisture from liquid yeast to create a
product called "crumbled yeast," which is sold in 50-
pound bags. The next processing step extrudes the
yeast to make a product that remains fully hydrated,
yet fine enough to press into the small cakes you see
for sale in supermarkets labeled "cake yeast." Further
processing yields dried, powdered yeast, called active
dry yeast. (The same process is used to make other
dry yeasts, including rapid-rise and instant yeasts,
although these products start with different strains of
yeast. For more information on rapid-rise and instant
yeast, see page 354.)

We rely on active dry yeast and rapid-rise yeast in
our recipes since these products are the most widely
available. If you want to use cake yeast, also called
fresh-active, or compressed, yeast, you'll need twice
as much yeast as recommended in the recipe. Note
that cake yeast is highly perishable and must be
refrigerated.

Starting with the correct ingredients is part of the
puzzle when making good bread. Proper technique
is equally important. Our experience in the test
kitchen has revealed the importance of several issues.

First of all, most bread doughs do not require
lengthy kneading. In fact, we have found that kneading bread for 10 or 15 minutes can often produce an
inferior loaf. Often the kneading that occurs in the
food processor (coupled with a minute or two on a
floured surface to bring the dough together in a ball)
will suffice. Likewise, when using a standing mixer,
pay careful attention to the recommended mixing
speeds and kneading times.

If you are kneading by hand, resist the temptation
to add too much flour to a dough or you risk making the texture dry. (This temptation is one reason
why we prefer to knead bread dough in a standing
mixer or food processor when possible.) In many
recipes, the dough will at first seem very sticky, as if
it needs more flour. However, as it rises, the dough
hydrates—that is, the water becomes more evenly
distributed—and the texture becomes very soft and
smooth. So, do not add more flour unless the dough
really seems much too wet. One way to avoid adding
more flour is to slightly moisten your hands to prevent sticking. You will also produce a slightly drier

loaf if you substitute regular sugar for honey in a bread recipe without increasing the water.

On rare occasions, you may find that a loaf does not rise properly. Check to make sure that the expiration date on your yeast has not passed. Another possibility is that the water was too hot and killed the yeast. (Water used to make bread should be no hotter than 115 degrees.) Poor rising may also mean that you have added too much flour or placed the bread in a cool, drafty spot. To cure the latter situation, heat your oven for 10 minutes at 200 degrees and turn it off; the oven can now be used as a proofing box. A microwave oven can also be used as a proofing box. To do so, nearly fill a two-cup Pyrex measure with water, place it in the microwave, and bring the water to a boil. Now place the dough (which should be in a bowl covered with plastic wrap) into the microwave oven with the measuring cup. The preheated water will keep the microwave oven at the proper temperature for rising.

We prefer to let bread rise in a straight-sided plastic container. Dough needs to be contained while it ferments, not spread out in a big bowl. (You may use a bowl, just don't use one that is too large.) A container or bowl two to three times the size of the dough is perfect. If you use a container, you can mark the outside of it to indicate the original volume of the dough, which makes it easy to gauge the point at which the dough has doubled.

If you are shaping the dough and are not pleased

EQUIPMENT: Standing Mixer

Years ago, free-standing mixers were a kitchen staple. Grandma probably had a "mixmaster," which is a generic term for a free-standing mixer, though it is actually a brand name for units manufactured by Sunbeam. For a while, these large machines went out of favor as new food processors and more powerful hand mixers, which were better suited for many of the tasks of standing mixers, became available. If all you want to do is whip egg whites or cream, or if you only make cakes from a mix, you don't really need a heavy-duty standing mixer.

However, if you like to bake, a standing mixer permits maximum flexibility. Models with the most options, such as a whisk, paddle, and dough hook, will open up the most possibilities for baking everything from cakes and cookies to breads.

Perhaps the best use for standing mixers is for mixing and kneading bread dough. Standing mixers knead perfectly in about one-third the time of hand kneading, and with far more control and satisfaction than bread machines. (Hand-held mixers lack the stability and power to do a good job.) Some large food processors can knead bread dough, but they can only handle relatively small batches of dough.

Unfortunately, not all brands of standing mixers are helpful kitchen allies. In the process of testing seven of the top-selling standing mixers, we found that some models are simply too difficult and frustrating to work with to make them worthwhile purchases. Outdated engineering and poorly designed beaters and bowls made it a challenge, rather than a pleasure, to prepare baked goods in several of the models we used.

On the other hand, three of the seven models were outstanding, and making cakes, cookies, and bread with them was enjoyable and gratifying. The Rival Select was exceptional, performing every task flawlessly. The two KitchenAid models we tested were outstanding as well, although the Rival's dough hook is better designed and kneaded bread dough more quickly. These three models are also the most expensive of the group, costing $300 to $400. Are they worth it? Plainly and simply, yes. Each is designed for endurance, so it makes sense to spend the money up front, since you will derive years of use and pleasure from these models.

Both the Rival Select and the two KitchenAid mixers operate by "planetary action," in which a wide, flat beater (called the paddle) moves around a stationary bowl. This proved the most effective way of blending ingredients, since the paddle reaches the sides as well as the center of the bowl and gathers particles quickly. As a result, there is little need to stop the machine and scrape the sides of the bowl.

Another critical point of comparison among the mixers was stability. The Rival and KitchenAid models are heavy and barely vibrate even when put to the test of mixing stiff cookie and bread dough. A standing mixer you have to hold with one or two hands is not a labor-saving device.

The Rival and the KitchenAids were the best at kneading bread dough, performing the task quickly, smoothly, and efficiently, with the motors showing not the slightest sign of strain and without spilling any flour. All three models had the weight, stability, and power needed to make smooth, elastic, tender dough.

with your efforts, simply let the dough rest for a few minutes, covered with a damp cloth. The dough will then be sufficiently rested to be shaped a second time. Otherwise, the dough can become elastic and difficult to manage.

It should be noted that the length of time the bread is in the oven has a tremendous effect on texture and quality. Most cookbooks tell you to tap the bottom of a loaf of bread to see if it is done. (Supposedly, a loaf will sound hollow when done.) This is, at best, an inexact method. We find it is much better to use an instant-read thermometer. When baking freestanding loaves, insert the thermometer into the middle of the bottom of the loaf and then halfway up. For bread baked in a loaf pan, insert the thermometer into one end of the loaf, angling it down toward the middle. This method produces the same reading as poking through the bottom of the loaf without having to remove the bread from the pan.

Note that different types of bread should be baked to different internal temperatures. The recipe for Rustic Country Bread on page 362, for example, requires an internal temperature of 210 degrees because the dough is extremely wet. In contrast, Cinnamon Swirl Bread (page 371) starts with a much drier dough and should be baked to an internal temperature of 185 to 190 degrees.

AMERICAN SANDWICH BREAD

AMERICAN LOAF BREADS ARE QUITE DIFFERent from their European cousins, primarily because they contain fat in the form of milk and melted butter. This produces a more tender crumb and a softer loaf particularly well-suited to sandwiches, for which less assertive bread works best (notwithstanding the current ill-conceived trend of using thick slabs of focaccia with dainty fixings). As we discovered during the testing process, this is not just an exercise in convenience. American loaf bread is every bit as inspiring as those toothier imports—there is nothing like a fresh-from-the-oven loaf cut into slabs and slathered with butter and honey.

These days, many home cooks might choose to use a bread machine to make this type of bread. In our experience, this method produces a crust that is mediocre at best and an interior of unpredictable quality—that is, all too often, cakelike. As for purchasing this type of bread at the store, it's actually not that easy. Most gourmet shops don't carry a basic sandwich bread. Of course, many people who might enjoy making terrific sandwich bread at home don't even try it because they think it takes most of a day. So we set out to develop a good, solid recipe that could be done in two hours, start to finish, including baking time.

For many home cooks, the other great impedi-

EQUIPMENT: Food Processor

Spending several hundred dollars on a standing mixer may not be an option. In that case, you may want to buy a good food processor and try to use it for everything, including bread kneading. An inexpensive hand-held mixer can handle (if not as well) most of the other tasks usually reserved for a standing mixer, including whipping cream or beating cake batter.

So how to go about buying a food processor that can handle pesto as well as bread dough? We evaluated seven food processors based on the results in five general categories: chopping and grinding, slicing, grating, pureeing, and kneading.

We found that most food processors chop, grind, slice, grate, and puree at least minimally well. Of course, there are differences in models, but they were not as dramatic as the results of our bread-kneading tests.

A food processor won't really knead bread fully, but the dry and wet ingredients come together beautifully to form the dough. If a recipe calls for a smooth, satiny ball of dough, you will have to knead the dough by hand on the counter after processing; however, the kneading time should be just a few minutes.

We found that successful kneading in a food processor was linked directly to large bowl size as well as to the weight of the base. The 11-cup machines were best because they provided ample space for the ball of dough to move around. A heavy base provided stability, and the nods went to KitchenAid and Cuisinart, with their substantial, 10-pound-plus bases. Luckily, these machines also did the best job on the other basic food processor tests.

ment to making bread at home is the notion of kneading bread by hand. To find out if this was essential, we used a standard American loaf bread recipe and tested hand-kneaded bread against bread kneaded by machine—both in a standing mixer and a food processor—to find out if hand kneading makes better bread. The results were eye-opening. The hand-kneaded loaf was not as good as the two loaves kneaded by machine. It was denser, did not rise as well, and the flavor was lacking the pleasant yeastiness found in the other loaves. After some additional testing and discussion, we hit on a reasonable explanation: When kneading by hand, most home cooks cannot resist the temptation of adding too much additional flour, because bread dough is notoriously sticky. In a machine, however, you add no additional flour, and the resulting bread has the correct proportion of liquid to flour.

Now that we knew that kneading this kind of bread by machine was actually preferable to doing it by hand, we set out to refine the techniques. We wanted to include separate recipes for a standing mixer and a food processor, given that many home kitchens have one or the other, but not both.

Starting with the standing mixer, we tested the dough hook versus the paddle attachment. (Some recipes use the paddle for part or all of the kneading process.) The hook turned out to be vastly preferable, as dough quickly got caught in the paddle, requiring frequent starting and stopping to free it. We also found that a medium-speed setting is better than a slow setting. Although the hook appears to move at an alarming rate, the resulting centrifugal force throws the dough off the hook, resulting in a more thorough kneading. At slower speeds, the dough has a tendency to cling to the hook like a child on a tire swing.

Next we turned to the food processor. This method, to our surprise, was very successful, although the dough did require about four minutes of hand kneading at the finish. (A food processor does not knead as thoroughly as a standing mixer.) Using a metal blade, we pulsed the dry ingredients to combine them. Then, with the machine running, we added the liquid ingredients through the feed tube and processed the dough until it formed a rough ball. After a rest of two minutes, we processed the dough a second time, for about 30 seconds, and then

removed it to a lightly floured counter for hand kneading. We also tested the recipe without any hand kneading and found the resulting bread inferior—coarser in texture, with less rise.

We also noted that the action of the food processor was quite different from that of the standing mixer. A relatively dry dough had worked well in the mixer because it was less likely to stick to the dough hook. However, in the food processor a slightly wetter dough seemed preferable, as the metal blade stretched and pulled it better than a dry dough, which ended up simply being cut into pieces. Therefore, to improve the performance of the food processor, we added two tablespoons of water to the dough.

In addition, we found that the difference in action between food processor and mixer called for different types of flour. The reason for this has to do with the difference in protein content of the two types of flour. Bread flour, which has a high protein content, requires a thorough, slow kneading process to properly develop the gluten. This type of kneading action does occur in a mixer, so bread flour worked well there. In the rapid kneading of the food processor, however, all-purpose flour, with its lower protein content, worked better.

With our dough and kneading methods set, we turned to oven temperatures and baking times. When we baked our bread at oven temperatures of 350, 375, and 400 degrees, the two higher temperatures overcooked the crust by the time the inside of the loaf was done. Again, unlike most European breads, this American loaf is prone to quick browning because it contains milk, butter, and honey.

To determine the proper baking time, you have to figure out how to decide when your bread is done. After testing bread taken from the oven at internal temperatures of 190, 195, and 200 degrees, the 195-degree reading was clearly the winner. The lower temperature produced dense bread, and the higher temperature produced dry, overcooked bread.

As stated above, one of the objectives in developing this recipe was to produce bread as quickly as possible. Our first thought was to use rapid-rise yeast, even though we were certain that it would produce inferior bread—another example of technology run amok.

However, not only did the rapid-rise yeast greatly

reduce rising times, but, in a blind tasting, the bread actually tasted better. (See "Rapid-Rise Yeast," below.) To further speed this process, we preheated the oven to 200 degrees for 10 minutes, turned it off, then used it as our proofing box, allowing the dough to rise in a very warm, draft-free environment. Next, we tried heating the milk and water to jump-start the yeast. When the liquids were too hot, well over 130

INGREDIENTS: Rapid-Rise Yeast

We taste-tested our recipe for American Sandwich Bread with eight different yeasts: Fleischmann's Rapid Rise Yeast, Fleischmann's Active Dry Yeast, Fleischmann's Cake Yeast, Red Star Quick-Rise, King Arthur Regular Instant Yeast, King Arthur Special Instant Yeast, Fleischmann's Instant Yeast, and Red Star Instant Yeast. (We should note that many of these yeasts are recommended for breads quite different from the all-purpose American loaf tested; the results might be quite different with another recipe.)

The surprising winner of our minitasting was Fleischmann's Instant Yeast, with Fleischmann's Cake Yeast and Fleischmann's Rapid Rise Yeast close seconds. The instant yeast is not always available in supermarkets ("instant" yeast is not the same as "rapid-rise," which is more commonly available), and cake yeast can also be somewhat difficult to locate.

The most startling result from this taste test, however, was that while Fleischmann's Rapid Rise came out near the top, the regular Fleischmann's Active Yeast placed dead last. It should be noted that the rising methods were also different—we placed the doughs made with rapid-rise yeast in a warmed oven for just 40 minutes, whereas breads made with the regular active yeast took about two hours when left to rise on top of the stove. The faster rise, in fact, yielded more flavor and produced a noticeably sweeter bread. One theory is that a rapid rise provides less time for the creation of the acidic byproducts of fermentation, hence a sweeter loaf. It is also true that rapid-rise yeast has superior enzyme activity, which converts starches to sugar faster than regular-rise varieties.

But even taking all of these factors into account, it still seems logical that a longer, gentler rise would allow the dough more time to produce complex flavors. This may be true for a European-style loaf that contains nothing more than flour, yeast, salt, and water. But an American bread contains both fat (milk and butter) and sugar (honey) so that the complexity of flavors, which would be evident in a plainer loaf, is easily missed here. Even more to the point, though, is the fact that rapid-rise yeast is not necessarily an inferior product. Yeast is a plant, not bacteria, and different varieties have quite different qualities, as do different varieties of, say, roses. Rapid-rise yeast has been genetically engineered to reproduce the best characteristics of yeasts from around the world. Although genetic engineering often results in loss of flavor, our blind taste tests confirmed that in this case it produced an excellent product.

As for why the yeast works faster, there are two primary reasons. Besides the more rapid enzyme activity described above, rapid-rise yeast also has an open, porous structure, which means that it absorbs liquid instantly. When rapid-rise yeast was introduced to consumers, they had difficulty with it because they continued to follow habit rather than the manufacturer's directions—that is, they proofed the yeast in water rather than mixing it directly into the flour. Because of its efficiency, the yeast dissolved in water rapidly ran out of food (starch) and died before the rising process was complete.

To correct this problem, scientists went back and added more starch to the mix, providing enough food for the yeast to survive proofing. Today, however, most yeast does not have to be proofed. Proofing used to serve two functions. First, it was an indicator of the health of the yeast. Today, yeast is both refrigerated and marked with an expiration date for freshness. (Note that these expiration dates should be taken seriously. We tried baking a loaf with yeast that was one month past expiration, and the rising times were double those experienced with fresh yeast. The resulting loaf was denser, with a smaller rise.) Second, although most yeast consists of dead cells encapsulating live cells, the dead cells need to dissolve before the live cells start working. This hydration process occurs quickly when yeast and water are mixed together, but it will also occur in short order in the dough mixture during kneading. For our American sandwich bread, therefore, we have opted not to proof the yeast but to mix it directly into the warm liquid to speed up rising time. However, feel free to mix yeast in with the flour for any bread recipe if a few extra minutes of rising time is not an issue.

Although proofing is not necessary, keep in mind that the temperature of the water or milk is crucial. Dry yeast will die either in ice water or in liquids at 125 degrees or higher (some yeasts can live up to 170 degrees). When testing recipes, we found that hot milk often killed off the yeast and therefore suggest using warm milk (about 110 degrees). We also use warm water at the same temperature in many recipes.

degrees, we had some failures because the yeast was killed by the excess heat. We did find, however, that when we warmed the liquids to about 110 degrees, the rising times were reduced by 5 to 10 minutes. These three changes brought the first rise down to 40 minutes and the second rise to a mere 20. Now we could make homemade bread in two hours, including kneading, both risings, and the baking time, which for us was no more than 40 minutes.

At the end of two months of testing, we had produced a terrific loaf of bread in just two hours, start to finish. Using rapid-rise yeast, we kneaded the dough in a standing mixer for 10 minutes (and then by hand for a mere 15 seconds). We then let it rise in a warmed oven for 40 to 50 minutes, at which point we gently shaped it and placed it in a loaf pan.

The second rise took 20 to 30 minutes, after which we baked the dough at a moderate 350 degrees for about 40 minutes, or until the internal temperature reached 195 degrees.

Master Recipe for American Sandwich Bread

MAKES ONE 9-INCH LOAF

This recipe uses a standing electric mixer; a variation below gives instructions for using a food processor. You can hand-knead the dough, but we found it's easy to add too much flour during this stage, resulting in a somewhat tougher loaf. If you don't have bread flour, you can use all-purpose flour. To promote a crisp crust, we found it best to place a loaf pan filled with boiling water in the oven as the bread bakes.

3½	cups bread flour, plus extra for work surface
2	teaspoons salt
1	cup warm milk (110 degrees)
⅓	cup warm water (110 degrees)
2	tablespoons butter, melted
3	tablespoons honey
1	package (about 2¼ teaspoons) rapid-rise yeast

1. Adjust oven rack to low position and heat oven to 200 degrees. Once oven temperature reaches 200 degrees, maintain heat 10 minutes, then turn off oven heat.

2. Mix flour and salt in bowl of standing mixer fitted with dough hook. Mix milk, water, butter, honey, and yeast in 1-quart Pyrex liquid measuring cup. Turn machine to low and slowly add liquid. When dough comes together, increase speed to medium and mix until dough is smooth and satiny, stopping machine two or three times to scrape dough from hook if necessary, about 10 minutes. Turn dough onto lightly floured work surface; knead to form smooth, round ball, about 15 seconds.

3. Place dough in very lightly oiled container or bowl, rubbing dough around bowl to lightly coat. Cover with plastic wrap; place in warm oven until dough doubles in size, 40 to 50 minutes.

4. Gently press dough into rectangle 1 inch thick and no longer than 9 inches. With a long side facing you, roll dough firmly into cylinder, pressing with your fingers to make sure dough sticks to itself. Turn dough seam side up and pinch it closed. Place dough in greased 9 x 5 x 3-inch loaf pan and press it gently so it touches all four sides of pan.

5. Cover with plastic wrap; set aside in warm spot until dough almost doubles in size, 20 to 30 minutes. Heat oven to 350 degrees and place an empty loaf pan on bottom rack. Bring 2 cups water to boil.

6. Remove plastic wrap from filled loaf pan and place pan in oven. Immediately, pour heated water into empty loaf pan; close oven door. Bake until instant-read thermometer inserted at angle from short end just above pan rim into center of loaf reads 195 degrees, about 40 to 50 minutes. Remove bread from pan, transfer to a wire rack, and cool to room temperature. Slice and serve.

➤ VARIATIONS

American Sandwich Bread Kneaded in a Food Processor

American Sandwich Bread made in the food processor was slightly better made with all-purpose flour, but no matter what flour you use, add an extra two tablespoons of water to the dry ingredients. The food processor blade kneads the softer dough more effectively. During the hand-kneading phase, you may need to add a little flour to make a workable dough. To ensure a tender bread, however, add as little as possible.

Follow Master Recipe for American Sandwich Bread, substituting equal amount of all-purpose flour for the bread flour and increasing the warm water by 2 tablespoons. Mix flour and salt in bowl of food processor fitted with steel blade. Add liquid ingredients; process until rough ball forms. Let dough rest 2 minutes. Process 35 seconds. Turn dough onto lightly floured work surface and knead by hand until dough is smooth and satiny, 4 to 5 minutes. Continue with Master Recipe.

Slow-Rise American Sandwich Bread

If you do not have rapid-rise yeast on hand, try this slow-rise variation.

Follow Master Recipe for American Sandwich Bread, substituting an equal amount of dry active yeast for the rapid-rise yeast. Let dough rise at room temperature, instead of in the warm oven, until almost doubled (about 2 hours for first rise and 45 to 60 minutes for second rise).

Buttermilk Sandwich Bread

Follow Master Recipe for American Sandwich Bread, bringing water to boil rather than 110 degrees. Substitute cold buttermilk for the warm milk, adding it to the hot water. (The mixing of hot water and cold buttermilk should bring the liquid to the right temperature—about 110 degrees—for adding the yeast.) Increase first rise to 50–60 minutes.

Oatmeal Sandwich Bread

To turn this loaf into oatmeal-raisin bread, simply knead ¾ cup of raisins, tossed with 1 tablespoon of flour, into dough after it comes out of food processor or mixer.

Bring ¾ cup water to boil in small saucepan. Add ¾ cup rolled oats; cook to soften slightly, about 90 seconds. Follow Master Recipe for American Sandwich Bread, decreasing flour from 3½ to 2¾ cups, adding cooked oatmeal to flour, and omitting warm water from wet ingredients.

Cornmeal Sandwich Bread

Bring ½ cup water to boil in small saucepan. Slowly whisk in ¼ cup cornmeal. Cook, stirring constantly, until mixture thickens, about 1 minute. Follow Master Recipe for American Sandwich Bread, decreasing flour from 3½ to 3¼ cups, decreasing milk from 1 cup to ¾ cup, and adding cornmeal mixture to flour (before incorporating liquids).

Anadama Bread

Follow recipe for Cornmeal Sandwich Bread, substituting molasses for the honey.

WHOLE WHEAT BREAD

IF ASKED TO DESCRIBE THE PERFECT LOAF of whole wheat bread, you might say that it should be wheaty but not grainy, chewy but not tough, dense but not heavy, and full-flavored but not overpowering. In fact, you might come to the conclusion, as we did, that the perfect loaf of whole wheat bread is hard to define. While there are literally hundreds of different types of loaves that use at least some whole wheat flour, earning the distinction of being a shining example of whole wheat bread is another matter entirely.

We decided to make a few loaves from various cookbooks just to explore the range of possibilities, starting with recipes from five of our favorite bread books. A recipe for an Italian walnut bread was terrific but clearly a rustic European loaf, not the distinctly American whole wheat bread we were looking for. Other recipes were bitter, had odd flavors, or had too many other grains or flours to qualify as whole wheat. Still others were too dense, too salty, or not sweet enough, an important element for enhancing the rich flavor of the wheat flour.

We went back to the drawing board to create a master recipe that had the elements we liked best from each of the test breads. The recipe we started with contained 1 tablespoon of yeast, 2⅓ cups of warm water, 4 cups of whole wheat flour, 1¼ cups of all-purpose flour, ¼ cup of rye flour (to add complexity of flavor), 1 teaspoon of salt, and 2 tablespoons of honey.

The initial results from this recipe were good, but not great. The bread was too dense, and it needed a boost of both salt and honey for flavor. So we made a new loaf in which we doubled the amount of both yeast and honey and punched up the salt to two teaspoons. The taste-test results were encouraging, and the loaf was even better when we tried making it again, using ½ tablespoon less yeast and adding ¼ cup of melted butter for flavor. But some problems remained. The texture was still too dense for our taste, and the flavor was a bit generic, reminiscent of what one might find at a diner, served with two individually wrapped pats of butter.

Having already tested a higher amount of yeast, we suspected that the texture might be improved by using a drier dough, which tends to produce a lighter bread. We therefore increased the total amount of flour from 5½ cups to 6 cups. We then varied the proportion of whole wheat flour to white to rye. The loaf with a slightly higher amount of whole wheat than white flour, and with some rye flour was the best of the lot, and actually quite good.

Now we were close, but the bread still lacked the proper texture and wheatiness we expected from a whole wheat loaf. So we turned to one of our favorite bread books, *The Book of Bread* (HarperPerennial, 1982) by Evan and Judith Jones, and discovered that one of their whole wheat bread recipes contained wheat germ. As it turned out, this simple addition—a mere quarter cup of wheat germ—made a terrific difference in our loaf, producing a nutty flavor and slightly more complex texture. We liked it so much· that we tried a loaf with a half cup of wheat germ, which turned out to be the ideal amount.

Into our thirtieth loaf at this point, we decided to press on with the issue of sweeteners. We tend to use honey in bread doughs, but we also made loaves with a variety of other sweeteners, including one-quarter cup of each of the following: white sugar, dark brown sugar, maple syrup, malt, and molasses. We also tested half quantities of malt and molasses paired with an equal amount of honey. Oddly, it was hard to differentiate the flavors added by the sweeteners. That said, though, the honey version was generally picked by our tasters as number one, with a nice, clean, sweet flavor and moist texture.

We went on to try different fats. We sampled loaves made with vegetable oil (a noticeable lack of flavor), melted lard (a strong flavor but unwelcome in this recipe), the standard melted butter (by far the best: good texture, sweet flavor), cold butter kneaded into the dough (denser, not as moist), and the addition of a whole egg (grainy, gritty texture—almost cottony).

Having found the dough recipe we wanted, we proceeded to test the variables of kneading, rising, and baking.

One of the most interesting tests involved kneading times. Using a standing mixer, we kneaded for 8, 12, and 16 minutes, respectively, with no discernible difference in the finished loaves. Because whole-wheat flour contains so much protein, a reasonable amount of gluten is formed as long as the ingredients are quite thoroughly mixed together. With this recipe, it matters little whether the kneading is done by machine or by hand, for a short time or a long time.

Our final recipe calls for an initial rising of just under one hour (a relatively short rising time owing to the relatively high amount of yeast). We tested a shorter rising time of only 30 minutes, but the resulting loaf was dense and dry. For the second rise, after the dough has been shaped, we found that 20 to 30 minutes was best. When left to rise for longer than this, the dough baked up into a light loaf with an unwelcome cottony texture and a crust that had separated from the rest of the loaf, causing a rippled effect.

We were also curious about rising methods. To promote flavor, many bread recipes start with a sponge, which is nothing more than yeast, water, and flour, mixed together and allowed to stand for anywhere from one hour to overnight. As the yeast culture grows, it is thought that the depth of flavor is developed.

We tried two tests of the sponge method. A one-hour sponge produced a light bread, with a soft, cottony texture and mild flavor. A four-hour sponge had a nice rise but evidenced no improvement in flavor.

Finally, we tested a bread that rose three times (instead of the regulation two-rise system), and this loaf, with a slightly more developed flavor, edged out the basic recipe (only two rises) for first place. However, the difference was very subtle and deemed not to be worth the extra time.

Although we were confident about oven temperatures and baking times, we tested them to be sure. As we had expected, the 375-degree oven worked best. A 350-degree oven turned out doughy bread, while a 400-degree oven produced a loaf with a slightly burned bottom. To determine when a loaf is properly cooked, we used an instant-read thermometer inserted from one end into the middle of the loaf; for a free-form loaf, simply insert the thermometer from the bottom to the middle of the loaf.

An internal temperature of 205 degrees proved ideal; at lower temperatures the bread was undercooked.

We also wondered if the introduction of steam into the oven would affect the crust. Although we liked the crust created without any steam, we tried adding boiling water to a pan in the oven and also spritzed water on the loaf as it baked, neither of which made any discernible difference in this recipe.

It did occur to us that perhaps the brand of whole wheat flour might make a difference. We had performed all of our tests to this point with King Arthur flour. So we tried Arrowhead Mills Stone Ground Whole Wheat. This flour produced a loaf with a nice wheat flavor, but it was lighter in both color and texture. Next we made a loaf using Hodgson Mill Whole Wheat Graham Flour, which produced a wonderful loaf with a terrific, nutty flavor. Graham flour is a bit coarser and perhaps flakier than regular whole wheat flour and, as we noted in our testing, provides a nuttier flavor. It is named after its inventor, Sylvester Graham. Although the King Arthur was also very good, we felt that the Hodgson flour was best suited for this recipe.

Whole Wheat Bread with Wheat Germ and Rye

MAKES 2 LOAVES

Because kneading this wet, sticky dough can cause damage to lower-horsepower mixers, it's best to use a heavy-duty standing mixer. For those with less powerful mixers, be especially sure to use the low rather than the medium speed during kneading, or proceed instead with the instructions for hand kneading. This recipe makes too much dough to knead in a food processor.

2 ⅓	cups warm water (110 degrees)
1 ½	tablespoons active dry yeast
¼	cup honey
4	tablespoons unsalted butter, melted
2 ½	teaspoons salt
¼	cup rye flour
½	cup toasted wheat germ
3	cups whole wheat flour, preferably Hodgson Mill Whole Wheat Graham Flour
2¾	cups all-purpose flour, plus extra for work surface

1. In bowl of standing mixer, mix water, yeast, honey, butter, and salt with rubber spatula. Mix in rye flour, wheat germ, and 1 cup each of whole wheat and white flours.

2. Using dough hook attachment, mix in remaining flours on low speed until dough is smooth and elastic, about 8 minutes. Transfer dough to floured work surface. Knead just long enough to confirm dough is soft and smooth, about 30 seconds.

3. Place dough in lightly greased container or bowl; cover with plastic wrap or damp kitchen towel. Let rise in warm draft-free area until dough has doubled in volume, about 1 hour.

4. Heat oven to 375 degrees. Gently punch down dough and divide into two equal pieces. Gently press each piece into an oblong rectangle, about 1 inch thick and no longer than length of pan. With long side of dough facing you, roll firmly into cylinder, pressing down to make sure that dough sticks to itself. Turn dough seam side up and pinch it closed. Place each cylinder of dough into a greased 9 x 5 x 3-inch loaf pan, pressing dough gently so it touches all four sides of pan. Cover shaped dough; let rise until almost doubled in volume, 20 to 30 minutes.

5. Bake until instant-read thermometer inserted into loaf center reads 205 degrees, 35 to 45 minutes. Transfer bread immediately from baking pans to wire rack; cool to room temperature.

➤ VARIATION
Hand-Kneaded Whole Wheat Bread

Follow recipe for Whole Wheat Bread with Wheat Germ and Rye, mixing water, yeast, honey, butter, salt, rye flour, and wheat germ in large mixing bowl. Mix 2¾ cups each of whole wheat and white flours in separate bowl, reserving ¼ cup whole wheat flour. Add 3½ cups of the flour mixture to wet ingredients; beat with wooden spoon 5 minutes. Beat in another 1½ cups of the flour mixture to make thick dough. Turn dough onto work surface that has been sprinkled with some of the reserved flour. Knead, adding as little of remaining flour as necessary, to form soft, elastic dough, about 5 minutes. Continue with step 3.

RUSTIC COUNTRY BREAD

FLOUR, WATER, YEAST, AND SALT. THAT'S about as simple as it gets in the kitchen, or so we thought when we set out to discover a reliable home recipe for a crusty, full-textured, European-style country bread. This is the kind of bread that is a main course all by itself; the first bite hits you with a heady burst of crackle and chew, an inspired whiff of yeast, and a hint of sourness.

Our first task was to determine which of the four types of country bread to test. These four types result from four different methods of leavening the bread: with a natural starter (a mixture of flour and water are left out for 24 hours, during which time the mixture attracts natural yeast spores from the air), a mixed starter (the starter in this case is a piece of dough reserved from a previously made kneaded batch), a standard yeast starter (where yeast is dissolved in warm water and then added to the dry ingredients), or a sponge starter (a "sponge" of flour, water, and yeast is left to ferment, then additional flour, water, and other ingredients are added in).

The first and second methods are inconvenient for home cooks. The third method does not provide enough time for the flavor to develop. The last method proved to be a good compromise.

In the *Chez Panisse Cookbook* (Random House, 1988), Paul Bertolli suggests making a sponge, covering it, and letting it sit out overnight before making the dough. We decided to follow this method. In his recipe, however, he uses only one-quarter of the sponge as a starter for his bread, reserving the rest for use in future loaves. Since most home cooks don't have the patience to keep a starter going in the refrigerator, we decided to deviate from his recipe by using the entire sponge.

This approach worked well. As we had expected, there was more flavor than with a quick rise using a greater amount of yeast. In fact, we only used half a teaspoon of dry yeast (most recipes call for up to a tablespoon) for six cups of flour. We also varied the sponge recipe by increasing the percentage of whole wheat flour, using equal amounts of whole wheat and white flour for added flavor and texture.

The next element to consider was water. Professional bakers know that a high water content produces more texture and chew. To figure out the percentage of water in a bread recipe (as a percentage of the flour weight), simply calculate the weight, in grams, of water in the recipe (each cup of water weighs 237.5 grams) and divide that by the weight of the flour (there are 130 grams in one cup of flour). After some research, we figured that a water content of 68 percent would be about right. The theory was that the higher percentage of water—most bread recipes run around 60 percent—would improve the chew. We tried this formula and got mediocre results. It was good bread, but without the big-league chew we wanted.

We then visited Iggy's Bakery just outside of Boston. The bread they make has a big chew, big crust, and big flavor. The chief baker told us we needed to push the water level even higher. He pointed to the plastic vats filled with rising dough. This dough was a sticky mass that would just about pour. This was a breakthrough. Our idea of bread dough had been a nonstick satin ball, easy to handle and more solid than liquid. But this stuff puddled and pulled, shimmered and shook. At Iggy's, they use a mixture of three flours—high protein, whole wheat, and rye—for optimum flavor and texture.

Back in the test kitchen, we increased the water percentage to near-dangerous levels. The revised recipe now had 2½ cups of water to 6 cups of flour, which brought the percentage of water to flour up to a whopping 76 percent, a percentage so high it borders on heresy. However, this high percentage was slightly counteracted by the fact that almost 30 percent of the total flour used was whole wheat and rye. We chose these flours for flavor, but both also absorb more water than white flour does.

Professional bakers use giant mixers and special shaping machines that easily handle very moist dough. Using consumer equipment in our test kitchen, the bread stuck to our hands, the wooden counter, the bowl, the damp dishtowel, and even the heavily floured peel (the shovellike tool used to get breads in and out of the oven). We tried to knead the dough by hand, but this was almost impossible without adding lots of additional flour. But at the end of the day, the bread was vastly improved. Although a bit sticky, the inside had cavernous air holes and some real chew.

We now turned our attention more closely to the flour. Up until now, we had been using a professional baker's bread flour, which has a very high level of protein (about 14 percent). We decided to try both a regular bread flour and an all-purpose flour to see if protein content would have a noticeable affect on the finished product. The all-purpose flour yielded an extremely wet, unworkable dough, and the bread flour was wetter than the high-protein loaf but still workable. Of most interest, however, was the fact that these lower-protein flours produced a chewier, crustier loaf, although we felt that the loaf made with all-purpose flour was a little too tough. After additional testing, it became clear that we had to adjust the recipe to accommodate the lower-protein flours, which can't absorb as much water as higher-protein flour. When we reduced the amount of water used in our "regular" bread flour dough to 2⅓ cups, the results were even better. Since this flour is sold in supermarkets, we decided to use it in our recipe.

Kneading by hand was not our first choice (it can be done, however). We tried using a food processor with the metal blade, which worked fine except that our $250 machine sounded like a lawnmower in a dense patch of weeds; all that was missing was a curl of blue smoke and the smell of burning rubber. The machine simply could not handle 6 cups of quick-sand. We tried the recipe in two half-batches, which worked pretty well. We found that leaving the metal blade in the processor between batches is best (you won't get absolutely all of the first batch out of the processor bowl), otherwise your hands will get sticky and dough may ooze out around the center core of the bowl during the second batch. We also learned that the machine works great for the first 25 to 30 seconds and then starts to slow down. Our processor can just about handle it (although it seemed compelled to walk across the counter like a dog off its leash). We recommend that you process for no more than 30 seconds, which is enough time to knead the dough, and we recommend this method only for home cooks with a good heavy-duty processor.

The best solution was a heavy-duty standing mixer with a dough hook. We simply threw in the ingredients, mixed them briefly with a large, stiff rubber spatula, and then turned the machine on at the lowest setting for 15 minutes. When done, we transferred the dough to an oiled bowl to rise for about 2 hours, or until tripled in volume. Allowing the dough to triple in volume both improves flavor and helps the dough to develop more "muscle," which helps the bread to maintain its shape when baked.

Even after the dough was kneaded, it was a problem to handle. For the first rise, simply use a rubber spatula to transfer the wet dough to an oiled bowl or plastic tub. After rising for about 2 hours, use the same spatula to transfer the dough onto a lightly floured surface. Now flour both your hands and the dough (the latter lightly). Press the dough very gently into a round and then fold into a ball. Note that you should handle the dough as little as possible at this point both because it is still a little sticky (you'll be tempted to add extra flour) and because excessive handling is bad for rustic bread—you want an irregular texture with lots of air holes. This point goes for all bread making: strong kneading after the first rise will harm the delicate structure of the dough.

The best way to move the dough from here on in is to use a large dough scraper, two metal spatulas, or a thin floured cookie sheet. The dough is now transferred, smooth side down, into a colander or a basket that has been lined with a piece of muslin or linen that has been well-floured. The flour should be rubbed into the fabric so the dough will not stick. A banneton is a cloth-lined woven basket designed just for this purpose. You can purchase one or try making your own. Muslin (which is cheaper than linen) comes in different grades from fine (the most expensive) to coarse (the least expensive). Use the cheaper variety to line your basket, and make sure that it is 100 percent cotton and unbleached. A real banneton has the linen or muslin sewn right into the basket, an optional refinement. The basket we used was 4 inches high, 7 inches wide across the bottom, and 12 inches wide across the top. A colander is also a perfectly good option. It works well because it allows for air flow (the dough is more likely to stick to the muslin when sitting in a bowl).

For its second rise the dough needs to be covered. We tried a damp dishtowel, but this simply stuck to the dough. It was like unwrapping a piece of salt water taffy on a hot day. Aluminum foil was the test winner because the dough is less likely to stick, and it allows the dough to breathe and thus keeps it from rising too much. If the dough rises too much at this point you will end up with a fluffy texture (plastic wrap, for example, will cause too much rising). The foil will give the dough shape and allow you to transfer it easily to the peel when the second rise is completed.

We also wanted to test varying the amount of salt as well as the impact of other ingredients. Most recipes with six cups of flour use two teaspoons of salt, and this amount is just right. Next, we decided to try a little sweetness to both boost flavor and promote browning of the crust (sugar promotes browning). When we added two tablespoons of honey, the flavor was a bit better and the crust turned a rich nut-brown.

The last major issue was the crust. The key, according to most experts, is steam. Just to test this theory, we baked one loaf with no steam at all, and the crust was thin and unappealing. This bread does need steam, but there are many ways in which to provide it. Some bakers use a spritzer and mist the outside of the dough every few minutes. Others throw ice cubes on the floor of the oven. Still others pour hot water into a pan at the beginning of baking. Our tests showed that hot water is the best option. We tested spritzing the bread every few minutes and the results were poor—a thin, pliable crust.

As for the ice cube method, why throw ice into an oven where you want lots of heat? Our tests confirmed that ice cubes lower oven temperature much more than hot water does, and a head-to-head test also proved that you get a better crust with hot water versus ice cubes. (A note to those who count themselves among the ice cube flingers: You could blow out the heating element in an electric oven if you don't throw the ice into a container. This also goes for throwing tap water onto the floor of the oven).

When adding a pan of hot water to the oven, be sure to use a small preheated pan and place it on a separate, lower rack in the oven. The theory among bread pros is that you want steam immediately, in the first few minutes of baking. A cold pan will not do the trick—the hot water will just sit there. By using enough water, two cups, you get both instant steam and enough residual water to maintain a nice steamy environment throughout the cooking process. A preheated pan will, however, vaporize some of the hot water in seconds, which leads to the issue of safety. Use thick oven mitts and a long-sleeved shirt when pouring the hot water into the pan. In sum: Use hot water, preheat the pan, and don't ever open the oven door for the first 20 minutes of baking—you'll let out steam.

Most recipes state that the bread should be baked to an internal temperature of 190 degrees. This produces undercooked bread, at least as far as our recipe goes. This bread needs to reach 210 degrees (use an instant-read thermometer pushed halfway into the bottom of the loaf). An undercooked loaf will be sticky inside and will not have developed the very dark brown crust we're after. If you do not have an instant-read thermometer, just bake the bread until the crust starts to turn brownish-black in spots.

We also tested starting oven temperature. We first started the bread off in a 500-degree oven and then immediately turned the heat down to 400 degrees on the theory that the higher temperature offsets the drop in temperature caused by opening the oven door and adding the dough (the dough absorbs a great deal of heat quickly). The resulting crust was thin and disappointing. We also tested actually baking the bread at 500 degrees for the first 15 minutes and then reducing the temperature to 400. The crust was scorched. It cooked so fast that the interior had no time to cook properly. The best baking temperature turned out to be a constant 450 degrees.

Some final refinements: We found that cornmeal is vastly better than flour for coating a peel, especially when working with a wet dough. The dough will slide off easily. Also, use a very quick backward jerk when removing the peel.

Rustic Country Bread

MAKES I LARGE ROUND LOAF

Whole wheat and rye flours contribute to this bread's full flavor, and extra oven time gives the bread its thick crust. Because of its high water content, the bread will be gummy if pulled from the oven too soon. To ensure the bread's doneness, make sure its internal temperature reads 210 degrees by inserting an instant-read thermometer into the bottom of the loaf. Also look at the crust—it should be very dark brown, almost black. Because the dough is so sticky, a heavy-duty standing mixer is best for kneading, but food processor and hand-kneading instructions follow this recipe. Keep in mind that rising times vary depending on kitchen temperature (the times listed below are minimums). You can vary the texture by increasing or decreasing the flour. For bread with a finer crumb and less chewy texture, increase the flour by ¼ cup increments. For coarser, chewier bread, decrease the flour by the same increments. You will need baking tiles or a stone (see page 334 for more information) for this recipe.

SPONGE

½	teaspoon active dry yeast (not rapid rise)
I	cup water (room temperature)
I	cup bread flour
I	cup whole wheat flour

DOUGH

3 ½	cups bread flour
½	cup rye flour
I ⅓	cups water (room temperature)
2	tablespoons honey
2	teaspoons salt
	Coarse cornmeal for sprinkling on peel

1. FOR THE SPONGE: Stir yeast into water in a medium bowl until dissolved. Mix in flours with a rubber spatula to create a stiff, wet dough. Cover with plastic wrap; let sit at room temperature for at least 5 hours, preferably overnight. (Can be refrigerated up to 24 hours; return to room temperature before continuing with recipe.)

2. FOR THE DOUGH: Mix flours, water, honey, and sponge in the bowl of an electric mixer with a rubber spatula. Knead dough, using the dough hook attachment, on lowest speed until dough is smooth, about 15 minutes, adding salt during the final 3 minutes. Transfer dough to a large, lightly oiled container or bowl. Cover with plastic wrap; let rise until tripled in size, at least 2 hours.

3. Turn dough onto lightly floured surface. Dust dough top and hands with flour. Lightly press dough into a round by folding edges of dough into middle from top, right, bottom, and left, sequentially, then gathering it loosely together. Transfer dough, smooth side down, to a colander or basket lined with heavily floured muslin or linen. Cover loosely with a large sheet of aluminum foil; let dough rise until almost doubled in size, at least 45 minutes.

4. Meanwhile, adjust oven rack to low-center position and arrange baking tiles to form a surface that is at least 18 x 12 inches or place a large baking stone on rack. On lowest oven rack, place a small baking pan or cast-iron skillet to hold water. Heat oven to 450 degrees.

5. Liberally sprinkle coarse cornmeal over the entire surface of peel. Invert dough onto peel and remove muslin. Use scissors or a serrated knife to cut three slashes on dough top.

6. Slide dough from peel onto tiles or stone; remove peel with a quick backward jerk. Carefully add 2 cups hot water to preheated pan. Bake until instant-read thermometer inserted in bread bottom registers 210 degrees and crust is very dark brown, 35 to 40 minutes, turning bread around after 25 minutes if not browning evenly. Turn oven off, open door, and let bread remain in oven 10 minutes longer. Remove, then let cool to room temperature before slicing, about 2 hours. To crisp crust, bake cooled bread in a 450 degree oven for 10 minutes.

> VARIATIONS

Rustic Country Bread Kneaded in a Food Processor

Make sponge as directed in recipe for Rustic Country Bread. Mix half the sponge and half the flours and honey in a food processor fitted with the metal blade. Pulse until roughly blended, 3 to 4 one-second pulses. With the machine running, add half the water (⅔ cup) slowly through the feed tube; process until dough forms a ball. Let sit for 3 minutes, then add half the salt and process to form a smooth dough, about 30 seconds longer. Transfer dough to a large lightly oiled container or bowl, leaving metal blade in the processor (some dough will remain under the blade). Repeat process with remaining half of the ingredients. Proceed with recipe as directed.

Rustic Country Bread Kneaded by Hand

Make sponge as directed in recipe for Rustic Country Bread. Place sponge and all dough ingredients, except 2 cups of the bread flour, in a large bowl. Stir the mixture with a wooden spoon to develop the gluten, about 5 minutes. Work in reserved flour and then turn out onto a floured board. Knead by hand for 5 minutes, incorporating no more than an additional ¼ cup of flour as you work. The dough will be very wet and sticky. Proceed with recipe.

JEWISH RYE BREAD

JEWISH RYE, A.K.A. NEW YORK RYE, IS ONE of our favorite breads. We love its tang and chew. Unfortunately, it's difficult to find good Jewish rye these days. The mass-produced varieties in supermarkets (and even the rye bread at our local Jewish bakery in Boston) are too refined, fluffy, and soft, with only a hint of rye flavor. The rye bread we hanker for should be slightly moist and chewy but not too dense. It should have a tight, uneven crumb, a hard, thin, almost brittle crust, and a tangy rye flavor. Perhaps most important, the bread shouldn't become soggy or limp when stacked with a pile of pastrami.

We discovered a myriad of rye bread recipes during our research. Not just the Jewish varieties, but Old World recipes containing buttermilk, sour cream, mashed potato, molasses, ginger, and even sauerkraut. Intriguing as these variations were, we stuck to the basics: rye and white flours, water, a sweetener, salt, fat, and caraway seeds. Working with these ingredients, we identified three variables that we thought would affect the texture and flavor of the bread: the method of leavening, the type of rye flour, and the ratio of rye to white flour.

We focused first on two basic methods for leavening the dough, both of which are practical for home cooks. The sponge starter method (which we used in our rustic country bread) involves first mixing a small amount of flour, water, and yeast, then leaving this starter to ferment for a defined period of time. More flour and water are then added to make the dough. In the second method, yeast and water are mixed and when the yeast dissolves the mixture is added directly to make the dough.

Using a variety of cookbook rye bread recipes, we did side-by-side testing of the sponge and direct methods. We found the sponge method clearly preferable. Because the slow rise allows time for the creation of fermentation byproducts that add flavor, this method produced a bread with strong, tangy flavor and a chewy, pleasantly uneven texture. We also liked the way the bread made using the sponge method maintained its moistness during storage. The bread made with the direct method had a tighter web of holes and a more even crumb.

We also tested different sponge fermentation times, including half an hour, 2½ hours, and overnight. As we increased the fermentation time, the rise was faster, the bread baked higher, the crumb was more uneven, the bread was chewier, and the flavor was stronger. The sponge fermentation time can, therefore, be varied to taste, with 2½ hours being the minimum. We prefer an overnight sponge fermentation, and we find that the initial intense and slightly sour rye flavor improves with cooling and storage. However, we were looking for more chew and a sharper tang than even the longest fermentation time could give. In search of this, we turned to the choice and ratio of different flours.

We suspected that different rye flours might affect the texture and flavor of the rye bread. However, many rye bread recipes don't even specify the type of rye flour to use. Up to this point all of our testing had been done using a whole grain rye flour. We now proceeded to round up the rest of the nationally available rye flours: light rye, medium rye, and pumpernickel. The breads they produced were dramatically different. We preferred the breads made with King Arthur light rye and Pillsbury medium rye, both of which had an earthy, tangy flavor with a slight springiness.

Following the successes with these two flours, we moved on to test different ratios of rye to white flour. Rye flour alone does not contain enough gluten-forming proteins to make the bread rise adequately, so some protein-rich wheat flour must be used as well. When water is mixed with wheat flour, the proteins glutenin and gliadin bind to each other and to the water molecules to form gluten. Kneading shapes the protein/gluten into elastic sheets that trap and hold air and the gases produced by the yeast, the combination of which allows the bread to rise.

Our test recipe had 3 cups of rye flour and 4½ cups of all-purpose unbleached white flour. As we reduced the rye flour (increasing the white flour proportionally), the breads became significantly lighter, softer, and less chewy. As one tester said, they were too "bready." With 4 cups of rye flour and 3½ cups of white flour, the bread was too heavy and dense. We settled on 3½ cups of rye flour to 4½ cups of white flour. This produced a rye bread with a perfect balance of tang, chew, and moistness.

From here on, it was all about fine-tuning. We wanted to test some supporting and flavoring ingredients. After baking 20 or so loaves (some with caraway seeds and some without), it became clear that rye bread just isn't rye bread without caraway seeds. We have to admit that before this testing, we had confused the flavor of caraway with rye. Rye gives the bread its earthy, tangy, and fruity character, while caraway adds pepper and spice. Too much caraway is overpowering. Too little caraway and the bread seems incomplete. Two tablespoons is just about right.

We tried substituting honey, molasses, or malt in place of the two tablespoons of sugar in our test recipe. The malt and molasses added a bitter flavor, although we did prefer the honey over the sugar. The bread made with sugar was slightly drier. When we tried increasing the amount of sweetener, the bread tasted too sweet, and this confused the other flavors.

We also experimented with several different types of fat in the bread, including butter, Crisco, and oil. With such a small amount of fat in the recipe, the differences were barely discernible, so we opted to stick with vegetable oil. We even tried using no fat at all, but it was not a good idea—a relatively small amount of fat, about two tablespoons per loaf, goes a long way to soften and moisten the bread.

Finally, we decided to try adding rye flakes—rye kernels that are steamed and then rolled flat to form flakes similar to oat flakes—to the bread dough. The flakes added a nice boost of rye flavor and a bit of extra chew, but they had an unattractive raw appearance. We then tried adding them to the sponge, rather than the dough. This was just the trick: the rye flakes softened up during the rise and lost their rough appearance.

Throughout the testing we noticed that working with rye dough is different from working with wheat dough. The most obvious difference is the rye dough's slimy tackiness and its lack of elasticity. It bears more resemblance to molding clay slightly puffed up with air than to a stretchy and springy bread dough. The visual and textural cues that guide the wheat bread baker don't hold true with rye bread.

Rye doughs contain a cereal gum called pentosane, which makes the dough very slimy, sticky, and difficult to mix. Because rye dough is so sticky, the temptation is to add more flour, but we found that this made the bread dry and coarse. Using wet hands made it easier to remove the dough from the bowl and dough hook. We use a tablespoon or two of flour to aid in shaping the dough into a ball, which is then placed in a greased container to rise. From there on it is more manageable.

Rye dough's lack of elasticity results from the low gluten content of rye flour. Some references claim it has so little gluten that the dough should be kneaded longer to allow the gluten to develop. So we tested kneading the dough for 5, 10, 15, and 20 minutes. At 5 minutes the dough was very sticky, soft, and inelastic, yet the bread rose the highest and had the strongest, springiest, and most moist texture. As we increased the kneading time, the bread became more fluffy and soft, characteristics we did not want in a rye bread. So we found that, contrary to conventional wisdom, 5 minutes of kneading produced the best results.

Like most doughs, rye dough is given two rises. Most recipes suggest letting the dough double in volume during both the first and second rises. The first takes from 1¼ hours to 2 hours.

It is easy to gauge the first rise in a straight-sided container, as the dough doubles in height. After the first rise, the dough should be gently punched down and shaped into loaves. The second rise is more difficult to gauge, since the dough is on a baking sheet and a doubling in volume is less apparent. During the second rise, we found that the dough develops a bloated appearance and tends to spread out rather than up. This spread is actually a crucial indicator of proper rising; if the dough hasn't started to spread out, it's not ready. Underrisen rye dough does not bake as high and can have a "blowout" in which the soft inner dough of a partially baked bread slips out from the developing crust. As soon as the dough has that bloated look and starts to spread, get it in the oven—overrising reduces oven rise.

As a final touch, we wanted to develop the shiny, brittle crust that is the hallmark of Jewish rye. In our research, we found numerous methods designed to achieve this, including egg yolks on their own, egg whites on their own or mixed with water or milk, a mixture of cornstarch and water, and a mixture of potato starch and water. The most interesting (and authentic) approach is the potato starch/water mixture applied to the loaf as it is removed from the oven. We found, however, that this liquid gave the bread a milky white coating rather than a clear sheen. All the other recommended methods involve glazing the dough before it is baked. After trying them all, we found that preglazing with one egg white mixed with one tablespoon of milk worked best.

Deli-Style Rye Bread

MAKES 1 LARGE LOAF OR
2 SMALLER LOAVES

Because this dough requires so much flour (a whopping 8 cups), it is best kneaded in a heavy-duty standing mixer. The rye flakes add flavor to the bread, but if unavailable, they can be omitted from the recipe.

SPONGE

²/₃	cup rye flakes (optional)
2 ¾	cups water (room temperature)
1½	teaspoons dry active yeast
2	tablespoons honey
3	cups unbleached all-purpose or bread flour

DOUGH

1½	cups unbleached all-purpose or bread flour
3½	cups rye flour, such as Pillsbury medium rye or King Arthur light rye
2	tablespoons caraway seeds
2	tablespoons vegetable oil
1	tablespoon salt
	Cornmeal for sprinkling

GLAZE

1	egg white
1	tablespoon milk

1. FOR THE SPONGE: Heat oven to 350 degrees; toast rye flakes on small baking sheet until fragrant and golden brown, about 10–12 minutes. Cool to room temperature. Mix water, yeast, honey, rye flakes, and flour in the large mixing bowl of a heavy-duty mixer to form a thick batter. Cover with plastic wrap, and let sit until bubbles form over entire surface, at least 2½ hours. (Can stand at room temperature overnight.)

2. FOR THE BREAD: Stir all-purpose flour, 3¼ cups rye flour, caraway seeds, oil, and salt into the sponge. With standing mixer fitted with dough hook and set on low, knead dough, adding the remaining ¼ cup rye flour once the dough becomes cohesive; knead until smooth yet sticky, about 5 minutes. With moistened hands, transfer dough to a well-floured counter, knead it into a smooth ball, then place in a lightly greased container or bowl. Cover with plastic wrap and let rise at warm room temperature until doubled in size, 1¼ to 2 hours.

3. Generously sprinkle cornmeal on a large baking sheet. Turn dough onto a lightly floured work surface and press it into 12 x 9-inch rectangle. (For two smaller loaves, halve the dough, pressing each portion into a 9 x 6½-inch rectangle.) With one of the long sides facing you, roll dough into a 12-inch (or 9-inch) log, seam side up. Pinch seam with fingertips to seal. Turn dough seam side down, and with fingertips, seal ends by tucking dough into the loaf. Carefully transfer shaped loaf (or loaves) to prepared baking sheet, cover loosely with greased plastic wrap, and let rise until dough looks bloated and dimply and starts to spread out, 60 to 75 minutes. Adjust oven rack to lower center position and heat oven to 425 degrees.

4. **FOR THE GLAZE:** Whisk egg white and milk together and brush over sides and top of loaf (loaves). Right before baking, make 6 or 7 slashes, ½-inch-deep, on dough top(s) with a serrated knife or single-edge razor blade. Bake for 15 minutes, then lower oven temperature to 400 degrees and bake until golden brown and an instant-read thermometer inserted in center of the loaf registers 200 degrees, 15 to 20 minutes for small loaves and 25 to 30 for larger loaf. Transfer to a wire rack and cool to room temperature. Slice and serve.

INGREDIENTS: RYE FLOUR

To produce the same light, holey, moist, and springy bread we developed, you will have to use exactly the same kind of rye flour that we used. This is because rye flours vary radically. In fact, there are no federal or industry standards to dictate their composition. What one miller calls a light rye flour another will call medium rye flour; what one miller labels medium might be another's pumpernickel and another's whole grain.

What differentiates one rye flour from the other is not only how finely they are milled but also which part of the hulled rye berry is milled. The berry consists of the bran (the outer covering), the germ (the seedling plant within the grain from which the rye sprouts), and the endosperm (the inner part of the kernel consisting mostly of starch and small amounts of protein).

We had the best luck getting the airy rye bread we were looking for by using flours milled only from the endosperm. These included King Arthur's light rye and Pillsbury's medium rye. These chalky-colored flours have a light, fine texture, much like white flour. In general, bread made with rye flour that contains even a trace of bran will be heavier because the bran particles tend to slice the strands of gluten, which give breads their elasticity.

King Arthur's "medium rye" contains traces of germ and bran as well as the endosperm of the berry. This flour produced a bread with earthy flavors and only a slight spring. Arrowhead Mills' "whole grain rye" produced a similar bread, although it is ground from the whole berry. King Arthur's "pumpernickel" flour and Hodgson Mills' "whole grain, stone ground medium" rye flour are also ground from the whole berry, but not as finely. Specks of bran are visible in these two coarse flours, which look much like sand. They produced dense, dry, and grainy breads.

BAGELS

THE BEST WAY TO EAT A BAGEL IS PLAIN AND unadorned, still warm from the oven. When eaten plain, you can linger on the details: the complex, yeasty aroma; the golden crust, stubbled with the crispy fermentation bubbles that bakers call fish eyes; the tenaciously chewy interior.

If you live in New York (and maybe some other large cities, although some bagel fans would argue that good bagels don't exist outside of New York), you can get great bagels. But what about everyone who lives in the rest of the country? What was needed, we decided, was a simple process for baking delicious, attractive, authentic bagels at home.

Looking at all the recipes we could get our hands on, we developed a fairly typical one, using bread flour, salt, sugar, yeast, and water, reasoning that the bread flour would give the bagels the chewy texture we were looking for. Following the procedure outlined in all the recipes, we kneaded the dough and then allowed it to rise for about an hour. Next we shaped it into rings, risen again, boiled, and finally baked the bagels.

Rather than plump, smooth, golden brown bagels, we ended up with small, dense hockey pucks, with crusts that were dull, wrinkled, and mottled brown. The flavor was bland and unappealing. We had our work cut out for us.

We decided that the first issue we needed to address was appearance. One problem we had encountered in forming the bagels was that after the first rise, the dough was somewhat grainy and loose. Instead of stretching easily, it was more inclined to tear. Forming bagels at this stage, as all the recipes we came across advocated, tended to result in a lumpy, uneven crust.

To overcome this difficulty, we tried forming the bagels immediately after we kneaded the dough, letting the rings rise until puffy, then boiling and baking as before. This approach turned out to be an improvement in terms of handling the dough, and also in the appearance of the bagels. However, they were still small and tough.

We began to question our choice of flour. We figured that bread flour, with about 13 percent protein content, was probably an improvement over all-purpose flour, with 10 to 12 percent protein content. We knew that the higher protein level would lead to the formation of more gluten, that network of elastic protein strands that traps the carbon dioxide released by the activity of the yeast, allowing bread to rise. It stood to reason, then, that a higher-protein flour would rise better, thus yielding a bagel that was plumper and had a finer, chewier texture.

The next flour up the scale in terms of protein content is high-gluten, a flour produced by the milling of high-protein wheat. High-gluten flour has the highest protein content of any flour, usually around 14 percent, and is the flour of choice at most professional bagel bakeries and pizza parlors. We made our next batch of bagels using high-gluten flour and saw a difference the moment we removed the dough from the mixer. This dough was satiny smooth and much more elastic than the dough made with bread flour. And the bagels made with high-gluten flour were larger and rose higher. In addition, the crust was smoother and more attractive. The interior structure of these bagels was also better—lighter and chewier.

We were getting close now, but the bagels were still a bit flat on the bottom. A little fiddling around with the water-to-flour ratio quickly solved that problem. Initially, we were treating the bagel dough like any other bread dough, trying to achieve a smooth, slightly tacky consistency. A few test batches using less water in relation to flour revealed that a stiff, drier dough produces a firmer-textured, even chewier bagel. "Dry," however, may not be the most appropriate word to use in describing the correct consistency. A dough with the right consistency will be smooth and elastic, though somewhat firm. After the dough has come together in the first five minutes of mixing, it should not stick to your finger when pressed. And when you have completely kneaded the dough, a piece about the size of a golf ball should hold its shape and should not sag.

With the shape and texture of the bagels very much improved, we turned to the issue of flavor. Traditionally, bagels are placed in a specially designed refrigerator, called a retarder, for several hours or overnight after being formed. This practice allows for a slower, more natural fermentation. It is during this retarding process that bagels develop most of their flavor. We wanted to test the impact of retarding, so after mixing and forming a batch of bagels, we placed them in the refrigerator overnight. The results were both dramatic and surprising.

The most obvious change in the bagels was in their size. What had gone into the refrigerator as tight, shapely rings of dough came out as flaccid blobs. The yeast fermentation had continued unabated, and the bagels had overrisen. We finished the boiling and baking process anyway.

In spite of being overlarge and flat-bottomed, these overrisen bagels were a vast improvement over our previous attempts. When we sliced one open, we were greeted by a heavenly aroma. This was more than just flour, salt, and yeast! The long, slow fermentation process the bagels had undergone had yielded the complex flavor and aroma we were seeking. So retarding really was crucial for great bagel flavor. We were even more surprised by the other effects of retarding: the crust of these bagels had taken on a dark, reddish sheen, and the surface was covered in crispy fish eyes.

So what was actually happening to the bagels during retarding? The primary mechanism involved is bacterial fermentation. At lower temperatures, yeast fermentation is suppressed, and the lactobacilli bacteria naturally present in the flour and the yeast begin to produce a variety of organic acids, primarily lactic acid and acetic acid. These organic acids, the same acids present in a healthy sourdough culture, give the dough a more complex flavor. The fish eyes are a result of the same bacterial reaction, which breaks down some of the gluten in the dough. The weakened gluten structure on the surface of the bagels allows the formation of fermentation bubbles. The richer, reddish brown color of the crust was the result of another chemical process, the Maillard, or browning, reaction. During the retarding process, enzymes produced by the bacteria convert wheat starch into simple sugars and protein into peptides and amino acids. As the product loses moisture during baking, the reaction between these sugars and the amino acids—the Maillard reaction—produces a rich brown crust.

In subsequent tests, we lowered the yeast level in our recipe by a full half. We also lowered the temperature of the water we used in the dough to control the activity of the yeast. Initially, we had been proofing the active dry yeast in 110-degree water as recommended on the package. We ultimately decided against dissolving the yeast before adding it to the flour and in favor of using 80-degree water.

Experimenting with different retarding times, we eventually concluded that a period of 13 to 18 hours is best for a balance between flavor and crust development. Less time and the flavor did not develop as fully, although a short retarding time is better than none. More than 18 hours and we began to notice some adverse effects on the bagels, such as an excessive darkening of the crust, the formation of large bubbles inside the bagels, and the development of too many fermentation bubbles on the surface.

Boiling the dough, which is the most unusual step in the bagel-making process, is responsible for the bagel's unique characteristics—the shiny crust and chewy texture. Boiling a bagel before baking it serves three purposes. Most important, it sets the shape of the bagel by cooking the surface and killing off some of the yeast in the outer layer of dough. This helps to limit the expansion of the bagel when it is baked. A

bagel that is not boiled, we discovered, will expand into a round ball in the heat of the oven. The second function of the boiling process is to give the bagel its characteristic shine. When you boil the bagel, starches on the surface become gelatinized. These starches then cook to a crispy, shiny coating in the oven. The third purpose of boiling is to activate the yeast in the inner layers of dough, which has been made sluggish by the retarding process.

All of the home recipes we reviewed recommended boiling the bagels for a period of one to four minutes. We tried the whole range of suggested times and found, surprisingly, that a shorter boil of about 30 seconds yielded the best results. Bagels boiled for four minutes had noticeably less shine and were not as plump as those boiled for 30 seconds. We surmised that the bagels boiled for four minutes had developed such a thick crust that they were unable to expand fully in the oven.

SHAPING BAGELS

1. Form each dough ball into a rope 11 inches long by rolling it under your outstretched palms. Do not taper the ends of the rope. Overlap the ends of the rope about 1½ inches and pinch the entire overlapped area firmly together. If the ends of the rope do not want to stick together, you can dampen them slightly.

2. Place the loop of dough around the base of your fingers and, with the overlap under your palm, roll the rope several times, applying firm pressure to seal the seam. The bagel should be roughly the same thickness all the way around.

Master Recipe for Plain Bagels
MAKES 8 BAGELS

Because bagel dough is much drier and stiffer than bread dough, it takes longer for the ingredients to cohere during mixing. For this same reason, we recommend that you neither double the recipe nor try to knead the dough by hand. Most good natural foods stores carry barley malt syrup. High-gluten flour might be more difficult to find. You can order both the syrup and the flour from the King Arthur Flour Baker's Catalogue (800-827-6836). See the illustrations at left for tips on shaping bagels.

4	cups high-gluten flour
2	teaspoons salt
1	tablespoon barley malt syrup or powder
1½	teaspoons active dry yeast
1¼	cups lukewarm water (80 degrees)
3	tablespoons cornmeal, for dusting baking sheet

1. Mix flour, salt, and malt in bowl of standing mixer fitted with dough hook. Add yeast and water; mix at lowest speed until dough looks scrappy, like shreds just beginning to come together, about 4 minutes. Increase to speed to low; continue mixing until dough is cohesive, smooth, and stiff, 8 to 10 minutes.

2. Turn dough onto work surface; divide into 8

portions, about 4 ounces each. Roll pieces into smooth balls and cover with towel or plastic wrap to rest for 5 minutes.

3. Form each dough ball into a rope 11 inches long by rolling it under your outstretched palms. Do not taper ends of rope. Shape rope into circle, overlapping ends of rope about 1½ inches. Pinch overlapped area firmly together, dampening slightly if ends won't stick. Place loop of dough around base of your fingers and, with the overlap under your palm, roll rope several times, applying firm pressure to seal seam. The bagel should be roughly the same thickness all the way around. Place bagels on cornmeal-dusted baking sheet, cover tightly with plastic wrap, and refrigerate overnight (12 to 18 hours).

4. About 20 minutes before baking, remove dough rings from refrigerator. Adjust oven rack to center position and heat oven to 450 degrees. Fill large soup kettle with 3-inch depth of water; bring to rapid boil.

5. Working four at a time, drop dough rings into boiling water, stirring and submerging loops with Chinese skimmer or slotted spoon, until very slightly puffed, 30 to 35 seconds. Remove rings from water; transfer to wire rack, bottom side down, to drain.

6. Transfer boiled rings, rough side down, to baking sheet lined with parchment paper or to baking stone. Bake until deep golden brown and crisp, about 14 minutes. Use tongs to transfer to wire rack to cool. Serve warm or at room temperature.

➤ VARIATIONS

Topped Bagels

Topping ingredients stick to the bagels best when applied to the dough rings just as they come out of the boiling water, while still wet and sticky.

Follow Master Recipe for Plain Bagels, dunking bagels into ½ cup raw sesame seeds, poppy or caraway seeds, dehydrated onion or garlic flakes, or sea or kosher salt while they are still wet and sticky (at end of step 5, after draining).

Everything Bagels

Follow recipe for Topped Bagels, dunking bagels into mixture of 2 tablespoons each sesame and poppy seeds and 1 tablespoon each caraway seeds, sea or kosher salt, dehydrated onion flakes, and dehydrated garlic flakes.

Cinnamon Raisin Bagels

Follow Master Recipe for Plain Bagels, mixing 1 teaspoon vanilla extract, 1 tablespoon ground cinnamon, and ½ cup raisins into flour, salt, and malt in step 1.

CINNAMON SWIRL BREAD

SOMETIMES THE HEAVENLY SMELL OF CINNAmon swirl bread emanating from the oven is the best part of the bread. Often after baking there are gaps between the swirls of cinnamon filling and bread, and the filling is prone to leaking out and burning in the pan.

We wanted to solve these problems when developing our recipe. We also wanted the baked texture to be moist and light, yet firm enough to be sliced fresh the first day and toasted for a few days after. To achieve the best texture and crust, we knew we needed to perfect the baking time and temperature as well as fine-tune the ingredients. While we were at it, we decided to use this recipe to develop a technique for the ever-popular cinnamon rolls.

To get our bearings, we tried a range of yeast bread recipes, from rich brioche-type formulas with a high proportion of eggs, butter, and sugar to recipes for lean, white sandwich-style bread. When these first breads were tasted, everyone was drawn to the richer versions, as expected. However, for a more versatile bread that could be cut into thin or thick slices and toasted, we decided on a formula that was a compromise between the two.

We began our tests by focusing on milk, eggs, and sugar—the ingredients that most affect richness and texture. We tested loaves using all milk, all water, and a combination. All milk yielded a denser texture than we wanted; water had the opposite effect, producing a loaf that was too lean. An equal combination of milk and water was the answer. To lighten the texture a little bit more, we increased the eggs in our original recipe to two. Eggs contribute to the evenness of the crumb as well as to color and flavor, but using more than two produced a crumb that was too light and airy for this type of bread.

Our final measurements of sugar and butter resulted in a crumb that was tender and soft the first day and retained some moisture for two to three days. The amount of sugar—one-third cup per loaf—is just enough to add flavor to the bread without competing with the filling. Of course, since butter also contributes color and richness, we knew that to some extent the amount was a personal preference. For the everyday loaf we were after, we tested from two to eight tablespoons per loaf and settled on four; using more than that resulted in a loaf that was fattier than we wanted.

We tried adding yeast by the direct method (dissolving yeast in warm liquid and adding the remaining ingredients) and also by the rapid-mix method (mixing yeast with dry ingredients and then adding warm liquids), and found very little difference in the quality of the loaf. The rapid-mix method is quicker and works especially well with rapid-rise yeast. The direct method involves an extra step, but the doughs using this method took 20 minutes less for their first rise. Regardless of the method you use, just remember that you'll kill the yeast if you use any liquid above 125 degrees. When mixing yeast with water initially, the recommended temperature is 110 degrees.

We tested a range of flours, from bleached all-purpose to bread, and found surprisingly little difference. We detected a slight mushiness in bread made with bleached flour, and bread flour produced a slightly coarser texture, which was not objectionable. Overall, the breads made with unbleached all-purpose flours consistently tasted the best, with a fine, even crumb and a pleasant chew. (For more information on flour in general and bleaching in particular see page 416.)

Almost more important than the type of flour used is the total amount. Depending on a number of factors, including how humid it is, the exact size of the eggs, and how precisely the liquids are measured, the dough will take anywhere from 3¼ to 3¾ cups of flour. Any of the doughs we made could have taken the full amount or more if we forced it in, but when we did, the resulting loaves were dry. We had the best results when we held out the last half-cup of flour, adding it only as necessary, little by little, at the end while kneading, either by hand or machine. To test the dough to determine if the flour level is correct, squeeze it using your entire hand (completely clean with no dough clinging to it) and release it.

When the dough does not stick to your hand, the kneading is complete. Even if the dough still feels soft, resist the temptation to add more flour.

Now that we had perfected the dough, we were ready to tackle filling, rolling, and shaping the loaf. For the filling, we tried both brown and white sugar mixed with cinnamon. Although we like the taste of brown sugar, we finally had to rule it out because it melted more readily and leaked through the dough in places during baking.

The amount of filling was determined by one factor besides taste. We discovered that using much more than one-quarter cup of the cinnamon-sugar mixture resulted in small separations between the filling and the bread because the excess sugar prevented the dough from cohering. We eventually discovered that one-quarter cup of sugar mixed with five teaspoons of cinnamon resulted in a tasty bread with no gaps.

Rolling and shaping the dough into a loaf are crucial steps. To create swirls in the finished bread and end up with a loaf that would fit into a 9-inch loaf pan, we rolled the dough out evenly into a rectangle 8 inches wide and 18 inches long. When we rolled the dough out longer than this, it was so thin that the filling popped through the edges in some places. Rolling the dough up evenly and closely was also important. When we rolled the dough too tightly, the filling popped through; rolling too loosely produced an uneven loaf and gaps between the swirls and the bread. Finally, we found that we could prevent the filling from leaking and burning in the pan while baking if we pinched the edges of the bottom seam and the ends of the roll together very tightly.

Getting the dough mixed, risen, and shaped still doesn't guarantee great bread. Rising time is also crucial. In fact, finding the proper rising time entirely solved the problem of gaps in the bread. When we allowed the shaped loaf to rise just to the top of the pan, the baked bread was dense and did not have a fully risen, attractive shape. But when we allowed the unbaked loaf to rise too much, 1½ inches or more above the pan, we ended up with those unwanted gaps between dough and filling. Our overrisen loaves also collapsed in the oven. Allowing the dough to rise just 1 inch above the top of a 9-inch loaf pan before baking resulted in a perfectly shaped loaf with no gaps.

To determine the best baking temperature, we first tested the bread in a slow oven (300 to 325 degrees). Because this allowed the unbaked loaf too long a time to continue to rise before the yeast died (at an internal temperature of 140 degrees), the bread rose too much and lost its shape. A hotter oven (375 to 425 degrees) resulted in a loaf that was too brown on the outside before it was cooked through. Since our bread formula contained milk, eggs, and sugar, all browning agents, we found that a moderate oven (350 degrees) baked the most evenly.

We tested final internal temperatures between 180 and 210 degrees and found 185 to 190 to be the ideal range. Technically, bread is not totally finished baking until all the steam has evaporated and it has cooled completely on a rack, so resist the temptation to cut the bread while it's hot. The pressure of the knife will compress the loaf and you'll end up with a doughy slice.

Cinnamon Swirl Bread

MAKES 1 LOAF

If you like, the dough can be made one day, refrigerated overnight, then shaped, allowed to rise, and baked the next day. This recipe also doubles easily.

ENRICHED BREAD DOUGH

½ cup milk
4 tablespoons (½ stick) unsalted butter, cut into ½-inch pieces
1 package (2¼ teaspoons) dry active yeast
½ cup warm water (110 degrees)
⅓ cup sugar
2 large eggs
1½ teaspoons salt
3¼–3¾ cups unbleached all-purpose flour

FILLING

¼ cup sugar
5 teaspoons ground cinnamon
Milk for brushing

GLAZE

1 large egg
2 teaspoons milk

1. Heat milk and butter in small saucepan over medium heat until butter melts. Cool to lukewarm (about 110 degrees).

2. Meanwhile, sprinkle yeast over warm water in bowl of standing mixer fitted with paddle. Beat in sugar and eggs and mix at low speed to blend. Add salt, lukewarm milk mixture, 2 cups of flour; mix at medium speed until thoroughly blended, about 1 minute. Switch to dough hook attachment. Add 1¼ cups flour, and knead at medium-low speed, adding more flour sparingly if dough sticks to sides of bowl, until dough is smooth and comes away from sides of bowl, about 10 minutes.

3. Turn dough onto work surface. Squeeze dough with a clean dry hand. If dough is sticky, knead in up to ½ additional cup flour to form a smooth, soft, elastic dough. Transfer dough to a large, very lightly oiled plastic container or bowl. Cover top of container with plastic wrap and let rise until double in size, 2 to 2½ hours. (Ideal rising temperature is 75 degrees.) After rise, punch down center of dough once (can be refrigerated, covered, up to 18 hours). Making sure not to fold or misshape dough, turn it onto unfloured work surface; let dough rest, to relax, about 10 minutes.

4. Grease sides and bottom of 9 x 5 x 3-inch loaf pan. Mix sugar and cinnamon in small bowl.

5. Press dough neatly into an evenly shaped 6 x 8-inch rectangle. With short side of dough facing you, roll dough with rolling pin into evenly shaped 8 x 18-inch rectangle (flour counter lightly if dough sticks). Brush dough liberally with milk. Sprinkle filling evenly over dough, leaving ½-inch border on far end. Starting at end closest to you, roll up dough, pinching dough gently with fingertips to make sure it is tightly sealed. To keep loaf from stretching beyond 9 inches, use hands to occasionally push ends in as dough is rolled. When you reach the end, use fingertips to pinch the dough ends together very tightly to form a secure seam. With seam side facing up, push in center of ends. Firmly pinch dough at either end together to seal sides of loaf.

6. Place loaf, seam side down, into prepared pan; press lightly to flatten. Cover top of pan loosely with plastic wrap and set aside to rise. Let rise until dough is 1 inch above top of pan, about 1½ hours, or about 1 hour longer if dough has been refrigerated. As

dough nears top of pan, adjust oven rack to center position and heat oven to 350 degrees.

7. Meanwhile, in small bowl, whisk together egg and milk. Gently brush loaf top with egg mixture.

8. Bake until loaf is golden brown and instant-read thermometer pushed through from top end into center of loaf registers 185 to 190 degrees, 30 to 35 minutes. Remove bread from pan and cool on its side on wire rack until room temperature, at least 45 minutes. (Can be double-wrapped in plastic wrap and stored at room temperature for four days or frozen up to three months.)

➤ VARIATIONS

Cinnamon Swirl Bread Kneaded by Hand

Follow recipe for Cinnamon Swirl Bread, sprinkling yeast over water in large bowl in step 2. Use wooden spoon to incorporate the other ingredients as directed. When dough comes together, turn it onto lightly floured surface and knead until smooth and elastic, 12 to 15 minutes, adding more flour if necessary. Transfer dough to lightly oiled container and follow rising instructions.

Cinnamon Swirl Rolls

MAKES I DOZEN

This recipe starts with the same bread dough but adds a richer filling and sweet icing.

I   recipe Enriched Bread Dough

FILLING
⅓   cup sugar
2   tablespoons ground cinnamon
     Milk for brushing
½   cup raisins, golden or dark (optional)
½   cup chopped nuts of choice

ICING
I ¼ cups confectioners' sugar, sifted
2   tablespoons milk
½   teaspoon vanilla extract

1. Follow steps 1 through 3 in recipe for Cinnamon Swirl Bread.

2. Grease 13 x 9-inch baking pan. Mix sugar and cinnamon in small bowl.

3. Roll dough with rolling pin into an evenly shaped 12 x 16-inch rectangle. Brush dough liberally with milk and sprinkle with an even layer of cinnamon-sugar mixture, leaving a ½-inch border along one of the long sides. Sprinkle raisins and/or chopped nuts over cinnamon mixture. Roll, beginning with the long side of the rectangle. Use both hands to pinch dough with fingertips as you go, sealing edges firmly to form a seam. (Do not seal ends.)

4. Using dental floss, cut formed roll in half, cut each half in half again, and then cut each piece into 3 rolls for a total of 12 rolls. Space rolls evenly in greased baking pan, leaving some space between them.

5. Cover loosely with plastic and allow to rise until double in size (rolls will touch), about 1 hour. When rolls are almost fully risen, adjust oven rack to center position and heat oven to 350 degrees.

6. Bake until golden brown and thermometer inserted in center roll registers 185 to 190 degrees, 25 to 30 minutes. Invert rolls onto wire rack. Cool to room temperature, 20 to 30 minutes.

7. Whisk sugar, milk, and vanilla in small bowl until smooth. Reinvert rolls and place rack over piece of parchment or wax paper. When rolls have cooled to room temperature, drizzle icing off end of large spoon and over rolls. Cut or pull apart to separate, and serve.

15

MUFFINS, BISCUITS, AND QUICK BREADS

MUFFINS, BISCUITS, AND QUICK BREADS, such as cornbread and Irish soda bread, have a number of elements in common. All of these baked goods can be quickly prepared (the batter or dough can usually be assembled in the time it takes to pre-heat the oven) and quickly baked. This sets them far apart from yeast breads, which must rise for hours on the counter. Chemical leaveners (baking soda and baking powder) are speedy and reliable.

There are several methods commonly used to assemble quick breads. The most common, often referred to as the quick bread method, calls for mea-suring wet and dry ingredients separately, pouring wet into dry, then mixing them together as quickly as possible. Batters for pancakes, popovers, and most quick breads rely on this approach. A second tech-nique, often called the creaming method and more common to cake batters, starts with creaming the butter and sugar until light and fluffy. Eggs and fla-vorings are beaten in, then the dry and liquid ingre-dients are alternately added. A third possibility comes from the biscuit- and pie dough–making tradition, in which cold fat is cut into the dry ingredients with fingertips, forks, a pastry blender, or the blade of a food processor. Once the mixture has achieved a cornmeal-like texture with pea-sized flecks, liquid is added and quickly mixed in.

We have tested these three mixing methods on many of the recipes in this chapter. Often, we have found that the same ingredients will bake up quite differently depending on how they are combined.

In addition to mixing methods, it's also important to pay attention to the choice of flours and leaven-ers in these recipes. The protein content of the flour

INGREDIENTS: Baking Soda and Baking Powder

Muffins, biscuits, and quick breads, as well as cookies, cakes, pan-cakes, and waffles, get their rise from chemical leaveners—baking soda and baking powder—rather than yeast. Chemical leavenings react with acids to produce carbon dioxide, the gas that causes these baked goods to rise.

To do its work, baking soda relies on an acid in the recipe, such as buttermilk or molasses. It's important to use the right amount of baking soda in recipes. Use more baking soda than can be neu-tralized by the acidic ingredient, and you'll end up with a metallic-tasting, coarse-crumbed quick bread or cake. One cup of butter-milk is needed to neutralize one-half teaspoon of baking soda.

Baking powder is nothing more than baking soda (about one-quarter to one-third of the total makeup) mixed with a dry acid and double-dried cornstarch. The cornstarch absorbs moisture and keeps the two elements apart during storage, preventing pre-mature production of the gas. When baking powder becomes wet, the acid comes into contact with the baking soda, producing carbon dioxide. Most commercial baking powders are "double-acting." In other words, they contain two kinds of acids—one that produces a carbon dioxide reaction at room temperature, the other responding only to heat.

In contrast, baking soda is only single-acting, as is homemade baking powder, which contains only one acid, cream of tartar. Baking soda reacts immediately on contact with an acid.

In a cake, for example, it is important to have an early release of carbon dioxide during the batter preparation so that small bubbles will be created to form the foundation of the cell struc-ture. These cells expand during baking because of additional car-bon dioxide production caused by the action of the second leav-ening acid, and the dough firms up into the final cake structure. Therefore, double-acting baking powder is essential. In a cookie batter, however, especially one that has a good deal of structure from butter and eggs, the double-acting issue is less critical.

Since baking powder is nothing more than baking soda and acid, it's easy to convert a recipe from baking powder and milk to baking soda and buttermilk. Just divide the amount of baking powder by four to determine how much baking soda you should use and substitute buttermilk. For example, in a recipe calling for two teaspoons of baking powder and one cup of milk, you could substitute one-half teaspoon of baking soda and one cup of but-termilk. There would be taste and textural differences, it is true, but the leavening action would be about the same.

One final note about baking soda: You may not want it to neutralize all the buttermilk's acidity. If you want to taste the buttermilk, you can substitute baking powder for some or all of the baking soda. Since baking powder has its own built-in acid to react with, the acidity of the buttermilk is allowed to come through. For example, in a recipe that calls for one-half teaspoon of baking soda and one cup of buttermilk, the baking soda could be replaced with two teaspoons of baking powder. The leaven-ing result would be the same, but the baked good would have a tangier flavor.

can greatly affect the texture in these simple baked goods. (For more information on flour, see page 416.) Chemical leaveners (that is, baking soda and baking powder) are key elements in quick bread recipes. See page 374 for more information on these ingredients.

This chapter also includes a trio of breakfast dishes—pancakes, waffles, and French toast. Pancakes and waffles are chemically leavened quick breads that are cooked on a griddle or in an iron rather than in the oven. French toast, which does not contain any chemical leavener, is not, technically, a quick bread. However, since many of the same cooking issues apply to pancakes, waffles, and French toast, we have grouped all three of these recipes at the end of this chapter.

MUFFINS

HAVE YOU EVER TRIED TO BAKE A BATCH OF those jumbo muffins you see in bakeries and specialty coffee shops these days? If you follow most cookbook recipes, you won't get what you're looking for. We weren't satisfied with our results, and we've tried scores of recipes. Some muffins came out flat-topped or misshapen. Other batches were either rich and leaden or dense and dry. The best were pleasant, but not outstanding.

Our standards, admittedly, were high. We weren't looking for a "healthy" muffin to incorporate in our daily diet. We wanted a really great weekend muffin, one that would make brunch guests covet the recipe. This muffin had to have it all. It needed rich, full flavor with a thin, crisp crust protecting its fragile, tender crumb. What's more, this muffin had to be a real looker, too. We would settle for nothing less than a perfectly round, mushroomlike cap with a pronounced, crisp overhang.

Working with a conservative six-muffin recipe, we decided to start our tests with mixing techniques. Our review of recipes pointed to the three possible methods introduced on the previous page (quick bread method, creaming method, and the biscuit/pie dough method). Although the recipe we were working with at this point was way too lean (the muffins were small, dry, tough, and unappetizing), it did have one thing going for it—the creaming method. The creamed-batter muffins we had made thus far were more tender-crumbed than their competitors. (For more information on these tests, see page 378.)

With the mixing method semidecided, we moved on to testing individual ingredients. Because our original formula was too dry and savory, we increased the butter and sugar, then moved on to testing the primary ingredient: flour. We made muffins with cake flour, unbleached flour, bleached flour, and an equal mix of cake flour and bleached all-purpose flour.

The batter made with cake flour was incredibly loose compared with the other batters, resulting in muffins that were squat, wet, and greasy. They also lacked a distinct, crisp outer crust. Muffins baked with half cake and half all-purpose were a step up from the cake flour muffins, but their texture was a tad wet and greasy and they lacked the beautiful shape of those made entirely with all-purpose flour. Although the all-purpose flour formula still needed work, both all-purpose muffins we had made were shapely and fairly tender, with a nice contrast between crust and crumb. After our flour tests, we decided that the formula needed more sugar for added flavor.

By now our formula was beginning to take shape, and we were ready to test liquids. We made muffins using low-fat milk, whole milk, half-and-half, cream, powdered milk plus water (common in commercial baking), buttermilk, yogurt, and sour cream. Leavening adjustments were made (reducing the amount of baking powder and including baking soda) for all the buttermilk, yogurt, and sour cream muffins.

The thin liquids—low-fat milk, whole milk, powdered milk, and half-and-half—naturally produced thin batters that baked into smooth-topped muffins. They looked more like cupcakes. Low-fat milk muffins were soufflé-shaped with straight sides and flat tops.

The thicker liquids—cream, buttermilk, low-fat yogurt, and sour cream—delivered thicker batters and muffins with rounded, textured tops. The higher-fat muffins, particularly those made with sour cream and cream, were squatty, dense, heavy, and wet. The buttermilk muffins were good, but the yogurt-enriched were even better, giving us a rough-textured rounded top, a sweet-tangy flavor, and a light, tender crumb.

Now that we had a working base, we started adding fruits and flavorings. Three additional adjustments to the recipe came during this part of the testing. Although the sugar level seemed right in the plain muffin, the addition of tart fruit and other ingredients made the muffins seem not sweet enough. We found that increasing the sugar again helped immensely in both the plain and fruit variations. We also found that one more tablespoon of butter gave us additional tenderness without weighting down the muffin. Increasing the batter by one-third—from a two-cup flour to a three-cup flour recipe—gave us not only a beautifully rounded top but a nice big lip. This base worked with all of the following variations, so you should feel free to plug in your own favorites.

As a final question, we wondered if it matters which fat you use to grease a muffin tin. To find out, we baked muffins in an ungreased muffin tin, one that had been coated in butter, one in shortening, one in oil, and a final in vegetable cooking spray. Only those baked in ungreased muffin tins were unacceptable, displaying tough, leathery crusts. Although differences were subtle, we preferred the flavor of the muffins baked in buttered tins. The oil-coated muffins felt and tasted greasy. For ease and speed, vegetable cooking spray took first place.

INGREDIENTS: Homemade Baking Powder

Unlike baking soda, which keeps forever, baking powder begins to react and lose its potency the instant you open the can and expose the contents to humidity in the air. For maximum leavening power, we recommend buying baking powder in the smallest can available, dating the can when opened, and discarding the contents after three months.

The alternative, uncommon but hardly daunting, is to make your own baking powder. Simply combine one-quarter teaspoon of baking soda, one-half teaspoon of cream of tartar, and one-quarter teaspoon of cornstarch. This homemade baking powder works well in recipes that require only a brief lift as soon as the batter is prepared, such as waffles or some cookies. Do not use homemade baking powder in recipes that require long, slow rising in the oven, such as cakes.

A few recipes advised against muffin papers, warning that muffins would not rise as high. We also saw a couple of recipes with instructions to grease the bottom, but not the sides, of the muffin cups. So we tested three batches of muffins—one baked in papers, one baked in greased cups, and a final batch baked in cups in which only the bottoms were greased.

We observed differences in shape more than height in the three sets of muffins. Those baked in papers were, indeed, shorter than those baked right in the cup, but they also had a more rounded, filled-out look than the other two muffins. But we still disliked muffin papers for other reasons. When peeling off the papers, we lost a good portion of the muffin. Muffin papers also keep the muffins' sides from browning as well as those baked right in the cup. We observed no difference between those baked in cups that had been greased completely and those baked in cups with greased bottoms only.

Master Recipe for Basic Muffins

MAKES 1 DOZEN LARGE MUFFINS

To cinnamon-coat muffin tops, dip warm muffins in melted butter, then in mixture of one-half cup granulated sugar and two teaspoons ground cinnamon.

3	cups all-purpose flour
1	tablespoon baking powder
½	teaspoon baking soda
½	teaspoon salt
10	tablespoons unsalted butter, softened
1	cup minus 1 tablespoon granulated sugar
2	large eggs
1½	cups plain low-fat yogurt
	Vegetable cooking spray or additional unsalted butter for greasing muffin tins

1. Adjust oven rack to lower-middle position and heat oven to 375 degrees. Whisk flour, baking powder, baking soda, and salt together in medium bowl; set aside.

2. Cream butter and sugar with electric mixer on medium-high speed until light and fluffy, about 2 minutes. Add eggs, one at a time, beating well after each addition. Beat in one-half of dry ingredients.

Beat in one-third of yogurt. Beat in remaining dry ingredients in two batches, alternating with yogurt, until incorporated.

3. Spray 12-cup muffin tin with vegetable cooking spray or coat lightly with butter. Divide batter evenly among cups. Bake until muffins are golden brown, 25 to 30 minutes. Set on wire rack to cool slightly, about 5 minutes. Remove muffins from tin and serve warm.

➤ VARIATIONS

Mocha Chip Muffins

Follow Master Recipe for Basic Muffins, dissolving 3 tablespoons instant espresso powder in yogurt and folding 1 cup chocolate chips into finished batter.

Apricot Almond Muffins

Follow Master Recipe for Basic Muffins, creaming 1 ounce (3 tablespoons) almond paste with butter and sugar and folding 1½ cups finely diced dried apricots into finished batter. Sprinkle each top with portion of ½ cup sliced almonds.

Raspberry Almond Muffins

Follow Master Recipe for Basic Muffins, creaming 1 ounce (3 tablespoons) almond paste with butter and sugar. Spoon one-half portion of batter into each muffin cup. With small spoon, make well in center of each cup of dough. Spoon 1 to 1½ teaspoons raspberry (or any flavored) jam into each well. Fill with remaining batter.

Cranberry-Walnut-Orange Muffins

Follow Master Recipe for Basic Muffins, adding 1 teaspoon grated orange zest to butter-sugar mixture and folding 1½ cups coarsely chopped fresh or frozen cranberries and ¾ cup coarsely chopped walnuts into finished batter.

Lemon Blueberry Muffins

Follow Master Recipe for Basic Muffins, adding 1 teaspoon grated lemon zest to butter-sugar mixture and folding 1½ cups blueberries that have been tossed in 1 tablespoon flour into finished batter.

Lemon Poppy Seed Muffins

Follow Master Recipe for Basic Muffins, adding 3 tablespoons poppy seeds to dry ingredients and 1 tablespoon grated lemon zest to butter-sugar mixture. While muffins are baking, heat ¼ cup granulated sugar and ¼ cup lemon juice from 2 small lemons in small saucepan until sugar dissolves and mixture forms light syrup, 3 to 4 minutes. Brush warm syrup over warm muffins and serve.

Banana Walnut Muffins

Follow Master Recipe for Basic Muffins, adding ½ teaspoon grated nutmeg to dry ingredients, substituting 1 cup packed light brown sugar for granulated sugar, and folding 1½ cups finely diced bananas (about 3 small) and ¾ cup chopped walnuts into finished batter.

BRAN MUFFINS

MOST ANY MUFFIN CAN BE MADE AS A VARIA-tion on our recipe for Basic Muffins. Bran muffins, however, require a different formula. While most muffins have a buttery, delicate yellow crumb, bran muffins should be dark, rich, hearty, and moist.

There are two basic types of bran muffins—"refrigerator" muffins and muffins based on a classic batter. The batter for the refrigerator muffins, which contains bran cereal, is simply mixed together and then stored in the refrigerator until you are ready to bake. The second type is made by combining ingredients according to the creaming method (just like putting together a butter cake batter) or the quick bread method (mixing dry ingredients with a whisked liquid mixture).

When we baked and compared batches of both muffin varieties, it was immediately obvious that the classic muffins, made with wheat bran, far exceeded the refrigerator type in taste, texture, and appearance. Compared with the wheat bran muffins, the cereal-based bran muffins had a muddy look, a somewhat rubbery texture, and an oddly chewy quality. The bran flavor was dull and muted, and they lacked that all-around depth we expected from a bran muffin. By contrast, the classic bran muffins tasted deeply of bran and had a better (although still far from perfect) texture.

Next we compared muffins made with the creaming and the quick bread method. As with regular muffins, we found that creaming the butter and sugar together and then alternately stirring in wet and dry ingredients created a fuller, more tender muffin.

With the mixing method decided, we moved on to the ingredients. In a standard muffin batter composed of flour, sugar, leavening, eggs, flavorings, milk, and fat, the batter's volume is built on a higher proportion of flour relative to fat and liquid. But when you reduce a portion of the flour to accommodate the bran, you disrupt the balance of liquid and dry ingredients, because wheat bran isn't actually absorbed into the batter the way flour is. This means that you need to rework the proportion of liquid and dry ingredients.

To understand this dynamic, it is important to know a bit about bran. Bran, the exterior covering of wheat kernels, is milled into flakes. These flakes, known as wheat bran, are high in insoluble fiber. As a result, they are actually suspended in the batter, making a denser muffin. The bran flakes also tend to dry out and "break up" the batter, in much the same way that chocolate chips or nuts break up the batter in cookies.

When we started baking the muffins, we used a whopping two cups of bran. You could probably imagine the result: Dry, crumbly muffins that tasted (and acted) just like sawdust. After much fine-tuning, we found that we could achieve a fuller, more tempered flavor and a pleasing texture by replacing a little of the all-purpose flour with whole wheat flour. This allowed us to cut the bran down to one-and-one-half cups without losing the flavor we wanted.

After many tests with individual ingredients, we concluded that bran muffins are best made by juggling a proper amount of wheat bran with all-purpose and whole wheat flour; adding buttermilk and sour cream for smoothness and moisture; using butter as the fat for creaming; and brightening the batter with vanilla extract, spices, and molasses if needed.

Finally, we noticed that bran muffins tend to overbake in a flash. A tray of muffins are baked through when they retract ever so slightly from the sides of the cups and the tops spring back very gently on being touched. Don't look for an active spring. The muffins will still be baked through even if a wooden pick withdrawn from the centers has a few moist crumbs clinging to it.

SCIENCE: Why Creamed Butter Works Best

Practically every pancake and quick bread recipe cautions not to overmix the batter once wet and dry ingredients have been combined. Better, most authors reason, to leave streaks of flour in the batter than to overdevelop the flour's gluten, resulting in smaller, denser, and tougher muffins.

Because we found the standard creaming method (creaming butter and sugar, then alternately beating in dry and wet ingredients) to deliver a lighter, more tender muffin than the gingerly mixed quick-bread method, we were puzzled. In the creaming method, the flour was beaten by machine up to two minutes, depending on the recipe. If overbeating caused gluten development and tough muffins, why were these muffins tender?

The explanation is fairly straightforward. In the creaming process butter is first aerated with sugar; then fat- and moisture-rich eggs are beaten into the mix. Dry ingredients are added, alternately with the wet ingredients.

In most creamed butter recipes, a good portion of the flour (in our recipe, it's half) is added to the creamed butter mixture before the wet ingredients. That way, the fat from the butter and egg coats most of the flour, preventing any gluten formation. The remaining flour and wet ingredients are added alternately at this point, stimulating only a part of the flour's gluten. Certainly some of the flour's gluten must be activated; otherwise the muffin would have no structure at all.

In the quick-bread method, all wet ingredients and fats are added at once, denying the flour an opportunity to be coated with fat. We naturally questioned why the quick-bread method couldn't approximate the creaming method of coating the flour with fat first. So we made a batch of muffins, mixing the dry ingredients, then adding melted butter and the eggs to disperse the fat. When the flour was sufficiently coated, we stirred in the yogurt.

The muffins were just as tender as those made using the creamed method. But because the batter had not been aerated by the mixer, they lacked the height of the mixer muffins. So when you're short on time, you can achieve more tender muffins by simply mixing the butter and eggs into the dry ingredients. The muffins will not rise high enough to develop a lip, but their texture and flavor will be fine. When perfection counts, get out the mixer.

Bran Muffins

MAKES 1 DOZEN MUFFINS

Wheat bran is available at natural food stores. It is also available in supermarkets in boxes labeled Quaker Unprocessed Bran.

1 ¼	cups all-purpose flour
¼	cup whole wheat flour
1 ¼	teaspoons baking powder
½	teaspoon baking soda
¾	teaspoon salt
1 ¼	teaspoons ground cinnamon
¾	teaspoon ground allspice
½	teaspoon freshly grated nutmeg
7	tablespoons unsalted butter, softened
½	cup plus 2 tablespoons packed dark brown sugar
2	large eggs
2 ½	teaspoons vanilla extract
3	tablespoons unsulphured molasses
¼	cup sour cream
1	cup plus 3 tablespoons buttermilk
1 ½	cups wheat bran
1	cup raisins

1. Adjust oven rack to lower-middle position and heat oven to 375 degrees. Whisk flours, baking powder, baking soda, salt, and spices together in medium bowl; set aside.

2. Cream butter with mixer on medium speed until light and fluffy, 1 to 2 minutes. Add brown sugar, increase speed to medium-high, and beat until combined and fluffy, about 1 minute longer. Add eggs one at a time, beating thoroughly before adding the next. Beat in vanilla, molasses, and sour cream until thoroughly combined and creamy, about 1 minute longer. Reduce speed to low; beat in buttermilk and half the flour mixture until combined, about 1 minute. Beat in remaining flour mixture until incorporated and slightly curdled looking, about 1 minute longer, scraping sides of bowl as necessary. Stir in bran and raisins.

3. Spray 12-cup muffin tin with vegetable cooking spray or coat lightly with butter. Divide batter evenly among cups. Bake until a toothpick inserted into center withdraws cleanly or with a few moist particles adhering to it, about 25 minutes. Set on wire rack to cool slightly, about 5 minutes. Remove muffins from tin and serve warm.

BISCUITS

WHILE MANY PEOPLE THINK OF "BISCUITS" as a single category, there are actually two distinct varieties—soft, fluffy mounds and flaky, high-rising cylinders. If you know which type you prefer, it is easy to tailor your ingredients and cooking method to produce it.

In our testing, we found that the flour you begin with has a great effect on the biscuit you end up with. The main factor here is the proportion of starch to protein in the flour. Low-protein, or "soft," flour encourages a tender, cakelike texture, while high-protein, or "strong," flour promotes crisper, chewier results.

This means that for fluffy biscuits you should use a soft flour, such as White Lily brand (favored for biscuit making throughout the South), or a blend of low-protein, all-purpose flour, such as Pillsbury, and plain cake flour, which is extremely soft. For flaky biscuits, on the other hand, you need dough with a lot of structure to produce a multilayered, well-defined shape, so "strong" flour is called for. For the best results, use a high-protein brand of all-purpose, such as King Arthur, or combine relatively soft Pillsbury all-purpose with bread flour, which is very strong. (See page 416 for more information on the types and properties of flours.)

Fat also plays an important role, since it makes biscuits (and other pastries) more tender, moist, smooth, and tasty. Butter, of course, delivers the best flavor, but lard and shortening make for more tender biscuits, so you have to balance these two factors, again depending on the type of biscuit you want. Since flaky biscuits are handled a fair amount—handling activates gluten and makes a potentially less tender product—we found it best to use two parts butter (for flavor) to one part shortening or lard (for texture). For fluffy biscuits, which are handled less during preparation, you can use all butter without worrying too much about the texture.

We discovered that a proportion of one-half cup fat to two cups of flour provides the best balance of tenderness and richness with structure. If you use less fat, your biscuits will rise well, but they will be tough and dry. If you use more, your biscuits will have a lovely texture but they may end up a bit squat.

After mixing flour and leavening, you must "rub" the fat into the dry ingredients, making a dry, coarse mixture akin to large bread crumbs or rolled oats, with some slightly bigger lumps mixed in. This rubbing may seem unimportant, but in fact it is crucial to proper rising of the biscuits. Gas released by the leavening during baking must have a space in which to collect; if the texture of the dough is homogeneous, the gas will simply dissipate. Melting fat particles create convenient spaces in which the gas can collect, form a bubble, and produce rising. Proper rubbing breaks the fat into tiny bits and disperses it throughout the dough. As the fat melts during baking, its place is taken up by gas and steam, which expand and push the dough up. The wider the dispersal of the fat, the more even the rising of the dough.

If, however, the fat softens and binds with the dry ingredients during rubbing, it forms a pasty goo, the spaces collapse, and the biscuits become leaden. To produce light, airy biscuits, the fat must remain cold and firm, which means rubbing must be deft and quick. Traditionally, biscuit makers pinch the cut-up fat into the dry ingredients, using only their fingertips—never the whole hand, which is too hot—and they pinch hard and fast, practically flinging the little bits of flour and fat into the bowl after each pinch. Less experienced cooks turned to the use of two knives, scraped in opposite directions, or to a bow-shaped pastry blender. We prefer to use the food processor for this task: pulsing the dry ingredients and fat is fast and almost foolproof.

After cutting in the fat, liquid is added and the dough is stirred, just until the ingredients are bound, using a light hand so the gluten will not become activated. Flaky biscuits can be challenging at this point. If the dough is even a bit too dry and firm, the biscuits will fail to rise properly and will be dry. If the dough is too wet and soft, the biscuits will spread and lose their shape. Since dough consistency is critical in flaky biscuits, follow our recipe carefully the first few times you make them, paying particular attention to the feel of the dough.

Fluffy biscuits are best formed by gently batting gobs of dough between lightly floured hands. If the work surface, the dough, and the cutter are generously floured, fluffy biscuits can be rolled and cut; but the softness of the dough makes this a tricky procedure, and the extra flour and handling will make the biscuits heavier and somewhat dense.

Flaky biscuits must be rolled out and cut for proper appearance and texture. For extra flakiness, we shape the dough into a rectangle, fold it up, and roll it a second time. This technique, which is also used to make puff pastry, sandwiches the particles of fat between sheets of dough, which separate into layers during baking. Use a light touch with the rolling pin or the biscuits will be small and tough.

When you begin cutting, so as not to flatten the edges of the biscuits and cause a low or lopsided rise, very lightly grease the cutter and dip it in flour; after the first biscuit has been made, the cutter should be floured (though not greased) before each cut. Press into the dough with one decisive punch and cut as close together and as close to the edges as possible in order to generate few scraps.

It's best to bake both kinds of biscuits on ungreased sheets to give them a firm foundation from which to rise. Spacing them closely gives them support, which improves the rise, and helps keep them moist. (But don't jam the biscuits right up against each other or the ones in the middle will not bake through.) We brush biscuits with plenty of butter, which not only promotes browning and improves flavor but also produces a lovely, tender crust. Brushing with milk gives an even deeper color but leaves a shiny, slightly tough glaze that we find less attractive. Of course, biscuits will also brown, if not quite so well, when not brushed at all.

Because they need quick heat, biscuits are best baked in the middle of the oven. Placed too close to the bottom, they burn on the underside and remain pale on top; set too near the oven roof, they do not rise well because the outside hardens into a shell before the inside has had a chance to rise properly. As soon as they are a light brown, they are done. Be careful, as overcooking will dry them out. Biscuits are always at their best when served as soon as they come out of the oven. The dough, however, may be made some hours in advance and baked when needed; they will still rise well.

Fluffy Biscuits
MAKES I DOZEN BISCUITS

If you are using yogurt instead of buttermilk in this recipe, note that 8 ounces of yogurt equals 1 cup plus 2 tablespoons, not 1 cup as you might expect. Make sure that your oven rack is set at the center position. Baked too low, your biscuits will likely end up with burned bottoms.

- 1 cup all-purpose flour
- 1 cup plain cake flour
- 2 teaspoons baking powder
- ½ teaspoon baking soda
- 1 teaspoon sugar
- ½ teaspoon salt
- 8 tablespoons (1 stick) unsalted butter, chilled and cut into ¼-inch cubes, plus 2 tablespoons melted for brushing tops
- ¾ cup cold buttermilk or ¾ cup plus 2 tablespoons low-fat or whole-milk plain yogurt
- 2–3 tablespoons additional buttermilk (or milk), if needed

1. Adjust oven rack to middle position and heat the oven to 450 degrees.

2. Mix or pulse flours, baking powder, baking soda, sugar, and salt in a large bowl or the workbowl of a food processor fitted with steel blade. With your fingertips, a pastry blender, 2 knives, or steel blade of the food processor, mix, cut, or process butter into the dry ingredients until mixture resembles coarse meal with a few slightly larger butter lumps.

3. If making by hand, stir in buttermilk with a rubber spatula or fork until mixture forms into soft, slightly sticky ball. If dough feels firm and dry bits are not gathering into a ball, sprinkle dough clumps with additional tablespoon of buttermilk (or milk for the yogurt dough). Be careful not to overmix. If using food processor, pulse until dough gathers into moist clumps. Remove from food processor bowl and form into rough ball.

4. With lightly floured hands, divide dough into 12 equal portions. Lightly pat a portion of dough back and forth a few times between floured hands until it begins to form a ball, then pat lightly with cupped hands to form a rough ball. Repeat with remaining dough, placing formed dough rounds 1

inch apart on ungreased cookie sheet. Brush dough tops with melted butter. (May be covered with plastic wrap and refrigerated for up to 2 hours.) Bake until biscuit tops are light brown, 10 to 12 minutes. Serve immediately.

Flaky Biscuits
MAKES 16 BISCUITS

After stirring in the milk, this dough should feel very soft and moist, but you should be able to hold it briefly between lightly floured hands without its sticking. If it turns out wet and sticky, return it to the bowl and sprinkle it with 2 to 4 tablespoons additional flour (of any kind) on all sides, gently patting in the flour with your palm. Let the dough rest another half-minute before removing it to your work surface. It is best to discard the dough that is left over from the second cutting, as biscuits made with thrice-recycled dough tend to be tough and flat. If you don't want to use a biscuit cutter, form the dough into a neat eight-inch square and cut it into little squares or triangles with a knife. This eliminates all scraps and thus all the problems of re-rolling. No matter how they are cut, these biscuits are best served at once, though leftovers may be wrapped and refrigerated for a day, then reheated for a few minutes in a 350-degree oven.

- 2 cups high-protein all-purpose flour, such as King Arthur, or 1 cup low-protein unbleached all-purpose flour, such as Pillsbury, and 1 cup bread flour
- 1 tablespoon baking powder
- ¾ teaspoon salt
- 5 tablespoons unsalted butter, chilled and cut into ¼-inch cubes, plus 2 tablespoons melted for brushing tops
- 3 tablespoons vegetable shortening or lard, chilled
- ¾ cup cold milk

1. Adjust oven rack to middle position and heat oven to 450 degrees.

2. Mix flour, baking powder, and salt in a large bowl or the workbowl of a food processor fitted with steel blade. Add butter; with your fingertips, a pastry blender, 2 knives, or steel blade of a food processor, mix, cut, or process butter and shortening into dry ingredients, until the mixture resembles dry oatmeal.

(Transfer food processor mixture to a large bowl.)

3. Stir in milk with a rubber spatula or fork until dry ingredients are just moistened. Let dough rest for 1 minute, then transfer it to a well-floured work surface.

4. Roll dough into rough 6 x 10-inch rectangle. With long edge of dough facing you, fold in both short ends of dough so that they meet in center; then fold dough in half by width, forming a package of dough four layers thick. Once again, roll the dough into a 6 x 10-inch rectangle, about ½ inch thick.

5. Using a lightly greased and floured 2-inch cutter, stamp, with one decisive punch per round, 4 rows of 3 dough rounds, cutting them close together to generate as few scraps as possible. Dip cutter into flour before each new cut. Push the scraps of dough together so that their edges join; firmly pinch the edges with fingertips to make a partial seal. Pat the dough into small rectangle, fold it as before, and re-roll until ½ inch thick. Cut out 3 or 4 more biscuits.

6. Place dough rounds 1½ inches apart on an ungreased baking sheet; brush dough tops with melted butter. (May be covered with plastic wrap and refrigerated up to 3 hours.)

7. Bake until biscuits are lightly browned, 10 to 12 minutes. Serve immediately.

➤ VARIATIONS

Cheddar Biscuits

Decrease butter to 5 tablespoons in Fluffy Biscuits or to 3 in Flaky Biscuits. After the fat has been cut or processed into the flour, add 1 cup shredded extra-sharp cheddar cheese (4 ounces); toss lightly, then stir in liquid.

Herb Biscuits

Split these and use them as a base for rich scrambled eggs or chicken stews, or serve them as biscuits plain and simple.

Follow recipe for Fluffy Biscuits, adding 3 tablespoons minced fresh parsley leaves or 2 tablespoons parsley and 1 tablespoon of either minced fresh tarragon or dill leaves after the fat has been cut or processed into the flour.

SCONES

SCONES, THE QUINTESSENTIAL TEA CAKE OF the British Isles, are delicate, fluffy biscuits, which may come as a surprise to Americans—the clunky mounds of oven-baked sweetened dough called rock cakes by the English are often called scones in our restaurants and coffee shops. Unlike rock cakes, in which dough is dropped from a spoon onto a baking sheet, traditional scones are quickly rolled or patted out and cut into rounds or wedges.

Almost all scone recipes call for the same proportion of dry to liquid ingredients—2 cups of dry to ¾ cup of wet. We started our testing by focusing on the flour. We made a composite recipe with bread flour, with all-purpose flour, and with cake flour. The differences in outcome were astonishing. The scones made with bread flour were heavy and tough. The scones made with all-purpose flour were lighter and much more flavorful. Cake flour produced scones that were doughy in the center, with a raw taste and poor texture.

After trying scones made with butter and with lard, we decided we preferred the rich flavor of butter. (If we made scones commercially we might reconsider that; day-old scones made with lard hold up better. The preservative effects of different fats, along with lower cost, may be why store-bought scones are often made with margarine or other hydrogenated fats.) Although the amount of solid fat can be varied, most recipes use ¼ cup fat to 2 cups flour, and we found that proportion to be just right.

The choice of liquid can also profoundly affect the flavor of a scone. It is possible to use skim milk, but if you're cooking with butter, why bother? We tested various liquids and found that milk made the best scones that were tender yet still light. Cream makes deliciously rich scones that are tender but quite heavy, more like cake than a biscuit. We tried adding an egg to the dough but found that this, too, made the scones too heavy and rich.

As for leavener, we have found that commercial double-acting baking powder can have a harsh flavor in scones. It also tends to be used in too much quantity in many scone recipes. Therefore, we use homemade, single-acting baking powder, made with two parts (one teaspoon) cream of tartar to one part (one-half teaspoon) baking soda; it produces a scone that is sweeter and less soapy-flavored than those made with commercial double-acting baking powder.

In traditional recipes, one to two tablespoons of sugar is enough to sweeten an entire batch of scones. American scones tend to be far sweeter than the British versions, which are usually sweetened with toppings such as jam. Americans seem to eat their scones like muffins, without anything more than a smear of butter, so the sweetness is baked in. We prefer the British approach, but you may increase the sugar if you like, adding up to ¼ cup.

Finally, all scones can be glazed before baking with a brush dipped in a little beaten egg or milk. Glazes don't contribute to flavor, but they do deepen the color and make the scones look most appetizing. Glazing also makes it easier for sugar to stick, if sprinkling the surface appeals to you. In addition to milk or beaten egg, scones may also be glazed with heavy cream.

The line from "Patty-cake, Patty-cake" that demands "make me a cake as fast as you can" must refer to scones. The secret to making a good scone is to work the dough quickly and lightly and to immediately bake it in a preheated oven. Speed is of the essence to prevent toughening of the dough; it is also important when using a homemade single-acting baking powder for a leavener, since you want the powder to do its work in the oven, not before baking. The whole process shouldn't take more than 30 minutes, from mixing the ingredients together to pulling the finished scones out of the oven.

Scones can be mixed by hand or with a food processor. (The processor is used to cut fat into flour; minimal hand mixing is required afterward.) We found machine-made dough to be identical to that made entirely by hand.

Do remember to thoroughly preheat the oven, as it is the intense heat that makes the scones rise. Other guidelines are to have the dough as wet as you can handle and, when using a scone or biscuit cutter, don't wiggle it—just place it on the dough and push straight down.

Sweet Milk Scones
MAKES 8 OR 9 SCONES

Work the dough quickly, don't overmix, and put the dough rounds into the heated oven as soon as possible. If you like, brush scones with a little beaten egg or milk just before they go into the oven. Scones are best served warm and fresh, split open, and topped with thick homemade strawberry or raspberry jam and clotted cream (or crème fraîche, mascarpone, or whipped cream).

2	cups all-purpose flour
1	teaspoon cream of tartar
½	teaspoon baking soda
½	teaspoon salt
1–2	tablespoons sugar (optional)
4	tablespoons unsalted butter, chilled and cut into ½-inch pieces
¾	cup whole milk

1. Adjust oven rack to middle position and heat oven to 450 degrees.

2. Whisk flour, cream of tartar, baking soda, salt, and sugar (if using) together in large bowl, or measure into workbowl of a food processor fitted with steel blade; pulse until blended. With fingertips, pastry blender, 2 knives, or steel blade of a food processor, cut or process butter into flour mixture until mixture resembles coarse meal with a few slightly larger butter lumps.

3. If making by hand, make a well in the center and pour in milk. Working quickly, blend ingredients together with a rubber spatula into a soft, slightly wet dough. If using a food processor, pour milk though feed tube; pulse until dough just starts to gather into a rough ball (do not overprocess or scones will be tough). Turn dough onto a well-floured work surface.

4. Quickly roll dough to thickness of ½ inch. Use a lightly greased and floured 3-inch biscuit cutter to stamp dough with one decisive punch, cutting close together to generate as few scraps as possible. Dip cutter into flour as often as necessary to keep dough from sticking. Push scraps of dough together so that edges join; firmly pinch edges with fingertips to make a partial seal. Pat this remaining dough to ½ inch thick; continue to cut 3-inch rounds. Place

dough rounds 1½ inches apart on a greased baking sheet. Bake until scones are lightly browned, 10 to 12 minutes. Serve immediately.

➤ VARIATIONS
Scones with Dried Fruit
Follow recipe for Sweet Milk Scones, adding ⅓ to ½ cup raisins or currants to dry ingredients.

Ginger Scones
Follow recipe for Sweet Milk Scones, adding ½ cup chopped crystallized ginger to dry ingredients.

Cheese Scones
These make an excellent accompaniment to salads or soups.

Follow recipe for Sweet Milk Scones, omitting sugar. Stir or pulse in ½ cup grated aged cheddar or Cheshire cheese just before adding wet ingredients.

Citrus Honey-Nut Scones
MAKES 9 OR 10 SCONES
Follow recipe for Sweet Milk Scones, adding ¼ cup finely chopped walnuts and 2 tablespoons minced lemon zest to dry ingredients and omitting sugar. If using food processor, pulse walnuts with dry ingredients, then pulse in the minced lemon zest just before adding the butter. Replace milk with mixture of ½ cup milk, ¼ cup orange juice, and 2 tablespoons honey.

POPOVERS

POPOVERS SEEM MAGICAL. MADE FROM A simple, thin batter of eggs, flour, milk, and melted butter, they pop up in the oven to triple their original height with no help from leavening of any sort. (The recipe list for popovers reads more like a crêpe batter, but because they are served in the fashion of muffins and biscuits, we have included them in this chapter.)

So how does a batter without any chemical leavening rise so high? This amazing feat is actually the result of two factors. A hot oven and a pan that is deeper than it is wide cause the steam released during baking to make a giant bubble, which is contained by a structure created by the starches and proteins in the batter.

We set out to discover how to make the ideal popover: one that pops up high with a thin, crusty exterior and a relatively dry interior with threads of custardy dough. Surprisingly in a recipe so simple, this meant testing a large number of variations of both ingredients and technique.

First we looked for the best ratio of eggs to milk and flour. Starting with two large eggs, we worked our way up to four extra-large eggs while keeping the amount of milk and flour constant. We found that two extra-large eggs provided enough fat and protein to pop reliably and well without overwhelming the popover with an eggy flavor.

Next we tested the butter. Some recipes call for up to four tablespoons of melted butter in the pan. But after varying the quantity from less than one tablespoon up to the full four tablespoons, we concluded that only a thin film of butter was needed in the pan.

We then tried making popovers with and without melted butter in the batter. Both ways worked, and our taste panel was evenly divided on which method tasted better. Those who like a custard texture preferred the butterless version; those who prefer a crisp exterior and maximum pop liked the buttered batter. We decided that a batter with a minimal amount of melted butter (one tablespoon) produced the most consistent and best-tasting result.

With the proportions of ingredients set, we tested the recipe again to see how it would change with four different kinds of flour: bleached all-purpose flour, unbleached all-purpose flour, cake flour, and whole wheat flour. Bleached and unbleached all-purpose flour both gave good results, while whole wheat and cake flour both produced heavy muffins that never really popped.

With the ingredient list completed, we turned to other variables in the recipe—oven temperature, baking time, and baking container.

We started by sticking to one oven temperature—400 degrees. But after much experimentation, we found that the optimum was baking first at 450 for 20 minutes to achieve maximum height and then at 350 for 15 to 20 minutes more to achieve the right texture. Many recipes recommend piercing just-baked popovers with a sharp knife and putting them back in the oven for a few minutes to dry the interior and thus prevent collapse. We found this to be unnecessary when popovers are cooked using the two-temperature method.

To test the effect of the pan, we tried a 6-bowl popover pan; a 6-bowl crown muffin pan; deep porcelain ramekins; and the old tried-and-true 12-hole muffin tin. The surprise winner was the humble muffin tin. Deep, six-bowl popover pans (like the tinned-steel and Silverstone models) use the same amount of batter as a standard, 12-hole muffin tin. But each "hole" in the popover pans is larger, and the batter is poured into any pan up to somewhere between the half and two-thirds mark. What we discovered was that a given amount of batter would produce the same size popovers whether it was portioned out to 6 deep bowls or 12 shallower ones! This means that the popovers cooked in the 12-hole muffin tin popped twice as much as the other popovers. Therefore, the popovers made in the muffin tin were lighter, and when opened, their interiors were indistinguishable from the heavier popovers.

We also tried cooking popovers in both hot and cold pans and in preheated and cold ovens. Surprisingly, all variations worked, although there is some sacrifice in pop when using cold pans in a cold oven. The best results came from room-temperature batter poured into sizzling-hot pans and cooked in a preheated oven.

Popovers

MAKES 1 DOZEN POPOVERS

This batter can be made ahead and refrigerated for up to four days. If you're making it ahead, bring it to room temperature and stir well before pouring it into a hot pan.

1	cup all-purpose flour
1/4	teaspoon salt
1	cup whole milk
2	extra-large eggs
1	tablespoon unsalted butter, melted, plus additional melted butter, vegetable oil, or vegetable oil spray for greasing pan

1. Adjust oven rack to low position and heat oven to 450 degrees. Place empty muffin or popover tin in oven to heat while making batter.

2. Whisk flour and salt together in medium bowl.

In a 2-cup Pyrex measuring cup, lightly whisk together milk, eggs, and butter. Pour wet ingredients into dry ingredients all at once; whisk until just blended. Pour batter into measuring cup for easy pouring.

3. Remove hot pan from oven; lightly grease interior of each cup and pan rim.

4. Fill each cup half-full with batter. Bake without opening oven door for 20 minutes. Lower heat to 350 degrees and continue to bake until popovers are rich brown in color, 15 to 20 minutes longer. Serve warm.

CORNBREAD

WHILE ALL CORNBREADS ARE QUICK TO make and bake, there are two very distinct types: Northern and Southern. Southerners use 100 percent white cornmeal, and they like their cornbread crumbly, dry, and flat—about one inch thick. Most Northerners prefer sweeter, lighter, and higher golden cornbreads, which they achieve by adding a little sugar and combining white flour and yellow cornmeal. Both types of cornbread sport a brown crust, although Southern cornbread crusts are also crisp and crunchy.

Since there are cooks who are attached to each style, we decided to develop recipes for two kinds of cornbread. One should be tender and fluffy but not too sweet, something akin to cake but not too rich. This Northern-style cornbread would be good enough to eat on its own. For Southern-style cornbread, we envisioned something drier, more crumbly. It would be perfect with a bowl of soup or a pot of greens. For both recipes, choosing the right cornmeal would be crucial.

Large commercial mills use huge steel rollers to grind dent corn (a hard, dry corn) into cornmeal. This is how Quaker, the leading supermarket brand, is produced. But some smaller mills scattered around the United States grind with millstones; this product is called stone-ground cornmeal. (If water is used as an energy source, the cornmeal may be labeled "water-ground"). Stone-ground cornmeal is usually a bit coarser than cornmeal processed through steel rollers.

Besides differences in milling methods, smaller

millers often choose not to degerm, or remove all the germ, cleanly. This makes their product closer to a whole-grain cornmeal. If the color is uniform, the germ has been removed. A stone-ground cornmeal with some germ will have flecks that are both lighter and darker than the predominant color, whether that's yellow or white.

In our tests, we found the texture of cornbreads made with stone-ground meals to be more interesting, since the cornmeals were not of a uniform grind. More important, we found that cornbreads made with stone-ground cornmeal tasted much better than those made with the standard Quaker cornmeal.

The higher moisture and oil content of stone-ground cornmeal causes it to go rancid within weeks. If you buy some, wrap it tightly in plastic or put it into a moisture-proof container, then refrigerate or freeze it. Degerminated cornmeals, such as Quaker, keep for a year, if stored in a dry, cool place.

NORTHERN CORNBREAD

IN PERFECTING HOMEMADE NORTHERN cornbread, we aimed for a high-rising, moist bread, one with a rich corn taste and handsome golden color. Among other things, we wanted to find the right proportion of cornmeal to flour, the correct type and amount of chemical leavening, and the ideal amount of sugar. During our baking of 43 batches of cornbread using varying ingredients, mixing techniques, and baking temperatures and times, we uncovered some surprises.

In testing aspects of the dry ingredients, we found that the proportion of cornmeal to flour was key. The best flavor, texture, and rise resulted from a 1:1 ratio of cornmeal to all-purpose flour. If we added more cornmeal, the texture coarsened, and the cornbread baked flatter. Using more flour than cornmeal resulted in a less intense corn flavor and a cake-like texture.

All-purpose, unbleached flour easily won out over plain cake flour and whole wheat flour. All-purpose flour yielded the tallest cornbreads. Cake flour produced a doughy cornbread that collapsed. Whole wheat flour masked some corn flavor and made the cornbread too dense and gritty.

We had thought we would like a fairly sweet Northern cornbread. We sure changed our opinion fast. The recipes we examined ranged from one tablespoon of sugar to eight, so we started with two and adjusted up and down. More sugar made the cornbread taste like a dessert. In test batches without sugar, though, we missed it. In the end, four teaspoons of sugar was the right amount for our cornbread.

The leavening we used would depend on whether we used milk or buttermilk in the mixture, so we postponed a final decision on that dry ingredient. Finally, in tests with and without salt, we found that adding one-half teaspoon helped bring out the corn flavor and balanced the sweetness.

We had now assembled the dry ingredients. At this point, most cornbread recipes instruct the cook to add the wet ingredients-egg, milk, and fat-to the dry ones. We first tested for the number of eggs. Two eggs tasted the best. Three eggs rated as too eggy, and one left things a bit dry. The eggs added moisture and helped the cornbread rise higher; the yolks contributed to the golden interior and rich taste.

Our next set of tests focused on buttermilk and milk. Buttermilk contributed a rich, luscious taste that highlighted the corn flavor, although its use also resulted in a coarser and heavier texture. Buttermilk also placed the cornbread squarely in the bread corner—it no longer hinted at dessert. Cornbreads made with milk tasted fine but lacked richness, although the lighter texture and softer yellow color were appealing. To remedy this, we decided to use a combination of buttermilk and milk. A half-milk/half-buttermilk combination baked into the best cornbread, with a wonderful taste, light texture, handsome yellow-gold interior, high rise, and a brown crust with some crunch.

Next, we tested the fats. Butter outranked the other contenders. Vegetable oil, vegetable shortening, and margarine tasted boring and lackluster, and lard seemed out of place in this recipe. A couple of tasters enjoyed the flavor of bacon fat at first, but after a few more bites found it overpowering. We discovered that we liked a cornbread made with butter, but not too much. Two tablespoons per batch was enough. More butter was too heavy and started to interfere with the corn flavor. Cornbread made with less lacked richness.

Most recipes instruct the cook to add the melted

butter last. Is this necessary? To find out, we tried several experiments. First we creamed the softened butter, then added the remaining ingredients. The top of this cornbread looked pebbled and not very appetizing. Next, we melted the butter, then stirred in all the other ingredients. Now the cornbread was heavy and too moist. Finally, we added the melted butter last. This method produced the best-tasting and most attractive cornbread. We detected no difference when we used hot or warm melted butter as long as we mixed it in fast.

Armed with our basic ingredients and their order into the mixing bowl, we then asked ourselves two questions. How long do we mix the batter, and with what? We learned to mix quickly, just to combine the dry and wet ingredients (if overmixed the cornbread will be tough), and added another 10 or 12 strokes to distribute the melted butter quickly and evenly. As for the proper tool, we found that a fork left clumps of dry cornmeal at the bottom of the bowl, while a whisk, egg beaters, or electric mixer was overkill. We rated a wooden spoon as the best and easiest-to-use tool.

To obtain the light texture and high rise of Northern cornbread, some type of chemical leavening is required. As we experimented with baking soda and baking powder, the two typical leavenings for cornbread, we discovered that three or four teaspoons of baking powder produced the tallest cornbreads, but that these breads were lacking in corny taste. Cornbreads made with 100 percent baking soda sported darker, more deeply golden brown top crusts and a stronger array of interior colors: a deeper golden or yellow overall color, with flecks of deep orange and yellow.

Hoping to produce a bread with the color provided by baking soda and the high rise caused by baking powder, we combined the two chemical leavenings. After tinkering with various amounts of each, we found that two teaspoons of baking powder plus one-half teaspoon of baking soda yielded a tall rise, golden color, and the best taste. When we increased the baking soda, we noted a mushy, soapy taste, which meant that the available acid in the batter was not neutralizing the extra leavening, so we stuck with the one-half teaspoon.

With our recipe now in hand, we looked at two final variables: the type of baking pan and oven temperature. Our goal was a Northern cornbread with an evenly browned crust and a moist interior.

A crisp, crunchy crust is an essential feature of Southern-style cornbread, so a cast-iron skillet is the preferred pan for cooking it. For the more tender Northern cornbreads, however, metal baking pans are the best choice. We tried using a glass pan, but the cornbread overbaked and became hard around the edges, a common problem with glass pans, which tend to overheat.

As for oven temperature, we found that cornbreads baked at 350 degrees and 375 degrees had very thick, heavy crusts because they took a long time to form. A 425-degree oven worked best for our Northern cornbread. At this higher temperature, the crust formed more quickly and the whole cornbread baked faster, resulting in a crisper crust and lighter-textured cornbread.

Golden Northern Cornbread
MAKES 9 SERVINGS

This cornbread is moist and light, with the rich taste of corn. Use stone-ground yellow cornmeal for the best taste and texture. Stone-ground cornmeal can be recognized by its light and dark flecks.

1	cup yellow cornmeal, preferably stone-ground
1	cup all-purpose flour
2	teaspoons baking powder
1/2	teaspoon baking soda
4	teaspoons sugar
1/2	teaspoon salt
2	large eggs
2/3	cup buttermilk
2/3	cup milk
2	tablespoons unsalted butter, melted, plus extra softened butter for greasing pan

1. Adjust oven rack to center position and heat oven to 425 degrees. Grease a 9-inch square metal pan.

2. Whisk cornmeal, flour, baking powder, baking soda, sugar, and salt together in large bowl. Push dry ingredients up side of bowl to make a well.

3. Crack eggs into well and stir lightly with wooden spoon, then add buttermilk and milk. Stir

wet and dry ingredients quickly until almost combined. Add melted butter; stir until ingredients are just combined.

4. Pour batter into greased pan. Bake until top is golden brown and lightly cracked and edges have pulled away from side of pan, about 25 minutes.

5. Transfer pan to wire rack to cool slightly, 5 to 10 minutes. Cut cornbread into squares and serve warm. (Pan can be wrapped in foil up to 1 day. Reheat cornbread in a 350-degree oven for 10 to 15 minutes.)

➤ VARIATIONS

Golden Cornbread with Cheddar

Follow recipe for Golden Northern Cornbread, omitting sugar. After adding butter, quickly fold in 1 cup (2½ ounces) shredded cheddar or Monterey Jack cheese.

Golden Cornbread with Chiles

Follow recipe for Golden Northern Cornbread, omitting sugar. After adding butter, quickly fold in 1 small jalapeño, stemmed, seeded, and minced, for mild chile flavor. For more heat, use up to two jalapeños that have been stemmed and minced but not seeded.

Golden Cornbread with Bacon

To end up with the ½ cup bacon needed for this recipe, cut 8 ounces sliced bacon into small dice, then fry in large skillet until well-browned and crisp. Drain, cool, then set aside until ready to fold into batter.

Follow recipe for Golden Northern Cornbread, omitting sugar. After adding butter, quickly fold in ½ cup crumbled bacon bits.

SOUTHERN CORNBREAD

ALTHOUGH THE TWO INGREDIENT LISTS MAY look similar, the cornbreads of the North and South are as different as Boston and Birmingham. White, not yellow, is the cornmeal of choice for Southern-style cornbread. Unlike Northerners, Southerners use only trace amounts of flour, if any, and if sugar is included it is treated like salt, to be measured out in teaspoons rather than by the cup. Buttermilk moistens, bacon drippings enrich, and a combination of baking powder and soda provides lift.

Classic Southern cornbread batter is poured into a scorching hot, greased cast-iron skillet, which causes it to develop a thin, shattery-crisp crust as the bread bakes. At its best, this bread is moist and tender, with the warm fragrance of the cornfield and the subtle flavor of the dairy in every bite. It is the best possible accompaniment to soups, salads, chilis, and stews. So we set out to create a recipe for it that would be foolproof.

We began by testing 11 different cornmeals in one simple Southern cornbread recipe. Before the cornmeal tests, we would have bet that color was a regional idiosyncrasy that had little to do with flavor. But tasting proved otherwise. Cornbreads made with yellow cornmeal consistently had a more potent corn flavor than those made with white meal.

Although we didn't want Southern cornbread to taste like dessert, we wondered whether a little sugar might enhance the corn flavor. So we made three batches—one with no sugar, one with two teaspoons, and one with a heaping tablespoon. The higher-sugar bread was really too sweet for Southern cornbread, but 2 teaspoons of sugar seemed to enhance the natural sweetness of the corn without calling attention to itself.

Most Southern-style cornbread batters are made with just buttermilk, but we found recipes calling for the full range of acidic and sweet dairy products—buttermilk, sour cream, yogurt, milk, and cream—and made batches with each of them. We still loved the pure, straightforward flavor of the buttermilk-based cornbread, but the batch made with sour cream was actually more tasty and baked into a more attractive shape.

At this point we began to feel a little uneasy about where we were taking this bread. A couple of teaspoons of sugar might be overlooked; yellow cornmeal was a big blow; but the sour cream felt like we were crossing the border, giving up our claim to a recipe for Southern cornbread.

So far all of our testing had been done with a composite recipe under which most Southern cornbread recipes seemed to fall. There were two recipes, however, that didn't quite fit the mold—one very rich and one very lean—and now seemed like the right time to give them a try.

After rejecting the rich version as closer to spoon-bread, a soufflelike dish, than cornbread, we went to the other extreme. In this simple version, boiling water is stirred into the cornmeal, then modest amounts of milk, egg, butter, salt, and baking powder are stirred into the resulting cornmeal mush and the whole thing is baked. So simple, so lean, so humble, so backwater, this recipe would have been easy to pass over. But given our options at this point, we decided to give it a quick test. Just one bite completely changed the direction of our pursuit. Unlike anything we had tasted so far, the crumb of this cornbread was incredibly moist and fine and bursting with corn flavor, all with no flour and virtually no fat.

We were pleased, but since the foundation of this bread was cornmeal mush, the crumb was actually more mushy than moist. In addition, the baking powder, the only dry ingredient left, got stirred into the wet batter at the end. This just didn't feel right.

After a few unsuccessful attempts to make this cornbread less mushy, we started thinking that this great idea was a bust. In a last attempt to salvage it, we decided to make mush out of only half the cornmeal and mix the remaining cornmeal with the leavener. To our relief, the bread made this way was much improved. Decreasing the mush even further—from a half to a third of the cornmeal—gave us exactly what we were looking for. We made the new, improved cornbread with buttermilk and mixed a bit of baking soda with the baking powder, and it tasted even better. Finally our recipe was starting to feel Southern again. Although we still preferred yellow cornmeal and a sprinkle of sugar, we had achieved a moist, tender, rather fine-crumbed bread without flour, and a nicely shaped one at that, without sour cream, thus avoiding two ingredients that would have interfered with the strong corn flavor we wanted.

With this new recipe in hand, we performed a few final tests. Our recipe called for 1 tablespoon of butter, but many Southern cornbreads call for no more fat than is needed to grease the pan. We tried vegetable oil, peanut oil, shortening, butter, and bacon drippings, as well as a batch with no fat at all. To our delight, the cornbread with no added fat was as moist and delicious as the other breads. Butter and bacon drippings, however, were pleasant flavor additions, so we kept a little in our recipe.

Before conducting these cornbread tests, we didn't think it was possible to bake cornbread in too hot an oven, but after tasting breads baked on the bottom rack of a 475-degree oven, we found that a dark brown crust makes bitter bread. We moved the rack up a notch, reduced the oven temperature to 450 degrees, and were thus able to cook many loaves of bread and pans of muffins to golden brown perfection.

One final question: Do you need to heat up the skillet before adding the batter? If you're not a Southerner, the answer is no. Although the bread will not be as crisp in an unheated pan, it will ultimately brown up with a longer baking time. If you are a Southerner, of course, the answer is yes. More than the color of the meal or the presence of sugar or flour, cornbread becomes Southern when the batter hits the hot fat in a cast-iron skillet.

Southern Cornbread

MAKES 8 SERVINGS

Unlike its sweet, cakey Northern counterpart, Southern cornbread is thin, crusty, and decidedly savory. Though some styles of Southern cornbread are dry and crumbly, we favor this dense, moist, tender version. Cornmeal mush of just the right texture is essential to this bread. Make sure that the water is at a rapid boil when it is added to the cornmeal. Though we prefer to make cornbread in a preheated cast-iron skillet, a 9-inch round cake pan or 9-inch square baking pan, greased lightly with butter and not preheated, will also produce acceptable results if you double the recipe and bake the bread for 25 minutes.

4	teaspoons bacon drippings or 1 teaspoon vegetable oil plus 1 tablespoon melted butter
1	cup yellow cornmeal, preferably stone-ground
2	teaspoons sugar
1/2	teaspoon salt
1	teaspoon baking powder
1/4	teaspoon baking soda
1/3	cup rapidly boiling water
3/4	cup buttermilk
1	large egg, beaten lightly

1. Adjust oven rack to lower-middle position and heat oven to 450 degrees. Set 8-inch cast-iron skillet with bacon fat (or vegetable oil) in heating oven.

2. Measure ⅓ cup cornmeal into medium bowl. Whisk remaining cornmeal, sugar, salt, baking powder, and baking soda together in small bowl; set aside.

3. Pour boiling water all at once into the ⅓ cup cornmeal; stir to make a stiff mush. Whisk in buttermilk gradually, breaking up lumps until smooth, then whisk in egg. When oven is preheated and skillet very hot, stir dry ingredients into mush mixture until just moistened. Carefully remove skillet from oven. Pour hot bacon fat from pan (or melted butter) into batter and stir to incorporate, then quickly pour batter into heated skillet. Bake until golden brown, about 20 minutes. Remove from oven and instantly turn cornbread onto wire rack; cool for 5 minutes, then serve immediately.

Banana Bread

OVERRIPE BANANAS ON THE KITCHEN counter are an excellent excuse to make banana bread. However, many banana breads are flat, gritty, or heavy. Worse, some loaves taste only remotely of bananas. Good banana bread is soft and tender with plenty of banana flavor and crunchy toasted walnuts. It should be moist and light, something so delicious that you look forward to the bananas on the counter turning soft and mushy.

In our testing, we found it very important to pay close attention to the condition of the bananas. Sweet, older, darkly speckled bananas infused the bread with both moisture and flavor, which meant that the bread, whether still warm or day-old, succeeded with less butter (minus two tablespoons) than the amount used in most recipes (a half-cup).

We also experimented with the way we prepared the banana for the batter: slightly mashed, mashed well, and pureed. Loaves with slightly mashed bananas left chunks of fruit. We preferred a smoother texture, but pureeing the bananas turned out to be a bad idea, because the batter did not rise as well. Leavener probably escaped before the thin batter developed enough structure to trap gases. Bananas well-mashed by hand kept the batter thick.

We still wanted more moisture in the bread, so we tried mixing in milk, buttermilk, sour cream, and plain yogurt. Sour cream added richness, but it also made for a heavy texture and an unattractive, pebbly crust. Milk added little flavor and created a slick crust. Buttermilk added a delightful tang, but yogurt let the banana flavor stand out. And because yogurt has more solids than buttermilk, it made for a somewhat more solid loaf, which we preferred.

While the added yogurt softened the bread's crumb, we still sought a more delicate, open grain. So we decided to experiment with various mixing methods to see how they affected the final texture. We considered the quick bread method (dry ingredients mixed in one bowl, liquids in another, with the two then gently stirred together) and the creaming method (butter and sugar creamed together, dry and wet ingredients then alternately mixed in).

The creaming method created a soft texture (reminiscent of butter cake) and good volume from the whipped sugar and butter. However, its lighter color looked less appetizing next to the golden-brown loaf achieved with the quick bread method. The quick bread method produced a delicate texture, too, and the less consistent crumb looked hearty and delicious. It also rose more than the creamed loaf. All in all, it was a better choice.

Take caution when mixing, though. When we stirred the wet and the dry ingredients into a smooth batter, the loaves turned out small and tough. Flour contains protein, and when protein mixes with water, gluten develops. The more you stir with a spoon, the more the gluten proteins arrange into long, orderly bundles. These bundles create an elastic batter that resists changing shape and cannot rise as well. To minimize gluten development, fold together the wet and dry ingredients gently, just until the dry ingredients are moistened. The batter should still be thick and chunky, but without any streaks of unincorporated flour.

Banana Bread

MAKES ONE 9-INCH LOAF

Greasing and flouring only the bottom of a regular loaf pan causes the bread to cling to the sides and rise higher. If using a nonstick loaf pan, on which the sides are very slick, grease and flour the sides as well as the bottom. Either way, use a loaf pan that measures nine inches long, five inches across, and three inches deep.

9-22-02
I used pecans
un toasted &
no fat lemon yogurt

MUFFINS, BISCUITS, AND QUICK BREADS

2   cups all-purpose flour

¾   cup sugar

¾   teaspoon baking soda

½   teaspoon salt

1¼   cups toasted walnuts, chopped coarse (about 1 cup)

3   very ripe, soft, darkly speckled large bananas, mashed well (about 1½ cups)

¼   cup plain yogurt

2   large eggs, beaten lightly

6   tablespoons butter, melted and cooled

1   teaspoon vanilla extract

1. Adjust oven rack to lower-middle position and heat oven to 350 degrees. Grease and flour bottom only of regular loaf pan, or grease and flour bottom and sides of nonstick loaf pan; set aside. *Did sides*.

2. Whisk flour, sugar, baking soda, salt, and walnuts together in large bowl; set aside.

3. Mix mashed bananas, yogurt, eggs, butter, and vanilla with wooden spoon in medium bowl. Lightly fold banana mixture into dry ingredients with rubber spatula until just combined and batter looks thick and chunky. Scrape batter into prepared loaf pan; bake until loaf is golden brown and toothpick inserted in center comes out clean, about 55 minutes. Cool in pan for 5 minutes, then transfer to wire rack. Serve warm or at room temperature.

➤ VARIATIONS

Banana-Chocolate Bread

Follow recipe for Banana Bread, reducing sugar to 10 tablespoons and mixing 2½ ounces grated bittersweet chocolate (a heaping ½ cup) into dry ingredients.

Banana-Coconut Bread with Macadamia Nuts

Adjust oven rack to middle position and heat oven to 350 degrees. Toast ½ cup flaked, sweetened coconut and 1 cup chopped macadamia nuts on small cookie sheet, stirring every 2 minutes, until golden brown, about 6 minutes. Follow recipe for Banana Bread, substituting toasted macadamias and coconut for walnuts.

Orange-Spice Banana Bread

Follow recipe for Banana Bread, adding 1 teaspoon ground cinnamon, ¼ teaspoon grated nutmeg, and 2 tablespoons grated orange zest to dry ingredients.

IRISH SODA BREAD

RICH, SWEET AMERICAN-STYLE IRISH SODA bread is filled with raisins and caraway seed. It is delicious, but its uses are limited to snacking. Authentic Irish soda bread has a tender, dense crumb and rough-textured, crunchy crust. It is versatile enough to be served with butter and jam at breakfast, for sandwiches at lunch, or alongside the evening meal. We set out to devise a recipe for this leaner, more savory style of soda bread.

As we looked over a multitude of recipes for soda bread, we found that they fell into two categories. The American versions contained eggs, butter, and sugar in varying amounts along with caraway seed, raisins, and a multitude of other flavorings. But most Irish cookbooks combined only four ingredients: flour (white and/or whole wheat), baking soda, salt, and buttermilk.

Flour, being the predominant ingredient, seemed like a good place to start in our investigative baking. Because of Ireland's climate, the wheat grown there is a "soft," or low-protein, variety. While not suitable for strong European-style yeast breads, this flour is perfect for chemically leavened breads. This is basically because flour with a lower protein content produces a finer crumb and more tender product, key for breads that don't have the light texture provided when yeast is used as the leavener.

After suffering through several tough, heavy loaves made with unbleached all-purpose flour, we started exploring different proportions of cake flour—a low-protein flour—and all-purpose flour. And, in fact, the bread did become more tender and a little lighter with the addition of some cake flour. As the ratio of cake to all-purpose exceeded 1:1, however, the bread became much more compact and heavy, with an undesirable mouthfeel: 1 cup of cake flour to 3 cups of bleached all-purpose flour proved best.

Because the liquid-to-dry ratio is important in determining dough texture and bread moistness, we decided to test buttermilk next. (We also knew that the amount of this acidic liquid would have a direct effect on the amount of baking soda we would be able to use. As mentioned when discussing other recipes, baking soda reacts with acids such as those in buttermilk to provide leavening; however, if there is too much soda, some remains intact in the bread, giving it a slightly metallic taste.) As it turned out, bread made with 1¾ or 1⅔ cups of buttermilk produced bread that was doughy, almost gummy. With 1½ cups, the dough was firmer yet still moist—and the resulting bread was no longer doughy. (If you don't have buttermilk on hand, yogurt can be substituted for an equally delicious bread with a slightly rougher crust and lighter texture.)

With the amount of buttermilk decided upon, we were now ready to explore the amount and type of leavening used. After trying various combinations of baking soda, baking powder, and cream of tartar, we found that 1½ teaspoons of soda, combined with an equal amount of cream of tartar, provided just the right amount of lift for a bread that was light but not airy. Relying on cream of tartar (rather than the acidity in the buttermilk) to react with the baking soda allows the tangy buttermilk flavor to come through.

Unfortunately, the flavor of these basic loaves was mediocre at best, lacking depth and dimension, and they were also a bit tough. Traditionally, very small amounts of sugar and/or butter are sometimes added to soda bread, so, starting with sugar, we baked loaves with one and two tablespoons. Two tablespoons of sugar added just the flavor balance that was needed without making the bread sweet. It was only with the introduction of butter, though, that the loaves began to lose their toughness and become outstanding. Still, we really wanted to maintain the integrity of this basic bread and avoid making it too rich. After trying tests with from one to four tablespoons of unsalted butter, two tablespoons proved a clear winner. This bread was tender but not crumbly, compact but not heavy. More than two tablespoons of butter began to shift the flavor balance of the bread and add unnecessary richness.

We were getting very close to our goal, but the crust was still too hard, thick, and crumbly. We wanted crunch, but crispness and tenderness as well.

In our research, we came upon various techniques for modifying the crust. Some dealt with the way the bread was baked, while others concentrated on how the bread was treated after baking. Trying to inhibit the formation of a thick crust by covering the bread with a bowl during the first 30 minutes of baking helped some, but the resulting bread took longer to bake and was paler and uneven in color. Using a large flowerpot and clay dish to simulate a cloche (a covered earthenware dish specifically designed for baking bread) again gave us a bread that didn't color well, even with both preheating the tray and buttering the dough.

But the next test, which, by no coincidence, closely simulated historical cooking methods for Irish soda bread, was a breakthrough. Baking the loaf in a well-buttered Dutch oven or cast-iron pot, covered only for the first 30 minutes, produced a well-risen loaf with an even, golden crust that was thin and crisp yet still had a bit of chew.

We realized, however, that not everyone has a cast-iron pot available, so we explored ways of softening the crust after baking. Wrapping the bread in a clean tea towel as soon as it emerged from the oven helped soften the crust, while a slightly damp tea towel softened it even more. The best technique, though, was to brush the warm loaf with some melted butter. This gave it an attractive sheen as well as a delicious, buttery crust with just enough crunch. Although we liked the crust of the bread baked in the Dutch oven a little better, the ease of baking it on a baking sheet made the loaf brushed with butter a more practical option.

Finally, make sure that you cool the bread for at least 30 to 40 minutes before serving. If cut when too hot, the bread will be dense and slightly doughy.

Classic Irish Soda Bread
MAKES 1 LOAF

Fresh out of the oven, this bread is a great accompaniment to soups or stews, and leftovers make fine toast. With their flavorful grains and additions, the variations can stand alone.

3	cups low-protein all-purpose flour, such as Pillsbury, plus more for work surface
1	cup cake flour
2	tablespoons sugar
1½	teaspoons baking soda
1½	teaspoons cream of tartar

1½   teaspoons salt

2   tablespoons unsalted butter, softened, plus

    1 tablespoon melted butter for crust

1½   cups buttermilk

1. Adjust oven rack to upper-middle position and heat oven to 400 degrees. Whisk flours, sugar, baking soda, cream of tartar, and salt together in large bowl. Work softened butter into dry ingredients with fork or fingertips until texture resembles coarse crumbs.

2. Add buttermilk and stir with a fork just until dough begins to come together. Turn out onto flour-coated work surface; knead until dough just becomes cohesive and bumpy, 12 to 14 turns. (Do not knead until dough is smooth, or bread will be tough.)

3. Pat dough into a round about 6 inches in diameter and 2 inches high; place on greased or parchment-lined baking sheet. Score dough by cutting cross shape on top of loaf.

4. Bake until golden brown and a skewer inserted into center of loaf comes out clean or internal temperature reaches 180 degrees, 40 to 45 minutes. Remove from oven and brush with melted butter; cool to room temperature, 30 to 40 minutes.

➤ VARIATIONS

Irish Brown Soda Bread

Unlike the Classic Irish Soda Bread dough, which is dry, this dough is extremely sticky.

1¾   cups low-protein all-purpose flour, such as Pillsbury, plus more for work surface

1¼   cups whole wheat flour

½   cup cake flour

½   cup toasted wheat germ

3   tablespoons brown sugar

1½   teaspoons baking soda

1½   teaspoons cream of tartar

1½   teaspoons salt

2   tablespoons unsalted butter, softened, plus

    1 tablespoon melted butter for crust

1½   cups buttermilk

1. Adjust oven rack to upper-middle position and heat oven to 400 degrees. Whisk flours, wheat germ, brown sugar, baking soda, cream of tartar, and salt together in large bowl. Work softened butter into dry

ingredients with fork or fingertips until texture resembles coarse crumbs.

2. Add buttermilk and stir with a fork just until dough begins to come together. Turn out onto flour-coated work surface; knead until dough just becomes cohesive and bumpy, 12 to 14 turns. (Do not knead until dough is smooth, or bread will be tough.)

3. Pat dough into a round about 6 inches in diameter and 2 inches high; place on greased or parchment-lined baking sheet. Score dough by cutting cross shape on top of loaf.

4. Bake until golden brown and a skewer inserted into center of loaf comes out clean or internal temperature reaches 190 degrees, 45 to 55 minutes. Remove from oven and brush with melted butter; cool to room temperature, 30 to 40 minutes.

Oatmeal-Walnut Soda Bread

2½   cups old-fashioned oats

1¾   cups buttermilk

2   cups low-protein all-purpose flour, such as Pillsbury, plus more for work surface

½   cup cake flour

½   cup whole wheat flour

¼   cup brown sugar

1½   teaspoons baking soda

1½   teaspoons cream of tartar

1½   teaspoons salt

2   tablespoons unsalted butter, softened, plus

    1 tablespoon melted butter for crust

1   cup walnuts, toasted

1. Place 2 cups oats in medium bowl. Add buttermilk and soak for 1 hour.

2. Adjust oven rack to upper-middle position and heat oven to 400 degrees. Whisk flours, remaining ½ cup oats, brown sugar, baking soda, cream of tartar, and salt together in large bowl. Work softened butter into dry ingredients with fork or fingertips until texture resembles coarse crumbs.

3. Add buttermilk-soaked oats and nuts and stir with a fork just until dough begins to come together. Turn out onto flour-coated work surface; knead until dough just becomes cohesive and bumpy, 12 to 14 turns. (Do not knead until dough is smooth, or bread will be tough.)

4. Pat dough into a round about 6 inches in diam-

eter and 2 inches high; place on greased or parchment-lined baking sheet. Score dough by cutting cross shape on top of loaf.

5. Bake until golden brown and a skewer inserted into center of loaf comes out clean or internal temperature reaches 190 degrees, 45 to 55 minutes. Remove from oven and brush with melted butter; cool to room temperature, 30 to 40 minutes.

American-Style Soda Bread with Raisins and Caraway

3	cups low-protein all-purpose flour, such as Pillsbury, plus more for work surface
1	cup cake flour
1/4	cup sugar
1 1/2	teaspoons baking soda
1 1/2	teaspoons cream of tartar
1 1/2	teaspoons salt
4	tablespoons unsalted butter, softened, plus 1 tablespoon melted butter for crust
1 1/4	cups buttermilk
1	large egg, lightly beaten
1	cup raisins
1	tablespoon caraway seeds

1. Adjust oven rack to upper-middle position and heat oven to 400 degrees. Whisk flours, sugar, baking soda, cream of tartar, and salt together in large bowl. Work softened butter into dry ingredients

with fork or fingertips until texture resembles coarse crumbs.

2. Combine buttermilk and egg with a fork. Add buttermilk-egg mixture, raisins, and caraway and stir with a fork just until dough begins to come together. Turn out onto flour-coated work surface; knead until dough just becomes cohesive and bumpy, 12 to 14 turns. (Do not knead until dough is smooth, or bread will be tough.)

3. Pat dough into a round about 6 inches in diameter and 2 inches high; place on greased or parchment-lined baking sheet. Score dough by cutting cross shape on top of loaf.

4. Bake, covering bread with aluminum foil if it is browning too much, until golden brown and a skewer inserted into center of loaf comes out clean or internal temperature reaches 170 degrees, 40 to 45 minutes. Remove from oven and brush with melted butter; cool to room temperature, 30 to 40 minutes.

PANCAKES

PANCAKES ARE FAST AND SIMPLE, BUT IF THEY are also to be good, there are a few things you have to get right. First, the batter has to be the right texture. Runny batters cook into crêpes; thick batters—particularly those made with buttermilk—can cook up wet and heavy. Second, the griddle needs to be the right temperature. An overly hot skillet delivers a cake with a scorched exterior and raw interior, while a cool skillet gives the cake a hard, thick crust and a dry interior. But one of the most crucial issues with pancakes—as with all quick breads, really—is getting the leavening right. Too much baking powder or soda in a batter can result in metallic- or soapy-flavored pancakes—the taste equivalent of fingernails scraping across a blackboard.

Our goal, then, was clear: a light, fluffy, moist, and flavorful pancake. We started our testing by examining the type of flour. We tested a working recipe (using milk and baking powder) with all-purpose flour, cake flour, and a combination of the two. We knew a higher-gluten product, such as bread flour, would not deliver the tender pancakes we sought.

We noted immediately that the batters made with cake flour were significantly thinner than those

---

SCIENCE: A Light Hand

While testing the various ingredients in our Classic Irish Soda Bread, we discovered that the way the dough is handled while you are mixing it is as crucial as the amount and type of leavening used. Because baking soda begins reacting immediately with the cream of tartar, and does not provide the big second rise you get with double-acting baking powder, it is important to mix the dough quickly and not too vigorously. If you mix too slowly or too enthusiastically, too much carbon dioxide will be formed and will dissipate during the mixing process; not enough will then be produced during baking to provide the proper rise. Extended kneading also overdevelops the gluten in the flour, toughening the bread. It's no wonder that in Ireland a baker who produces a superior loaf of soda bread is traditionally said to have "a light hand," a great compliment.

---

made from regular all-purpose. Although neither batch rose nearly as high as it should have (we were not yet using enough baking powder), the cake flour pancakes were particularly crêpelike. The cake flour didn't appear to be strong enough to support the pancakes' weighty structure. Although the all-purpose pancakes looked and tasted flat at this point as well, their higher gluten content made them more substantial, yet still tender. The combination cake and all-purpose flour pancakes offered no advantages that would warrant pulling two boxes of flour down from the cupboard.

Thinking that perhaps our original formula was responsible for the poor performance of the cake flour, we continued trying cake flour as our formula evolved. But never once did we feel that it outperformed all-purpose flour.

With the flour issue resolved, we decided to work on the pancakes' flavor and texture. From past experience, we were certain that buttermilk was the quickest way to boost flavor, so we made the original formula with buttermilk and baking soda rather than milk and baking powder. We were amazed at the textural difference in the batter. Substituting an equal amount of buttermilk for the milk gave us a batter so thick that it had to be spooned, rather than poured, onto the griddle. We thinned the batter with a little milk, but the cooked cakes were too wet and, to our disappointment, lacked that flavor depth and dairy tang we thought we'd get from the buttermilk.

We had simply traded problems with buttermilk. Milk had given us thin batter and thin cakes. Buttermilk gave us thicker batter, but leaden cakes. Although we thought the flour/buttermilk ratio was partially responsible for the pancakes' heaviness, we knew it was time to deal with baking powder and soda. We were certain that these leavenings were at least partially responsible for the cakes' wet, heavy texture and were fully responsible for the buttermilk's unimpressive flavor performance.

We knew that one-half teaspoon of baking soda would neutralize our one cup of buttermilk. (For more on chemical leaveners, see page 374.) But we also recalled that prior to our leavening research we had been unimpressed with the flavor of the pancakes made with this very combination. So we thought perhaps we should switch to baking pow-

der. If baking powder and buttermilk were used in a batter, the baking powder would react with its own acid, allowing the full flavor of the buttermilk to come through. We had our next set of tests. To determine just which leavening, or what combination of leavenings, worked best with the buttermilk, we made three batches of batter: one with two teaspoons of baking powder, another with one-half teaspoon of baking soda, and a final batch with one-quarter teaspoon of baking soda and one teaspoon of baking powder.

Pancakes made from all three batters rose beautifully on the griddle. The all–baking powder pancakes were pale-colored and very finely textured—almost gummy. Compared with the other two varieties of pancake, they were tougher. They also tasted salty (which we attributed to the acid salt in the baking powder), and they had a tinny, metallic aftertaste. The buttermilk/dairy flavor really came through, but almost too much. Rather than tasting mildly tangy, these pancakes were almost sour.

The all–baking soda pancakes were more yellow in color. They were tender with a coarser crumb, and they weren't too salty, as were the baking powder pancakes. Although pleasant enough on their own, however, when compared with the other two varieties, they lacked flavor.

The combination baking powder/baking soda pancakes offered a good balance. They displayed the good qualities of the other two types of pancakes, without any of the negative side effects. The small amount of baking soda (one-quarter teaspoon) gave the cakes a coarser crumb and made them light and tender. Since some of the buttermilk's remaining acid was not neutralized, the pancakes also had a pleasant dairy tang. The baking powder helped with the rise, but since it was busy reacting with its own acid, it had allowed the buttermilk flavor to pass through.

We were getting close to perfect pancakes. Although our pancakes were relatively light, they weren't exactly fluffy. Ideal for waffles, our batter was too thick for pancakes; they came out slightly wet. We wanted our pancakes to look like the ones on the Bisquick box—the kind that spring back into shape when cut. At this point ours didn't—the tops stuck to the bottoms when cut with a fork.

INGREDIENTS: Maple Syrup

What's pancakes (or waffles or French toast for that matter) without maple syrup? We wondered how the consumer should buy maple syrup. By grade? By source (is Vermont syrup really better than the rest)? We also wondered if any of the pancake syrups—those supermarket staples made with a tiny percentage of maple syrup—were demonstrably better than the others.

In general, a maple syrup's grade is determined by the period during which it was made (the sugaring season lasts from February to early April). Technically, the grades of maple syrup are measured by the amount of light that can pass through the syrup. Straight from the tree, maple sap is clear, consisting of about 98 percent water and 2 percent sugar. To make maple syrup, the water has to be boiled off to a concentration of 66 percent sugar. (This means boiling off about 39 gallons of water to get one gallon of syrup.)

Early in the season, maple syrups tend to be near-transparent because the sugar molecules in the boiled-down sap are able to reflect much light. As temperatures warm outside, wild yeasts in the sap begin feeding on and breaking down the sugar. As a result, light can be absorbed. So as the season progresses, the syrup darkens.

This breakdown of sugar also affects flavor. If maple sap is concentrated without boiling (by freeze-drying, for example), the syrup will taste sweet but otherwise have little flavor. The flavor we perceive as "maple" is actually the result of chemical reactions that occur when the sap is boiled. One of the two primary flavor notes is derived from the compounds that form when sugar molecules break down. The process is similar to caramelizing. This may explain why the darker syrups produced later in the season have more of the caramel notes distinct to maple syrup. The second flavor note is vanilla, which is produced from compounds in the sap that the tree uses to make wood.

While vanilla and caramel are essential maple flavor elements, the full flavor of maple is far more complex. One producer's syrup can vary from a neighbor's because of differences in the soil, the tree chemistry, or the method of heating the sap.

The season's earliest sap flow produces Grade A light, or "Fancy," as it is called in Vermont. Honey gold and near-transparent, it has a pronounced sweetness and a delicate vanilla flavor. Grade A light can be the most expensive syrup and is not typically found in supermarkets. While it takes no more energy to produce than the other grades, its higher price was estab-lished more than 100 years ago, when "sugaring" was about just that—turning maple syrup into sugar. The lighter syrup made a finer sugar, so it sold at a higher cost, which simply never changed. Today Grade A light syrups are primarily used to make maple sugar candies.

The season's second syrup is Grade A medium amber. This has a warmer caramel color with a medium-strength flavor. It is generally touted as the syrup for pancakes. Right on the heels of medium amber is Grade A dark amber, which is slightly deeper in color and has a more pronounced flavor.

After the ambers falls Grade B, the darkest and typically least expensive of the syrups on the market. It is traditionally considered cooking grade because of its strength of flavor. Only Vermont makes Grade B syrup for consumer table use. Other states make a similar syrup but only sell it in bulk to the food industry because it is deemed too strong and too dark. Some whole foods stores carry it in bulk.

Lastly, there is a Grade C, characterized by strong, almost molasses-like flavor. Sold only to the food industry, Grade C is used in pancake syrups.

Of the nine samples in our tasting, tasters decided that if they had the choice, they would reach for the Vermont "B" syrup in the tasting to drizzle on their pancakes. Most tasters were won over by the depth of flavor and the dark rum color of the syrup. Many wrote comments such as "tastes real." And unlike many of the syrups, which lost their distinction when poured on a waffle, this one's bold characteristics held up.

The close runner-up in our tasting was a Grade A dark amber. Overall, tasters preferred the dark amber syrups to the medium ambers, which failed to spark tasters' interest, apparently because they were not bold enough. Not surprisingly, then, tasters flat-out rejected the one "Fancy" grade syrup we included in the tasting.

None of our results indicated syrup made from one region or state is superior to another, and industry experts agreed that it is difficult, if not impossible, to determine by taste where a syrup is made.

Because pancake syrups far outsell real maple syrups, we decided to do an additional tasting of the three top-selling national pancake syrups. The high scorer was Aunt Jemima, which is made of high fructose corn syrup, with just four percent maple syrup. We found that even this low percentage of maple syrup gave Aunt Jemima a decent maple flavor. It was superior to the other pancake syrups, one made with less maple syrup and the other with none.

We tried fixing the problem by thinning the batter with milk. To our one cup of buttermilk we added enough milk to make a semipourable batter. But adding more liquid to the batter wasn't the answer. The pancakes just became wetter. What ultimately worked for us was not adding, but substituting, one-quarter cup of milk for one-quarter cup of the buttermilk. Using three-quarters of a cup of buttermilk and one-quarter cup of milk lightened the batter and gave us fluffy pancakes.

As we reviewed the results of these leavening and liquid tests, we wondered if we could perhaps get away with even less baking powder. We made a batch of batter with the three-quarters cup buttermilk and one-quarter cup milk, a quarter teaspoon of baking soda, and a reduced measure of baking powder: one-half teaspoon. The pancakes rose as beautifully as if they had been made with the full teaspoon, they looked light and fluffy, and they tasted great.

Though we were pleased at this point, we wanted to run a final few tests with the secondary ingredients—eggs and butter—and to determine the fastest way to mix up a lumpless batter.

A number of pancake recipes called for separating the egg and mixing the yolk into the batter. The white was whipped, then folded into the already-mixed batter. We noticed right off that the batter made by this method was stiff, requiring us to spoon it onto the griddle. The resulting pancakes, though, were airy and tender. We liked this style of pancake enough to make it a variation but found it a little too delicate for a cake with the nickname "flapjack."

Since we were happy with our pancake's flavor and texture, we knew we didn't want to increase the butter in the recipe, but it's always worth trying to reduce fat these days. So we made the batter with only one tablespoon of butter, only to find the cooked pancakes a bit tougher than those made with two tablespoons of butter.

Enough experiments have been done in the test kitchen to prove the importance of getting in and out of the mixing phase as quickly as possible. (The more you mix a quick-bread batter, the more you develop the flour's gluten, and the tougher the resulting cake or bread.) We found the quickest way to incorporate the wet ingredients into the dry ingredients was to dump the milk mixture all at once into the flour mixture, then quickly mix it with a whisk. This method guaranteed us a virtually lumpless batter within seconds every time.

Light and Fluffy Pancakes

SERVES 3 TO 4

(MAKES ABOUT EIGHT 3-INCH PANCAKES)

This batter serves four perfectly for a light weekday breakfast. You may want to double the recipe for weekend pancake making, when appetites are larger. If you happen to be using salted butter or buttermilk, you may want to cut back a bit on the salt. If you don't have any buttermilk, mix three-quarters cup of room-temperature milk with one tablespoon of lemon juice and let it stand for five minutes. Substitute this "clabbered milk" for the three-quarters cup of buttermilk and one-quarter cup of milk in this recipe. Since this milk mixture is not as thick as buttermilk, the batter and resulting pancakes will not be as thick.

1	cup all-purpose flour
2	teaspoons sugar
1/2	teaspoon salt
1/2	teaspoon baking powder
1/4	teaspoon baking soda
3/4	cup buttermilk
1/4	cup milk (plus a tablespoon or so extra if batter is too thick)
1	large egg, separated
2	tablespoons unsalted butter, melted
	Vegetable oil for brushing griddle

1. Whisk dry ingredients in medium bowl. Pour buttermilk and milk into 2-cup Pyrex measuring cup. Whisk egg white into milk mixture. Mix yolk with melted butter, then stir into milk mixture. Dump wet ingredients into dry ingredients all at once; whisk until just mixed.

2. Meanwhile, heat griddle or large skillet over medium-high heat. Brush griddle generously with oil. When water splashed on surface sizzles, pour batter, about 1/4 cup at a time, onto griddle, making sure not to overcrowd. When pancake bottoms are brown and top surface starts to bubble, 2 to 3 minutes, flip cakes and cook until remaining side has browned, 1 to 2 minutes longer. Re-oil the skillet and repeat for the next batch of pancakes.

➤ VARIATIONS

Blueberry Pancakes

Follow recipe for Light and Fluffy Pancakes, pouring a little less than ¼ cup batter at a time onto griddle. Starting with ½ cup blueberries, drop about seven blueberries on top of each pancake. Proceed as directed in Master Recipe.

Whole Wheat Pancakes

Follow recipe for Light and Fluffy Pancakes, substituting ½ cup whole wheat flour for ½ cup of the all-purpose flour.

Toasted Pecan Pancakes

Heat pan over medium heat. Add ¼ cup pecans, chopped fairly fine; toast, shaking pan frequently, until nuts are fragrant, 3 to 5 minutes. Follow recipe for Light and Fluffy Pancakes, stirring pecans into dry ingredients along with wet ingredients.

Featherweight Pancakes

Whisking the egg whites gives pancakes an especially light texture. Don't bother with a hand mixer for beating one egg white. By the time you've assembled the mixer, you could be folding the hand-whipped egg white into the batter. Don't make the mistake of using too small a bowl, either. The egg needs space to aerate, so use a whisk and a large metal bowl.

Follow recipe for Light and Fluffy Pancakes, whisking egg white in large bowl to stiff peaks. Gently fold egg white into completed batter and continue with recipe, spooning rather than pouring batter onto griddle.

SCIENCE: Handling Melted Butter

Although some say that the egg and milk in pancakes need to be brought to room temperature before making the batter, we found our pancakes made from eggs and milk right out of the refrigerator to be just fine. The only problem we ran into was trying to whisk the melted butter into these cold ingredients. The cold milk and egg caused the butter to harden, and the mixture turned lumpy. While these lumps do dissolve when the pancakes are cooked, we think that the butter is more evenly distributed when stirred into the batter if it does not lump up.

Instead of stirring the whole egg into the milk, we separated the egg, added the white to the milk, but whisked the yolk into the melted butter before stirring it into the milk. This simple technique allowed us to add melted butter to cold ingredients.

Why does this work? The yolk is made up of lipoproteins, or fat proteins. The fat in the yolk mixes easily with the butter. The proteins, which are water soluble, help the fat disperse easily into the liquid.

WAFFLES

OUR IDEAL WAFFLE HAS A CRISP, WELL-browned exterior with a moist, fluffy interior. It should be like a rich, just-cooked soufflé encased in a flavorful crust. After testing more than 15 recipes, we realized that our ideal waffle requires a thick batter, so the outside can become crisp while the inside remains custardy. Also, a good waffle must be quickly cooked, since slow cooking evens out the cooking rate within the waffle and the center overcooks.

Many waffle batters are too thin, usually because the proportion of milk to flour—at one cup of each—is too high. Such thin batter results in a disappointing, gummy-textured waffle with a dry, unappealing interior. We have found that seven-eighths cup of buttermilk, or three-quarters cup of sweet milk, to one cup of flour is a far better proportion.

Most recipes omit buttermilk entirely, or at best list it as an option. Yet we found that buttermilk is absolutely crucial. Why? Because buttermilk and baking soda create a much thicker batter than the alternative, sweet milk and baking powder. We eventually found a way to make good waffles with sweet milk (reduce the amount of liquid and use homemade baking powder for a thicker batter), but buttermilk waffles will always taste better.

Although you don't need baking powder when baking with buttermilk (baking powder depends on cream of tartar, an acidic ingredient, for its rising power; cream of tartar is unnecessary in the presence of acidic buttermilk), many recipes call for it. But when we eliminated the baking powder, we found that the waffles cooked up crisper. Out of curiosity, we also tried to make a waffle with buttermilk and baking powder, eliminating the baking soda. The waffle was inedible by any standard, since there was too much acid and not enough baking soda.

Because crispness is so important in waffles, we tried substituting cornmeal for a bit of the flour and found that one tablespoon per cup of flour adds extra crackle. We also experimented with the addition of cake flour but found that it produces a finer crumb and a more tender product. The waffle lacked desirable contrast between a crisp exterior and the creamy interior.

We felt obliged to attempt making a waffle without melted butter. This created a bland, tasteless product with a limp exterior. Vegetable oil produced as much crispness as butter but could not provide the same good flavor.

Some waffle recipes call for separating the egg and then whipping the white and folding it into the mixed batter. We made waffles this way and found that folding in beaten egg whites is an improvement. The batter is glossier, and the waffle is fluffier inside. If you cut through a cooked waffle made with beaten egg whites, you can actually see pockets of air trapped inside. The same examination made with a whole-egg waffle reveals a flatter, more consistent texture.

Look at a number of waffle recipes and you'll see a wide range of recommendations as to how to combine ingredients. One author carefully mixes with a whisk until the liquid and dry ingredients are just combined; another throws everything into the bowl of an electric mixer and cranks up the horsepower. But most have this in common: they add all of the liquid ingredients at once. This practice necessitates overmixing and usually results in clumps of unmoistened flour. When we used a whisk to combine the ingredients until they were smooth, the batter was thin and the waffle tough.

The objective in all this is to moisten the flour thoroughly, not to create a smooth batter, and for this there is no question that a gentle hand is crucial. This is the technique that worked best for us: Whisk together the dry ingredients, whisk together the liquid ingredients, then pour the liquid ingredients into the dry ingredients very slowly, mixing gently with a rubber spatula. Use a thin steady stream, as you would when you add oil to vinegar for salad dressing. When most of the liquid has been added, the batter becomes thicker; switch to a folding motion, similar to that used in folding egg whites, to finally combine and moisten the batter. Then continue folding as you add the beaten egg white.

When you cook waffles, remember that darker waffles are better than lighter ones. In scientific terms, this is due to the Maillard reaction, which refers to the reaction and subsequent transformation of carbohydrates at high temperatures. The browning reaction promotes the development of flavor. Waffles should be cooked until medium-brown, not lightly tanned. Toasty brown waffles will also stay crisper

---

SCIENCE: Why Commercial Baking Powder Doesn't Work in Waffles

Baking powder is made from two major elements: an acid (cream of tartar, for example) and baking soda. The cream of tartar provides acidity and the baking soda provides the rise. Baking powder is used when there is no natural acidity in the batter—that is, you are using sweet milk without the addition of an acidic ingredient such as yogurt or buttermilk.

When baking soda comes in contact with a moist, acidic environment, carbon dioxide gas is produced, which in turn provides "rise." This chemical reaction is quite pronounced in a buttermilk batter—buttermilk contains lactic acid, which reacts strongly with the soda, generating a thick, spongy batter in seconds.

Because sweet milk reacts less strongly with baking powder, the batter remains thin. This is partially because most baking powder is "double-acting," which means that manufacturers use two different acidic ingredients. One works (creates carbon dioxide gas) at room temperature, and the other works at higher temperatures (above 120 degrees). Baking powder is designed to create gas slowly so that a cake, for example, will have time to bake and set before all of the bubbles dissipate.

In our tests, it was clear that most of the rise with baking powder occurs at oven temperatures. Since waffles are cooked so quickly, baking powder is not well-suited to this type of batter; the amount of "room-temperature" acid it can provide is insufficient. With waffles you want a lot of room-temperature reaction, and therefore it's best, when using sweet milk, to make your own recipe for baking powder, using cream of tartar and baking soda.

longer than manila-colored waffles, which are likely to become soggy by the time they get to the table.

Just don't overdo it—the perfect waffle is still moist and creamy inside.

Best Buttermilk Waffles

MAKES 3 TO 4,
DEPENDING ON SIZE OF WAFFLE IRON

The secret to great waffles is a thick batter, so don't expect a pourable batter. The optional cornmeal adds a pleasant crunch to the finished waffle. This recipe can be doubled or tripled.

1	cup all-purpose flour
1	tablespoon cornmeal (optional)
1/2	teaspoon salt
1/4	teaspoon baking soda
1	egg, separated
7/8	cup buttermilk
2	tablespoons unsalted butter, melted

1. Heat waffle iron. Whisk dry ingredients together in a medium bowl. Whisk yolk with buttermilk and butter.

2. Beat egg white until it just holds a 2-inch peak.

3. Add liquid ingredients to dry ingredients in a thin steady stream while mixing gently with a rubber spatula. (Do not add liquid faster than you can incorporate it into the batter.) Toward end of mixing, use a folding motion to incorporate ingredients. Gently fold egg white into batter.

4. Spread appropriate amount of batter onto waffle iron. Following manufacturer's instructions, cook waffle until golden brown, 2 to 5 minutes. Serve immediately. (In a pinch, you can keep waffles warm on a wire rack in a 200-degree oven for up to 5 minutes.)

VARIATION
Almost-As-Good-As-Buttermilk Waffles
MAKES 3 TO 4

If you're out of buttermilk, we offer this sweet-milk variation. By making your own baking powder using baking soda and cream of tartar and by cutting back on the quantity of milk, you can make a thick, quite respectable batter.

Follow recipe for Best Buttermilk Waffles, adding 1/2 teaspoon cream of tartar to the dry ingredients and substituting a scant 3/4 cup milk for the buttermilk.

EQUIPMENT: Waffle Irons

We tested eight brands of waffle iron and found that all irons are definitely not the same. They vary widely in quality, even within the same price range. As a result, choosing the right iron is critical. Even the best batter can make poor waffles if poured into an inferior iron.

The top-rated iron was made by Vitantonio. This iron yields perfect waffles in just two minutes. The bottom-rated Toastmaster family-size iron (which turns out four waffles at a time) can take 10 minutes to crank out rubbery discs better suited to sporting events than breakfast.

So what makes the Vitantonio waffle iron so good? This machine achieves a temperature of 470 degrees when fully preheated, as compared with 400 to 450 degrees in other irons. The higher working temperature means crisper waffles in less time.

You might think a large iron, capable of making four waffles at once, would get the designated waffle chef out of the kitchen faster and let him or her eat with everyone else. Not so. Every large iron we tested took at least 6 minutes (and in one case 10 minutes) to make a single batch. In that time, the top-rated Vitantonio can crank our three or four perfectly crisp, well-browned waffles.

FRENCH TOAST

FRENCH TOAST (OR PAIN PERDU, "LOST bread") started out as a simple way to use up old bread by dipping it in a beaten egg and frying it. Many current recipes deviate little from that, calling for a couple of eggs and a touch of milk. Those recipes, though, produce a toast that tastes mostly of fried egg and that, depending on the amount of liquid, is either overly soggy or still dry in the middle.

We wanted something quite different: bread that was crisp and buttery on the outside, soft and custardlike inside. We wanted to taste a balance of flavors rather than just eating egg. We wanted our French toast to be sweet enough to eat with only a sprinkling of confectioners' sugar, but not so sweet that we couldn't top it with syrup or macerated fruit if we chose to.

We started testing with a simple formula: two eggs beaten with one-half cup of milk to soak four slices of three-quarter-inch-thick, day-old French bread. From this starting point, we wanted to settle first on which bread works best for French toast, but that proved to be the hardest part of the testing. At first, it seemed simple. One-inch-thick bread of any sort was too thick; it either soaked up too much liquid and didn't cook through, or it stayed dry in the middle with shorter soaking. So we stuck with three-quarter-inch bread and started trying various baguettes, supermarket breads, challah and brioche, and a dense white bread.

At the end of these tests, we thought we had the answer. Challah was clearly best, adding a lot of flavor and richness, staying generally crisp outside and somewhat moist inside—not perfect, but likely to improve with changes in the liquid component. Baguette slices and slices of a high-quality Italian bread, so long as they weren't more than a day old, came in second. Hard-to-find brioche was only acceptable. Brioche can vary widely in quality, and our open-textured version failed to take up the liquid evenly. Dense white bread simply tasted like fried bread, so it rated near the bottom. Presliced sandwich bread was acceptable in a pinch, although just barely. Worst, though, was the supermarket bakery version of French or Italian bread. Spongy and flabby, this bread simply fell apart when we took it out of the liquid. For the moment, the bread issue seemed resolved. So, using challah for testing, we moved on to the liquids.

Because we didn't want our French toast to be too eggy, we first tried dropping one egg from the test recipe. That decision showed an immediate improvement, yielding a finished product that was crispier outside but still soft inside. To be sure that fewer eggs made for a better result, we tried going the opposite way, using 3 eggs to ½ cup milk. That confirmed it: More egg seems to create a barrier on the outside of the bread, causing the interior to stay dry while the outside ends up tasting like fried egg.

The next logical step seemed to be to increase the milk, given that a higher proportion of milk to egg had worked so far. A jump to one cup of milk made the bread too wet inside, but it was better than one-half cup. Three-quarters cup of milk proved to be ideal, as the toast stayed custardlike inside and fairly crisp outside.

Throughout the egg and milk testings, the basic recipe had tasted flat, and we had been looking for-

ward to the final tests, when we would add other ingredients. We first tried salt, and that gave the recipe a big boost: Adding one-quarter teaspoon of salt made a toast that finally had some taste. We added sugar next, which also made a great difference. At last, we added vanilla. Few recipes call for it, but two teaspoons pull everything together, balancing the flavors.

After all this, we had a French toast that was better than any we could remember, yet still not ideal. It was fairly crisp, but not the texture we wanted: an almost deep-fried crispness. We knew the sugar helped, but there had to be something else. More butter in the skillet (until now we'd been using 1½ tablespoons to 4 pieces of bread) only made the challah greasier, and heat higher than medium to medium-high simply burned it. When one editor mentioned a French toast version she'd once had in which the bread was dipped in pancake batter, plus a recipe that called for a pinch of flour, it got us thinking about what flour could do. Ultimately, what it did was solve the puzzle.

At first we liked one tablespoon of flour to help get the exterior extra crisp and not greasy, but in later testings we noted that this made the breads somewhat soggy inside; yet when we went up to two tablespoons, the bread became tough. So we started trying more flour—but with butter added to keep the bread from toughening. And after a few more tests, we finally had fabulous French toast: A batter with one-third cup of flour balanced by two tablespoons of melted butter gets the outside of the challah evenly crisped and brown and lets just enough moisture through to the interior to keep it custardlike but not heavy.

A few other tests answered some final questions. We tried cooking in all kinds of skillets and ended up liking cast iron best, with a regular (not nonstick) skillet a close second. Using medium heat with one tablespoon of butter worked well with these skillets; nonstick skillets made the bread too greasy, even with less butter and other heat settings.

Unfortunately, our perfect French toast recipe worked wonders with challah but failed with chewy French or Italian breads. While we strongly recommend using challah if you can, we know it's less likely to be the day-old bread people have on hand. So we worked out a separate recipe for French and Italian breads, but we recommend it with a caveat: If you're using soft supermarket-style French bread or sliced white sandwich bread, go with the challah recipe.

With a chewier, drier French or Italian loaf, however, the high amount of flour in the batter used for challah prevented needed moisture from soaking into the bread. Also, the exterior had a harder time crisping because the rougher surface of this somewhat open-textured bread didn't make good contact with the pan. To get the interior moist, we tried dropping some of the flour; to get the exterior crisped, we tried again with a two-egg recipe. Neither trick worked. In the end, more tests showed that the recipe needed even more milk for a custardlike interior and just one tablespoon of flour to aid in crisping; with this little flour, the batter needed no butter.

French Toast for Challah or Sandwich Bread

MAKES 4 TO 5 SLICES FROM CHALLAH OR
6 TO 8 SLICES FROM SANDWICH BREAD

Though thick-sliced challah is best for French toast, you can substitute high-quality, presliced sandwich bread. Flipping challah is easiest with tongs, but a spatula works best with sandwich bread. To speed the cooking of large quantities, heat two or more skillets to brown a few batches at once. To vary the flavor of the batter, add three-quarters teaspoon ground cinnamon or one-half teaspoon ground nutmeg with the dry ingredients, or substitute almond extract for the vanilla.

1	large egg
2	tablespoons unsalted butter, melted, plus extra for frying
¾	cup milk
2	teaspoons vanilla extract
2	tablespoons sugar
⅓	cup all-purpose flour
¼	teaspoon salt
4–5	slices day-old challah, ¾ inch thick, or 6 to 8 slices day-old sandwich bread

1. Heat 10- to 12-inch skillet (preferably cast iron) over medium heat for 5 minutes. Meanwhile, beat egg lightly in shallow pan or pie plate; whisk in butter, then milk and vanilla, and finally sugar, flour, and salt, continuing to whisk until smooth. Soak bread without oversaturating, about 40 seconds per side for challah or 30 seconds per side for sandwich bread. Pick up bread and allow excess batter to drip off; repeat with remaining slices.

2. Swirl 1 tablespoon butter in hot skillet. Transfer prepared bread to skillet; cook until golden brown, about 1 minute 45 seconds on first side and 1 minute on the second. Serve immediately. Continue, adding 1 tablespoon butter to skillet for each new batch.

French Toast for Firm European-Style Bread

MAKES 4 TO 8 SLICES, DEPENDING
ON THE LOAF

Less flour in this recipe allows the batter to penetrate more easily into drier, chewier French or Italian loaves.

1	large egg
1	cup milk
2	teaspoons vanilla extract
2	tablespoons sugar
1	tablespoon all-purpose flour
¼	teaspoon salt
4–8	slices firm, day-old European-style bread, such as French or Italian, ¾ inch thick
	Unsalted butter to grease skillet (about 1 tablespoon per batch)

1. Heat 10- to 12-inch skillet (preferably cast iron) over medium heat for 5 minutes. Meanwhile, beat egg lightly in shallow pan or pie plate; whisk in milk and vanilla, and then sugar, flour, and salt, continuing to whisk until smooth. Soak bread without oversaturating, about 30 seconds per side. Pick up bread and allow excess batter to drip off; repeat with remaining slices.

2. Swirl 1 tablespoon butter in hot skillet. Transfer prepared bread to skillet; cook until golden brown, about 2 minutes on first side and 1 minute and 15 seconds on the second. Serve immediately. Continue, adding 1 tablespoon butter to skillet for each new batch.

16

EGGS

EGGS ARE AN ESSENTIAL INGREDIENT IN most desserts and are used in numerous savory recipes, everything from egg salad (see page 57) to stuffings for the holiday turkey. Eggs add a rich flavor and silky texture to hundreds of dishes.

Depending on the breed of the hen and her size, a chicken egg can weigh as much as three ounces or as little as one ounce. Size is not necessarily a reflection of quality, nor is the color of the shell. The average weight of one egg for each of the common sizes is as follows: jumbo (2½ ounces), extra-large (2¼ ounces), large (2 ounces), and medium (1¾ ounces).

We generally use large eggs in this book. However, you may use other sizes if you approximate the total weight by relying on the figures listed above. For instance, replace four large eggs (which weigh 8 ounces), with three jumbo eggs (7½ ounces) rather than four jumbo eggs (10 ounces).

No matter the size, the egg consists of two parts that can function quite differently in recipes. The white, or albumen, consists primarily of water (about 90 percent) and layers of protein. It begins to coagulate at 144 degrees, ahead of the yolk. The yolk is where most of the fat and cholesterol in the egg is located. The yolk also contains most of the vitamins and nutrients, as well as lecithin, the emulsifier that gives sauces with eggs their smooth texture. The yolk begins to coagulate at 149 degrees. (For more information on the thickening power of the egg, see page 516.)

In recent years, there have been numerous outbreaks of intestinal illness traced to eggs contaminated with salmonella. Although the odds of getting a bad egg are quite low (some experts estimate that 1 in 10,000 eggs is contaminated with the bacteria), it makes sense to take some precautions. This is especially true if you are cooking for the young, the elderly, women who are pregnant, or for people with compromised immune systems.

Thorough cooking of eggs, to at least 160 degrees, will kill any salmonella that is present. Since it is hard to use an instant-read thermometer on scrambled eggs, you will have to rely on visual clues. Given the thickening temperatures mentioned above, you should cook all eggs until fully set if you are concerned about salmonella. Note that there are recipes in this book (such as mayonnaise) that we feel are best made with raw eggs. You may want to avoid these dishes if you are concerned about egg safety.

Eggs should always be refrigerated to prolong their shelf life. Since the door is actually the warmest spot in most refrigerators, you should keep eggs in their container and store them on one of the shelves. The shelves are likely to be colder and the box acts as a layer of insulation around the eggs.

This chapter considers the egg for breakfast, the way most American are likely to eat them. Recipes for scrambled and poached eggs, omelets, and frittatas are included. Perhaps the most important thing you can do to ensure success when cooking these egg dishes is to use a nonstick skillet. Of course, you can make scrambled eggs in a conventional pan, but you have to use more fat and you always run the risk of losing half your eggs to the pan. A nonstick skillet requires a fraction of the fat so you end up tasting the egg, not the butter or oil.

Many Americans can't imagine eggs without bacon. See page 239 for information on buying and cooking bacon. See pages 57–58 for information about hard-boiled eggs.

SCRAMBLED EGGS

SCRAMBLED EGGS SHOULD BE A DREAMY mound of big, softly wobbling curds, yellow as a legal pad, glistening, a hairsbreadth away from being undercooked. When cut, the eggs should be cooked enough to hold their shape but soft enough to eat with a spoon.

We first tested beating the eggs to see if this made a difference in the final outcome. Our advice is to stop

---

EQUIPMENT: Nonstick Skillet

We tested the major brands of nonstick skillets and particularly liked pans from All-Clad and Calphalon. Both pans are sturdy but not overly heavy. For instance, many enameled cast-iron pans weigh close to five pounds and are hard to maneuver. A pan that weighs two to three pounds is much easier to control and still heavy enough to heat evenly. When shopping, make sure the handle is comfortable and preferably heat-resistant. A hollowed-out metal handle or a handle with a removable plastic sheath is ideal.

muscling the raw eggs into a tight froth. We found that overbeating can cause premature coagulation of the eggs' protein—even without heat! Too much beating can make eggs tough before they hit the pan. For a smooth yellow color and no streaks of white, we whip eggs in a medium-sized bowl with a fork and stop while the bubbles are large. For 10 or 12 eggs, we've found that a balloon whisk works just fine.

Before beating, the eggs get a few additions—salt, pepper, and either milk or water. Compared side by side, we found that scrambled eggs made with water are less flavorful, don't fluff as nicely, form wrinkled curds, and aren't as soft as those made with milk. With its traces of sugar, proteins, and fats, milk has a wonderful pillowy effect and helps create large curds—the bigger you can get the curds, the more steam you'll trap inside, for puff all the way to the table.

We tried most of the pans in our kitchen and discovered that a nonstick surface is best for scrambled eggs. As always, a heavy-bottomed skillet is preferable. Cheap, thin pans overheat and are difficult to control on high heat. Thicker pans may take longer to heat up, but they hold heat evenly without hot spots.

Pan size is important, too. When we used a 10-inch skillet for two eggs, the batter spread out so thinly that while we were busy moving one area of the eggs, another area overcooked. We found that the more the eggs are contained, the bigger the curds. An 8-inch skillet kept the two-egg batter at a depth of about ¼ inch, and the curds came out nice and plump.

We've tried cooking scrambled eggs over medium heat but the eggs got tough, dried out, and overcoagulated, like a badly made meringue that "weeps." A hot pan will begin to cook eggs instantaneously, for the quickest coagulation. The tradeoff for using high heat is absolute vigilance in making sure the eggs are off the heat before serious damage is done.

Keeping the eggs in constant, steady motion also helps keep them from overcooking. You don't want to beat the eggs, but they should be gently stirred as they cook. A wooden or plastic spatula works best; use the flat edge to snowplow a two- to three-inch swath of eggs across the pan in one pass. The idea is to slowly push, lift, and fold. Two eggs should cook into big curds in about 30 seconds.

When are the eggs done? The idea behind big voluptuous curds is to trap steam. The larger the curds,

the more steam is pocketed inside, and the more the eggs will continue to cook once off the heat. We like scrambled eggs soft and juicy, so they look positively undone when we make that final fold and push them out of the pan. But if you get the eggs off the heat when they're still juicy, you'll always get lush scrambled eggs with big curds that melt in your mouth.

Fluffy Scrambled Eggs

SERVES 4

These eggs cook very quickly, so it's important to be ready to eat before you start to cook them.

8	large eggs
½	teaspoon salt
	Several grinds of ground black pepper
½	cup milk
I	tablespoon butter

1. Crack eggs into a medium bowl. Add salt, pepper, and milk. Whip with a fork until streaks are gone and color is pure yellow; stop beating while the bubbles are still large.

2. Meanwhile, put butter in a 10-inch nonstick skillet, then set the pan over high heat. When the butter foams, swirl it around and up the sides of the pan. Before foam completely subsides, pour in beaten eggs. With a wooden or plastic spatula, push eggs from one side of the pan to the other, slowly but deliberately, lifting and folding eggs as they form into curds, until eggs are nicely clumped into a single mound, but remain shiny and wet, 1½ to 2 minutes. Serve immediately.

> VARIATIONS

Two Scrambled Eggs

Season 2 eggs with ⅛ teaspoon salt, 1 grind of pepper, and 2 tablespoons milk. Heat only 1½ teaspoons butter and use 8-inch skillet. Cooking time is only 30 to 45 seconds.

Four Scrambled Eggs

Season 4 eggs with ¼ teaspoon salt, 2 grinds of pepper, and ¼ cup milk. Heat ¾ tablespoon butter and use a 10-inch skillet. Cooking time is about 1 minute.

Twelve Scrambled Eggs
Season 12 eggs with ¾ teaspoon salt, 6 grinds of pepper, and ¾ cup milk. Heat 1½ tablespoons butter and use a 12-inch skillet. Cooking time is 2½ to 3 minutes.

POACHED EGGS

POACHING IS A GREAT WAY TO TREAT AN EGG, provided you know the best way to poach. Eggs don't respond well to random acts of culinary violence. Cast them about like a raft at sea in water that's too hot and too rough, and they will get revenge by tightening, toughening, getting stringy, or falling apart.

A poached egg should be something quite different: a lovely, tender white pouch cooked evenly all the way through. The top of the egg yolk should look a little pink, and, when cut, the yolk should run just a little. The whites that surround it should glisten and jiggle a little like baked custard, and the cooking liquid should be left with no stray strands of egg white.

We suspected that part of the problem with many poached egg recipes was the pot. Most recipes call for a deep saucepan, but we wondered if the eggs would be easier to control in a shallow skillet. We decided to test a three-quart saucepan against an eight-inch nonstick skillet with flared sides, which we figured might make it easier to maneuver the eggs.

The first advantage of the skillet quickly becomes clear: The shallower water comes to a boil more quickly, making poached eggs a speedy proposition. Second, an egg meets the bottom of a skillet sooner than it does the bottom of a pot just a few inches taller. This gives the egg an early floor on which to land gently, before it has a chance to build up any velocity. The sooner the egg is on solid ground, the quicker the whites hold together and the less likely they are to become stringy.

To get enough water in a skillet, it is necessary to fill the pan almost to the rim. We found that the highest heat possible on impact sets egg whites most quickly. Because water is the cooking medium, that means 212 degrees Fahrenheit. This high heat also helps the yolks to hurry up and cook.

Even with these measures, however, whites can still become ragged (the process is called feathering). Most experts suggest treating the water with vinegar to lower the pH of the water. We found that adding vinegar does in fact reduce feathering. The lower pH of the water lowers the temperature at which the whites and yolks set, which means that after the initial dunk into boiling water, the egg can cook in water that's slightly cooler and, hence, calmer.

In fact, we found that poached eggs come out best when the water is not at a boil. The eggs should be added to boiling water, but for the actual cooking time, we've concluded that absolutely still water, as long as it's very hot, will poach an egg just the same. So we turn off the heat and cover the skillet. Without all the agitation of simmering or boiling water, the eggs cook up better looking every time.

During the 3½ to 4 minutes that it takes the captured heat to cook the eggs, the temperature of the covered water drops only about 20 degrees. This means that poaching eggs in residual heat eliminates the need to simmer, which can create rough waters that cause the egg to partially disintegrate. It also outwits home stoves that run "hot" and can't hold a simmer.

With our technique down, we focused on some smaller issues. Heavily salted water, we found, makes the eggs taste better than lightly salted water. We use at least one full teaspoon in the filled skillet; otherwise the eggs are bland.

The next question is how to get the eggs into the boiling water without breaking them apart. Cracking the egg onto a saucer is often mentioned in old

POACHING EGGS

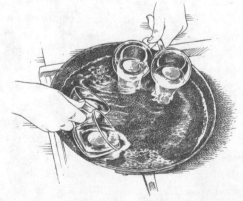

To get four eggs into simmering water at the same time, crack each into a small cup with a handle. Lower lips of each cup just into the water at same time and then tip eggs into the pan.

recipes, but you lose a lot of control as the slithery egg and gravity derail your aim. Cracked into a small cup, the egg stays in one piece through its entire descent into purgatory. Each egg should be cracked into its own cup before the water boils. It may seem easier to refill the same cup over and over with a freshly cracked egg than to wash two or four or more once the eggs are done, but you use a lot of precious time when you crack and pour the eggs one at a time. If the eggs aren't in the water within seconds of each other, you'll have to keep track of which egg went in when, a nearly impossible proposition.

When time's up, we use an oval-bowled slotted spoon to get the eggs out of the poaching liquid. The spoon mimics the shape of the egg so it can nestle comfortably. A skimmer picks the egg up nicely, but we find the eggs roll around dangerously on the flat skimmer.

We let the egg "drip-dry" by holding it aloft briefly over the skillet. For really dry eggs a paper towel blots to the last drop. We actually like a little of the cooking water to come with the poached eggs, the better to taste the vinegar. Pass the salt and pepper and a bottle of Tabasco, and the poached eggs are ready to eat.

Poached Eggs
SERVES 2

Poached eggs take well to any number of accompaniments. Try serving them on a bed of grated mild cheddar or Monterey Jack cheese or creamed spinach; in a pool of salsa; on a thick slice of tomato topped with a slice of Bermuda onion; on a potato pancake; or simply with plain buttered toast. See the illustration on page 406 for a tip on getting four eggs into boiling water at the same time.

4   large eggs, each cracked into a small handled cup
1   teaspoon salt, plus more to taste
2   tablespoons distilled white vinegar
    Ground black pepper

1. Fill 8- to 10-inch nonstick skillet nearly to rim with water, add 1 teaspoon salt and vinegar, and bring mixture to boil over high heat.

2. Lower lips of each cup just into water at once; tip eggs into boiling water, cover, and remove from heat. Poach until yolks are medium-firm, exactly 4 minutes. For firmer yolks (or for extra-large or

jumbo eggs), poach 4½ minutes; for looser yolks (or for medium eggs), poach 3 minutes.

3. With slotted spoon, carefully lift and drain each egg over skillet. Season to taste with salt and pepper and serve immediately.

OMELETS

MANY PEOPLE HAVE BEEN LED TO BELIEVE that you must be a trained chef to turn out a decent omelet. The truth is, while this may once have been the case, nonstick pans now make omelets a cinch. And that's good news, because omelets are a satisfying dish that can be made quickly—and with almost anything you happen to have on hand.

A big part of the omelet mystique centers around the pan in which it is cooked. Traditional omelet pans are made of heavy iron with an absolutely flat bottom and sloping sides to help ease the omelet out of the pan. These pans are carefully seasoned before use to prevent the omelet from sticking; to prevent rusting, they are never washed thereafter—just wiped out with a towel.

It is true that the proper pan is essential to good omelet making. Today, however, that pan is a nonstick skillet; it is already "seasoned" to prevent sticking and requires no special care. It just needs to be the right size for the job.

The traditional technique for cooking omelets involves a number of fairly tricky arm motions that take practice to master—stirring with a flat fork in a circular motion until the egg mixture has thickened, tapping the handle to dislodge the set eggs, and sliding the omelet up one side of the pan. However, the nonstick pan makes most of this unnecessary.

Using two eggs and a half tablespoon of butter (olive oil is also delicious and works just fine) for each omelet, we tested the classic technique to determine the simplest way to cook an omelet without compromising the taste. The vehicle was a nine-inch nonstick pan with sloping sides; the flat bottom of the pan measures about five inches.

In our first series of tests we determined how best to beat the eggs and which utensil to use—most classic recipes merely dictate that the eggs be "completely incorporated," although some say "beat until frothy" and others "beat until barely combined." We tried three methods of mixing the eggs: beating them lightly with a fork to barely combine the yolk and white; beating more vigorously with a fork to completely mix them; and using a whisk to beat them until they turned frothy. The easiest and best method is to mix the eggs with a fork until they're well mixed; this gives the omelet a more uniform texture than if the eggs are beaten less. Beating with a whisk simply doesn't improve the texture.

The next step was to determine the best heat for cooking. Since many egg preparations call for gentle heat, we wondered if low heat would make a more tender omelet. It doesn't. All it does is slow down the cooking process. Medium-high to high heat cooks the eggs quickly, helping you to achieve the true omelet, what the famed French chef Escoffier called "scrambled eggs enclosed in a coating of coagulated egg," with a lovely brown exterior.

We also tried adding liquid to the eggs, using a bit less than a tablespoon each of water, milk, and cream in three separate egg mixtures. We found that the addition of any liquid helps the omelet remain moist in the event of overcooking, but it detracts from the flavor of the eggs. Water and milk merely lessen the purity of the eggs, while cream really competes and even overwhelms the flavor of the eggs.

We then investigated the necessity of stirring the eggs as they cooked. The classic technique is to stir them until they thicken, then pull in the edges to finish. We also tested pulling in the edges until the omelet was set without any stirring. The results were clear. Stirring breaks up and integrates the cooked egg with the soft portions, giving the finished omelet a very consistent texture and a smooth appearance. If the eggs are not stirred during cooking, the omelet has a less homogeneous texture and a more uneven exterior. Stirring also shortens the cooking time.

We tried various methods of getting the omelet out of the pan, both with and without utensils. The technique of tapping the handle to slide the omelet up in the pan is one of the trickiest in cooking. But with a nonstick pan you can use a simple jerk of the handle to accomplish the same thing. Folding is easiest with a spatula; you can make the final fold as you turn the omelet out of the pan.

If you are flavoring the omelet with herbs, a dry grated cheese, or a small dice of onion or sweet pep-

per, just whisk the ingredient into the egg mixture. Add chunkier fillings just after the omelet has set, before you fold it. For a filling that must be cooked first, you can simply pour the egg mixture over the cooked filling, then cook and fold the two together.

Master Recipe for Basic Omelet

SERVES 1

This basic omelet can be flavored as you like. Some of our favorite omelet variations follow this recipe.

2	large eggs
	Salt and freshly ground black pepper
1½	teaspoons butter

1. In a small bowl, lightly beat eggs and a pinch of salt and pepper with a fork until mixed.

2. Heat butter in an 8- or 9-inch nonstick pan over medium-high heat. When butter stops foaming and just begins to color, pour in eggs. Wait a few seconds until edges of omelet begin to set. Then stir in a circular motion with the flat of a fork until eggs are thickened but not completely set. Use a wooden spoon or spatula to pull cooked egg at side of pan in toward center; tilt pan toward that side so that the uncooked eggs run to edge of pan. Repeat until omelet is just set but still moist on top. Cook omelet a few more seconds to brown bottom.

3. To fold omelet, jerk the pan sharply away from you a few times to slide omelet up far side of pan. Use a fork or spatula to fold the far edge in toward the center of the pan. Grasp pan as far down the handle as possible; rest far edge of pan on serving plate and gently roll omelet onto plate so that near edge folds in toward the center as you do this. Use a fork or spatula to tuck in any edges. Serve immediately.

➤ VARIATIONS

Smoked Salmon Omelet

Follow Master Recipe through step 2. Just before folding, sprinkle 1 teaspoon minced fresh dill, chive, or scallion green over entire omelet, then place 2 tablespoons thin-sliced smoked salmon strips over center third of omelet. Fold and turn out as directed.

Cheese Omelet

Make omelet according to Master Recipe. If using a hard grating cheese like Parmesan, beat 1 tablespoon grated cheese into eggs before cooking. If using softer cheeses, such as Monterey Jack, cheddar, or soft goat cheese, sprinkle over center third of omelet just before folding. Fold and turn out as directed.

Mixed Herb Omelet

Mince equal parts fresh parsley, chives (or scallion green), tarragon, and chervil (if available) to yield 1 tablespoon. Beat eggs with herbs. Make omelet according to Master Recipe.

FRITTATAS

FOR THOSE WHO LOVE THE IDEA OF OMELETS but can't handle the execution, there are frittatas, an Italian dish consisting of eggs and a filling, but requiring no fancy pan work.

To make an omelet, you must place a filling on top of partially set eggs, wait a second for the eggs to set further, then turn the contents out onto a serving plate in one graceful swoop. This technique is not hard, but it does take some practice. For a frittata, you simply prepare the filling in a pan, pour the eggs on top, and cook until the eggs are set. The difference in preparation yields different results: While an omelet is soft, delicate, and slightly runny, a frittata is tender but firm. An omelet encases its filling while a frittata incorporates it evenly throughout. Aside from simplicity, frittatas have another advantage: They're delicious hot, cold, or at room temperature—so you don't have to sweat the timing as you do with most omelets, which must be served warm.

Since few cookbooks agree on a method for making frittatas, we tested a number of techniques to determine which would consistently yield a frittata that was moist but not runny, firm but not tough, and light but substantial. The filling would need to meld with the eggs, not overwhelm them. To get the results we desired, we had to find the optimal ratio of eggs to cooking fat to pan size, as well as the best proportion of filling to eggs.

To discover the best proportion of eggs to pan size to filling to cooking fat, we began with the recipes in Italian cookbooks, most of which called for six eggs and roughly two tablespoons of oil for a frittata for four. None of the recipes specified pan size, but having eaten very thin frittatas in Italy, we guessed the pan was at least 12 inches.

Two tablespoons of oil proved to be too much in the first version we tested; the frittata tasted of the oil when the oil should mainly have just facilitated the cooking. Also, the frittata was very thin, almost crêpe-like, which we liked but which didn't seem substantial enough for a lunch or supper dish. To retest, we cut the oil in half, to one tablespoon, and used a 10-inch skillet. This turned out to be the right proportion for firm, flavorful frittatas when the filling had few ingredients. However, when the filling had more substantial ingredients, such as mushrooms, potatoes, or asparagus, we found that it was better to return to the original two tablespoons of oil.

To determine the ideal amount of filling, we decided to judge it by sight, adding only enough to cover the bottom of the pan. We didn't want to risk having the filling overwhelm the eggs, and it just seemed sensible that a layer spread across the pan would be adequate for flavor and substance. This approach turned out to be correct, amounting to about two-thirds cup of filling for a 10-inch skillet.

To keep the preparation as simple as possible, we began each test by sautéing the ingredients for the filling in the same nonstick pan in which we would cook the frittata. Then we beat the eggs lightly and poured them over the filling, stirring them with a fork to distribute the white and yolk evenly, then proceeded with the following cooking methods, getting the results described:

Stove top only: Judging from the old cookbooks we have from Italy, this is the original method. Once we'd poured the eggs into the pan, we cooked them over medium-low heat until all but the top was set. To set the top, we flipped the frittata with a large spatula, a move that called for a lot of dexterity and that involved the risk of tearing. The next time, we covered the pan with a heat-resistant plate. This caused the underside to overcook and turn tough.

Oven only: Once we'd poured the eggs into the pan, we placed the pan in the center of a 375-degree oven for 30 minutes. The frittata cooked evenly and looked impressive, puffing up a bit and turning golden brown. But it was on the dry side. Hoping to keep it moist, we tinkered with the following: oven temperature (lowering it to 350 degrees), placement of the pan (putting it on a lower rack), and timing (baking it for 20 to 25 minutes). Cooked at the lower temperature, the frittata was still dry. Cooked at the lower temperature in the lower part of the oven, it set unevenly, with parts still runny while others were dry. Cooking it for a shorter period of time left part of it uncooked.

Starting on the stove top and finishing under the broiler: We cooked the frittata on the stove until all but the top was set. Then we placed the pan under a preheated broiler three inches from the heat for about forty seconds.

Provided you work swiftly to keep the frittata from overcooking, this method ties for the best, making a slightly crispy outer layer but leaving the inside creamy and moist. The only reason we don't rate this method absolute tops is because of the care you have to take not to burn the top; broiling adds an element of stress to what's meant to be an entirely casual process.

Starting on the stove top and finishing in the oven: We found this method best overall. Instead of going under the broiler as above, the nearly set frittata is placed in the upper third of a 350-degree oven for two to four minutes. While the top won't turn crispy as it would under the broiler, it sets evenly. Moreover, there's more leeway before the frittata burns or dries out.

We found that nonstick skillets with ovenproof handles are best for frittatas. Conventional skillets require so much oil to prevent sticking that frittatas cooked in them are likely to be greasy. Eggs often cook more evenly in a nonstick pan because they won't cling to the surface in various places.

Master Recipe for Frittata

SERVES 4

Cheese and herbs are the simplest additions to a frittata.

I	tablespoon extra-virgin olive oil or unsalted butter
1/2	small onion, I medium scallion, or I medium shallot, chopped fine
2	tablespoons minced fresh herb leaves, such as parsley, basil, dill, tarragon, or mint
2	tablespoons to 1/3 cup grated cheese of your

choice (1/2 to I ounce)

1/4	teaspoon salt
1/4	teaspoon ground black pepper
6	large eggs, lightly beaten

1. Adjust oven rack to upper-middle position and heat oven to 350 degrees.

2. Heat oil or butter in 10-inch nonstick, ovenproof skillet over medium heat. Swirl skillet to distribute evenly over bottom and sides. Add onion and sauté until softened, 3 to 4 minutes. Stir in herbs.

3. Meanwhile, stir cheese, salt, and pepper into eggs.

4. Pour mixture into skillet; stir lightly with fork until eggs start to set. Once bottom is firm, use thin, plastic spatula to lift frittata edge closest to you. Tilt skillet slightly toward you so that uncooked egg runs underneath. Return skillet to level position and swirl gently to evenly distribute egg. Continue cooking about 40 seconds, then lift edge again, repeating process until egg on top is no longer runny.

5. Transfer skillet to oven; bake until frittata top is set and dry to the touch, 2 to 4 minutes, making sure to remove frittata as soon as top is just set.

6. Run spatula around skillet edge to loosen frittata; invert onto serving plate. Serve warm, at room temperature, or chilled.

➤ VARIATIONS

Asparagus Frittata with Mint and Parmesan

2	tablespoons extra-virgin olive oil or unsalted butter
I	shallot, minced
I	tablespoon minced fresh mint leaves
2	tablespoons minced fresh parsley leaves
1/3	pound asparagus, ends trimmed, spears cut into I-inch pieces and blanched until crisp-tender
5	tablespoons grated Parmesan cheese
1/4	teaspoon salt
1/4	teaspoon ground black pepper
6	large eggs, lightly beaten

1. Adjust oven rack to upper-middle position and heat oven to 350 degrees.

2. Heat oil or butter in 10-inch nonstick skillet over medium heat. Swirl skillet to distribute evenly over bottom and sides. Add shallot; sauté until soft-

ened, 3 to 4 minutes. Add mint, parsley, and aspara-gus; toss to coat with oil. Spread in single layer.

3. Meanwhile, stir 3 tablespoons cheese, salt, and pepper into eggs.

4. Complete frittata following steps 4, 5, and 6 in Master Recipe, sprinkling remaining 2 tablespoons cheese over frittata before baking.

Frittata with Leek and Potatoes

2	tablespoons extra-virgin olive oil or unsalted butter
I	large leek, white part only, rinsed and sliced thin
2	medium red potatoes (8 ounces), boiled until tender, drained, and cut into medium dice
2	tablespoons minced fresh parsley leaves
⅓	cup shredded Emmentaler cheese
¼	teaspoon salt
¼	teaspoon ground black pepper
6	large eggs, lightly beaten

1. Adjust oven rack to upper-middle position and heat oven to 350 degrees.

2. Heat oil or butter in 10-inch nonstick skillet over medium heat. Swirl skillet to distribute evenly over bottom and sides. Add leek; sauté until softened, 5 to 6 minutes. Add potatoes and parsley; toss to coat with oil. Spread in single layer.

3. Meanwhile, stir cheese, salt, and pepper into eggs.

4. Complete frittata following steps 4, 5, and 6 of Master Recipe.

Feta Cheese Frittata with Olives and Sun-Dried Tomatoes

I	tablespoon extra-virgin olive oil
I	small garlic clove, peeled and flattened
I	tablespoon minced fresh basil leaves
I	tablespoon minced fresh oregano leaves
¼	cup sun-dried tomatoes packed in oil, chopped coarse
¼	cup oil-cured olives, pitted and minced
⅓	cup crumbled feta cheese
¼	teaspoon ground black pepper
6	large eggs, lightly beaten

1. Adjust oven rack to upper-middle position and heat oven to 350 degrees.

2. Heat oil and garlic in 10-inch nonstick skillet over medium heat. Remove garlic from skillet as it begins to color. Swirl skillet to distribute oil evenly over bottom and sides. Add herbs, tomatoes, and olives; stir to coat with oil. Spread in single layer.

3. Meanwhile, stir cheese and pepper into eggs.

4. Complete frittata following steps 4, 5, and 6 in Master Recipe.

QUICHE

QUICHE IS AT BASE AN EGG DISH, ALBEIT enriched with dairy and baked in pie pastry. There is no dispute about the characteristics of an ideal quiche: It must have a tender, buttery pastry case embracing a velvety smooth custard that is silken on the tongue and neither too rich nor too lean. Our prebaked pie dough (page 485) makes an excellent crust, but we wondered about the ideal filling. We tried every probable and improbable custard combi-nation, from whole eggs and whole milk to whole eggs with half-and-half to whole eggs with half milk and half heavy cream to eggs with several added yolks and all heavy cream.

The leanest of these mixtures tasted so, and we rejected it as boring, with no creamy mouthfeel. The one with half-and-half was not as rich as you might think because the liquid contains just 11.7 percent butterfat; it was OK, but not great. The mixture con-taining half whole milk and half heavy cream was significantly richer, because heavy cream contains three times the butterfat (an average of 36 percent) added to the approximately 3.7 percent fat of the whole milk. Whole eggs, extra yolks, and all heavy cream produced a custard that was just too much of a good thing: overpoweringly rich and too creamy.

The best mixture—a medium-rich custard with good mouthfeel, fine taste, and a good set—com-bined two whole eggs with two yolks, one cup of milk, and one cup of heavy cream. Baked in our favorite crust, it was just what we were looking for: a custard that was creamy but not cloyingly rich, with excellent mouthfeel and perfect set, its tender skin a luscious golden brown hue. It puffed slightly while baking and settled neatly as it cooled.

Of course, baking temperature is also an impor-tant factor in regulating custard texture. High heat toughens egg proteins and shrinks the albumen, separating, or curdling, the mixture and squeezing out the water instead of keeping the egg in perfect suspension. Moderate heat proved best.

We tested different quiche formulas at temperatures ranging from 325 degrees to 400 degrees. We found 350 degrees to be slightly slow; by the time the custard had set, the top, which was a pallid yellow, had developed into a chewy skin. On the theory that warming the liquid in the custard would shorten baking time and keep the custard smoother, we tried heating the milk to 100 degrees before whisking in the eggs. Indeed, this custard set a few minutes faster, but it was otherwise unremarkable and still had a pallid color on top. We found that baking at 375 degrees was exactly right, setting the custard gently enough to maintain its creamy consistency, yet hot enough to brown the top before it dried out and became rubbery.

As a test for doneness, we advise watching the oven, not the clock. What you're looking for is a light golden brown coloring on the quiche surface, which may puff up slightly as it bakes. A knife blade inserted about one inch from the edge should come out clean; the center may still be slightly liquid, but internal heat will finish the baking and it will solidify when cool. If your test blade comes out clean in the center, the quiche may already be slightly overbaked and should be removed from the oven at once. Be sure to set the baked quiche on a wire rack to cool so that air circulates all around it, preventing condensation on the bottom. Allowing the quiche to cool until it is either warm or at room temperature also lets the custard settle before serving. The cooler the quiche, the more neatly it will slice and the easier it will be to serve.

Quiche Lorraine
SERVES 8

The center will be surprisingly soft when the quiche comes out of the oven, but the filling will continue to set (and sink somewhat) as it cools. If the pie shell has been previously baked and cooled, place the pie shell in the preheating oven for about five minutes to warm it, taking care that it does not burn. Because ingredients in the variations that follow are bulkier, the amount of custard mixture has been reduced to prevent overflow.

I	recipe American Pie Dough for Prebaked Pie Shell (page 485), prepared through step 4
8	ounces (about 8 slices) bacon, cut into ½-inch pieces
2	large eggs, plus 2 large yolks
I	cup whole milk
I	cup heavy cream
½	teaspoon salt
½	teaspoon ground white pepper
	Pinch grated nutmeg
4	ounces Gruyère cheese, grated (about I cup)

1. Adjust oven rack to middle position and heat oven to 375 degrees. Partially bake pie shell as directed in step 5 on page 485.

2. Meanwhile, fry bacon in skillet over medium heat until crisp and brown, about 5 minutes. Transfer with slotted spoon to paper towel–lined plate. Whisk all remaining ingredients except cheese in medium bowl.

3. As soon as pie shell comes out of the oven, spread cheese and bacon evenly over bottom of pie shell and set shell on oven rack. Pour in custard mixture to ½ inch below crust rim. Bake until lightly golden brown, a knife blade inserted about one inch from the edge comes out clean, and center feels set but soft like gelatin, 32 to 35 minutes. Transfer quiche to rack to cool. Serve warm or at room temperature.

➤ VARIATIONS
Crabmeat Quiche
Follow recipe for Quiche Lorraine, reducing quantities of milk and cream to ¾ cup each. Add 2 tablespoons dry sherry and a pinch of cayenne pepper to custard mixture. Substitute 8 ounces (1 cup) cooked crabmeat tossed with 2 tablespoons chopped fresh chives for bacon and cheese.

Leek and Goat Cheese Quiche
Sauté white part of 2 medium leeks (washed thoroughly and cut into ½-inch dice, about 2 cups) in 2 tablespoons unsalted butter over medium heat until soft, 5 to 7 minutes. Follow recipe for Quiche Lorraine, reducing quantities of milk and cream to ¾ cup each. Omit bacon; substitute 4 ounces mild goat cheese, broken into ½-inch pieces, for Gruyère. Add leeks with cheese.

17

COOKIES, BROWNIES, AND BARS

MAKING COOKIES AND BROWNIES IS AMERICA'S favorite kind of baking project. Not only are results usually quite good, but the time, effort, and skills required are usually minimal. Ingredient lists draw heavily on pantry staples as well as refrigerated items (like butter and eggs) that can be found in most reasonably stocked kitchens.

Most cookie doughs are prepared in the same fashion. The butter is creamed with the sugar until light and creamy. The eggs and other liquids (vanilla or other extracts) are added. Finally, the flour and other dry ingredients, which have been sifted or stirred together, are added.

This process sounds easy (and it is), but there is some important science here. The butter must be properly creamed in order to incorporate the right amount of air into the fat. In our tests, we've consistently found that cookies made with creamed butter bake higher and have a lighter texture than those made with butter that is not creamed. (Brownies are meant to be dense and fudgy, so melted butter is fine in this recipe.) We also found that creaming the butter with sugar adds more air than beating the butter alone. That's because the sharp edges of the sugar crystals physically aerate the butter by cutting small air pockets in the fat.

In most cases, the first step is to soften the butter. Chilled butter (at 35 degrees, the temperature of most refrigerators) is too cold to combine with other ingredients. We found that cookies made with cold butter are often flat because not enough air is whipped into the butter during creaming. Ideally, an hour or two before you want to make cookies, remove the butter from the refrigerator and let it warm to about 65 degrees. Butter starts to melt at 68 degrees, so the stick should still be a bit firm when pressed.

If you have forgotten to soften the butter, don't use the microwave to bring it up to room temperature. The microwave will melt the butter in places. Instead, we found it best to cut the butter into very small bits so they will warm up quickly. By the time you have preheated the oven and assembled and measured the remaining ingredients, the butter should be close to 65 degrees.

Butter and sugar can be creamed by hand, but an electric mixer (either handheld or standing) is quicker and yields superior results. Most cooks don't cream the butter and sugar long enough and don't get as much volume as they should. The beating times for recipes in this chapter are for an electric mixer. If you beat the butter and sugar with a wooden spoon, the times will be several minutes longer, depending on your hand strength and speed. When the butter and sugar have lightened in color and become fluffy, you can stop.

Once the butter and sugar are creamed, most recipes call for the addition of eggs and vanilla or other liquids. Make sure the eggs are at room temperature so they don't cause the batter to curdle.

(Let the eggs sit out on the counter for an hour or two, or warm them in a bowl of hot tap water for five minutes). At this point, the dry ingredients can be stirred into the batter. We found it is perfectly fine to use an electric mixer—although many recipes call for combining the ingredients by hand at this stage—just make sure the speed is set to low.

In many old-fashioned recipes, the flour, leavener, and salt are sifted together before being added to the batter. This was necessary when flour was often lumpy straight from the bag. Because modern flour is presifted, however, we find this step to be unnecessary for making cookies. (Cakes, however, are a different matter.) We simply mix the dry ingredients together in a bowl (a whisk does this well) to make sure that the leavener and salt will be evenly distributed in the batter.

When making cookies there are two dry ingredients that we like to sift. Cocoa powder and confectioners' sugar often have small lumps. We find that sifting breaks up these lumps and does an excellent job of mixing the cocoa or powdered sugar with the other dry ingredients.

The final step in the dough-making process is to add solid ingredients, like chocolate chips and nuts. These should be stirred in by hand since a mixer might break them apart.

There are several ways to manipulate a finished dough in order to change the appearance or texture of the baked cookies. (No matter how the dough is shaped, you can inhibit spreading in the oven—and thus prevent the cookies from becoming too thin—by chilling the dough in the refrigerator for at least one hour.)

The quickest way to get the dough into the oven

is to drop it from a spoon directly onto a cookie sheet. Because the pieces of dough are not round, they spread unevenly in the oven. The result is cookies with thin, crisp edges and thicker centers.

For molded or shaped cookies, each piece of dough is rolled into a ball or otherwise manipulated by hand before being placed on a cookie sheet. When rolled into a ball, the dough is often also rolled in sugar before being baked. Shaping the dough into a ball promotes even spreading and thickness in the baked cookies.

The third option is rolling and cutting. This method is used to guarantee a thin, crisp cookie suit-

able for decoration. Rolled-and-cut cookies have an even thickness from edge to edge and usually snap rather than bend.

When shaping cookies, make sure to measure the batter so that all of the cookies will be the same size and will bake at the same rate. Make sure to leave enough room between pieces of dough for cookies to spread in the oven. Two inches is usually a safe distance.

Once cookies are in the oven, we find it best to reverse the top and bottom sheets and also rotate each sheet from back to front at the halfway point of the baking time to promote even cooking. If you like your cookies soft and chewy, underbake them

---

EQUIPMENT: Tools for Making Cookies

While cookie making generally doesn't require any fancy equipment, there are some basic items you will need. Besides a large bowl, you will need some sort of implement to mix the cookie dough. A wooden spoon is adequate for this task, although a mixer will beat more air into the butter and produce better cookies. There are two basic types of mixers. Handheld mixers lack the power to knead bread (you need a standing mixer for that), but are fine for cookie doughs. Of course, you can use a standing mixer (see page 351) if you like.

When shopping for a handheld mixer, look for models that have thin, curved wire beaters rather than the old-fashioned kind with thick posts down the center. This new design does a better job of driving food down into the bowl, improving the efficiency of the mixer while reducing splattering. Wire beaters are also much less likely to become clogged when mixing stiff cookie doughs.

In our testing, we also found that mixers with handles that slant up to the front fit the hand better and cause less arm stress than those with handles that are parallel to the beaters. We tested nine mixers and found the KitchenAid to be the best choice.

Once the dough is mixed, it's ready for the cookie sheet. Most cookie sheets have the same basic design. They are a piece of metal that is usually slightly longer than it is wide. (A standard size is 16 inches long and 14 inches across.) Some are dark, some are light. Some have rims on all four sides. Others have rims on one or two sides but otherwise have flat edges. We tested 11 sheets in a variety of materials and came to some surprising conclusions.

First of all, shiny light-colored sheets do a better job of evenly browning the bottoms of cookies than dark sheets. Most of the dark sheets are nonstick, and we found that these pans tend to

overbrown cookies. Shiny, sliver sheets heat much more evenly, and if sticking is a concern we simply use parchment paper. Parchment paper also keeps the bottom of the cookies from overbrowning.

In our testing, we also came to prefer sheets with at least one rimless edge. This way we could slide a whole sheet of parchment paper onto a cooling rack without actually touching the hot paper. (When cooled, the cookies can be peeled away from the paper.) The open edge also makes it possible to slide cookies on a rack, rather than lifting them onto the rack and possibly dropping them. Our favorite cookie sheet is made by Kaiser out of tinned steel. At just $7, it was also the cheapest sheet we tested.

A final note about lining cookie sheets with parchment. Even when sticking is not an issue, we still use parchment paper. It makes cleanup a snap, and we can reuse cookie sheets for subsequent batches without having to wash them first. When parchment is essential, the recipe directions call for it. Otherwise, use parchment at your discretion.

Cooling racks are just as important as cookie sheets and parchment paper. These often-neglected items are essential because they allow air to circulate under and around the cookies as they cool. Cookies cooled on a closed sheet might stick or become soggy. Choose a cooling rack that is large and sturdy. Some models have thin wires running in a single direction, but we prefer racks with crosswoven pieces of metal that form a fairly tight grid. These racks, sometimes called icing racks, are usually fairly sturdy. Also, the holes in the grid are very small, making it impossible for cookies to slide through onto the counter, something that often occurs on racks with wires that run in just one direction.

INGREDIENTS: Flour

We wanted to know if there was a single all-purpose flour that would be best for those who keep only one kind of flour in the pantry. So we stocked our test kitchen shelves with many bags of many brands of all-purpose flour and started a bake-off that eventually stretched over some six months. We ended up preparing two kinds of cookies, pie pastry, biscuits, cake, muffins, and bread with nine brands of flour, often making several batches of each.

Before we began testing, we turned to experts in both grain science and baking science to find out what we should be looking for. Many of these sources began by pointing out that all-purpose flour is not necessarily a premium product. Most wheat that is milled is made into specialized flours used on a large-scale commercial level. All-purpose is designed to be used in a wide range of recipes written for home cooks who do not have the kind of high-intensity mixers or the expertise necessary to use the specialized flours made for commercial bakeries.

There are a number of choices a flour company must make when milling all-purpose flour that will influence the way its product performs in recipes. For starters, there is the essence of the flour, the wheat itself. All-purpose flour is typically made from either hard red winter wheat, soft red winter wheat, or a combination of the two. Of the flours we used in the taste tests, five were made from hard winter wheat, one was made of soft wheat, and three were a mix of soft and hard.

Perhaps the primary difference between these types of wheat—and, consequently, in the flours made from them—is the variation in protein content. Hard winter wheat is about 10 to 13 percent protein, and soft wheat about 8 to 10 percent. Mixtures of the two wheats are somewhere in between.

High-protein flours are generally recommended for yeasted products and other baked goods that require a lot of structural support. The reason is that the higher the protein level in a flour, the greater the formation of gluten. The sheets that gluten forms in dough are elastic enough to move with the gas released by yeast but also sturdy enough to prevent that gas from escaping, so the dough doesn't deflate. Lower-protein flours, on the other hand, are recommended for chemically leavened baked goods. This is because baking powder and baking soda are quick leaveners. They lack the endurance of yeast, which can force the naturally resistant gluten sheets to expand. Gluten can overpower quick leaveners, causing the final baked product to fall flat.

A second important difference in flours is whether they are bleached or not. Technically, all all-purpose flours are bleached. Carotenoid pigments in wheat lend a faint yellowish tint to freshly milled flour. But in a matter of about 12 weeks, these pigments oxidize, undergoing the same chemical process that turns a sliced apple brown. In this case, yellowish flour changes to a whiter hue (though not stark white). Early in this century, as the natural bleaching process came to be understood, scientists identified methods to chemically expedite and intensify it. Typically, all-purpose flours are bleached with either benzoyl peroxide or chlorine gas. The latter not only bleaches the flour but also alters the flour proteins, making them less inclined to form strong gluten. Today consumers prefer chemically bleached flour over unbleached because they associate the whiter color with higher quality.

While the protein guidelines make eminently good sense, to our surprise, the results of our tests did not always correspond. The biscuit test did reveal a certain progression from light, cake-like biscuits produced by the lowest-protein flours to coarser, heavier biscuits produced by the higher-protein flours. But our tasters liked all of the biscuits, except for one that had stale flavors. Another trend we noticed was that lower-protein flours spread more in tests of chocolate chip cookies and muffins.

As an overall category, the four bleached flours in our tests in fact did not perform as well as the unbleached flours and were regularly criticized for tasting flat or carrying "off" flavors, often described as metallic. These characteristics, however, were more difficult to detect in recipes that contained a high proportion of ingredients other than flour. Coincidentally, our cake tests and chocolate chip cookie tests (both sugary recipes) were the two tests in which off flavors carried by the bleached flour went undetected or were considered faint.

Despite the variations and subtleties, however, the good news is that we did end up with two flours we can recommend wholeheartedly. Both King Arthur and Pillsbury unbleached flours regularly made for highly recommended baked goods, producing a more consistent range of preferred products than the other seven flours in the taste tests. If you are going to have only one flour in the house, our advice is to choose one of these two.

No matter the type or brand, we measure all flour by the dip-and-sweep method. Dip a metal or plastic dry measure into a bag of flour so that the cup is overflowing with flour. Then use a knife or icing spatula to level off the flour, sweeping the excess back into the bag. Short of weighing flour (which is what professional bakers do), this measuring method is your best guarantee of using the right amount of flour. Spooning the flour into the measuring cup aerates it, and you might end up with as much as 25 percent less flour by weight.

slightly and allow the cookies to firm up on the baking sheets for several minutes before transferring them to a cooling rack.

When making second and third batches, do not place dough directly onto hot cookie sheets. This causes excess spreading and uneven baking because it will probably take you a few minutes to get all the dough on the sheet.

Most cookies taste best the day they are made. That said, most cookies can also be stored with only minimal loss in freshness. Soft, chewy cookies may dry out a bit and harden after a few days, but they will retain their flavor.

If you want to keep cookies for several days, we suggest storing them in a metal tin at room temperature. In our testing, we found that you can restore just-baked freshness to chewy cookies by wrapping a single cookie in a sheet of paper towel and microwaving it until soft, 15 to 25 seconds. Cool microwaved cookies before serving. This technique works best with oversized cookies like peanut butter and oatmeal that should be chewy and a bit soft. Do not try this with cookies that should be crisp.

CHOCOLATE CHIP COOKIES

CHOCOLATE CHIP COOKIES COME IN VARIOUS styles, with significant differences in texture, size, and flavor. The dough is a basic sugar cookie, in which some of the granulated sugar has been replaced by brown sugar, which gives them a caramel flavor. Of course, the dough is also studded with chocolate chips and, often, nuts.

Traditional recipes follow the Tollhouse cookie model, made famous on packages of Nestlé chocolate chips. This recipe dates back to the 1930s when Ruth Wakefield, owner of the Toll House Inn in Whitman, Massachusetts, cut up a chocolate bar and added the pieces to a cookie dough. She eventually sold the recipe to Nestlé, which introduced the chocolate morsel in 1939.

These cookies are on the small side (about 2 inches in diameter). The edges are thin, crisp, and golden brown. The center of the cookie is thicker and will bend when the cookies are warm but hardens as the cookies cool and snaps after several hours. The center

---

INGREDIENTS: Chocolate Chips

Chips have a lower cocoa butter content than chocolate bars, which keeps them from becoming too liquidy when baked. Often the cocoa butter is replaced by sugar, which is why we found many chocolate chips in our tasting of various brands to be quite sweet. We found that the chips that tasted best straight out of the bag tasted best in cookies. Nestlé, Guittard, Ghirardelli, and Tropical Source (a brand sold in natural food stores) all received high marks. Those chips which excelled were noted for a balance of bitterness, sweetness, and smoothness—and turned out to hold a few curious secrets.

In the spectrum of chocolates, chips are generally considered the least refined. The most refined would be a coating chocolate, also known as couverture, an extremely glossy chocolate usually found only in specialty candy-making shops and primarily used by pastry chefs in confections. Chocolate chips lack the fluidity necessary for the technical and detailed work of a pastry chef, such as molds and truffles, or even for the thin, glossy effect of a simple chocolate-dipped strawberry. For example, a bowl of melted couverture will pour out smoothly, like cream, but a bowl of melted chips will slide sluggishly like glue. This high viscosity and low fluidity

are what make the chip shape possible. When squeezed through a nozzle onto a moving belt in the factory, the chocolate quickly sets up into a pert morsel rather than collapsing into a small blob.

The chip that rated second in our tasting defied the unspoken standard for chip shape. Guittard grinds and blends its chip chocolate like it does its couverture. This helps to develop the flavor. The tradeoff, however, is that the chip is too fluid to hold the tightly pointed shape of a typical chip. Even so, some of our tasters liked the larger size and unorthodox disc shape of the chip.

The top-rated chip, Tropical Source, did showcase the typical pointed shape, but like the Guittard chip, it had an unusually high cocoa butter content. The average chip is 27 percent cocoa butter, but both Guittard and Tropical Source chips contain 30 percent. Cocoa butter is renowned for providing the melt-in-your-mouth lusciousness of chocolate. Because it is costly, though, most chocolate chip manufacturers limit the cocoa butter content. Tasters typically had to agitate chips between their tongues and the roofs of their mouths or even bite into some to break them down. Guittard and Tropical Source stood out because they melted more smoothly than the rest.

of this cookie is often cakey, but should not be dry.

The original recipe calls for equal parts of brown and granulated sugar. We found that we like the caramel flavor that the brown sugar gives this cookie and have increased the ratio of brown to granulated sugar to two to one. Modern Tollhouse cookie recipes often omit the water that was part of the original. We found that the water makes the cookies a bit more moist and should be added.

An attractive variation on the traditional chocolate chip cookie that some bake shops and cookie stores have recently made their reputations on—not to mention a lot of money—is the oversized cookie. Unlike the traditional cookies made at home, these cookies are thick right from the edge to the center. They are also chewy, even a bit soft. Although we knew at the outset that molding the dough rather than dropping it into uneven blobs would be essential to achieving an even thickness, we didn't realize how challenging making them really chewy would be.

We added more flour or ground oats (as some recipes suggest), which helped the cookies hold their shape and remain thick but also made the texture cakey and dry rather than chewy. When we tried liquid sweeteners, such as molasses and corn syrup, the dough spread too much in the oven and the cookies baked up thin.

At this point in our testing, we decided to experiment with the butter. Some chewy cookies start with melted rather than creamed butter. In its solid state, butter is an emulsion of butter and water. When butter is melted, the fat and water molecules separate. When melted butter is added to a dough, the proteins in the flour immediately grab onto the freed water molecules to form elastic sheets of gluten. The gluten makes a cookie chewy.

Our first attempt with melted butter was disappointing. The dough was very soft from all the liquid, and the cookies baked up greasy. Because the dough was having a hard time absorbing the liquid fat, we reduced the amount of butter from sixteen to twelve tablespoons. We also reduced the number of eggs from two to one to make the dough stiffer.

The cookies were chewy at this point, but they became somewhat tough as they cooled, and after a few hours they were hard. Fat acts as a tenderizer and by reducing the amount of butter in the recipe we

had limited its ability to keep the cookies soft. The only other source of fat is the egg. Since our dough was already soft enough and probably could not stand the addition of too much more liquid, we decided to add another yolk (which contains all the fat) and leave out the white. The dough was still stiff enough to shape. When baked, the cookies were thick and chewy and they remained that way when they cooled. Finally, we had the perfect recipe.

Traditional Chocolate Chip Cookies

MAKES ABOUT 60 COOKIES

This is our take on the classic Tollhouse cookie, thin and crisp around the edges, thicker and a bit cakier in the middle. The dough can be baked on ungreased sheets, but lining the sheets with parchment will make cleanup easier. When the cookies come out of the oven, they are very soft. Let them cool on the sheets for a minute or two before transferring them to a rack.

2 ¼	cups all-purpose flour
1	teaspoon salt
1	teaspoon baking soda
½	pound (2 sticks) unsalted butter, softened
1	cup light or dark brown sugar, packed
½	cup granulated sugar
2	large eggs
1	teaspoon vanilla extract
½	teaspoon water
2	cups semisweet chocolate chips
1	cup coarsely chopped walnuts or pecans

1. Adjust oven racks to upper- and lower-middle positions and heat oven to 375 degrees. Whisk flour, salt, and baking soda together in medium bowl; set aside.

2. Either by hand or with electric mixer, cream together butter and sugars until light and fluffy, about 3 minutes with mixer set at medium speed. Scrape sides of bowl with rubber spatula. Add eggs, vanilla, and water. Beat until combined, about 40 seconds. Scrape sides of bowl.

3. Add dry ingredients and beat at low speed until just combined, 15 to 20 seconds. Add chocolate chips and nuts and stir until combined.

4. Drop batter by tablespoons onto ungreased

cookie sheets, spacing pieces of dough about 1 inch apart. Bake, reversing position of cookie sheets halfway through baking (from top to bottom and front to back), until cookies are light golden brown and outer edges begin to crisp, 8 to 10 minutes. Cool cookies on sheets for 1 to 2 minutes before transferring to cooling racks with wide spatula.

➤ VARIATION

Cocoa Chocolate Chip Cookies

We like these chocolaty cookies with extra nuts. They won't spread as much in the oven, so drop the batter by generous tablespoons onto the baking sheet. We tried both dutched and natural cocoa in this recipe. We thought the dutched cocoa gave the cookies a slightly stronger chocolate flavor, but both types of cocoa worked fine.

Follow recipe for Traditional Chocolate Chip Cookies, decreasing flour to 2 cups and sifting ½ cup cocoa powder with other dry ingredients. Increase nuts to 1½ cups. Drop batter by generous tablespoons on cookie sheets and bake 10 to 12 minutes.

Thick and Chewy Chocolate Chip Cookies

MAKES ABOUT 18 LARGE COOKIES

These oversized cookies are chewy and thick, like many of the chocolate chip cookies sold in gourmet shops and cookie stores. They rely on melted butter and an extra yolk to keep their texture soft. These cookies are best served warm from the oven but will retain their texture even when cooled. To ensure the proper texture, cool the cookies on the cookie sheet. Oversized cookie sheets allow you to get all the dough into the oven at one time. If you're using small- *er cookie sheets, put fewer cookies on each sheet and bake them in batches. See the illustrations below for tips on shaping these cookies.*

2	cups plus 2 tablespoons all-purpose flour
½	teaspoon baking soda
½	teaspoon salt
12	tablespoons (1½ sticks) unsalted butter, melted and cooled until warm
1	cup light or dark brown sugar, packed
½	cup granulated sugar
1	large egg plus 1 egg yolk
2	teaspoons vanilla extract
1–1½	cups semisweet chocolate chips

1. Adjust oven racks to upper- and lower-middle positions and heat oven to 325 degrees. Line two large cookie sheets with parchment paper.

2. Whisk flour, baking soda, and salt together in medium bowl; set aside.

3. Either by hand or with electric mixer, mix butter and sugars until thoroughly blended. Beat in egg, yolk, and vanilla until combined. Add dry ingredients and beat at low speed just until combined. Stir in chips to taste.

4. Roll scant ¼ cup dough into ball. Holding dough ball in fingertips of both hands, pull into two equal halves. Rotate halves 90 degrees and, with jagged surfaces facing up, join halves together at their base, again forming a single ball, being careful not to smooth dough's uneven surface. Place formed dough onto cookie sheet, leaving 2½ inches between each ball.

5. Bake, reversing position of cookie sheets

SHAPING THICK CHOCOLATE CHIP COOKIES

 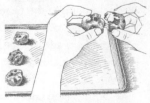  

1. Creating a jagged surface on each dough ball gives the finished cookies an attractive appearance. Start by rolling a scant ¼ cup of dough into a smooth ball.

2. Holding the dough ball in the fingertips of both hands, pull the dough apart into two equal halves.

3. Each half will have a jagged surface where it was ripped from the other. Rotate each piece 90 degrees so that the jagged surface faces up.

4. Jam the halves back together into one ball so that the top surface remains jagged.

halfway through baking (from top to bottom and front to back), until cookies are light golden brown and outer edges start to harden yet centers are still soft and puffy, 15 to 18 minutes. Cool cookies on sheets. When cooled, peel cookies from parchment.

➤ VARIATIONS

Chocolate Chip Cookies with Coconut and Toasted Almonds

Follow recipe for Thick and Chewy Chocolate Chip Cookies, adding 1½ cups sweetened dried coconut and 1 cup toasted sliced almonds along with chips.

Black and White Chocolate Chip Cookies with Pecans

Follow recipe for Thick and Chewy Chocolate Chip Cookies, substituting ½ cup white chocolate chips for ½ cup of semisweet chips. Add 1 cup chopped pecans with chips.

INGREDIENTS: Sugar

Granulated sugar is a key ingredient in almost every cookie recipe on the planet. Besides adding sweetness, sugar provides some structure and chew. In fact, very chewy cookies generally have quite a lot of sugar in them.

Many cookie recipes also call for brown sugar, which is granulated sugar with a small percentage of molasses added for flavor and color. (Light brown sugar contains 3.5 percent molasses; dark brown sugar has 6.5 percent molasses.) Brown sugar lends a caramel flavor that is welcome in many cookies. Dark brown sugar has a slightly stronger caramel flavor, but in most cookie recipes the differences are slight. Unless noted, use either light or dark in the recipes in this book.

When measuring brown sugar, it is important to pack the sugar into the dry measure for accurate measurement. We like to use the back of a smaller measure to press brown sugar into the cup.

Confectioners' sugar is used in cookies where tenderness and a fine crumb are important. Confectioners' sugar is made by pulverizing granulated sugar and combining it with a little cornstarch (about 3 percent of the total weight) to prevent it from clumping. Because of its fine, powdery consistency, this sugar gives cookies a melt-in-your-mouth texture. Note that small lumps can still form in the box, so we recommend sifting confectioners' sugar before combining it with other ingredients.

PEANUT BUTTER COOKIES

THERE ARE SEVERAL STYLES OF PEANUT butter cookie. Some are thin and candyish; others are dry and crumbly. For us, the best peanut butter cookie is crisp around the edges, chewy in the center, and slightly puffed. The flavor is buttery and sweet, with a strong hit of peanuts.

We started our tests by focusing on the fat. We quickly determined that butter accentuated the peanut flavor, while margarine and Crisco diminished it. Crisco did make the cookie chewier in the center, but we felt the added chewiness was not worth the loss in peanut flavor. We tried peanut oil (thinking this might boost the overall peanut flavor), but the resulting texture was dry and sandy.

From these early tests, we also noticed that peanut butter types replicated the results we found with fats. Natural peanut butters, with a layer of oil on top, made the cookies sandy. Commercial brands, which contain partially hydrogenated vegetable oils that are similar to Crisco, helped the cookie rise and achieve a crisper edge and chewier center. We tested both smooth and chunky peanut butter and felt that the chunky styles contributed more peanut flavor.

We tried using more peanut butter to boost the peanut flavor (we even used all peanut butter and no butter), but we still could not get a strong enough peanut flavor. Also, the texture suffered as we removed the butter from our working recipe. The cookies were sandy and almost like shortbread. Butter was crucial for lightness and a chewy texture. Clearly, we would need peanuts as well as peanut butter. We found that chopped peanuts tend to slip out of the dough. We then ground them in the food processor and worked them directly into the dough, which greatly improved the peanut flavor.

Salt brings out the flavor of peanuts (salted roasted peanuts taste better than unsalted nuts), and we found that salt also helped bring out the flavor of the peanuts in the cookies. In fact, we found it best to use both salted nuts and salted butter for the strongest peanut flavor.

At this point, we focused our attention on the sweetener. We had been using granulated sugar and now began to wonder if a liquid sweetener might make the cookies chewier. We tried molasses and corn syrup, but they could not beat granulated sugar. We tried brown sugar but found the resulting cookies to be too sweet and candyish. However, because the brown sugar did make the cookies taste nuttier, we decided to test half brown sugar and half granulated sugar. This turned out to be ideal, giving the cookies a mild praline flavor that highlighted the flavor of the peanuts.

We found that the amount of flour in the dough also affected the peanut flavor. Too little flour made the cookies taste greasy and not very peanutty. As we increased the flour, the peanut flavor intensified. Too much flour, however, and the cookies became dry. Slightly more flour than butter and peanut butter combined proved to be the right amount.

Peanut Butter Cookies

MAKES ABOUT 3 DOZEN COOKIES

These cookies have a strong peanut flavor that comes from extra-crunchy peanut butter (in our taste test we preferred Jif) as well as from roasted salted peanuts that are ground in a food processor and worked into the dough. In our testing, we found that salted butter brings out the flavor of the nuts. If using unsalted butter, increase the salt to one teaspoon.

2½	cups all-purpose flour
½	teaspoon baking soda
½	teaspoon baking powder
½	teaspoon salt
½	pound (2 sticks) salted butter, softened
1	cup brown sugar, packed
1	cup granulated sugar
1	cup extra-crunchy peanut butter, preferably Jif, at room temperature
2	large eggs
2	teaspoons vanilla extract
1	cup roasted salted peanuts, ground in food processor to resemble bread crumbs, about 14 pulses

1. Adjust ovens rack to upper- and lower-middle positions and heat oven to 350 degrees. Line two large cookie sheets with parchment paper.

2. Whisk flour, baking soda, baking powder, and salt together in medium bowl; set aside.

3. Either by hand or with electric mixer, beat butter until creamy. Add sugars; beat until fluffy, about 3 minutes with electric mixer, stopping to scrape down bowl as necessary. Beat in peanut butter until fully incorporated, then eggs, one at a time, then vanilla. Gently stir dry ingredients into peanut butter mixture. Add ground peanuts; stir gently until just incorporated.

4. Working with generous 2 tablespoons each time, roll dough into 2-inch balls. Place balls on parchment-lined cookie sheets, leaving 2½ inches between each ball. Press each dough ball twice with dinner fork dipped in cold water to make crisscross design.

5. Bake, reversing position of cookie sheets halfway through baking time (from top to bottom racks and back to front), until cookies are puffed and slightly brown along edges but not on top, 10 to 12 minutes. (Cookies will not look fully baked.) Cool cookies on cookie sheet until set, about 4 minutes, then transfer to wire rack with wide spatula to cool completely.

➤ VARIATION

Peanut Butter Chocolate Chip Cookies
Follow recipe for Peanut Butter Cookies, adding 1½ cups semisweet chocolate chips with ground nuts.

OATMEAL COOKIES

WHEN DEVELOPING THIS RECIPE, WE WANTED an oversized cookie that was chewy and moist. Most oatmeal cookies seem dry to us, and the flavor of the oats seems too weak. Many recipes don't call for enough oats, and spices often overwhelm the flavor of the oats that are there.

The flavor issues were easily solved with some testing. We experimented with various amounts of oats and found that in order to have a real oat flavor, we needed a ratio of 2 cups of oats for every cup of flour—far more oats than in most recipes.

To keep the focus on the oats, we decided to eliminate the cinnamon, a common ingredient in these cookies, because it was overpowering the oats. We wanted some spice, however, and chose nutmeg, which has a cleaner, subtler flavor that we liked with oats.

Our cookies tasted good at this point, but we needed to work on the texture. In our tests, we found that a high proportion of butter to flour helped to keep the cookies moist. We settled on 2 parts butter to 3 parts flour.

We found that shaping the dough into two-inch balls (rather than dropping the meager rounded tablespoon called for in most recipes) helped keep the cookies more moist and chewy, especially in the center, which remains a bit underbaked in an oversized cookie. Smaller cookies are considerably drier and more cakelike, something we did not want in an oatmeal cookie.

Our final tests involved the sugar. We experimented with various amounts and found that adding a full cup each of both brown and granulated sugar delivered the best results, a cookie that was especially moist and rich. Sugar makes baked goods more moist and tender because it helps them hold onto water during the baking process. In addition, sugar encourages exterior browning, which promotes crispness.

Big and Chewy Oatmeal–Raisin Cookies

MAKES ABOUT 18 LARGE COOKIES

If you prefer a less sweet cookie, you can reduce the white sugar by one-quarter cup, but you will lose some crispness. Do not overbake these cookies. The edges should be brown, but the rest of the cookie should be very light in color. Parchment paper makes for easy cookie removal and cleanup, but it is not a necessity. If you don't use parchment, cool the cookies on the baking sheet for two minutes before transferring them to a cooling rack.

1½	cups all-purpose flour
½	teaspoon salt
½	teaspoon baking powder
¼	teaspoon freshly grated nutmeg
½	pound (2 sticks) unsalted butter, softened
1	cup light brown sugar, packed
1	cup granulated sugar
2	large eggs
3	cups rolled oats
1½	cups raisins (optional)

1. Adjust oven racks to low and middle positions and heat oven to 350 degrees. Line two large cookie sheets with parchment paper.

2. Whisk flour, salt, baking powder, and nutmeg together in medium bowl.

3. Either by hand or with electric mixer, beat butter until creamy. Add sugars; beat until fluffy, about 3 minutes. Beat in eggs one at a time.

4. Stir dry ingredients into butter-sugar mixture with wooden spoon or large rubber spatula. Stir in oats and optional raisins.

5. Working with generous 2 tablespoons of dough each time, roll dough into 2-inch balls. Place balls on parchment-lined cookie sheet, leaving at least 2 inches between each ball.

6. Bake until cookie edges turn golden brown, 22 to 25 minutes. (Halfway during baking, turn cookie sheets from front to back and also switch them from top to bottom.) Slide cookies, on parchment, to cooling rack. Let cool at least 30 minutes before peeling cookie from parchment.

➤ VARIATIONS
Date Oatmeal Cookies
Follow recipe for Big and Chewy Oatmeal Cookies, substituting 1½ cups chopped dates for raisins.

Ginger Oatmeal Cookies
Follow recipe for Big and Chewy Oatmeal Cookies, adding ¾ teaspoon ground ginger to flour and other dry ingredients and omitting raisins.

Chocolate Chip Oatmeal Cookies
Follow recipe for Big and Chewy Oatmeal Cookies, omitting nutmeg and substituting 1½ cups semisweet chocolate chips for raisins.

Nut Oatmeal Cookies
Follow recipe for Big and Chewy Oatmeal Cookies, decreasing flour to 1⅓ cups and adding ¼ cup ground almonds and 1 cup chopped walnut pieces along with oats. (Almonds can be ground in food processor or blender.) Omit raisins.

Orange and Almond Oatmeal Cookies
Follow recipe for Big and Chewy Oatmeal Cookies, omitting raisins and adding 2 tablespoons minced orange zest and 1 cup toasted chopped almonds (toast nuts in 350-degree oven for 5 minutes) along with oats.

[handwritten notes in margins:]
10/21/01 mine made 24 very large cookies. Excellent!
I lightly broke & stirred together & added at same time

MOLASSES-SPICE COOKIES

MANY MOLASSES-SPICE COOKIES ARE REALLY gingersnaps. They are hard and dry and not nearly sweet enough. We wanted to create an oversized cookie that was especially soft and chewy. We also wanted the cookie to have a strong molasses flavor with a good hit of sweetness. We started by testing the sweetener, assuming that the molasses would be the key to the puzzle.

We quickly found that too much molasses will impart a bitter quality to the cookies. Cookies made with a lot of molasses may be soft and chewy, but they won't taste very good. We tried cutting back on the amount of molasses, but the cookies were too bland.

Brown sugar, which is made with a small amount of molasses, proved to be the answer. Unlike straight molasses, brown sugar has no harsh flavors. After several tests, we settled on the following formula as the ideal compromise between sweetness and good molasses flavor: ½ cup each of dark brown sugar and granulated sugar, along with ⅓ cup of molasses.

We found that using a fair amount of sweetener helped make the cookies soft and chewy. Our other trick was to underbake the cookies a bit. Even with all the sweetener, these cookies can become hard if overbaked. Since the color of the cookies is so dark, err on the side of underbaking.

Molasses-spice cookies need to have a good spice flavor as well. Cinnamon, ginger, cloves, and allspice are the usual choices in most recipes. We especially like the

---

INGREDIENTS: Cinnamon

True cinnamon, which is made from the dried bark of a tropical evergreen tree called *Cinnamomum zeylanicum*, has been all but unavailable in the United States for almost 100 years. Early in the twentieth century, this spice became very popular for medicinal uses in Europe, and its cost skyrocketed.

A century ago, American merchants began importing cassia, which is the bark of a related tropical evergreen, *Cinnamomum cassia*. Because of this, Americans have grown used to and prefer the stronger, fuller flavors of cassia.

While there is just one true cinnamon, commonly called Ceylon cinnamon, there are a number of different cassias, typically identified by their place of origin. Some spice merchants will indicate this on their labels, but most supermarket brands do not, nor can you tell by appearance which variety you are buying. We decided to hold a blind tasting of all the cinnamons, the true and the not-so-true, to see if we have been missing out on something.

As predicted by our research, the one true cinnamon sample was unlike the cassias. While most tasters did not find anything offensive about it, it was, ironically, often downgraded for not tasting "cinnamon-y." While subdued, its flavor was complex, with notes of citrus and clove.

As for the cassias, almost half of those sampled in our tasting were Indonesian cassia (also known as Korintje cassia), a variety that comprises the overwhelming majority of so-called cinnamon sold in the United States today. While some of these Indonesian cassias were notably spicy and bitter, the common denominator among those which the tasters liked was a solid, familiar cinna-

mon flavor that was relatively strong and had no off flavors.

The cassia that particularly grabbed the tasters came from China. Chinese cassia tends to have a stronger, sweeter flavor than Indonesian cassia. Both the samples in our tasting were also notably spicy, reminding many tasters of Red Hots candy. Penzeys Chinese cassia, which was anything but meek, secured the top ranking as excellent overall.

The second favorite sample was a Vietnamese cassia. Vietnamese cassias, which only recently became available in the United States with the relaxing of the U.S. trade embargo, tend to be expensive and hold a reputation for being the "world's finest." The two Vietnamese samples in our tasting, though, were quite different from each other. Penzeys Extra Fancy Vietnamese cassia finished second overall with big yet balanced flavors and a subtle complexity. The other Vietnamese cassia in our tasting, McCormick/Schilling Premium cinnamon, was also well-received by tasters, but not for any kind of flavor intensity. Instead, they liked it for being light and sweet, with faint spice notes.

Whether cinnamon or cassia, the characteristic flavors and aromas of these spices come from their essential oils, which in turn are composed of hundreds of chemical compounds. One of the reasons that Ceylon or "true" cinnamon is so different from cassia is that the main components of its essential oils are different. The chemical compound cinnamaldehyde gives cassia its characteristic flavor. While Ceylon cinnamon contains cinnamaldehyde, it also contains a significant amount of eugenol, the chemical compound the gives cloves their aroma and flavor.

flavor of the cinnamon and ginger in these cookies. The cloves are good, but they can dominate if used too freely. We settled on ¾ teaspoon as the right amount. Allspice is more problematic. In small amounts, this spice can sharpen the molasses flavor without seeming obtrusive, but we found that adding more than ¼ teaspoon made the cookies harsh and even bitter.

Molasses-Spice Cookies

MAKES ABOUT 20 LARGE COOKIES

These oversized cookies are especially attractive, with a rich, dark color, almost perfectly round edges, a surface marked with deep cracks, and an even thickness from the edge to the center. They stay incredibly soft and chewy, even days after they are baked. It is important to underbake the cookies (they won't look done when you take them out of the oven) and then let them firm up as they cool on the baking sheet. If you overbake the cookies, they will become dry and crisp.

2 ¼	cups all-purpose flour
2	teaspoons baking soda
½	teaspoon salt
1 ½	teaspoons ground cinnamon
1	teaspoon ground ginger
¾	teaspoon ground cloves
¼	teaspoon ground allspice
12	tablespoons (1 ½ sticks) unsalted butter, softened
½	cup dark brown sugar, packed
½	cup granulated sugar, plus ⅓ cup for rolling cookies
1	large egg
1	teaspoon vanilla extract
⅓	cup unsulphured molasses

1. Adjust racks to upper- and lower-middle positions and heat oven to 375 degrees. Whisk flour, baking soda, salt, and spices together in medium bowl; set aside.

2. Either by hand or with electric mixer, cream butter, brown sugar, and ½ cup granulated sugar until light and fluffy, about 3 minutes with mixer set at medium speed. Scrape sides of bowl with rubber spatula. Add egg, vanilla extract, and molasses. Beat until combined, about 30 seconds. Scrape sides of bowl.

3. Add dry ingredients and beat at low speed until just combined, about 30 seconds.

4. Place remaining ⅓ cup granulated sugar in shallow bowl. Working with 2 tablespoons of dough each time, roll dough into 1¾-inch balls. Roll balls in sugar and place on ungreased cookie sheets, spacing them 1½ to 2 inches apart.

5. Bake, reversing position of cookie sheets (from top to bottom and front to back) halfway through baking, until outer edges begin to set and centers are soft and puffy, 11 to 13 minutes. Cool cookies on sheets for 2 to 3 minutes before transferring to cooling racks with wide spatula.

➤ VARIATIONS

Molasses-Spice Cookies with Orange Zest

These cookies have orange zest in the dough as well as in the sugar coating. The zest in the sugar coating prevents the sugar from melting completely and clumps up a bit. The result is a frosted orange appearance that is quite attractive.

Follow recipe for Molasses-Spice Cookies, stirring 2 teaspoons grated orange zest into dough after dry ingredients have been incorporated. Place ⅓ cup sugar for coating dough in step 4 in food processor. Add 1 teaspoon grated orange zest and process until sugar becomes yellow and zest is evenly distributed, about 10 seconds. Roll dough balls in orange sugar, gently shaking off excess.

Glazed Molasses-Spice Cookies

Follow recipe for Molasses-Spice Cookies, preparing and baking cookies as directed. When cookies have

DRIZZLING ICING OVER COOKIES

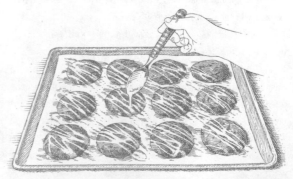

Using a spoon to drizzle glaze over the cookies is fast and efficient. Place the cooled cookies back onto a cooled baking sheet. (Line the cookie sheet with parchment paper to speed cleanup, if you like.) Dip the spoon into the glaze and move the spoon over the cookies so that the glaze drizzles down onto them. Continue to dip the spoon into the glaze as needed.

cooled, sift 1¼ cups confectioners' sugar and then whisk with 2 tablespoons milk until smooth. Dip spoon into glaze and drizzle over cookies (see illustration on page 424).

SNICKERDOODLES

WITH THEIR CRINKLY TOPS AND LIBERAL dusting of cinnamon sugar, chewy snickerdoodles are a favorite in New England. The name is a corruption of a German word that translates as "crinkly noodles."

Traditionally, a snickerdoodle has a subtle tang or sour undertone that contrasts with the cinnamon sugar coating. Most recipes rely on baking soda and cream of tartar as the leavening agent for two reasons. First, the baking soda provides the characteristic tang. Second, the baking soda and cream of tartar cause the cookie to rise very quickly and then to collapse somewhat. The result is the characteristic crinkly top.

We tested both baking powder and the baking soda/cream of tartar combination. As we expected, the latter is essential to this cookie. Double-acting baking powder caused the cookies to rise too much in the oven. The leavening power of baking soda and cream of tartar is short-lived by comparison, so the cookies rise and then fall rather quickly. To make the cookies especially tangy, we found it helpful not to add vanilla. The vanilla can take away from the sourness, which is fairly subtle.

We noticed that most of the recipes we tested were not nearly chewy enough. We found that increasing the sugar helped, but we wondered why some traditional snickerdoodle recipes contained vegetable shortening or Crisco. Although we generally don't recommend using shortening in cookies (it does not taste as good as butter), we thought it might be worth trying in this case. Unlike butter, which contains about 18 percent water, shortening is 100 percent fat. The water in butter evaporates in the oven and helps the cookies to spread. Since shortening does not contain water, in theory it should help reduce spread in the oven and keep cookies thick and chewy.

Our tests revealed that this bit of common culinary wisdom is in fact true. However, you don't need to use all or even half shortening for the desired effect. When we used 1 part shortening to 1 part butter, we felt the flavor of the cookie was lacking. After several attempts, we discovered that just 1 part shortening for every 3 parts butter is enough to keep the cookies chewy. At this level, the butter flavor still dominates.

Snickerdoodles

MAKES ABOUT 30 COOKIES

These old-fashioned cookies are dusted with cinnamon sugar and have a good contrast between crisp exterior and soft, chewy interior.

2 ¼	cups all-purpose flour
2	teaspoons cream of tartar
I	teaspoon baking soda
½	teaspoon salt
12	tablespoons (1½ sticks) unsalted butter, softened
¼	cup vegetable shortening
1½	cups granulated sugar, plus 3 tablespoons for rolling cookies
2	large eggs
I	tablespoon ground cinnamon for rolling cookies

1. Adjust oven racks to upper- and lower-middle positions and heat oven to 400 degrees. Grease cookie sheets or line with parchment paper.

2. Whisk flour, cream of tartar, baking soda, and salt together in medium bowl; set aside.

3. Either by hand or electric mixer, cream butter, shortening, and 1½ cups sugar until combined, 1 to 1½ minutes with electric mixer set at medium speed. Scrape down sides of bowl with rubber spatula. Add eggs. Beat until combined, about 30 seconds.

4. Add dry ingredients and beat at low speed until just combined, about 20 seconds.

5. Mix remaining 3 tablespoons sugar with cinnamon in shallow bowl. Working with scant 2 tablespoons of dough each time, roll dough into 1½-inch balls. Roll balls in cinnamon sugar and place on cookie sheet, spacing them 2 to 2½ inches apart.

6. Bake, reversing position in oven halfway through baking time (from top rack to bottom and front to back), until edges of cookies are beginning to set and centers are soft and puffy, 9 to 11 minutes. Let cookies cool on cookie sheet 2 to 3 minutes before transferring them to cooling rack with wide spatula.

NUT CRESCENT COOKIES

NUT CRESCENTS, COATED IN A PASTY LAYER of melting confectioners' sugar, can taste like stale, dry, floury, flavorless little chokeballs. They often fall short of the buttery, nutty, slightly crisp, slightly crumbly, melt-in-your-mouth nuggets they should be.

But that is a shame. Nut crescents are very much an "adult" cookie, low on sweetness, simple in flavor, and the perfect accompaniment to a cup of coffee or tea. When they are well-made, they are delicious.

We gathered recipe after recipe. These cookies, round and crescent-shaped, go by different names: Viennese crescents, butterballs, and Mexican wedding cakes, as well as almond, pecan, or walnut crescents. All the recipes are surprisingly similar, differing mainly in the amount and type of sugar and nuts. The standard ratio of butter to flour is 1 cup to 2 cups, which our testing confirmed is right on. Across the board, the ingredients are simple: flour, sugar, butter, and nuts. Some add vanilla extract and salt.

We first zeroed in on the sugar, testing the effects of granulated, confectioners', and superfine sugar in the dough. Granulated sugar yielded a cookie that was tasty but also coarse in both texture and appearance. Cookies made with confectioners' sugar were very tender, light, and fine-textured. Superfine, however, proved superior, producing cookies that were delicate, lightly crisp, and superbly tender, with a true melt-in-your-mouth quality. In a side-by-side tasting, the cookies made with superfine sugar were nuttier and purer in flavor, while the cornstarch in the confectioners' sugar bogged down the flavor and left a faint pastiness in the mouth.

While superfine sugar is best in the dough, by definition the exterior of nut crescents must be coated with confectioners' sugar. When to give the baked cookies their coat of confectioners' sugar is a matter of some debate. Some recipes said to dust or dip them when they're still hot or warm. The sugar melts a bit, and then they're usually given a second coat to even out their appearance and form a thicker coating. But we didn't like the layer of melting moistened confectioners' sugar, concealed or not. It formed a thin skin that was pasty and gummy and didn't dissolve on the tongue with the same finesse as a fine, powdery coat.

We found it better to wait until the cookies had cooled to room temperature before rolling them twice (for optimum coverage) in confectioners' sugar.

During the nut testing, we concluded that what affected the cookies most was not the taste of the nuts but whether they were oily or dry. The flavor of oily nuts like walnuts and pecans is strong and distinct. They are also easy to chop and grind, and, when finely ground, they become quite oily, which is a definite advantage when making nut crescents. The oils actually tenderize the cookies, making them incredibly delicate. Dry nuts like almonds and hazelnuts are rather subdued by comparison, although they can be toasted to eke out their maximum flavor and crunchiness. This is not to say that crescents made with almonds and hazelnuts aren't delicious—they just don't melt in your mouth with the same abandon as do those made with pecans and walnuts.

So ground, oily nuts would be essential. But we wondered whether a handful of chopped nuts might give the cookies a pleasant bite. A combination of one cup finely chopped and three-quarters cup ground nuts was the tasters' choice. This formula

SHAPING CRESCENT COOKIES

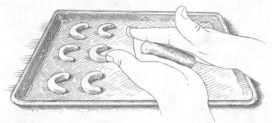

1. Working with 1 tablespoon of dough each time, roll the dough into 1¼-inch balls. Roll each ball between palms into a rope that measures approximately 3½ inches long.

2. Place the ropes on an ungreased cookie sheet and shape each rope into a half circle.

yielded cookies that were tender, flavorful, and slightly crunchy.

Recipes suggested baking temperatures ranging from a ridiculously low 300 degrees to a hot 400 degrees. At 375 degrees, the cookies browned too quickly, while at 300, they never achieved a nice golden hue, even after nearly half an hour of baking. Clearly the answer lay somewhere in between. Our cookie-baking experience told us that many delicate, rich doughs like to bake at lower temperatures, and these cookies were no exception. Cookies baked at 350 degrees were good, but those baked at 325 degrees had a smoother, finer appearance, and were more tender and evenly textured and colored.

Pecan or Walnut Crescent Cookies

MAKES ABOUT 4 DOZEN COOKIES

You can buy superfine sugar in most grocery stores. You can also process regular granulated sugar to superfine consistency in about 30 seconds in the workbowl of a food processor fitted with a steel blade. See the illustrations on page 426 for tips on shaping these cookies.

2	cups whole pecans or walnuts, chopped fine
2	cups bleached all-purpose flour
¾	teaspoon salt
½	pound (2 sticks) unsalted butter, softened
⅓	cup superfine sugar
1½	teaspoons vanilla extract
1½	cups confectioners' sugar for rolling cooled cookies

1. Adjust oven racks to upper- and lower-middle positions and heat oven to 325 degrees. Mix 1 cup chopped nuts, flour, and salt in medium bowl; set aside. In workbowl of a food processor fitted with a steel blade, process remaining chopped nuts until the texture of coarse cornmeal, 10 to 15 seconds (do not overprocess; you should have about ¾ cup ground nuts); stir into flour mixture and set aside. (To finely grind chopped nuts by hand, roll them between two large sheets plastic wrap with rolling pin, applying moderate pressure, until broken down to coarse cornmeal-like texture).

2. Either by hand or with electric mixer, cream butter and sugar until light and creamy, about 1½

minutes with mixer set at medium; beat in vanilla. Scrape sides and bottom of bowl with rubber spatula; add flour mixture and beat at low speed until dough just begins to come together but still looks scrappy, about 15 seconds. Scrape sides and bottom of bowl again with rubber spatula; continue beating at low speed until dough is cohesive, 6 to 9 seconds longer. Do not overbeat.

3. Working with about 1 tablespoon dough at a time, roll dough into 1¼-inch balls. Roll each ball between hands into rope that measures 3½ inches long. Shape ropes into crescents on ungreased cookie sheets, spacing them 1 to 1½ inches apart.

4. Bake, reversing position of cookie sheets (from top rack to bottom and front to back) halfway through baking, until tops are pale golden and bottoms are just beginning to brown, 17 to 19 minutes. Cool cookies on sheets about 2 minutes before transferring them to cooling rack with wide spatula.

5. Cool cookies to room temperature, about 30 minutes. Working with three or four cookies at a time, roll cookies in confectioners' sugar to coat them thoroughly. Gently shake off excess. (They can be stored in an airtight container up to 5 days.) Before serving, roll cookies in confectioners' sugar a second time to ensure a thick coating, and tap off excess.

➤ VARIATION
Almond or Hazelnut Crescent Cookies
Toast hazelnuts or almonds in a preheated 350-degree oven until very lightly browned, stirring twice during baking, 12 to 14 minutes.

Follow recipe for Pecan or Walnut Crescent Cookies, substituting 2 cups toasted, skinned hazelnuts or a scant 1¾ cups toasted, whole blanched almonds for pecans or walnuts. If using almonds, add ½ teaspoon almond extract along with vanilla extract.

SUGAR COOKIES

SUGAR COOKIES ARE THE SIMPLEST COOKIE you can make. Although the ingredient list is short (butter, flour, sugar, eggs, vanilla, leavener, and salt), this cookie can be especially delicious when made right. However, sugar cookies can also be bland and boring. There are no chips or nuts to offer distractions, so the dough itself must be delicious. Our ideal sugar cookie is sweet and buttery, with a soft, chewy texture.

We started testing by focusing on the type and amount of sugar. Some recipes call for confectioners' sugar, but we found that these cookies were too crumbly and not chewy at all. We tried adding some brown sugar, but the caramel flavor felt like a variation to us. It did not deliver the clean, sweet, buttery flavor we wanted for a master recipe. Granulated sugar (and a lot of it) proved to be the best sweetener for flavor and texture.

We next focused on the flour. After several tests we settled on a ratio of 1 cup butter to 2 cups flour. This recipe calls for slightly less flour than many others to allow the buttery flavor to dominate. Cutting the flour made the dough a tad soft, but we reduced the eggs from two in our working recipe down to one and that solved the problem. Reducing the egg also seemed to bring out the flavor of the butter.

We tried baking powder as well as cream of tartar and baking soda. (There are no acidic ingredients in this cookie, so plain baking soda would not work properly.) We felt that the baking powder gave this cookie the cleanest flavor. Several tasters noted a slightly sour flavor in the cookies made with cream

---

INGREDIENTS: Vanilla Extract

Vanilla extract is added to most cookie doughs, but it is especially important in a simple sugar cookie. A sugar cookie made without vanilla will taste a bit bland and flat.

So does it matter which brand of extract you buy? The answer is no. When we tested vanilla extracts several years ago, the results were so shocking that we retested again and again. It turns out that most people, including pastry chefs, can't even tell the difference between a cookie made with vanilla extract and a cookie made with the imitation stuff, which is derived from wood pulp, let alone the differences among brands of real vanilla.

The differences between real and imitation were more apparent in our tasting of custards. However, in a cookie the quantities of extract are so small and the other ingredients are so flavorful that these differences are hard to detect. But since we are generally loath to recommend ersatz products and since the price differential between real and fake vanilla is fairly small, we opt for the real thing, even if it's hard to taste the difference.

---

of tartar and baking soda.

Our final tests concerned the vanilla. We tried leaving it out and really noticed the difference in this simple cookie. For the best flavor, we found it necessary to use two teaspoons. With less vanilla, the cookies tasted flat or bland.

Sugar Cookies

MAKES ABOUT 30 COOKIES

This is the simplest cookie imaginable, with the flavors of butter, sugar, and vanilla at the fore. The edges are firm, but the center is soft and chewy.

2	cups all-purpose flour
1	teaspoon baking powder
½	teaspoon salt
½	pound (2 sticks) unsalted butter, softened
1	cup granulated sugar, plus ¼ cup for rolling cookies
1	large egg
2	teaspoons vanilla extract

1. Adjust oven racks to upper- and lower-middle position and heat oven to 375 degrees. Whisk flour, baking powder, and salt together in medium bowl; set aside.

2. Either by hand or with electric mixer, cream butter and 1 cup sugar until light and fluffy, about 3 minutes with mixer set at medium speed. Scrape sides of bowl with rubber spatula. Add egg and vanilla extract. Beat until combined, about 30 seconds. Add dry ingredients and beat at low speed until just combined, about 30 seconds.

3. Place remaining ¼ cup sugar in shallow bowl. Working with 1½ tablespoons of dough each time, roll dough into 1½ inch balls. Roll balls in sugar and place on ungreased cookie sheets, spacing balls 2 to 2½ inches apart.

4. Butter bottom of drinking glass with flat bottom that measures about 2 inches across. Dip bottom of glass in remaining sugar and flatten balls of dough with bottom of glass until ⅜ to ½ inch thick and about 1¾ inches in diameter. Dip bottom of glass into sugar after every two or three cookies.

5. Bake, reversing positions of cookie sheets halfway through baking time, until edges of cookies

are pale golden, 10 to 11 minutes. Let cookies cool on cookie sheet 2 to 3 minutes before transferring to cooling rack with wide spatula.

➤ VARIATIONS

Sugar Cookies with Ginger

Follow recipe for Sugar Cookies, whisking 1 teaspoon ground ginger with dry ingredients. Stir 1 tablespoon chopped crystallized ginger into finished dough.

Sugar Cookies with Lime Zest

Follow recipe for Sugar Cookies, adding 1 teaspoon grated lime zest along with egg. Place ¼ cup sugar for coating dough in step 3 in food processor. Add 1 teaspoon grated lime zest and process until sugar becomes green and zest is evenly distributed, about 10 seconds. Roll dough balls in lime sugar, gently shaking off excess.

ROLLED BUTTER COOKIES

ROLLED BUTTER COOKIES ARE BASICALLY sugar cookies made with more flour (the dough has to be sturdy enough to withstand rolling, cutting, and decorating) and without any chemical leavener (you don't want rolled cookies to rise much or they lose their shape). These two minor changes create all kinds of flavor and texture problems.

Each year, we make holiday cookies and always think they look better than they taste. We decided to solve this problem by developing an all-purpose holiday cookie dough that could be subjected to endless flavor variations. Of course, the dough had to be easy to handle, but first and foremost the cookies had to taste great. We wanted a cookie that was at once crisp and tender, light and sturdy. As if that weren't enough, we also wanted a clear, buttery flavor. Was it possible to combine all of these characteristics in the same cookie?

Despite the many differences in rolled cookie recipes, we found that most have the same basic ingredients: flour, sugar, fat, egg, and vanilla. Of course, there are still significant differences. Some recipes use less egg and compensate with milk, cream, or sour cream. Others add chemical leaveners to lighten the cookies. And the basic ingredients certainly vary. What kind of flour should be used? Is granulated or confectioners' sugar better? Is the best cookie made with butter, shortening, oil, or a combination of some sort?

To understand the role of each of these many possible ingredients, we developed a composite formula, based on a review of scores of cookie recipes, to use in our testing. The recipe was as follows: three-quarters cup flour, one-quarter cup each sugar and unsalted butter, one large egg yolk, one-half teaspoon vanilla, and a pinch of salt.

With the basic recipe in hand, we proceeded to substitute different flours, sugars, fats, and egg parts as well as to vary the quantities of each. Following the formula, we also made doughs with different leaveners as well as with milk, cream, and sour cream standing in for part of the egg. Curious about whether fresh vanilla bean might make a more flavorful cookie, we scraped flecks of vanilla into a batch. Finally, in an attempt to lighten the cookies without chemical leaveners, we tried cutting butter into flour rather than creaming it with the sugar. The melting butter bits, we speculated, would create spaces between the set flour, creating a lighter, crisper cookie without a leavener lift.

From these initial tests, we learned that our original formula wasn't far off the mark. Although the recipe did need refining, none of the extra ingredients we had added were necessary.

Using cake flour, adding cornstarch for part of the flour, and relying on smaller quantities of flour all made the cookies too tender and fragile, as did substituting confectioners' sugar for granulated sugar. Cookies made with shortening and oil were sandy-textured and lacked flavor.

Although baking powder and soda helped lighten the cookies, we found their distinct flavors to be too distracting. Using half of a whole egg, rather than just the yolk, made the cookies brittle rather than crisp. Substituting milk and cream for part of the egg made moist, difficult doughs, and the resulting cookies tasted hard and stale, while sour cream neither helped nor hurt the outcome. Cookies flecked with fresh vanilla bean looked promising, but any flavor difference was absolutely imperceptible in the finished cookies. Finally, cutting the butter into the flour resulted in cookies with a nice texture but a disastrous, pocked appearance, as if they had a rash.

Now that we felt sure we were using just the right ingredients in the right proportion, we needed to make sure that the recipe could easily be multiplied to produce a big batch of cookies. We quadrupled the recipe, using three cups of flour, one cup of sugar, one cup of butter, two teaspoons of vanilla extract, and one-quarter teaspoon salt. We did change the egg. In the original formula, one egg yolk made sense because half an egg delivered brittle cookies. Working in larger quantities allowed us to try a whole egg plus two yolks rather than four yolks.

Right off, we found that cookies made with three cups of flour tasted dry and not very buttery. To solve this problem, we reduced the flour by one-half cup, eliminating one of the two yolks to compensate for the loss of dry ingredients. Since the dough seemed wet enough with just one whole egg, we didn't add the remaining extra yolk. The flavor of these reduced-flour cookies was excellent because the reduced amount of flour intensified the buttery flavor. Once again, though, we found that whole egg alone made brittle, hard cookies. Adding the egg yolk back into the cookie dough made it more tender without making it too wet, and increasing the salt to one-half teaspoon balanced the relatively high sugar quantity. Cookies with even two tablespoons less sugar threw off that tender/crisp texture and accentuated the flouriness.

We ran across a recipe that called for superfine sugar. Using the food processor, we turned granulated sugar into superfine and made a batch of cookies. This finer-grained sugar quite naturally gave the cookies a lightness and fineness of texture that we liked better.

A generous amount of butter guaranteed rich flavor. The extra yolk saved the cookies from brittleness. The superfine sugar made the cookies light and tender, but, unlike cornstarch or confectioners' sugar, it kept them durable and sturdy. We like this cookie recipe. No gimmicks. Just simple ingredients in the right proportions.

Master Recipe for Rolled Butter Cookies

MAKES ABOUT 7 DOZEN 2½-INCH COOKIES ROLLED TO ⅛ INCH THICK

We found that dough rolled three times does indeed bake into a tougher cookie. So get as many dough shapes as you can out of each sheet; we suggest that you donate dough that's been rolled more than twice to someone who needs rolling practice.

½   pound (2 sticks) unsalted butter, softened

1   cup superfine sugar, or granulated sugar processed in food processor for 30 seconds

½   teaspoon salt

1   large egg plus 1 yolk

2   teaspoons vanilla extract

2½   cups all-purpose flour, plus extra for work surface

1. Either by hand or with electric mixer, cream butter, sugar, and salt until light and fluffy, about 3 minutes with mixer set at medium speed. Add yolk, beat well, then add whole egg and vanilla; continue beating until well incorporated. Add flour; beat at low speed until flour is just mixed in. Divide dough in half and wrap in plastic wrap. Refrigerate until firm, at least 1 hour. (Can be refrigerated up to 2 days or double-wrapped and frozen 1 month.)

2. Adjust oven racks to upper- and lower-middle positions and heat oven to 375 degrees. Remove one disk of dough from refrigerator and cut in half. Return unused portion of dough to refrigerator.

3. Lightly flour work surface; roll dough to ⅛ inch thick, using thin metal spatula to loosen dough. Sprinkle surface lightly with flour as needed to keep dough from sticking.

4. Cut or form dough into desired shape. Place dough shapes ½ inch apart on parchment-lined cookie sheet. Bake, reversing cookie sheets (from top to bottom and back to front) halfway through baking time, until evenly golden brown, 6 to 8 minutes.

5. Use thin-bladed spatula to immediately transfer cookies to cooling rack. Cool to room temperature. Repeat rolling, cutting, and baking remaining dough. Decorate cooled cookies, if desired, and transfer to airtight container (can be stored up to 3 weeks).

➤ VARIATIONS

Cornmeal-Citrus Cookies

Follow Master Recipe, adding 1 teaspoon finely grated lemon or orange zest to creamed butter, sugar, and salt and substituting 1 cup fine cornmeal for 1 cup of the flour.

Chocolate Cinnamon Cookies

Follow Master Recipe, adding 1 ounce melted and cooled unsweetened chocolate to creamed butter, sugar, and salt. Substitute ¼ cup cocoa for ¼ cup of the flour and mix in ¼ teaspoon cinnamon to flour-cocoa mixture.

Lemon Butter Cookies

Follow Master Recipe, adding 2 teaspoons finely grated lemon zest to creamed butter, sugar, and salt.

Lemon-Poppy Seed Cookies

Follow Master Recipe, adding 2 teaspoons finely grated lemon zest to creamed butter, sugar, and salt, and stirring 2 tablespoons poppy seeds into finished dough.

Orange Butter Cookies

Follow Master Recipe, adding 1 teaspoon finely grated orange zest to creamed butter, sugar, and salt.

Orange-Nut Cookies

Follow Master Recipe, adding 1 teaspoon finely grated orange zest and 1 cup finely ground walnuts, pecans, or hazelnuts to creamed butter, sugar, and salt.

Spice Cookies

Follow Master Recipe, substituting 1 cup packed light brown sugar for superfine sugar and adding ¾ teaspoon ground cinnamon, ½ teaspoon ground ginger, ¼ teaspoon ground nutmeg, ¼ teaspoon ground allspice, and ⅛ teaspoon ground cloves to flour.

Coconut Cookies

Follow Master Recipe, stirring 1 cup toasted, flaked, sweetened coconut into finished batter.

Ginger Cookies

Follow Master Recipe, adding 1 teaspoon ground ginger to flour and stirring 6 tablespoons finely minced crystallized ginger into finished dough.

Butterscotch Cookies

Follow Master Recipe, substituting 1 cup packed light brown sugar for superfine sugar.

COOKIE GLAZES

THERE ARE SEVERAL WAYS TO APPLY A THIN glaze to cooled holiday cookies. Here are some ideas.

➤ Use a butter knife or small icing spatula to spread the glaze over the entire surface of each cookie.

➤ Dip part of the cookie into a bowl filled with the glaze, allowing the excess glaze to drop back into the bowl and then placing the cookie on a rack until the glaze has set.

➤ Use the tines of a fork to drizzle the glaze over a batch of cookies on a rack (place parchment paper underneath to speed clean-up).

➤ Fill a pastry bag fitted with a writing tip with glaze.

Lemon, Orange, or Plain Glaze

MAKES ABOUT ¾ CUP

Lemon juice or orange juice gives the glaze a mild citrus flavor and color. Milk is more neutral in flavor and produces a bright white glaze. If you decide to color the glaze, cut back a bit on the liquid unless using color pastes.

I	cup confectioners' sugar
5–6	teaspoons lemon or orange juice or milk

Mix sugar and liquid in small bowl, adding just enough liquid to make spreadable or pourable glaze. Use immediately or cover with sheet of plastic wrap directly on surface of glaze to keep it from hardening.

All-Purpose Chocolate Glaze

MAKES ½ CUP

Because the glaze hardens as it cools, you may need to warm it several times during decorating.

4	ounces bittersweet or semisweet chocolate
4	tablespoons unsalted butter
I	tablespoon corn syrup

Melt chocolate and butter in medium bowl set over pan of almost simmering water. Stir in corn syrup. Proceed with decorating.

BISCOTTI

DESPITE THEIR ELEGANT APPEARANCE, THE twice-baked Italian cookies known as biscotti are easy to make. A longer-than-average baking time yields a uniquely crunchy texture and also gives them an unusually long shelf life. Together, these factors make biscotti an excellent choice for home bakers. To find out how to make the very best biscotti, we decided to test and compare the dozens of traditional recipes that are out there. The results were surprising.

Most recipes have a fairly constant ratio of sugar to flour to flavorings. The major difference in the recipes is the type and quantity of fat used, which varied dramatically. It is this "fat factor," we discovered, that has the most dramatic effect on the taste, texture, and shelf life of the resulting biscotti.

There are three styles of biscotti based on the fat content. The richest variety contains butter and eggs. The most traditional recipes contain whole eggs, sometimes supplemented by additional yolks, but no butter. The leanest biscotti contain just egg whites—no yolks or butter. We tested all three varieties and found differences in texture and taste.

In the matter of texture, we found that recipes containing butter produced satisfyingly crunchy biscuits that were nonetheless somewhat softer and richer—more cookielike—when compared with those not containing butter. We also discovered that recipes using whole eggs only, without additional yolks, were noticeably less cakelike, with a more straightforward crunch. (Biscotti with whole eggs and additional yolks were more like those with butter.) On the other end of the scale, the biscotti made with egg whites only—no butter or yolks—produced the driest and crispiest cookies, reminiscent of hard candy. In fact, these cookies were so hard that they might present the risk of cracking a tooth if eaten without dunking in milk or coffee first. We liked biscotti made with butter and with whole eggs but rejected those made with just whites.

In the matter of taste, the fresh-baked biscotti containing butter provided a superior and irresistibly rich flavor. On the other hand, the biscotti made with whole eggs but no additional yolks or butter resulted in the truest delivery—lean and direct—of the flavorings in these cookies. Because both styles of biscotti—those with whole eggs and those with eggs

and butter—had their merits, we decided to include recipes for both.

We found that storage and shelf life were also directly affected by fat content. As we experimented with different doughs, we noticed that recipes using butter initially had the best taste and texture but lost their full flavor and satisfying crunch after only one day, as the butter baked into the cookies began to go stale. Recipes with eggs but no butter held up better in both categories as the days went by. They seemed to get even better with time; they tasted great and remained very crisp after a week and, if stored properly, would keep for several weeks.

Whatever the amount and type of fat they contain, all biscotti recipes share the common characteristics of quick preparation time and a relatively long baking time. For most recipes, preparation involves simply mixing the wet ingredients with a whisk in one bowl, whisking the dry ingredients together in another bowl, then folding the dry into the wet, while adding flavorings. Because they are baked twice, however, the total baking time for biscotti is longer than for regular cookies; first they are baked in flat loaves for 30 to 40 minutes, then sliced and baked again for an additional 10 to 15 minutes. This double-baking technique ensures a very low moisture content, contributing enormously to this cookie's great potential for storage—the primary reason bakers go to all this trouble in the first place.

As for flavorings, there are literally dozens of different combinations used in biscotti, since the plain dough adapts beautifully to various pairings. Some of the best flavor combinations date from the late Middle Ages, when sea trade became very active and many new and varied ingredients became available to cooks and bakers. Medieval sailors and explorers such as Columbus and Marco Polo relied on these biscuits for energy and nourishment. Zests of citrus fruits, native to southern Italy and other parts of the northern Mediterranean, were combined with exotic dry spices such as cinnamon, cloves, and ginger. Dried and candied fruits were used, along with local and foreign varieties of nuts such as walnuts, hazelnuts, almonds, pistachios, and sesame seeds.

The batter may at first appear rather sticky, but resist the urge to dust with flour: too much and the biscotti will become heavy and dense. It is preferable to use a rubber spatula, waxed paper, or plastic wrap if you have trouble handling the dough. One final note: Biscotti must be completely cooled before storage to ensure that all the moisture has escaped.

Lemon-Anise Biscotti

MAKES 3 TO 4 DOZEN COOKIES

A Sicilian specialty, this recipe (without butter) produces a relatively hard biscuit—perfect with an afternoon cup of coffee. They are also delicious dunked in a glass of sherry, Marsala, or Vin Santo.

2	cups all-purpose flour
1	teaspoon baking powder
1/4	teaspoon salt
1	cup sugar
2	large eggs
1/4	teaspoon vanilla extract
1	tablespoon minced zest from 1 lemon
1	tablespoon anise seed

1. Adjust oven rack to middle position and heat oven to 350 degrees. Whisk flour, baking powder, and salt together in medium bowl; set aside.

2. Whisk sugar and eggs in a large bowl to a light lemon color; stir in vanilla, lemon zest, and anise seed. Sprinkle dry ingredients over egg mixture, then fold in until dough is just combined.

3. Halve dough and turn each portion onto an oiled cookie sheet covered with parchment. Using floured hands, quickly stretch each portion of dough into a rough 13 x 2-inch log, placing them about 3 inches apart on the cookie sheet. Pat each dough shape to smooth it. Bake, turning pan once, until loaves are golden and just beginning to crack on top, about 35 minutes.

4. Cool the loaves for 10 minutes; lower oven temperature to 325 degrees. Cut each loaf diagonally into 3/8-inch slices with a serrated knife. Lay the slices flat, about 1/2 inch apart, on the cookie sheet and return them to the oven. Bake, turning over each cookie halfway through baking, until crisp and golden brown on both sides, about 15 minutes. Transfer biscotti to wire rack and cool completely. (Biscotti can be stored in an airtight container for at least 1 month.)

Spiced Biscotti

MAKES 4 TO 5 DOZEN COOKIES

If you like, macerate 3/4 cup currants, chopped raisins, or dates in 1/4 cup brandy or Marsala for at least 1 hour. Drain and fold into the dough in step 2, adding a teaspoon or so of the macerating liquid to the dough. This recipe contains additional yolks and is bit richer than the preceding biscotti.

2 1/4	cups all-purpose flour
1	teaspoon baking powder
1/2	teaspoon baking soda
1/4	teaspoon salt
1/4	teaspoon ground white pepper
1/2	teaspoon ground cloves
1/2	teaspoon ground cinnamon
1/4	teaspoon ground ginger
1	cup sugar
2	large eggs plus 2 yolks
1/2	teaspoon vanilla extract

1. Adjust oven rack to middle position and heat oven to 350 degrees. Whisk flour, baking powder, baking soda, salt, and spices together in medium bowl; set aside.

2. Whisk sugar and eggs in a large bowl to a light lemon color; stir in vanilla. Sprinkle dry ingredients over egg mixture, then fold in until dough is just combined.

3. Halve dough and turn each portion onto an oiled cookie sheet covered with parchment. Using floured hands, quickly stretch each portion of dough into a rough 13 x 2-inch log, placing them about 3 inches apart on the cookie sheet. Pat each dough shape to smooth it. Bake, turning pan once, until loaves are golden and just beginning to crack on top, about 35 minutes.

4. Cool the loaves for 10 minutes; lower oven temperature to 325 degrees. Cut each loaf diagonally into 3/8-inch slices with a serrated knife. Lay the slices flat, about 1/2 inch apart, on the cookie sheet and return them to the oven. Bake, turning over each cookie halfway through baking, until crisp and golden brown on both sides, about 15 minutes. Transfer biscotti to wire rack and cool completely. (Biscotti can be stored in an airtight container for at least 1 month.)

Orange-Almond Biscotti

MAKES 3 TO 4 DOZEN

The addition of a small amount of butter produces a richer, more cookielike texture. Although they will keep for two weeks in an airtight container, these biscotti are especially good when eaten the same day they are baked. You can substitute toasted hazelnuts for the almonds in this recipe.

2	cups all-purpose flour
1	teaspoon baking powder
¼	teaspoon salt
4	tablespoons unsalted butter, softened
1	cup sugar
2	large eggs
½	teaspoon vanilla extract
¼	teaspoon almond extract
¾	cup whole almonds with skins, toasted, cooled, and chopped coarse
2	tablespoons minced zest from 1 orange

1. Adjust oven rack to middle position and heat oven to 350 degrees. Whisk flour, baking powder, and salt together in medium bowl; set aside.

2. Either by hand or with electric mixer, cream butter and sugar together until light and smooth, about 2 minutes with mixer set at medium speed. Beat in eggs one at a time, then extracts. Stir in almonds and zest. Sprinkle dry ingredients over egg mixture, then fold in until dough is just mixed.

3. Halve dough and turn each portion onto an oiled cookie sheet covered with parchment. Using floured hands, quickly stretch each portion of dough into a rough 13 x 2-inch log, placing them about 3 inches apart on the cookie sheet. Pat each dough shape to smooth it. Bake, turning pan once, until loaves are golden and just beginning to crack on top, about 35 minutes.

4. Cool the loaves for 10 minutes; lower oven temperature to 325 degrees. Cut each loaf diagonally into ⅜-inch slices with a serrated knife. Lay the slices flat, about ½ inch apart, on the cookie sheet and return them to the oven. Bake, turning over each cookie halfway through baking, until crisp and golden brown on both sides, about 15 minutes. Transfer biscotti to wire rack and cool completely. (Biscotti can be stored in an airtight container for 2 weeks.)

BROWNIES

OUR GOAL WAS SIMPLE. WE DID NOT WANT A fancy brownie. We wanted chocolate pure and simple baked into a substantial but not leaden brownie. Our ideal brownie would have contrasting textures—a dense, fudgy center and a crackly, crisp top.

Even novice bakers know how to make brownies—just combine chocolate, butter, sugar, eggs, and flour. But cookbook authors are not content to leave well enough alone. We researched dozens of recipes and started our testing by examining some of the more unusual leads we uncovered. We used brown sugar instead of the traditional white sugar and ended up with brownies that tasted burned from over-caramelization. For extra moistness, we replaced some of the sugar with corn syrup and the result was a dull chocolate flavor and puffy, cakelike texture. We added all manner of dairy—milk, sour cream, buttermilk— but each toned down the chocolate flavor and gave the brownies a light, cakey texture. We beat eggs and sugar for 15 minutes to increase aeration and build structure but ended up with tough, hard bricks. We separated eggs and folded whites beaten to soft peaks into the batter to produce souffléd brownies.

All this fruitless testing convinced us that the basic recipe—with chocolate, butter, sugar, eggs, and flour—was best. But we still had some questions about the ratio of ingredients as well as the baking time. We also wondered what kind of flour we should use and whether we should melt or cream the butter. In the course of perfecting our recipe, we addressed these fundamental issues.

Basic brownies begin with melted chocolate that has been cooled slightly so as not to "cook" the eggs. However, some recipes call for the butter to be melted along with the chocolate, while others instruct you to cream softened butter and sugar and then add eggs and melted chocolate.

In recipes without leavening, creaming the butter does create a slightly fluffier brownie; the sharp sugar crystals separate fat molecules in the butter, adding more air to the batter.

At a sampling of brownies made with melted and creamed butter, a majority of tasters preferred the latter. The improvement was so slight, however, it hardly seemed worth the loss of spontaneity. Brownies are spur-of-the-moment baking at its best.

By the time butter softens, the craving may pass. We decided to melt the butter, then see if there were other techniques we could use to compensate for the slightly heavier texture.

After the melted butter and chocolate have cooled a bit—they don't need to be at room temperature, but should not be hot either—sugar is added. At this point the mixture will appear grainy. Next, eggs and vanilla are beaten in. The batter thickens and becomes smoother with the addition of the eggs, and the teaspoon of vanilla highlights the chocolate. The final step is to combine and add the dry ingredients.

The most unusual ingredient in our recipe is baking powder. Many classic recipes omit chemical leavening, and we were initially adverse to adding any. Our brownies, however, were a bit leaden, especially when we decided to melt the butter and not cream it, and the addition of ½ teaspoon baking powder provided the contrasting textures we associate with the perfect brownie—a crackly top that lifts gently from the fudgy center.

We also compared brownies made with all-purpose and plain (not self-rising) cake flour. All-purpose flour yields taller brownies that are more cakey and tough. In contrast, brownies made with cake flour have a tender, melt-in-your-mouth quality, which we prefer.

We found recipes that call for as little as ¼ cup of flour and as much as 1⅓ cups for an eight-inch pan. Brownies made with less than ⅔ cup cake flour were too greasy, while those made with more were too dry.

In tests with and without salt, we found that the presence of just a quarter teaspoon helps balance the sweetness. A brief whisk of the dry ingredients—sifting is unnecessary—distributes them evenly and provides a bit of aeration. If you feel the need to jazz up brownies, fold a half cup or so of chopped pecans or walnuts into the batter along with the dry ingredients.

Even a few extra minutes in the oven can turn the best batter into dry brownies. The problem is complicated by the imprecise results of the "tooth-

INGREDIENTS: Unsweetened Chocolate

Many American desserts have traditionally been made with unsweetened chocolate. Brownies, frostings, and fudge, for example, start with unsweetened chocolate, also called baking chocolate or chocolate liquor.

Chocolate liquor is simply cocoa beans that have been fermented, roasted, shelled, and then ground into a molten paste and cooled in forms to make bars or squares. Nothing else is added—no sugar or milk. By law, the cocoa butter content can vary only from 50 percent to 58 percent. The differences in content between brands are fairly slight.

We wondered if the brand of baking chocolate would make a difference in our baking. Because it's very difficult to taste baking chocolate as is, we decided to make two different preparations with each brand. We made a simple blender frosting (sugar, boiling water, butter, and chocolate) as well as our basic brownie recipe.

Nestlé took top honors in the brownie tasting (by a wide margin) and finished second among the frostings. It was the clear favorite. Guittard, Merckens, Ghirardelli, Van Leer, and Baker's finished fairly close together.

Hershey's and Callebaut showed quite poorly. The low ranking of Hershey's, an inexpensive mass-market brand, may not be much of a surprise, but our panel was shocked at the last-place finish of Callebaut, an expensive Belgian chocolate

that many professional bakers use.

Our panel detected some real style differences, especially in the chocolates at the top and bottom of the list. Sourcing as well as blending and roasting can affect the final flavor of chocolate liquor. Some companies obviously want a spicier flavor, while others are aiming for a more neutral or middle-of-the-road approach.

Our panel of tasters favored samples with a strong, clean chocolate flavor. With a high proportion of chocolate and no cooking involved, distinct character traits were easy to detect in the frostings. Chocolates with unusual flavors (especially coconut, cherry, and cinnamon tones) showed poorly in the frosting tasting.

However, when it came time to taste brownies, some of these oddities faded. Such was the case with Baker's, which zoomed from last place among the frostings to fourth among the brownies. Flour, eggs, sugar, and the effects of baking masked many individual peculiarities in chocolate samples. Brownies also require less chocolate than frosting.

Familiarity may also be a factor affecting the results. So many Americans grew up eating brownies made with Baker's that this assertive chocolate in some sense defines brownies. In contrast, several premium chocolates, especially Callebaut, were considered too mild in the brownies.

pick test." Batter around the outer edge of the pan cooks much faster and can appear dry after only 15 minutes. The center of the pan can remain moist even after 30 minutes, when the brownies are way overdone.

We recommend using two visual clues to determine when brownies should be removed from the oven. First, check to see if the center is set. After 15 minutes, the center should still wobble or jiggle when the pan is moved. After 20 minutes, however, the center should be gently set. At this point, stick a toothpick or cake tester into the batter halfway between center and edge of the pan—the middle of the pan should always remain fairly moist. If the toothpick comes out clean (a few fudge crumbs are OK, but the batter should not be liquidy), the brownies are done.

In many cases, the brownies will not be completely cooked after 20 minutes. If the toothpick comes out covered with batter, bake the brownies another 2 to 4 minutes. However, if a toothpick comes out moist after 24 minutes, resist the temptation to keep baking. The ideal brownie is moist—even slightly underdone.

Basic Brownies

MAKES 12 BROWNIES

To melt the chocolate and butter in a microwave oven, microwave chocolate alone at 50 percent power for 2 minutes. Stir chocolate, add butter, and continue microwaving at 50 percent for another 2 minutes, stopping to stir the mixture after 1 minute. If chocolate is not entirely melted, microwave an additional 30 seconds at 50 percent power. Make sure to cool the melted chocolate and butter for about 10 minutes—it can be warm to the touch but not hot. Batter can be doubled and divided evenly between two 8-inch pans or poured into one 13 x 9-inch pan. If using one large pan, bake for about 26 minutes.

8	tablespoons (1 stick) unsalted butter
2	ounces unsweetened chocolate
2/3	cup cake flour
1/2	teaspoon baking powder
1/4	teaspoon salt
1	cup sugar
2	large eggs
1	teaspoon vanilla extract
1/2	cup chopped nuts (optional)

1. Adjust oven rack to middle position and heat oven to 350 degrees. In medium, heatproof bowl set over a pan of almost simmering water, melt chocolate and butter, stirring occasionally until mixture is smooth. (Alternatively, melt chocolate and butter in microwave oven. See instructions above.) Set mixture aside to cool.

2. Whisk flour, baking powder, and salt together in small bowl; set aside.

3. Whisk sugar into cooled chocolate mixture. Whisk in eggs and vanilla, then fold in flour mixture (and nuts if using) until just combined.

4. Pour batter into greased 8-inch-square metal baking dish; bake until toothpick inserted halfway between center and edge of pan comes out with a few fudgy crumbs, about 20 minutes. If batter coats toothpick, return pan to oven and bake 2 to 4 minutes more. Cool brownies completely in pan set on a wire rack. Cut into squares and serve. (Pan can be wrapped in plastic, then foil, for up to 2 days. To preserve moistness, cut and remove brownies only as needed.)

CREAM CHEESE BROWNIES

FOR MANY DESSERT LOVERS, NOTHING COULD be better than a rich, fudgy brownie with generous dollops of cheesecake baked inside. The ideal cream cheese brownie should be distinctly a brownie, but with a swirl of cream cheese filling in every bite. We wanted the brownie portion of the bar to have a rich, soft texture that would complement the lush cream cheese filling, yet at the same time contrast its soft interior with a thin, crisp (but not overbaked) crust. These brownies would taste intensely chocolate, with a tangy filling that could hold its own against such a dominant partner.

Our Basic Brownies are thin, moist squares, with a good chocolate flavor and a fine, tender crumb—in other words, classic brownies. Add cream cheese batter to the equation, however, and the chief assets of these brownies become liabilities. When paired with dense, tangy cream cheese, the brownie's fine cake-flour crumb did not provide enough structure to suspend the filling; its otherwise pleasant chocolate flavor lacked intensity; and, finally, the amount of batter did not produce a tall enough bar for cream cheese brownies. To make this brownie batter more suitable for its cream cheese partner, we needed to strengthen its structure, infuse it with more chocolate flavor, and give it a bit more height.

To this end, we increased our Basic Brownie recipe by half (for added height), used all-purpose flour instead of cake flour (for strengthened structure), and threw in an extra ounce of unsweetened chocolate (for a more intense chocolate flavor). Baking the increased amount of batter (1½ times the original recipe) in the same size pan solved the height problem. The extra height, however, accentuated the brownie's cakey qualities. Desiring a denser, softer texture, we made the brownies again, this time returning the flour and baking powder to the original amounts, but leaving the eggs and vanilla at the increased quantities. This equation created a dense but relatively dry brownie. The increased amount of unsweetened chocolate, while making the brownie more intensely flavored, also caused it to taste bitter.

From previous chocolate experiments, we deduced that the unsweetened chocolate might be at the root of our harsh, bitter brownies. We made three pans of brownies—one with all unsweetened chocolate, another with all bittersweet chocolate, and a third with a combination of the two, adjusting the sugar as necessary. The brownies made with unsweetened chocolate alone were dry and crumbly, with a slightly bitter finish. On the other hand, the brownies created with all bittersweet chocolate were too soft and gooey. A combination of unsweetened and bittersweet chocolate corrected the texture and flavor deficiencies and delivered a perfect cream cheese brownie base—intensely chocolate, soft, lush, with just a hint of structure.

What's the reason behind this unusual result? Unlike unsweetened chocolate, bittersweet chocolate (as well as semisweet chocolate, which can be used interchangeably with bittersweet) contains lecithin, a sticky emulsifier that is responsible for chocolate's creamy mouthfeel. It makes sense that these smoother, creamier sweetened varieties would bake into gooier, chewier brownies. Because unsweetened chocolate contains no lecithin, brownies made with this ingredient tend to be drier and more crumbly.

Second, during the manufacture of sweetened chocolates, sugar and chocolate are heated together so that the sugar dissolves and the cocoa butter melts, bonding the two together. Unsweetened chocolate contains no sugar, so larger quantities of granulated sugar must be mixed with the chocolate just before baking. These undissolved sugar granules remain distinct and separate in the batter. Sugar is hygroscopic (that is, it readily takes up and retains moisture), which causes the undissolved granules to absorb moisture during baking, resulting in a drier, more crumbly brownie. Because brownies are so rich in chocolate, the types of chocolate used in the cream cheese brownie batter create dramatic differences in the recipe.

Fortunately, the cream cheese filling was much simpler to develop than the brownie batter. We were looking for an intensely flavored filling, but we found that other common cheesecake ingredients like sour cream, butter, and cream simply diluted the intense cream cheese flavor we were after. As it turned out, we only needed to add an egg yolk, a quarter cup of sugar, and a couple of drops of vanilla extract to an eight-ounce package of cream cheese to achieve the flavor and texture we were seeking.

To determine the best way to incorporate the filling into the batter, we experimented with four options: We spread a thin layer of cream cheese filling between two layers of brownie batter. We sandwiched dollops of the cream cheese filling between the two layers of brownie batter. We sandwiched dollops of the cream cheese filling between two layers of brownie batter, then swirled them with a knife. Finally, twice we alternated a layer of brownie batter with a layer of cream cheese filling dollops that we then swirled with a knife. The final technique—which created a visible swirl of light on dark and evenly distributed the filling throughout the brownies—was the winner.

This ultrathick brownie, with its delicate filling, needed to be baked at a relatively low oven temperature. Brownies baked at 350 degrees burned at the edges, requiring the crusts to be trimmed, or turned out hard and inedible. At 325 degrees, however, the problem was solved: The brownies baked evenly. By putting a foil sling coated with cooking spray in the bottom of the pan before we added the batter, we were able to remove the brownies from the pan almost immediately after baking, which made cooling, cutting, and serving the brownies a breeze.

Cream Cheese Brownies

MAKES 16 BROWNIES

Knowing when to remove a pan of brownies from the oven is the only difficult part about baking them. If you wait until an inserted toothpick comes out clean, the brownies are overcooked. But if a toothpick inserted in the middle of the pan comes out with fudgy crumbs, remove the pan immediately.

To melt the chocolate and butter in a microwave oven, microwave chocolate alone at 50 percent power for 2 minutes. Stir chocolate; add butter; and continue microwaving at 50 percent for another 2 minutes, stopping to stir the mixture after 1 minute. If chocolate is not entirely melted, microwave an additional 30 seconds at 50 percent power.

BROWNIE BASE

⅔	cup all-purpose flour
¼	teaspoon salt
½	teaspoon baking powder
2	ounces unsweetened chocolate
4	ounces bittersweet or semisweet chocolate
8	tablespoons (1 stick) unsalted butter
1	cup sugar
2	teaspoons vanilla extract
3	large eggs

CREAM CHEESE FILLING

8	ounces cream cheese, at room temperature
¼	cup sugar
½	teaspoon vanilla extract
1	egg yolk

1. **FOR THE BROWNIE BASE:** Adjust oven rack to lower-middle position and heat oven to 325 degrees. Whisk flour, salt, and baking powder together in small bowl; set aside. Coat an 8-inch-square baking pan with cooking spray. Fit a 16 x 8-inch sheet of aluminum foil in bottom of pan. (Foil overhangs both sides of the pan; use as handles to remove baked brownies from pan.) Coat foil with cooking spray.

2. In a medium heatproof bowl set over a pan of almost simmering water, melt chocolate and butter, stirring occasionally until mixture is smooth. (Alternatively, melt chocolate and butter in micro-

wave oven. See instructions in note above.) Remove melted chocolate mixture from heat; whisk in 1 cup sugar and 2 teaspoons vanilla; cool slightly. Whisk in 3 eggs, one at a time, fully incorporating each before adding the next. Continue whisking until mixture is completely smooth. Add dry ingredients; whisk until just incorporated.

3. **FOR THE CREAM CHEESE FILLING:** In a small bowl, beat cream cheese with remaining ¼ cup sugar, ½ teaspoon vanilla, and egg yolk until of even consistency.

4. **TO FINISH:** Pour half the brownie batter into prepared pan. Drop half the cream cheese mixture, by spoonfuls, over batter. Repeat, layering remaining brownie batter and cream cheese filling. Use blade of a table knife or a spoon handle to gently swirl batter and cream cheese filling, creating a marbled effect.

5. Bake until edges of brownies have puffed slightly, center feels not quite firm when touched lightly, and a toothpick or cake tester inserted into center comes out with several moist, fudgy crumbs adhering to it, 50 to 60 minutes.

6. Cool brownies in pan on a wire rack for 5 minutes. Use foil sling handles to lift brownies from pan. Place brownies on wire rack; allow them to cool to room temperature. Refrigerate until chilled, at least 3 hours. (To hasten cooling, place brownies in the freezer for about 1½ hours.) Cut into squares and serve. (To keep them from drying out, do not cut brownies until ready to serve. Can be wrapped, uncut, in plastic wrap, then foil, and refrigerated up to 5 days.)

LEMON BARS

LEMON SQUARES (OR BARS, AS WE LIKE TO refer to them, since it seems to give you permission to cut them into other than perfect squares) are a favorite classic American bar cookie. In this style of cookie, a bottom layer, or "crust," is pressed into a pan, prebaked, then topped with a filling. The cookies are baked again, then cut into bars.

Lemon bars are easy to make—but that doesn't mean it's easy to get them just the way you want them. Whether from bakeries or home recipes, many versions are too sweet and lack true lemon flavor. The topping might be too gummy or too starchy; it might be skimpy relative to the amount of crust, or piled so high the bar doesn't hold its shape when cut. We have sampled crusts that are too thin, too dry, or too brittle; some lack flavor and others have so much fat they leave a greasy taste in your mouth.

With these variables in mind, we set out to develop a recipe for a lemon bar with a tender, melt-in-your-mouth crust that has a good balance of sweetness and richness. The lemon topping needed to have a true, vibrant lemon taste, a light texture, and good mouthfeel. We also wanted to find just the right balance between filling and crust in terms of both texture and flavor. In addition, we wanted a good, clean cut when serving, without the crust crumbling or the topping falling over. Last but not least, since lemon bars are a casual treat to make without a lot of fuss, we wanted a recipe that was simple and straightforward.

We knew that flour, butter, and sugar would be the main ingredients of the bottom layer. We also knew that since we wanted a cookie or shortbread texture rather than a pastry-type crust, we would need a fair amount of sugar. No liquid would be necessary because we weren't trying to create the little pockets of steam that produce flakiness and layering in pastry.

Our first challenges were to decide the proportion of flour to butter and the amount, as well as the type, of sugar. We decided, after several taste tests, that a bit more than 12 tablespoons of butter and a little less than two cups of flour were just right.

Since sugar affects tenderness as well as sweetness, the amount and type of sugar needed to be determined along with the butter. Brown sugar proved too rich for tasters' palates, while granulated sugar produced a crust that was a bit brittle and gritty. The best, most tender texture came from confectioners' sugar. To achieve the delicate crumb and melt-in-your-mouth quality of shortbread, we also added a bit of cornstarch to our formula.

Having decided on the basic ingredients, we began to investigate ways to combine and bake them. For most cookies and one type of pastry, the fat and sugar are creamed together in the first step. The alternative is to start by cutting the fat into the flour with your fingertips or a food processor, which is common in most pastry crusts. After testing both methods, we decided that because of the proportion of flour to butter and the absence of liquid, the sec-

ond method was best suited for this crust. Cutting the butter into the flour created a crumbly mixture that could be pressed into the pan. To make sure we would end up with an evenly baked crust that was not soggy, we found it necessary to prebake the crust. Through trial and error, we discovered that the standard temperature of 350 degrees worked best.

Now that we had decided on a formula for the crust and the best techniques for making it, we needed to learn how much to make so that it would be in the right proportion to the filling. The bottom layer must not only provide support for the topping but also balance the lemony taste. A crust that was about ¼-inch thick provided the right foundation for the amount of filling we wanted, which ended up being about one-third inch in depth.

The usual method for making the lemon layer of these sweet bars is to mix eggs, sugar, lemon, and flour, pour it over the prebaked crust, and bake until set. Our next step was to determine the amount of fresh lemon juice we would need for a clear, tart lemon flavor. We knew that 2 tablespoons of lemon juice, the minimum amount in the recipes we had researched, would not produce the zing we were after, and initial tests proved this to be true. The flavor was bland and uninteresting. We kept adding more, finally ending up with 11 tablespoons of juice and 2 teaspoons of zest. Even tasters who initially thought this amount made the filling too lemony eventually decided they liked it.

This agreement notwithstanding, we eventually decided that we wanted a topping that was just a little less intense, so we tried adding other liquids. Water thinned out the lemon filling too much, and heavy cream not only adversely affected the lightness but also cut the lemony taste. Adding a small amount of whole milk, though, seemed to balance the flavor with the texture. We also found that baking the topping at a slightly lower temperature than was used for the crust (325 degrees rather than 350 degrees) helped produce a smooth texture, since eggs do not curdle when cooked at lower temperatures.

In our first round of tests, we thought it was unnecessary to thicken the filling with flour. After more tests, though, we discovered two very good reasons to use it. First, some of the fillings baked without flour seemed to have a mealy texture after cooling, a result of the eggs being exposed to the oven heat during baking. Second, toppings made without flour became watery after sitting for only an hour or so. Adding just a small amount of flour solved both these problems without adding any starchy taste—buffering the eggs produced a smooth texture and effectively halted the "weeping."

Now we had only one last problem to solve. During all our tests, the filling would inevitably shift and stick to the sides of the pan, which made it difficult to cut the bars along the edges. We solved this problem by lining the pan with paper, either parchment or waxed, the sides as well as the bottom. We cut two pieces to fit the pan, one for each direction, and held them in place with a small amount of butter. After baking, we lifted the uncut lemon bars from the pan by holding onto the edges of the paper. Because the paper could be cut or peeled away from the sides of the bars and there was no obstruction from the pan edges, we found it easy to cut the bars into even, presentable pieces, using either a knife or a large pizza wheel. A sifting of powdered sugar, and we had perfect lemon bars.

Lemon Bars

MAKES ABOUT TWO DOZEN
1 1/2- TO 2-INCH SQUARES

The lemon filling must be added to a warm crust. The 30-minute chilling and 20-minute baking of the crust should allow plenty of time to prepare the filling. If not, make the filling first and stir to blend just before pouring it into the crust. Any leftover bars can be sealed in plastic wrap and refrigerated for up to 2 days.

CRUST

1 3/4	cups all-purpose flour
2/3	cup confectioners' sugar, plus extra to decorate finished bars
1/4	cup cornstarch
3/4	teaspoon salt
12	tablespoons (1 1/2 sticks) unsalted butter, softened and cut into 1-inch pieces, plus extra for greasing pan

LEMON FILLING

4	large eggs, beaten lightly
1 1/3	cups granulated sugar
3	tablespoons all-purpose flour
2	teaspoons finely grated zest from two large lemons
2/3	cup juice from 3 to 4 large lemons, strained
1/3	cup whole milk
1/8	teaspoon salt

1. FOR THE CRUST: Adjust oven rack to middle position and heat oven to 350 degrees. Lightly butter a 13 by 9-inch baking dish and line with one sheet parchment or wax paper. Dot paper with butter, then lay second sheet crosswise over it.

2. Pulse flour, confectioners' sugar, cornstarch, and salt in workbowl of food processor fitted with steel blade. Add butter and process to blend, 8 to 10 seconds, then pulse until mixture is pale yellow and resembles coarse meal, about three 1-second bursts. (To do this by hand, mix flour, confectioners' sugar, cornstarch, and salt in medium bowl. Freeze butter and grate it on large holes of box grater into flour mixture. Toss butter pieces to coat. Rub pieces between your fingers for a minute, until flour turns pale yellow and coarse.) Sprinkle mixture into lined pan, pressing firmly with fingers into even, 1/4-inch layer over entire pan bottom and about 1/2 inch up sides. Refrigerate for 30 minutes, then bake until golden brown, about 20 minutes.

3. FOR THE FILLING: Meanwhile, whisk eggs, sugar, and flour in medium bowl, then stir in lemon zest, lemon juice, milk, and salt to blend well.

4. TO FINISH: Reduce oven temperature to 325 degrees. Stir filling mixture to reblend; pour into warm crust. Bake until filling feels firm when touched lightly, about 20 minutes. Transfer pan to wire rack; cool to near room temperature, at least 30 minutes. Grasp edges of the lengthwise piece of parchment or waxed paper and lift the bars onto a cutting board. Fold paper down and cut into serving-size bars, wiping knife or pizza wheel clean between cuts, as necessary. Sieve confectioners' sugar over bars, if desired.

18

CAKES

CAKE MAKING REQUIRES PRECISION AND careful attention to detail. A slight mismeasurement of ingredients or the failure to follow a specific beating instruction can have drastic consequences in terms of flavor and texture. Over the years, we have developed a list of general tips designed to head off the mistakes that home cooks might otherwise make.

Proper oven temperature is always important, especially when baking a cake, so periodically check your oven temperature with an oven thermometer. If your oven is too hot, the sides of the cake will set before the middle does, and the cake will hump or crack. If your oven is too cold, the air will escape from the batter before the batter begins to set, and the cake will have a coarse texture and may even fall.

You should own two sets of cake pans—two that measure eight inches across and two that measure nine across. Some recipes call for eight-inch cake pans, others for nine-inch pans. Use the correct size. If the pans are too large, they overheat the rim of the cake, causing the same sorts of problems as an overheated oven. If the pans are too small, batter may rise right out of them. Choose sturdy aluminum pans with absolutely vertical sides. Do not use disposable foil pans, which often produce misshapen cakes.

Generously grease the pans with shortening (Crisco)—not butter—and coat them well with flour. Solid vegetable shortening, such as Crisco, is 100 percent fat and won't leave gaps. Butter contains water, which when it evaporates may leave greaseless gaps to which cake batter can stick. The flour holds the shortening in place and keeps the batter from seeping through to the pan bottom. We find that shiny cake pans are almost always nonstick, so there is no need for parchment paper liners. If you are using an older pan with a dull finish, as an extra pre-caution you may want to grease the pan, line the bottom with a piece of parchment or waxed paper, grease the paper, and then flour the pan and paper.

Have all ingredients, especially butter, eggs, and milk, at room temperature. Chilled ingredients do not emulsify well, which leads to a dense cake, and cold butter won't even mix into a batter. Very warm ingredients may cause air cells in creamed butter to dissolve. Unless specified otherwise in a recipe, all ingredients should register between 65 and 70 degrees on an instant-read thermometer. Let butter soften on the counter for about an hour before creaming. The sticks should give when pressed, but still hold their shape with no signs of melting.

To quickly bring eggs to room temperature, submerge uncracked eggs in a bowl of warm water for 5 to 10 minutes. Since separating eggs is somewhat easier when they are cold, you may want to separate the eggs first and then let them warm up while you assemble and measure the remaining ingredients. You may also place a bowl or measuring cup filled with yolks or whites in a bowl of warm water if necessary.

Unless otherwise noted, measure flour carefully by the dip-and-sweep method. Dip the measuring cup into the container of flour, scoop out a heaping cupful, and then level the top with the straight edge of a butter knife or icing spatula. Do not shake, tap, or pack the cup. If the cup is not completely filled on the first try, dump the flour back into the container and dip again.

Give pans enough space in the oven. Cakes placed too close together will rise toward each other and end up lopsided. Cakes placed too close to the oven walls won't rise as high on the side nearest the wall. Keep pans at least three inches from each other and the oven walls and on the middle rack of the oven.

INGREDIENTS: Cake Flour

Cake flour gives many cakes their delicate, tender crumb. While all-purpose flour is made from hard wheat (at least in part) and contains between 10 and 12 percent protein, cake flour is made from soft wheat and typically has just 8 to 10 percent protein. Less protein means less gluten formation and a more tender crumb.

Most supermarkets sell two kinds of cake flour—self-rising and plain. Self-rising cake flour contains salt and baking powder and is meant to be a convenience product. However, we would rather choose the amount and type of leavener that goes into our baking. For instance, self-rising flour would have disastrous results in a cake that calls for buttermilk and therefore needs baking soda rather than baking powder as the leavener. (For more on leaveners, see page 374.) To avoid this kind of problem, we always use plain cake flour.

If your oven is small, stagger the pans on racks set at the upper-middle and lower-middle positions to allow for proper air circulation.

Use your finger and a cake tester to judge when layers are done. Cakes should be baked until firm in the center when lightly pressed and a cake needle or toothpick inserted in the center comes out clean or with just a crumb or two adhering. If the tester comes out perfectly clean, the cake is probably over-cooked and dry.

ANGEL FOOD CAKE

AT ITS BEST, AN ANGEL FOOD CAKE SHOULD be tall and perfectly shaped, have a snowy-white, tender crumb, and be encased in a thin, delicate, golden crust. Although most angel food cakes contain no more than six ingredients, there are literally hundreds of variations on this basic theme. The type of flour used, the baking temperature, the type of sugar, and even the use of baking powder—a serious transgression according to most experts—are all in dispute. What is not in dispute is that angel food cake requires a delicate balance of ingredients and proper cooking techniques. If leavened with just beaten egg whites (as is the custom), this cake can be fickle.

An angel food cake is distinguished by its lack of egg yolks, chemical leaveners, and fat. Other cakes also use beaten egg whites for leaveners, but there are differences. Chiffon cake (page 446) contains egg yolks, which makes for a slightly heavier, moister cake. Sponge cake (page 449) also includes whole or separated eggs; it, too, is denser and more yellow than angel food cake.

The six ingredients found in every angel food cake are egg whites, sugar, flour, cream of tartar, salt, and flavorings. Most recipes start by beating the egg whites. (Save all the yolks for making custards.) Mixer speed is critical for well-beaten whites. We found that starting at high speed will produce quick but inconsistent results. To create the most stable foam, beat the whites at low speed to break them up into a froth. Add the cream of tartar and salt, increase the speed to medium, and beat until the whites form very soft, billowy mounds. When large bubbles stop appearing around the edges, and with the mixer still on medium, begin adding the sugar, a tablespoon at a time, until all the sugar has been incorporated and the whites are shiny and form soft peaks when the beater is lifted. The mass should still flow slightly when the bowl is tilted. Do not beat until the peaks are stiff—we found that this makes it difficult to fold in the flour, deflating the whites and therefore reducing volume.

Because there is no fat in angel food cake, sugar is critical to its taste and texture. We tested confectioners' sugar and found that the cornstarch in it—which is added to the sugar—makes the cake too dense. Superfine sugar is simply too fine, making a soft cake with little substance. We found that granulated sugar is best in this recipe.

Flour sets the cake batter, but because it also adds weight, the flour should be as light and airy as possible. We found that cake flour, which is finer than all-purpose flour, is easier to incorporate into the beaten whites without deflating them. The lower protein content of cake flour results in a more delicate, tender crumb, which we preferred. No matter what kind of flour is used, we found sifting to be essential; it makes the flour lighter in texture and easier to incorporate into the whites. We sift the flour twice—once before measuring and once before adding it to the beaten whites—for maximum lightness.

Sugar, flour, egg whites, and cream of tartar will

INGREDIENTS: Cream of Tartar

Cream or tartar was once known as the secret ingredient in angel food cakes. A common solid salt of tartaric acid, this substance acts as a stabilizer when beating egg whites and produces a higher, lighter-textured cake. The acidity in cream of tartar also acts as a bleach, helping to make a snowy-white cake. (Lemon juice works in the same way, which is why we add some to the batter.)

We found that cream of tartar does not increase the volume of the beaten whites, as many sources suggest. It does, however, make the foam less prone to overcoagulation during beating by slightly lowering the pH of the egg whites from about 9 to 8 (that is, the mixture becomes more acidic). Chemically, the cream of tartar adds hydrogen ions, creating a more stable molecular structure. In our tests, batters made with cream of tartar held onto more of their volume when the dry ingredients were added and therefore baked up higher.

INGREDIENTS : Butter

Simply put, butter is overwhipped or churned cream. In cream, globules of fat protected by a phospholipid membrane float about in a suspension of water. When cream is agitated or churned, the fat globules collide with one another, causing the membranes to break. The freed fat globules then begin to clump together, trapping little pockets of water along with the broken membrane pieces and some intact fat crystals. After the cream is churned into a semisolid mass of butter, any remaining liquid is drawn off as buttermilk. So what begins as an oil-in-water emulsion known as cream is reversed to a water-in-oil emulsion known as butter.

All butter must consist of at least 80 percent milk fat, according to U.S. Department of Agriculture standards. Most commercial butters do not exceed this. European butters and Hotel Bar's Plugrá are exceptions, with anywhere from 82 to 88 percent milk fat. All butters contain about 2 percent milk solids, and the remainder is water.

In addition to standardizing butter composition, the USDA closely and frequently inspects butter-manufacturing plants for sanitation and grades batches of retail butter to make sure they are made with high-quality sweet cream.

If a cream is not up to the potential of grade AA butter (the highest grade), a dairy will typically use it in cheese, ice cream, or other products that do not demand the clean, delicate flavor of the highest quality cream. Supermarkets can also sell Grade A butter, which is downgraded for having a slightly acidic flavor.

You can be sure that a Grade AA butter originated in premium form because of tight government standards on the quality of butter. Unfortunately, though, by the time you go to purchase it, you have no way of knowing how long or under what conditions it was sitting in frozen storage or in a market. And you cannot estimate its age by its expiration date, because there are no industry standards for such information. Each brand differs. So even if your butter is used before its expiration date or even immediately after purchase, you cannot be guaranteed the good taste of fresh butter.

Grade AA butter can easily deteriorate before purchase if improperly shipped or stored at the market. Butter can also spoil in your refrigerator, turning rancid from the oxidation of fatty acids. Exposure to air or light are particular culprits, which explains why Land O Lakes takes the precaution of wrapping its unsalted butter in foil.

The fats in butter are vulnerable not only to oxidation but also to picking up odors. They are particularly susceptible at warmer temperatures, but can take on odors even when they are chilled or frozen. For this reason, we suggest not storing butter in a refrigerator's butter compartment, which tends to be warmer because it's inside the door. To find out how much of a difference this made, we stored one stick of butter in its original wrapper in the butter compartment and one in the center of the refrigerator. After one week, the butter in the compartment had begun to pick up off flavors, while the one stored in the center still tasted fresh.

Butter is a crucial ingredient in most baked goods, especially cakes. To find out if the brand of butter makes a difference, we made our basic yellow cake with eight different butters. All the cakes received high ratings, and the scores were within close range of one another. Tasters confessed it was difficult to really taste the butter in the cakes.

We also used the eight butters in a rich buttercream frosting made with softened butter, confectioners' sugar, and some milk. Most of these frostings were well-liked (some more than others), but the one made with Plugrá (a higher-fat butter) was head and shoulders above the others for both a pleasant, delicate butter flavor and an airy texture. The other high-fat butter, Celles Sur Belle, scored well but was not judged to have as light a texture as the Plugrá. In this one instance, the butter is such an important ingredient and the recipe is so simple that a higher-fat butter created a noticeable difference in both flavor and texture.

Overall, however, we recommend that you pay more attention to the condition in which you buy the butter and the conditions under which you store it than to the particular brand. Purchase your butter from a store you can depend on and that has a high turnover of products. The best way to store butter is sealed in an airtight plastic bag in your freezer, pulling out sticks as you need them. Butter will keep in the freezer for several months, and in the refrigerator for no more than two or three weeks.

One final note about butter. We use unsalted butter in our test kitchen. We like its sweet, delicate flavor and prefer to add our own salt to recipes. We find that the quality of salted butter is often inferior and that each manufacturer adds a different amount of salt, which makes recipe writing difficult. While you can certainly get away with using salted butter in some savory recipes (as long as you adjust the total amount of salt in the recipe), we strongly recommend using unsalted butter when baking.

produce a good-looking angel food cake that is sweet but bland. Salt is added for flavor and also helps stabilizes the beaten whites. Other common additions are vanilla or almond extract (we like to add both), which add flavor without changing the basic chemistry of the batter. You can add grated citrus zest or a little citrus juice (we prefer the latter because zest can mar the perfectly soft, white texture of the cake). We found that high-fat flavorings, such as grated chocolate and nuts, greatly affect the cake's texture, and we prefer to stick with simpler flavorings.

We tried using some baking powder for added leavening and stability but found that the resulting cake was not as white and had a coarser crumb. Adding baking powder felt like cheating. If you separate and beat the egg whites properly, there should be no need to add baking powder.

Our most intriguing experiment involved oven temperatures. We baked the same recipe in the same pan at 300, 325, 350, and 375 degrees, baking each until the cake tested done with a skewer and the top bounced back when pressed lightly. Surprisingly, all cooked evenly, but the cakes baked at 350 and 375 degrees had a thicker, darker crust while the cakes baked at 300 and 325 degrees had a more desirable, delicate, evenly pale golden crust. After many tastings, we decided that 325 degrees was the ideal temperature.

The best tool we found to remove an angel food cake from the pan is a thin, flexible, nonserrated knife that is at least five inches long. Tilt the pan at a right angle to the counter to make it easy to work the knife around the sides. Insert the knife between the crust and the pan, pressing hard against the side of the pan, and work your way all around the cake. To cut around the central core of a tube pan, use a long, thin skewer. Invert the pan so that the cake slides out, then peel off the parchment or wax paper. If using a pan with a removable bottom, slide the knife blade between the cake and the pan to release it. Present the cake bottom side up, sitting on its wide, crustier top, with the delicate and more easily sliced crust facing up.

To cut the cake, use a long, serrated knife, and pull it back and forth with a gentle sawing motion. When we tried using the specially made tool for cutting angel food cake—a row of prongs attached to a bar—it mashed and squashed this tender cake.

Angel Food Cake
SERVES 10 TO 12

Sift both the cake flour and granulated sugar before measuring to eliminate any lumps and ensure the lightest possible texture. See page 446 for more information about choosing the right pan for this recipe.

1	cup sifted plain cake flour
1 ½	cups sifted granulated sugar
12	large egg whites, room temperature
1	teaspoon cream of tartar
¼	teaspoon salt
1 ½	teaspoons vanilla extract
1 ½	teaspoons lemon juice
½	teaspoon almond extract

1. Adjust oven rack to lower-middle position and heat oven to 325 degrees. Have ready an ungreased large tube pan (9-inch diameter and 16-cup capacity), preferably with a removable bottom. If pan bottom is not removable, line with parchment or wax paper.

2. Whisk flour and ¾ cup sugar in small bowl. Place remaining ¾ cup sugar in another small bowl next to mixer.

SCIENCE: Beating Egg Whites

When egg whites are beaten, they produce a foam much like soap bubbles or the head on a beer. Like most other foams, egg whites, which are liquid, create a latticework structure through agitation. This structure traps pockets of air or gas, which in turn form a series of bubbles. Stable foams (eggs whites are particularly stable) have two things in common—the liquid that traps the gas is very strong, and the bubbles are very small.

Egg whites are particularly well-suited to producing stable foam because they are so thick and viscous. The heat of the oven causes the trapped air to expand, causing the entire structure to rise. A specific protein in egg whites, called ovalbumin, does its work in the oven, helping to further set the structure of the foam and keep it from falling.

It's important for cooks to remember that they can control the size of the bubbles produced when egg whites are beaten. Start beating the whites at low speed to produce small bubbles, then increase the speed to encourage the development of a stable foam with small bubbles.

3. Beat egg whites with electric mixer at low speed until just broken up and beginning to froth. Add cream of tartar and salt and beat at medium speed until whites form very soft, billowy mounds. With the mixer still at medium speed, beat in ¾ cup sugar, 1 tablespoon at a time, until all sugar is added and whites are shiny and form soft peaks. Add vanilla, lemon juice, and almond extract and beat until just blended.

4. Place flour-sugar mixture in sifter set over wax paper. Sift flour mixture over whites, about 3 tablespoons at a time, and gently fold in, using a large rubber spatula. Sift any flour-sugar mixture that falls onto paper back into bowl with whites.

5. Gently scrape batter into pan, smooth top with spatula, and give pan a couple of raps on the counter to release any large air bubbles.

6. Bake until cake is golden brown and top springs back when pressed firmly, 50 to 60 minutes.

7. If cake pan has feet, invert pan onto them. If not, invert pan over neck of bottle so air can circulate all around it. Allow to cool completely for 2 to 3 hours.

8. To unmold, run a knife around edges, being careful not to dislodge golden crust. Pull cake out of pan and cut the same way around the removable bottom to release, or peel off parchment or wax paper if using. Place cake, bottom side up, on platter. Cut slices by sawing gently with a serrated knife. Serve cake the day it is made.

~~~~~~

EQUIPMENT: Tube Pan

The traditional pan for angel food cake is a tall tube pan with a central column. The central tube exposes more batter to the heat, helps the center of the cake rise, and dries out the cake evenly. In addition, a tube pan creates more of the lightly caramelized, macaroonlike outer crust that we like so much.

We were curious to learn if we could improvise by using a deep cake pan that measures eight inches across and three inches from bottom to top. We baked our batter three times in this pan. Each time the center of the cake fell. Our conclusion: the batter needs the center surface area of the tube to cling to as it bakes and cools.

We recommend using a tube pan with a removable bottom. If you don't have one, you will need to line your pan with parchment or wax paper. An angel food cake pan is never greased—you want the batter to climb up the sides, which will not happen if the surface is slick.

~~~~~~

CHIFFON CAKE

ON ANY GIVEN DAY THERE MUST HAVE BEEN at least a thousand chiffon cakes hanging upside down to cool in the gleaming kitchens of postwar America. The cake seemed not to have come from an oven but rather from out of a dream: a mile high and light as a feather, yet also tender and moist, qualities that angel food and sponge cakes typically lack.

And chiffon cake was modern. It was made with vegetable oil—a brand new idea in 1950—and so required none of the tedious creaming and incremental adding of ingredients demanded by butter cakes. One simply mixed flour, sugar, baking powder, egg yolks, water, and oil as if making a pancake batter, then folded in stiffly beaten egg whites. The whipping of the whites— "they should be much stiffer than for angel food or meringue," warned Betty Crocker— was the only tricky feat required, and even this was no longer an arduous task. More than a few households could boast a snappy new electric mixer.

Chiffon cake was invented in 1927 by the aptly named Harry Baker, a Los Angeles insurance salesman turned caterer who had been wholesaling fudge from the kitchen of the apartment he shared with his aging mother. When the cake became a featured attraction at the Brown Derby, then the restaurant of the stars, Baker converted a spare room into his top-secret bakery, fitted it with 12 tin hot-plate ovens, and personally baked 42 cakes a day. The cakes sold for a remarkable two dollars each to prestigious hostesses and the MGM and RKO studio commissaries.

Baker kept his recipe a secret for 20 years. Finally, having been evicted from his apartment and fearing memory loss, the usually reclusive Baker trekked uninvited to Minneapolis to sell his recipe to General Mills. After much dickering, a deal was cut. There ensued considerable testing, but with only a couple of minor changes to the technique and a new name—"chiffon cake"—the cake appeared before the American public in a 1948 pamphlet called "Betty Crocker Chiffon," containing 14 recipes and variations in addition to umpteen icings, fillings, serving ideas, and helpful hints. It was an instant hit and became one of the most popular cakes of the time.

Like the Hollywood stars of the 1920s who were the first to taste Harry Baker's secret-recipe cakes, we have been delighted by the uniquely light yet full richness and deep flavor of this American invention. But we also know that chiffon cakes can be dry or cottony. Ideally, chiffon cake should be moist and tender with a rich flavor. To perfect this twentieth-century classic, we decided to go back to Betty Crocker's version, as first put before the public by General Mills in 1948.

With the exception of the chocolate variation, all of Betty Crocker's original chiffon cakes call for 2¼ cups sifted cake flour (which translates into about 1⅔ cups as measured by the dip-and-sweep method), 1½ cups sugar, one tablespoon baking powder, one teaspoon salt, one-half cup oil, five egg yolks, three-quarters cup water or other liquid, one cup egg whites (seven to eight large), and one-half teaspoon cream of tartar.

We made a plain, an orange, and a walnut chiffon cake according to the original formula and found that we had three complaints. The cakes were a bit dry—cottony and fluffy rather than moist and foamy, the way we thought chiffon cakes should be—and they seemed to lack flavor, punch, pizzazz. In addition, the cakes rose a bit too high for the pan, a consequence of the downsizing of tube pans, from 18 to 16 cups, that took place around 1970.

Since fat increases perceived moistness and also transmits flavor, we thought that adding more oil might help, but it did not. An orange chiffon cake made with an additional quarter cup of oil (up from one-half cup) turned out not only dry and flavorless but also greasy and heavy, an outcome that was as unexpected as it was disappointing.

We increased the number of eggs, and the cakes, even though they were lighter and richer than Betty Crocker's original, still tasted dry. We instinctively felt that adding more liquid would be a poor idea, but at this point we felt we had no choice but to try. Unfortunately, increasing the water from three-quarters cup to one cup made the texture gummy and heavy—and the cake still managed to taste dry!

There was now only one ingredient left to play with, the flour. Since the problem was dryness, the flour obviously had to be decreased, but we knew from our experience with other sponge-type cakes that decreasing the flour could have very messy consequences. We might end up with a rubbery sponge or, worse, with a demonic soufflé that heaved plops of batter onto the floor of the oven.

Whenever a sponge-type cake decides to collapse or explode, the culprit is the same: a lack of structure. Since eggs as well as flour provide structure, we reasoned that we could compensate for a decrease in flour by adding an extra egg yolk. We made an orange chiffon cake using the Betty Crocker formula but decreasing the flour by one-third cup and increasing the yolks from five to six. The effect was magical. Instead of being fluffy, cottony, and crumbly, the cake was wonderfully moist and so tremblingly tender that slices flopped over at the middle if cut too thin. And the moistness transmitted all of the taste that had been lacking in our first experiments.

The cake, however, was not quite perfect. Evidently the structure was borderline, and so the cake rose very high, spilling over onto the lip of the pan. This made it difficult to cut the cake free from the pan without tearing the top crust. Furthermore, because its top was humped, the cake did not sit flat when turned upside down onto a serving plate. We figured that removing an egg white would help to shrink the cake, but we feared that it might also undercut the structure to the point where the cake wouldn't rise at all. Nonetheless, we gave the idea a try. The resulting cake was lovely coming out of the oven, risen just to the top of the pan and perfectly flat—but its perfection was illusory. We hung the cake upside down to cool and started to clean up the kitchen when we heard a soft plop: The cake had fallen out of the pan.

Once we had taken a few nibbles of the mess, our fears were confirmed. The cake was pasty and overly moist. There was simply not enough structure to hold it together. It had to have that egg white. But perhaps, we thought, using an extra egg yolk in place of that white would save the structure but prevent the excess puffiness. Unfortunately, when we tried this formula, our test cake bulged almost as much as the one we had made with five yolks and eight whites, though it didn't fall out of the pan, which meant that it had sufficient structure.

At this point a chiffon cake recipe that we had seen in Carole Walter's *Great Cakes* (Ballantine, 1991) came to mind. Rather than whipping all of the egg whites, Walter mixed some of them, unbeaten, into the dry ingredients along with the yolks, water, and oil. Thus she incorporated less air into the batter, which should, we reasoned, make for a smaller cake. We tried Walter's technique using seven eggs, two of them added whole to the batter and five of them separated with the whites beaten. Eureka! At last we had the perfect chiffon cake: moist, tender, flavorful, and just the right size for the pan.

Master Recipe for Chiffon Cake

SERVES 12

In the original recipes for chiffon cake published by General Mills, the directions for beating the egg whites read, "WHIP until whites form very stiff peaks. They should be much stiffer than for angel food or meringue. DO NOT UNDERBEAT." These instructions, with their anxiety-inducing capitalized words, are well taken. If the whites are not very stiff, the cake will not rise properly, and the bottom will be heavy, dense, wet, and custardlike. Better to overbeat than underbeat. After all, if you overbeat the egg whites and they end up dry and "blocky," you can simply smudge and smear the recalcitrant blobs with the flat side of the spatula to break up the clumps.

1 ½	cups sugar
1 ⅓	cups plain cake flour
2	teaspoons baking powder
½	teaspoon salt
7	large eggs, 2 left whole, 5 separated, room temperature
½	cup vegetable oil
1	tablespoon vanilla extract
½	teaspoon almond extract
½	teaspoon cream of tartar

1. Adjust rack to lower-middle position and heat oven to 325 degrees. Whisk sugar, flour, baking powder, and salt together in large bowl (at least 4-quart size). Whisk in two whole eggs, five egg yolks (reserve whites), ¾ cup water, oil, and extracts until batter is just smooth.

2. Pour reserved egg whites into large bowl; beat at low speed with electric mixer until foamy, about 1 minute. Add cream of tartar, gradually increase speed to medium-high, then beat whites until very thick and stiff, just short of dry, 9 to 10 minutes with

handheld mixer and 5 to 7 minutes in standing mixer. With large rubber spatula, fold whites into batter, smearing in any blobs of white that resist blending with flat side of spatula.

3. Pour batter into ungreased large tube pan (9-inch diameter, 16-cup capacity). Rap pan against countertop five times to rupture any large air pockets. If using two-piece pan, grasp on both sides with your hands while firmly pressing down on the tube with thumbs to keep batter from seeping underneath pan during this rapping process. Wipe off any batter that may have dripped or splashed onto inside walls of pan with paper towel.

4. Bake cake until wire cake tester inserted in center comes out clean, 55 to 65 minutes. Immediately turn cake upside down to cool. If pan does not have prongs around rim for elevating cake, invert pan over bottle or funnel, inserted through tube. Let cake hang until completely cool, about 2 hours.

5. To unmold, turn pan upright. Run frosting spatula or thin knife around pan's circumference between cake and pan wall, always pressing against the pan. Use cake tester to loosen cake from tube. For one-piece pan, bang it on counter several times, then invert over serving plate. For two-piece pan, grasp tube and lift cake out of pan. If glazing the cake, use a fork or a paring knife to gently scrape all the crust off the cake. Loosen cake from pan bottom with spatula or knife, then invert cake onto plate. (Can be wrapped in plastic and stored at room temperature 2 days or refrigerated 4 days.)

➤ VARIATIONS

Banana-Nut Chiffon Cake
Follow Master Recipe for Chiffon Cake, decreasing baking powder to 1¼ teaspoons and adding ¼ teaspoon baking soda. Decrease water to ⅔ cup and vanilla to 1 teaspoon; omit almond extract. Fold in 1 cup very finely mashed bananas (about 2 large or 3 medium) and ½ cup very finely ground toasted walnuts or pecans to batter before folding in whites. Increase baking time to 60 to 70 minutes.

Chocolate Marble Chiffon Cake
Combine ¼ cup unsweetened cocoa powder and 2 tablespoons firmly packed dark brown sugar in small bowl. Stir in 3 tablespoons boiling water, mixing

until smooth. Follow Master Recipe for Chiffon Cake, equally dividing batter into two separate bowls. Mix scant ½ cup of one batter portion into cocoa mixture, then partially fold this mixture back into the batter from which it came. Sieve or sift 3 tablespoons cake flour over the now-chocolate batter and continue to fold until just mixed. Pour half the white and then half the chocolate batter into pan; repeat. Do not rap pan against countertop.

Date-Spice Chiffon Cake

Follow Master Recipe for Chiffon Cake, substituting 1½ cups firmly packed dark brown sugar for white sugar and adding ¾ cup chopped or snipped dates, 2 teaspoons ground cinnamon, ½ teaspoon ground nutmeg, and ¼ teaspoon ground cloves to dry ingredients. Rather than mixing, process dry ingredients in workbowl of food processor fitted with metal blade until dates are reduced to ⅛-inch bits and any lumps of brown sugar are pulverized. Continue with Master Recipe, omitting almond extract.

Lemon or Lemon-Coconut Chiffon Cake

Follow Master Recipe for Chiffon Cake, substituting ½ teaspoon baking soda for baking powder, decreasing water to ⅔ cup and vanilla to 1 teaspoon, and omitting almond extract. Along with vanilla, add grated zests of 2 large lemons and 2 tablespoons strained lemon juice. (For Lemon-Coconut Chiffon Cake, proceed as above, adding ⅔ to 1 cup lightly packed sweetened flaked coconut, chopped a bit with chef's knife, to batter before folding in whites.)

Mocha-Nut Chiffon Cake

Follow Master Recipe for Chiffon Cake, substituting ¾ cup brewed espresso-strength coffee for the water and omitting almond extract. Add ½ cup finely chopped toasted walnuts and 1 ounce grated unsweetened baking chocolate to batter before folding in whites.

Orange or Cranberry-Orange Chiffon Cake

Follow Master Recipe for Chiffon Cake, substituting 2 tablespoons grated orange zest and ¾ cup strained orange juice for the water, decreasing vanilla to 1 teaspoon, and omitting almond extract. (For Cranberry-Orange Chiffon Cake, proceed as above, adding 1 cup cranberries, chopped to ⅛-inch flecks in food processor, and ½ cup finely chopped toasted walnuts to batter before folding in whites.)

Glaze for Chiffon Cake
ENOUGH FOR 1 CAKE

Since lumps in the confectioners' sugar don't dissolve completely in the liquid, they really show up once the cake is glazed. Unless you are certain that your sugar is lump-free, better to sift it. Before you glaze the cake, the crumbs must be scraped. With a fork or paring knife, gently scrape all the crust off the cake. To keep the serving plate from becoming smudged with glaze, slip small pieces of waxed paper beneath the cake edge all along the bottom. If making the milk variation, stir in one-half teaspoon of lemon juice to cut the intense sweetness.

- 4 tablespoons unsalted butter, melted
- 4–5 tablespoons orange juice, lemon juice, milk, or coffee (for date-spice or mocha-nut variations)
- 2 cups sifted confectioners' sugar

Beat butter, 4 tablespoons of the liquid, and sugar in medium bowl until smooth. Let glaze stand 1 minute, then try spreading a little on cake. If cake threatens to tear, thin glaze with up to 1 tablespoon more liquid. A little at a time, spread glaze over cake top, letting excess dribble down sides. Let cake stand until glaze dries, about 30 minutes. If you like, spread dribbles (before they have a chance to harden) to make a thin, smooth coat.

SPONGE CAKE

SPONGE CAKE IS THE BEST CHOICE FOR Boston Cream Pie, that misnamed yellow layer cake filled with custard and drizzled with chocolate icing. It is also delicious in simple layer cakes filled with jam or lemon custard. Ideally, sponge cake is lighter than the standard butter-based layer cake, with a springy but delicate texture that stands up nicely to a rich custard filling and a sweet chocolate glaze. It should not be dry or tough, the curse of many classic sponge cakes, nor should it be difficult to make. We were seeking a basic building-block cake recipe, just as dependable and useful as a classic American layer cake.

There are several kinds of sponge or "foam" cakes, so named because they depend on eggs (whole or separated) beaten to a foam to provide lift and structure. They all use egg foam for structure, but they differ in two ways: whether fat (butter or milk) is added and whether the foam is made from whole eggs, egg whites, or a combination.

A French foam cake, called génoise, is made by whipping whole eggs and calls for a small amount of melted butter. We made several génoise and the cakes were delicate but springy, light but firm—all in all, very good. But, as we soon discovered, a génoise is anything but simple. This aerated mixture is dependent on the temperature of the ingredients, the ratio of eggs to flour, and even the speed with which the cake is put into the oven. During testing, we discovered that if the milk was added at room temperature (not hot, as is suggested in most recipes), or if the eggs were a bit over- or underbeaten, the cake would not rise properly. This makes for a professional baker's cake, not the simple everyday cake recipe we were looking for.

Our next thought was to turn to an American sponge cake. It differs from a génoise only in that little or no fat is added and some or all of the egg whites are beaten separately, which delivers a more stable batter and thus a more foolproof recipe.

We started by making a classic American sponge cake, which adds no fat in the form of butter or milk and calls for eight beaten egg whites folded into four beaten egg yolks. The cake certainly was light, but it lacked flavor, and the texture was dry and a bit chewy. To solve these problems, we turned to a recipe for a hot-milk sponge cake, in which a small amount of melted butter and hot milk are added to the whole-egg foam. This cake turned out much better on all counts. The added fat provided not only flavor but also tenderized the crumb. This particular recipe also used fewer eggs than our original sponge cake recipe.

We were now working with a master recipe that used three-quarters cup cake flour, one teaspoon baking powder, three-quarters cup sugar, and five eggs. We started by separating out all five whites and found that the cake was too light, its insufficient structure resulting in a slightly sunken center. We then separated out and beat just three of the whites, and the resulting cake was excellent. When all-purpose flour was substituted for cake flour, the cake had more body and was a bit tougher than the version with cake flour. We then tried different proportions of the two flours, finally settling on a 2:1 ratio of cake flour to all-purpose. We also tested to find the proper ratio of eggs to flour and found that five eggs to three-quarters cup flour (we tested one-half cup and a full cup) was best. Five eggs also turned out to

SCIENCE: Egg Foams

Our recipe for sponge cake, which is a "foam" cake, depends on the proper aeration of both whole eggs and egg whites. When egg whites are beaten into a foam, their proteins partially unwind around air bubbles, lining the bubbles with protein strands that are loosely connected to one another. When the batter is heated, the bubbles increase in size, and the loose, elastic strands of protein allow this expansion without breaking their bonds. (If egg whites are overbeaten, on the other hand, the protein strands become inelastic and the mixture cannot expand.) This aeration is a good thing for leavening, but it creates a less stable overall structure since the protein has been partially denatured through beating.

A whole-egg foam is even more sensitive and unstable than an egg-white foam because it is based on the process of emulsification and not, like egg whites, on a film of protein that traps air. During emulsification, tiny bubbles of air become suspended in the liquid of the egg through the medium of the lecithin in the eggs. This produces a very fragile and complex structure, since water and air are not naturally inclined to bond.

Folding an egg-white foam into a whole-egg foam increases the protein content of the batter, which makes it more stable because of the air-protein construction. The beaten egg whites also set at a lower temperature than the whole-egg foam, which means that the cake firms up more quickly during baking. We also decided to add flour, a stabilizing influence, to this mixture before adding melted butter and milk, additional fats that often destabilize egg foams.

be appropriate: Six eggs produced an "eggy" cake, while four eggs resulted in a lower rise and a cake with a bit less flavor.

We had thought that the baking powder might be optional, but it turned out to be essential to a properly risen cake. Although angel food and classic sponge cakes, which use no added fat, do not require chemical leavening, in this sponge cake the addition of milk and melted butter combined with the relatively small amount of beaten egg whites in proportion to the flour make baking powder necessary.

Two tablespoons of melted butter was just the right amount; three tablespoons made the cake a bit oily and the butter flavor too prominent. As for the milk, three tablespoons was best; larger quantities resulted in a wet, mushy texture.

With our basic recipe in hand, we played with the order of the steps. Beating the whole-egg foam first, and then the whites, allowed the relatively fragile foam to deteriorate, producing less rise. We found that beating the whites first was vastly better. After much experimentation, we also found it best to fold together, all at the same time, the beaten whole eggs, the beaten whites, and the flour, and then, once the mixture was about half-mixed, to add the warm butter and milk. This eliminated the possibility that the liquid would damage the egg foam and also made the temperature of the butter/milk mixture less important than it was with a génoise.

Determining when a sponge cake is properly cooked is a little more difficult than it is with a regular American layer cake. A sponge cake should provide some resistance and not feel as if one just touched the top of a soufflé. Another good test is color. The top of the cake should be a nice light brown, not pale golden or a dark, rich brown.

We also tested the best way to handle the cake once out of the oven. When left to cool in a baking pan, the cake shrinks away from the sides and the edges become uneven. Quickly removing it onto a cooling rack works well, but it's tricky, because the cake pan is very hot. We discovered that the best method is to place the hot cake pan on a towel, cover it with a plate, and then use the towel to invert the cake. Finally, reinvert the cake and slip it back onto a cooling rack.

Foolproof Sponge Cake

MAKES TWO 8- OR 9-INCH CAKES

The egg whites should be beaten to soft, glossy, billowy peaks. If beaten until too stiff, they will be very difficult to fold into the whole-egg mixture.

½	cup plain cake flour
¼	cup all-purpose flour
1	teaspoon baking powder
¼	teaspoon salt
3	tablespoons milk
2	tablespoons unsalted butter
½	teaspoon vanilla extract
5	large eggs, room temperature
¾	cup sugar

1. Adjust oven rack to lower-middle position and heat oven to 350 degrees. Grease two 8- or 9-inch cake pans and cover pan bottoms with rounds of parchment paper. Whisk flours, baking powder, and salt in a medium bowl (or sift onto waxed paper). Heat milk and butter in a small saucepan over low heat until butter melts. Remove from heat and add vanilla; cover and keep warm.

2. Separate three of the eggs, placing whites in bowl of standing mixer fitted with whisk attachment (or large mixing bowl if using hand mixer) and reserving the 3 yolks plus remaining 2 whole eggs in another mixing bowl. Beat the 3 whites on low speed until whites are foamy. Increase mixer speed to medium and gradually add 6 tablespoons of the sugar; continue to beat whites to soft, moist peaks. (Do not overbeat.) If using a standing mixer, transfer egg whites to a large bowl and add yolk/whole-egg mixture to mixing bowl.

3. Beat yolk/whole-egg mixture with remaining 6 tablespoons sugar. Beat on medium-high speed until eggs are very thick and a pale yellow color, about 5 minutes. Add beaten eggs to whites.

4. Sprinkle flour mixture over beaten eggs and whites; fold very gently 12 times with a large rubber spatula. Make a well in one side of batter and pour milk mixture into bowl. Continue folding until batter shows no trace of flour and whites and whole eggs are evenly mixed, about 8 additional strokes.

5. Immediately pour batter into prepared baking pans; bake until cake tops are light brown and feel firm and spring back when touched, about 16 minutes for 9-inch cake pans and 20 minutes for 8-inch cake pans.

6. Immediately run a knife around pan perimeter to loosen cake. Cover pan with large plate. Using a towel, invert pan and remove pan from cake. Peel off parchment. Reinvert cake from plate onto rack. Repeat with remaining cake and continue with one of the recipes that follow.

Boston Cream Pie

SERVES 8

Why is this cake called Boston cream pie? It seems that the cake does indeed have its roots in Boston, where it developed in the middle of the nineteenth century. Modern baking experts believe that since pies predated cakes in the American kitchen, pie pans were simply more common kitchen equipment than cake pans. Hence the name pie was originally given to this layer cake.

I	recipe Foolproof Sponge Cake

PASTRY CREAM

2	cups milk
6	large egg yolks
½	cup sugar
¼	teaspoon salt
¼	cup cornstarch, sifted
I	teaspoon vanilla extract
I	tablespoon rum
2	tablespoons unsalted butter, optional

RICH CHOCOLATE GLAZE

I	cup heavy cream
¼	cup light corn syrup
8	ounces semisweet chocolate, chopped into small pieces
½	teaspoon vanilla

1. FOR THE PASTRY CREAM: Heat milk in a small saucepan until hot but not simmering. Whisk yolks, sugar, and salt in a large saucepan until mixture is thick and lemon-colored, 3 to 4 minutes. Add cornstarch; whisk to combine. Slowly whisk in hot milk.

Cook milk mixture over medium-low heat, whisking constantly and scraping pan bottom and sides as you stir, until mixture thickens to a thick pudding consistency and loses all traces of raw starch flavor, about 10 minutes. Off heat, stir in vanilla, rum, and butter (if using) and transfer to another container to cool to room temperature, placing a piece of plastic wrap directly on surface of mixture to prevent skin from forming. Refrigerate pastry cream until firm. (Can be refrigerated overnight.) To ensure that pastry cream does not thin out, do not whisk once it has set.

2. FOR THE GLAZE: Bring cream and corn syrup to a full simmer over medium heat in a medium saucepan. Off heat, add chocolate; cover and let stand for 8 minutes. (If chocolate has not completely melted, return saucepan to low heat; stir constantly until melted.) Add vanilla; stir very gently until mixture is smooth. Cool until tepid so that a spoonful drizzled back into pan mounds slightly. (Glaze can be refrigerated to speed up cooling process, stirring every few minutes to ensure even cooling.)

3. While glaze is cooling, place one cake layer on a cardboard round on cooling rack set over waxed paper. Carefully spoon pastry cream over cake and spread evenly up to cake edge. Place the second layer on top, making sure layers line up properly.

4. Pour glaze over middle of top layer and let flow down cake sides. Use a metal spatula, if necessary, to completely coat cake. Use a small needle to puncture air bubbles. Let sit until glaze fully sets, about 1 hour. Serve.

Blackberry Jam Cake

SERVES 8

I	recipe Foolproof Sponge Cake
I	jar (8 ounces) blackberry jam
	Confectioners' sugar for dusting

Place one cake layer on a cardboard round on a sheet of waxed paper. Evenly spread jam over cake. Place second layer over jam, making sure layers line up properly. Sieve confectioners' sugar over cake and serve.

Sponge Cake with Rich Lemon Filling

SERVES 8

1   recipe Foolproof Sponge Cake

RICH LEMON FILLING

¾   cup sugar
¼   cup cornstarch
⅛   teaspoon salt
1   cup cold water
4   large egg yolks
2   teaspoons finely grated zest and ⅓ cup juice from 2 lemons
2   tablespoons unsalted butter
     Confectioners' sugar for dusting

1. FOR THE FILLING: Bring sugar, cornstarch, salt, and water to simmer in a large nonreactive saucepan over medium heat, whisking occasionally at beginning of process and more frequently as mixture begins to thicken. When mixture starts to simmer and turn translucent, whisk in egg yolks, two at a time. Whisk in zest, then lemon juice, and finally butter. Bring mixture to a steady simmer, whisking constantly. Remove from heat, and transfer to another container to cool to room temperature, placing a piece of plastic wrap directly on the surface of the filling to prevent a skin from forming. Let stand to room temperature. (Can be refrigerated overnight.) To ensure that lemon filling does not thin out, do not whisk or vigorously stir once it has set.

2. Place one cake layer on a cardboard round on a sheet of waxed paper. Carefully spoon filling over layer and spread evenly up to cake edge. Place the second layer on top, making sure layers line up properly. Sieve confectioners' sugar over cake and serve.

POUND CAKE

UNLIKE THEIR MODERN DESCENDANTS, classic pound cakes contain no chemical leavening. Instead, they depend for lightness on the innate puffing power of eggs and on the air incorporated into the batter through beating. This gives these cakes (which take their name from what is believed to be their original ingredients—a pound each of flour, sugar, butter, and eggs) a wonderful flavor, but can cause problems with texture. After testing 31 old-style pound cake recipes, however, we have found one that is perfect in every regard—and, because the cake is made without a speck of baking powder— it tastes of pure butter and eggs.

We embarked on this orgy of baking knowing that the main difficulty with pound cakes of the classic type is textural. Cakes might be said to have five "texture points": moist/dry, soft/hard, dense/porous, light/heavy, rich/plain. To the contemporary taste, cakes must be relatively moist and soft; the three remaining texture points are negotiable.

The problem with pound cake is that we ask it to be moist and soft, on the one hand, but also dense, light, and rich on the other. This is an extremely difficult texture to achieve unless one resorts to baking powder, with its potent chemical magic. Air-leavened cakes that are light and soft also tend to be porous and plain, as in sponge or angel cakes; moist and dense cakes inevitably also turn out heavy, as in the various syrup-soaked bundt cakes that are so popular. From pound cake we ask all things.

In our early experiments, our interest was in comparing the merits of the three major mixing methods for pound cake. Accordingly, we prepared all of the cakes with exactly one-half pound each of flour, sugar, butter, and eggs. When we got what looked to be a promising result, we also tried adding varying amounts of liquid in the hope of achieving perfection.

The first mixing method we tried is probably the most common, and it produced good cakes, but not great ones. It entails creaming the butter, sugar, and egg yolks into a fluff, adding the flour, and then folding in the stiffly beaten egg whites. But the cakes were a little tough, dry, and heavy, and they did not taste quite rich enough. We next tried adding some of the sugar to the egg whites during beating to give the whites more strength and puffing power. This did make the cakes lighter and more tender, but we still found them dry and insufficiently rich. Adding one-quarter cup of liquid, as older cookbooks recommend, made the cakes moister but also turned them rubbery.

In French cookbooks, pound cake is generally mixed like génoise. The eggs and sugar are first whipped into a fluffy mass, and then the flour and butter (melted or softened to the consistency of mayonnaise) are folded in. Although we tried several variations on this method, adding liquid at different points in the process, beating the yolks and whites separately, we got generally similar results. All the cakes were good—moist, soft, and fairly light—but they were also crumbly and coarse-grained, a little, in fact, like génoise. In short, all of the cakes failed the density test. This may well be the French understanding of pound cake, but it is not ours.

The simplest, most straightforward method of making pound cake involves beating the butter and sugar to a fluffy cream, adding the eggs (whole) one at a time, creaming the batter some more, and then mixing in the flour. No matter how we tried to work this method—adding and withholding liquid, beating the batter after putting in the flour (as some old cookbooks recommend)—we got simply awful results. The cakes were rubber doorstops.

Having thus far failed to make a perfect pound cake with any mixing method, we turned our attention to the ingredients themselves. In our readings of old cookbooks, we had long noted that pound cake, in the period of its greatest popularity, was rarely made with precisely one pound each of flour, sugar, butter, and eggs; nor were these necessarily the only ingredients used. For example, Eliza Leslie, the Julia Child of the 1830s–1840s, specifies a "small pound of flour" (around 14 ounces), "a large pound of sugar" (perhaps 18 ounces), and somewhat better than one-half cup of liquid (eggs plus brandy, sherry, or rose water). Leslie's fiddling with the flour and sugar are atypical, but her use of one-half cup liquid is virtually invariable in pound cake recipes written before 1850. Meanwhile, other authors play around with the eggs. In *The Virginia House-Wife* (1824), Mary Randolph specifies a dozen eggs; in her time, 10 eggs were generally considered to weigh one pound. Susannah Carter, an English author whose cookery book was published in America in 1772, calls for six whole eggs and six yolks. Carter's idea to use extra yolks eventually proved a cornerstone in our own recipe.

Before tinkering with the sacrosanct pound formula, we decided to consult some modern cookbooks. We could hardly believe what we found in Flo Braker's *The Simple Art of Perfect Baking* (Morrow, 1985). Her

classic pound cake is mixed in a way very similar to the third method we had tried, the one that we had found disastrous! We made her pound cake exactly as directed, and it turned out, indeed, to be the very best one we had baked so far. What made the difference?

First of all, Braker refined the mixing method. Instead of adding whole eggs one at a time to the creamed butter and sugar, she directs that the eggs first be lightly beaten in a bowl and then added by tablespoons to the butter mixture. The butter and sugar mixture is evidently incapable of absorbing whole eggs; the mixture "curdles" and all the air is let out, resulting in tough, shrunken, wet pound cakes. But dribbling in the egg a little at a time preserves the emulsion—Braker cannily compares the process to making mayonnaise—and allows all the air to be retained, making for a light, soft, tender cake. In baking, everything is in the details.

We also noted that Braker slightly modified the one-pound-each proportions. Her recipe, a "half-pound" cake like the ones we had been working with, calls for roughly 7 ounces of flour, 9 ounces of sugar, and 5 eggs (10 ounces weighed with the shells, the usual method of computation, or 8¾ ounces weighed without). She calls for 8 ounces of butter, the standard amount, and no added liquid other than almond and vanilla extracts. What a brilliant formula this is. Decreasing the flour makes the cake moister; increasing the sugar makes it more tender and, of course, sweeter; and adding an extra egg adds both moistness and lightness while at the same time compensating for the loss of structure caused by removing a little of the flour.

For many people, Braker's Viceroy Pound Cake will prove to be the only pound cake recipe they will ever need. It is a truly wonderful cake. We were hoping, however, to make a slightly denser cake. Adding liquid to Braker's pound cake made it rubbery; increasing the butter by a mere two tablespoons made it heavy. We tried any number of other small modifications, all to no avail, until finally we remembered Carter's recipe, with those extra egg yolks. Because they contain lecithin, yolks are good emulsifiers and thus help the batter retain air, making the cake light. Their fattiness contributes richness, tenderness, and moistness, while tamping the batter down a bit and thus militating against too fluffy an effect. Finally, the deep yellow of egg yolks gives the cake a beautiful golden color. Herewith is our own version of the perfect classic pound cake, inspired by gifted bakers living two centuries apart.

Master Recipe for Classic Pound Cake

SERVES 8 TO 10

You may double the recipe and bake the cake in a large nonstick bundt pan (14-cup capacity); the baking time remains the same. The recipe also makes four miniature pound cakes; use four two-cup pans and reduce baking time to 40 minutes. Though best when freshly baked, the cake will keep reasonably well for four to five days.

½	pound (2 sticks) unsalted butter, softened
1⅓	cups sugar
3	large eggs, plus 3 large yolks, room temperature
1½	teaspoons vanilla extract
1½	teaspoons water
½	teaspoon salt
1½	cups plain cake flour

1. Adjust oven rack to center position and heat oven to 325 degrees. Grease a 9 x 5 x 3½-inch loaf pan (7½-cup capacity) with vegetable shortening or spray. Line bottom and sides of pan with parchment paper by placing two pieces of paper, one lengthwise and one crosswise, into pan.

2. Beat butter in bowl of electric mixer set at medium-high speed until smooth and shiny, about 15 seconds. With machine still on, take about 30 seconds to sprinkle in sugar. Beat mixture until light, fluffy, and almost white, 4 to 5 minutes, stopping mixer once or twice to scrape down sides of bowl.

3. Mix eggs, yolks, vanilla, and water in a 2-cup glass measure with a pour spout. With mixer set at medium-high speed, add egg mixture to butter/sugar mixture in a very slow, thin stream. Finally, beat in salt.

4. Remove bowl from mixer stand. Turn ½ cup of flour into sieve or shaker; sprinkle it over batter. Fold gently with rubber spatula, scraping up from bottom of the bowl, until flour is incorporated. Repeat twice more, adding flour in ½-cup increments.

5. Scrape batter into prepared pan, smoothing top with a spatula or wooden spoon. Bake until cake needle or tester inserted into crack running along

top comes out clean, 70 to 80 minutes. Let cake rest in pan for 5 minutes, then invert onto wire rack. Place second wire rack on cake bottom, then turn cake top side up. Cool to room temperature, remove and discard parchment, wrap cake in plastic, then in foil. Store cake at room temperature.

➤ VARIATIONS

Ginger Pound Cake

Follow Master Recipe for Classic Pound Cake, adding 3 tablespoons very finely minced candied ginger, 1½ teaspoons ground ginger, and ½ teaspoon mace along with the salt.

Citrus Pound Cake

Follow Master Recipe for Classic Pound Cake, adding any of the following along with the salt: the grated zests of 2 lemons, the grated zest of 1 orange, or the grated zest of 1 lemon and 1 orange. You can replace the water and vanilla extract with 1 tablespoon orange or lemon blossom water.

CRUMB COFFEE CAKE

YEAST COFFEE CAKES ARE DELICIOUS, but are time-consuming to prepare. Coffee cakes that rely on baking powder rarely prove tasty enough to merit even a modest effort. There is, however, one coffee cake that is both delicious and quick enough for the bleary-eyed Sunday-morning baker: crumb coffee cake.

Our goal for this cake was to create the simplest recipe possible. Crumb coffee cake is nothing more than a single layer of buttery yellow cake topped with crumbs made from sugar, flour, and butter.

We had seen recipes that used the same flour-sugar batter mixture for the topping and as the basis of the batter. We were intrigued. Although these recipes might seem odd, they do make some sense. Cake batters and crumb toppings are composed of the same basic ingredients—namely flour, sugar, and butter. The main difference between the two is that cake batters contain liquid, which binds the protein and starch in flour into a springy, cohesive mass, while crumb toppings are made without liquid and thus remain loose. A recipe that derives both cake

1-12-03
Easy and delicious
I used 1/2 cup nonfat peaches & cream yogurt & 1/4 cup half and half
added an extra TB butter or so to crumb mixture.
cooked a minute too long

and crumbs from the same basic mixture seemed like a great way to simplify the preparation process.

We baked up cakes from several sources but were disappointed. First of all, there were not nearly enough crumbs (this problem was easily remedied). The bigger issue was the lack of contrast between the batter and the topping. Either the cake was too brown or the crumbs were insipid—they needed the molasses flavor of brown sugar. We devised a two-tone cake (a yellow cake topped with dark brown crumbs) by making the initial crumb mixture with white sugar and then adding brown sugar to the topping crumbs only.

Other problems proved trickier to solve, however. None of the recipes that we tested were quite buttery enough, but when we tried adding more butter to the batter the cake became too weak to support the crumbs and collapsed in the center. Increasing the flour shored up the cake but also made it dry and puffy, sort of like a bland yellow layer cake.

We knew that adding a bit more buttermilk (our liquid of choice) would strengthen the structure by promoting the gelatinization of the starch in the flour, but we resisted this option because we thought the resulting batter would be too liquid to hold fruit (an ingredient in some variations) in suspension. When we finally bit the bullet and put a little more buttermilk in, we were pleasantly surprised. The batter was less stiff and easier to beat, and we found that a thorough beating aerated and emulsified the ingredients, making the batter wonderfully thick and fluffy. Even with a goodly quantity of butter added, the cake with more buttermilk rose perfectly, and the solids stayed firmly suspended.

Master Recipe for Quick Crumb Coffee Cake

SERVES 8 TO 10

This cake is best eaten on the day it is baked, though it may be made a day ahead. The batter is quite heavy, so you may prefer to beat it with an electric mixer at medium-high speed for a minute or so rather than whisk it by hand.

- 1 tablespoon dry bread crumbs
- 2 cups all-purpose flour
- 1 cup plus 2 tablespoons sugar
- 1 teaspoon salt
- 10 tablespoons (1 1/4 sticks) unsalted butter, softened
- 1 teaspoon baking powder
- 1/2 teaspoon baking soda
- 3/4 cup buttermilk or low-fat (not nonfat) plain yogurt, room temperature
- 1 large egg, room temperature
- 1 teaspoon vanilla extract
- 3/4 cup (3 ounces) walnuts or pecans, finely chopped
- 1/2 cup dark brown sugar, firmly packed
- 1 teaspoon ground cinnamon

1. Adjust oven rack to center position and heat oven to 350 degrees. Generously grease bottom and lightly grease sides of 10-inch springform pan. Sprinkle bottom of pan with dry bread crumbs, then shake lightly to coat. Tap out excess crumbs.

2. Whisk flour, sugar, and salt in large mixing bowl until blended. Add butter and cut with whisk until mixture resembles coarse crumbs. Remove 1 cup to separate bowl.

3. Whisk baking powder and soda into mixture remaining in large mixing bowl. Add buttermilk or yogurt, egg, and vanilla; whisk vigorously until batter is thick, smooth, fluffy, and frostinglike, 1½ to 2 minutes. Using a rubber spatula, scrape batter into prepared pan and smooth top.

4. Add nuts, brown sugar, and cinnamon to reserved crumbs of flour, sugar, and butter; toss with a fork or your hands until blended. Sprinkle over batter, pressing lightly so that mixture adheres. Bake cake until center is firm and cake tester comes out clean, 50 to 55 minutes. Transfer cake to rack; remove pan sides. Let cake cool completely, about 2 hours, before serving. When completely cooled, cake can be slid off pan bottom onto serving plate.

VARIATIONS

Apple-Cinnamon Coffee Cake

Peel and core 2 medium-large Granny Smith apples and cut into 1/4-inch dice. Heat 1 tablespoon butter in a 10-inch skillet (preferably nonstick) over high heat until golden. Add apples, cover, and cook over high heat, stirring frequently, until they are dry and very tender, 2 to 3 minutes. Remove from heat, sprinkle apples with 2 tablespoons sugar, and lightly toss until glazed. Cool to room temperature. Follow Master Recipe for Quick Crumb Coffee Cake, adding 1 teaspoon cinnamon with the baking powder and soda, and folding the apples into the finished batter.

Coconut Chocolate Chip Coffee Cake

Follow Master Recipe for Quick Crumb Coffee Cake, substituting firmly packed light brown sugar for white sugar and stirring 1 cup miniature chocolate chips into finished batter. For topping, decrease nuts to ½ cup, substitute light brown sugar for dark, omit cinnamon, and add 1 cup sweetened flaked coconut.

Raspberry-Almond Coffee Cake

Follow Master Recipe for Quick Crumb Coffee Cake, adding 1 teaspoon pure almond extract along with vanilla. Turn batter into pan. Beat ½ cup seedless raspberry jam until smooth and fluid, then carefully spread it over the batter with the back of a teaspoon. For crumb topping, substitute ¾ cup (4 ounces) ground almonds for walnuts or pecans and ½ cup white sugar for dark brown sugar; omit cinnamon. Add 1 large egg yolk and 1 teaspoon pure almond extract to topping and mix with a fork. Thoroughly knead mixture with your fingers until the color is uniform.

FRUIT UPSIDE-DOWN CAKE

THE IDEAL FRUIT UPSIDE-DOWN CAKE HAS a glistening, caramelized, deep amber topping encasing plump fruit on top of a flavorful, tender butter cake. The proportions and textures must also marry well, providing the perfect balance of topping, fruit, and cake in each bite.

Unfortunately, when we tested the standard recipes, we were left with pale, blond, anemic-looking desserts consisting of fruit and topping that just sat on the cake component, not melding with it at all.

We set out to determine what proportions of brown sugar topping, fruit, and batter and what techniques worked most harmoniously. We also wanted to see if a master recipe could be developed that would support a variety of fresh fruits, including pineapple, plums, and peaches, in place of the more common canned pineapple.

Most recipes for this cake, including the original and the current recipe from Dole's test kitchen (where the recipe was first developed in 1925), combine brown sugar and butter for the topping by melting the butter, adding the brown sugar, and immediately proceeding to the fruit. This is why these cakes turn out very blond and light in taste. We knew we wanted a darker, richer, caramelized topping, so we opted to try the technique used in recipes that follow the method of tarte Tatin, in which the sugar and butter combination is lightly caramelized on top of the stove before the fruit is added.

We tested butter combined with granulated sugar, light brown sugar, and a combination of white and brown. The traditional brown sugar won out, since it added an extra complexity to the final taste. As far as proportions were concerned, we settled on ¼ cup of butter to ¾ cup of brown sugar. The proportions were right, and by simmering and stirring for a few minutes to really meld the butter and sugar and produce a slightly reduced caramel, we hit the mark.

Coincidentally, this important step of caramelizing and thickening the topping affected unmolding as well. If the butter and sugar for the topping were simply stirred together, the cake, after being turned out of the pan, had a greasy top, with fruit that tended to alternately stick or fall off to the sides. By cooking the topping first, we discovered that the unmolded cakes consistently yielded beautiful-looking tops with fruit that stayed put and never stuck.

We assumed initially that using fresh pineapple would be a problem and that we might end up preferring the ease of canned fruit. To our surprise, the fresh pineapple worked wonderfully with little preparation.

Fresh peaches and plums were also excellent and easy to prepare; we simply pitted and sliced them into thin half-inch wedges—no peeling was necessary. Mangoes required a bit more work because they had to be peeled as well as pitted and sliced but were wonderfully delicious. For all fruits, the slices were placed in concentric circles, filling up the pan in the same way as the pineapple slices.

Having arrived at the proper topping and the right approach to each fruit, we turned to the question of the cake batter. Our aim was to make a cake that tasted good in its own right and that would physically support the fruit and caramelized topping, yet not detract from it. The proportions of cake to topping also had to be just right, and the cake had to meld with the topping and fruit to present a unified whole.

We thought a classic butter-type cake would work best, but we also had a notion that a light, low-fat sponge cake might balance well with the rich topping. We theorized that the syrupy caramel and fruit juices would be soaked up by the intentionally dryish sponge. We were pretty sure that a rich pound cake would be too heavy, but we decided to try both of these extremes first to establish whether or not they were even in the running.

We began with the sponge, and the results were poor. Its excessive dryness in juxtaposition to the unctuous topping did not make a happy pairing texturally. The pound cake similarly placed poorly in tastings; its heaviness prevented it from melding with the topping, and its extra butteriness competed with the caramel. We knew the ideal lay somewhere in between, so the next tests would be with butter cakes.

We began by using all-purpose flour, whole eggs, and milk. The cake texture was a bit coarse, so we went on to try cake flour and separating of the eggs in both separate and combined tests. We found that the differences between flours in this cake were negligible but that the separated eggs improved the texture dramatically. When the whites were whipped separately and folded in, the resulting cake was extremely tender, with a crumb so fine that it was almost too velvety. The combination of all-purpose flour and separated eggs was a winner. To give the cake a slightly coarser crumb and help balance the rich topping, we added three tablespoons of cornmeal.

The milk helped to produce a smooth, moist cake and batter, but we wanted to detour and try buttermilk because it often works so well in butter cake recipes. We thought the sharp flavor might also offset the sweetness of the topping. We reduced the amount of baking powder and added baking soda to offset the acidic nature of the buttermilk. The cakes baked well and looked fine, but a more open crumb, a byproduct of the baking soda, was not right for this cake.

As far as flavorings were concerned, we had always thought vanilla should be included, and it did provide the butter cake with a rounder, fuller flavor. We experimented with cinnamon and ginger, which were interesting, and lemon zest added a nice tangy flavor, but all of these additions veered away from what we thought a very basic pineapple upside-down cake should taste like. Vanilla was necessary, but no other flavoring was required.

While we had discovered early on the value of the caramelized topping to easier unmolding, we also came to understand that the length of the cooling period is crucial. In short, the best procedure is to remove the cake from the oven when done, let it sit for two minutes on a rack, then flip it over onto a plate. This minimal cooling time allows the caramelized top to solidify enough to keep it from flowing down off the top after unmolding yet not so much that the caramelized sugar is allowed to set, which would lead to unmolding problems. If any fruit does stick, it is easy enough to remove manually and place it properly on the cake top.

Master Recipe for Fruit Upside-Down Cake

SERVES 8 TO 10

Using a 9 x 3-inch round pan to bake the cake gives it straight sides. If you prefer slightly flared sides on your cake, bake it in a 10-inch cast-iron skillet, which streamlines the process in three ways. First, the skillet need not be buttered; second, the caramel topping can be prepared in it directly; and third, the total baking time is cut to 50 minutes, which is 10 to 15 minutes faster than the cake pan.

TOPPING

4	tablespoons unsalted butter, plus more for cake pan
¾	cup light brown sugar
1	recipe Fruit for Upside-Down Cake (see chart, next page)

CAKE

1½	cups all-purpose flour
1½	teaspoons baking powder
3	tablespoons cornmeal
½	teaspoon salt
8	tablespoons (1 stick) unsalted butter, softened
1	cup plus 2 tablespoons granulated sugar
4	large eggs, separated, room temperature
1½	teaspoons vanilla extract
⅔	cup milk

1. FOR THE TOPPING: Butter bottom and sides of 9 x 3-inch round cake pan. Melt 4 tablespoons butter in medium saucepan over medium heat; add brown sugar and cook, stirring occasionally, until mixture is foamy and pale, 3 to 4 minutes. Pour mixture into prepared cake pan; swirl pan to distribute evenly. Arrange fruit slices in concentric circles over topping; set aside.

2. FOR THE CAKE: Adjust oven rack to lower-middle position and heat oven to 350 degrees. Whisk flour, baking powder, cornmeal, and salt together in medium bowl; set aside. Cream butter in large bowl with electric mixer at medium speed. Gradually add 1 cup sugar; continue beating until light and fluffy, about 2 minutes. Beat in yolks and vanilla (scraping sides of bowl with rubber spatula if necessary); reduce speed to low and add dry mixture and milk, alternately in three or four batches, beginning and ending with dry ingredients, until batter is just smooth.

3. Beat egg whites in large bowl at low speed until frothy. Increase speed to medium-high; beat to soft peaks. Gradually add 2 tablespoons sugar; continue to beat to stiff peaks. Fold one-quarter of beaten whites into batter with large rubber spatula to lighten. Fold in remaining whites until no white streaks remain. Gently pour batter into pan and spread evenly on top of fruit, being careful not to

Fruit for Upside-Down Cake

Our favorite fruits for upside-down cakes are peaches, nectarines, and plums (all of which are stone fruits), mangoes, and, of course, pineapple. Below are instructions to prepare enough of each fruit for one upside-down cake.

FRUIT	QUANTITY	PREPARATION
Peaches or Nectarines	4 medium	Halve fruits pole to pole; remove stone. Cut each half into slices ½ inch thick.
Plums	5 medium	Halve fruits pole to pole; remove stone (cutting halves in half again, if needed). Cut into slices ½ inch thick.
Mangoes	2 medium	Peel and pit. Cut flesh into slices ¼ inch thick.
Pineapple	1 small	Stem, peel, quarter, and core. Cut each quarter into pieces ⅜ inch thick.

disperse fruit. Bake until top is golden and toothpick inserted into cake center (not fruit, which remains gooey) comes out clean, 60 to 65 minutes.

4. Rest cake on rack for 2 minutes. Slide a paring knife around the edge of the cake to loosen it from the pan. Place a serving platter over the pan and hold tightly. Invert the cake onto the platter. Carefully remove the cake pan. If any fruit sticks to pan bottom, remove and position on top of cake.

FLOURLESS CHOCOLATE CAKE

TO OUR KNOWLEDGE, FLOURLESS CHOCOLATE cake is the only dessert that is named for a missing ingredient. Besides this, the word "cake" stretches the point in describing this very popular dessert; although some recipes replace flour or crumbs with ground nuts, the quintessence of the genre contains only chocolate, butter, and eggs—nothing that could conceivably be called a dry ingredient. The result is more confection than cake, like a dense baked mousse or chocolate cheesecake, with butter replacing cheese.

Although the ingredient choices are limited—chocolate, butter, and eggs, sometimes sugar, and sometimes liquid such as water, coffee, or liqueur—the proportions as well as mixing and baking methods differed considerably in the recipes we researched.

We selected and baked six recipes that represented the array of choices. The results were staggering in their variety. One resembled a flourless fudge brownie, one was more like an ultradense, creamy custard, and one was a pouffy, fallen soufflé-like affair. Some were very bittersweet, others quite sweet. All, however, had the richness and intensity of a confection.

Although the desserts were almost all very enticing, we were quickly able to define our criteria for the ultimate flourless chocolate cake. We wanted something dense, moist, and ultrachocolatey, but with some textural finesse. We wanted a mouthfeel and texture somewhere between a substantial marquise au chocolat—that dense, buttery, and just slightly aerated chocolate mousse with a characteristic dry but creamy texture—and a heavy New York–style cheesecake, which requires the mouth to work for just a second before the stuff melts and dissolves with sublime flavor. We wanted the flavor and character of good, eating-quality chocolate to reign supreme, with no unnecessary sweetness and not even the slightest grain of sugar on the palate. In short, we wanted an intense bittersweet "adult" dessert, not a piece of fudge or a brownie or a thick chocolate pudding—and certainly nothing fluffy.

Some recipes used unsweetened chocolate instead of semisweet or bittersweet, but we rejected this idea after tasting just one cake made with unsweetened chocolate. Neither flavor nor texture were smooth or silky enough for this type of dessert, and there was a slight chalky sensation on the palate. This made perfect sense. Unsweetened chocolate is coarse and needs high heat to blend perfectly with the sugar required to sweeten it. It is most successful in desserts with a cakey or fudgy texture, when perfect smoothness is unnecessary. Hot fudge sauce made with unsweetened chocolate is smooth because it is cooked to a temperature high enough to melt the sugar and change the physical properties of the chocolate. But our flourless chocolate cake is more like chocolate mousse, chocolate truffles, or ganache—ingredients are few, cooked very gently, and the results must be perfectly smooth. Made to be nibbled, semisweet and bittersweet chocolates are incomparably smooth, refined so that chocolate and sugar are intimately married and every particle is smaller than the human palate can detect.

The next decision had to do with the baking temperature and whether or not a water bath was indicated. The original recipe for this now-popular dessert was flawed by hard, crumbly edges—surely caused by baking for a short time at a high temperature without a water bath. We tried a similar recipe baked at a high temperature for a short time but in a water bath. It was creamier by far, but we could taste raw egg. We guessed that, like cheesecake, this dessert required a longer baking time at a lower temperature in a water bath to allow the interior to reach a safe temperature without overcooking the edges. We found that 325 degrees in a water bath produced a successful sample.

The trick in baking this cake, however, was knowing when to stop. Just like cheesecake, our flourless chocolate cake must be taken from the oven when the center still jiggles and looks quite underdone, as it continues to cook after it comes out of the oven.

At first we used a thermometer to make sure that the center of the cake had reached the safe temperature of 160 degrees (that is, any salmonella bacteria present in the eggs would be killed). But this cake was clearly overbaked—the texture was dryish and chalky. Knowing that a temperature of at least 140 degrees held for five minutes also killed salmonella bacteria, we let the cake reach 140 degrees and then left it in the oven for five more minutes. It was overbaked as well. After trying four, three, and two extra minutes in the oven, we finally realized that if we removed the cake at 140 degrees it would stay at or even above 140 degrees for at least five minutes (thus killing off salmonella) as the heat from the edges of the cake penetrated the center. The results were perfect.

Before determining the perfect quantities of butter and eggs for a pound of chocolate, we decided to test textures. We were pretty sure that the ultimate cake would need some form of aeration from beaten eggs to achieve the texture that we wanted. In the first test, we whisked the eggs over gentle heat to warm them (as for a génoise), and then beat them until about triple in volume and the consistency of soft whipped cream. We then folded the whipped eggs into the warm chocolate and butter in three parts. In the second test, we separated the eggs and whisked the yolks into the warm chocolate and butter and then beat the whites to a meringue before folding them in. In the third test, we simply whisked the eggs, one by one, into the warm chocolate and butter, as though making a custard.

The sample made with eggs simply whisked into the melted chocolate and butter was dense and smooth like a very rich custard or crème brûlée. Our definition of the ultimate flourless chocolate cake ruled this version out. The cake with beaten whole eggs differed from the one with yolks and meringue more than we expected. Surprisingly, the difference in flavor was greater than the difference in texture. Whole beaten eggs produced a dessert with nicely blended flavors, while the cake with separated eggs tasted as though the ingredients had not been completely integrated. Along the way, we realized that we could eliminate the step of warming the eggs before beating them, since cold eggs produce a denser foam with smaller bubbles, which in turn gave the cake a more velvety texture.

Ultimate Flourless Chocolate Cake

SERVES 12 TO 16

Even though the cake may not look done, pull it from the oven when an instant-read thermometer registers 140 degrees. (Make sure not to let tip of thermometer hit the bottom of the pan.) It will continue to firm up as it cools. If you use a 9-inch springform pan instead of the preferred 8-inch, reduce the baking time to 18 to 20 minutes. See page 462 for more information about choosing a particular brand of chocolate for this recipe. We like the pure flavor of chocolate. However, coffee or liqueur (choose something that tastes like nuts, coffee, or oranges) can be added if desired.

8	large eggs, cold
1	pound bittersweet or semisweet chocolate, coarsely chopped
½	pound (2 sticks) unsalted butter, cut into ½-inch chunks
¼	cup strong coffee or liqueur (optional) Confectioners' sugar or cocoa powder for decoration

1. Adjust oven rack to lower-middle position and heat oven to 325 degrees. Line bottom of 8-inch springform pan with parchment and grease pan sides. Cover pan underneath and along sides with sheet of heavy-duty foil and set in large roasting pan. Bring kettle of water to boil.

2. Beat eggs with handheld mixer at high speed until volume doubles to approximately 1 quart, about 5 minutes. Alternatively, beat in bowl of electric mixer fitted with wire whip attachment at medium speed to achieve same result, about 5 minutes.

3. Meanwhile, melt chocolate and butter (adding coffee or liqueur, if using) in large heatproof bowl set over pan of almost simmering water, until smooth and very warm (about 115 degrees on an instant-read thermometer), stirring once or twice. (For the microwave, melt chocolate at 50 percent power for 2 minutes, stir, add butter, and continue heating at 50 percent power, stirring every minute, until chocolate and butter have melted and are smooth, another 2 to 3 minutes total.) Fold ⅓ of egg foam into chocolate mixture using large rubber spatula until only a few streaks of egg are visible; fold in half of remaining foam, then last of remaining foam, until mixture is totally homogenous.

4. Scrape batter into prepared springform pan and smooth surface with rubber spatula. Set roasting pan on oven rack and pour in enough boiling water to come about halfway up side of springform pan. Bake until cake has risen slightly, edges are just beginning to set, a thin glazed crust (like a brownie) has formed on surface, and an instant-read thermometer inserted halfway through center of cake registers 140 degrees, 22 to 25 minutes. Remove cake pan from water bath and set on wire rack; cool to room temperature. Cover and refrigerate overnight to mellow (can be covered and refrigerated for up to 4 days).

5. About 30 minutes before serving, remove springform pan sides, invert cake on sheet of waxed paper, peel off parchment pan liner, and turn cake right side up on serving platter. Sieve light sprinkling of confectioners' sugar or unsweetened cocoa powder over cake to decorate, if desired.

FALLEN CHOCOLATE CAKE

THE "FALLEN CHOCOLATE CAKE," AN UNDER-cooked-in-the-center mound of intense, buttery chocolate cake, which ranges from a dense, brownie-like consistency to something altogether more ethereal, is the restaurant dessert of the moment. When cutting-edge international chef Jean-Georges Vongerichten serves several hundred of these desserts every night in his three New York restaurants, you know something is afoot.

Having tasted Jean-Georges' recipe on a number of occasions and having also tried this dessert at other trendy eateries, we became intrigued with the notion of turning a restaurant show stopper into a practical recipe for home cooks. We knew that the ingredient list was short and suspected that the techniques would be relatively simple, but, since restaurant recipes rarely work at home, it was clear that a great deal of culinary translation awaited us.

The first step, since this recipe concept encompasses a wide range of styles from half-cooked batter to a chocolate sponge cake, was to organize a tasting in the test kitchen to decide exactly what we were looking for. We made three variations: the Warm, Soft Chocolate Cake from Jean-Georges, Fallen Chocolate Cake from the restaurant Olives, created by chef-owner Todd English, and an old favorite entitled Fallen Chocolate Soufflé Cake, published by Richard Sax, a well-known food writer.

Sax's recipe, which is baked in a tube pan rather than in a ramekin, was quite delicious and soufflélike in texture. However, it lacked the intense whack of chocolate and the rich, buttery texture of the other two desserts. The recipe from Olives was the heaviest of the lot, very good but quite similar to an undercooked brownie. Jean-Georges' cake was the tasting panel's favorite, with the most intense chocolate flavor, a relatively light texture, and a very runny center. We then wondered if we might be able to capture some of the ethereal lightness of Sax's cake with the rich taste and buttery mouthfeel of Jean-Georges' dessert.

First we had to decide on the basic preparation method. There were two choices. We could beat the egg yolks and whites separately and then fold them together, or we could beat whole eggs and sugar to create a thick foam. The latter method proved superior, as it delivered the rich, moist texture we were looking for as well as making the recipe simpler. That left us with a recipe that consisted of melting chocolate; beating whole eggs, sugar, and flavorings into a foam; and then folding the two together, perhaps with a little flour or ground nuts for extra body.

Our next step was to determine what amounts of each ingredient made the best cake. After considerable testing, we decided that one-half cup of melted butter made the dessert considerably more moist. Some

INGREDIENTS: Bittersweet and Semisweet Chocolate

There is substantial confusion caused by the terms "bittersweet chocolate" and "semisweet chocolate." No industry or federal definitions exist for these terms—both fall under the broad category of dark chocolate. Companies that make both bittersweet and semisweet chocolate reserve the latter term for their slightly sweeter product. However, we have found that one company's bittersweet may in fact have more sugar in it than another company's semisweet. After years of baking with both kinds of dark chocolate, we have concluded that bittersweet and semisweet chocolates can be used interchangeably in recipes, with minor differences in flavor.

The labels on bittersweet and semisweet chocolate have the same list of ingredients: sugar, chocolate liquor, cocoa butter, lecithin (a natural emulsifier), and vanilla. But the quality of the cocoa bean, the roasting levels, amounts of cocoa butter and sugar, and the "conching," or amalgamation, of all the ingredients determine the ultimate taste and texture of the chocolate. Because there is such a high percentage of chocolate in our flourless chocolate cake recipe, we decided to conduct tests to determine how different brands affected the outcome. For our tests, we chose semisweet chocolate from Van Leer, Callebaut, and Ghirardelli, three specialty brands that tested well in a tasting of chocolates, as well as two supermarket brands, Baker's and Nestle's.

Five cakes, each using one of the chosen brands, were baked according to the recipe. For these tests, we omitted the addition of coffee or liqueur so we could concentrate on the pure chocolate flavor. The baked cakes were judged for their taste and texture. We were specifically looking for depth of chocolate flavor, mouthfeel, creaminess, underlying flavors, sweetness, and density.

Because of the subtleties in chocolate, it was not surprising that our tests revealed different preferences and opinions when the complex taste of chocolate in these cakes was evaluated.

Overall, the cake made with Ghirardelli chocolate received the most positive comments, such as "creamy taste, true chocolate flavor, and velvety texture." Callebaut was also highly praised for its "rich chocolate taste, aroma, and silky texture." Tasters liked the creamy texture of the cake made with Van Leer, but what one tester found to be "a balanced and intriguing taste," another found to be bland. Nestle's and Baker's appealed to some for the "mousselike" texture they imparted and also for the "coffee and fruitiness" in their taste. A higher level of sweetness was also mentioned by everyone when tasting the cakes made with these chocolates.

None of the brands tested were ruled out for use as an ingredient in this recipe, but clearly there were differences in the textures and, especially, the tastes. Individual preferences, and perhaps availability, will dictate which brand you choose. If a deep, rich, chocolate taste is important, you'll probably reach for a specialty brand. If you prefer sweetness and light, a supermarket brand will suit your needs.

recipes use no flour or very little (Jean-Georges, for instance, uses only four teaspoons), but we finally settled on two tablespoons. The amount of chocolate was key and highly variable, running from a mere 4 ounces to a high of 12 ounces in English's recipe. Eight ounces provided a good jolt of chocolate without being overbearing.

The eggs, however, were perhaps the most crucial element. We tested six whole eggs (light and airy sponge-cake texture), four whole eggs plus four yolks (moist and dark), and the winning combination of four whole eggs plus one yolk (rich but light, moist, intense, and dark).

When baking these desserts in ramekins at 450 degrees, as called for in the Jean-Georges recipe, we found that the tops were slightly burned and the center was a bit too runny. At 350 degrees, the dessert took on a more cakelike quality and was also drier. Four hundred degrees was best, yielding a light, cakelike perimeter around a moist well of intense chocolate. (When using a cake pan rather than ramekins, though, we found it best to set the oven at 375 degrees.)

At this point we had the recipe pretty well in order. To finish the translation from restaurant to home kitchen, however, we still had some work to do. The biggest obstacle was the amount of last-minute cooking. No one wants to run out to the kitchen during dinner and whip up an egg foam. Having had some experience with preparing chocolate soufflés ahead of time, we tested pouring the batter into the ramekins, refrigerating them, and then baking them during dinner. This worked, the batter holding for up to eight hours. Although the filled ramekins can be taken directly from the refrigerator to the oven with reasonably good results, they rise better if allowed to sit at room temperature for 30 minutes before baking.

We also wondered if most folks have eight ramekins at home. Therefore, we developed variations using both 8- and 9-inch springform pans. As an added benefit for the home cook we discovered that, in cake form, this dessert can be baked up to one hour before serving, remaining warm right in the pan. (In a pinch, this dessert can be held up to two hours in the pan, but it will become slightly more dense as it cools.)

Individual Fallen Chocolate Cakes
SERVES 8

To melt the chocolate and butter in a microwave oven, heat chocolate alone at 50 percent power for 2 minutes; stir chocolate, add butter, and continue heating at 50 percent for another 2 minutes, stopping to stir after 1 minute. If chocolate is not yet entirely melted, heat an additional 30 seconds at 50 percent power.

8	tablespoons (1 stick) unsalted butter, plus extra for ramekins
8	ounces bittersweet or semisweet chocolate, coarsely chopped
4	large eggs, plus 1 large yolk, room temperature
1	teaspoon vanilla extract
¼	teaspoon salt
½	cup sugar
2	tablespoons all-purpose flour, plus extra for ramekins
	Confectioners' sugar or unsweetened cocoa powder for decoration, optional
	Whipped cream for serving, optional

1. Adjust oven rack to center position and heat oven to 400 degrees. Generously butter and flour eight 6-ounce ramekins or Pyrex custard/baking cups; tap out excess flour and position ramekins on shallow roasting pan, jelly-roll pan, or baking sheet. Meanwhile, melt 8 tablespoons butter and chocolate in medium heatproof bowl set over a pan of almost-simmering water, stirring once or twice, until smooth; remove from heat. (Or melt chocolate and butter in microwave oven. See instructions above.)

2. Beat eggs, yolk, vanilla, salt, and sugar at highest speed in bowl of a standing mixer fitted with whisk attachment until volume nearly triples, color is very light, and mixture drops from beaters in a smooth, thick stream, about 5 minutes. (Alternatively, beat for 10 minutes using a handheld electric mixer and large mixing bowl.) Scrape egg mixture over melted chocolate and butter; sprinkle flour over egg mixture. Gently fold egg and flour into chocolate until mixture is uniformly colored. Ladle or pour batter into prepared ramekins. (Can be covered lightly with plastic wrap and refrigerated up to

8 hours. Return to room temperature for 30 minutes before baking.)

3. Bake until cakes have puffed about ½ inch above rims of ramekins, have a thin crust on top, and jiggle slightly at center when ramekins are shaken very gently, 12 to 13 minutes. Run a paring knife around inside edges of ramekins to loosen cakes and invert onto serving plates; cool for 1 minute and lift off ramekins. Sieve light sprinkling of confectioners' sugar or cocoa powder over cakes to decorate, if desired, and serve immediately with optional whipped cream.

➤ VARIATIONS
Fallen Chocolate Cake
SERVES 8 TO 10

One large chocolate cake can be prepared in a springform pan. Do not use a regular cake pan, as the cake will be impossible to remove once baked. Though the cake is best when served warm, within about 30 minutes of being unmolded, it can also be held in the pan for up to two hours.

Follow recipe for Individual Fallen Chocolate Cakes, substituting an 8- or 9-inch springform pan for ramekins. Decrease baking temperature to 375 degrees and bake until cake looks puffed, a thin top crust has formed, and center jiggles slightly when pan is shaken gently, 22 to 25 minutes for 9-inch pan or 27 to 30 minutes for 8-inch pan. Cool cake for 15 minutes, run a paring knife around inside edge of pan, and remove pan sides. Sieve light sprinkling of confectioners' sugar or unsweetened cocoa powder over cake to decorate, if desired, just before serving, and serve warm, with optional whipped cream.

Orange Chocolate Cakes
Follow recipe for Individual Fallen Chocolate Cakes or Fallen Chocolate Cake, folding 1 tablespoon finely grated zest from 2 medium oranges and 2 tablespoons orange liqueur (such as Grand Marnier or Triple Sec) into beaten egg and melted chocolate mixture.

CHEESECAKE

PERFECT CHEESECAKE HAS MORE TO DO WITH texture than flavor. Some cheesecakes are firm and dense, like a classic New York–style cheesecake. Others are rich, lush, and creamy, almost like a thick custard. Still others are as light and airy as meringue. Each style has its own following. One person's lush is another's wimpy; one person's fluffy is another's spongy; and one's dense is another's dry.

It was clear from the beginning that there could be no single ideal cheesecake recipe. In our informal cheesecake polls, all three textural styles came up as favorites. Our goal was to develop a basic cheesecake whose texture could be altered with a simple ingredient change or baking method. To better understand exactly what affects cheesecake's texture, we tested the key ingredients—cream cheese, eggs, cream, and sour cream—as well as a variety of baking methods and temperatures. After three days of testing, not only had we come up with the lush, creamy cheesecake we preferred, we had also figured out how to lighten the texture or make it more dense to suit other preferences.

To clearly determine the role of each ingredient, we made all cakes from a simple recipe with cream cheese, sugar, eggs, vanilla, and a little lemon zest. Since cream cheese is, after all, the cornerstone in cheesecake, we started with this ingredient. We tested cakes made with fresh cream cheese and regular Philadelphia brand commercial cream cheese, as well as Philadelphia's Neufchâtel (one-third less fat), light (50 percent less fat), and no-fat cream cheeses.

Fresh cream cheese was not available locally, so we resorted to mail order at $5.50 per pound plus overnight mail charges. Although this softer, creamier, tangy cheese was our first choice for spreading over a bagel, it proved too unstable for baking. Unlike any of the other cakes, the one made with fresh cream cheese baked up grainy, having broken or curdled slightly. The fresh cheese was simply too fragile for baking. Philadelphia brand cream cheese, on the other hand, was firmer and denser in texture than fresh cream cheese. Baked exactly the same way, this cake was smooth and creamy, superior to cake made with fresh cream cheese.

Unlike real cream cheese, which melts like butter in your mouth, low-fat and no-fat varieties cling to the tongue. The cakes made from these cheeses also baked differently from those made with regular cream cheese. The Philly Neufchâtel brand, which is whiter, softer, and more watery than regular cream cheese, baked more quickly as well. Even though it was pulled from the oven 10 minutes sooner than any of the other cheesecakes, it cracked. The cake made with this cheese was also harder and more crumbly than that made with regular cream cheese.

Philly no-fat cream cheese developed a rubbery skin and several mudlike shallow cracks during baking. Underneath the skin, the cake was soft and chalky in texture with an unpleasant artificial taste. Of all the cakes we made during those three days, it was the only one we actually threw away. And although not nearly as bad as the no-fat cream cheese version, the light cream cheese cake tasted artificial as well. It was deceptively creamy at first, but an unmistakable dustiness lingered on the tongue.

Egg quantity differed with cheesecake recipes. To see just how many eggs a cheesecake would need, we made cakes with virtually every egg combination that made sense, starting with a cheesecake made with all egg whites and ending with one made with all yolks. We should have used blindfolds to taste these cheesecakes, for their hues ranged from vivid yellow to pale cream, corresponding directly to egg quantity.

What we learned from our egg experiments is that a good cheesecake needs a combination of egg whites and yolks. The all–egg-white cheesecake was dry. Fortunately, the other extreme—an all-yolk cheesecake—didn't produce the best result either. The all-yolk cakes, and the ones made with whole eggs plus extra yolks, seemed to push this dessert into the custard category. The cakes were rich, heavy, and pleasantly eggy—but hardly cheesecake. Four whole eggs made the cake creamy and tender without tasting overly rich and custardy.

It made sense that folding whipped egg whites into the batter would lighten the cheesecake's texture. So, during our egg tests, we confirmed our suspicions. Instead of beating whole eggs into the batter, we separated the eggs, beating the yolks into the cream cheese and sugar, then folding in the whipped whites just before baking. Though our master recipe was still in process, we could see that this technique of whipping the egg whites and folding them into the batter led to a light and airy texture, one of the three textures we were looking for.

The simple cream cheese–only cakes we had been baking were perfect for testing individual ingredients, but as a real dessert, they were lacking. Their relatively dry texture needed softening, and their flat flavor

needed rounding. Our next set of tests—adding different ratios of sour cream and heavy cream to the cheesecake batter—made us realize the importance of these two supporting ingredients. We had hoped to develop a cheesecake formula using either just cream or just sour cream because we didn't want a recipe calling for small quantities of each unless it was really necessary. But we found that it was.

In an attempt to drop the sour cream from our recipe, we tried substituting lemon juice. The resulting cake was pleasant, but too distinctly lemon-flavored. Another option, topping the cheesecake with sour cream rather than incorporating it into the batter, seemed to us an extra step designed exclusively for hiding those unsightly center cracks. Our plan was to lose the cracks, not cover them up.

So we went back to experimenting with various ratios of these two ingredients. Cream gives cheesecake that velvety, smooth texture, but too much of it and you begin to mask the cream cheese flavor. Sour cream supports the underlying tang of the cream cheese, but, if overdone, it takes over as the dominant flavor. You need a little of each—cream for texture and sour cream for flavor. Too much of both and you end up with a rich, characterless dessert. After many experiments, we ended up using one-quarter cup of each.

Now that we had a good batter, we wanted to keep it from baking up grainy and cracked. From previous cheesecake testing, we were water bath converts. We already knew that a water bath protects a cake from harsh, direct heat that can cause it to overcook, crack, and sink. But we also knew that this method has its drawbacks.

If there were a better way, we were open. Would baking the cake over a pan of water work just as well as a water bath, or bain-marie? Would a dry method at a lower heat turn out as velvety-textured a cake as a bain-marie? Here was our chance to find out.

Starting with the more straightforward cooking methods, we baked three different cakes at 325 degrees for one hour. We baked the first cake in a dry oven. The second cake was baked over a pan of water placed on the rack below. The third cake was baked in a water bath. Predictably, the dry-baked cheesecake puffed up like a soufflé, developing hairline cracks around the perimeter toward the end of baking. Its top was quite brown. As it cooled, though, it developed that familiar center crack. We tasted the cake at room temperature. A large area around the perimeter of the cake was as grainy as a broken hollandaise—the eggs had clearly overcooked. Only the very center of the cake was smooth and creamy.

The cheesecake baked over the pan of water was a step up from the dry-baked cake. Like the dry cake, it developed hairline cracks around the perimeter. It souffléed throughout, though, not just around the edges. As it cooled, it developed only a tiny center crack. Its surface was cream-colored with a few brown spots. The very outer edges of the cake were overcooked, but the large center area was soft and creamy.

The cake baked in the water bath was perfect: no cracks, no sinking, no spotting. Its texture around the outer edges was just as creamy as it was in the center.

A number of recipes instruct the cook to leave the cake in a turned-off oven once it has cooked. This technique, they say, keeps the cake from deflating. Although we never had problems with cheesecake deflation, we came to like this method for a different reason. We turned off the oven when the cake was just slightly underdone in the center. The tame heat of the turned-off oven allowed our cakes to fully set without overcooking.

We were almost there. We had the lush and creamy and the light and fluffy cakes perfected, but we had not come up with a crack-free, smooth-textured, dense cheesecake. We knew that moist heat could not deliver this style of cheesecake. It needed gentle, dry heat to evaporate some of the cake's moisture without overcooking the eggs. So we tried baking cakes for less time and at lower temperatures. Reduced oven time still delivered cracked cakes. Lower oven temperatures produced cakes that were not creamy enough to compete with our soft, lush cakes but not dense enough to offer a contrast. We finally decided to try the absurd.

During our research, we had come across a really odd baking method in *Villas at Table* (Harper & Row, 1988). In his recipe for Lindy's Cheesecake, author Jim Villas instructs the cook to bake the cake dry in a blistering 500-degree oven for the first 12 minutes, then 200 degrees for one hour longer. So skeptical were we of this method that we at first decided not even to waste the cream cheese. If cakes crack under more moderate conditions, we rea-

soned, then how could a cake baked in this environment stand a chance? Nevertheless, we followed Villas's instructions, reducing the time the cake spent at 500 degrees to 10 minutes to compensate for the lesser amount of cream cheese in our recipe. After 10 minutes, we peered in at a beautifully puffed cake. We held the oven door open until the inside reduced to 200 degrees and baked the cake for another hour. The finished cake was beautiful. The high heat had caused the graham cracker crumbs to brown nicely and the eggs to puff. The low heat had gently cooked the cake, keeping the eggs from overcooking. The dry heat had allowed the cake to slowly dehydrate, creating that dense yet creamy texture we were seeking. Finally, we had a cheesecake to suit every taste.

Rich and Creamy Cheesecake
SERVES 12 TO 16

Rather than wrapping foil around the exterior of the pan, we prefer to line the removable bottom with foil, put the bottom back in the pan, foil side up, and then pull the excess foil up around the side of the pan. This method prevents water from seeping in from the bath and also makes it easy to slip the baked cheesecake off the bottom of the pan.

1	tablespoon unsalted butter, melted
3	tablespoons graham cracker crumbs
2	pounds cream cheese
1¼	cups sugar
4	large eggs, room temperature
1	teaspoon zest from small lemon, minced
2	teaspoons vanilla extract
¼	cup heavy cream
¼	cup sour cream

1. Adjust oven rack to middle position and heat oven to 325 degrees. Line bottom of 9-inch springform pan with foil, tuck foil underneath pan bottom, assemble pan, then pull foil around side of pan. Brush bottom and sides with butter. Sprinkle crumbs over bottom. Tilt pan in all directions to coat evenly with crumbs. Cover pan underneath and along sides with sheet of heavy-duty foil and set in large roasting pan. Bring kettle of water to boil for water bath.

2. Meanwhile, beat cream cheese in bowl of electric mixer until smooth. Gradually add sugar and

beat on medium speed until sugar dissolves, about 3 minutes. Add eggs, one at a time, beating until just incorporated and scraping down after each addition. (If you don't scrape down the bowl after each egg, cream cheese that sticks to the bowl will ultimately show up as lumps in the batter.) Add zest and vanilla and beat until just incorporated. Remove bowl from mixer; stir in cream and sour cream.

3. Pour batter into prepared pan. Set roasting pan on oven rack and pour in enough boiling water to come about halfway up side of springform pan. Bake until perimeter of cake is set but center jiggles like Jell-O when pan is tapped, 55 to 60 minutes. Turn off heat and leave oven door ajar, using a long-handled kitchen fork or spoon to hold it open for 1 hour longer. Remove springform pan from water bath and set on wire rack; cool to room temperature. Cover and refrigerate until chilled, at least 4 hours. (Can be refrigerated up to 4 days.)

➤ VARIATIONS

Light and Airy Cheesecake

Follow recipe for Rich and Creamy Cheesecake, separating eggs. Add yolks, rather than whole eggs, at instructed time. Continue with recipe, stirring in cream and sour cream. Beat egg whites to soft peaks. Fold whites into batter, pour into prepared pan, and bake, reducing cooking time to 45 to 50 minutes.

Dense and Firm Cheesecake

Follow recipe for Rich and Creamy Cheesecake, disregarding instructions for water bath. Bake cake at 500 degrees for 10 minutes. Reduce oven temperature to 200 degrees (leave oven door open until oven temperature reduces). Bake until cheesecake perimeter is set but center jiggles like Jell-O when pan is tapped, about 1 hour longer. Continue with cooling instructions in basic recipe.

LAYER CAKES

LAYER CAKES ARE THE "FANCIEST" KIND OF cake a home cook is likely to make, but they are also the most rewarding. The combination of tender cake and rich, creamy frosting is worth the extra effort. There are three basic kinds of layer cakes: those starting with yellow or butter cake layers, those starting with white cake layers, and those starting with chocolate cake layers.

While the batter for a layer cake is prepared much like any other cake, layer cakes do require some special assembling skills. We find it best to cool cake layers in their pans, then on racks. Grease racks with nonstick vegetable spray to keep cake layers from sticking to them and do not frost the layers until they are completely cooled. Cake layers are best frosted the day they are made. However, layers may be wrapped tightly in plastic and stored at room temperature for a day. For longer storage, freeze wrapped layers for up to one month. Defrost them on the counter and unwrap them just before frosting.

Most cakes taste best the day they are made. However, it is possible to keep a frosted cake fresh for a day or so if it is stored in a cake stand with a tight-fitting lid. As an alternative, you may also place a cake on a flat platter and cover it with an inverted large bowl. If the frosting is made with cream or your kitchen is very hot, refrigerate the cake and then bring it to room temperature before serving. Otherwise, keep the cake on the counter.

YELLOW CAKE

YELLOW CAKE HAS ALWAYS BEEN A BROAD category, but most of the recipes for making it are very similar. For example, in *The Boston Cook Book,* published in 1884, Mary Lincoln, one of Fannie Farmer's colleagues at the Boston Cooking School, outlined several recipes for yellow cake. But she singled out one as "the foundation for countless varieties of cake, which are often given in cook books under different names." Mrs. Lincoln's master cake formula turns out to be similar to what we today call a 1-2-3-4 cake, made with one cup of butter, two cups of sugar, three cups of (sifted) cake flour, and four eggs, plus milk and small amounts of baking powder, vanilla, and salt.

As it turns out, things have not changed much since more than a century ago: When analyzed, most of the yellow cake recipes in today's cookbooks are 1-2-3-4 cakes or something very similar.

So when we set out in search of the perfect yellow cake, the first thing we did was bake a 1-2-3-4 cake. It wasn't a bad cake, it just wasn't very interesting. Instead of melting in the mouth, the cake seemed crumbly, sugary, and a little hard. The crust was tacky and separated from the underlying cake. Above all, the cake lacked flavor. It did not taste of butter and eggs, as all plain cakes ought to, but instead seemed merely sweet.

Before tinkering with the ingredients, we decided to try a different mixing method. We had mixed our 1-2-3-4 cake in the classic way, first beating the butter and sugar until light and fluffy, then adding the eggs one at a time, and finally adding the dry ingredients and milk alternately. Now we wanted to try mixing the batter by the so-called two-stage method, developed by General Mills and Pillsbury in the 1940s and later popularized by Rose Levy Beranbaum in *The Cake Bible* (Morrow, 1988).

In the two-stage method, the flour, sugar, baking powder, and salt are combined, the butter and about two-thirds of the milk and eggs are added, and the batter is beaten until thick and fluffy, about a minute. Then, in the second stage, the rest of the milk and eggs are poured in and the batter is beaten about half a minute more. The two-stage method is simpler, quicker, and more nearly foolproof than the conventional creaming method.

The results exceeded our expectations. The two-stage method is often touted for the tender texture it promotes in cakes, and our two-stage 1-2-3-4 cake was indeed tender. But, more important, its consistency was improved. Whereas the conventionally mixed 1-2-3-4 cake had been crumbly, this cake was fine-grained and melting, and, interestingly enough, it did not seem overly sweet. Even the crust was improved. It was still a bit coarse, but only slightly sticky. This was a cake with a texture that we truly liked.

The problem was the taste. The cake still didn't have any. In fact, oddly enough, it seemed to have less taste than the conventionally mixed version. Certainly it had less color. The 1-2-3-4 cake, it seemed, conformed to a typical cake pattern—as the texture lightened, the taste and color faded.

After trying to remedy the taste deficit by playing around with the ingredients in many ways—primarily adjusting the amounts and proportions of the sugar and eggs—we finally recalled a recipe called Bride's Cake in Mrs. Rorer's *New Cook Book*, published exactly a century ago. This is basically an egg-white pound cake—made of a pound each of flour, sugar, butter, and egg whites—with a cup of milk and a little chemical leavening added. What would happen, we wondered, if we made Mrs. Rorer's cake with whole eggs instead of egg whites? It seemed worth a try.

SCIENCE: To Sift or Not to Sift?

Sifting flour is a chore. This is especially true when sifting into a measuring cup, since inevitably you end up sifting twice as much as you need to fill the cup. We suspected that many bakers skip this step, thinking it insignificant, so we thought we'd look into its importance.

The technique we usually use for measuring flour is the dip-and-sweep method, mentioned in the introduction and recommended for most of the recipes in this chapter. It involves simply scooping up the dry ingredient with the measuring cup and leveling the mound with a straight edge. Actually, this is a relatively imprecise method. When we asked six different people to dip and sweep one cup of flour in our test kitchen, there was a variance of half an ounce in the weight of the flour they measured out. Most recipes would not suffer adverse results in the end product from this relatively small difference. In a recipe such as our yellow cake recipe, however, where the precise balancing of ingredients is key to success, the exact amount of flour is critical. Sifting the flour into a measuring cup produces more consistent measurements; when the same six dip-and-sweepers sifted one cup of flour, the weight variance was less than one-fifth of an ounce.

Sifting also reduces the overall amount of flour (in weight) that goes into the recipe. Because sifting aerates the flour, one cup of sifted cake flour weighs in at about three ounces, whereas one cup of cake flour measured with the dip-and-sweep method weighs around four ounces. This difference translates into about a whopping one-fourth cup more of dipped and swept flour in this recipe. So what? you may wonder. To find out, we baked two cakes according to this recipe, one with sifted flour and one with dipped and swept flour. The cake made with sifted flour baked up perfectly flat, a dream to frost and layer since it required no trimming or leveling. The cake made with dipped and swept flour, however, mounded in the center and, though still very tasty, was also a bit drier.

We cut all of Mrs. Rorer's ingredients by half—that is, we made a half-pound cake, so that the batter would fit into two standard 9 by 1½-inch round layer pans—and when mixing the batter we followed the two-stage method.

The resulting cake was richer, more flavorful, and generally more interesting than any of the 1-2-3-4 cakes we had baked, but it was not perfect. The layers were low, and the cake was just a tad dense and rough on the tongue (though not rubbery, thank goodness). We had several options. We could try to open up the crumb by adding more milk and baking powder; we could try to lighten the cake up with an extra egg or a couple of extra yolks; or we could try to increase the volume and tenderize the texture by adding a few more ounces of sugar. We tried all three strategies. The last one—the extra sugar—did the trick. This cake was fine-grained, soft, and melting, and it tasted of butter and eggs. It had elegance and finesse and yet was still sturdy enough to withstand the frosting process.

Both the 1-2-3-4 cake and our improved yellow cake based on Mrs. Rorer's recipe are made with a half pound each of butter and eggs. But while the 1-2-3-4 cake contains three cups of sifted cake flour and one cup of milk, our improved yellow cake contains just 2¼ cups of sifted cake flour and only ½ cup of milk. So, while the 1-2-3-4 cake contains, by weight, three ounces more flour and milk than butter and eggs, our yellow cake contains three ounces less flour and milk than butter and eggs. This difference in basic proportions, as it turns out, makes a tremendous difference in texture and taste.

Rich and Tender Yellow Cake

MAKES TWO 9-INCH CAKES

Adding the butter pieces to the mixing bowl one at a time prevents the dry ingredients from flying up and out of the bowl. This yellow cake works with any of the frostings that follow.

4	large eggs, room temperature
½	cup whole milk, room temperature
2	teaspoons vanilla extract
2¼	cups sifted plain cake flour
1½	cups sugar
2	teaspoons baking powder

¾ teaspoon salt

½ pound (2 sticks) unsalted butter, softened, each stick cut into 8 pieces

1. Adjust oven rack to lower-middle position and heat oven to 350 degrees. Generously grease two 9 by 1½-inch cake pans with vegetable shortening and cover pan bottoms with rounds of parchment paper or wax paper. Grease parchment rounds, dust cake pans with flour, and tap out excess.

2. Beat eggs, milk, and vanilla with fork in small bowl; measure out 1 cup of this mixture and set aside. Combine flour, sugar, baking powder, and salt in bowl of standing mixer fitted with paddle attachment; mix on lowest speed to blend, about 30 seconds. With mixer still running at lowest speed, add butter one piece at a time; mix until butter and flour begin to clump together and look sandy and pebbly, with pieces about the size of peas, 30 to 40 seconds after all butter is added. Add reserved 1 cup of egg mixture and mix at lowest speed until incorporated, 5 to 10 seconds. Increase speed to medium-high and beat until light and fluffy, about 1 minute. Add remaining egg mixture (about ½ cup) in slow steady stream, about 30 seconds. Stop mixer and thoroughly scrape sides and bottom of bowl. Beat on medium-high until thoroughly combined and batter looks slightly curdled, about 15 seconds longer. (To mix using hand mixer, whisk flour, sugar, baking powder, and salt in large bowl. Add butter pieces and cut into the flour mixture with a pastry blender. Add reserved 1 cup of egg mixture; beat with hand mixer at lowest speed until incorporated, 20 to 30 seconds. Increase speed to high, add remaining egg mixture, and beat until light and fluffy, about 1 minute. Stop mixer and thoroughly scrape sides and bottom of bowl. Beat at high speed 15 seconds longer.)

3. Divide batter equally between prepared cake pans; spread to sides of pan and smooth with rubber spatula. Bake until cake tops are light golden and skewer inserted in center comes out clean, 20 to 25 minutes. (Cakes may mound slightly but will level when cooled.) Cool on rack 10 minutes. Run a knife around pan perimeter to loosen. Invert cake onto large plate, peel off parchment, and reinvert onto lightly greased rack. Cool completely before icing.

4. Assemble and frost cake (see pages 470–471).

Coffee Buttercream Frosting

MAKES ABOUT 3 CUPS

If you prefer not to use the raw egg the texture will be less smooth.

1½	tablespoons instant coffee
1½	tablespoons water
1½	tablespoons vanilla extract
¾	pound (3 sticks) unsalted butter, softened
3	cups confectioners' sugar
1	large egg, beaten, or 3 tablespoons milk

1. Dissolve coffee in water and add vanilla in small bowl; set aside. Beat butter in bowl of electric mixer fitted with paddle attachment on medium speed until fluffy, about 1 minute. Reduce speed to low and add sugar, 1 cup at a time, beating 15 seconds between each addition. Increase speed to medium and beat until smooth, about 3 minutes.

2. Add coffee mixture and egg or milk; beat on low speed to combine. Scrape sides and bottom of bowl with rubber spatula. Increase speed to medium and beat until fluffy, 3 to 4 minutes. (Buttercream may be covered and kept at room temperature for several hours or refrigerated in an airtight container for a week. Bring to room temperature before using.)

➤ VARIATIONS

Orange Buttercream Frosting

Follow recipe for Coffee Buttercream Frosting, omitting instant coffee and vanilla, substituting 3 tablespoons orange juice for water, and adding 1 tablespoon grated orange zest along with egg or milk.

Lemon Buttercream Frosting

Follow recipe for Coffee Buttercream Frosting, omitting instant coffee and vanilla, substituting 1½ tablespoons lemon juice for water, and adding 1½ tablespoons grated lemon zest along with egg or milk.

FROSTING A LAYER CAKE

1. Using four rectangular pieces of parchment paper, form an empty square on top of a cake platter.

2. Place cake on parchment. Place about one cup of icing in the center of the cake and, with an icing spatula, spread the icing to the edge of the cake, then level the icing.

3. Place second cake layer on top, making sure layers are aligned. Frost the top in the same manner as the first layer.

4. Holding the icing spatula perpendicular to the platter, frost the sides of the cake. Smooth the frosting on the top to level the ridge that forms around the edge.

5. If desired, lightly press nuts on sides of cake, letting the excess fall onto the parchment. Allow about one cup of nuts to work with; some will be left over once the parchment is removed and the excess is poured off.

6. Carefully pull out the pieces of parchment from beneath the cake.

Chocolate Cream Frosting

MAKES ABOUT 3 CUPS

1½	cups heavy cream
16	ounces bittersweet or semisweet chocolate, chopped fine
⅓	cup corn syrup
1	teaspoon vanilla extract

Place chocolate in heatproof bowl. Bring heavy cream to boil in small saucepan over medium-high heat; pour over chocolate. Add corn syrup and let stand 3 minutes. Whisk gently until smooth; stir in vanilla. Refrigerate 1 to 1½ hours, stirring every 15 minutes, until mixture reaches spreadable consistency.

ALL-PURPOSE BIRTHDAY CAKE

WHITE LAYER CAKES HAVE BEEN THE CLASSIC birthday cake for more than a hundred years. White cake is simply a basic butter cake made with egg whites instead of whole eggs. The whites produce the characteristic color, and they also make the cake soft and fine-grained, a bit like pound cake but much lighter and more delicate. Unfortunately, the white cakes we have baked over the years, although good enough, always fell short of our high expectations. They came out a little dry and chewy—one might say cottony—and we noticed that they were riddled with tunnels and small holes. What was going wrong?

Early on, we suspected the mixing method might be to blame. We had always mixed white cakes according to standard cookbook procedure—that is, we had creamed the butter and sugar, added the flour and milk alternately, and finally folded in stiffly beaten egg whites. Because this mixing method brings the flour into direct contact with liquid, it encourages the flour to form the elastic protein, gluten. When beaten, gluten forms a stretchy net of ropelike fibers that not only make the cake tough, but also press the air cells together into holes and tunnels. Cookbook recipes generally recommend deft, gentle handling of the batter to minimize gluten formation, but it seemed that no matter how little we beat or how delicately we folded, the cakes did not improve.

In trying to avoid an "overglutenized" cake batter, we ordinarily use the so-called two-stage mixing method. This method entails creaming the flour, butter, and sugar together (rather than just the butter and sugar) before adding the eggs and other liquid ingredients. Because the flour is mixed with butter at the start, it is partially waterproofed, and thus less prone to develop gluten. In the case of white cake, however, we could not bring ourselves to try this method because it uses unbeaten eggs, and every traditional recipe for white cake calls for stiffly beaten egg whites folded into the batter at the end. Surely the cake's special texture depended on beating the whites first, we thought. So we stuck with the creaming method and tried to improve the results by fiddling with the proportions. Into the garbage went a dozen cakes.

Luckily, we happened upon a recipe called Old-Fashioned White Cake in the 1943 edition of the *Joy of Cooking*. The recipe called for working the butter into the flour with one's fingertips, as when making pie crust, and then whisking in beaten egg whites. We were intrigued: Here was a two-stage white cake, but with the beaten egg whites we thought were necessary. Upon testing, the cake indeed proved to be more tender than the others we had made, and it also had a finer crumb. After a few more experiments, we eventually arrived at a white cake that we thought very good—but, alas, still not quite perfect. There were still those holes.

We were stumped and might have stayed stumped if we had not been paying particularly close attention one day while we were folding egg whites into a soufflé batter. As the rubber spatula drew the egg whites up from the bottom of the bowl and over the top of the batter, we noticed how coarse and bubbly the whites were, even though they were not overbeaten and had seemed perfectly smooth and thick when taken from the mixer just moments before. Could it be that beaten egg whites, instead of promoting an ethereal texture in white cakes, actually formed large air pockets and caused those unsightly holes?

We tried the "old-fashioned" recipe again, only this time we simply mixed the egg whites with the milk before beating them into the flour-and-butter mixture. The results were fantastic. The cake was not only fine-grained and holeless, but to our surprise, it was also larger and lighter than the ones we'd prepared with beaten whites. And the method couldn't be simpler, quicker, or more nearly failureproof. The two-stage method had proved, after all, to be the way to go.

Of course we were curious to know the reason for this surprising outcome, so we did some boning up on egg whites. Apparently, beating has something of the same effect on egg whites that cooking does. Both beating and heating cause some of the individual protein strands to uncoil, whereupon they bump into each other and start linking up into an increasingly tight, dense web. It is this linking process that causes cooked whites to coagulate and beaten whites to stiffen. The problem, then, with putting beaten egg whites into a batter is that the whites have, in this respect, already been partially cooked. Because of this, the whites do not mix well with the rest of the batter and tend instead to create large air pockets when the cake bakes. Unbeaten egg whites, on the other hand, mix easily with the rest of the ingredients. When, during baking, they set and stiffen, they provide the structure necessary to hold the fine air bubbles beaten into the batter by creaming. The result is a wonderfully velvety cake, perfect for that birthday person.

Classic White Layer Cake with Butter Frosting and Raspberry-Almond Filling

SERVES 12

If you have forgotten to bring the milk and egg white mixture to room temperature, set the bottom of the glass measure containing it in a sink of hot water and stir until the mixture feels cool rather than cold, around 65 degrees. Cake layers can be wrapped and stored for one day; frosting can be covered with plastic wrap and set aside at room temperature for several hours. Once assembled, the cake should be covered with an inverted bowl or cake cover and refrigerated. Under its coat of frosting, it will remain fresh for two to three days. Bring it to room temperature before serving. There is enough frosting to pipe a border around the base and top of the cake. If you want to decorate the cake more elaborately, you should make one and a half times the frosting recipe. You may also substitute lemon curd for the raspberry jam in the filling.

CLASSIC WHITE CAKE

I	**cup milk, room temperature**

¾	**cup egg whites (about 6 large or 5 extra large), room temperature**
2	**teaspoons almond extract**
I	**teaspoon vanilla extract**
2¼	**cups plain cake flour**
1¾	**cups sugar**
4	**teaspoons baking powder**
I	**teaspoon salt**
12	**tablespoons (1½ sticks) unsalted butter, softened**

BUTTER FROSTING

½	**pound (2 sticks) unsalted butter, softened**
I	**pound (4 cups) confectioners' sugar**
I	**tablespoon vanilla extract**
I	**tablespoon milk**
	Pinch salt

RASPBERRY-ALMOND FILLING

½	**cup blanched slivered almonds, toasted and chopped coarse**
⅓	**cup seedless raspberry jam**

1. **FOR THE CAKE:** Adjust oven rack to middle position and heat oven to 350 degrees. Generously grease two 9 by 1½-inch or 2-inch round cake pans with vegetable shortening and cover pan bottoms with rounds of parchment paper or wax paper. Grease parchment rounds, dust cake pans with flour, and tap out excess.

2. Pour milk, egg whites, and extracts into 2-cup glass measure, and mix with fork until blended.

3. Mix cake flour, sugar, baking powder, and salt in bowl of electric mixer at slow speed. Add butter; continue beating at slow speed until mixture resembles moist crumbs, with no powdery ingredients remaining.

4. Add all but ½ cup of milk mixture to crumbs and beat at medium speed (or high speed if using handheld mixer) for 1½ minutes. Add remaining ½ cup of milk mixture and beat 30 seconds more. Stop mixer and scrape sides of bowl. Return mixer to medium (or high) speed and beat 20 seconds longer.

5. Divide batter evenly between two prepared cake pans; using rubber spatula, spread batter to pan walls and smooth tops. Arrange pans at least 3 inches from the oven walls and 3 inches apart. (If oven is

small, place pans on separate racks in staggered fashion to allow for air circulation.) Bake until cake needle or toothpick inserted in the center comes out clean, 23 to 25 minutes.

6. Let cakes rest in pans for 3 minutes. Loosen from sides of pans with a knife, if necessary, and invert onto greased cake racks. Reinvert onto additional greased racks. Let cool completely, about 1½ hours.

7. FOR THE FROSTING: Beat butter, confectioners' sugar, vanilla, milk, and salt in bowl of electric mixer at slow speed until sugar is moistened. Increase speed to medium (high if using handheld mixer); beat, stopping twice to scrape down bowl, until creamy and fluffy, about 1½ minutes. Avoid overbeating, or frosting will be too soft to pipe.

8. FOR THE FILLING: Before assembling cake, set aside ¾ cup frosting for decoration. Spread small dab of frosting in center of cake plate to anchor cake, and set down one cake layer. Combine ½ cup remaining frosting with almonds in small bowl and spread over first layer. Carefully spread jam on top, then cover with second cake layer. Spread frosting over top and sides of cake (see page 470). Pipe reserved frosting around perimeter of cake or top.

CHOCOLATE LAYER CAKE

RECIPES FOR CHOCOLATE LAYER CAKE CAN be maddening. One promises an especially fudgy and rich cake, the next guarantees a light and tender one, the third pledges the best-ever devil's food cake—whatever "devil's food" might be. The secret to the recipe, we are told, is Dutch-process cocoa, or dark brown sugar, or sour cream, or buttermilk, or some special mixing method—so on and so forth. If you've made as many chocolate cakes as we have over the years, you can fill in the blanks yourself.

Finally, you make the cake, and you think, well, it is a little fudgy, or tender, or a little like devil's food, or whatever. But isn't it also very much like the chocolate cake you made just the other week, from a recipe that called for very different ingredients and promised some very other kind of result?

We set out to make sense of this muddle. After baking and comparing dozens of different chocolate cakes, we have devised a master recipe and four variations that produce five truly distinctive chocolate layer cakes. In the process, we discovered a couple of general principles that apply to whatever type of chocolate layer cake you are making. Perhaps more important, we also learned a great deal about how various ingredients function and what results they produce, so that each of these recipes delivers exactly the type of chocolate cake it promises.

To carry out these experiments, we needed a base from which to begin. We chose as a master recipe a perennial favorite among all chocolate cakes, which we call Velvet Devil's Food Layer Cake.

This cake is extremely soft and tender, as well as pleasantly sweet (we find very bitter chocolate cakes hard to swallow—literally). We also find it appealing because this cake delivers a potent chocolate punch. The "velvet" in the title suggests the cake's texture as well as distinguishing it from what we take to be a more classic devil's food, which is sweeter and decidedly spongy, even a tad chewy. We also chose Velvet Devil's Food Layer Cake because it is basically a standard yellow butter cake with some of the flour replaced by cocoa. Because it follows a simple, familiar pattern, the recipe is easy to change by varying ingredients and techniques.

Bakers can (and do) argue endlessly over whether cocoa-based chocolate cakes are best made with standard American cocoa, such as Hershey's, or with a European-style cocoa, such as Droste, that has been alkalized, or "Dutched," to neutralize some of the natural acid.

To settle this question, we prepared several recipes using both types of cocoa—and found that there was not an enormous difference. Cakes made with Hershey's were a little blacker and had a slight bitter edge; in the Droste cakes, the chocolate flavor was perhaps a bit mellower, but also fainter. But these distinctions were minor, and the bottom line was that we liked cakes made with both natural and Dutched cocoas just fine.

A second cocoa experiment, however, proved much more conclusive. In cakes made with cocoa and water, the chocolate flavor was much stronger and the color twice as dark when the cocoa was first dissolved in boiling water rather than simply being mixed into the batter dry. We therefore recommend following this procedure in any cocoa-based chocolate cake in which water is the liquid.

Next, we sought to discover the effects of substituting unsweetened baking chocolate or semisweet chocolate for cocoa. Following standard substitution tables, we prepared the master recipe using three ounces of unsweetened chocolate in place of the cocoa, subtracting three tablespoons of butter to compensate for the fat in the chocolate. We also made the master recipe with five ounces of semisweet chocolate in lieu of cocoa, cutting the butter by two tablespoons and the sugar by six tablespoons. These cakes were neither as moist nor as flavorful as those made with cocoa.

Our second—and most extensive—set of experiments concerned the effect of dairy liquids on the cake. We checked out everything from sweet milk to buttermilk to yogurt to sour cream.

When we replaced the water in our recipe with milk, we got a cake that we liked a great deal. As we had predicted, the chocolate flavor was somewhat muted, but to some tastes, this would be for the better. The cake was a little less tender and more crumbly than the one made with water, but on the plus side, it also felt pleasantly substantial in the mouth. Milk produced the kind of chocolate cake that we remember from childhood, so we call this milk-based variation Old-Fashioned Chocolate Layer Cake.

Further experiments revealed that neither dissolving the cocoa in hot milk nor cooking the cocoa and milk together made for an appreciably stronger flavor than simply adding the cocoa to the batter dry. Evidently, dissolving the cocoa in boiling liquid only improves its flavor if the liquid in question is water.

Buttermilk and yogurt proved to be far more problematic ingredients. In our myriad tests, both had a paradoxical effect on texture, on the one hand velvetizing the crumb and adding a nice moistness, but on the other compacting the cakes and making them seem a little hard and chewy and also a bit pasty. Taste, though, was the real issue. While milk had a gentling effect on the flavor of chocolate, buttermilk and yogurt nearly killed it.

By testing various cookbook recipes, we eventually learned how to use buttermilk in such a way as to maximize its tenderizing qualities without obliterating all chocolate taste. One solution is to make your cake with a great deal of sugar; sugar speeds melting, and rapid melting intensifies flavor. Thus the Classic Devil's Food Layer Cake, which like other standard devil's food recipes is high in sugar, derives a lovely moist sponginess from buttermilk while retaining a good chocolate pungency. We discovered that extra fat also mitigates the chocolate-blocking effects of buttermilk, though fat seems at the same time to undercut buttermilk's tenderizing properties, resulting in a fudgy texture.

Finally, if you actually prefer a chocolate cake with a mild flavor, buttermilk can be very helpful, for the velvetiness it imparts reinforces the flavor impression you are trying to create. The trick, we think, is to use the buttermilk in sparing quantities. The German Chocolate-Style Layer Cake is a reconfiguration of a cake popularly made with German sweet chocolate and a cup or more of buttermilk. We are not particularly fond of the cake made according to the standard recipe, but when the buttermilk is reduced, the cake turns out quite nicely.

Having tested the master recipe using buttermilk in place of water, we next tried replacing some of the water with sour cream, at the same time decreasing the butter to compensate for the milk fat in sour cream. Like buttermilk, sour cream made for a more velvety crumb, but there was a marked difference in degree—the sour cream cake was so feathery and soft as to seem almost puddinglike.

The effects of sour cream on flavor were complicated. It did make for a less pungent chocolate taste, but at the same time it imparted a pleasing, lingering mellowness. Strangely enough, it seemed to sweeten the cake rather than making it more tart, as buttermilk had. Sour cream and buttermilk, of course, are two very different things, so perhaps we shouldn't have been so surprised by the results. In our fifth variation, Sour Cream Fudge Layer Cake, we use the unique properties of sour cream to produce a cake with a dense yet melting texture and a rich taste.

Our final set of experiments concerned leavening, which presented us with a fascinating set of problems. In several of the earlier tests, we had noticed that the master recipe and the Old-Fashioned Chocolate Layer Cake developed a slight hump during baking, which subsided upon cooling. This phenomenon often results from insufficient leavening, so we tried increasing the baking soda from one-half teaspoon to three-quarters teaspoon. Sure enough, the cakes rose higher and were more level, and they were also lighter and softer in texture without seeming excessively crumbly or porous. We also noted that the cakes were considerably darker. A little research revealed why. As pH increases (in other words, the mixture becomes less acidic), the pigments in cocoa turn from blondish to brownish to black; if you add enough soda, you will eventually induce a reddish cast in cocoa cakes, which is how the name devil's food arose.

Initially, we were pleased by the results of adding extra soda, but then we noticed something else. Tasting one of the cakes, we detected a musty, peculiar flavor. The musty taste, more commonly described as soapiness, is caused by using more baking soda than can be neutralized by the available acid in a batter. In both the master recipe and the old-fashioned variation, the cocoa supplies the only acid present. But in the devil's food variation, additional acid is provided by the buttermilk, which in turn neutralizes the extra one-quarter teaspoon baking soda. It is not essential to add the extra baking soda to classic devil's food cake, but you might as well, since the soda produces greater volume and also tames the slightly distracting tang of the buttermilk.

Master Recipe for Chocolate Layer Cake
(Velvet Devil's Food Layer Cake with Coffee Buttercream Frosting)
SERVES 12

This cake's texture is both soft and dense, similar to chocolate pound cake, only softer and lighter. Its flavor is intensely chocolate, yet pleasantly sweet. The substantial coffee-flavored buttercream stands up to the cake's dense texture and balances the rich chocolate flavor.

VELVET DEVIL'S FOOD CAKE

½ cup nonalkalized (natural) cocoa powder, such as Hershey's

2 teaspoons instant espresso or instant coffee

1 cup boiling water

2 teaspoons vanilla extract

12 tablespoons (1½ sticks) unsalted butter, softened

1¼ cups sugar

2 large eggs, room temperature

1¼ cups all-purpose flour

½ teaspoon baking soda

½ teaspoon salt

1 recipe Coffee Buttercream Frosting (page 470)

1. FOR THE CAKE: Adjust oven rack to center position and heat oven to 350 degrees. Generously grease two 8 by 1½-inch round cake pans with vegetable shortening and cover pan bottoms with rounds of parchment paper or waxed paper. Grease parchment rounds, dust cake pans with flour, and tap out excess.

2. Mix cocoa and instant coffee in small bowl; add boiling water and mix until smooth. Cool to room temperature, then stir in vanilla.

3. Beat butter in bowl of electric mixer set at medium-high speed until smooth and shiny, about 30 seconds. Gradually sprinkle in sugar; beat until mixture is fluffy and almost white, 3 to 5 minutes. Add eggs one at a time, beating 1 full minute after each addition.

4. Whisk flour, baking soda, and salt in medium bowl. With mixer on lowest speed, add about ⅓ of dry ingredients to batter, followed immediately by about ⅓ of cocoa mixture; mix until ingredients are almost incorporated into batter. Repeat process twice more. When batter appears blended, stop mixer and scrape bowl sides with rubber spatula. Return mixer to low speed; beat until batter looks satiny, about 15 seconds longer.

5. Divide batter evenly between pans. With rubber spatula, spread batter to pan sides and smooth top. Bake cakes until they feel firm in center when lightly pressed and skewer comes out clean or with just a crumb or two adhering, 23 to 30 minutes. Transfer pans to wire racks; cool for 10 minutes. Run knife around perimeter of each pan, invert cakes onto racks, and peel off paper liners. Reinvert cakes onto additional racks; cool completely before frosting.

6. Assemble and frost the cake (see page 470).

VARIATIONS
Classic Devil's Food Layer Cake with Whipped Cream

The increased sugar quantity in this recipe results in an extremely tender cake—it almost falls apart at the touch of a fork—yet when you chew it, it turns out to be resilient and spongy. Since this batter rises higher, make sure to use 9 by 1½-inch round cake pans rather than the 8-inch ones called for in the master recipe. Sweeter and lighter than the Velvet Devil's Food Layer Cake, this cake is appropriately paired with lightly sweetened whipped cream.

CLASSIC DEVIL'S FOOD CAKE

- ½ cup nonalkalized (natural) cocoa powder, such as Hershey's
- 2 teaspoons instant espresso or instant coffee
- 1 cup boiling water
- ¾ cup firmly packed dark brown sugar
- ½ cup plain yogurt or buttermilk
- 2 teaspoons vanilla extract
- 8 tablespoons (1 stick) unsalted butter, softened
- 1¼ cups sugar
- 2 large eggs, room temperature
- 1¼ cups all-purpose flour
- ¾ teaspoon baking soda
- ½ teaspoon salt

WHIPPED CREAM FROSTING

- 2½ cups heavy cream, chilled
- ¾ cup confectioners' sugar, sifted
- 1 teaspoon vanilla extract

1. **FOR THE CAKE:** Adjust oven rack to center position and heat oven to 350 degrees. Generously grease two 9 by 1½-inch round cake pans with vegetable shortening and cover pan bottoms with rounds of parchment paper or waxed paper. Grease parchment rounds, dust cake pans with flour, and tap out excess.

2. Mix cocoa and instant coffee in small bowl; add boiling water and mix until smooth. Stir in brown sugar and yogurt or buttermilk. Cool to room temperature, then stir in vanilla.

3. Beat butter in bowl of electric mixer set at medium-high speed until smooth and shiny, about 30 seconds. Gradually sprinkle in sugar; beat until mixture is fluffy and almost white, 3 to 5 minutes. Add eggs one at a time, beating 1 full minute after each addition.

4. Whisk flour, baking soda, and salt in medium bowl. With mixer on lowest speed, add about one-third of dry ingredients to batter, followed immediately by about one-third of cocoa mixture; mix until

ingredients are almost incorporated into batter. Repeat process twice more. When batter appears blended, stop mixer and scrape bowl sides with rubber spatula. Return mixer to low speed; beat until batter looks satiny, about 15 seconds longer.

5. Divide batter evenly between pans. With rubber spatula, spread batter to pan sides and smooth top. Bake cakes until they feel firm in center when lightly pressed and skewer comes out clean or with just a crumb or two adhering, 23 to 30 minutes. Transfer pans to wire racks; cool for 10 minutes. Run knife around perimeter of each pan, invert cakes onto racks, and peel off paper liners. Reinvert cakes onto additional racks; cool completely before frosting.

6. **FOR THE FROSTING:** Beat cream at medium speed in an electric mixer until thickened. Add sugar and vanilla; beat until stiff.

7. Assemble and frost the cake immediately (see page 470).

Old-Fashioned Chocolate Layer Cake with Chocolate Cream Frosting

Unlike our two devil's food cakes, which are almost like chocolate in the form of cake, this one resembles a traditional yellow cake with a great deal of chocolate added. The milk slightly mutes the chocolate flavor while giving the cake a sturdy, pleasantly crumbly texture. Cream enriches the frosting, making it compatible with this less assertive chocolate cake.

OLD-FASHIONED CHOCOLATE CAKE

- 12 tablespoons (1½ sticks) unsalted butter, softened
- 1¼ cups sugar
- 2 large eggs, room temperature
- 1¼ cups all-purpose flour
- ½ teaspoon baking soda
- ½ teaspoon salt
- ½ cup nonalkalized (natural) cocoa powder, such as Hershey's
- 2 teaspoons instant espresso or instant coffee
- 1 cup plus 2 tablespoons milk
- 2 teaspoons vanilla extract
- 1 recipe Chocolate Cream Frosting (page 471)

1. **FOR THE CAKE:** Adjust oven rack to center position and heat oven to 350 degrees. Generously

grease two 8 by 1½-inch round cake pans with vegetable shortening and cover pan bottoms with rounds of parchment paper or waxed paper. Grease parchment rounds, dust cake pans with flour, and tap out excess.

2. Beat butter in bowl of electric mixer set at medium-high speed until smooth and shiny, about 30 seconds. Gradually sprinkle in sugar; beat until mixture is fluffy and almost white, 3 to 5 minutes. Add eggs one at a time, beating 1 full minute after each addition.

3. Whisk flour, baking soda, salt, cocoa, and instant espresso in medium bowl. Combine milk and vanilla in measuring cup. With mixer on lowest speed, add about one-third of dry ingredients to batter, followed immediately by about one-third of milk mixture; mix until ingredients are almost incorporated into batter. Repeat process twice more. When batter appears blended, stop mixer and scrape bowl sides with rubber spatula. Return mixer to low speed; beat until batter looks satiny, about 15 seconds longer.

4. Divide batter evenly between pans. With rubber spatula, spread batter to pan sides and smooth top. Bake cakes until they feel firm in center when lightly pressed and skewer comes out clean or with just a crumb or two adhering, 23 to 30 minutes. Transfer pans to wire racks; cool for 10 minutes. Run knife around perimeter of each pan, invert cakes onto racks, and peel off paper liners. Reinvert cakes onto additional racks; cool completely before frosting.

5. Assemble and frost the cake (see page 470).

German Chocolate Layer Cake with Coconut-Pecan Filling

Buttermilk gives this cake a pleasantly mild chocolate flavor with a very light, soft texture. The pecan and coconut filling provides textural contrast. Be sure to divide batter evenly between pans as cakes will rise high.

GERMAN CHOCOLATE CAKE

¼ cup nonalkalized (natural) cocoa powder, such as Hershey's
2 teaspoons instant espresso or instant coffee
⅓ cup boiling water
⅓ cup buttermilk or plain yogurt
2 teaspoons vanilla extract

12 tablespoons (1½ sticks) unsalted butter, softened
1¼ cups sugar
3 large eggs, room temperature
1¼ cups all-purpose flour
½ teaspoon baking soda
½ teaspoon salt

COCONUT-PECAN FILLING

4 large egg yolks
1 cup sugar
¼ teaspoon salt
8 tablespoons (1 stick) unsalted butter, softened
1 cup heavy cream
1 teaspoon vanilla extract
1½ cups chopped pecans, toasted
7 ounces (about 2 cups lightly packed) sweetened flaked coconut

1. **FOR THE CAKE:** Adjust oven rack to center position and heat oven to 350 degrees. Generously grease two 8 by 1½-inch round cake pans with vegetable shortening and cover pan bottoms with rounds of parchment paper or waxed paper. Grease parchment rounds, dust cake pans with flour, and tap out excess.

2. Mix cocoa and instant coffee in small bowl; add boiling water and mix until smooth. Cool to room temperature, then stir in buttermilk and vanilla.

3. Beat butter in bowl of electric mixer set at medium-high speed until smooth and shiny, about 30 seconds. Gradually sprinkle in sugar; beat until mixture is fluffy and almost white, 3 to 5 minutes. Add eggs one at a time, beating 1 full minute after each addition.

4. Whisk flour, baking soda, and salt in medium bowl. With mixer on lowest speed, add about one-third of dry ingredients to batter, followed immediately by about one-third of cocoa mixture; mix until ingredients are almost incorporated into batter. Repeat process twice more. When batter appears blended, stop mixer and scrape bowl sides with rubber spatula. Return mixer to low speed; beat until batter looks satiny, about 15 seconds longer.

5. Divide batter evenly between pans. With rubber spatula, spread batter to pan sides and smooth top. Bake cakes until they feel firm in center when lightly pressed and skewer comes out clean or with just a crumb or two adhering, 23 to 30 minutes.

Transfer pans to wire racks; cool for 10 minutes. Run knife around perimeter of each pan, invert cakes onto racks, and peel off paper liners. Reinvert cakes onto additional racks; cool completely before frosting.

6. FOR THE FILLING: Mix egg yolks, sugar, and salt in a medium bowl; beat in butter, then gradually beat cream and vanilla into mixture. Pour into medium, nonreactive saucepan and cook over low heat, stirring constantly until mixture is puffy and just begins to thicken, 15 to 20 minutes. Pour mixture into a medium bowl and cool to room temperature. Stir in pecans and coconut.

7. TO ASSEMBLE: Halve each cake round to make four layers for the completed cake. Place one of the cake bottoms on a serving plate. Spread about 1 cup filling over cake half. Place another halved cake round over filling. Repeat this stacking and spreading process with remaining filling and cake, ending with a final layer of filling.

Sour Cream Fudge Layer Cake with Chocolate Butter Icing

Sour cream gives this cake its smooth, rich chocolate taste with a dense yet melting texture, almost like fudge. An equally intense chocolate icing stands up to the rich cake. Since this batter rises fairly high, make sure to use 9 by 1½-inch round cake pans rather than the 8-inch ones called for in the master recipe. It is best not to refrigerate this cake, but if you do, cut it while cold, then let slices come to room temperature before serving.

SOUR CREAM FUDGE CAKE

I	cup nonalkalized (natural) cocoa powder, such as Hershey's
2	teaspoons instant espresso or instant coffee
I	cup boiling water
½	cup sour cream
2	teaspoons vanilla extract
½	pound (2 sticks) unsalted butter, softened
I ¾	cups sugar
2	large eggs, room temperature
I ¼	cups all-purpose flour
¾	teaspoon baking soda
½	teaspoon salt

CHOCOLATE BUTTER ICING

9	ounce bittersweet or semisweet chocolate
8	tablespoons (I stick) unsalted butter
⅓	cup light corn syrup

1. FOR THE CAKE: Adjust oven rack to center position and heat oven to 350 degrees. Generously grease two 9 by 1½-inch round cake pans with vegetable shortening and cover pan bottoms with rounds of parchment paper or waxed paper. Grease parchment rounds, dust cake pans with flour, and tap out excess.

2. Mix cocoa and instant coffee in small bowl; add boiling water and mix until smooth. Cool to room temperature, then stir in sour cream and vanilla.

3. Beat butter in bowl of electric mixer set at medium-high speed until smooth and shiny, about 30 seconds. Gradually sprinkle in sugar; beat until mixture is fluffy and almost white, 3 to 5 minutes. Add eggs one at a time, beating 1 full minute after each addition.

4. Whisk flour, baking soda, and salt in medium bowl. With mixer on lowest speed, add about one-third of dry ingredients to batter, followed immediately by about one-third of cocoa mixture; mix until ingredients are almost incorporated into batter. Repeat process twice more. When batter appears blended, stop mixer and scrape bowl sides with rubber spatula. Return mixer to low speed; beat until batter looks satiny, about 15 seconds longer.

5. Divide batter evenly between pans. With rubber spatula, spread batter to pan sides and smooth top. Bake cakes until they feel firm in center when lightly pressed and skewer comes out clean or with just a crumb or two adhering, 23 to 30 minutes. Transfer pans to wire racks; cool for 10 minutes. Run knife around perimeter of each pan, invert cakes onto racks, and peel off paper liners. Reinvert cakes onto additional racks; cool completely before frosting.

6. FOR THE ICING: Melt chocolate and butter in a medium bowl set over pan of almost-simmering water. Stir in corn syrup. Set bowl of chocolate mixture over a larger bowl of ice water, stirring occasionally, until the icing is just thick enough to spread.

7. Assemble and frost the cake (see page 470).

19

PIES AND TARTS

AMERICAN PIE DOUGH FOR FRUIT PIES

MAKING GOOD PIE CRUST CAN BE A SIMPLE procedure, but almost everyone who has tried can tell horror stories of crusts that turned out hard, soggy, flavorless, oversalted, underbaked, too crumbly, or unworkable. Advice is easy to come by: One expert says that butter is the secret to perfect crust; others swear by vegetable shortening, lard, even canola oil. Some omit salt, some omit sugar, some insist that working the dough by hand is essential, some use cake flour in addition to all-purpose flour, some freeze the dough, some do away with the rolling pin…and so on.

Simple as it can be, pie crust—essentially a combination of flour, water, and fat—raises numerous questions: What are the ideal proportions of the main ingredients? What else should be added for character? What methods should be used to combine these ingredients?

The most controversial ingredient in pastry is fat. We've found that all-butter crusts have good taste, but they are not as flaky and fine-textured as those made with some shortening, which are our favorites. All-shortening crusts have great texture but lack flavor; oil-based crusts are flat and entirely unappealing; and those made with lard are not only heavy and strongly flavored but are out of favor owing to health issues. We've experimented with a variety of combinations and ultimately settled on a proportion of three parts butter to two parts shortening as optimal for both flavor and texture.

There's a reason shortening works: Vegetable shortenings such as Crisco are made from vegetable oil that has been hydrogenated in order to incorporate air and to raise its melting point above room temperature. (This is much the same process as "creaming" butter and sugar, with the sharp sugar crystals cut into the fat to create pockets of air.) The absence of hydrogenation is why regular vegetable oil, which holds no more air than water, makes for poor pie doughs, whereas Crisco, which is about 10 percent gas, does a good job of lightening and tenderizing.

We also experimented with the relative proportions of fat and flour and finally settled on a ratio of two parts flour to one part fat. This ratio results in a relatively high-fat crust (you will find other recipes containing four parts of flour to one part of fat). But we found that the two-to-one proportion produces crusts that are easy to work and, when baked, are more tender and flavorful than any other.

The protein content of flour is important in any sort of baking. Bread flour, which is high in protein, produces a strong, elastic dough. Low-protein pastry flour makes for a soft, tender crumb, the best for cakes. Pie crusts fall in between and thus are best made with all-purpose flour, a combination of bread and cake flours. No matter what we've tried—substituting cornstarch for part of the all-purpose flour (a cookie-baking trick that increases tenderness), adding a quarter teaspoon of baking powder to increase rise, and mixing cake flour with the all-purpose flour (again, to increase tenderness)—we've always come back to plain old all-purpose flour.

We also tackled the proportions of salt and sugar, which were much easier to resolve. After testing amounts ranging from a quarter teaspoon to as much as two tablespoons, we settled on one teaspoon salt and two tablespoons sugar for a double-crust pie, amounts that enhance the flavor of the dough without shouting out their presence.

We experimented with a variety of liquid ingredients, such as buttermilk, milk, and cider vinegar, a common ingredient in many pastry recipes. No liquid additions improved our basic recipe, so we recommend that you stick with ice water.

You can make a pie dough by hand, but the food processor is faster and easier and does the best job of cutting the fat into the flour. Cut the butter in cubes. Pulse the butter and flour together five times, then add the shortening and pulse four more times. Proper mixing is important: If you undermix, the crusts will shrink when baked and became hard and crackly. If you overprocess, you'll get a crumbly cookielike dough.

When you've combined the flour and fat, dump the dough into a bowl and add the ice water. Use a rubber spatula and a folding motion to mix in the water, which exposes all of the dough to moisture without overworking it, something that can happen if the dough is left in the food processor and the water is pulsed in. Using a spatula to incorporate water allows you to minimize the amount of water used (less water means a more tender dough) and reduces the likelihood of overworking the dough.

Once you have a ball of dough, divide it in half, flatten each piece into a disk, wrap each one in plastic wrap, and rest the dough balls in the refrigerator for 30 minutes. You can let the dough rest for longer (an hour is best if the weather is warm), but then let it warm up slightly before attempting to roll it.

This dough is easy to roll if you follow a few basic guidelines. Flour the work surface very lightly; too much flour will be absorbed by the dough and cause it to toughen. If the dough seems too soft to roll, refrigerate it rather than adding more flour.

American Pie Dough for Fruit Pies

FOR ONE DOUBLE-CRUST 9-INCH PIE
See page 482 for specific rolling directions.

2½	cups all-purpose flour, plus extra for dusting dough and work surface
1	teaspoon salt
2	tablespoons sugar
12	tablespoons unsalted butter, chilled, cut into ¼-inch pieces
8	tablespoons all-vegetable shortening, chilled
6–8	tablespoons ice water

1. Mix flour, salt, and sugar in food processor fitted with steel blade. Scatter butter pieces over flour mixture, tossing to coat butter with a little of the flour. Cut butter into flour with five 1-second pulses. Add shortening and continue cutting in until flour is pale yellow and resembles coarse cornmeal, with butter bits no larger than small peas, about four more 1-second pulses. Turn mixture into medium bowl.

2. Sprinkle 6 tablespoons ice water over mixture. With blade of rubber spatula, use folding motion to mix. Press down on dough with broad side of spatula until dough sticks together, adding up to 2 tablespoon more ice water if it will not come together. Divide dough into two balls and flatten each into 4-inch-wide disk. Dust disks lightly with flour, wrap each in plastic, and refrigerate at least 30 minutes, or up to 2 days, before rolling.

➤ VARIATION
Firm American Pie Dough for Decorative Edging

This crust has less flavor and a firmer texture than the master recipe, but decorative edging will hold up nicely in the oven.

Follow recipe for American Pie Dough for Fruit Pies, using just 8 tablespoons butter and 6 tablespoons shortening. Reduce ice water to about 5 tablespoons.

EQUIPMENT: Pie Plates

Pie plates come in a variety of shapes and sizes as well as materials. We tested the three main types of pie plates—glass, ceramic, and metal—and found that a Pyrex glass pie plate did the best job of browning the crust, both when filled and baked blind. Several metal pie plates also browned quite well, but the glass pie plate has a number of other advantages.

Because you can see through a Pyrex plate, it's easy to judge just how brown the bottom crust has become during baking. With a metal pie plate, it's easy to pull the pie out of the oven too soon, when the bottom crust is still quite pale. A second feature we like about the traditional Pyrex plate is the wide rim, which makes the plate easier to take in and out of the oven and also supports fluted edges better than thin rims. Finally, because glass is nonreactive, you can store a pie filled with acidic fruit and not worry about metal giving the fruit an off flavor.

Pyrex pie plates do heat up more quickly than metal pie plates, so pies may be done a bit sooner than you think, especially if you are following a recipe that was tested in a metal plate. All the times in our recipes are based on baking in a glass pie plate; if baking in metal you may need to add two to three minutes for empty crusts and five minutes for filled pies.

AMERICAN PIE DOUGH FOR PREBAKED PIE SHELL

BAKING AN UNFILLED PIE PASTRY, COMMONLY called blind baking, can turn out to be the ultimate culinary nightmare. Without the weight of a filling, a pastry shell set into a hot oven can shrink dramatically, fill with air pockets, and puff up like a linoleum floor after a flood. The result? A shrunken, uneven shell that can hold only part of the filling intended for it.

ROLLING OUT PIE DOUGH

No matter what kind of pie crust you are making (single, double, or lattice top), follow these directions before proceeding to specific directions on that type of crust.

1. Sprinkle a couple of tablespoons of flour over the work surface and the top of the dough. To roll, apply light pressure to the dough with a rolling pin and work from the center outwards to avoid rolling over the same area more than necessary.

2. Every thirty seconds or so, slide a bench scraper under the dough to make sure it is not sticking to the work surface. Rotate the dough a quarter turn and continue rolling out. Rotating the dough like this ensures that the dough will be thinned to a uniform thickness and form a perfect circle.

3. To make sure that you've rolled the dough to the right size, place the pie plate upside down on top of it; the diameter of the dough should be 2 inches greater than that of the pie plate.

4. When the dough has reached the correct size, fold it into quarters. Place the folded dough in an empty pie plate, making sure the folded point of the dough is in the center of the plate. Unfold gently.

5. Lift the edge of the dough with one hand and ease the pastry along the bottom into the corners with the other hand; repeat around the circumference of the pan. Do not stretch the dough. Proceed with appropriate steps, depending on whether you are making a single- or double-crust pie or a lattice top.

FOR A SINGLE-CRUST PIE

1. Use kitchen scissors to trim the dough to within ½ inch of the lip of the pan all the way around.

2. Tuck the overhanging dough back under itself so the folded edge extends ¼ inch beyond the pan lip. Press it firmly to seal.

3. The pie crust is ready for a decorative edge. The simplest thing to do is to press the tines of a fork against the dough to flatten it against the rim of the pie plate.

We started with our favorite pie dough recipe (see page 481) and began to investigate the effects of resting the dough (in the refrigerator or the freezer), docking it (pricking the dough before it bakes), and weighting the crust as it bakes to keep it anchored in place. All three tricks are used by professional bakers to prevent common problems encountered when blind-baking a crust.

We found that refrigeration does the best job of preventing shrinkage. Pastry shrinkage is caused by gluten. Simply put, when you add water to the proteins in flour, elastic strands of gluten are formed. The strands of gluten in the dough get stretched during the rolling process, and if they are not allowed to relax after rolling, the pastry will snap back like a rubber band when baked, resulting in a shrunken, misshapen shell. Resting allows the tension in the taut strands of dough to ease so that they remain stretched and do not shrink back when heated.

This process does not occur, however, when the dough is immediately placed in the freezer to rest after rolling. When frozen, the water in the crust solidifies, freezing the gluten in place so it is not free to relax. As a result, when you bake the dough the tense, stretched strands of gluten snap back, causing the crust to shrink.

We might have concluded that pie dough should be refrigerated and not frozen if we hadn't noticed that the frozen crusts, although shrunken, were much flakier than the refrigerated crusts. Pastry is made up of layers of dough (protein and starch from the flour combined with water) and fat. Dough and fat have different heat capacities. When you place the pastry in the oven after freezing it (rather than just refrigerating it), the dough heats up and starts to set relatively quickly in comparison to the time it takes for the butter to melt and then vaporize, since butter has a much higher proportion of water than the dough. As a result, by the time the water in the butter starts to turn to steam, the dough is well into its setting phase. The air spaces occupied by the frozen butter, now that it has largely turned to steam, hold their shape because the dough is far along in the baking process.

Dough that you have refrigerated, on the other hand, is not as well set by the time the butter vaporizes; hence the air pockets disappear, the soft dough simply sinking into the spaces left by the butter. We came to a simple conclusion: First refrigerate the pie shell to relax the gluten, thus solving the problem of shrinkage during baking, then pop the dough in the freezer to improve flakiness.

This bit of science led to one other fascinating discovery. It is common knowledge that lard or vegetable shortening such as Crisco produces very flaky doughs. In fact, we use a combination of butter and shortening in our recipe because of the improvement in texture over an all-butter crust. The explanation for this phenomenon is simple. Lard and Crisco don't melt as quickly as butter when heated. Therefore, they retain their shape as the dough sets up, keeping the layers of pastry separated.

While this combination-chilling method prevents shrinkage, ballooning can occur when air pockets form beneath the crust. Typically, bakers dock (or prick) the dough with the tines of a fork before it goes into the oven. However, we found that docking was not necessary as long as the dough is weighted. Since weighting is a must—it not only prevents ballooning but keeps the shell, especially the sides, in place as it bakes—we do not dock pastry dough.

Some professional bakers swear by "official" pie weights, while others make do with rice or dried beans. We found that metal or ceramic pie weights do a better job than rice or beans. They are heavier and therefore more effective at preventing the pastry from puffing. Pie weights are also better heat conductors and promote more thorough browning of the pastry.

We got the most consistent results and even browning by baking in the middle rack at a constant 375 degrees. At higher temperatures the pastry was prone to overbrowning and burned in spots, while lower temperatures caused the edges to brown well before the bottom. More important than temperature and placement, though, was cooking time.

There are two stages in prebaking. In the first stage, the dough is baked with a lining and weights. This stage usually takes about 17 minutes; the objective is to cook the dough until it sets, at which point it can hold its shape without assistance. When the dough loses its wet look, turns off-white from its original pale yellow, and the edges just start to take on a very light brown color, the dough is set. If you have any doubts, carefully (the dough is hot) touch the side of the shell to make sure that the crust is firm. If you remove the pie weights too soon, the

FOR A DOUBLE-CRUST PIE

1. Refrigerate pie plate with dough while preparing filling. Place filling into shell. Roll out the second piece of dough and use a bench scraper to wrap the dough around the rolling pin.

2. Unroll the dough over the filled pie, making sure to center the piece of dough on the pie plate.

3. Use kitchen scissors to trim the overhanging edges of the top and bottom crusts to about 1/2 inch.

4. For a neat edge that stays sealed, press the edges of the top and bottom crusts together. The folded edge should be flush with the lip of the pie plate.

5. Finish the formation of the double crust by pressing the edges with a fork or fluting them (as shown) to seal well.

6. Use a sharp knife to cut vents in the top crust.

FOR A LATTICE-TOP PIE

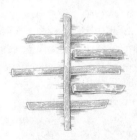

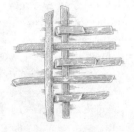

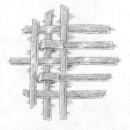

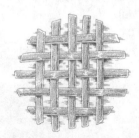

1. Refrigerate pie plate with bottom crust. Prepare filling. Roll out top crust, but cut it into ten strips, each 1/2 inch wide. Lay five strips horizontally across piece of waxed paper. Fold second and fourth strips in half and place a strip of dough in center, at right angles to the other strips.

2. Unfold the second and fourth strips so they lie on top of the vertical strip. Fold back the first, third, and fifth horizontal strips. Position a second strip of dough vertically, next to first vertical strip.

3. Unfold the first, third, and fifth strips. Fold back the second and fourth strips and add a third vertical strip of dough. Unfold the strips.

4. Repeat this process on the other side, alternating folds and adding two more strips of dough (you will have a total of ten, five running each way). Slide the lattice onto a filled pie shell. Trim off the excess lattice ends, fold the rim of the shell up and over the lattice strips, and crimp.

dough sides will slip down, ruining the pie shell.

For the second stage, the foil and weights are removed, and the baking continues. At this point, if you are going to fill the pie shell and then bake it again, as for pumpkin or pecan pie or quiches, you should bake it until it is just lightly browned, about 9 minutes. Pie shells destined for fillings that require little or no further cooking, such as cream and lemon meringue pies, should be baked for about 15 minutes.

American Pie Dough for Prebaked Pie Shell

FOR A SINGLE-CRUST 9-INCH PIE

See page 482 for more information about rolling out the dough.

1¼	cups all-purpose flour, plus extra for dusting dough and work surface
½	teaspoon salt
1	tablespoon sugar
4	tablespoons unsalted butter, chilled, cut into ¼-inch pieces
3	tablespoons all-vegetable shortening, chilled
4–5	tablespoons ice water

1. Pulse flour, salt, and sugar in workbowl of food processor fitted with steel blade. Scatter butter pieces over flour mixture, tossing to coat with flour. Cut butter into flour with five 1-second pulses. Add shortening and continue cutting in until flour is pale yellow and resembles coarse cornmeal, with butter bits no larger than small peas, about four more 1-second pulses. Turn mixture into medium bowl.

2. Sprinkle 4 tablespoons ice water over mixture. With blade of rubber spatula, use folding motion to mix. Press down on mixture with broad side of spatula until dough sticks together, adding up to 1 tablespoon more ice water if it will not come together. Shape dough into ball, squeezing two or three times with hands until cohesive, then flatten into 4-inch-wide disk. Dust lightly with flour, wrap in plastic, and refrigerate at least 30 minutes, or up to 2 days, before rolling.

3. Remove dough from refrigerator; let stand at room temperature to soften slightly, about 10 minutes if dough has chilled for 30 minutes, about 20 minutes if it has chilled overnight. (The dough should be pliable. Use your hands to squeeze the dough; if you can squeeze it without applying too much pressure, it is ready to roll.) Roll dough on lightly floured work surface to a 12-inch disk about ⅛ inch thick. Fold dough in quarters, then place dough point in center of pie pan. Unfold dough.

4. Working around circumference of pan, press dough carefully into pan by gently lifting dough edges with one hand while pressing around pan bottom with other hand. Trim edge to ½ inch beyond pan lip. Tuck this rim of dough underneath itself so that folded edge is about ¼ inch beyond pan lip; flute dough in your own fashion. Refrigerate pie shell for 40 minutes and then freeze for 20 minutes.

5. Meanwhile, adjust oven rack to middle position and heat oven to 375 degrees. Press doubled 12-inch square of aluminum foil inside dough shell; evenly distribute 1 cup or 12 ounces ceramic or metal pie weights over foil. Bake, leaving foil and weights in place until dough dries out, about 17 minutes. Carefully remove foil and weights by gathering sides of foil and pulling up and out. For partially baked crust, continue baking until lightly golden brown, about 9 minutes more; for fully baked crust, continue baking until deep golden brown, about 15 minutes more. Transfer to wire rack to cool as directed in individual recipes.

➤ VARIATION

Prebaked Pie Dough Coated with Graham Cracker Crumbs

Custard fillings, such as those used in lemon meringue pie and cream pies, are tough on crisp crusts. After much experimentation, we found that rolling out the pie dough in graham cracker crumbs promotes browning and crisps the crust. It also adds a wonderful graham flavor that complements the lemon and cream pie fillings without masking the character of the dough itself.

Follow recipe for American Pie Dough for Prebaked Pie Shell, sprinkling work surface when rolling out dough with 2 tablespoons graham cracker crumbs. Sprinkle more crumbs over dough itself. Continue sprinkling additional crumbs underneath and on top of dough as it is rolled, making sure to coat dough heavily with crumbs. You will use a total of about ½ cup crumbs. Fit graham-cracker-coated dough into pie plate as directed and bake fully.

Some flaky pie crust recipes call for an egg, which adds structure, color, and flavor. We discovered that a whole egg or just a yolk also dramatically increases the amount of ballooning, that is, the crust puffing up all over. Here is why it happens.

When you bake a traditional pie pastry without egg, moisture from the water and butter vaporizes and forms steam. As the steam rises and expands, it slightly separates the dough into the delicate, flaky layers desired for a good pie crust. Add egg to this finely balanced equation for flakiness, though, and you get too much lifting power.

Like baking soda, eggs contain a natural leavening known as bicarbonate. Heat causes bicarbonate to break down into water vapor and carbon dioxide, the latter of which contributes to the exaggerated ballooning effect. The ballooning effect is compounded by the coagulation of the egg's protein as it cooks. This creates a tougher pastry that prevents the steam and carbon dioxide from escaping; instead they stretch the pastry, causing ballooning. In essence, a good flaky crust results from a controlled amount of puffing. In the case of an egg-based pie pastry dough, however, the effect is exaggerated, and the results are unwelcome, unless a richer, eggier crust is desired for flavor reasons.

Classic Apple Pie

COOKS WHO SLATHER THE APPLES WITH cinnamon, sugar, and a starchy thickener do themselves and the apples a disservice, so we set out to make a pie in which the apples shine through. We started by examining the choice of apples for the filling. We tested the nine best-selling apples, figuring that we wanted a recipe that would work with apples commonly available in supermarkets throughout the year.

We determined that Granny Smith and McIntosh both have excellent qualities; the former is tart with good texture and the latter has excellent flavor. But each of them also has drawbacks. A pie made with just Grannies was too sour and a bit dull in flavor, while an all-McIntosh pie was too soft, more like applesauce than apple pie. A pie made with both varieties, however, was outstanding. The Grannies hold up well during cooking, the Macs add flavor, and the mushy texture of the Macs becomes a virtue in this setting, providing a nice base for the harder Grannies and soaking up some of the juice.

If you are making this pie during the fall apple season, when many local varieties may be available, follow the recipe using all Macoun, Royal Gala, Empire, Winesap, Rhode Island Greening, or Cortland apples. Unlike the Granny Smith, these are well-balanced apples that work well on their own without thickeners or the addition of McIntosh.

We have always used butter in our pies. In fact, we used to use up to six tablespoons in a deep dish pie, cutting this back to a more modest two tablespoons over the years. But when we taste-tested pies with and without butter, the leaner pies won hands down. Butter simply dulls the fresh taste of apples. Lemon juice, however, is absolutely crucial to a good apple pie. With a proper balance of sweet and tart, a good apple pie tastes like a crisp October morning rather than a muggy August afternoon. In the end, we settled on 1½ tablespoons of lemon juice and one teaspoon of zest.

Even a cursory review of apple pie recipes reveals a wide range of preferences for thickeners, with flour, tapioca, and cornstarch being the most common. We did try flour and tapioca and found that they overthickened the pie. A bit of tart, thin juice gives the pie a breath of the orchard, whereas a thick, syrupy texture is dull. In the end, we prefer not to thicken the filling for our apple pie.

Many cookbooks claim that letting apples sit in a bowl with the sugar, lemon juice, and spices, otherwise known as macerating, is key in developing flavors and juice. We found, however, that this simply caused the apples to dry out, making them rubbery and unpleasant. In addition, the apples themselves lose flavor, having exuded all of their fruitiness into the juice. So macerating, a common step in apple pie making, was clearly out.

In many apple pies, the top crust sets up quickly, leaving an air space between it and the apples, which reduce in volume as they cook. With our crust recipe, however, this is not an issue. Sufficient shortening is cut into the flour so that the crust sinks down onto the apples as they cook. We did notice, however, that this high ratio of shortening produces a very flaky crust, one that is not easily cut into perfect slices. In addition, because there is still a fair amount of juice, which we find essential for good flavor, the filling may spread slightly once the pie is cut into individual slices.

Apple Pie

SERVES 8

For more detailed instructions on rolling out the pie dough, see page 482. The pie is best eaten when cooled almost to room temperature, or even the next day.

1	recipe American Pie Dough for Fruit Pies (page 481)
2	pounds Granny Smith apples (4 medium)
2	pounds McIntosh apples (4 medium)
¾	cup plus 1 tablespoon sugar
1½	tablespoons juice and 1 teaspoon zest from one medium lemon
¼	teaspoon salt
¼	teaspoon ground nutmeg
¼	teaspoon ground cinnamon
⅛	teaspoon ground allspice
1	egg white, beaten lightly

1. Prepare and shape dough into two disks as directed. Refrigerate until needed.

2. Remove one piece of dough from refrigerator. If stiff and very cold, let stand until dough is cool but malleable. Adjust oven rack to center position and heat oven to 425 degrees.

3. Roll one dough disk on a lightly floured surface into a 12-inch circle. Fold dough in quarters, then place dough point in center of 9-inch Pyrex regular or deep dish pie pan. Unfold dough.

4. Gently press dough into sides of pan, leaving portion that overhangs lip of pie plate in place. Refrigerate while preparing fruit.

5. Peel, core, and cut apples into ½- to ¾-inch slices and toss with ¾ cup sugar, lemon juice and zest, salt, and spices. Turn fruit mixture, including juices, into chilled pie shell and mound slightly in center.

6. Roll out second dough disk and place over filling. Trim top and bottom edges to ½ inch beyond pan lip. Tuck this rim of dough underneath itself so

---

EQUIPMENT: Tools for Preparing Apples

As we sliced our way through more than 100 pounds of apples en route to developing these apple pie recipes, the easiest way to peel, core, and slice apples became a hotly debated subject. We began to wonder about all those kitchen gadgets designed to help with some or all phases of apple preparation. Glancing through some catalogs, we came across apple corers, corer/slicers, and a fancy crank-operated gizmo that peels, cores, and slices in a single motion. In addition, we found small paring knives with special curved blades, called bird's beak knives, specifically designed for peeling round fruits. We decided to give them all a try.

None of us were fans of the apple corer, which handles only one step of the peeling, coring, and slicing process and does not perform even that task well. Most corers have a diameter between three-quarters and seven-eighths of an inch (ours was three-quarters), which is too small to consistently remove all of the seeds and the seed cavity.

The next gadget we tried was the corer/slicer, which is designed to accomplish two steps of the apple prep process. After peeling the apple, you plunge the corer/slicer down through the fruit to core and slice it. However, we had the same problem with bits of the seed cavity being left in the flesh, and we were stuck with thicker slices than we wanted.

Several companies market crank-operated apple paring machines that handle all three parts of the job. After the machine

is attached to a table or counter, you spear an apple on a three-pronged fork, which is attached to a rod that you turn with the crank. As the handle is turned, the apple moves forward, coming into contact with a peeling blade mounted on a spring-loaded arm. This allows the blade to adjust to the contours of the apple as it moves past. The apple then passes by a second blade that both cores and slices.

While it was something of an improvement, this machine didn't wow us. It works best with very hard, fresh fruit. Some of our Macs were less than perfectly firm, and the peeling blade slid right over the skin, failing to do its job. When the peeling blade did work well on a firm Granny Smith, it showered us with apple juice as it peeled.

We then went back to the tried-and-true method, using a paring knife. We tested the straight-edged paring knife against the curved blade bird's beak model, but none of the testers found the bird's beak to be significantly easier to use or more effective.

Yet the debate was still not settled. Those of us on staff who were trained in formal cooking programs all learned to quarter the apple first and then peel, core, and slice each quarter separately. Others among us peel the apple intact, spiraling down from top to bottom, then quarter, core, and slice. After some practice with the spiral peeling method, even the trained cooks among us converted, finding it easier and quicker to peel the apple whole, then proceed.

---

that folded edge is flush with pan lip. Flute edging or press with fork tines to seal. Cut four slits on dough top. If pie dough is very soft, place in freezer for 10 minutes. Brush egg white onto top of crust and sprinkle evenly with remaining 1 tablespoon sugar.

7. Bake until top crust is golden, about 25 minutes. Reduce oven temperature to 375 degrees; continue baking until juices bubble and crust is deep golden brown, 30 to 35 minutes longer.

8. Transfer pie to wire rack; cool to almost room temperature, at least 4 hours.

➤ VARIATIONS

Apple Pie with Crystallized Ginger
Follow recipe for Apple Pie, adding 3 tablespoons chopped crystallized ginger to apple mixture.

Apple Pie with Dried Fruit
Macerate 1 cup raisins, dried sweet cherries, or dried cranberries in the lemon juice and 1 tablespoon Apple Jack, brandy, or cognac. Follow recipe for Apple Pie, adding macerated dried fruit and liquid to apple mixture.

Apple Pie with Fresh Cranberries
Follow recipe for Apple Pie, increasing sugar to 1 cup and adding 1 cup fresh or frozen cranberries to apple mixture.

Do-Ahead Fresh-Baked Apple Pie
We have been asked many times about whether an unbaked pie could be frozen and then baked days or weeks later. We tried this after two weeks and six weeks. The two-week pie was flatter than the freshly baked version, the flavor was a bit muted, and the apples were slightly on the spongy side. Nevertheless, we all felt that the results were good, a reasonable sacrifice in the name of convenience. However, the pie frozen for six weeks was a disaster, resulting in soft, foamy apples and a lackluster, greasy crust.

Follow recipe for Apple Pie through step 6, but do not brush with egg or sprinkle with sugar. Place pie on baking sheet and freeze for two to three hours, then cover it with a double layer of plastic wrap, and return it to the freezer for no more than two weeks. To bake, remove the pie from the freezer, brush it with the egg wash, sprinkle with sugar, and place directly into a preheated oven. After baking it for the usual 55 minutes, reduce the oven to 325 degrees, cover the pie with foil so as not to overcook the crust, and bake for an additional 20 to 25 minutes.

SUMMER FRUIT PIE
SUMMER FRUIT PIES TRADITIONALLY RELY on the use of flour or cornstarch to thicken the fresh blueberry, cherry, peach, or strawberry-rhubarb filling. However, we find these thickeners to be problematic. Cornstarch thickens well, but at a price: In our tests, it yielded dull fruit, lacking in bright flavor and noticeably less acid. As a result, the mixture tasted sweeter and heavier.

The flour resulted in fruit that was similarly unsatisfying in appearance and taste, and it also had another failing: Two tablespoons was not enough to

SCIENCE: How Starches Work

In its natural state, starch exists in the form of essentially insoluble granules. These granules only begin to absorb water with the introduction of energy in the form of heat. As the water begins to seep into the granules, they swell and begin to bump into one another, so that the mixture thickens. The solution reaches its thickest point just past the gelatinization stage, which occurs between 175 and 205 degrees. At this point, the granules begin to leak amylose and amylopectin starches into the liquid. These molecules, particularly the long amylose chains, form a web that traps the swollen granules, thickening the liquid even further.

At a temperature somewhere near boiling, however, the granules have swollen to their maximum size and burst open. This bursting has two consequences: It allows most of the starch molecules to escape, and it also forces the water that had been absorbed by the granules to escape back into the mixture. As a result, the mixture begins to thin out again. Obviously, this is not desirable, so manufacturers further process starches, such as Minute Tapioca, to keep the granules from bursting. This also provides a creamier, more pleasant texture during thickening. The processing also makes starches less vulnerable to the work of acids such as lemon juice, which can impair thickening properties.

firm up the fruit well. To give flour another chance, we ran a test using four tablespoons. This time, the fruit was gummy and almost inedible. As it turns out, this is because flour, unlike the other thickeners, contains proteins and other components as well as starch. As a result, it takes at least twice as much flour by volume to create the same degree of thickening as cornstarch. This amount of flour will adversely affect your cherry or blueberry pie—you can taste it.

By contrast, the samples of fruit thickened with the root starches, arrowroot and tapioca, were clear and bright in appearance, and the flavor of the fruit came through clearly. Of the two, tapioca thickens a little better and is much cheaper, so it is our favorite.

During additional testing we found that the amount of tapioca should be varied depending on the juiciness of the berries. If you like a juicier pie, three tablespoons of tapioca is an adequate amount for six cups of fresh blueberries, for example. If you like a really firm pie with no juices, five tablespoons is the correct amount.

Mixing the fruit and tapioca together works fine if placing a regular top crust on the pie. However, when we made a lattice-top pie, we found that the tapioca on top of the fruit baked into hard bits that once in our mouths felt like Tic-Tacs. For an open or lattice-top pie, we suggest mixing all of the tapioca with three-quarters of the fruit, filling the pie, and then adding the balance of the fruit on top.

Summer Fruit Pie

SERVES 8

For more detailed instructions on rolling out the pie dough, see page 482.

1	recipe American Pie Dough for Fruit Pies (page 481)
1	recipe from Fillings for Summer Fruit Pies (see table below)
2	tablespoons unsalted butter, cut into small pieces

Fillings for Summer Fruit Pies

Combine the ingredients for a specific filling in a large bowl for use in the summer fruit pie recipe above. Allow the fruit mixture to macerate for fifteen minutes before scraping the mixture into the pie plate. You may use frozen blueberries or cherries in this recipe (frozen peaches and strawberries are quite watery), measuring the fruit when frozen but letting it thaw before making the filling. If you don't follow this procedure, you run the risk of partially cooked fruit and undissolved tapioca.

FRUIT	QUANTITY	SUGAR	TAPIOCA	FLAVORINGS
Blueberries	3 pints (6 cups) rinsed and picked over (or 36 ounces frozen)	¾ to 1 cup	3 to 4 tablespoons	2 teaspoons lemon juice 1 teaspoon grated lemon zest ¼ teaspoon ground allspice Pinch grated nutmeg
Cherries	6 cups (about 3 pounds) stemmed and pitted (or 36 ounces frozen)	¾ to 1 cup (use higher amount with sour cherries)	3 to 4 tablespoons (use higher amount with sour cherries)	2 teaspoons lemon juice 1 teaspoon grated lemon zest ⅛ teaspoon ground allspice ⅛ teaspoon ground cinnamon ⅛ teaspoon almond extract 1 tablespoon brandy
Peaches	6 cups (about 3 pounds) peeled, pitted, and sliced	¼ to ½ cup granulated sugar with ½ cup brown sugar	3 to 4 tablespoons	2 teaspoons lemon juice 1 teaspoon grated lemon zest ¼ teaspoon ground allspice ¼ teaspoon grated nutmeg ¼ teaspoon salt 1 tablespoon minced crystallized ginger
Strawberry-Rhubarb	3 cups hulled and sliced strawberries with 3 cups rhubarb, trimmed and cut into 1-inch pieces	¾ to 1 cup	3 to 4 tablespoons	2 teaspoons lemon juice 1 tablespoon grated orange zest ¼ teaspoon vanilla extract

1. Prepare and shape dough into two disks as directed. Refrigerate until needed.

2. Remove one piece of dough from refrigerator. If stiff and very cold, let stand until dough is cool but malleable. Adjust oven rack to center position and heat oven to 400 degrees.

3. Roll one dough disk on a lightly floured surface into a 12-inch circle. Fold dough in quarters, then place dough point in center of 9-inch Pyrex regular or deep dish pie pan. Unfold dough.

4. Gently press dough into sides of pan, leaving portion that overhangs lip of pie plate in place.

5. Prepare fruit filling and let stand for 15 minutes. Turn fruit mixture, including juices, into pie shell. Scatter butter pieces over fruit. Refrigerate until ready to top with remaining dough.

6. Roll out second dough disk and place over filling. Trim top and bottom edges to ½ inch beyond pan lip. Tuck this rim of dough underneath itself so that folded edge is flush with pan lip. Flute edging or press with fork tines to seal. Cut four slits on dough top. If pie dough is very soft, place in freezer for 10 minutes before baking.

7. Place pie on baking sheet to catch any drips; bake until top crust is golden, 20 to 25 minutes. Reduce oven temperature to 350 degrees and continue to bake until juices bubble and crust is golden brown, 30 to 40 minutes longer.

8. Transfer pie to wire rack; let cool to almost room temperature so juices have time to thicken, from 1 to 2 hours. Serve that day.

INGREDIENTS: Tapioca

Cornstarch is made from corn, rice starch from rice, wheat starch from wheat, and arrowroot from the root of the arrowroot plant. But the source of tapioca, our favorite thickener for summer fruit pies, is not quite so obvious: It comes from the root of the cassava plant. Also called manioc, this plant is grown throughout most of the tropical world and is harvested when its roots are about 6 to 12 inches long. The starchy root can be boiled and eaten, and in many countries it takes the place of rice or potatoes in the diet.

To make what we know as tapioca, the starch is separated from the cellulose in the root. Pearl tapioca is made from tapioca starch that is heated into pearls. To create Minute Tapioca, the starch is partially gelatinized and then pasted together into pellets to improve its thickening powers.

PUMPKIN PIE

A PUMPKIN PIE IS NO MORE THAN A VARIATION on custard pie, and it presents the baker with the same challenge—making the crust crisp while developing a filling that is firm but still tender. After baking countless pumpkin pies, we found it necessary to take a threefold approach.

First, we began baking our crusts almost completely before filling them; that way we knew they started out crisp. Next, we made sure that both shell and filling were hot when we assembled the pie, so the custard could begin to firm up almost immediately rather than soaking into the pastry. Finally, we baked the pie quickly, in the bottom of the oven, where the bottom of the crust is exposed to the most intense heat. (Baking in the top of the oven exposes the rim of the crust to the most intense heat, while baking in the middle fails to expose the crust to intense heat from any source.)

Because it sets the filling quickly, high oven heat works to the advantage of all custard pies; the quicker the pie gets out of the oven, the less likely the filling is to soak into the crust and make it soggy. But baking at high heat also has its perils—when overbaked, custard will curdle, becoming grainy and watery. No matter what the heat level, however, curdling can be averted if the pie is taken out of the oven immediately once the center thickens to the point where it no longer sloshes but instead wiggles like gelatin when the pan is gently shaken. Residual heat will finish the cooking outside the oven. Because the presence of the pumpkin dilutes the egg proteins and therefore interferes with curdling, you have a window of about five minutes between "set" and "curdled," considerably longer than with most other custards.

Two other features of our recipe provide further insurance against curdling. First, because the filling is hot when it is put into the shell, the center cooks quickly; this means that the edges, which receive the most direct heat, are less likely to become overcooked. Second, as with many older recipes, this recipe calls for heavy cream as well as milk and a goodly quantity of sugar. These ingredients not only improve the flavor, but they also protect the texture, since both fat and sugar serve to block the curdling reaction.

Fresh pumpkin is so difficult to use that few modern cooks go down this road. Canned pumpkin is surprisingly good, and, given a little special treatment, it can be as tasty as fresh. One problem with canned pumpkin is its fibrous nature, which is easily corrected by pureeing it in a food processor. You can freshen the taste of canned pumpkin by cooking it with the sugar and spices before combining it with the custard ingredients. As the pumpkin simmers, you can actually smell the unwelcome canned odor give way to the sweet scent of fresh squash. This is a small but delightful culinary miracle.

Pumpkin Pie
SERVES 8

The key to this recipe is timing. Start preparing the filling when you put the pie shell in the oven. The pie may be served slightly warm, chilled, or at room temperature, which is our preference. The pie is fine by itself but much improved by a dollop of the brandied whipped cream.

1	recipe American Pie Dough for Prebaked Pie Shell (page 485), prepared through step 4
2	cups (16 ounces) plain canned pumpkin puree
1	cup packed dark brown sugar
2	teaspoons ground ginger
2	teaspoons ground cinnamon
1	teaspoon fresh grated nutmeg
1/4	teaspoon ground cloves
1/2	teaspoon salt
2/3	cup heavy cream
2/3	cup milk
4	large eggs

BRANDIED WHIPPED CREAM

1 1/3	cups heavy cream, chilled
2	tablespoons sugar
1	tablespoon brandy

1. Adjust oven rack to lower and middle positions and heat oven to 375 degrees. Partially bake pie shell on middle rack as directed in step 5 on page 485.

2. Meanwhile, process pumpkin puree, brown sugar, spices, and salt in a food processor fitted with steel blade for 1 minute. Transfer pumpkin mixture to 3-quart heavy-bottomed saucepan; bring it to a sputtering simmer over medium-high heat. Cook pumpkin, stirring constantly, until thick and shiny, about 5 minutes.

3. As soon as pie shell comes out of oven, increase oven temperature to 400 degrees. Whisk heavy cream and milk into pumpkin and bring to a bare simmer. Process eggs in food processor until whites and yolks are mixed, about 5 seconds. With motor running, slowly pour about half of hot pumpkin mixture through feed tube. Stop machine and scrape in remaining pumpkin. Process 30 seconds longer.

4. Immediately pour warm filling into hot pie shell. (Ladle any excess filling into pie after it has baked for 5 minutes or so—by this time filling will have settled.) Bake pie on lower rack until filling is puffed, dry-looking, and lightly cracked around edges, and center wiggles like gelatin when pie is gently shaken, about 25 minutes. Cool on a wire rack for at least 1 hour.

5. FOR THE WHIPPED CREAM: When ready to serve the pie, beat cream and sugar in electric mixer at medium speed to soft peaks; add brandy. Beat to stiff peaks. Accompany each wedge of pie with a dollop of whipped cream.

PECAN PIE

PECAN PIE TYPICALLY PRESENTS A COUPLE of problems. First, this pie is often too sweet, both in an absolute sense and in relation to its other flavors, which are overwhelmed by the sugariness. This problem is easily remedied by lowering the amount of sugar.

The other major complaint has to do with texture. Pecan pies too often turn out to be curdly and separated, and the weepy filling turns the bottom crust soggy and leathery. The fact that the undercrust usually seems underbaked to begin with doesn't help matters.

Pecan pie should be wonderfully soft and smooth, almost like a cream pie. Taking the pie out of the oven before it is completely set helps achieve this texture. The pie continues to cook after being removed from the oven, as heat travels from the edges to the middle by conduction. And since pecan pies are composed largely of sugar and butter, cooling serves to make them still more solid.

A hot oven is a disaster with pecan pie. At 375 degrees and above, the edges of the filling solidified before the center had even thickened. A moderate oven (325 to 350 degrees) is better, but a slow oven

(250 to 300 degrees) turned out to be the best—yielding, but with a nicely thickened center without any hardened edges.

There was a problem, however. Pies baked at very low temperatures took so long to firm up that the crusts turned soggy, even when the shells were thoroughly prebaked. Furthermore, the filling tended to separate into a jellylike layer on the bottom with a frothy cap on top. At this point, we tried adding hot filling to the crust, which was also hot. When we tried this, we cut the baking time by close to half and fixed the problems of soggy crust and separated filling.

We tested pies made with whole pecan halves, chopped pecans, and a combination of chopped and whole nuts. We had no problem deciding our preference. We found whole pecans too much of a mouthful, and we had difficulty cutting through them with a fork as we consumed a slice. Chopped nuts are easier to slice through and eat.

Toasting the nuts beforehand is a major improvement. We toasted the nuts in the oven while it was preheating in preparation for baking the crust. Toasting takes about seven minutes, but the nuts should be watched carefully and stirred from time to time to prevent burning. Be sure to let them cool to lukewarm before chopping them, or they will crumble. Use a knife rather than a food processor, which tends to cut the nuts too fine.

Pecan Pie

SERVES 8

If you want warm pie, cool the pie thoroughly so that it sets completely, then warm it in a 250-degree oven for about 15 minutes and slice.

I	recipe American Pie Dough for Prebaked Pie Shell (page 485), prepared through step 4
6	tablespoons unsalted butter, cut into 1-inch pieces
I	cup packed dark brown sugar
½	teaspoon salt
3	large eggs
¾	cup light corn syrup
I	tablespoon vanilla extract
2	cups pecans (8 ounces), toasted and chopped into small pieces

1. Adjust oven rack to middle position and heat oven to 375 degrees. Partially bake pie shell as directed in step 5 on page 485.

2. Meanwhile, melt butter in medium heatproof bowl set in skillet of water maintained at just below simmer. Remove bowl from skillet; mix in sugar and salt with wooden spoon until butter is absorbed. Beat in eggs, then corn syrup and vanilla. Return bowl to hot water; stir until mixture is shiny and hot to the touch, about 130 degrees. Remove from heat; stir in pecans.

3. As soon as pie shell comes out of oven, decrease oven temperature to 275 degrees. Pour pecan mixture into hot pie shell.

4. Bake until center feels set yet soft, like gelatin, when gently pressed, 50 to 60 minutes. Transfer pie to rack; let cool completely, at least 4 hours. Serve pie at room temperature or warm, with lightly sweetened whipped cream or vanilla ice cream.

➤ VARIATIONS
Triple Chocolate Chunk Pecan Pie

I	recipe American Pie Dough for Prebaked Pie Shell (page 485), prepared through step 4
3	tablespoons unsalted butter, cut into 1-inch pieces
¾	cup packed dark brown sugar
½	teaspoon salt
2	large eggs
½	cup light corn syrup
I	teaspoon vanilla extract
I	cup pecans (4 ounces), toasted and chopped into small pieces
2	ounces each semisweet, milk, and white chocolate, cut into ¼-inch pieces

1. Adjust oven rack to middle position and heat oven to 375 degrees. Partially bake pie shell as directed in step 5 on page 485.

2. Meanwhile, melt butter in medium heatproof bowl set in skillet of water maintained at just below simmer. Remove bowl from skillet; mix in sugar and salt with wooden spoon until butter is absorbed. Beat in eggs, then corn syrup and vanilla. Return bowl to hot water; stir until mixture is shiny and hot to the touch, about 130 degrees. Remove from heat; stir in pecans.

3. As soon as pie shell comes out of oven, decrease

oven temperature to 275 degrees. Pour pecan mixture into hot pie shell. Scatter chocolate pieces over filling. Press pieces into filling with back of spoon.

4. Bake until center feels set yet soft, like gelatin, when gently pressed, 55 to 65 minutes. Transfer pie to rack; let cool completely, at least 4 hours. Serve pie at room temperature or warm, with lightly sweetened whipped cream or vanilla ice cream.

Maple Pecan Pie

More liquid than corn syrup, maple syrup yields a softer, more custardlike pie. Toasted walnuts can be substituted for pecans.

I	recipe American Pie Dough for Prebaked Pie Shell (page 485), prepared through step 4
4	tablespoons unsalted butter, cut into 1-inch pieces
½	cup sugar
½	teaspoon salt
3	large eggs
I	cup maple syrup
I ½	cups pecans (6 ounces), toasted and chopped into small pieces

1. Adjust oven rack to middle position and heat oven to 375 degrees. Partially bake pie shell as directed in step 5 on page 485.

2. Meanwhile, melt butter in medium heatproof bowl set in skillet of water maintained at just below simmer. Remove bowl from skillet; mix in sugar and salt with wooden spoon until butter is absorbed. Beat in eggs, then maple syrup. Return bowl to hot water; stir until mixture is shiny and hot to the touch, about 130 degrees. Remove from heat; stir in pecans.

3. As soon as pie shell comes out of oven, decrease oven temperature to 275 degrees. Pour pecan mixture into hot pie shell.

4. Bake until center feels set yet soft, like gelatin, when gently pressed, 50 to 60 minutes. Transfer pie to rack; let cool completely, at least 4 hours. Serve pie at room temperature or warm, with lightly sweetened whipped cream or vanilla ice cream.

LEMON MERINGUE PIE

THE IDEAL LEMON MERINGUE PIE HAS A RICH filling that balances the airy meringue without detracting from the flavor of lemon. The lemon filling should be soft but not runny, firm enough to cut but not stiff and gelatinous. Finally, the meringue itself should not break down and puddle on the bottom or "weep" on top—not even on rainy days.

The ingredients in lemon meringue pie have remained constant for some time: sugar, water (or sometimes milk), cornstarch (sometimes mixed with flour), egg yolks, lemon juice (and usually zest), and a little butter. To our tastes, the straightforward lemon flavor of the water-based filling is pleasant, but it is also one-dimensional, lacking depth. Milk, however, subdues the lemon flavor. The solution is to rely primarily on water and a lot egg yolks (we use six rather than the more conventional three), eliminating the milk altogether. This has another benefit: The addition of egg yolks allows you to cut back on both sugar (which acts as a softener at a certain level) and cornstarch and still achieve a firm yet tender filling.

The meringue is much more tricky. On any given day it can shrink, bead, puddle, deflate, burn, sweat, break down, or turn rubbery. Most cookbooks don't even attempt to deal with the problems of meringue. They follow the standard recipe—granulated sugar and cream of tartar beaten slowly into the egg whites—assuming, apparently, that there is no way around the flaws. After making 30-something lemon meringue pies, we're not sure we blame anyone for skirting the issue. For as easy as it was to figure out the perfect lemon filling, the meringue remains, finally, only a manageable mystery.

The puddling underneath the meringue is from undercooking. Undercooked whites break down and return to their liquid state. The beading on top of the pie is from overcooking. This near-the-surface overcooking of the meringue causes the proteins in the egg white to coagulate, squeezing out moisture, which then surfaces as tears or beads. This double dilemma might seem insurmountable, but we hit upon a solution.

If the filling is piping hot when the meringue is applied, the underside of the meringue will not undercook; if the oven temperature is relatively low, the top of the meringue won't overcook. Baking the pie in a relatively cool oven also produces the best-looking, most evenly browned meringue. To further stabilize the meringue, we like to beat in a tiny bit of cornstarch; if you do this, the meringue will not weep, even on hot, humid days.

Lemon Meringue Pie
SERVES 8

As soon as the filling is made, cover it with plastic wrap to keep it hot and then start working on the meringue topping. You want to add hot filling to the pie shell, apply the meringue topping, and then quickly get the pie into the oven.

LEMON FILLING

1	cup sugar
¼	cup cornstarch
⅛	teaspoon salt
1½	cups cold water
6	large egg yolks
1	tablespoon grated zest and ½ cup juice from 2 or 3 lemons
2	tablespoons unsalted butter

MERINGUE TOPPING

1	tablespoon cornstarch
⅓	cup water
¼	teaspoon cream of tartar
½	cup sugar
4	large egg whites
½	teaspoon vanilla extract

1	recipe Prebaked Pie Dough Coated with Graham Cracker Crumbs (page 485), fully baked and cooled completely.

1. **FOR THE FILLING:** Mix sugar, cornstarch, salt, and water in a large, nonreactive saucepan. Bring mixture to simmer over medium heat, whisking occasionally at beginning of the process and more frequently as mixture begins to thicken. When mixture starts to simmer and turn translucent, whisk in egg yolks, two at a time. Whisk in zest, then lemon juice, and finally butter. Bring mixture to a good simmer, whisking constantly. Remove from heat,

place plastic wrap directly on surface of filling to keep hot and prevent skin from forming.

2. **FOR THE MERINGUE:** Mix cornstarch with water in small saucepan; bring to simmer, whisking occasionally at beginning and more frequently as mixture thickens. When mixture starts to simmer and turn translucent, remove from heat. Let cool while beating egg whites.

3. Heat oven to 325 degrees. Mix cream of tartar and sugar together. Beat egg whites and vanilla until frothy. Beat in sugar mixture, 1 tablespoon at a time, until sugar is incorporated and mixture forms soft peaks. Add cornstarch mixture, 1 tablespoon at a time; continue to beat meringue to stiff peaks. Remove plastic from lemon filling and return to very low heat during last minute or so of beating meringue (to ensure filling is hot).

4. Pour hot filling into pie shell. Using a rubber spatula, immediately distribute meringue evenly around edge and then center of pie to keep it from sinking into filling (see figure 1, below). Make sure meringue attaches to pie crust to prevent shrinking (see figure 2). Use back of spoon to create peaks all over meringue. Bake pie until meringue is golden brown, about 20 minutes. Transfer to wire rack and cool to room temperature. Serve that day.

APPLYING A MERINGUE TOPPING

1. Start by placing dabs of meringue evenly around the edge of the pie. Once the edge of the pie is covered with meringue, fill in the center of the pie with the remaining meringue.

2. Use a rubber spatula to anchor the meringue to the edge of the crust or it may pull away and shrink in the oven.

KEY LIME PIE

THE STANDARD RECIPE FOR CONDENSED MILK Key lime pie is incredibly short and simple: beat four egg yolks, add a 14-ounce can of sweetened condensed milk, and then stir in one-half cup of lime juice and a tablespoon of grated lime zest. Pour it all into a graham cracker crust and chill it until firm, about two hours. Top the pie with sweetened whipped cream and serve.

It would be lovely if this recipe worked, but we found that it doesn't. Although the filling does set firm enough to yield clean-cut slices, it has a loose, "slurpy" consistency. We tried to fix the consistency by beating the yolks until thick, as some recipes direct, but this did not help. Nor did it help to dribble in the lime juice rather than adding it all at once, as other recipes suggest. We also made the filling with only two yolks and with no yolks at all (such "eggless" versions of the recipe do exist), but this yielded even thinner fillings.

Still, the time spent mixing Key lime pie fillings in various ways was not a total loss. While in the heat of experimenting, we inadvertently threw the lime zest into a bowl in which we had already placed the egg yolks. When we whisked up the yolks, they turned green, and the whole filling ended up tinted a lovely shade of pale lime.

Having found the mix-and-chill method wanting, we decided to try baking the pie, as some recipes suggest. We used the same ingredients as we had before and simply baked the pie until the filling stiffened slightly, about 15 minutes in a moderate oven. The difference between the baked pie (which was really a custard) and the unbaked pie (which had merely been a clabber) was remarkable. The baked filling was thick, creamy, and unctuous, reminiscent of cream pie. It also tasted more pungent and complex than the raw fillings had, perhaps because the heat of the oven released the flavorful oils in the lime zest.

The filling is fairly tart and must be overset by whipped cream that has been generously sweetened. Since granulated sugar can cause graininess at high levels, we opt for confectioners' sugar in the whipped cream topping for this pie.

Key Lime Pie

SERVES 8

If you prefer, you can use the Prebaked Pie Dough Coated with Graham Cracker Crumbs (see page 485), but we like the simple graham cracker crust in this recipe.

LIME FILLING

- 4 teaspoons grated zest plus ½ cup strained juice from 3 to 4 limes
- 4 large egg yolks
- 1 14-ounce can sweetened condensed milk

GRAHAM CRACKER CRUST

- 11 full-size graham crackers, processed to fine crumbs (1¼ cups)
- 3 tablespoons granulated sugar
- 5 tablespoons unsalted butter, melted

WHIPPED CREAM TOPPING

- ¾ cup heavy cream, chilled
- ¼ cup confectioners' sugar
- ½ lime, sliced paper thin and dipped in sugar (optional)

INGREDIENTS: Limes

True Key limes, *Citrus aurantifolia*, have not been a significant commercial crop in this country since storms destroyed the Florida groves early in this century. However, a few growers have recently begun to revive the crop, and Key limes occasionally show up in supermarkets. Most food writers seem to like Key lime juice much better than Persian lime juice, but they give wildly divergent reasons for their preference. One book describes Key limes as "sourer and more complex" than their supermarket cousins. But another writer holds that Key limes differ from Persian limes in being more "mild" and "delicate."

We'd love to be able to say that Key lime juice made all the difference in the world, but it didn't. To our testers, it tasted pretty much the same as the juice of supermarket limes. Key limes are a nuisance to zest and squeeze, for they are thin-skinned, full of seeds, and generally little bigger than walnuts. You need only three or four Persian limes to make a Key lime pie, but you will need up to a dozen Key limes. So despite the name of the pie, we actually find the juice of Persian limes preferable as an ingredient.

1. FOR THE FILLING: Whisk zest and yolks in medium bowl until tinted light green, about 2 minutes. Beat in milk, then juice; set aside at room temperature to thicken.

2. FOR THE CRUST: Adjust oven rack to center position and heat oven to 325 degrees. Mix crumbs and sugar in medium bowl. Add butter; stir with fork until well blended. Scrape mixture into 9-inch pie pan; press crumbs over bottom and up sides of pan to form even crust. Bake until lightly browned and fragrant, about 15 minutes. Transfer pan to wire rack; cool to room temperature, about 20 minutes.

3. Pour lime filling into crust; bake until center is set, yet wiggly when jiggled, 15 to 17 minutes. Return pie to wire rack; cool to room temperature. Refrigerate until well chilled, at least 3 hours. (Can be covered with lightly oiled or oil-sprayed plastic wrap laid directly on filling and refrigerated up to 1 day.)

4. FOR THE WHIPPED CREAM: Up to 2 hours before serving, whip cream in medium bowl to very soft peaks. Adding confectioners' sugar 1 tablespoon at a time, continue whipping to just-stiff peaks. Decoratively pipe whipped cream over filling or spread evenly with rubber spatula. Garnish with optional sugared lime slices and serve.

➤ VARIATION

Key Lime Pie with Meringue Topping

We prefer to top Key lime pie with whipped cream, but meringue is another option.

Follow recipe for Key Lime Pie, replacing Whipped Cream Topping with Meringue Topping from recipe for Lemon Meringue Pie on page 494. Bake pie only 7 minutes, then apply meringue gently, first spreading a ring around the outer edge to attach the meringue to the crust, then filling in the center. Return pie to oven and bake 20 minutes more.

VANILLA CREAM PIE

CREAM PIE HAS ALMOST UNIVERSAL APPEAL, with enough flavoring options—vanilla, chocolate, banana, coconut, and butterscotch—to satisfy almost everyone. The key is to create a filling that is soft and creamy yet stiff enough to be cut cleanly. It's not as easy as it sounds.

In our tests, adding flour left us with a filling that was too soft. Gelatin made for a rubbery filling, and tapioca, which works well in fruit pies, produced a filling with the texture of stewed okra. Only cornstarch coupled with egg yolks (whole eggs yielded a grainy texture) gave us the proper results.

The dairy component is also vital. Cream is simply too rich for a pie that already contains butter and

---

SCIENCE: How Key Lime Pie Thickens

The extraordinarily high acid content of limes and the unique properties of sweetened condensed milk are responsible for the fact that lime pie filling will thicken without cooking.

The acid in the lime juice does its work by causing the proteins in both the egg yolks and the condensed milk to coil up and bond together. This effect is similar to that of heat. The same process can be observed in the Latin American dish seviche, in which raw fish is "cooked" simply by being pickled in lime juice.

But this process does not work well with just any kind of milk; it requires both the sweetness and the thickness of sweetened condensed milk. This canned product is made by boiling the moisture out of fresh milk and then adding sugar. Because the milk has been evaporated, or condensed, it is thick enough to stiffen into a sliceable filling when clabbered by the lime juice. The sugar, meanwhile, plays the crucial role of separating, or "greasing," the protein strands so that they do not bond too tightly. If they did, the result would be a grainy or curdled filling rather than a smooth and creamy one. Of course, a liquidy, curdly filling is exactly what one would get if one tried to use fresh milk instead of canned, because fresh milk lacks the crucial added sugar and is also much thinner.

We discovered that cream is not a viable substitute for sweetened condensed milk either. It does not curdle the way milk does because its fat, like the sugar in condensed milk, acts as a buffer to the lime juice. Cream is roughly 50 percent liquid, however, and thus it will only thicken, not stiffen, when clabbered.

eggs. Skim milk tastes thin and lacks the creamy texture we wanted. Both 2 percent and whole milk work well, but they are even better when combined with a bit of evaporated milk, which adds a rich, round, caramel flavor. The basic vanilla cream filling also benefits greatly from the use of a vanilla bean in place of extract.

When making a cream filling for a pie, some cooks heat the sugar, cornstarch, and milk to a simmer, gradually add some of this mixture to the yolks to stabilize them, and then add the stabilized yolks to the rest of the simmering milk. We found that this process, called tempering the eggs, is not necessary in this recipe. You can dump everything except the flavorings and butter into a saucepan and cook, stirring often, until the mixture begins to bubble. This method is simpler, and because the cornstarch prevents the eggs from curdling, it isn't that risky.

Developing a filling with great body as well as flavor is important, as is preventing that filling from turning the prebaked crust soggy. Unlike most pies, the filling does not bake in the crust. The moist, fluid filling is simply poured into the crust and chilled. We found two procedures that help to keep the crust crisp.

Coating the dough with graham cracker crumbs as it is rolled out produces an especially crisp, browned pie shell. It also helps to pour filling into the crust while the filling is warm but not quite hot. Hot filling keeps the crust crisp, but because it is still quite liquid when poured into the crust, it settles compactly and falls apart when sliced. Warm filling, having had a chance to set a bit, mounds when poured into the crust and slices beautifully. What's more, it won't make the crust soggy.

Whatever you do, don't wait until the filling has cooled to scrape it into the pie shell. Cooled filling turned soupy and moistened our once-crisp crust. You can't disturb the filling once the starch bonds have completely set. If you break the starch bonds, you destroy the filling's structure. Those who have tried stirring liqueur into a chilled pastry cream may have been confronted with similar results. When we stirred the cold filling to put it into the crust, we broke the starch bonds so that the filling went from stiff to runny. We learned a major lesson. You can cool the filling to warm, but once it has set, don't stir it.

Vanilla Cream Pie

SERVES 8

For this pie, warm (but not hot) filling is poured into a fully baked, cooled crust. The filled pie is then refrigerated until thoroughly chilled and topped with whipped cream.

CREAM FILLING

- ½ cup plus 2 tablespoons sugar
- ¼ cup cornstarch
- ⅛ teaspoon salt
- 5 large egg yolks, lightly beaten
- 2 cups 2 percent or whole milk
- ½ cup evaporated milk
- ½ vanilla bean, about 3 inches long, split lengthwise
- 2 tablespoons unsalted butter
- 1–2 teaspoons brandy
- 1 recipe Prebaked Pie Shell Coated with Graham Cracker Crumbs (page 485), fully baked and cooled completely

WHIPPED CREAM TOPPING

- 1 cup heavy cream, chilled
- 1 tablespoon sugar
- 1 teaspoon vanilla extract

1. FOR THE FILLING: Whisk sugar, cornstarch, and salt in medium saucepan. Add yolks, then immediately but gradually whisk in milk and evaporated milk. Drop in vanilla bean. Cook over medium heat, stirring frequently at first, then constantly, as mixture starts to thicken and begins to simmer, 8 to 10 minutes. Once mixture simmers, continue to cook, stirring constantly, for 1 minute longer. Remove pan from heat; whisk in butter and brandy. Remove vanilla bean, scrape out seeds, and whisk them back into filling.

2. Pour filling into shallow pan (another pie pan works well). Put plastic wrap directly over filling surface to prevent skin from forming; cool until warm, 20 to 30 minutes. Pour warm filling into pie shell and, once again, place sheet of plastic wrap directly over filling surface. Refrigerate pie until completely chilled, at least 3 hours.

3. FOR THE WHIPPED CREAM: Beat cream and sugar in electric mixer at medium speed to soft peaks; add vanilla. Continue to beat to barely stiff peaks. Spread

over filling and refrigerate pie until ready to serve.

➤ VARIATIONS

Chocolate Cream Pie

Follow recipe for Vanilla Cream Pie, omitting vanilla bean. Add 2 tablespoons unsweetened cocoa to cornstarch mixture and stir in 4 ounces good-quality semisweet or bittersweet chocolate and 1 teaspoon vanilla extract with butter and brandy.

Coconut Cream Pie

Adjust oven rack to lower-middle position and heat oven to 300 degrees. Scatter 1¼ cups sweetened flaked coconut in 9-inch square pan. Bake, stirring occasionally, until evenly golden brown, 20 to 25 minutes. Cool to room temperature. Follow recipe for Vanilla Cream Pie, stirring 1 cup of the coconut

---

INGREDIENTS: Evaporated Milk

As an ingredient, evaporated milk offers cooks a subtle, sweet flavor that can deepen the overall taste of many dishes. The process that yields evaporated milk has four parts.

First, pasteurized milk is "forewarmed," a process of heating the milk to about 200 degrees then cooling it to between 36 and 39 degrees. This procedure both softens the milk proteins and increases the stability of the concentrated product during the sterilization process to come.

Next, the milk is evaporated under a vacuum, reducing its water content by 60 percent. In step three, the milk is homogenized by forcing it through a tiny nozzle at very high pressure onto a hard surface, breaking the fat globules down to about one-quarter of their original size and dispersing them evenly throughout.

In the fourth step, heat sterilization, the evaporated milk takes on its telltale trait—a soft, flavorful note of caramel. The milk is poured into cans, sealed, and heated to almost 240 degrees, destroying any dangerous bacteria and stabilizing the product for an extended shelf life. The high temperature reached during this process, coupled with the greater than usual concentration of lactose (milk sugar), causes the sugar to undergo some browning, which imparts the delicate caramel sweetness.

Unopened cans of evaporated milk can be stored at a cool room temperature—for 9 months for the skimmed product and 12 months for the whole—but must be refrigerated and consumed within five to seven days once opened.

---

into filling once butter has melted. Continue with recipe, sprinkling remaining toasted coconut over whipped cream topping.

Banana Cream Pie

The safest and best place for the banana slices is sandwiched between two layers of filling. If sliced over the pie shell, the bananas tend to moisten the crust; if sliced over the filling top or mashed and folded into the filling, they turn brown faster.

Follow recipe for Vanilla Cream Pie, spooning half the warm filling into baked and cooled pie shell. Peel 2 medium bananas and slice them over filling. Top with remaining filling. Continue with recipe.

Butterscotch Cream Pie

Whisking the milk slowly into the brown sugar mixture keeps the sugar from lumping. Don't worry if the sugar does lump—it will dissolve as the milk heats—but make sure not to add the egg-cornstarch mixture until the sugar completely dissolves.

BUTTERSCOTCH FILLING

¼	cup cornstarch
¼	teaspoon salt
½	cup evaporated milk
5	large egg yolks
6	tablespoons unsalted butter
1	cup packed light brown sugar
2	cups whole milk
1½	teaspoons vanilla extract
1	recipe Prebaked Pie Shell Coated with Graham Cracker Crumbs (page 485), fully baked and cooled completely

WHIPPED CREAM TOPPING

1	cup heavy cream, chilled
1	tablespoon sugar
1	teaspoon vanilla extract

1. FOR THE FILLING: Dissolve cornstarch and salt in evaporated milk; whisk in egg yolks and set aside.

2. Meanwhile, heat butter and brown sugar in medium saucepan over medium heat until candy thermometer registers 220 degrees, about 5 minutes. Gradually whisk in whole milk. Once sugar

dissolves, gradually whisk in cornstarch mixture. Continue cooking until mixture comes to boil; cook 1 minute longer. Turn off heat, then stir in vanilla. Pour filling into shallow pan (another pie pan works well). Put plastic wrap directly over filling surface to prevent skin from forming; cool until warm, 20 to 30 minutes. Pour filling into pie shell and, once again, place sheet of plastic wrap over filling surface. Refrigerate until completely chilled, at least 3 hours.

3. **FOR THE WHIPPED CREAM:** Beat cream and sugar in electric mixer at medium speed to soft peaks; add vanilla. Continue to beat to barely stiff peaks. Spread over filling and refrigerate pie until ready to serve.

FREE-FORM FRUIT TART

THE ELEMENTS OF A FRUIT TART ARE THE same, no matter what fruit is being used: A tender, fragile, and slightly sweet crust is spread with a small amount of pastry cream, which is in turn covered with a selection of fresh, raw fruit. A glaze, although not essential, may be used to highlight both the flavor and appearance of the fruit.

A free-form tart simplifies the process by eliminating the need for a tart pan with removable sides. Instead, you simply form the dough into the shape that you wish; edges are created with the crimping maneuver familiar to bakers of pie crusts.

A fruit tart requires a dough that is different from that used for a classic American pie. This dessert is French in origin and relies on an all-butter crust that has been enriched with egg. Tart doughs are usually wrapped and chilled, or at least rested, at two stages. In both cases, resting helps to limit gluten development in the dough and to hydrate the starch in the flour, which prevents toughness and excessive distortion in the baked dough.

Because of the high butter and egg content of this dough, docking (piercing the dough with holes before baking) is important. During baking, water trapped in the dough begins to evaporate, causing steam to accumulate in the tiny spaces previously occupied by the butter, which has melted. These spaces inflate and distort the tart crust if the crust is not docked. This is particularly important with a free-form crust, such as the one used here, which has no pan to help maintain its shape.

If the quantity of pastry cream we specify seems small, remember that too much pastry cream makes the tart overly rich; excess pastry cream will also ooze out between the fruit, making the tart look sloppy.

In this recipe, we eliminate the painstaking process of thin-slicing fruit and arranging it in careful concentric circles. Instead, a variety of fruits are simply tossed together and then spooned on top of the pastry cream layer.

Any fruit normally served uncooked is perfect for this type of tart, with the exception of those that discolor quickly, such as apples, pears, bananas, peaches, and apricots. Good candidates include blackberries, blueberries, raspberries, strawberries, seedless grapes, kiwis, oranges, mangoes, and papayas. The first three berries can be simply rinsed and dried prior to use; strawberries should be hulled and halved; grapes should be halved if large; kiwis peeled, halved, and sliced; oranges peeled and sectioned; and mangoes and papayas peeled, pitted, and sliced thinly.

Although the crust can be baked and pastry cream can be made a day ahead, a fruit tart is best assembled just before serving, ensuring a crisp crust and a fruit juice–free custard.

Free-Form Fruit Tart

SERVES 8

If you prefer, you can fashion the dough into a square or rectangular base rather than a disk. Just make sure that the dough has been rolled about ⅛ inch thick and that you flute the edges so that the shell will be able to hold the pastry cream in place. See the illustration on page 484 for more information on fluting pastry dough.

FREE-FORM PASTRY SHELL

1¼ cups all-purpose flour, plus extra for dusting dough and parchment paper

2 tablespoons sugar

⅛ teaspoon salt

⅛ teaspoon baking powder

7 tablespoons unsalted butter, chilled, cut into ½-inch pieces

1 large egg beaten with 1 tablespoon water

EASY PASTRY CREAM

3	tablespoons sugar
2	tablespoons all-purpose flour
	Pinch of salt
¾	cup milk
1	large egg
1	egg yolk
1	teaspoon vanilla extract
1	tablespoon unsalted butter, softened
2	teaspoons orange liqueur or Kirsch

GLAZED FRUIT

| 6 | cups mixed fruit |
| ¼ | cup apple jelly |

1. FOR THE SHELL: Mix flour, sugar, salt, and baking powder in workbowl of food processor fitted with steel blade. Scatter butter over dry ingredients. Pulse until mixture resembles coarse cornmeal. Turn mixture into medium bowl.

2. Add egg mixture. With blade of rubber spatula, use folding motion to mix. Press down on mixture with broad side of spatula until dough sticks together, adding up to 1 tablespoon more water if it will not come together. Shape dough into ball, squeezing two or three times with hands until cohesive, then flatten into 4-inch-wide disk. Dust lightly with flour, wrap in plastic, and refrigerate at least 1 hour, or up to 2 days, before rolling.

3. Remove dough from refrigerator; let stand at room temperature to soften slightly, about 10 minutes if dough has chilled for 30 minutes, about 20 minutes if it has chilled overnight. (The dough should be pliable. Use your hands to squeeze the dough; if you can squeeze it without having to apply too much pressure, it is ready to roll.) Roll dough on lightly floured piece of parchment paper to a

12½-inch disk about ⅛ inch thick.

4. Slide parchment paper and dough onto cookie sheet. Using a plate or cardboard disk as a guide, trim dough to a 12-inch disk. Fold dough about ½ inch up around perimeter of disk. Flute edge of tart dough by pressing thumb and index finger of one hand about ½ inch apart on the outside lip while using index finger (or knuckle) of other hand to lightly press an indentation into space between thumb and finger; repeat around the perimeter of the dough. Using a table fork, prick dough at ½-inch intervals. Cover with plastic wrap; place in freezer until firm, about 20 minutes. (If you have the time, dough can be refrigerated until well chilled, at least 3 hours and up to 3 days.)

5. Adjust oven rack to center position and heat oven to 400 degrees. Bake shell, lowering heat immediately to 350, until golden brown, about 20 minutes. Slide tart shell on parchment to a wire rack; cool to room temperature.

6. FOR THE PASTRY CREAM: Whisk sugar, flour, and salt together in a 1- to 1½-quart nonreactive saucepan. Whisk in milk, then egg and yolk. Heat mixture over low heat, whisking constantly, until pastry cream thickens and comes to a boil. Boil, whisking constantly, for 15 seconds.

7. Remove from heat; whisk in vanilla and butter. Scrape pastry cream into a nonreactive bowl and press plastic wrap against the surface. Refrigerate until cold, at least 1 hour. (Can be refrigerated overnight.)

8. Stir liqueur into pastry cream, then spread pastry cream evenly over tart shell.

8. FOR THE FRUIT: Toss fruit in a bowl, then spoon over pastry cream.

9. Heat jelly in a small saucepan. Using a funnel if necessary, pour warm jelly into a heat-safe atomizer. Mist fruit evenly with apple glaze. Serve immediately.

20

CRISPS, COBBLERS, AND OTHER FRUIT DESSERTS

THERE IS AN ASTONISHING ARRAY OF OLD-fashioned American desserts that consist of fruit baked with bread, cake crumbs, flour and butter, oats, crackers, and the like. In the days when home cooks were frugal, these desserts were an easy way to use up stale leftovers while providing a bit of variety in terms of texture and flavor.

Most of these simple desserts have funny names that are hard to keep straight. While regional differences exist, most American cookbooks agree on the following formulations:

BETTY Fruit is combined with buttered bread (or sometimes cake) crumbs and baked. Similar to a crisp, except that crumbs are usually layered with fruit instead of placed all on top. Also called a brown betty.

BUCKLE Fruit is mixed with simple yellow cake batter and baked. Cake batter can be topped with streusel crumbs.

COBBLER Fruit is topped with a crust, which can be made from cookie dough, pie pastry, or biscuit topping, and baked. If made from biscuit or cookie dough, the topping can be dropped over the fruit for a cobbled appearance.

CRISP Fruit is topped with a "rubbed" mixture of butter, sugar, and flour, then baked. Topping often includes nuts or oats.

CRUMBLE An English term for crisp, usually made with oats.

GRUNT Fruit is topped with biscuit dough, covered, and baked so that biscuits steam rather than bake. Texture is akin to dumplings and is often gummy. Sometimes made on top of the stove. Also called a slump.

PANDOWDY Fruit is covered with pastry dough and baked. Dough is cut, scored, and pressed into fruit. Sometimes crust is pressed into fruit during baking; other recipes "dowdy" the crust after baking.

PLATE CAKE Fruit is topped with rolled biscuit dough and baked. When done, dessert is flipped and biscuit topping becomes bottom crust.

SHORTCAKE Often grouped with crisps, cobblers, and such, this dessert is made with fruit that has not been baked. Rather, the fruit is macerated and then layered between split biscuits with whipped cream.

SLUMP See Grunt.

The following pages contain recipes for our favorite American fruit desserts. All are an excellent alternative to pies and tarts, especially when you're pressed for time.

FRUIT CRISP

THERE IS SELDOM ANYTHING CRISP ABOUT most crisps. This simple baked dessert, made from sweetened fruit topped with a combination of sugar, butter, and flour, almost invariably comes out of the oven with a soggy top crust. A few recipes go so far as to refer to this classic dish as a crunch, a term that has no bearing on the flat, dull, overly sweetened crumble that serves as a streusel topping for the fruit.

We tried covering fruit with sweetened and buttered oats as well as plain toppings without oats or nuts and were unimpressed. None of these toppings merited the name "crisp." We found that spices (we recommend cinnamon and nutmeg) and nuts (particularly whole almonds or pecans) are essential. The spices add flavor to the topping, while the nuts give it some texture and much-needed crunch. We find that the food processor does the best job of making the topping, although you can also use your fingers or a fork.

Firm fruits, such as apples, pears, nectarines, peaches, and plums, work best in crisps and betties. Berries are quite watery and will make the topping soggy if used alone. However, they will work in combination with firmer fruits. If you like, replace up to one cup of the fruit in the fillings with an equal amount of berries. We think that raspberries are especially good with apples, while blueberries work nicely with peaches.

Our tests revealed that when using apples, a combination of Granny Smith and McIntosh apples works best. The McIntosh apples have a good flavor and cook down to form a thick sauce. The Granny Smiths cut some of the sweetness and hold their shape.

We found it unnecessary to thicken the fruit in all but two cases. Plums are a bit watery and benefit from the addition of a little quick-cooking tapioca. Peaches will thicken up on their own but need some help when blueberries are added to the mix. Juices thrown off by any of the other fruits will evaporate or thicken nicely without causing the topping to become soft.

As for flavoring the fruit, we found one quarter cup of sugar to be adequate, especially since the toppings are fairly sweet. We also like to add some lemon juice and zest. One half teaspoon of grated gingerroot makes a nice addition to any of the following fillings.

Fruit Crisp

SERVES 4 TO 6

A dollop of whipped cream or vanilla ice cream is always welcome, especially if serving the crisp warm.

6	tablespoons all-purpose flour
¼	cup packed light brown sugar
¼	cup granulated sugar
¼	teaspoon ground cinnamon
¼	teaspoon ground nutmeg
¼	teaspoon salt
5	tablespoons unsalted butter, chilled, cut into ½-inch pieces
¾	cup coarsely chopped nuts
I	recipe Fruit Fillings for Crisps and Betties (see table below)

1. Pulse flour, sugars, spices, and salt in workbowl of food processor. Add butter and pulse 10 times, about 4 seconds each pulse. The mixture will first look like dry sand, with large lumps of butter, then like coarse cornmeal. Add nuts, then pulse again, four to five times, about 1 second each pulse. Topping should look like slightly clumpy wet sand. Be sure not to overmix or mixture will become too wet and homogeneous. Refrigerate topping while preparing fruit, at least 15 minutes.

2. Adjust oven rack to lower-middle position and heat oven to 375 degrees. Scrape fruit mixture with rubber spatula into 8-inch square (2-quart) baking pan or 9-inch round deep dish pie plate. Distribute chilled topping evenly over fruit.

3. Bake for 40 minutes. Increase oven temperature to 400 degrees and continue baking until fruit is bubbling and topping turns deep golden brown, about 5 minutes more. Serve warm. (Crisp can be set aside at room temperature for a few hours and then reheated in a warm oven just before serving.)

> VARIATIONS

Fruit Crisp with Hand-Mixed Topping

A food processor is better suited to mixing the buttery topping for a crisp, but the job may be done by hand. To mix by hand, allow butter pieces to sit at room temperature for 5 minutes. Meanwhile, mix flour, brown sugar, granulated sugar, cinnamon, nutmeg, and salt in medium bowl. Add butter; toss to coat. Pinch butter chunks and dry mixture between fingertips until mixture looks like crumbly wet sand. Add ¾ cup finely chopped nuts (not coarsely chopped, as with food processor method) and toss to distribute evenly. Proceed with step 2 of Fruit Crisp recipe, refrigerating topping while preparing fruit.

Fruit Fillings for Crisps and Betties

Combine the ingredients for a specific filling in a bowl and use as directed in the Fruit Crisp recipe (above) or Brown Betty recipe (page 504).

FRUIT	QUANTITY	PREPARATION	SUGAR	FLAVORINGS
Apples	2½ to 3 pounds (half Granny Smiths and half McIntosh)	Peel, quarter, core, and cut into 1-inch chunks	¼ cup	1½ tablespoons lemon juice ½ teaspoon grated lemon zest
Peaches/ Nectarines	2½ to 3 pounds	Peel, pit, and cut into ⅓-inch wedges	¼ cup	1½ tablespoons lemon juice ½ teaspoon grated lemon zest
Pears	2½ to 3 pounds	Peel, halve, core, and cut into 1-inch chunks	¼ cup	1½ tablespoons lemon juice ½ teaspoon grated lemon zest
Plums	2½ to 3 pounds	Pit and cut into ⅓-inch wedges	¼ cup	1½ tablespoons lemon juice ½ teaspoon grated lemon zest 1 tablespoon quick-cooking tapioca

Fruit Crisp for a Crowd

Follow recipe for Fruit Crisp, doubling all ingredients and using a 13 by 9-inch baking pan. Bake for 55 minutes at 375 degrees without increasing the oven temperature. Serves 10.

Brown Betty

SERVES 4 TO 6

Betties are similar to crisps, with two exceptions. Traditionally, the streusel topping is made from buttered bread crumbs and layered in the middle of the fruit as well as on top. We like the idea of using buttered bread crumbs but find that the crumbs become soggy when layered in the middle of the fruit. Our solution is to sprinkle them on top of the fruit only.

4	slices firm white sandwich bread (about 4 ounces), torn into large pieces and pulsed in food processor to yield 2 cups coarse crumbs
1/4	cup packed light brown sugar
2	tablespoons granulated sugar
1/4	teaspoon ground cinnamon
3	tablespoons unsalted butter, melted
1	recipe Fruit Fillings for Crisps and Betties (page 503)

1. Adjust oven rack to middle position and heat oven to 375 degrees. Toss bread crumbs, sugars, and cinnamon with melted butter in medium bowl. Rub with fingers to combine.

2. Scrape fruit mixture with rubber spatula into 8-inch square (2-quart) baking pan or 9-inch round deep dish pie plate. Sprinkle topping evenly over fruit.

3. Bake until crumbs turn deep golden brown, juices bubble, and fruit is tender, 40 to 45 minutes. Serve warm.

FRUIT COBBLERS

UNLIKE CRISPS, WHICH ARE NECESSARILY on the dry side so that the topping will remain crunchy, cobblers ought to be juicy. In our research, we found recipes for the usual pastry- and biscuit-topped fruit, but we also saw custardy clafouti-style desserts, fruits baked in sweet pancake batters, and double-crusted, juicy pies, all confidently called cobbler. Among the many, we isolated three cobbler styles—toppings of butter cookie dough, biscuit (shortcake), and pastry—we wanted to investigate.

Before refining the toppings, we first wanted to understand the dynamics of the fruit. While there is little need to thicken the fruit for a crisp or a betty, we found that cobblers are a different matter. Because the fruit usually cooks under a thick blanket of dough or pastry, the excess fruit juices cannot evaporate. Also, many cobblers are traditionally made with berries, which are quite watery. To keep cobblers from becoming a soggy, soupy mess, it is necessary to thicken the fruit.

For a natural, thin, silky syrup, we prefer cornstarch, arrowroot, or potato starch. Used in small quantities, we found it difficult to tell much difference between the three. Though they all worked equally well at unobtrusively thickening fruit juices, we recommend cornstarch because it is the most widely available. Flour turned the juices cloudy, and tapioca can actually thicken the fruit too much and give it a jammy consistency. Neither is recommended in cobblers.

We found that each fruit requires a different amount of thickener based on its liquid content. At one extreme, apples and pears were so dry that we ultimately added water to make them juicy enough. At the other end, sour cherries were too watery, demanding more thickener than other fruits. Soft berries (strawberries, blackberries, and raspberries, but not blueberries) need more thickener than fleshier fruits like peaches and plums.

As for sweetening, most fruits benefit from the addition of sugar, since they are too tart when baked without. Sweet toppings and ice cream only make unsweetened fruit seem even more tart. We found that sugar is also crucial in thickening the fruit juices into a light syrup.

After extensive testing, we devised formulas for preparing, thickening, and sweetening 13 fruits for cobblers (see page 507). Each preparation yields 5 to 6 cups of fruit filling. Adjust the sweetener level depending on ripeness of fruit and individual tastes. Different cobbler toppings contain different amounts of sugar. See individual recipes for suggestions on choosing the lower or higher amount of sugar listed in the fruit filling directions.

Fruits may be combined if desired. Adjust amounts of thickener and sweetener as needed. For example, to make blackberry-apricot filling, use two-and-a-half teaspoons cornstarch and about a half cup of sugar to balance differences between the two formulas.

While summer's tree-ripened fruits make the best cobblers, there is an alternative if you are baking out of season. We tried making our cobblers with IQF (individually quick frozen) fruits, and to our surprise, most of the frozen fruits made respectable-looking and -tasting cobblers. As a matter of fact, frozen blueberries held their shape and flavor better than out-of-season Chilean imports. Frozen strawberries, rhubarb, blackberries, raspberries, and sour cherries all worked well. There were a few exceptions, though. Frozen peach slices lacked the juiciness and perfume of fresh ones. Frozen dark sweet cherries were flavorless when baked, but so were the fresh ones. Tart cherries, fresh or frozen, are more suited to baking. Preparation is embarrassingly simple—just snip the bag and dump it in a bowl. Cobblers made with unthawed frozen fruit need a little extra oven time, so bake them for the maximum time in the suggested time range.

Any of the cobbler recipes that follow can be doubled and baked in a 13 by 9-inch dish. You may need to increase the baking time by five minutes.

Cobbler with Butter Cookie Dough Topping

SERVES 4 TO 6

Although a bit unconventional, the sweet, sugar cookie topping is our favorite. Spoonfuls of dough are dropped over the fruit filling and melt in the oven to form a golden brown crust with bits of fruit and juices bursting through in places. The topping is quite sweet, so go lightly on the sugar in the fruit filling.

¹/₂	cup all-purpose flour
¹/₄	teaspoon baking powder
	Pinch salt
8	tablespoons unsalted butter, room temperature
¹/₂	cup sugar
I	large egg yolk (use whole egg if doubling recipe)
¹/₄	teaspoon vanilla extract
I	recipe Fruit Fillings for Cobblers (page 507)

1. Preheat oven to 375 degrees. Mix flour, baking powder, and salt together in small bowl and set aside.

2. Beat butter and sugar until light and fluffy, about 1 minute with electric mixer or 3 minutes by hand. Beat in egg yolk and vanilla until smooth. Stir in dry ingredients until just combined.

2. Scrape fruit mixture with rubber spatula into 8-inch square (2-quart) baking pan or 9-inch round deep dish pie plate. Drop cookie dough topping by heaping tablespoons evenly over fruit. Make sure that pieces of batter are not touching or clumping together in one spot.

4. Bake until golden brown, 45 to 55 minutes. Serve warm. (Cobbler can be kept at room temperature for several hours and reheated just before serving.)

Cobbler with Rich Shortcake Topping

SERVES 4 TO 6

Because the biscuit easily absorbs juices, this shortcake topping is best with berries. There's no sugar in the biscuit topping (just a dusting on top), so make sure to sweeten the fruit adequately by using the upper amount listed in filling recipes.

I	cup all-purpose flour
I ¹/₂	teaspoons baking powder
¹/₄	teaspoon salt
4	tablespoons unsalted butter, chilled, cut into ¹/₄-inch pieces
2	tablespoons vegetable shortening, chilled
7	tablespoons milk
I	recipe Blackberry, Blueberry, Raspberry, or Strawberry Filling for Cobblers (page 507)
I	tablespoon sugar

1. Preheat oven to 375 degrees. Mix flour, baking powder, and salt in workbowl of food processor. Scatter butter pieces over mixture, tossing to coat butter with dry ingredients. Cut butter into dry ingredients with five pulses of food processor, 1 second each. Add vegetable shortening; continue cutting in until flour is pale yellow and resembles coarse cornmeal, with butter bits no larger than small peas, about four more 1-second pulses. Turn mixture into medium bowl.

PEELING AND PITTING A MANGO

1. A sharp paring knife makes it easy to peel a mango. Start by removing a thin slice from one end of the mango so that it sits flat on a work surface.

2. Hold the mango cut-side down, and remove the skin in thin strips, working from top to bottom.

3. Once the peel has been completely removed, cut down along the side of the flat pit to remove the flesh from one side of the mango. Do the same thing on the other side of the pit.

4. Trim around the pit to remove any remaining flesh. The flesh can now be sliced or chopped as needed.

PEELING PEACHES

1. To remove the skin from peaches and other stone fruits, bring a small saucepan of water to a boil. Add the peaches and simmer, turning once or twice, for 30 seconds. Remove the peaches with a slotted spoon or Chinese skimmer and transfer them to a bowl of ice water to stop the cooking process.

2. When cool enough to handle, remove the peaches from the water and peel away the skin with your fingers.

CORING A PEAR

1. Cut the fruit in half from stem to blossom end. Use a melon baller to cut around the central core with a circular motion.

2. Draw the melon baller from the central core to the top of the pear, removing the interior portion of the stem as you go.

3. Use the melon baller to remove the blossom end as well.

2. Pour 6 tablespoons milk into flour mixture. Mix with rubber spatula until large clumps form. Turn mixture onto work surface; lightly knead until mixture just comes together. Place dough on sheet of plastic wrap and press into either square or circle, depending on whether using square or round pan. (Can be refrigerated for up to 2 hours.)

3. Scrape fruit mixture with rubber spatula into 8-inch square (2-quart) baking pan or 9-inch round deep dish pie plate. Roll dough on lightly floured work surface to 10-inch square or circle. Lay dough over prepared fruit; tuck excess dough in between pan side and fruit. (The tucked portion of the crust will be soft, in contrast to the golden brown top crust.) Brush dough with remaining tablespoon of milk; sprinkle biscuit topping with sugar. Cut four 2-inch air vents in dough top.

4. Bake until golden brown, 45 to 55 minutes. Serve warm.

➤ VARIATIONS
Plate Cake

This New England favorite is nothing more than a short-cake-topped cobbler turned upside down just before serving. The juices drip down over the biscuit, which forms a plate of sorts that holds the fruit.

Follow recipe for Cobbler with Rich Shortcake Topping, cooling baked cobbler on rack for 10 min-

Fruit Fillings for Cobblers

Combine the ingredients for a specific filling in a bowl and use as directed in the cobbler recipes on pages 505 through 510.

FRUIT	QUANTITY	PREPARATION	CORNSTARCH	SUGAR	FLAVORINGS
Apples	1¾ pounds tart, firm (such as Granny Smiths)	Peel, quarter, core, and cut into thick slices	2 teaspoons dissolved in ¼ cup water	⅓ to ½ cup	½ teaspoon ground cinnamon 1 teaspoon vanilla extract 1 tablespoon brandy
Apricots	1¾ pounds	Halve and pit	2 teaspoons	½ to ⅔ cup	1 teaspoon vanilla extract ½ teaspoon almond extract
Blackberries	2 pints fresh (or 24 ounces frozen)	Rinse if using fresh	1 tablespoon	⅓ to ½ cup	1 teaspoon vanilla extract
Blueberries	2 pints fresh (or 24 ounces frozen)	Rinse and pick over if using fresh	2 teaspoons	½ to ⅔ cup	½ teaspoon ground cinnamon 1 teaspoon vanilla extract
Mangoes	3 pounds	Peel, pit, and cut into thick slices	2 teaspoons	⅓ cup	¼ teaspoon ground ginger
Peaches/ Nectarines	1¾ pounds	Peel, pit, and cut into thick slices	2 teaspoons	⅓ to ½ cup	Pinch cloves 1 teaspoon vanilla extract 1 tablespoon brandy
Pears	1¾ pounds	Peel, quarter, core, and cut into thick slices	2 teaspoons	⅓ to ½ cup	¼ teaspoon ground ginger or grated nutmeg 1 teaspoon vanilla extract
Plums	1¾ pounds	Pit and quarter	2 teaspoons	½ to ⅔ cup	½ teaspoon ground cinnamon 1 teaspoon vanilla extract
Raspberries	2 pints fresh (or 24 ounces frozen)	Rinse if using fresh	1 tablespoon	½ to ⅔ cup	1 teaspoon vanilla extract
Sour Cherries	1¾ pounds fresh (or 24 ounces frozen)	Stem and pit if using fresh	1½ tablespoons	⅔ to ¾ cup	2 teaspoons almond extract 1 tablespoon kirsch
Strawberries or Strawberry/ Rhubarb	2 pints fresh (or 24 ounces frozen or 10 ounces each frozen strawberries and rhubarb)	Stem and rinse fresh strawberries, leave small and medium whole, halve large berries; cut rhubarb into ⅓-inch chunks	1 tablespoon	⅓ to ½ cup (use greater amount with rhubarb)	1 teaspoon vanilla extract

REMOVING THE PEEL AND PITH FROM AN ORANGE

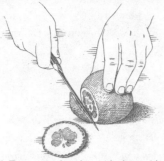

1. To remove the white pith along with the colored peel from oranges and grapefruits, it is necessary to use a knife rather than your hands. Start by trimming a thin slice from either end so that the fruit will sit flat on a counter.

2. Using a sharp paring knife, cut down around the orange to remove the peel and pith in long slices. Try to follow the outline of the fruit as closely as possible.

PEELING AND CORING A PINEAPPLE

1. A pineapple can seem daunting to peel and core. We find the following method to be the easiest. Start by trimming the ends of the pineapple so that it will sit flat on a counter. Cut the pineapple through the ends into four quarters.

2. Lay each quarter cut side up on a work surface, and slide a knife between the skin and flesh to remove the skin.

3. Stand each peeled quarter on end and slice off the portion of the tough, light-colored core that is attached to the quarter. The pineapple can now be sliced or chopped as needed.

PEELING RHUBARB

1. Rhubarb stalks, especially thick ones, are often covered with a stringy outside layer that should be removed before cooking. Cut away and discard the inedible leaves. Trim both ends of the stalk and then partially slice a thin disk from the bottom of the stalk, being careful not to cut all the way through. Gently pull the partially attached disk away from the stalk, pull back the outer peel, and discard.

2. Make a second cut partially through the bottom of the stalk in the reverse direction. Pull back the peel on the other side of the stalk and discard. The rhubarb is now ready to be sliced or chopped as needed.

utes. Run knife around edges of pan to loosen dough. Place large serving plate on top of pan and quickly invert so that biscuit rests on the plate with the fruit and juices on top. Spoon any fruit remaining in pan over shortcake. Cool 10 minutes, cut into pieces, and serve immediately.

Cobbler with Individual Biscuit Topping

A cobbler may be topped with individual biscuits rather than a seamless shortcake topping.

Follow recipe for Cobbler with Rich Shortcake Topping, increasing biscuit recipe by one half. Roll biscuit dough ¾ inch thick and use 2½-inch biscuit cutter to punch out dough rounds. You should be able to cut nine rounds. Top fruit filling with individual biscuits, making sure to space biscuits evenly over filling. Brush with milk, sprinkle with sugar, and bake as directed.

Cobbler with Dropped Biscuit Topping

Instead of rolling out the biscuit dough, you can pinch off pieces and drop them over the fruit, as with the cookie dough topping. The result is a rustic cobbler with fruit peeking through the biscuit topping.

Follow recipe for Cobbler with Rich Shortcake Topping until dough comes together. Pinch off walnut-sized pieces of dough and arrange them evenly over the fruit filling so that they do not touch each other. Do not brush with milk or sprinkle with sugar. Bake as directed.

Cobbler with Flaky Pie Pastry Topping

SERVES 4 TO 6

You can effortlessly achieve a nice contrast between soft- and crisp-textured crust by tucking the pastry between the fruit and pan wall. The fruit juices keep the side crust tender while the dry oven heat crisps up the top.

1	cup all-purpose flour
¼	teaspoon salt
2	tablespoons sugar
6	tablespoons unsalted butter, chilled, cut into ¼-inch pieces
2	tablespoons vegetable shortening, chilled
2–3	tablespoons ice water
1	recipe Fruit Fillings for Cobblers (page 507)
1	tablespoon milk (or water)

1. Mix flour, salt, and 1 tablespoon sugar in workbowl of food processor. Scatter butter pieces over mixture, tossing to coat butter with dry ingredients. Cut butter into dry ingredients with five 1-second pulses. Add shortening; continue cutting in until flour is pale yellow and resembles coarse cornmeal, with butter bits no larger than small peas, about four more 1-second pulses. Turn mixture into medium bowl.

2. Sprinkle 2 tablespoons ice water over flour mixture. Using rubber spatula, fold water into mixture. Then press down on mixture with broad side of spatula until dough sticks together, adding up to 1 tablespoon more water if dough will not come together. Place dough on sheet of plastic wrap and press into either square or circle, depending on whether using square or round pan. Refrigerate while preparing fruit, at least 15 minutes. (Can be refrigerated for up to 2 days.)

3. Preheat oven to 375 degrees. Scrape fruit mixture with rubber spatula into 8-inch square (2-quart) baking pan or 9-inch round deep dish pie plate. Roll dough on lightly floured work surface to 10-inch square or circle. Lay dough over prepared fruit; tuck excess dough in between pan side and fruit. Brush dough with milk; sprinkle with remaining tablespoon sugar. Cut four 2-inch air vents in dough top.

4. Bake until golden brown, 45 to 55 minutes. Serve warm.

➤ VARIATION
Pandowdy

The crust in most pandowdy recipes is quite soggy, especially if the crust is pressed into the fruit halfway through baking, as is the custom. We prefer a contrast between crisp and tender crust. To achieve this balance, we "dowdy" the crust after it is fully baked. We then press the edges of the scored crust into the fruit; don't completely submerge the pieces or they will become soggy.

Follow recipe for Cobbler with Flaky Pie Pastry Topping, baking until golden brown. Remove pan from oven and score crust lengthwise and crosswise to form 2-inch squares. Use the edge of large spoon or metal spatula to press edges of crust squares down into fruit. Because the crust will soften quickly, this dessert is best served when still warm.

SHORTCAKES

SHORTCAKES MAY SEEM SIMILAR TO CRISPS and cobblers, but there is one important difference—the fruit is not cooked. For a true shortcake, sweetened fruit is spread between a split biscuit. A dollop or two of whipped cream is also added. The contrast of the cool fruit, warm and crisp biscuit halves, and chilled whipped cream places this dessert in a category by itself.

Since the fruit is not cooked, frozen fruit is not an option. The fruit must be ripe as well. Half-ripe berries will bake up fine in a pandowdy but will make a second-rate shortcake. Also, because the fruit is not baked, only softer fruits are appropriate. A pear or apple shortcake does not make sense.

We find that two types of fruit, stone fruit and berries, are soft enough and have enough flavor to be used uncooked in a shortcake. Stone fruits, such as apricots, mangoes, nectarines, peaches, and plums, should be sliced thin and sugared to release some of their juices. The peels must be removed from mangoes but can be left on the other fruits if desired.

Fresh berries are also suitable for use in shortcakes. We don't like quartered or sliced strawberries in shortcakes—they often slide off the split biscuit—but we don't like the look of a crushed fruit shortcake either. So we found a happy compromise by slicing most of the strawberries and then crushing the remaining portion of the berry mixture to unify the sliced fruit. This technique works with other berries, except that some berries are mashed and others are left whole since they are quite small. Either way, the thick puree will anchor the remaining whole or sliced fruit so that it won't slip off the split biscuit.

Our testing for this recipe revolved mostly around the biscuit. We tried four very different sweetened biscuits at the outset—a baking powder version with fat cut into flour, baking powder, salt, and sugar, and then moistened with milk; buttermilk biscuits with buttermilk in place of milk and baking soda substituted for part of the baking powder; cream biscuits, with heavy cream standing in for the milk and some of the fat; and egg-enriched cream biscuits with an egg and half-and-half replacing the milk.

After sampling each, we felt that the egg-enriched biscuits had the advantage. Even with the added sugar, the baking powder and buttermilk biscuits seemed more at home in a bread basket than on a dessert plate. The cream biscuits were good looking, but gummy inside. The egg and half-and-half biscuits were finer-textured and more cakelike.

With our general direction settled, we then tested individual ingredients. Because biscuits should be tender, we assumed that low-protein cake flour would deliver the best results. Defying our predictions, the cake flour biscuit came in last, with a meltingly tender yet powdery and dry texture that was too much like shortbread. There was not enough gluten in this flour to support all the fat.

Shortcakes made with all-purpose flour were tender, moist, and cakelike. They were our clear favorites, besting a combination of cake and all-purpose flours as well as the plain cake flour.

We then experimented with liquids, figuring that the egg might be crucial but maybe not the half-and-half that won in our initial test. Buttermilk made the biscuits too savory, while heavy cream made them squat and dense. Milk was fine, but the richer flavor of half-and-half makes it our first choice.

With the ingredient list settled, we focused on technique. The pastry cutter works well, but cutting the butter into small cubes beforehand can be a problem. If the butter is soft enough to cut easily, then it's too soft for the pastry and must be refrigerated or frozen (plus it tends to stick to the knife). If the butter is hard enough for the pastry, then it's difficult to cut.

Some cooks have cold fingertips, perfect for cutting butter into flour by hand, but many people don't, and soften the butter too much in the process. The food processor is foolproof and is our preferred method for mixing biscuits. For cooks without a food processor, we suggest freezing the butter and then using a box grater to cut it into the flour.

When testing dough shaping, we made an interesting discovery. Although hand-formed biscuits look attractive and rustic, we found they were fairly easy to overwork, since warm hands can cause the dough's surface butter to melt. Using a biscuit cutter requires less handling, and dough rounds cut this way develop a natural crack around the circumference during baking, making them easy to split by hand. We also realized we didn't need a rolling pin. Patting the dough to a thickness of three-quarters of an inch on a floured work surface was fast and simple.

After cutting six perfect rounds of dough, you can reknead the scraps and repeat the cutting process to get one or two more rounds. These shortcakes will be a little tougher and less attractive than those from the first cutting.

Shortcakes

SERVES 6

Start the recipe by preparing the fruit, then set the fruit aside while preparing biscuits to allow the juices to become syrupy.

1	recipe Fruit Fillings for Shortcakes (at right)
2	cups all-purpose flour, plus more for work surface and biscuit cutter
1	tablespoon baking powder
1/2	teaspoon salt
5	tablespoons sugar
8	tablespoons unsalted butter, chilled, cut into 1/2-inch pieces
1	large egg, lightly beaten
1/2	cup plus 1 tablespoon half-and-half or milk
1	large egg white, lightly beaten
2	cups Whipped Cream (page 512)

1. Prepare fruit and set aside to macerate for at least 30 minutes and up to 2 hours.

2. Adjust oven rack to lower-middle position and heat oven to 425 degrees. Mix flour, baking powder, salt, and 3 tablespoons sugar in workbowl of food processor. Scatter butter pieces over mixture, tossing to coat butter with dry ingredients. Cut butter into dry ingredients with five 1-second pulses. Continue cutting in butter until flour is pale yellow and resembles coarse cornmeal, with butter bits no larger than small peas, about four more 1-second pulses. Turn mixture into medium bowl.

3. Mix beaten egg with half-and-half; pour into bowl with flour mixture. Combine with rubber spatula until large clumps form. Turn mixture onto floured work surface and lightly knead until it comes together.

4. Pat dough with fingertips into 9 by 6-inch rectangle about 3/4 inch thick, being careful not to overwork dough. Flour a 2¾-inch biscuit cutter; cut out 6 dough rounds. Place rounds 1 inch apart on small baking sheet; brush tops with egg white and sprinkle with remaining 2 tablespoons sugar. (Can be covered and refrigerated for up to 2 hours before baking.)

5. Bake until biscuits are golden brown, 12 to 14 minutes. Place baking sheet on wire rack; cool cakes until warm, about 10 minutes.

6. When biscuits have cooled slightly, look for a natural crack around the circumference of the biscuits. Gently insert your fingers into the crack and split the biscuits in half crosswise. Place each cake bottom on individual serving plate. Spoon portion of fruit and then dollop of whipped cream over each cake bottom. Cap with cake top and serve immediately.

Fruit Fillings for Shortcakes

Although the fruit used to fill a pie, crisp, or cobbler is simply mixed together, shortcakes made with berries require an extra step—crushing 3 cups of the fruit with a potato masher. Once this fruit has been crushed, mix in the remaining 5 cups of fruit (sliced if using strawberries) and the sugar.

Stone fruits are merely sliced (without crushing) and sugared. With both berries and stone fruits, set the prepared filling aside for at least 30 minutes and up to 2 hours to macerate.

FRUIT	QUANTITY	SUGAR
Blackberries	8 cups (3 cups mashed, remaining berries whole)	6 tablespoons
Blueberries	8 cups stemmed (3 cups mashed, remaining berries whole)	6 tablespoons
Mangoes	8 cups (4 to 5 pounds), peeled, pitted, and sliced thin	6 tablespoons
Peaches/ Nectarines	8 cups (3 to 4 pounds), pitted and sliced thin	6 tablespoons
Plums	8 cups (about 3 pounds), pitted and sliced thin	6 tablespoons
Strawberries	8 cups hulled (3 cups mashed, remaining berries sliced)	6 tablespoons

➤ VARIATIONS

Cornmeal Shortcakes

These pale yellow cakes work well with blueberries.

Follow recipe for Shortcakes, replacing ½ cup of flour with ½ cup yellow cornmeal.

Ginger Shortcakes

These spiced shortcakes taste best with peaches or mangoes.

Follow recipe for Shortcakes, adding ½ teaspoon ground ginger and 1 tablespoon minced crystallized ginger to dry ingredients.

Whipped Cream

MAKES ABOUT 2 CUPS

Many sources suggest sweetening cream with confectioners' sugar to ensure that the sugar dissolves. In our tests with lightly sweetened whipped cream, regular granulated sugar dissolved just fine as long as it was added before beating, not after. When making a highly sweetened whipped cream topping (with more than two tablespoons of sugar per cup of heavy cream), it is best to use fine confectioners' sugar to prevent the possibility of grittiness.

I   cup (½ pint) heavy cream, chilled, preferably pasteurized or pasteurized organic
I   tablespoon granulated sugar
I   teaspoon vanilla extract

1. Chill nonreactive, deep 1- to 1½-quart bowl and beaters for a handheld mixer in freezer for at least 20 minutes.

2. Add cream, sugar, and vanilla to chilled bowl. Beat on low speed until small bubbles form, about 30 seconds. Increase speed to medium and continue beating until beaters leave a trail, about 30 seconds. Increase speed to high and continue beating until cream is smooth, thick, and nearly doubled in volume, about 20 seconds for soft peaks or about 30 seconds for stiff peaks. If necessary, finish beating by hand to adjust consistency. Serve immediately or spoon into fine sieve or strainer set over measuring cup and refrigerate for up to 8 hours.

INGREDIENTS: Cream

Supermarkets offer several creams for whipping. We tested them side by side and found pasteurized organic heavy cream to be our favorite. It delivers the sweetest cream flavor, and although it pours the thinnest, it whips up to double its volume.

Regular pasteurized heavy cream is thicker and has a richer mouthfeel, owing no doubt to additives intended to bulk up the texture. However, it is not as sweet and does not whip as well as organic cream.

Finally, we tried ultrapasteurized heavy cream and were disappointed. While it is the thickest by far out of the container, its volume increases by just 50 percent when whipped because the high temperatures required for ultrapasteurizing destroy some of the proteins and enzymes that promote whipping. The higher heat (which prolongs shelf life) also leaves the cream with a slightly cooked taste. Ultrapasteurized has become the "standard" in many markets, but pasteurized cream delivers better flavor and volume every time and is worth searching out. Note that whipping times will be slightly longer if using ultrapasteurized cream.

BAKED APPLES

MANY APPLES SPLIT OR BECOME TOO MUSHY when baked. The ideal baked apple holds its shape during baking and softens and remains moist without becoming mushy. We tested nine apple varieties to see how they would hold up and taste when baked. Among common varieties, only Golden Delicious apples rated well. McIntosh were mushy and Red Delicious and Granny Smiths were too dry. Several lesser known varieties also baked up nicely, including Baldwin, Cortland, Ida Red, and Northern Spy.

To allow steam to escape and to keep the apples from bursting in the oven, we found it helpful to remove a strip of skin around the apple's stem with a vegetable peeler. To fill the apples, you must remove the core. The easiest way to core a whole apple thoroughly is with a melon baller. Start at the stem end and use the melon baller to scoop out and remove the core. Just be careful not to puncture the blossom end.

Baked apples require a moderate oven heat of 350 degrees; higher temperatures can cause apples to split. To keep the apples moist, baste them with apple cider, our preferred choice because it reinforces the apple flavor, every 15 minutes. Serve warm with whipped cream or ice cream if desired.

Baked Apples

SERVES 4

4	large apples, with strip of skin peeled from stem end, then rinsed, dried, and cored
½	cup sugar
½	teaspoon ground cinnamon
	About 1 cup apple cider

1. Heat oven to 350 degrees. Place apples in 8-inch square or 9-inch round glass or ceramic baking dish or pie pan. Mix sugar and cinnamon in small bowl. Sprinkle mixture over apples and inside of cavities. Pour in enough cider so that liquid comes ½ inch up sides of pan.

2. Bake, basting every 15 minutes, until apples are tender when pierced with thin, sharp knife or cake tester, 45 to 55 minutes. Be careful not to overbake or skins will split, causing apples to lose their shape. Serve apples warm with some pan juices. (Can be cooled to room temperature, covered, and refrigerated for 2 days. Reheat before serving.)

➤ VARIATIONS

Brown Sugar Baked Apples

Follow recipe for Baked Apples, replacing white sugar with brown sugar and adding 1 teaspoon vanilla extract to cider before pouring into pan.

Baked Apples with Walnut–Raisin Filling

Combine 4 teaspoons softened butter and ¼ cup each dark raisins and chopped walnuts. Follow recipe for Baked Apples, filling each apple cavity with ¼ of mixture. Sprinkle apples with cinnamon–sugar and proceed as directed.

POACHED FRUIT

UNLIKE OTHER COOKING METHODS, POACHing leaves intact the shape, texture, and basic flavor of fruit, while improving its tenderness and enhancing its flavor. The cooking medium is a simple syrup made with water and sugar. We found that most syrups are too sweet. After extensive testing, we chose a fairly light syrup made with three parts liquid to one part sugar. This light syrup does not have the body of syrup made with more sugar, but it also is not cloyingly sweet.

In our testing, we also kept reducing the cooking time to keep the fruit from becoming mushy. Eventually, we eliminated cooking altogether. As long as the fruit is ripe, we recommend the following method: Bring the syrup ingredients to a boil, add the fruit, turn off the heat, cover the pan, and set aside until the syrup has reached room temperature. By this time the fruit will be tender, and there is no chance that it will have become mushy. If poaching underripe fruit, you should simmer the fruit in the syrup for several minutes, then turn off the heat and cover the pan. Either way, when the fruit is tender, chill and serve.

To Prepare Fruit for Poaching

The following quantities will yield the 2 pounds needed for a single recipe of Poached Fruit. Fruits may be combined if desired. For example, use 2 oranges and 6 figs to yield the necessary 2 pounds.

FRUIT	QUANTITY	PREPARATION
Apples	5 medium	Peel, quarter, and core
Apricots	12 medium	Halve and pit
Cherries	2 pounds	Stem and pit
Figs	12 fresh	Stem and halve lengthwise
Oranges	4 medium	Remove rind and pith with sharp knife and cut crosswise into rounds ½ inch thick
Peaches/ Nectarines	5 medium	Peel, halve, and pit
Pears	4 medium	Peel, halve, and core
Pineapple	1 medium	Trim ends, quarter, peel, core, and cut into pieces 2 inches thick
Plums	9 medium	Halve and pit

Poached Fruit

SERVES 4 TO 6

Other ingredients, such as spices, herbs, or wine, can be added to the syrup (see To Flavor Poaching Liquid, right).

1½	cups water
½	cup sugar
2	pounds ripe fruit (see To Prepare Fruit for Poaching on page 513)

1. Combine water and sugar in medium saucepan. Bring to boil and simmer, stirring occasionally, until sugar dissolves completely, about 5 minutes.

2. While syrup is cooking, prepare fruit. Add fruit to pan, turn off heat, cover, and set aside until mixture returns to room temperature, about 30 minutes. Transfer fruit and syrup to airtight container. Refrigerate until well chilled, at least 2 hours and up to 3 days.

3. To serve, spoon portions of fruit and syrup into individual bowls.

➤ VARIATIONS

Peaches Poached in Spiced Red Wine

Follow recipe for Poached Fruit, replacing water with 1½ cups fruity red wine. Add 1 cinnamon stick, 2 cloves, and 1 long strip of lemon zest to wine along with sugar.

Poached Pears with Vanilla and Star Anise

Follow recipe for Poached Fruit, adding 1 whole vanilla bean and 2 pieces star anise to syrup. When cooled, vanilla bean may be removed, washed, and reused.

To Flavor Poaching Liquid

Use these ingredients singly or in combination as desired. Unless otherwise noted, add the flavorings to the poaching liquid along with the sugar.

LIQUORS AND LIQUEURS A small amount of the eau de vie of the same fruit—such as Framboise with raspberries—enhances the flavor of most poached fruits. Add it after the fruit has cooled to room temperature and use sparingly. Start with no more than 1 tablespoon and add according to taste. Note that the bitterness of the alcohol will quickly overwhelm the sweetness of the fruit.

In addition to eaux de vie, the following liquors may be used, especially with the fruits listed with them: bourbon (apples or pears), Framboise (figs, plums, raspberries, or strawberries), Grand Marnier (all fruit), kirsch (all fruit), and rum (white with delicate and/or acidic fruit; dark with apples and pears).

CITRUS ZEST Strip zest from one lemon or orange with vegetable peeler.

FRUIT JUICE Replace half the water with orange, white grape, raspberry, apple, or other juice.

HERBS Add several sprigs fresh rosemary, thyme, lemon verbena, or mint.

SPICES Add any of the following alone or in combination: 1 cinnamon stick, 2 cloves, 10 black peppercorns, 2 pieces star anise, several slices fresh gingerroot.

VANILLA BEAN Add 1 whole bean. Don't split the bean unless you want the fruit to be covered with tiny black specks. Whole beans can be removed from the syrup when cooled, then washed, dried, and reused.

WINES Replace all or part of the water with red, white, or even rosé wine. Red and rosé wines are good with apricots, cherries, peaches, pears, plums, and strawberries. White wine is best with apples, oranges, pears, and pineapple. Fortified wines, such as port and Madeira, may be used in smaller amounts and are especially good with pears.

21

PUDDINGS, CUSTARDS, AND SOUFFLÉS

THIS CHAPTER INCLUDES A RANGE OF creamy desserts meant to be eaten with a spoon—everything from chocolate pudding and chocolate mousse to crème caramel. In most cases, eggs provide the structure and texture in these desserts. (Bread provides the structure for summer puddings, and the starch released by the rice thickens rice pudding.) How the eggs are handled makes the difference between a silky, creamy custard and one that is lumpy or grainy.

Most custards and puddings are made with eggs, sugar, and some sort of dairy—milk, half-and-half, and/or cream. As the custard is heated, individual protein molecules in the eggs begin to unfold and stretch out. (Think of a bird's nest of dried pasta; when it is cooked, the individual strands of pasta unwind and stretch out.) Once unfolded, the molecules become more likely to bond, and as they bond, water molecules become trapped between them, causing the custard to thicken. The problem with egg custards is that overcooking (that is, overheating) results in more frenzied, tighter bonding that forces the water molecules out of the fragile framework and causes the proteins to clump together. This process is called curdling.

There are several ways to prevent curdling. The first is the judicious use of heat. When a custard reaches 185 to 190 degrees, the proteins bond together so extensively that they form clumps and the eggs curdle—in effect, they become scrambled eggs.

Because of this dynamic, the speed with which you heat the custard mixtures is very important. If the eggs are heated quickly, they won't thicken until well into the 170-degree range, sometimes just before 180 degrees (a safe place to stop heating custards), leaving little time for thickening before curdling. If the eggs are heated slowly, though, thickening can start at 150 degrees and continue slowly as the custard heats past 160 and 170 degrees. Slow, gentle heat, then, is the best—and probably the only—way to succeed with custards. This is especially true of a custard made without cornstarch, such as crème brûlée.

Cornstarch and sugar molecules in a custard are very large and therefore come between unwound egg proteins during cooking, in effect blocking, at least temporarily, their attempts to bond. While sugar molecules are only moderately effective at this task, cornstarch produces dramatic results. Puddings with cornstarch can be heated well above 180 degrees without any curdling; that's because the starch molecules are incredibly effective at keeping the unwound egg proteins from joining together. This explains why chocolate pudding (which contains cornstarch) can be cooked to 200 degrees, while a French custard such as crème brûlée or crème caramel, made without cornstarch, will curdle if cooked past 180 degrees.

You might wonder why we don't just add cornstarch to these recipes. Unfortunately, cornstarch can leave a slightly grainy residue in these simple custards. When chocolate or other flavorings are added to pudding, the tongue is less likely to notice the cornstarch. The other reason is that cornstarch causes custards and puddings to set quite firmly. The starch absorbs excess water and causes puddings to become especially thick. Crème brûlée and crème caramel would loose their wobbly, just-set texture if cornstarch were added.

Many custard-based desserts are cooked in a water bath, or bain-marie. The science here is fairly simple. If ramekins filled with custard are baked in a roasting pan filled with water, the water limits their exposure to direct heat. In effect, the boiling point of water (212 degrees at sea level) sets a limit on the internal temperature these custards can reach. A lower internal temperature means less risk of curdling or oversetting. The water bath also evens out the heat distribution within each ramekin, protecting the outside layers from cooking too quickly.

CHOCOLATE PUDDING

ON A MAP OF DESSERTS, CHOCOLATE PUDding can be located as the chocolate version of a classic cornstarch custard. Typically, a cornstarch custard is made by cooking a mixture of sugar, cornstarch, eggs (or egg yolks), a bit of salt, and a dairy liquid in a saucepan on the stove top until thickened. Butter (which is optional) and vanilla extract are added off the heat.

The choicest chocolate pudding should taste deeply of chocolate and dairy ingredients, be thickened to a soft suppleness, and sweetened just enough to support the chocolate bouquet. The correct balance of dairy and chocolate should make the dessert rich but not cloying and exceptionally smooth on the tongue.

With voluptuous as the key word, we set out to create a pudding that would bring together all of these factors. We determined that a pudding based on three cups of liquid would yield enough for six ramekin-size servings.

From early tests, we concluded that a pudding mixture needs to be pampered by sifting the dry ingredients (sugar, cornstarch, and cocoa powder) before combining them with the liquids to make the liquid-thickener amalgamation as smooth as possible in the beginning. We also learned that to achieve a gorgeous texture, it is important to monitor the strength of the heat beneath the saucepan and to use a reasonably slow hand to stir (not whisk or beat) the pudding mixture as it approaches the thickening point, then continue to slowly stir the pudding as it cooks for two minutes. More vigorous beating can break down the starch granules built up during the thickening process. We also found that it helped to strain the finished pudding through a fine-meshed sieve for a suave, smooth texture.

With these points in mind, we began to test individual ingredients. We made puddings with all milk, two-thirds milk and one-third heavy cream, two-thirds milk and one-third light cream, half milk and half heavy cream, half milk and half light cream, and all light cream. The clear winner was the leaner blend of milk and light cream, which was rich but not overwhelming and mixed well with the chocolate.

Now we were ready to begin building the chocolate taste. We started with three ounces of unsweetened chocolate alone, but that proved inadequate. An ounce or two more of semisweet chocolate added only a nuance of flavor; an ounce or two of bittersweet chocolate raised the chocolate meter slightly, but not enough. At this point, we turned to cocoa powder to see if it would develop, sharpen, and polish the chocolate flavor. Fortunately, it did. We eventually settled on using two tablespoons of cocoa powder in the pudding, along with a combination of unsweetened and bittersweet chocolate.

One nagging problem remained: Although the density, dairy ingredients, and chocolate intensity were right on the mark, the pudding finished with a certain chalkiness on the tongue. To remedy this problem, we replaced the unsweetened chocolate with bittersweet chocolate, adjusting the sugar to balance out the sweetness. Now the pudding was smooth and silky. There are two reasons for the pudding's successful textural change with the use of bittersweet chocolate. First, unsweetened chocolate has a lower percentage of cocoa butter than the bittersweet variety. Second, bittersweet chocolate contains some milk solids and lecithin (an emulsifier), both of which create a smoother, creamier texture and mouthfeel.

Double Chocolate Pudding

SERVES 4 TO 6

To melt the chocolate, chop and place it in a heatproof bowl set over a pan of almost simmering water, stirring once or twice until smooth. You can also melt the chocolate in a microwave at 50 percent power for 3½ minutes, stopping to stir after 2 minutes. If the chocolate is not yet completely melted, heat up to 30 seconds more at 50 percent power. Serve the pudding with whipped cream, if desired.

2	tablespoons Dutch-processed cocoa powder
2	tablespoons cornstarch
⅔	cup sugar
⅛	teaspoon salt
1	cup light cream
3	large egg yolks
2	cups whole milk
6	ounces bittersweet or semisweet chocolate, melted (see note above) and cooled slightly
1	tablespoon unsalted butter, softened
2	teaspoons vanilla extract

1. Sift cocoa powder, cornstarch, sugar, and salt into large heavy-bottomed saucepan. Slowly whisk in light cream, followed by yolks, then milk. Stir in chocolate. (Chocolate will form clumps that smooth with cooking.)

2. Bring mixture to boil over medium-high heat, stirring constantly with whisk, scraping bottom and sides of pot. Pudding will gradually darken and thicken. Reduce heat to medium and cook, stirring gently but constantly with wooden spoon until pudding very thickly coats spoon or instant-read thermometer registers about 200 degrees, 1½ to 2 minutes.

3. Pass pudding through fine-mesh strainer into medium bowl, pressing with rubber spatula. Leave residue in strainer. Stir butter and vanilla into pudding. Serve warm or directly cover surface of pudding with plastic wrap, cool 30 minutes, and refrigerate.

RICE PUDDING

AT ITS BEST, RICE PUDDING IS SIMPLE AND lightly sweet, and it tastes of its primary component: rice. At its worst, the rice flavor is lost to cloying sweetness, condensed dairy, and a pasty, leaden consistency.

Right from the start we agreed on the qualities of the ideal candidate: intact, tender grains bound loosely in a subtly sweet, milky sauce. We were looking for a straightforward stove-top rice pudding, in which both the texture and flavor of the primary ingredient would stand out.

We decided to check out the cooking medium and method first. For our first experiment, we prepared and tasted eight existing recipes for rice pudding, each using a different combination of water, milk, and cream and each with varying ratios of rice to liquid. The tasting revealed that cooking the rice in milk or cream obscured the rice flavor, while a cooking medium of water emphasized it. The most appealing balance of rice flavor and satisfying, but not too rich consistency derived from cooking the rice in two cups of water until it was all absorbed, then adding equal parts (2½ cups each) of whole milk and half-and-half to make the pudding. The whole milk alone made the pudding too thin, but the milk and half-and-half together imparted just the right degree of richness. Eggs, butter, whipped cream, and heavy cream—on their own or in combination—overpowered the flavor of the rice.

We also tried a couple of variations in the cooking method, such as covering the pot or not, and using a double boiler. The double boiler lengthened the cooking time by 25 minutes and turned out a pudding that was gummy and too sweet. By far the best results came from cooking the rice and water in a covered pot first, followed by simmering the cooked rice uncovered in the dairy mixture. The texture of this pudding was just what we wanted—distinct, tender grains in a smooth sauce that tasted of milk rather than reduced cream. We found we could cut 10 minutes off the total cooking time by simmering the rice in the water and dairy mixture together, rather than sequentially, but this approach sacrificed the texture of the grains and resulted in a pudding that our tasters described as overly dense and sweet.

Now it was time to try different kinds of rice. We tested the readily available varieties: supermarket brands of long- and medium-grain white (such as Goya, which distributes both of these types nationally), arborio (a superstarchy Italian medium-grain white used to make risotto), and basmati (an aromatic long-grain white).

All rice contains two types of starch, called amylose and amylopectin, but they are present in different concentrations in different kinds of rice. Arborio, with its high level of amylopectin, made a stiff, gritty pudding. On the other end of the starch scale, long-grain rice, which is high in amylose starch, cooked up separate and fluffy. But the puddings made with long-grain rice were a little too thin for our liking (although not objectionable), while the flavor of the basmati was too perfumy, overwhelming the milk. Medium-grain rice, which has a high proportion of amylopectin (but less than short-grain), cooked up a little moister and stickier than long-grain. This type proved ideal for our rice pudding, which turned out creamy-textured and tasting distinctly of rice and milk. As a final test, we made a pudding with rice that had been refrigerated overnight. Unfortunately, the result was liquidy and grainy without discernible rice flavor.

Simple Stove-Top Rice Pudding

SERVES 6 TO 8

We prefer pudding made from medium-grain rice, but long-grain is perfectly acceptable if that's what you happen to have on hand.

¼	teaspoon salt
1	cup medium- or long-grain rice
2½	cups whole milk
2½	cups half-and-half
⅔	cup sugar
1¼	teaspoons vanilla extract

1. Bring 2 cups water to boil in large, heavy-bottomed pot (at least 3 quarts) or small soup kettle (4 to 5 quarts). Stir in salt and rice; cover and simmer over low heat, stirring once or twice until water is almost fully absorbed, 15 to 20 minutes.

2. Add milk, half-and-half, and sugar. Increase heat to medium-high to bring to simmer, then reduce heat to maintain simmer. Cook uncovered, stirring frequently, until mixture starts to thicken, about 30 minutes. Reduce heat to low and continue to cook, stirring every couple of minutes to prevent sticking and scorching, until a spoon is just able to stand up in the pudding, about 15 minutes longer.

3. Remove from heat and stir in vanilla extract. Cool and serve at room temperature or chilled. (Can be covered with plastic wrap on surface of pudding and then refrigerated up to 2 days.)

➤ VARIATIONS

Rice Pudding with Orange and Toasted Almonds

Follow recipe for Simple Stove-Top Rice Pudding, adding ⅓ cup slivered almonds that have been toasted until just golden and fragrant in small heavy skillet over medium heat (4 to 5 minutes with frequent stirring) and 2 teaspoons grated orange zest along with vanilla extract.

Rice Pudding with Cinnamon and Dried Fruit

Follow recipe for Simple Stove-Top Rice Pudding, adding ½ cup dried fruit (such as raisins, cranberries, cherries, or chopped prunes or apricots) and 1 teaspoon ground cinnamon along with vanilla extract.

BREAD PUDDING

RECIPES FOR BREAD PUDDING ARE FOUND in virtually all European home cooking. Most are simply a mixture of bread, milk and/or cream, sugar, eggs, and flavorings. So what's to discover? Well, the styles vary tremendously, from a baked custard with slices of French bread on top (such as the famous Coach House Bread Pudding, one of James Beard's favorite recipes) to a rich, treacly pudding with sauce, really more of a pudding cake.

Our previous encounters with bread puddings had been decidedly mixed. Since we were not certain which style appealed to us most, we decided to work our way through every version we could find. We consumed every conceivable sort of bread pudding: those in which the bread seemed to have melted into the custard; dry slices of bread that were slightly moistened, sweetened, and baked; puddings shot through with a surfeit of ingredients, including raisins, pecans, orange zest, coconut, and, in one less than memorable instance, pineapple chunks.

This massive intake of calories yielded some valuable clues. We discovered that we wanted a real contrast between the crust and the filling in both texture and flavor; without this contrast, we found this to be a dull little dessert, all pudding and no chew. We also knew that the choice of bread was going to be crucial. Whereas some loaves simply melted into the custard, tough, rustic breads seemed too muscular to succumb to the soft embrace of milk, cream, and eggs. The consistency of the "pudding" was also important, our tastes tending to land halfway between a custard and a sauce.

The balance between bread and filling was going to be critical as well. Some recipes were dry from too much bread; others used so little that it disappeared during baking. The pudding and the bread needed to be distinct but well integrated; we were not favorably inclined toward bread puddings that were nothing more than egg custards topped with bread. We wanted a modest amount of sugar, not something that would indulge the indefatigable sweet tooth of a child. Finally, we decided to dispense with a sauce; the pudding would be plenty rich without it, and a sauce would add extra work to a recipe that cries out for simplicity.

First, we tackled the bread. We tried rustic Italian, a fine-textured French pullman loaf, Pepperidge Farm raisin bread, supermarket Italian bread, challah, brioche, and potato bread. The winners were the French loaf (this was not a baguette but more of a dense sandwich loaf), the fine, dense texture holding up well during cooking, and a quality American-style white bread purchased from a local baker. Pepperidge Farm Hearty White will do in a pinch if you depend entirely on supermarket bread. More tender loaves such as challah and brioche were too soft and spongy. Really tough rustic loaves with heavy crusts and excessive chew should also be avoided, since this type of bread will not soften sufficiently during soaking and baking.

In the course of our testing we also discovered that there was no point in removing the crusts other than for appearance, that using stale or dried bread did not make a difference, and that we preferred cubes over sliced bread since they were easier to measure (8 cups is a more precise measurement than 8 slices) and to work with (large slices tended to curl at the corners when baked). Finally, we tested buttering the bread and found that this added an excessive amount of fat and was unnecessary.

We discovered that the key to a crisp, crunchy top layer was to separate two cups of the cubed bread and place them on top of the pudding just before baking. Brushing these cubes with melted butter added a rich color to the dessert. To provide more contrast between the topping and the filling, we also decided to sprinkle the pudding with cinnamon and two tablespoons of sugar just before it was placed in the oven. This gave the bread topping a flavor distinct from that of the nutmeg-laced custard.

As for the custard, what we wanted, as stated above, was something rich, silky, not simply a thin egg custard. It turned out after many tests that half milk and half cream was about right. Although many recipes use only two or three eggs, we finally agreed on four whole eggs plus one yolk for a rich pudding. The amount of sugar was a matter of some dispute in the tasting, some people preferring a full cup, others a more modest ¾ cup. A low oven temperature, 325 degrees, was best. Although a water bath seemed to provide a slightly improved texture, we opted not to include it in the final recipe because the extra work didn't seem worth the effort.

Determining just when to remove the pudding turned out to be a bit of a trick. Overcooking results in a dry, unappealing custard, and undercooking makes for a very loose sauce. After two scores or more of tests, we determined that the bread pudding should wobble like a Jell-O mold. (Remember that it will continue to cook after it's removed from the oven.) Another tip is to remove the pudding from the oven before it has a chance to inflate and rise up high in the pan. Actually, it is done just when this

process begins, when the edges of the pudding start their upward climb. A knife inserted in the center should not come out clean but be partially coated with half-set custard.

Rich Bread Pudding with Crisp Cinnamon-Sugar Topping

SERVES 8 TO 10

A firm, white American-style bakery loaf gives the best texture to this pudding. In a pinch, however, use Pepperidge Farm Hearty White Bread. Avoid chewy, crusty European-style breads because they do not soften properly in the custard. If desired, serve this pudding with softly whipped cream.

CINNAMON SUGAR

| 2 | tablespoons sugar |
| ½ | teaspoon ground cinnamon |

BREAD PUDDING

4	large eggs, plus 1 large yolk
¾	cup sugar
2½	cups whole milk
2½	cups heavy cream
3	tablespoons bourbon
1	tablespoon vanilla extract
¾	teaspoon fresh ground nutmeg
¼	teaspoon salt
12	ounces (about ½ loaf) good quality American-style white bread, sliced ⅜ inch thick and cut into 1½-inch-square pieces (about 8 cups)
1½	tablespoons unsalted butter, melted, plus extra for greasing pan

1. FOR THE CINNAMON SUGAR: Mix sugar and cinnamon in small bowl; set aside.

2. FOR THE PUDDING: Adjust oven rack to lower-middle position and heat oven to 325 degrees. Butter 13 x 9-inch baking dish.

3. Whisk eggs, yolk, and sugar in a large bowl to blend well. Whisk in milk, cream, bourbon, vanilla extract, nutmeg, and salt. Stir in 6 cups bread cubes; mix thoroughly to moisten. Let stand 20 minutes.

4. Pour mixture into prepared baking dish. Scatter remaining 2 cups bread pieces on top, pushing down

gently to partially submerge. Brush exposed bread with melted butter and sprinkle with cinnamon sugar. Bake until pudding is deep golden brown, is beginning to rise up sides of baking dish, and jiggles very slightly at the center when shaken, about 45 to 50 minutes. Let cool until set but still warm, about 45 minutes. Serve.

➤ VARIATION

Rich Bread Pudding with Raisins and Walnuts

Follow recipe for Rich Bread Pudding, increasing bourbon to ⅓ cup. Soak ¾ cup raisins in bourbon until moistened and plumped, 20 to 25 minutes. Stir plumped raisins, any remaining bourbon, and 1 cup chopped walnuts into soaked bread mixture before transferring to baking dish.

SUMMER FRUIT PUDDING

SUMMER PUDDING DOESN'T FIT THE RICH, creamy, silky pudding archetype. In this classic English dessert, ripe, fragrant, lightly sweetened berries are gently cooked to coax out their juices, which are used to soak and soften slices of bread to make them meld with the fruit. This mélange of berries and bread is usually weighted down with heavy cans, then chilled overnight until it is a cohesive-enough mass to be unmolded.

We have always been intrigued by this "pudding," drawn in by its rustic, unaffected appeal. Unfortunately, many summer puddings are sweet, and the bread often seems to stand apart from the fruit, as if it were just a casing. We wanted sweet-tart berries and bread that melded right into them.

In a typical summer pudding, berries fill a bowl or mold of some sort that has been neatly lined with crustless bread. Some recipes say to line the bowl with full slices, laying them flat against the bottom and sides of the bowl. Others have you cutting the slices down into triangles and rectangles and arranging them such that when unmolded they form an attractive pattern. Well, trimming the crusts is easy, but trimming the bread to fit the mold, then lining the bowl with it is fussy. After having made a cou-

ple of puddings, we quickly grew tired of this technique—it seemed to undermine the simplicity of the dessert.

We came across a couple of recipes that called for layering the bread right in with the berries instead of using it to line the bowl. Not only is this bread-on-the-inside method easier, but a summer pudding made in this fashion looks spectacular—the berries on the outside are brilliant jewels. Meanwhile, the layers of bread on the inside almost melt into the fruit.

Our next adjustment to this recipe was losing the bowl as a mold. We switched instead to a loaf pan. Its rectangular shape requires less trimming of bread slices, and, once unmolded, the pudding better retains its shape. Besides, this version was simply more beautiful than a round one made in a bowl. When we tried making individual summer puddings in ramekins, we found them to be hardly more labor-intensive in assembly than a single large serving. Sure, you have to cut out rounds of bread to fit the ramekins, but a cookie cutter makes easy work of it, and individual servings transform this humble dessert into an elegant one. The individual puddings are also easily served: you simply unmold them onto a plate; there's no slicing or scooping involved.

With the form set, we moved on to the ingredients. For the four pints of berries we were using, three-quarters cup of sugar was a good amount of sweetener. Lemon juice, we found, perked up the berry flavors and rounded them out. We then sought alternatives to cooking the fruit in an attempt to preserve its freshness. We mashed first some of and then all of the berries with sugar. We tried cooking only a portion of the fruit with sugar. We macerated the berries with sugar. None of these methods worked. These puddings, even after being weighted and chilled overnight, had an unwelcome crunchy, raw quality. The berries need a gentle cooking to make their texture more yielding, more puddinglike, if you will. But don't worry—five minutes is all it takes, not even long enough to heat up the kitchen.

So far, we had been using a mix of strawberries, raspberries, blueberries, and blackberries and were pleased with the variety of flavors, textures, and colors. Strawberries made up the bulk, contributing the most substance and sweetness. Raspberries easily break down with the gentle cooking, providing much juice along with their distinct flavor. Blackberries and blueberries are more resistant; they retain their shape and unique textures. And their deep color is a beautiful addition, like sapphires in a pool of rubies.

The next obvious ingredient to investigate was the bread. We tried six different kinds as well as pound cake (for which we were secretly rooting). Hearty, coarse-textured sandwich bread and a rustic French loaf were too tough and tasted fermented and yeasty. Soft, pillowy sandwich bread became soggy and lifeless when soaked with juice. The pound cake, imbibed with berry juice, turned into wet sand and had the textural appeal of sawdust. A good-quality white sandwich bread that had a medium texture, somewhere between Wonder Bread and Pepperidge Farm, was good, but there were two very clear winners: challah and potato bread. Their even, tight-crumbed, tender texture and light sweetness were a perfect match for the berries. Challah, available in the bakery section of most grocery stores, is usually sold in unsliced braided loaves and therefore makes for irregular slices. We sidestepped this complication and chose to go with potato bread, which tastes every bit as good as challah in this recipe but comes in convenient bagged and sliced loaves, like sandwich bread.

Most summer pudding recipes call for stale bread. And for good reason. Fresh bread, we found, when soaked with those berry juices, turns to mush. You might not think this would be so noticeable with the bread layered between all those berries, but every single taster remarked that the pudding made with fresh bread was soggy and gummy. On the other hand, stale bread absorbs some of the juices and melds with the berries but still maintains some structural integrity. We tried different degrees of staleness. A day-old loaf was still too fresh, but bread left out long enough to become completely dry easily cracked and crumbled under the cookie cutter or bread knife. We found that simply leaving slices out overnight until they were dry to the touch but still somewhat pliable resulted in bread that was easy to cut and also tasted good in the pudding.

We encountered a few recipes with instructions to butter the bread. Since pound cake doesn't work in a summer pudding, we thought that this might be a nice way of adding a subtle richness. Wrong. The coating of butter prevented the juices from thoroughly permeating the bread and also dulled the vibrant flavor of the berries.

Probably the oddest thing about summer pudding is the fact that it is weighted as it chills. What, we wondered, does this do for the texture? And how long does the pudding need to chill? We made several and chilled them with and without weights for 4, 8, 24, and 30 hours. The puddings chilled for 4 hours tasted of underripe fruit—you could sense that they would be good if only given more time. The bread was barely soaked through, and the berries barely clung together. At 8 hours the pudding was at its peak: the berries tasted fresh and held together, while the bread melted right into them. Twenty-four hours and the pudding was still good, though a hairsbreadth duller in color and flavor. After 30 hours the pudding was well past its prime and began to smell and taste fermented.

No matter how long they chilled, the summer puddings without weights were loose. They didn't hold together after unmolding, the fruit was less cohesive, and the puddings less pleasurable to eat.

Individual Summer Berry Puddings
SERVES 6

Stale the bread for this recipe by leaving it out overnight; it should be dry to the touch but not brittle. Otherwise, put the slices on a rack in a single layer into a 200-degree oven for 50 to 60 minutes, turning them once halfway through. For this recipe, you will need six 6-ounce ramekins and a round cookie cutter of slightly smaller diameter than the ramekins. If you don't have the right size cutter, use a paring knife and the bottom of a ramekin (most ramekins taper towards the bottom) as a guide for trimming the rounds. Challah is the second choice for bread, but will probably require cutting into about ½-inch-thick slices. If both potato bread and challah are unavailable, use a good-quality white sandwich bread with a dense, soft texture. Summer pudding can be made up to 24 hours before serving, but any longer and the berries begin to lose their freshness. Lightly sweetened whipped cream is the perfect accompaniment to summer pudding. See the illustrations on page 523 for tips on assembly.

2   pints strawberries, rinsed, hulled, and sliced
I   pint raspberries
½   pint blueberries
½   pint blackberries
¾   cup sugar
2   tablespoons juice from I lemon
12   slices stale potato bread, challah, or other white bread (see note on page 522)

1. Heat strawberries, raspberries, blueberries, blackberries, and sugar in large nonreactive saucepan over medium heat, stirring occasionally, until berries begin to release their juice and sugar has dissolved, about 5 minutes. Off heat, stir in lemon juice; let cool to room temperature.

2. While berries are cooling, use cookie cutter to cut out 12 bread rounds that are slightly smaller in diameter than ramekins.

3. Spray six 6-ounce ramekins with vegetable cooking spray and place on rimmed cookie sheet. Following illustrations below, assemble, cover, and

weight summer puddings and refrigerate for at least 8 and up to 24 hours.

4. Remove weights, cookie sheet, and plastic wrap. Run paring knife around perimeter of each ramekin, unmold into individual bowls, and serve.

➤ VARIATION
Large Summer Berry Pudding
SERVES 6 TO 8
To ensure that this larger pudding unmolds in one piece, use a greased loaf pan lined with plastic wrap. Because there is no need to cut out rounds for this version, you will need only about 8 bread slices, depending on their size.

Follow recipe for Individual Summer Berry Puddings through step 1. While berries are cooling, remove crusts from bread slices and trim so slices will fit in single layer in 9 by 5-inch loaf pan. (You will need about 2½ slices per layer and a total of three layers.) Line loaf pan with plastic wrap. Make sure wrap lies flat against surface of pan, leaving no air space. Place loaf pan on rimmed cookie sheet, and

ASSEMBLING SUMMER BERRY PUDDINGS

1. For individual summer puddings, cut out rounds of bread with a cookie cutter.

2. With a slotted spoon, place about ¼ cup of fruit into the bottoms of greased 6-ounce ramekins that have been placed on a cookie sheet.

3. Lightly soak a round of bread in the juices and place on top of the fruit in the ramekin.

4. Divide the remaining fruit among the ramekins (about ½ cup more per ramekin).

5. Lightly soak a round of bread and place on top of fruit; it should sit above the lip of the ramekin. Pour any remaining juices over top bread layer, and cover the ramekins loosely with plastic wrap.

6. Place a second cookie sheet on top, then weight with several heavy cans.

use slotted spoon to place about 2 cups of fruit into bottom of pan. Lightly soak enough bread slices for one layer in fruit juices and place on top of fruit. Repeat with two more layers of fruit and bread. Top with remaining juices, cover loosely with a second sheet of plastic wrap, and weight with a second cookie sheet and several heavy cans. To unmold, remove outer plastic wrap and invert onto serving platter. Lift off loaf pan, remove plastic wrap lining, slice, and serve.

CRÈME BRÛLÉE

OUR OBJECTIVE WAS SIMPLE—FIND THE PERfect recipe for classic crème brûlée. Our standards were high—we wanted a custard that was light, firm, smooth, creamy, sweet, fragrant, and slightly eggy, with a brown sugar crust that was both delicate and crisp. Our execution was to be efficient—we wanted to create a recipe that could be made as easily and as quickly as possible.

As we attempted to reach this elusive goal, trying some 36 variations along the way, we found that the process was one of exclusion, not inclusion. The fewest ingredients, fewest steps, and simplest cooking techniques delivered the best results.

Probably the biggest challenge in making crème brûlée is getting the texture of the custard right. In consulting dozens of recipes, we found a surprising number of options for the custard ingredients, including variations on the eggs (either yolks only or whole eggs), the sugar (white, brown, or none at all), the flavorings (vanilla, rum, kirsch, various liqueurs, instant espresso, cinnamon, and grated nutmeg), and, most important, the cream (heavy, whipping, or half-and-half). Further variations could be found in the cooking techniques, such as what temperature to use for the cream (the range was from boiling to chilled) and whether to cook the custard on the stove top or in the oven.

We experimented with every possible variation and found that the most crucial were the type of cream, the cooking time and temperature, and the cooking method (stove top or oven).

We started with a simple, traditional crème brûlée recipe that called for two cups of heavy cream to be boiled for one minute, beaten into four egg yolks, returned to the fire over low flame (in a double boiler if desired), then stirred until nearly boiling. The mixture is then poured into a greased baking dish, chilled, covered with a thin layer of brown sugar, caramelized under the broiler, chilled again, and served.

We began by making separate versions of this recipe using all three types of cream and cooking them in the oven, on top of the stove in a pan, and on top of the stove in a double boiler.

The custard made with heavy cream, which contains between 36 and 40 percent fat, was way too rich; half-and-half, with between 10½ and 18 percent fat, made a watery custard. Whipping cream (sometimes called light whipping cream), which is between 30 and 36 percent fat, gave the custard the smooth, sweet, balanced flavor and texture we wanted.

After this first set of tests, we also dismissed cooking the custard on the stove top in a saucepan, since the results were so poor. The double boiler was not much better, but we decided to try some variations before giving up on this more forgiving method.

We found that stirring constantly, which is necessary to keep the heat evenly distributed in a double boiler, where the heat all comes from the bottom, makes thickening more difficult. As you stir, you actually break apart the egg proteins as they attempt to bond to each other. While this is fine for a custard like crème anglaise that should be thin enough to pour, crème brûlée has to be dense.

We weren't surprised by the results we got on top of the stove. Custard science (see page 516 for more details) tells us that the best results are obtained when eggs are heated slowly and gently. The stove top heats the custard much too fast; even if you can remove the pan before the custard curdles, the mixture has spent so little time warming up (a custard on the stove can zoom from 100 to 180 degrees in minutes) that the eggs cannot properly thicken the liquid. At this point, it seemed time to move on to the oven.

We first tried placing uncooked and uncovered custards in a warm water bath, called a bain-marie, in a cold oven, turned the heat to 250 degrees, and baked for 80 minutes. This first attempt at oven-cooking was a disaster. The custard did not set right, it cooked unevenly, and it was too runny.

Meanwhile, the brown sugar toppings absorbed moisture when caramelized and turned into iron plates. More lessons learned.

We next tried covering and cooking the custard for 15 minutes in a warm water bath in a preheated 350-degree oven. When these custards had been cooked, chilled, topped, caramelized, chilled again, and finally served, we knew we were getting close to reaching our goal.

As a final test, we compared uncovered custards cooked in a bain-marie with those cooked without a water bath in a 300-degree oven. Dry heat caused the baked custards to set like omelets. Cooking the custards in a bain-marie keeps their temperature from rising above 212 degrees; this low temperature guarantees that the custard approaches its set point slowly and therefore thickens gradually. At this lower temperature, the custards cooked in the water bath were also silkier than those baked in a 350-degree oven. As a final refinement, we lowered the oven temperature to 275 degrees and increased the cooking time to 45 minutes. Even better.

Had we exhausted all the custard options? Not yet! We decided to fiddle with the temperature of the cream. Until now, we'd always boiled the cream for a minute or so and then mixed it into the yolk-sugar mixture. This time we tried our recipe with scalded cream, room temperature cream, and chilled cream straight from the fridge. We were pleasantly surprised to find that the chilled cream sample was richer, smoother, and more velvety than its scalded or room temperature counterparts.

Adding hot cream certainly raises the temperature of the eggs very quickly. Since the secret to perfect crème brûlée is very slow heat, the use of chilled cream fit in with the rest of our results.

While working on the custard variations, we also experimented with the caramelized sugar topping. The first recipe we had tried called for a brown sugar topping so thick that it formed a barrier difficult to penetrate with a spoon. We soon realized that two teaspoons of brown sugar per crème brûlée gave the best coverage and depth for even, controllable, and consistent caramelization.

We also tested the relative merits of light and dark brown sugar for the topping. On our first try, the dark brown sugar topping burned quickly, was too hard, and didn't taste as good as the topping made with light brown sugar. But the light brown sugar topping was not perfect either, so we decided to try drying both light and dark brown sugar for 15 minutes in a 250-degree oven before sprinkling over the chilled custards. Predrying the brown sugar significantly improved its taste, texture, and appearance when caramelized. Predried dark brown sugar gave the topping a richer flavor that was superior to the light brown sugar topping, just the reverse of when the sugars were not predried.

It seems that drying brown sugar in the oven removes moisture as well as some of the lumps, which makes it easier to sprinkle and allows it to coat more evenly. Also, since the caramelization process involves melting the sugar and then evaporating some of its water, having less water in the brown sugar before it is run under the broiler undoubtedly helps get the process going. A dried sugar topping needs less time under the broiler, so the dark brown sugar, with its richer flavor, can be used without the danger of burning or becoming too hard.

Perfect Crème Brûlée
SERVES 6

This recipe is incredibly simple to prepare. In fact, since we don't heat the cream, you can get the custard into the oven in five minutes.

1	tablespoon unsalted butter, softened
6	large egg yolks, chilled
6	tablespoons white sugar
1½	cups whipping cream, chilled
4	tablespoons dark brown sugar

1. Adjust oven rack to center position and heat oven to 275 degrees. Butter six ½-cup ramekins or six ⅔-cup custard cups and set them in a glass baking pan.

2. Whisk yolks in medium bowl until slightly thickened. Add white sugar and whisk until dissolved. Whisk in cream, then pour mixture into prepared ramekins.

3. Set baking pan on oven rack and pour warm water into pan to come halfway up the ramekins. Bake uncovered until custards are just barely set, about 45 minutes.

4. Remove baking pan from oven, leaving ramekins in the hot water; cool to room temperature. Cover each ramekin with plastic wrap and refrigerate until chilled, at least 2 hours. (Can be covered and refrigerated overnight.)

5. While custards are cooling, spread brown sugar in a small baking pan; set in turned-off (but still warm) oven until sugar dries, about 20 minutes. Transfer sugar to a small zipper-lock freezer bag; seal bag and crush sugar fine with a rolling pin. Store sugar in an airtight container until ready to top custards.

6. Adjust oven rack to the next-to-the-highest position and heat broiler. Remove chilled ramekins from refrigerator, uncover, and evenly spread each with 2 teaspoons dried sugar. Set ramekins in a baking pan. Broil, watching constantly and rotating pan for even caramelization, until toppings are brittle, 2 to 3 minutes, depending on heat intensity.

7. Refrigerate crème brûlées to rechill custard, about 30 minutes. Brown sugar topping will start to deteriorate in about 1 hour.

CRÈME CARAMEL

CRÈME CARAMEL IS A DECEPTIVELY SIMPLE classic French dessert. Made with just a few ingredients that are readily available (sugar, eggs, and milk or cream), it is similar in construction and flavor to other baked custards. This dessert is slightly lighter and a little less sweet than a standard baked custard, but what really makes it special is the caramel sauce.

For us, though, what made a perfect crème caramel was texture. We wanted a custard that was creamy and tender enough to melt in our mouths, yet firm enough to unmold without collapsing on the serving plate. We were also looking for a mellow flavor that was neither too rich nor too eggy.

As for the caramel, we learned one lesson early on: it's not for wimps. If we got nervous and took it off the heat too early, we had a pale, insipid, overly sweet caramel; if we braved it out for too long, we ended up with a bitter, dark, inedible sauce. But the caramel we were looking for was somewhere between the two: a rich, honey-colored sauce with just the right amount of sweetness and complexity.

The first thing we discovered in our research was

that the most important part of the recipe is the proportion of egg whites to egg yolks. Too many whites produced a custard that was almost solid and rubbery; too few egg whites, on the other hand, and our custard collapsed. After much tinkering, we came up with what we consider the ideal ratio: 3 whole eggs to 2 yolks—in other words, 3 whites to 5 yolks. The resulting custard was tender yet not overly rich and firm enough to unmold easily.

Next, we examined the question of what liquid to use. Since we were making a classic crème caramel, our choices were limited to milk, heavy cream, light cream, and half-and-half. We made our initial custard using milk alone, but it tasted far too thin. Our custard with heavy cream and milk, on the other hand, was creamy but too rich. The high fat content of the cream caused the custard to coat our mouths as we ate, and the custard tasted less of eggs than of rich cream. Half-and-half was better, yet left us wanting something slightly richer. Light cream solved our problem. A mixture of equal parts of milk and light cream gave us just that extra edge of richness, creamy enough to satisfy both ourselves and our tasters.

Our experiments with sugar were less extensive, since we had decided at the beginning that a crème caramel custard should be less sweet than a custard meant to be eaten unadorned. To us, that made the dessert more interesting and sophisticated. We initially used six tablespoons of sugar for the three cups of liquid in the recipe and were quite satisfied, but some tasters felt that this custard was bland. We then tried using one-half cup of sugar for the same amount of liquid. Opinions were divided on this custard. Some palates still wanted an even sweeter custard, so we tried two-thirds of a cup. This slightly sweeter custard became the new favorite for the majority, but if you prefer a less sweet custard, simply cut the sugar down to one-half cup.

There are basically two methods of making caramel. In the dry method, you use only sugar, cooking it slowly until it melts and caramelizes. The wet method uses a combination of water and sugar. The sugar begins to dissolve in the water, then the mixture is simmered until the water evaporates and the sugar caramelizes. We never successfully produced a smooth caramel with the dry method, so we opted for the wet as a way of increasing the margin of success.

We had good success with the wet method, but it was a bit tricky and left us wondering if there was a foolproof method. At this point we remembered an interesting recipe in Shirley Corriher's *Cookwise* (Morrow, 1997). To her basic water and sugar mixture, Corriher added corn syrup and lemon juice. The corn syrup added another type of sugar (glucose) to the table sugar (sucrose) and the lemon juice (an acid) broke down the table sugar, making the dreaded crystallization difficult. This yielded great results every time. Even when crystallization occurred along the edges of the pan during the cooking process, as often happens to many home cooks, the caramel in the pan was still clear and perfect with no crystallization at all, time after time. We now had the foolproof caramel we had wanted.

Once our caramel was done, we poured it directly into our molds. While some cookbooks advised buttering the molds, we found this step both unnecessary and ill-advised: the butter solidified when cold and left the custard greasy. We then followed the common advice to pour the caramel into the molds, coat the bottom evenly, and then tilt the molds to coat the sides. An accident with hot caramel burning our fingers while the molds were tilted caused us to question this particular bit of advice. (A bowl of ice water nearby—a useful thing to have when you are making caramel or any type of candy—saved the day for the burned finger.) We started to coat only the bottoms of the mold, reasoning that the caramel sinks to the bottom of the mold while baking anyway. When we unmolded the custards, the caramel still poured evenly over the tops of the custards. It was an easier and safer method.

How you bake crème caramel and how long you bake it can make the difference between a great dessert and a mediocre, or even disappointing, one. After considerable experimentation, we determined that baking the custards at 350 degrees in a bain-marie, or water bath, to maintain an even, gentle heating environment, produced custards that were creamy and smooth.

As a final experiment, we decided to try lining the baking pan with a towel before adding the molds or the water. We found this step in a couple of recipes and initially dismissed it as not worth the bother. At this point, however, our testing produced custards that were wonderful, but still had bubbles from overcooking near the bottom. We reasoned that the towel might absorb some of the heat from the bottom, preventing the custards from overcooking in this area. Custards baked with the towel contained significantly fewer bubbles, so we judged them worth the effort.

Classic Crème Caramel

SERVES 8

Though you can make one large crème caramel, we find that custards baked in individual ramekins cook faster, are more evenly textured, and unmold more easily. You can vary the amount of sugar in the custard to suit your taste. Most tasters preferred the full two-thirds cup, but you can reduce that amount to as little as one-half cup to create a greater contrast between the custard and the sweetness of the caramel. Cook the caramel in a pan with a light-colored interior, since a dark surface makes it difficult to judge the color of the syrup. Caramel can leave a real mess in a pan, but it is easy to clean. Simply boil lots of water in the pan for 5 to 10 minutes to loosen the hardened caramel.

CARAMEL SAUCE

1	cup sugar
⅓	cup water
2	tablespoons corn syrup
¼	teaspoon juice from one lemon

CUSTARD

1½	cups whole milk
1½	cups light cream
3	large eggs, plus 2 large yolks
⅔	cup sugar
1½	teaspoons vanilla extract
	Pinch salt

1. FOR THE CARAMEL: In a medium nonreactive saucepan and without stirring, bring sugar, water, corn syrup, and lemon juice to simmer over medium-high heat, wiping sides of pan with wet cloth to remove any sugar crystals that might cause syrup to turn grainy. Continue to cook until syrup turns from clear to golden, swirling pan gently to ensure even browning, about 8 minutes. Continue to cook, swirling pan gently and constantly, until large, slow

bubbles on mixture's surface turn honey-caramel in color, 4 to 5 minutes longer. Remove pan immediately from heat and, working quickly but carefully (the caramel is above 300 degrees and will burn you if it touches your skin), pour a portion of the caramel into each of 8 ungreased 6-ounce ovenproof ramekins. Allow caramel to cool and harden, about 15 minutes. (Can be covered with plastic wrap and refrigerated for up to 2 days; return to room temperature before adding custard.)

2. FOR THE CUSTARD: Adjust oven rack to center position and heat oven to 350 degrees. Heat milk and cream, stirring occasionally, in medium saucepan over medium heat until steam appears and/or an instant-read thermometer held in the liquid registers 160 degrees, 6 to 8 minutes; remove from heat. Meanwhile, gently whisk eggs, yolks, and sugar in large bowl until just combined. Off heat, gently whisk warm milk mixture, vanilla, and salt into eggs until just combined but not at all foamy. Strain mixture through fine mesh sieve into large measuring cup or container with pouring spout; set aside.

3. Bring 2 quarts water to boil in kettle. Meanwhile, fold dish towel to fit bottom of large baking dish or roasting pan and position in pan. Divide reserved custard mixture among ramekins; place filled ramekins on towel in pan (making sure they do not touch) and set pan on oven rack. Fill pan with boiling water to reach halfway up ramekins; cover entire pan loosely with aluminum foil so steam can escape. Bake until a paring knife inserted halfway between center and edge of the custards comes out clean, 35 to 40 minutes. Transfer custards to wire rack; cool to room temperature (Can be covered with plastic wrap and refrigerated up to 2 days.)

4. To unmold, slide a paring knife around entire mold perimeter, pressing knife against the side of the dish. Hold serving plate over top of ramekin and invert; set plate on work surface and shake ramekin gently to release custard. Serve immediately.

➤ VARIATIONS
Large Crème Caramel
Follow recipe for Classic Crème Caramel, pouring caramel and custard into 1½-quart straight-sided soufflé dish rather than individual ramekins. Fill roasting pan with boiling water to reach halfway up

sides of soufflé dish; increase baking time to 70 to 75 minutes or until an instant-read thermometer inserted in center of custard registers 175 degrees.

Espresso Crème Caramel
Espresso beans ground in a coffee grinder would be too fine and impart too strong a coffee flavor to the custard. Instead, crush the beans lightly with the bottom of a heavy saucepan.

Follow recipe for Classic Crème Caramel, heating ½ cup lightly crushed espresso coffee beans with milk and cream mixture until steam appears and/or an instant-read thermometer held in the liquid registers 160 degrees, 6 to 8 minutes. Off heat, cover and steep until coffee flavor has infused milk and cream, about 15 minutes. Strain out beans and continue with recipe, reducing vanilla extract to 1 teaspoon.

CHOCOLATE MOUSSE

CHOCOLATE MOUSSE IS ONE OF AMERICA'S best-known desserts, a standby of cooks who want to create something with the allure of French baking but without the difficulty of, say, a gâteau Saint-Honoré. However, exactly what makes a chocolate mousse a chocolate mousse turned out to be something of a mystery.

When we went to cookbooks, we found that all the recipes for this dessert started with chocolate and eggs, but that's where the similarity ended. Most of the recipes added some other elements, most frequently (but not always) butter, sugar, and cream. In addition, all sorts of different flavorings could be present, apparently at the whim of the individual cook.

So we started by setting some standards of our own. We wanted a creamy mousse and a deep chocolate flavor, but we didn't want either of these aspects to dominate. Chocolate flavor is essential, yes, but when we crave a solid-chocolate experience, we'd rather have a flourless chocolate cake instead of one of the sticky, heavy chocolate mousses we tested from some cookbooks. In taking this position we were therefore able to eliminate one whole folder's worth of obviously leaden recipes. At the other extreme, diet chocolate mousse is a contradiction in terms. When we want more air than flavor, there are meringues and sponge cakes.

As a starting point, we turned to the most basic definition of chocolate mousse that we could find. Surprisingly, it was in a book by the late British cookbook author Elizabeth David. In her *French Provincial Cooking* (Harper & Row, 1962), she refers to the "old and reliable formula for chocolate mousse—four yolks beaten into four ounces of bitter chocolate, and the four whipped whites folded in." We decided to stick with the four eggs, then test mousses using varying amounts and proportions of the other possible ingredients, including not only the chocolate that David's bare-bones recipe specified but also the butter, cream, sugar, and flavorings that other cookbooks recommended.

Because chocolate mousse derives almost all of its flavor from the starring ingredient, we first wanted to see how much chocolate in proportion to eggs would give us a flavor we liked. Because chocolate contains sugar, as well as saturated fat in the form of cocoa butter, the amount of chocolate affects the texture of the final mousse as well.

We started with David's four ounces of chocolate to four eggs. While we liked it, we found it somewhat lacking in chocolate flavor. Six ounces of chocolate provided a much richer flavor. In the spirit of experimentation, we upped the chocolate again, adding eight ounces to our next mousse. At that level, however, the chocolate was too predominant, giving the mousse an underlying edge of bitterness that seemed inappropriate. We settled on six ounces.

Because most of the French recipes we had found in our cookbook research used butter to some degree, we next tried adding unsalted butter to the mixture. We discovered that it did make the mousse denser and gave it a rich mouthfeel. With one ounce of butter, the four-egg mousse was airy and light. Two ounces of butter gave it more creaminess and density without obliterating the lightness. When we moved up to four and six ounces of butter, the mousses took on a solid, trufflelike consistency and were so rich they could only be eaten in very small amounts, so we stuck with the two ounces.

Cooks have often used whipped cream as a garnish for chocolate mousse. Many newer recipes add it to the mousse itself, so we tried some variations with whipped cream (and no butter) to determine the effect. Whipped cream, like the butter, made the mousse a little denser in texture and it also softened the flavor, taking some of the deep chocolate hit out of the finished dish. Although chocolate fanatics can stop reading right here, we wanted a more balanced flavor and thus found this effect useful and desirable. One-half cup of heavy cream, whipped and folded in, smoothed out the flavor without diluting the chocolate impression by much.

Having tested butter and cream separately, we decided to try the ultimate creamy mousse, one with both butter and cream. To do this, we made 18 different mousses for another informal tasting. The version with two ounces of butter and a half cup of whipped cream was the clear winner.

Because chocolates vary so much in sugar content, and because sugar is also a structural element in mousse, the recipes we encountered varied widely in the type and quantity of sugar specified. While your choice of chocolate will determine exactly how much sugar you need, we got a nicely balanced flavor using two tablespoons of sugar with most bittersweet and semisweet chocolates (three tablespoons actually made the chocolate flavor weaker, and didn't seem any sweeter). Professional dessert chefs stock superfine sugar to ensure that it dissolves completely, but we had no difficulties in several tests with ordinary granulated sugar.

We next tested various flavoring liquids, including strong coffee and a variety of liquors and liqueurs. Not surprisingly, all such additions made the final product less firm. More than two tablespoons of such liquid (in addition to the teaspoon of vanilla extract) started to make the mousse slightly soupy, and more than two tablespoons of any alcohol-based liquid overwhelmed the flavor as well. If you prefer a stronger alcohol kick, we recommend you try whipping some additional liqueur into a whipped cream topping.

About half the recipes we researched called for whisking the egg yolks one by one into the chocolate mixture, and this was the technique we had been using to standardize our other ingredients. We had set aside another, more time-consuming approach to the egg yolks, in which they are beaten with some sugar until lightened in texture and color, then added to the chocolate. When we got around to trying a recipe that followed this procedure with the yolks, the volume of the mousse increased by as much as one-fourth, and the texture was much lighter and more airy.

Nonetheless, in a side-by-side test, we preferred the flavor of mousse made with unbeaten yolks. As with recipes made with extra whipped cream, more air in the mousse meant less flavor per mouthful. So this time, the easier technique was also the winner.

Chocolate Mousse

SERVES 6 TO 8

For an extra creamy chocolate mousse, fold in one cup of heavy cream that's been whipped instead of the one-half cup called for here. Make this mousse at least 2 hours before you wish to serve it to let the flavors develop, but serve it within 24 hours because the flavor and texture will begin to deteriorate.

6	ounces bittersweet or semisweet chocolate, chopped coarse
4	tablespoons unsalted butter
	Pinch salt
1	teaspoon vanilla extract
2	tablespoons strong coffee or 4 teaspoons brandy, orange-flavored liqueur, or light rum
4	large eggs, separated
2	tablespoons sugar
½	cup heavy cream, plus extra for garnish

1. Melt chocolate in medium bowl set over large saucepan of barely simmering water or in uncovered Pyrex measuring cup microwaved at 50 percent heat for 3 minutes, stirring once at 2-minute mark. Whisk butter into melted chocolate, 1 tablespoon at a time; stir in salt, vanilla, and coffee or liquor until completely incorporated. Whisk in yolks one at a time, making sure that each is fully incorporated before adding the next; set chocolate mixture aside.

2. Stir egg whites in clean mixing bowl set over saucepan of hot water until slightly warm, 1 to 2 minutes; remove bowl from saucepan. Beat with electric mixer set at medium speed until soft peaks form. Raise mixer speed to high and slowly add sugar; beat to soft peaks. Whisk a quarter of the beaten whites into chocolate mixture to lighten it, then gently fold in remaining whites.

3. Whip cream to soft peaks; gently fold into mousse. Spoon portions of mousse into six to eight individual serving dishes or goblets. Cover and refrigerate to blend flavors, at least 2 hours. (Can be covered and refrigerated up to 24 hours.) Serve with additional whipped cream.

Chocolate Soufflé

WHAT IS THE PERFECT SOUFFLÉ? IT IS A soufflé that has a crusty exterior packed with flavor, a dramatic rise above the rim, an airy but substantial outer layer, and a rich, loose center that is not completely set. A great soufflé must also convey a true mouthful of flavor, bursting with the bright, clear taste of the main ingredient. In a chocolate soufflé, the chocolate high notes should be clear and strong. A balancing act between egg whites, chocolate, yolks, and butter is the essence of a great chocolate soufflé.

A primary consideration when trying to create such a soufflé is what to use as the "base," the mixture that gives substance and flavor to the soufflé as opposed to the airiness and "lift" provided by the whipped egg whites. The base can be a béchamel (a classic French sauce made with equal amounts of butter and flour, whisked with milk over heat), pastry cream (egg yolks beaten with sugar and then heated with milk), or a bouilli (flour cooked with milk or water until thickened). After trying several versions of each of these options, we found that we consistently preferred the béchamel base. It provided the soufflé with good chocolate flavor and a puffed yet substantial texture. By contrast, the versions made with pastry cream and bouillie were too dense and puddinglike for our tasters' palates.

After a week of refining a recipe using a béchamel base, we thought the soufflé was good but that the chocolate was muted by the milk used in the béchamel. We removed the flour from our recipe, separated the eggs (whipping the whites separately), more than doubled the amount of chocolate, used six whole eggs, and reduced the amount of butter. This approach resulted in a base of egg yolks beaten with sugar until thick. This gave the soufflé plenty of volume but eliminated the milk, the ingredient that was holding back the chocolate. The result was fantastic—the most intense chocolate dessert we had ever tasted.

Our chocolate soufflé now had the intense flavor we had been looking for, but we still weren't completely happy with the texture because the outer layer was a bit cakey. After several more experiments, though, we discovered that adding two egg whites resolved the problem, giving the soufflé more lift and a better texture.

We now moved on to check other variables, including oven temperature, a water bath, and the dish in which to bake the soufflé.

For most recipes a 25-degree variance in oven temperature is not crucial, so we were surprised to discover the dramatic impact it had on our soufflé. Our initial oven temperature was 375 degrees, but to be sure this temperature was optimum, we tested both 350 and 400 degrees as well. The higher oven temperature resulted in an overcooked exterior and an undercooked interior, while the lower temperature did not brown the exterior enough to provide good flavor and also produced a texture that was too even, given that we were looking for a loose center at the point at which the exterior was nicely cooked. We decided to stick with 375 degrees.

A water bath was a truly awful idea. When we tested it, the outer crust of the soufflé turned out wet, with a gelatinlike appearance, and the soufflé did not rise well.

One factor we found to be of surprising importance was the baking dish. We tried using a standard casserole dish for one of the tests, and the soufflé rose right out of the dish onto the floor of the oven! The problem was that the dish did not have the perfectly straight sides of a soufflé dish. It pays to make sure that you are using a real soufflé dish.

We also tested the theory that a chilled soufflé dish improves the rise, and discovered that it did cause chocolate soufflés to rise higher but made little difference with nonchocolate soufflés.

During the course of all this testing, we also found a chocolate soufflé will give you three indications of when it is done: when you can smell the chocolate, when it stops rising, and when only the very center of the top jiggles when gently shaken. Of course, these are all imprecise methods. If you are not sure if your soufflé is done, simply take two large spoons, pull open the top of the soufflé, and peek inside. If the center is still soupy, simply put the dish back in the oven! Much to our surprise, this in no way harmed the soufflé.

For years, we had heard rumors about chefs who had devised secret recipes for chocolate soufflés that are prepared ahead of time, then refrigerated or frozen, and baked at the last minute. We wanted to develop just such a recipe to take the last-minute worry out of soufflés for busy cooks.

For the first test, we tried both refrigerating and freezing the soufflé batter in individual ramekins. (We had discovered through earlier testing that individual soufflés hold up much better in the refrigerator or freezer than a full recipe held in a soufflé dish.) When we baked them, the refrigerated soufflés were a disaster (they hardly rose at all and were very wet inside), but the frozen versions worked fairly well. However, they were cakelike, without the loose center we were seeking.

For the second test, we heated the sugar used in the recipe with two tablespoons of water just to the boiling stage and added it to the yolks while beating. Although this produced more volume, the final soufflé was only slightly better than that in the first test.

Finally, we also added two tablespoons of confectioners' sugar to the whites. This version was a great success, producing a soufflé that was light and airy with an excellent rise and a nice wet center. The actual texture of the whites changed as they were beaten, becoming stable enough so they held up better during freezing. We did find that these soufflés ended up with a domed top, but by increasing the oven temperature to 400 degrees, this problem was solved. We had our make-ahead soufflé at last.

Chocolate Soufflé

SERVES 6 TO 8

Individual soufflés are an alternative to making a single large one. To make them, completely fill eight 8-ounce ramekins with the chocolate mixture, making sure to clean each rim with a wet paper towel, and reduce baking time to 16–18 minutes. For a mocha-flavored soufflé, add one tablespoon of instant coffee powder dissolved in one tablespoon of hot water when adding the vanilla to the chocolate mixture. If you like the microwave, melt the chocolate at 50 percent power for three minutes, stirring in the butter after two minutes.

5	tablespoons unsalted butter (1 tablespoon softened, remaining 4 tablespoons cut into ½-inch chunks)
1	tablespoon plus ⅓ cup sugar
8	ounces bittersweet or semisweet chocolate, chopped coarse
⅛	teaspoon salt
½	teaspoon vanilla extract
1	tablespoon Grand Marnier
6	large egg yolks
8	large egg whites
¼	teaspoon cream of tartar

1. Adjust oven rack to lower-middle position and heat oven to 375 degrees. Butter inside of 2-quart soufflé dish with the tablespoon of softened butter, then coat inside of dish evenly with the tablespoon of sugar; refrigerate until ready to use.

2. Melt chocolate and remaining butter in medium bowl set over pan of simmering water. Turn off heat, stir in salt, vanilla, and liqueur; set aside.

3. In medium bowl, beat yolks and remaining sugar with electric mixer set on medium speed until

thick and pale yellow, about 3 minutes. Fold into chocolate mixture. Clean beaters.

4. In medium bowl, beat whites with electric mixer set on medium speed until foamy. Add cream of tartar and continue to beat on high speed to stiff, moist peaks. (Mixture should just hold the weight of a raw egg in the shell when the egg is placed on top.)

5. Vigorously stir one-quarter of whipped whites into chocolate mixture. Gently fold remaining whites into mixture until just incorporated. Spoon mixture into prepared dish; bake until exterior is set but interior is still a bit loose and creamy, about 25 minutes. (Soufflé is done when fragrant and fully risen. Use two large spoons to pull open the top and peek inside. If not yet done, place back in oven.) Serve immediately.

VARIATION
Make-Ahead Chocolate Soufflé

This technique works only for the individual chocolate soufflés, which can be made and frozen up to two days before baking.

Follow instructions for Chocolate Soufflé, coating eight 1-cup ramekins with butter and sugar. Rather than beating sugar with yolks, bring sugar and 2 tablespoons water to boil in small saucepan, then simmer until sugar dissolves. With mixer running, slowly add this sugar syrup to egg yolks; beat until mixture triples in volume, about 3 minutes. Beat egg whites until frothy; add cream of tartar and beat to soft peaks; add 2 tablespoons confectioners' sugar; continue beating to stiff peaks. Fill each ramekin almost to rim, wiping excess filling from rim with wet paper towel. Cover and freeze until firm, at least 3 hours. Increase oven temperature to 400 degrees; bake until fully risen, 16 to 18 minutes. Do not overbake.

CHILLED LEMON SOUFFLÉ

BASED ON A CLASSIC BAVARIAN CREAM, chilled lemon soufflé is most often a mixture of a custard base, gelatin, whipped cream, beaten egg whites, sugar, and lemon flavorings. But like any good mongrel American classic, "chilled lemon soufflé" covers a wide range of recipes, from baked pudding cakes, which are cooled and served at room temperature, to nothing more than lemon juice, sugar, and beaten whites, with no egg yolks and no whipped cream.

Despite its various guises, how should it taste? For us, a chilled lemon soufflé is an unusual marriage of cream and foam, of sweet and sour, of high lemony notes and lingering, rich custard. It starts at the tip of the tongue with the sharp tingle of lemon zest and then slides slowly down the throat, filling the mouth with cream and pudding and a soft, long finish. At least that's what it is supposed to do. The question is, how can a home cook make this delicate balance of ingredients and technique turn out just right? We set out to test as many recipes as possible to find out.

For starters, we hauled out as many recipes as we could find and quickly discovered that there are five basic approaches to this dessert. The most elaborate begins with a custard base that is then combined with gelatin, whipped cream, and beaten egg whites. Many recipes, however, leave out the custard, using only beaten egg yolks and sugar as the base, while some classic French versions of this dish also leave out the egg whites. Other recipes omit the egg yolks altogether, using just sugar, lemon juice, whipped cream, and beaten egg whites. If the whipped cream is eliminated in a further act of reductionism, you have what is known as a lemon snow pudding. We also looked up recipes for lemon mousse and found that mousse is usually made without gelatin, the key ingredient in chilled lemon soufflé.

We began our testing with the simplest approach, just beaten egg whites, gelatin, sugar, and lemon juice. The result was a foamy confection, much like being served a mound of beaten egg whites. This dessert needed some fat for texture and flavor. We then thought we would try a recipe with whipped cream as well. This was quite good, rated number 1 by some tasters. It had lots of lemon punch but a somewhat airy, foamy texture that called for a bit more fat. Next, we added beaten egg yolks to the mixture, perhaps the most common approach to chilled lemon soufflé, but the texture of this version of the dessert was tough. We tried a second variation on this theme and were still unsatisfied with the texture. We then left out the egg whites and produced

a dense, rubbery lemon dome, the sort of dessert that might hold up nicely in Death Valley in July. Finally, we started with a custard base made with sugar, egg yolks, milk, lemon juice, and gelatin and then added this to the whipped cream and beaten whites. This was highly rated, but the lemon flavor was a bit muted.

Upon reviewing the test results, we decided that a compromise might be reached between the two test winners. The lemon juice/whipped cream/beaten egg-white dessert was light and lemony but too foamy; the custard base dessert had a better finish and mouthfeel but was lacking the bright, clear flavor of lemon. We worked up a new master recipe that called for softening one package of gelatin over a half cup of lemon juice. (We tried two packages of gelatin and ended up with a rubbery orb.) Next, a cup of milk was heated with sugar while we beat two egg yolks with an extra two tablespoons of sugar. The milk and the beaten yolks were combined on top of the stove and heated until the mixture began to steam. Finally, the cooled custard was folded into three-quarters cup of whipped heavy cream, and six beaten egg whites were folded into the result. This was the best variation to date, but it still needed a few refinements.

First, we cut back the whites to five from six to give the dessert a bit less air and more substance. Next, we added just one-quarter teaspoon of cornstarch to the custard mixture to prevent the yolks from curdling too easily. We then wondered if either lemon oil or lemon extract might be better than zest, so we made a side-by-side comparison. We settled on the zest, since it produced a more complex range of flavors. We also discovered that to maintain a more consistent texture it was better to whisk a small part of the beaten egg whites into the custard base before folding the mixture together.

Although many recipes call for using individual ramekins, we preferred to make one large and impressive soufflé. To make it look even more like its baked cousin, we added a simple collar of aluminum foil and increased the recipe to the point where it would rise above the rim of the dish, much like a real soufflé. We were also curious about how well this dessert would hold up in the refrigerator. After one day, it was still good but slightly foamy, losing the creamy, tender undercurrent that is the hallmark of this dessert when well made. After two days, it quickly deteriorated. This is one dessert that is best served the day it is made.

Chilled Lemon Soufflé
SERVES 4 TO 6

To make this lemon soufflé "soufflé" over the rim of the dish, use a 1-quart soufflé dish and make a foil collar for it as follows: Cut a piece of foil 3 inches longer than the cir-cumference of the soufflé dish and fold it lengthwise into fourths. Wrap the foil strip around the upper half of the souf-flé dish and secure the overlap with tape. Tape the collar to the soufflé dish as necessary to prevent it from slipping. Spray the inside of the foil collar with vegetable cooking spray. When ready to serve, carefully remove the collar.

For those less concerned with appearance, this dessert can be served from any 1½-quart serving bowl. For best texture, serve the soufflé after 1½ hours of chilling. It may be chilled up to 6 hours; though the texture will stiffen slightly because of the gelatin, it will taste just as good.

½	cup lemon juice from 2 or 3 lemons, plus 2½ teaspoons grated zest (grate before juicing)
1	¼-ounce packet unflavored gelatin
1	cup whole milk
¾	cup sugar
5	large egg whites, plus 2 yolks, room temperature
¼	teaspoon cornstarch
¾	cup heavy cream

1. Place lemon juice in small nonreactive bowl; sprinkle gelatin over. Set aside.

2. Heat milk and ½ cup of the sugar in medium saucepan over medium-low heat, stirring occasional-ly, until steaming and sugar is dissolved, about 5 min-utes. Meanwhile, whisk together yolks, 2 tablespoons sugar, and cornstarch in medium bowl until pale yel-low and thickened. Whisking constantly, gradually add hot milk to yolks. Return milk and egg mixture to saucepan and cook, stirring constantly, over medium-low heat until foam has dissipated to a thin layer and mixture thickens to consistency of heavy cream and registers 185 degrees on instant-read thermometer, about 4 minutes. Strain into medium bowl; stir in lemon juice mixture and zest. Set bowl of custard in large bowl of ice water; stir occasionally to cool.

3. While custard mixture is chilling, in bowl of standing mixer fitted with whisk attachment (or in large mixing bowl if using hand mixer), beat egg whites on medium speed until foamy, about 1 minute. Increase speed to medium-high; gradually add remaining 2 tablespoons sugar and continue to beat until glossy and whites hold soft peaks when beater is lifted, about 2 minutes longer. Do not over-beat. Remove bowl containing custard mixture from ice water bath; gently whisk in about one-third of egg whites, then fold in remaining whites with large rubber spatula until almost no white streaks remain.

4. In same mixer bowl (washing not necessary), with mixer fitted with whisk attachment, beat cream on medium-high speed until soft peaks form when beater is lifted, 2 to 3 minutes. Fold cream into cus-tard and egg-white mixture until no white streaks remain. Pour into prepared soufflé dish or bowl. Chill until set but not stiff, about 1½ hours (can be refrigerated up to 6 hours, see note at left); remove foil collar, if using, and serve.

> VARIATION

Chilled Lemon Soufflé with White Chocolate
The white chocolate in this variation subdues the lemony kick. The difference is subtle, but the sweeter, richer flavor and texture was popular among tasters.

Follow recipe for Chilled Lemon Soufflé, adding 2 ounces chopped white chocolate to warm custard before adding lemon juice mixture and zest. Stir until melted and fully incorporated.

INDEX